The Oxford Spanish Dictionary and Grammar

Second edition

D0054741

Dictionary
Christine Lea

Second edition edited by
Carol Styles Carvajal
Michael Britton
Jane Horwood

Grammar
John Butt

OXFORD

UNIVERSITY PRESS

Great Clarendon Street, Oxford OX2 6DP

Oxford University Press is a department of the University of Oxford.
It furthers the University's objective of excellence in research, scholarship,
and education by publishing worldwide in

Oxford New York

Auckland Bangkok Buenos Aires Cape Town Chennai
Dar es Salaam Delhi Hong Kong Istanbul Karachi Kolkata
Kuala Lumpur Madrid Melbourne Mexico City Mumbai Nairobi
São Paulo Shanghai Taipei Tokyo Toronto

Oxford is a registered trade mark of Oxford University Press
in the UK and in certain other countries

Published in the United States
by Oxford University Press Inc., New York

Dictionary © Oxford University Press, 1993, 2001
Grammar © Oxford University Press, 1996, 2000

The moral rights of the author have been asserted

Database right Oxford University Press (maker)

This combined edition first published 1997
Second edition published 2001

British Library Cataloguing in Publication Data

Data available

Library of Congress Cataloging in Publication Data

Data available

ISBN 0-19-860388-6

10 9 8 7 6 5

Printed in Great Britain by
Clays Ltd, St Ives plc

General Contents

contents

Dictionary Contents

Introduction

The wordlist of this new edtion has been comprehensively revised to reflect recent additions to both languages and to cover such topics as computing and the Internet. A further new feature of the dictionary is the special status given to more complex grammatical words which provide the basic structure of both languages. Boxed entries in the text for these *function words* provide extended treatment, including notes to warn of possible pitfalls.

The dictionary has an easy-to-use, streamlined layout. Bullets separate each new part of speech within an entry. Nuances of sense or usage are pinpointed by indicators or by typical collocates with which the word frequently occurs. Extra help is given in the form of symbols to mark the register of words and phrases. An exclamation mark ▣ indicates colloquial language, and a cross ▣ indicates slang.

Each English headword is followed by its phonetic transcription between slashes. The symbols used are those of the International Phonetic Alphabet. Pronunciation is also shown for derivatives and compounds where it is not easily deduced from that of a headword. The rules for pronunciation of Spanish are given on page ix.

The swung dash (∿) is used to replace a headword or that part of a headword preceding the vertical bar (|).

In both English and Spanish only irregular plurals are given. Normally Spanish nouns and adjectives ending in an unstressed vowel form the plural by adding *s* (e.g. *libro, libros*). Nouns and adjectives ending in a stressed vowel or a consonant add *es* (e.g. *rubí, rubíes, pared, paredes*). An accent on the final syllable is not required when *es* is added (e.g. *nación, naciones*). Final *z* becomes *ces* (e.g. *vez, veces*).

Spanish nouns and adjectives ending in *o* form the feminine by changing the final *o* to *a* (e.g. *hermano, hermana*). Most Spanish nouns and adjectives ending in anything other than final *o* do not have a separate feminine form, with the exception of those denoting nationality etc.; these add *a* to the masculine singular form (e.g. *español, española*). An accent on the final syllable is then not required (e.g. *inglés, inglesa*). Adjectives ending in *án*, *ón*, or *or* behave like those denoting nationality, with the following exceptions: *inferior, mayor, mejor, menor, peor, superior*, where the feminine has the same form as the masculine.

Spanish verb tables will be found after the A-Z dictionary and before the grammar.

The Spanish alphabet

In Spanish *ñ* is considered a separate letter and in the Spanish–English section, therefore, is alphabetized after *ny*.

Proprietary terms

This dictionary includes some words which have, or are asserted to have, proprietary status as trademarks. Their inclusion does not imply that they have acquired for legal purposes a non-proprietary or general significance, nor any other judgement concerning their legal status. In cases where the editorial staff have some evidence that a word has proprietary status this is indicated in the entry for that word by the symbol (P), but no judgement concerning the legal status of such words is made or implied thereby.

Pronunciation of Spanish

Vowels

a between pronunciation of *a* in English *cat* and *arm*
e like *e* in English *bed*
i like *ee* in English *see* but a little shorter
o like *o* in English *hot* but a little longer
u like *oo* in English *too*
y when a vowel is as Spanish **i**

Consonants

b (1) in initial position or after a nasal consonant is like English *b*
   (2) in other positions is between English *b* and English *v*
c (1) before **e** or **i** is like *th* in English *thin*. In Latin American Spanish is like English *s*.
   (2) in other positions is like *c* in English *cat*
ch like *ch* in English *chip*
d (1) in initial position, after nasal consonants and after **l** is like English *d*
   (2) in other positions is like *th* in English *this*
f like English *f*
g (1) before **e** or **i** is like *ch* in Scottish *loch*
   (2) in initial position is like *g* in English *get*
   (3) in other positions is like (2) but a little softer
h silent in Spanish but see also **ch**
j like *ch* in Scottish *loch*
k like English *k*
l like English *l* but see also **ll**
ll like *lli* in English *million*
m like English *m*
n like English *n*
ñ like *ni* in English *opinion*
p like English *p*
q like English *k*
r rolled or trilled
s like *s* in English *sit*
t like English *t*
v (1) in initial position or after a nasal consonant is like English *b*
   (2) in other positions is between English *b* and English *v*
w like Spanish **b** or **v**
x like English *x*
y like English *y*
z like *th* in English *thin*

Abbreviations

adjective	*a*	adjetivo
abbreviation	*abbr/abrev*	abreviatura
administration	*admin*	administración
adverb	*adv*	adverbio
American	*Amer*	americano
anatomy	*Anat*	anatomía
architecture	*Archit/Arquit*	arquitectura
definite article	*art def*	artículo definido
indefinite article	*art indef*	artículo indefinido
astrology	*Astr*	astrología
motoring	*Auto*	automóvil
auxiliary	*aux*	auxiliar
aviation	*Aviat/Aviac*	aviación
biology	*Biol*	biología
botany	*Bot*	botánica
British	*Brit*	británico
commerce	*Com*	comercio
conjunction	*conj*	conjunción
cookery	*Culin*	cocina
electricity	*Elec*	electricidad
school	*Escol*	enseñanza
Spain	*Esp*	España
feminine	*f*	femenino
familiar	*fam*	familiar
figurative	*fig*	figurado
philosophy	*Fil*	filosofía
photography	*Foto*	fotografía
geography	*Geog*	geografía
geology	*Geol*	geología
grammar	*Gram*	gramática
humorous	*hum*	humorístico
interjection	*int*	interjección
interrogative	*inter*	interrogativo
invariable	*invar*	invariable
legal, law	*Jurid*	jurídico
Latin American	*LAm*	latinoamericano
language	*Lang*	lengua(je)
masculine	*m*	masculino
mathematics	*Mat(h)*	matemáticas
mechanics	*Mec*	mecánica
medicine	*Med*	medicina

Mexico	*Mex*	México
military	*Mil*	militar
music	*Mus*	música
mythology	*Myth*	mitología
noun	*n*	nombre
nautical	*Naut*	náutica
oneself	*o. s.*	uno mismo, se
proprietary term	*P*	marca registrada
pejorative	*pej*	peyorativo
philosophy	*Phil*	filosofía
photography	*Photo*	fotografía
plural	*pl*	plural
politics	*Pol*	política
possessive	*poss*	posesivo
past participle	*pp*	participio pasado
prefix	*pref*	prefijo
preposition	*prep*	preposición
present participle	*pres p*	participio de presente
pronoun	*pron*	pronombre
psychology	*Psych*	psicología
past tense	*pt*	tiempo pasado
railroad	*Rail*	ferrocarril
relative	*rel*	relativo
religion	*Relig*	religión
school	*Schol*	enseñanza
singular	*sing*	singular
slang	*sl*	argot
someone	*s. o.*	alguien
something	*sth*	algo
subjunctive	*subj*	subjuntivo
technical	*Tec*	técnico
television	*TV*	televisión
university	*Univ*	universidad
auxiliary verb	*v aux*	verbo auxiliar
verb	*vb*	verbo
intransitive verb	*vi*	verbo intransitivo
pronominal verb	*vpr*	verbo pronominal
transitive verb	*vt*	verbo transitivo
transitive & intransitive verb	*vti*	verbo transitivo e intransitivo
vulgar	*vulg*	vulgar

Aa

a

● *preposición*

Note that **a** followed by **el** becomes **al**, e.g. **vamos al cine**

····▶ (dirección) to. **fui a México** I went to Mexico. **muévete a la derecha** move to the right

····▶ (posición) **se sentaron a la mesa** they sat at the table. **al lado del banco** next to the bank. **a orillas del río** on the banks of the river

····▶ (distancia) **queda a 5 km** it's 5 km away. **a pocos metros de aquí** a few metres from here

····▶ (fecha) **hoy estamos a 5** today is the 5th. **¿a cuánto estamos?**, (LAm) **¿a cómo estamos?** what's the date?

····▶ (hora, momento) at. **a las 2** at 2 o'clock. **a fin de mes** at the end of the month. **a los 21 años** at the age of 21; (después de) after 21 years

····▶ (precio) **¿a cómo están las peras?** how much are the pears? **están a 500 pesetas el kilo** they're 500 pesetas a kilo. **salen a 30 pesetas cada uno** they work out at 30 pesetas each

····▶ (medio, modo) **fuimos a pie** we went on foot. **hecho a mano** handmade. **pollo al horno** (LAm) roast chicken

····▶ (cuando precede al objeto directo de persona) *no se traduce*. **conocí a Juan** I met Juan. **quieren mucho a sus hijos** they love their children very much

····▶ (con objeto indirecto) to. **se lo di a Juan** I gave it to Juan. **le vendí el coche a mi amigo** I sold my friend the car, I sold the car to my friend. **se lo compré a mi madre** I bought it from my mother; (para) I bought it for my mother

➡ Cuando la preposición **a** se emplea precedida de ciertos verbos como **empezar, faltar, ir, llegar** etc., ver bajo el respectivo verbo

ábaco *m* abacus

abadía *f* abbey

abajo *adv* (down) below; (dirección) down(wards); (en casa) downstairs. ● *int* down with. **~ de** (LAm) under (neath). **calle ~** down the street. **el ~ firmante** the undersigned. **escaleras ~** down the stairs. **la parte de ~** the bottom (part). **los de ~** those at the bottom. **más ~** further down

abalanzarse [10] *vpr* rush (**hacia** towards)

abanderado *m* standard-bearer; (Mex, en fútbol) linesman

abandon|ado *adj* abandoned; (descuidado) neglected; *<persona>* untidy. **~ar** *vt* leave *<un lugar>*; abandon *<persona, cosa>*. ● *vi* give up. □ **~arse** *vpr* give in; (descuidarse) let o.s. go. **~o** *m* abandonment; (estado) neglect

abani|car [7] *vt* fan. **~co** *m* fan

abaratar *vt* reduce

abarcar [7] *vt* put one's arms around, embrace; (comprender) embrace

abarrotar *vt* overfill, pack full

abarrotes *mpl* (LAm) groceries; (tienda) grocer's shop

abast|ecer [11] *vt* supply. **~ecimiento** *m* supply; (acción) supplying. **~o** *m* supply. **no dar ~o** be unable to cope (**con** with)

abati|do *a* depressed. **~miento** *m* depression

abdicar [7] *vt* give up. ● *vi* abdicate

abdom|en *m* abdomen. **~inal** *a* abdominal

abec|é *m* Ⓘ alphabet, ABC. **~edario** *m* alphabet

abedul *m* birch (tree)

abej|a *f* bee. **~orro** *m* bumble-bee

aberración *f* aberration

abertura *f* opening

abeto *m* fir (tree)

abierto *pp* ⇒ABRIR. ● *a* open

abism|al *a* abysmal; (profundo) deep. ~**ar** *vt* throw into an abyss; (fig, abatir) humble. □ ~**arse** *vpr* be absorbed (**en** in), be lost (**en** in). ~**o** *m* abyss; (fig, diferencia) world of difference

ablandar *vt* soften.□ ~**se** *vpr* soften

abnega|ción *f* self-sacrifice. ~**do** *a* self-sacrificing

abochornar *vt* embarrass. □ ~**se** *vpr* feel embarrassed

abofetear *vt* slap

aboga|cía *f* law. ~**do** *m* lawyer, solicitor; (ante tribunal superior) barrister (Brit), attorney (Amer). ~**r** [12] *vi* plead

abolengo *m* ancestry

aboli|ción *f* abolition. ~**cionismo** *m* abolitionism. ~**cionista** *m* & *f* abolitionist. ~**r** [24] *vt* abolish

abolla|dura *f* dent. ~**r** *vt* dent

abolsado *a* baggy

abomba|do *a* convex; (LAm, atontado) dopey. ~**r** *vt* make convex. □ ~**rse** *vpr* (LAm, descomponerse) go bad

abominable *a* abominable

abona|ble *a* payable. ~**do** *a* paid. ● *m* subscriber. ~**r** *vt* pay; (en agricultura) fertilize. □ ~**rse** *vpr* subscribe. ~**o** *m* payment; (estiércol) fertilizer; (a un periódico) subscription

aborda|ble *a* reasonable; <*persona*> approachable. ~**je** *m* boarding. ~**r** *vt* tackle <*un asunto*>; approach <*una persona*>; (Naut) come alongside; (Mex, Aviac) board

aborigen *a* & *m* native

aborrec|er [11] *vt* loathe. ~**ible** *a* loathsome. ~**ido** *a* loathed. ~**i-miento** *m* loathing

abort|ar *vi* have a miscarriage. ~**ivo** *a* abortive. ~**o** *m* miscarriage; (voluntario) abortion. **hacerse un** ~**o** have an abortion

abotonar *vt* button (up). □ ~**se** *vpr* button (up)

abovedado *a* vaulted

abrasa|dor *a* burning. ~**r** *vt* burn. □ ~**rse** *vpr* burn

abraz|ar *vt* [10] embrace. ~**arse** *vpr* embrace. ~**o** *m* hug. **un fuerte** ~**o de** (en una carta) with best wishes from

abre|botellas *m invar* bottle-opener. ~**cartas** *m invar* paper-knife. ~**latas** *m invar* tin opener (Brit), can opener

abrevia|ción *f* abbreviation; (texto abreviado) abridged text. ~**do** *a* brief; <*texto*> abridged. ~**r** *vt* abbreviate; abridge <*texto*>; cut short <*viaje etc*>. ● *vi* be brief. ~**tura** *f* abbreviation

abrig|ado *a* <*lugar*> sheltered; <*persona*> well wrapped up. ~**ador** *a* (Mex, ropa) warm. ~**ar** [12] *vt* shelter; cherish <*esperanza*>; harbour <*duda, sospecha*>. □ ~**arse** *vpr* (take) shelter; (con ropa) wrap up. ~**o** *m* (over)coat; (lugar) shelter

abril *m* April. ~**eño** *a* April

abrillantar *vt* polish

abrir (*pp* **abierto**) *vt/i* open. □ ~**se** *vpr* open; (extenderse) open out; <*el tiempo*> clear

abrochar *vt* do up; (con botones) button up

abruma|dor *a* overwhelming. ~**r** *vt* overwhelm

abrupto *a* steep; (áspero) harsh

abrutado *a* brutish

absentismo *m* absenteeism

absolución *f* (Relig) absolution; (Jurid) acquittal

absolut|amente *adv* absolutely, completely. ~**o** *a* absolute. **en** ~**o** (not) at all. ~**orio** *a* of acquittal

absolver [2] (*pp* **absuelto**) *vt* (Relig) absolve; (Jurid) acquit

absor|bente *a* absorbent; (fig, interesante) absorbing. ~**ber** *vt* absorb. ~**ción** *f* absorption. ~**to** *a* absorbed

abstemio *a* teetotal. ● *m* teetotaller

absten|ción *f* abstention. □ ~**erse** [40] *vpr* abstain, refrain (**de** from)

abstinencia *f* abstinence

abstra|cción *f* abstraction. ~**cto** *a* abstract. ~**er** [41] *vt* abstract. □ ~**erse** *vpr* be lost in thought. ~**ído** *a* absent-minded

absuelto *a* (Relig) absolved; (Jurid) acquitted

absurdo *a* absurd. ● *m* absurd thing

abuche|ar *vt* boo. **~o** *m* booing

abuel|a *f* grandmother. **~o** *m* grandfather. **~os** *mpl* grandparents

ab|ulia *f* apathy. **~úlico** *a* apathetic

abulta|do *a* bulky. **~r** *vt* (fig, exagerar) exaggerate. ● *vi* be bulky

abunda|ncia *f* abundance. **nadar en la ~ncia** be rolling in money. **~nte** *a* abundant, plentiful. **~r** *vi* be plentiful

aburguesarse *vpr* become middle-class

aburri|do *a* (*con estar*) bored; (*con ser*) boring. **~dor** *a* (LAm) boring. **~miento** *m* boredom; (cosa pesada) bore. **~r** *vt* bore. □ **~rse** *vpr* get bored

abus|ar *vi* take advantage. **~ar de la bebida** drink too much. **~ivo** *a* excessive. **~o** *m* abuse

acá *adv* here. **~ y allá** here and there. **de ~ para allá** to and fro. **de ayer ~** since yesterday. **más ~** nearer

acaba|do *a* finished; (perfecto) perfect. ● *m* finish. **~r** *vt/i* finish. □ **~rse** *vpr* finish; (agotarse) run out; (morirse) die. **~r con** put an end to. **~r de** (+ *infinitivo*) have just (+ *pp*). **~ de llegar** he has just arrived. **~r por** (+ *infinitivo*) end up (+ *gerundio*). **¡se acabó!** that's it!

acabóse *m* **ser el ~** be the end, be the limit

acad|emia *f* academy. **~émico** *a* academic

acallar *vt* silence

acalora|do *a* heated; *<persona>* hot. □ **~rse** *vpr* get hot; (fig, excitarse) get excited

acampar *vi* camp

acantilado *m* cliff

acapara|r *vt* hoard; (monopolizar) monopolize. **~miento** *m* hoarding; (monopolio) monopolizing

acariciar *vt* caress; *<animal>* stroke; *<idea etc>* nurture

ácaro *m* mite

acarre|ar *vt* transport; *<desgracias etc>* cause. **~o** *m* transport

acartona|do *a* *<piel>* wizened. □ **~rse** *vpr* (ponerse rígido) go stiff; *<piel>* become wizened

acaso *adv* maybe, perhaps. ● *m* chance. **~ llueva mañana** perhaps it will rain tomorrow. **por si ~** (just) in case

acata|miento *m* compliance (de with). **~r** *vt* comply with

acatarrarse *vpr* catch a cold, get a cold

acaudalado *a* well off

acceder *vi* agree; (tener acceso) have access

acces|ible *a* accessible; *<persona>* approachable. **~o** *m* access, entry; (Med, ataque) attack

accesorio *a & m* accessory

accident|ado *a* *<terreno>* uneven; (agitado) troubled; *<persona>* injured. **~al** *a* accidental. □ **~arse** *vpr* have an accident. **~e** *m* accident

acci|ón *f* (incl Jurid) action; (hecho) deed; (Com) share. **~onar** *vt* work. ● *vi* gesticulate. **~onista** *m & f* shareholder

acebo *m* holly (tree)

acech|ar *vt* lie in wait for. **~o** *m* spying. **al ~o** on the look-out

aceit|ar *vt* oil; (Culin) add oil to. **~e** *m* oil. **~e de oliva** olive oil. **~te de ricino** castor oil. **~era** *f* cruet; (para engrasar) oilcan. **~ero** *a* oil. **~oso** *a* oily

aceitun|a *f* olive. **~ado** *a* olive. **~o** *m* olive tree

acelera|dor *m* accelerator. **~r** *vt* accelerate; (fig) speed up, quicken

acelga *f* chard

acent|o *m* accent; (énfasis) stress. **~uación** *f* accentuation. **~uar** [21] *vt* stress; (fig) emphasize. □ **~uarse** *vpr* become noticeable

acepción *f* meaning, sense

acepta|ble *a* acceptable. **~ción** *f* acceptance; (éxito) success. **~r** *vt* accept

acequia *f* irrigation channel

acera *f* pavement (Brit), sidewalk (Amer)

acerca de *prep* about

acerca|miento *m* approach; (fig) reconciliation. ∼**r** [7] *vt* bring near. □ ∼**rse** *vpr* approach

acero *m* steel. ∼ **inoxidable** stainless steel

acérrimo *a* (fig) staunch

acert|ado *a* right, correct; (apropiado) appropriate. ∼**ar** [1] *vt* (adivinar) get right, guess. ● *vi* get right; (en el blanco) hit. ∼**ar a** happen to. ∼**ar con** hit on. ∼**ijo** *m* riddle

achacar [7] *vt* attribute

achacoso *a* sickly

achaque *m* ailment

achatar *vt* flatten

achicar [7] *vt* make smaller; (fig, ▯, empequeñecer) belittle; (Naut) bale out. □ ∼**rse** *vpr* become smaller; (humillarse) be intimidated

achicharra|r *vt* burn; (fig) pester. □ ∼**rse** *vpr* burn

achichincle *m & f* (Mex) hanger-on

achicopalado *a* (Mex) depressed

achicoria *f* chicory

achiote *m* (LAm) annatto

achispa|do *a* tipsy. □ ∼**rse** *vpr* get tipsy

achulado *a* cocky

acicala|do *a* dressed up. ∼**r** *vt* dress up. □ ∼**rse** *vpr* get dressed up

acicate *m* spur

acidez *f* acidity; (Med) heartburn

ácido *a* sour. ● *m* acid

acierto *m* success; (idea) good idea; (habilidad) skill

aclama|ción *f* acclaim; (aplausos) applause. ∼**r** *vt* acclaim; (aplaudir) applaud

aclara|ción *f* explanation. ∼**r** *vt* lighten *<colores>*; (explicar) clarify; (enjuagar) rinse. ● *vi <el tiempo>* brighten up. □ ∼**rse** *vpr* become clear. ∼**torio** *a* explanatory

aclimata|ción *f* acclimatization, acclimation (Amer). ∼**r** *vt* acclimatize, acclimate (Amer). □ ∼**rse** *vpr* become acclimatized, become acclimated (Amer)

acné *m* acne

acobardar *vt* intimidate. □ ∼**se** *vpr* lose one's nerve

acocil *m* (Mex) freshwater shrimp

acog|edor *a* welcoming; *<ambiente>* friendly. ∼**er** [14] *vt* welcome; (proteger) shelter; (recibir) receive. □ ∼**erse** *vpr* take refuge. ∼**ida** *f* welcome; (refugio) refuge

acolcha|do *a* quilted. ∼**r** *vt* quilt, pad

acomedido *a* (Mex) obliging

acomet|er *vt* attack; (emprender) undertake ∼**ida** *f* attack

acomod|ado *a* well off. ∼**ador** *m* usher. ∼**adora** *f* usherette. ∼**ar** *vt* arrange; (adaptar) adjust. ● *vi* be suitable. □ ∼**arse** *vpr* settle down; (adaptarse) conform

acompaña|miento *m* accompaniment. ∼**nte** *m & f* companion; (Mus) accompanist. ∼**r** *vt* go with; (hacer compañía) keep company; (adjuntar) enclose

acondicionar *vt* fit out; (preparar) prepare

aconseja|ble *a* advisable. ∼**do** *a* advised. ∼**r** *vt* advise. □ ∼**rse** *vpr* ∼**rse con** consult

acontec|er [11] *vi* happen. ∼**i-miento** *m* event

acopla|miento *m* coupling; (Elec) connection. ∼**r** *vt* fit; (Elec) connect; (Rail) couple

acorazado *a* armour-plated. ● *m* battleship

acord|ar [2] *vt* agree (upon); (decidir) decide; (recordar) remind. □ ∼**arse** *vpr* remember. ∼**e** *a* in agreement; (Mus) harmonious. ● *m* chord

acorde|ón *m* accordion. ∼**onista** *m & f* accordionist

acordona|do *a <lugar>* cordoned off; *<zapatos>* lace-up. ∼**r** *vt* lace (up); (rodear) cordon off

acorralar *vt* round up *<animales>*; corner *<personas>*

acortar *vt* shorten; cut short *<permanencia>*. □ ∼**se** *vpr* get shorter

acos|ar *vt* hound; (fig) pester. ∼**o** *m* pursuit; (fig) pestering

acostar [2] *vt* put to bed; (Naut) bring alongside. ● *vi* (Naut) reach land. □ ∼**se** *vpr* go to bed; (echarse) lie down. ∼**se con** (fig) sleep with

acostumbra|do *a* (habitual) usual. ~**do a** used to. ~**r** *vt* get used. **me ha** ~**do a levantarme por la noche** he's got me used to getting up at night. ● *vi*. ~**r a** be accustomed to. **acostumbro a comer a la una** I usually have lunch at one o'clock. □ ~**rse** *vpr* become accustomed, get used

acota|ción *f* (nota) margin note; (en el teatro) stage direction; (cota) elevation mark. ~**miento** *m* (Mex) hard shoulder

acrecentar [1] *vt* increase. □ ~**se** *vpr* increase

acredita|do *a* reputable; (Pol) accredited. ~**r** *vt* prove; accredit <*diplomático*>; (garantizar) guarantee; (autorizar) authorize. □ ~**rse** *vpr* make one's name

acreedor *a* worthy (**de** of). ● *m* creditor

acribillar *vt* (a balazos) riddle (**a** with); (a picotazos) cover (**a** with); (fig, a preguntas etc) bombard (**a** with)

acr|obacia *f* acrobatics. ~**obacias aéreas** aerobatics. ~**óbata** *m & f* acrobat. ~**obático** *a* acrobatic

acta *f* minutes; (certificado) certificate

actitud *f* posture, position; (fig) attitude, position

activ|ar *vt* activate; (acelerar) speed up. ~**idad** *f* activity. ~**o** *a* active. ● *m* assets

acto *m* act; (ceremonia) ceremony. **en el** ~ immediately

act|or *m* actor. ~**riz** *f* actress

actuación *f* action; (conducta) behaviour; (Theat) performance

actual *a* present; <*asunto*> topical. ~**idad** *f* present; (de asunto) topicality. **en la** ~**idad** (en este momento) currently; (hoy en día) nowadays. ~**idades** *fpl* current affairs. ~**ización** *f* modernization. ~**izar** [10] *vt* modernize. ~**mente** *adv* now, at the present time

actuar [21] *vi* act. ~ **de** act as

acuarel|a *f* watercolour. ~**ista** *m & f* watercolourist

acuario *m* aquarium. **A**~ Aquarius

acuartelar *vt* quarter, billet; (mantener en cuartel) confine to barracks

acuático *a* aquatic

acuchillar *vt* slash; stab <*persona*>

acuci|ante *a* urgent. ~**ar** *vt* urge on; (dar prisa a) hasten. ~**oso** *a* keen

acudir *vi*. ~ **a** go to; (asistir) attend; turn up for <*a una cita*>. ~ **en auxilio** go to help

acueducto *m* aqueduct

acuerdo *m* agreement. ● *vb* ⇒ACORDAR. **¡de** ~**!** OK! **de** ~ **con** in accordance with. **estar de** ~ agree. **ponerse de** ~ agree

acuesto *vb* ⇒ACOSTAR

acumula|dor *m* accumulator. ~**r** *vt* accumulate. □ ~**rse** *vpr* accumulate

acunar *vt* rock

acuñar *vt* mint, coin

acupuntura *f* acupuncture

acurrucarse [7] *vpr* curl up

acusa|do *a* accused; (destacado) marked. ● *m* accused. ~**r** *vt* accuse; (mostrar) show; (denunciar) denounce; acknowledge <*recibo*>

acuse *m*. ~ **de recibo** acknowledgement of receipt

acus|ica *m & f* 🆒 telltale. ~**ón** *m* 🆒 telltale

acústic|a *f* acoustics. ~**o** *a* acoustic

adapta|ble *a* adaptable. ~**ción** *f* adaptation. ~**dor** *m* adapter. ~**r** *vt* adapt; (ajustar) fit. □ ~**rse** *vpr* adapt o.s.

adecua|do *a* suitable. ~**r** *vt* adapt, make suitable

adelant|ado *a* advanced; <*niño*> precocious; <*reloj*> fast. **por** ~**ado** in advance. ~**amiento** *m* advance (ment); (Auto) overtaking. ~**ar** *vt* advance, move forward; (acelerar) speed up; put forward <*reloj*>; (Auto) overtake. ● *vi* advance, go forward; <*reloj*> gain, be fast. □ ~**arse** *vpr* advance, move forward; <*reloj*> gain; (Auto) overtake. ~**e** *adv* forward. ● *int* come in!; (¡siga!) carry on! **más** ~**e** (lugar) further on; (tiempo) later on. ~**o** *m* advance; (progreso) progress

adelgaza|miento *m* slimming. ~**r** [10] *vt* make thin; lose <*kilos*>. ● *vi* lose weight; (adrede) slim. □ ~**rse** *vpr* lose weight; (adrede) slim

ademán *m* gesture. **en** ~ **de** as if to.
ademanes *mpl* (modales) manners.

además *adv* besides; (también) also;
(lo que es más) what's more. ~ **de** besides

adentr|arse *vpr*. ~**arse en** pene-
trate into; study thoroughly *<tema
etc>*. ~**o** *adv* in(side). ~ **de** (LAm)
in(side). **mar** ~**o** out at sea. **tierra** ~**o**
inland

adepto *m* supporter

aderez|ar [10] *vt* flavour *<bebidas>*;
(condimentar) season; dress *<ensala-
da>*. ~**o** *m* flavouring; (con condi-
mentos) seasoning; (para ensalada)
dressing

adeud|ar *vt* owe. ~**o** *m* debit

adhe|rir [4] *vt/i* stick. □ ~**rirse** *vpr*
stick; (fig) follow. ~**sión** *f* adhesion;
(fig) support. ~**sivo** *a & m* adhesive

adici|ón *f* addition. ~**onal** *a* add-
itional. ~**onar** *vt* add

adicto *a* addicted. ● *m* addict; (seguidor) follower

adiestra|do *a* trained. ~**miento**
m training. ~**r** *vt* train. □ ~**rse** *vpr*
practise

adinerado *a* wealthy

adiós *int* goodbye!; (al cruzarse con alguien) hello!

adit|amento *m* addition; (accesorio)
accessory. ~**ivo** *m* additive

adivin|anza *f* riddle. ~**ar** *vt* fore-
tell; (acertar) guess. ~**o** *m* fortune-
teller

adjetivo *a* adjectival. ● *m* adjective

adjudica|ción *f* award. ~**r** [7] *vt*
award. □ ~**rse** *vpr* appropriate.
~**tario** *m* winner of an award

adjunt|ar *vt* enclose. ~**o** *a* enclosed;
(auxiliar) assistant. ● *m* assistant

administra|ción *f* administra-
tion; (gestión) management. ~**dor** *m*
administrator; (gerente) manager.
~**dora** *f* administrator; manager-
ess. ~**r** *vt* administer. ~**tivo** *a* ad-
ministrative

admira|ble *a* admirable. ~**ción** *f*
admiration. ~**dor** *m* admirer. ~**r** *vt*
admire; (sorprender) amaze. □ ~**rse**
vpr be amazed

admi|sibilidad *f* admissibility.
~**sible** *a* acceptable. ~**sión** *f* admission; (aceptación) acceptance. ~**tir**
vt admit; (aceptar) accept

adobar *vt* (Culin) pickle; (condimentar)
marinade

adobe *m* sun-dried brick

adobo *m* pickle; (condimento) marinade

adoctrinar *vt* indoctrinate

adolecer [11] *vi*. ~ **de** suffer from

adolescen|cia *f* adolescence. ~**te**
a adolescent. ● *m & f* teenager, adolescent

adonde *adv* where

adónde *adv* where?

adop|ción *f* adoption. ~**tar** *vt*
adopt. ~**tivo** *a* adoptive; *<hijo>*
adopted; *<patria>* of adoption

adoqu|ín *m* paving stone; (imbécil)
idiot. ~**inado** *m* paving. ~**inar** *vt*
pave

adora|ción *f* adoration. ~**r** *vt* adore

adormec|er [11] *vt* send to sleep;
(fig, calmar) calm, soothe. □ ~**erse**
vpr fall asleep; *<un miembro>* go to
sleep. ~**ido** *a* sleepy; *<un miembro>*
numb

adormilarse *vpr* doze

adorn|ar *vt* adorn (**con**, **de** with).
~**o** *m* decoration

adosar *vt* lean (**a** against); (Mex,
adjuntar) to enclose

adquiri|r [4] *vt* acquire; (comprar)
purchase. ~**sición** *f* acquisition;
(compra) purchase. ~**sitivo** *a* pur-
chasing

adrede *adv* on purpose

adrenalina *f* adrenalin

aduan|a *f* customs. ~**ero** *a* cus-
toms. ● *m* customs officer

aducir [47] *vt* allege

adueñarse *vpr* take possession

adul|ación *f* flattery. ~**ador** *a* flat-
tering. ● *m* flatterer. ~**ar** *vt* flatter

ad|ulterar *vt* adulterate. ~**últero** *a*
adulterous. ~**ulterio** *m* adultery

adulto *a & m* adult, grown-up

advenedizo *a & m* upstart

advenimiento *m* advent, arrival;
(subida al trono) accession

adverbio *m* adverb

advers|ario *m* adversary. **~idad** *f* adversity. **~o** *a* adverse, unfavourable

advert|encia *f* warning. **~ir** [4] *vt* warn; (notar) notice

adviento *m* Advent

adyacente *a* adjacent

aéreo *a* air; *<foto>* aerial; *<ferrocarril>* overhead

aeróbico *a* aerobic

aerodeslizador *m* hovercraft

aero|lito *m* meteorite. **~moza** *f* (LAm) flight attendant. **~puerto** *m* airport. **~sol** *m* aerosol

afab|ilidad *f* affability. **~le** *a* affable

afamado *a* famous

af|án *m* hard work; (deseo) desire. **~nador** *m* (Mex) cleaner. **~anar** *vt* ▣ pinch ▣. □ **~anarse** *vpr* strive (en, por to)

afear *vt* disfigure, make ugly; (censurar) censure

afecta|ción *f* affectation. **~do** *a* affected. **~r** *vt* affect

afect|ivo *a* sensitive. **~o** *m* (cariño) affection. ● *a*. **~o a** attached to. **~uoso** *a* affectionate. **con un ~uoso saludo** (en cartas) with kind regards. **suyo ~ísimo** (en cartas) yours sincerely

afeita|do *m* shave. **~dora** *f* electric razor. **~r** *vt* shave. □ **~rse** *vpr* shave, have a shave

afeminado *a* effeminate. ● *m* effeminate person

aferrar *vt* grasp. □ **~se** *vpr* to cling (a to)

afianza|miento *m* (refuerzo) strengthening; (garantía) guarantee. □ **~r** [10] *vpr* become established

afiche *m* (LAm) poster

afici|ón *f* liking; (conjunto de aficionados) fans. **por ~ón** as a hobby. **~onado** *a* keen (a on), fond (a of). ● *m* fan. **~onar** *vt* make fond. □ **~onarse** *vpr* take a liking to

afila|do *a* sharp. **~dor** *m* knifegrinder. **~r** *vt* sharpen

afilia|ción *f* affiliation. **~do** *a* affiliated. □ **~rse** *vpr* become a member (a of)

afín *a* similar; (contiguo) adjacent; *<personas>* related

afina|ción *f* (Auto, Mus) tuning. **~do** *a* (Mus) in tune. **~dor** *m* tuner. **~r** *vt* (afilar) sharpen; (Auto, Mus) tune. □ **~rse** *vpr* become thinner

afincarse [7] *vpr* settle

afinidad *f* affinity; (parentesco) relationship by marriage

afirma|ción *f* affirmation. **~r** *vt* make firm; (asentir) affirm. □ **~rse** *vpr* steady o.s. **~tivo** *a* affirmative

aflicción *f* affliction

afligi|do *a* distressed. **~r** [14] *vt* distress. □ **~rse** *vpr* distress o.s.

aflojar *vt* loosen; (relajar) ease. ● *vi* let up. □ **~se** *vpr* loosen

aflu|encia *f* flow. **~ente** *a* flowing. ● *m* tributary. **~ir** [17] *vi* flow (a into)

afónico *a* hoarse

aforismo *m* aphorism

aforo *m* capacity

afortunado *a* fortunate, lucky

afrancesado *a* Frenchified

afrenta *f* insult; (vergüenza) disgrace

África *f* Africa. **~ del Sur** South Africa

africano *a* & *m* African

afrodisíaco, afrodisiaco *a* & *m* aphrodisiac

afrontar *vt* bring face to face; (enfrentar) face, confront

afuera *adv* out(side) **¡~!** out of the way! **~ de** (LAm) outside. **~s** *fpl* outskirts

agachar *vt* lower. □ **~se** *vpr* bend over

agalla *f* (de los peces) gill. **~s** *fpl* (fig) guts

agarradera *f* (LAm) handle

agarr|ado *a* (fig, ▣) mean. **~ar** *vt* grasp; (esp LAm) take; (LAm, pillar) catch. □ **~arse** *vpr* hold on; (▣, reñirse) have a fight. **~ón** *m* tug; (LAm ▣, riña) row

agarrotar *vt* tie tightly; *<el frío>* stiffen; garotte *<un reo>*. □ **~se** *vpr* go stiff; (Auto) seize up

agasaj|ado *m* guest of honour. **~ar** *vt* look after well. **~o** *m* good treatment

agazaparse *vpr* crouch

agencia *f* agency. ~ **de viajes** travel agency. ~ **inmobiliaria** estate agency (Brit), real estate agency (Amer). □ ~**rse** *vpr* find (out) for o.s.

agenda *f* diary (Brit), appointment book (Amer); (programa) agenda

agente *m* agent; (de policía) policeman. ●*f* agent; (de policía) policewoman. ~ **de aduanas** customs officer. ~ **de bolsa** stockbroker

ágil *a* agile

agili|dad *f* agility. ~**zación** *f* speeding up. ~**zar** *vt* speed up

agita|ción *f* waving; (de un líquido) stirring; (intranquilidad) agitation. ~**do** *a* <*el mar*> rough; (fig) agitated. ~**dor** *m* (Pol) agitator

agitar *vt* wave; shake <*botellas etc*>; stir <*líquidos*>; (fig) stir up. □ ~**se** *vpr* wave; <*el mar*> get rough; (fig) get excited

aglomera|ción *f* agglomeration; (de tráfico) traffic jam. ~**r** *vt* amass. □ ~**rse** *vpr* form a crowd

agnóstico *a & m* agnostic

agobi|ante *a* <*trabajo*> exhausting; <*calor*> oppressive. ~**ar** *vt* weigh down; (fig, abrumar) overwhelm. ~**o** *m* weight; (cansancio) exhaustion; (opresión) oppression

agolparse *vpr* crowd together

agon|ía *f* death throes; (fig) agony. ~**izante** *a* dying; <*luz*> failing. ~**izar** [10] *vi* be dying

agosto *m* August. **hacer su** ~ feather one's nest

agota|do *a* exhausted; (todo vendido) sold out; <*libro*> out of print. ~**dor** *a* exhausting. ~**miento** *m* exhaustion. ~**r** *vt* exhaust. □ ~**rse** *vpr* be exhausted; <*existencias*> sell out; <*libro*> go out of print

agracia|do *a* attractive; (que tiene suerte) lucky. ~**r** *vt* make attractive

agrada|ble *a* pleasant, nice. ~**r** *vt/i* please. **esto me** ~ I like this

agradec|er [11] *vt* thank <*persona*>; be grateful for <*cosa*>. ~**ido** *a* grateful. ¡**muy** ~**ido!** thanks a lot! ~**imiento** *m* gratitude

agrado *m* pleasure; (amabilidad) friendliness

agrandar *vt* enlarge; (fig) exaggerate. □ ~**se** *vpr* get bigger

agrario *a* agrarian, land; <*política*> agricultural

agrava|nte *a* aggravating. ●*f* additional problem. ~**r** *vt* aggravate; (aumentar el peso) make heavier. □ ~**rse** *vpr* get worse

agravi|ar *vt* offend; (perjudicar) wrong. ~**o** *m* offence

agredir [24] *vt* attack. ~ **de palabra** insult

agrega|do *m* aggregate; (diplomático) attaché. ~**r** [12] *vt* add; appoint <*persona*>. □ ~**se** *vpr* to join

agres|ión *f* aggression; (ataque) attack. ~**ividad** *f* aggressiveness. ~**ivo** *a* aggressive. ~**or** *m* aggressor

agreste *a* country; <*terreno*> rough

agriar *regular, o raramente* [20] *vt* sour. □ ~**se** *vpr* turn sour; (fig) become embittered

agr|ícola *a* agricultural. ~**icultor** *m* farmer. ~**icultura** *f* agriculture, farming

agridulce *a* bitter-sweet; (Culin) sweet-and-sour

agrietar *vt* crack. □ ~**se** *vpr* crack; <*piel*> chap

agrio *a* sour. ~**s** *mpl* citrus fruits

agro|nomía *f* agronomy. ~**pecuario** *a* farming

agrupa|ción *f* group; (acción) grouping. ~**r** *vt* group. □ ~**rse** *vpr* form a group

agruras *fpl* (Mex) heartburn

agua *f* water; (lluvia) rain; (marea) tide; (vertiente del tejado) slope. ~ **abajo** downstream. ~ **arriba** upstream. ~ **bendita** holy water. ~ **corriente** running water. ~ **de colonia** eau-de-cologne. ~ **dulce** fresh water. ~ **mineral con gas** fizzy mineral water. ~ **mineral sin gas** still mineral water. ~ **potable** drinking water. ~ **salada** salt water. **hacer** ~ (Naut) leak. **se me hizo** ~ **la boca** (LAm) it made my mouth water

aguacate *m* avocado pear; (árbol) avocado pear tree

aguacero *m* downpour, heavy shower

aguado *a* watery; (Mex, aburrido) boring

agua|fiestas *m & f invar* spoilsport, wet blanket. **~mala** *f* (Mex), **~mar** *m* jellyfish. **~marina** *f* aquamarine

aguant|ar *vt* put up with, bear; (sostener) support. ● *vi* hold out. □ **~arse** *vpr* restrain o.s. **~e** *m* patience; (resistencia) endurance

aguar [15] *vt* water down

aguardar *vt* wait for. ● *vi* wait

agua|rdiente *m* (cheap) brandy. **~rrás** *m* turpentine, turps 🔒

agud|eza *f* sharpness; (fig, perspicacia) insight; (fig, ingenio) wit. **~izar** [10] *vt* sharpen. □ **~izarse** *vpr* <enfermedad> get worse. **~o** *a* sharp; <ángulo, enfermedad> acute; <voz> high-pitched

agüero *m* omen. **ser de mal ~** be a bad omen

aguijón *m* sting; (vara) goad

águila *f* eagle; (persona perspicaz) astute person; (Mex, de moneda) heads. **¿~ o sol?** heads or tails?

aguileño *a* aquiline

aguinaldo *m* Christmas box; (LAm, paga) Christmas bonus

aguja *f* needle; (del reloj) hand; (Arquit) steeple. **~s** *fpl* (Rail) points

agujer|ear *vt* make holes in. **~o** *m* hole

agujetas *fpl* stiffness; (Mex, de zapatos) shoe laces. **tener ~** be stiff

aguzado *a* sharp

ah *int* ah!, oh!

ahí *adv* there. **~ nomás** (LAm) just there. **de ~ que** that is why. **por ~** that way; (aproximadamente) thereabouts

ahija|da *f* god-daughter, godchild. **~do** *m* godson, godchild. **~dos** *mpl* godchildren

ahínco *m* enthusiasm; (empeño) insistence

ahog|ado *a* (en el agua) drowned; (asfixiado) suffocated. **~ar** [12] *vt* (en el agua) drown; (asfixiar) suffocate; put out <fuego>. □ **~arse** *vpr* (en el agua) drown; (asfixiarse) suffocate. **~o** *m* breathlessness; (fig, angustia) distress

ahondar *vt* deepen. ● *vi* go deep. **~ en** (fig) examine in depth. □ **~se** *vpr* get deeper

ahora *adv* now; (hace muy poco) just now; (dentro de poco) very soon. **~ bien** however. **~ mismo** right now. **de ~ en adelante** from now on, in future. **por ~** for the time being

ahorcar [7] *vt* hang. □ **~se** *vpr* hang o.s.

ahorita *adv* (esp LAm 🔒) now. **~ mismo** right now

ahorr|ador *a* thrifty. **~ar** *vt* save. □ **~arse** *vpr* save o.s. **~o** *m* saving. **~os** *mpl* savings

ahuecar [7] *vt* hollow; fluff up <colchón>; deepen <la voz>

ahuizote *m* (Mex) scourge

ahuma|do *a* (Culin) smoked; (de colores) smoky. **~r** *vt* (Culin) smoke; (llenar de humo) fill with smoke. ● *vi* smoke. □ **~rse** *vpr* become smoky; <comida> acquire a smoky taste

ahuyentar *vt* drive away; banish <pensamientos etc>

aimará *a & m* Aymara. ● *m & f* Aymara indian

airado *a* annoyed

aire *m* air; (viento) breeze; (corriente) draught; (aspecto) appearance; (Mus) tune, air. **~ acondicionado** air-conditioning. **al ~ libre** outdoors. **darse ~s** give o.s. airs. **~ar** *vt* air; (ventilar) ventilate; (fig, publicar) make public. □ **~arse** *vpr*. **salir para ~arse** go out for some fresh air

airoso *a* graceful; (exitoso) successful

aisla|do *a* isolated; (Elec) insulated. **~dor** *a* (Elec) insulating. **~nte** *a* insulating. **~r** [23] *vt* isolate; (Elec) insulate

ajar *vt* crumple; (estropear) spoil

ajedre|cista *m & f* chess-player. **~z** *m* chess

ajeno *a* (de otro) someone else's; (de otros) other people's; (extraño) alien

ajetre|ado *a* hectic, busy. **~o** *m* bustle

ají *m* (LAm) chilli; (salsa) chilli sauce

aj|illo *m* garlic. **al ~illo** cooked with garlic. **~o** *m* garlic. **~onjolí** *m* sesame

ajuar *m* furnishings; (de novia) trousseau; (de bebé) layette

ajust|ado *a* right; <*vestido*> tight. **~ar** *vt* fit; (adaptar) adapt; (acordar) agree; settle <*una cuenta*>; (apretar) tighten. ● *vi* fit. □ **~arse** *vpr* fit; (adaptarse) adapt o.s.; (acordarse) come to an agreement. **~e** *m* fitting; (adaptación) adjustment; (acuerdo) agreement; (de una cuenta) settlement

al = **a** + **el**

ala *f* wing; (de sombrero) brim.● *m* & *f* (deportes) winger

alaba|nza *f* praise. **~r** *vt* praise

alacena *f* cupboard (Brit), closet (Amer)

alacrán *m* scorpion

alambr|ada *f* wire fence. **~ado** *m* (LAm) wire fence. **~e** *m* wire. **~e de púas** barbed wire

alameda *f* avenue; (plantío de álamos) poplar grove

álamo *m* poplar. **~ temblón** aspen

alarde *m* show. **hacer ~ de** boast of

alarga|do *a* long. **~dor** *m* extension. **~r** [12] *vt* lengthen; stretch out <*mano etc*>; (dar) give, pass. □ **~rse** *vpr* get longer

alarido *m* shriek

alarm|a *f* alarm. **~ante** *a* alarming. **~ar** *vt* alarm, frighten. □ **~arse** *vpr* be alarmed. **~ista** *m* & *f* alarmist

alba *f* dawn

albacea *m* & *f* executor

albahaca *f* basil

albanés *a* & *m* Albanian

Albania *f* Albania

albañil *m* builder; (que coloca ladrillos) bricklayer

albarán *m* delivery note

albaricoque *m* apricot. **~ro** *m* apricot tree

albedrío *m* will. **libre ~** free will

alberca *f* tank, reservoir; (Mex, piscina) swimming pool

alberg|ar [12] *vt* (alojar) put up; <*vivienda*> house; (dar refugio) shelter. □ **~arse** *vpr* stay; (refugiarse) shelter. **~ue** *m* accommodation; (refugio) shelter. **~ue de juventud** youth hostel

albino *a* & *m* albino

albóndiga *f* meatball, rissole

albornoz *m* bathrobe

alborot|ado *a* excited; (aturdido) hasty. **~ador** *a* rowdy. ● *m* troublemaker. **~ar** *vt* disturb, upset. ● *vi* make a racket. □ **~arse** *vpr* get excited; <*el mar*> get rough. **~o** *m* row, uproar

álbum *m* (*pl* **~es** *o* **~s**) album

alcachofa *f* artichoke

alcald|e *m* mayor. **~esa** *f* mayoress. **~ía** *f* mayoralty; (oficina) mayor's office

alcance *m* reach; (de arma, telescopio etc) range; (déficit) deficit

alcancía *f* money-box; (LAm, de niño) piggy bank

alcantarilla *f* sewer; (boca) drain

alcanzar [10] *vt* (llegar a) catch up; (coger) reach; catch <*un autobús*>; <*bala etc*> strike, hit. ● *vi* reach; (ser suficiente) be enough. **~ a** manage

alcaparra *f* caper

alcázar *m* fortress

alcoba *f* bedroom

alcoh|ol *m* alcohol. **~ol desnaturalizado** methylated spirits, meths **~ólico** *a* & *m* alcoholic. **~olímetro** *m* Breathalyser . **~olismo** *m* alcoholism

alcornoque *m* cork-oak; (persona torpe) idiot

aldaba *f* door-knocker

aldea *f* village. **~ano** *a* village. ● *m* villager

alea|ción *f* alloy. **~r** *vt* alloy

aleatorio *a* uncertain

aleccionar *vt* instruct

aledaños *mpl* outskirts

alega|ción *f* allegation; (LAm, disputa) argument. **~r** [12] *vt* claim; (Jurid) plead. ● *vi* (LAm) argue. **~ta** *f* (Mex) argument. **~to** *m* plea

alegoría *f* allegory

alegr|ar *vt* make happy; (avivar) brighten up. □ **~arse** *vpr* be happy; (emborracharse) get merry. **~e** *a* happy; (achispado) merry, tight. **~ía** *f* happiness

aleja|do *a* distant. **~amiento** *m* removal; (entre personas) estrangement; (distancia) distance. ~r *vt* remove; (ahuyentar) get rid of; (fig, apartar) separate. □ ~**rse** *vpr* move away

alemán *a* & *m* German

Alemania *f* Germany. ~ **Occidental** (historia) West Germany. ~ **Oriental** (historia) East Germany

alenta|dor *a* encouraging. ~**r** [1] *vt* encourage. ● *vi* breathe

alerce *m* larch

al|ergia *f* allergy. ~**érgico** *a* allergic

alero *m* (del tejado) eaves

alerta *a* alert. ¡~! look out! estar ~ be alert; (en guardia) be on the alert. ~**r** *vt* alert

aleta *f* wing; (de pez) fin

aletarga|do *a* lethargic. ~**r** [12] *vt* make lethargic. □ ~**rse** *vpr* become lethargic

alet|azo *m* (de un ave) flap of the wings; (de un pez) flick of the fin. ~**ear** *vi* flap its wings, flutter

alevosía *f* treachery

alfab|ético *a* alphabetical. ~**etizar** [10] *vt* alphabetize; teach to read and write. ~**eto** *m* alphabet. ~**eto Morse** Morse code

alfalfa *f* alfalfa

alfarería *f* pottery. ~**ero** *m* potter

alféizar *m* (window)sill

alférez *m* second lieutenant

alfil *m* (en ajedrez) bishop

alfile|r *m* pin. ~**tero** *m* pincushion; (estuche) pin-case

alfombr|a *f* (grande) carpet; (pequeña) rug, mat. ~**ado** *a* (LAm) carpeted. ~**ar** *vt* carpet. ~**illa** *f* rug, mat; (Med) type of measles

alforja *f* saddle-bag

algarabía *f* hubbub

algas *fpl* seaweed

álgebra *f* algebra

álgido *a* (fig) decisive

algo *pron* something; (en frases interrogativas, condicionales) anything. ● *adv* rather. ¿~ **más?** anything else? ¿quieres tomar ~? would you like a drink?; (de comer) would you like something to eat?

algod|ón *m* cotton. ~**ón de azúcar** candy floss (Brit), cotton candy (Amer).

~**ón hidrófilo** cotton wool. ~**onero** *a* cotton. ● *m* cotton plant

alguacil *m* bailiff

alguien *pron* someone, somebody; (en frases interrogativas, condicionales) anyone, anybody

alguno *a* (delante de nombres masculinos en singular **algún**) some; (en frases interrogativas, condicionales) any; (pospuesto al nombre en frases negativas) at all. **no tiene idea alguna** he hasn't any idea at all. **alguna que otra vez** from time to time. **algunas veces, alguna vez** sometimes. ● *pron* one; (en plural) some; (alguien) someone

alhaja *f* piece of jewellery; (fig) treasure. ~**s** *fpl* jewellery

alharaca *f* fuss

alhelí *m* wallflower

alia|do *a* allied. ● *m* ally. ~**nza** *f* alliance; (anillo) wedding ring. ~**r** [20] *vt* combine. □ ~**rse** *vpr* be combined; (formar una alianza) form an alliance

alias *adv* & *m* alias

alicaído *a* (fig, débil) weak; (fig, abatido) depressed

alicates *mpl* pliers

aliciente *m* incentive; (de un lugar) attraction

alienado *a* mentally ill

aliento *m* breath; (ánimo) courage

aligerar *vt* make lighter; (aliviar) alleviate, ease; (apresurar) quicken

alijo *m* (de contrabando) consignment

alimaña *f* pest. ~**s** *fpl* vermin

aliment|ación *f* diet; (acción) feeding. ~**ar** *vt* feed; (nutrir) nourish. ● *vi* be nourishing. □ ~**arse** *vpr* feed (con, de on). ~**icio** *a* nourishing. **productos** *mpl* ~**icios** foodstuffs. ~**o** *m* food. ~**os** *mpl* (Jurid) alimony

alinea|ción *f* alignment; (en deportes) line-up. ~**r** *vt* align, line up

aliñ|ar *vt* (Culin) season; dress <*ensalada*>. ~**o** *m* seasoning; (para ensalada) dressing

alioli *m* garlic mayonnaise

alisar *vt* smooth

alistar *vt* put on a list; (Mil) enlist. □ ~**se** *vpr* enrol; (Mil) enlist; (LAm, prepararse) get ready

alivi|ar *vt* lighten; relieve *<dolor, etc>*; (🅧, hurtar) steal, pinch 🅣. □ **~arse** *vpr* *<dolor>* diminish; *<persona>* get better. **~o** *m* relief

aljibe *m* tank

allá *adv* (over) there. ¡**~** él! that's his business. **~ fuera** out there. **~ por 1970** back in 1970. **el más ~** the beyond. **más ~** further on. **más ~ de** beyond. **por ~** that way

allana|miento *m.* **~miento** (de morada) breaking and entering; (LAm, por la autoridad) raid. **~r** *vt* level; remove *<obstáculos>*; (fig) iron out *<dificultades etc>*; break into *<una casa>*; (LAm, por la autoridad) raid

allega|do *a* close. ● *m* close friend; (pariente) close relative. **~r** [12] *vt* collect

allí *adv* there; (tiempo) then. **~ fuera** out there. **por ~** that way

alma *f* soul; (habitante) inhabitant

almac|én *m* warehouse; (LAm, tienda) grocer's shop; (de un arma) magazine. **~enes** *mpl* department store. **~enaje** *m* storage; (derechos) storage charges. **~enar** *vt* store; stock up with *<provisiones>*

almanaque *m* almanac

almeja *f* clam

almendr|a *f* almond. **~ado** *a* almond-shaped. **~o** *m* almond tree

alm|íbar *m* syrup. **~ibarar** *vt* cover in syrup

almid|ón *m* starch. **~onado** *a* starched; (fig, estirado) starchy

almirante *m* admiral

almizcle *m* musk. **~ra** *f* muskrat

almohad|a *f* pillow. **consultar con la ~a** sleep on it. **~illa** *f* small cushion. **~ón** *m* large pillow, bolster

almorranas *fpl* haemorrhoids, piles

alm|orzar [2 & 10] *vt* (a mediodía) have for lunch; (desayunar) have for breakfast. ● *vi* (a mediodía) have lunch; (desayunar) have breakfast. **~uerzo** *m* (a mediodía) lunch; (desayuno) breakfast

alocado *a* scatter-brained

aloja|miento *m* accommodation. **~r** *vt* put up. □ **~rse** *vpr* stay

alondra *f* lark

alpaca *f* alpaca

alpargata *f* canvas shoe, espadrille

alpin|ismo *m* mountaineering, climbing. **~ista** *m & f* mountaineer, climber. **~o** *a* Alpine

alpiste *m* birdseed

alquil|ar *vt* (tomar en alquiler) hire *<vehículo>*, rent *<piso, casa>*; (dar en alquiler) hire (out) *<vehículo>*, rent (out) *<piso, casa>*. **se alquila** to let (Brit), for rent (Amer.) **~er** *m* (acción — de alquilar un piso etc) renting; (— de alquilar un vehículo) hiring; (precio — por el que se alquila un piso etc) rent; (— por el que se alquila un vehículo) hire charge. **de ~er** for hire

alquimi|a *f* alchemy. **~sta** *m* alchemist

alquitrán *m* tar

alrededor *adv* around. **~ de** around; (con números) about. **~es** *mpl* surroundings; (de una ciudad) outskirts

alta *f* discharge

altaner|ía *f* (arrogancia) arrogance. **~o** *a* arrogant, haughty

altar *m* altar

altavoz *m* loudspeaker

altera|ble *a* changeable. **~ción** *f* change, alteration. **~r** *vt* change, alter; (perturbar) disturb; (enfadar) anger, irritate. □ **~rse** *vpr* change, alter; (agitarse) get upset; (enfadarse) get angry; *<comida>* go off

altercado *m* argument

altern|ar *vt/i* alternate. □ **~arse** *vpr* take turns. **~ativa** *f* alternative. **~ativo** *a* alternating. **~o** *a* alternate; (Elec) alternating

Alteza *f* (título) Highness

altibajos *mpl* (de terreno) unevenness; (fig) ups and downs

altiplanicie *f*, **altiplano** *m* high plateau

altisonante *a* pompous

altitud *f* altitude

altiv|ez *f* arrogance. **~o** *a* arrogant

alto *a* high; *<persona, edificio>* tall; *<voz>* loud; (fig, elevado) lofty; (Mus) *<nota>* high(-pitched); (Mus) *<voz, instrumento>* alto; *<horas>* early. ● *adv* high; (de sonidos) loud(ly). ● *m* height; (de un edificio) top floor; (viola)

viola; (voz) alto; (parada) stop. ● *int*
halt!, stop! **en lo ~ de** on the top of.
tiene 3 metros de ~ it is 3 metres
high

altoparlante *m* (esp LAm) loudspeaker

altruis|mo *m* altruism. **~ta** *a* al-
truistic. ● *m & f* altruist

altura *f* height; (Aviac, Geog) altitude;
(de agua) depth; (fig, cielo) sky. **a estas
~s** at this stage. **tiene 3 metros de ~**
it is 3 metres high

alubia *f* (haricot) bean

alucinación *f* hallucination

alud *m* avalanche

aludi|do *a* in question. **darse por
~do** take it personally. **no darse por
~do** turn a deaf ear. **~r** *vi* mention

alumbra|do *a* lit. ● *m* lighting.
~miento *m* lighting; (parto) child-
birth. **~r** *vt* light

aluminio *m* aluminium (Brit), alumi-
num (Amer)

alumno *m* pupil; (Univ) student

aluniza|je *m* landing on the moon.
~r [10] *vi* land on the moon

alusi|ón *f* allusion. **~vo** *a* allusive

alza *f* rise. **~da** *f* (de caballo) height;
(Jurid) appeal. **~do** *a* raised; (Mex, so-
berbio) vain; *<precio>* fixed. **~mien-
to** *m* (Pol) uprising. **~r** [10] *vt* raise,
lift (up); raise *<precios>*. □ **~rse** *vpr*
(Pol) rise up

ama *f* lady of the house. **~ de casa**
housewife. **~ de cría** wet-nurse. **~
de llaves** housekeeper

amab|ilidad *f* kindness. **~le** *a*
kind; (simpático) nice

amaestra|do *a* trained. **~r** *vt*
train

amag|ar [12] *vt* (mostrar intención de)
make as if to; (Mex, amenazar) threat-
en. ● *vi* threaten; *<algo bueno>* be in
the offing. **~o** *m* threat; (señal) sign;
(Med) symptom

amainar *vi* let up

amalgama *f* amalgam. **~r** *vt* amalgamate

amamantar *vt/i* breast-feed; *<ani-
mal>* to suckle

amanecer *m* dawn. ● *vi* dawn;
<persona> wake up. **al ~** at dawn, at

daybreak. □ **~se** *vpr* (Mex) stay up
all night

amanera|do *a* affected. □ **~rse**
vpr become affected

amansar *vt* tame; break in *<un ca-
ballo>*; soothe *<dolor etc>*. □ **~se** *vpr*
calm down

amante *a* fond. ● *m & f* lover

amapola *f* poppy

amar *vt* love

amara|je *m* landing on water; (de
astronave) splash-down. **~r** *vi* land on
water; *<astronave>* splash down

amarg|ado *a* embittered. **~ar** [12]
vt make bitter; embitter *<persona>*.
□ **~arse** *vpr* become bitter. **~o** *a*
bitter. **~ura** *f* bitterness

amariconado *a* 🅣 effeminate

amarill|ento *a* yellowish; *<tez>* sal-
low. **~o** *a & m* yellow

amarra|s *fpl.* **soltar las ~s** cast off.
~do *a* (LAm) mean. **~r** *vt* moor; (esp
LAm, atar) tie. □ **~rse** *vpr* LAm tie up

amas|ar *vt* knead; (acumular) to
amass. **~ijo** *m* dough; (acción) knead-
ing; (fig, 🅣, mezcla) hotchpotch

amate *m* (Mex) fig tree

amateur *a & m & f* amateur

amazona *f* Amazon; (jinete) horse-
woman

ámbar *m* amber

ambici|ón *f* ambition. **~onar** *vt* as-
pire to. **~onar ser** have an ambition
to be. **~oso** *a* ambitious. ● *m* ambitious person

ambidextro *a* ambidextrous. ● *m*
ambidextrous person

ambient|ar *vt* give an atmosphere
to. □ **~arse** *vpr* adapt o.s. **~e** *m* atmosphere; (entorno) environment

ambig|üedad *f* ambiguity. **~uo** *a*
ambiguous

ámbito *m* sphere; (alcance) scope

ambos *a & pron* both

ambulancia *f* ambulance

ambulante *a* travelling

ambulatorio *m* out-patients' department

amedrentar *vt* frighten, scare.
□ **~se** *vpr* be frightened

amén *m* amen. ● *int* amen! **en un decir ~** in an instant

amenaza *f* threat. ~**r** [10] *vt* threaten

amen|idad *f* pleasantness. ~**izar** [10] *vt* brighten up. ~**o** *a* pleasant

América *f* America. ~ Central Central America. ~ **del Norte** North America. ~ **del Sur** South America. ~ **Latina** Latin America

american|a *f* jacket. ~**ismo** *m* Americanism. ~**o** *a* American

amerita|do *a* (LAm) meritorious. ~**r** *vt* (LAm) deserve

amerizaje *m* ⇒AMARAJE

ametralla|dora *f* machine-gun. ~**r** *vt* machine-gun

amianto *m* asbestos

amig|a *f* friend; (novia) girl-friend; (amante) lover. ~**able** *a* friendly. ~**ablemente** *adv* amicably

am|ígdala *f* tonsil. ~**igdalitis** *f* tonsillitis

amigo *a* friendly. ● *m* friend; (novio) boyfriend; (amante) lover. **ser** ~ **de** be fond of. **ser muy** ~**s** be close friends

amilanar *vt* daunt. □ ~**se** *vpr* be daunted

aminorar *vt* lessen; reduce <*velocidad*>

amist|ad *f* friendship. ~**ades** *fpl* friends. ~**oso** *a* friendly

amn|esia *f* amnesia. ~**ésico** *a* amnesiac

amnist|ía *f* amnesty. ~**iar** [20] *vt* grant an amnesty to

amo *m* master; (dueño) owner

amodorrarse *vpr* feel sleepy

amoldar *vt* mould; (adaptar) adapt; (acomodar) fit. □ ~**se** *vpr* adapt

amonestar *vt* rebuke, reprimand; (anunciar la boda) publish the banns

amoniaco, **amoníaco** *m* ammonia

amontonar *vt* pile up; (fig, acumular) accumulate. □ ~**se** *vpr* pile up; <*gente*> crowd together

amor *m* love. ~**es** *mpl* (relaciones amorosas) love affairs. ~ **propio** pride. **con mil** ~**es, de mil** ~**es** with (the greatest of) pleasure. **hacer el** ~ make love. **por (el)** ~ **de Dios** for God's sake

amoratado *a* purple; (de frío) blue

amordazar [10] *vt* gag; (fig) silence

amorfo *a* amorphous, shapeless

amor|ío *m* affair. ~**oso** *a* loving; <*cartas*> love; (LAm), encantador) cute

amortajar *vt* shroud

amortigua|dor *a* deadening. ● *m* (Auto) shock absorber. ~**r** [15] *vt* deaden <*ruido*>; dim <*luz*>; cushion <*golpe*>; tone down <*color*>

amortiza|ble *a* redeemable. ~**ción** *f* (de una deuda) repayment; (de bono etc) redemption. ~**r** [10] *vt* repay <*una deuda*>

amotinar *vt* incite to riot. □ ~**se** *vpr* rebel; (Mil) mutiny

ampar|ar *vt* help; (proteger) protect. □ ~**arse** *vpr* seek protection; (de la lluvia) shelter. ~**o** *m* protection; (de la lluvia) shelter. **al** ~**o de** under the protection of

amperio *m* ampere, amp

amplia|ción *f* extension; (photo) enlargement. ~**r** [20] *vt* enlarge, extend; (photo) enlarge

amplifica|ción *f* amplification. ~**dor** *m* amplifier. ~**r** [7] amplify

ampli|o *a* wide; (espacioso) spacious; <*ropa*> loose-fitting. ~**tud** *f* extent; (espaciosidad) spaciousness; (espacio) space

ampolla *f* (Med) blister; (de medicamento) ampoule, phial

ampuloso *a* pompous

amputar *vt* amputate; (fig) delete

amueblar *vt* furnish

amuleto *m* charm, amulet

amuralla|do *a* walled. ~**r** *vt* build a wall around

anacr|ónico *a* anachronistic. ~**onismo** *m* anachronism

anales *mpl* annals

analfabet|ismo *m* illiteracy. ~**o** *a & m* illiterate

analgésico *a* analgesic. ● *m* pain-killer

an|álisis *m invar* analysis. ~**álisis de sangre** blood test. ~**alista** *m & f* analyst. ~**alítico** *a* analytical. ~**alizar** [10] *vt* analyze

an|alogía *f* analogy. ~**álogo** *a* analogous

anaranjado *a* orangey

an|arquía f anarchy. **~árquico** a anarchic. **~arquismo** m anarchism. **~arquista** a anarchistic. ● m & f anarchist

anat|omía f anatomy. **~ómico** a anatomical

anca f haunch; (parte superior) rump; (▣, nalgas) bottom. **en ~s** (LAm) on the crupper

ancestro m ancestor

ancho a wide; <ropa> loose-fitting; (fig) relieved; (demasiado grande) too big; (ufano) smug. ● m width; (Rail) gauge. **a mis anchas, a sus anchas** etc comfortable, relaxed. **tiene 3 metros de ~** it is 3 metres wide

anchoa f anchovy

anchura f width; (medida) measurement

ancian|o a elderly, old. ● m elderly man, old man. **~a** f elderly woman, old woman. **los ~os** old people

ancla f anchor. **echar ~s** drop anchor. **levar ~s** weigh anchor. **~r** vi anchor

andad|eras fpl (Mex) baby-walker. **~or** m baby-walker

Andalucía f Andalusia

andaluz a & m Andalusian

andamio m platform. **~s** mpl scaffolding

and|anzas fpl adventures. **~ar** [25] vt (recorrer) cover, go. ● vi walk; <máquina> go, work; (estar) be; (moverse) move. **~ar a caballo** (LAm) ride a horse. **~ar en bicicleta** (LAm) ride a bicycle. **¡anda!** go on!, come on! **~ar por** be about. □ **~arse** vpr (LAm, en imperativo) **¡ándate!** go away!. ● m walk. **~ariego** a fond of walking

andén m platform

Andes mpl. **los ~** the Andes

andin|o a Andean. **~ismo** m (LAm) mountaineering, climbing. **~ista** m & f (LAm) mountaineer, climber

andrajo m rag. **~so** a ragged

anduve vb ⇒ANDAR

anécdota f anecdote

anecdótico a anecdotal

anegar [12] vt flood. □ **~rse** vpr be flooded, flood

anejo a ⇒ANEXO

an|emia f anaemia. **~émico** a anaemic

anest|esia f anaesthesia; (droga) anaesthetic. **~esiar** vt anaesthetize. **~ésico** a & m anaesthetic. **~esista** m & f anaesthetist

anex|ar vt annex. **~o** a attached. ● m annexe

anfibio a amphibious. ● m amphibian

anfiteatro m amphitheatre; (en un teatro) upper circle

anfitri|ón m host. **~ona** f hostess

ángel m angel; (encanto) charm

angelical a, **angélico** a angelic

anglna f. **~ de pecho** angina (pectoris). **tener ~s** have tonsillitis

anglicano a & m Anglican

angl|icismo m Anglicism. **~ófilo** a & m Anglophile. **~ohispánico** a Anglo-Spanish. **~osajón** a & m Anglo-Saxon

angosto a narrow

angu|ila f eel. **~la** f elver, baby eel

ángulo m angle; (rincón, esquina) corner; (curva) bend

angusti|a f anguish. **~ar** vt distress; (inquietar) worry. □ **~arse** vpr get distressed; (inquietarse) get worried. **~oso** a anguished; (que causa angustia) distressing

anhel|ar vt (+ nombre) long for; (+ verbo) long to. **~o** m (fig) yearning

anidar vi nest

anill|a f ring. **~o** m ring. **~o de boda** wedding ring

ánima f soul

anima|ción f (de personas) life; (de cosas) liveliness; (bullicio) bustle; (en el cine) animation. **~do** a lively; <sitio etc> busy. **~dor** m host. **~dora** f hostess; (de un equipo) cheerleader

animadversión f ill will

animal a animal; (fig, ▣, torpe) stupid. ● m animal; (fig, ▣, idiota) idiot; (fig, ▣, bruto) brute

animar vt give life to; (dar ánimo) encourage; (dar vivacidad) liven up. □ **~se** vpr (decidirse) decide; (ponerse alegre) cheer up. **¿te animas a ir al cine?** do you feel like going to the cinema?

ánimo *m* soul; (mente) mind; (valor) courage; (intención) intention. ¡~! come on!, cheer up! **dar ~s** encourage

animos|idad *f* animosity. **~o** *a* brave; (resuelto) determined

aniquilar *vt* annihilate; (acabar con) ruin

anís *m* aniseed; (licor) anisette

aniversario *m* anniversary

anoche *adv* last night, yesterday evening

anochecer [11] *vi* get dark. **anochecí en Madrid** I was in Madrid at dusk. ● *m* nightfall, dusk. **al ~** at nightfall

anodino *a* bland

an|omalía *f* anomaly. **~ómalo** *a* anomalous

an|onimato *m* anonymity. **~ónimo** *a* anonymous; <sociedad> limited. ● *m* (carta) anonymous letter

anormal *a* abnormal. ● *m* & *f* 🄸 idiot. **~idad** *f* abnormality

anota|ción *f* (nota) note; (acción de poner notas) annotation. **~r** *vt* (poner nota) annotate; (apuntar) make a note of; (LAm) score <un gol>

anquilosa|miento *m* (fig) paralysis. □ **~rse** *vpr* become paralyzed

ansi|a *f* anxiety, worry; (anhelo) yearning. **~ar** [20] *vt* long for. **~edad** *f* anxiety. **~oso** *a* anxious; (deseoso) eager

antag|ónico *a* antagonistic. **~onismo** *m* antagonism. **~onista** *m* & *f* antagonist

antaño *adv* in days gone by

antártico *a* & *m* Antarctic

ante *prep* in front of, before; (frente a) in the face of; (en vista de) in view of. ● *m* elk; (piel) suede. **~anoche** *adv* the night before last. **~ayer** *adv* the day before yesterday. **~brazo** *m* forearm

antece|dente *a* previous. ● *m* antecedent. **~dentes** *mpl* history, background. **~dentes penales** criminal record. **~der** *vt* precede. **~sor** *m* predecessor; (antepasado) ancestor

antelación *f* (advance) notice. **con ~** in advance

antemano *adv*. **de ~** beforehand

antena *f* antenna; (radio, TV) aerial

antenoche *adv* (LAm) the night before last

anteoj|eras *fpl* blinkers. **~jo** *m* telescope. **~os** *mpl* binoculars; (LAm, gafas) glasses, spectacles. **~os de sol** sunglasses

ante|pasados *mpl* forebears, ancestors. **~poner** [34] *vt* put in front (a of); (fig) put before, prefer. **~proyecto** *m* preliminary sketch; (fig) blueprint

anterior *a* previous; (delantero) front. **~idad** *f*. **con ~idad** previously. **con ~idad a** prior to

antes *adv* before; (antiguamente) in the past; (mejor) rather; (primero) first. **~ de** before. **~ de ayer** the day before yesterday. **~ de que +** *subj* before. **~ de que llegue** before he arrives. **~ cuanto ~, lo ~ posible** as soon as possible

anti|aéreo *a* anti-aircraft. **~biótico** *a* & *m* antibiotic. **~ciclón** *m* anticyclone

anticip|ación *f*. **con ~ación** in advance. **con media hora de ~ación** half an hour early. **~ado** *a* advance. **por ~ado** in advance. **~ar** *vt* bring forward; advance <dinero>. □ **~arse** *vpr* be early. **~o** *m* (dinero) advance; (fig) foretaste

anti|conceptivo *a* & *m* contraceptive. **~congelante** *m* antifreeze

anticua|do *a* old-fashioned. **~rio** *m* antique dealer

anticuerpo *m* antibody

antídoto *m* antidote

anti|estético *a* ugly. **~faz** *m* mask

antig|ualla *f* old relic. **~uamente** *adv* formerly; (hace mucho tiempo) long ago. **~üedad** *f* antiquity; (objeto) antique; (en un empleo) length of service. **~uo** *a* old; <ruinas> ancient; <mueble> antique

Antillas *fpl*. **las ~** the West Indies

antílope *m* antelope

antinatural *a* unnatural

antip|atía *f* dislike; (cualidad de antipático) unpleasantness. **~ático** *a* unpleasant, unfriendly

anti|semita *m & f* anti-Semite. ~**séptico** *a & m* antiseptic. ~**social** *a* antisocial

antítesis *f invar* antithesis

antoj|adizo *a* capricious. □ ~**arse** *vpr* fancy. **se le** ~**a un caramelo** he fancies a sweet. ~**itos** *mpl* (Mex) snacks bought at street stands. ~**o** *m* whim; (de embarazada) craving

antología *f* anthology

antorcha *f* torch

antro *m* (fig) dump, hole. ~ **de perversión** den of iniquity

antrop|ología *f* anthropology. ~**ólogo** *m* anthropologist

anua|l *a* annual. ~**lidad** *f* annuity. ~**lmente** *adv* yearly. ~**rio** *m* yearbook

anudar *vt* tie, knot. □ ~**se** *vpr* tie

anula|ción *f* annulment, cancellation. ~**r** *vt* annul, cancel. ● *a* <*dedo*> ring. ● *m* ring finger

anunci|ante *m & f* advertiser. ~**ar** *vt* announce; advertise <*producto comercial*>; (presagiar) be a sign of. ~**o** *m* announcement; (para vender algo) advertisement, advert 🄴; (cartel) poster

anzuelo *m* (fish)hook; (fig) bait. **tragar el** ~ swallow the bait

añadi|dura *f* addition. **por** ~**dura** in addition. ~**r** *vt* add

añejo *a* <*vino*> mature

añicos *mpl.* **hacer(se)** ~ smash to pieces

año *m* year. ~ **bisiesto** leap year. ~ **nuevo** new year. **al** ~ per year, a year. **¿cuántos** ~**s tiene?** how old is he? **tiene 5** ~**s** he's 5 (years old). **el** ~ **pasado** last year. **el** ~ **que viene** next year. **entrado en** ~**s** elderly. **los** ~**s 60** the sixties

añora|nza *f* nostalgia. ~**r** *vt* miss

apabulla|nte *a* overwhelming. ~**r** *vt* overwhelm

apacible *a* gentle; <*clima*> mild

apaciguar [15] *vt* pacify; (calmar) calm; relieve <*dolor etc*>. □ ~**se** *vpr* calm down

apadrinar *vt* sponsor; be godfather to <*a un niño*>

apag|ado *a* extinguished; <*color*> dull; <*aparato eléctrico, luz*> off;

<*persona*> lifeless; <*sonido*> muffled. ~**ar** [12] *vt* put out <*fuego, incendio*>; turn off, switch off <*aparato eléctrico, luz*>; quench <*sed*>; muffle <*sonido*>. □ ~**arse** *vpr* <*fuego, luz*> go out; <*sonido*> die away. ~**ón** *m* blackout

apalabrar *vt* make a verbal agreement; (contratar) engage

apalear *vt* winnow <*grano*>; beat <*alfombra, frutos, persona*>

apantallar *vt* (Mex) impress

apañar *vt* (arreglar) fix; (remendar) mend; (agarrar) grasp, take hold of. □ ~**se** *vpr* get along, manage

apapachar *vt* (Mex) cuddle

aparador *m* sideboard; (Mex, de tienda) shop window

aparato *m* apparatus; (máquina) machine; (doméstico) appliance; (teléfono) telephone; (radio, TV) set; (ostentación) show, pomp. ~**so** *a* showy, ostentatious; <*caída*> spectacular

aparca|miento *m* car park (Brit), parking lot (Amer). ~**r** [7] *vt/i* park

aparear *vt* mate <*animales*>. □ ~**se** *vpr* mate

aparecer [11] *vi* appear. □ ~**se** *vpr* appear

aparej|ado *a.* **llevar** ~**ado, traer** ~**ado** mean, entail. ~**o** *m* (avíos) equipment; (de caballo) tack; (de pesca) tackle

aparent|ar *vt* (afectar) feign; (parecer) look. ● *vi* show off. ~**a 20 años** she looks like she's 20. ~**e** *a* apparent

apari|ción *f* appearance; (visión) apparition. ~**encia** *f* appearance; (fig) show. **guardar las** ~**encias** keep up appearances

apartado *a* separated; (aislado) isolated. ● *m* (de un texto) section. ~ **(de correos)** post-office box, PO box

apartamento *m* apartment, flat (Brit)

apart|ar *vt* separate; (alejar) move away; (quitar) remove; (guardar) set aside. □ ~**arse** *vpr* leave; (quitarse de en medio) get out of the way; (aislarse) cut o.s. off. ~**e** *adv* apart; (por separado) separately; (además) besides. ● *m* aside; (párrafo) new paragraph. ~**e de**

apart from. **dejar** ~e leave aside. **eso** ~e apart from that

apasiona|do *a* passionate; (entusiasta) enthusiastic; (falto de objetividad) biased. ● *m*. ~do de lover. ~**miento** *m* passion. ~**r** *vt* excite. □ ~**rse** *vpr* be mad (**por** about); (ser parcial) become biased

ap|atía *f* apathy. ~**ático** *a* apathetic

apea|dero *m* (Rail) halt. □ ~**rse** *vpr* get off

apechugar [12] *vi* Ⓣ ~ **con** put up with

apedrear *vt* stone

apeg|ado *a* attached (**a** to). ~**o** *m* Ⓣ attachment. **tener** ~**o a** be fond of

apela|ción *f* appeal. ~**r** *vi* appeal; (recurrir) resort (**a** to). ● *vt* (apodar) call. ~**tivo** *m* (nick)name

apellid|ar *vt* call. □ ~**arse** *vpr* be called. **¿cómo te apellidas?** what's your surname? ~**o** *m* surname

apelmazarse *vpr* <*lana*> get matted

apenar *vt* sadden; (LAm, avergonzar) embarrass. □ ~**se** *vpr* be sad; (LAm, avergonzarse) be embarrassed

apenas *adv* hardly, scarcely; (Mex, sólo) only. ● *conj* (esp LAm, en cuanto) as soon as. ~ **si** Ⓣ hardly

ap|éndice *m* appendix. ~**endicitis** *f* appendicitis

apergaminado *a* <*piel*> wrinkled

aperitivo *m* (bebida) aperitif; (comida) appetizer

aperos *mpl* implements; (de labranza) agricultural equipment; (LAm, de un caballo) tack

apertura *f* opening

apesadumbrar *vt* upset. □ ~**se** *vpr* sadden

apestar *vt* infect. ● *vi* stink (**a** of)

apet|ecer [11] *vi*. **¿te** ~**ece una copa?** do you fancy a drink? do you feel like a drink?. **no me** ~**ece** I don't feel like it. ~**ecible** *a* attractive. ~**ito** *m* appetite; (fig) desire. ~**itoso** *a* appetizing

apiadarse *vpr* feel sorry (**de** for)

ápice *m* (nada, en frases negativas) anything. **no ceder un** ~ not give an inch

apilar *vt* pile up

apiñar *vt* pack in. □ ~**se** *vpr* <*personas*> crowd together; <*cosas*> be packed tight

apio *m* celery

aplacar [7] *vt* placate; soothe <*dolor*>

aplanar *vt* level. ~ **calles** (LAm Ⓣ) loaf around

aplasta|nte *a* overwhelming. ~**r** *vt* crush. □ ~**rse** *vpr* flatten o.s.

aplau|dir *vt* clap, applaud; (fig) applaud. ~**so** *m* applause; (fig) praise

aplaza|miento *m* postponement. ~**r** [10] *vt* postpone; defer <*pago*>

aplica|ble *a* applicable. ~**ción** *f* application. ~**do** *a* <*persona*> diligent. ~**r** [7] *vt* apply. ● *vi* (LAm, a un puesto) apply (for). □ ~**rse** *vpr* apply o.s.

aplom|ado *a* composed. ~**o** *m* composure

apocado *a* timid

apocar [7] *vt* belittle <*persona*>. □ ~**se** *vpr* feel small

apodar *vt* nickname

apodera|do *m* representative. □ ~**rse** *vpr* seize

apodo *m* nickname

apogeo *m* (fig) height

apolilla|do *a* moth-eaten. □ ~**rse** *vpr* get moth-eaten

apolítico *a* non-political

apología *f* defence

apoltronarse *vpr* settle o.s. down

apoplejía *f* stroke

aporrear *vt* hit, thump; beat up <*persona*>

aport|ación *f* contribution. ~**ar** *vt* contribute. ~**e** *m* (LAm) contribution

aposta *adv* on purpose

apostar[1] [2] *vt/i* bet

apostar[2] *vt* station. □ ~**se** *vpr* station o.s.

apóstol *m* apostle

apóstrofo *m* apostrophe

apoy|ar *vt* lean (**en** against); (descansar) rest; (asentar) base; (reforzar) support. □ ~**arse** *vpr* lean, rest. ~**o** *m* support

apreci|able *a* appreciable; (digno de estima) worthy. ~**ación** *f* appreci-

ation; (valoración) appraisal. ~**ar** *vt*
value; (estimar) appreciate. ~**o** *m* appraisal; (fig) esteem

apremi|ante *a* urgent, pressing.
~**ar** *vt* urge; (obligar) compel; (dar prisa
a) hurry up. ● *vi* be urgent. ~**o** *m*
urgency; (obligación) obligation

aprender *vt/i* learn. □ ~**se** *vpr*
learn

aprendiz *m* apprentice. ~**aje** *m*
learning; (período) apprenticeship

aprensi|ón *f* apprehension; (miedo)
fear. ~**vo** *a* apprehensive, fearful

apresar *vt* seize; (capturar) capture

aprestar *vt* prepare. □ ~**se** *vpr*
prepare

apresura|do *a* in a hurry; (hecho
con prisa) hurried. ~**r** *vt* hurry.
□ ~**rse** *vpr* hurry up

apret|ado *a* tight; (difícil) difficult;
(tacaño) stingy, mean. ~**ar** [1] *vt*
tighten; press <*botón*>; squeeze
<*persona*>; (comprimir) press down. ●
vi be too tight. □ ~**arse** *vpr* crowd
together. ~**ón** *m* squeeze. ~**ón de
manos** handshake

aprieto *m* difficulty. **verse en un** ~
be in a tight spot

aprisa *adv* quickly

aprisionar *vt* trap

aproba|ción *f* approval. ~**r** [2] *vt*
approve (of); pass <*examen*>. ● *vi*
pass

apropia|ción *f* appropriation.
~**do** *a* appropriate. ~**rse** *vpr*. ~**rse
de** appropriate, take

aprovecha|ble *a* usable. ~**do** *a*
(aplicado) diligent; (ingenioso) resource-
ful; (oportunista) opportunist. **bien**
~**do** well spent. ~**miento** *m* advantage; (uso) use. ~**r** *vt* take advantage
of; (utilizar) make use of. ● *vi* make
the most of it. **¡que aproveche!** enjoy
your meal! □ ~**rse** *vpr*. ~**rse de**
take advantage of

aprovisionar *vt* provision (con, de
with). □ ~**se** *vpr* stock up

aproxima|ción *f* approximation;
(proximidad) closeness; (en la lotería)
consolation prize. ~**damente** *adv*
roughly, approximately. ~**do** *a* approximate, rough. ~**r** *vt* bring near;

(fig) bring together <*personas*>.
□ ~**rse** *vpr* come closer, approach

apt|itud *f* suitability; (capacidad) abil-
ity. ~**o** *a* (capaz) capable; (adecuado)
suitable

apuesta *f* bet

apuesto *m* handsome. ● *vb* ⇒APOS-
TAR [1]

apuntalar *vt* shore up

apunt|ar *vt* aim <*arma*>; (señalar)
point at; (anotar) make a note of, note
down; (inscribir) enrol; (en el teatro)
prompt. ● *vi* (con un arma) to aim (**a**
at). □ ~**arse** *vpr* put one's name
down; score <*triunfo, tanto etc*>. ~**e**
m note; (bosquejo) sketch. **tomar** ~**s**
take notes

apuñalar *vt* stab

apur|ado *a* difficult; (sin dinero) hard
up; (LAm, con prisa) in a hurry. ~**ar** *vt*
(acabar) finish; drain <*vaso etc*>; (causar vergüenza) embarrass; (LAm, apresurar) hurry. □ ~**arse** *vpr* worry; (LAm,
apresurarse) hurry up. ~**o** *m* tight
spot, difficult situation; (vergüenza)
embarrassment; (estrechez) hardship,
want; (LAm, prisa) hurry

aquejar *vt* afflict

aquel *a* (*f* **aquella**, *mpl* **aquellos**,
fpl **aquellas**) that; (en plural) those

aquél *pron* (*f* **aquélla**, *mpl* **aquéllos**, *fpl* **aquéllas**) that one; (en plural) those

aquello *pron* that; (asunto) that business

aquí *adv* here. **de** ~ from here. **de** ~
a 15 días in a fortnight's time. ~
mismo right here. **de** ~ **para allá** to
and fro. **de** ~ **que** that is why. **hasta**
~ until now. **por** ~ around here

aquietar *vt* calm (down)

árabe *a* & *m* & *f* Arab; (lengua) Arab-
ic

Arabia *f* Arabia. ~ **Saudita**, ~ **Saudí**
Saudi Arabia

arado *m* plough. ~**r** *m* ploughman

arancel *m* tariff; (impuesto) duty.
~**ario** *a* tariff

arandela *f* washer

araña *f* spider; (lámpara) chandelier.
~**r** *vt* scratch

arar *vt* plough

arbitra|je *m* arbitration; (en deportes) refereeing. **~r** *vt/i* arbitrate; (en fútbol etc) referee; (en tenis etc) umpire

arbitr|ariedad *f* arbitrariness. **~ario** *a* arbitrary. **~io** *m* (free) will

árbitro *m* arbitrator; (en fútbol etc) referee; (en tenis etc) umpire

árbol *m* tree; (eje) axle; (palo) mast. **~ genealógico** family tree. **~ de Navidad** Christmas tree

arbol|ado *m* trees. **~eda** *f* wood

arbusto *m* bush

arca *f* (caja) chest. **~ de Noé** Noah's ark

arcada *f* arcade; (de un puente) arch; (náuseas) retching

arcaico *a* archaic

arce *m* maple (tree)

arcén *m* (de autopista) hard shoulder; (de carretera) verge

archipiélago *m* archipelago

archiv|ador *m* filing cabinet. **~ar** *vt* file (away). **~o** *m* file; (de documentos históricos) archives

arcilla *f* clay

arco *m* arch; (Elec, Mat) arc; (Mus, arma) bow; (LAm, en fútbol) goal. **~ iris** rainbow

arder *vi* burn; (LAm, escocer) sting; (fig, de ira) seethe. **estar que arde** be very tense

ardid *m* trick, scheme

ardiente *a* burning

ardilla *f* squirrel

ardor *m* heat; (fig) ardour; (LAm, escozor) smarting. **~ de estómago** heartburn

arduo *a* arduous

área *f* area

arena *f* sand; (en deportes) arena; (en los toros) (bull)ring. **~ movediza** quicksand

arenoso *a* sandy

arenque *m* herring. **~ ahumado** kipper

arete *m* (Mex) earring

Argel *m* Algiers. **~ia** *f* Algeria

Argentina *f* Argentina

argentino *a* Argentinian, Argentine. ● *m* Argentinian

argolla *f* ring. **~ de matrimonio** (LAm) wedding ring

arg|ot *m* slang. **~ótico** *a* slang

argucia *f* cunning argument

argüir [19] *vt* (probar) prove, show; (argumentar) argue. ● *vi* argue

argument|ación *f* argument. **~ar** *vt/i* argue. **~o** *m* argument; (de libro, película etc) story, plot

aria *f* aria

aridez *f* aridity, dryness

árido *a* arid, dry. **~s** *mpl* dry goods

Aries *m* Aries

arisco *a* unfriendly

arist|ocracia *f* aristocracy. **~ócrata** *m & f* aristocrat. **~ocrático** *a* aristocratic

aritmética *f* arithmetic

arma *f* arm, weapon; (sección) section. **~ de fuego** firearm. **~da** *f* navy; (flota) fleet. **~do** *a* armed (**de** with). **~dura** *f* armour; (de gafas etc) frame; (Tec) framework. **~mentismo** *m* build up of arms. **~mento** *m* arms, armaments; (acción de armar) armament. **~r** *vt* arm (**de** with); (montar) put together. **~r un lío** kick up a fuss

armario *m* cupboard; (para ropa) wardrobe (Brit), closet (Amer)

armatoste *m* huge great thing

armazón *m & f* frame(work)

armiño *m* ermine

armisticio *m* armistice

armonía *f* harmony

armónica *f* harmonica, mouth organ

armoni|oso *a* harmonious. **~zar** [10] *vt* harmonize. ● *vi* harmonize; *<personas>* get on well (**con** with); *<colores>* go well (**con** with)

arn|és *m* armour. **~eses** *mpl* harness

aro *m* ring, hoop

arom|a *m* aroma; (de flores) scent; (de vino) bouquet. **~ático** *a* aromatic

arpa *f* harp

arpía *f* harpy; (fig) hag

arpillera *f* sackcloth, sacking

arpón *m* harpoon

arquear *vt* arch, bend. □ **~se** *vpr* arch, bend

arque|ología *f* archaeology. ~**ológico** *a* archaeological. ~**ólogo** *m* archaeologist

arquero *m* archer; (LAm, en fútbol) goalkeeper

arquitect|o *m* architect. ~**ónico** *a* architectural. ~**ura** *f* architecture

arrabal *m* suburb; (barrio pobre) poor area. ~**es** *mpl* outskirts. ~**ero** *a* suburban; (de modales groseros) common

arraiga|do *a* deeply rooted. ~**r** [12] *vi* take root. □ ~**rse** *vpr* take root; (fig) settle

arran|car [7] *vt* pull up <*planta*>; pull out <*diente*>; (arrebatar) snatch; (Auto) start. ● *vi* start. □ ~**carse** *vpr* pull out. ~**que** *m* sudden start; (Auto) start; (fig) outburst

arras *fpl* security; (en boda) coins

arrasar *vt* level, smooth; raze to the ground <*edificio etc*>; (llenar) fill to the brim. ● *vi* (en deportes) sweep to victory; (en política) win a landslide victory

arrastr|ar *vt* pull; (por el suelo) drag (along); give rise to <*consecuencias*>. ● *vi* trail on the ground. □ ~**arse** *vpr* crawl; (humillarse) grovel. ~**e** *m* dragging; (transporte) haulage. **estar para el ~e** 🔲 be done in

arre *int* gee up! ~**ar** *vt* urge on

arrebat|ado *a* (irreflexivo) impetuous. ~**ar** *vt* snatch (away); (fig) win (over); captivate <*corazón etc*>. □ ~**arse** *vpr* get carried away. ~**o** *m* (de cólera etc) fit; (éxtasis) extasy

arrech|ar *vt* (LAm 🔲, enfurecer) to infuriate. □ ~**se** *vpr* get furious. ~**o** *a* furious

arrecife *m* reef

arregl|ado *a* neat; (bien vestido) well-dressed; (LAm, amañado) fixed. ~**ar** *vt* arrange; (poner en orden) tidy up; sort out <*asunto, problema etc*>; (reparar) mend. □ ~**arse** *vpr* (solucionarse) get sorted out; (prepararse) get ready; (apañarse) manage, make do; (ponerse de acuerdo) come to an agreement. ~**árselas** manage, get by. ~**o** *m* (incl Mus) arrangement; (acción de reparar) repair; (acuerdo) agreement; (solución) solution. **con ~o a** according to

arrellanarse *vpr* settle o.s. (**en** into)

arremangar [12] *vt* roll up <*mangas*>; tuck up <*falda*>. □ ~**se** *vpr* roll up one's sleeves

arremeter *vi* charge (**contra** at); (atacar) attack

arremolinarse *vpr* mill about; <*el agua*> to swirl

arrenda|dor *m* landlord. ~**dora** *f* landlady. ~**miento** *m* renting; (contrato) lease; (precio) rent. ~**r** [1] *vt* (dar casa en alquiler) let; (dar cosa en alquiler) hire out; (tomar en alquiler) rent. ~**tario** *m* tenant

arreos *mpl* tack

arrepenti|miento *m* repentance, regret. ~**rse** [4] *vpr* (retractarse) to change one's mind; (lamentarse) be sorry. ~**rse de** regret; repent of <*pecados*>

arrest|ar *vt* arrest, detain; (encarcelar) imprison. ~**o** *m* arrest; (encarcelamiento) imprisonment

arriar [20] *vt* lower <*bandera, vela*>

arriba *adv* up; (dirección) up(wards); (en casa) upstairs. ● *int* up with; (¡levántate!) up you get!; (¡ánimo!) come on! **¡~ España!** long live Spain! **~ de** (LAm) on top of. ~ **mencionado** aforementioned. **calle ~** up the street. **de ~ abajo** from top to bottom. **de 100 pesetas para ~** over 100 pesetas. **escaleras ~** upstairs. **la parte de ~** the top part. **los de ~** those at the top. **más ~** higher up

arrib|ar *vi* <*barco*> reach port; (esp LAm, llegar) arrive. ~**ista** *m & f* social climber. ~**o** *m* (esp LAm) arrival

arriero *m* muleteer

arriesga|do *a* risky; <*person*> daring. ~**r** [12] *vt* risk; (aventurar) venture. □ ~**rse** *vpr* take a risk

arrim|ar *vt* bring close(r). □ ~**arse** *vpr* come closer, approach; (apoyarse) lean (a on). ~**o** *m* protection. **al ~o de** with the help of

arrincona|do *a* forgotten; (acorralado) cornered. ~**r** *vt* put in a corner; (perseguir) corner (arrumbar) put aside. □ ~**rse** *vpr* become a recluse

arrocero *a* rice

arrodillarse *vpr* kneel (down)

arrogan|cia *f* arrogance; (orgullo) pride. **~te** *a* arrogant; (orgulloso) proud

arroj|ar *vt* throw; (emitir) give off, throw out; (producir) produce. ● *vi* (esp LAm, vomitar) throw up. □ **~arse** *vpr* throw o.s. **~o** *m* courage

arrollar *vt* roll (up); (atropellar) run over; (vencer) crush

arropar *vt* wrap up; (en la cama) tuck up. □ **~se** *vpr* wrap (o.s.) up

arroy|o *m* stream; (de una calle) gutter. **~uelo** *m* small stream

arroz *m* rice. **~ con leche** rice pudding. **~al** *m* rice field

arruga *f* (en la piel) wrinkle, line; (en tela) crease. **~r** [12] *vt* wrinkle; crumple *<papel>*; crease *<tela>*. □ **~rse** *vpr* *<la piel>* become wrinkled; *<tela>* crease, get creased

arruinar *vt* ruin; (destruir) destroy. □ **~se** *vpr* *<persona>* be ruined

arrullar *vt* lull to sleep. ● *vi* *<palomas>* coo

arrumbar *vt* put aside

arsenal *m* (astillero) shipyard; (de armas) arsenal; (fig) mine

arsénico *m* arsenic

arte *m* (*f en plural*) art; (habilidad) skill; (astucia) cunning. **bellas ~s** fine arts. **con ~** skilfully. **malas ~s** trickery. **por amor al ~** for the fun of it

artefacto *m* device

arteria *f* artery; (fig, calle) main road

artesan|al *a* craft. **~ía** *f* handicrafts. **objeto** *m* **de ~ía** traditional craft object. **~o** *m* artisan, craftsman

ártico *a* Arctic. **Á~** *m*. **el Á~** the Arctic

articula|ción *f* joint; (pronunciación) articulation. **~do** *a* articulated; *<lenguaje>* articulate. **~r** *vt* articulate

artículo *m* article. **~s** *mpl* (géneros) goods. **~ de exportación** export product. **~ de fondo** editorial, leader

artífice *m & f* artist; (creador) architect

artifici|al *a* artificial. **~o** *m* (habilidad) skill; (dispositivo) device; (engaño) trick

artiller|ía *f* artillery. **~o** *m* artilleryman, gunner

artilugio *m* gadget

artimaña *f* trick

art|ista *m & f* artist. **~ístico** *a* artistic

artritis *f* arthritis

arveja *f* (LAm) pea

arzobispo *m* archbishop

as *m* ace

asa *f* handle

asado *a* roast(ed) ● *m* roast (meat), joint; (LAm, reunión) barbecue. **~o a la parrilla** grilled meat; (LAm) barbecued meat

asalariado *a* salaried. ● *m* employee

asalt|ante *m* attacker; (de un banco) robber. **~ar** *vt* storm *<fortaleza>*; attack *<persona>*; raid *<banco etc>*; (fig) *<duda>* assail; (fig) *<idea etc>* cross one's mind. **~o** *m* attack; (robo) robbery; (en boxeo) round

asamblea *f* assembly; (reunión) meeting

asar *vt* roast. □ **~se** *vpr* be very hot. **~ a la parrilla** grill; (LAm) barbecue. **~ al horno** (sin grasa) bake; (con grasa) roast

asbesto *m* asbestos

ascend|encia *f* descent; (LAm, influencia) influencia. **~ente** *a* ascending. **~er** [1] *vt* promote. ● *vi* go up, ascend; *<cuenta etc>* come to, amount to; (ser ascendido) be promoted. **~iente** *m & f* ancestor; (influencia) influence

ascens|ión *f* ascent; (de grado) promotion. **día** *m* **de la A~ión** Ascension Day. **~o** *m* ascent; (de grado) promotion

ascensor *m* lift (Brit), elevator (Amer). **~ista** *m & f* lift attendant (Brit), elevator operator (Amer)

asco *m* disgust. **dar ~** be disgusting; (fig, causar enfado) be infuriating. **estar hecho un ~** be disgusting. **me da ~** it makes me feel sick. **¡qué ~!** how disgusting! **ser un ~** be disgusting

ascua *f* ember. **estar en ~s** be on tenterhooks

asea|do *a* clean; (arreglado) neat. ∼**r** *vt* (lavar) wash; (limpiar) clean; (arreglar) tidy up

asedi|ar *vt* besiege; (fig) pester. ∼**o** *m* siege

asegura|do *a & m* insured. ∼**dor** *m* insurer. ∼**r** *vt* secure, make safe; (decir) assure; (concertar un seguro) insure; (preservar) safeguard. □ ∼**rse** *vpr* make sure

asemejarse *vpr* be alike

asenta|do *a* situated; (arraigado) established. ∼**r** [1] *vt* place; (asegurar) settle; (anotar) note down; (Mex, afirmar) state. □ ∼**rse** *vpr* settle; (estar situado) be situated; (esp LAm, sentar cabeza) settle down

asentir [4] *vi* agree (a to). ∼ **con la cabeza** nod

aseo *m* cleanliness. ∼**s** *mpl* toilets

asequible *a* obtainable; *<precio>* reasonable; *<persona>* approachable

asesin|ar *vt* murder; (Pol) assassinate. ∼**ato** *m* murder; (Pol) assassination. ∼**o** *m* murderer; (Pol) assassin

asesor *m* adviser, consultant. ∼**ar** *vt* advise. □ ∼**arse** *vpr*. ∼**arse con** consult. ∼**ía** *f* consultancy; (oficina) consultant's office

asfalt|ado *a* asphalt. ∼**ar** *vt* asphalt. ∼**o** *m* asphalt

asfixia *f* suffocation. ∼**nte** *a* suffocating. ∼**r** *vt* suffocate. □ ∼**rse** *vpr* suffocate

así *adv* (de esta manera) like this, like that. ● *a* such. ∼ ∼ so-so. ∼ **como** just as. ∼ **como** ∼, (LAm) ∼ **nomás** just like that. ∼ ... **como** both ... and. ∼ **pues** so. ∼ **que** so; (en cuanto) as soon as. ∼ **sea** so be it. ∼ **y todo** even so. **aun** ∼ even so. **¿no es** ∼? isn't that right? **si es** ∼ if that is the case. **y** ∼ **(sucesivamente)** and so on

Asia *f* Asia

asiático *a & m* Asian

asidero *m* handle; (fig, pretexto) excuse

asidu|amente *adv* regularly. ∼**o** *a & m* regular

asiento *m* seat; (en contabilidad) entry. ∼ **delantero** front seat. ∼ **trasero** back seat

asignar *vt* assign; allot *<porción, tiempo etc>*

asignatura *f* subject. ∼ **pendiente** (Escol) failed subject; (fig) matter still to be resolved

asil|ado *m* inmate; (Pol) refugee. ∼**o** *m* asylum; (fig) shelter; (de ancianos etc) home. **pedir** ∼**o político** ask for political asylum

asimétrico *a* asymmetrical

asimila|ción *f* assimilation. ∼**r** *vt* assimilate

asimismo *adv* also; (igualmente) in the same way, likewise

asir [45] *vt* grasp

asist|encia *f* attendance; (gente) people (present); (en un teatro etc) audience; (ayuda) assistance. ∼**encia médica** medical care. ∼**enta** *f* (mujer de la limpieza) charwoman. ∼**ente** *m & f* assistant. ∼**ente social** social worker. ∼**ido** *a* assisted. ∼**ir** *vt* assist, help. ● *vi*. ∼**ir a** attend, be present at

asm|a *f* asthma. ∼**ático** *a & m* asthmatic

asno *m* donkey; (fig) ass

asocia|ción *f* association; (Com) partnership. ∼**do** *a* associated; *<socio>* associate. ● *m* associate. ∼**r** *vt* associate; (Com) take into partnership. □ ∼**rse** *vpr* associate; (Com) become a partner

asolar [1] *vt* devastate

asomar *vt* show. ● *vi* appear, show. □ ∼**se** *vpr* *<persona>* lean out (**a**, **por** of); *<cosa>* appear

asombr|ar *vt* (pasmar) amaze; (sorprender) surprise. □ ∼**arse** *vpr* be amazed; (sorprenderse) be surprised. ∼**o** *m* amazement, surprise. ∼**oso** *a* amazing, astonishing

asomo *m* sign. **ni por** ∼ by no means

aspa *f* cross, X-shape; (de molino) (windmill) sail. **en** ∼ X-shaped

aspaviento *m* show, fuss. ∼**s** *mpl* gestures. **hacer** ∼**s** make a big fuss

aspecto *m* look, appearance; (fig) aspect

aspereza *f* roughness; (de sabor etc) sourness

áspero *a* rough; *<sabor etc>* bitter

aspersión *f* sprinkling

aspiración *f* breath; (deseo) ambition

aspirador *m*, **aspiradora** *f* vacuum cleaner

aspira|nte *m & f* candidate. ～**r** *vt* breathe in; *<máquina>* suck up. ● *vi* breathe in; *<máquina>* suck. ～**r a** aspire to

aspirina *f* aspirin

asquear *vt* sicken. ● *vi* be sickening. □ ～**se** *vpr* be disgusted

asqueroso *a* disgusting

asta *f* spear; (de la bandera) flagpole; (cuerno) horn. **a media** ～ at half-mast. ～**bandera** *f* (Mex) flagpole

asterisco *m* asterisk

astilla *f* splinter. ～**s** *fpl* firewood

astillero *m* shipyard

astringente *a & m* astringent

astr|o *m* star. ～**ología** *f* astrology. ～**ólogo** *m* astrologer. ～**onauta** *m & f* astronaut. ～**onave** *f* spaceship. ～**onomía** *f* astronomy. ～**ónomo** *m* astronomer

astu|cia *f* cleverness; (ardid) cunning trick. ～**to** *a* astute; (taimado) cunning

asumir *vt* assume

asunción *f* assumption. **la A**～ the Assumption

asunto *m* (cuestión) matter; (de una novela) plot; (negocio) business. ～**s** *mpl* **exteriores** foreign affairs. **el** ～ **es que** the fact is that

asusta|dizo *a* easily frightened. ～**r** *vt* frighten. □ ～**rse** *vpr* be frightened

ataca|nte *m & f* attacker. ～**r** [7] *vt* attack

atad|o *a* tied. ● *m* bundle. ～**ura** *f* tie

ataj|ar *vi* take a short cut; (Mex, en tenis) pick up the balls. ● *vt* (LAm, agarrar) catch. ～**o** *m* short cut

atañer [22] *vt* concern

ataque *m* attack; (Med) fit, attack. ～ **al corazón** heart attack. ～ **de nervios** fit of hysterics

atar *vt* tie. □ ～**se** *vpr* tie up

atarantar *vt* (LAm) fluster. □ ～**se** *vpr* (LAm) get flustered

atardecer [11] *vi* get dark. ● *m* dusk. **al** ～ at dusk

atareado *a* busy

atasc|ar [7] *vt* block; (fig) hinder. □ ～**arse** *vpr* get stuck; *<tubo etc>* block. ～**o** *m* blockage; (Auto) traffic jam

ataúd *m* coffin

atav|iar [20] *vt* dress up. □ ～**iarse** *vpr* dress up, get dressed up. ～**ío** *m* dress, attire

atemorizar [10] *vt* frighten. □ ～**se** *vpr* be frightened

atención *f* attention; (cortesía) courtesy, kindness; (interés) interest. ¡～! look out!. **llamar la** ～ attract attention, catch the eye; **prestar** ～ pay attention

atender [1] *vt* attend to; (cuidar) look after. ● *vi* pay attention

atenerse [40] *vpr* abide (**a** by)

atentado *m* (ataque) attack; (afrenta) affront (**contra** to). ～ **contra la vida de uno** attempt on s.o.'s life

atentamente *adv* attentively; (con cortesía) politely; (con amabilidad) kindly. **lo saluda** ～ (en cartas) yours faithfully

atentar *vi*. ～ **contra** threaten. ～ **contra la vida de uno** make an attempt on s.o.'s life

atento *a* attentive; (cortés) polite; (amable) kind

atenua|nte *a* extenuating. ● *f* extenuating circumstance. ～**r** [21] *vt* attenuate; (hacer menor) diminish, lessen

ateo *a* atheistic. ● *m* atheist

aterciopelado *a* velvety

aterra|dor *a* terrifying. ～**r** *vt* terrify

aterriza|je *m* landing. ～**je forzoso** emergency landing. ～**r** [10] *vt* land

aterrorizar [10] *vt* terrify

atesorar *vt* hoard; amass *<fortuna>*

atesta|do *a* packed, full up. ● *m* sworn statement. ～**r** *vt* fill up, pack; (Jurid) testify

atestiguar [15] *vt* testify to; (fig) prove

atiborrar *vt* fill, stuff. □ ～**se** *vpr* stuff o.s.

ático *m* attic

atina|do *a* right; (juicioso) wise, sensible. **~r** *vt/i* hit upon; (acertar) guess right

atizar [10] *vt* poke; (fig) stir up

atlántico *a* Atlantic. **el (océano) A~** the Atlantic (Ocean)

atlas *m* atlas

atl|eta *m & f* athlete. **~ético** *a* athletic. **~etismo** *m* athletics

atmósfera *f* atmosphere

atole *m* (LAm) boiled maize drink

atolladero *m* bog; (fig) tight corner

atolondra|do *a* scatter-brained; (aturdido) stunned. **~r** *vt* fluster; (pasmar) stun. □ **~rse** *vpr* get flustered

at|ómico *a* atomic. **~omizador** *m* spray, atomizer

átomo *m* atom

atónito *m* amazed

atonta|do *a* stunned; (tonto) stupid. **~r** *vt* stun. □ **~rse** *vpr* get confused

atorar *vt* (esp LAm) to block; (Mex, sujetar) secure. □ **~rse** *vpr* (esp LAm, atragantarse) choke; (atascarse) get blocked; *<puerta>* get jammed

atormentar *vt* torture. □ **~rse** *vpr* worry, torment o.s.

atornillar *vt* screw on

atosigar [12] *vt* pester

atraca|dor *m* mugger; (de banco) bank robber. **~r** [7] *vt* dock; (arrimar) bring alongside; hold up *<banco>*; mug *<persona>*. ● *vi <barco>* dock

atracci|ón *f* attraction. **~ones** *fpl* entertainment, amusements

atrac|o *m* hold-up, robbery. **~ón** *m*. **darse un ~ón** stuff o.s. (**de** with)

atractivo *a* attractive. ● *m* attraction; (encanto) charm

atraer [41] *vt* attract

atragantarse *vpr* choke (**con** on). **la historia se me atraganta** I can't stand history

atrancar [7] *vt* bolt *<puerta>*. □ **~se** *vpr* get stuck

atrapar *vt* catch; (encerrar) trap

atrás *adv* back; (tiempo) previously, before. **años ~** years ago. **~ de** (LAm) behind. **dar un paso ~** step backwards. **hacia ~, para ~** backwards

atras|ado *a* behind; *<reloj>* slow; (con deudas) in arrears; *<país>* back-

ward. **llegar ~ado** (esp LAm) arrive late. **~ar** *vt* put back *<reloj>*; (demorar) delay, postpone. ● *vi <reloj>* be slow. □ **~arse** *vpr* be late; *<reloj>* be slow; (quedarse atrás) fall behind. **~o** *m* delay; (de un reloj) slowness; (de un país) backwardness. **~os** *mpl* (Com) arrears

atravesa|do *a* lying across. **~r** [1] *vt* cross; (traspasar) go through (poner transversalmente) lay across. □ **~rse** *vpr* lie across; (en la garganta) get stuck, stick

atrayente *a* attractive

atrev|erse *vpr* dare. **~erse con** tackle. **~ido** *a* daring; (insolente) insolent. **~imiento** *m* daring; (descaro) insolence

atribu|ción *f* attribution. **~ciones** *fpl* authority. **~uir** [17] *vt* attribute; confer *<función>*. □ **~irse** *vpr* claim

atribulado *a* afflicted

atributo *m* attribute

atril *m* lectern; (Mus) music stand

atrocidad *f* atrocity. **¡qué ~!** how awful!

atrofiarse *vpr* atrophy

atropell|ado *a* hasty. **~ar** *vt* knock down; (por encima) run over; (empujar) push aside; (fig) outrage, insult. □ **~arse** *vpr* rush. **~o** *m* (Auto) accident; (fig) outrage

atroz *a* appalling; (fig) atrocious

atuendo *m* dress, attire

atún *m* tuna (fish)

aturdi|do *a* bewildered; (por golpe) stunned. **~r** *vt* bewilder; *<golpe>* stun; *<ruido>* deafen

auda|cia *f* boldness, audacity. **~z** *a* bold

audi|ble *a* audible. **~ción** *f* hearing; (prueba) audition. **~encia** *f* audience; (tribunal) court; (sesión) hearing

auditor *m* auditor. **~io** *m* audience; (sala) auditorium

auge *m* peak; (Com) boom

augur|ar *vt* predict; *<cosas>* augur. **~io** *m* prediction. **con nuestros mejores ~ios para** with our best wishes for. **mal ~** bad omen

aula *f* class-room; (Univ) lecture room

aull|ar [23] *vi* howl. **~ido** *m* howl

aument|ar *vt* increase; magnify
<*imagen*>. ● *vi* increase. ∼**o** *m* in-
crease; (de sueldo) rise

aun *adv* even. ∼ **así** even so. ∼ **cuando** although. **más** ∼ even more. **ni** ∼
not even

aún *adv* still, yet. ∼ **no ha llegado** it
still hasn't arrived, it hasn't arrived
yet

aunar [23] *vt* join. □ ∼**se** *vpr* join together

aunque *conj* although, (even)
though

aúpa *int* up! **de** ∼ wonderful

aureola *f* halo

auricular *m* (de teléfono) receiver.
∼**es** *mpl* headphones

aurora *f* dawn

ausen|cia *f* absence. **en** ∼**cia de** in
the absence of. □ ∼**tarse** *vpr* leave.
∼**te** *a* absent. ● *m* & *f* absentee; (Jurid) missing person. ∼**tismo** *m* (LAm)
absenteeism

auspici|ador *m* sponsor. ∼**ar** *vt*
sponsor. ∼**o** *m* sponsorship; (signo)
omen. **bajo los** ∼**s de** sponsored by

auster|idad *f* austerity. ∼**o** *a* aus-
tere

austral *a* southern

Australia *m* Australia

australiano *a* & *m* Australian

Austria *f* Austria

austriaco, **austríaco** *a* & *m*
Austrian

aut|enticar [7] authenticate. ∼**en-
ticidad** *f* authenticity. ∼**éntico** *a*
authentic

auto *m* (Jurid) decision; (orden) order;
(Auto, 🔲) car. ∼**s** *mpl* proceedings

auto|abastecimiento *m* self-
sufficiency. ∼**biografía** *f* autobiography

autobús *m* bus. **en** ∼ by bus

autocar *m* (long-distance) bus,
coach (Brit)

autocontrol *m* self-control

autóctono *a* indigenous

auto|determinación *f* self-deter-
mination. ∼**didacta** *a* self-taught.
● *m* & *f* self-taught person. ∼**escuela** *f* driving school. ∼**financia-
miento** *m* self-financing

autógrafo *m* autograph

autómata *m* robot

autom|ático *a* automatic. ● *m*
press-stud. ∼**atización** *f* automa-
tion

automotor *m* diesel train

autom|óvil *a* motor. ● *m* car.
∼**ovilismo** *m* motoring. ∼**ovilista**
m & *f* driver, motorist

aut|onomía *f* autonomy. ∼**onómi-
co** *a*, ∼**ónomo** *a* autonomous

autopista *f* motorway (Brit), free-
way (Amer)

autopsia *f* autopsy

autor *m* author. ∼**a** *f* author(ess)

autori|dad *f* authority. ∼**tario** *a*
authoritarian

autoriza|ción *f* authorization.
∼**do** *a* authorized, official; <*opinión
etc*> authoritative. ∼**r** [10] *vt* authorize

auto|rretrato *m* self-portrait.
∼**servicio** *m* self-service restaurant. ∼**stop** *m* hitch-hiking. **hacer**
∼**stop** hitch-hike

autosuficiente *a* self-sufficient

autovía *f* dual carriageway

auxili|ar *a* auxiliary; <*profesor*> as-
sistant. ● *m* & *f* assistant. ● *vt* help.
∼**o** *m* help. **¡**∼**o!** help! **en** ∼**o de** in
aid of. **pedir** ∼**o** shout for help. **primeros** ∼**os** first aid

Av. *abrev* (**Avenida**) Ave

aval *m* guarantee

avalancha *f* avalanche

avalar *vt* guarantee

aval|uar *vt* [21] (LAm) value. ∼**úo** *m*
valuation

avance *m* advance; (en el cine) trailer. ∼**s** *mpl* (Mex) trailer

avanzar [10] *vt* move forward. ● *vi*
advance

avar|icia *f* avarice. ∼**icioso** *a*,
∼**iento** *a* greedy; (tacaño) miserly.
∼**o** *a* miserly. ● *m* miser

avasallar *vt* dominate

Avda. *abrev* (**Avenida**) Ave

ave *f* bird. ∼ **de paso** (incl fig) bird of
passage. ∼ **de rapiña** bird of prey

avecinarse *vpr* approach

avejentar *vt* age

avellan|a *f* hazel-nut. **~o** *m* hazel (tree)

avemaría *f* Hail Mary

avena *f* oats

avenida *f* (calle) avenue

avenir [53] *vt* reconcile. □ **~se** *vpr* come to an agreement; (entenderse) get on well (**con** with)

aventaja|do *a* outstanding. **~r** *vt* be ahead of; (superar) surpass

avent|ar [1] *vt* fan; winnow <*grano etc*>; (Mex, lanzar) throw; (Mex, empujar) push. □ **~arse** *vpr* (Mex) throw o.s.; (atreverse) dare. **~ón** *m* (Mex) ride, lift (Brit)

aventur|a *f* adventure. **~a amorosa** love affair. **~ado** *a* risky. **~ero** *a* adventurous. ● *m* adventurer

avergonzar [10 & 16] *vt* shame; (abochornar) embarrass. □ **~se** *vpr* be ashamed; (abochornarse) be embarrassed

aver|ía *f* (Auto) breakdown; (en máquina) failure. **~iado** *a* broken down. □ **~iarse** [20] *vpr* break down

averigua|ción *f* inquiry; (Mex, disputa) argument. **~r** [15] *vt* find out. ● *vi* (Mex) argue

aversión *f* aversion (**a, hacia, por** to)

avestruz *m* ostrich

avia|ción *f* aviation; (Mil) air force. **~dor** *m* (piloto) pilot

av|ícola *a* poultry. **~icultura** *f* poultry farming

avidez *f* eagerness, greed

ávido *a* eager, greedy

avinagra|do *a* sour. □ **~rse** *vpr* go sour; (fig) become embittered

avi|ón *m* aeroplane (Brit), airplane (Amer); (Mex, juego) hopscotch. **~ona-zo** *m* (Mex) plane crash

avis|ar *vt* warn; (informar) notify, inform; call <*médico etc*>. **~o** *m* warning; (comunicación) notice; (LAm, anuncio, cartel) advertisement; (en televisión) commercial. **estar sobre ~o** be on the alert. **sin previo ~o** without prior warning

avisp|a *f* wasp. **~ado** *a* sharp. **~ero** *m* wasps' nest; (fig) mess. **~ón** *m* hornet

avistar *vt* catch sight of

avivar *vt* stoke up <*fuego*>; brighten up <*color*>; arouse <*interés, pasión*>; intensify <*dolor*>. □ **~se** *vpr* revive; (animarse) cheer up; (LAm, despabilarse) wise up

axila *f* armpit, axilla

axioma *m* axiom

ay *int* (de dolor) ouch!; (de susto) oh!; (de pena) oh dear! **¡~ de ti!** poor you!

aya *f* governess, child's nurse

ayer *adv* yesterday. ● *m* past. **antes de ~** the day before yesterday. **~ por la mañana**, (LAm) **~ en la mañana** yesterday morning

ayuda *f* help, aid. **~ de cámara** valet. **~nta** *f*, **~nte** *m* assistant; (Mil) adjutant. **~r** *vt* help

ayun|ar *vi* fast. **~as** *fpl*. **estar en ~as** have had nothing to eat or drink; (fig, 🄸) be in the dark. **~o** *m* fasting

ayuntamiento *m* town council, city council; (edificio) town hall

azabache *m* jet

azad|a *f* hoe. **~ón** *m* (large) hoe

azafata *f* air hostess

azafate *m* (LAm) tray

azafrán *m* saffron

azahar *m* orange blossom; (del limonero) lemon blossom

azar *m* chance; (desgracia) misfortune. **al ~** at random. **por ~** by chance. **~es** *mpl* ups and downs

azaros|amente *adv* hazardously. **~o** *a* hazardous, risky; <*vida*> eventful

azorar *vt* embarrass. □ **~rse** *vpr* be embarrassed

Azores *fpl*. **las ~** the Azores

azotador *m* (Mex) caterpillar

azot|ar *vt* whip, beat; (Mex, puerta) slam. **~e** *m* whip; (golpe) smack; (fig, calamidad) calamity

azotea *f* flat roof

azteca *a* & *m* & *f* Aztec

az|úcar *m* & *f* sugar. **~ucarado** *a* sweet, sugary. **~ucarar** *vt* sweeten. **~ucarero** *m* sugar bowl

azucena *f* (white) lily

azufre *m* sulphur

azul *a* & *m* blue. **~ado** *a* bluish. **~ marino** navy blue

azulejo *m* tile

azuzar [10] *vt* urge on, incite

Bb

bab|a f spittle. **~ear** vi drool, slobber; <niño> dribble. **caérsele la ~a a uno** be delighted. **~eo** m drooling; (de un niño) dribbling. **~ero** m bib

babor m port. **a ~** to port, on the port side

babosa f slug

babosada f (Mex) drivel

babos|ear vt slobber over; <niño> dribble over. ● vi (Mex) day dream. **~o** a slimy; (LAm, tonto) silly

babucha f slipper

baca f luggage rack

bacalao m cod

bache m pothole; (fig) bad patch

bachillerato m school-leaving examination

bacteria f bacterium

bagaje m. **~ cultural** cultural knowledge; (de un pueblo) cultural heritage

bahía f bay

bail|able a dance. **~aor** m Flamenco dancer. **~ar** vt/i dance. **ir a ~ar** go dancing. **~arín** m dancer. **~arina** f dancer; (de ballet) ballerina. **~e** m dance; (actividad) dancing. **~e de etiqueta** ball

baja f drop, fall; (Mil) casualty. **~ por maternidad** maternity leave. **darse de ~** take sick leave. **~da** f slope; (acto de bajar) descent; (camino) way down. **~r** vt lower; (llevar abajo) get down; go down <escalera>; bow <la cabeza>. ● vi go down; <temperatura, precio> fall. □ **~rse** vpr pull down <pantalones>. **~r(se) de** get out of <coche>; get off <autobús, caballo, tren, bicicleta>

bajeza f vile deed

bajío m shallows; (de arena) sandbank; (LAm, terreno bajo) low-lying area

bajo a low; (de estatura) short, small; <cabeza, ojos> lowered; (humilde) humble, low; (vil) vile, low; <voz> low; (Mus) deep. ● m lowland; (Mus) bass. ● adv quietly; <volar> low. ● prep under. **~ cero** below zero. **~ la lluvia** in the rain. **los ~s** (LAm) ground floor (Brit), first floor (Amer); **los ~s fondos** the underworld

bajón m sharp drop; (de salud) sudden decline

bala f bullet; (de algodón etc) bale. (LAm, en atletismo) shot. **como una ~** like a shot. **lanzamiento de ~** (LAm) shot put

balada f ballad

balan|ce m balance; (documento) balance sheet; (resultado) outcome. **~cear** vt balance. □ **~cearse** vpr swing. **~ceo** m swinging. **~cín** m rocking chair; (de niños) seesaw. **~za** f scales; (Com) balance

balar vi bleat

balazo m (disparo) shot; (herida) bullet wound

balboa f (unidad monetaria panameña) balboa

balbuc|ear vt/i stammer; <niño> babble. **~eo** m stammering; (de niño) babbling. **~ir** [24] vt/i stammer; <niño> babble

balcón m balcony

balda f shelf

balde m bucket. **de ~** free (of charge). **en ~** in vain

baldío a <terreno> waste

baldosa f (floor) tile; (losa) flagstone

bale|ar a Balearic. **las (Islas) B~ares** the Balearics, the Balearic Islands. ● vt (LAm) to shoot. **~o** m (LAm, tiroteo) shooting

balero m (Mex) cup and ball toy; (rodamiento) bearing

balido m bleat; (varios sonidos) bleating

balística f ballistics

baliza f (Naut) buoy; (Aviac) beacon

ballena f whale

ballet /ba'le/ (pl ~s) m ballet

balneario m spa; (con playa) seaside resort

balompié m soccer, football (Brit)

bal|ón *m* ball. **~oncesto** *m* basketball. **~onmano** *m* handball. **~onvolea** *m* volleyball

balotaje *m* (LAm) voting

balsa *f* (de agua) pool; (plataforma flotante) raft

bálsamo *m* balsam; (fig) balm

baluarte *m* (incl fig) bastion

bambalina *f* drop curtain. **entre ~s** behind the scenes

bambole|ar *vi* sway. □ **~arse** *vpr* sway; <*mesa etc*> wobble; <*barco*> rock. **~o** *m* swaying; (de mesa etc) wobbling; (de barco) rocking

bambú *m* (*pl* **~es**) bamboo

banal *a* banal. **~ldad** *f* banality

banan|a *f* (esp LAm) banana. **~ero** *a* banana. **~o** *m* (LAm) banana tree

banc|a *f* banking; (conjunto de bancos) banks; (en juegos) bank; (LAm, asiento) bench. **~ario** *a* a bank, banking. **~arrota** *f* bankruptcy. **hacer ~arrota, lr a la ~arrota** go bankrupt. **~o** *m* (asiento) bench; (Com) bank; (bajío) sandbank; (de peces) shoal

banda *f* (incl Mus, Radio) band; (Mex, para el pelo) hair band; (raya ancha) stripe; (cinta ancha) sash; (grupo) gang, group. **~ sonora** sound-track. **~da** *f* (de pájaros) flock; (de peces) shoal

bandeja *f* tray

bandejón *m* (Mex) central reservation (Brit), median strip (Amer)

bander|a *f* flag. **~illa** *f* banderilla. **~ear** *vt* stick the banderillas in. **~ero** *m* banderillero. **~ín** *m* pennant, small flag

bandido *m* bandit

bando *m* edict, proclamation; (facción) camp, side. **~s** *mpl* banns. **pasarse al otro ~** go over to the other side

bandolero *m* bandit

bandoneón *m* large accordion

banjo *m* banjo

banquero *m* banker

banquete *m* banquet; (de boda) wedding reception

banquillo *m* bench; (Jurid) dock; (taburete) footstool

bañ|ador *m* (de mujer) swimming costume; (de hombre) swimming trunks. **~ar** *vt* bath <*niño*>; (Culin, recubrir) coat. □ **~arse** *vpr* go swimming, have a swim; (en casa) have a bath. **~era** *f* bath (tub). **~ista** *m & f* bather. **~o** *m* bath; (en piscina, mar etc) swim; (cuarto) bathroom; (LAm, wáter) toilet; (bañera) bath(tub); (capa) coat (ing)

baqueano, (LAm) **baquiano** *m* guide

bar *m* bar

baraja *f* pack of cards. **~r** *vt* shuffle; juggle <*cifras etc*>; consider <*posibilidades*>; (Mex, explicar) explain

baranda, barandilla *f* rail; (de escalera) banisters

barat|a *f* (Mex) sale. **~ija** *f* trinket. **~illo** *m* junk shop; (géneros) cheap goods. **~o** *a* cheap. ● *adv* cheap(ly)

barba *f* chin; (pelo) beard

barbacoa *f* barbecue; (carne) barbecued meat

barbari|dad *f* atrocity; (🔲, mucho) awful lot 🔲. **¡qué ~dad!** how awful! **~e** *f* barbarity; (fig) ignorance. **~smo** *m* barbarism

bárbaro *a* barbaric, cruel; (bruto) uncouth; (🔲, estupendo) terrific 🔲 ● *m* barbarian. **¡qué ~!** how marvellous!

barbear *vt* (Mex, lisonjear) suck up to

barbecho *m*. **en ~** fallow

barber|ía *f* barber's (shop). **~o** *m* barber; (Mex, adulador) creep

barbilla *f* chin

barbitúrico *m* barbiturate

barbudo *a* bearded

barca *f* (small) boat. **~ de pasaje** ferry. **~za** *f* barge

barcelonés *a* of Barcelona, from Barcelona. ● *m* native of Barcelona

barco *m* boat; (navío) ship. **~ cisterna** tanker. **~ de vapor** steamer. **~ de vela** sailing boat. **ir en ~** go by boat

barda *f* (Mex) wall; (de madera) fence

barítono *a & m* baritone

barman *m* (*pl* **~s**) barman

barniz *m* varnish; (para loza etc) glaze; (fig) veneer. **~ar** [10] *vt* varnish; glaze <*loza etc*>

barómetro *m* barometer

bar|ón *m* baron. **~onesa** *f* baroness

barquero *m* boatman

barquillo m wafer; (Mex, de helado) ice-cream cone

barra f bar; (pan) loaf of French bread; (palanca) lever; (de arena) sandbank; (LAm, de hinchas) supporters. ~ **de labios** lipstick

barrabasada f mischief, prank

barraca f hut; (vivienda pobre) shack, shanty

barranco m ravine, gully; (despeñadero) cliff, precipice

barrer vt sweep; thrash <rival>

barrera f barrier. ~ **del sonido** sound barrier

barriada f district; (LAm, barrio marginal) slum

barrial m (LAm) quagmire

barrida f sweep; (LAm, redada) police raid

barrig|a f belly. ~**ón** a, ~**udo** a pot-bellied

barril m barrel

barrio m district, area. ~**s bajos** poor quarter, poor area. **el otro** ~ (fig, 🅷) the other world. ~**bajero** a vulgar, common

barro m mud; (arcilla) clay; (arcilla cocida) earthenware

barroco a Baroque. ● m Baroque style

barrote m bar

bartola f. **tirarse a la** ~ take it easy

bártulos mpl things. **liar los** ~ pack one's bags

barullo m racket; (confusión) confusion. **a** ~ galore

basar vt base. □ ~**se** vpr. ~**se en** be based on

báscula f scales

base f base; (fig) basis, foundation. **a** ~ **de** thanks to; (mediante) by means of; (en una receta) mainly consisting of. ~ **de datos** database. **partiendo de la** ~ **de, tomando como** ~ on the basis of

básico a basic

basílica f basilica

básquetbol, basquetbol m (LAm) basketball

bastante

● adjetivo/pronombre

····► (suficiente) enough. **¿hay** ~**s sillas?** are there enough chairs? **ya tengo** ~ I have enough already

····► (mucho) quite a lot. **vino** ~ **gente** quite a lot of people came. **tiene** ~**s amigos** he has quite a lot of friends **¿te gusta?- sí,** ~ do you like it? - yes, quite a lot

● adverbio

····► (suficientemente) enough. **no has estudiado** ~ you haven't studied enough. **no es lo** ~ **inteligente** he's not clever enough (**como para** to)

····► **bastante** + adjetivo/adverbio (modificando la intensidad) quite, fairly. **parece** ~ **simpático** he looks quite friendly. **es** ~ **fácil de hacer** it's quite easy to do. **canta** ~ **bien** he sings quite well

····► **bastante** con verbo (considerablemente) quite a lot. **el lugar ha cambiado** ~ the place has changed quite a lot

bastar vi be enough. **¡basta!** that's enough! **basta con decir que** suffice it to say that. **basta y sobra** that's more than enough

bastardilla f italics

bastardo a & m bastard

bastidor m frame; (Auto) chassis. ~**es** mpl (en el teatro) wings. **entre** ~**es** behind the scenes

basto a coarse. ~**s** mpl (naipes) clubs

bast|ón m walking stick; (de esquí) ski pole. ~**onazo** m blow with a stick; (de mando) staff of office

basur|a f rubbish, garbage (Amer); (en la calle) litter. ~**al** m (LAm, lugar) rubbish dump. ~**ero** m dustman (Brit), garbage collector (Amer); (sitio) rubbish dump; (Mex, recipiente) dustbin (Brit), garbage can (Amer)

bata f dressing-gown; (de médico etc) white coat; (esp LAm, de baño) bathrobe

batahola f (LAm) pandemonium

batall|a f battle. ~**a campal** pitched battle. **de** ~**a** everyday. ~**ador** a fighting. ● m fighter. ~**ar** vi battle, fight. ~**ón** m battalion.

batata f sweet potato

bate *m* bat. **~ador** *m* batter; (cricket) batsman. **~ar** *vi* bat

batería *f* battery; (Mus) drums. ● *m* & *f* drummer. **~ de cocina** kitchen utensils, pots and pans

baterista *m* & *f* drummer

batido *a* beaten; <*nata*> whipped. ● *m* batter; (bebida) milk shake. **~ra** *f* (food) mixer

batir *vt* beat; break <*récord*>; whip <*nata*>. **~ palmas** clap. □ **~se** *vpr* fight

batuta *f* baton. **llevar la ~** be in command, be the boss

baúl *m* trunk

bauti|smal *a* baptismal. **~smo** *m* baptism, christening. **~zar** [10] *vt* baptize, christen. **~zo** *m* christening

baya *f* berry

bayeta *f* cloth

bayoneta *f* bayonet

baza *f* (naipes) trick; (fig) advantage. **meter ~** interfere

bazar *m* bazaar

bazofia *f* revolting food; (fig) rubbish

beato *a* blessed; (piadoso) devout; (pey) overpious

bebé *m* baby

beb|edero *m* drinking trough; (sitio) watering place. **~edizo** *m* potion; (veneno) poison. **~edor** *m* heavy drinker. **~er** *vt/i* drink. **~ida** *f* drink. **~ido** *a* drunk

beca *f* grant, scholarship. **~do** *m* (LAm) scholarship holder, scholar. **~r** [7] *vt* give a scholarship to. **~rio** *m* scholarship holder, scholar

beige /beis, beʒ/ *a* & *m* beige

béisbol, (Mex) **beisbol** *m* baseball

belén *m* crib, nativity scene

belga *a* & *m* & *f* Belgian

Bélgica *f* Belgium

bélico *a*, **belicoso** *a* warlike

bell|eza *f* beauty. **~o** *a* beautiful. **~as artes** *fpl* fine arts

bellota *f* acorn

bemol *m* flat. **tener (muchos) ~es** be difficult

bend|ecir [46] (*pero imperativo* **bendice**, *futuro, condicional y pp*

regulares) *vt* bless. **~ición** *f* blessing. **~ito** *a* blessed; (que tiene suerte) lucky; (feliz) happy

benefactor *m* benefactor

benefic|encia *f* charity. **de ~encia** charitable. **~iar** *vt* benefit. □ **~iarse** *vpr* benefit. **~iario** *m* beneficiary; (de un cheque etc) payee. **~io** *m* benefit; (ventaja) advantage; (ganancia) profit, gain. **~ioso** *a* beneficial

benéfico *a* beneficial; (de beneficencia) charitable

ben|evolencia *f* benevolence. **~évolo** *a* benevolent

bengala *f* flare. **luz** *f* **de ~** flare

benigno *a* kind; (moderado) gentle, mild; <*tumor*> benign

berberecho *m* cockle

berenjena *f* aubergine (Brit), eggplant (Amer)

berr|ear *vi* <*animales*> bellow; <*niño*> bawl. **~ido** *m* bellow; (de niño) bawling

berrinche *m* temper; (de un niño) tantrum

berro *m* watercress

besamel(a) *f* white sauce

bes|ar *vt* kiss. □ **~arse** *vpr* kiss (each other). **~o** *m* kiss

bestia *f* beast; (bruto) brute; (idiota) idiot. **~ de carga** beast of burden. **~l** *a* bestial, animal; (fig, 🎁) terrific. **~lidad** *f* (acción brutal) horrid thing; (insensatez) stupidity

besugo *m* red bream

besuquear *vt* cover with kisses

betabel *f* (Mex) beetroot

betún *m* (para el calzado) shoe polish

biberón *m* feeding-bottle

Biblia *f* Bible

bibliografía *f* bibliography

biblioteca *f* library; (mueble) bookcase. **~ de consulta** reference library. **~rio** *m* librarian

bicarbonato *m* bicarbonate

bicho *m* insect, bug; (animal) small animal, creature. **~ raro** odd sort

bici *f* 🎁 bike. **~cleta** *f* bicycle. **ir en ~cleta** cycle. **~moto** (LAm) moped

bidé, **bidet** *m* /bi'ðe/ bidet

bidón *m* drum, can

bien *adv* well; (muy) very, quite; (correctamente) right; (de buena gana) willingly. ● *m* good; (efectos) property. ¡∼! fine!, OK!, good! ∼... (o) ∼ either... or. ¡está ∼! fine!, alright!; (basta) that is enough!. **más** ∼ rather. ¡muy ∼! good! **no** ∼ as soon as. ¡qué ∼! marvellous!, great! ⚏. **si** ∼ although

bienal *a* biennial

bien|aventurado *a* fortunate. ∼**estar** *m* well-being. ∼**hablado** *a* well-spoken. ∼**hecho** *m* benefactor. ∼**intencionado** *a* well-meaning

bienio *m* two year-period

bienvenid|a *f* welcome. **dar la** ∼**a** **a** **uno** welcome s.o. ∼**o** *a* welcome. ¡∼o! welcome!

bifurca|ción *f* junction. □ ∼**rse** [7] *vpr* fork; (rail) branch off

b|igamia *f* bigamy. ∼**ígamo** *a* bigamous. ● *m* bigamist

bigot|e *m* moustache. ∼**ón** *a* (Mex), ∼**udo** *a* with a big moustache

bikini *m* bikini

bilingüe *a* bilingual

billar *m* billiards

billete *m* ticket; (de banco) (bank) note (Brit), bill (Amer). ∼ **de ida y vuelta** return ticket (Brit), round-trip ticket (Amer). ∼ **sencillo** single ticket (Brit), one-way ticket (Amer). ∼**ra** *f*, ∼**ro** *m* wallet, billfold (Amer)

billón *m* billion (Brit), trillion (Amer)

bi|mensual *a* fortnightly, twice-monthly. ∼**mestral** *a* two-monthly. ∼**mestre** *m* two-month period. ∼**motor** *a* twin-engined. ● *m* twin-engined plane

binoculares *mpl* binoculars

bi|ografía *f* biography. ∼**ográfico** *a* biographical

bi|ología *f* biology. ∼**ológico** *a* biological. ∼**ólogo** *m* biologist

biombo *m* folding screen

biopsia *f* biopsy

biplaza *m* two-seater

biquini *m* bikini

birlar *vt* ⚏ steal, pinch ⚏

bis *m* encore. ¡∼! encore! **vivo en el 3** ∼ I live at 3A

bisabuel|a *f* great-grandmother. ∼**o** *m* great-grandfather. ∼**os** *mpl* great-grandparents

bisagra *f* hinge

bisiesto *a*. **año** *m* ∼ leap year

bisniet|a *f* great-granddaughter. ∼**o** *m* great-grandson. ∼**os** *mpl* great-grandchildren

bisonte *m* bison

bisoño *a* inexperienced

bisté, bistec *m* steak

bisturí *m* scalpel

bisutería *f* imitation jewellery, costume jewellery

bitácora *f* binnacle

bizco *a* cross-eyed

bizcocho *m* sponge (cake)

bizquear *vi* squint

blanc|a *f* white woman; (Mus) minim. ∼**o** *a* white; *<tez>* fair. ● *m* white; (persona) white man; (espacio) blank; (objetivo) target. **dar en el** ∼**o** hit the mark. **dejar en** ∼**o** leave blank. **pasar la noche en** ∼**o** have a sleepless night. ∼**ura** *f* whiteness

blandir [24] *vt* brandish

bland|o *a* soft; *<carácter>* weak; (cobarde) cowardly; *<carne>* tender. ∼**ura** *f* softness; (de la carne) tenderness

blanque|ar *vt* whiten; whitewash *<paredes>*; bleach *<tela>*; launder *<dinero>*. ● *vi* turn white. ∼**o** *m* whitening; (de dinero) laundering

blasón *m* coat of arms

bledo *m*. **me importa un** ∼ I couldn't care less

blinda|je *m* armour (plating). ∼**r** *vt* armour(-plate)

bloc *m* (*pl* ∼**s**) pad

bloque *m* block; (Pol) bloc. **en** ∼ **en bloc**. ∼**ar** *vt* block; (Mil) blockade; (Com) freeze. ∼**o** *m* blockade; (Com) freezing

blusa *f* blouse

bob|ada *f* silly thing. **decir** ∼**adas** talk nonsense. ∼**ería** *f* silly thing

bobina *f* reel; (Elec) coil

bobo *a* silly, stupid. ● *m* idiot, fool

boca f mouth; (fig, entrada) entrance; (de buzón) slot; (de cañón) muzzle. ~ abajo face down. ~ arriba face up. a ~ de jarro point-blank. con la ~ abierta dumbfounded. se me hizo la ~ agua it made my mouth water

bocacalle f junction. la primera ~ a la derecha the first turning on the right

bocad|illo m (filled) roll; (🄵, comida ligera) snack. ~o m mouthful; (mordisco) bite; (de caballo) bit

boca|jarro. a ~jarro point-blank. ~manga f cuff

bocanada f puff; (de vino etc) mouthful; (ráfaga) gust

bocaza m & f invar big-mouth

boceto m sketch; (de proyecto) outline

bochinche m row; (alboroto) racket. ~ro a (LAm) rowdy

bochorno m sultry weather; (fig, vergüenza) embarrassment. ¡qué ~! how embarrassing!. ~so a oppressive; (fig) embarrassing

bocina f horn; (LAm, auricular) receiver. tocar la ~ sound one's horn. ~zo m toot

boda f wedding

bodeg|a f cellar; (de vino) wine cellar; (LAm, almacén) warehouse; (de un barco) hold. ~ón m cheap restaurant; (pintura) still life

bodoque m & f (🄵, tonto) thickhead; (Mex, niño) kid

bofes mpl lights. echar los ~ slog away

bofet|ada f slap; (fig) blow. ~ón m punch

boga f (moda) fashion. estar en ~ be in fashion, be in vogue. ~r [12] vt row. ~vante m (crustáceo) lobster

Bogotá f Bogotá

bogotano a from Bogotá. ● m native of Bogotá

bohemio a & m Bohemian

bohío m (LAm) hut

boicot m (pl ~s) boycott. ~ear vt boycott. ~eo m boycott. hacer un ~ boycott

boina f beret

bola f ball; (canica) marble; (mentira) fib; (Mex, reunión desordenada) rowdy party; (Mex, montón). una ~ de a bunch of; (Mex, revolución) revolution; (Mex, brillo) shine

boleadoras (LAm) fpl bolas

bolear vt (Mex) polish, shine

bolera f bowling alley

bolero m (baile, chaquetilla) bolero; (fig, 🄵, mentiroso) liar; (Mex, limpiabotas) bootblack

bole|ta f (LAm, de rifa) ticket; (Mex, de notas) (school) report; (Mex, electoral) ballot paper. ~taje m (Mex) tickets. ~tería f (LAm) ticket office; (de teatro, cine) box office. ~tero m (LAm) ticket-seller

boletín m bulletin; (publicación periódica) journal; (de notas) report

boleto m (esp LAm) ticket; (Mex, de avión) (air) ticket. ~ de ida y vuelta, (Mex) ~ redondo return ticket (Brit), round-trip ticket (Amer). ~ sencillo single ticket (Brit), one-way ticket (Amer)

boli m 🄸 Biro (P), ball-point pen

boliche m (juego) bowls; (bolera) bowling alley

bolígrafo m Biro (P), ball-point pen

bolillo m bobbin; (Mex, pan) (bread) roll

bolívar m (unidad monetaria venezolana) bolívar

Bolivia f Bolivia

boliviano a Bolivian. ● m Bolivian; (unidad monetaria de Bolivia) boliviano

boll|ería f baker's shop. ~o m roll; (con azúcar) bun

bolo m skittle; (Mex, en bautizo) coins. ~s mpl (juego) bowling

bols|a f bag; (Mex, bolsillo) pocket; (Mex, de mujer) handbag; (Com) stock exchange; (cavidad) cavity. ~a de agua caliente hot-water bottle. ~illo m pocket. de ~illo pocket. ~o m (de mujer) handbag. ~o de mano, ~o de viaje (overnight) bag

bomba f bomb; (máquina) pump; (noticia) bombshell. ~ de aceite (Auto) oil pump. ~ de agua (Auto) water pump. pasarlo ~ have a marvellous time

bombachos mpl baggy trousers, baggy pants (Amer)

bombarde|ar vt bombard; (desde avión) bomb. **~o** m bombardment; (desde avión) bombing. **~ro** m (avión) bomber

bombazo m explosion

bombear vt pump

bombero m fireman. **cuerpo** m **de ~s** fire brigade (Brit), fire department (Amer)

bombilla f (light) bulb; (LAm, para mate) pipe for drinking maté

bombín m pump; ([T], sombrero) bowler (hat) (Brit), derby (Amer)

bombo m (tambor) bass drum. **a ~ y platillos** with a lot of fuss

bomb|ón m chocolate; (Mex, malvavisco) marshmallow. **~ona** f gas cylinder

bonachón a easygoing; (bueno) good-natured

bonaerense a from Buenos Aires. ● m native of Buenos Aires

bondad f goodness; (amabilidad) kindness; (del clima) mildness. **tenga la ~ de** would you be kind enough to. **~oso** a kind

boniato m sweet potato

bonito a nice; (mono) pretty. **¡muy ~!, ¡qué ~!** that's nice!, very nice!. ● m bonito

bono m voucher; (título) bond. **~ del Tesoro** government bond

boñiga f dung.

boqueada f gasp. **dar la última ~** be dying

boquerón m anchovy

boquete m hole; (brecha) breach

boquiabierto a open-mouthed; (fig) amazed, dumbfounded. **quedarse ~** be amazed

boquilla f mouthpiece; (para cigarrillos) cigarette-holder; (filtro de cigarillo) tip

borbotón m. **hablar a borbotones** gabble. **salir a borbotones** gush out

borda|do a embroidered. ● m embroidery. **~r** vt embroider

bord|e m edge; (de carretera) side; (de plato etc) rim; (de un vestido) hem. **al ~e de** on the edge of; (fig) on the brink of. **~ear** vt go round; (fig) border on. **~illo** m kerb (Brit), curb (esp Amer)

bordo. **a ~** on board

borla f tassel

borrach|era f drunkenness. **pegarse una ~era** get drunk. **~ín** m drunk; (habitual) drunkard. **~o** a drunk. ● m drunkard. **estar ~o** be drunk. **ser ~o** be a drunkard

borrador m rough draft; (de contrato) draft; (para la pizarra) (black)board rubber; (goma) eraser

borrar vt rub out; (tachar) cross out; delete <información>

borrasc|a f depression; (tormenta) storm. **~oso** a stormy

borrego m year-old lamb; (Mex, noticia falsa) canard

borrico m donkey; (fig, [T]) ass

borrón m smudge; (de tinta) inkblot. **~ y cuenta nueva** let's forget about it!

borroso a blurred; (fig) vague

bos|coso a wooded. **~que** m wood, forest

bosquej|ar vt sketch; outline <plan>. **~o** m sketch; (de plan) outline

bosta f dung

bostez|ar [10] vi yawn. **~o** m yawn

bota f boot; (recipiente) wineskin

botana f (Mex) snack, appetizer

botánic|a f botany. **~o** a botanical. ● m botanist

botar vt launch; bounce <pelota>; (esp LAm, tirar) throw away. ● vi bounce

botarate m irresponsible person; (esp LAm, derrochador) spendthrift

bote m boat; (de una pelota) bounce; (lata) tin, can; (vasija) jar. **~ de la basura** (Mex) rubbish bin (Brit), trash can (Amer). **~ salvavidas** lifeboat. **de ~ en ~** packed

botella f bottle

botica f chemist's (shop) (Brit), drugstore (Amer). **~rio** m chemist (Brit), druggist (Amer)

botijo m earthenware jug

botín m half boot; (de guerra) booty; (de ladrones) haul

botiquín m medicine chest; (de primeros auxilios) first aid kit

bot|ón *m* button; (yema) bud; (LAm, insignia) badge. **~ones** *m invar* bellboy (Brit), bellhop (Amer)

bóveda *f* vault

boxe|ador *m* boxer. **~ar** *vi* box. **~o** *m* boxing

boya *f* buoy; (corcho) float. **~nte** *a* buoyant

bozal *m* (de perro etc) muzzle; (de caballo) halter

bracear *vi* wave one's arms; (nadar) swim, crawl

bracero *m* seasonal farm labourer

braga(s) *f(pl)* panties, knickers (Brit)

bragueta *f* flies

bram|ar *vi* bellow. **~ido** *m* bellowing

branquia *f* gill

bras|a *f* ember. **a la ~a** grilled. **~ero** *m* brazier

brasier *m* (Mex) bra

Brasil *m*. (el) **~** Brazil

brasile|ño *a & m* Brazilian. **~ro** *a & m* (LAm) Brazilian

bravío *a* wild

brav|o *a* fierce; (valeroso) brave; *<mar>* rough. **¡~!** *int* well done! bravo! **~ura** *f* ferocity; (valor) bravery

braz|a *f* fathom. **nadar a ~a** swim breast-stroke. **~ada** *f* (en natación) stroke. **~alete** *m* bracelet; (brazal) arm-band. **~o** *m* arm; (de caballo) foreleg; (rama) branch. **~o derecho** right-hand man. **del ~o** arm in arm

brea *f* tar, pitch

brebaje *m* potion; (pej) concoction

brecha *f* opening; (Mil) breach; (Med) gash. **~ generacional** generation gap. **estar en la ~** be in the thick of it

brega *f* struggle. **andar a la ~** work hard

breva *f* early fig

breve *a* short. **en ~** soon, shortly. **en ~s momentos** soon. **~dad** *f* shortness

brib|ón *m* rogue, rascal. **~onada** *f* dirty trick

brida *f* bridle

brigad|a *f* squad; (Mil) brigade. **~ier** *m* brigadier (Brit), brigadier-general (Amer)

brill|ante *a* bright; (lustroso) shiny; *<persona>* brilliant. ● *m* diamond. **~ar** *vi* shine; (centellear) sparkle. **~o** *m* shine; (brillantez) brilliance; (centelleo) sparkle. **sacar ~o** polish. **~oso** *a* (LAm) shiny

brinc|ar [7] *vi* jump up and down. **~o** *m* jump. **dar un ~o, pegar un ~o** jump

brind|ar *vt* offer. ● *vi*. **~ar por** toast, drink a toast to. **~is** *m* toast

br|ío *m* energy; (decisión) determination. **~ioso** *a* spirited; (garboso) elegant

brisa *f* breeze

británico *a* British. ● *m* Briton, British person

brocha *f* paintbrush; (para afeitarse) shaving-brush

broche *m* clasp, fastener; (joya) brooch; (Mex, para el pelo) hairslide (Brit), barrete (Amer)

brocheta *f* skewer; (plato) kebab

brócoli *m* broccoli

brom|a *f* joke. **~a pesada** practical joke. **en ~a** in fun. **ni de ~a** no way. **~ear** *vi* joke. **~ista** *a* fond of joking. ● *m & f* joker

bronca *f* row; (reprensión) telling-off; (LAm, rabia) foul mood. **dar ~ a uno** bug s.o.

bronce *m* bronze; (LAm) brass. **~ado** *a* bronze; (por el sol) tanned. **~ar** *vt* tan *<piel>*. □ **~arse** *vpr* get a suntan

bronquitis *f* bronchitis

brot|ar *vi* (plantas) sprout; (Med) break out; *<líquido>* gush forth; *<lágrimas>* well up. **~e** *m* shoot; (Med) outbreak

bruces: **de ~** face down(wards). **caer de ~** fall flat on one's face

bruj|a *f* witch. **~ería** *f* witchcraft. **~o** *m* wizard, magician. ● *a* (Mex) broke

brújula *f* compass

brum|a *f* mist; (fig) confusion. **~oso** *a* misty, foggy

brusco *a* (repentino) sudden; *<persona>* brusque

Bruselas *f* Brussels

brusquedad *f* roughness; (de movimiento) abruptness

brut|al *a* brutal. **~alidad** *f* brutality; (estupidez) stupidity. **~o** *a* ignorant; (tosco) rough; *<peso, sueldo>* gross

bucal *a* oral; *<lesión>* mouth

buce|ar *vi* dive; (nadar) swim under water. **~o** *m* diving; (natación) underwater swimming

bucle *m* ringlet

budín *m* pudding

budis|mo *m* Buddhism. **~ta** *m & f* Buddhist

buen ⇒BUENO

buenaventura *f* good luck; (adivinación) fortune

bueno *a* (delante de nombre masculino en singular **buen**) good; (agradable) nice; *<tiempo>* fine. ● *int* well!; (de acuerdo) OK!, very well! ¡buena la has hecho! you've gone and done it now! ¡buenas noches! good night! ¡buenas tardes! (antes del atardecer) good afternoon!; (después del atardecer) good evening! ¡~s días! good morning! estar de buenas be in a good mood. por las buenas willingly. ¡qué bueno! (LAm) great!

Buenos Aires *m* Buenos Aires

buey *m* ox

búfalo *m* buffalo

bufanda *f* scarf

bufar *vi* snort

bufete *m* (mesa) writing-desk; (despacho) lawyer's office

buf|o *a* comic. **~ón** *a* comical. ● *m* buffoon; (Historia) jester

buhardilla *f* attic; (ventana) dormer window

búho *m* owl

buhonero *m* pedlar

buitre *m* vulture

bujía *f* (Auto) spark plug

bulbo *m* bulb

bulevar *m* avenue, boulevard

Bulgaria *f* Bulgaria

búlgaro *a & m* Bulgarian

bull|a *f* noise. **~icio** *m* hubbub; (movimiento) bustle. **~icioso** *a* bustling; (ruidoso) noisy

bullir [22] *vi* boil; (burbujear) bubble; (fig) bustle

bulto *m* (volumen) bulk; (forma) shape; (paquete) package; (maleta etc) piece of luggage; (protuberancia) lump

buñuelo *m* fritter

BUP *abrev* (**Bachillerato Unificado Polivalente**) secondary school education

buque *m* ship, boat

burbuj|a *f* bubble.. **~ear** *vi* bubble; *<vino>* sparkle

burdel *m* brothel

burdo *a* rough, coarse; *<excusa>* clumsy

burgu|és *a* middle-class, bourgeois. ● *m* middle-class person. **~esía** *f* middle class, bourgeoisie

burla *f* taunt; (broma) joke; (engaño) trick. **~r** *vt* evade. □ **~rse** *vpr*. **~rse de** mock, make fun of

burlesco *a* (en literatura) burlesque

burlón *a* mocking

bur|ocracia *f* bureaucracy; (Mex, funcionariado) civil service. **~ócrata** *m & f* bureaucrat; (Mex, funcionario) civil servant. **~ocrático** *a* bureaucratic; (Mex) *<empleado>* government

burro *a* stupid; (obstinado) pigheaded. ● *m* donkey; (fig) ass

bursátil *a* stock-exchange

bus *m* bus

busca *f* search. a la **~** de in search of. en **~** de in search of. ● *m* beeper

buscapleitos *m & f invar* (LAm) trouble-maker

buscar [7] *vt* look for. ● *vi* look. buscársela ask for it; ir a **~** a uno fetch s.o.

búsqueda *f* search

busto *m* bust

butaca *f* armchair; (en el teatro etc) seat

buzo *m* diver

buzón *m* postbox (Brit), mailbox (Amer)

Cc

C/ *abrev* (**Calle**) St, Rd

cabal *a* exact; (completo) complete. **no estar en sus ~es** not be in one's right mind

cabalga|dura *f* mount, horse. **~r** [12] *vt* ride. ● *vi* ride, go riding. **~ta** *f* ride; (desfile) procession

caballa *f* mackerel

caballerango *m* (Mex) groom

caballeresco *a* gentlemanly. **literatura** *f* **caballeresca** books of chivalry

caballer|ía *f* mount, horse. **~iza** *f* stable. **~izo** *m* groom

caballero *m* gentleman; (de orden de caballería) knight; (tratamiento) sir. **~so** *a* gentlemanly

caballete *m* (del tejado) ridge; (para mesa) trestle; (de pintor) easel

caballito *m* pony. **~ del diablo** dragonfly. **~ de mar** sea-horse. **~s** *mpl* (carrusel) merry-go-round

caballo *m* horse; (del ajedrez) knight; (de la baraja española) queen. **~ de fuerza** horsepower. **a ~** on horseback

cabaña *f* hut

cabaret /kaba're/ *m* (*pl* **~s**) nightclub

cabecear *vi* nod off; (en fútbol) head the ball; *<caballo>* toss its head

cabecera *f* (de la cama) headboard; (de la mesa) head; (en un impreso) heading

cabecilla *m* ringleader

cabello *m* hair. **~s** *mpl* hair

caber [28] *vi* fit (en into). **no cabe duda** there's no doubt

cabestr|illo *m* sling. **~o** *m* halter

cabeza *f* head; (fig, inteligencia) intelligence. **andar de ~** have a lot to do. **~da** *f* nod. **dar una ~da** nod off. **~zo** *m* butt; (en fútbol) header

cabida *f* capacity; (extensión) area; (espacio) room. **dar ~ a** have room for, accommodate

cabina *f* (de pasajeros) cabin; (de pilotos) cockpit; (electoral) booth; (de camión) cab. **~ telefónica** telephone box (Brit), telephone booth (Amer)

cabizbajo *a* crestfallen

cable *m* cable

cabo *m* end; (trozo) bit; (Mil) corporal; (mango) handle; (Geog) cape; (Naut) rope. **al ~ de** after. **de ~ a rabo** from beginning to end. **llevar a ~** carry out

cabr|a *f* goat. **~iola** *f* jump, skip. **~itilla** *f* kid. **~ito** *m* kid

cábula *m* (Mex) crook

cacahuate, (Mex) **cacahuete** *m* peanut

cacalote *m* (Mex) crow

cacao *m* (planta y semillas) cacao; (polvo) cocoa; (fig) confusion

cacarear *vt* boast about. ● *vi* *<gallo>* crow; *<gallina>* cluck

cacería *f* hunt. **ir de ~** go hunting

cacerola *f* saucepan, casserole

cacharro *m* (earthenware) pot; (coche estropeado) wreck; (cosa inútil) piece of junk; (chisme) thing. **~s** *mpl* pots and pans

cachear *vt* frisk

cachemir *m*, **cachemira** *f* cashmere

cacheo *m* frisking

cachetada *f* (LAm) slap

cache|te *m* slap; (esp LAm, mejilla) cheek. **~tear** *vt* (LAm) slap. **~tón** *a* (LAm) chubby-cheeked

cachimba *f* pipe

cachiporra *f* club, truncheon

cachivache *m* piece of junk. **~s** *mpl* junk

cacho *m* bit, piece; (LAm, cuerno) horn

cachondeo *m* 🔲 joking, joke

cachorro *m* (perrito) puppy; (de león, tigre) cub

cachucha *f* (Mex) cup

caciqu|e *m* cacique, chief; (Pol) local political boss; (hombre poderoso) tyrant. **~il** *a* despotic. **~ismo** *m* despotism

caco *m* thief

cacofonía *f* cacophony

cacto *m*, **cactus** *m invar* cactus

cada *a invar* each, every. ~ **uno** each one, everyone. **uno de** ~ **cinco** one in five. ~ **vez más** more and more

cadáver *m* corpse

cadena *f* chain; (TV) channel. ~ **de fabricación** production line. ~ **de montañas** mountain range. ~ **perpetua** life imprisonment

cadera *f* hip

cadete *m* cadet

caduc|ar [7] *vi* expire. ~**idad** *f*. **fecha** *f* **de** ~**idad** sell-by date. ~**o** *a* outdated

cae|r [29] *vi* fall. **dejar** ~**r** drop. **este vestido no me** ~ **bien** this dress doesn't suit me. **hacer** ~**r** knock over. **Juan me** ~ **bien** I like Juan. **su cumpleaños cayó en martes** his birthday fell on a Tuesday. □ ~**rse** *vpr* fall (over). **se le cayó** he dropped it

café *m* coffee; (cafetería) café; (Mex, marrón) brown. ● *a*. **color** ~ coffee-coloured. ~ **con leche** white coffee. ~ **cortado** coffee with a little milk. ~ **negro** (LAm) expresso. ~ **solo** black coffee

cafe|ína *f* caffeine. ~**tal** *m* coffee plantation. ~**tera** *f* coffee-pot. ~**tería** *f* café. ~**tero** *a* coffee

caíd|a *f* fall; (disminución) drop; (pendiente) slope. ~**o** *a* fallen

caigo *vb* ⇒CAER

caimán *m* cayman, alligator

caj|a *f* box; (de botellas) case; (ataúd) coffin; (en tienda) cash desk; (en supermercado) check-out; (en banco) cashier's desk. ~**a de ahorros** savings bank. ~**a de cambios** gearbox. ~**a de caudales**, ~**a fuerte** safe. ~**a registradora** till. ~**ero** *m* cashier. ~**ero automático** cash dispenser. ~**etilla** *f* packet. ~**ita** *f* small box. ~**ón** *m* (de mueble) drawer; (caja grande) crate; (LAm, ataúd) coffin; (Mex, en estacionamiento) parking space. **ser de** ~**ón** be obvious. ~**uela** *f* (Mex) boot (Brit), trunk (Amer)

cal *m* lime

cala *f* cove

calaba|cín *m*, ~**cita** *f* (Mex) courgette (Brit), zucchini (Amer). ~**za** *f* pumpkin; (fig, 🎓, idiota) idiot. **dar** ~**zas a uno** give s.o. the brush-off

calabozo *m* prison; (celda) cell

calado *a* soaked. **estar** ~ **hasta los huesos** be soaked to the skin. ● *m* (Naut) draught

calamar *m* squid

calambre *m* cramp

calami|dad *f* calamity, disaster. ~**toso** *a* calamitous

calaña *f* sort

calar *vt* soak; (penetrar) pierce; (fig, penetrar) see through; rumble <*persona*>; sample <*fruta*>. □ ~**se** *vpr* get soaked; <*zapatos*> leak; (Auto) stall

calavera *f* skull; (Mex, Auto) taillight

calcar [7] *vt* trace; (fig) copy

calcet|a *f*. **hacer** ~ knit. ~**ín** *m* sock

calcetín *m* sock

calcinar *vt* burn

calcio *m* calcium

calcomanía *f* transfer

calcula|dor *a* calculating. ~**dora** *f* calculator. ~**r** *vt* calculate; (suponer) reckon, think; (imaginar) imagine

cálculo *m* calculation; (Med) stone

caldear *vt* heat, warm. □ ~**se** *vpr* get hot

caldera *f* boiler

calderilla *f* small change

caldo *m* stock; (sopa) clear soup, broth

calefacción *f* heating. ~ **central** central heating

caleidoscopio *m* kaleidoscope

calendario *m* calendar; (programa) schedule

calent|ador *m* heater. ~**amiento** *m* warming; (en deportes) warm-up. ~**ar** [1] *vt* heat; (templar) warm. □ ~**arse** *vpr* get hot; (templarse) warm up; (LAm, enojarse) get mad. ~**ura** *f* fever, (high) temperature. ~**uriento** *a* feverish

calibr|ar *vt* calibrate; (fig) weigh up. ~**e** *m* calibre; (diámetro) diameter; (fig) importance

calidad *f* quality; (condición) capacity. **en** ~ **de** as

calidez f (LAm) warmth

cálido a warm

caliente a hot; <habitación, ropa> warm; (LAm, enojado) angry

califica|ción f qualification; (evaluación) assessment; (nota) mark. ~**do** a (esp LAm) qualified; (mano de obra) skilled. ~**r** [7] vt qualify; (evaluar) assess; mark <examen etc>. ~**r de** describe as, label

cáliz m chalice; (Bot) calyx

caliz|a f limestone. ~**o** a lime

calla|do a quiet. ~**r** vt silence; keep <secreto>; hush up <asunto>. ● vi be quiet, keep quiet, shut up 🔟. □ ~**rse** vpr be quiet, keep quiet, shut up 🔟 ¡**cállate!** be quiet!, shut up! 🔟

calle f street, road; (en deportes, autopista) lane. ~ **de dirección única** one-way street. ~ **mayor** high street, main street. **de** ~ everyday. ~**ja** f narrow street. ~**jear** vi hang out on the streets. ~**jero** a street. ● m street plan. ~**jón** m alley. ~**ón sin salida** dead end. ~**juela** f back street, side street

call|ista m & f chiropodist. ~**o** m corn, callus. ~**os** mpl tripe. ~**osidad** f callus

calm|a f calm. ¡~**a!** calm down!. **en** ~**a** calm. **perder la** ~**a** lose one's composure. ~**ante** m tranquilizer; (para el dolor) painkiller. ~**ar** vt calm; (aliviar) soothe. ● vi <viento> abate. □ ~**arse** vpr calm down; <viento> abate. ~**o** a calm. ~**oso** a calm; (🔟, flemático) slow

calor m heat; (afecto) warmth. **hace** ~ it's hot. **tener** ~ be hot. ~**ía** f calorie. ~**ífero** a heat-producing. ~**ico** a calorific

calumni|a f calumny; (oral) slander; (escrita) libel. ~**ar** vt slander; (por escrito) libel. ~**oso** a slanderous; <cosa escrita> libellous

caluroso a warm; <clima> hot

calv|a f bald head; (parte sin pelo) bald patch. ~**icie** f baldness. ~**o** a bald

calza f wedge

calzada f road; (en autopista) carriageway

calza|do a wearing shoes. ● m footwear, shoe. ~**dor** m shoehorn. ~**r** [10] vt put shoes on; (llevar) wear. ¿**qué número calza Vd?** what size shoe do you take? ● vi wear shoes. □ ~**rse** vpr put on

calz|ón m shorts. ~**ones** mpl shorts; (LAm, ropa interior) panties. ~**oncillos** mpl underpants

cama f bed. ~ **de matrimonio** double bed. ~ **individual** single bed. **guardar** ~ stay in bed

camada f litter

camafeo m cameo

camaleón m chameleon

cámara f (aposento) chamber; (fotográfica) camera. ~ **fotográfica** camera. **a** ~ **lenta** in slow motion

camarad|a m & f colleague; (de colegio) schoolfriend; (Pol) comrade. ~**ería** f camaraderie

camarer|a f chambermaid; (de restaurante etc) waitress. ~**o** m waiter

camarógrafo m cameraman

camarón m shrimp

camarote m cabin

cambi|able a changeable; (Com etc) exchangeable. ~**ante** a variable; <persona> moody. ~**ar** vt change; (trocar) exchange ● vi change. ~ **de idea** change one's mind. □ ~**arse** vpr change. ~**o** m change; (Com) exchange rate; (moneda menuda) (small) change; (Auto) gear. **en** ~**o** on the other hand

camello m camel

camellón m (Mex) traffic island

camerino m dressing room

camilla f stretcher

camin|ante m traveller. ~**ar** vt/i walk. ~**ata** f long walk. ~**o** m road; (sendero) path, track; (dirección, ruta) way. ~**o de** towards, on the way to. **abrir** ~**o** make way. **a medio** ~**o, a la mitad del** ~**o** half-way. **de** ~**o** on the way

cami|ón m lorry; (Mex, autobús) bus. ~**onero** m lorry-driver; (Mex, de autobús) bus driver. ~**oneta** f van; (LAm, coche familiar) estate car

camis|a f shirt. ~ **de fuerza** straitjacket. ~**ería** f shirtmaker's. ~**eta**

f T-shirt; (ropa interior) vest. **~ón** *m* nightdress

camorra *f* 🇮 row. **buscar ~** look for a fight

camote *m* (LAm) sweet potato

campamento *m* camp. **de ~** *a* camping

campan|a *f* bell. **~ada** *f* stroke. **~ario** *m* bell tower, belfry. **~illa** *f* bell

campaña *f* campaign

campe|ón *a & m* champion. **~onato** *m* championship

campes|ino *a* country. ● *m* peasant. **~tre** *a* country

camping /'kampin/ *m* (*pl* **~s**) camping; (lugar) campsite. **hacer ~** go camping

camp|iña *f* countryside. **~o** *m* country; (agricultura, fig) field; (de fútbol) pitch; (de golf) course. **~osanto** *m* cemetery

camufla|je *m* camouflage. **~r** *vt* camouflage

cana *f* grey hair, white hair. **peinar ~s** be getting old

Canadá *m.* **el ~** Canada

canadiense *a & m & f* Canadian

canal *m* (incl TV) channel; (artificial) canal; (del tejado) gutter. **~ de la Mancha** English Channel. **~ de Panamá** Panama Canal. **~ón** *m* (horizontal) gutter; (vertical) drain-pipe

canalla *f* rabble. ● *m* (fig, 🇮) swine. **~da** *f* dirty trick

canapé *m* sofa, couch; (Culin) canapé

Canarias *fpl.* **las** (**islas**) **~** the Canary Islands, the Canaries

canario *a* of the Canary Islands. ● *m* native of the Canary Islands; (pájaro) canary

canast|a *f* (large) basket **~illa** *f* small basket; (para un bebé) layette. **~illo** *m* small basket. **~o** *m* (large) basket

cancela|ción *f* cancellation. **~r** *vt* cancel; write off <*deuda*>

cáncer *m* cancer. **C~** Cancer

cancha *f* court; (LAm, de fútbol, rugby) pitch, ground

canciller *m* chancellor; (LAm, ministro) Minister of Foreign Affairs

canci|ón *f* song. **~ón de cuna** lullaby. **~onero** *m* song-book

candado *m* padlock

candel|a *f* candle. **~abro** *m* candelabra. **~ero** *m* candlestick

candente *a* (rojo) red-hot; (fig) burning

candidato *m* candidate

candidez *f* innocence; (ingenuidad) naivety

cándido *a* naive

candil *m* oil lamp. **~ejas** *fpl* footlights

candor *m* innocence; (ingenuidad) naivety

canela *f* cinnamon

cangrejo *m* crab. **~ de río** crayfish

canguro *m* kangaroo. ● *m & f* (persona) baby-sitter

caníbal *a & m & f* cannibal

canica *f* marble

canijo *a* weak; (Mex, terco) stubborn; (Mex, intenso) incredible

canilla *f* (LAm) shinbone

canino *a* canine. ● *m* canine (tooth)

canje *m* exchange. **~ar** *vt* exchange

cano *a* grey. **de pelo ~** grey-haired

canoa *f* canoe

can|ónigo *m* canon. **~onizar** [10] *vt* canonize

canoso *a* grey-haired

cansa|do *a* tired; (que cansa) tiring. **~dor** (LAm) tiring. **~ncio** *m* tiredness. **~r** *vt* tire; (aburrir) bore. ● *vi* be tiring; (aburrir) get boring. □ **~rse** *vpr* get tired

canta|nte *a* singing. ● *m & f* singer. **~or** *m* Flamenco singer. **~r** *vt/i* sing. **~rlas claras** speak frankly. ● *m* singing; (poema) poem

cántaro *m* pitcher. **llover a ~s** pour down

cante *m* folk song. **~ flamenco, ~ jondo** Flamenco singing

cantera *f* quarry

cantidad *f* quantity; (número) number; (de dinero) sum. **una ~ de** lots of

cantimplora *f* water-bottle

cantina *f* canteen; (Rail) buffet; (LAm, bar) bar

cant|inela *f* song. **~o** *m* singing; (canción) chant; (borde) edge; (de un cuchillo) blunt edge. **~o rodado** boulder; (guijarro) pebble. **de ~o** on edge

canturre|ar *vt/i* hum. **~o** *m* humming

canuto *m* tube

caña *f* (planta) reed; (del trigo) stalk; (del bambú) cane; (de pescar) rod; (de la bota) leg; (vaso) glass. **~ de azúcar** sugar-cane. **~da** *f* ravine; (camino) track; (LAm, arroyo) stream

cáñamo *m* hemp. **~ indio** cannabis

cañ|ería *f* pipe; (tubería) piping. **~o** *m* pipe, tube; (de fuente) jet. **~ón** *m* (de pluma) quill; (de artillería) cannon; (de arma de fuego) barrel; (desfiladero) canyon. **~onera** *f* gunboat

caoba *f* mahogany

ca|os *m* chaos. **~ótico** *a* chaotic

capa *f* layer; (de pintura) coat; (Culin) coating; (prenda) cloak; (más corta) cape; (Geol) stratum

capaci|dad *f* capacity; (fig) ability. **~tar** *vt* qualify, enable; (instruir) train

caparazón *m* shell

capataz *m* foreman

capaz *a* capable, able

capcioso *a* sly, insidious

capellán *m* chaplain

caperuza *f* hood; (de bolígrafo) cap

capilla *f* chapel

capital *a* capital, very important. ● *m* (dinero) capital. ● *f* (ciudad) capital. **~ de provincia** county town. **~ino** *a* (LAm) of/from the capital. **~ismo** *m* capitalism. **~ista** *a* & *m* & *f* capitalist. **~izar** [10] *vt* capitalize

capit|án *m* captain; (de pesquero) skipper. **~anear** *vt* lead, command; skipper *<pesquero>*; captain *<un equipo>*

capitel *m* (Arquit) capital

capitulaci|ón *f* surrender. **~ones** *fpl* marriage contract

capítulo *m* chapter; (de serie) episode

capó *m* bonnet (Brit), hood (Amer)

capón *m* (pollo) capon

caporal *m* (Mex) foreman

capot|a *f* (de mujer) bonnet; (Auto) folding top; (de cochecito) hood. **~e** *m* cape; (Mex, de coche) bonnet (Brit), hood (Amer)

capricho *m* whim. **~so** *a* capricious, whimsical

Capricornio *m* Capricorn

cápsula *f* capsule

captar *vt* harness *<agua>*; grasp *<sentido>*; capture *<atención>*; win *<confianza>*; (radio) pick up

captura *f* capture. **~r** *vt* capture

capucha *f* hood

capullo *m* bud; (de insecto) cocoon

caqui *m* khaki

cara *f* face; (de una moneda) heads; (de un objeto) side; (aspecto) look, appearance; (descaro) cheek. **~ a** facing. **~ a ~** face to face. **~ dura** ⇒ CARADURA. **~ o cruz** heads or tails. **dar la ~ a** face up to. **hacer ~ a** face. **tener mala ~** look ill. **volver la ~** look the other way

carabela *f* caravel

carabina *f* carbine; (fig, 🆃, señora) chaperone

caracol *m* snail; (de mar) winkle; (LAm, concha) conch; (de pelo) curl. **¡~es!** Good Heavens!. **~a** *f* conch

carácter *m* (*pl* **caracteres**) character; (índole) nature. **con ~ de** as

característic|a *f* characteristic. **~o** *a* characteristic, typical

caracteriza|do *a* characterized; (prestigioso) distinguished. **~r** [10] *vt* characterize

caradura *f* cheek, nerve. ● *m* & *f* cheeky person

caramba *int* good heavens!

carambola *f* (en billar) cannon; (Mex, choque múltiple) pile-up. **de ~** by pure chance

caramelo *m* sweet (Brit), candy (Amer); (azúcar fundido) caramel

caraqueño *a* from Caracas

carátula *f* (de disco) sleeve (Brit), jacket (Amer); (de vídeo) case; (de libro) cover; (Mex, del reloj) face

caravana *f* caravan; (de vehículos) convoy; (Auto) long line, traffic jam; (remolque) caravan (Brit), trailer (Amer); (Mex, reverencia) bow

caray *int* 🆃 good heavens!

carb|ón *m* coal; (para dibujar) charcoal. **~ de leña** charcoal. **~oncillo** *m* charcoal. **~onero** *a* coal. ● *m* coal-merchant. **~onizar** [10] *vt* (fig) burn (to a cinder). **~ono** *m* carbon

carbura|dor *m* carburettor. **~nte** *m* fuel

carcajada *f* guffaw. **reírse a ~s** roar with laughter. **soltar una ~** burst out laughing

cárcel *f* prison, jail

carcelero *m* jailer

carcom|er *vt* eat away; (fig) undermine. □ **~erse** *vpr* be eaten away; (fig) waste away

cardenal *m* cardinal; (contusión) bruise

cardiaco, **cardíaco** *a* cardiac, heart

cardinal *a* cardinal

cardo *m* thistle

carear *vt* bring face to face <*personas*>; compare <*cosas*>

care|cer [11] *vi.* **~cer de** lack. **~cer de sentido** not to make sense. **~ncia** *f* lack. **~nte** *a* lacking

care|ro *a* pricey. **~stía** *f* (elevado) high cost

careta *f* mask

carey *m* tortoiseshell

carga *f* load; (fig) burden; (acción) loading; (de barco, avión) cargo; (de tren) freight; (de arma) charge; (Elec, ataque) charge; (obligación) obligation. **llevar la ~ de algo** be responsible for sth. **~da** *f* (Mex, Pol) supporters. **~do** *a* loaded; (fig) burdened; <*atmósfera*> heavy; <*café*> strong; <*pila*> charged. **~mento** *m* load; (acción) loading; (de un barco) cargo. **~r** [12] *vt* load; (fig) burden; (Elec, atacar) charge; fill <*pluma etc*>. ● *vi* load. **~r con** carry. □ **~rse** *vpr* <*pila*> charge. **~rse de** to load s.o. down with

cargo *m* (puesto) post; (acusación) charge. **a ~ de** in the charge of. **hacerse ~ de** take responsibility for. **tener ~ a su ~** be in charge of

carguero *m* (Naut) cargo ship

caria|do *a* decayed. □ **~rse** *vpr* decay

caribeño *a* Caribbean

caricatura *f* caricature

caricia *f* caress; (a animal) stroke

caridad *f* charity. **¡por ~!** for goodness sake!

caries *f invar* tooth decay; (lesión) cavity

cariño *m* affection; (caricia) caress. **~ mío** my darling. **con mucho ~** (en carta) with love from. **tener ~ a** be fond of. **tomar ~ a** become fond of. **~so** *a* affectionate

carisma *m* charisma

caritativo *a* charitable

cariz *m* look

carmesí *a* & *m* crimson

carmín *m* (de labios) lipstick; (color) red

carnal *a* carnal. **primo ~** first cousin

carnaval *m* carnival. **~esco** *a* carnival

carne *f* meat; (Anat, de frutos, pescado) flesh. **~ de cerdo** pork. **~ de cordero** lamb. **~ de gallina** goose pimples. **~ molida** (LAm), **~ picada** mince (Brit), ground beef (Amer). **~ de ternera** veal. **~ de vaca** beef. **me pone la ~ de gallina** it gives me the creeps. **ser de ~ y hueso** be only human

carné, **carnet** *m* card. **~ de conducir** driving licence (Brit), driver's license (Amer) **~ de identidad** identity card. **~ de manejar** (LAm) driving license (Brit), driver's license (Amer). **~ de socio** membership card

carnero *m* ram

carnicer|ía *f* butcher's (shop); (fig) massacre. **~o** *a* carnivorous. ● *m* butcher

carnívoro *a* carnivorous. ● *m* carnivore

carnoso *a* fleshy; <*pollo*> meaty

caro *a* expensive. ● *adv* dear, dearly. **costar ~ a uno** cost s.o. dear.

carpa *f* carp; (LAm, tienda) tent

carpeta *f* folder, file. **~zo** *m*. **dar ~zo a** shelve

carpinter|ía *f* carpentry. **~o** *m* carpenter, joiner

carraspe|ar *vi* clear one's throat. **~ra** *f*. **tener ~ra** have a frog in one's throat

carrera *f* run; (prisa) rush; (concurso) race; (estudios) degree course; (profesión) career; (de taxi) journey

carreta f cart. **~da** f cartload

carrete m reel; (película) film

carretear vi (LAm) taxi

carretera f road. **~ de circunvalación** bypass, ring road. **~ nacional** A road (Brit), highway (Amer)

carretilla f wheelbarrow

carril m lane; (Rail) rail

carrito m (en supermercado, para equipaje) trolley (Brit), cart (Amer)

carro m cart; (LAm, coche) car; (Mex, vagón) coach. **~ de combate** tank. **~cería** f (Auto) bodywork

carroña f carrion

carroza f coach, carriage; (en desfile de fiesta) float

carruaje m carriage

carrusel m merry-go-round

cart|a f letter; (lista de platos) menu; (lista de vinos) list; (Geog) map; (naipe) card. **~a blanca** free hand. **~a de crédito** letter of credit. **~earse** vpr correspond

cartel m poster; (letrero) sign. **~era** f hoarding; (en periódico) listings; (LAm en escuela, oficina) notice board (Brit), bulletin board (Amer). **de ~** celebrated

carter|a f wallet; (de colegial) satchel; (para documentos) briefcase; (LAm, de mujer) handbag (Brit), purse (Amer). **~ista** m & f pickpocket

cartero m postman, mailman (Amer)

cartílago m cartilage

cartilla f first reading book. **~ de ahorros** savings book. **leerle la ~ a uno** tell s.o. off

cartón m cardboard

cartucho m cartridge

cartulina f card

casa f house; (hogar) home; (empresa) firm. **~ de huéspedes** boardinghouse. **~ de socorro** first aid post. **ir a ~** go home. **salir de ~** go out

casaca f jacket

casado a married. **los recién ~os** the newly-weds

casa|mentero m matchmaker. **~miento** m marriage; (ceremonia) wedding. **~r** vt marry. □ **~rse** vpr get married

cascabel m small bell; (de serpiente) rattle

cascada f waterfall

casca|nueces m invar nutcrackers. **~r** [7] vt crack <nuez, huevo>; (pegar) beat. □ **~rse** vpr crack

cáscara f (de huevo, nuez) shell; (de naranja) peel; (de plátano) skin

cascarrabias a invar grumpy

casco m helmet; (de cerámica etc) piece, fragment; (cabeza) scalp; (de barco) hull; (envase) empty bottle; (de caballo) hoof; (de una ciudad) part, area

cascote m piece of rubble. **~s** mpl rubble

caserío m country house; (poblado) hamlet

casero a home-made; (doméstico) domestic; (amante del hogar) home-loving; <reunión> family. ● m owner; (vigilante) caretaker

caseta f hut; (puesto) stand. **~ de baño** bathing hut

casete m & f cassette

casi adv almost, nearly; (en frases negativas) hardly. **~ ~** very nearly. **~ nada** hardly any. **¡~ nada!** is that all? **~ nunca** hardly ever

casill|a f hut; (en ajedrez etc) square; (en formulario) box; (compartimento) pigeonhole. **~ electrónica** e-mail address. **~ero** m pigeonholes; (compartimento) pigeonhole

casino m casino; (club social) club

caso m case. **el ~ es que** the fact is that. **en ~ de** in the event of. **en cualquier ~** in any case, whatever happens. **en ese ~** in that case. **en todo ~** in any case. **en último ~** as a last resort. **hacer ~ de** take notice of. **poner por ~** suppose

caspa f dandruff

casquivana f flirt

cassette m & f cassette

casta f (de animal) breed; (de persona) descent; (grupo social) caste

castaña f chestnut

castañetear vi <dientes> chatter

castaño a chestnut; <ojos> brown. ● m chestnut (tree)

castañuela f castanet

castellano *a* Castilian. ● *m* (persona) Castilian; (lengua) Castilian, Spanish. ~**parlante** *a* Castilian-speaking, Spanish-speaking. ¿**habla Vd** ~? do you speak Spanish?

castidad *f* chastity

castig|ar [12] *vt* punish; (en deportes) penalize. ~**o** *m* punishment; (en deportes) penalty

castillo *m* castle

cast|izo *a* traditional; (puro) pure. ~**o** *a* chaste

castor *m* beaver

castrar *vt* castrate

castrense *m* military

casual *a* chance, accidental. ~**idad** *f* chance, coincidence. **dar la** ~**idad** happen. **de** ~**idad, por** ~**idad** by chance. ¡**qué** ~**idad!** what a coincidence!. ~**mente** *adv* by chance; (precisamente) actually

cataclismo *m* cataclysm

catador *m* taster

catalán *a & m* Catalan

catalizador *m* catalyst

cat|alogar [12] *vt* catalogue; (fig) classify. ~**álogo** *m* catalogue

Cataluña *f* Catalonia

catamarán *m* catamaran

catapulta *f* catapult

catar *vt* taste, try

catarata *f* waterfall, falls; (Med) cataract

catarro *m* cold

cat|ástrofe *m* catastrophe. ~**astrófico** *a* catastrophic

catecismo *m* catechism

cátedra *f* (en universidad) professorship, chair; (en colegio) post of head of department

catedral *f* cathedral

catedrático *m* professor; (de colegio) teacher, head of department

categ|oría *f* category; (clase) class. **de** ~**oría** important. **de primera** ~**oría** first-class. ~**órico** *a* categorical

cat|olicismo *m* catholicism. ~**ólico** *a* (Roman) Catholic ● *m* (Roman) Catholic

catorce *a & m* fourteen

cauce *m* river bed; (fig, artificial) channel

caucho *m* rubber

caudal *m* (de río) volume of flow; (riqueza) wealth. ~**oso** *a* <*río*> large

caudillo *m* leader

causa *f* cause; (motivo) reason; (Jurid) trial. **a** ~ **de, por** ~ **de** because of. ~**r** *vt* cause

cautel|a *f* caution. ~**oso** *a* cautious, wary

cauterizar [10] *vt* cauterize

cautiv|ar *vt* capture; (fig, fascinar) captivate. ~**erio** *m*, ~**idad** *f* captivity. ~**o** *a & m* captive

cauto *a* cautious

cavar *vt/i* dig

caverna *f* cave, cavern

caviar *m* caviare

cavidad *f* cavity

caza *f* hunting; (con fusil) shooting; (animales) game. ● *m* fighter. **andar a** (**la**) ~ **de** be in search of. ~ **mayor** game hunting. **dar** ~ chase, go after. **ir de** ~ go hunting/shooting. ~**dor** *m* hunter. ~**dora** *f* jacket. ~**r** [10] *vt* hunt; (con fusil) shoot; (fig) track down; (obtener) catch, get

caz|o *m* saucepan; (cucharón) ladle. ~**oleta** *f* (small) saucepan. ~**uela** *f* casserole

cebada *f* barley

ceb|ar *vt* fatten (up); bait <*anzuelo*>; prime <*arma de fuego*>. ~**o** *m* bait; (de arma de fuego) charge

cebol|la *f* onion. ~**eta** *f* spring onion (Brit), scallion (Amer). ~**ino** *m* chive

cebra *f* zebra

cece|ar *vi* lisp. ~**o** *m* lisp

cedazo *m* sieve

ceder *vt* give up; (transferir) transfer. ● *vi* give in; (disminuir) ease off; (romperse) give way, collapse. **ceda el paso** give way (Brit), yield (Amer)

cedro *m* cedar

cédula *f* bond. ~ **de identidad** identity card

CE(E) *abrev* (**Comunidad (Económica) Europea**) E(E)C

ceg|ador *a* blinding. ~**ar** [1 & 12] *vt* blind; (tapar) block up. □ ~**arse** *vpr* be blinded (**de** by). **~uera** _f_ blindness

ceja _f_ eyebrow

cejar _vi_ give way

celada _f_ ambush; (fig) trap

cela|dor _m_ (de cárcel) prison warder; (de museo etc) security guard. **~r** _vt_ watch

celda _f_ cell

celebra|ción _f_ celebration. **~r** _vt_ celebrate; (alabar) praise. □ **~rse** _vpr_ take place

célebre _a_ famous

celebridad _f_ fame; (persona) celebrity

celest|e _a_ heavenly; _<vestido>_ pale blue. **azul ~e** sky-blue. **~ial** _a_ heavenly

celibato _m_ celibacy

célibe _a_ celibate

celo _m_ zeal; (de las hembras) heat; (de los machos) rut; (cinta adhesiva) Sellotape (P) (Brit), Scotch (P) tape (Amer). **~s** _mpl_ jealousy. **dar ~s** make jealous. **tener ~s** be jealous

celofán _m_ cellophane

celoso _a_ conscientious; (que tiene celos) jealous

celta _a_ & _m_ (lengua) Celtic. ● _m_ & _f_ Celt

célula _f_ cell

celular _a_ cellular. ● _m_ (LAm) mobile phone

celulosa _f_ cellulose

cementerio _m_ cemetery

cemento _m_ cement; (hormigón) concrete; (LAm, cola) glue

cena _f_ dinner; (comida ligera) supper

cenag|al _m_ marsh, bog; (fig) tight spot. **~oso** _a_ boggy

cenar _vt_ have for dinner; (en cena ligera) have for supper. ● _vi_ have dinner; (tomar cena ligera) have supper

cenicero _m_ ashtray

ceniza _f_ ash

censo _m_ census. **~ electoral** electoral roll

censura _f_ censure; (de prensa etc) censorship. **~r** _vt_ censure; censor _<prensa etc>_

centavo _a_ & _m_ hundredth; (moneda) centavo

centell|a _f_ flash; (chispa) spark. **~ar**, **~ear** _vi_ sparkle

centena _f_ hundred. **~r** _m_ hundred. **a ~res** by the hundred. **~rio** _a_ centenarian. ● _m_ centenary; (persona) centenarian

centeno _m_ rye

centésim|a _f_ hundredth. **~o** _a_ hundredth

cent|ígrado _a_ centigrade, Celsius. ● _m_ centigrade. **~igramo** _m_ centigram. **~ilitro** _m_ centilitre. **~ímetro** _m_ centimetre

céntimo _a_ hundredth. ● _m_ cent

centinela _f_ sentry

centolla _f_, **centollo** _m_ spider crab

central _a_ central. ● _f_ head office. **~ de correos** general post office. **~ eléctrica** power station. **~ nuclear** nuclear power station. **~ telefónica** telephone exchange. **~ita** _f_ switchboard

centraliza|ción _f_ centralization. **~r** [10] _vt_ centralize

centrar _vt_ centre

céntrico _a_ central

centrífugo _a_ centrifugal

centro _m_ centre. **~ comercial** shopping centre (Brit), shopping mall (Amer)

Centroamérica _f_ Central America

centroamericano _a_ & _m_ Central American

ceñi|do _a_ tight. **~r** [5 & 22] _vt_ take _<corona>_; _<vestido>_ cling to. □ **~rse** _vpr_ limit o.s. (**a** to)

ceñ|o _m_ frown. **fruncir el ~o** frown. **~udo** _a_ frowning

cepill|ar _vt_ brush; (en carpintería) plane. **~o** _m_ brush; (en carpintería) plane. **~o de dientes** toothbrush

cera _f_ wax

cerámic|a _f_ ceramics; (materia) pottery; (objeto) piece of pottery. **~o** _a_ ceramic

cerca _f_ fence; (de piedra) wall. ● _adv_ near, close. **~ de** close to, close up, closely

cercan|ía *f* nearness, proximity. ~**ías** *fpl* vicinity. **tren** *m* **de** ~**ías** local train. ~**o** *a* near, close.

cercar [7] *vt* fence in, enclose; *<gente>* surround; (asediar) besiege

cerciorar *vt* convince. □ ~**se** *vpr* make sure

cerco *m* (asedio) siege; (círculo) ring; (LAm, valla) fence; (LAm, seto) hedge

cerdo *m* pig; (carne) pork

cereal *m* cereal

cerebr|al *a* cerebral. ~**o** *m* brain; (persona) brains

ceremoni|a *f* ceremony. ~**al** *a* ceremonial. ~**oso** *a* ceremonious

cerez|a *f* cherry. ~**o** *m* cherry tree

cerill|a *f* match. ~**o** *m* (Mex) match

cern|er [1] *vt* sieve. □ ~**erse** *vpr* hover. ~**idor** *m* sieve

cero *m* nought, zero; (fútbol) nil (Brit), zero (Amer); (tenis) love; (persona) nonentity

cerquillo *m* (LAm, flequillo) fringe (Brit), bangs (Amer)

cerra|do *a* shut, closed; (espacio) shut in, enclosed; *<cielo>* overcast; *<curva>* sharp. ~**dura** *f* lock; (acción de cerrar) shutting, closing. ~**jero** *m* locksmith. ~**r** [1] *vt* shut, close; (con llave) lock; (cercar) enclose; turn off *<grifo>*; block up *<agujero etc>*. ● *vi* shut, close. □ ~**rse** *vpr* shut, close; *<herida>* heal. ~**r con llave** lock

cerro *m* hill

cerrojo *m* bolt. **echar el** ~ bolt

certamen *m* competition, contest

certero *a* accurate

certeza, **certidumbre** *f* certainty

certifica|do *a* *<carta etc>* registered. ● *m* certificate. ~**r** [7] *vt* certify

certitud *f* certainty

cervatillo, **cervato** *m* fawn

cerve|cería *f* beerhouse, bar; (fábrica) brewery. ~**za** *f* beer. ~**za de barril** draught beer. ~**za rubia** lager

cesa|ción *f* cessation, suspension. ~**nte** *a* redundant. ~**r** *vt* stop. ● *vi* stop, cease; (dejar un empleo) resign. **sin** ~**r** incessantly

cesárea *f* caesarian (section)

cese *m* cessation; (de un empleo) dismissal. ~ **del fuego** (LAm) ceasefire

césped *m* grass, lawn

cest|a *f* basket. ~**o** *m* basket. ~**o de los papeles** waste-paper basket

chabacano *a* common; *<chiste etc>* vulgar. ● *m* (Mex, albaricoque) apricot

chabola *f* shack. ~**s** *fpl* shanty town

cháchara *f* 🔲 chatter; (Mex, objetos sin valor) junk

chacharear *vt* (Mex) sell. ● *vi* 🔲 chatter

chacra *f* (LAm) farm

chal *m* shawl

chalado *a* 🔲 crazy

chalé *m* house (with a garden), villa

chaleco *m* waistcoat, vest (Amer). ~ **salvavidas** life-jacket

chalet *m* (*pl* ~**s**) house (with a garden), villa

chalote *m* shallot

chamac|a *f* (esp Mex) girl. ~**o** *m* (esp Mex) boy

chamarra *f* sheepskin jacket; (Mex, chaqueta corta) jacket

chamb|a *f* (Mex, trabajo) work. **por** ~**a** by fluke. ~**ear** *vi* (Mex, 🔲) work

champán *m*, **champaña** *m* & *f* champagne

champiñón *m* mushroom

champú *m* (*pl* ~**es** *o* ~**s**) shampoo

chamuscar [7] *vt* scorch

chance *m* (esp LAm) chance

chancho *m* (LAm) pig

chanchullo *m* 🔲 swindle, fiddle 🔲

chanclo *m* clog; (de caucho) rubber overshoe

chándal *m* (*pl* ~**s**) tracksuit

chantaje *m* blackmail. ~**ar** *vt* blackmail

chanza *f* joke

chapa *f* plate, sheet; (de madera) plywood; (de botella) metal top; (carrocería) bodywork; (LAm cerradura) lock. ~**do** *a* plated. ~**do a la antigua** old-fashioned. ~**do en oro** gold-plated

chaparro *a* (LAm) short, squat

chaparrón *m* downpour

chapopote *m* (Mex) tar

chapotear *vi* splash

chapucero *a* <*persona*> slapdash; <*trabajo*> shoddy

chapulín *m* (Mex) locust; (saltamontes) grasshopper

chapurrar, chapurrear *vt* have a smattering of, speak a little

chapuza *f* botched job; (trabajo ocasional) odd job

chaquet|a *f* jacket. **cambiar de** ~**a** change sides. ~**ón** *m* three-quarter length coat

charc|a *f* pond, pool. ~**o** *m* puddle, pool

charcutería *f* delicatessen

charla *f* chat; (conferencia) talk. ~**dor** *a* talkative. ~**r** *vi* 🔟 chat. ~**tán** *a* talkative. ● *m* chatterbox; (vendedor) cunning hawker; (curandero) charlatan

charol *m* varnish; (cuero) patent leather. ~**a** *f* (Mex) tray

charr|a *f* (Mex) horsewoman, cowgirl. ~**o** *m* (Mex) horseman, cowboy

chascar [7] *vt* crack <*látigo*>; click <*lengua*>; snap <*dedos*>. ● *vi* <*madera*> creak. ~ **con la lengua** click one's tongue

chasco *m* disappointment

chasis *m* (Auto) chassis

chasqu|ear *vt* crack <*látigo*>; click <*lengua*>; snap <*dedos*>. ● *vi* <*madera*> creak. ~ **con la lengua** click one's tongue. ~**ido** *m* crack; (de la lengua) click; (de los dedos) snap

chatarra *f* scrap iron; (fig) scrap

chato *a* <*nariz*> snub; <*objetos*> flat. ● *m* wine glass

chav|a *f* (Mex) girl, lass. ~**al** *m* 🔟 boy, lad. ~**o** *m* (Mex) boy, lad.

checa|da *f* (Mex) check; (Mex, Med) checkup. ~**r** [7] *vt* (Mex) check; (vigilar) check up on. ~**r tarjeta** clock in

checo *a* & *m* Czech. ~**slovaco** *a* & *m* (History) Czechoslovak

chelín *m* shilling

chelo *m* cello

cheque *m* cheque. ~ **de viaje** traveller's cheque. ~**ar** *vt* check; (LAm) check in <*equipaje*>. ~**o** *m* check; (Med) checkup. ~**ra** *f* chequebook

chévere *a* (LAm) great

chica *f* girl; (criada) maid, servant

chicano *a* & *m* Chicano, Mexican-American

chícharo *m* (Mex) pea

chicharra *f* cicada; (timbre) buzzer

chichón *m* bump

chicle *m* chewing-gum

chico *a* 🔟 small; (esp LAm, de edad) young. ● *m* boy. ~**s** *mpl* children

chicoria *f* chicory

chifla|do *a* 🔟 crazy, daft. ~**r** *vt* whistle at, boo. ● *vi* (LAm) whistle; (🔟, gustar mucho) **me chifla el chocolate** I'm mad about chocolate. □ ~**rse** *vpr* be mad (**por** about)

chilango *a* (Mex) from Mexico City

chile *m* chilli

Chile *m* Chile

chileno *a* & *m* Chilean

chill|ar *vi* scream, shriek; <*ratón*> squeak; <*cerdo*> squeal. ~**ido** *m* scream, screech. ~**ón** *a* noisy; <*colores*> loud; <*sonido*> shrill

chimenea *f* chimney; (hogar) fireplace

chimpancé *m* chimpanzee

china *f* Chinese (woman)

China *f* China

chinche *m* drawing-pin (Brit), thumbtack (Amer); (insecto) bedbug; (fig) nuisance. ~**eta** *f* drawing-pin (Brit), thumbtack (Amer)

chinela *f* slipper

chino *a* Chinese; (Mex rizado) curly. ● *m* Chinese (man); (Mex, de pelo rizado) curly-haired person

chipriota *a* & *m* & *f* Cypriot

chiquero *m* pen; (LAm, pocilga) pigsty (Brit), pigpen (Amer)

chiquillo *a* childish. ● *m* child, kid 🔟

chirimoya *f* custard apple

chiripa *f* fluke

chirri|ar [20] *vi* creak; <*frenos*> screech; <*pájaro*> chirp. ~**do** *m* creaking; (de frenos) screech; (de pájaros) chirping

chis *int* sh!, hush!; (🔟, para llamar a uno) hey!, psst!

chism|e *m* gadget, thingumajig 🔟; (chismorreo) piece of gossip. ~**es** *mpl* things, bits and pieces. **~orreo** *m* gossip. **~oso** *a* gossipy.● *m* gossip

chisp|a *f* spark; (pizca) drop; (gracia) wit; (fig) sparkle. **estar que echa ~a(s)** be furious. **~eante** *a* sparkling. **~ear** *vi* spark; (lloviznar) drizzle; (fig) sparkle. **~orrotear** *vt* throw out sparks; <*fuego*> crackle; <*aceite*> spit

chistar *vi.* **ni chistó** he didn't say a word. **sin ~** without saying a word

chiste *m* joke, funny story. **tener ~** be funny

chistera *f* top hat

chistoso *a* funny

chiva|rse *vpr* tip-off; <*niño*> tell. **~tazo** *m* tip-off. **~to** *m* informer; (niño) telltale

chivo *m* kid; (LAm, macho cabrío) billy goat

choca|nte *a* shocking; (Mex desagradable) unpleasant. **~r** [7] *vt* clink <*vasos*>; (LAm) crash <*vehículo*>. **¡chócala!** give me five! ● *vi* collide, hit. **~r con**, **~r contra** crash into

choch|ear *vi* be gaga. **~o** *a* gaga; (fig) soft

chocolate *m* chocolate. **tableta** *f* **de ~** bar of chocolate

chófer, (LAm) **chofer** *m* chauffeur; (conductor) driver

cholo *a* & *m* (LAm) half-breed

chopo *m* poplar

choque *m* collision; (fig) clash; (eléctrico) shock; (Auto, Rail etc) crash, accident; (sacudida) jolt

chorizo *m* chorizo

chorro *m* jet, stream; (caudal pequeño) trickle; (fig) stream. **a ~** <*avión*> jet. **a ~os** (fig) in abundance

chovinista *a* chauvinistic. ● *m* & *f* chauvinist

choza *f* hut

chubas|co *m* squall, heavy shower. **~quero** *m* raincoat, anorak

chuchería *f* trinket

chueco *a* (LAm) crooked

chufa *f* tiger nut

chuleta *f* chop

chulo *a* cocky; (bonito) lovely (Brit), neat (Amer); (Mex, atractivo) cute. ● *m* tough guy; (proxeneta) pimp

chup|ada *f* suck; (al helado) lick; (al cigarro) puff. **~ado** *a* skinny; (fácil) very easy. **~ar** *vt* suck; puff at <*cigarro etc*>; (absorber) absorb. **~ete** *m* dummy (Brit), pacifier (Amer). **~ón** *m* sucker; (LAm) dummy (Brit), pacifier (Amer); (Mex, del biberón) teat

churro *m* fritter; mess

chusma *f* riff-raff

chut|ar *vi* shoot. **~e** *m* shot

cianuro *m* cyanide

cibernética *f* cibernetics

cicatriz *f* scar. **~ar** [10] *vt/i* heal. □ **~arse** *vpr* heal

cíclico *a* cyclic(al)

ciclis|mo *m* cycling. **~ta** *a* cycle. ● *m* & *f* cyclist

ciclo *m* cycle; (de películas, conciertos) season; (de conferencias) series

ciclomotor *m* moped

ciclón *m* cyclone

ciego *a* blind. ● *m* blind man, blind person. **a ciegas** in the dark

cielo *m* sky; (Relig) heaven; (persona) darling. **¡~s!** good heavens!, goodness me!

ciempiés *m invar* centipede

cien *a* a hundred. **~ por ~** one hundred per cent

ciénaga *f* bog, swamp

ciencia *f* science; (fig) knowledge. **~s** *fpl* (Univ etc) science. **~s empresariales** business studies. **a ~ cierta** for certain

cieno *m* mud

científico *a* scientific. ● *m* scientist

ciento *a* & *m* a hundred, one hundred. **~s de** hundreds of. **por ~** per cent

cierre *m* fastener; (acción de cerrar) shutting, closing; (LAm, cremallera) zip, zipper (Amer)

cierro *vb* ⇒CERRAR

cierto *a* certain; (verdad) true. **estar en lo ~** be right. **lo ~ es que** the fact is that. **no es ~** that's not true. **¿no es ~?** isn't that right? **por ~** by the way. **si bien es ~ que** although

ciervo *m* deer

cifra *f* figure, number; (cantidad) sum. **en ~** coded, in code. **~do** *a* coded. **~r** *vt* code; place *<esperanzas>*

cigala *f* crayfish

cigarra *f* cicada

cigar|illera *f* cigarette box; (de bolsillo) cigarette case. **~illo** *m* cigarette. **~o** *m* (cigarrillo) cigarette; (puro) cigar

cigüeña *f* stork

cilantro *m* coriander

cil|índrico *a* cylindrical. **~indro** *m* cylinder

cima *f* top; (fig) summit

cimbr|ear *vt* shake. □ **~earse** *vpr* sway. **~onada** *f*, **~onazo** *m* (LAm) jolt; (de explosión) blast

cimentar [1] *vt* lay the foundations of; (fig, reforzar) strengthen

cimientos *mpl* foundations

cinc *m* zinc

cincel *m* chisel. **~ar** *vt* chisel

cinco *a* & *m* five; (en fechas) fifth

cincuent|a *a* & *m* fifty; (quincuagési-mo) fiftieth. **~ón** *a* in his fifties

cine *m* cinema; (local) cinema (Brit), movie theater (Amer). **~asta** *m* & *f* film maker (Brit), movie maker (Amer). **~matográfico** *a* film (Brit), movie (Amer)

cínico *a* cynical. ● *m* cynic

cinismo *m* cynicism

cinta *f* ribbon; (película) film (Brit), movie (Amer); (para grabar, en carreras) tape. **~ aislante** insulating tape. **~ métrica** tape measure. **~ virgen** blank tape

cintur|a *f* waist. **~ón** *m* belt. **~ón de seguridad** safety belt. **~ón salva-vidas** lifebelt

ciprés *m* cypress (tree)

circo *m* circus

circuito *m* circuit; (viaje) tour. **~ ce-rrado** closed circuit. **corto ~** short circuit

circula|ción *f* circulation; (vehícu-los) traffic. **~r** *a* circular. ● *vi* circu-late; *<líquidos>* flow; (conducir) drive; (caminar) walk; *<autobús>* run

círculo *m* circle. **~ vicioso** vicious circle. **en ~** in a circle

circunci|dar *vt* circumcise. **~sión** *f* circumcision

circunferencia *f* circumference

circunflejo *m* circumflex

circunscri|bir (*pp* **circunscrito**) *vt* confine. □ **~birse** *vpr* confine o.s. (a to). **~pción** *f* (distrito) district. **~pción electoral** constituency

circunspecto *a* circumspect

circunstancia *f* circumstance

circunv|alar *vt* bypass. **~olar** *vt* [2] circle

cirio *m* candle

ciruela *f* plum. **~ pasa** prune

ciru|gía *f* surgery. **~jano** *m* sur-geon

cisne *m* swan

cisterna *f* tank, cistern

cita *f* appointment; (entre chico y chica) date; (referencia) quotation. **~ción** *f* quotation; (Jurid) summons. **~do** *a* aforementioned. **~r** *vt* make an ap-pointment with; (mencionar) quote; (Jurid) summons. □ **~rse** *vpr* ar-range to meet

cítara *f* zither

ciudad *f* town; (grande) city. **~ bal-neario** (LAm) coastal resort. **~ perdi-da** (Mex) shanty town. **~ universita-ria** university campus. **~anía** *f* citi-zenship; (habitantes) citizens. **~ano** *a* civic. ● *m* citizen, inhabitant

cívico *a* civic

civil *a* civil. ● *m* & *f* civil guard; (persona no militar) civilian

civiliza|ción *f* civilization. **~r** [10] *vt* civilize. □ **~rse** *vpr* become civil-ized

civismo *m* community spirit

clam|ar *vi* cry out, clamour. **~or** *m* clamour; (protesta) outcry. **~oroso** *a* noisy; (éxito) resounding

clandestino *a* clandestine, secret; *<periódico>* underground

clara *f* (de huevo) egg white

claraboya *f* skylight

clarear *vi* dawn; (aclarar) brighten up

clarete *m* rosé

claridad *f* clarity; (luz) light

clarifica|ción *f* clarification. **~r** [7] *vt* clarify

clar|ín *m* bugle. **~inete** *m* clarinet. **~inetista** *m & f* clarinettist

clarividen|cia *f* clairvoyance; (fig) far-sightedness. **~te** *a* clairvoyant; (fig) far-sighted

claro *a* clear; (luminoso) bright; <colores> light; <líquido> thin. ● *m* (en bosque etc) clearing; (espacio) gap. ● *adv* clearly. ● *int* of course! ¡~ que sí! yes, of course! ¡~ que no! of course not!

clase *f* class; (tipo) kind, sort; (aula) classroom. **~ media** middle class. **~ obrera** working class. **~ social** social class. **dar ~s** teach

clásico *a* classical; (típico) classic. ● *m* classic

clasifica|ción *f* classification; (deportes) league. **~r** [7] *vt* classify; (seleccionar) sort

claudicar [7] give in

claustro *m* cloister; (Univ) staff

claustrof|obia *f* claustrophobia. **~óbico** *a* claustrophobic

cláusula *f* clause

clausura *f* closure; (ceremonia) closing ceremony. **~r** *vt* close

clava|do *a* fixed; (con clavo) nailed. **es ~do a su padre** he's the spitting image of his father. ● *m* (LAm) dive. **~r** *vt* knock in <clavo>; stick in <cuchillo>; (fijar) fix; (juntar) nail together

clave *f* key; (Mus) clef; (instrumento) harpsichord. **~cín** *m* harpsichord

clavel *m* carnation

clavícula *f* collarbone, clavicle

clav|ija *f* peg; (Elec) plug. **~o** *m* nail; (Culin) clove

claxon *m* /'klakson/ (*pl* ~s) horn

clemencia *f* clemency, mercy

clementina *f* clementine

cleptómano *m* kleptomaniac

clerical *a* clerical

clérigo *m* priest

clero *m* clergy

cliché *m* cliché; (Foto) negative

cliente *m* customer; (de médico) patient; (de abogado) client. **~la** *f* clientele, customers; (de médico) patients

clim|a *m* climate; (ambiente) atmosphere. **~ático** *a* climatic. **~atizado** *a* air-conditioned

clínic|a *f* clinic. **~o** *a* clinical

cloaca *f* drain, sewer

cloro *m* chlorine

club *m* (*pl* ~s o ~es) club

coacci|ón *f* coercion. **~onar** *vt* coerce

coagular *vt* coagulate; clot <sangre>; curdle <leche>. □ **~se** *vpr* coagulate; <sangre> clot; <leche> curdle

coalición *f* coalition

coarta|da *f* alibi. **~r** *vt* hinder; restrict <libertad etc>

cobard|e *a* cowardly. ● *m* coward. **~ía** *f* cowardice

cobert|izo *m* shed. **~ura** *f* covering

cobij|a *f* (Mex, manta) blanket. **~as** *fpl* (LAm, ropa de cama) bedclothes. **~ar** *vt* shelter. □ **~arse** *vpr* (take) shelter. **~o** *m* shelter

cobra *f* cobra

cobra|dor *m* collector; (de autobús) conductor. **~r** *vt* collect; (ganar) earn; charge <precio>; cash <cheque>; (recuperar) recover. ● *vi* be paid

cobr|e *m* copper. **~izo** *a* coppery

cobro *m* collection; (de cheque) cashing; (pago) payment. **presentar al ~** cash

cocaína *f* cocaine

cocción *f* cooking; (Tec) firing

coc|er [2 & 9] *vt/i* cook; (hervir) boil; (Tec) fire. **~ido** *m* stew

coche *m* car, automobile (Amer); (de tren) coach, carriage; (de bebé) pram (Brit), baby carriage (Amer). **~-cama** sleeper. **~ fúnebre** hearse. **~ restaurante** dining-car. **~s de choque** dodgems. **~ra** *f* garage; (de autobuses) depot

cochin|ada *f* dirty thing. **~o** *a* dirty, filthy. ● *m* pig

cociente *m* quotient. **~ intelectual** intelligence quotient, IQ

cocin|a *f* kitchen; (arte) cookery, cuisine; (aparato) cooker. **~a de gas** gas cooker. **~a eléctrica** electric cooker. **~ar** *vt/i* cook. **~ero** *m* cook

coco *m* coconut; (árbol) coconut palm; (cabeza) head; (que mete miedo) bogeyman. **comerse el ~** think hard

cocoa *f* (LAm) cocoa

cocodrilo *m* crocodile

cocotero *m* coconut palm

cóctel *m* (*pl* ~s *o* ~es) cocktail

cod|azo *m* nudge (with one's elbow). ~**ear** *vt/i* elbow, nudge. □ ~**arse** *vpr* rub shoulders (**con** with)

codici|a *f* greed. ~**ado** *a* coveted, sought after. ~**ar** *vt* covet. ~**oso** *a* greedy

código *m* code. ~ **de la circulación** Highway Code

codo *m* elbow; (dobladura) bend. ~ **a** ~ side by side. **hablar (hasta) por los** ~**s** talk too much

codorniz *m* quail

coeficiente *m* coefficient. ~ **intelectual** intelligence quotient, IQ

coerción *f* constraint

coetáneo *a* & *m* contemporary

coexist|encia *f* coexistence. ~**ir** *vi* coexist

cofradía *f* brotherhood

cofre *m* chest; (Mex, capó) bonnet (Brit), hood (Amer)

coger [14] *vt* (esp Esp) take; catch <*tren, autobús, pelota, catarro*>; (agarrar) take hold of; (del suelo) pick up; pick <*frutos etc*>. □ ~**se** *vpr* trap, catch; (agarrarse) hold on

cogollo *m* (de lechuga etc) heart; (brote) bud

cogote *m* nape; (LAm, cuello) neck

cohech|ar *vt* bribe. ~**o** *m* bribery

cohe|rente *a* coherent. ~**sión** *f* cohesion

cohete *m* rocket

cohibi|do *a* shy; (inhibido) awkward; (incómodo) awkward. ~**r** *vt* inhibit; (incomodar) make s.o. feel embarrassed. □ ~**rse** *vpr* feel inhibited

coincid|encia *f* coincidence. **dar la** ~**encia** happen. ~**ir** *vt* coincide

coje|ar *vt* limp; <*mueble*> wobble. ~**ra** *f* lameness

coj|ín *m* cushion. ~**inete** *m* small cushion

cojo *a* lame; <*mueble*> wobbly. ● *m* lame person

col *f* cabbage. ~**es de Bruselas** Brussel sprouts

cola *f* tail; (fila) queue; (para pegar) glue. **a la** ~ at the end. **hacer** ~ queue (up) (Brit), line up (Amer). **tener** ~, **traer** ~ have serious consequences

colabora|ción *f* collaboration. ~**dor** *m* collaborator. ~**r** *vi* collaborate

colada *f* washing. **hacer la** ~ do the washing

colador *m* strainer

colapso *m* collapse; (fig) standstill

colar [2] *vt* strain; pass <*moneda falsa etc*>. ● *vi* <*líquido*> seep through; (fig) be believed. □ ~**se** *vpr* slip; (en una cola) jump the queue; (en fiesta) gatecrash

colch|a *f* bedspread. ~**ón** *m* mattress. ~**oneta** *f* air bed; (en gimnasio) mat.

colear *vi* wag its tail; <*asunto*> not be resolved. **vivito y coleando** alive and kicking

colecci|ón *f* collection. ~**onar** *vt* collect. ~**onista** *m* & *f* collector

colecta *f* collection

colectivo *a* collective

colega *m* & *f* colleague

colegi|al *m* schoolboy. ~**ala** *f* schoolgirl. ~**o** *m* school; (de ciertas profesiones) college. ~**o mayor** hall of residence

cólera *m* cholera. ● *f* anger, fury. **montar en** ~ fly into a rage

colérico *a* furious, irate

colesterol *m* cholesterol

coleta *f* pigtail

colga|nte *a* hanging. ● *m* pendant. ~**r** [2 & 12] *vt* hang; hang out <*ropa lavada*>; hang up <*abrigo etc*>; put down <*teléfono*>. ● *vi* hang; (teléfono) hang up. □ ~**rse** *vpr* hang o.s. **dejar a uno** ~**do** let s.o. down

colibrí *m* hummingbird

cólico *m* colic

coliflor *f* cauliflower

colilla *f* cigarette end

colina *f* hill

colinda|nte *a* adjoining. ~**r** *vt* border (**con** on)

colisión *f* collision, crash; (fig) clash

collar *m* necklace; (de perro) collar

colmar *vt* fill to the brim; try <*pa-ciencia*>; (fig) fulfill. ~ **a uno de atenciones** lavish attention on s.o.

colmena *f* beehive, hive

colmillo *m* eye tooth, canine (tooth); (de elefante) tusk; (de carnívoro) fang

colmo *m* height. **ser el** ~ be the limit, be the last straw

coloca|ción *f* positioning; (empleo) job, position. ~**r** [7] *vt* put, place; (buscar empleo) find work for. □ ~**rse** *vpr* find a job

Colombia *f* Colombia

colombiano *a & m* Colombian

colon *m* colon

colón *m* (unidad monetaria de Costa Rica y El Salvador) colon

colon|ia *f* colony; (comunidad) community; (agua de colonia) cologne; (Mex, barrio) residential suburb. ~**a de verano** holiday camp. ~**iaje** *m* (LAm) colonial period. ~**ial** *a* colonial. ~**ialista** *m & f* colonialist. ~**ización** *f* colonization. ~**izar** [10] colonize. ~**o** *m* colonist, settler; (labrador) tenant farmer

coloqui|al *a* colloquial. ~**o** *m* conversation; (congreso) conference

color *m* colour. **de** ~ colour. **en** ~(**es**) <*fotos, película*> colour. ~**ado** *a* (rojo) red. ~**ante** *m* colouring. ~**ear** *vt/i* colour. ~**ete** *m* blusher. ~**ido** *m* colour

colosal *a* colossal; (fig, 🅹, magnífico) terrific

columna *f* column; (Anat) spine. ~ **vertebral** spinal column; (fig) backbone

columpi|ar *vt* swing. □ ~**arse** *vpr* swing. ~**o** *m* swing

coma *f* comma; (Mat) point. ● *m* (Med) coma

comadre *f* (madrina) godmother; (amiga) friend. ~**ar** *vi* gossip

comadreja *f* weasel

comadrona *f* midwife

comal *m* (Mex) griddle

comand|ancia *f* command. ~**ante** *m & f* commander. ~**o** *m* command; (Mil, soldado) commando; (de terroristas) cell

comarca *f* area, region

comba *f* bend; (juguete) skipping-rope; (de viga) sag. **saltar a la** ~ skip. □ ~**rse** *vpr* bend; <*viga*> sag

combat|e *m* combat; (pelea) fight. ~**iente** *m* fighter. ~**ir** *vt/i* fight

combina|ción *f* combination; (enlace) connection; (prenda) slip. ~**r** *vt* combine; put together <*colores*>

combustible *m* fuel

comedia *f* comedy; (cualquier obra de teatro) play; (LAm, telenovela) soap (opera)

comedi|do *a* restrained; (LAm, atento) obliging. □ ~**rse** [5] *vpr* show restrain

comedor *m* dining-room; (restaurante) restaurant

comensal *m* companion at table, fellow diner

comentar *vt* comment on; discuss <*tema*>; (mencionar) mention. ~**io** *m* commentary; (observación) comment. ~**ios** *mpl* gossip. ~**ista** *m & f* commentator

comenzar [1 & 10] *vt/i* begin, start

comer *vt* eat; (a mediodía) have for lunch; (esp LAm, cenar) have for dinner; (corroer) eat away; (en ajedrez) take. ● *vi* eat; (a mediodía) have lunch; (esp LAm, cenar) have dinner. **dar de** ~ a feed. □ ~**se** *vpr* eat (up)

comerci|al *a* commercial; <*ruta*> trade; <*nombre, trato*> business. ● *m* (LAm) commercial, ad. ~**ante** *m* trader; (de tienda) shopkeeper. ~**ar** *vi* trade (**con** with, **en** in); (con otra persona) do business. ~**o** *m* commerce; (actividad) trade; (tienda) shop; (negocios) business

comestible *a* edible. ~**s** *mpl* food. **tienda de** ~**s** grocer's (shop) (Brit), grocery (Amer)

cometa *m* comet. ● *f* kite

comet|er *vt* commit; make <*falta*>. ~**ido** *m* task

comezón *m* itch

comicios *mpl* elections

cómico *a* comic; (gracioso) funny. ● *m* comic actor; (humorista) comedian

comida *f* food; (a mediodía) lunch; (esp LAm, cena) dinner; (acto) meal

comidilla *f*. **ser la** ~ **del pueblo** be the talk of the town

comienzo *m* beginning, start

comillas *fpl* inverted commas

comil|ón *a* greedy. **~ona** *f* feast

comino *m* cumin. **(no) me importa un ~** I couldn't care less

comisar|ía *f* police station. **~io** *m* commissioner; (deportes) steward

comisión *f* assignment; (organismo) commission, committee; (Com) commission

comisura *f* corner. **~ de los labios** corner of the mouth

comité *m* committee

como *prep* as; (comparación) like. ● *adv* about. ● *conj* as. **~ quieras** as you like. **~ si** as if

cómo

● *adverbio*

····▸ how. **¿~ se llega?** how do you get there? **¿~ es de alto?** how tall is it? **sé ~ pasó** I know how it happened

! Cuando **cómo** va seguido del verbo **llamar** se traduce por *what*, p. ej. **¿~ te llamas?** *what's your name?*

····▸ **cómo + ser** (sugiriendo descripción) **¿~ es su marido?** what's her husband like?; (físicamente) what does her husband look like? **no sé ~ es la comida** I don't know what the food's like

····▸ (por qué) why. **¿~ no actuaron antes?** why didn't they act sooner?

····▸ (pidiendo que se repita) sorry?, pardon? **¿~? no te escuché** sorry? I didn't hear you

····▸ (en exclamaciones) **¡~ llueve!** it's really pouring! **¡~! ¿que no lo sabes?** what! you mean you don't know? **¡~ no!** of course!

cómoda *f* chest of drawers

comodidad *f* comfort. **a su ~** at your convenience

cómodo *a* comfortable; (conveniente) convenient

comoquiera *conj*. **~ que sea** however it may be

compacto *a* compact; (denso) dense; <*líneas etc*> close

compadecer [11] *vt* feel sorry for. **□ ~se** *vpr*. **~se de** feel sorry for

compadre *m* godfather; (amigo) friend

compañ|ero *m* companion; (de trabajo) colleague; (de clase) classmate; (pareja) partner. **~ía** *f* company. **en ~ía de** with

compara|ble *a* comparable. **~ción** *f* comparison. **~r** *vt* compare. **~tivo** *a & m* comparative

comparecer [11] *vi* appear

comparsa *f* group. ● *m & f* (en el teatro) extra

compartim(i)ento *m* compartment

compartir *vt* share

compás *m* (instrumento) (pair of) compasses; (ritmo) rhythm; (división) bar (Brit), measure (Amer); (Naut) compass. **a ~** in time

compasi|ón *f* compassion, pity. **tener ~ón de** feel sorry for. **~vo** *a* compassionate

compatib|ilidad *f* compatibility. **~le** *a* compatible

compatriota *m & f* compatriot

compendio *m* summary

compensa|ción *f* compensation. **~ción por despido** redundancy payment. **~r** *vt* compensate

competen|cia *f* competition; (capacidad) competence; (poder) authority; (incumbencia) jurisdiction. **~te** *a* competent

competi|ción *f* competition. **~dor** *m* competitor. **~r** [5] *vi* compete

compinche *m* accomplice; (▣, amigo) friend, mate ▣

complac|er [32] *vt* please. **□ ~erse** *vpr* be pleased. **~iente** *a* obliging; <*marido*> complaisant

complej|idad *f* complexity. **~o** *a & m* complex

complement|ario *a* complementary. **~o** *m* complement; (Gram) object, complement

complet|ar *vt* complete. **~o** *a* complete; (lleno) full; (exhaustivo) comprehensive

complexión *f* build

complica|ción f complication; (esp AmL, implicación) involvement. ~**r** [7] vt complicate; involve <persona>. □ ~**rse** vpr become complicated; (implicarse) get involved

cómplice m & f accomplice

complot m (pl ~s) plot

compon|ente a component. ● m component; (miembro) member. ~**er** [34] vt make up; (Mus, Literatura etc) write, compose; (esp LAm, reparar) mend; (LAm) set <hueso>; settle <estómago>. □ ~**erse** vpr be made up; (arreglarse) get better. ~**érselas** manage

comporta|miento m behaviour. □ ~**rse** vpr behave. ~**rse mal** misbehave

composi|ción f composition. ~**tor** m composer

compostura f composure; (LAm, arreglo) repair

compota f stewed fruit

compra f purchase. ~ **a plazos** hire purchase. **hacer la(s)** ~**(s)** do the shopping. **ir de** ~**s** go shopping. ~**dor** m buyer. ~**r** vt buy. ~**venta** f buying and selling; (Jurid) sale and purchase contract. **negocio** m **de** ~**venta** second-hand shop

compren|der vt understand; (incluir) include. ~**sión** f understanding. ~**sivo** a understanding

compresa f compress; (de mujer) sanitary towel

compr|esión f compression. ~**imido** a compressed. ● m pill, tablet. ~**imir** vt compress

comproba|nte m proof; (recibo) receipt. ~**r** vt check; (demostrar) prove

comprom|eter vt compromise; (arriesgar) jeopardize. □ ~**eterse** vpr compromise o.s.; (obligarse) agree to; <novios> get engaged. ~**etido** a <situación> awkward, delicate; <autor> politically committed. ~**iso** m obligation; (apuro) predicament; (cita) appointment; (acuerdo) agreement. **sin** ~**iso** without obligation

compuesto a compound; <persona> smart. ● m compound

computa|ción f (esp LAm) computing. **curso** m **de** ~**ción** computer course. ~**dor** m, ~**dora** f computer. ~**r** vt calculate. ~**rizar, computerizar** [10] vt computerize

cómputo m calculation

comulgar [12] vi take Communion

común a common; (compartido) joint. **en** ~ in common. **por lo** ~ generally. ● m. **el** ~ **de** most

comunal a communal

comunica|ción f communication. ~**do** m communiqué. ~**do de prensa** press release. ~**r** [7] vt communicate; (informar) inform; (LAm, por teléfono) put through. **está** ~**ndo** <teléfono> it's engaged. □ ~**rse** vpr communicate; (ponerse en contacto) get in touch. ~**tivo** a communicative

comunidad f community. ~ **de vecinos** residents' association. **C**~ **(Económica) Europea** European (Economic) Community. **en** ~ together

comunión f communion; (Relig) (Holy) Communion

comunis|mo m communism. ~**ta** a & m & f communist

con prep with; (+ infinitivo) by. ~ **decir la verdad** by telling the truth. ~ **que** so. ~ **tal que** as long as

concebir [5] vt/i conceive

conceder vt concede, grant; award <premio>; (admitir) admit

concej|al m councillor. ~**ero** m (LAm) councillor. ~**o** m council

concentra|ción f concentration; (Pol) rally. ~**r** vt concentrate; assemble <personas>. □ ~**rse** vpr concentrate

concep|ción f conception. ~**to** m concept; (opinión) opinion. **bajo ningún** ~**to** in no way

concerniente a. **en lo** ~ **a** with regard to

concertar [1] vt arrange; agree (upon) <plan>

concesión f concession

concha f shell; (carey) tortoiseshell

conciencia f conscience; (conocimiento) awareness. ~ **limpia** clear conscience. ~ **sucia** guilty conscience. **a** ~ **de que** fully aware that. **en** ~ honestly. **tener** ~ **de** be aware

of. **tomar** ∼ **de** become aware of. ∼**r**
vt make aware. ∼**rse** *vpr* become
aware

concientizar [10] *vt* (esp LAm)
make aware. □ ∼**se** *vpr* become
aware

concienzudo *a* conscientious

concierto *m* concert; (acuerdo)
agreement; (Mus, composición) concerto

concilia|ción *f* reconciliation. ∼**r**
vt reconcile. ∼**r el sueño** get to sleep.
□ ∼**rse** *vpr* gain

concilio *m* council

conciso *m* concise

conclu|ir [17] *vt* finish; (deducir) con-
clude. ● *vi* finish, end. ∼**sión** *f* conclusion. ∼**yente** *a* conclusive

concord|ancia *f* agreement. ∼**ar**
[2] *vt* reconcile. ● *vi* agree. ∼**e** *a* in
agreement. ∼**ia** *f* harmony

concret|amente *adv* specifically,
to be exact. ∼**ar** *vt* make specific.
∼**arse** *vpr* become definite; (limitarse)
confine o.s. ∼**o** *a* concrete; (determinado) specific, particular. **en** ∼**o** definite; (concretamente) to be exact; (en resumen) in short. ● *m* (LAm, hormigón)
concrete

concurr|encia *f* concurrence; (reu-
nión) audience. ∼**ido** *a* crowded,
busy. ∼**ir** *vi* meet; ; (coincidir) agree.
∼ **a** (asistir a) attend

concurs|ante *m* & *f* competitor,
contestant. ∼**ar** *vi* compete, take
part. ∼**o** *m* competition; (ayuda) help

cond|ado *m* county. ∼**e** *m* earl,
count

condena *f* sentence. ∼**ción** *f* con-
demnation. ∼**do** *m* convicted person. ∼**r** *vt* condemn; (Jurid) convict

condensa|ción *f* condensation.
∼**r** *vt* condense

condesa *f* countess

condescende|ncia *f* condescen-
sion; (tolerancia) indulgence. ∼**r** [1] *vi*
agree; (dignarse) condescend

condici|ón *f* condition. **a** ∼**ón de**
(que) on condition that. ∼**onal** *a*
conditional. ∼**onar** *vt* condition

condiment|ar *vt* season. ∼**o** *m*
seasoning

condolencia *f* condolence

condominio *m* joint ownership;
(LAm, edificio) block of flats (Brit), condominium (esp Amer)

condón *m* condom

condonar *vt* (perdonar) reprieve;
cancel <*deuda*>

conducir [47] *vt* drive <*vehículo*>;
carry <*electricidad, gas, agua*>. ● *vi*
drive; (fig, llevar) lead. ¿**a qué condu-**
ce? what's the point? □ ∼**se** *vpr* behave

conducta *f* behaviour

conducto *m* pipe, tube; (Anat) duct.
por ∼ **de** through. ∼**r** *m* driver; (jefe)
leader; (Elec) conductor

conduzco *vb* ⇒CONDUCIR

conectar *vt/i* connect

conejo *m* rabbit

conexión *f* connection

confabularse *vpr* plot

confecci|ón *f* (de trajes) tailoring;
(de vestidos) dressmaking. ∼**ones** *fpl*
clothing, clothes. **de** ∼**ón** ready-to-
wear. ∼**onar** *vt* make

confederación *f* confederation

conferencia *f* conference; (al teléfono) long-distance call; (Univ) lecture.
∼ **en la cima,** ∼ **(en la) cumbre** summit conference. ∼**nte** *m* & *f* lecturer

conferir [4] *vt* confer; award <*pre-*
mio>

confes|ar [1] *vt/i* confess. □ ∼**arse**
vpr confess. ∼**ión** *f* confession. ∼**io-**
nario *m* confessional. ∼**or** *m* con-
fessor

confeti *m* confetti

confia|do *a* trusting; (seguro de sí
mismo) confident. ∼**nza** *f* trust; (en sí
mismo) confidence; (intimidad) familiarity. ∼**r** [20] *vt* entrust. ● *vi*. ∼**r en**
trust

confiden|cia *f* confidence, secret.
∼**cial** *a* confidential. ∼**te** *m* confi-
dant. ● *f* confidante

conf|ín *m* border. ∼**ines** *mpl* outer-
most parts. ∼**inar** *vt* confine; (desterrar) banish

confirma|ción *f* confirmation. ∼**r**
vt confirm

confiscar [7] *vt* confiscate

confit|ería *f* sweet-shop (Brit), candy
store (Amer). ∼**ura** *f* jam

conflict|ivo *a* difficult; *<época>* troubled; (polémico) controversial. **~o** *m* conflict

confluencia *f* confluence

conform|ación *f* conformation, shape. **~ar** *vt* (acomodar) adjust. ● *vi* agree. □ **~arse** *vpr* conform. **~e** *a* in agreement;(contento) happy, satisfied; (según) according (con to). **~e a** in accordance with, according to. ● *conj* as. ● *int* OK!. **~idad** *f* agreement; (tolerancia) resignation. **~ista** *m & f* conformist

conforta|ble *a* comfortable. **~nte** *a* comforting. **~r** *vt* comfort

confronta|ción *f* confrontation. **~r** *vt* confront

confu|ndir *vt* (equivocar) mistake, confuse; (mezclar) mix up, confuse; (turbar) embarrass. □ **~ndirse** *vpr* become confused; (equivocarse) make a mistake. **~sión** *f* confusion; (vergüenza) embarrassment. **~so** *a* confused; (borroso) blurred

congela|do *a* frozen. **~dor** *m* freezer. **~r** *vt* freeze

congeniar *vi* get on

congesti|ón *f* congestion. **~ona-do** *a* congested. □ **~onarse** *vpr* become congested

congoja *f* distress; (pena) grief

congraciarse *vpr* ingratiate o.s.

congratular *vt* congratulate

congrega|ción *f* gathering; (Relig) congregation. □ **~rse** [12] *vpr* gather, assemble

congres|ista *m & f* delegate, member of a congress. **~o** *m* congress, conference. **C~** Parliament. **C~o de los Diputados** Chamber of Deputies

cónico *a* conical

conifer|a *f* conifer. **~o** *a* coniferous

conjetura *f* conjecture, guess. **~r** *vt* conjecture, guess

conjuga|ción *f* conjugation. **~r** [12] *vt* conjugate

conjunción *f* conjunction

conjunto *a* joint. ● *m* collection; (Mus) band; (ropa) suit, outfit. **en ~** altogether

conjurar *vt* exorcise; avert *<peligro>*. ● *vi* plot, conspire

conllevar *vt* to entail

conmemora|ción *f* commemoration. **~r** *vt* commemorate

conmigo *pron* with me

conmo|ción *f* shock; (tumulto) upheaval. **~** **cerebral** concussion. **~cionar** *vt* shock. **~ver** [2] *vt* shake; (emocionar) move

conmuta|dor *m* switch; (LAm, de teléfonos) switchboard. **~r** *vt* exchange

connota|ción *f* connotation. **~do** *a* (LAm, destacado) distinguished. **~r** *vt* connote

cono *m* cone

conoc|edor *a & m* expert. **~er** [11] *vt* know; (por primera vez) meet; (reconocer) recognize, know. **se conoce que** apparently. **dar a ~er** make known. □ **~erse** *vpr* know o.s.; *<dos personas>* know each other; (notarse) be obvious. **~ido** *a* well-known. ● *m* acquaintance. **~imiento** *m* knowledge; (sentido) consciousness. **sin ~imiento** unconscious. **tener ~imiento de** know about

conozco *vb* ⇒CONOCER

conque *conj* so

conquista *f* conquest. **~dor** *a* conquering. ● *m* conqueror; (de América) conquistador. **~r** *vt* conquer, win

consabido *a* usual, habitual

consagra|ción *f* consecration. **~r** *vt* consecrate; (fig) devote. □ **~rse** *vpr* devote o.s.

consanguíneo *m* blood relation

consciente *a* conscious

consecuen|cia *f* consequence; (coherencia) consistency. **a ~cia de** as a result of. **~te** *a* consistent

consecutivo *a* consecutive

conseguir [5 & 13] *vt* get, obtain; (lograr) manage; achieve *<objetivo>*

consej|ero *m* adviser; (miembro de consejo) member. **~o** *m* piece of advice; (Pol) council. **~o de ministros** cabinet

consenso *m* assent, consent

consenti|do *a* *<niño>* spoilt. **~miento** *m* consent. **~r** [4] *vt* allow; spoil *<niño>*. ● *vi* consent

conserje *m* porter, caretaker. **~ría** *f* porter's office

conserva f (mermelada) preserve; (en lata) tinned food. **en ~** tinned (Brit), canned. **~ción** f conservation; (de alimentos) preservation

conservador a & m (Pol) conservative

conservar vt keep; preserve <alimentos>. □ **~se** vpr keep; <costumbre> survive

conservatorio m conservatory

considera|ble a considerable. **~ción** f consideration; (respeto) respect. **de ~ción** serious. **de mi ~ción** (LAm, en cartas) Dear Sir. **~do** a considerate; (respetado) respected. **~r** vt consider; (respetar) respect

consigna f order; (para equipaje) left luggage office (Brit), baggage room (Amer); (eslogan) slogan

consigo pron (él) with him; (ella) with her; (Ud, Uds) with you; (uno mismo) with o.s.

consiguiente a consequent. **por ~** consequently

consist|encia f consistency. **~ente** a consisting (en of); (firme) solid; (LAm, congruente) consistent. **~ir** vi. **~ en** consist of; (radicar en) be due to

consola|ción f consolation. **~r** [2] vt console, comfort. □ **~rse** vpr console o.s.

consolidar vt consolidate. □ **~se** vpr consolidate

consomé m clear soup, consommé

consonante a consonant. ● f consonant

consorcio m consortium

conspira|ción f conspiracy. **~dor** m conspirator. **~r** vi conspire

consta|ncia f constancy; (prueba) proof; (LAm, documento) written evidence. **~nte** a constant. **~r** vi be clear; (figurar) appear, figure; (componerse) consist. **hacer ~r** state; (por escrito) put on record. **me ~ que** I'm sure that. **que conste que** believe me

constatar vt check; (confirmar) confirm

constipa|do m cold. ● a. **estar ~do** have a cold; (LAm, estreñido) be constipated. □ **~rse** vpr catch a cold

constitu|ción f constitution; (establecimiento) setting up. **~cional** a constitutional. **~ir** [17] vt constitute; (formar) form; (crear) set up, establish. □ **~irse** vpr set o.s. up (en as). **~tivo** a, **~yente** a constituent

constru|cción f construction. **~ctor** m builder. **~ir** [17] vt construct; build <edificio>

consuelo m consolation

consuetudinario a customary

cónsul m & f consul

consulado m consulate

consult|a f consultation. **horas** fpl **de ~a** surgery hours. **obra** f **de ~a** reference book. **~ar** vt consult. **~orio** m surgery

consumar vt complete; commit <crimen>; carry out <robo>; consummate <matrimonio>

consum|ición f consumption; (bebida) drink; (comida) food. **~ición mínima** minimum charge. **~ido** a <persona> skinny, wasted. **~idor** m consumer. **~ir** vt consume. □ **~irse** vpr <persona> waste away; <vela, cigarillo> burn down; <líquido> dry up. **~ismo** m consumerism. **~o** m consumption; (LAm, en restaurante etc) (bebida) drink; (comida) food. **~o mínimo** minimum charge

contab|ilidad f book-keeping; (profesión) accountancy. **~le** m & f accountant

contacto m contact. **ponerse en ~ con** get in touch with

conta|do a. **al ~** cash. **~s** a pl few. **tiene los días ~s** his days are numbered. **~dor** m meter; (LAm, persona) accountant

contagi|ar vt infect <persona>; pass on <enfermedad>; (fig) contaminate. **~o** m infection; (directo) contagion. **~oso** a infectious; (por contacto directo) contagious

contamina|ción f contamination, pollution. **~r** vt contaminate, pollute

contante a. **dinero** m **~** cash

contar [2] vt count; tell <relato>. **se cuenta que** it's said that. ● vi count. **~ con** rely on, count on. □ **~se** vpr be included (**entre** among)

contempla|ción f contemplation. **sin ~ciones** unceremoniously. **~r** vt look at; (fig) contemplate

contemporáneo a & m contemporary

conten|er [40] vt contain; hold <respiración>. □ **~erse** vpr contain o.s. ● m contents

content|ar vt please. □ **~arse** vpr. **~arse con** be satisfied with, be pleased with. **~o** a (alegre) happy; (satisfecho) pleased

contesta|ción f answer. **~dor** m. **~ automático** answering machine. **~r** vt/i answer; (replicar) answer back

contexto m context

contienda f conflict; (lucha) contest

contigo pron with you

contiguo a adjacent

continen|tal a continental. **~te** m continent

continu|ación f continuation. **a ~ación** immediately after. **~ar** [21] vt continue, resume. ● vi continue. **~idad** f continuity. **~o** a continuous; (frecuente) continual. **corriente** f **~a** direct current

contorno m outline; (de árbol) girth; (de caderas) measurement. **~s** mpl surrounding area

contorsión f contortion

contra prep against. **en ~** against. ● m cons. ● f snag. **llevar la ~** contradict

contraata|car [7] vt/i counterattack. **~que** m counter-attack

contrabaj|ista m & f double-bass player. **~o** m double-bass; (persona) double-bass player

contraband|ista m & f smuggler. **~o** m contraband

contracción f contraction

contrad|ecir [46] vt contradict. **~icción** f contradiction. **~ictorio** a contradictory

contraer [41] vt contract. **~ matrimonio** marry. □ **~se** vpr contract

contralto m counter tenor. ● f contralto

contra|mano. a ~ in the wrong direction. **~partida** f compensation. **~pelo. a ~** the wrong way

contrapes|ar vt counterweight. **~o** m counterweight

contraproducente a counterproductive

contrari|a f. **llevar la ~a** contradict. **~ado** a upset; (enojado) annoyed. **~ar** [20] vt upset; (enojar) annoy. **~edad** f setback; (disgusto) annoyance. **~o** a contrary (a to); <dirección> opposite. **al ~o** on the contrary. **al ~o de** contrary to. **de lo ~o** otherwise. **por el ~o** on the contrary. **ser ~o a** be opposed to, be against

contrarrestar vt counteract

contrasentido m contradiction

contraseña f (palabra) password; (en cine) stub

contrast|ar vt check, verify. ● vi contrast. **~e** m contrast; (en oro, plata) hallmark

contratar vt contract <servicio>; hire, take on <empleados>; sign up <jugador>

contratiempo m setback; (accidente) mishap

contrat|ista m & f contractor. **~o** m contract

contraven|ción f contravention. **~ir** [53] vt contravene

contraventana f shutter

contribu|ción f contribution; (tributo) tax. **~ir** [17] vt/i contribute. **~yente** m & f contributor; (que paga impuestos) taxpayer

contrincante m rival, opponent

control m control; (vigilancia) check; (lugar) checkpoint. **~ar** vt control; (vigilar) check. □ **~se** vpr control s.o.

controversia f controversy

contundente a <arma> blunt; <argumento> convincing

contusión f bruise

convalec|encia f convalescence. **~er** [11] vi convalesce. **~iente** a & m & f convalescent

convalidar vt recognize <título>

convenc|er [9] vt convince. **~imiento** m conviction

convenci|ón f convention. **~onal** a conventional

conveni|encia f convenience; (aptitud) suitability. **~ente** a suitable; (aconsejable) advisable; (provechoso) useful. **~o** m agreement. **~r** [53] vt agree. ● vi agree (**en** on); (ser conveniente) be convenient for, suit; (ser aconsejable) be advisable

convento m (de monjes) monastery; (de monjas) convent

conversa|ción f conversation. **~ciones** fpl talks. **~r** vi converse, talk

conver|sión f conversion. **~so** a converted. ● m convert. **~tible** a convertible. ● m (LAm) convertible. **~tir** [4] vt convert. □ **~tirse** vpr. **~tirse en** turn into; (Relig) convert

convic|ción f conviction. **~to** a convicted

convida|do m guest. **~r** vt invite

convincente a convincing

conviv|encia f coexistence; (de parejas) life together. **~ir** vi live together; (coexistir) coexist

convocar [7] vt call <huelga, elecciones>; convene <reunión>; summon <personas>

convulsión f convulsion

conyugal a marital, conjugal; <vida> married

cónyuge m spouse. **~s** mpl married couple

coñac m (pl **~s**) brandy

coopera|ción f cooperation. **~r** vi cooperate. **~tiva** f cooperative. **~tivo** a cooperative

coordinar vt coordinate

copa f glass; (deportes, fig) cup; (de árbol) top. **~s** fpl (naipes) hearts. **tomar una ~** have a drink

copia f copy. **~ en limpio** fair copy. **sacar una ~** make a copy. **~r** vt copy

copioso a copious; <lluvia, nevada etc> heavy

copla f verse; (canción) folksong

copo m flake. **~ de nieve** snowflake. **~s de maíz** cornflakes

coquet|a f flirt; (mueble) dressing-table. **~ear** vi flirt. **~o** a flirtatious

coraje m courage; (rabia) anger

coral a choral. ● m coral; (Mus) chorale

coraza f cuirass; (Naut) armour-plating; (de tortuga) shell

coraz|ón m heart; (persona) darling. **sin ~ón** heartless. **tener buen ~ón** be good-hearted. **~onada** f hunch; (impulso) impulse

corbata f tie, necktie (esp Amer). **~ de lazo** bow tie

corche|a f quaver. **~te** m fastener, hook and eye; (gancho) hook; (paréntesis) square bracket

corcho m cork. **~lata** f (Mex) (crown) cap

corcova f hump. **~do** a hunchbacked

cordel m cord, string

cordero m lamb

cordial a cordial, friendly. ● m tonic. **~idad** f cordiality, warmth

cordillera f mountain range

córdoba m (unidad monetaria de Nicaragua) córdoba

cordón m string; (de zapatos) lace; (cable) cord; (fig) cordon. **~ umbilical** umbilical cord

coreografía f choreography

corista f (bailarina) chorus girl

cornet|a f bugle; (Mex, de coche) horn. **~ín** m cornet

cornudo a horned. ● m cuckold

coro m (Arquit, Mus) choir; (en teatro) chorus

corona f crown; (de flores) wreath, garland. **~ción** f coronation. **~r** vt crown

coronel m colonel

coronilla f crown. **estar hasta la ~** be fed up

corpora|ción f corporation. **~l** a <castigo> corporal; <trabajo> physical

corpulento a stout

corral m farmyard. **aves** fpl **de ~** poultry

correa f strap; (de perro) lead; (cinturón) belt

correc|ción f correction; (cortesía) good manners. **~to** a correct; (cortés) polite

corre|dizo a running. **nudo** m **~dizo** slip knot. **puerta** f **~diza** sliding door. **~dor** *m* runner; (pasillo) corridor; (agente) agent, broker. **~dor de coches** racing driver

corregir [5 & 14] *vt* correct

correlación *f* correlation

correo *m* post, mail; (persona) courier; (LAm, oficina) post office. **~s** *mpl* post office. **~ electrónico** e-mail. **echar al ~** post

correr *vt* run; (mover) move; draw *<cortinas>*. ● *vi* run; *<agua, electricidad etc>* flow; *<tiempo>* pass. □ **~se** *vpr* (apartarse) move along; *<colores>* run

correspond|encia *f* correspondence. **~er** *vi* correspond; (ser adecuado) be fitting; (contestar) reply; (pertenecer) belong; (incumbir) fall to. □ **~erse** *vpr* (amarse) love one another. **~iente** *a* corresponding

corresponsal *m* correspondent

corrid|a *f* run. **~a de toros** bullfight. **de ~a** from memory. **~o** *a* (continuo) continuous

corriente *a* *<agua>* running; *<monedas, publicación, cuenta, año>* current; (ordinario) ordinary. ● *f* current; (de aire) draught; (fig) tendency. ● *m* current month. **al ~** (al día) up-to-date; (enterado) aware

corr|illo *m* small group. **~o** *m* circle

corroborar *vt* corroborate

corroer [24 & 37] *vt* corrode; (Geol) erode; (fig) eat away

corromper *vt* corrupt, rot *<materia>*. □ **~se** *vpr* become corrupted; *<materia>* rot; *<alimentos>* go bad

corrosi|ón *f* corrosion. **~vo** *a* corrosive

corrupción *f* corruption; (de materia etc) rot

corsé *m* corset

corta|do *a* cut; *<carretera>* closed; *<leche>* curdled; (avergonzado) embarrassed; (confuso) confused. ● *m* coffee with a little milk. **~dura** *f* cut. **~nte** *a* sharp; *<viento>* biting; *<frío>* bitter. **~r** *vt* cut; (recortar) cut out; (aislar, separar, interrumpir) cut off. ● *vi* cut; *<novios>* break up. □ **~rse** *vpr* cut o.s.; *<leche etc>* curdle; (fig) be embarrassed. **~rse el pelo** have one's

hair cut. **~rse las uñas** cut one's nails. **~uñas** *m invar* nail-clippers

corte *m* cut; (de tela) length. **~ de luz** power cut. **~ y confección** dressmaking. ● *f* court; (LAm, tribunal) Court of Appeal. **hacer la ~** court. **las C~s** the Spanish parliament. **la C~ Suprema** the Supreme Court

cortej|ar *vt* court. **~o** *m* (de rey etc) entourage. **~o fúnebre** cortège, funeral procession

cortés *a* polite

cortesía *f* courtesy

corteza *f* bark; (de queso) rind; (de pan) crust

cortijo *m* farm; (casa) farmhouse

cortina *f* curtain

corto *a* short; (apocado) shy. **~ de** short of. **~ de alcances** dim, thick. **~ de vista** short-sighted. **a la corta o a la larga** sooner or later. **quedarse ~** fall short; (miscalcular) underestimate. **~circuito** *m* short circuit

Coruña *f*. **La ~** Corunna

cosa *f* thing; (asunto) business; (idea) idea. **como si tal ~** just like that; (como si no hubiera pasado nada) as if nothing had happened. **decirle a uno cuatro ~s** tell s.o. a thing or two

cosecha *f* harvest; (de vino) vintage. **~r** *vt* harvest

coser *vt* sew; sew on *<botón>*; stitch *<herida>*. ● *vi* sew. □ **~se** *vpr* stick to s.o.

cosmético *a & m* cosmetic

cósmico *a* cosmic

cosmo|polita *a & m & f* cosmopolitan. **~s** *m* cosmos

cosquillas *fpl*. **dar ~** tickle. **hacer ~** tickle. **tener ~** be ticklish

costa *f* coast. **a ~ de** at the expense of. **a toda ~** at any cost

costado *m* side

costal *m* sack

costar [2] *vt* cost. ● *vi* cost; (resultar difícil) to be hard. **~ caro** be expensive. **cueste lo que cueste** at any cost

costarricense *a & m*, **costarriqueño** *a & m* Costa Rican

cost|as *fpl* (Jurid) costs. **~e** *m* cost. **~ear** *vt* pay for; (Naut) sail along the coast

costero a coastal

costilla f rib; (chuleta) chop

costo m cost. **~so** a expensive

costumbre f custom; (de persona) habit. **de ~** usual; (como adv) usually

costur|a f sewing; (línea) seam; (confección) dressmaking. **~era** f dressmaker. **~ero** m sewing box

cotejar vt compare

cotidiano a daily

cotille|ar vt gossip. **~o** m gossip

cotiza|ción f quotation, price. **~r** [10] vt (en la bolsa) quote. ● vi pay contributions. □ **~rse** vpr fetch; (en la bolsa) stand at; (fig) be valued

coto m enclosure; (de caza) preserve. **~ de caza** game preserve

cotorr|a f parrot; (fig) chatterbox. **~ear** vi chatter

coyuntura f joint

coz f kick

cráneo m skull

cráter m crater

crea|ción f creation. **~dor** a creative. ● m creator. **~r** vt create

crec|er [11] vi grow; (aumentar) increase; <río> rise. **~ida** f (de río) flood. **~ido** a <persona> grown-up; <número> large, considerable; <plantas> fully-grown. **~iente** a growing; <luna> crescent. **~imiento** m growth

credencial f document. ● a. **cartas** fpl **~es** credentials

credibilidad f credibility

crédito m credit; (préstamo) loan. **digno de ~** reliable

credo m creed

crédulo a credulous

cre|encia f belief. **~er** [18] vt/i believe; (pensar) think. **~o que no** I don't think so, I think not. **~o que sí** I think so. **no ~o** I don't think so. **¡ya lo ~o!** I should think so!. □ **~erse** vpr consider o.s. **no me lo ~o** I don't believe it. **~íble** a credible

crema f cream; (Culin) custard; (LAm, de la leche) cream. **~ batida** (LAm) whipped cream. **~ bronceadora** suntan cream

cremallera f zip (Brit), zipper (Amer)

crematorio m crematorium

crepitar vi crackle

crepúsculo m twilight

crespo a frizzy; (LAm, rizado) curly. ● m (LAm) curl

cresta f crest; (de gallo) comb

creyente m believer

cría f breeding; (animal) baby animal. **las ~s** the young

cria|da f maid, servant. **~dero** m (de pollos etc) farm; (de ostras) bed; (Bot) nursery. ● m servant. **~dor** m breeder. **~nza** f breeding. **~r** [20] vt suckle; grow <plantas>; breed <animales>; (educar) bring up (Brit), raise (esp Amer). □ **~rse** vpr grow up

criatura f creature; (niño) baby

crim|en m (serious) crime; (asesinato) murder; (fig) crime. **~inal** a & m & f criminal

crin f mane

crío m child

criollo a Creole; (LAm), <música, comida> traditional. ● m Creole; (LAm, nativo) Peruvian, Chilean etc

crisantemo m chrysanthemum

crisis f invar crisis

crispar vt twitch; (⬛, irritar) annoy. **~le los nervios a uno** get on s.o.'s nerves

cristal m crystal; (Esp, vidrio) glass; (Esp, de una ventana) pane of glass. **limpiar los ~es** (Esp) clean the windows. **~ino** a crystalline; (fig) crystal-clear. **~izar** [10] crystallize. □ **~izarse** vpr crystallize

cristian|dad f Christendom. **~ismo** m Christianity. **~o** a Christian. **ser ~o** be a Christian. ● m Christian

cristo m crucifix

Cristo m Christ

criterio m criterion; (discernimiento) judgement; (opinión) opinion

cr|ítica f criticism; (reseña) review. **~iticar** [7] vt criticize. **~ítico** a critical. ● m critic

croar vi croak

crom|ado a chromium-plated. **~o** m chromium, chrome

crónic|a f chronicle; (de radio, TV) report; (de periódico) feature. **~a deportiva** sport section. **~o** a chronic

cronista *m & f* reporter

cronología *f* chronology

cron|ometrar *vt* time. **~ómetro** *m* (en deportes) stop-watch

croqueta *f* croquette

cruce *m* crossing; (de calles, carreteras) crossroads; (de peatones) (pedestrian) crossing

crucial *a* crucial

crucifi|car [7] *vt* crucify. **~jo** *m* crucifix

crucigrama *m* crossword (puzzle)

crudo *a* raw; (fig) harsh. ● *m* crude (oil)

cruel *a* cruel. **~dad** *f* cruelty

cruji|do *m* (de seda, de hojas secas) rustle; (de muebles) creak. **~r** *vi* <seda, hojas secas> rustle; <muebles> creak

cruz *f* cross; (de moneda) tails. **~ gamada** swastika. **la C~ Roja** the Red Cross

cruza|da *f* crusade. **~r** [10] *vt* cross; exchange <palabras>. □ **~rse** *vpr* cross; (pasar en la calle) pass each other. **~rse con** pass

cuaderno *m* exercise book; (para apuntes) notebook

cuadra *f* (caballeriza) stable; (LAm, distancia) block

cuadrado *a & m* square

cuadragésimo *a* fortieth

cuadr|ar *vt* square. ● *vi* suit; <cuentas> tally. □ **~arse** *vpr* (Mil) stand to attention; (fig) dig one's heels in. **~ilátero** *m* quadrilateral; (Boxeo) ring

cuadrilla *f* group; (pandilla) gang

cuadro *m* square; (pintura) painting; (Teatro) scene; (de números) table; (de mando etc) panel; (conjunto del personal) staff. **~ de distribución** switchboard. **a ~s, de ~s** check. **¡qué ~!, ¡vaya un ~!** what a sight!

cuadrúpedo *m* quadruped

cuádruple *a & m* quadruple

cuajar *vt* congeal <sangre>; curdle <leche>; (llenar) fill up. ● *vi* <nieve> settle; (fig, 🔟) work out. **cuajado de** full of. □ **~se** *vpr* coagulate; <sangre> clot; <leche> curdle

cual *pron.* **el ~, la ~** etc (animales y cosas) that, which; (personas, sujeto) who, that; (personas, objeto) whom. ● *a* (LAm, qué) what. **~ si** as if. **cada ~** everyone. **lo ~** which. **por lo ~** because of which. **sea ~ sea** whatever

cuál *pron* which

cualidad *f* quality

cualquiera *a* (delante de nombres **cualquier,** *pl* **cualesquiera**) any. ● *pron* (*pl* **cualesquiera**) anyone, anybody; (cosas) whatever, whichever. **un ~** a nobody. **una ~** a slut

cuando *adv* when. ● *conj* when; (si) if. **~ más** at the most. **~ menos** at the least. **aun ~** even if. **de ~ en ~** from time to time

cuándo *adv & conj* when. **¿de ~ acá?, ¿desde ~?** since when? **¡~ no!** (LAm) as usual!, typical!

cuant|ía *f* quántity; (extensión) extent. **~ioso** *a* abundant. **~o** *a* as much ... as, as many ... as. ● *pron* as much as, as many as. ● *adv* as much as. **~o antes** as soon as possible. **~o más, mejor** the more the merrier. **en ~o** as soon as. **en ~o a** as for. **por ~o** since. **unos ~os** a few, some

cuánto *a* (interrogativo) how much?; (interrogativo en plural) how many?; (exclamativo) what a lot of! ● *pron* how much?; (en plural) how many? ● *adv* how much. **¿~ mides?** how tall are you? **¿~ tiempo?** how long? **¡~ tiempo sin verte!** it's been a long time! **¿a ~s estamos?** what's the date today? **un Sr. no sé ~s** Mr So-and-So

cuáquero *m* Quaker

cuarent|a *a & m* forty; (cuadragésimo) fortieth. **~ena** *f* (Med) quarantine. **~ón** *a* about forty

cuaresma *f* Lent

cuarta *f* (palmo) span

cuartel *m* (Mil) barracks. **~ general** headquarters

cuarteto *m* quartet

cuarto *a* fourth. ● *m* quarter; (habitación) room. **~ de baño** bathroom. **~ de estar** living room. **~ de hora** quarter of an hour. **estar sin un ~** be broke. **y ~** (a) quarter past

cuarzo *m* quartz

cuate *m* (Mex) twin; (amigo) friend; (①, tipo) guy

cuatro *a* & *m* four. **~cientos** *a* & *m* four hundred

Cuba *f* Cuba

cuba|libre *m* rum and Coke (P). **~no** *a* & *m* Cuban

cúbico *a* cubic

cubículo *m* cubicle

cubiert|a *f* cover; (neumático) tyre; (Naut) deck. **~o** *a* covered; *<cielo>* overcast. ● *m* place setting, piece of cutlery; (en restaurante) cover charge. **a ~o** under cover

cubilete *m* bowl; (molde) mould; (para los dados) cup

cubis|mo *m* cubism. **~ta** *a* & *m* & *f* cubist

cubo *m* bucket; (Mat) cube

cubrecama *m* bedspread

cubrir (*pp* **cubierto**) *vt* cover; fill *<vacante>*. □ **~se** *vpr* cover o.s.; (ponerse el sombrero) put on one's hat; *<el cielo>* cloud over, become overcast

cucaracha *f* cockroach

cuchar|a *f* spoon. **~ada** *f* spoonful. **~adita** *f* teaspoonful. **~illa**, **~ita** *f* teaspoon. **~ón** *m* ladle

cuchichear *vi* whisper

cuchill|a *f* large knife; (de carnicero) cleaver; (hoja de afeitar) razor blade. **~ada** *f* stab; (herida) knife wound. **~o** *m* knife

cuchitril *m* (fig) hovel

cuclillas: **en ~** *adv* squatting

cuco *a* shrewd; (mono) pretty, nice. ● *m* cuckoo

cucurucho *m* cornet

cuello *m* neck; (de camisa) collar. **cortar(le) el ~ a uno** cut s.o.'s throat

cuenc|a *f* (del ojo) (eye) socket; (Geog) basin. **~o** *m* hollow; (vasija) bowl

cuenta *f* count; (acción de contar) counting; (cálculo) calculation; (factura) bill; (en banco, relato) account; (de collar) bead. **~ corriente** current account, checking account (Amer). **dar ~ de** give an account of. **darse ~ de** realize. **en resumidas ~s** in short. **por mi propia ~** on my own account. **tener en ~** bear in mind

cuentakilómetros *m invar* milometer

cuent|ista *m* & *f* story-writer; (de mentiras) fibber. **~o** *m* story; (mentira) fib, tall story. **~ de hadas** fairy tale. ● *vb* ⇒CONTAR

cuerda *f* rope; (más fina) string; (Mus) string. **~ floja** tightrope. **dar ~ a** wind up *<un reloj>*

cuerdo *a* *<persona>* sane; *<acción>* sensible

cuerno *m* horn

cuero *m* leather; (piel) skin; (del grifo) washer. **~ cabelludo** scalp. **en ~s** (vivos) stark naked

cuerpo *m* body

cuervo *m* crow

cuesta *f* slope, hill. **~ abajo** downhill. **~ arriba** uphill. **a ~s** on one's back

cuestión *f* matter; (problema) problem; (cosa) thing

cueva *f* cave

cuida|do *m* care; (preocupación) worry. **~do!** watch out!. **tener ~do** be careful. **~doso** *a* careful. **~r** *vt* look after. ● *vi*. **~r de** look after. □ **~rse** *vpr* look after o.s. **~rse de** be careful to

culata *f* (de revólver, fusil) butt. **~zo** *m* recoil

culebr|a *f* snake. **~ón** *m* soap opera

culinario *a* culinary

culminar *vi* culminate

culo *m* ① bottom; (LAm vulg) arse (Brit vulg), ass (Amer vulg)

culpa *f* fault. **echar la ~** blame. **por ~ de** because of. **tener la ~** be to blame (de for). **~bilidad** *f* guilt. **~ble** *a* guilty. ● *m* & *f* culprit. **~r** *vt* blame (de for)

cultiv|ar *vt* farm; grow *<plantas>*; (fig) cultivate. **~o** *m* farming; (de plantas) growing

cult|o *a* *<persona>* educated. ● *m* cult; (homenaje) worship. **~ura** *f* culture. **~ural** *a* cultural

culturismo *m* body-building

cumbre *f* summit

cumpleaños *m invar* birthday

cumplido *a* perfect; (cortés) polite. ● *m* compliment. **de ~** courtesy. **por**

~ out of a sense of duty. ~**r** *a* reliable

cumpli|miento *m* fulfilment; (de ley) observance; (de orden) carrying out. ~**r** *vt* carry out; observe *<ley>*; serve *<condena>*; reach *<años>*; keep *<promesa>*. **hoy cumple 3 años** he's 3 (years old) today. ● *vi* do one's duty. **por ~r** as a mere formality. □ ~**rse** *vpr* expire; (realizarse) be fulfilled

cuna *f* cradle; (fig, nacimiento) birthplace

cundir *vi* spread; (rendir) go a long way

cuneta *f* ditch

cuña *f* wedge

cuñad|a *f* sister-in-law. ~**o** *m* brother-in-law

cuño *m* stamp. **de nuevo ~** new

cuota *f* quota; (de sociedad etc) membership, fee; (LAm, plazo) instalment; (Mex, peaje) toll

cupe *vb* ⇒CABER

cupo *m* cuota; (LAm, capacidad) room; (Mex, plaza) place

cupón *m* coupon

cúpula *f* dome

cura *f* cure; (tratamiento) treatment. ● *m* priest. ~**ción** *f* healing. ~**ndero** *m* faith-healer. ~**r** *vt* (incl Culin) cure; dress *<herida>*; (tratar) treat; (fig) remedy; tan *<pieles>*. □ ~**rse** *vpr* get better

curios|ear *vi* pry; (mirar) browse. ~**idad** *f* curiosity. ~**o** *a* curious; (raro) odd, unusual. ● *m* onlooker; (fisgón) busybody

curita *f* (LAm) (sticking) plaster

curriculum (vitae) *m* curriculum vitae, CV

cursar *vt* issue; (estudiar) study

cursi *a* pretentious, showy

cursillo *m* short course

cursiva *f* italics

curso *m* course; (Univ etc) year. **en ~** under way; *<año etc>* current

cursor *m* cursor

curtir *vt* tan; (fig) harden. □ ~**se** *vpr* become tanned; (fig) become hardened

curv|a *f* curve; (de carretera) bend. ~**ar** *vt* bend; bow *<estante>*. ~**arse** *vpr* bend; *<estante>* bow; *<madera>* warp. ~**ilíneo** *a* curvilinear; *<mujer>* curvaceous. ~**o** *a* curved

cúspide *f* top; (fig) pinnacle

custodi|a *f* safe-keeping; (Jurid) custody. ~**ar** *vt* guard; (guardar) look after. ~**o** *m* guardian

cutáneo *a* skin

cutis *m* skin, complexion

cuyo *pron* (de persona) whose, of whom; (de cosa) whose, of which. **en ~ caso** in which case

Dd

dactilógrafo *m* typist

dado *m* dice. ● *a* given. ~ **que** since, given that

daltónico *a* colour-blind

dama *f* lady. ~ **de honor** bridesmaid. ~**s** *fpl* draughts (Brit), checkers (Amer)

damasco *m* damask; (LAm, fruta) apricot

danés *a* Danish. ● *m* Dane; (idioma) Danish

danza *f* dance; (acción) dancing. ~**r** [10] *vt/i* dance

dañ|ar *vt* damage. □ ~**se** *vpr* get damaged. ~**ino** *a* harmful. ~**o** *m* damage; (a una persona) harm. ~**os y perjuicios** damages. **hacer ~o** a harm, hurt. **hacerse ~o** hurt o.s.

dar [26] *vt* give; bear *<frutos>*; give out *<calor>*; strike *<la hora>*. ● *vi* give. **da igual** it doesn't matter. **¡dale!** go on! **da lo mismo** it doesn't matter. ~ **a** *<ventana>* look on to; *<edificio>* face. ~ **a luz** give birth. ~ **con** meet *<persona>*; find *<cosa>*. **¿qué más da?** it doesn't matter! □ ~**se** *vpr* have *<baño>*. **dárselas de** make o.s. out to be. ~**se por** consider o.s.

dardo *m* dart

datar *vi*. ~ **de** date from

dátil *m* date

dato *m* piece of information. ~**s** *mpl* data, information. ~**s personales** personal details

de

● *preposición*

Note that **de** before **el** becomes **del**, e.g. **es del norte**

····➤ (contenido, material) of. **un vaso de agua** a glass of water. **es de madera** it's made of wood

····➤ (pertenencia) **el coche de Juan** Juan's car. **es de ella** it's hers. **es de María** it's María's. **las llaves del coche** the car keys

····➤ (procedencia, origen, época) from. **soy de Madrid** I'm from Madrid. **una llamada de Lima** a call from Lima. **es del siglo V** it's from the 5th century

····➤ (causa, modo) **se murió de cáncer** he died of cancer. **temblar de miedo** to tremble with fear. **de dos en dos** two by two

····➤ (parte del día, hora) **de noche** at night. **de madrugada** early in the morning. **las diez de la mañana** ten (o'clock) in the morning. **de 9 a 12** from 9 to 12

····➤ (en oraciones pasivas) by. **rodeado de agua** surrounded by water. **va seguido de coma** it's followed by a comma. **es de Mozart** it's by Mozart

····➤ (al especificar) **el cajón de arriba** the top drawer. **la clase de inglés** the English lesson. **la chica de verde** the girl in green. **el de debajo** the one underneath

····➤ (en calidad de) as. **trabaja de oficinista** he works as a clerk. **vino de chaperón** he came as a chaperon

····➤ (en comparaciones) than. **pesa más de un kilo** it weighs more than a kilo

····➤ (con superlativo) **el más alto del mundo** the tallest in the world. **el mejor de todos** the best of all

····➤ (sentido condicional) if. **de haberlo sabido** if I had known. **de continuar así** if this goes on

⮕ Cuando la preposición **de** se emplea como parte de expresiones como **de prisa, de acuerdo** etc., y de nombres compuestos como **hombre de negocios, saco de dormir** etc., ver bajo el respectivo nombre

deambular *vi* roam (**por** about)

debajo *adv* underneath. ~ **de** under (neath). **el de** ~ the one underneath. **por** ~ underneath. **por** ~ **de** below

debat|e *m* debate. ~**ir** *vt* debate

deber *vt* owe. ● *v aux* have to, must; (en condicional) should. **debo marcharme** I must go, I have to go. ● *m* duty. ~**es** *mpl* homework. □ ~**se** *vpr*. ~**se a** be due to

debido *a* due; (correcto) proper. ~ **a** due to. **como es** ~ as is proper

débil *a* weak; <sonido> faint; <luz> dim

debili|dad *f* weakness. ~**tar** *vt* weaken. □ ~**tarse** *vpr* weaken, get weak

débito *m* debit. ~ **bancario** (LAm) direct debit

debutar *vi* make one's debut

década *f* decade

deca|dencia *f* decline. ~**dente** *a* decadent. ~**er** [29] *vi* decline; (debilitarse) weaken. ~**ido** *a* in low spirits. ~**imiento** *m* decline, weakening

decano *m* dean; (miembro más antiguo) senior member

decapitar *vt* behead

decena *f* ten. **una** ~ **de** about ten

decencia *f* decency

decenio *m* decade

decente *a* decent; (decoroso) respectable; (limpio) clean, tidy

decepci|ón *f* disappointment. ~**onar** *vt* disappoint

decidi|do *a* decided; <persona> determined, resolute. ~**r** *vt* decide; settle <cuestión etc>. ● *vi* decide. □ ~**rse** *vpr* make up one's mind

decimal *a & m* decimal

décimo *a & m* tenth. ● *m* (de lotería) tenth part of a lottery ticket

decir [46] *vt* say; (contar) tell. ● *m* saying. ~ **que no** say no. ~ **que sí** say yes. **dicho de otro modo** in other words. **dicho y hecho** no sooner said than done. **¿dígame?** can I help you? **¡dígame!** (al teléfono) hello! **digamos**

let's say. **es** ~ that is to say. **mejor dicho** rather. **¡no me digas!** you don't say!, really! **por así** ~, **por** ~**lo así** so to speak, as it were. **querer** ~ mean. **se dice que** it is said that, they say that

decisi|ón f decision. ~**vo** a decisive

declara|ción f declaration; (a autoridad, prensa) statement. ~**ción de renta** income tax return. ~**r** vt/i declare. □ ~**rse** vpr declare o.s.; <epidemia etc> break out

declinar vt turn down; (Gram) decline

declive m slope; (fig) decline. **en** ~ sloping

decola|je m (LAm) take-off. ~**r** vi (LAm) take off

decolorarse vpr become discoloured, fade

decora|ción f decoration. ~**do** m (en el teatro) set. ~**r** vt decorate. ~**tivo** a decorative

decoro m decorum. ~**so** a decent, respectable

decrépito a decrepit

decret|ar vt decree. ~**o** m decree

dedal m thimble

dedica|ción f dedication. ~**r** [7] vt dedicate; devote <tiempo>. □ ~**rse** vpr. ~**rse a** devote o.s. to. **¿a qué se dedica?** what does he do? ~**toria** f dedication

dedo m finger; (del pie) toe. ~ **anular** ring finger. ~ **corazón** middle finger. ~**gordo** thumb; (del pie) big toe. ~ **índice** index finger. ~ **meñique** little finger. ~ **pulgar** thumb

deduc|ción f deduction. ~**ir** [47] vt deduce; (descontar) deduct

defect|o m fault, defect. ~**uoso** a defective

defen|der [1] vt defend. ~**sa** f defence. □ ~**derse** vpr defend o.s. ~**sivo** a defensive. ~**sor** m defender. **abogado** m ~**sor** defence counsel

defeño m (Mex) person from the Federal District

deficien|cia f deficiency. ~**cia mental** mental handicap. ~**te** a poor, deficient. ● m & f. ~**te mental** mentally handicapped person

déficit m invar deficit

defini|ción f definition. ~**do** a defined. ~**r** vt define. ~**tivo** a definitive. **en** ~**tiva** all in all

deform|ación f deformation; (de imagen etc) distortion. ~**ar** vt deform; distort <imagen, metal>. □ ~**arse** vpr go out of shape. ~**e** a deformed

defraudar vt defraud; (decepcionar) disappoint

defunción f death

degenera|ción f degeneration; (cualidad) degeneracy. ~**do** a degenerate. ~**r** vi degenerate

degollar [16] vt cut s.o.'s throat

degradar vt degrade; (Mil) demote. □ ~**se** vpr demean o.s..

degusta|ción f tasting. ~**r** vt taste

dehesa f pasture

deja|dez f slovenliness; (pereza) laziness. ~**do** a slovenly; (descuidado) slack, negligent. ~**r** vt leave; (abandonar) abandon; give up <estudios>; (prestar) lend; (permitir) let. ~**r a un lado** leave aside. ~**r de** stop

dejo m aftertaste; (tonillo) slight accent; (toque) touch

del = **de** + **el**

delantal m apron

delante adv in front. ~ **de** in front of. **de** ~ front. ~**ra** f front; (de teatro etc) front row; (ventaja) lead; (de equipo) forward line. **llevar la** ~**ra** be in the lead. ~**ro** a front. ● m forward

delat|ar vt denounce. ~**or** m informer

delega|ción f delegation; (oficina) regional office; (Mex, comisaría) police station. ~**do** m delegate; (Com) agent, representative. ~**r** [12] vt delegate

deleit|ar vt delight. ~**e** m delight

deletrear vt spell (out)

delfín m dolphin

delgad|ez f thinness. ~**o** a thin; (esbelto) slim. ~**ucho** a skinny

delibera|ción f deliberation. ~**do** a deliberate. ~**r** vi deliberate (**sobre** on)

delicad|eza f gentleness; (fragilidad) frailty; (tacto) tact. **falta de** ~**eza** tactlessness. **tener la** ~ **de** have the courtesy to. **~o** *a* delicate; (refinado) refined; (sensible) sensitive

delici|a *f* delight. **~oso** *a* delightful; *<sabor etc>* delicious

delimitar *vt* delimit

delincuen|cia *f* delinquency. **~te** *m & f* criminal, delinquent

delinquir [8] *vi* commit a criminal offence

delir|ante *a* delirious. **~ar** *vi* be delirious; (fig) talk nonsense. **~io** *m* delirium; (fig) frenzy

delito *m* crime, offence

demacrado *a* haggard

demagogo *m* demagogue

demanda *f* demand; (Jurid) lawsuit. **~do** *m* defendant. **~nte** *m & f* (Jurid) plaintiff. **~r** *vt* (Jurid) sue; (LAm, requerir) require

demarcación *f* demarcation

demás *a* rest of the, other. ● *pron* rest, others. **lo ~** the rest. **por ~** extremely. **por lo ~** otherwise

demas|ía *f.* **en ~ía** in excess. **~iado** *a* too much; (en plural) too many. ● *adv* too much; (con adjetivo) too

demen|cia *f* madness. **~te** *a* demented, mad

dem|ocracia *f* democracy. **~ócrata** *m & f* democrat. **~ocrático** *a* democratic

demol|er [2] *vt* demolish. **~ición** *f* demolition

demonio *m* devil, demon. ¡**~s**! hell! ¿**cómo ~s**? how the hell? ¡**qué ~s**! what the hell!

demora *f* delay. **~r** *vt* delay. ● *vi* stay on. □ **~rse** *vpr* be too long; (LAm, cierto tiempo). **se ~ una hora en llegar** it takes him an hour to get there

demostra|ción *f* demonstration, show. **~r** [2] *vt* demonstrate; (mostrar) show; (probar) prove. **~tivo** *a* demonstrative

dengue *m* dengue fever

denigrar *vt* denigrate

dens|idad *f* density. **~o** *a* dense, thick

denta|dura *f* teeth. **~dura postiza** dentures, false teeth. **~l** *a* dental

dent|era *f.* **darle ~era a uno** set s.o.'s teeth on edge. **~ífrico** *m* toothpaste. **~ista** *m & f* dentist

dentro *adv* inside; (de un edificio) indoors. **~ de** in. **~ de poco** soon. **por ~** inside

denuncia *f* report; (acusación) accusation. **~r** *vt* report; *<periódico etc>* denounce

departamento *m* department; (LAm, apartamento) flat (Brit), apartment (Amer)

depend|encia *f* dependence; (sección) section; (oficina) office. **~encias** *fpl* buildings. **~er** *vi* depend (**de** on). **~ienta** *f* shop assistant. **~iente** *a* dependent (**de** on). ● *m* shop assistant

depila|r *vt* depilate. **~torio** *a* depilatory

deplora|ble *a* deplorable. **~r** *vt* deplore, regret

deponer [34] *vt* remove from office; depose *<rey>*; lay down *<armas>*. ● *vi* give evidence

deporta|ción *f* deportation. **~r** *vt* deport

deport|e *m* sport. **hacer ~e** take part in sports. **~ista** *m* sportsman. ● *f* sportswoman. **~ivo** *a* sports. ● *m* sports car

dep|ositante *m & f* depositor. **~ositar** *vt* deposit; (poner) put, place. **~ósito** *m* deposit; (almacén) warehouse; (Mil) depot; (de líquidos) tank

depravado *a* depraved

deprecia|ción *f* depreciation. **~r** *vt* depreciate. □ **~rse** *vpr* depreciate

depr|esión *f* depression. **~imido** *a* depressed. **~imir** *vt* depress. □ **~imirse** *vpr* get depressed

depura|ción *f* purification. **~do** *a* refined. **~r** *vt* purify; (Pol) purge; refine *<estilo>*

derech|a *f* (mano) right hand; (lado) right. **a la ~a** on the right; (hacia el lado derecho) to the right. **~ista** *a* right-wing. ● *m & f* right-winger. **~o** *a* right; (vertical) upright; (recto) straight. ● *adv* straight. **todo ~o**

straight on. ● *m* right; (Jurid) law; (lado) right side. ∼**os** *mpl* dues. ∼**os de autor** royalties

deriva *f* drift. **a la** ∼ drifting, adrift

deriva|do *a* derived. ● *m* derivative, by-product. ∼**r** *vt* divert. ● *vi*. ∼**r de** derive from, be derived from. □ ∼**rse** *vpr*. ∼**se de** be derived from

derram|amiento *m* spilling. ∼**amiento de sangre** bloodshed. ∼**ar** *vt* spill; shed *<lágrimas>*. □ ∼**arse** *vpr* spill. ∼**e** *m* spilling; (pérdida) leakage; (Med) discharge; (Med, de sangre) haemorrhage

derretir [5] *vt* melt

derribar *vt* knock down; bring down, overthrow *<gobierno etc>*

derrocar [7] *vt* bring down, overthrow *<gobierno etc>*

derroch|ar *vt* squander. ∼**e** *m* waste

derrot|a *f* defeat. ∼**ar** *vt* defeat. ∼**ado** *a* defeated. ∼**ero** *m* course

derrumba|r *vt* knock down. □ ∼**rse** *vpr* collapse; *<persona>* go to pieces

desabotonar *vt* unbutton, undo. □ ∼**se** *vpr* come undone; *<persona>* undo

desabrido *a* tasteless; *<persona>* surly; (LAm) dull

desabrochar *vt* undo. □ ∼**se** *vpr* come undone; *<persona>* undo

desacato *m* defiance; (Jurid) contempt of court

desac|ertado *a* ill-advised; (erróneo) wrong. ∼**ierto** *m* mistake

desacreditar *vt* discredit

desactivar *vt* defuse

desacuerdo *m* disagreement

desafiar [20] *vt* challenge; (afrontar) defy

desafina|do *a* out of tune. ∼**r** *vi* be out of tune. □ ∼**rse** *vpr* go out of tune

desafío *m* challenge; (a la muerte) defiance; (combate) duel

desafortunad|amente *adv* unfortunately. ∼**o** *a* unfortunate

desagrada|ble *a* unpleasant. ∼**r** *vt* displease. ● *vi* be unpleasant. **me** ∼ **el sabor** I don't like the taste

desagradecido *a* ungrateful

desagrado *m* displeasure. **con** ∼ unwillingly

desagüe *m* drain; (acción) drainage. **tubo** *m* **de** ∼ drain-pipe

desahog|ado *a* roomy; (acomodado) comfortable. ∼**ar** [12] *vt* vent. □ ∼**arse** *vpr* let off steam. ∼**o** *m* comfort; (alivio) relief

desahuci|ar *vt* declare terminally ill *<enfermo>*; evict *<inquilino>*. ∼**o** *m* eviction

desair|ar *vt* snub. ∼**e** *m* snub

desajuste *m* maladjustment; (desequilibrio) imbalance

desal|entador *a* disheartening. ∼**entar** [1] *vt* discourage. ∼**iento** *m* discouragement

desaliñado *a* slovenly

desalmado *a* heartless

desalojar *vt* *<ocupantes>* evacuate; *<policía>* to clear; (LAm) evict *<inquilino>*

desampar|ado *a* helpless; *<lugar>* unprotected. ∼**ar** *vt* abandon. ∼**o** *m* helplessness; (abandono) lack of protection

desangrar *vt* bleed. □ ∼**se** *vpr* bleed

desanima|do *a* down-hearted. ∼**r** *vt* discourage. □ ∼**rse** *vpr* lose heart

desapar|ecer [11] *vi* disappear; *<efecto>* wear off. ∼**ecido** *a* missing. ● *m* missing person. ∼**ición** *f* disappearance

desapego *m* indifference

desapercibido *a*. **pasar** ∼ go unnoticed

desaprobar [2] *vt* disapprove of

desarm|able *a* collapsible; *<estante>* easy to dismantle. ∼**ar** *vt* disarm; (desmontar) dismantle; take apart; (LAm) take down *<carpa>*. ∼**e** *m* disarmament

desarraig|ado *a* rootless. ∼**ar** [12] *vt* uproot. ∼**o** *m* uprooting

desarregl|ar *vt* mess up; (alterar) disrupt. ∼**o** *m* disorder

desarroll|ar *vt* develop. □ ∼**arse** *vpr* (incl Foto) develop; *<suceso>* take place. ∼**o** *m* development

desaseado *a* dirty; (desordenado) untidy

desasosiego *m* anxiety; (intranquilidad) restlessness

desastr|ado *a* scruffy. **~e** *m* disaster. **~oso** *a* disastrous

desatar *vt* untie; (fig, soltar) unleash. □ **~se** *vpr* come undone; to undo <*zapatos*>

desatascar [7] *vt* unblock

desaten|der [1] *vt* not pay attention to; neglect <*deber etc*>. **~to** *a* inattentive; (descortés) discourteous

desatin|ado *a* silly. **~o** *m* silliness; (error) mistake

desatornillar *vt* unscrew

desautorizar [10] *vt* declare unauthorized; discredit <*persona*>; (desmentir) deny

desavenencia *f* disagreement

desayun|ar *vt* have for breakfast. ● *vi* have breakfast. **~o** *m* breakfast

desazón *m* (fig) unease

desbandarse *vpr* (Mil) disband; (dispersarse) disperse

desbarajust|ar *vt* mess up. **~e** *m* mess

desbaratar *vt* spoil; (Mex) mess up <*papeles*>

desbloquear *vt* clear; release <*mecanismo*>; unfreeze <*cuenta*>

desbocado *a* <*caballo*> runaway; <*escote*> wide

desbordarse *vpr* overflow; <*río*> burst its banks

descabellado *a* crazy

descafeinado *a* decaffeinated. ● *m* decaffeinated coffee

descalabro *m* disaster

descalificar [7] *vt* disqualify; (desacreditar) discredit

descalz|ar [10] *vt* take off <*zapatos*>. **~o** *a* barefoot

descampado *m* open ground. al **~** (LAm) in the open air

descans|ado *a* rested; <*trabajo*> easy. **~ar** *vt/i* rest. **~illo** *m* landing. **~o** *m* rest; (del trabajo) break; (LAm, rellano) landing; (en deportes) half-time; (en el teatro etc) interval

descapotable *a* convertible

descarado *a* cheeky; (sin vergüenza) shameless

descarg|a *f* unloading; (Mil, Elec) discharge. **~ar** [12] *vt* unload; (Mil, Elec) discharge; (Informática) download. **~o** *m* (recibo) receipt; (Jurid) evidence

descaro *m* cheek, nerve

descarriarse [20] *vpr* go the wrong way; <*res*> stray; (fig) go astray

descarrila|miento *m* derailment. **~r** *vi* be derailed. □ **~se** *vpr* (LAm) be derailed

descartar *vt* rule out

descascararse *vpr* <*pintura*> peel; <*taza*> chip

descen|dencia *f* descent; (personas) descendants. **~der** [1] *vt* go down <*escalera etc*>. ● *vi* go down; <*temperatura*> fall, drop; (provenir) be descended (de from). **~diente** *m & f* descendent. **~so** *m* descent; (de temperatura, fiebre etc) fall, drop

descifrar *vt* decipher; decode <*clave*>

descolgar [2 & 12] *vt* take down; pick up <*el teléfono*>. □ **~se** *vpr* lower o.s.

descolor|ar *vt* discolour, fade. **~ido** *a* discoloured, faded; <*persona*> pale

descomp|oner [34] *vt* break down; decompose <*materia*>; upset <*estómago*>; (esp LAm, estropear) break; (esp LAm, desarreglar) mess up. □ **~onerse** *vpr* decompose; (esp LAm, estropearse) break down; <*persona*> feel sick. **~ostura** *f* (esp LAm, de máquina) breakdown; (esp LAm, náuseas) sickness; (esp LAm, diarrea) diarrhoea; (LAm, falla) fault. **~uesto** *a* decomposed; (encolerizado) angry; (esp LAm, estropeado) broken. estar **~uesto** (del estómago) have diarrhoea

descomunal *a* enormous

desconc|ertante *a* disconcerting. **~ertar** [1] *vt* disconcert; (dejar perplejo) puzzle. □ **~ertarse** *vpr* be put out, be disconcerted

desconectar *vt* disconnect

desconfia|do *a* distrustful. **~nza** *f* distrust, suspicion. **~r** [20] *vi*. **~r de** mistrust; (no creer) doubt

descongelar *vt* defrost; (Com) unfreeze

desconoc|er [11] *vt* not know, not recognize. ~**ido** *a* unknown; (cambiado) unrecognizable. ● *m* stranger. ~**imiento** *m* ignorance

desconsidera|ción *f* lack of consideration. ~**do** *a* inconsiderate

descons|olado *a* distressed. ~**uelo** *m* distress; (tristeza) sadness

desconta|do *a*. dar por ~**do** (que) take for granted (that). ~**r** [2] *vt* discount; deduct *<impuestos etc>*

descontento *a* unhappy (con with), dissatisfied (con with). ● *m* discontent

descorazonar *vt* discourage. □ ~**se** *vpr* lose heart

descorchar *vt* uncork

descorrer *vt* draw *<cortina>*. ~ **el cerrojo** unbolt the door

descort|és *a* rude, discourteous. ~**esía** *f* rudeness

descos|er *vt* unpick. □ ~**erse** *vpr* come undone. ~**ido** *a* unstitched

descrédito *m* disrepute. **ir en** ~ **de** damage the reputation of

descremado *a* skimmed

descri|bir (*pp* **descrito**) *vt* describe. ~**pción** *f* description

descuartizar [10] *vt* cut up

descubierto *a* discovered; (no cubierto) uncovered; *<vehículo>* open-top; *<piscina>* open-air; *<cielo>* clear; *<cabeza>* bare. ● *m* overdraft. **poner al** ~ expose

descubri|miento *m* discovery. ~**r** (*pp* **descubierto**) *vt* discover; (destapar) uncover; (revelar) reveal; unveil *<estatua>*. □ ~**rse** *vpr* (quitarse el sombrero) take off one's hat

descuento *m* discount; (del sueldo) deduction

descuid|ado *a* careless; *<aspecto etc>* untidy; (desprevenido) unprepared. ~**ar** *vt* neglect. ● *vi* not worry. ¡~**a**! don't worry!. □ ~**arse** *vpr* be careless ~**o** *m* carelessness; (negligencia) negligence

desde *prep* (lugar etc) from; (tiempo) since, from. ~ **ahora** from now on. ~ **hace un mes** for a month. ~ **luego** of course. ~ **Madrid hasta Barcelona** from Madrid to Barcelona. ~ **niño** since childhood

desdecirse [46] *vpr*. ~ **de** take back *<palabras etc>*; go back on *<promesa>*

desd|én *m* scorn. ~**eñable** *a* insignificant. **nada** ~**eñable** significant. ~**eñar** *vt* scorn

desdicha *f* misfortune. **por** ~ unfortunately. ~**do** *a* unfortunate

desdoblar *vt* (desplegar) unfold

desear *vt* want; wish *<suerte etc>*. **le deseo un buen viaje** I hope you have a good journey. **¿qué desea Vd?** can I help you?

desech|able *a* disposable. ~**ar** *vt* throw out; (rechazar) reject. ~**o** *m* waste

desembalar *vt* unpack

desembarcar [7] *vt* unload. ● *vi* disembark

desemboca|dura *f* (de río) mouth; (de calle) opening. ~**r** [7] *vi*. ~**r en** *<río>* flow into; *<calle>* lead to

desembolso *m* payment

desembragar [12] *vi* declutch

desempaquetar *vt* unwrap

desempat|ar *vi* break a tie. ~**e** *m* tie-breaker

desempeñ|ar *vt* redeem; play *<papel>*; hold *<cargo>*; perform, carry out *<deber etc>*. □ ~**arse** *vpr* (LAm) perform. ~**arse bien** manage well. ~**o** *m* redemption; (de un deber, una función) discharge; (LAm, actuación) performance

desemple|ado *a* unemployed. ● *m* unemployed person. **los** ~**ados** the unemployed. ~**o** *m* unemployment

desencadenar *vt* unchain *<preso>*; unleash *<perro>*; (causar) trigger. □ ~**se** *vpr* be triggered off; *<guerra etc>* break out

desencajar *vt* dislocate; (desconectar) disconnect. □ ~**se** *vpr* become dislocated

desenchufar *vt* unplug

desenfad|ado *a* uninhibited; (desenvuelto) self-assured. ~**o** *m* lack of inhibition; (desenvoltura) self-assurance

desenfocado *a* out of focus

desenfren|ado *a* unrestrained. ~**o** *m* licentiousness

desenganchar *vt* unhook; uncouple *<vagón>*

desengañ|ar *vt* disillusion. □ ~**arse** *vpr* become disillusioned; (darse cuenta) realize. ~**o** *m* disillusionment, disappointment

desenlace *m* outcome

desenmascarar *vt* unmask

desenredar *vt* untangle. □ ~**se** *vpr* untangle

desenro|llar *vt* unroll, unwind. ~**scar** [7] *vt* unscrew

desentend|erse [1] *vpr* want nothing to do with. ~**ido** *m*. **hacerse el ~ido** (fingir no oír) pretend not to hear; (fingir ignorancia) pretend not to know

desenterrar [1] *vt* exhume; (fig) unearth

desentonar *vi* be out of tune; *<colores>* clash

desenvoltura *f* ease; (falta de timidez) confidence

desenvolver [2] (*pp* **desenvuelto**) *vt* unwrap; expound *<idea etc>*. □ ~**se** *vpr* perform; (manejarse) manage

deseo *m* wish, desire. ~**so** *a* eager. **estar ~so de** be eager to

desequilibr|ado *a* unbalanced. ~**io** *m* imbalance

des|ertar *vt* desert; (Pol) defect. ~**értico** *a* desert-like. ~**ertor** *m* deserter; (Pol) defector

desespera|ción *f* despair. ~**do** *a* desperate; (enfurecer) infuriating. ~**r** *vt* drive to despair. □ ~**rse** *vpr* despair

desestimar *vt* (rechazar) reject

desfachat|ado *a* brazen, shameless. ~**ez** *f* nerve, cheek

desfallec|er [11] *vt* weaken. ● *vi* become weak; (desmayarse) faint. ~**imiento** *m* weakness; (desmayo) faint

desfasado *a* out of phase; *<idea>* outdated; *<persona>* out of touch

desfavorable *a* unfavourable

desfil|adero *m* narrow mountain pass; (cañón) narrow gorge. ~**ar** *vi* march (past). ~**e** *m* procession, parade. ~**e de modelos** fashion show

desgana *f*, (LAm) **desgano** *m* (falta de apetito) lack of appetite; (Med) weakness, faintness; (fig) unwillingness

desgarr|ador *a* heart-rending. ~**ar** *vt* tear; (fig) break *<corazón>*. ~**o** *m* tear, rip

desgast|ar *vt* wear away; wear out *<ropa>*. □ ~**arse** *vpr* wear away; *<ropa>* be worn out; *<persona>* wear o.s. out. ~**e** *m* wear

desgracia *f* misfortune; (accidente) accident; **por ~** unfortunately. **¡qué ~!** what a shame!. ~**do** *a* unlucky; (pobre) poor. ● *m* unfortunate person, poor devil Ⓣ

desgranar *vt* shell *<habas etc>*

desgreñado *a* ruffled, dishevelled

deshabitado *a* uninhabited; *<edificio>* unoccupied

deshacer [31] *vt* undo; strip *<cama>*; unpack *<maleta>*; (desmontar) take to pieces; break *<trato>*; (derretir) melt; (disolver) dissolve. □ ~**se** *vpr* come undone; (disolverse) dissolve; (derretirse) melt. ~**se de algo** get rid of sth. ~**se en lágrimas** dissolve into tears. ~**se por hacer algo** go out of one's way to do sth

desheredar *vt* disinherit

deshidratarse *vpr* become dehydrated

deshielo *m* thaw

deshilachado *a* frayed

deshincha|do *a* *<neumático>* flat. ~**r** *vt* deflate; (Med) reduce the swelling in. □ ~**rse** *vpr* go down

deshollinador *m* chimney sweep

deshon|esto *a* dishonest; (obsceno) indecent. ~**ra** *f* disgrace. ~**rar** *vt* dishonour

deshora *f*. **a ~** out of hours. **comer a ~s** eat between meals

deshuesar *vt* bone *<carne>*; stone *<fruta>*

desidia *f* slackness; *<pereza>* laziness

desierto *a* deserted. ● *m* desert

designar *vt* designate; (fijar) fix

desigual *a* unequal; *<terreno>* uneven; (distinto) different. ~**dad** *f* inequality

desilusi|ón *f* disappointment; (pérdida de ilusiones) disillusionment. ~**onar** *vt* disappoint; (quitar las ilusiones) disillusion. □ ~**onarse** *vpr* be disappointed; (perder las ilusiones) become disillusioned

desinfecta|nte *m* disinfectant. ~**r** *vt* disinfect

desinflar *vt* deflate. □ ~**se** *vpr* go down

desinhibido *a* uninhibited

desintegrar *vt* disintegrate. □ ~**se** *vpr* disintegrate

desinter|és *m* lack of interest; (generosidad) unselfishness. ~**esado** *a* uninterested; (liberal) unselfish

desistir *vi*. ~ de give up

desleal *a* disloyal. ~**tad** *f* disloyalty

desligar [12] *vt* untie; (separar) separate; (fig, librar) free. □ ~**se** *vpr* break away; (de un compromiso) free o.s. (de from)

desliza|dor *m* (Mex) hang glider. ~**r** [10] *vt* slide, slip. □ ~**se** *vpr* slide, slip; <*patinador*> glide; <*tiempo*> slip by, pass; (fluir) flow

deslucido *a* tarnished; (gastado) worn out; (fig) undistinguished

deslumbrar *vt* dazzle

desmadr|arse *vpr* get out of control. ~**e** *m* excess

desmán *m* outrage

desmanchar *vt* (LAm) remove the stains from

desmantelar *vt* dismantle; (despojar) strip

desmaquillador *m* make-up remover

desmay|ado *a* unconscious. □ ~**arse** *vpr* faint. ~**o** *m* faint

desmedido *a* excessive

desmemoriado *a* forgetful

desmenti|do *m* denial. ~**r** [4] *vt* deny; (contradecir) contradict

desmenuzar [10] *vt* crumble; shred <*carne etc*>

desmerecer [11] *vi*. no ~ de compare favourably with

desmesurado *a* excessive; (enorme) enormous

desmonta|ble *a* collapsible; <*armario*> easy to dismantle; (separable) removable. ~**r** *vt* (quitar) remove; (desarmar) dismantle, take apart. ● *vi* dismount

desmoralizar [10] *vt* demoralize

desmoronarse *vpr* crumble; <*edificio*> collapse

desnatado *a* skimmed

desnivel *m* unevenness; (fig) difference, inequality

desnud|ar *vt* strip; undress, strip <*persona*>. □ ~**arse** *vpr* undress. ~**ez** *f* nudity. ~**o** *a* naked; (fig) bare. ● *m* nude

desnutri|ción *f* malnutrition. ~**do** *a* undernourished

desobed|ecer [11] *vt* disobey. ~**iencia** *f* disobedience

desocupa|do *a* <*asiento etc*> vacant, free; (sin trabajo) unemployed; (ocioso) idle. ~**r** *vt* vacate; (vaciar) empty; (desalojar) clear

desodorante *m* deodorant

desolado *a* desolate; <*persona*> sorry, sad

desorbitante *a* excessive

desorden *m* disorder, untidiness; (confusión) confusion. ~**ado** *a* untidy. ~**ar** *vt* disarrange, make a mess of

desorganizar [10] *vt* disorganize; (trastornar) disturb

desorienta|do *a* confused. ~**r** *vt* disorientate. □ ~**rse** *vpr* lose one's bearings

despabila|do *a* wide awake; (listo) quick. ~**r** *vt* (despertar) wake up; (avivar) wise up. □ ~**rse** *vpr* wake up; (avivarse) wise up

despach|ar *vt* finish; (tratar con) deal with; (atender) serve; (vender) sell; (enviar) send; (despedir) fire. ~**o** *m* dispatch; (oficina) office; (venta) sale; (de localidades) box office

despacio *adv* slowly

despampanante *a* stunning

desparpajo *m* confidence; (descaro) impudence

desparramar *vt* scatter; spill <*líquidos*>

despavorido *a* terrified

despecho *m* spite. **a ~ de** in spite of. **por ~** out of spite

despectivo *a* contemptuous; *<sentido etc>* pejorative

despedazar [10] *vt* tear to pieces

despedi|da *f* goodbye, farewell. **~da de soltero** stag-party. **~r** [5] *vt* say goodbye to, see off; dismiss *<empleado>*; evict *<inquilino>*; (arrojar) throw; give off *<olor etc>*. □ **~rse** *vpr* say goodbye (**de** to)

despeg|ar [12] *vt* unstick. ● *vi* *<avión>* take off. **~ue** *m* take-off

despeinar *vt* ruffle the hair of

despeja|do *a* clear; *<persona>* wide awake. **~r** *vt* clear; (aclarar) clarify. ● *vi* clear. □ **~rse** *vpr* (aclararse) become clear; *<tiempo>* clear up

despellejar *vt* skin

despensa *f* pantry, larder

despeñadero *m* cliff

desperdici|ar *vt* waste. **~o** *m* waste. **~os** *mpl* rubbish

desperta|dor *m* alarm clock. **~r** [1] *vt* wake (up); (fig) awaken. □ **~rse** *vpr* wake up

despiadado *a* merciless

despido *m* dismissal

despierto *a* awake; (listo) bright

despilfarr|ar *vt* waste. **~o** *m* squandering; (gasto innecesario) extravagance

despintarse *vpr* (Mex) run

despista|do *a* (con estar) confused; (con ser) absent-minded. **~r** *vt* throw off the scent; (fig) mislead. □ **~rse** *vpr* go wrong; (fig) get confused

despiste *m* mistake; (confusión) muddle

desplaza|miento *m* displacement; (de opinión etc) swing, shift. **~r** [10] *vt* displace. □ **~rse** *vpr* travel

desplegar [1 & 12] *vt* open out; spread *<alas>*; (fig) show

desplomarse *vpr* collapse

despoblado *m* deserted area

despoj|ar *vt* deprive *<persona>*; strip *<cosa>*. **~os** *mpl* remains; (de res) offal; (de ave) giblets

despreci|able *a* despicable; *<cantidad>* negligible. **~ar** *vt* des-

pise; (rechazar) scorn. **~o** *m* contempt; (desaire) snub

desprender *vt* remove; give off *<olor>*. □ **~se** *vpr* fall off; (fig) part with; (deducirse) follow

despreocupa|do *a* unconcerned; (descuidado) careless. □ **~rse** *vpr* not worry

desprestigiar *vt* discredit

desprevenido *a* unprepared. **pillar a uno ~** catch s.o. unawares

desproporcionado *a* disproportionate

desprovisto *a*. **~ de** lacking in, without

después *adv* after, afterwards; (más tarde) later; (a continuación) then. **~ de** after. **~ de comer** after eating. **~ de todo** after all. **~ (de) que** after. **poco ~** soon after

desquit|arse *vpr* get even (**de** with). **~e** *m* revenge

destaca|do *a* outstanding. **~r** [7] *vt* emphasize. ● *vi* stand out. □ **~rse** *vpr* stand out. **~se en** excel at

destajo *m*. **trabajar a ~** do piecework

destap|ar *vt* uncover; open *<botella>*. □ **~arse** *vpr* reveal one's true self. **~e** *m* (fig) permissiveness

destartalado *a* *<coche>* clapped-out; *<casa>* ramshackle

destello *m* sparkle; (de estrella) twinkle; (fig) glimmer

destemplado *a* discordant; *<nervios>* frayed

desteñir [5 & 22] *vt* fade. ● *vi* fade; *<color>* run. □ **~se** *vpr* fade; *<color>* run

desterra|do *m* exile. **~r** [1] *vt* banish

destetar *vt* wean

destiempo *m*. **a ~** at the wrong moment; (Mus) out of time

destierro *m* exile

destil|ar *vt* distil. **~ería** *f* distillery

destin|ar *vt* destine; (nombrar) post. **~atario** *m* addressee. **~o** *m* (uso) use, function; (lugar) destination; (suerte) destiny. **con ~o a** (going) to

destituir [17] *vt* dismiss

destornilla|dor *m* screwdriver. ~**r** *vt* unscrew

destreza *f* skill

destroz|ar [10] *vt* destroy; (fig) shatter. ~**os** *mpl* destruction, damage

destru|cción *f* destruction. ~**ir** [17] *vt* destroy

desus|ado *a* old-fashioned; (insólito) unusual. ~**o** *m* disuse. **caer en** ~**o** fall into disuse

desvalido *a* needy, destitute

desvalijar *vt* rob; ransack *<casa>*

desvalorizar [10] *vt* devalue

desván *m* loft

desvanec|er [11] *vt* make disappear; (borrar) blur; (fig) dispel. □ ~**erse** *vpr* disappear; (desmayarse) faint. ~**imiento** *m* (Med) faint

desvariar [20] *vi* be delirious; (fig) talk nonsense

desvel|ar *vt* keep awake. □ ~**arse** *vpr* stay awake, have a sleepless night. ~**o** *m* sleeplessness

desvencijado *a* *<mueble>* rickety

desventaja *f* disadvantage

desventura *f* misfortune. ~**do** *a* unfortunate

desverg|onzado *a* impudent, cheeky. ~**üenza** *f* impudence, cheek

desvestirse [5] *vpr* undress

desv|iación *f* deviation; (Auto) diversion. ~**iar** [20] *vt* divert; deflect *<pelota>*. □ ~**iarse** *vpr* *<carretera>* branch off; (del camino) make a detour; (del tema) stray. ~**ío** *m* diversion

desvivirse *vpr*. ~**se por** be completely devoted to; (esforzarse) go out of one's way to

detall|ar *vt* relate in detail. ~**e** *m* detail; (fig) gesture. **al** ~**e** retail. **entrar en** ~**es** go into detail. **¡qué** ~**e!** how thoughtful! ~**ista** *m & f* retailer

detect|ar *vt* detect. ~**ive** *m* detective

deten|ción *f* stopping; (Jurid) arrest; (en la cárcel) detention. ~**er** [40] *vt* stop; (Jurid) arrest; (encarcelar) detain; (retrasar) delay. □ ~**erse** *vpr* stop; (entretenerse) spend a lot of time.

~**idamente** *adv* at length. ~**ido** *a* (Jurid) under arrest. ● *m* prisoner

detergente *a & m* detergent

deterior|ar *vt* damage, spoil. □ ~**arse** *vpr* deteriorate. ~**o** *m* deterioration

determina|ción *f* determination; (decisión) decison. ~**nte** *a* decisive. ~**r** *vt* determine; (decidir) decide

detestar *vt* detest

detrás *adv* behind; (en la parte posterior) on the back. ~ **de** behind. **por** ~ at the back; (por la espalda) from behind

detrimento *m* detriment. **en** ~ **de** to the detriment of

deud|a *f* debt. ~**or** *m* debtor

devalua|ción *f* devaluation. ~**r** [21] *vt* devalue. □ ~**se** *vpr* depreciate

devastador *a* devastating

devoción *f* devotion

devol|ución *f* return; (Com) repayment, refund. ~**ver** [5] (*pp* **devuelto**) *vt* return; (Com) repay, refund. ● *vi* be sick

devorar *vt* devour

devoto *a* devout; *<amigo etc>* devoted. ● *m* admirer

di *vb* ⇒DAR, DECIR

día *m* day. ~ **de fiesta** (public) holiday. ~ **del santo** saint's day. ~ **feriado** (LAm), ~ **festivo** (public) holiday. **al** ~ up to date. **al** ~ **siguiente** (on) the following day. **¡buenos** ~**s!** good morning! **de** ~ by day. **el** ~ **de hoy** today. **el** ~ **de mañana** tomorrow. **un** ~ **sí y otro no** every other day. **vivir al** ~ live from hand to mouth

diab|etes *f* diabetes. ~**ético** *a* diabetic

diab|lo *m* devil. ~**lura** *f* mischief. ~**ólico** *a* diabolical

diadema *f* diadem

diáfano *a* diaphanous; *<cielo>* clear

diafragma *m* diaphragm

diagn|osis *f* diagnosis. ~**osticar** [7] *vt* diagnose. ~**óstico** *m* diagnosis

diagonal *a & f* diagonal

diagrama *m* diagram

dialecto *m* dialect

di|alogar [12] *vi* talk. **~álogo** *m* dialogue; (Pol) talks

diamante *m* diamond

diámetro *m* diameter

diana *f* reveille; (blanco) bull's-eye

diapositiva *f* slide, transparency

diario *a* daily. ● *m* newspaper; (libro) diary. **a ~o** daily. **de ~o** everyday, ordinary

diarrea *f* diarrhoea

dibuj|ante *m* draughtsman. ●*f* draughtswoman. **~ar** *vt* draw. **~o** *m* drawing. **~os animados** cartoons

diccionario *m* dictionary

dich|a *f* happiness. **por ~a** fortunately. **~o** *a* said; (tal) such. ● *m* saying. **~o y hecho** no sooner said than done. **mejor ~o** rather. **propiamente ~o** strictly speaking. **~oso** *a* happy; (afortunado) fortunate

diciembre *m* December

dicta|do *m* dictation. **~dor** *m* dictator. **~dura** *f* dictatorship. **~men** *m* opinion; (informe) report. **~r** *vt* dictate; pronounce *<sentencia etc>*; (LAm) give *<clase>*

didáctico *a* didactic

dieci|nueve *a* & *m* nineteen. **~ocho** *a* & *m* eighteen. **~séis** *a* & *m* sixteen. **~siete** *a* & *m* seventeen

diente *m* tooth; (de tenedor) prong; (de ajo) clove. **~ de león** dandelion. **hablar entre ~s** mumble

diestro *a* right-handed; (hábil) skillful

dieta *f* diet

diez *a* & *m* ten

diezmar *vt* decimate

difamación *f* (con palabras) slander; (por escrito) libel

diferen|cia *f* difference; (desacuerdo) disagreement. **~ciar** *vt* differentiate between. □ **~ciarse** *vpr* differ. **~te** *a* different; (diversos) various

diferido *a* (TV etc). **en ~** recorded

dif|ícil *a* difficult; (poco probable) unlikely. **~icultad** *f* difficulty. **~icultar** *vt* make difficult

difteria *f* diphtheria

difundir *vt* spread; (TV etc) broadcast

difunto *a* late, deceased. ● *m* deceased

difusión *f* spreading

dige|rir [4] *vt* digest. **~stión** *f* digestion. **~stivo** *a* digestive

digital *a* digital; (de los dedos) finger

dign|arse *vpr* deign to. **~atario** *m* dignitary. **~idad** *f* dignity. **~o** *a* honourable; (decoroso) decent; (merecedor) worthy (**de** of). **~ de elogio** praiseworthy

digo *vb* ⇒DECIR

dije *vb* ⇒DECIR

dilatar *vt* expand; (Med) dilate; (prolongar) prolong. □ **~se** *vpr* expand; (Med) dilate; (extenderse) extend; (Mex, demorarse) be late

dilema *m* dilemma

diligen|cia *f* diligence; (gestión) job; (carruaje) stagecoach. **~te** *a* diligent

dilucidar *vt* clarify; solve *<misterio>*

diluir [17] *vt* dilute

diluvio *m* flood

dimensión *f* dimension; (tamaño) size

diminut|ivo *a* & *m* diminutive. **~o** *a* minute

dimitir *vt/i* resign

Dinamarca *f* Denmark

dinamarqués *a* Danish. ● *m* Dane

dinámic|a *f* dynamics. **~o** *a* dynamic

dinamita *f* dynamite

dínamo *m* dynamo

dinastía *f* dynasty

diner|al *m* fortune. **~o** *m* money. **~o efectivo** cash. **~o suelto** change

dinosaurio *m* dinosaur

dios *m* god. **~a** *f* goddess. **¡D~ mío!** good heavens! **¡gracias a D~!** thank God!

diplom|a *m* diploma. **~acia** *f* diplomacy. **~ado** *a* qualified. □ **~arse** *vpr* (LAm) graduate. **~ático** *a* diplomatic. ● *m* diplomat

diptongo *m* diphthong

diputa|ción *f* delegation. **~ción provincial** county council. **~do** *m* deputy; (Pol, en España) member of the Cortes; (Pol, en Inglaterra) Member of Parliament; (Pol, en Estados Unidos) congressman

dique *m* dike

direc|ción *f* direction; (señas) address; (los que dirigen) management; (Pol) leadership; (Auto) steering. ~**ción prohibida** no entry. ~**ción única** one-way. ~**ta** *f* (Auto) top gear. ~**tiva** *f* board; (Pol) executive committee. ~**tivas** *fpl* guidelines. ~**to** *a* direct; *<línea>* straight; *<tren>* through. **en** ~**to** (TV etc) live. ~**tor** *m* director; (Mus) conductor; (de escuela) headmaster; (de periódico) editor; (gerente) manager. ~**tora** *f* (de escuela etc) headmistress. ~**torio** *m* board of directors; (LAm, de teléfonos) telephone directory

dirig|ente *a* ruling. ● *m & f* leader; (de empresa) manager. ~**ir** [14] *vt* direct; (Mus) conduct; run *<empresa etc>*; address *<carta etc>*. □ ~**irse** *vpr* make one's way; (hablar) address

disciplina *f* discipline. ~**r** *vt* discipline. ~**rio** *a* disciplinary

discípulo *m* disciple; (alumno) pupil

disco *m* disc; (Mus) record; (deportes) discus; (de teléfono) dial; (de tráfico) sign; (Rail) signal. ~ **duro** hard disk. ~ **flexible** floppy disk

disconforme *a* not in agreement

discord|e *a* discordant. ~**ia** *f* discord

discoteca *f* discothèque, disco 🆃; (colección de discos) record collection

discreción *f* discretion

discrepa|ncia *f* discrepancy; (desacuerdo) disagreement. ~**r** *vi* differ

discreto *a* discreet; (moderado) moderate

discrimina|ción *f* discrimination. ~**r** *vt* (distinguir) discriminate between; (tratar injustamente) discriminate against

disculpa *f* apology; (excusa) excuse. **pedir** ~**s** apologize. ~**r** *vt* excuse, forgive. □ ~**rse** *vpr* apologize

discurs|ar *vi* speak (**sobre** about). ~**o** *m* speech

discusión *f* discussion; (riña) argument

discuti|ble *a* debatable. ~**r** *vt* discuss; (contradecir) contradict. ● *vi* argue (**por** about)

disecar [7] *vt* stuff; (cortar) dissect

diseminar *vt* disseminate, spread

disentir [4] *vi* disagree (**de** with, **en** on)

diseñ|ador *m* designer. ~**ar** *vt* design. ~**o** *m* design; (fig) sketch

disertación *f* dissertation

disfraz *m* fancy dress; (para engañar) disguise. ~**ar** [10] *vt* dress up; (para engañar) disguise. □ ~**arse** *vpr*. ~**arse de** dress up as; (para engañar) disguise o.s. as.

disfrutar *vt* enjoy. ● *vi* enjoy o.s. ~ **de** enjoy

disgust|ar *vt* displease; (molestar) annoy. □ ~**arse** *vpr* get annoyed, get upset; *<dos personas>* fall out. ~**o** *m* annoyance; (problema) trouble; (riña) quarrel; (dolor) sorrow, grief

disidente *a & m & f* dissident

disimular *vt* conceal. ● *vi* pretend

disipar *vt* dissipate; (derrochar) squander

dislocarse [7] *vpr* dislocate

disminu|ción *f* decrease. ~**ir** [17] *vi* diminish

disolver [2] (*pp* **disuelto**) *vt* dissolve. □ ~**se** *vpr* dissolve

dispar *a* different

disparar *vt* fire; (Mex, pagar) buy. ● *vi* shoot (**contra** at)

disparate *m* silly thing; (error) mistake. **decir** ~**s** talk nonsense. **¡qué** ~**!** how ridiculous!

disparidad *f* disparity

disparo *m* (acción) firing; (tiro) shot

dispensar *vt* give; (eximir) exempt. ● *vi*. **¡Vd dispense!** forgive me

dispers|ar *vt* scatter, disperse. □ ~**arse** *vpr* scatter, disperse. ~**ión** *f* dispersion. ~**o** *a* scattered

dispon|er [34] *vt* arrange; (Jurid) order. ● *vi*. ~**er de** have; (vender etc) dispose of. □ ~**erse** *vpr* prepare (**a** to). ~**ibilidad** *f* availability. ~**ible** *a* available

disposición *f* arrangement; (aptitud) talent; (disponibilidad) disposal; (Jurid) order, decree. ~ **de ánimo** frame of mind. **a la** ~ **de** at the disposal of. **a su** ~ at your service

dispositivo *m* device

dispuesto *a* ready; *<persona>* disposed (a to); (servicial) helpful

disputa *f* dispute; (pelea) argument

disquete *m* diskette, floppy disk

dista|ncia *f* distance. **a ~ncia** from a distance. **guardar las ~ncias** keep one's distance. **~nciar** *vt* space out; distance *<amigos>*. □ **~nciarse** *vpr* *<dos personas>* fall out. **~nte** *a* distant. **~r** *vi* be away; (fig) be far. **~ 5 kilómetros** it's 5 kilometres away

distin|ción *f* distinction; (honor) award. **~guido** *a* distinguished. **~guir** [13] *vt/i* distinguish. □ **~guirse** *vpr* distinguish o.s.; (diferenciarse) differ. **~tivo** *a* distinctive. ● *m* badge. **~to** *a* different, distinct

distra|cción *f* amusement; (descuido) absent-mindedness, inattention. **~er** [41] *vt* distract; (divertir) amuse. □ **~erse** *vpr* amuse o.s.; (descuidarse) not pay attention. **~ído** *a* (desatento) absent-minded

distribu|ción *f* distribution. **~idor** *m* distributor. **~ir** [17] *vt* distribute

distrito *m* district

disturbio *m* disturbance

disuadir *vt* deter, dissuade

diurno *a* daytime

divagar [12] *vi* digress; (hablar sin sentido) ramble

diván *m* settee, sofa

diversi|dad *f* diversity. **~ficar** [7] *vt* diversify

diversión *f* amusement, entertainment; (pasatiempo) pastime

diverso *a* different

diverti|do *a* amusing; (que tiene gracia) funny. **~r** [4] *vt* amuse, entertain. □ **~rse** *vpr* enjoy o.s.

dividir *vt* divide; (repartir) share out

divino *a* divine

divisa *f* emblem. **~s** *fpl* currency

divisar *vt* make out

división *f* division

divorci|ado *a* divorced. ● *m* divorcee. **~ar** *vt* divorce. □ **~arse** *vpr* get divorced. **~o** *m* divorce

divulgar [12] *vt* spread; divulge *<secreto>*

dizque *adv* (LAm) apparently; (supuestamente) supposedly

do *m* C; (solfa) doh

dobl|adillo *m* hem; (de pantalón) turn-up (Brit), cuff (Amer). **~ar** *vt* double; (plegar) fold; (torcer) bend; turn *<esquina>*; dub *<película>*. ● *vi* turn; *<campana>* toll. □ **~arse** *vpr* double; (curvarse) bend. **~e** *a* double. ● *m* double. **el ~e** twice as much (de, que as). **~egar** [12] *vt* (fig) force to give in. □ **~egarse** *vpr* give in

doce *a* & *m* twelve. **~na** *f* dozen

docente *a* teaching. ● *m* & *f* teacher

dócil *a* obedient

doctor *m* doctor. **~ado** *m* doctorate

doctrina *f* doctrine

document|ación *f* documentation, papers. **~al** *a* & *m* documentary. **~o** *m* document. **D~o Nacional de Identidad** national identity card

dólar *m* dollar

dol|er [2] *vi* hurt, ache; (fig) grieve. **me duele la cabeza** I have a headache. **le duele el estómago** he has (a) stomach-ache. **~or** *m* pain; (sordo) ache; (fig) sorrow. **~or de cabeza** headache. **~or de muelas** toothache. **~oroso** *a* painful

domar *vt* tame; break in *<caballo>*

dom|esticar [7] *vt* domesticate. **~éstico** *a* domestic

domicili|ar *vt*. **~ar los pagos** pay by direct debit. **~o** *m* address. **~o particular** home address. **reparto a ~** home delivery service

domina|nte *a* dominant; *<persona>* domineering. **~r** *vt* dominate; (contener) control; (conocer) have a good command of. ● *vi* dominate. □ **~rse** *vpr* control o.s.

domingo *m* Sunday

dominio *m* authority; (territorio) domain; (fig) command

dominó *m* (*pl* **~s**) dominoes; (ficha) domino

don *m* talent, gift; (en un sobre) Mr. **~ Pedro** Pedro

donación *f* donation

donaire *m* grace, charm

dona|nte *m & f* (de sangre) donor. **~r** *vt* donate

doncella *f* maiden; (criada) maid

donde *adv* where

dónde *adv* where?; (LAm, cómo) how; ¿hasta **~**? how far? ¿por **~**? whereabouts?; (por qué camino?) which way? ¿a **~** vas? where are you going? ¿de **~** eres? where are you from?

dondequiera *adv.* **~** que wherever. por **~** everywhere

doña *f* (en un sobre) Mrs. **~** María María

dora|do *a* golden; (cubierto de oro) gilt. **~r** *vt* gilt; (Culin) brown

dormi|do *a* asleep. quedarse **~do** fall asleep; (no despertar) oversleep. **~r** [6] *vt* send to sleep. **~r la siesta** have an afternoon nap, have a siesta. ● *vi* sleep. □ **~rse** *vpr* fall asleep. **~tar** *vi* doze. **~torio** *m* bedroom

dors|al *a* back. ● *m* (en deportes) number. **~o** *m* back. nadar de **~** (Mex) do (the) backstroke

dos *a & m* two. de **~** en **~** in twos, in pairs. los **~**, las **~** both (of them). **~cientos** *a & m* two hundred

dosi|ficar [7] *vt* dose; (fig) measure out. **~s** *f invar* dose

dot|ado *a* gifted. **~ar** *vt* give a dowry; (proveer) provide (de with). **~e** *m* dowry

doy *vb* ⇒DAR

dragar [12] *vt* dredge

drama *m* drama; (obra de teatro) play. **~turgo** *m* playwright

drástico *a* drastic

droga *f* drug. **~dicto** *m* drug addict. **~do** *m* drug addict. **~r** [12] *vt* drug. □ **~rse** *vpr* take drugs

droguería *f* hardware store

ducha *f* shower. □ **~rse** *vpr* have a shower

dud|a *f* doubt. poner en **~a** question. sin **~a** (alguna) without a doubt. **~ar** *vt/i* doubt. **~oso** *a* doubtful; (sospechoso) dubious

duelo *m* duel; (luto) mourning

duende *m* imp

dueñ|a *f* owner, proprietress; (de una pensión) landlady. **~o** *m* owner, proprietor; (de una pensión) landlord

duermo *vb* ⇒DORMIR

dul|ce *a* sweet; <agua> fresh; (suave) soft, gentle. ● *m* (LAm) sweet. **~zura** *f* sweetness; (fig) gentleness

duna *f* dune

dúo *m* duet, duo

duplica|do *a* duplicated. por **~** in duplicate. ● *m* duplicate. **~r** [7] *vt* duplicate. □ **~rse** *vpr* double

duque *m* duke. **~sa** *f* duchess

dura|ción *f* duration, length. **~dero** *a* lasting. **~nte** *prep* during; (medida de tiempo) for. **~** todo el año all year round. **~r** *vi* last

durazno *m* (LAm, fruta) peach

dureza *f* hardness; (Culin) toughness; (fig) harshness

duro *a* hard; (Culin) tough; (fig) harsh. ● *adv* (esp LAm) hard. ● *m* five-peseta coin

Ee

e *conj* and

ebrio *a* drunk

ebullición *f* boiling

eccema *m* eczema

echar *vt* throw; post <carta>; give off <olor>; pour <líquido>; (expulsar) expel; (de recinto) throw out; fire <empleado>; (poner) put on; get <gasolina>; put out <raíces>; show <película>. **~** a start. **~** a perder spoil. **~** de menos miss. **~se atrás** (fig) back down. echárselas de feign. □ **~se** *vpr* throw o.s.; (tumbarse) lie down

eclesiástico *a* ecclesiastical

eclipse *m* eclipse

eco *m* echo. hacerse **~** de echo

ecolog|ía *f* ecology. **~ista** *m & f* ecologist

economato *m* cooperative store

econ|omía *f* economy; (ciencia) economics. **~ómico** *a* economic; (no caro) inexpensive. **~omista** *m & f* economist. **~omizar** [10] *vt/i* economize

ecuación *f* equation

ecuador *m* equator. **el E~** the Equator. **E~** (país) Ecuador

ecuánime *a* level-headed; (imparcial) impartial

ecuatoriano *a & m* Ecuadorian

ecuestre *a* equestrian

edad *f* age. **~ avanzada** old age. **E~ de Piedra** Stone Age. **E~ Media** Middle Ages. **¿qué ~ tiene?** how old is he?

edición *f* edition; (publicación) publication

edicto *m* edict

edific|ación *f* building. **~ante** *a* edifying. **~ar** [7] *vt* build; (fig) edify. **~io** *m* building; (fig) structure

edit|ar *vt* edit; (publicar) publish. **~or** *a* publishing. ● *m* editor; (que publica) publisher. **~orial** *a* editorial. ● *m* leading article. ● *f* publishing house

edredón *m* duvet

educa|ción *f* upbringing; (modales) (good) manners; (enseñanza) education. **falta de ~ción** rudeness, bad manners. **~do** *a* polite. **bien ~do** polite. **mal ~do** rude. **~r** [7] *vt* bring up; (enseñar) educate. **~tivo** *a* educational

edulcorante *m* sweetener

EE.UU. *abrev* (**Estados Unidos**) USA

efect|ivamente *adv* really; (por supuesto) indeed. **~ivo** *a* effective; (auténtico) real. ● *m* cash. **~o** *m* effect; (impresión) impression. **en ~o** really; (como respuesta) indeed. **~os** *mpl* belongings; (Com) goods. **~uar** [21] *vt* carry out; make <*viaje, compras etc*>

efervescente *a* effervescent; <*bebidas*> fizzy

efica|cia *f* effectiveness; (de persona) efficiency. **~z** *a* effective; <*persona*> efficient

eficien|cia *f* efficiency. **~te** *a* efficient

efímero *a* ephemeral

efusi|vidad *f* effusiveness. **~vo** *a* effusive; <*persona*> demonstrative

egipcio *a & m* Egyptian

Egipto *m* Egypt

ego|ísmo *m* selfishness, egotism. **~ísta** *a* selfish

egresar *vi* (LAm) graduate; (de colegio) leave school, graduate Amer

eje *m* axis; (Tec) axle

ejecu|ción *f* execution; (Mus) performance. **~tar** *vt* carry out; (Mus) perform; (matar) execute. **~tivo** *m* executive

ejempl|ar *a* exemplary; (ideal) model. ● *m* specimen; (libro) copy; (revista) issue, number. **~ificar** [7] *vt* exemplify. **~o** *m* example. **dar (el) ~o** set an example. **por ~o** for example

ejerc|er [9] *vt* exercise; practise <*profesión*>; exert <*influencia*>. ● *vi* practise. **~icio** *m* exercise; (de profesión) practice. **hacer ~icios** take exercise. **~itar** *vt* exercise

ejército *m* army

ejido *m* (Mex) cooperative

ejote *m* (Mex) green bean

....

el ⋮

....

● *artículo definido masculino* (*pl* **los**)

> The masculine article **el** is also used before feminine nouns which begin with stressed **a** or **ha**, e.g. **el ala derecha**, **el hada madrina**. Also, preceded by **de** becomes **del** and preceded by **a** becomes **al**

····▸ the. **el tren de las seis** the six o'clock train. **el vecino de al lado** the next-door neighbour. **cerca del hospital** near the hospital

No se traduce en los siguientes casos:

····▸ (con nombre abstracto, genérico) **el tiempo vuela** time flies. **odio el queso** I hate cheese. **el hilo es muy durable** linen is very durable

····▸ (con colores, días de la semana) **el rojo está de moda** red is in fashion. **el lunes es fiesta** Monday is a holiday

····▸ (con algunas instituciones) **termino el colegio mañana** I finish school tomorrow. **lo ingresaron en el hospital** he was admitted to hospital

····▸ (con nombres propios) **el Sr. Díaz** Mr Díaz. **el doctor Lara** Doctor Lara

····▸ (antes de infinitivo) **es muy cuidadosa en el vestir** she takes great care in the way she dresses. **me di cuenta al verlo** I realized when I saw him

••••➤ (con partes del cuerpo, artículos personales) *se traduce por un posesivo.* **apretó el puño** he clenched his fist. **tienes el zapato desatado** your shoe is undone

••••➤ **el + de. es de Pedro** it's Pedro's. **el del sombrero** the one with the hat

••••➤ **el + que** (persona) **el que me atendió** the one who served me. (cosa) **el que se rompió** the one that broke.

••••➤ **el + que** + *subjuntivo* (quienquiera) whoever. **el que gane la lotería** whoever wins the lottery. (cualquiera) whichever. **compra el que sea más barato** buy whichever is cheaper

él *pron* (persona) he; (persona con prep) him; (cosa) it. **es de ~** it's his

elabora|ción *f* elaboration; (fabricación) manufacture. **~r** *vt* elaborate; manufacture *<producto>*; (producir) produce

el|asticidad *f* elasticity. **~ástico** *a & m* elastic

elec|ción *f* choice; (de político etc) election. **~ciones** *fpl* (Pol) election. **~tor** *m* voter. **~torado** *m* electorate. **~toral** *a* electoral; *<campaña>* election

electrici|dad *f* electricity. **~sta** *m & f* electrician

eléctrico *a* electric; *<aparato>* electrical

electri|ficar [7] *vt*, electrify. **~zar** [10] *vt* electrify

electrocutar *vt* electrocute. □ **~se** *vpr* be electrocuted

electrodoméstico *a* electrical appliance

electrónic|a *f* electronics. **~o** *a* electronic

elefante *m* elephant

elegan|cia *f* elegance. **~te** *a* elegant

elegía *f* elegy

elegi|ble *a* eligible. **~do** *a* chosen. **~r** [5 & 14] *vt* choose; (por votación) elect

element|al *a* elementary; (esencial) fundamental. **~o** *m* element; (persona) person, bloke (Brit, 🆃). **~os** *mpl* (nociones) basic principles

elenco *m* (en el teatro) cast

eleva|ción *f* elevation; (de precios) rise, increase; (acción) raising. **~dor** *m* (Mex) lift (Brit), elevator (Amer). **~r** *vt* raise; (promover) promote

elimina|ción *f* elimination. **~r** *vt* eliminate; (Informática) delete. **~toria** *f* preliminary heat

élite /e'lit, e'lite/ *f* elite

ella *pron* (persona) she; (persona con prep) her; (cosa) it. **es de ~** it's hers. **~s** *pron pl* they; (con prep) them. **es de ~s** it's theirs

ello *pron* it

ellos *pron pl* they; (con prep) them. **es de ~** it's theirs

elocuen|cia *f* eloquence. **~te** *a* eloquent

elogi|ar *vt* praise. **~o** *m* praise

elote *m* (Mex) corncob; (Culin) corn on the cob

eludir *vt* avoid, elude

emanar *vi* emanate (de from); (originarse) originate (de from, in)

emancipa|ción *f* emancipation. **~r** *vt* emancipate. □ **~rse** *vpr* become emancipated

embadurnar *vt* smear

embajad|a *f* embassy. **~or** *m* ambassador

embalar *vt* pack

embaldosar *vt* tile

embalsamar *vt* embalm

embalse *m* reservoir

embaraz|ada *a* pregnant. ● *f* pregnant woman. **~ar** [10] *vt* get pregnant. **~o** *m* pregnancy; (apuro) embarrassment; (estorbo) hindrance. **~oso** *a* awkward, embarrassing

embar|cación *f* vessel. **~cadero** *m* jetty, pier. **~car** [7] *vt* load *<mercancías etc>*. □ **~carse** *vpr* board. **~carse en** (fig) embark upon

embargo *m* embargo; (Jurid) seizure. **sin ~** however

embarque *m* loading; (de pasajeros) boarding

embaucar [7] *vt* trick

embelesar *vt* captivate

embellecer [11] *vt* make beautiful

embesti|da *f* charge. **~r** [5] *vt/i* charge

emblema *m* emblem

embolsarse *vpr* pocket

embonar *vt* (Mex) fit

emborrachar *vt* get drunk. □ ~**se** *vpr* get drunk

emboscada *f* ambush

embotar *vt* dull

embotella|miento *m* (de vehículos) traffic jam. ~**r** *vt* bottle

embrague *m* clutch

embriag|arse [12] *vpr* get drunk. ~**uez** *f* drunkenness

embrión *m* embryo

embroll|ar *vt* mix up; involve <*persona*>. □ ~**arse** *vpr* get into a muddle; (en un asunto) get involved. ~**o** *m* tangle; (fig) muddle

embruj|ado *a* bewitched; <*casa*> haunted. ~**ar** *vt* bewitch. ~**o** *m* spell

embrutecer [11] *vt* brutalize

embudo *m* funnel

embuste *m* lie. ~**ro** *a* deceitful. ● *m* liar

embuti|do *m* (Culin) sausage. ~**r** *vt* stuff

emergencia *f* emergency

emerger [14] *vi* appear, emerge

emigra|ción *f* emigration. ~**nte** *a* & *m* & *f* emigrant. ~**r** *vi* emigrate

eminen|cia *f* eminence. ~**te** *a* eminent

emisario *m* emissary

emi|sión *f* emission; (de dinero) issue; (TV etc) broadcast. ~**sor** *a* issuing; (TV etc) broadcasting. ~**sora** *f* radio station. ~**tir** *vt* emit, give out; (TV etc) broadcast; cast <*voto*>; (poner en circulación) issue

emoci|ón *f* emotion; (excitación) excitement. ¡qué ~**ón**! how exciting!. ~**onado** *a* moved. ~**onante** *a* exciting; (conmovedor) moving. ~**onar** *vt* move. □ ~**onarse** *vpr* get excited; (conmoverse) be moved

emotivo *a* emotional; (conmovedor) moving

empacar [7] *vt* (LAm) pack

empacho *m* indigestion

empadronar *vt* register. □ ~**se** *vpr* register

empalagoso *a* sickly; <*persona*> cloying

empalizada *f* fence

empalm|ar *vt* connect, join. ● *vi* meet. ~**e** *m* junction; (de trenes) connection

empan|ada *f* (savoury) pie; (LAm, individual) pasty. ~**adilla** *f* pasty

empantanarse *vpr* become swamped; <*coche*> get bogged down

empañar *vt* steam up; (fig) tarnish. □ ~**se** *vpr* steam up

empapar *vt* soak. □ ~**se** *vpr* get soaked

empapela|do *m* wallpaper. ~**r** *vt* wallpaper

empaquetar *vt* package

emparedado *m* sandwich

emparentado *a* related

empast|ar *vt* fill <*muela*>. ~**e** *m* filling

empat|ar *vi* draw. ~**e** *m* draw

empedernido *a* confirmed; <*bebedor*> inveterate

empedrar [1] *vt* pave

empeine *m* instep

empeñ|ado *a* in debt; (decidido) determined (en to). ~**ar** *vt* pawn; pledge <*palabra*>. □ ~**arse** *vpr* get into debt; (estar decidido a) be determined (en to). ~**o** *m* pledge; (resolución) determination. **casa** *f* **de** ~**s** pawnshop. ~**oso** *a* (LAm) hardworking

empeorar *vt* make worse. ● *vi* get worse. □ ~**se** *vpr* get worse

empequeñecer [11] *vt* become smaller; (fig) belittle

empera|dor *m* emperor. ~**triz** *f* empress

empezar [1 & 10] *vt/i* start, begin. **para** ~ to begin with

empina|do *a* <*cuesta*> steep. ~**r** *vt* raise. □ ~**rse** *vpr* <*persona*> stand on tiptoe

empírico *a* empirical

emplasto *m* plaster

emplaza|miento *m* (Jurid) summons; (lugar) site. ~**r** [10] *vt* summon; (situar) site

emple|ada *f* employee; (doméstica) maid. ~**ado** *m* employee. ~**ar** *vt* use; employ <*persona*>; spend <*tiempo*>. □ ~**arse** *vpr* get a job. ~**o** *m* use; (trabajo) employment; (puesto) job

empobrecer [11] *vt* impoverish. □ ~**se** *vpr* become poor

empoll|ar *vt* incubate <*huevos*>; (▣, estudiar) cram Ⓣ. ● *vi* <*ave*> sit; <*estudiante*> ▣ cram. ~**ón** *m* ▣ swot (Brit Ⓣ), grind (Amer Ⓣ)

empolvarse *vpr* powder

empotra|do *a* built-in, fitted. ~**r** *vt* fit

emprende|dor *a* enterprising. ~**r** *vt* undertake; set out on <*viaje*>. ~**rla con uno** pick a fight with s.o.

empresa *f* undertaking; (Com) company, firm. ~**rio** *m* businessman; (patrón) employer; (de teatro etc) impresario

empuj|ar *vt* push. ~**e** *m* (fig) drive. ~**ón** *m* push, shove

empuña|dura *f* handle. ~**r** *vt* take up <*pluma, espada*>

emular *vt* emulate

en *prep* in; (sobre) on; (dentro) inside, in; (medio de transporte) by. ~ **casa** at home. ~ **coche** by car. ~ **10 días** in 10 days. **de pueblo** ~ **pueblo** from town to town

enagua *f* petticoat

enajena|ción *f* alienation. ~**ción mental** insanity. ~**r** *vt* alienate; (volver loco) derange

enamora|do *a* in love. ● *m* lover. ~**r** *vt* win the love of. □ ~**rse** *vpr* fall in love (**de** with)

enano *a* & *m* dwarf

enardecer [11] *vt* inflame. □ ~**se** *vpr* get excited (**por** about)

encabeza|do *m* (Mex) headline. ~**miento** *m* heading; (de periódico) headline. ~**r** [10] *vt* head; lead <*revolución etc*>

encabritarse *vpr* rear up

encadenar *vt* chain; (fig) tie down

encaj|ar *vt* fit; fit together <*varias piezas*>. ● *vi* fit; (cuadrar) tally. □ ~**arse** *vpr* put on. ~**e** *m* lace; (Com) reserve

encaminar *vt* direct. □ ~**se** *vpr* make one's way

encandilar *vt* dazzle; (estimular) stimulate

encant|ado *a* enchanted; <*persona*> delighted. **¡~ado!** pleased to meet you! ~**ador** *a* charming. ~**amiento** *m* spell. ~**ar** *vt* bewitch; (fig) charm, delight. **me** ~**a la leche** I love milk. ~**o** *m* spell; (fig) delight

encapricharse *vpr.* ~ **con** take a fancy to

encarar *vt* face; (LAm) stand up to <*persona*>. □ ~**se** *vpr.* ~**se con** stand up to

encarcelar *vt* imprison

encarecer [11] *vt* put up the price of. □ ~**se** *vpr* become more expensive

encarg|ado *a* in charge. ● *m* manager, person in charge. ~**ar** [12] *vt* entrust; (pedir) order. □ ~**arse** *vpr* take charge (**de** of). ~**o** *m* job; (Com) order; (recado) errand. **hecho de** ~**o** made to measure

encariñarse *vpr.* ~ **con** take to, become fond of

encarna|ción *f* incarnation. ~**do** *a* incarnate; (rojo) red; <*uña*> ingrowing. ● *m* red

encarnizado *a* bitter

encarpetar *vt* file; (LAm, dar carpetazo) shelve

encarrilar *vt* put back on the rails; (fig) direct, put on the right track

encasillar *vt* classify; (fig) pigeonhole

encauzar [10] *vt* channel

enceguecer *vt* [11] (LAm) blind

encend|edor *m* lighter. ~**er** [1] *vt* light; switch on, turn on <*aparato eléctrico*>; start <*motor*>; (fig) arouse. □ ~**erse** *vpr* light; <*aparato eléctrico*> come on; (excitarse) get excited; (ruborizarse) blush. ~**ido** *a* lit; <*aparato eléctrico*> on; (rojo) bright red. ● *m* (Auto) ignition

encera|do *a* waxed. ● *m* (pizarra) blackboard. ~**r** *vt* wax

encerr|ar [1] *vt* shut in; (con llave) lock up; (fig, contener) contain. ~**ona** *f* trap

enchilar *vt* (Mex) add chili to

enchinar *vt* (Mex) perm

enchuf|ado *a* switched on. ~**ar** *vt* plug in; fit together <*tubos etc*>. ~**e** *m* socket; (clavija) plug; (de tubos etc) joint; (Ⅱ, influencia) contact. **tener ~e** have friends in the right places

encía *f* gum

enciclopedia *f* encyclopaedia

encierro *m* confinement; (cárcel) prison

encim|a *adv* on top; (arriba) above. **~ de** on, on top of; (sobre) over; (además de) besides, as well as. **por ~** on top; (*a la ligera*) superficially. **por ~ de todo** above all. **~ar** *vt* (Mex) stack up. **~era** *f* worktop

encina *f* holm oak

encinta *a* pregnant

enclenque *a* weak; (enfermizo) sickly

encoger [14] *vt* shrink; (contraer) contract. □ **~se** *vpr* shrink. **~erse de hombros** shrug one's shoulders

encolar *vt* glue; (pegar) stick

encolerizar [10] *vt* make angry. □ **~se** *vpr* get furious

encomendar [1] *vt* entrust

encomi|ar *vt* praise. **~o** *m* praise. **~oso** *a* (LAm) complimentary

encono *m* bitterness, ill will

encontra|do *a* contrary, conflicting. **~r** [2] *vt* find; (tropezar con) meet. □ **~rse** *vpr* meet; (hallarse) be. **no ~rse** feel uncomfortable

encorvar *vt* hunch. □ **~se** *vpr* stoop

encrespa|do *a* <pelo> curly; <mar> rough. **~r** *vt* curl <pelo>; make rough <mar>

encrucijada *f* crossroads

encuaderna|ción *f* binding. **~dor** *m* bookbinder. **~r** *vt* bind

encub|ierto *a* hidden. **~rir** (*pp* **encubierto**) *vt* hide, conceal; cover up <delito>; shelter <delincuente>

encuentro *m* meeting; (en deportes) match; (Mil) encounter

encuesta *f* survey; (investigación) inquiry

encumbrado *a* eminent; (alto) high

encurtidos *mpl* pickles

endeble *a* weak

endemoniado *a* possessed; (muy malo) wretched

enderezar [10] *vt* straighten out; (poner vertical) put upright; (fig, arreglar) put right, sort out; (dirigir) direct. □ **~se** *vpr* straighten out

endeudarse *vpr* get into debt

endiablado *a* possessed; (malo) terrible; (difícil) difficult

endosar *vt* endorse <cheque>

endulzar [10] *vt* sweeten; (fig) soften

endurecer [11] *vt* harden. □ **~se** *vpr* harden

enemi|go *a* enemy. ● *m* enemy. **~stad** *f* enmity. **~star** *vt* make an enemy of. □ **~starse** *vpr* fall out (con with)

en|ergía *f* energy. **~érgico** *a* <persona> lively; <decisión> forceful

energúmeno *m* madman

enero *m* January

enésimo *a* nth, umpteenth Ⅱ

enfad|ado *a* angry; (molesto) annoyed. **~ar** *vt* make cross, anger; (molestar) annoy. □ **~arse** *vpr* get angry; (molestarse) get annoyed. **~o** *m* anger; (molestia) annoyance

énfasis *m invar* emphasis, stress. **poner ~** stress, emphasize

enfático *a* emphatic

enferm|ar *vi* fall ill. □ **~arse** *vpr* (LAm) fall ill. **~edad** *f* illness. **~era** *f* nurse. **~ería** *f* sick bay; (carrera) nursing. **~ero** *m* (male) nurse. **~izo** *a* sickly. **~o** *a* ill. ● *m* patient

enflaquecer [11] *vt* make thin. ● *vi* lose weight

enfo|car [7] *vt* shine on; focus <lente>; (fig) approach. **~que** *m* focus; (fig) approach

enfrentar *vt* face, confront; (poner frente a frente) bring face to face. □ **~se** *vpr*. **~se con** confront; (en deportes) meet

enfrente *adv* opposite. **~ de** opposite. **de ~** opposite

enfria|miento *m* cooling; (catarro) cold. **~r** [20] *vt* cool (down); (fig) cool down. □ **~rse** *vpr* go cold; (fig) cool off

enfurecer [11] *vt* infuriate. □ **~se** *vpr* get furious

engalanar *vt* adorn. □ **~se** *vpr* dress up

enganchar *vt* hook; hang up *<ropa>*. □ **~se** *vpr* get caught; (Mil) enlist

engañ|ar *vt* deceive, trick; (ser infiel) be unfaithful. □ **~arse** *vpr* be wrong, be mistaken; (no admitir la verdad) deceive o.s. **~o** *m* deceit, trickery; (error) mistake. **~oso** *a* deceptive; *<persona>* deceitful

engarzar [10] *vt* string *<cuentas>*; set *<joyas>*

engatusar *vt* Ⅰ coax

engendr|ar *vt* father; (fig) breed. **~o** *m* (monstruo) monster; (fig) brainchild

englobar *vt* include

engomar *vt* glue

engordar *vt* fatten, gain *<kilo>*. ● *vi* get fatter, put on weight

engorro *m* nuisance

engranaje *m* (Auto) gear

engrandecer [11] *vt* (enaltecer) exalt, raise

engrasar *vt* grease; (con aceite) oil; (ensuciar) get grease on

engreído *a* arrogant

engullir [22] *vt* gulp down

enhebrar *vt* thread

enhorabuena *f* congratulations. dar la ~ congratulate

enigm|a *m* enigma. **~ático** *a* enigmatic

enjabonar *vt* soap. □ **~se** *vpr* to soap o.s.

enjambre *m* swarm

enjaular *vt* put in a cage

enjuag|ar [12] *vt* rinse. **~ue** *m* rinsing; (para la boca) mouthwash

enjugar [12] *vt* wipe (away)

enjuiciar *vt* pass judgement on

enjuto *a* *<persona>* skinny

enlace *m* connection; (matrimonial) wedding

enlatar *vt* tin, can

enlazar [10] *vt* link; tie together *<cintas>*; (Mex, casar) marry

enlodar *vt*, **enlodazar** [10] *vt* cover in mud

enloquecer [11] *vt* drive mad. ● *vi* go mad. □ **~se** *vpr* go mad

enlosar *vt* (con losas) pave; (con baldosas) tile

enmarañar *vt* tangle (up), entangle; (confundir) confuse. □ **~se** *vpr* get into a tangle; (confundirse) get confused

enmarcar [7] *vt* frame

enm|endar *vt* correct. □ **~endarse** *vpr* mend one's way. **~ienda** *f* correction; (de ley etc) amendment

enmohecerse [11] *vpr* (con óxido) go rusty; (con hongos) go mouldy

enmudecer [11] *vi* be dumbstruck; (callar) fall silent

ennegrecer [11] *vt* blacken

ennoblecer [11] *vt* ennoble; (fig) add style to

enoj|adizo *a* irritable. **~ado** *a* angry; (molesto) annoyed. **~ar** *vt* anger; (molestar) annoy. □ **~arse** *vpr* get angry; (molestarse) get annoyed. **~o** *m* anger; (molestia) annoyance. **~oso** *a* annoying

enorgullecerse [11] *vpr* be proud

enorm|e *a* huge, enormous. **~emente** *adv* enormously. **~idad** *f* immensity; (de crimen) enormity

enraizado *a* deeply rooted

enrarecido *a* rarefied

enred|adera *f* creeper. **~ar** *vt* tangle (up), entangle; (confundir) confuse; (involucrar) involve. □ **~arse** *vpr* get tangled; (confundirse) get confused; *<persona>* get involved (con with). **~o** *m* tangle; (fig) muddle, mess

enrejado *m* bars

enriquecer [11] *vt* make rich; (fig) enrich. □ **~se** *vpr* get rich

enrojecerse [11] *vpr* *<persona>* go red, blush

enrolar *vt* enlist

enrollar *vt* roll (up), wind *<hilo etc>*

enroscar [7] *vt* coil; (atornillar) screw in

ensalad|a *f* salad. armar una ~a make a mess. **~era** *f* salad bowl. **~illa** *f* Russian salad

ensalzar [10] *vt* praise; (enaltecer) exalt

ensambla|dura *f*, **ensamblaje** *m* (acción) assembling; (efecto) joint. **~r** *vt* join

ensanch|ar *vt* widen; (agrandar) enlarge. □ ~**arse** *vpr* get wider. ~**e** *m* widening

ensangrentar [1] *vt* stain with blood

ensañarse *vpr*. ~ **con** treat cruelly

ensartar *vt* string <*cuentas etc*>

ensay|ar *vt* test; rehearse <*obra de teatro etc*>. ~**o** *m* test, trial; (composición literaria) essay

enseguida *adv* at once, immediately

ensenada *f* inlet, cove

enseña|nza *f* education; (acción de enseñar) teaching. ~**nza media** secondary education. ~**r** *vt* teach; (mostrar) show

enseres *mpl* equipment

ensillar *vt* saddle

ensimismarse *vpr* be lost in thought

ensombrecer [11] *vt* darken

ensordecer [11] *vt* deafen. ● *vi* go deaf

ensuciar *vt* dirty. □ ~**se** *vpr* get dirty

ensueño *m* dream

entablar *vt* (empezar) start

entablillar *vt* put in a splint

entallar *vt* tailor <*un vestido*>. ● *vi* fit

entarimado *m* parquet; (plataforma) platform

ente *m* entity, being; (🄵, persona rara) weirdo; (Com) firm, company

entend|er [1] *vt* understand; (opinar) believe, think. ● *vi* understand. ~**er de** know about. **a mi** ~**er** in my opinion. **dar a** ~**er** hint. **darse a** ~**er** (LAm) make o.s. understood □ ~**erse** *vpr* make o.s. understood; (comprenderse) be understood. ~**erse con** get on with. ~**ido** *a* understood; (enterado) well-informed. **no darse por** ~**ido** pretend not to understand. ● *interj* agreed!, OK! 🄵. ~**imiento** *m* understanding

entera|do *a* well-informed; (que sabe) aware. **darse por** ~**do** take the hint. ~**r** *vt* inform (de of). □ ~**rse** *vpr*. ~**rse de** find out about, hear of. ¡**entérate!** listen! **¿te** ~**s?** do you understand?

entereza *f* (carácter) strength of character

enternecer [11] *vt* (fig) move, touch. □ ~**se** *vpr* be moved, be touched

entero *a* entire, whole. **por** ~ entirely, completely

enterra|dor *m* gravedigger. ~**r** [1] *vt* bury

entibiar *vt* (enfriar) cool; (calentar) warm (up). □ ~**se** *vpr* (enfriarse) cool down; (fig) cool; (calentarse) get warm

entidad *f* entity; (organización) organization; (Com) company; (importancia) significance

entierro *m* burial; (ceremonia) funeral

entona|ción *f* intonation. ~**r** *vt* in tone; sing <*nota*>. ● *vi* (Mus) be in tune; <*colores*> match. □ ~**rse** *vpr* (emborracharse) get tipsy

entonces *adv* then. **en aquel** ~ at that time, then

entorn|ado *a* <*puerta*> ajar; <*ventana*> slightly open. ~**o** *m* environment; (en literatura) setting

entorpecer [11] *vt* dull; slow down <*tráfico*>; (dificultar) hinder

entra|da *f* entrance; (incorporación) admission, entry; (para cine etc) ticket; (de datos, Tec) input; (de una comida) starter. **de** ~**da** right away. ~**do** *a*. ~**do en años** elderly. **ya** ~**da la noche** late at night. ~**nte** *a* next, coming

entraña *f* (fig) heart. ~**s** *fpl* entrails; (fig) heart. ~**ble** *a* <*cariño*> deep; <*amigo*> close. ~**r** *vt* involve

entrar *vt* (traer) bring in; (llevar) take in. ● *vi* go in, enter; (venir) come in, enter; (empezar) start, begin; (incorporarse) join. ~ **en**, (LAm) ~ **a** go into

entre *prep* (dos personas o cosas) between; (más de dos) among(st)

entre|abierto *a* half-open. ~**abrir** (*pp* **entreabierto**) *vt* half open. ~**acto** *m* interval. ~**cejo** *m* forehead. **fruncir el** ~**cejo** frown. ~**cerrar** [1] *vt* (LAm) half close. ~**cortado** *a* <*voz*> faltering; <*respiración*> laboured. ~**cruzar** [10] *vt* intertwine

entrega *f* handing over; (de mercancías etc) delivery; (de novela etc) instalment; (dedicación) commitment. ~**r** [12] *vt* deliver; (dar) give; hand in <*deberes*>; hand over <*poder*>. □ ~**rse** *vpr* surrender, give o.s. up; (dedicarse) devote o.s. (**a** to)

entre|lazar [10] *vt* intertwine. ~**més** *m* hors-d'oeuvre; (en el teatro) short comedy. ~**mezclar** *vt* intermingle

entrena|dor *m* trainer. ~**miento** *m* training. ~**r** *vt* train. □ ~**rse** *vpr* train

entre|pierna *f* crotch. ~**piso** *m* (LAm) mezzanine. ~**sacar** [7] *vt* pick out. ~**suelo** *m* mezzanine. ~**tanto** *adv* meanwhile. ~**tejer** *vt* interweave

entrepiso *m* (LAm) mezzanine

entresacar [7] *vt* pick out

entresuelo *m* mezzanine

entretanto *adv* meanwhile

entretejer *vt* interweave

entreten|ción *f* (LAm) entertainment. ~**er** [40] *vt* entertain, amuse; (detener) delay, keep. □ ~**erse** *vpr* amuse o.s.; (tardar) delay, linger. ~**ido** *a* (con ser) entertaining; (con estar) busy. ~**imiento** *m* entertainment

entrever [43] *vt* make out, glimpse

entrevista *f* interview; (reunión) meeting. □ ~**rse** *vpr* have an interview

entristecer [11] *vt* sadden, make sad. □ ~**se** *vpr* grow sad

entromet|erse *vpr* interfere. ~**ido** *a* interfering

entumec|erse [11] *vpr* go numb. ~**ido** *a* numb

enturbiar *vt* cloud

entusi|asmar *vt* fill with enthusiasm; (gustar mucho) delight. □ ~**asmarse** *vpr*. ~**asmarse con** get enthusiastic about. ~**asmo** *m* enthusiasm. ~**asta** *a* enthusiastic. ● *m & f* enthusiast

enumerar *vt* enumerate

envalentonar *vt* encourage. □ ~**se** *vpr* become bolder

envas|ado *m* packaging; (en latas) canning; (en botellas) bottling. ~**ar** *vt* package; (en latas) tin, can; (en botellas) bottle. ~**e** *m* packing; (lata) tin, can; (botella) bottle

envejec|er [11] *vt* make (look) older. ● *vi* age, grow old. □ ~**erse** *vpr* age, grow old

envenenar *vt* poison

envergadura *f* importance

envia|do *m* envoy; (de la prensa) correspondent. ~**r** [20] *vt* send

enviciarse *vpr* become addicted (**con** to)

envidi|a *f* envy; (celos) jealousy. ~**ar** *vt* envy, be envious of. ~**oso** *a* envious; (celoso) jealous. **tener** ~**a a** envy

envío *m* sending, dispatch; (de mercancías) consignment; (de dinero) remittance. ~ **contra reembolso** cash on delivery. **gastos** *mpl* **de** ~ postage and packing (costs)

enviudar *vi* be widowed

env|oltura *f* wrapping. ~**olver** [2] (*pp* **envuelto**) *vt* wrap; (cubrir) cover; (rodear) surround; (fig, enredar) involve. ~**uelto** *a* wrapped (up)

enyesar *vt* plaster; (Med) put in plaster

épica *f* epic

épico *a* epic

epid|emia *f* epidemic. ~**émico** *a* epidemic

epil|epsia *f* epilepsy. ~**éptico** *a* epileptic

epílogo *m* epilogue

episodio *m* episode

epístola *f* epistle

epitafio *m* epitaph

época *f* age; (período) period. **hacer** ~ make history, be epoch-making

equidad *f* equity

equilibr|ado *a* (well-)balanced. ~**ar** *vt* balance. ~**io** *m* balance; (de balanza) equilibrium. ~**ista** *m & f* tightrope walker

equinoccio *m* equinox

equipaje *m* luggage (esp Brit), baggage (esp Amer)

equipar *vt* equip; (de ropa) fit out

equiparar *vt* make equal; (comparar) compare

equipo *m* equipment; (de personas) team

equitación f riding

equivale|nte a equivalent. ~r [42] vi be equivalent; (significar) mean

equivoca|ción f mistake, error. ~do a wrong. □ ~rse vpr make a mistake; (estar en error) be wrong, be mistaken. ~rse de be wrong about. ~rse de número dial the wrong number. si no me equivoco if I'm not mistaken

equívoco a equivocal; (sospechoso) suspicious ● m misunderstanding; (error) mistake

era f era. ● vb ⇒SER

erario m treasury

erección f erection

eres vb ⇒SER

erguir [48] vt raise. □ ~se vpr raise

erigir [14] vt erect. □ ~se vpr. ~se en set o.s. up as; (llegar a ser) become

eriza|do a prickly. □ ~rse [10] vpr stand on end; (LAm) <persona> get goose pimples

erizo m hedgehog; (de mar) sea urchin. ~ de mar sea urchin

ermita f hermitage. ~ño m hermit

erosi|ón f erosion. ~onar vt erode

er|ótico a erotic. ~otismo m eroticism

err|ar [1] (la i inicial pasa a ser y) vt miss. ● vi wander; (equivocarse) make a mistake, be wrong. ~ata f misprint. ~óneo a erroneous, wrong. ~or m error, mistake. estar en un ~or be wrong, be mistaken

eruct|ar vi belch. ~o m belch

erudi|ción f learning, erudition. ~to a learned; <palabra> erudite

erupción f eruption; (Med) rash

es vb ⇒SER

esa a ⇒ESE

ésa pron ⇒ÉSE

esbelto a slender, slim

esboz|ar [10] vt sketch, outline. ~o m sketch, outline

escabeche m brine. en ~ pickled

escabroso a <terreno> rough; <asunto> difficult; (atrevido) crude

escabullirse [22] vpr slip away

escafandra f diving-suit

escala f scale; (escalera de mano) ladder; (Aviac) stopover. hacer ~ en

stop at. vuelo sin ~s non-stop flight. ~da f climbing; (Pol) escalation. ~r vt climb; break into <una casa>. ● vi climb, go climbing

escaldar vt scald

escalera f staircase, stairs; (de mano) ladder. ~ de caracol spiral staircase. ~ de incendios fire escape. ~ de tijera step-ladder. ~ mecánica escalator

escalfa|do a poached. ~r vt poach

escalinata f flight of steps

escalofrío m shiver. tener ~s be shivering

escalón m step, stair; (de escala) rung

escalope m escalope

escam|a f scale; (de jabón, de la piel) flake. ~oso a scaly; <piel> flaky

escamotear vt make disappear; (robar) steal, pinch

escampar vi stop raining

esc|andalizar [10] vt scandalize, shock. □ ~andalizarse vpr be shocked. ~ándalo m scandal; (alboroto) commotion, racket. armar un ~ make a scene. ~andaloso a scandalous; (alborotador) noisy

escandinavo a & m Scandinavian

escaño m bench; (Pol) seat

escapa|da f escape; (visita) flying visit. ~r vi escape. dejar ~r let out. □ ~rse vpr escape; <líquido, gas> leak

escaparate m (shop) window

escap|atoria f (fig) way out. ~e m (de gas, de líquido) leak; (fuga) escape; (Auto) exhaust

escarabajo m beetle

escaramuza f skirmish

escarbar vt scratch; pick <dientes, herida>; (fig, escudriñar) pry (en into). □ ~se vpr pick

escarcha f frost. ~do a <fruta> crystallized

escarlat|a a invar scarlet. ~ina f scarlet fever

escarm|entar [1] vt teach a lesson to. ● vi learn one's lesson. ~iento m punishment; (lección) lesson

escarola f endive

escarpado a steep

escas|ear *vi* be scarce. ~**ez** *f* scarcity, shortage; (pobreza) poverty. ~**o** *a* scarce; (poco) little; (muy justo) barely. ~**o de** short of

escatimar *vt* be sparing with

escayola *f* plaster

esc|ena *f* scene; (escenario) stage. ~**enario** *m* stage; (fig) scene. ~**énico** *a* stage. ~**enografía** *f* set design

esc|epticismo *m* scepticism. ~**éptico** *a* sceptical. ● *m* sceptic

esclarecer [11] *vt* (fig) throw light on, clarify

esclav|itud *f* slavery. ~**izar** [10] *vt* enslave. ~**o** *m* slave

esclusa *f* lock; (de presa) floodgate

escoba *f* broom

escocer [2 & 9] *vi* sting

escocés *a* Scottish. ● *m* Scot

Escocia *f* Scotland

escog|er [14] *vt* choose. ~**ido** *a* chosen; <mercancía> choice; <clientela> select

escolar *a* school. ● *m* schoolboy. ● *f* schoolgirl

escolta *f* escort

escombros *mpl* rubble

escond|er *vt* hide. □ ~**erse** *vpr* hide. ~**idas** *fpl* (LAm, juego) hide-and-seek. **a** ~**idas** secretly. ~**ite** *m* hiding place; (juego) hide-and-seek. ~**rijo** *m* hiding place

escopeta *f* shotgun

escoria *f* slag; (fig) dregs .

escorpión *m* scorpion

Escorpión *m* Scorpio

escot|ado *a* low-cut. ~**e** *m* low neckline. **pagar a** ~**e** share the expenses

escozor *m* stinging

escri|bano *m* clerk. ~**bir** (*pp* **escrito**) *vt/i* write. ~**bir a máquina** type. **¿cómo se escribe...?** how do you spell...? □ ~**birse** *vpr* write to each other. ~**to** *a* written. **por** ~**to** in writing. ● *m* document. ~**tor** *m* writer. ~**torio** *m* desk; (oficina) office; (LAm, en una casa) study. ~**tura** *f* (hand)writing; (Jurid) deed

escr|úpulo *m* scruple. ~**upuloso** *a* scrupulous

escrut|ar *vt* scrutinize; count <votos>. ~**inio** *m* count

escuadr|a *f* (instrumento) square; (Mil) squad; (Naut) fleet. ~**ón** *m* squadron

escuálido *a* skinny

escuchar *vt* listen to; (esp LAm, oír) hear. ● *vi* listen

escudo *m* shield. ~ **de armas** coat of arms

escudriñar *vt* examine

escuela *f* school. ~ **normal** teachers' training college

escueto *a* simple

escuincle *m* (Mex 🏵) kid 🏵

escul|pir *vt* sculpture. ~**tor** *m* sculptor. ~**tora** *f* sculptress. ~**tura** *f* sculpture

escupir *vt/i* spit

escurr|eplatos *m* *invar* plate rack. ~**idizo** *a* slippery. ~**ir** *vt* drain; wring out <ropa>. ● *vi* drain; <ropa> drip. □ ~**irse** *vpr* slip

ese *a* (*f* **esa**) that; (*mpl* **esos**, *fpl* **esas**) those

ése *pron* (*f* **ésa**) that one: (*mpl* **ésos**, *fpl* **ésas**) those; (primero de dos) the former

esencia *f* essence. ~**l** *a* essential. **lo** ~**l** the main thing

esf|era *f* sphere; (de reloj) face. ~**érico** *a* spherical

esf|orzarse [2 & 10] *vpr* make an effort. ~**uerzo** *m* effort

esfumarse *vpr* fade away; <persona> vanish

esgrim|a *f* fencing. ~**ir** *vt* brandish; (fig) use

esguince *m* sprain

eslabón *m* link

eslavo *a* Slavic, Slavonic

eslogan *m* slogan

esmalt|ar *vt* enamel. ~**e** *m* enamel. ~**e de uñas** nail polish

esmerado *a* careful; <persona> painstaking

esmeralda *f* emerald

esmer|arse *vpr* take care (**en** over). ~**o** *m* care

esmero *m* care

esmoquin (*pl* **esmóquines**) *m* dinner jacket, tuxedo (Amer)

esnob *a invar* snobbish. ● *m & f (pl* ~**s**) snob. ~**ismo** *m* snobbery

esnórkel *m* snorkel

eso *pron* that. ¡~ **es!** that's it! ~ **mismo** exactly. **a** ~ **de** about. **en** ~ at that moment. ¿**no es** ~? isn't that right? **por** ~ that's why. **y** ~ **que** even though

esos *a pl* ⇒ESE

ésos *pron pl* ⇒ÉSE

espabila|do *a* bright; (despierto) awake. ~**r** *vt* (avivar) brighten up; (despertar) wake up. □ ~**rse** *vpr* wake up; (avivarse) wise up; (apresurarse) hurry up

espaci|al *a* space. ~**ar** *vt* space out. ~**o** *m* space. ~**oso** *a* spacious

espada *f* sword. ~**s** *fpl* (en naipes) spades

espaguetis *mpl* spaghetti

espald|a *f* back. **a** ~**as de uno** behind s.o.'s back. **volver la(s)** ~**a(s) a uno** give s.o. the cold shoulder. ~**illa** *f* shoulder-blade

espant|ajo *m*, ~**apájaros** *m invar* scarecrow. ~**ar** *vt* frighten; (ahuyentar) frighten away. □ ~**arse** *vpr* be frightened; (ahuyentarse) be frightened away. ~**o** *m* terror; (horror) horror. ¡**qué** ~**o!** how awful! ~**oso** *a* horrific; (terrible) terrible

España *f* Spain

español *a* Spanish. ● *m* (persona) Spaniard; (lengua) Spanish. **los** ~**es** the Spanish. ~**izado** *a* Hispanicized

esparadrapo *m* (sticking) plaster

esparcir [9] *vt* scatter; (difundir) spread. □ ~**rse** *vpr* be scattered; (difundirse) spread; (divertirse) enjoy o.s.

espárrago *m* asparagus

espasm|o *m* spasm. ~**ódico** *a* spasmodic

espátula *f* spatula; (en pintura) palette knife

especia *f* spice

especial *a* special. **en** ~ especially. ~**idad** *f* speciality (Brit), specialty (Amer). ~**ista** *a & m & f* specialist. ~**ización** *f* specialization. □ ~**izarse** [10] *vpr* specialize. ~**mente** *adv* especially

especie *f* kind, sort; (Biol) species. **en** ~ in kind

especifica|ción *f* specification. ~**r** [7] *vt* specify

específico *a* specific

espect|áculo *m* sight; (de circo etc) show. ~**acular** *a* spectacular. ~**ador** *m & f* spectator

espectro *m* spectre; (en física) spectrum

especula|dor *m* speculator. ~**r** *vi* speculate

espej|ismo *m* mirage. ~**o** *m* mirror. ~**o retrovisor** (Auto) rear-view mirror

espeluznante *a* horrifying

espera *f* wait. **a la** ~ waiting (de for). ~**nza** *f* hope. ~**r** *vt* hope; (aguardar) wait for; expect <*visita, carta, bebé*>. **espero que no** I hope not. **espero que sí** I hope so. ● *vi* (aguardar) wait. □ ~**rse** *vpr* hang on; (prever) expect

esperma *f* sperm

esperpento *m* fright

espes|ar *vt/i* thicken. □ ~**arse** *vpr* thicken. ~**o** *a* thick. ~**or** *m* thickness

espetón *m* spit

esp|ía *f* spy. ~**iar** [20] *vt* spy on. ● *vi* spy

espiga *f* (de trigo etc) ear

espina *f* thorn; (de pez) bone; (Anat) spine. ~ **dorsal** spine

espinaca *f* spinach

espinazo *m* spine

espinilla *f* shin; (Med) blackhead; (LAm, grano) spot

espino *m* hawthorn. ~**so** *a* thorny; (fig) difficult

espionaje *m* espionage

espiral *a & f* spiral

esp|iritista *m & f* spiritualist. ~**íritu** *m* spirit; (mente) mind. ~**iritual** *a* spiritual

espl|éndido *a* splendid; <*persona*> generous. ~**endor** *m* splendour

espolear *vt* spur (on)

espolvorear *vt* sprinkle

esponj|a *f* sponge. ~**oso** *a* spongy

espont|aneidad *f* spontaneity. ~**áneo** *a* spontaneous

esporádico *a* sporadic

espos|a f wife. ∼**as** fpl handcuffs. ∼**ar** vt handcuff. ∼**o** m husband

espuela f spur; (fig) incentive

espum|a f foam; (en bebidas) froth; (de jabón) lather; (de las olas) surf. echar ∼**a** foam, froth. ∼**oso** a <vino> sparkling

esqueleto m skeleton; (estructura) framework

esquema m outline

esquí m (pl ∼**is**, ∼**íes**) ski; (deporte) skiing. ∼**iar** [20] vi ski

esquilar vt shear

esquimal a & m Eskimo

esquina f corner

esquiv|ar vt avoid; dodge <golpe>. ∼**o** a elusive

esquizofrénico a & m schizophrenic

esta a ⇒ESTE

ésta pron ⇒ÉSTE

estab|ilidad f stability. ∼**le** a stable

establec|er [11] vt establish. □ ∼**erse** vpr settle; (Com) set up. ∼**imiento** m establishment

establo m cattleshed

estaca f stake

estación f station; (del año) season. ∼ **de invierno** winter (sports) resort. ∼ **de servicio** service station

estaciona|miento m parking; (LAm, lugar) car park (Brit), parking lot (Amer). ∼**r** vt station; (Auto) park. ∼**rio** a stationary

estadía f (LAm) stay

estadio m stadium; (fase) stage

estadista m statesman. ● f stateswoman

estadístic|a f statistics; (cifra) statistic. ∼**o** a statistical

estado m state; (Med) condition. ∼ **civil** marital status. ∼ **de ánimo** frame of mind. ∼ **de cuenta** bank statement. ∼ **mayor** (Mil) staff. **en buen** ∼ in good condition

Estados Unidos mpl United States

estadounidense a American, United States. ● m & f American

estafa f swindle. ∼**r** vt swindle

estafeta f (oficina de correos) (sub-) post office

estala|ctita f stalactite. ∼**gmita** f stalagmite

estall|ar vi explode; <olas> break; <guerra etc> break out; (fig) burst. ∼**ar en llanto** burst into tears. ∼**ar de risa** burst out laughing. ∼**ido** m explosion; (de guerra etc) outbreak

estamp|a f print; (aspecto) appearance. ∼**ado** a printed. ● m printing; (motivo) pattern; (tela) cotton print. ∼**ar** vt stamp; (imprimir) print

estampido m bang

estampilla f (LAm, de correos) (postage) stamp

estanca|do a stagnant. ∼**r** [7] vt stem. □ ∼**rse** vpr stagnate

estancia f stay; (cuarto) large room

estanco a watertight. ● m tobacconist's (shop)

estandarte m standard, banner

estanque m pond; (depósito de agua) (water) tank

estanquero m tobacconist

estante m shelf. ∼**ría** f shelves; (para libros) bookcase

estaño m tin

estar [27]

● verbo intransitivo

····➤ to be. ¿**cómo estás?** how are you?. **estoy enfermo** I'm ill. **está muy cerca** it's very near. ¿**está Pedro?** is Pedro in? ¿**cómo está el tiempo?** what's the weather like? **ya estamos en invierno** it's winter already

····➤ (quedarse) to stay. **sólo** ∼**é una semana** I'll only be staying for a week. **estoy en un hotel** I'm staying in a hotel

····➤ (con fecha) ¿**a cuánto estamos?** what's the date today? **estamos a 8 de mayo** it's the 8th of May.

····➤ (en locuciones) ¿**estamos?** all right? **¡ahí está!** that's it! ∼ **por** (apoyar a) to support; (LAm, encontrarse a punto de) to be about to; (quedar por) **eso está por verse** that remains to be seen. **son cuentas que están por pa-gar** they're bills still to be paid

● verbo auxiliar

····▸ (con gerundio) **estaba estudiando** I was studying

····▸ (con participio) **está condenado a muerte** he's been sentenced to death. **está mal traducido** it's wrongly translated.

□ **estarse** *verbo pronominal* to stay. **no se está quieto** he won't stay still

⇒ Cuando el verbo **estar** forma parte de expresiones como **estar de acuerdo, estar a la vista, estar constipado,** etc., ver bajo el respectivo nombre o adjetivo

estatal *a* state

estático *a* static

estatua *f* statue

estatura *f* height

estatuto *m* statute; (norma) rule

este *a* <*región*> eastern; <*viento, lado*> east. ● *m* east. ● *a* (*f* **esta**) this; (*mpl* **estos**, *fpl* **estas**) these; (LAm, como muletilla) well, er

éste *pron* (*f* **ésta**) this one; (*mpl* **éstos**, *fpl* **éstas**) these; (segundo de dos) the latter

estela *f* wake; (de avión) trail; (Arquit) carved stone

estera *f* mat; (tejido) matting

est|éreo *a* stereo. **~ereofónico** *a* stereo, stereophonic

estereotipo *m* stereotype

estéril *a* sterile; <*terreno*> barren

esterilla *f* mat

esterlina *a*. **libra** *f* **~** pound sterling

estético *a* aesthetic

estiércol *m* dung; (abono) manure

estigma *m* stigma. **~s** *mpl* (Relig) stigmata

estil|arse *vpr* be used. **~o** *m* style; (en natación) stroke. **~ mariposa** butterfly. **~ pecho** (LAm) breaststroke. **por el ~o** of that sort

estilográfica *f* fountain pen

estima *f* esteem. **~do** *a* <*amigo, colega*> valued. **~do señor** (en cartas) Dear Sir. **~r** *vt* esteem; have great respect for <*persona*>; (valorar) value; (juzgar) consider

est|imulante *a* stimulating. ● *m* stimulant. **~imular** *vt* stimulate; (incitar) incite. **~ímulo** *m* stimulus

estir|ado *a* stretched; <*persona*> haughty. **~ar** *vt* stretch; (fig) stretch out. **~ón** *m* pull, tug; (crecimiento) sudden growth

estirpe *m* stock

esto *pron neutro* this; (este asunto) this business. **en ~** at this point. **en ~ de** in this business of. **por ~** therefore

estofa|do *a* stewed. ● *m* stew. **~r** *vt* stew

estómago *m* stomach. **dolor** *m* **de ~** stomach ache

estorb|ar *vt* obstruct; (molestar) bother. ● *vi* be in the way. **~o** *m* hindrance; (molestia) nuisance

estornud|ar *vi* sneeze. **~o** *m* sneeze

estos *a mpl* ⇒ESTE

éstos *pron mpl* ⇒ÉSTE

estoy *vb* ⇒ESTAR

estrabismo *m* squint

estrado *m* stage; (Mus) bandstand

estrafalario *a* eccentric; <*ropa*> outlandish

estrago *m* devastation. **hacer ~os** devastate

estragón *m* tarragon

estrambótico *a* eccentric; <*ropa*> outlandish

estrangula|dor *m* strangler; (Auto) choke. **~r** *vt* strangle

estratagema *f* stratagem

estrat|ega *m* & *f* strategist. **~egia** *f* strategy. **~égico** *a* strategic

estrato *m* stratum

estrech|ar *vt* make narrower; take in <*vestido*>; embrace <*persona*>. **~ar la mano a uno** shake hands with s.o. □ **~arse** *vpr* become narrower; (abrazarse) embrace. **~ez** *f* narrowness. **~eces** *fpl* financial difficulties. **~o** *a* narrow; <*vestido etc*> tight; (fig, íntimo) close. **~o de miras** narrow-minded. ● *m* strait(s)

estrella *f* star. **~ de mar** starfish. **~ado** *a* starry

estrellar *vt* smash; crash <*coche*>. □ **~se** *vpr* crash (**contra** into)

estremec|er [11] *vt* shake. □ **~erse** *vpr* shake; (de emoción etc) tremble (**de** with). **~imiento** *m* shaking

estren|ar *vt* wear for the first time <*vestido etc*>; show for the first time <*película*>. □ **~arse** *vpr* make one's début. **~o** *m* (de película) première; (de obra de teatro) first night; (de persona) debut

estreñi|do *a* constipated. **~miento** *m* constipation

estrés *m* stress

estría *f* groove; (de la piel) stretch mark

estribillo *m* (incl Mus) refrain

estribo *m* stirrup; (de coche) step. perder los **~s** lose one's temper

estribor *m* starboard

estricto *a* strict

estridente *a* strident, raucous

estrofa *f* stanza, verse

estropajo *m* scourer

estropear *vt* damage; (plan) spoil; ruin <*ropa*>. □ **~se** *vpr* be damaged; (averiarse) break down; <*ropa*> get ruined; <*fruta etc*> go bad; (fracasar) fail

estructura *f* structure. **~l** *a* structural

estruendo *m* roar; (de mucha gente) uproar

estrujar *vt* squeeze; wring (out) <*ropa*>; (fig) drain

estuario *m* estuary

estuche *m* case

estudi|ante *m & f* student. **~antil** *a* student. **~ar** *vt* study. **~o** *m* study; (de artista) studio. **~oso** *a* studious

estufa *f* heater; (Mex, cocina) cooker

estupefac|iente *m* narcotic. **~to** *a* astonished

estupendo *a* marvellous; <*persona*> fantastic; ¡**~**! that's great!

est|upidez *f* stupidity; (acto) stupid thing. **~úpido** *a* stupid

estupor *m* amazement

estuve *vb* ⇒ESTAR

etapa *f* stage. por **~s** in stages

etc *abrev* (**etcétera**) etc. **~étera** *adv* et cetera

etéreo *a* ethereal

etern|idad *f* eternity. **~o** *a* eternal

étic|a *f* ethics. **~o** *a* ethical

etimología *f* etymology

etiqueta *f* ticket, tag; (ceremonial) etiquette. de **~** formal

étnico *a* ethnic

eucalipto *m* eucalyptus

eufemismo *m* euphemism

euforia *f* euphoria

Europa *f* Europe

europeo *a & m* European

eutanasia *f* euthanasia

evacua|ción *f* evacuation. **~r** [21] *vt* evacuate

evadir *vt* avoid; evade <*impuestos*>. □ **~se** *vpr* escape

evaluar [21] *vt* assess; evaluate <*datos*>

evangeli|o *m* gospel. **~sta** *m & f* evangelist; (Mex, escribiente) scribe

evapora|ción *f* evaporation. □ **~rse** *vpr* evaporate; (fig) disappear

evasi|ón *f* evasion; (fuga) escape. **~vo** *a* evasive

evento *m* event; (caso) case

eventual *a* possible. **~idad** *f* eventuality

eviden|cia *f* evidence. poner en **~cia a uno** show s.o. up. **~ciar** *vt* show. □ **~ciarse** *vpr* be obvious. **~te** *a* obvious. **~temente** *adv* obviously

evitar *vt* avoid; (ahorrar) spare; (prevenir) prevent

evocar [7] *vt* evoke

evoluci|ón *f* evolution. **~onar** *vi* evolve; (Mil) manoeuvre

ex *pref* ex-, former

exacerbar *vt* exacerbate

exact|amente *adv* exactly. **~itud** *f* exactness. **~o** *a* exact; (preciso) accurate; (puntual) punctual. ¡**~**! exactly!

exagera|ción *f* exaggeration. **~do** *a* exaggerated. **~r** *vt/i* exaggerate

exalta|do *a* exalted; (excitado) (over-)excited; (fanático) hot-headed. **~r** *vt* exalt. □ **~rse** *vpr* get excited

exam|en *m* exam, examination. **∼inar** *vt* examine. □ **∼inarse** *vpr* take an exam

exasperar *vt* exasperate. □ **∼se** *vpr* get exasperated

excarcela|ción *f* release (from prison). **∼r** *vt* release

excava|ción *f* excavation. **∼dora** *f* digger. **∼r** *vt* excavate

excede|ncia *f* leave of absence. **∼nte** *a & m* surplus. **∼r** *vi* exceed. □ **∼rse** *vpr* go too far

excelen|cia *f* excellence; (tratamiento) Excellency. **∼te** *a* excellent

exc|entricidad *f* eccentricity. **∼éntrico** *a & m* eccentric

excepci|ón *f* exception. **∼onal** *a* exceptional. **a ∼ón de, con ∼ón de** except (for)

except|o *prep* except (for). **∼uar** [21] *vt* except

exces|ivo *a* excessive. **∼o** *m* excess. **∼o de equipaje** excess luggage (esp Brit), excess baggage (esp Amer)

excita|ción *f* excitement. **∼r** *vt* excite; (incitar) incite. □ **∼rse** *vpr* get excited

exclama|ción *f* exclamation. **∼r** *vi* exclaim

exclu|ir [17] *vt* exclude. **∼sión** *f* exclusion. **∼siva** *f* sole right; (reportaje) exclusive (story). **∼sivo** *a* exclusive

excomu|lgar [12] *vt* excommunicate. **∼nión** *f* excommunication

excremento *m* excrement

excursi|ón *f* excursion, outing. **∼onista** *m & f* day-tripper

excusa *f* excuse; (disculpa) apology. **presentar sus ∼s** apologize. **∼r** *vt* excuse

exento *a* exempt; (libre) free

exhalar *vt* exhale, breath out; give off *<olor etc>*

exhaust|ivo *a* exhaustive. **∼o** *a* exhausted

exhibi|ción *f* exhibition; (demostración) display. **∼cionista** *m & f* exhibitionist. **∼r** *vt* exhibit. □ **∼rse** *vpr* show o.s.; (hacerse notar) draw attention to o.s.

exhumar *vt* exhume; (fig) dig up

exig|encia *f* demand. **∼ente** *a* demanding. **∼ir** [14] *vt* demand

exiguo *a* meagre

exil|(i)ado *a* exiled. ● *m* exile. □ **∼(i)arse** *vpr* go into exile. **∼io** *m* exile

exim|ente *m* reason for exemption; (Jurid) grounds for acquittal. **∼ir** *vt* exempt

existencia *f* existence. **∼s** *fpl* stock. **∼lismo** *m* existentialism

exist|ente *a* existing. **∼ir** *vi* exist

éxito *m* success. **no tener ∼** fail. **tener ∼** be successful

exitoso *a* successful

éxodo *m* exodus

exonerar *vt* exonerate

exorbitante *a* exorbitant

exorci|smo *m* exorcism. **∼zar** [10] *vt* exorcise

exótico *a* exotic

expan|dir *vt* expand; (fig) spread. □ **∼dirse** *vpr* expand. **∼sión** *f* expansion. **∼sivo** *a* expansive

expatria|do *a & m* expatriate. □ **∼rse** *vpr* emigrate; (exiliarse) go into exile

expectativa *f* prospect; (esperanza) expectation. **estar a la ∼** be waiting

expedi|ción *f* expedition; (de documento) issue; (de mercancías) dispatch. **∼ente** *m* record, file; (Jurid) proceedings. **∼r** [5] *vt* issue; (enviar) dispatch, send. **∼to** *a* clear; (LAm, fácil) easy

expeler *vt* expel

expend|edor *m* dealer. **∼dor automático** vending machine. **∼io** *m* (LAm) shop; (venta) sale

expensas *fpl* (Jurid) costs. **a ∼ de** at the expense of. **a mis ∼** at my expense

experiencia *f* experience

experiment|al *a* experimental. **∼ar** *vt* test, experiment with; (sentir) experience. **∼o** *m* experiment

experto *a & m* expert

expiar [20] *vt* atone for

expirar *vi* expire

explanada *f* levelled area; (paseo) esplanade

explayarse *vpr* speak at length; (desahogarse) unburden o.s. (**con** to)

explica|ción *f* explanation. **~r** [7] *vt* explain. □ **~rse** *vpr* understand; (hacerse comprender) explain o.s. **no me lo explico** I can't understand it

explícito *a* explicit

explora|ción *f* exploration. **~dor** *m* explorer; (muchacho) boy scout. **~r** *vt* explore

explosi|ón *f* explosion; (fig) outburst. **~onar** *vt* blow up. **~vo** *a* & *m* explosive

explota|ción *f* working; (abuso) exploitation. **~r** *vt* work *<mina>*; farm *<tierra>*; (abusar) exploit. ● *vi* explode

expone|nte *m* exponent. **~r** [34] *vt* expose; display *<mercancías>*; present *<tema>*; set out *<hechos>*; exhibit *<cuadros etc>*; (arriesgar) risk. ● *vi* exhibit. □ **~rse** *vpr*. **~se a que** run the risk of

exporta|ción *f* export. **~dor** *m* exporter. **~r** *vt* export

exposición *f* exposure; (de cuadros etc) exhibition; (de hechos) exposition

expres|ar *vt* express. □ **~arse** *vpr* express o.s. **~ión** *f* expression. **~ivo** *a* expressive; (cariñoso) affectionate

expreso *a* express. ● *m* express; (café) expresso

exprimi|dor *m* squeezer. **~r** *vt* squeeze

expropiar *vt* expropriate

expuesto *a* on display; *<lugar etc>* exposed; (peligroso) dangerous. **estar ~ a** be exposed to

expuls|ar *vt* expel; throw out *<persona>*; send off *<jugador>*. **~ión** *f* expulsion

exquisito *a* exquisite; (de sabor) delicious

éxtasis *m invar* ecstasy

extend|er [1] *vt* spread (out); (ampliar) extend; issue *<documento>*. □ **~erse** *vpr* spread; *<paisaje etc>* extend, stretch. **~ido** *a* spread out; (generalizado) widespread; *<brazos>* outstretched

extens|amente *adv* widely; (detalladamente) in full. **~ión** *f* extension; (área) expanse; (largo) length. **~o** *a* extensive

extenuar [21] *vt* exhaust

exterior *a* external, exterior; (del extranjero) foreign; *<aspecto etc>* outward. ● *m* outside, exterior; (países extranjeros) abroad

extermin|ación *f* extermination. **~ar** *vt* exterminate. **~io** *m* extermination

externo *a* external; *<signo etc>* outward. ● *m* day pupil

extin|ción *f* extinction. **~guidor** *m* (LAm) fire extinguisher. **~guir** [13] *vt* extinguish. □ **~guirse** *vpr* die out; *<fuego>* go out. **~to** *a* *<raza etc>* extinct. **~tor** *m* fire extinguisher

extirpar *vt* eradicate; remove *<tumor>*

extorsión *f* extortion

extra *a invar* extra; (de buena calidad) good-quality; *<huevos>* large. **paga** *f* **~** bonus

extracto *m* extract

extradición *f* extradition

extraer [41] *vt* extract

extranjero *a* foreign. ● *m* foreigner; (países) foreign countries. **del ~** from abroad. **en el ~, por el ~** abroad

extrañ|ar *vt* surprise; (encontrar extraño) find strange; (LAm, echar de menos) miss. □ **~arse** *vpr* be surprised (**de** at). **~eza** *f* strangeness; (asombro) surprise. **~o** *a* strange. ● *m* stranger

extraoficial *a* unofficial

extraordinario *a* extraordinary

extrarradio *m* outlying districts

extraterrestre *a* extraterrestrial. ● *m* alien

extravagan|cia *f* oddness, eccentricity. **~te** *a* odd, eccentric

extrav|iado *a* lost. **~iar** [20] *vt* lose. □ **~iarse** *vpr* get lost; *<objetos>* go missing. **~ío** *m* loss

extremar *vt* take extra *<precauciones>*; tighten up *<vigilancia>*. □ **~se** *vpr* make every effort

extremeño *a* from Extremadura

extrem|idad *f* end. **~idades** *fpl* extremities. **~ista** *a* & *m* & *f* extremist. **~o** *a* extreme. ● *m* end; (colmo) extreme. **en ~o** extremely. **en último ~o** as a last resort

extrovertido *a* & *m* extrovert
exuberan|cia *f* exuberance. **~te** *a* exuberant
eyacular *vt/i* ejaculate

....

F f

....

fa *m* F; (solfa) fah
fabada *f* bean and pork stew
fábrica *f* factory. **marca** *f* **de ~** trade mark
fabrica|ción *f* manufacture. **~ción en serie** mass production. **~nte** *m* & *f* manufacturer. **~r** [7] *vt* manufacture
fábula *f* fable; (mentira) fabrication
fabuloso *a* fabulous
facci|ón *f* faction. **~ones** *fpl* (de la cara) features
faceta *f* facet
facha *f* (🄵, aspecto) look. **~da** *f* façade
fácil *a* easy; (probable) likely
facili|dad *f* ease; (disposición) aptitude. **~dades** *fpl* facilities. **~tar** *vt* facilitate; (proporcionar) provide
factible *a* feasible
factor *m* factor
factura *f* bill, invoice. **~r** *vt* (hacer la factura) invoice; (Aviat) check in
faculta|d *f* faculty; (capacidad) ability; (poder) power. **~tivo** *a* optional
faena *f* job. **~s domésticas** housework
faisán *m* pheasant
faja *f* (de tierra) strip; (corsé) corset; (Mil etc) sash
fajo *m* bundle; (de billetes) wad
falda *f* skirt; (de montaña) side
falla *f* fault; (defecto) flaw. **~ humana** (LAm) human error. **~r** *vi* fail. **me falló** he let me down. **sin ~r** without fail. ● *vt* (errar) miss
fallec|er [11] *vi* die. **~ido** *m* deceased
fallido *a* vain; (fracasado) unsuccessful

fallo *m* (defecto) fault; (error) mistake. **~ humano** human error; (en certamen) decision; (Jurid) ruling

falluca *f* (Mex) smuggled goods

fals|ear *vt* falsify, distort. **~ificación** *f* forgery. **~ificador** *m* forger. **~ificar** [7] *vt* forge. **~o** *a* false; (falsificado) forged; <*joya*> fake

falt|a *f* lack; (ausencia) absence; (escasez) shortage; (defecto) fault, defect; (culpa) fault; (error) mistake; (en fútbol etc) foul; (en tenis) fault. **a ~a de** for lack of. **echar en ~a** miss. **hacer ~a** be necessary. **me hace ~a** I need. **sacar ~as** find fault. **~o** *a* lacking (**de** in

....

faltar

● *verbo intransitivo*

! Cuando el verbo **faltar** va precedido del complemento indirecto **le** (o **les, nos** etc) el sujeto en español pasa a ser el objeto en inglés p.ej: **les falta experiencia** *they lack experience*

••••➤ (no estar) to be missing **¿quién falta?** who's missing? **falta una de las chicas** one of the girls is missing. **al abrigo le faltan 3 botones** the coat has three buttons missing. **~ a algo** (no asistir) to be absent from sth; (no acudir) to miss sth

••••➤ (no haber suficiente) **va a ~ leche** there won't be enough milk. **nos faltó tiempo** we didn't have enough time

••••➤ (no tener) **le falta cariño** he lacks affection

••••➤ (hacer falta) **le falta sal** it needs more salt. **¡es lo que nos faltaba!** that's all we needed!

••••➤ (quedar) **¿te falta mucho?** are you going to be much longer? **falta poco para Navidad** it's not long until Christmas. **aún falta mucho** (distancia) there's a long way to go yet **¡no faltaba más!** of course!

....

fama *f* fame; (reputación) reputation

famélico *a* starving

familia *f* family; (hijos) children. ~ **numerosa** large family. ~**r** *a* familiar; (de la familia) family; (sin ceremonia) informal; *<lenguaje>* colloquial. ● *m* & *f* relative. ~**ridad** *f* familiarity. □ ~**rizarse** [10] *vpr* become familiar (con with)

famoso *a* famous

fanático *a* fanatical. ● *m* fanatic

fanfarr|ón *a* boastful. ● *m* braggart. ~**onear** *vi* show off

fango *m* mud. ~**so** *a* muddy

fantasía *f* fantasy. de ~ fancy; *<joya>* imitation

fantasma *m* ghost

fantástico *a* fantastic

fardo *m* bundle

faringe *f* pharynx

farmac|éutico *m* chemist (Brit), pharmacist, druggist (Amer). ~**ia** *f* (ciencia) pharmacy; (tienda) chemist's (shop) (Brit), pharmacy

faro *m* lighthouse; (Aviac) beacon; (Auto) headlight

farol *m* lantern; (de la calle) street lamp. ~**a** *f* street lamp

farr|a *f* partying. ~**ear** *vi* (LAm) go out partying

farsa *f* farce. ~**nte** *m* & *f* fraud

fascículo *m* instalment

fascinar *vt* fascinate

fascis|mo *m* fascism. ~**ta** *a* & *m* & *f* fascist

fase *f* phase

fastidi|ar *vt* annoy; (estropear) spoil. □ ~**arse** *vpr* *<máquina>* break down; hurt *<pierna>*; (LAm, molestarse) get annoyed. ¡**para que te ~es!** so there!. ~**o** *m* nuisance; (aburrimiento) boredom. ~**oso** *a* annoying

fatal *a* fateful; (mortal) fatal; (ⒻⒾ, pésimo) terrible. ~**idad** *f* fate; (desgracia) misfortune

fatig|a *f* fatigue. ~**ar** [12] *vt* tire. □ ~**arse** *vpr* get tired. ~**oso** *a* tiring

fauna *f* fauna

favor *m* favour. **a** ~ **de**, **en** ~ **de** in favour of. **haga el** ~ **de** would you be so kind as to, please. **por** ~ please

favorec|er [11] *vt* favour; *<vestido, peinado etc>* suit. ~**ido** *a* favoured

favorito *a* & *m* favourite

faz *f* face

fe *f* faith. **dar** ~ **de** certify. **de buena** ~ in good faith

fealdad *f* ugliness

febrero *m* February

febril *a* feverish

fecha *f* date. **a estas** ~**s** now; (todavía) still. **hasta la** ~ so far. **poner la** ~ date. ~**r** *vt* date

fecund|ación *f* fertilization. ~**ación artificial** artificial insemination. ~**ar** *vt* fertilize. ~**o** *a* fertile; (fig) prolific

federa|ción *f* federation. ~**l** *a* federal

felici|dad *f* happiness. ~**dades** *fpl* best wishes; (congratulaciones) congratulations. ~**tación** *f* letter of congratulation. ¡~**taciones!** (LAm) congratulations! ~**tar** *vt* congratulate

feligrés *m* parishioner

feliz *a* happy; (afortunado) lucky. ¡**Felices Pascuas!** Happy Christmas! ¡**F~ Año Nuevo!** Happy New Year!

felpudo *m* doormat

fem|enil *a* (Mex) women's. ~**inino** *a* feminine; *<equipo>* women's; (Biol, Bot) female. ● *m* feminine. ~**inista** *a* & *m* & *f* feminist

fen|omenal *a* phenomenal. ~**ómeno** *m* phenomenon; (monstruo) freak

feo *a* ugly; (desagradable) nasty. ● *adv* (LAm, mal) bad

feria *f* fair; (verbena) carnival; (Mex, cambio) small change. ~**do** *m* (LAm) public holiday

ferment|ar *vt/i* ferment. ~**o** *m* ferment

fero|cidad *f* ferocity. ~**z** *a* fierce

férreo *a* iron; *<disciplina>* strict

ferreter|ía *f* hardware store, ironmonger's (Brit). ~**o** *m* hardware dealer, ironmonger (Brit)

ferro|carril *m* railway (Brit), railroad (Amer). ~**viario** *a* rail. ● *m* railwayman (Brit), railroader (Amer)

fértil *a* fertile

fertili|dad *f* fertility. ~**zante** *m* fertilizer. ~**zar** [10] *vt* fertilize

ferv|iente *a* fervent. **~or** *m* fervour

festej|ar *vt* celebrate; entertain *<persona>*. **~o** *m* celebration

festiv|al *m* festival. **~idad** *f* festivity. **~o** *a* festive. ● *m* public holiday

fétido *a* stinking

feto *m* foetus

fiable *a* reliable

fiado *m*. **al ~** on credit. **~r** *m* (Jurid) guarantor

fiambre *m* cold meat. **~ría** *f* (LAm) delicatessen

fianza *f* (dinero) deposit; (objeto) surety. **bajo ~** on bail

fiar [20] *vt* (vender) sell on credit. ● *vi* give credit. **ser de ~** be trustworthy. □ **~se** *vpr*. **~se de** trust

fibra *f* fibre. **~ de vidrio** fibreglass

fic|ción *f* fiction. **~ticio** *a* fictitious; (falso) false

fich|a *f* token; (tarjeta) index card; (en juegos) counter. **~ar** *vt* open a file on. **estar ~ado** have a (police) record. **~ero** *m* card index

fidedigno *a* reliable

fidelidad *f* faithfulness. **alta ~** hi-fi 🔲, high fidelity

fideos *mpl* noodles

fiebre *f* fever. **~ del heno** hay fever. **tener ~** have a temperature

fiel *a* faithful; *<memoria, relato etc>* reliable. ● *m* believer; (de balanza) needle. **los ~es** the faithful

fieltro *m* felt

fier|a *f* wild animal. **~o** *a* fierce

fierro *m* (LAm) metal bar; (hierro) iron

fiesta *f* party; (día festivo) holiday. **~s** *fpl* celebrations

figura *f* figure; (forma) shape. **~r** *vi* appear; (destacar) show off. □ **~rse** *vpr* imagine. **¡figúrate!** just imagine!

fij|ación *f* fixing; (obsesión) fixation. **~ar** *vt* fix; establish *<residencia>*. □ **~arse** *vpr* (poner atención) pay attention; (percatarse) notice. **¡fíjate!** just imagine! **~o** *a* fixed; (firme) stable; (permanente) permanent. ● *adv*. **mirar ~o** stare

fila *f* line; (de soldados etc) file; (en el teatro, cine etc) row; (cola) queue. **ponerse en ~** line up

filántropo *m* philanthropist

filat|elia *f* stamp collecting, philately. **~élico** *a* philatelic. ● *m* stamp collector, philatelist

filete *m* fillet

filial *a* filial. ● *f* subsidiary

Filipinas *fpl*. **las (islas) ~** the Philippines

filipino *a* Philippine, Filipino

filmar *vt* film; shoot *<película>*

filo *m* edge; (de hoja) cutting edge. **al ~ de las doce** at exactly twelve o'clock. **sacar ~ a** sharpen

filología *f* philology

filón *m* vein; (fig) gold-mine

fil|osofía *f* philosophy. **~ósofo** *m* philosopher

filtr|ar *vt* filter. □ **~arse** *vpr* filter; *<dinero>* disappear; *<noticia>* leak. **~o** *m* filter; (bebida) philtre. **~ solar** sunscreen

fin *m* end; (objetivo) aim. **~ de semana** weekend. **a ~ de** in order to. **a ~ de cuentas** at the end of the day. **a ~ de que** in order that. **a ~es de** at the end of. **al ~** finally. **al ~ y al cabo** after all. **dar ~ a** end. **en ~** in short. **por ~** finally. **sin ~** endless

final *a* final. ● *m* end. ● *f* final. **~idad** *f* aim. **~ista** *m* & *f* finalist. **~izar** [10] *vt* finish. ● *vi* end

financi|ación *f* financing; (fondos) funds; (facilidades) credit facilities. **~ar** *vt* finance. **~ero** *a* financial. ● *m* financier

finca *f* property; (tierras) estate; (rural) farm; (de recreo) country house

fingir [14] *vt* feign; (simular) simulate. ● *vi* pretend. □ **~se** *vpr* pretend to be

finlandés *a* Finnish. ● *m* (persona) Finn; (lengua) Finnish

Finlandia *f* Finland

fino *a* fine; (delgado) thin; *<oído>* acute; (de modales) refined; (sútil) subtle

firma *f* signature; (acto) signing; (empresa) firm

firmar *vt/i* sign

firme *a* firm; (estable) stable, steady; *<color>* fast. ● *m* (pavimento) (road) surface. ● *adv* hard. **~za** *f* firmness

fisc|al *a* fiscal, tax. ● *m & f* public prosecutor. **~o** *m* treasury

fisg|ar [12] *vi* snoop (around). **~ón** *a* nosy. ● *m* snooper

físic|a *f* physics. **~o** *a* physical. ● *m* physique; (persona) physicist

fisonomista *m & f.* **ser buen ~** be good at remembering faces

fistol *m* (Mex) tiepin

flaco *a* thin, skinny; (débil) weak

flagelo *m* scourge

flagrante *a* flagrant. **en ~** red-handed

flama *f* (Mex) flame

flamante *a* splendid; (nuevo) brand-new

flamear *vi* flame; <bandera etc> flap

flamenco *a* flamenco; (de Flandes) Flemish. ● *m* (ave) flamingo; (música etc) flamenco; (idioma) Flemish

flan *m* crème caramel

flaqueza *f* thinness; (debilidad) weakness

flauta *f* flute

flecha *f* arrow. **~zo** *m* love at first sight

fleco *m* fringe; (Mex, en el pelo) fringe (Brit), bangs (Amer)

flem|a *f* phlegm. **~ático** *a* phlegmatic

flequillo *m* fringe (Brit), bangs (Amer)

fletar *vt* charter; (LAm, transportar) transport

flexible *a* flexible

flirte|ar *vi* flirt. **~o** *m* flirting

floj|ear *vi* flag; (holgazanear) laze around. **~o** *a* loose; (poco fuerte) weak; (perezoso) lazy

flor *f* flower. **la ~ y nata** the cream. **~a** *f* flora. **~ecer** [11] *vi* flower, bloom; (fig) flourish. **~eciente** *a* (fig) flourishing. **~ero** *m* flower vase. **~ista** *m & f* florist

flot|a *f* fleet. **~ador** *m* float; (de niño) rubber band. **~ar** *vi* float. **~e. a ~e** afloat

fluctua|ción *f* fluctuation. **~r** [21] *vi* fluctuate

flu|idez *f* fluidity; (fig) fluency. **~ido** *a* fluid; (fig) fluent. ● *m* fluid. **~ir** [17] *vi* flow

fluoruro *m* fluoride

fluvial *a* river

fobia *f* phobia

foca *f* seal

foco *m* focus; (lámpara) floodlight; (LAm, de coche) (head)light; (Mex, bombilla) light bulb

fogón *m* cooker; (LAm, fogata) bonfire

folio *m* sheet

folklórico *a* folk

follaje *m* foliage

follet|ín *m* newspaper serial. **~o** *m* pamphlet

follón *m* Ⓘ mess; (alboroto) row; (problema) trouble

fomentar *vt* promote; boost <ahorro>; stir up <odio>

fonda *f* (pensión) boarding-house; (LAm, restaurant) cheap restaurant

fondo *m* bottom; (de calle, pasillo) end; (de sala etc) back; (de escenario, pintura etc) background. **~s** *mpl* funds, money. **a ~** thoroughly. **en el ~** deep down

fonétic|a *f* phonetics. **~o** *a* phonetic

fontanero *m* plumber

footing /'futin/ *m* jogging

forastero *m* stranger

forcejear *vi* struggle

forense *a* forensic. ● *m & f* forensic scientist

forjar *vt* forge. □ **~se** *vpr* forge; build up <ilusiones>

forma *f* form; (contorno) shape; (modo) way; (Mex, formulario) form. **~s** *fpl* conventions. **de todas ~s** anyway. **estar en ~** be in good form. **~ción** *f* formation; (educación) training. **~l** *a* formal; (de fiar) reliable; (serio) serious. **~lidad** *f* formality; (fiabilidad) reliability; (seriedad) seriousness. **~r** *vt* form; (componer) make up; (enseñar) train. □ **~rse** *vpr* form; (desarrollarse) develop; (educarse) to be educated. **~to** *m* format

formidable *a* formidable; (muy grande) enormous

fórmula *f* formula; (sistema) way. **~ de cortesía** polite expression

formular *vt* formulate; make <queja etc>. **~io** *m* form

fornido *a* well-built

forr|ar *vt* (en el interior) line; (en el exterior) cover. **~o** *m* lining; (cubierta) cover

fortale|cer [11] *vt* strengthen. **~za** *f* strength; (Mil) fortress; (fuerza moral) fortitude

fortuito *a* fortuitous; *<encuentro>* chance

fortuna *f* fortune; (suerte) luck

forz|ar [2 & 10] *vt* force; strain *<vista>*. **~osamente** *adv* necessarily. **~oso** *a* necessary

fosa *f* ditch; (tumba) grave. **~s nasales** nostrils

fósforo *m* phosphorus; (cerilla) match

fósil *a & m* fossil

foso *m* ditch; (en castillo) moat; (de teatro) pit

foto *f* photo. **sacar ~s** take photos

fotocopia *f* photocopy. **~dora** *f* photocopier. **~r** *vt* photocopy

fotogénico *a* photogenic

fot|ografía *f* photography; (Foto) photograph. **~ografiar** [20] *vt* photograph. **~ógrafo** *m* photographer

foul /faul/ *m* (*pl* **~s**) (LAm) foul

frac *m* (*pl* **~s** o **fraques**) tails

fracas|ar *vi* fail. **~o** *m* failure

fracción *f* fraction; (Pol) faction

fractura *f* fracture. **~r** *vt* fracture. □ **~rse** *vpr* fracture

fragan|cia *f* fragrance. **~te** *a* fragrant

frágil *a* fragile

fragmento *m* fragment; (de canción etc) extract

fragua *f* forge. **~r** [15] *vt* forge; (fig) concoct. ● *vi* set

fraile *m* friar; (monje) monk

frambuesa *f* raspberry

franc|és *a* French. ● *m* (persona) Frenchman; (lengua) French. **~esa** *f* Frenchwoman

Francia *f* France

franco *a* frank; (evidente) marked; (Com) free. ● *m* (moneda) franc

francotirador *m* sniper

franela *f* flannel

franja *f* border; (banda) stripe; (de terreno) strip

franque|ar *vt* clear; (atravesar) cross; pay the postage on *<carta>*. **~o** *m* postage

franqueza *f* frankness

frasco *m* bottle; (de mermelada etc) jar

frase *f* phrase; (oración) sentence. **~ hecha** set phrase

fratern|al *a* fraternal. **~idad** *f* fraternity

fraud|e *m* fraud. **~ulento** *a* fraudulent

fray *m* brother, friar

frecuen|cia *f* frequency. **con ~cia** frequently. **~tar** *vt* frequent. **~te** *a* frequent

frega|dero *m* sink. **~r** [1 & 12] *vt* scrub; wash *<los platos>*; mop *<el suelo>*; (LAm, 🔲, molestar) annoy

freír [51] (*pp* **frito**) *vt* fry. □ **~se** *vpr* fry; *<persona>* roast

frenar *vt* brake; (fig) check

frenético *a* frenzied; (furioso) furious

freno *m* (de caballería) bit; (Auto) brake; (fig) check

frente *m* front. **~ a** opposite. **~ a ~** face to face. **al ~** at the head; (hacia delante) forward. **chocar de ~** crash head on. **de ~ a** (LAm) facing. **hacer ~ a** face *<cosa>*; stand up to *<persona>*. ● *f* forehead. **arrugar la ~** frown

fresa *f* strawberry

fresc|o *a* (frío) cool; (reciente) fresh; (descarado) cheeky. ● *m* fresh air; (frescor) coolness; (mural) fresco; (persona) impudent person. **al ~o** in the open air. **hacer ~o** be cool. **tomar el ~o** get some fresh air. **~or** *m* coolness. **~ura** *f* freshness; (frío) coolness; (descaro) cheek

frialdad *f* coldness; (fig) indifference

fricci|ón *f* rubbing; (fig, Tec) friction; (masaje) massage. **~onar** *vt* rub

frigidez *f* frigidity

frígido *a* frigid

frigorífico *m* fridge, refrigerator

frijol *m* (LAm) bean. **~es refritos** (Mex) fried purée of beans

frío *a & m* cold. **tomar ~** catch cold. **hacer ~** be cold. **tener ~** be cold

frito *a* fried; (🔲, harto) fed up. **me tiene ~** I'm sick of him

fr|ivolidad f frivolity. **∼ívolo** a frivolous

fronter|a f border, frontier. **∼izo** a border; <*país*> bordering

frontón m pelota court; (pared) fronton

frotar vt rub; strike <*cerilla*>

fructífero a fruitful

fruncir [9] vt gather <*tela*>. **∼ el ceño** frown

frustra|ción f frustration. **∼r** vt frustrate. □ **∼rse** vpr (fracasar) fail. **quedar ∼do** be disappointed

frut|a f fruit. **∼al** a fruit. **∼ería** f fruit shop. **∼ero** m fruit seller; (recipiente) fruit bowl. **∼icultura** f fruit-growing. **∼o** m fruit

fucsia f fuchsia. ● m fuchsia

fuego m fire. **∼s artificiales** fireworks. **a ∼ lento** on a low heat. **tener ∼** have a light

fuente f fountain; (manantial) spring; (plato) serving dish; (fig) source

fuera adv out; (al exterior) outside; (en otra parte) away; (en el extranjero) abroad. **∼ de** outside; (excepto) except for, besides. **por ∼** on the outside. ● vb ⇒IR y SER

fuerte a strong; <*color*> bright; <*sonido*> loud; <*dolor*> severe; (duro) hard; (grande) large; <*lluvia, nevada*> heavy. ● m fort; (fig) strong point. ● adv hard; (con hablar etc) loudly; <*llover*> heavily; (mucho) a lot

fuerza f strength; (poder) power; (en física) force; (Mil) forces. **∼ de voluntad** will-power. **a ∼ de** by (dint of). **a la ∼** by necessity. **por ∼** by force; (por necesidad) by necessity. **tener ∼s para** have the strength to

fuese vb ⇒IR y SER

fug|a f flight, escape; (de gas etc) leak; (Mus) fugue. □ **∼arse** [12] vpr flee, escape. **∼az** a fleeting. **∼itivo** a & m fugitive

fui vb ⇒IR, SER

fulano m so-and-so. **∼, mengano y zutano** every Tom, Dick and Harry

fulminar vt (fig, con mirada) look daggers at

fuma|dor a smoking. ● m smoker. **∼r** vt/i smoke. **∼r en pipa** smoke a pipe. □ **∼rse** vpr smoke. **∼rada** f puff of smoke

funci|ón f function; (de un cargo etc) duty; (de teatro) show, performance. **∼onal** a functional. **∼onar** vi work, function. **no ∼ona** out of order. **∼onario** m civil servant

funda f cover. **∼ de almohada** pillow-case

funda|ción f foundation. **∼mental** a fundamental. **∼mentar** vt base (en on). **∼mento** m foundation. **∼r** vt found; (fig) base. □ **∼rse** vpr be based

fundi|ción f melting; (de metales) smelting; (taller) foundry. **∼r** vt melt; smelt <*metales*>; cast <*objeto*>; blend <*colores*>; (fusionar) merge; (Elec) blow; (LAm) seize up <*motor*>. □ **∼rse** vpr melt; (unirse) merge

fúnebre a funeral; (sombrío) gloomy

funeral a funeral. ● m funeral. **∼es** mpl funeral

funicular a & m funicular

furg|ón m van. **∼oneta** f van

fur|ia f fury; (violencia) violence. **∼ibundo** a furious. **∼ioso** a furious. **∼or** m fury

furtivo a furtive. **cazador ∼** poacher

furúnculo m boil

fusible m fuse

fusil m rifle. **∼ar** vt shoot

fusión f melting; (unión) fusion; (Com) merger

fútbol m, (Mex) **futbol** m football

futbolista m & f footballer

futur|ista a futuristic. ● m & f futurist. **∼o** a & m future

G g

gabardina f raincoat

gabinete m (Pol) cabinet; (en museo etc) room; (de dentista, médico etc) consulting room

gaceta f gazette

gafa f hook. **∼s** fpl glasses, spectacles. **∼s de sol** sunglasses

gaf|ar *vt* 🔲 bring bad luck to. **~e** *m* jinx

gaita *f* bagpipes

gajo *m* segment

gala *f* gala. **~s** *fpl* finery, best clothes. **estar de ~** be dressed up. **hacer ~ de** show off

galán *m* (en el teatro) (romantic) hero; (enamorado) lover

galante *a* gallant. **~ar** *vt* court. **~ría** *f* gallantry

galápago *m* turtle

galardón *m* award

galaxia *f* galaxy

galera *f* galley

galer|ía *f* gallery. **~ía comercial** (shopping) arcade. **~ón** *m* (Mex) hall

Gales *m* Wales. **país de ~** Wales

gal|és *a* Welsh. ● *m* Welshman; (lengua) Welsh. **~esa** *f* Welshwoman

galgo *m* greyhound

Galicia *f* Galicia

galimatías *m invar* gibberish

gallard|ía *f* elegance. **~o** *a* elegant

gallego *a & m* Galician

galleta *f* biscuit (Brit), cookie (Amer)

gall|ina *f* hen, chicken; (fig, 🔲) coward. **~o** *m* cock

galón *m* gallon; (cinta) braid; (Mil) stripe

galop|ar *vi* gallop. **~e** *m* gallop

gama *f* scale; (fig) range

gamba *f* prawn (Brit), shrimp (Amer)

gamberro *m* hooligan

gamuza *f* (piel) chamois leather; (de otro animal) suede

gana *f* wish, desire; (apetito) appetite. **de buena ~** willingly. **de mala ~** reluctantly. **no me da la ~** I don't feel like it. **tener ~s de** (+ *infinitivo*) feel like (+ *gerundio*)

ganad|ería *f* cattle raising; (ganado) livestock. **~o** *m* livestock. **~o lanar** sheep. **~o porcino** pigs. **~o vacuno** cattle

gana|dor *a* winning. ● *m* winner. **~ncia** *f* gain; (Com) profit. **~r** *vt* earn; (en concurso, juego etc) win; (alcanzar) reach. ● *vi* (vencer) win; (mejorar) improve. **~rle a uno** beat s.o. **~rse la vida** earn a living. **salir ~ndo** come out better off

ganch|illo *m* crochet. **hacer ~illo** crochet. **~o** *m* hook; (LAm, colgador) hanger. **tener ~o** be very attractive

ganga *f* bargain

ganso *m* goose

garabat|ear *vt/i* scribble. **~o** *m* scribble

garaje *m* garage

garant|e *m & f* guarantor. **~ía** *f* guarantee. **~izar** [10] *vt* guarantee

garapiña *f* (Mex) pineapple squash. **~do** *a*. **almendras** *fpl* **~das** sugared almonds

garbanzo *m* chick-pea

garbo *m* poise; (de escrito) style. **~so** *a* elegant

garganta *f* throat; (Geog) gorge

gárgaras *fpl*. **hacer ~** gargle

garita *f* hut; (de centinela) sentry box

garra *f* (de animal) claw; (de ave) talon

garrafa *f* carafe

garrafal *a* huge

garrapata *f* tick

garrapat|ear *vi* scribble. **~o** *m* scribble

garrote *m* club, cudgel; (tormento) garrotte

gar|úa *f* (LAm) drizzle. **~uar** *vi* [21] (LAm) drizzle

garza *f* heron

gas *m* gas. **con ~** fizzy. **sin ~** still

gasa *f* gauze

gaseosa *f* fizzy drink

gas|óleo *m* diesel. **~olina** *f* petrol (Brit), gasoline (Amer), gas (Amer). **~olinera** *f* petrol station (Brit), gas station (Amer)

gast|ado *a* spent; <vestido etc> worn out. **~ador** *m* spendthrift. **~ar** *vt* spend; (consumir) use; (malgastar) waste; (desgastar) wear out; wear <vestido etc>; crack <broma>. □ **~arse** *vpr* wear out. **~o** *m* expense; (acción de gastar) spending

gastronomía *f* gastronomy

gat|a *f* cat. **a ~as** on all fours. **~ear** *vi* crawl

gatillo *m* trigger

gat|ito *m* kitten. **~o** *m* cat. **dar ~o por liebre** take s.o. in

gaucho *m* Gaucho

gaveta *f* drawer

gaviota *f* seagull

gazpacho *m* gazpacho

gelatina *f* gelatine; (jalea) jelly

gema *f* gem

gemelo *m* twin. ∼**s** *mpl* (anteojos) binoculars; (de camisa) cuff-links

gemido *m* groan

Géminis *m* Gemini

gemir [5] *vi* moan; <*animal*> whine, howl

gen *m*, **gene** *m* gene

geneal|ogía *f* genealogy. ∼**ógico** *a* genealogical. **árbol** *m* ∼**ógico** family tree

generaci|ón *f* generation. ∼**onal** *a* generation

general *a* general. **en** ∼ in general. **por lo** ∼ generally. ● *m* general. ∼**izar** [10] *vt/i* generalize. ∼**mente** *adv* generally

generar *vt* generate

género *m* type, sort; (Biol) genus; (Gram) gender; (en literatura etc) genre; (producto) product; (tela) material. ∼**s de punto** knitwear. ∼ **humano** mankind

generos|idad *f* generosity. ∼**o** *a* generous

genétic|a *f* genetics. ∼**o** *a* genetic

geni|al *a* brilliant; (divertido) funny. ∼**o** *m* temper; (carácter) nature; (talento, persona) genius

genital *a* genital. ∼**es** *mpl* genitals

gente *f* people; (nación) nation; (⊞, familia) family, folks; (Mex, persona) person. ● *a* (LAm) respectable; (amable) kind

gentil *a* charming. ∼**eza** *f* kindness. **tener la** ∼**eza de** be kind enough to

gentío *m* crowd

genuflexión *f* genuflection

genuino *a* genuine

ge|ografía *f* geography. ∼**ográfico** *a* geographical.

ge|ología *f* geology. ∼**ólogo** *m* geologist

geom|etría *f* geometry. ∼**étrico** *a* geometrical

geranio *m* geranium

geren|cia *f* management. ∼**ciar** *vt* (LAm) manage. ∼**te** *m* & *f* manager

germen *m* germ

germinar *vi* germinate

gestación *f* gestation

gesticula|ción *f* gesticulation. ∼**r** *vi* gesticulate

gesti|ón *f* step; (administración) management. ∼**onar** *vt* take steps to arrange; (dirigir) manage

gesto *m* expression; (ademán) gesture; (mueca) grimace

gibraltareño *a* & *m* Gibraltarian

gigante *a* gigantic. ● *m* giant. ∼**sco** *a* gigantic

gimn|asia *f* gymnastics. ∼**asio** *m* gymnasium, gym ⊞. ∼**asta** *m* & *f* gymnast. ∼**ástic** *a* gymnastic

gimotear *vi* whine

ginebra *f* gin

ginecólogo *m* gynaecologist

gira *f* tour. ∼**r** *vt* spin; draw <*cheque*>; transfer <*dinero*>. ● *vi* rotate, go round; <*en camino*> turn

girasol *m* sunflower

gir|atorio *a* revolving. ∼**o** *m* turn; (Com) draft; (locución) expression. ∼**o postal** money order

gitano *a* & *m* gypsy

glacia|l *a* icy. ∼**r** *m* glacier

glándula *f* gland

glasear *vt* glaze; (Culin) ice

glob|al *a* global; (fig) overall. ∼**o** *m* globe; (aerostato, juguete) balloon

glóbulo *m* globule

gloria *f* glory; (placer) delight. □ ∼**rse** *vpr* boast (**de** about)

glorieta *f* square; (Auto) roundabout (Brit), (traffic) circle (Amer)

glorificar [7] *vt* glorify

glorioso *a* glorious

glotón *a* gluttonous. ● *m* glutton

gnomo /'nomo/ *m* gnome

gob|ernación *f* government. **Ministerio** *m* **de la G**∼**ernación** Home Office (Brit), Department of the Interior (Amer). ∼**ernador** *a* governing. ● *m* governor. ∼**ernante** *a* governing. ● *m* & *f* leader. ∼**ernar** [1] *vt* govern. ∼**ierno** *m* government

goce *m* enjoyment

gol *m* goal

golf *m* golf

golfo *m* gulf; (niño) urchin; (holgazán) layabout

golondrina *f* swallow

golos|ina *f* titbit; (dulce) sweet. **~o** *a* fond of sweets

golpe *m* blow; (puñetazo) punch; (choque) bump; (de emoción) shock; (⊠, atraco) job 🆃; (en golf, en tenis, de remo) stroke. **~ de estado** coup d'état. **~ de fortuna** stroke of luck. **~ de vista** glance. **~ militar** military coup. **de ~** suddenly. **de un ~** in one go. **~ar** *vt* hit; (dar varios golpes) beat; (con mucho ruido) bang; (con el puño) punch. ● *vi* knock

goma *f* rubber; (para pegar) glue; (banda) rubber band; (de borrar) eraser. **~a de mascar** chewing gum. **~a espuma** foam rubber

gord|a *f* (Mex) small thick tortilla. **~o** *a* <persona> (con ser) fat; (con estar) have put on weight; <carne> fatty; (grueso) thick; (grande) large, big. ● *m* first prize. **~ura** *f* fatness; (grasa) fat

gorila *f* gorilla

gorje|ar *vi* chirp. **~o** *m* chirping

gorra *f* cap. **~ de baño** (LAm) bathing cap

gorrión *m* sparrow

gorro *m* cap; (de niño) bonnet. **~ de baño** bathing cap

got|a *f* drop; (Med) gout. **ni ~a** nothing. **~ear** *vi* drip. **~era** *f* leak

gozar [10] *vt* enjoy. ● *vi*. **~ de** enjoy

gozne *m* hinge

gozo *m* pleasure; (alegría) joy. **~so** *a* delighted

graba|ción *f* recording. **~do** *m* engraving, print; (en libro) illustration. **~dora** *f* tape-recorder. **~r** *vt* engrave; record <discos etc>

graci|a *f* grace; (favor) favour; (humor) wit. **~as** *fpl* thanks. **¡~as!** thank you!, thanks! **dar las ~as** thank. **hacer ~a** amuse; (gustar) please. **¡muchas ~as!** thank you very much! **tener ~a** be funny. **~oso** *a* funny. ● *m* fool, comic character

grad|a *f* step. **~as** *fpl* stand(s). **~ación** *f* gradation. **~o** *m* degree; (Escol) year (Brit), grade (Amer). **de buen ~o** willingly

gradua|ción *f* graduation; (de alcohol) proof. **~do** *m* graduate. **~l** *a*

gradual. **~r** [21] *vt* graduate; (regular) adjust. □ **~rse** *vpr* graduate

gráfic|a *f* graph. **~o** *a* graphic. ● *m* graph

gram|ática *f* grammar. **~atical** *a* grammatical

gramo *m* gram, gramme (Brit)

gran *a véase* GRANDE

grana *f* (color) deep red

granada *f* pomegranate; (Mil) grenade

granate *m* (color) maroon

Gran Bretaña *f* Great Britain

grande *a* (delante de nombre en singular **gran**) big, large; (alto) tall; (fig) great; (LAm, de edad) grown up. **~za** *f* greatness

grandioso *a* magnificent

granel *m*. **a ~** in bulk; (suelto) loose; (fig) in abundance

granero *m* barn

granito *m* granite; (grano) small grain

graniz|ado *m* iced drink. **~ar** [10] *vi* hail. **~o** *m* hail

granj|a *f* farm. **~ero** *m* farmer

grano *m* grain; (semilla) seed; (de café) bean; (Med) spot. **~s** *mpl* cereals

granuja *m & f* rogue

grapa *f* staple. **~r** *vt* staple

gras|a *f* grease; (Culin) fat. **~iento** *a* greasy

gratifica|ción *f* (de sueldo) bonus; (recompensa) reward. **~r** [7] *vt* reward

grat|is *adv* free. **~itud** *f* gratitude. **~o** *a* pleasant **~uito** *a* free; (fig) uncalled for

grava|men *m* tax; (carga) burden; (sobre inmueble) encumbrance. **~r** *vt* tax; (cargar) burden

grave *a* serious; <voz> deep; <sonido> low; <acento> grave. **~dad** *f* gravity

gravilla *f* gravel

gravitar *vi* gravitate; (apoyarse) rest (**sobre** on); <peligro> hang (**sobre** over)

gravoso *a* costly

graznar *vi* <cuervo> caw; <pato> quack; honk <ganso>

Grecia *f* Greece

gremio *m* union

greña f mop of hair

gresca f rumpus; (riña) quarrel

griego a & m Greek

grieta f crack

grifo m tap, faucet (Amer)

grilletes mpl shackles

grillo m cricket. **~s** mpl shackles

gringo m (LAm) foreigner; (norteamericano) Yankee 🔲

gripe f flu

gris a grey. ● m grey; (🔲, policía) policeman

grit|ar vi shout. **~ería** f, **~erío** m uproar. **~o** m shout; (de dolor, sorpresa) cry; (chillido) scream. **dar ~s** shout

grosella f redcurrant. **~ negra** blackcurrant

groser|ía f rudeness; (ordinariez) coarseness; (comentario etc) coarse remark; (palabra) swearword. **~o** a coarse; (descortés) rude

grosor m thickness

grotesco a grotesque

grúa f crane

grueso a thick; <persona> fat, stout. ● m thickness; (fig) main body

grumo m lump

gruñi|do m grunt; (de perro) growl. **~r** [22] vi grunt; <perro> growl

grupa f hindquarters

grupo m group

gruta f grotto

guacamole m guacamole

guadaña f scythe

guaje m (Mex) gourd

guajolote m (Mex) turkey

guante m glove

guapo a good-looking; <chica> pretty; (elegante) smart

guarda m & f guard; (de parque etc) keeper. **~barros** m invar mudguard. **~bosque** m gamekeeper. **~costas** m invar coastguard vessel. **~espaldas** m invar bodyguard. **~meta** m goalkeeper. **~r** vt keep; (proteger) protect; (en un lugar) put away; (reservar) save, keep. □ **~rse** vpr. **~rse de** (+ infinitivo) avoid (+ gerundio). **~rropa** m wardrobe; (en local público) cloakroom. **~vallas** m invar (LAm) goalkeeper

guardería f nursery

guardia f guard; (policía) policewoman; (de médico) shift. **G~ Civil** Civil Guard. **~ municipal** police. **estar de ~** be on duty. **estar en ~** be on one's guard. **montar la ~** mount guard. ● m policeman. **~ jurado** m & f security guard. **~ de tráfico** m traffic policeman. ● f traffic policewoman

guardián m guardian; (de parque etc) keeper; (de edificio) security guard

guar|ecer [11] vt (albergar) give shelter to. □ **~ecerse** vpr take shelter. **~ida** f den, lair; (de personas) hideout

guarn|ecer [11] vt (adornar) adorn; (Culin) garnish. **~ición** m adornment; (de caballo) harness; (Culin) garnish; (Mil) garrison; (de piedra preciosa) setting

guas|a f joke. **~ón** a humorous. ● m joker

Guatemala f Guatemala

guatemalteco a & m Guatemalan

guateque m party, bash

guayab|a f guava; (dulce) guava jelly. **~era** f lightweight jacket

gubernatura f (Mex) government

güero a (Mex) fair

guerr|a f war; (método) warfare. **dar ~a** annoy. **~ero** a warlike; (belicoso) fighting. ● m warrior. **~illa** f band of guerrillas. **~illero** m guerrilla

guía m & f guide. ● f guidebook; (de teléfonos) directory

guiar [20] vt guide; (llevar) lead; (Auto) drive. □ **~se** vpr be guided (por by)

guijarro m pebble

guillotina f guillotine

guind|a f morello cherry. **~illa** f chilli

guiñapo m rag; (fig, persona) wreck

guiñ|ar vt/i wink. **~o** m wink. **hacer ~os** wink

gui|ón m hyphen, dash; (de película etc) script. **~onista** m & f scriptwriter

guirnalda f garland

guisado m stew

guisante m pea. **~ de olor** sweet pea

guis|ar vt/i cook. **~o** m stew

guitarr|a *f* guitar. **∼ista** *m* & *f* guitarist

gula *f* gluttony

gusano *m* worm; (larva de mosca) maggot

gustar

● *verbo intransitivo*

! Cuando el verbo **gustar** va precedido del complemento indirecto **le** (o **les, nos** etc), el sujeto en español pasa a ser el objeto en inglés. **me gusta mucho la música** *I like music very much.* **le gustan los helados** *he likes ice cream.* **a Juan no le gusta** *Juan doesn't like it* (or *her* etc)

····➤ **gustar** + *infinitivo.* **les gusta ver televisión** they like watching television

····➤ **gustar que** + *subjuntivo.* **me ∼ía que vinieras** I'd like you to come. **no le gusta que lo corrijan** he doesn't like being corrected. **¿te ∼ía que te lo comprara?** would you like me to buy it for you?

····➤ **gustar de algo** to like sth. **gustan de las fiestas** they like parties

····➤ (tener acogida) to go down well. **ese tipo de cosas siempre gusta** those sort of things always go down well. **el libro no gustó** the book didn't go down well

····➤ (en frases de cortesía) to wish. **como guste** as you wish. **cuando gustes** whenever you wish

● *verbo transitivo*

····➤ (LAm, querer) **¿gusta un café?** would you like a coffee? **¿gustan pasar?** would you like to come in?

□ **gustarse** *verbo pronominal* to like each other

gusto *m* taste; (placer) pleasure. **a ∼** comfortable. **a mi ∼** to my liking. **buen ∼** good taste. **con mucho ∼** with pleasure. **dar ∼** please. **mucho ∼** pleased to meet you. **∼so** *a* tasty; (de buen grado) willingly

gutural *a* guttural

ha *vb* ⇒HABER

haba *f* broad bean

Habana *f.* **La ∼** Havana

habano *m* (puro) Havana

haber *v aux* [30] have. ● *v impersonal* (*presente* s & *pl* **hay,** *imperfecto* s & *pl* **había,** *pretérito* s & *pl* **hubo**). **hay una carta para ti** there's a letter for you. **hay 5 bancos en la plaza** there are 5 banks in the square. **hay que hacerlo** it must be done, you have to do it. **he aquí** here is, here are. **no hay de qué** don't mention it, not at all. **¿qué hay?** (¿qué pasa?) what's the matter?; (¿qué tal?) how are you?

habichuela *f* bean

hábil *a* skilful; (listo) clever; <*día*> working; (Jurid) competent

habili|dad *f* skill; (astucia) cleverness; (Jurid) competence. **∼tar** *vt* qualify

habita|ción *f* room; (dormitorio) bedroom; (en biología) habitat. **∼ción de matrimonio,** **∼ción doble** double room. **∼ción individual,** **∼ción sencilla** single room. **∼do** *a* inhabited. **∼nte** *m* inhabitant. **∼r** *vt* live in. ● *vi* live

hábito *m* habit

habitua|l *a* usual, habitual; <*cliente*> regular. **∼r** [21] *vt* accustom. □ **∼rse** *vpr.* **∼rse a** get used to

habla *f* speech; (idioma) language; (dialecto) dialect. **al ∼** (al teléfono) speaking. **ponerse al ∼ con** get in touch with. **∼dor** *a* talkative. ● *m* chatterbox. **∼duría** *f* rumour. **∼durías** *fpl* gossip. **∼nte** *a* speaking. ● *m* & *f* speaker. **∼r** *vt* speak. ● *vi* speak, talk (**con** to); (Mex, por teléfono) call. **¡ni ∼r!** out of the question! **se ∼ español** Spanish spoken

hacend|ado *m* landowner; (LAm) farmer. **∼oso** *a* hard-working

hacer [31]

● *verbo transitivo*

····➤ to do. **¿qué haces?** what are you doing? **~ los deberes** to do one's homework. **no sé qué ~** I don't know what to do. **hazme un favor** can you do me a favour?

····➤ (fabricar, preparar, producir) to make. **me hizo un vestido** she made me a dress. **~ un café** to make a (cup of) coffee. **no hagas tanto ruido** don't make so much noise

····➤ (construir) to build <*casa, puente*>

····➤ **hacer que uno haga algo** to make s.o. do sth. **haz que se vaya** make him leave. **hizo que se equivocara** he made her go wrong

····➤ **hacer hacer algo** to have sth done. **hizo arreglar el techo** he had the roof repaired

⇒ Cuando el verbo **hacer** se emplea en expresiones como **hacer una pregunta, hacer trampa** etc., ver bajo el respectivo nombre

● *verbo intransitivo*

····➤ (actuar, obrar) to do. **hiciste bien en llamar** you did the right thing to call. **¿cómo haces para parecer tan joven?** what do you do to look so young?

····➤ (fingir, simular) **hacer como que** to pretend. **hizo como que no me conocía** he pretended not to know me. **haz como que estás dormido** pretend you're asleep

····➤ **hacer de** (en teatro) to play the part of; (ejercer la función de) to act as

····➤ (LAm, sentar) **tanta sal hace mal** so much salt is not good for you. **dormir le hizo bien** the sleep did him good. **el pepino me hace mal** cucumber doesn't agree with me

● *verbo impersonal*

····➤ (hablando del tiempo atmosférico) to be. **hace sol** it's sunny. **hace 3 grados** it's 3 degrees

····➤ (con expresiones temporales) **hace una hora que espero** I've been waiting for an hour. **llegó hace 3 días** he arrived 3 days ago. **hace mucho tiempo** a long time ago. **hasta hace poco** until recently

□ **hacerse** *verbo pronominal*

····➤ (para sí) to make o.s. <*falda, café*>

····➤ (hacer que otro haga) **se hizo la permanente** she had her hair permed. **me hice una piscina** I had a swimming pool built

····➤ (convertirse en) to become. **se hicieron amigos** they became friends

····➤ (acostumbrarse) **~se a algo** to get used to sth

····➤ (fingirse) to pretend. **~se el enfermo** to pretend to be ill

····➤ (moverse) to move. **hazte para atrás** move back

····➤ **hacerse de** (LAm) to make <*amigo, dinero*>

hacha *f* axe; (antorcha) torch

hacia *prep* towards; (cerca de) near; (con tiempo) at about. **~ abajo** downwards. **~ arriba** upwards. **~ atrás** backwards. **~ las dos** (at) about two o'clock

hacienda *f* country estate; (en LAm) ranch; **la ~ pública** the Treasury. **Ministerio** *m* **de H~** Ministry of Finance; (en Gran Bretaña) Exchequer; (en Estados Unidos) Treasury

hada *f* fairy. **el ~ madrina** the fairy godmother

hago *vb* ⇒HACER

Haití *m* Haiti

halag|ar [12] *vt* flatter. **~üeño** *a* flattering; (esperanzador) promising

halcón *m* falcon

halla|r *vt* find; (descubrir) discover. □ **~rse** *vpr* be. **~zgo** *m* discovery

hamaca *f* hammock; (asiento) deckchair

hambr|e *f* hunger; (de muchos) famine. **tener ~e** be hungry. **~iento** *a* starving

hamburguesa *f* hamburger

harag|án *a* lazy, idle. ● *m* layabout. **~anear** *vi* laze around

harap|iento *a* in rags. **~o** *m* rag

harina *f* flour

hart|ar *vt* (fastidiar) annoy. **me estás ~ando** you're annoying me. □ **~arse** *vpr* (llenarse) gorge o.s. (de on); (cansarse) get fed up (de with).

∼**o** *a* full; (cansado) tired; (fastidiado) fed up (**de** with). ● *adv* (LAm) (muy) very; (mucho) a lot

hasta *prep* as far as; (en el tiempo) until, till; (Mex) not until. ● *adv* even. ¡∼ **la vista!** goodbye!, see you! ▣ ¡∼ **luego!** see you later! ¡∼ **mañana!** see you tomorrow! ¡∼ **pronto!** see you soon!

hast|iar [20] *vt* (cansar) weary, tire; (aburrir) bore. □ ∼**iarse** *vpr* get fed up (**de** with). ∼**ío** *m* weariness; (aburrimiento) boredom

haya *f* beech (tree). ● *vb* ⇒HABER

hazaña *f* exploit

hazmerreír *m* laughing stock

he *vb* ⇒HABER

hebilla *f* buckle

hebra *f* thread; (fibra) fibre

hebreo *a* & *m* Hebrew

hechi|cera *f* witch. ∼**cería** *f* witchcraft. ∼**cero** *m* wizard. ∼**zar** [10] *vt* cast a spell on; (fig) captivate. ∼**zo** *m* spell; (fig) charm

hech|o *pp de* **hacer**. ● *a* (manufacturado) made; (terminado) done; <*vestidos etc*> ready-made; (Culin) done. ● *m* fact; (acto) deed; (cuestión) matter; (suceso) event. **de** ∼**o** in fact. ∼**ura** *f* making; (forma) form; (del cuerpo) build; (calidad de fabricación) workmanship

hed|er [1] *vi* stink. ∼**iondez** *f* stench. ∼**iondo** *a* stinking, smelly. ∼**or** *m* stench

hela|da *f* frost. ∼**dera** *f* (LAm) fridge, refrigerator. ∼**dería** *f* ice-cream shop. ∼**do** *a* freezing; (congelado) frozen; (LAm, bebida) chilled. ● *m* ice-cream. ∼**r** [1] *vt/i* freeze. **anoche heló** there was a frost last night. □ ∼**rse** *vpr* freeze

helecho *m* fern

hélice *f* propeller

helicóptero *m* helicopter

hembra *f* female; (mujer) woman

hemorr|agia *f* haemorrhage. ∼**oides** *fpl* haemorrhoids

hendidura *f* crack, split; (Geol) fissure

heno *m* hay

heráldica *f* heraldry

hered|ar *vt/i* inherit. ∼**era** *f* heiress. ∼**ero** *m* heir. ∼**itario** *a* hereditary

herej|e *m* heretic. ∼**ia** *f* heresy

herencia *f* inheritance; (fig) heritage

heri|da *f* injury; (con arma) wound. ∼**do** *a* injured; (con arma) wounded; (fig) hurt. ● *m* injured person. ∼**r** [4] *vt* injure; (con arma) wound, (fig) hurt. □ ∼**rse** *vpr* hurt o.s.

herman|a *f* sister. ∼**a política** sister-in-law. ∼**astra** *f* stepsister. ∼**astro** *m* stepbrother. ∼**o** *m* brother. ∼**o político** brother-in-law. ∼**os** *mpl* brothers; (chicos y chicas) brothers and sisters. ∼**os gemelos** twins

hermético *a* hermetic; (fig) watertight

hermos|o *a* beautiful; (espléndido) splendid. ∼**ura** *f* beauty

héroe *m* hero

hero|ico *a* heroic. ∼**ína** *f* heroine; (droga) heroin. ∼**ísmo** *m* heroism

herr|adura *f* horseshoe. ∼**amienta** *f* tool. ∼**ero** *m* blacksmith

herv|idero *m* (fig) hotbed; (multitud) throng. ∼**ir** [4] *vt/i* boil. ∼**or** *m* (fig) ardour. **romper el** ∼ come to the boil

hiberna|ción *f* hibernation. ∼**r** *vi* hibernate

híbrido *a* & *m* hybrid

hice *vb* ⇒HACER

hidalgo *m* nobleman

hidrata|nte *a* moisturizing. ∼**r** *vt* hydrate; <*crema etc*> moisturize

hidráulico *a* hydraulic

hid|roavión *m* seaplane. ∼**oeléctrico** *a* hydroelectric. ∼**ofobia** *f* rabies. ∼**ófobo** *a* rabid. ∼**ógeno** *m* hydrogen

hiedra *f* ivy

hielo *m* ice

hiena *f* hyena

hierba *f* grass; (Culin, Med) herb. **mala** ∼ weed. ∼**buena** *f* mint

hierro *m* iron

hígado *m* liver

higi|ene *f* hygiene. ∼**énico** *a* hygienic

hig|o *m* fig. ∼**uera** *f* fig tree

hij|a *f* daughter. **~astra** *f* stepdaughter. **~astro** *m* stepson. **~o** *m* son. **~os** *mpl* sons; (chicos y chicas) children

hilar *vt* spin. **~ delgado** split hairs

hilera *f* row; (Mil) file

hilo *m* thread; (Elec) wire; (de líquido) trickle; (lino) linen

hilv|án *m* tacking. **~anar** *vt* tack; (fig) put together

himno *m* hymn. **~ nacional** anthem

hincapié *m*. hacer **~ en** stress, insist on

hincar [7] *vt* drive *<estaca>* (en into). □ **~se** *vpr*. **~se de rodillas** kneel down

hincha *f* ⬛ grudge. ● *m & f* (⬛, aficionado) fan

hincha|do *a* inflated; (Med) swollen. **~r** *vt* inflate, blow up. □ **~rse** *vpr* swell up; (fig, ⬛, comer mucho) gorge o.s. **~zón** *f* swelling

hinojo *m* fennel

hiper|mercado *m* hypermarket. **~sensible** *a* hypersensitive. **~tensión** *f* high blood pressure

hípic|a *f* horse racing. **~o** *a* horse

hipn|osis *f* hypnosis. **~otismo** *m* hypnotism. **~otizar** [10] *vt* hypnotize

hipo *m* hiccup. **tener ~** have hiccups

hipo|alérgeno *a* hypoallergenic. **~condríaco** *a & m* hypochondriac

hip|ocresía *f* hypocrisy. **~ócrita** *a* hypocritical. ● *m & f* hypocrite

hipódromo *m* racecourse

hipopótamo *m* hippopotamus

hipoteca *f* mortgage. **~r** [7] *vt* mortgage

hip|ótesis *f* *invar* hypothesis. **~otético** *a* hypothetical

hiriente *a* offensive, wounding

hirsuto *a* *<barba>* bristly; *<pelo>* wiry

hispánico *a* Hispanic

Hispanoamérica *f* Spanish America

hispano|americano *a* Spanish American. **~hablante** *a* Spanish-speaking

hist|eria *f* hysteria. **~érico** *a* hysterical

hist|oria *f* history; (relato) story; (excusa) tale, excuse. **pasar a la ~oria** go down in history. **~oriador** *m* historian. **~órico** *a* historical. **~orieta** *f* tale; (con dibujos) strip cartoon

hito *m* milestone

hizo *vb* ⇒HACER

hocico *m* snout

hockey /'(x)oki/ *m* hockey. **~ sobre hielo** ice hockey

hogar *m* home; (chimenea) hearth. **~eño** *a* domestic; *<persona>* home-loving

hoguera *f* bonfire

hoja *f* leaf; (de papel, metal etc) sheet; (de cuchillo, espada etc) blade. **~ de afeitar** razor blade. **~lata** *f* tin

hojaldre *m* puff pastry

hojear *vt* leaf through

hola *int* hello!

Holanda *f* Holland

holand|és *a* Dutch. ● *m* Dutchman; (lengua) Dutch. **~esa** *f* Dutchwoman. **los ~eses** the Dutch

holg|ado *a* loose; (fig) comfortable. **~ar** [2 & 12] *vi*. **huelga decir que** needless to say. **~azán** *a* lazy. ● *m* idler. **~ura** *f* looseness; (fig) comfort

hollín *m* soot

hombre *m* man; (especie humana) man(kind). ● *int* Good Heavens!; (de duda) well. **~ de negocios** businessman. **~ rana** frogman

hombr|era *f* shoulder pad. **~o** *m* shoulder

homenaje *m* homage, tribute. **rendir ~ a** pay tribute to

home|ópata *m* homoeopath. **~opatía** *f* homoeopathy. **~opático** *a* homoeopathic

homicid|a *a* murderous. ● *m & f* murderer. **~io** *m* murder

homosexual *a & m & f* homosexual. **~idad** *f* homosexuality

hond|o *a* deep. **~onada** *f* hollow

Honduras *f* Honduras

hondureño *a & m* Honduran

honest|idad *f* honesty. **~o** *a* honest

hongo *m* fungus; (LAm, Culin) mushroom; (venenoso) toadstool

hon|or *m* honour. **~orable** *a* honourable. **~orario** *a* honorary. **~orarios** *mpl* fees. **~ra** *f* honour; (buena fama) good name. **~radez** *f* honesty. **~rado** *a* honest. **~rar** *vt* honour

hora *f* hour; (momento puntual) time; (cita) appointment. **~ pico, ~ punta** rush hour. **~s** *fpl* **de trabajo** working hours. **~s** *fpl* **extraordinarias** overtime. **~s** *fpl* **libres** free time. **a estas ~s** now. **¿a qué ~?** (at) what time? **a última ~** at the last moment. **de última ~** last-minute. **en buena ~** at the right time. **media ~** half an hour. **pedir ~** to make an appointment. **¿qué ~ es?** what time is it?

horario *a* hourly. ● *m* timetable. **~ de trabajo** working hours

horca *f* gallows

horcajadas *fpl*. **a ~** astride

horchata *f* tiger-nut milk

horizont|al *a & f* horizontal. **~e** *m* horizon

horma *f* mould; (para fabricar calzado) last; (para conservar su forma) shoe-tree. **de ~ ancha** broad-fitting

hormiga *f* ant

hormigón *m* concrete

hormigue|ar *vi* tingle; (bullir) swarm. **me ~a la mano** I've got pins and needles in my hand. **~o** *m* tingling; (fig) anxiety

hormiguero *m* anthill; (de gente) swarm

hormona *f* hormone

horn|ada *f* batch. **~illa** *f* (LAm) burner. **~illo** *m* burner; (cocina portátil) portable electric cooker. **~o** *m* oven; (para cerámica etc) kiln; (Tec) furnace

horóscopo *m* horoscope

horquilla *f* pitchfork; (para el pelo) hairpin

horr|endo *a* awful. **~ible** *a* horrible. **~ipilante** *a* terrifying. **~or** *m* horror; (atrocidad) atrocity. **¡qué ~or!** how awful!. **~orizar** [10] *vt* horrify. □ **~orizarse** *vpr* be horrified. **~oroso** *a* horrifying

hort|aliza *f* vegetable. **~elano** *m* market gardener

hosco *a* surly

hospeda|je *m* accommodation. **~r** *vt* put up. □ **~rse** *vpr* stay

hospital *m* hospital. **~ario** *a* hospitable. **~idad** *f* hospitality

hostal *m* boarding-house

hostería *f* inn

hostia *f* (Relig) host

hostigar [12] *vt* whip; (fig, molestar) pester

hostil *a* hostile. **~idad** *f* hostility

hotel *m* hotel. **~ero** *a* hotel. ● *m* hotelier

hoy *adv* today. **~ (en) día** nowadays. **~ por ~** at the present time. **de ~ en adelante** from now on

hoy|o *m* hole. **~uelo** *m* dimple

hoz *f* sickle

hube *vb* ⇒HABER

hucha *f* money box

hueco *a* hollow; *<palabras>* empty; *<voz>* resonant; *<persona>* superficial. ● *m* hollow; (espacio) space; (vacío) gap

huelg|a *f* strike. **~a de brazos caídos** sit-down strike. **~a de hambre** hunger strike. **declararse en ~a** come out on strike. **~uista** *m & f* striker

huella *f* footprint; (de animal, vehículo etc) track. **~ digital** fingerprint

huelo *vb* ⇒OLER

huérfano *a* orphaned. ● *m* orphan. **~ de** without

huert|a *f* market garden (Brit), truck farm (Amer); (terreno de regadío) irrigated plain. **~o** *m* vegetable garden; (de árboles frutales) orchard

hueso *m* bone; (de fruta) stone

huésped *m* guest; (que paga) lodger

huesudo *a* bony

huev|a *f* roe. **~o** *m* egg. **~o duro** hard-boiled egg. **~o escalfado** poached egg. **~o estrellado, ~o frito** fried egg. **~o pasado por agua** boiled egg. **~os revueltos** scrambled eggs. **~o tibio** (Mex) boiled egg

hui|da *f* flight, escape. **~dizo** *a* (tímido) shy; (esquivo) elusive

huipil *m* (Mex) traditional embroidered smock

huir *vi* [17] flee, run away; (evitar). **~ de** avoid. **me huye** he avoids me

huitlacoche *m* (Mex) edible black fungus

hule *m* oilcloth; (Mex, goma) rubber

human|idad *f* mankind; (fig) humanity. **~itario** *a* humanitarian. **~o** *a* human; (benévolo) humane

humareda *f* cloud of smoke

humed|ad *f* dampness; (en meteorología) humidity; (gotitas de agua) moisture. **~ecer** [11] *vt* moisten. □ **~ecerse** *vpr* become moist

húmedo *a* damp; *<clima>* humid; *<labios>* moist; (mojado) wet

humi|ldad *f* humility. **~lde** *a* humble. **~llación** *f* humiliation. **~llar** *vt* humiliate. □ **~llarse** *vpr* lower o.s.

humo *m* smoke; (vapor) steam; (gas nocivo) fumes. **~s** *mpl* airs

humor *m* mood, temper; (gracia) humour. **estar de mal ~** be in a bad mood. **~ista** *m & f* humorist. **~ístico** *a* humorous

hundi|miento *m* sinking. **~r** *vt* sink; destroy *<persona>*. □ **~rse** *vpr* sink; *<edificio>* collapse

húngaro *a & m* Hungarian

Hungría *f* Hungary

huracán *m* hurricane

huraño *a* unsociable

hurgar [12] *vi* rummage (**en** through). □ **~se** *vpr*. **~se la nariz** pick one's nose

hurra *int* hurray!

hurtadillas *fpl*. **a ~** stealthily

hurt|ar *vt* steal. **~o** *m* theft; (cosa robada) stolen object

husmear *vt* sniff out; (fig) pry into

huyo *vb* ⇒HUIR

....

....

iba *vb* ⇒IR

ibérico *a* Iberian

iberoamericano *a & m* Latin American

iceberg /iθ'ber/ *m* (*pl* **~s**) iceberg

ictericia *f* jaundice

ida *f* outward journey; (partida) departure. **de ~ y vuelta** *<billete>* return (Brit), round-trip (Amer); *<viaje>* round

idea *f* idea; (opinión) opinion. **cambiar de ~** change one's mind. **no tener la más remota ~, no tener la menor ~** not have the slightest idea, not have a clue ⊡

ideal *a & m* ideal. **~ista** *m & f* idealist. **~izar** [10] *vt* idealize

idear *vt* think up, conceive; (inventar) invent

ídem *pron & adv* the same

idéntico *a* identical

identi|dad *f* identity. **~ficación** *f* identification. **~ficar** [7] *vt* identify. □ **~ficarse** *vpr* identify o.s. **~ficarse con** identify with

ideol|ogía *f* ideology. **~ógico** *a* ideological

idílico *a* idyllic

idilio *m* idyll

idiom|a *m* language. **~ático** *a* idiomatic

idiosincrasia *f* idiosyncrasy

idiot|a *a* idiotic. ● *m & f* idiot. **~ez** *f* stupidity

idolatrar *vt* worship; (fig) idolize

ídolo *m* idol

idóneo *a* suitable (**para** for)

iglesia *f* church

iglú *m* igloo

ignora|ncia *f* ignorance. **~nte** *a* ignorant. ● *m* ignoramus. **~r** *vt* not know, be unaware of; (no hacer caso de) ignore

igual *a* equal; (mismo) the same; (similar) like; (llano) even; (liso) smooth. ● *adv* the same. ● *m* equal. **~ que** (the same) as. **al ~ que** the same as. **da ~, es ~** it doesn't matter. **sin ~** unequalled

igual|ar *vt* make equal; equal *<éxito, récord>*; (allanar) level. □ **~arse** *vpr* be equal. **~dad** *f* equality. **~mente** *adv* equally; (también) also, likewise; (respuesta de cortesía) the same to you

ilegal *a* illegal

ilegible *a* illegible

ilegítimo *a* illegitimate

ileso *a* unhurt

ilícito a illicit

ilimitado a unlimited

ilógico a illogical

ilumina|ción f illumination; (alumbrado) lighting. ~**r** vt light (up). □ ~**rse** vpr light up

ilusi|ón f illusion; (sueño) dream; (alegría) joy. **hacerse** ~**ones** build up one's hopes. **me hace** ~**ón** I'm thrilled; I'm looking forward to <algo en el futuro>. ~**onado** a excited. ~**onar** vt give false hope. □ ~**onarse** vpr have false hopes

ilusionis|mo m conjuring. ~**ta** m & f conjurer

iluso a naive. ● m dreamer. ~**rio** a illusory

ilustra|ción f learning; (dibujo) illustration. ~**do** a learned; (con dibujos) illustrated. ~**r** vt explain; (instruir) instruct; (añadir dibujos etc) illustrate. □ ~**rse** vpr acquire knowledge. ~**tivo** a illustrative

ilustre a illustrious

imagen f image; (TV etc) picture

imagina|ble a imaginable. ~**ción** f imagination. ~**r** vt imagine. □ ~**rse** vpr imagine. ~**rio** m imaginary. ~**tivo** a imaginative

imán m magnet

imbécil a stupid. ● m & f idiot

imborrable a indelible; <recuerdo etc> unforgettable

imita|ción f imitation. ~**r** vt imitate

impacien|cia f impatience. □ ~**tarse** vpr lose one's patience. ~**te** a impatient

impacto m impact; (huella) mark. ~ **de bala** bullet hole

impar a odd

imparcial a impartial. ~**idad** f impartiality

impartir vt impart, give

impasible a impassive

impávido a fearless; (impasible) impassive

impecable a impeccable

impedi|do a disabled. ~**mento** m impediment. ~**r** [5] vt prevent; (obstruir) hinder

impenetrable a impenetrable

impensa|ble a unthinkable. ~**do** a unexpected

impera|r vi prevail. ~**tivo** a imperative; <necesidad> urgent

imperceptible a imperceptible

imperdible m safety pin

imperdonable a unforgivable

imperfec|ción f imperfection. ~**to** a imperfect

imperi|al a imperial. ~**alismo** m imperialism. ~**o** m empire; (poder) rule. ~**oso** a imperious

impermeable a waterproof. ● m raincoat

impersonal a impersonal

impertinen|cia f impertinence. ~**te** a impertinent

imperturbable a imperturbable

ímpetu m impetus; (impulso) impulse; (violencia) force

impetuos|idad f impetuosity. ~**o** a impetuous

implacable a implacable

implantar vt introduce

implica|ción f implication. ~**r** [7] vt implicate; (significar) imply

implícito a implicit

implorar vt implore

impon|ente a imposing; 🔟 terrific. ~**er** [34] vt impose; (requerir) demand; deposit <dinero>. □ ~**erse** vpr (hacerse obedecer) assert o.s.; (hacerse respetar) command respect; (prevalecer) prevail. ~**ible** a taxable

importa|ción f importation; (artículo) import. ~**ciones** fpl imports. ~**dor** a importing. ● m importer

importa|ncia f importance. ~**nte** a important; (en cantidad) considerable. ~**r** vt import; (ascender a) amount to. ● vi be important, matter. **¿le** ~**ría...?** would you mind...? **no** ~ it doesn't matter

importe m price; (total) amount

importun|ar vt bother. ~**o** a troublesome; (inoportuno) inopportune

imposib|ilidad f impossibility. ~**le** a impossible. **hacer lo** ~**le para** do all one can to

imposición f imposition; (impuesto) tax

impostor m impostor

impoten|cia f impotence. ~**te** a impotent

impracticable a impracticable; (intransitable) unpassable

imprecis|ión f vagueness; (error) inaccuracy. ~**o** a imprecise

impregnar vt impregnate; (empapar) soak

imprenta f printing; (taller) printing house, printer's

imprescindible a indispensable, essential

impresi|ón f impression; (acción de imprimir) printing; (tirada) edition; (huella) imprint. ~**onable** a impressionable. ~**onante** a impressive; (espantoso) frightening. ~**onar** vt impress; (negativamente) shock; (conmover) move; (Foto) expose. □ ~**onarse** vpr be impressed; (negativamente) be shocked; (conmover) be moved

impresionis|mo m impressionism. ~**ta** a & m & f impressionist

impreso a printed. ● m form. ~**s** mpl printed matter. ~**ra** f printer

imprevis|ible a unforeseeable. ~**to** a unforeseen

imprimir (pp **impreso**) vt print <libro etc>

improbab|ilidad f improbability. ~**le** a unlikely, improbable

improcedente a inadmissible; <conducta> improper; <despido> unfair

improductivo a unproductive

improperio m insult. ~**s** mpl abuse

impropio a improper

improvis|ación f improvisation. ~**ado** a improvised. ~**ar** vt improvise. ~**o** a. **de** ~**o** unexpectedly

impruden|cia f imprudence. ~**te** a imprudent

imp|udicia f indecency; (desvergüenza) shamelessness. ~**údico** a indecent; (desvergonzado) shameless. ~**udor** m indecency; (desvergüenza) shamelessness

impuesto a imposed. ● m tax. ~ **a la renta** income tax. ~ **sobre el valor agregado** (LAm), ~ **sobre el valor añadido** VAT, value added tax

impuls|ar vt propel; drive <persona>; boost <producción etc>. ~**ivi-dad** f impulsiveness. ~**ivo** a impulsive. ~**o** m impulse

impun|e a unpunished. ~**idad** f impunity

impur|eza f impurity. ~**o** a impure

imputa|ción f charge. ~**r** vt attribute; (acusar) charge

inaccesible a inaccessible

inaceptable a unacceptable

inactiv|idad f inactivity. ~**o** a inactive

inadaptado a maladjusted

inadecuado a inadequate; (inapropiado) unsuitable

inadmisible a inadmissible; (inaceptable) unacceptable

inadvertido a distracted. **pasar** ~ go unnoticed

inagotable a inexhaustible

inaguantable a unbearable

inaltera|ble a impassive; <color> fast; <convicción> unalterable. ~**do** a unchanged

inapreciable a invaluable; (imperceptible) imperceptible

inapropiado a inappropriate

inasequible a out of reach

inaudito a unprecedented

inaugura|ción f inauguration. ~**l** a inaugural. ~**r** vt inaugurate

inca a & m & f Inca. ~**ico** a Inca

incalculable a incalculable

incandescente a incandescent

incansable a tireless

incapa|cidad f incapacity; (física) disability. ~**citado** a disabled. ~**citar** vt incapacitate. ~**z** a incapable

incauto a unwary; (fácil de engañar) gullible

incendi|ar vt set fire to. □ ~**arse** vpr catch fire. ~**ario** a incendiary. ● m arsonist. ~**o** m fire

incentivo m incentive

incertidumbre f uncertainty

incesante a incessant

incest|o m incest. ~**uoso** a incestuous

inciden|cia f incidence; (efecto) impact; (incidente) incident. ~**tal** a incidental. ~**te** m incident

incidir *vi* fall (**en** into); (influir) influence

incienso *m* incense

incierto *a* uncertain

incinera|dor *m* incinerator. ~**r** *vt* incinerate; cremate *<cadáver>*

incipiente *a* incipient

incisi|ón *f* incision. ~**vo** *a* incisive. ● *m* incisor

incitar *vt* incite

inclemen|cia *f* harshness. ~**te** *a* harsh

inclina|ción *f* slope; (de la cabeza) nod; (fig) inclination. ~**r** *vt* tilt; (inducir) incline. ~**rse** *vpr* lean; (en saludo) bow; (tender) be inclined (**a** to)

inclu|ido *a* included; *<precio>* inclusive. ~**ir** [17] *vt* include; (en cartas) enclose. ~**sión** *f* inclusion. ~**sive** *adv* inclusive. **hasta el lunes** ~**sive** up to and including Monday. ~**so** *adv* even

incógnito *a* unknown. **de** ~ incognito

incoheren|cia *f* incoherence. ~**te** *a* incoherent

incoloro *a* colourless

incomestible *a*, **incomible** *a* uneatable, inedible

incomodar *vt* inconvenience; (causar vergüenza) make feel uncomfortable. □ ~**se** *vpr* feel uncomfortable; (enojarse) get angry

incómodo *a* uncomfortable; (inconveniente) inconvenient

incomparable *a* incomparable

incompatib|ilidad *f* incompatibility. ~**le** *a* incompatible

incompeten|cia *f* incompetence. ~**te** *a* & *m* & *f* incompetent

incompleto *a* incomplete

incompren|dido *a* misunderstood. ~**sible** *a* incomprehensible. ~**sión** *f* incomprehension

incomunicado *a* cut off; *<preso>* in solitary confinement

inconcebible *a* inconceivable

inconcluso *a* unfinished

incondicional *a* unconditional

inconfundible *a* unmistakable

incongruente *a* incoherent; (contradictorio) inconsistent

inconmensurable *a* immeasurable

inconscien|cia *f* unconsciousness; (irreflexión) recklessness. ~**te** *a* unconscious; (irreflexivo) reckless

inconsecuente *a* inconsistent

inconsistente *a* flimsy

inconsolable *a* unconsolable

inconstan|cia *f* lack of perseverance. ~**te** *a* changeable; *<persona>* lacking in perseverance; (voluble) fickle

incontable *a* countless

incontenible *a* irrepressible

incontinen|cia *f* incontinence. ~**te** *a* incontinent

inconvenien|cia *f* inconvenience. ~**te** *a* inconvenient; (inapropiado) inappropriate; (incorrecto) improper. ● *m* problem; (desventaja) drawback

incorpora|ción *f* incorporation. ~**r** *vt* incorporate; (Culin) add. □ ~**rse** *vpr* sit up; join *<sociedad, regimiento etc>*

incorrecto *a* incorrect; (descortés) discourteous

incorregible *a* incorrigible

incorruptible *a* incorruptible

incrédulo *a* sceptical; *<mirada, gesto>* incredulous

increíble *a* incredible

increment|ar *vt* increase. ~**o** *m* increase

incriminar *vt* incriminate

incrustar *vt* encrust

incuba|ción *f* incubation. ~**dora** *f* incubator. ~**r** *vt* incubate; (fig) hatch

incuestionable *a* unquestionable

inculcar [7] *vt* inculcate

inculpar *vt* accuse

inculto *a* uneducated

incumplimiento *m* non-fulfilment; (de un contrato) breach

incurable *a* incurable

incurrir *vi*. ~ **en** incur *<gasto>*; fall into *<error>*; commit *<crimen>*

incursión *f* raid

indagar [12] *vt* investigate

indebido *a* unjust; *<uso>* improper

indecen|cia *f* indecency. ~**te** *a* indecent

indecible *a* indescribable

indecis|ión *f* indecision. **~o** *a* (con ser) indecisive; (con estar) undecided

indefenso *a* defenceless

indefini|ble *a* indefinable. **~do** *a* indefinite; (impreciso) undefined

indemnizar [10] *vt* compensate

independ|encia *f* independence. **~iente** *a* independent. **~izarse** [10] *vpr* become independent

indes|cifrable *a* indecipherable. **~criptible** *a* indescribable

indeseable *a* undesirable

indestructible *a* indestructible

indetermina|ble *a* indeterminable. **~do** *a* indeterminate; *<tiempo>* indefinite

India *f*. la **~** India

indica|ción *f* indication; (señal) signal. **~ciones** *fpl* directions. **~dor** *m* indicator; (Tec) gauge. **~r** [7] *vt* show, indicate; (apuntar) point at; (hacer saber) point out; (aconsejar) advise. **~tivo** *a* indicative. ● *m* indicative; (al teléfono) dialling code

índice *m* index; (dedo) index finger; (catálogo) catalogue; (indicación) indication; (aguja) pointer

indicio *m* indication, sign; (vestigio) trace

indiferen|cia *f* indifference. **~te** *a* indifferent. **me es ~te** it's all the same to me

indígena *a* indigenous. ● *m & f* native

indigen|cia *f* poverty. **~te** *a* needy

indigest|ión *f* indigestion. **~o** *a* indigestible

indign|ación *f* indignation. **~ado** *a* indignant. **~ar** *vt* make indignant. □ **~arse** *vpr* become indignant. **~o** *a* unworthy; (despreciable) contemptible

indio *a & m* Indian

indirect|a *f* hint. **~o** *a* indirect

indisciplinado*a* undisciplined

indiscre|ción *f* indiscretion. **~to** *a* indiscreet

indiscutible *a* unquestionable

indisoluble *a* indissoluble

indispensable *a* indispensable

indisp|oner [34] *vt* (enemistar) set against. □ **~onerse** *vpr* fall out; (ponerse enfermo) fall ill. **~osición** *f* indisposition. **~uesto** *a* indisposed

individu|al *a* individual; *<cama>* single. ● *m* (en tenis etc) singles. **~alidad** *f* individuality. **~alista** *m & f* individualist. **~alizar** [10] *vt* individualize. **~o** *m* individual

índole *f* nature; (clase) type

indolen|cia *f* indolence. **~te** *a* indolent

indoloro *a* painless

indomable *a* untameable

inducir [47] *vt* induce. **~ a error** be misleading

indudable *a* undoubted

indulgen|cia *f* indulgence. **~te** *a* indulgent

indult|ar *vt* pardon. **~o** *m* pardon

industria *f* industry. **~l** *a* industrial. ● *m & f* industrialist. **~lización** *f* industrialization. **~lizar** [10] *vt* industrialize

inédito *a* unpublished; (fig) unknown

inefable *a* indescribable

ineficaz *a* ineffective; *<sistema etc>* inefficient

ineficiente *a* inefficient

ineludible *a* inescapable, unavoidable

inept|itud *f* ineptitude. **~o** *a* inept

inequívoco *a* unequivocal

inercia *f* inertia

inerte *a* inert; (sin vida) lifeless

inesperado *a* unexpected

inestable *a* unstable

inestimable *a* inestimable

inevitable *a* inevitable

inexistente *a* non-existent

inexorable *a* inexorable

inexper|iencia *f* inexperience. **~to** *a* inexperienced

inexplicable *a* inexplicable

infalible *a* infallible

infam|ar *vt* defame. **~atorio** *a* defamatory. **~e** *a* infamous; (fig, 🄴, muy malo) awful. **~ia** *f* infamy

infancia *f* infancy

infant|a *f* infanta, princess. **~e** *m* infante, prince. **~ería** *f* infantry. **~il** *a* children's; *<población>* child; *<actitud etc>* childish, infantile

infarto *m* heart attack

infec|ción *f* infection. **~cioso** *a* infectious. **~tar** *vt* infect. □ **~tarse** *vpr* become infected. **~to** *a* infected; ⚇ disgusting

infeli|cidad *f* unhappiness. **~z** *a* unhappy

inferior *a* inferior. ● *m & f* inferior. **~idad** *f* inferiority

infernal *a* infernal, hellish

infestar *vt* infest; (fig) inundate

infi|delidad *f* unfaithfulness. **~el** *a* unfaithful

infierno *m* hell

infiltra|ción *f* infiltration. □ **~rse** *vpr* infiltrate

ínfimo *a* lowest; *<calidad>* very poor

infini|dad *f* infinity. **~tivo** *m* infinitive. **~to** *a* infinite. ● *m*. **el ~to** the infinite; (en matemáticas) infinity. **~dad de** countless

inflación *f* inflation

inflama|ble *a* (in)flammable **~ción** *f* inflammation. **~r** *vt* set on fire; (fig, Med) inflame. □ **~rse** *vpr* catch fire; (Med) become inflamed

inflar *vt* inflate; blow up *<globo>*; (fig, exagerar) exaggerate

inflexi|ble *a* inflexible. **~ón** *f* inflexion

influ|encia *f* influence (en on). **~ir** [17] *vt* influence. ● *vi*. **~ en** influence. **~jo** *m* influence. **~yente** *a* influential

informa|ción *f* information; (noticias) news; (en aeropuerto etc) information desk; (de teléfonos) directory enquiries. **~dor** *m* informant

informal *a* informal; *<persona>* unreliable

inform|ante *m & f* informant. **~ar** *vt/i* inform. □ **~arse** *vpr* find out. **~ática** *f* information technology, computing. **~ativo** *a* informative; *<programa>* news. **~atizar** [10] *vt* computerize

informe *a* shapeless. ● *m* report. **~s** *fpl* references, information

infracción *f* infringement. **~ de tráfico** traffic offence

infraestructura *f* infrastructure

infranqueable *a* impassable; (fig) insuperable

infrarrojo *a* infrared

infringir [14] *vt* infringe

infructuoso *a* fruitless

ínfulas *fpl*. **darse ~** give o.s. airs. **tener ~ de** fancy o.s. as

infundado *a* unfounded

infu|ndir *vt* instil. **~sión** *f* infusion

ingeni|ar *vt* invent. **~árselas para** find a way to

ingenier|ía *f* engineering. **~o** *m* engineer

ingenio *m* ingenuity; (agudeza) wit; (LAm, de azúcar) refinery. **~so** *a* ingenious

ingenu|idad *f* naivety. **~o** *a* naive

Inglaterra *f* England

ingl|és *a* English. ● *m* Englishman; (lengua) English. **~esa** *f* Englishwoman. **los ~eses** the English

ingrat|itud *f* ingratitude. **~o** *a* ungrateful; (desagradable) thankless

ingrediente *m* ingredient

ingres|ar *vt* deposit. ● *vi*. **~ar en** come in, enter; join *<sociedad>*. **~o** *m* entrance; (de dinero) deposit; (en sociedad, hospital) admission. **~os** *mpl* income

inh|ábil *a* unskilful; (no apto) unfit. **~abilidad** *f* unskilfulness; (para cargo) ineligibility

inhabitable *a* uninhabitable

inhala|dor *m* inhaler. **~r** *vt* inhale

inherente *a* inherent

inhibi|ción *f* inhibition. **~r** *vt* inhibit

inhóspito *a* inhospitable

inhumano *a* inhuman

inici|ación *f* beginning. **~al** *a & f* initial. **~ar** *vt* initiate; (comenzar) begin, start. **~ativa** *f* initiative. **~o** *m* beginning

inigualado *a* unequalled

ininterrumpido *a* uninterrupted

injert|ar *vt* graft. **~to** *m* graft

injuri|a *f* insult. **~ar** *vt* insult. **~oso** *a* insulting

injust|icia *f* injustice. **~o** *a* unjust, unfair

inmaculado *a* immaculate

inmaduro *a* unripe; *<persona>* immature

inmediaciones *fpl.* **las ~** the vicinity, the surrounding area

inmediat|amente *adv* immediately. **~o** *a* immediate; (contiguo) next. **de ~o** immediately

inmejorable *a* excellent

inmemorable *a* immemorial

inmens|idad *f* immensity. **~o** *a* immense

inmersión *f* immersion

inmigra|ción *f* immigration. **~nte** *a & m & f* immigrant. **~r** *vt* immigrate

inminen|cia *f* imminence. **~te** *a* imminent

inmiscuirse [17] *vpr* interfere

inmobiliario *a* property

inmolar *vt* sacrifice

inmoral *a* immoral. **~idad** *f* immorality

inmortal *a* immortal. **~izar** [10] *vt* immortalize

inmóvil *a* immobile

inmueble *a.* **bienes ~s** property

inmund|icia *f* filth. **~o** *a* filthy

inmun|e *a* immune. **~idad** *f* immunity. **~ización** *f* immunization. **~izar** [10] *vt* immunize

inmuta|ble *a* unchangeable. □ **~rse** *vpr* be perturbed. **sin ~rse** unperturbed

innato *a* innate

innecesario *a* unnecessary

innegable *a* undeniable

innova|ción *f* innovation. **~r** *vi* innovate. ● *vt* make innovations in

innumerable *a* innumerable

inocen|cia *f* innocence. **~tada** *f* practical joke. **~te** *a* innocent. **~tón** *a* naïve

inocuo *a* innocuous

inodoro *a* odourless. ● *m* toilet

inofensivo *a* inoffensive

inolvidable *a* unforgettable

inoperable *a* inoperable

inoportuno *a* untimely; *<comentario>* ill-timed

inoxidable *a* stainless

inquiet|ar *vt* worry. □ **~arse** *vpr* get worried. **~o** *a* worried; (agitado) restless. **~ud** *f* anxiety

inquilino *m* tenant

inquirir [4] *vt* enquire into, investigate

insaciable *a* insatiable

insalubre *a* unhealthy

insatisfecho *a* unsatisfied; (descontento) dissatisfied

inscri|bir (*pp* **inscrito**) *vt* (en registro) register; (en curso) enrol; (grabar) inscribe. □ **~birse** *vpr* register. **~pción** *f* inscription; (registro) registration

insect|icida *m* insecticide. **~o** *m* insect

insegur|idad *f* insecurity. **~o** *a* insecure; *<ciudad>* unsafe, dangerous

insemina|ción *f* insemination. **~r** *vt* inseminate

insensato *a* foolish

insensible *a* insensitive

inseparable *a* inseparable

insertar *vt* insert

insidi|a *f* malice. **~oso** *a* insidious

insigne *a* famous

insignia *f* badge; (bandera) flag

insignificante *a* insignificant

insinu|ación *f* insinuation. **~ante** *a* insinuating. **~ar** [21] *vt* imply; insinuate *<algo ofensivo>*. □ **~arse** *vpr*. **~ársele a** make a pass at

insípido *a* insipid

insist|encia *f* insistence. **~ente** *a* insistent. **~ir** *vi* insist; (hacer hincapié) stress

insolación *f* sunstroke

insolen|cia *f* rudeness, insolence. **~te** *a* rude, insolent

insólito *a* unusual

insolven|cia *f* insolvency. **~te** *a & m & f* insolvent

insomn|e *a* sleepless. ● *m & f* insomniac. **~io** *m* insomnia

insondable *a* unfathomable

insoportable *a* unbearable

insospechado *a* unexpected

insostenible *a* untenable

inspec|ción *f* inspection. ~**cionar** *vt* inspect. ~**tor** *m* inspector

inspira|ción *f* inspiration. ~**r** *vt* inspire. □ ~**rse** *vpr* be inspired

instala|ción *f* installation. ~**r** *vt* install. □ ~**rse** *vpr* settle

instancia *f* request. **en última** ~ as a last resort

instant|ánea *f* snapshot. ~**áneo** *a* instantaneous; *<café etc>* instant. ~**e** *m* instant. **a cada** ~**e** constantly. **al** ~**e** immediately

instaura|ción *f* establishment. ~**r** *vt* establish

instiga|ción *f* instigation. ~**dor** *m* instigator. ~**r** [12] *vt* instigate; (incitar) incite

instint|ivo *a* instinctive. ~**o** *m* instinct

institu|ción *f* institution. ~**cional** *a* institutional. ~**ir** [17] *vt* establish. ~**to** *m* institute; (Escol) (secondary) school. ~**triz** *f* governess

instru|cción *f* education; (Mil) training. ~**cciones** *fpl* instruction. ~**ctivo** *a* instructive; *<película etc>* educational. ~**ctor** *m* instructor. ~**ir** [17] *vt* instruct, teach; (Mil) train

instrument|ación *f* instrumentation. ~**al** *a* instrumental. ~**o** *m* instrument; (herramienta) tool

insubordina|ción *f* insubordination. ~**r** *vt* stir up. □ ~**rse** *vpr* rebel

insuficien|cia *f* insufficiency; (inadecuación) inadequacy. ~**te** *a* insufficient

insufrible *a* insufferable

insular *a* insular

insulina *f* insulin

insulso *a* tasteless; (fig) insipid

insult|ar *vt* insult. ~**o** *m* insult

insuperable *a* insuperable; (inmejorable) unbeatable

insurgente *a* insurgent

insurrec|ción *f* insurrection. ~**to** *a* insurgent

intachable *a* irreproachable

intacto *a* intact

intangible *a* intangible

integra|ción *f* integration. ~**l** *a* integral; (completo) complete; (incorporado) built-in; *<pan>* wholemeal (Brit), wholewheat (Amer). ~**r** *vt* make up

integridad *f* integrity; (entereza) wholeness

íntegro *a* complete; (fig) upright

intelect|o *m* intellect. ~**ual** *a & m & f* intellectual

inteligen|cia *f* intelligence. ~**te** *a* intelligent

inteligible *a* intelligible

intemperie *f.* **a la** ~ in the open

intempestivo *a* untimely

intenci|ón *f* intention. **con doble** ~**ón** implying sth else. ~**onado** *a* deliberate. **bien** ~**onado** well-meaning. **mal** ~**onado** malicious. ~**onal** *a* intentional

intens|idad *f* intensity. ~**ificar** [7] *vt* intensify. ~**ivo** *a* intensive. ~**o** *a* intense

intent|ar *vt* try. ~**o** *m* attempt; (Mex, propósito) intention

inter|calar *vt* insert. ~**cambio** *m* exchange. ~**ceder** *vt* intercede

interceptar *vt* intercept

interdicto *m* ban

inter|és *m* interest; (egoísmo) self-interest. ~**esado** *a* interested; (parcial) biassed; (egoísta) selfish. ~**esante** *a* interesting. ~**esar** *vt* interest; (afectar) concern. ● *vi* be of interest. □ ~**esarse** *vpr* take an interest (**por** in)

interfer|encia *f* interference. ~**ir** [4] *vi* interfere

interfono *m* intercom

interino *a* temporary; *<persona>* acting. ● *m* stand-in; (médico) locum

interior *a* interior; *<comercio etc>* domestic. ● *m* inside. **Ministerio del** I~ Home Office (Brit), Department of the Interior (Amer)

interjección *f* interjection

inter|locutor *m* speaker. ~**mediario** *a & m* intermediary. ~**medio** *a* intermediate. ● *m* interval

interminable *a* interminable

intermitente *a* intermittent. ● *m* indicator

internacional *a* international

intern|ado *m* (Escol) boarding-school. **~ar** *vt* (en manicomio) commit; (en hospital) admit. □ **~arse** *vpr* penetrate

Internet *m* Internet

interno *a* internal; (Escol) boarding. ● *m* (Escol) boarder

interponer [34] *vt* interpose. □ **~se** *vpr* intervene

int|erpretación *f* interpretation. **~erpretar** *vt* interpret; (Mús etc) play. **~érprete** *m* interpreter; (Mus) performer

interroga|ción *f* interrogation; (signo) question mark. **~r** [12] *vt* question. **~tivo** *a* interrogative

interru|mpir *vt* interrupt; cut off *<suministro>*; cut short *<viaje etc>*; block *<tráfico>*. **~pción** *f* interruption. **~ptor** *m* switch

inter|sección *f* intersection. **~urbano** *a* inter-city; *<llamada>* long-distance

intervalo *m* interval; (espacio) space. **a ~s** at intervals

interven|ir [53] *vt* control; (Med) operate on. ● *vi* intervene; (participar) take part. **~tor** *m* inspector; (Com) auditor

intestino *m* intestine

intim|ar *vi* become friendly. **~idad** *f* intimacy

intimidar *vt* intimidate

íntimo *a* intimate; *<amigo>* close. ● *m* close friend

intolera|ble *a* intolerable. **~nte** *a* intolerant

intoxicar [7] *vt* poison

intranquilo *a* worried

intransigente *a* intransigent

intransitable *a* impassable

intransitivo *a* intransitive

intratable *a* impossible

intrépido *a* intrepid

intriga *f* intrigue. **~nte** *a* intriguing. **~r** [12] *vt* intrigue

intrincado *a* intricate

intrínseco *a* intrinsic

introduc|ción *f* introduction. **~ir** [47] *vt* introduce; (meter) insert. □ **~irse** *vpr* get into

intromisión *f* interference

introvertido *a* introverted. ● *m* introvert

intruso *m* intruder

intui|ción *f* intuition. **~r** [17] *vt* sense. **~tivo** *a* intuitive

inunda|ción *f* flooding. **~r** *vt* flood

inusitado *a* unusual

in|útil *a* useless; (vano) futile. **~utilidad** *f* uselessness

invadir *vt* invade

inv|alidez *f* invalidity; (Med) disability. **~álido** *a & m* invalid

invariable *a* invariable

invas|ión *f* invasion. **~or** *a* invading. ● *m* invader

invencible *a* invincible

inven|ción *f* invention. **~tar** *vt* invent

inventario *m* inventory

invent|iva *f* inventiveness. **~ivo** *a* inventive. **~or** *m* inventor

invernadero *m* greenhouse

invernal *a* winter

inverosímil *a* implausible

inversión *f* inversion; (Com) investment

inverso *a* inverse; (contrario) opposite. **a la inversa** the other way round. **a la inversa de** contrary to

invertir [4] *vt* reverse; (Com) invest; put in *<tiempo>*

investidura *f* investiture

investiga|ción *f* investigation; (Univ) research. **~dor** *m* investigator; (Univ) researcher. **~r** [12] *vt* investigate; (Univ) research

investir [5] *vt* invest

invicto *a* unbeaten

invierno *m* winter

inviolable *a* inviolate

invisible *a* invisible

invita|ción *f* invitation. **~do** *m* guest. **~r** *vt* invite. **te invito a una copa** I'll buy you a drink

invocar [7] *vt* invoke

involuntario *a* involuntary

invulnerable *a* invulnerable

inyec|ción *f* injection. **~tar** *vt* inject

ir [49]

● *verbo intransitivo*

····➤ to go. **fui a verla** I went to see her. **ir a pie** to go on foot. **ir en coche** to go by car. **vamos a casa** let's go home. **fue (a) por el pan** he went to get some bread

! Cuando la acción del verbo **ir** significa trasladarse hacia o con el interlocutor la traducción es *to come*, p.ej: **¡ya voy!** *I'm coming!* **yo voy contigo** *I'll come with you*

····➤ (estar) to be. **iba con su novio** she was with her boyfriend. **¿cómo te va?** how are you?

····➤ (sentar) to suit. **ese color no le va** that colour doesn't suit her. **no me va ni me viene** I don't mind at all

····➤ (Méx, apoyar) **irle a** to support. **le va al equipo local** he supports the local team

····➤ (en exclamaciones) **¡vamos!** come on! **¡vaya!** what a surprise!; (contrariedad) oh, dear! **¡vaya noche!** what a night! **¡qué va!** nonsense!

⟹ Cuando el verbo intransitivo se emplea con expresiones como **ir de paseo, ir de compras, ir tirando** etc., ver bajo el respectivo nombre, verbo etc.

● *verbo auxiliar*

····➤ **ir a** + *infinitivo* (para expresar futuro, propósito) to be going to + *infinitive;* (al prevenir) **no te vayas a caer** be careful you don't fall. **no vaya a ser que llueva** in case it rains. (en sugerencias) **vamos a dormir** let's go to sleep. **vamos a ver** let's see

····➤ **ir** + *gerundio*. **ve arreglándote** start getting ready. **el tiempo va mejorando** the weather is gradually getting better.

□ **irse** *verbo pronominal*

····➤ to go. **vete a la cama** go to bed. **se ha ido a casa** he's gone home

····➤ (marcharse) to leave. **se fue sin despedirse** he left without saying goodbye. **se fue de casa** she left home

ira *f* anger. **∼cundo** *a* irascible

Irak *m* Iraq

Irán *m* Iran

iraní *a* & *m* & *f* Iranian

iraquí *a* & *m* & *f* Iraqi

iris *m* (Anat) iris

Irlanda *f* Ireland

irland|és *a* Irish. ● *m* Irishman; (lengua) Irish. **∼esa** *f* Irishwoman. **los ∼eses** the Irish

ir|onía *f* irony. **∼ónico** *a* ironic

irracional *a* irrational

irradiar *vt* radiate

irreal *a* unreal. **∼idad** *f* unreality

irrealizable *a* unattainable

irreconciliable *a* irreconcilable

irreconocible *a* unrecognizable

irrecuperable *a* irretrievable

irreflexión *f* impetuosity

irregular *a* irregular. **∼idad** *f* irregularity

irreparable *a* irreparable

irreprimible *a* irrepressible

irreprochable *a* irreproachable

irresistible *a* irresistible

irrespetuoso *a* disrespectful

irresponsable *a* irresponsible

irriga|ción *f* irrigation. **∼r** [12] *vt* irrigate

irrisorio *a* derisory

irrita|ble *a* irritable. **∼ción** *f* irritation. **∼r** *vt* irritate. □ **∼rse** *vpr* get annoyed

irrumpir *vi* burst (en in)

isla *f* island. **las I∼s Británicas** the British Isles

islámico *a* Islamic

islandés *a* Icelandic. ● *m* Icelander; (lengua) Icelandic

Islandia *f* Iceland

isleño *a* island. ● *m* islander

Israel *m* Israel

israelí *a* & *m* Israeli

Italia *f* Italy

italiano *a* & *m* Italian

itinerario *a* itinerary

IVA *abrev* (**impuesto sobre el valor agregado** (LAm), **impuesto sobre el valor añadido**) VAT

izar [10] *vt* hoist

izquierd|a *f*. **la** ~**a** the left hand; (Pol) left. **a la** ~**a** on the left; (con movimiento) to the left. **de** ~**a** left-wing. ~**ista** *m & f* leftist. ~**o** *a* left

....

Jj

....

ja *int* ha!

jabalí *m* (*pl* ~**es**) wild boar

jabalina *f* javelin

jab|ón *m* soap. ~**onar** *vt* soap. ~**onoso** *a* soapy

jaca *f* pony

jacinto *m* hyacinth

jactarse *vpr* boast

jadea|nte *a* panting. ~**r** *vi* pant

jaguar *m* jaguar

jaiba *f* (LAm) crab

jalar *vt* (LAm) pull

jalea *f* jelly

jaleo *m* row, uproar. **armar un** ~ kick up a fuss

jalón *m* (LAm, tirón) pull; (Mex 🆒, trago) drink; (Mex, tramo) stretch

jamás *adv* never. **nunca** ~ never ever

jamelgo *m* nag

jamón *m* ham. ~ **de York** boiled ham. ~ **serrano** cured ham

Japón *m*. **el** ~ Japan

japonés *a & m* Japanese

jaque *m* check. ~ **mate** checkmate

jaqueca *f* migraine

jarabe *m* syrup

jardín *m* garden. ~ **de la infancia**, (Mex) ~ **de niños** kindergarten, nursery school

jardiner|ía *f* gardening. ~**o** *m* gardener

jarr|a *f* jug. **en** ~**as** with hands on hips. ~**o** *m* jug. **caer como un** ~**o de agua fría** come as a shock. ~**ón** *m* vase

jaula *f* cage

jauría *f* pack of hounds

jazmín *m* jasmine

jef|a *f* boss. ~**atura** *f* leadership; (sede) headquarters. ~**e** *m* boss; (Pol etc) leader. ~**e de camareros** head waiter. ~**e de estación** station-master. ~**e de ventas** sales manager

jengibre *m* ginger

jer|arquía *f* hierarchy. ~**árquico** *a* hierarchical

jerez *m* sherry. **al** ~ with sherry

jerga *f* coarse cloth; (argot) jargon

jerigonza *f* jargon; (galimatías) gibberish

jeringa *f* syringe; (LAm 🆒, molestia) nuisance. ~**r** [12] *vt* (fig, 🆒, molestar) annoy

jeroglífico *m* hieroglyph(ic)

jersey *m* (*pl* ~**s**) jersey

Jesucristo *m* Jesus Christ. **antes de** ~ BC, before Christ

jesuita *a & m* Jesuit

Jesús *m* Jesus. ● *int* good heavens!; (al estornudar) bless you!

jícara *f* (Mex) gourd

jilguero *m* goldfinch

jinete *m & f* rider

jipijapa *m* panama hat

jirafa *f* giraffe

jirón *m* shred, tatter

jitomate *m* (Mex) tomato

jorna|da *f* working day; (viaje) journey; (etapa) stage. ~**l** *m* day's wage. ~**lero** *m* day labourer

joroba *f* hump. ~**do** *a* hunchbacked. ● *m* hunchback. ~**r** *vt* 🆒 annoy

jota *f* letter J; (danza) jota, popular dance. **ni** ~ nothing

joven (*pl* **jóvenes**) *a* young. ● *m* young man. ● *f* young woman

jovial *a* jovial

joy|a *f* jewel. ~**as** *fpl* jewellery. ~**ería** *f* jeweller's (shop). ~**ero** *m* jeweller; (estuche) jewellery box

juanete *m* bunion

jubil|ación *f* retirement. ~**ado** *a* retired. ~**ar** *vt* pension off. □ ~**arse** *vpr* retire. ~**eo** *m* jubilee

júbilo *m* joy

judaísmo *m* Judaism

judía *f* Jewish woman; (alubia) bean. ~ **blanca** haricot bean. ~ **escarlata** runner bean. ~ **verde** French bean

judicial *a* judicial
judío *a* Jewish. ● *m* Jewish man
judo *m* judo
juego *m* play; (de mesa, niños) game; (de azar) gambling; (conjunto) set. **estar en ~** be at stake. **estar fuera de ~** be offside. **hacer ~** match. **~s** *mpl* malabares juggling. **J~s** *mpl* **Olímpicos** Olympic Games. ● *vb* ⇒JUGAR
juerga *f* spree
jueves *m invar* Thursday
juez *m* judge. **~ de instrucción** examining magistrate. **~ de línea** linesman
juga|dor *m* player; (habitual, por dinero) gambler. **~r** [3] *vt* play. ● *vi* play; (apostar fuerte) gamble. □ **~rse** *vpr* risk. **~r al fútbol**, (LAm) **~r fútbol** play football
juglar *m* minstrel
jugo *m* juice; (de carne) gravy; (fig) substance. **~so** *a* juicy; (fig) substantial
juguet|e *m* toy. **~ear** *vi* play. **~ón** *a* playful
juicio *m* judgement; (opinión) opinion; (razón) reason. **a mi ~** in my opinion. **~so** *a* wise
juliana *f* vegetable soup
julio *m* July
junco *m* rush, reed
jungla *f* jungle
junio *m* June
junt|a *f* meeting; (consejo) board, committee; (Pol) junta; (Tec) joint. **~ar** *vt* join; (reunir) collect. □ **~arse** *vpr* join; <*gente*> meet. **~o** *a* joined; (en plural) together. **~o a** next to. **~ura** *f* joint
jura|do *a* sworn. ● *m* jury; (miembro de jurado) juror. **~mento** *m* oath. **prestar ~mento** take an oath. **~r** *vt/i* swear. **~r en falso** commit perjury. **jurárselas a uno** have it in for s.o.
jurel *m* (type of) mackerel
jurídico *a* legal
juris|dicción *f* jurisdiction. **~prudencia** *f* jurisprudence
justamente *a* exactly; (con justicia) fairly
justicia *f* justice
justifica|ción *f* justification. **~r** [7] *vt* justify

justo *a* fair, just; (exacto) exact; <*ropa*> tight. ● *adv* just. **~ a tiempo** just in time
juven|il *a* youthful. **~tud** *f* youth; (gente joven) young people
juzga|do *m* (tribunal) court. **~r** [12] *vt* judge. **a ~r por** judging by

Kk

kilo *m*, **kilogramo** *m* kilo, kilogram
kil|ometraje *m* distance in kilometres, mileage. **~ométrico** *a* 🄸 endless. **~ómetro** *m* kilometre. **~ómetro cuadrado** square kilometre
kilovatio *m* kilowatt
kiosco *m* kiosk

Ll

la

● *artículo definido femenino* (*pl* **las**)
····➤ the. **la flor azul** the blue flower. **la casa de al lado** the house next door. **cerca de la iglesia** near the church
No se traduce en los siguientes casos:
····➤ (con nombre abstracto, genérico) **la paciencia es una virtud** patience is a virtue. **odio la leche** I hate milk. **la madera es muy versátil** wood is very versatile
····➤ (con algunas instituciones) **termino la universidad mañana** I finish university tomorrow. **no va nunca a la iglesia** he never goes to church. **está en la cárcel** he's in jail
····➤ (con nombres propios) **la Sra. Díaz** Mrs Díaz. **la doctora Lara** doctor Lara
····➤ (antes de infinitivo) **es muy cuidadosa en el vestir** she takes great care in the way she dresses. **me di cuenta al**

verla I realized when I saw her

····➤ (con partes del cuerpo, artículos personales) *se traduce por un posesivo.* **apretó la mano** he clenched his fist. **tienes la camisa desabrochada** your shirt is undone

····➤ **la + de.** **es la de Ana** it's Ana's. **la del sombrero** the one with the hat

····➤ **la + que** (persona) **la que me atendió** the one who served me. (cosa) **la que se rompió** the one that broke

····➤ **la + que** + *subjuntivo* (quienquiera) whoever. **la que gane pasará a la final** whoever wins will go to the final. (cualquiera) whichever. **compra la que sea más barata** buy whichever is cheaper

laberinto *m* labyrinth, maze
labia *f* gift of the gab
labio *m* lip
labor *f* work. ~**es de aguja** needlework. ~**es de ganchillo** crochet. ~**es de punto** knitting. ~**es domésticas** housework. ~**able** *a* working. ~**ar** *vi* work
laboratorio *m* laboratory
laborioso *a* laborious
laborista *a* Labour. ● *m & f* member of the Labour Party
labra|do *a* worked; *<madera>* carved; *<metal>* wrought; *<tierra>* ploughed. ~**dor** *m* farmer; (obrero) farm labourer. ~**nza** *f* farming. ~**r** *vt* work; carve *<madera>*; cut *<piedra>*; till *<la tierra>*. □ ~**rse** *vpr.* ~**rse un porvenir** carve out a future for o.s.
labriego *m* peasant
laca *f* lacquer
lacayo *m* lackey
lacio *a* straight; (flojo) limp
lacón *m* shoulder of pork
lacónico *a* laconic
lacr|ar *vt* seal. ~**e** *m* sealing wax
lactante *a* *<niño>* still on milk
lácteo *a* milky. **productos** *mpl* ~**s** dairy products
ladear *vt* tilt. □ ~**se** *vpr* lean
ladera *f* slope
ladino *a* astute

lado *m* side. **al** ~ near. **al** ~ **de** next to, beside. **de** ~ sideways. **en todos** ~**s** everywhere. **los de al** ~ the next door neighbours. **por otro** ~ on the other hand. **por todos** ~**s** everywhere. **por un** ~ on the one hand
ladr|ar *vi* bark. ~**ido** *m* bark
ladrillo *m* brick
ladrón *m* thief, robber; (de casas) burglar
lagart|ija *f* (small) lizard. ~**o** *m* lizard
lago *m* lake
lágrima *f* tear
lagrimoso *a* tearful
laguna *f* small lake; (fig, omisión) gap
laico *a* lay
lament|able *a* deplorable; (que da pena) pitiful; *<pérdida>* sad. ~**ar** *vt* be sorry about. □ ~**arse** *vpr* lament; (quejarse) complain. ~**o** *m* moan
lamer *vt* lick
lámina *f* sheet; (ilustración) plate; (estampa) picture card
lamina|do *a* laminated. ~**r** *vt* laminate
lámpara *f* lamp. ~ **de pie** standard lamp
lamparón *m* stain
lampiño *a* beardless; *<cuerpo>* hairless
lana *f* wool. **de** ~ wool(len)
lanceta *f* lancet
lancha *f* boat. ~ **motora** motor boat. ~ **salvavidas** lifeboat
langost|a *f* (de mar) lobster; (insecto) locust. ~**ino** *m* king prawn
languide|cer [11] *vi* languish. ~**z** *f* languor
lánguido *a* languid; (decaído) listless
lanilla *f* nap; (tela fina) flannel
lanudo *a* woolly; *<perro>* shaggy
lanza *f* lance, spear
lanza||llamas *m invar* flamethrower. ~**miento** *m* throw; (acción de lanzar) throwing; (de proyectil, de producto) launch. ~**miento de peso**, (LAm) ~**miento de bala** shot put. ~**r** [10] *vt* throw; (de un avión) drop; launch *<proyectil, producto>.* □ ~**rse** *vpr* throw o.s.
lapicero *m* (propelling) pencil

lápida f tombstone; (placa conmemorativa) memorial tablet

lapidar vt stone

lápiz m pencil. ~ **de labios** lipstick. a ~ in pencil

lapso m lapse

larg|a f. **a la** ~**a** in the long run. **dar** ~**as** put off. ~**ar** [12] vt (Naut) let out; (🔲, dar) give; 🔲 deal <bofetada etc>. □ ~**arse** vpr 🔲 beat it 🔲. ~**o** a long. ● m length. ¡~**o**! go away! **a lo** ~**o** lengthwise. **a lo** ~**o de** along. **tener 100 metros de** ~**o** be 100 metres long

laring|e f larynx. ~**itis** f laryngitis

larva f larva

las art def fpl the. véase tb LA. ● pron them. ~ **de** those, the ones. ~ **de Vd** your ones, yours. ~ **que** whoever, the ones

láser m laser

lástima f pity; (queja) complaint. **da** ~ **verlo así** it's sad to see him like that. **ella me da** ~ I feel sorry for her. ¡**qué** ~! what a pity!

lastim|ado a hurt. ~**ar** vt hurt. □ ~**arse** vpr hurt o.s. ~**ero** a doleful. ~**oso** a pitiful

lastre m ballast; (fig) burden

lata f tinplate; (envase) tin (esp Brit), can; (🔲, molestia) nuisance. **dar la** ~ be a nuisance. ¡**qué** ~! what a nuisance!

latente a latent

lateral a side, lateral

latido m beating; (cada golpe) beat

latifundio m large estate

latigazo m (golpe) lash; (chasquido) crack

látigo m whip

latín m Latin. **saber** ~ 🔲 know what's what 🔲

latino a Latin. **L**~**américa** f Latin America. ~**americano** a & m Latin American

latir vi beat; <herida> throb

latitud f latitude

latón m brass

latoso a annoying; (pesado) boring

laúd m lute

laureado a honoured; (premiado) prize-winning

laurel m laurel; (Culin) bay

lava f lava

lava|ble a washable. ~**bo** m washbasin; (retrete) toilet. ~**dero** m sink. ~**do** m washing. ~**do de cerebro** brainwashing. ~**do en seco** drycleaning. ~**dora** f washing machine. ~**ndería** f laundry. ~**ndería automática** launderette, laundromat (esp Amer). ~**platos** m & f invar dishwasher. ● m (Mex, fregadero) sink. ~**r** vt wash. ~**r en seco** dryclean. □ ~**rse** vpr have a wash. ~**rse las manos** (incl fig) wash one's hands. ~**tiva** f enema. ~**vajillas** m invar dishwasher; (detergente) washing-up liquid (Brit), dishwashing liquid (Amer)

laxante a & m laxative

lazada f bow

lazarillo m guide for a blind person

lazo m knot; (lazada) bow; (fig, vínculo) tie; (con nudo corredizo) lasso; (Mex, cuerda) rope

le pron (acusativo, él) him; (acusativo, Vd) you; (dativo, él) (to) him; (dativo, ella) (to) her; (dativo, cosa) (to) it; (dativo, Vd) (to) you

leal a loyal; (fiel) faithful. ~**tad** f loyalty; (fidelidad) faithfulness

lección f lesson

leche f milk; (golpe) bash. ~ **condensada** condensed milk. ~ **desnatada** skimmed milk. ~ **en polvo** powdered milk. ~ **sin desnatar** whole milk. **tener mala** ~ be spiteful. ~**ra** f (vasija) milk jug. ~**ría** f dairy. ~**ro** a milk, dairy. ● m milkman

lecho m (en literatura) bed. ~ **de río** river bed

lechoso a milky

lechuga f lettuce

lechuza f owl

lect|or m reader; (Univ) language assistant. ~**ura** f reading

leer [18] vt/i read

legación f legation

legado m legacy; (enviado) legate

legajo m bundle, file

legal a legal. ~**idad** f legality. ~**izar** [10] vt legalize; (certificar) authenticate. ~**mente** adv legally

legar [12] vt bequeath

legible *a* legible

legi|ón *f* legion. **~onario** *m* legionary

legisla|ción *f* legislation. **~dor** *m* legislator. **~r** *vi* legislate. **~tura** *f* term (of office); (año parlamentario) session; (LAm, cuerpo) legislature

leg|itimidad *f* legitimacy. **~ítimo** *a* legitimate; (verdadero) real

lego *a* lay; (ignorante) ignorant. ● *m* layman

legua *f* league

legumbre *f* vegetable

lejan|ía *f* distance. **~o** *a* distant

lejía *f* bleach

lejos *adv* far. **~ de** far from. **a lo ~** in the distance. **desde ~** from a distance, from afar

lema *m* motto

lencería *f* linen; (de mujer) lingerie

lengua *f* tongue; (idioma) language. **irse de la ~** talk too much. **morderse la ~** hold one's tongue

lenguado *m* sole

lenguaje *m* language

lengüeta *f* (de zapato) tongue. **~da** *f*, **~zo** *m* lick

lente *f* lens. **~s** *mpl* glasses. **~s de contacto** contact lenses

lentej|a *f* lentil. **~uela** *f* sequin

lentilla *f* contact lens

lent|itud *f* slowness. **~o** *a* slow

leñ|a *f* firewood. **~ador** *m* woodcutter. **~o** *m* log

Leo *m* Leo

le|ón *m* lion. **~ona** *f* lioness

leopardo *m* leopard

leotardo *m* thick tights

lepr|a *f* leprosy. **~oso** *m* leper

lerdo *a* dim; (torpe) clumsy

les *pron* (acusativo) them; (acusativo, Vds) you; (dativo) (to) them; (dativo, Vds) (to) you

lesbiana *f* lesbian

lesi|ón *f* wound. **~onado** *a* injured. **~onar** *vt* injure; (dañar) damage

letal *a* lethal

let|árgico *a* lethargic. **~argo** *m* lethargy

letr|a *f* letter; (escritura) handwriting; (de una canción) words, lyrics. **~a de** cambio bill of exchange. **~a de imprenta** print. **~ado** *a* learned. **~ero** *m* notice; (cartel) poster

letrina *f* latrine

leucemia *f* leukaemia

levadura *f* yeast. **~ en polvo** baking powder

levanta|miento *m* lifting; (sublevación) uprising. **~r** *vt* raise, lift; (construir) build; (recoger) pick up. □ **~rse** *vpr* get up; (ponerse de pie) stand up; (erguirse, sublevarse) rise up

levante *m* east; (viento) east wind

levar *vt*. **~ anclas** weigh anchor

leve *a* light; *<sospecha etc>* slight; *<enfermedad>* mild; (de poca importancia) trivial. **~dad** *f* lightness; (fig) slightness

léxico *m* vocabulary

lexicografía *f* lexicography

ley *f* law; (parlamentaria) act

leyenda *f* legend

liar [20] *vt* tie; (envolver) wrap up; roll *<cigarrillo>*; (fig, confundir) confuse; (fig, enredar) involve. □ **~se** *vpr* get involved

libanés *a & m* Lebanese

libelo *m* (escrito) libellous article; (Jurid) petition

libélula *f* dragonfly

libera|ción *f* liberation. **~dor** *a* liberating. ● *m* liberator

liberal *a & m & f* liberal. **~idad** *f* liberality

liber|ar *vt* free. **~tad** *f* freedom. **~tad de cultos** freedom of worship. **~tad de imprenta** freedom of the press. **~tad provisional** bail. **en ~tad** free. **~tador** *m* liberator. **~tar** *vt* free

libertino *m* libertine

libido *f* libido

libio *a & m* Libyan

libra *f* pound. **~ esterlina** pound sterling

Libra *m* Libra

libra|dor *m* (Com) drawer. **~r** *vt* free; (de un peligro) save. □ **~rse** *vpr* free o.s. **~rse de** get rid of

libre *a* free. **estilo ~** (en natación) freestyle. **~ de impuestos** tax-free

librea *f* livery

libr|ería f bookshop (Brit), bookstore (Amer); (mueble) bookcase. ~**ero** m bookseller; (Mex, mueble) bookcase. ~**eta** f notebook. ~**o** m book. ~**o de bolsillo** paperback. ~**o de ejercicios** exercise book. ~**o de reclamaciones** complaints book

licencia f permission; (documento) licence. ~**do** m graduate; (Mex, abogado) lawyer. ~ **para manejar** (Mex) driving licence. ~**r** vt (Mil) discharge; (echar) dismiss. ~**tura** f degree

licencioso a licentious

licitar vt bid for

lícito a legal; (permisible) permissible

licor m liquor; (dulce) liqueur

licua|dora f blender. ~**r** [21] liquefy; (Culin) blend

lid f fight. **en buena** ~ by fair means. ~**es** fpl matters

líder m leader

liderato m, **liderazgo** m leadership

lidia f bullfighting; (lucha) fight. ~**r** vt/i fight

liebre f hare

lienzo m linen; (del pintor) canvas; (muro, pared) wall

liga f garter; (alianza) league; (LAm, gomita) rubber band. ~**dura** f bond; (Mus) slur; (Med) ligature. ~**mento** m ligament. ~**r** [12] vt bind; (atar) tie; (Mus) slur. ● vi mix. ~**r con** (fig) pick up. □ ~**rse** vpr (fig) commit o.s.

liger|eza f lightness; (agilidad) agility; (rapidez) swiftness; (de carácter) fickleness. ~**o** a light; (rápido) quick; (ágil) agile; (superficial) superficial; (de poca importancia) slight. ● adv quickly. **a la ~a** lightly, superficially

liguero m suspender belt

lija f dogfish; (papel de lija) sandpaper. ~**r** vt sand

lila f lilac. ● m (color) lilac

lima f file; (fruta) lime. ~**duras** fpl filings. ~**r** vt file (down)

limita|ción f limitation. ~**do** a limited. ~**r** vt limit. ~**r con** border on. ~**tivo** a limiting

límite m limit. ~ **de velocidad** speed limit

limítrofe a bordering

lim|ón m lemon; (Mex) lime. ~**ona-da** f lemonade

limosn|a f alms. **pedir** ~**a** beg. ~**ear** vi beg

limpia|botas m invar bootblack. ~**parabrisas** m invar windscreen wiper (Brit), windshield wiper (Amer). ~**pipas** m invar pipe-cleaner. ~**r** vt clean; (enjugar) wipe. ~**vidrios** m invar (LAm) window cleaner.

limpi|eza f cleanliness; (acción de limpiar) cleaning. ~**eza en seco** dry-cleaning. ~**o** a clean; <cielo> clear; (fig, honrado) honest; (neto) net. **pasar a** ~**o**, (LAm) **pasar en** ~**o** make a fair copy. ● adv fairly. **jugar** ~**o** play fair

linaje m lineage; (fig, clase) kind

lince m lynx

linchar vt lynch

lind|ar vi border (**con** on). ~**e** f boundary. ~**ero** m border

lindo a pretty, lovely. **de lo** ~ 🄳 a lot

línea f line. **en** ~**s generales** broadly speaking. **guardar la** ~ watch one's figure

lingote m ingot

lingü|ista m & f linguist. ~**ística** f linguistics. ~**ístico** a linguistic

lino m flax; (tela) linen

linterna f lantern; (de bolsillo) torch, flashlight (Amer)

lío m bundle; (jaleo) fuss; (embrollo) muddle; (amorío) affair

liquida|ción f liquidation; (venta especial) sale. ~**r** vt liquify; (Com) liquidate; settle <cuenta>

líquido a liquid; (Com) net. ● m liquid; (Com) cash

lira f lyre; (moneda italiana) lira

líric|a f lyric poetry. ~**o** a lyric(al)

lirio m iris

lirón m dormouse; (fig) sleepyhead. **dormir como un** ~ sleep like a log

lisiado a crippled

liso a smooth; <pelo> straight; <tierra> flat; (sencillo) plain

lisonj|a f flattery. ~**eador** a flattering. ● m flatterer. ~**ear** vt flatter. ~**ero** a flattering

lista f stripe; (enumeración) list. ~ **de correos** poste restante. **a** ~**s** striped.

pasar ∼ take the register. **∼do** *a* striped

listo *a* clever; (preparado) ready

listón *m* strip; (en saltos) bar; (Mex, cinta) ribbon

litera *f* (en barco, tren) berth; (en habitación) bunk bed

literal *a* literal

litera|rio *a* literary. **∼tura** *f* literature

litig|ar [12] *vi* dispute; (Jurid) litigate. **∼io** *m* dispute; (Jurid) litigation

litografía *f* (arte) lithography; (cuadro) lithograph

litoral *a* coastal. ● *m* coast

litro *m* litre

lituano *a & m* Lithuanian

liturgia *f* liturgy

liviano *a* fickle; (LAm, de poco peso) light

lívido *a* livid

llaga *f* wound; (úlcera) ulcer

llama *f* flame; (animal) llama

llamada *f* call

llama|do *a* called. ● *m* (LAm) call. **∼miento** *m* call. **∼r** *vt* call; (por teléfono) phone. ● *vi* call; (golpear en la puerta) knock; (tocar el timbre) ring. **∼r por teléfono** phone, telephone. □ **∼rse** *vpr* be called. **¿cómo te ∼s?** what's your name?

llamarada *f* sudden blaze; (fig, de pasión etc) outburst

llamativo *a* flashy; <*color*> loud; <*persona*> striking

llamear *vi* blaze

llano *a* flat, level; <*persona*> natural; (sencillo) plain. ● *m* plain

llanta *f* (Auto) (wheel) rim; (LAm, neumático) tyre

llanto *m* crying

llanura *f* plain

llave *f* key; (para tuercas) spanner; (LAm, del baño etc) tap (Brit), faucet (Amer); (Elec) switch. **∼ inglesa** monkey wrench. **cerrar con ∼** lock. **echar la ∼** lock up. **∼ro** *m* key-ring

llega|da *f* arrival. **∼r** [12] *vi* arrive, come; (alcanzar) reach; (bastar) be enough. **∼r a** (conseguir) manage to. **∼r a saber** find out. **∼r a ser** become. **∼r hasta** go as far as

llen|ar *vt* fill (up); (rellenar) fill in; (cubrir) cover (**de** with). **∼o** *a* full. ● *m* (en el teatro etc) full house. **de ∼** entirely

lleva|dero *a* tolerable. **∼r** *vt* carry; (inducir, conducir) lead; (acompañar) take; wear <*ropa*>. **¿cuánto tiempo ∼s aquí?** how long have you been here? **llevo 3 años estudiando inglés** I've been studying English for 3 years. □ **∼rse** *vpr* take away; win <*premio etc*>; (comprar) take. **∼rse bien** get on well together

llor|ar *vi* cry; <*ojos*> water. **∼iquear** *vi* whine. **∼iqueo** *m* whining. **∼o** *m* crying. **∼ón** *a* whining. ● *m* crybaby. **∼oso** *a* tearful

llov|er [2] *vi* rain. **∼izna** *f* drizzle. **∼iznar** *vi* drizzle

llueve *vb* ⇒LLOVER

lluvi|a *f* rain; (fig) shower. **∼oso** *a* rainy; <*clima*> wet

lo *art def neutro.* ∼ **importante** what is important, the important thing. ● *pron* (él) him; (cosa) it. ∼ **que** what, that which

loa *f* praise. **∼ble** *a* praiseworthy. **∼r** *vt* praise

lobo *m* wolf

lóbrego *a* gloomy

lóbulo *m* lobe

local *a* local. ● *m* premises. **∼idad** *f* locality; (de un espectáculo) seat; (entrada) ticket. **∼izar** [10] *vt* find, locate

loción *f* lotion

loco *a* mad, crazy. ● *m* lunatic. ∼ **de alegría** mad with joy. **estar ∼ por** be crazy about. **volverse ∼** go mad

locomo|ción *f* locomotion. **∼tora** *f* locomotive

locuaz *a* talkative

locución *f* expression

locura *f* madness; (acto) crazy thing. **con ∼** madly

locutor *m* broadcaster

lod|azal *m* quagmire. **∼o** *m* mud

lógic|a *f* logic. **∼o** *a* logical

logr|ar *vt* get; win <*premio*>. ∼ **hacer** manage to do. **∼o** *m* achievement; (de premio) winning; (éxito) success

loma *f* small hill

lombriz *f* worm

lomo *m* back; (de libro) spine. ~ **de cerdo** loin of pork

lona *f* canvas

loncha *f* slice; (de tocino) rasher

londinense *a* from London. ● *m* Londoner

Londres *m* London

loneta *f* thin canvas

longaniza *f* sausage

longev|idad *f* longevity. ~**o** *a* long-lived

longitud *f* length; (Geog) longitude

lonja *f* slice; (de tocino) rasher; (Com) market

lord *m* (*pl* **lores**) lord

loro *m* parrot

los *art def mpl* the. *véase tb* EL. ● *pron* them. ~ **de Antonio** Antonio's. ~ **que** whoever, the ones

losa *f* (baldosa) flagstone. ~ **sepulcral** tombstone

lote *m* share; (de productos) batch; (terreno) plot (Brit), lot (Amer)

lotería *f* lottery

loto *m* lotus

loza *f* crockery; (fina) china

lozano *a* fresh; <*vegetación*> lush; <*persona*> healthy-looking

lubrica|nte *a* lubricating. ● *m* lubricant. ~**r** [7] *vt* lubricate

lucero *m* bright star. ~ **del alba** morning star

lucha *f* fight; (fig) struggle. ~**dor** *m* fighter. ~**r** *vi* fight; (fig) struggle

lucid|ez *f* lucidity. ~**o** *a* splendid

lúcido *a* lucid

luciérnaga *f* glow-worm

lucimiento *m* brilliance

lucir [11] *vt* (fig) show off. ● *vi* shine; <*joya*> sparkle; (LAm, mostrarse) look. □ ~**se** *vpr* (fig) shine, excel; (presumir) show off

lucr|ativo *a* lucrative. ~**o** *m* gain

luego *adv* then; (más tarde) later (on); (Mex, pronto) soon. ● *conj* therefore. ~ **que** as soon as. **desde** ~ of course

lugar *m* place; (espacio libre) room. ~ **común** cliché. **dar** ~ **a** give rise to. **en** ~ **de** instead of. **en primer** ~ first. **hacer** ~ make room. **tener** ~ take place. ~**eño** *a* local, village

lugarteniente *m* deputy

lúgubre *a* gloomy

lujo *m* luxury. **de** ~ luxury. ~**so** *a* luxurious

lujuria *f* lust

lumbago *m* lumbago

lumbre *f* fire; (luz) light

luminoso *a* luminous; (fig) bright; <*letrero*> illuminated

luna *f* moon; (espejo) mirror. ~ **de miel** honeymoon. **claro de** ~ moonlight. **estar en la** ~ be miles away. ~**r** *a* lunar. ● *m* mole; (en tela) spot

lunes *m invar* Monday

lupa *f* magnifying glass

lustr|abotas *m invar* (LAm) bootblack. ~**ar** *vt* shine, polish. ~**e** *m* shine; (fig, esplendor) splendour. **dar** ~**e a**, **sacar** ~**e a** polish. ~**oso** *a* shining

luto *m* mourning. **estar de** ~ be in mourning

luz *f* light; (electricidad) electricity. **luces altas** (LAm) headlights on full beam. **luces bajas** (LAm), **luces cortas** dipped headlights. **luces antiniebla** fog light. **luces largas** headlights on full beam. **a la** ~ **de** in the light of. **a todas luces** obviously. **dar a** ~ give birth. **hacer la** ~ **sobre** shed light on. **sacar a la** ~ bring to light

Mm

macabro *a* macabre

macaco *m* macaque (monkey)

macanudo *a* 🅵 great🅵

macarrones *mpl* macaroni

macerar *vt* macerate <*fruta*>; marinade <*carne etc*>

maceta *f* mallet; (tiesto) flowerpot

machacar [7] *vt* crush. ● *vi* go on (**sobre** about)

machamartillo. **a** ~ *adj* ardent; (como adv) firmly

machet|azo *m* blow with a machete; (herida) wound from a machete. ~**e** *m* machete

mach|ista *m* male chauvinist. **~o** *a* male; (varonil) macho

machu|car [7] *vt* bruise; (aplastar) crush. **~cón** *m* (LAm) bruise

macizo *a* solid. ● *m* mass; (de plantas) bed

madeja *f* skein

madera *m* (vino) Madeira. ● *f* wood; (naturaleza) nature. **~ble** *a* yielding timber. **~men** *m* woodwork

madero *m* log; (de construcción) timber

madona *f* Madonna

madr|astra *f* stepmother. **~e** *f* mother. **~eperla** *f* mother-of-pearl. **~eselva** *f* honeysuckle

madrigal *m* madrigal

madriguera *f* den; (de conejo) burrow

madrileño *a* of Madrid. ● *m* person from Madrid

madrina *f* godmother; (en una boda) matron of honour

madrug|ada *f* dawn. de **~ada** at dawn. **~ador** *a* who gets up early. ● *m* early riser. **~ar** [12] *vi* get up early

madur|ación *f* maturing; (de fruta) ripening. **~ar** *vt/i* mature; *<fruta>* ripen. **~ez** *f* maturity; (de fruta) ripeness. **~o** *a* mature; *<fruta>* ripe

maestr|ía *f* skill; (Univ) master's degree. **~o** *m* master; (de escuela) schoolteacher

mafia *f* mafia

magdalena *f* fairy cake (Brit), cup cake (Amer)

magia *f* magic

mágico *a* magic; (maravilloso) magical

magist|erio *m* teaching (profession); (conjunto de maestros) teachers. **~rado** *m* magistrate; (juez) judge. **~ral** *a* teaching; (bien hecho) masterly. **~ratura** *f* magistracy

magn|animidad *f* magnanimity. **~ánimo** *a* magnanimous. **~ate** *m* magnate, tycoon

magnavoz *m* (Mex) megaphone

magnético *a* magnetic

magneti|smo *m* magnetism. **~zar** [10] *vt* magnetize

magn|ificar *vt* extol; (LAm) magnify *<objeto>*. **~ificencia** *f* magnificence. **~ífico** *a* magnificent. **~itud** *f* magnitude

magnolia *f* magnolia

mago *m* magician; (en cuentos) wizard

magro *a* lean; *<tierra>* poor

magulla|dura *f* bruise. **~r** *vt* bruise. □ **~rse** *vpr* bruise

mahometano *a* Islamic

maíz *m* maize, corn (Amer)

majada *f* sheepfold; (estiércol) manure; (LAm) flock of sheep

majader|ía *f* silly thing. **~o** *m* idiot. ● *a* stupid

majest|ad *f* majesty. **~uoso** *a* majestic

majo *a* nice

mal *adv* badly; (poco) poorly; (difícilmente) hardly; (equivocadamente) wrongly; (desagradablemente) bad. ● *a*. estar **~** be ill; (anímicamente) be in a bad way; (incorrecto) be wrong. estar **~ de** (escaso de) be short of. *véase tb* MALO. ● *m* evil; (daño) harm; (enfermedad) illness. **~ que bien** somehow (or other). de **~ en peor** from bad to worse. hacer **~** en be wrong to. ¡menos **~**! thank goodness!

malabaris|mo *m* juggling. **~ta** *m* & *f* juggler

mala|consejado *a* ill-advised. **~costumbrado** *a* spoilt. **~crianza** *f* (LAm) rudeness. **~gradecido** *a* ungrateful

malagueño *a* of Málaga. ● *m* person from Málaga

malaria *f* malaria

Malasia *f* Malaysia

malavenido *a* incompatible

malaventura *a* unfortunate

malayo *a* Malay(an)

malbaratar *vt* sell off cheap; (malgastar) squander

malcarado *a* nasty looking

malcriado *a* *<niño>* spoilt

maldad *f* evil; (acción) wicked thing

maldecir [46] (*pero imperativo* **maldice**, *futuro y condicional regulares, pp* **maldecido** *o* **maldito**) *vt* curse. ● *vi* curse; speak ill (**de** of)

maldi|ciente *a* backbiting; (que blasfema) foul-mouthed. **~ción** *f* curse. **~to** *a* damned. ¡**~to sea!** damn (it)!

maleab|ilidad *f* malleability. **~le** *a* malleable

malea|nte *m* criminal. **~r** *vt* damage; (pervertir) corrupt. □ **~rse** *vpr* be spoilt; (pervertirse) be corrupted

malecón *m* breakwater; (embarcadero) jetty; (Rail) embankment; (LAm, paseo marítimo) seafront

maledicencia *f* slander

mal|eficio *m* curse. **~éfico** *a* evil

malestar *m* discomfort; (fig) uneasiness

malet|a *f* (suit)case. **hacer la ~a** pack (one's case). **~ero** *m* porter; (Auto) boot, trunk (Amer). **~ín** *m* small case; (para documentos) briefcase

mal|evolencia *f* malevolence. **~évolo** *a* malevolent

maleza *f* weeds; (matorral) undergrowth

mal|gastar *vt* waste. **~hablado** *a* foul-mouthed. **~hechor** *m* criminal. **~humorado** *a* bad-tempered

malici|a *f* malice; (picardía) mischief. □ **~arse** *vpr* suspect. **~oso** *a* malicious; (pícaro) mischievous

maligno *a* malignant; *<persona>* evil

malintencionado *a* malicious

malla *f* mesh; (de armadura) mail; (de gimnasia) leotard

Mallorca *f* Majorca.

mallorquín *a* & *m* Majorcan

malmirado *a* (con estar) frowned upon

malo *a* (*delante de nombre masculino en singular* **mal**) bad; (enfermo) ill. **~ de** difficult to. **estar de malas** (malhumorado) be in a bad mood; (LAm, con mala suerte) be out of luck. **lo ~ es que** the trouble is that. **por las malas** by force

malogr|ar *vt* waste; (estropear) spoil. □ **~arse** *vpr* fall through

maloliente *a* smelly

malpensado *a* nasty, malicious

malsano *a* unhealthy

malsonante *a* ill-sounding; (grosero) offensive

malt|a *f* malt. **~eada** *f* (LAm) milk shake. **~ear** *vt* malt

maltr|atar *vt* ill-treat; (pegar) batter; mistreat *<juguete etc>*. **~echo** *a* battered

malucho *a* 🅳 under the weather

malva *f* mallow. (color de) **~** *a invar* mauve

malvado *a* wicked

malvavisco *m* marshmallow

malversa|ción *f* embezzlement. **~dor** *a* embezzling. ● *m* embezzler. **~r** *vt* embezzle

Malvinas *fpl.* **las (islas) ~** the Falklands, the Falkland Islands

mama *f* mammary gland; (de mujer) breast

mamá *f* mum; (usado por niños) mummy

mama|da *f* sucking. **~r** *vt* suck; (fig) grow up with. ● *vi <bebé>* feed; *<animal>* suckle. **dar de ~** breastfeed

mamario *a* mammary

mamarracho *m* clown; (cosa ridícula) (ridiculous) sight; (cosa mal hecha) botch; (cosa fea) mess. **ir hecho un ~** look a sight

mameluco *m* (LAm) overalls; (de niño) rompers

mamífero *a* mammalian. ● *m* mammal

mamila *f* (Mex) feeding bottle

mamotreto *m* (libro) hefty volume; (armatoste) huge thing

mampara *f* screen

mampostería *f* masonry

mamut *m* mammoth

manada *f* herd; (de lobos) pack; (de leones) pride. **en ~** in crowds

mana|ntial *m* spring; (fig) source. **~r** *vi* flow; (fig) abound. ● *vt* drip with

manaza *f* big hand

mancha *f* stain; (en la piel) blotch. **~do** *a* stained; (sucio) dirty; *<animal>* spotted. **~r** *vt* stain; (ensuciar) dirty. □ **~rse** *vpr* get stained; (ensuciarse) get dirty

manchego *a* of la Mancha. ● *m* person from la Mancha

manchón *m* large stain

mancilla *f* blemish. ∼**r** *vt* stain

manco *a* (de una mano) one-handed; (de las dos manos) handless; (de un brazo) one-armed; (de los dos brazos) armless

mancomun|adamente *adv* jointly. ∼**ar** *vt* unite; (Jurid) make jointly liable. □ ∼**arse** *vpr* unite. ∼**idad** *f* union

manda *f* (Mex) religious offering

manda|dero *m* messenger. ∼**do** *m* (LAm) shopping; (diligencia) errand. **hacer los** ∼**dos** (LAm) do the shopping. ∼**miento** *m* order; (Relig) commandment. ∼**r** *vt* order; (enviar) send; (gobernar) rule. ● *vi* be in command. **¿mande?** (Mex) pardon?

mandarin|a *f* (naranja) mandarin (orange). ∼**o** *m* mandarin tree

mandat|ario *m* attorney; (Pol) head of state. ∼**o** *m* mandate; (Pol) term of office

mandíbula *f* jaw

mando *m* command. ∼ **a distancia** remote control. **al** ∼ **de** in charge of. **altos** ∼**s** *mpl* high-ranking officers

mandolina *f* mandolin

mandón *a* bossy

manducar [7] *vt* 🄳 stuff oneself with

manecilla *f* hand

manej|able *a* manageable. ∼**ar** *vt* use; handle *<asunto etc>*; (fig) manage; (LAm, conducir) drive. □ ∼**arse** *vpr* get by. ∼**o** *m* handling. ∼**os** *mpl* scheming

manera *f* way. ∼**s** *fpl* manners. **de alguna** ∼ somehow. **de** ∼ **que** so (that). **de ninguna** ∼ by no means. **de otra** ∼ otherwise. **de todas** ∼**s** anyway

manga *f* sleeve; (tubo de goma) hose; (red) net; (para colar) filter; (LAm, de langostas) swarm

mango *m* handle; (fruta) mango. ∼**near** *vt* boss about. ● *vi* (entrometerse) interfere

manguera *f* hose(pipe)

manguito *m* muff

maní *m* (*pl* ∼**es**) (LAm) peanut

manía *f* mania; (antipatía) dislike. **tener la** ∼ **de** have an obsession with

maniaco *a*, **maníaco** *a* maniac (al). ● *m* maniac

maniatar *vt* tie s.o.'s hands

maniático *a* maniac(al); (obsesivo) obsessive; (loco) crazy; (delicado) finicky

manicomio *m* lunatic asylum

manicura *f* manicure; (mujer) manicurist

manido *a* stale

manifesta|ción *f* manifestation, sign; (Pol) demonstration. ∼**nte** *m* demonstrator. ∼**r** [1] *vt* show; (Pol) state. □ ∼**rse** *vpr* show; (Pol) demonstrate

manifiesto *a* clear; *<error>* obvious; *<verdad>* manifest. ● *m* manifesto

manilargo *a* light-fingered

manilla *f* (de cajón etc) handle; (de reloj) hand. ∼**r** *m* handlebar(s)

maniobra *f* manoeuvre. ∼**r** *vt* operate; (Rail) shunt. ● *vt/i* manoeuvre. ∼**s** *fpl* (Mil) manoeuvres

manipula|ción *f* manipulation. ∼**r** *vt* manipulate

maniquí *m* dummy. ● *m & f* model

mani|rroto *a & m* spendthrift. ∼**ta** *f*, (LAm) ∼**to** *m* little hand

manivela *f* crank

manjar *m* delicacy

mano *f* hand; (de animales) front foot; (de perros, gatos) front paw. ∼ **de obra** work force. ∼**s arriba!** hands up! **a** ∼ by hand; (próximo) handy. **a** ∼ **derecha** on the right. **de segunda** ∼ second hand. **echar una** ∼ lend a hand. **tener buena** ∼ **para** be good at. ● *m* (LAm, 🄳) mate (Brit), buddy (Amer)

manojo *m* bunch

manose|ar *vt* handle. ∼**o** *m* handling

manotada *f*, **manotazo** *m* slap

manote|ar *vi* gesticulate. ∼**o** *m* gesticulation

mansalva: **a** ∼ *adv* without risk

mansarda *f* attic

mansión *f* mansion. ∼ **señorial** stately home

manso *a* gentle; *<animal>* tame

manta *f* blanket

mantec|a *f* fat. ∼**oso** *a* greasy

mantel *m* tablecloth; (del altar) altar cloth. ~**ería** *f* table linen

manten|er [40] *vt* support; (conservar) keep; (sostener) maintain. □ ~**erse** *vpr* support o.s.; (permanecer) remain. ~**se de/con** live off. ~**imiento** *m* maintenance

mantequ|era *f* butter churn. ~**illa** *f* butter

mant|illa *f* mantilla. ~**o** *m* cloak. ~**ón** *m* shawl

manual *a & m* manual

manubrio *m* crank; (LAm, de bicicleta) handlebars

manufactura *f* manufacture. ~**r** *vt* manufacture, make

manuscrito *a* handwritten. ● *m* manuscript

manutención *f* maintenance

manzana *f* apple; (de edificios) block. ~ **de Adán** (LAm) Adam's apple. ~**r** *m* (apple) orchard

manzan|illa *f* camomile tea. ● *m* manzanilla, pale dry sherry. ~**o** *m* apple tree

maña *f* skill. ~**s** *fpl* cunning

mañan|a *f* morning. ~**a por la** ~**a** tomorrow morning. **pasado** ~**a** the day after tomorrow. **en la** ~**a** (LAm), **por la** ~**a** in the morning. ● *m* future. ● *adv* tomorrow. ~**ero** *a* who gets up early. ● *m* early riser

mañoso *a* clever; (astuto) crafty; (LAm, caprichoso) difficult

mapa *m* map

mapache *m* racoon

maqueta *f* scale model

maquiladora *f* (Mex) cross-border assembly plant

maquilla|je *m* make-up. ~**r** *vt* make up. □ ~**rse** *vpr* make up

máquina *f* machine; (Rail) engine. ~ **de afeitar** shaver. ~ **de escribir** typewriter. ~ **fotográfica** camera

maquin|ación *f* machination. ~**al** *a* mechanical. ~**aria** *f* machinery. ~**ista** *m & f* operator; (Rail) engine driver

mar *m & f* sea. **alta** ~ high seas. **la** ~ **de** 🆃 lots of

maraña *f* thicket; (enredo) tangle; (embrollo) muddle

maratón *m & f* marathon

maravill|a *f* wonder. **a las mil** ~**as**, **de** ~**as** marvellously. **contar/decir** ~**as de** speak wonderfully of. **hacer** ~**as** work wonders. ~**ar** *vt* astonish. □ ~**arse** *vpr* be astonished (**de** at). ~**oso** *a* marvellous, wonderful

marca *f* mark; (de coches etc) make; (de alimentos, cosméticos) brand; (Deportes) record. ~ **de fábrica** trade mark. **de** ~ brand name; (fig) excellent. **de** ~ **mayor** 🆃 absolute. ~**do** *a* marked. ~**dor** *m* marker; (Deportes) scoreboard. ~**r** [7] *vt* mark; (señalar) show; score *<un gol>*; dial *<número de teléfono>*. ● *vi* score

marcha *f* (incl Mus) march; (Auto) gear; (desarrollo) course; (partida) departure. **a toda** ~ at full speed. **dar/hacer** ~ **atrás** put into reverse. **poner en** ~ start; (fig) set in motion

marchante *m* (*f* **marchanta**) art dealer; (Mex, en mercado) stall holder

marchar *vi* go; (funcionar) work, go; (Mil) march. □ ~**se** *vpr* leave

marchit|ar *vt* wither. □ ~**arse** *vpr* wither. ~**o** *a* withered

marcial *a* martial

marciano *a & m* Martian

marco *m* frame; (moneda alemana) mark; (deportes) goal-posts

marea *f* tide. ~**do** *a* sick; (en el mar) seasick; (aturdido) dizzy; (borracho) drunk. ~**r** *vt* make feel sick; (aturdir) make feel dizzy; (confundir) confuse. □ ~**rse** *vpr* feel sick; (en un barco) get seasick; (estar aturdido) feel dizzy; (irse la cabeza) feel faint; (emborracharse) get slightly drunk; (confundirse) get confused

marejada *f* swell; (fig) wave

mareo *m* sickness; (en el mar) seasickness; (aturdimiento) dizziness; (confusión) muddle

marfil *m* ivory

margarina *f* margarine

margarita *f* daisy; (cóctel) margarita

marg|en *m* margin; (de un camino) side. ● *f* (de un río) bank. ~**inado** *a* excluded. ● *m* outcast. **al** ~**en** (fig) outside. ~**inal** *a* marginal. ~**inar** *vt* (excluir) exclude; (fijar márgenes) set margins

mariachi *m* (Mex) (música popular de Jalisco) Mariachi music; (conjunto) Mariachi band; (músico) Mariachi musician

maric|a *m* 🔲 sissy 🔲. ~**ón** *m* 🔲 homosexual, queer 🔲; (LAm, cobarde) wimp

marido *m* husband

mariguana *f*, **marihuana** *f* marijuana

marimacho *f* mannish woman

marimba *f* (type of) drum (LAm, especie de xilofón) marimba

marin|a *f* navy; (barcos) fleet; (cuadro) seascape. ~**a de guerra** navy. ~**a mercante** merchant navy. ~**ería** *f* seamanship; (marineros) sailors. ~**ero** *a* marine; <*barco*> seaworthy. ● *m* sailor. **a la** ~**era** in tomato and garlic sauce. ~**o** *a* marine

marioneta *f* puppet. ~**s** *fpl* puppet show

maripos|a *f* butterfly. ~**a nocturna** moth. ~**ear** *vi* be fickle; (galantear) flirt. ~**ón** *m* flirt

mariquita *f* ladybird (Brit), ladybug (Amer). ● *m* 🔲 sissy 🔲

mariscador *m* shell-fisher

mariscal *m* marshal

maris|car *vt* fish for shellfish. ~**co** *m* seafood, shellfish. ~**quero** *m* (pescador de mariscos) seafood fisherman; (vendedor de mariscos) seafood seller

marital *a* marital; <*vida*> married

marítimo *a* maritime; <*ciudad etc*> coastal, seaside

marmita *f* cooking pot

mármol *m* marble

marmota *f* marmot

maroma *f* rope; (Mex, voltereta) somersault

marqu|és *m* marquess. ~**esa** *f* marchioness. ~**esina** *f* glass canopy; (en estadio) roof

marran|a *f* sow. ~**ada** *f* filthy thing; (cochinada) dirty trick. ~**o** *a* filthy. ● *m* hog

marrón *a & m* brown

marroqu|í *a & m & f* Moroccan. ● *m* (leather) morocco. ~**inería** *f* leather goods

Marruecos *m* Morocco

marsopa *f* porpoise

marsupial *a & m* marsupial

marta *f* marten

martajar *vt* (Mex) crush <*maíz*>

Marte *m* Mars

martes *m invar* Tuesday. ~ **de carnaval** Shrove Tuesday

martill|ar *vt* hammer. ~**azo** *m* blow with a hammer. ~**ear** *vt* hammer. ~**eo** *m* hammering. ~**o** *m* hammer

martín pescador *m* kingfisher

martinete *m* (del piano) hammer; (ave) heron

martingala *f* (ardid) trick

mártir *m & f* martyr

martir|io *m* martyrdom; (fig) torment. ~**izar** [10] *vt* martyr; (fig) torment, torture

marxis|mo *m* Marxism. ~**ta** *a & m & f* Marxist

marzo *m* March

más *adv & a* (comparativo) more; (superlativo) most. ~ **caro** dearer. ~ **doloroso** more painful. **el** ~ **caro** the dearest; (de dos) the dearer. **el** ~ **curioso** the most curious; (de dos) the more curious. ● *prep* plus. ● *m* plus (sign). ~ **bien** rather. ~ **de** (cantidad indeterminada) more than. ~ **o menos** more or less. ~ **que** more than. ~ **y** ~ more and more. **a lo** ~ at (the) most. **dos** ~ **dos** two plus two. **de** ~ too many. **es** ~ moreover. **nadie** ~ nobody else. **no** ~ no more

masa *f* mass; (Culin) dough. **en** ~ en masse

masacre *f* massacre

masaj|e *m* massage. ~**ear** *vt* massage. ~**ista** *m* masseur. ● *f* masseuse

mascada *f* (Mex) scarf

mascar [7] *vt* chew

máscara *f* mask

mascar|ada *f* masquerade. ~**illa** *f* mask. ~**ón** *m* (Naut) figurehead

mascota *f* mascot

masculin|idad f masculinity. ～**o** a masculine; <*sexo*> male. ● m masculine

mascullar [3] vt mumble

masilla f putty

masivo a massive, large-scale

mas|ón m Freemason. ～**onería** f Freemasonry. ～**ónico** a Masonic

masoquis|mo m masochism. ～**ta** a masochistic. ● m & f masochist

mastica|ción f chewing. ～**r** [7] vt chew

mástil m (Naut) mast; (de bandera) flagpole; (de guitarra, violín) neck

mastín m mastiff

mastodonte m mastodon; (fig) giant

masturba|ción f masturbation. □ ～**rse** vpr masturbate

mata f (arbusto) bush; (LAm, planta) plant

matad|ero m slaughterhouse. ～**or** a killing. ● m (torero) matador

matamoscas m invar fly swatter

mata|nza f killing. ～**r** vt kill <*personas*>; slaughter <*reses*>. ～**rife** m butcher. □ ～**rse** vpr kill o.s.; (en un accidente) be killed; (Mex, para un examen) cram. ～**rse trabajando** work like mad

mata|polillas m invar moth killer. ～**rratas** m invar rat poison

matasanos m invar quack

matasellos m invar postmark

mate a matt. ● m (ajedrez) (check) mate (LAm, bebida) maté

matemátic|as fpl mathematics, maths (Brit), math (Amer). ～**o** a mathematical. ● m mathematician

materia f matter; (material) material; (LAm, asignatura) subject. ～ **prima** raw material. **en** ～ **de** on the question of

material a & m material. ～**idad** f material nature. ～**ismo** m materialism. ～**ista** a materialistic. ● m & f materialist; (Mex, constructor) building contractor. ～**izar** [10] vt materialize. □ ～**izarse** vpr materialize. ～**mente** adv materially; (absolutamente) absolutely

matern|al a maternal; <*amor*> motherly. ～**idad** f motherhood; (hospital) maternity hospital; (sala) maternity ward. ～**o** a motherly; <*lengua*> mother

matin|al a morning. ～**ée** m matinée

matiz m shade; (fig) nuance. ～**ación** f combination of colours. ～**ar** [10] vt blend <*colores*>; (introducir variedad) vary; (teñir) tinge (**de** with)

mat|ón m bully; (de barrio) thug. ～**onismo** m bullying; (de barrio) thuggery

matorral m scrub; (conjunto de matas) thicket

matraca f rattle. **dar** ～ pester

matraz m flask

matriarca f matriarch. ～**do** m matriarchy. ～**l** a matriarchal

matr|ícula f (lista) register, list; (inscripción) registration; (Auto) registration number; (placa) licence plate. ～**icular** vt register. □ ～**icularse** vpr enrol, register

matrimoni|al a matrimonial. ～**o** m marriage; (pareja) married couple

matriz f matrix; (molde) mould; (Anat) womb, uterus

matrona f matron; (partera) midwife

matutino a morning

maull|ar vi miaow. ～**ido** m miaow

mausoleo m mausoleum

maxilar a maxillary. ● m jaw(bone)

máxim|a f maxim. ～**e** adv especially. ～**o** a maximum; <*punto*> highest. ● m maximum

maya f daisy. ● a Mayan. ● m & f (persona) Maya

mayo m May

mayonesa f mayonnaise

mayor a (más grande, comparativo) bigger; (más grande, superlativo) biggest; (de edad, comparativo) older; (de edad, superlativo) oldest; (adulto) grown-up; (principal) main, major; (Mus) major. ● m & f (adulto) adult. **al por** ～ wholesale. ～**al** m foreman. ～**azgo** m entailed estate

mayordomo m butler

mayor|ía f majority. ~**ista** m & f wholesaler. ~**itario** a majority; <socio> principal. ~**mente** adv especially

mayúscul|a f capital (letter). ~**o** a capital; (fig, grande) big

mazacote m hard mass

mazapán m marzipan

mazmorra f dungeon

mazo m mallet; (manojo) bunch; (LAm, de naipes) pack (Brit), deck (Amer)

mazorca f cob. ~ **de maíz** corncob

me pron (acusativo) me; (dativo) (to) me; (reflexivo) (to) myself

mecánic|a f mechanics. ~**o** a mechanical. ● m mechanic

mecani|smo m mechanism. ~**zación** f mechanization. ~**zar** [10] vt mechanize

mecanograf|ía f typing. ~**iado** a typed, typewritten. ~**iar** [20] vt type

mecanógrafo m typist

mecate m (Mex) string; (más grueso) rope

mecedora f rocking chair

mecenas m & f invar patron

mecer [9] vt rock; swing <columpio>. □ ~**se** vpr rock; (en un columpio) swing

mecha f (de vela) wick; (de explosivo) fuse. ~**s** fpl highlights

mechar vt stuff, lard

mechero m (cigarette) lighter

mechón m (de pelo) lock

medall|a f medal. ~**ón** m medallion; (relicario) locket

media f stocking; (promedio) average. **a** ~**s** half each

mediación f mediation

mediado a half full; (a mitad de) halfway through. ~**s** mpl. **a** ~**s de marzo** in mid-March

mediador m mediator

medialuna f (pl **medialunas**) croissant

median|amente adv fairly. ~**a** f (Auto) central reservation (Brit), median strip (Amer). ~**era** f party wall. ~**ero** a <muro> party. ~**o** a medium; (mediocre) average, mediocre

medianoche f (pl **mediasnoches**) midnight; (Culin) type of roll

mediante prep through, by means of

mediar vi mediate; (llegar a la mitad) be halfway through; (interceder) intercede (por for)

medic|ación f medication. ~**amento** m medicine. ~**ina** f medicine. ~**inal** a medicinal

medición f measurement

médico a medical. ● m doctor. ~ **de cabecera** GP, general practitioner

medid|a f measurement; (unidad) measure; (disposición) measure, step; (prudencia) moderation. **a la** ~**a** made to measure. **a** ~**a que** as. **en cierta** ~**a** to a certain extent. ~**or** m (LAm) meter

medieval a medieval. ~**ista** m & f medievalist

medio a half (a); (mediano) average. **dos horas y media** two and a half hours. ~ **litro** half a litre. **las dos y media** half past two. ● m middle; (Math) half; (manera) means; (en deportes) half(-back). **en** ~ in the middle (de of). **por** ~ **de** through. ~ **ambiente** m environment

medioambiental a environmental

mediocr|e a mediocre. ~**idad** f mediocrity

mediodía m midday, noon; (sur) south

medioevo m Middle Ages

Medio Oriente m Middle East

medir [5] vt measure; weigh up <palabras etc>. ● vi measure, be. **¿cuánto mide de alto?** how tall is it? □ ~**se** vpr (moderarse) measure o.s.; (Mex, probarse) try on

medita|bundo a thoughtful. ~**ción** f meditation. ~**r** vt think about. ● vi meditate

mediterráneo a Mediterranean

Mediterráneo m Mediterranean

médium m & f medium

médula f marrow

medusa f jellyfish

megáfono m megaphone

megalómano m megalomaniac

mejicano a & m Mexican

Méjico m Mexico

mejilla *f* cheek

mejillón *m* mussel

mejor *a & adv* (comparativo) better; (superlativo) best. ~ **dicho** rather. **a lo** ~ perhaps. **tanto** ~ so much the better. ~**a** *f* improvement. ~**able** *a* improvable. ~**amiento** *m* improvement

mejorana *f* marjoram

mejorar *vt* improve, better. ● *vi* get better. □ ~**se** *vpr* get better

mejunje *m* mixture

melanc|olía *f* melancholy. ~**ólico** *a* melancholic

melaza *f* molasses

melen|a *f* long hair; (de león) mane. ~**udo** *a* long-haired

melindr|es *mpl* affectation. **hacer** ~**es con la comida** be picky about food. ~**oso** *a* affected

mellizo *a & m* twin

melocot|ón *m* peach. ~**onero** *m* peach tree

mel|odía *f* melody. ~**ódico** *a* melodic. ~**odioso** *a* melodious

melodram|a *m* melodrama. ~**ático** *a* melodramatic

melómano *m* music lover

melón *m* melon

meloso *a* sickly-sweet; *<canción>* slushy

membran|a *f* membrane. ~**oso** *a* membranous

membrete *m* letterhead

membrill|ero *m* quince tree. ~**o** *m* quince

memo *a* stupid. ● *m* idiot

memorable *a* memorable

memorando *m*, **memorándum** *m* notebook; (nota) memorandum, memo

memori|a *f* memory; (informe) report; (tesis) thesis. ~**as** *fpl* (autobiografía) memoirs. **de** ~**a** by heart; *<citar>* from memory. ~**al** *m* memorial. ~**ón** *m* good memory. ~**zación** *f* memorizing. ~**zar** [10] *vt* memorize

menaje *m* household goods. ~ **de cocina** kitchenware

menci|ón *f* mention. ~**onado** *a* aforementioned. ~**onar** *vt* mention

mendi|cidad *f* begging. ~**gar** [12] *vt* beg for. ● *vi* beg. ~**go** *m* beggar

mendrugo *m* piece of stale bread

mene|ar *vt* wag *<rabo>*; shake *<cabeza>*; wiggle *<caderas>*. □ ~**arse** *vpr* move; (con inquietud) fidget; (balancearse) swing). ~**o** *m* movement; *<sacudida>* shake

menester *m* occupation. **ser** ~ be necessary. ~**oso** *a* needy

menestra *f* vegetable stew

mengano *m* so-and-so

mengua *f* decrease; (falta) lack. ~**do** *a* diminished. ~**nte** *a* *<luna>* waning; *<marea>* ebb. ~**r** [15] *vt/i* decrease, diminish

meningitis *f* meningitis

menjurje *m* mixture

menopausia *f* menopause

menor *a* (más pequeño, comparativo) smaller; (más pequeño, superlativo) smallest; (más joven, comparativo) younger; (más joven, superlativo) youngest; (Mus) minor. ● *m & f* (menor de edad) minor. **al por** ~ retail

menos *a* (comparativo) less; (comparativo, con plural) fewer; (superlativo) least; (superlativo, con plural) fewest. ● *adv* (comparativo) less; (superlativo) least. ● *prep* except. **al** ~ at least. **a** ~ **que** unless. **las dos** ~ **diez** ten to two. **ni mucho** ~ far from it. **por lo** ~ at least. ~**cabar** *vt* lessen; (fig, estropear) damage. ~**cabo** *m* lessening. ~**preciable** *a* contemptible. ~**preciar** *vt* despise. ~**precio** *m* contempt

mensaje *m* message. ~**ro** *m* messenger

menso *a* (LAm, ▣) stupid

menstru|ación *f* menstruation. ~**al** *a* menstrual. ~**ar** [21] *vi* menstruate

mensual *a* monthly. ~**idad** *f* monthly pay; (cuota) monthly payment

mensurable *a* measurable

menta *f* mint

mental *a* mental. ~**idad** *f* mentality. ~**mente** *adv* mentally

mentar [1] *vt* mention, name

mente *f* mind

mentecato *a* stupid. ● *m* idiot

mentir [4] *vi* lie. **~a** *f* lie. **~ijillas** *fpl*. de **~ijillas** for a joke. **~oso** *a* lying. ● *m* liar

mentís *m invar* denial

mentor *m* mentor

menú *m* menu

menud|ear *vi* happen frequently; (Mex, Com) sell retail. **~encia** *f* trifle. **~encias** *fpl* (LAm) giblets. **~eo** *m* (Mex) retail trade. **~illos** *mpl* giblets. **~o** *a* small; *<lluvia>* fine. **a ~o** often. **~os** *mpl* giblets

meñique *a <dedo>* little. ● *m* little finger

meollo *m* (médula) marrow; (de tema etc) heart

merca|chifle *m* hawker; (fig) profiteer. **~der** *m* merchant. **~dería** *f* (LAm) merchandise. **~do** *m* market. **M~do Común** Common Market. **~do negro** black market

mercan|cía(s) *f(pl)* goods, merchandise. **~te** *a* merchant. ● *m* merchant ship. **~til** *a* mercantile, commercial. **~tilismo** *m* mercantilism

merced *f* favour. **su/vuestra ~** your honour

mercenario *a* & *m* mercenary

mercer|ía *f* haberdashery (Brit), notions (Amer). **~io** *m* mercury

mercurial *a* mercurial

Mercurio *m* Mercury

merec|edor *a* worthy (de of). **~er** [11] *vt* deserve. □ **~erse** *vpr* deserve. **~idamente** *adv* deservedly. **~ido** *a* well deserved. **~imiento** *m* (mérito) merit

merend|ar [1] *vt* have as an afternoon snack. ● *vi* have an afternoon snack. **~ero** *m* snack bar; (lugar) picnic area

merengue *m* meringue

meridi|ano *a* midday; (fig) dazzling. ● *m* meridian. **~onal** *a* southern. ● *m* southerner

merienda *f* afternoon snack

merino *a* merino

mérito *m* merit; (valor) worth

meritorio *a* praiseworthy. ● *m* unpaid trainee

merluza *f* hake

merma *f* decrease. **~r** *vt/i* decrease, reduce

mermelada *f* jam

mero *a* mere; (Mex, verdadero) real. ● *adv* (Mex, precisamente) exactly; (Mex, casi) nearly. ● *m* grouper

merode|ador *m* prowler. **~ar** *vi* prowl

mes *m* month

mesa *f* table; (para escribir o estudiar) desk. **poner la ~** lay the table

mesarse *vpr* tear at one's hair

meser|a *f* (LAm) waitress. **~o** *m* (LAm) waiter

meseta *f* plateau; (descansillo) landing

Mesías *m* Messiah

mesilla *f*, **mesita** *f* small table. **~ de noche** bedside table

mesón *m* inn

mesoner|a *f* landlady. **~o** *m* landlord

mestiz|aje *m* crossbreeding. **~o** *a* *<persona>* half-caste; *<animal>* cross-bred. ● *m* (persona) half-caste; (animal) cross-breed

mesura *f* moderation. **~do** *a* moderate

meta *f* goal; (de una carrera) finish

metabolismo *m* metabolism

metafísic|a *f* metaphysics. **~o** *a* metaphysical

met|áfora *f* metaphor. **~afórico** *a* metaphorical

met|al *m* metal; (de la voz) timbre. **~ales** *mpl* (instrumentos de latón) brass. **~álico** *a* *<objeto>* metal; *<sonido>* metallic

metal|urgia *f* metallurgy. **~úrgico** *a* metallurgical

metamorfosis *f invar* metamorphosis

metedura de pata *f* blunder

mete|órico *a* meteoric. **~orito** *m* meteorite. **~oro** *m* meteor. **~orología** *f* meteorology. **~orológico** *a* meteorological. **~orólogo** *m* meteorologist

meter *vt* put; score *<un gol>*; (enredar) involve; (causar) make. □ **~se** *vpr* get involved (**en** in); (entrometerse) meddle. ∼**se con uno** pick a quarrel with s.o.

meticulos|idad *f* meticulousness. ∼**o** *a* meticulous

metida de pata *f* (LAm) blunder

metido *m* reprimand. ● *a.* ∼ **en años** getting on. **estar** ∼ **en algo** be involved in sth. **estar muy** ∼ **con uno** be well in with s.o.

metódico *a* methodical

metodis|mo *m* Methodism. ∼**ta** *a* & *m* & *f* Methodist

método *m* method

metodología *f* methodology

metraje *m* length. **de largo** ∼ <*película*> feature

metrall|a *f* shrapnel. ∼**eta** *f* submachine gun

métric|a *f* metrics. ∼**o** *a* metric; <*verso*> metrical

metro *m* metre; (tren) underground (Brit), subway (Amer). ∼ **cuadrado** square metre

metrónomo *m* metronome

metr|ópoli *f* metropolis. ∼**opolitano** *a* metropolitan. ● *m* metropolitan; (tren) underground (Brit), subway (Amer)

mexicano *a* & *m* Mexican

México *m* Mexico. ∼ **D. F.** Mexico City

mezcal *m* (Mex) mescal

mezc|la *f* (acción) mixing; (substancia) mixture; (argamasa) mortar. ∼**lador** *m* mixer. ∼**lar** *vt* mix; shuffle <*los naipes*>. □ ∼**larse** *vpr* mix; (intervenir) interfere. ∼**olanza** *f* mixture

mezquin|dad *f* meanness. ∼**o** *a* mean; (escaso) meagre. ● *m* mean person

mezquita *f* mosque

mi *a* my. ● *m* (Mus) E; (solfa) mi

mí *pron* me

miau *m* miaow

mica *f* (silicato) mica

mico *m* (long-tailed) monkey

microbio *m* microbe

micro|biología *f* microbiology. ∼**cosmos** *m invar* microcosm. ∼**film(e)** *m* microfilm

micrófono *m* microphone

microonda *f* microwave. ∼**s** *m invar* microwave oven

microordenador *m* microcomputer

micros|cópico *a* microscopic. ∼**copio** *m* microscope. ∼**urco** *m* long-playing record

miedo *m* fear (**a** for). **dar** ∼ frighten. **morirse de** ∼ be scared to death. **tener** ∼ be frightened. ∼**so** *a* fearful

miel *f* honey

miembro *m* limb; (persona) member

mientras *conj* while. ● *adv* meanwhile. ∼ **que** whereas. ∼ **tanto** in the meantime

miércoles *m invar* Wednesday. ∼ **de ceniza** Ash Wednesday

mierda *f* (vulgar) shit

mies *f* ripe, grain

miga *f* crumb; (fig, meollo) essence. ∼**jas** *fpl* crumbs; (sobras) scraps. ∼**r** [12] *vt* crumble

migra|ción *f* migration. ∼**torio** *a* migratory

mijo *m* millet

mil *a* & *m* a/one thousand. ∼**es de** thousands of. ∼ **novecientos noventa y nueve** nineteen ninety-nine. ∼ **pesetas** a thousand pesetas

milagro *m* miracle. ∼**so** *a* miraculous

milen|ario *a* millenial. ∼**io** *m* millennium

milésimo *a* & *m* thousandth

mili *f* 🄳 military service. ∼**cia** *f* soldiering; (gente armada) militia

mili|gramo *m* milligram. ∼**litro** *m* millilitre

milímetro *m* millimetre

militante *a* & *m* & *f* activist

militar *a* military. ● *m* soldier. ∼**ismo** *m* militarism. ∼**ista** *a* militaristic. ● *m* & *f* militarist. ∼**izar** [10] *vt* militarize

milla *f* mile

millar *m* thousand. **a** ∼**es** by the thousand

mill|ón *m* million. **un** ∼**ón de libros** a million books. ∼**onada** *f* fortune. ∼**onario** *m* millionaire. ∼**onésimo** *a* & *m* millionth

milonga *f popular dance and music from the River Plate region*

milpa *f* (Mex) maize field, cornfield (Amer)

milpies *m invar* woodlouse

mimar *vt* spoil

mimbre *m & f* wicker. □ ~**arse** *vpr* sway. ~**ra** *f* osier. ~**ral** *m* osier-bed

mimetismo *m* mimicry

mímic|a *f* mime. ~**o** *a* mimic

mimo *m* mime; (*a un niño*) spoiling; (caricia) cuddle

mimosa *f* mimosa

mina *f* mine. ~**r** *vt* mine; (fig) undermine

minarete *m* minaret

mineral *m* mineral; (mena) ore. ~**ogía** *f* mineralogy. ~**ogista** *m & f* mineralogist

miner|ía *f* mining. ~**o** *a* mining. ● *m* miner

miniatura *f* miniature

minifundio *m* smallholding

minimizar [10] *vt* minimize

mínim|o *a & m* minimum. **como** ~ at least. ~**um** *m* minimum

minino *m* ⓘ cat, puss ⓘ

minist|erial *a* ministerial; *<reunión>* cabinet. ~**erio** *m* ministry. ~**ro** *m* minister

minor|ía *f* minority. ~**idad** *f* minority. ~**ista** *m & f* retailer

minuci|a *f* trifle. ~**osidad** *f* thoroughness. ~**oso** *a* thorough; (detallado) detailed

minúscul|a *f* lower case letter. ~**o** *a* tiny

minuta *f* draft copy; (de abogado) bill

minut|ero *m* minute hand. ~**o** *m* minute

mío *a & pron* mine. **un amigo** ~ a friend of mine

miop|e *a* short-sighted. ● *m & f* short-sighted person. ~**ía** *f* short-sightedness

mira *f* sight; (fig, intención) aim. **a la** ~ on the lookout. **con** ~**s a** with a view to. ~**da** *f* look. **echar una** ~**da a** glance at. ~**do** *a* careful with money; (comedido) considerate. **bien** ~**do** highly regarded. **no estar bien** ~**do** be frowned upon. ~**dor** *m* viewpoint. ~**miento** *m* consideration. ~**r** *vt* look at; (observar) watch; (considerar) consider. ~**r fijamente** a stare at. ● *vi* look *<edificio etc>*. ~ **hacia** face. □ ~**rse** *vpr <personas>* look at each other

mirilla *f* peephole

miriñaque *m* crinoline

mirlo *m* blackbird

mirón *a* nosey. ● *m* nosey-parker; (espectador) onlooker

mirto *m* myrtle

misa *f* mass. ~**l** *m* missal

misántropo *m* misanthropist

miscelánea *f* miscellany; (Mex, tienda) corner shop (Brit), small general store (Amer)

miser|able *a* very poor; (lastimoso) miserable; (tacaño) mean. ~**ia** *f* extreme poverty; (suciedad) squalor

misericordi|a *f* pity; (piedad) mercy. ~**oso** *a* merciful

mísero *a* miserable; (tacaño) mean; (malvado) wicked

misil *m* missile

misi|ón *f* mission. ~**onero** *m* missionary

misiva *f* missive

mism|ísimo *a* very same. ~**o** *a* same; (después de pronombre personal) myself, yourself, himself, herself, itself, ourselves, yourselves, themselves; (enfático) very. ● *adv.* **ahora** ~ right now. **aquí** ~ right here. **lo** ~ the same

misterio *m* mystery. ~**so** *a* mysterious

míst|ica *f* mysticism. ~**o** *a* mystical. ● *m* mystic

mistifica|ción *f* mystification. ~**r** [7] *vt* mystify

mitad *f* half; (centro) middle. **cortar algo por la** ~ cut sth in half

mitigar [12] *vt* mitigate; quench *<sed>*; relieve *<dolor etc>*

mitin *m*, **mitín** *m* meeting

mito *m* myth. ~**logía** *f* mythology. ~**lógico** *a* mythological

mitón *m* mitten

mitote *m* (Mex) Aztec dance

mixt|o *a* mixed. **educación mixta** coeducation

mobiliario *m* furniture

moce|dad *f* youth. ~**río** *m* young people. ~**tón** *m* strapping lad. ~**tona** *f* strapping girl

mochales *a invar.* **estar** ~ be round the bend

mochila *f* rucksack

mocho *a* blunt. ● *m* butt end

mochuelo *m* little owl

moción *f* motion

moco *m* mucus. **limpiarse los** ~**s** blow one's nose

moda *f* fashion. **estar de** ~ be in fashion. ~**l** *a* modal. ~**les** *mpl* manners. ~**lidad** *f* kind

model|ado *m* modelling. ~**ador** *m* modeller. ~**ar** *vt* model; (fig, configurar) form. ~**o** *m & f* model

módem *m* modem

modera|ción *f* moderation. ~**do** *a* moderate. ~**r** *vt* moderate; reduce <*velocidad*>. □ ~**rse** *vpr* control oneself

modern|idad *f* modernity. ~**ismo** *m* modernism. ~**ista** *m & f* modernist. ~**izar** [10] *vt* modernize. ~**o** *a* modern; (a la moda) fashionable

modest|ia *f* modesty. ~**o** *a* modest

módico *a* moderate

modifica|ción *f* modification. ~**r** [7] *vt* modify

modismo *m* idiom

modist|a *f* dressmaker. ~**o** *m* designer

modo *m* manner, way; (Gram) mood; (Mus) mode. ~ **de ser** character. **de** ~ **que** so that. **de ningún** ~ certainly not. **de todos** ~**s** anyhow. **ni** ~ (LAm) no way

modorra *f* drowsiness

modula|ción *f* modulation. ~**dor** *m* modulator. ~**r** *vt* modulate

módulo *m* module

mofa *f* mockery. □ ~**rse** *vpr*. ~**rse de** make fun of

mofeta *f* skunk

moflet|e *m* chubby cheek. ~**udo** *a* with chubby cheeks

mohín *m* grimace. **hacer un** ~ pull a face

moho *m* mould; (óxido) rust. ~**so** *a* mouldy; <*metales*> rusty

moisés *m* Moses basket

mojado *a* wet

mojar *vt* wet; (empapar) soak; (humedecer) moisten, dampen

mojigat|ería *f* prudishness. ~**o** *m* prude. ● *a* prudish

mojón *m* boundary post; (señal) signpost

molar *m* molar

mold|e *m* mould; (aguja) knitting needle. ~**ear** *vt* mould, shape; (fig) form. ~**ura** *f* moulding

mole *f* mass, bulk. ● *m* (Mex, salsa) chili sauce with chocolate and sesame

mol|écula *f* molecule. ~**ecular** *a* molecular

mole|dor *a* grinding. ● *m* grinder. ~**r** [2] grind

molest|ar *vt* annoy; (incomodar) bother. ¿**le** ~**a que fume?** do you mind if I smoke? ● *vi* be a nuisance. **no** ~**ar** do not disturb. □ ~**arse** *vpr* bother; (ofenderse) take offence. ~**ia** *f* bother, nuisance; (inconveniente) inconvenience; (incomodidad) discomfort. ~**o** *a* annoying; (inconveniente) inconvenient; (ofendido) offended

molicie *f* softness; (excesiva comodidad) easy life

molido *a* ground; (fig, muy cansado) worn out

molienda *f* grinding

molin|ero *m* miller. ~**ete** *m* toy windmill. ~**illo** *m* mill; (juguete) toy windmill. ~**o** *m* mill. ~ **de agua** watermill. ~**o de viento** windmill

molleja *f* gizzard

mollera *f* (de la cabeza) crown; (fig, sesera) brains

molusco *m* mollusc

moment|áneamente *adv* momentarily. ~**áneo** *a* (breve) momentary; (pasajero) temporary. ~**o** *m* moment; (ocasión) time. **al** ~**o** at once. **de** ~**o** for the moment

momi|a *f* mummy. ~**ficar** [7] *vt* mummify. □ ~**ficarse** *vpr* become mummified

monacal *a* monastic

monada *f* beautiful thing; (niño bonito) cute kid; (acción tonta) silliness

monaguillo *m* altar boy

mon|arca *m* & *f* monarch. **~arquía** *f* monarchy. **~árquico** *a* monarchical

monasterio *m* monastery

monda *f* peeling; (piel) peel. **~dientes** *m invar* toothpick. **~adura** *f* peeling; (piel) peel. **~ar** *vt* peel *<fruta etc>*. **~o** *a* (sin pelo) bald

mondongo *m* innards

moned|a *f* coin; (de un país) currency. **~ero** *m* purse (Brit), change purse (Amer)

monetario *a* monetary

mongolismo *m* Down's syndrome

monigote *m* weak character; (muñeco) rag doll; (dibujo) doodle

monitor *m* monitor

monj|a *f* nun. **~e** *m* monk. **~il** *a* nun's; (como de monja) like a nun

mono *m* monkey; (sobretodo) overalls. ● *a* pretty

monocromo *a* & *m* monochrome

monóculo *m* monocle

mon|ogamia *f* monogamy. **~ógamo** *a* monogamous

monogra|fía *f* monograph. **~ma** *m* monogram

mon|ologar [12] *vi* soliloquize. **~ólogo** *m* monologue

monoplano *m* monoplane

monopoli|o *m* monopoly. **~zar** [10] *vt* monopolize

monos|ilábico *a* monosyllabic. **~ílabo** *m* monosyllable

monoteís|mo *m* monotheism. **~ta** *a* monotheistic. ● *m* & *f* monotheist

mon|otonía *f* monotony. **~ótono** *a* monotonous

monseñor *m* monsignor

monstruo *m* monster. **~sidad** *f* monstrosity; (atrocidad) atrocity. **~so** *a* monstrous

monta *f* mounting; (valor) total value

montacargas *m invar* service lift (Brit), service elevator (Amer)

monta|dor *m* fitter. **~je** *m* assembly; (Cine) montage; (teatro) staging, production

montañ|a *f* mountain. **~a rusa** roller coaster. **~ero** *a* mountaineer.

~és *a* mountain. ● *m* highlander. **~ismo** *m* mountaineering. **~oso** *a* mountainous

montaplatos *m invar* dumb waiter

montar *vt* ride; (subirse a) get on; (ensamblar) assemble; cock *<arma>*; set up *<una casa, un negocio>*. ● *vi* ride; (subirse) mount. **~ a caballo** ride a horse

monte *m* (montaña) mountain; (terreno inculto) scrub; (bosque) woodland. **~ de piedad** pawnshop

montepío *m* charitable fund for dependents

montés *a* wild

montevideano *a* & *m* Montevidean

montículo *m* hillock

montón *m* heap, pile. **a montones** in abundance. **un ~ de** loads of

montura *f* mount; (silla) saddle

monument|al *a* monumental; (fig, muy grande) enormous. **~o** *m* monument

monzón *m* & *f* monsoon

moñ|a *f* ribbon. **~o** *m* bun; (LAm, lazo) bow

moque|o *m* runny nose. **~ro** *m* Ⓣ handkerchief

moqueta *f* fitted carpet

moquillo *m* distemper

mora *f* mulberry; (de zarzamora) blackberry; (Jurid) default

morada *f* dwelling

morado *a* purple

morador *m* inhabitant

moral *m* mulberry tree. ● *f* morals. ● *a* moral. **~eja** *f* moral. **~idad** *f* morality. **~ista** *m* & *f* moralist. **~izador** *a* moralizing. ● *m* moralist. **~izar** [10] *vt* moralize

morar *vi* live

moratoria *f* moratorium

mórbido *a* soft; (malsano) morbid

morbo *m* illness. **~sidad** *f* morbidity. **~so** *a* unhealthy

morcilla *f* black pudding

morda|cidad *f* sharpness. **~z** *a* scathing

mordaza *f* gag

morde|dura f bite. ~**r** [2] vt bite; (Mex, exigir soborno a) extract a bribe from. ● vi bite. □ ~**rse** vpr bite o.s. ~**rse las uñas** bite one's nails

mordi|da f (Mex) bribe. ~**sco** m bite. ~**squear** vt nibble (at)

moreno a (con ser) dark; (de pelo obscuro) dark-haired; (de raza negra) dark-skinned; (con estar) brown, tanned

morera f white mulberry tree

moretón m bruise

morfema m morpheme

morfin|a f morphine. ~**ómano** m morphine addict

morfol|ogía f morphology. ~**ógi-co** a morphological

moribundo a dying

morir [6] (pp **muerto**) vi die; (fig, extinguirse) die away; (fig, terminar) end. ~ **ahogado** drown. □ ~**se** vpr die. ~**se de hambre** starve to death; (fig) be starving. **se muere por una flauta** she's dying to have a flute

morisco a Moorish. ● m Moor

morm|ón m Mormon. ~**ónico** a Mormon. ~**onismo** m Mormonism

moro a Moorish. ● m Moor

morral m (mochila) rucksack; (de cazador) gamebag; (para caballos) nosebag

morrillo m nape of the neck

morriña f homesickness

morro m snout

morrocotudo a 🅴 (tremendo) terrible; (estupendo) terrific 🅴

morsa f walrus

mortaja f shroud

mortal a & m & f mortal. ~**idad** f mortality. ~**mente** adv mortally

mortandad f loss of life; (Mil) carnage

mortecino a failing; <color> pale

mortero m mortar

mortífero a deadly

mortifica|ción f mortification. ~**r** [7] vt (atormentar) torment. □ ~**rse** vpr distress o.s.

mortuorio a death

mosaico m mosaic; (Mex, baldosa) floor tile

mosca f fly. ~**rda** f blowfly. ~**rdón** m botfly; (de cuerpo azul) bluebottle

moscatel a muscatel

moscón m botfly; (mosca de cuerpo azul) bluebottle

moscovita a & m & f Muscovite

mosque|arse vpr get cross. ~**o** m resentment

mosquete m musket. ~**ro** m musketeer

mosquit|ero m mosquito net. ~**o** m mosquito

mostacho m moustache

mostaza f mustard

mosto m must, grape juice

mostrador m counter

mostrar [2] vt show. □ ~**se** vpr (show oneself to) be. **se mostró muy amable** he was very kind

mota f spot, speck

mote m nickname

motea|do a speckled. ~**r** vt speckle

motejar vt call

motel m motel

motete m motet

motín m riot; (de tropas, tripulación) mutiny

motiv|ación f motivation. ~**ar** vt motivate. ~**o** m reason. **con** ~**o de** because of

motocicl|eta f motor cycle, motor bike 🅴. ~**ista** m & f motorcyclist

motoneta f (LAm) (motor) scooter

motor a motor. ● m motor, engine. ~ **de arranque** starter motor. ~**a** f motor boat. ~**ismo** m motorcycling. ~**ista** m & f motorist; (de una moto) motorcyclist. ~**izar** [10] vt motorize

motriz a motor

move|dizo a movable; (poco firme) unstable; <persona> fickle. ~**r** [2] vt move; shake <la cabeza>; (provocar) cause. □ ~**rse** vpr move; (darse prisa) hurry up

movi|ble a movable. ~**do** a moved; (Foto) blurred

móvil a mobile. ● m motive

movili|dad f mobility. ~**zación** f mobilization. ~**zar** [10] vt mobilize

movimiento m movement, motion; (agitación) bustle

moza f young girl. ~**lbete** m lad

mozárabe a Mozarabic. ● m & f Mozarab

moz|o *m* young boy. **~uela** *f* young girl. **~uelo** *m* young boy/lad

mucam|a *f* (LAm) servant. **~o** *m* (LAm) servant

muchach|a *f* girl; (sirvienta) servant, maid. **~o** *m* boy, lad

muchedumbre *f* crowd

mucho *a* a lot of; (en negativas, preguntas) much, a lot of. **~s** a lot of; (en negativas, preguntas) many, a lot of. ● *pron* a lot; (personas) many (people). **como ~** at the most. **ni ~ menos** by no means. **por ~ que** however much. ● *adv* a lot, very much; (tiempo) long, a long time

mucos|idad *f* mucus. **~o** *a* mucous

muda *f* change of clothing; (de animales) shedding. **~ble** *a* changeable; <personas> fickle. **~nza** *f* move, removal (Brit). **~r** *vt* change; shed <piel>. **~rse** *vpr* (de ropa) change one's clothes; (de casa) move (house)

mudéjar *a & m & f* Mudéjar

mud|ez *f* dumbness. **~o** *a* dumb; (callado) silent

mueble *a* movable. ● *m* piece of furniture. **~s** *mpl* furniture

mueca *f* grimace, face. **hacer una ~** pull a face

muela *f* back tooth, molar; (piedra de afilar) grindstone; (piedra de molino) millstone. **~ del juicio** wisdom tooth

muelle *a* soft. ● *m* spring; (Naut) wharf; (malecón) jetty

muérdago *m* mistletoe

muero *vb* ⇒MORIR

muert|e *f* death; (homicidio) murder. **~o** *a* dead. ● *m* dead person

muesca *f* nick; (ranura) slot

muestra *f* sample; (prueba) proof; (modelo) model; (señal) sign. **~rio** *m* collection of samples

muestro *vb* ⇒MOSTRAR

muevo *vb* ⇒MOVER

mugi|do *m* moo. **~r** [14] *vi* moo

mugr|e *m* dirt. **~iento** *a* dirty, filthy

mugrón *m* sucker

mujer *f* woman; (esposa) wife. ● *int* my dear! **~iego** *a* fond of the women. ● *m* womanizer. **~zuela** *f* prostitute

mula *f* mule. **~da** *f* drove of mules

mulato *a* of mixed race (black and white). ● *m* person of mixed race

mulero *m* muleteer

muleta *f* crutch; (toreo) stick with a red flag

mulli|do *a* soft. **~r** [22] *vt* soften

mulo *m* mule

multa *f* fine. **~r** *vt* fine

multi|color *a* multicoloured. **~copista** *m* duplicator. **~forme** *a* multiform. **~lateral** *a* multilateral. **~lingüe** *a* multilingual. **~millonario** *m* multimillionaire

múltiple *a* multiple

multiplic|ación *f* multiplication. **~ar** [7] *vt* multiply. □ **~arse** *vpr* multiply. **~idad** *f* multiplicity

múltiplo *m* multiple

multitud *f* multitude, crowd. **~inario** *a* mass; <concierto> with mass audience

mund|ano *a* wordly; (de la sociedad elegante) society. **~ial** *a* world-wide. **la segunda guerra ~ial** the Second World War. **~illo** *m* world, circles. **~o** *m* world. **todo el ~o** everybody

munición *f* ammunition; (provisiones) supplies

municip|al *a* municipal. **~alidad** *f* municipality. **~io** *m* municipality; (ayuntamiento) town council

muñe|ca *f* (Anat) wrist; (juguete) doll; (maniquí) dummy. **~co** *m* doll. **~quera** *f* wristband

muñón *m* stump

mura|l *a* mural, wall. ● *m* mural. **~lla** *f* (city) wall. **~r** *vt* wall

murciélago *m* bat

murga *f* street band

murmullo *m* (incl fig) murmur

murmura|ción *f* gossip. **~dor** *a* gossiping. ● *m* gossip. **~r** *vi* murmur; (criticar) gossip

muro *m* wall

murria *f* depression

mus *m* card game

musa *f* muse

musaraña *f* shrew

muscula|r _a_ muscular. **~tura** _f_ muscles

músculo _m_ muscle

musculoso _a_ muscular

muselina _f_ muslin

museo _m_ museum. **~ de arte** art gallery

musgo _m_ moss. **~so** _a_ mossy

música _f_ music

musical _a_ & _m_ musical

músico _a_ musical. ● _m_ musician

music|ología _f_ musicology. **~ólogo** _m_ musicologist

muslo _m_ thigh

mustio _a_ <_plantas_> withered; <_cosas_> faded; <_personas_> gloomy; (Mex, hipócrita) two-faced

musulmán _a_ & _m_ Muslim

muta|bilidad _f_ mutability. **~ción** _f_ mutation

mutila|ción _f_ mutilation. **~do** _a_ crippled. ● _m_ cripple. **~r** _vt_ mutilate; maim <_persona_>

mutis _m_ (en el teatro) exit. **~mo** _m_ silence

mutu|alidad _f_ mutuality; (asociación) friendly society. **~amente** _adv_ mutually. **~o** _a_ mutual

muy _adv_ very; (demasiado) too

....

Nn

....

nabo _m_ turnip

nácar _m_ mother-of-pearl

nac|er [11] _vi_ be born; <_pollito_> hatch out; <_planta_> sprout. **~ido** _a_ born. **recien ~ido** newborn. **~iente** _a_ <_sol_> rising. **~imiento** _m_ birth; (de río) source; (belén) crib. **lugar** _m_ **de ~imiento** place of birth

naci|ón _f_ nation. **~onal** _a_ national. **~onalidad** _f_ nationality. **~onalismo** _m_ nationalism. **~onalista** _m_ & _f_ nationalist. **~onalizar** [10] _vt_ nationalize. □ **~onalizarse** _vpr_ become naturalized

nada _pron_ nothing, not anything. ● _adv_ not at all. **¡~ de eso!** nothing of the sort! **antes que ~** first of all. **¡de ~!** (después de 'gracias') don't mention it! **para ~** (not) at all. **por ~ del mundo** not for anything in the world

nada|dor _m_ swimmer. **~r** _vi_ swim. **~r de espalda(s)** do (the) backstroke

nadería _f_ trifle

nadie _pron_ no one, nobody

nado _m_ (Mex) swimming. ● _adv_ **a ~** swimming

naipe _m_ (playing) card. **juegos** _mpl_ **de ~s** card games

nalga _f_ buttock. **~s** _fpl_ bottom. **~da** _f_ (Mex) smack on the bottom

nana _f_ lullaby

naranj|a _f_ orange. **~ada** _f_ orangeade. **~al** _m_ orange grove. **~ero** _m_ orange tree

narcótico _a_ & _m_ narcotic

nariz _f_ nose. **¡narices!** rubbish!

narra|ción _f_ narration. **~dor** _m_ narrator. **~r** _vt_ tell. **~tivo** _a_ narrative

nasal _a_ nasal

nata _f_ cream

natación _f_ swimming

natal _a_ native; <_pueblo etc_> home. **~idad** _f_ birth rate

natillas _fpl_ custard

nativo _a_ & _m_ native

nato _a_ born

natural _a_ natural. ● _m_ native. **~eza** _f_ nature. **~eza muerta** still life. **~idad** _f_ naturalness. **~ista** _a_ & _f_ naturalist. **~izar** [10] _vt_ naturalize. □ **~izarse** _vpr_ become naturalized. **~mente** _adv_ naturally. ● _int_ of course!

naufrag|ar [12] _vi_ <_barco_> sink; <_persona_> be shipwrecked; (fig) fail. **~io** _m_ shipwreck

náufrago _a_ shipwrecked. ● _m_ shipwrecked person

náuseas _fpl_ nausea. **dar ~s a uno** make s.o. feel sick. **sentir ~s** feel sick

náutico _a_ nautical

navaja _f_ penknife; (de afeitar) razor. **~zo** _m_ slash

naval _a_ naval

nave f ship; (de iglesia) nave. ~ **espacial** spaceship. **quemar las** ~**s** burn one's boats

navega|ble a navigable; <*barco*> seaworthy. ~**ción** f navigation; (tráfico) shipping. ~**dor** m (Informática) browser. ~**nte** m & f navigator. ~**r** [12] vi sail; (Informática) browse

Navid|ad f Christmas. ~**eño** a Christmas. **en** ~**ades** at Christmas. **¡feliz** ~**ad!** Happy Christmas! **por** ~**ad** at Christmas

nazi a & m & f Nazi. ~**smo** m Nazism

neblina f mist

nebuloso a misty; (fig) vague

necedad f foolishness. **decir** ~**es** talk nonsense. **hacer una** ~ do sth stupid

necesari|amente adv necessarily. ~**o** a necessary

necesi|dad f need; (cosa esencial) necessity; (pobreza) poverty. ~**dades** fpl hardships. **no hay** ~**dad** there's no need. **por** ~**dad** (out) of necessity. ~**tado** a in need (**de** of). ~**tar** vt need. ● vi. ~**tar de** need

necio a silly. ● m idiot

néctar m nectar

nectarina f nectarine

nefasto a unfortunate; <*consecuencia*> disastrous; <*influencia*> harmful

nega|ción f denial; (Gram) negative. ~**do** a useless. ~**r** [1 & 12] vt deny; (rehusar) refuse. □ ~**rse** vpr refuse (**a** to). ~**tiva** f (acción) denial; (acción de rehusar) refusal. ~**tivo** a & m negative

negligen|cia f negligence. ~**te** a negligent

negoci|able a negotiable. ~**ación** f negotiation. ~**ante** m & f dealer. ~**ar** vt/i negotiate. ~**ar en** trade in. ~**o** m business; (Com, trato) deal. ~**os** mpl business. **hombre** m **de** ~**os** businessman

negr|a f black woman; (Mus) crotchet. ~**o** a black; <*ojos*> dark. ● m (color) black; (persona) black man. ~**ura** f blackness. ~**uzco** a blackish

nen|a f little girl. ~**o** m little boy

nenúfar m water lily

neocelandés a from New Zealand. ● m New Zealander

neón m neon

nepotismo m nepotism

nervio m nerve; (tendón) sinew; (Bot) vein. ~**sidad** f, ~**sismo** m nervousness; (impaciencia) impatience. ~**so** a nervous; (de temperamento) highly-strung. **ponerse** ~**so** get nervous

neto a clear; <*verdad*> simple; (Com) net

neumático a pneumatic. ● m tyre

neumonía f pneumonia

neur|algia f neuralgia. ~**ología** f neurology. ~**ólogo** m neurologist. ~**osis** f neurosis. ~**ótico** a neurotic

neutr|al a neutral. ~**alidad** f neutrality. ~**alizar** [10] vt neutralize. ~**o** a neutral; (Gram) neuter

neva|da f snowfall. ~**r** [1] vi snow. ~**sca** f blizzard

nevera f refrigerator, fridge (Brit)

nevisca f light snowfall

nexo m link

ni conj. ~**...** ~ neither... nor. ~ **aunque** not even if. ~ **siquiera** not even. **sin...** ~ ... without ... or...

Nicaragua f Nicaragua

nicaragüense a & m & f Nicaraguan

nicho m niche

nicotina f nicotine

nido m nest; (de ladrones) den

niebla f fog. **hay** ~ it's foggy. **un día de** ~ a foggy day

niet|a f granddaughter. ~**o** m grandson. ~**os** mpl grandchildren

nieve f snow; (Mex, helado) sorbet

niki m polo shirt

nimi|edad f triviality. ~**o** a insignificant

ninfa f nymph

ningún ⇒ NINGUNO

ninguno a (*delante de nombre masculino en singular* **ningún**) no; (con otro negativo) any. **de ninguna manera, de ningún modo** by no means. **en ninguna parte** nowhere. **sin ningún amigo** without any friends.

● *pron* (de dos) neither; (de más de dos) none; (nadie) no-one, nobody

niñ|a *f* (little) girl. ~**era** *f* nanny. ~**ería** *f* childish thing. ~**ez** *f* childhood. ~**o** *a* childish. ● *m* (little) boy de ~**o** as a child. **desde** ~**o** from childhood

níquel *m* nickel

níspero *m* medlar

nitidez *f* clarity; (de foto, imagen) sharpness

nítido *a* clear; (foto, imagen) sharp

nitrógeno *m* nitrogen

nivel *m* level; (fig) standard. ~ **de vida** standard of living. ~**ar** *vt* level. □ ~**arse** *vpr* become level

no *adv* not; (como respuesta) no. ¿~? isn't it? **¡a que** ~! I bet you don't! **¡cómo** ~! of course! **Felipe** ~ **tiene hijos** Felipe has no children. **¡que** ~! certainly not!

nob|iliario *a* noble. ~**le** *a* & *m* & *f* noble. ~**leza** *f* nobility

noche *f* night. ~ **vieja** New Year's Eve. **de** ~ at night. **hacerse de** ~ get dark. **hacer** ~ spend the night. **media** ~ midnight. **en la** ~ (LAm), **por la** ~ at night

Nochebuena *f* Christmas Eve

noción *f* notion. **nociones** *fpl* rudiments

nocivo *a* harmful

nocturno *a* nocturnal; <clase> evening; <tren etc> night. ● *m* nocturne

nodriza *f* wet nurse

nogal *m* walnut tree; (madera) walnut

nómada *a* nomadic. ● *m* & *f* nomad

nombr|ado *a* famous; (susodicho) aforementioned. ~**amiento** *m* appointment. ~**ar** *vt* appoint; (citar) mention. ~**e** *m* name; (Gram) noun; (fama) renown. ~**e de pila** Christian name. **en** ~**e de** in the name of. **no tener** ~**e** be unspeakable. **poner de** ~**e** call

nomeolvides *m invar* forget-me-not

nómina *f* payroll

nomina|l *a* nominal. ~**tivo** *a* & *m* nominative. ~**tivo a** <cheque etc> made out to

non *a* odd. ● *m* odd number. **pares y** ~**es** odds and evens

nono *a* ninth

nordeste *a* <región> north-eastern; <viento> north-easterly. ● *m* north-east

nórdico *a* Nordic. ● *m* Northern European

noria *f* water-wheel; (en una feria) big wheel (Brit), Ferris wheel (Amer)

norma *f* rule

normal *a* normal. ● *f* teachers' training college. ~**idad** *f* normality (Brit), normalcy (Amer). ~**izar** [10] *vt* normalize. ~**mente** *adv* normally, usually

noroeste *a* <región> north-western; <viento> north-westerly. ● *m* north-west

norte *a* <región> northern; <viento, lado> north. ● *m* north; (fig, meta) aim

Norteamérica *f* (North) America

norteamericano *a* & *m* (North) American

norteño *a* northern. ● *m* northerner

Noruega *f* Norway

noruego *a* & *m* Norwegian

nos *pron* (acusativo) us; (dativo) (to) us; (reflexivo) (to) ourselves; (recíproco) (to) each other

nosotros *pron* we; (con prep) us

nost|algia *f* nostalgia; (de casa, de patria) homesickness. ~**álgico** *a* nostalgic

nota *f* note; (de examen etc) mark. **de** ~ famous. **de mala** ~ notorious. **digno de** ~ notable. ~**ble** *a* notable. ~**ción** *f* notation. ~**r** *vt* notice. **es de** ~**r** it should be noted. **hacerse** ~**r** stand out

notario *m* notary

notici|a *f* (piece of) news. ~**as** *fpl* news. **atrasado de** ~**as** behind with the news. **tener** ~**as de** hear from. ~**ario**, (LAm) ~**ero** *m* news

notifica|ción *f* notification. ~**r** [7] *vt* notify

notori|edad *f* notoriety. ~**o** *a* well-known; (evidente) obvious; (notable) marked

novato *a* inexperienced. ● *m* novice

novecientos *a* & *m* nine hundred

noved|ad *f* newness; (cosa nueva) innovation; (cambio) change; (moda) latest fashion. **llegar sin ~ad** arrive safely. **~oso** *a* novel

novel|a *f* novel. **~ista** *m* & *f* novelist

noveno *a* ninth

noventa *a* & *m* ninety; (nonagésimo) ninetieth

novia *f* girlfriend; (prometida) fiancée; (en boda) bride. **~r** *vi* (LAm) go out together. **~zgo** *m* engagement

novicio *m* novice

noviembre *m* November

novill|a *f* heifer. **~o** *m* bullock. **hacer ~os** play truant

novio *m* boyfriend; (prometido) fiancé; (en boda) bridegroom. **los ~s** the bride and groom

nub|arrón *m* large dark cloud. **~e** *f* cloud; (de insectos etc) swarm. **~lado** *a* cloudy, overcast. ● *m* cloud. **~lar** *vt* cloud. □ **~larse** *vpr* become cloudy; <vista> cloud over. **~oso** *a* cloudy

nuca *f* back of the neck

nuclear *a* nuclear

núcleo *m* nucleus

nudillo *m* knuckle

nudis|mo *m* nudism. **~ta** *m* & *f* nudist

nudo *m* knot; (de asunto etc) crux. **tener un ~ en la garganta** have a lump in one's throat. **~so** *a* knotty

nuera *f* daughter-in-law

nuestro *a* our. ● *pron* ours. **~ amigo** our friend. **un coche ~** a car of ours

nueva *f* (piece of) news. **~s** *fpl* news. **~mente** *adv* again

Nueva Zelanda, (LAm) **Nueva Zelandia** *f* New Zealand

nueve *a* & *m* nine

nuevo *a* new. **de ~** again. **estar ~** be as good as new

nuez *f* walnut. **~ de Adán** Adam's apple. **~ moscada** nutmeg

nul|idad *f* nullity; (fam, persona) dead loss fam. **~o** *a* useless; (Jurid) null and void

num|eración *f* numbering. **~eral** *a* & *m* numeral. **~erar** *vt* number. **~érico** *a* numerical

número *m* number; (arábigo, romano) numeral; (de zapatos etc) size; (billete de lotería) lottery ticket; (de publicación) issue. **sin ~** countless

numeroso *a* numerous

nunca *adv* never. **~ (ja)más** never again. **casi ~** hardly ever. **como ~** like never before. **más que ~** more than ever

nupcial *a* nuptial. **banquete ~** wedding breakfast

nutria *f* otter

nutri|ción *f* nutrition. **~do** *a* nourished, fed; (fig) large; <aplausos> loud; <fuego> heavy. **~r** *vt* nourish, feed; (fig) feed. **~tivo** *a* nutritious. **valor** *m* **~tivo** nutritional value

nylon *m* nylon

ñapa *f* (LAm) *extra goods given free*

ñato *adj* (LAm) snub-nosed

ñoñ|ería *f*, **~ez** *f* insipidity. **~o** *a* insipid; (tímido) bashful; (quisquilloso) prudish

o *conj* or. **~ bien** rather. **~... ~** either ... or

oasis *m invar* oasis

obed|ecer [11] *vt/i* obey. **~iencia** *f* obedience. **~iente** *a* obedient

obes|idad *f* obesity. **~o** *a* obese

obispo *m* bishop

obje|ción *f* objection. **~tar** *vt/i* object

objetivo *a* objective. ● *m* objective; (foto etc) lens

objeto *m* object. ~**r** *m* objector. ~**r de conciencia** conscientious objector

oblicuo *a* oblique

obliga|ción *f* obligation; (Com) bond. ~**do** *a* obliged; (forzoso) obligatory; ~**r** [12] *vt* force, oblige. □ ~**rse** *vpr*. ~**rse a** undertake to. ~**torio** *a* obligatory

oboe *m* oboe. ● *m & f* (músico) oboist

obra *f* work; (acción) deed; (de teatro) play; (construcción) building work. ~ **maestra** masterpiece. **en** ~**s** under construction. **por** ~ **de** thanks to. ~**r** *vt* do

obrero *a* labour; *<clase>* working. ● *m* workman; (de fábrica, construcción) worker

obscen|idad *f* obscenity. ~**o** *a* obscene

obscu... ⇒ oscu...

obsequi|ar *vt* lavish attention on. ~**ar con** give, present with. ~**o** *m* gift, present; (agasajo) attention. ~**oso** *a* obliging

observa|ción *f* observation. **hacer una** ~**ción** make a remark. ~**dor** *m* observer. ~**ncia** *f* observance. ~**r** *vt* observe; (notar) notice. ~**torio** *m* observatory

obses|ión *f* obsession. ~**ionar** *vt* obsess. ~**ivo** *a* obsessive. ~**o** *a* obsessed

obst|aculizar [10] *vt* hinder; hold up *<tráfico>*. ~**áculo** *m* obstacle

obstante: **no** ~ *adv* however, nevertheless; (como prep) in spite of

obstar *vi*. **eso no obsta para que vaya** that should not prevent him from going

obstina|do *a* obstinate. □ ~**rse** *vpr*. ~**rse en** (+ *infinitivo*) insist on (+ *gerundio*)

obstru|cción *f* obstruction. ~**ir** [17] *vt* obstruct

obtener [40] *vt* get, obtain

obtura|dor *m* (Foto) shutter. ~**r** *vt* plug; fill *<muela etc>*

obvio *a* obvious

oca *f* goose

ocasi|ón *f* occasion; (oportunidad) opportunity. **aprovechar la** ~**ón** take the opportunity. **con** ~**ón de** on the occasion of. **de** ~**ón** bargain; (usado) second-hand. **en** ~**ones** sometimes. **perder una** ~**ón** miss a chance. ~**onal** *a* chance. ~**onar** *vt* cause

ocaso *m* sunset; (fig) decline

occident|al *a* western. ● *m & f* westerner. ~**e** *m* west

océano *m* ocean

ochenta *a & m* eighty

ocho *a & m* eight. ~**cientos** *a & m* eight hundred

ocio *m* idleness; (tiempo libre) leisure time. ~**sidad** *f* idleness. ~**so** *a* idle; (inútil) pointless

oct|agonal *a* octagonal. ~**ágono** *m* octagon

octano *m* octane

octav|a *f* octave. ~**o** *a & m* eighth

octogenario *a & m* octogenarian

octubre *m* October

ocular *a* eye

oculista *m & f* ophthalmologist, ophthalmic optician

ocult|ar *vt* hide. □ ~**arse** *vpr* hide. ~**o** *a* hidden; (secreto) secret

ocupa|ción *f* occupation. ~**do** *a* occupied; *<persona>* busy. **estar** ~**do** *<asiento>* be taken; *<línea telefónica>* be engaged (Brit), be busy (Amer). ~**nte** *m & f* occupant. ~**r** *vt* occupy, take up *<espacio>*. □ ~**rse** *vpr* look after

ocurr|encia *f* occurrence, event; (idea) idea; (que tiene gracia) witty remark. ~**ir** *vi* happen. **¿qué** ~**e?** what's the matter? □ ~**irse** *vpr* occur. **se me** ~**e que** it occurs to me that

oda *f* ode

odi|ar *vt* hate. ~**o** *m* hatred. ~**oso** *a* hateful; *<persona>* horrible

oeste *a* *<región>* western; *<viento, lado>* west. ● *m* west

ofen|der *vt* offend; (insultar) insult. □ ~**derse** *vpr* take offence. ~**sa** *f* offence. ~**siva** *f* offensive. ~**sivo** *a* offensive

oferta *f* offer; (en subasta) bid. ~**s de empleo** situations vacant. **en** ~ on (special) offer

oficial *a* official. ● *m* skilled worker; (Mil) officer

oficin|a *f* office. ~**a de colocación** employment office. ~**a de turismo** tourist office. **horas** *fpl* **de** ~**a** business hours. ~**ista** *m & f* office worker

oficio *m* trade. ~**so** *a* (no oficial) unofficial

ofrec|er [11] *vt* offer; give *<fiesta, banquete etc>*; (prometer) promise. □ ~**erse** *vpr* *<persona>* volunteer. ~**imiento** *m* offer

ofrenda *f* offering. ~**r** *vt* offer

ofuscar [7] *vt* blind; (confundir) confuse. □ ~**se** *vpr* get worked up

oí|ble *a* audible. ~**do** *m* hearing; (Anat) ear. **al** ~**do** in one's ear. **de** ~**das** by hearsay. **conocer de** ~**das** have heard of. **de** ~**do** by ear. **duro de** ~**do** hard of hearing

oigo *vb* ⇒OÍR

oír [50] *vt* hear. **¡oiga!** listen!; (al teléfono) hello!

ojal *m* buttonhole

ojalá *int* I hope so! ● *conj* if only

ojea|da *f* glance. **dar una** ~**da a, echar una** ~**da a** have a quick glance at. ~**r** *vt* have a look at

ojeras *fpl* rings under one's eyes

ojeriza *f* ill will. **tener** ~ **a** have a grudge against

ojo *m* eye; (de cerradura) keyhole; (de un puente) span. **¡**~**!** careful!

ola *f* wave

olé *int* bravo!

olea|da *f* wave. ~**je** *m* swell

óleo *m* oil; (cuadro) oil painting

oleoducto *m* oil pipeline

oler [2] (*las formas que empezarían por* **ue** *se escriben* **hue**) *vt* smell. ● *vi* smell (**a** of). **me huele mal** (fig) it sounds fishy to me

olfat|ear *vt* sniff; scent *<rastro>*. ~**o** *m* (sense of) smell (fig) intuition

olimpiada *f*, **olimpíada** *f* Olympic games, Olympics

olímpico *a* Olympic; (fig, 🔟) total

oliv|a *f* olive. ~**ar** *m* olive grove. ~**o** *m* olive tree

olla *f* pot, casserole. ~ **a/de presión,** ~ **exprés** pressure cooker

olmo *m* elm (tree)

olor *m* smell. ~**oso** *a* sweet-smelling

olvid|adizo *a* forgetful. ~**ar** *vt* forget. □ ~**arse** *vpr* forget. ~**arse de** forget. **se me** ~**ó** I forgot. ~**o** *m* oblivion; (acto) omission

ombligo *m* navel

omi|sión *f* omission. ~**tir** *vt* omit

ómnibus *a* omnibus

omnipotente *a* omnipotent

omóplato *m*, **omoplato** *m* shoulder blade

once *a & m* eleven

ond|a *f* wave. ~**a corta** short wave. ~**a larga** long wave. **longitud** *f* **de** ~**a** wavelength. ~**ear** *vi* wave; *<agua>* ripple. ~**ulación** *f* undulation; (del pelo) wave. ~**ular** *vi* wave

onomásti|co *a* *<índice>* of names. ● *m* (LAm) saint's day. ~**ca** *f* saint's day

ONU *abrev* (**Organización de las Naciones Unidas**) UN

opac|ar [7] (LAm) make opaque; (deslucir) mar; (anular) overshadow. ~**o** *a* opaque; (fig) dull

opci|ón *f* option. ~**onal** *a* optional

ópera *f* opera

opera|ción *f* operation; (Com) transaction. ~**dor** *m* operator; (TV) cameraman; (Mex, obrero) machinist. ~**r** *vt* operate on; work *<milagro etc>*; (Mex) operate *<máquina>*. ● *vi* operate; (Com) deal. ~**rio** *m* machinist. □ ~**rse** *vpr* take place; (Med) have an operation. ~**torio** *a* operative

opereta *f* operetta

opin|ar *vi* express one's opinion. ● *vt* think. ~ **que** think that. **¿qué opinas?** what do you think? ~**ión** *f* opinion. **la** ~**ión pública** public opinion

opio *m* opium

opone|nte *a* opposing. ● *m & f* opponent. ~**r** *vt* oppose; offer *<resistencia>*; raise *<objeción>*. □ ~**rse** *vpr* be opposed; *<dos personas>* oppose each other

oporto *m* port (wine)

oportun|idad *f* opportunity; (cualidad de oportuno) timeliness; (LAm, ocasión) occasion. ~**ista** *m & f* opportunist. **~o** *a* opportune; (apropiado) suitable

oposi|ción *f* opposition. **~ciones** *fpl* public examination. **~tor** *m* candidate; (Pol) opponent

opres|ión *f* oppression; (ahogo) difficulty in breathing. **~ivo** *a* oppressive. **~or** *m* oppressor

oprimir *vt* squeeze; press *<botón etc>*; *<ropa>* be too tight for; (fig) oppress

optar *vi* choose. **~ por** opt for

óptic|a *f* optics; (tienda) optician's (shop). **~o** *a* optic(al). ● *m* optician

optimis|mo *m* optimism. **~ta** *a* optimistic. ● *m & f* optimist

óptimo *a* ideal; *<condiciones>* perfect

opuesto *a* opposite; *<opiniones>* conflicting

opulen|cia *f* opulence. **~to** *a* opulent

oración *f* prayer; (Gram) sentence

ora|dor *m* speaker. **~l** *a* oral

órale *int* (Mex) come on!; (de acuerdo) OK!

orar *vi* pray (**por** for)

órbita *f* orbit

orden *f* order. **~ del día** agenda. **órdenes** *fpl* **sagradas** Holy Orders. **a sus órdenes** (esp Mex) can I help you? **~ de arresto** arrest warrant. **en ~** in order. **por ~** in turn. **~ado** *a* tidy

ordenador *m* computer

ordena|nza *f* ordinance. ● *m* (Mil) orderly. **~r** *vt* put in order; (mandar) order; (Relig) ordain; (LAm, en restaurante) order

ordeñar *vt* milk

ordinario *a* ordinary; (grosero) common; (de mala calidad) poor-quality

orear *vt* air

orégano *m* oregano

oreja *f* ear

orfanato *m* orphanage

orfebre *m* goldsmith, silversmith

orfeón *m* choral society

orgánico *a* organic

organillo *m* barrel-organ

organismo *m* organism

organista *m & f* organist

organiza|ción *f* organization. **~dor** *m* organizer. **~r** [10] *vt* organize. □ **~rse** *vpr* get organized

órgano *m* organ

orgasmo *m* orgasm

orgía *f* orgy

orgullo *m* pride. **~so** *a* proud

orientación *f* orientation; (guía) guidance; (Archit) aspect

oriental *a & m & f* oriental

orientar *vt* position; advise *<persona>*. □ **~se** *vpr* point; *<persona>* find one's bearings

oriente *m* east

orificio *m* hole

orig|en *m* origin. **dar ~en a** give rise to. **~inal** *a* original; (excéntrico) odd. **~inalidad** *f* originality. **~inar** *vt* give rise to. **~inario** *a* original; (nativo) native. **ser ~inario de** come from. □ **~inarse** *vpr* originate; *<incendio>* start

orilla *f* (del mar) shore; (de río) bank; (borde) edge. **a ~s del mar** by the sea

orina *f* urine. **~l** *m* chamber-pot. **~r** *vi* urinate

oriundo *a* native. **ser ~ de** *<persona>* come from; *<especie etc>* native to

ornamental *a* ornamental

ornitología *f* ornithology

oro *m* gold. **~s** *mpl* Spanish card suit. **~ de ley** 9 carat gold. **hacerse de ~** make a fortune. **prometer el ~ y el moro** promise the moon

orquesta *f* orchestra. **~l** *a* orchestral. **~r** *vt* orchestrate

orquídea *f* orchid

ortiga *f* nettle

ortodoxo *a* orthodox

ortografía *f* spelling

ortopédico *a* orthopaedic

oruga *f* caterpillar

orzuelo *m* sty

os *pron* (acusativo) you; (dativo) (to) you; (reflexivo) (to) yourselves; (recíproco) (to) each other

osad|ía *f* boldness. **~o** *a* bold

oscila|ción *f* swinging; (de precios) fluctuation; (Tec) oscillation. **~r** *vi* swing; *<precio>* fluctuate; (Tec) oscillate

oscur|ecer [11] *vi* get dark. ● *vt* darken; (fig) obscure. □ **~ecerse** *vpr* grow dark; (nublarse) cloud over. **~idad** *f* darkness; (fig) obscurity. **~o** *a* dark; (fig) obscure. **a ~as** in the dark

óseo *a* bone

oso *m* bear. **~ de felpa, ~ de peluche** teddy bear

ostensible *a* obvious

ostent|ación *f* ostentation. **~ar** *vt* show off; (mostrar) show. **~oso** *a* ostentatious

osteópata *m & f* osteopath

ostión *m* (esp Mex) oyster

ostra *f* oyster

ostracismo *m* ostracism

Otan *abrev* (**Organización del Tratado del Atlántico Norte**) NATO, North Atlantic Treaty Organization

otitis *f* inflammation of the ear

otoño *m* autumn (Brit), fall (Amer)

otorga|miento *m* granting. **~r** [12] *vt* give; grant <*préstamo*>; (Jurid) draw up <*testamento*>

otorrinolaringólogo *m* ear, nose and throat specialist

································

otro, otra

● *adjetivo*

····▶ another; (con artículo, posesivo) other. **come ~ pedazo** have another piece. **el ~ día** the other day. **mi ~ coche** my other car. **otra cosa** something else. **otra persona** somebody else. **otra vez** again

····▶ (en plural) other; (con numeral) another. **en otras ocasiones** on other occasions. **~s 3 vasos** another 3 glasses

····▶ (siguiente) next. **al ~ día** the next day. **me bajo en la otra estación** I get off at the next station

● *pronombre*

····▶ (cosa) another one. **lo cambié por ~** I changed it for another one

····▶ (persona) someone else. **invitó a ~** she invited someone else

····▶ (en plural) (some) others. **tengo ~s en casa** I have (some) others at home. **~s piensan lo contrario** others think the opposite

····▶ (con artículo) **el ~** the other one. **los ~s** the others. **uno detrás del ~** one after the other. **los ~s no vinieron** the others didn't come. **esta semana no, la otra** not this week, next week. **de un día para el ~** from one day to the next

➡ Para usos complementarios ver **uno, tanto**

································

ovación *f* ovation

oval *a*, **ovalado** *a* oval

óvalo *m* oval

ovario *m* ovary

oveja *f* sheep; (hembra) ewe

overol *m* (LAm) overalls

ovillo *m* ball. **hacerse un ~** curl up

OVNI *abrev* (**objeto volante no identificado**) UFO

ovulación *f* ovulation

oxida|ción *f* rusting. **~r** *vi* rust. □ **~rse** *vpr* go rusty

óxido *m* rust; (en química) oxide

oxígeno *m* oxygen

oye *vb* ⇒ oíR

oyente *a* listening. ● *m & f* listener; (Univ) occasional student

ozono *m* ozone

································

Pp

································

pabellón *m* pavilion; (en jardín) summerhouse; (en hospital) block; (de instrumento) bell; (bandera) flag

pacer [11] *vi* graze

pachucho *a* <*fruta*> overripe; <*persona*> poorly

pacien|cia *f* patience. **perder la ~cia** lose patience. **~te** *a & m & f* patient

pacificar [7] *vt* pacify. □ **~se** *vpr* calm down

pacífico *a* peaceful. **el (Océano) P~** the Pacific (Ocean)

pacifis|mo *m* pacifism. **~ta** *a & m & f* pacifist

pact|ar *vi* agree, make a pact. **~o** *m* pact, agreement

padec|er [11] *vt/i* suffer (**de** from); (soportar) bear. **∼cer del corazón** have heart trouble. **∼imiento** *m* suffering

padrastro *m* stepfather

padre *a* ⓘ terrible; (Mex, estupendo) great. ● *m* father. **∼s** *mpl* parents

padrino *m* godfather; (en boda) *man who gives away the bride*

padrón *m* register. **∼ electoral** (LAm) electoral roll

paella *f* paella

paga *f* payment; (sueldo) pay. **∼dero** *a* payable

pagano *a & m* pagan

pagar [12] *vt* pay; pay for *<compras>*. ● *vi* pay. **∼é** *m* IOU

página *f* page

pago *m* payment

país *m* country; (ciudadanos) nation. **∼ natal** native land. **el P∼ Vasco** the Basque Country. **los P∼es Bajos** the Low Countries

paisaje *m* landscape, scenery

paisano *m* compatriot

paja *f* straw; (en texto) padding

pájaro *m* bird. **∼ carpintero** woodpecker

paje *m* page

pala *f* shovel; (para cavar) spade; (para basura) dustpan; (de pimpón) bat

palabr|a *f* word; (habla) speech. **pedir la ∼a** ask to speak. **tomar la ∼a** take the floor. **∼ota** *f* swear-word. **decir ∼otas** swear

palacio *m* palace

paladar *m* palate

palanca *f* lever; (fig) influence. **∼ de cambio** (**de velocidades**) gear lever (Brit), gear shift (Amer)

palangana *f* washbasin (Brit), washbowl (Amer)

palco *m* (en el teatro) box

palestino *a & m* Palestinian

paleta *f* (de pintor) palette; (de albañil) trowel

paleto *m* yokel

paliativo *a & m* palliative

palide|cer [11] *vi* turn pale. **∼z** *f* paleness

pálido *a* pale. **ponerse ∼** turn pale

palillo *m* (de dientes) toothpick; (para comer) chopstick

paliza *f* beating

palma *f* (de la mano) palm; (árbol) palm (tree); (de dátiles) date palm. **dar ∼s** clap. **∼da** *f* pat; (LAm) slap. **∼das** *fpl* applause

palmera *f* palm tree

palmo *m* span; (fig) few inches. **∼ a ∼** inch by inch

palmote|ar *vi* clap. **∼o** *m* clapping, applause

palo *m* stick; (de valla) post; (de golf) club; (golpe) blow; (de naipes) suit; (mástil) mast

paloma *f* pigeon; (blanca, símbolo) dove

palomitas *fpl* popcorn

palpar *vt* feel

palpita|ción *f* palpitation. **∼nte** *a* throbbing. **∼r** *vi* beat; (latir con fuerza) pound; *<vena, sien>* throb

palta *f* (LAm) avocado (pear)

paludismo *m* malaria

pamp|a *f* pampas. **∼ero** *a* of the pampas

pan *m* bread; (barra) loaf. **∼ integral** wholewheat bread, wholemeal bread (Brit). **∼ tostado** toast. **∼ rallado** breadcrumbs. **ganarse el ∼** earn one's living

pana *f* corduroy

panader|ía *f* bakery; (tienda) baker's (shop). **∼o** *m* baker

panal *m* honeycomb

panameño *a & m* Panamanian

pancarta *f* banner, placard

panda *m* panda

pander|eta *f* (small) tambourine. **∼o** *m* tambourine

pandilla *f* gang

panecillo *m* (bread) roll

panel *m* panel

panfleto *m* pamphlet

pánico *m* panic. **tener ∼** be terrified (a of)

panor|ama *m* panorama. **∼ámico** *a* panoramic

panque *m* (Mex) sponge cake

pantaletas *fpl* (Mex) panties, knickers (Brit)

pantalla *f* screen; (de lámpara) (lamp) shade

pantalón *m*, **pantalones** *mpl* trousers

pantano *m* marsh; (embalse) reservoir. **~so** *a* marshy

pantera *f* panther

panti *m*, (Mex) **pantimedias** *fpl* tights (Brit), pantyhose (Amer)

pantomima *f* pantomime

pantorrilla *f* calf

pantufla *f* slipper

panz|a *f* belly. **~udo** *a* pot-bellied

pañal *m* nappy (Brit), diaper (Amer)

paño *m* material; (de lana) woollen cloth; (trapo) cloth. **~o de cocina** dishcloth; (para secar) tea towel. **~o higiénico** sanitary towel. **en ~os menores** in one's underclothes

pañuelo *m* handkerchief; (de cabeza) scarf

papa *m* pope. ●*f* (LAm) potato. **~s fritas** (LAm) chips (Brit), French fries (Amer); (de paquete) crisps (Brit), chips (Amer)

papá *m* dad(dy). **~s** *mpl* parents. **P~ Noel** Father Christmas

papada *f* (de persona) double chin

papagayo *m* parrot

papalote *m* (Mex) kite

papanatas *m invar* simpleton

paparrucha *f* (tontería) silly thing

papaya *f* papaya, pawpaw

papel *m* paper; (en el teatro etc) role. **~ carbón** carbon paper. **~ de calcar** tracing paper. **~ de envolver** wrapping paper. **~ de plata** silver paper. **~ higiénico** toilet paper. **~ pintado** wallpaper. **~ secante** blotting paper. **~eo** *m* paperwork. **~era** *f* wastepaper basket. **~ería** *f* stationer's (shop). **~eta** *f* (para votar) (ballot) paper

paperas *fpl* mumps

paquete *m* packet; (bulto) parcel; (LAm, de papas fritas) bag; (Mex, problema) headache. **~ postal** parcel

Paquistán *m* Pakistan

paquistaní *a & m* Pakistani

par *a* <*número*> even. ●*m* couple; (dos cosas iguales) pair. **a ~es** two by two. **de ~ en ~** wide open. **~es y**

nones odds and evens. **sin ~** without equal. ●*f* par. **a la ~** (Com) at par. **a la ~ que** at the same time

para

● *preposición*

····➤ for. **es ~ ti** it's for you. **~ siempre** for ever. **¿~ qué?** what for? **~ mi cumpleaños** for my birthday

····➤ (con infinitivo) to. **es muy tarde ~ llamar** it's too late to call. **salió ~ para divertirse** he went out to have fun. **lo hago ~ ahorrar** I do it (in order) to save money

····➤ (dirección) **iba ~ la oficina** he was going to the office. **empújalo ~ atrás** push it back. **¿vas ~ casa?** are you going home?

····➤ (tiempo) by. **debe estar listo ~ el 5** it must be ready by the 5th. **~ entonces** by then

····➤ (LAm, hora) to. **son 5 para la una** it's 5 to one

····➤ **para que** so (that). **grité ~ que me oyera** I shouted so (that) he could hear me.

Note that **para que** is always followed by a verb in the subjunctive

parabienes *mpl* congratulations

parábola *f* (narración) parable

parabólica *f* satellite dish

para|brisas *m invar* windscreen (Brit), windshield (Amer). **~caídas** *m invar* parachute. **~caidista** *m & f* parachutist; (Mil) paratrooper. **~choques** *m invar* bumper (Brit), fender (Amer) (Rail) buffer

parad|a *f* (acción) stop; (lugar) bus stop; (de taxis) rank; (Mil) parade. **~ero** *m* whereabouts; (LAm, lugar) bus stop. **~o** *a* stationary; <*desempleado*> unemployed. **estar ~** (LAm, de pie) be standing

paradoja *f* paradox

parador *m* state-owned hotel

parafina *f* paraffin

paraguas *m invar* umbrella

Paraguay *m* Paraguay

paraguayo *a & m* Paraguayan

paraíso *m* paradise; (en el teatro) gallery

parelel|a *f* parallel (line). ~**as** *fpl* parallel bars. ~**o** *a & m* parallel

par|álisis *f invar* paralysis. ~**alítico** *a* paralytic. ~**alizar** [10] *vt* paralyse

paramilitar *a* paramilitary

páramo *m* bleak upland

parangón *m* comparison.

paraninfo *m* main hall

paranoi|a *f* paranoia. ~**co** *a* paranoiac

parar *vt/i* stop. **sin** ~ continuously. □ ~**se** *vpr* stop; (LAm, ponerse de pie) stand

pararrayos *m invar* lightning conductor

parásito *a* parasitic. ● *m* parasite

parcela *f* plot. ~**r** *vt* divide into plots

parche *m* patch

parcial *a* partial. **a tiempo** ~ part-time. ~**idad** *f* prejudice

parco *a* laconic; (sobrio) sparing, frugal

parear *vt* put into pairs

parec|er *m* opinion. **al** ~**er** apparently. **a mi** ~**er** in my opinion. ● *vi* [11] seem; (asemejarse) look like; (tener aspecto de) look. **me** ~**e** I think. ~**e fácil** it looks easy. **¿qué te** ~**e?** what do you think? **según** ~**e** apparently. □ ~**erse** *vpr* resemble, look like. ~**ido** *a* similar. **bien** ~**ido** good-looking. ● *m* similarity

pared *f* wall. ~ **por medio** next door. ~**ón** *m* (de fusilamiento) wall. **llevar al** ~**ón** shoot

parej|a *f* pair; (hombre y mujer) couple; (compañero) partner. ~**o** *a* the same; (LAm, sin desniveles) even; (LAm, liso) smooth; (Mex, equitativo) equal. ● *adv* (LAm) evenly

parente|la *f* relations. ~**sco** *m* relationship

paréntesis *m invar* parenthesis, bracket (Brit); (intervalo) break. **entre** ~ in brackets (Brit), in parenthesis; (fig) by the way

paria *m & f* outcast

paridad *f* equality; (Com) parity

pariente *m & f* relation, relative

parir *vt* give birth to. ● *vi* give birth

parisiense *a & m & f*, **parisino** *a & m* Parisian

parking /'parkin/ *m* car park (Brit), parking lot (Amer)

parlament|ar *vi* talk. ~**ario** *a* parliamentary. ● *m* member of parliament (Brit), congressman (Amer). ~**o** *m* parliament

parlanchín *a* talkative. ● *m* chatterbox

parlante *m* (LAm) loudspeaker

paro *m* stoppage; (desempleo) unemployment; (subsidio) unemployment benefit; (LAm, huelga) strike. ~ **cardíaco** cardiac arrest

parodia *f* parody

parpadear *vi* blink; <*luz*> flicker

párpado *m* eyelid

parque *m* park. ~ **de atracciones** funfair. ~ **infantil** playground. ~ **zoológico** zoo, zoological gardens

parquímetro *m* parking meter

parra *f* grapevine

párrafo *m* paragraph

parrilla *f* grill; (LAm, Auto) luggage rack. **a la** ~ grilled. ~**da** *f* grill

párroco *m* parish priest

parroquia *f* parish; (iglesia) parish church. ~**no** *m* parishioner; (cliente) customer

parte *m* (informe) report. **dar** ~ report. **de mi** ~ for me ● *f* part; (porción) share; (Jurid) party; (Mex, repuesto) spare (part). **de** ~ **de** from. **¿de** ~ **de quién?** (al teléfono) who's speaking? **en cualquier** ~ anywhere. **en gran** ~ largely. **en** ~ partly. **en todas** ~**s** everywhere. **la mayor** ~ the majority. **la** ~ **superior** the top. **ninguna** ~ nowhere. **por otra** ~ on the other hand. **por todas** ~**s** everywhere

partera *f* midwife

partición *f* division; (Pol) partition

participa|ción *f* participation; (noticia) announcement; (de lotería) share. ~**nte** *a* participating. ● *m & f* participant. ~**r** *vt* announce. ● *vi* take part

participio *m* participle

particular *a* particular; <*clase*> private. **nada de** ~ nothing special. ● *m* private individual.

partida f departure; (en registro) entry; (documento) certificate; (de mercancías) consignment; (juego) game; (de gente) group

partidario a & m partisan. ~ de in favour of

parti|do m (Pol) party; (encuentro) match, game; (LAm, de ajedrez) game. ~r vt cut; (romper) break; crack <nueces>. ● vi leave. a ~r de from. ~ de start from. □ ~rse vpr (romperse) break; (dividirse) split

partitura f (Mus) score

parto m labour. **estar de** ~ be in labour

parvulario m kindergarten, nursery school (Brit)

pasa f raisin. ~ **de Corinto** currant

pasa|da f passing; (de puntos) row. **de** ~**da** in passing. ~**dero** a passable. ~**dizo** m passage. ~**do** a past; <día, mes etc> last; (anticuado) old-fashioned; <comida> bad, off. ~**do maña**na the day after tomorrow. ~**dos tres días** after three days. ~**dor** m bolt; (de pelo) hair-slide

pasaje m passage; (pasajeros) passengers; (LAm, de avión etc) ticket. ~**ro** a passing. ● m passenger

pasamano(s) m handrail; (barandilla de escalera) banister(s)

pasamontañas m invar balaclava

pasaporte m passport

pasar vt pass; (atravesar) go through; (filtrar) strain; spend <tiempo>; show <película>; (tolerar) tolerate; give <mensaje, enfermedad>. ● vi pass; (suceder) happen; (ir) go; (venir) come; <tiempo> go by. ~ **de** have no interest in. ~**lo bien** have a good time. ~ **frío** be cold. ~ **la aspiradora** vacuum. ~ **por alto** leave out. **lo que pasa es que** the fact is that. **pase lo que pase** whatever happens. **¡pase Vd!** come in!, go in! **¡que lo pases bien!** have a good time! **¿qué pasa?** what's the matter?, what's happening? □ ~**se** vpr pass; <dolor> go away; <flores> wither; <comida> go bad; spend <tiempo>; (excederse) go too far

pasarela f footbridge; (Naut) gangway

pasatiempo m hobby, pastime

Pascua f (fiesta de los hebreos) Passover; (de Resurrección) Easter; (Navidad) Christmas. ~**s** fpl Christmas

pase m pass

pase|ante m & f passer-by. ~**ar** vt walk <perro>; (exhibir) show off. ● vi walk. **ir a** ~**ar, salir a** ~**ar** walk. □ ~**arse** vpr walk. ~**o** m walk; (en coche etc) ride; (calle) avenue. ~**o marítimo** promenade. **dar un** ~**o, ir de** ~ go for a walk. **¡vete a** ~**o!** Ⅱ get lost! Ⅱ

pasillo m corridor; (de cine, avión) aisle

pasión f passion

pasivo a passive

pasm|ar vt astonish. □ ~**arse** vpr be astonished

paso m step; (acción de pasar) passing; (camino) way; (entre montañas) pass; (estrecho) strait(s). ~ **a nivel** level crossing (Brit), grade crossing (Amer). ~ **de cebra** zebra crossing. ~ **de peatones** pedestrian crossing. ~ **elevado** flyover (Brit), overpass (Amer). **a cada** ~ at every turn. **a dos** ~**s** very near. **de** ~ in passing. **de** ~ **por** just passing through. **oír** ~**s** hear footsteps. **prohibido el** ~ no entry

pasota m & f drop-out

pasta f paste; (masa) dough; (▣, dinero) dough ▣. ~**s** fpl pasta; (pasteles) pastries. ~ **de dientes**, ~ **dentífrica** toothpaste

pastel m cake; (empanada) pie; (lápiz) pastel. ~**ería** f cake shop

pasteurizado a pasteurized

pastilla f pastille; (de jabón) bar; (de chocolate) piece

pasto m pasture; (hierba) grass; (LAm, césped) lawn. ~**r** m shepherd; (Relig) minister. ~**ra** f shepherdess

pata f leg; (pie de perro, gato) paw; (de ave) foot. ~**s arriba** upside down. **a cuatro** ~**s** on all fours. **meter la** ~ put one's foot in it. **tener mala** ~ have bad luck. ~**da** f kick. ~**lear** vi stamp one's feet; <niño pequeño> kick

patata f potato. ~**s fritas** chips (Brit), French fries (Amer); (de bolsa) (potato) crisps (Brit), (potato) chips (Amer)

patente *a* obvious. ● *f* licence

patern|al *a* paternal; *<cariño etc>* fatherly. **~idad** *f* paternity. **~o** *a* paternal; *<cariño etc>* fatherly

patético *a* moving

patillas *fpl* sideburns

patín *m* skate; (con ruedas) roller skate

patina|dor *m* skater. **~je** *m* skating. **~r** *vi* skate; (resbalar) slide; *<coche>* skid

patio *m* patio. **~ de butacas** stalls (Brit), orchestra (Amer)

pato *m* duck

patológico *a* pathological

patoso *a* clumsy

patraña *f* hoax

patria *f* homeland

patriarca *m* patriarch

patrimonio *m* patrimony; (fig) heritage

patri|ota *a* patriotic. ● *m & f* patriot. **~otismo** *m* patriotism

patrocin|ar *vt* sponsor. **~io** *m* sponsorship

patrón *m* (jefe) boss; (de pensión etc) landlord; (en costura) pattern

patrulla *f* patrol; (fig, cuadrilla) group. **~r** *vt/i* patrol

pausa *f* pause. **~do** *a* slow

pauta *f* guideline

paviment|ar *vt* pave. **~o** *m* pavement

pavo *m* turkey. **~ real** peacock

pavor *m* terror

payas|ada *f* buffoonery. **~o** *m* clown

paz *f* peace

peaje *m* toll

peatón *m* pedestrian

peca *f* freckle

peca|do *m* sin; (defecto) fault. **~dor** *m* sinner. **~minoso** *a* sinful. **~r** [7] *vi* sin

pech|o *m* chest; (de mujer) breast; (fig, corazón) heart. **dar el ~o a un niño** breast-feed a child. **tomar a ~o** take to heart. **~uga** *f* breast

pecoso *a* freckled

peculiar *a* peculiar, particular. **~idad** *f* peculiarity

pedal *m* pedal. **~ear** *vi* pedal

pedante *a* pedantic

pedazo *m* piece, bit. **a ~s** in pieces. **hacer(se) ~s** smash

pediatra *m & f* paediatrician

pedicuro *m* chiropodist

pedi|do *m* order; (LAm, solicitud) request. **~r** [5] *vt* ask for; (Com, en restaurante) order. ● *vi* ask. **~r prestado** borrow

pega|dizo *a* catchy. **~joso** *a* sticky

pega|mento *m* glue. **~r** [12] *vt* stick (on); (coser) sew on; give *<enfermedad etc>*; (juntar) join; (golpear) hit; (dar) give. **~r fuego a** set fire to. ● *vi* stick. □ **~rse** *vpr* stick; (pelearse) hit each other. **~tina** *f* sticker

pein|ado *m* hairstyle. **~ar** *vt* comb. □ **~arse** *vpr* comb one's hair. **~e** *m* comb. **~eta** *f* ornamental comb

p.ej. *abrev* (**por ejemplo**) e.g.

pelado *a* *<fruta>* peeled; *<cabeza>* bald; *<terreno>* bare

pela|je *m* (de animal) fur; (fig, aspecto) appearance. **~mbre** *m* (de animal) fur; (de persona) thick hair

pelar *vt* peel; shell *<habas>*; skin *<tomates>*; pluck *<ave>*

peldaño *m* step; (de escalera de mano) rung

pelea *f* fight; (discusión) quarrel. **~r** *vi* fight; (discutir) quarrel. □ **~rse** *vpr* fight; (discutir) quarrel

peletería *f* fur shop

peliagudo *a* difficult, tricky

pelícano *m* pelican

película *f* film (esp Brit), movie (esp Amer). **~ de dibujos animados** cartoon (film)

peligro *m* danger; (riesgo) hazard, risk. **poner en ~** endanger. **~so** *a* dangerous

pelirrojo *a* red-haired

pellejo *m* skin

pellizc|ar [7] *vt* pinch. **~o** *m* pinch

pelma *m & f*, **pelmazo** *m* bore, nuisance

pelo *m* hair. **no tener ~os en la lengua** be outspoken. **tomar el ~o a uno** pull s.o.'s leg

pelota *f* ball. **~ vasca** pelota. **hacer la ~ a uno** suck up to s.o.

pelotera *f* squabble

peluca *f* wig

peludo *a* hairy

peluquer|ía *f* hairdresser's. **~o** *m* hairdresser

pelusa *f* down

pena *f* sadness; *<lástima>* pity; (LAm, vergüenza) embarrassment; (Jurid) sentence. **~ de muerte** death penalty. **a duras ~s** with difficulty. **da ~ que** it's a pity that. **me da ~** it makes me sad. **merecer la ~** be worthwhile. **pasar ~s** suffer hardship. **¡qué ~!** what a pity! **valer la ~** be worthwhile

penal *a* penal; *<derecho>* criminal. ● *m* prison; (LAm, penalty) penalty. **~idad** *f* suffering; (Jurid) penalty. **~ty** *m* penalty

pendiente *a* hanging; *<cuenta>* outstanding; *<asunto etc>* pending. ● *m* earring. ● *f* slope

péndulo *m* pendulum

pene *m* penis

penetra|nte *a* penetrating; *<sonido>* piercing; *<viento>* bitter. **~r** *vt* penetrate; (fig) pierce. ● *vi*. **~r en** penetrate; (entrar) go into

penicilina *f* penicillin

pen|ínsula *f* peninsula. **~insular** *a* peninsular

penique *m* penny

penitencia *f* penitence; (castigo) penance

penoso *a* painful; (difícil) difficult; (LAm, tímido) shy; (LAm, embarazoso) embarrassing

pensa|do *a*. **bien ~do** all things considered. **menos ~do** least expected. **~dor** *m* thinker. **~miento** *m* thought. **~r** [1] *vt* think; (considerar) consider. **cuando menos se piensa** when least expected. **¡ni ~rlo!** no way! **pienso que sí** I think so. ● *vi* think. **~r en** think about. **~tivo** *a* thoughtful

pensi|ón *f* pension; (casa de huéspedes) guest-house. **~ón completa** full board. **~onista** *m* & *f* pensioner; (huésped) lodger

penúltimo *a* & *m* penultimate, last but one

penumbra *f* half-light

penuria *f* shortage. **pasar ~s** suffer hardship

peñ|a *f* rock; (de amigos) group; (LAm, club) folk club. **~ón** *m* rock. **el P~ón de Gibraltar** The Rock (of Gibraltar)

peón *m* labourer; (en ajedrez) pawn; (en damas) piece

peonza *f* (spinning) top

peor *a* (comparativo) worse; (superlativo) worst. ● *adv* worse. **de mal en ~** from bad to worse. **lo ~** the worst thing. **tanto ~** so much the worse

pepin|illo *m* gherkin. **~o** *m* cucumber. **(no) me importa un ~o** I couldn't care less

pepita *f* pip; (de oro) nugget

pequeñ|ez *f* smallness; (minucia) trifle. **~o** *a* small, little; (de edad) young; (menor) younger. ● *m* little one. **es el ~o** he's the youngest

pera *f* (fruta) pear. **~l** *m* pear (tree)

percance *m* mishap

percatarse *vpr*. **~ de** notice

perc|epción *f* perception. **~ibir** *vt* perceive; earn *<dinero>*

percha *f* hanger; (de aves) perch

percusión *f* percussion

perde|dor *a* losing. ● *m* loser. **~r** [1] *vt* lose; (malgastar) waste; miss *<tren etc>*. ● *vi* lose. □ **~rse** *vpr* get lost; (desaparecer) disappear; (desperdiciarse) be wasted; (estropearse) be spoilt. **echar(se) a ~r** spoil

pérdida *f* loss; (de líquido) leak; (de tiempo) waste

perdido *a* lost

perdiz *f* partridge

perd|ón *m* pardon, forgiveness. **pedir ~ón** apologize. ● *int* sorry! **~onar** *vt* excuse, forgive; (Jurid) pardon. **¡~one (Vd)!** sorry!

perdura|ble *a* lasting. **~r** *vi* last

perece|dero *a* perishable. **~r** [11] *vi* perish

peregrin|ación *f* pilgrimage. **~o** *a* strange. ● *m* pilgrim

perejil *m* parsley

perengano *m* so-and-so

perenne *a* everlasting; (Bot) perennial

perez|a *f* laziness. **~oso** *a* lazy

perfec|ción f perfection. **a la ~ción** perfectly, to perfection. **~cionar** vt perfect; (mejorar) improve. **~cionista** m & f perfectionist. **~to** a perfect; (completo) complete

perfil m profile; (contorno) outline. **~ado** a well-shaped

perfora|ción f perforation. **~dora** f punch. **~r** vt pierce, perforate; punch <papel, tarjeta etc>

perfum|ar vt perfume. □ **~arse** vpr put perfume on. **~e** m perfume, scent. **~ería** f perfumery

pericia f skill

perif|eria f (de ciudad) outskirts. **~érico** a <barrio> outlying. ● m (Mex, carretera) ring road

perilla f (barba) goatee

perímetro m perimeter

periódico a periodic(al). ● m newspaper

periodis|mo m journalism. **~ta** m & f journalist

período m, **periodo** m period

periquito m budgerigar

periscopio m periscope

perito a & m expert

perju|dicar [7] vt damage; (desfavorecer) not suit. **~dicial** a damaging. **~icio** m damage. **en ~icio de** to the detriment of

perla f pearl. **de ~s** adv very well

permane|cer [11] vi remain. **~ncia** f permanence; (estancia) stay. **~nte** a permanent. ● f perm. ● m (Mex) perm

permi|sivo a permissive. **~so** m permission; (documento) licence; (Mil etc) leave. **~so de conducir** driving licence (Brit), driver's license (Amer). **con ~so** excuse me. **~tir** vt allow, permit. ¿**me ~te?** may I? □ **~tirse** vpr allow s.o.

pernicioso a pernicious; <persona> wicked

perno m bolt

pero conj but. ● m fault; (objeción) objection

perogrullada f platitude

perpendicular a & f perpendicular

perpetrar vt perpetrate

perpetu|ar [21] vt perpetuate. **~o** a perpetual

perplejo a perplexed

perr|a f (animal) bitch; (moneda) coin, penny (Brit), cent (Amer); (rabieta) tantrum. **estar sin una ~a** be broke. **~era** f dog pound; (vehículo) dog catcher's van. **~o** a awful. ● m dog. **~o galgo** greyhound. **de ~os** awful

persa a & m & f Persian

perse|cución f pursuit; (política etc) persecution. **~guir** [5 & 13] vt pursue; (por ideología etc) persecute

persevera|nte a persevering. **~r** vi persevere

persiana f blind; (LAm, contraventana) shutter

persignarse vpr cross o.s.

persist|ente a persistent. **~ir** vi persist

person|a f person. **~as** fpl people. **~aje** m (persona importante) important figure; (de obra literaria) character. **~al** a personal. ● m staff. **~alidad** f personality. □ **~arse** vpr appear in person. **~ificar** [7] vt personify

perspectiva f perspective

perspica|cia f shrewdness; (de vista) keen eyesight. **~z** a shrewd; <vista> keen

persua|dir vt persuade. **~sión** f persuasion. **~sivo** a persuasive

pertenecer [11] vi belong

pértiga f pole. **salto** m **con ~** pole vault

pertinente a relevant

perturba|ción f disturbance. **~ción del orden público** breach of the peace. **~r** vt disturb; disrupt <orden>

Perú m. **el ~** Peru

peruano a & m Peruvian

perver|so a evil. ● m evil person. **~tir** [4] vt pervert

pesa f weight. **~dez** f weight; (de cabeza etc) heaviness; (lentitud) sluggishness; (cualidad de fastidioso) tediousness; (cosa fastidiosa) bore, nuisance

pesadilla f nightmare

pesado *a* heavy; *<sueño>* deep; *<viaje>* tiring; (duro) hard; (aburrido) boring, tedious

pésame *m* sympathy, condolences

pesar *vt* weigh. ● *vi* be heavy. ● *m* sorrow; (remordimiento) regret. **a ~ de (que)** in spite of. **pese a (que)** in spite of

pesca *f* fishing; (peces) fish; (pescado) catch. **ir de ~** go fishing. **~da** *f* hake. **~dería** *f* fish shop. **~dilla** *f* whiting. **~do** *m* fish. **~dor** *a* fishing. ● *m* fisherman. **~r** [7] *vt* catch. ● *vi* fish

pescuezo *m* neck

pesebre *m* manger

pesero *m* (Mex) minibus

peseta *f* peseta

pesimista *a* pessimistic. ● *m & f* pessimist

pésimo *a* very bad, awful

peso *m* weight; (moneda) peso. **~ bruto** gross weight. **~ neto** net weight. **al ~** by weight. **de ~** influential

pesquero *a* fishing

pestañ|a *f* eyelash. **~ear** *vi* blink

pest|e *f* plague; (hedor) stench. **~icida** *m* pesticide

pestillo *m* bolt; (de cerradura) latch

petaca *f* cigarette case; (Mex, maleta) suitcase

pétalo *m* petal

petardo *m* firecracker

petición *f* request; (escrito) petition

petirrojo *m* robin

petrificar [7] *vt* petrify

petr|óleo *m* oil. **~olero** *a* oil. ● *m* oil tanker

petulante *a* smug

peyorativo *a* pejorative

pez *f* fish; (substancia negruzca) pitch. **~ espada** swordfish

pezón *m* nipple

pezuña *f* hoof

piadoso *a* compassionate; (devoto) devout

pian|ista *m & f* pianist. **~o** *m* piano. **~o de cola** grand piano

piar [20] *vi* chirp

picad|a *f.* **caer en ~a** (LAm) nosedive. **~o** *a* perforated; *<carne>* minced (Brit), ground (Amer); (ofendido)

offended; *<mar>* choppy; *<diente>* bad. ● *m.* **caer en ~o** nosedive. **~ura** *f* bite, sting; (de polilla) moth hole

picaflor *m* (LAm) hummingbird

picante *a* hot; *<chiste etc>* risqué

picaporte *m* door-handle; (aldaba) knocker

picar [7] *vt* *<ave>* peck; *<insecto, pez>* bite; *<abeja, avispa>* sting; (comer poco) pick at; mince (Brit), grind (Amer) *<carne>*; chop (up) *<cebolla etc>*; (Mex, pinchar) prick. ● *vi* itch; *<ave>* peck; *<insecto, pez>* bite; *<sol>* scorch; *<comida>* be hot

picardía *f* craftiness; (travesura) naughty thing

pícaro *a* crafty; *<niño>* mischievous. ● *m* rogue

picazón *f* itch

pichón *m* pigeon; (Mex, novato) beginner

pico *m* beak; (punta) corner; (herramienta) pickaxe; (cima) peak. **y ~** (con tiempo) a little after; (con cantidad) a little more than. **~tear** *vt* peck; (🔲, comer) pick at

picudo *a* pointed

pido *vb* ⇒PEDIR

pie *m* foot; (Bot, de vaso) stem. **~ cuadrado** square foot. **a cuatro ~s** on all fours. **al ~ de la letra** literally. **a ~** on foot. **a ~(s) juntillas** (fig) firmly. **buscarle tres ~s al gato** split hairs. **de ~** standing (up). **de ~s a cabeza** from head to toe. **en ~** standing (up). **ponerse de ~** stand up

piedad *f* pity; (Relig) piety

piedra *f* stone; (de mechero) flint

piel *f* skin; (cuero) leather

pienso *vb* ⇒PENSAR

pierdo *vb* ⇒PERDER

pierna *f* leg

pieza *f* piece; (parte) part; (obra teatral) play; (moneda) coin; (habitación) room. **~ de recambio** spare part

pijama *m* pyjamas

pila *f* (montón) pile; (recipiente) basin; (eléctrica) battery. **~ bautismal** font. **~r** *m* pillar

píldora *f* pill

pilla|je *m* pillage. **~r** *vt* catch

pillo *a* wicked. ● *m* rogue

pilot|ar *vt* pilot. **~o** *m* pilot

pim|entero *m* (vasija) pepperpot. **~entón** *m* paprika; (LAm, fruto) pepper. **~ienta** *f* pepper. **grano** *m* de **~ienta** peppercorn. **~iento** *m* pepper

pináculo *m* pinnacle

pinar *m* pine forest

pincel *m* paintbrush. **~ada** *f* brushstroke. **la última ~ada** (fig) the finishing touch

pinch|ar *vt* pierce, prick; puncture <*neumático*>; (fig, incitar) push; (Med, 🛈) give an injection to. **~azo** *m* prick; (en neumático) puncture. **~itos** *mpl* kebab(s); (tapas) savoury snacks. **~o** *m* point

ping-pong *m* table tennis, pingpong

pingüino *m* penguin

pino *m* pine (tree)

pint|a *f* spot; (fig, aspecto) appearance. **tener ~a de** look like. **~ada** *f* graffiti. **~ar** *vt* paint. **no ~a nada** (fig) it doesn't count. □ **~arse** *vpr* put on make-up. **~or** *m* painter. **~oresco** *a* picturesque. **~ura** *f* painting; (material) paint

pinza *f* (clothes-)peg (Brit), clothespin (Amer); (de cangrejo etc) claw. **~s** *fpl* tweezers

piñ|a *f* pine cone; (fruta) pineapple. **~ón** *m* (semilla) pine nut

pío *a* pious. ● *m* chirp. **no decir ni ~** not say a word

piojo *m* louse

pionero *m* pioneer

pipa *f* pipe; (semilla) seed; (de girasol) sunflower seed

pique *m* resentment; (rivalidad) rivalry. **irse a ~** sink

piquete *m* picket; (Mex, herida) prick; (Mex, de insecto) sting

piragua *f* canoe

pirámide *f* pyramid

pirata *a invar* pirate. ● *m & f* pirate

Pirineos *mpl* **los ~** the Pyrenees

piropo *m* flattering comment

pirueta *f* pirouette

pirulí *m* lollipop

pisa|da *f* footstep; (huella) footprint. **~papeles** *m invar* paperweight. **~r** *vt* tread on. ● *vi* tread

piscina *f* swimming pool

Piscis *m* Pisces

piso *m* floor; (vivienda) flat (Brit), apartment (Amer); (de autobús) deck

pisotear *vt* trample (on)

pista *f* track; (fig, indicio) clue. **~ de aterrizaje** runway. **~ de baile** dance floor. **~ de carreras** racing track. **~ de hielo** ice-rink. **~ de tenis** tennis court

pistol|a *f* pistol. **~era** *f* holster. **~ero** *m* gunman

pistón *m* piston

pit|ar, (LAm) **~ear** *vt* whistle at; <*conductor*> hoot at; award <*falta*>. ● *vi* blow a whistle; (Auto) sound one's horn. **~ido** *m* whistle

pitill|era *f* cigarette case. **~o** *m* cigarette

pito *m* whistle; (Auto) horn

pitón *m* python

pitorre|arse *vpr*. **~arse de** make fun of. **~o** *m* teasing

pitorro *m* spout

piyama *m* (LAm) pyjamas

pizarr|a *f* slate; (en aula) blackboard. **~ón** *m* (LAm) blackboard

pizca *f* 🛈 tiny piece; (de sal) pinch. **ni ~** not at all

placa *f* plate; (con inscripción) plaque; (distintivo) badge. **~ de matrícula** number plate

place|ntero *a* pleasant. **~r** [32] *vi*. **haz lo que te plazca** do as you please. **me ~ hacerlo** I'm pleased to do it. ● *m* pleasure

plácido *a* placid

plaga *f* (also fig) plague. **~do** *a*. **~do de** filled with

plagio *m* plagiarism

plan *m* plan. **en ~ de** as

plana *f* page. **en primera ~** on the front page

plancha *f* iron; (lámina) sheet. **a la ~** grilled. **tirarse una ~** put one's foot in it. **~do** *m* ironing. **~r** *vt* iron. ● *vi* do the ironing

planeador *m* glider

planear *vt* plan. ● *vi* glide

planeta *m* planet

planicie *f* plain

planifica|ción *f* planning. **~r** [7] *vt* plan

planilla *f* (LAm) payroll; (personal) staff

plano *a* flat. ● *m* plane; (de edificio) plan; (de ciudad) street plan. **primer ~** foreground; (Foto) close-up

planta *f* (Anat) sole; (Bot, fábrica) plant; (plano) ground plan; (piso) floor. **~ baja** ground floor (Brit), first floor (Amer)

planta|ción *f* plantation. **~r** *vt* plant; deal *<golpe>*. **~r en la calle** throw out. □ **~rse** *vpr* stand; (fig) stand firm

plantear *vt* (exponer) expound; (causar) create; raise *<cuestión>*

plantilla *f* insole; (nómina) payroll; (personal) personnel

plaqué *m* plating. **de ~** plated

plástico *a* & *m* plastic

plata *f* silver; (fig, 🖫, dinero) money. **~ de ley** hallmarked silver

plataforma *f* platform

plátano *m* plane (tree); (fruta) banana. **platanero** *m* banana tree

platea *f* stalls (Brit), orchestra (Amer)

plateado *a* silver-plated; (color de plata) silver

pl|ática *f* talk. **~aticar** [7] *vi* (Mex) talk. ● *vt* (Mex) tell

platija *f* plaice

platillo *m* saucer; (Mus) cymbal. **~ volador** (LAm), **~ volante** flying saucer

platino *m* platinum. **~s** *mpl* (Auto) points

plato *m* plate; (comida) dish; (parte de una comida) course

platónico *a* platonic

playa *f* beach; (fig) seaside

plaza *f* square; (mercado) market (place); (sitio) place; (empleo) job. **~ de toros** bullring

plazco *vb* ⇒PLACER

plazo *m* period; (pago) instalment; (fecha) date. **comprar a ~s** buy on hire purchase (Brit), buy on the installment plan (Amer)

plazuela *f* little square

pleamar *f* high tide

pleb|e *f* common people. **~eyo** *a* & *m* plebeian. **~iscito** *m* plebiscite

plega|ble *a* pliable; *<silla>* folding. **~r** [1 & 12] *vt* fold. □ **~rse** *vpr* bend; (fig) yield

pleito *m* (court) case; (fig) dispute

plenilunio *m* full moon

plen|itud *f* fullness; (fig) height. **~o** *a* full. **en ~o día** in broad daylight. **en ~o verano** at the height of the summer

plieg|o *m* sheet. **~ue** *m* fold; (en ropa) pleat

plisar *vt* pleat

plom|ero *m* (LAm) plumber. **~o** *m* lead; (Elec) fuse. **con ~o** leaded. **sin ~o** unleaded

pluma *f* feather; (para escribir) pen. **~ atómica** (Mex) ballpoint pen. **~ estilográfica** fountain pen. **~je** *m* plumage

plum|ero *m* feather duster; (para plumas, lápices etc) pencil-case. **~ón** *m* down; (edredón) down-filled quilt

plural *a* & *m* plural. **en ~** in the plural

pluriempleo *m* having more than one job

plus *m* bonus

pluscuamperfecto *m* pluperfect

plusvalía *f* capital gain

pluvial *a* rain

pobla|ción *f* population; (ciudad) city, town; (pueblo) village. **~do** *a* populated. ● *m* village. **~r** [2] *vt* populate; (habitar) inhabit. □ **~rse** *vpr* get crowded

pobre *a* poor. ● *m* & *f* poor person; (fig) poor thing. **¡~cito!** poor (little) thing! **¡~ de mí!** poor (old) me! **~za** *f* poverty

pocilga *f* pigsty

poción *f* potion

poco

● *adjetivo/pronombre*

••••➤ **poco, poca** little, not much. **tiene poca paciencia** he has little patience. **¿cuánta leche queda? - poca** how much milk is there left? - not much

····▸ **pocos, pocas** few. **muy ~s días** very few days. **unos ~s dólares** a few dollars. **compré unos ~s** I bought a few. **aceptaron a muy ~s** very few (people) were accepted

····▸ **a ~ de llegar** soon after he arrived. **¡a ~ !** (Mex) really? **dentro de ~** soon. **~ a ~,** (LAm) **de a ~** gradually, little by little. **hace ~** recently, not long ago. **por ~** nearly. **un ~** (cantidad) a little; (tiempo) a while. **un ~ de** a (little) bit of, a little, some

● *adverbio*

····▸ (con verbo) not much. **lee muy ~** he doesn't read very much

····▸ (con adjetivo) **un lugar ~ conocido** a little known place. **es ~ inteligente** he's not very intelligent

> ❗ Cuando **poco** modifica a un adjetivo, muchas veces el inglés prefiere el uso del prefijo *un-*, p. ej. **poco amistoso** *unfriendly*. **poco agradecido** *ungrateful*

podar *vt* prune

poder [33] *v aux* be able to. **no voy a ~ terminar** I won't be able to finish. **no pudo venir** he couldn't come. **¿puedo hacer algo?** can I do anything? **¿puedo pasar?** may I come in?. **no ~ con** not be able to cope with; (no aguantar) not be able to stand. **no ~ más** be exhausted; (estar harto de algo) not be able to manage any more. **no ~ menos que** have no alternative but. **puede que** it is possible that. **puede ser** it is possible. **¿se puede ...?** may I...? ● *m* power. **en el ~** in power. **~es** *mpl* **públicos** authorities. **~oso** *a* powerful

podrido *a* rotten

po|ema *m* poem. **~esía** *f* poetry; (poema) poem. **~eta** *m & f* poet. **~ético** *a* poetic

polaco *a* Polish. ● *m* Pole; (lengua) Polish

polar *a* polar. **estrella ~** polestar

polea *f* pulley

pol|émica *f* controversy. **~emizar** [10] *vi* argue

polen *m* pollen

policía *f* police (force); (persona) policewoman. ● *m* policeman. **~co** *a* police; <*novela etc*> detective

policromo *a*, **polícromo** *a* polychrome

polideportivo *m* sports centre

polietileno *m* polythene

poligamia *f* polygamy

polígono *m* polygon

polilla *f* moth

polio(mielitis) *f* polio(myelitis)

polític|a *f* politics; (postura) policy; (mujer) politician. **~ interior** domestic policy. **~o** *a* political. **familia ~a** in-laws. ● *m* politician

póliza *f* (de seguros) policy

poll|o *m* chicken; (gallo joven) chick. **~uelo** *m* chick

polo *m* pole; (helado) ice lolly (Brit), Popsicle (P) (Amer); (juego) polo. **P~ norte** North Pole

Polonia *f* Poland

poltrona *f* armchair

polución *f* pollution

polv|areda *f* dust cloud; (fig, escándalo) uproar. **~era** *f* compact. **~o** *m* powder; (suciedad) dust. **~os** *mpl* powder. **en ~o** powdered. **estar hecho ~o** be exhausted. **quitar el ~o** dust

pólvora *f* gunpowder; (fuegos artificiales) fireworks

polvoriento *a* dusty

pomada *f* ointment

pomelo *m* grapefruit

pómez *a.* **piedra** *f* **~** pumice stone

pomp|a *f* bubble; (esplendor) pomp. **~as fúnebres** funeral. **~oso** *a* pompous; (espléndido) splendid

pómulo *m* cheekbone

ponchar *vt* (Mex) puncture

ponche *m* punch

poncho *m* poncho

ponderar *vt* (alabar) speak highly of

poner [34] *vt* put; put on <*ropa, obra de teatro, TV etc*>; lay <*la mesa, un huevo*>; set <*examen, deberes*>; (contribuir) contribute; give <*nombre*>; make <*nervioso*>; pay <*atención*>; show <*película, interés*>; open <*una tienda*>; equip <*una casa*>. **~ con** (al teléfono) put through to. **~ por escrito**

put into writing. ∼ **una multa** fine. **pongamos** let's suppose. ● *vi* lay. ▫ ∼**se** *vpr* (volverse) get; put on *‹ropa›*; *‹sol›* set. ∼**se a** start to. ∼**se a mal con uno** fall out with s.o.

pongo *vb* ⇒PONER

poniente *m* west; (viento) west wind

pont|ificar [7] *vi* pontificate. ∼**ífice** *m* pontiff

popa *f* stern

popote *m* (Mex) (drinking) straw

popul|acho *m* masses. ∼**ar** *a* popular; *‹costumbre›* traditional; *‹lenguaje›* colloquial. ∼**aridad** *f* popularity. ∼**arizar** [10] *vt* popularize.

póquer *m* poker

poquito *m*. un ∼ a little bit. ● *adv* a little

por

● *preposición*

····▸for. **es** ∼ **tu bien** it's for your own good. **lo compró** ∼ **5 dólares** he bought it for 5 dollars. **si no fuera** ∼ **ti** if it weren't for you. **vino** ∼ **una semana** he came for a week

➡ Para expresiones como por **la mañana**, por **la noche** etc., ver bajo el respectivo nombre

····▸(causa) because of. **se retrasó** ∼ **la lluvia** he was late because of the rain. **no hay trenes** ∼ **la huelga** there aren't any trains because of the strike

····▸(medio, agente) by. **lo envié** ∼ **correo** I sent it by post. **fue destruida** ∼ **las bombas** it was destroyed by the bombs

····▸(a través de) through. **entró** ∼ **la ventana** he got in through the window. **me enteré** ∼ **un amigo** I found out through a friend. ∼ **todo el país** throughout the country

····▸(a lo largo de) along. **caminar** ∼ **la playa** to walk along the beach. **cortar** ∼ **la línea de puntos** cut along the dotted line

····▸(proporción) per. **cobra 30 dólares** ∼ **hora** he charges 30 dollars per hour. **uno** ∼ **persona** one per person. **10** ∼ **ciento** 10 per cent

····▸(Mat) times. **dos** ∼ **dos** (**son**) **cuatro** two times two is four

····▸(modo) in. ∼ **escrito** in writing. **pagar** ∼ **adelantado** to pay in advance

➡ Para expresiones como por **dentro**, por **fuera** etc., ver bajo el respectivo adverbio

····▸(en locuciones) ∼ **más que** no matter how much. **¿**∼ **qué?** why? ∼ **si** in case. ∼ **supuesto** of course

porcelana *f* china

porcentaje *m* percentage

porcino *a* pig

porción *f* portion; (de chocolate) piece

pordiosero *m* beggar

porfia|do *a* stubborn. ∼**r** [20] *vi* insist

pormenor *m* detail

pornogr|afía *f* pornography. ∼**áfico** *a* pornographic

poro *m* pore; (Mex, puerro) leek. ∼**so** *a* porous

porque *conj* because; (para que) so that

porqué *m* reason

porquería *f* filth; (basura) rubbish; (grosería) dirty trick

porra *f* club

porrón *m* wine jug (with a long spout)

portaaviones *m invar* aircraft carrier

portada *f* (de libro) title page; (de revista) cover

portadocumentos *m invar* (LAm) briefcase

portador *m* bearer

portaequipaje(s) *m invar* boot (Brit), trunk (Amer); (encima del coche) roof-rack

portal *m* hall; (puerta principal) main entrance. ∼**es** *mpl* arcade

porta|ligas *m invar* suspender belt. ∼**monedas** *m invar* purse

portarse *vpr* behave

portátil *a* portable

portavoz *m* spokesman. ● *f* spokeswoman

portazo *m* bang. **dar un** ∼ slam the door

porte *m* transport; (precio) carriage; (LAm, tamaño) size. ~**ador** *m* carrier

portento *m* marvel

porteño *a* (from Buenos Aires

porter|ía *f* porter's lodge; (en deportes) goal. ~**o** *m* caretaker, porter; (en deportes) goalkeeper. ~**o automático** entryphone

pórtico *m* portico

portorriqueño *a* & *m* Puerto Rican

Portugal *m* Portugal

portugués *a* & *m* Portuguese

porvenir *m* future

posada *f* inn. dar ~ give shelter

posar *vt* put. ● *vi* pose. □ ~**se** *vpr* <*pájaro*> perch; <*avión*> land

posdata *f* postscript

pose|edor *m* owner; (de récord, billete, etc) holder. ~**er** [18] *vt* own; hold <*récord*>; have <*conocimientos*>. ~**sión** *f* possession. □ ~**sionarse** *vpr*. ~**sionarse de** take possession of. ~**sivo** *a* possessive

posgraduado *a* & *m* postgraduate

posguerra *f* post-war years

posib|ilidad *f* possibility. ~**le** *a* possible. de ser ~**le** if possible. en lo ~**le** as far as possible. si es ~**le** if possible

posición *f* position; (en sociedad) social standing

positivo *a* positive

poso *m* sediment

posponer [34] *vt* put after; (diferir) postpone

posta *f*. a ~ on purpose

postal *a* postal. ● *f* postcard

poste *m* pole; (de valla) post

póster *m* (*pl* ~**s**) poster

postergar [12] *vt* pass over; (diferir) postpone

posteri|dad *f* posterity. ~**or** *a* back; <*años*> later; <*capítulos*> subsequent. ~**ormente** *adv* later

postigo *m* door; (contraventana) shutter

postizo *a* false, artificial. ● *m* hairpiece

postrarse *vpr* prostrate o.s.

postre *m* dessert, pudding (Brit)

postular *vt* postulate; (LAm) nominate <*candidato*>

póstumo *a* posthumous

postura *f* position, stance

potable *a* drinkable; <*agua*> drinking

potaje *m* vegetable stew

potasio *m* potassium

pote *m* pot

poten|cia *f* power. ~**cial** *a* & *m* potential. ~**te** *a* powerful

potro *m* colt; (en gimnasia) horse

pozo *m* well; (hoyo seco) pit; (de mina) shaft; (fondo común) pool

práctica *f* practice. en la ~ in practice

practica|nte *m* & *f* nurse. ~**r** [7] *vt* practise; play <*deportes*>; (ejecutar) carry out

práctico *a* practical; (conveniente, útil) handy. ● *m* practitioner

prad|era *f* meadow; (terreno grande) prairie. ~**o** *m* meadow

pragmático *a* pragmatic

preámbulo *m* preamble

precario *a* precarious; <*medios*> scarce

precaución *f* precaution; (cautela) caution. con ~ cautiously

precaverse *vpr* take precautions

prece|ncia *f* precedence; (prioridad) priority. ~**nte** *a* preceding. ● *m* precedent. ~**r** *vt/i* precede

precepto *m* precept. ~**r** *m* tutor

precia|do *a* valued; <*don*> valuable. □ ~**rse** *vpr*. ~**rse de** pride o.s. on

precio *m* price. ~ de venta al público retail price. al ~ de at the cost of. no tener ~ be priceless. ¿qué ~ tiene? how much is it?

precios|idad *f* (cosa preciosa) beautiful thing. ¡es una ~**idad**! it's beautiful! ~**o** *a* precious; (bonito) beautiful

precipicio *m* precipice

precipita|ción *f* precipitation; (prisa) rush. ~**damente** *adv* hastily. ~**do** *a* hasty. ~**r** *vt* (apresurar) hasten; (arrojar) hurl. □ ~**rse** *vpr* throw o.s.; (correr) rush; (actuar sin reflexionar) act rashly

precis|amente *a* exactly. **~ar** *vt* require; (determinar) determine. **~ión** *f* precision. **~o** *a* precise; (necesario) necessary. **si es ~o** if necessary

preconcebido *a* preconceived

precoz *a* early; *<niño>* precocious

precursor *m* forerunner

predecesor *m* predecessor

predecir [46], (*pero imperativo* **pre-dice,** *futuro y condicional regulares*) *vt* foretell

predestinado *a* predestined

prédica *f* sermon

predicar [7] *vt/i* preach

predicción *f* prediction; (del tiempo) forecast

predilec|ción *f* predilection. **~to** *a* favourite

predisponer [34] *vt* predispose

predomin|ante *a* predominant. **~ar** *vi* predominate. **~io** *m* predominance

preeminente *a* pre-eminent

prefabricado *a* prefabricated

prefacio *m* preface

prefer|encia *f* preference; (Auto) right of way. **de ~encia** preferably. **~ente** *a* preferential. **~ible** *a* preferable. **~ido** *a* favourite. **~ir** [4] *vt* prefer

prefijo *m* prefix; (telefónico) dialling code

pregonar *vt* announce

pregunta *f* question. **hacer una ~** ask a question. **~r** *vt/i* ask (por about). □ **~rse** *vpr* wonder

prehistórico *a* prehistoric

preju|icio *m* prejudice. **~zgar** [12] *vt* prejudge

preliminar *a & m* preliminary

preludio *m* prelude

premarital *a*, **prematrimonial** *a* premarital

prematuro *a* premature

premedita|ción *f* premeditation. **~r** *vt* premeditate

premi|ar *vt* give a prize to; (recompensar) reward. **~o** *m* prize; (recompensa) reward. **~o gordo** jackpot

premonición *f* premonition

prenatal *a* antenatal

prenda *f* garment; (garantía) surety; (en juegos) forfeit. **en ~ de** as a token of. **~r** *vt* captivate. □ **~rse** *vpr* fall in love (**de** with)

prende|dor *m* brooch. **~r** *vt* capture; (sujetar) fasten; light *<cigarrillo>*; (LAm) turn on *<gas, radio, etc>*. ● *vi* catch; (arraigar) take root. □ **~se** *vpr* (encenderse) catch fire

prensa *f* press. **~r** *vt* press

preñado *a* pregnant; (fig) full

preocupa|ción *f* worry. **~do** *a* worried. **~r** *vt* worry. □ **~rse** *vpr* worry. **~rse de** look after

prepara|ción *f* preparation. **~do** *a* prepared. ● *m* preparation. **~r** *vt* prepare. □ **~rse** *vpr* get ready. **~tivos** *mpl* preparations. **~torio** *a* preparatory

preposición *f* preposition

prepotente *a* arrogant; *<actitud>* high-handed

prerrogativa *f* prerogative

presa *f* (cosa) prey; (embalse) dam

presagi|ar *vt* presage. **~o** *m* omen

presb|iteriano *a & m* Presbyterian. **~ítero** *m* priest

prescindir *vi.* **~ de** do without; (deshacerse de) dispense with

prescri|bir (*pp* **prescrito**) *vt* prescribe. **~pción** *f* prescription

presencia *f* presence; (aspecto) appearance. **en ~ de** in the presence of. **~r** *vt* be present at; (ver) witness

presenta|ble *a* presentable. **~ción** *f* presentation; (de una persona a otra) introduction. **~dor** *m* presenter. **~r** *vt* present; (ofrecer) offer; (entregar) hand in; (hacer conocer) introduce; show *<película>*. □ **~rse** *vpr* present o.s.; (hacerse conocer) introduce o.s.; (aparecer) turn up

presente *a* present; (actual) this. ● *m* present. **los ~s** those present. **tener ~** remember

presenti|miento *m* premonition. **~r** [4] *vt* have a feeling (**que** that)

preserva|r *vt* preserve. **~tivo** *m* condom

presiden|cia *f* presidency; (de asamblea) chairmanship. **~cial** *a* presidential. **~ta** *f* (woman) president. **~te** *m* president; (de asamblea) chairman. ~**te del gobierno** prime minister

presidi|ario *m* convict. ~**o** *m* prison

presidir *vt* be president of; preside over <*tribunal*>; chair <*reunión, comité*>

presi|ón *f* pressure. **a** ~**ón** under pressure. **hacer** ~**ón** press. ~**onar** *vt* press; (fig) put pressure on

preso *a*. **estar** ~ be in prison. **llevarse** ~ **a uno** take s.o. away under arrest. ● *m* prisoner

presta|do *a* (de uno) lent; (a uno) borrowed. **pedir** ~**do** borrow. ~**mista** *m & f* moneylender

préstamo *m* loan; (acción de pedir prestado) borrowing; (acción de prestar) lending

prestar *vt* lend; give <*ayuda etc*>; pay <*atención*>. □ ~**se** *vpr*. ~**se a** be open to; (ser apto) be suitable (**para** for)

prestidigita|ción *f* conjuring. ~**dor** *m* conjurer

prestigio *m* prestige. ~**so** *a* prestigious

presu|mido *a* conceited. ~**mir** *vi* show off. boast (**de** about). ~**nción** *f* conceit; (suposición) presumption. ~**nto** *a* alleged. ~**ntuoso** *a* conceited

presup|oner [34] *vt* presuppose. ~**uesto** *m* budget; (precio estimado) estimate

preten|cioso *a* pretentious. ~**der** *vt* try to; (afirmar) claim; (solicitar) apply for; (cortejar) court. ~**diente** *m* pretender; (a una mujer) suitor. ~**sión** *f* pretension; (aspiración) aspiration

pretérito *m* preterite, past

pretexto *m* pretext. **con el** ~ **de** on the pretext of

prevalecer [11] *vi* prevail (**sobre** over)

preven|ción *f* prevention; (prejuicio) prejudice. ~**ido** *a* ready; (precavido) cautious. ~**ir** [53] *vt* prevent; (advertir) warn. ~**tiva** *f* (Mex) amber light. ~**tivo** *a* preventive

prever [43] *vt* foresee; (planear) plan

previo *a* previous

previs|ible *a* predictable. ~**ión** *f* forecast; (prudencia) precaution

prima *f* (pariente) cousin; (cantidad) bonus

primario *a* primary

primavera *f* spring. ~**l** *a* spring

primer *a* ⇒PRIMERO. ~**a** *f* (Auto) first (gear); (en tren etc) first class. ~**o** *a* (*delante de nombre masculino en singular* **primer**) first; (mejor) best; (principal) leading. **la** ~**a fila** the front row. **lo** ~**o es** the most important thing is. ~**a enseñanza** primary education. **a** ~**os de** at the beginning of. **de** ~**a** first-class. ● *n* (the) first. ● *adv* first

primitivo *a* primitive

primo *m* cousin; 🄕 fool. **hacer el** ~ be taken for a ride

primogénito *a & m* first-born, eldest

primor *m* delicacy; (cosa) beautiful thing

primordial *a* fundamental; <*interés*> paramount

princesa *f* princess

principal *a* main. **lo** ~ **es que** the main thing is that

príncipe *m* prince

principi|ante *m & f* beginner. ~**o** *m* beginning; (moral, idea) principle; (origen) origin. **al** ~**o** at first. **a** ~**o(s) de** at the beginning of. **desde el** ~**o** from the start. **en** ~**o** in principle. ~**os** *mpl* (nociones) rudiments

prioridad *f* priority

prisa *f* hurry, haste. **a** ~ quickly. **a toda** ~ as quickly as possible. **darse** ~ hurry (up). **de** ~ quickly. **tener** ~ be in a hurry

prisi|ón *f* prison; (encarcelamiento) imprisonment. ~**onero** *m* prisoner

prismáticos *mpl* binoculars

priva|ción *f* deprivation. ~**da** *f* (Mex) private road. ~**do** *a* (particular) private. ~**r** *vt* deprive (**de** of). ~**tivo** *a* exclusive (**de** to)

privilegi|ado *a* privileged; (muy bueno) exceptional. ~**o** *m* privilege

pro *prep*. **en** ~ **de** for, in favour of. ● *m* advantage. **los** ~**s y los contras** the pros and cons

proa *f* bow

probab|ilidad f probability. **~le** a probable, likely. **~lemente** adv probably

proba|dor m fitting-room. **~r** [2] vt try; try on <ropa>; (demostrar) prove. ● vi try. □ **~rse** vpr try on

probeta f test-tube

problema m problem. **hacerse ~as** (LAm) worry

procaz a indecent

proced|encia f origin. **~ente** a (razonable) reasonable. **~ente de** (coming) from. **~er** m conduct. ● vi proceed. **~er contra** start legal proceedings against. **~er de** come from. **~imiento** m procedure; (sistema) process; (Jurid) proceedings

proces|ador m. **~ de textos** word processor. **~al** a procedural. **costas ~ales** legal costs. **~amiento** m processing; (Jurid) prosecution. **~amiento de textos** word-processing. **~ar** vt process; (Jurid) prosecute

procesión f procession

proceso m process; (Jurid) trial; (transcurso) course

proclamar vt proclaim

procrea|ción f procreation. **~r** vt procreate

procura|dor m attorney, solicitor; (asistente) clerk (Brit), paralegal (Amer). **~r** vt try; (obtener) obtain

prodigar [12] vt lavish

prodigio m prodigy; (maravilla) wonder; (milagro) miracle. **~ioso** a prodigious

pródigo a prodigal

produc|ción f production. **~ir** [47] vt produce; (causar) cause. □ **~irse** vpr (suceder) happen. **~tivo** a productive. **~to** m product. **~tos agrícolas** farm produce. **~tos alimenticios** foodstuffs. **~tos de belleza** cosmetics. **~tos de consumo** consumer goods. **~tor** m producer.

proeza f exploit

profan|ación f desecration. **~ar** vt desecrate. **~o** a profane

profecía f prophecy

proferir [4] vt utter; hurl <insultos etc>

profes|ión f profession. **~ional** a professional. **~or** m teacher; (en universidad) lecturer. **~orado** m teaching profession; (conjunto de profesores) staff

prof|eta m prophet. **~etizar** [10] vt/i prophesize

prófugo a & m fugitive

profund|idad f depth. **~o** a deep; (fig) profound. **poco ~** shallow

progenitor m ancestor

programa m programme; (de estudios) syllabus. **~ concurso** quiz show. **~ de entrevistas** chat show. **~ción** f programming; (TV etc) programmes; (en periódico) TV guide. **~r** vt programme. **~dor** m computer programmer

progres|ar vi (make) progress. **~ión** f progression. **~ista** a progressive. **~ivo** a progressive. **~o** m progress. **hacer ~os** make progress

prohibi|ción f prohibition. **~do** a forbidden. **prohibido fumar** no smoking. **~r** vt forbid. **~tivo** a prohibitive

prójimo m fellow man

prole f offspring

proletari|ado m proletariat. **~o** a & m proletarian

prol|iferación f proliferation. **~iferar** vi proliferate. **~ífico** a prolific

prolijo a long-winded

prólogo m prologue

prolongar [12] vt prolong; (alargar) lengthen. □ **~se** vpr go on

promedio m average. **como ~** on average

prome|sa f promise. **~ter** vt promise. ● vi show promise. □ **~terse** vpr <novios> get engaged. **~tida** f fiancée. **~tido** a promised; <novios> engaged. ● m fiancé

prominente f prominence

promiscu|idad f promiscuity. **~o** a promiscuous

promo|ción f promotion. **~tor** m promoter. **~ver** [2] vt promote; (causar) cause

promulgar [12] vt promulgate

pronombre m pronoun

pron|osticar [7] vt predict; forecast <tiempo>. **~óstico** m prediction; (del tiempo) forecast; (Med) prognosis

pront|itud f promptness. ~**o** a quick. ● adv quickly; (dentro de poco) soon; (temprano) early. **de** ~**o** suddenly. **por lo** ~**o** for the time being. **tan** ~**o como** as soon as

pronuncia|ción f pronunciation. ~**miento** m revolt. ~**r** vt pronounce; deliver <discurso>. □ ~**rse** vpr (declararse) declare o.s.; (sublevarse) rise up

propagación f propagation

propaganda f propaganda; (anuncios) advertising

propagar [12] vt/i propagate. □ ~**se** vpr spread

propasarse vpr go too far

propens|ión f inclination. ~**o** a inclined

propici|ar vt favour; (provocar) bring about. ~**o** a favourable

propie|dad f property. ~**tario** m owner

propina f tip

propio a own; (característico) typical; (natural) natural; (apropiado) proper. **el** ~ **médico** the doctor himself

proponer [34] vt propose; put forward <persona>. □ ~**se** vpr. ~**se hacer** intento to do

proporci|ón f proportion. ~**onado** a proportioned. ~**onal** a proportional. ~**onar** vt provide

proposición f proposition

propósito m intention. **a** ~ (adrede) on purpose; (de paso) by the way. **a** ~ **de** with regard to

propuesta f proposal

propuls|ar vt propel; (fig) promote. ~**ión** f propulsion. ~**ión a chorro** jet propulsion

prórroga f extension

prorrogar [12] vt extend

prosa f prose. ~**ico** a prosaic

proscri|bir (pp **proscrito**) vt exile; (prohibir) ban. ~**to** a banned. ● m exile; (bandido) outlaw

proseguir [5 & 13] vt/i continue

prospecto m prospectus; (de fármaco) directions for use

prosper|ar vi prosper; <persona> do well. ~**idad** f prosperity

próspero a prosperous. **¡P~ Año Nuevo!** Happy New Year!

prostit|ución f prostitution. ~**uta** f prostitute

protagonista m & f protagonist

prote|cción f protection. ~**ctor** a protective. ● m protector; (benefactor) patron. ~**ger** [14] vt protect. ~**gida** f protegée. ~**gido** a protected. ● m protegé

proteína f protein

protesta f protest; (manifestación) demonstration; (Mex, promesa) promise; (Mex, juramento) oath

protestante a & m & f Protestant

protestar vt/i protest

protocolo m protocol

provecho m benefit. **¡buen** ~! enjoy your meal! **de** ~ useful. **en** ~ **de** to the benefit of. **sacar** ~ **de** benefit from

proveer [18] (pp **proveído** y **provisto**) vt supply, provide

provenir [53] vi come (de from)

proverbi|al a proverbial. ~**o** m proverb

provincia f province. ~**l** a, ~**no** a provincial

provisional a provisional

provisto a provided (de with)

provoca|ción f provocation. ~**r** [7] vt provoke; (causar) cause. ~**tivo** a provocative

proximidad f proximity

próximo a next; (cerca) near

proyec|ción f projection. ~**tar** vt hurl; cast <luz>; show <película>. ~**til** m missile. ~**to** m plan. ~**to de ley** bill. **en** ~**to** planned. ~**tor** m projector

pruden|cia f prudence; (cuidado) caution. ~**te** a prudent, sensible

prueba f proof; (examen) test; (de ropa) fitting. **a** ~ on trial. **a** ~ **de** proof against. **a** ~ **de agua** waterproof. **poner a** ~ test

pruebo vb ⇒PROBAR

psicoan|álisis f psychoanalysis. ~**alista** m & f psychoanalyst. ~**alizar** [10] vt psychoanalyse

psic|ología *f* psychology. **~ológi-co** *a* psychological. **~ólogo** *m* psychologist. **~ópata** *m & f* psycho-path. **~osis** *f invar* psychosis

psiqu|e *f* psyche. **~iatra** *m & f* psychiatrist. **~iátrico** *a* psychiatric

psíquico *a* psychic

ptas, **pts** *abrev* (**pesetas**) pesetas

púa *f* sharp point; (Bot) thorn; (de erizo) quill; (de peine) tooth; (Mus) plectrum

pubertad *f* puberty

publica|ción *f* publication. **~r** [7] *vt* publish

publici|dad *f* publicity; (Com) advertising. **~tario** *a* advertising

público *a* public. ● *m* public; (de espectáculo etc) audience

puchero *m* cooking pot; (guisado) stew. **hacer ~s** (fig, 🄵) pout

pude *vb* ⇒PODER

pudor *m* modesty. **~oso** *a* modest

pudrir (*pp* **podrido**) *vt* rot; (fig, molestar) annoy. □ **~se** *vpr* rot

puebl|ecito *m* small village. **~eri-no** *m* country bumpkin. **~o** *m* town; (aldea) village; (nación) nation, people

puedo *vb* ⇒PODER

puente *m* bridge; (fig, 🄵) long weekend. **~ colgante** suspension bridge. **~ levadizo** drawbridge. **hacer ~** 🄵 have a long weekend

puerco *a* filthy; (grosero) coarse. ● *m* pig. **~ espín** porcupine

puerro *m* leek

puerta *f* door; (en deportes) goal; (de ciudad, en jardín) gate. **~ principal** main entrance. **a ~ cerrada** behind closed doors

puerto *m* port; (fig, refugio) refuge; (entre montañas) pass. **~ franco** free port

puertorriqueño *a & m* Puerto Rican

pues *adv* (entonces) then; (bueno) well. ● *conj* since

puest|a *f* setting; (en juegos) bet. **~a de sol** sunset. **~a en escena** staging. **~a en marcha** starting. **~o** *a* put; (vestido) dressed. ● *m* place; (empleo) position, job; (en mercado etc) stall. ● *conj*. **~o que** since

pugna *f* struggle. **~r** *vi*. **~r por** strive to

puja *f* struggle (**por** to); (en subasta) bid. **~r** *vt* struggle; (en subasta) bid

pulcro *a* neat

pulga *f* flea. **tener malas ~s** be bad-tempered

pulga|da *f* inch. **~r** *m* thumb; (del pie) big toe

puli|do *a* polished; *<modales>* refined. **~r** *vt* polish; (suavizar) smooth

pulla *f* gibe

pulm|ón *m* lung. **~onar** *a* pulmonary. **~onía** *f* pneumonia

pulpa *f* pulp

pulpería *f* (LAm) grocer's shop (Brit), grocery store (Amer)

púlpito *m* pulpit

pulpo *m* octopus

pulque *m* (Mex) pulque, alcoholic Mexican drink. **~ría** *f* bar

pulsa|ción *f* pulsation. **~dor** *m* button. **~r** *vt* press; (Mus) pluck

pulsera *f* bracelet

pulso *m* pulse; (firmeza) steady hand. **echar un ~** arm wrestle. **tomar el ~ a uno** take s.o.'s pulse

pulular *vi* teem with

puma *m* puma

puna *f* puna, high plateau

punitivo *a* punitive

punta *f* point; (extremo) tip. **estar de ~** be in a bad mood. **ponerse de ~ con uno** fall out with s.o. **sacar ~ a** sharpen

puntada *f* stitch

puntaje *m* (LAm) score

puntal *m* prop, support

puntapié *m* kick

puntear *vt* mark; (Mus) pluck; (LAm, en deportes) lead

puntería *f* aim; (destreza) markmanship

puntiagudo *a* pointed; (afilado) sharp

puntilla *f* (encaje) lace. **en ~s** (LAm), **de ~s** on tiptoe

punto *m* point; (señal, trazo) dot; (de examen) mark; (lugar) spot, place; (de taxis) stand; (momento) moment; (punto final) full stop (Brit), period (Amer); (puntada) stitch. **~ de vista** point of view. ~ **final** full stop (Brit), period (Amer). ~ **muerto** (Auto) neutral (gear). ~ **y aparte** full stop, new paragraph (Brit), period, new paragraph (Amer). ~ **y coma** semicolon. **a** ~ on time; (listo) ready. **a** ~ **de** on the point of. **de** ~ knitted. **dos** ~**s** colon. **en** ~ exactly. **hacer** ~ knit. **hasta cierto** ~ to a certain extent

puntuación f punctuation; (en deportes, acción) scoring; (en deportes, número de puntos) score

puntual a punctual; (exacto) accurate. ~**idad** f punctuality; (exactitud) accuracy

puntuar [21] vt punctuate; mark (Brit), grade (Amer) <examen>. ● vi score (points)

punza|da f sharp pain; (fig) pang. ~**nte** a sharp. ~**r** [10] vt prick

puñado m handful. **a** ~**s** by the handful

puñal m dagger. ~**ada** f stab

puñ|etazo m punch. ~**o** m fist; (de ropa) cuff; (mango) handle. **de su** ~**o (y letra)** in his own handwriting

pupa f (🔲, en los labios) cold sore

pupila f pupil

pupitre m desk

puré m purée; (sopa) thick soup. ~ **de papas** (LAm), ~ **de patatas** mashed potatoes

pureza f purity

purga f purge. ~**torio** m purgatory

puri|ficación f purification. ~**ificar** [7] vt purify. ~**sta** m & f purist. ~**tano** a puritanical. ● m puritan

puro a pure; <cielo> clear. **de pura casualidad** by sheer chance. **de** ~ **tonto** out of sheer stupidity. ● m cigar

púrpura f purple

pus m pus

puse vb ⇒PONER

pusilánime a fainthearted

puta f (vulg) whore

Qq

que pron rel (personas, sujeto) who; (personas, complemento) whom; (cosas) which, that. ● conj that. ¡~ **tengan Vds buen viaje!** have a good journey! ¡~ **venga!** let him come! ~ **venga o no venga** whether he comes or not. **creo** ~ **tiene razón** I think (that) he is right. **más** ~ more than. **lo** ~ what. **yo** ~ **tú** if I were you

qué a (con sustantivo) what; (con a o adv) how. ● pron what. ¡~ **bonito!** how nice!. **¿en** ~ **piensas?** what are you thinking about?

quebra|da f gorge; (paso) pass. ~**dizo** a fragile. ~**do** a broken; (Com) bankrupt. ● m (Math) fraction. ~**ntar** vt break; disturb <paz>. ~**nto** m (pérdida) loss; (daño) damage. ~**r** [1] vt break. ● vi break; (Com) go bankrupt. □ ~**rse** vpr break

quechua a Quechua. ● m & f Quechan. ● m (Lang) Quecha

quedar vi stay, remain; (estar) be; (haber todavía) be left. ~ **bien** come off well. □ ~**se** vpr stay. ~ **con** arrange to meet. ~ **en** agree to. ~ **en nada** come to nothing. ~ **por** (+ infinitivo) remain to be (+ pp) ·

quehacer m work. ~**es domésticos** household chores

quej|a f complaint; (de dolor) moan. □ ~**arse** vpr complain (de about); (gemir) moan. ~**ido** m moan

quema|do a burnt; (LAm, bronceado) tanned; (fig) annoyed. ~**dor** m burner. ~**dura** f burn. ~**r** vt/i burn. □ ~**rse** vpr burn o.s.; (consumirse) burn up; (con el sol) get sunburnt. ~**rropa** adv. **a** ~**rropa** point-blank

quena f Indian flute

quepo vb ⇒CABER

querella f (riña) quarrel, dispute; (Jurid) criminal action

quer|er [35] vt want; (amar) love; (necesitar) need. ~**er decir** mean. ● m love; (amante) lover. **como quiera que** however. **cuando quiera que**

whenever. **donde quiera** wherever. **¿quieres darme ese libro?** would you pass me that book? **¿quieres un helado?** would you like an ice-cream? **quisiera ir a la playa** I'd like to go to the beach. **sin ~er** without meaning to. **~ido** *a* dear; (amado) loved

querosén *m*, **queroseno** *m* kerosene

querubín *m* cherub

ques|adilla *f* (Mex) tortilla filled with cheese. **~o** *m* cheese

quetzal *m* (unidad monetaria ecuatoriana) quetzal

quicio *m* frame. **sacar de ~ a uno** infuriate s.o.

quiebra *f* (Com) bankruptcy

quien *pron rel* (sujeto) who; (complemento) whom

quién *pron interrogativo* (sujeto) who; (tras preposición) **¿con ~?** who with ?, to whom? **¿de ~ son estos libros?** whose are these books?

quienquiera *pron* whoever

quiero *vb* ⇒QUERER

quiet|o *a* still; (inmóvil) motionless; *<carácter etc>* calm. **~ud** *f* stillness

quijada *f* jaw

quilate *m* carat

quilla *f* keel

quimera *f* (fig) illusion

químic|a *f* chemistry. **~o** *a* chemical. ● *m* chemist

quince *a & m* fifteen. **~ días** a fortnight. **~na** *f* fortnight. **~nal** *a* fortnightly

quincuagésimo *a* fiftieth

quiniela *f* pools coupon. **~s** *fpl* (football) pools

quinientos *a & m* five hundred

quinquenio *m* (period of) five years

quinta *f* (casa) villa

quintal *m* a hundred kilograms

quinteto *m* quintet

quinto *a & m* fifth

quiosco *m* kiosk; (en jardín) summerhouse; (en parque etc) bandstand

quirúrgico *a* surgical

quise *vb* ⇒QUERER

quisquill|a *f* trifle; (camarón) shrimp. **~oso** *a* irritable; (exigente) fussy

quita|esmalte *m* nail polish remover. **~manchas** *m invar* stain remover. **~nieves** *m invar* snow plough. **~r** *vt* remove, take away; take off *<ropa>*; (robar) steal. **~ndo** (⊞, a excepción de) apart from. □ **~rse** *vpr* get rid of *<dolor>*; take off *<ropa>*. **~rse de** (no hacerlo más) stop. **~rse de en medio** get out of the way. **~sol** *m* sunshade

quizá(s) *adv* perhaps

quórum *m* quorum

Rr

rábano *m* radish. **~ picante** horseradish. **me importa un ~** I couldn't care less

rabi|a *f* rabies; (fig) rage. **~ar** *vi* (de dolor) be in great pain; (estar enfadado) be furious. **dar ~a** infuriate. **~eta** *f* tantrum

rabino *m* rabbi

rabioso *a* rabid; (furioso) furious

rabo *m* tail

racha *f* gust of wind; (fig) spate. **pasar por una mala ~** go through a bad patch

racial *a* racial

racimo *m* bunch

ración *f* share, ration; (de comida) portion

raciona|l *a* rational. **~lizar** [10] *vt* rationalize. **~r** *vt* (limitar) ration; (repartir) ration out

racis|mo *m* racism. **~ta** *a* racist

radar *m* radar

radiación *f* radiation

radiactiv|idad *f* radioactivity. **~o** *a* radioactive

radiador *m* radiator

radiante *a* radiant; (brillante) brilliant

radical *a & m & f* radical

radicar [7] *vi* lie (**en** in). □ ~**se** *vpr* settle

radio *m* radius; (de rueda) spoke; (LAm) radio. ● *f* radio. ~**actividad** *f* radioactivity. ~**activo** *a* radio-active. ~**difusión** *f* broadcasting. ~**emisora** *f* radio station. ~**escucha** *m* & *f* listener. ~**grafía** *f* radiography

radi|ólogo *m* radiologist. ~**oterapia** *f* radiotherapy

radioyente *m* & *f* listener

raer [36] *vt* scrape; (quitar) scrape off

ráfaga *f* (de viento) gust; (de ametralladora) burst

rafia *f* raffia

raído *a* threadbare

raíz *f* root. **a** ~ **de** as a result of. **echar raíces** (fig) settle

raja *f* split; (Culin) slice. ~**r** *vt* split. □ ~**rse** *vpr* split; (fig) back out

rajatabla. a ~ rigorously

ralea *f* sort

ralla|dor *m* grater. ~**r** *vt* grate

ralo *a* <*pelo*> thin

rama *f* branch. ~**je** *m* branches. ~**l** *m* branch

rambla *f* watercourse; (avenida) avenue

ramera *f* prostitute

ramifica|ción *f* ramification. □ ~**rse** [7] *vpr* branch out

ram|illete *m* bunch. ~**o** *m* branch; (de flores) bunch, bouquet

rampa *f* ramp, slope

rana *f* frog

ranch|era *f* (Mex) folk song. ~**ero** *m* cook; (Mex, hacendado) rancher. ~**o** *m* (LAm, choza) hut; (LAm, casucha) shanty; (Mex, hacienda) ranch

rancio *a* rancid; <*vino*> old; (fig) ancient

rango *m* rank

ranúnculo *m* buttercup

ranura *f* groove; (para moneda) slot

rapar *vt* shave; crop <*pelo*>

rapaz *a* rapacious; <*ave*> of prey

rapidez *f* speed

rápido *a* fast, quick. ● *adv* quickly. ● *m* (tren) express. ~**s** *mpl* rapids

rapiña *f* robbery. **ave** *f* **de** ~ bird of prey

rapsodia *f* rhapsody

rapt|ar *vt* kidnap. ~**o** *m* kidnapping; (de ira etc) fit

raqueta *f* racquet

rar|eza *f* rarity; (cosa rara) oddity. ~**o** *a* rare; (extraño) odd. **es** ~**o que** it is strange that. **¡qué** ~**o!** how strange!

ras. a ~ **de** level with

rasca|cielos *m invar* skyscraper. ~**r** [7] *vt* scratch; (raspar) scrape

rasgar [12] *vt* tear

rasgo *m* characteristic; (gesto) gesture; (de pincel) stroke. ~**s** *mpl* (facciones) features

rasguear *vt* strum

rasguñ|ar *vt* scratch. ~**o** *m* scratch

raso *a* <*cucharada etc*> level; <*vuelo etc*> low. **al** ~ in the open air. ● *m* satin

raspa|dura *f* scratch; (acción) scratching. ~**r** *vt* scratch; (rozar) scrape

rastr|a. a ~**as** dragging. ~**ear** *vt* track. ~**ero** *a* creeping. ~**illar** *vt* rake. ~**illo** *m* rake. ~**o** *m* track; (señal) sign. **ni** ~**o** not a trace

rata *f* rat

ratero *m* petty thief

ratifica|ción *f* ratification. ~**r** [7] *vt* ratify

rato *m* moment, short time. ~**s libres** spare time. **a** ~**s** at times. **a cada** ~ (LAm) always. **hace un** ~ a moment ago. **pasar un mal** ~ have a rough time

rat|ón *m* mouse. ~**onera** *f* mousetrap; (madriguera) mouse hole

raudal *m* torrent. **a** ~**les** in abundance

raya *f* line; (lista) stripe; (de pelo) parting. **a** ~**s** striped. **pasarse de la** ~ go too far. ~**r** *vt* scratch. ~**r en** border on

rayo *m* ray; (descarga eléctrica) lightning. ~ **de luna** moonbeam. ~ **láser** laser beam. ~**s X** X-rays

raza *f* race; (de animal) breed. **de** ~ <*caballo*> thoroughbred; <*perro*> pedigree

raz|ón *f* reason. **a** ~**ón de** at the rate of. **perder la** ~**ón** go out of one's mind. **tener** ~**ón** be right. ~**onable** *a* reasonable. ~**onamiento** *m* reasoning. ~**onar** *vt* reason out. ● *vi* reason

re *m* D; (solfa) re

reac|ción *f* reaction; (LAm, Pol) right wing. ~**ción en cadena** chain reaction. ~**cionario** *a & m* reactionary. ~**tor** *m* reactor; (avión) jet

real *a* real; (de rey etc) royal; *<hecho>* true. ● *m* real, old Spanish coin

realidad *f* reality; (verdad) truth. **en** ~ in fact. **hacerse** ~ come true

realis|mo *m* realism. ~**ta** *a* realistic. ● *m & f* realist

realiza|ción *f* fulfilment. ~**r** [10] *vt* carry out; make *<viaje>*; fulfil *<ilusión>*; (vender) sell. □ ~**rse** *vpr* *<sueño, predicción etc>* come true; *<persona>* fulfil o.s.

realzar [10] *vt* (fig) enhance

reanimar *vt* revive. □ ~**se** *vpr* revive

reanudar *vt* resume; renew *<amistad>*

reavivar *vt* revive

rebaja *f* reduction. **en** ~**s** in the sale. ~**do** *a* *<precio>* reduced. ~**r** *vt* lower; lose *<peso>*

rebanada *f* slice

rebaño *m* herd; (de ovejas) flock

rebasar *vt* exceed; (dejar atrás) leave behind; (Mex, Auto) overtake

rebatir *vt* refute

rebel|arse *vpr* rebel. ~**de** *a* rebellious; *<grupo>* rebel. ● *m* rebel. ~**día** *f* rebelliousness. ~**ión** *f* rebellion

rebosa|nte *a* brimming (**de** with). ~**r** *vi* overflow; (abundar) abound

rebot|ar *vt* bounce; (rechazar) repel. ● *vi* bounce; *<bala>* ricochet. ~**e** *m* bounce, rebound. **de** ~**e** on the rebound

reboz|ar [10] *vt* wrap up; (Culin) coat in batter. ~**o** *m* (LAm) shawl

rebusca|do *a* affected; (complicado) over-elaborate. ~**r** [7] *vt* search through

rebuznar *vi* bray

recado *m* errand; (mensaje) message

reca|er [29] *vi* fall back; (Med) relapse; (fig) fall. ~**ída** *f* relapse

recalcar [7] *vt* stress

recalcitrante *a* recalcitrant

recalentar [1] *vt* reheat; (demasiado) overheat

recámara *f* small room; (de arma de fuego) chamber; (Mex, dormitorio) bedroom

recambio *m* (Mec) spare (part); (de pluma etc) refill. **de** ~ spare

recapitular *vt* sum up

recarg|ar [12] *vt* overload; (aumentar) increase; recharge *<batería>*. ~**o** *m* increase

recat|ado *a* modest. ~**o** *m* prudence; (modestia) modesty. **sin** ~**o** openly

recauda|ción *f* (cantidad) takings. ~**dor** *m* tax collector. ~**r** *vt* collect

recel|ar *vt* suspect. ● *vi* be suspicious (**de** of). ~**o** *m* distrust; (temor) fear. ~**oso** *a* suspicious

recepci|ón *f* reception. ~**onista** *m & f* receptionist

receptáculo *m* receptacle

receptor *m* receiver

recesión *f* recession

receta *f* recipe; (Med) prescription

rechaz|ar [10] *vt* reject; defeat *<moción>*; repel *<ataque>*; (no aceptar) turn down. ~**o** *m* rejection

rechifla *f* booing

rechinar *vi* squeak. **le rechinan los dientes** he grinds his teeth

rechoncho *a* stout

recib|imiento *m* (acogida) welcome. ~**ir** *vt* receive; (acoger) welcome. ● *vi* entertain. □ ~**irse** *vpr* graduate. ~**o** *m* receipt. **acusar** ~**o** acknowledge receipt

reci|én *adv* recently; (LAm, hace poco) just. ~ **casado** newly married. ~ **nacido** newborn. ~**ente** *a* recent; (Culin) fresh

recinto *m* enclosure; (local) premises

recio *a* strong; *<voz>* loud. ● *adv* hard; (en voz alta) loudly

recipiente *m* receptacle. ● *m & f* recipient

recíproco *a* reciprocal; *<sentimiento>* mutual

recita|l *m* recital; (de poesías) reading. ~**r** *vt* recite

reclama|ción *f* claim; (queja) complaint. ~**r** *vt* claim. ● *vi* appeal

réclame *m* (LAm) advertisement

reclamo *m* (LAm) complaint

reclinar *vi* lean. □ ~**se** *vpr* lean

reclus|ión *f* imprisonment. ~**o** *m* prisoner

recluta *m & f* recruit. ~**miento** *m* recruitment. ~**r** *vt* recruit

recobrar *vt* recover. □ ~**se** *vpr* recover

recodo *m* bend

recog|er [14] *vt* collect; pick up *<cosa caída>*; (cosechar) harvest. □ ~**erse** *vpr* withdraw; (ir a casa) go home; (acostarse) go to bed. ~**ida** *f* collection; (cosecha) harvest

recomenda|ción *f* recommendation. ~**r** [1] *vt* recommend; (encomendar) entrust

recomenzar [1 & 10] *vt/i* start again

recompensa *f* reward. ~**r** *vt* reward

reconcilia|ción *f* reconciliation. ~**r** *vt* reconcile. □ ~**rse** *vpr* be reconciled

reconoc|er [11] *vt* recognize; (admitir) acknowledge; (examinar) examine. ~**imiento** *m* recognition; (admisión) acknowledgement; (agradecimiento) gratitude; (examen) examination

reconozco *vb* ⇒RECONOCER

reconquista *f* reconquest. ~**r** *vt* reconquer; (fig) win back

reconsiderar *vt* reconsider

reconstruir [17] *vt* reconstruct

récord /'rekor/ *m* (*pl* ~**s**) record

recordar [2] *vt* remember; (hacer acordar) remind. ● *vi* remember. **que yo recuerde** as far as I remember. **si mal no recuerdo** if I remember rightly

recorr|er *vt* tour *<país>*; go round *<zona, museo>*; cover *<distancia>*. ~ **mundo** travel all around the world. ~**ido** *m* journey; (trayecto) route

recort|ar *vt* cut (out). ~**e** *m* cutting (out); (de periódico etc) cutting

recostar [2] *vt* lean. □ ~**se** *vpr* lie down

recoveco *m* bend; (rincón) nook

recre|ación *f* recreation. ~**ar** *vt* recreate; (divertir) entertain. □ ~**arse** *vpr* amuse o.s. ~**ativo** *a* recreational. ~**o** *m* recreation; (Escol) break

recrudecer [11] *vi* intensify

recta *f* straight line. ~ **final** home stretch

rect|angular *a* rectangular. ~**ángulo** *a* rectangular; *<triángulo>* right-angled. ● *m* rectangle

rectifica|ción *f* rectification. ~**r** [7] *vt* rectify

rect|itud *f* straightness; (fig) honesty. ~**o** *a* straight; (fig, justo) fair; (fig, honrado) honest. **todo** ~**o** straight on. ● *m* rectum

rector *a* governing. ● *m* rector

recubrir (*pp* **recubierto**) *vt* cover (**con, de** with)

recuerdo *m* memory; (regalo) souvenir. ~**s** *mpl* (saludos) regards. ● *vb* ⇒RECORDAR

recupera|ción *f* recovery. ~**r** *vt* recover. ~**r el tiempo perdido** make up for lost time. □ ~**rse** *vpr* recover

recur|rir *vi.* ~**rir a** resort to *<cosa>*; turn to *<persona>*. ~**so** *m* resort; (medio) resource; (Jurid) appeal. ~**sos** *mpl* resources

red *f* network; (malla) net; (para equipaje) luggage rack; (Com) chain; (Elec, gas) mains. **la R**~ the Net

redac|ción *f* writing; (lenguaje) wording; (conjunto de redactores) editorial staff; (oficina) editorial office; (Escol, Univ) essay. ~**tar** *vt* write. ~**tor** *m* writer; (de periódico) editor

redada *f* catch; (de policía) raid

redecilla *f* small net; (para el pelo) hairnet

redentor *a* redeeming

redimir *vt* redeem

redoblar *vt* redouble; step up *<vigilancia>*

redomado *a* utter

redond|a *f* (de imprenta) roman (type); (Mus) semibreve (Brit), whole note (Amer). **a la** ~**a** around. ~**ear** *vt* round off. ~**el** *m* circle; (de plaza de toros) arena. ~**o** *a* round; (completo) complete; (Mex, boleto) return, round-trip (Amer). **en** ~**o** round; (categóricamente) flatly

reduc|ción f reduction. ~**ido** a reduced; (limitado) limited; (pequeño) small; <precio> low. ~**ir** [47] vt reduce. □ ~**irse** vpr be reduced; (fig) amount

reduje vb ⇒REDUCIR

redundan|cia f redundancy. ~**te** a redundant

reduzco vb ⇒REDUCIR

reembols|ar vt reimburse. ~**o** m repayment. **contra** ~**o** cash on delivery

reemplaz|ar [10] vt replace. ~**o** m replacement

refacci|ón f (LAm) refurbishment; (Mex, Mec) spare part. ~**onar** vt (LAm) refurbish. ~**onaria** f (Mex) repair shop

referencia f reference; (información) report. **con** ~ **a** with reference to. **hacer** ~ **a** refer to

referéndum m (pl ~**s**) referendum

referir [4] vt tell; (remitir) refer. □ ~**se** vpr refer. **por lo que se refiere a** as regards

refiero vb ⇒REFERIR

refilón. de ~ obliquely

refin|amiento m refinement. ~**ar** vt refine. ~**ería** f refinery

reflector m reflector; (proyector) searchlight

reflej|ar vt reflect. ~**o** a reflex. ● m reflection; (Med) reflex; (en el pelo) highlights

reflexi|ón f reflection. **sin** ~**ón** without thinking. ~**onar** vi reflect. ~**vo** a <persona> thoughtful; (Gram) reflexive

reforma f reform. ~**s** fpl (reparaciones) repairs. ~**r** vt reform. □ ~**rse** vpr reform

reforzar [2 & 10] vt reinforce

refrac|ción f refraction. ~**tario** a heat-resistant

refrán m saying

refregar [1 & 12] vt scrub

refresc|ar [7] vt refresh; (enfriar) cool. ● vi get cooler. □ ~**arse** vpr

refresh o.s. ~**o** m cold drink. ~**os** mpl refreshments

refrigera|ción f refrigeration; (aire acondicionado) air-conditioning; (de motor) cooling. ~**r** vt refrigerate; air-condition <lugar>; cool <motor>. ~**dor** m refrigerator

refuerzo m reinforcement

refugi|ado m refugee. □ ~**arse** vpr take refuge. ~**o** m refuge, shelter

refunfuñar vi grumble

refutar vt refute

regadera f watering-can; (Mex, ducha) shower

regala|do a as a present, free; (cómodo) comfortable. ~**r** vt give

regalo m present, gift

regañ|adientes. a ~**adientes** reluctantly. ~**ar** vt scold. ● vi moan; (dos personas) quarrel. ~**o** m (reprensión) scolding

regar [1 & 12] vt water

regata f boat race; (serie) regatta

regate|ar vt haggle over; (economizar) economize on. ● vi haggle; (en deportes) dribble. ~**o** m haggling; (en deportes) dribbling

regazo m lap

regenerar vt regenerate

régimen m (pl **regímenes**) regime; (Med) diet; (de lluvias) pattern

regimiento m regiment

regi|ón f region. ~**onal** a regional

regir [5 & 14] vt govern. ● vi apply, be in force

registr|ado a registered. ~**ar** vt register; (Mex) check in <equipaje>; (grabar) record; (examinar) search. □ ~**arse** vpr register; (darse) be reported. ~**o** m (acción de registrar) registration; (libro) register; (cosa anotada) entry; (inspección) search. ~**o civil** (oficina) registry office

regla f ruler; (norma) rule; (menstruación) period. **en** ~ in order. **por** ~ **general** as a rule. ~**mentación** f regulation. ~**mentar** vt regulate. ~**mentario** a regulation; <horario> set. ~**mento** m regulations

regocij|arse vpr be delighted. ~**o** m delight

regode|arse *vpr* (+ *gerundio*) delight in (+ *gerund*). ~**o** *m* delight

regordete *a* chubby

regres|ar *vi* return; (LAm) send back <*persona*>. □ ~**arse** *vpr* (LAm) return. ~**ivo** *a* backward. ~**o** *m* return

regula|ble *a* adjustable. ~**dor** *m* control. ~**r** *a* regular; (mediano) average; (no bueno) so-so. ● *vt* regulate; adjust <*volumen etc*>. ~**ridad** *f* regularity. **con** ~**ridad** regularly

rehabilita|ción *f* rehabilitation; (en empleo etc) reinstatement. ~**r** *vt* rehabilitate; (en cargo) reinstate

rehacer [31] *vt* redo; (repetir) repeat; rebuild <*vida*>. □ ~**se** *vpr* recover

rehén *m* hostage

rehogar [12] *vt* sauté

rehuir [17] *vt* avoid

rehusar *vt/i* refuse

reimpr|esión *f* reprinting. ~**imir** (*pp* **reimpreso**) *vt* reprint

reina *f* queen. ~**do** *m* reign. ~**nte** *a* ruling; (fig) prevailing. ~**r** *vi* reign; (fig) prevail

reincidir *vi* (Jurid) reoffend

reino *m* kingdom. **R**~ **Unido** United Kingdom

reintegr|ar *vt* reinstate <*persona*>; refund <*cantidad*>. □ ~**arse** *vpr* return. ~**o** *m* refund

reír [51] *vi* laugh. □ ~**se** *vpr* laugh. ~**se de** laugh at. **echarse a** ~ burst out laughing

reivindica|ción *f* claim. ~**r** [7] *vt* claim; (rehabilitar) restore

rej|a *f* grille; (verja) railing. **entre** ~**as** behind bars. ~**illa** *f* grille, grating; (red) luggage rack

rejuvenecer [11] *vt/i* rejuvenate. □ ~**se** *vpr* be rejuvenated

relaci|ón *f* connection; (trato) relation(ship); (relato) account; (lista) list. **con** ~**ón a**, **en** ~**ón a** in relation to. ~**onado** *a* related. **bien** ~**onado** well-connected. ~**onar** *vt* relate (con to). □ ~**onarse** *vpr* be connected; (tratar) mix (con with)

relaja|ción *f* relaxation; (aflojamiento) slackening. ~**do** *a* relaxed. ~**r** *vt* relax; (aflojar) slacken. □ ~**rse** *vpr* relax

relamerse *vpr* lick one's lips

relámpago *m* (flash of) lightning

relatar *vt* tell, relate

relativ|idad *f* relativity. ~**o** *a* relative

relato *m* tale; (relación) account

relegar [12] *vt* relegate. ~ **al olvido** consign to oblivion

relev|ante *a* outstanding. ~**ar** *vt* relieve; (substituir) replace. ~**o** *m* relief. **carrera** *f* **de** ~**os** relay race

relieve *m* relief; (fig) importance. **de** ~ important. **poner de** ~ emphasize

religi|ón *f* religion. ~**osa** *f* nun. ~**oso** *a* religious. ● *m* monk

relinch|ar *vi* neigh. ~**o** *m* neigh

reliquia *f* relic

rellano *m* landing

rellen|ar *vt* refill; (Culin) stuff; fill in <*formulario*>. ~**o** *a* full up; (Culin) stuffed. ● *m* filling; (Culin) stuffing

reloj *m* clock; (de bolsillo o pulsera) watch. ~ **de caja** grandfather clock. ~ **de pulsera** wrist-watch. ~ **de sol** sundial. ~ **despertador** alarm clock. ~**ería** *f* watchmaker's (shop). ~**ero** *m* watchmaker

reluci|ente *a* shining. ~**r** [11] *vi* shine; (destellar) sparkle

relumbrar *vi* shine

remach|ar *vt* rivet. ~**e** *m* rivet

remangar [12] *vt* roll up

remar *vi* row

remat|ado *a* (total) complete. ~**ar** *vt* finish off; (agotar) use up; (Com) sell off cheap; (LAm, subasta) auction; (en tenis) smash. ~**e** *m* end; (fig) finishing touch; (LAm, subastar) auction; (en tenis) smash. **de** ~**e** completely

remedar *vt* imitate

remedi|ar *vt* remedy; repair <*daño*>; (fig, resolver) solve. **no lo pude** ~**ar** I couldn't help it. ~**o** *m* remedy; (fig) solution; (LAm, medicamento) medicine. **como último** ~**o** as a last resort. **no hay más** ~**o** there's no other way. **no tener más** ~**o** have no choice

remedo *m* poor imitation

rem|endar [1] *vt* repair. ~**iendo** *m* patch

remilg|ado *a* fussy; (afectado) affected. **~o** *m* fussiness; (afectación) affectation. **~oso** *a* (Mex) fussy

reminiscencia *f* reminiscence

remisión *f* remission; (envío) sending; (referencia) reference

remit|e *m* sender's name and address. **~ente** *m* sender. **~ir** *vt* send; (referir) refer ● *vi* diminish

remo *m* oar

remoj|ar *vt* soak; (fig, 🔢) celebrate. **~o** *m* soaking. **poner a ~o** soak

remolacha *f* beetroot. **~ azucarera** sugar beet

remolcar [7] *vt* tow

remolino *m* swirl; (de aire etc) whirl

remolque *m* towing; (cabo) tow-rope; (vehículo) trailer. **a ~** on tow. **dar ~** a tow

remontar *vt* overcome. **~ el vuelo** soar up; *<avión>* gain height. □ **~se** *vpr* soar up; (en el tiempo) go back to

remord|er [2] *vi*. eso le remuerde he feels guilty for it. **me remuerde la conciencia** I have a guilty conscience. **~imiento** *m* remorse. **tener ~imientos** feel remorse

remoto *a* remote; *<época>* distant

remover [2] *vt* stir *<líquido>*; turn over *<tierra>*; (quitar) remove; (fig, activar) revive

remunera|ción *f* remuneration. **~r** *vt* remunerate

renac|er [11] *vi* be reborn; (fig) revive. **~imiento** *m* rebirth. **R~imiento** Renaissance

renacuajo *m* tadpole; (fig) tiddler

rencilla *f* quarrel

rencor *m* bitterness. **guardar ~ a** have a grudge against. **~oso** *a* resentful

rendi|ción *f* surrender. **~do** *a* submissive; (agotado) exhausted

rendija *f* crack

rendi|miento *m* performance; (Com) yield. **~r** [5] *vt* yield; (agotar) exhaust; pay *<homenaje>*; present *<informe>*. ● *vi* pay; (producir) produce. □ **~rse** *vpr* surrender

renegar [1 & 12] *vt* deny. ● *vi* grumble. **~r de** renounce *<fe etc>*; disown *<personas>*

renglón *m* line; (Com) item. **a ~ seguido** straight away

reno *m* reindeer

renombr|ado *a* renowned. **~e** *m* renown

renova|ción *f* renewal; (de edificio) renovation; (de mobiliario) complete change. **~r** *vt* renew; renovate *<edificio>*; change *<mobiliario>*

rent|a *f* income; (Mex, alquiler) rent. **~a vitalicia** (life) annuity. **~able** *a* profitable. **~ar** *vt* yield; (Mex, alquilar) rent, hire. **~ista** *m* & *f* person of independent means

renuncia *f* renunciation; (dimisión) resignation. **~r** *vi*. **~r a** renounce, give up; (dimitir) resign

reñi|do *a* hard-fought. **estar ~do con** be incompatible with *<cosa>*; be on bad terms with *<persona>*. **~r** [5 & 22] *vt* scold. ● *vi* quarrel

reo *m* & *f* (Jurid) accused; (condenado) convicted offender

reojo. **mirar de ~** look out of the corner of one's eye at

reorganizar [10] *vt* reorganize

repar|ación *f* repair; (acción) repairing (fig, compensación) reparation. **~ar** *vt* repair; (fig) make amends for; (notar) notice. ● *vi*. **~ar en** notice; (hacer caso de) pay attention to. **~o** *m* fault; (objeción) objection. **poner ~os** raise objections

repart|ición *f* distribution. **~idor** *m* delivery man. **~imiento** *m* distribution. **~ir** *vt* distribute, share out; deliver *<cartas, leche etc>*; hand out *<folleto, premio>*. **~o** *m* distribution; (de cartas, leche etc) delivery; (actores) cast

repas|ar *vt* go over; check *<cuenta>*; revise *<texto>*; (leer a la ligera) glance through; (coser) mend. ● *vi* revise. **~o** *m* revision; (de ropa) mending. **dar un ~o** look through

repatria|ción *f* repatriation. **~r** *vt* repatriate

repele|nte *a* repulsive. ● *m* insect repellent. **~r** *vt* repel

repent|e. **de ~** suddenly. **~ino** *a* sudden

repercu|sión *f* repercussion. ~**tir** *vi* reverberate; (fig) have repercussions (**en** on)

repertorio *m* repertoire

repeti|ción *f* repetition; (de programa) repeat. ~**damente** *adv* repeatedly. ~**r** [5] *vt* repeat; have a second helping of *<plato>*; (imitar) copy. ● *vi* have a second helping of

repi|car [7] *vt* ring *<campanas>*. ~**que** *m* peal

repisa *f* shelf. ~ **de chimenea** mantlepiece

repito *vb* ⇒REPETIR

replegarse [1 & 12] *vpr* withdraw

repleto *a* full up. ~ **de gente** packed with people

réplica *a* reply; (copia) replica

replicar [7] *vi* reply

repollo *m* cabbage

reponer [34] *vt* replace; revive *<obra de teatro>*; (contestar) reply. □ ~**se** *vpr* recover

report|aje *m* report; (LAm, entrevista) interview. ~**ar** *vt* yield; (LAm, denunciar) report. ~**e** *m* (Mex, informe) report; (Mex, queja) complaint. ~**ero** *m* reporter

repos|ado *a* quiet; (sin prisa) unhurried. ~**ar** *vi* rest; *<líquido>* settle. ~**o** *m* rest

repost|ar *vt* replenish. ● *vi* (Aviac) refuel; (Auto) fill up. ~**ería** *f* pastrymaking

reprender *vt* reprimand

represalia *f* reprisal. **tomar** ~**s** retaliate

representa|ción *f* representation; (en el teatro) performance. **en** ~**ción de** representing. ~**nte** *m* representative. ~**r** *vt* represent; perform *<obra de teatro>*; play *<papel>*; (aparentar) look. □ ~**rse** *vpr* imagine. ~**tivo** *a* representative

represi|ón *f* repression. ~**vo** *a* repressive

reprimenda *f* reprimand

reprimir *vt* supress. □ ~**se** *vpr* control o.s.

reprobar [2] *vt* condemn; (LAm, Univ, etc) fail

reproch|ar *vt* reproach. ~**e** *m* reproach

reproduc|ción *f* reproduction. ~**ir** [47] *vt* reproduce. ~**tor** *a* reproductive; *<animal>* breeding

reptil *m* reptile

rep|ública *f* republic. ~**ublicano** *a* & *m* republican

repudiar *vt* condemn; (Jurid) repudiate

repuesto *m* (Mec) spare (part). **de** ~ spare

repugna|ncia *f* disgust. ~**nte** *a* repugnant; *<olor>* disgusting. ~**r** *vt* disgust

repuls|a *f* rebuff. ~**ión** *f* repulsion. ~**ivo** *a* repulsive

reputa|ción *f* reputation. ~**do** *a* reputable. ~**r** *vt* consider

requeri|miento *m* request; (necesidad) requirement. ~**r** [4] *vt* require; summons *<persona>*

requesón *m* curd cheese

requete... *pref* extremely

requis|a *f* requisition; (confiscación) seizure; (inspección) inspection; (Mil) requisition. ~**ar** *vt* requisition; (confiscar) seize; (inspeccionar) inspect. ~**ito** *m* requirement

res *f* animal. ~ **lanar** sheep. ~ **vacuna** (vaca) cow; (toro) bull; (buey) ox. **carne de** ~ (Mex) beef

resabido *a* well-known; *<persona>* pedantic

resaca *f* undercurrent; (después de beber) hangover

resaltar *vi* stand out. **hacer** ~ emphasize

resarcir [9] *vt* repay; (compensar) compensate. □ ~**se** *vpr* make up for

resbal|adilla *f* (Mex) slide. ~**adizo** *a* slippery. ~**ar** *vi* slip; (Auto) skid; *<líquido>* trickle. □ ~**arse** *vpr* slip; (Auto) skid; *<líquido>* trickle. ~**ón** *m* slip; (de vehículo) skid. ~**oso** *a* (LAm) slippery

rescat|ar *vt* rescue; (fig) recover. ~**e** *m* ransom; (recuperación) recovery; (salvamento) rescue

rescoldo *m* embers

resecar [7] *vt* dry up. □ ~**se** *vpr* dry up

resenti|do a resentful. ~**miento** m resentment. □ ~**rse** vpr feel the effects; (debilitarse) be weakened; (ofenderse) take offence (**de** at)

reseña f summary; (de persona) description; (en periódico) report, review. ~**r** vt describe; (en periódico) report on, review

reserva f reservation; (provisión) reserve(s). **de** ~ in reserve. ~**ción** f (LAm) reservation. ~**do** a reserved. ~**r** vt reserve; (guardar) keep, save. □ ~**rse** vpr save o.s.

resfria|do m cold. □ ~**rse** vpr catch a cold

resguard|ar vt protect. □ ~**arse** vpr protect o.s.; (fig) take care. ~**o** m protection; (garantía) guarantee; (recibo) receipt

resid|encia f residence; (Univ) hall of residence (Brit), dormitory (Amer); (de ancianos etc) home. ~**encial** a residential. ~**ente** a & m & f resident. ~**ir** vi reside; (fig) lie (**en** in)

residu|al a residual. ~**o** m residue. ~**os** mpl waste

resigna|ción f resignation. □ ~**rse** vpr resign o.s. (**a** to)

resist|encia f resistence. ~**ente** a resistent. ~**ir** vt resist; (soportar) bear. ● vi resist. **ya no resisto más** I can't take it any more

resol|ución f resolution; (solución) solution; (decisión) decision. ~**ver** [2] (pp **resuelto**) resolve; solve <problema etc>. □ ~**verse** vpr resolve itself; (resultar bien) work out; (decidir) decide

resona|ncia f resonance. **tener** ~**ncia** cause a stir. ~**nte** a resonant; (fig) resounding. ~**r** [2] vi resound

resorte m spring; (Mex, elástico) elastic. **tocar** (**todos los**) ~**s** (fig) pull strings

respald|ar vt back; (escribir) endorse. □ ~**arse** vpr lean back. ~**o** m backing; (de asiento) back

respect|ar vi. **en lo que** ~**a** a with regard to. **en lo que a mí** ~**a** as far as I'm concerned. ~**ivo** a respective. ~**o** m respect. **al** ~**o** on this matter. (**con**) ~**o a** with regard to

respet|able a respectable. ● m audience. ~**ar** vt respect. ~**o** m respect. **faltar al** ~**o a** be disrespectful to. ~**uoso** a respectful

respir|ación f breathing; (ventilación) ventilation. ~**ar** vi breathe; (fig) breathe a sigh of relief. ~**o** m breathing; (fig) rest

respland|ecer [11] vi shine. ~**eciente** a shining. ~**or** m brilliance; (de llamas) glow

responder vi answer; (replicar) answer back; (reaccionar) respond. ~ **de** be responsible for. ~ **por uno** vouch for s.o.

responsab|ilidad f responsibility. ~**le** a responsible

respuesta f reply, answer

resquebrajar vt crack. □ ~**se** vpr crack

resquemor m (fig) uneasiness

resquicio m crack; (fig) possibility

resta f subtraction

restablecer [11] vt restore. □ ~**se** vpr recover

rest|ante a remaining. **lo** ~**nte** the rest. ~**ar** vt take away; (substraer) subtract. ● vi be left

restaura|ción f restoration. ~**nte** m restaurant. ~**r** vt restore

restitu|ción f restitution. ~**ir** [17] vt return; (restaurar) restore

resto m rest, remainder; (en matemática) remainder. ~**s** mpl remains; (de comida) leftovers

restorán m restaurant

restregar [1 & 12] vt rub

restri|cción f restriction. ~**ngir** [14] vt restrict, limit

resucitar vt resuscitate; (fig) revive. ● vi return to life

resuello m breath; (respiración) heavy breathing

resuelto a resolute

resulta|do m result (**en** in). ~**r** vi result; (salir) turn out; (dar resultado) work; (ser) be; (costar) come to

resum|en m summary. **en** ~**en** in short. ~**ir** vt summarize; (recapitular) sum up

resur|gir [14] *vi* reemerge; (fig) revive. **~gimiento** *m* resurgence. **~rección** *f* resurrection

retaguardia *f* (Mil) rearguard

retahíla *f* string

retar *vt* challenge

retardar *vt* slow down; (demorar) delay

retazo *m* remnant; (fig) piece, bit

reten|ción *f* retention. **~er** [40] *vt* keep; (en la memoria) retain; (no dar) withhold

reticencia *f* insinuation; (reserva) reluctance

retina *f* retina

retir|ada *f* withdrawal. **~ado** *a* remote; *<vida>* secluded; (jubilado) retired. **~ar** *vt* move away; (quitar) remove; withdraw *<dinero>*; (jubilar) pension off. □ **~arse** *vpr* draw back; (Mil) withdraw; (jubilarse) retire; (acostarse) go to bed. **~o** *m* retirement; (pensión) pension; (lugar apartado) retreat; (LAm, de apoyo, fondos) withdrawal

reto *m* challenge

retocar [7] *vt* retouch

retoño *m* shoot; (fig) kid

retoque *m* (acción) retouching; (efecto) finishing touch

retorc|er [2 & 9] *vt* twist; wring *<ropa>*. □ **~erse** *vpr* get twisted up; (de dolor) writhe. **~ijón** *m* (LAm) stomach cramp

retóric|a *f* rhetoric; (grandilocuencia) grandiloquence. **~o** *m* rhetorical

retorn|ar *vt/i* return. **~o** *m* return

retortijón *m* twist; (de tripas) stomach cramp

retractarse *vpr* retract. **~se de lo dicho** withdraw what one said

retransmitir *vt* repeat; (radio, TV) broadcast. **~ en directo** broadcast live

retras|ado *a* (con ser) mentally handicapped; (con estar) behind; *<reloj>* slow; (poco desarrollado) backward; (anticuado) old-fashioned. **~ar** *vt* delay; put back *<reloj>*; (retardar) slow down; (posponer) postpone. ● *vi* *<reloj>* be slow. □ **~arse** *vpr* be late; *<reloj>* be slow. **~o** *m* delay; (poco desarrollo) backwardness; (de reloj) slow-

ness. **traer ~o** be late. **~os** *mpl* arrears

retrato *m* portrait; (fig, descripción) description. **ser el vivo ~o de** be the living image of

retrete *m* toilet

retribu|ción *f* payment; (recompensa) reward. **~ir** [17] *vt* pay; (recompensar) reward; (LAm) return *<favor>*

retroce|der *vi* move back; (fig) back down. **~so** *m* backward movement; (de arma de fuego) recoil; (Med) relapse

retrógrado *a & m* (Pol) reactionary

retrospectivo *a* retrospective

retrovisor *m* rear-view mirror

retumbar *vt* echo; *<trueno etc>* boom

reum|a *m*, **reúma** *m* rheumatism. **~ático** *a* rheumatic. **~atismo** *m* rheumatism

reuni|ón *f* meeting; (entre amigos) reunion. **~r** [23] *vt* join together; (recoger) gather (together); raise *<fondos>*. □ **~rse** *vpr* meet; *<amigos etc>* get together

revalidar *vt* confirm; (Mex, estudios) validate

revalorizar [10] *vt*, (LAm) **revaluar** [21] *vt* revalue; increase *<pensiones>*. □ **~se** *vpr* appreciate

revancha *f* revenge; (en deportes) return match. **tomar la ~** get one's own back

revela|ción *f* revelation. **~do** *m* developing. **~dor** *a* revealing. **~r** *vt* reveal; (Foto) develop

revent|ar [1] *vi* burst; (tener ganas) be dying to. □ **~arse** *vpr* burst. **~ón** *m* burst; (Auto) blow out; (Mex, fiesta) party

reveren|cia *f* reverence; (de hombre, niño) bow; (de mujer) curtsy. **~ciar** *vt* revere. **~do** *a* (Relig) reverend. **~te** *a* reverent

revers|ible *a* reversible. **~o** *m* reverse; (de papel) back

revertir [4] *vi* revert (**a** to)

revés *m* wrong side; (de prenda) inside; (contratiempo) setback; (en deportes) backhand. **al ~** the other way round; (con lo de arriba abajo) upside down; (con lo de dentro fuera) inside out

revesti|miento *m* coating. **~r** [5] *vt* cover

revis|ar *vt* check; overhaul *<mecanismo>*; service *<coche etc>*; (LAm, equipaje) search. **~ión** *f* check(ing)); (Med) checkup; (de coche etc) service; (LAm, de equipaje) inspection. **~or** *m* inspector

revista *f* magazine; (inspección) inspection; (artículo) review; (espectáculo) revue. **pasar ~ a** inspect

revivir *vi* revive

revolcar [2 & 7] *vt* knock over. □ **~se** *vpr* roll around

revolotear *vi* flutter

revoltijo *m*, **revoltillo** *m* mess

revoltoso *a* rebellious; *<niño>* naughty

revoluci|ón *f* revolution. **~onar** *vt* revolutionize. **~onario** *a & m* revolutionary

revolver [2] (*pp* **revuelto**) *vt* mix; stir *<líquido>*; (desordenar) mess up

revólver *m* revolver

revuelo *m* fluttering; (fig) stir

revuelt|a *f* revolt; (conmoción) disturbance. **~o** *a* mixed up; *<líquido>* cloudy; *<mar>* rough; *<tiempo>* unsettled; *<huevos>* scrambled

rey *m* king. **los ~es** the king and queen. **los R~es Magos** the Three Wise Men

reyerta *f* brawl

rezagarse [12] *vpr* fall behind

rez|ar [10] *vt* say. ● *vi* pray; (decir) say. **~o** *m* praying; (oración) prayer

rezongar [12] *vi* grumble

ría *f* estuary

riachuelo *m* stream

riada *f* flood

ribera *f* bank

ribete *m* border; (fig) embellishment

rico *a* rich; (Culin, 🅣) good, nice. ● *m* rich person

rid|ículo *a* ridiculous. **~iculizar** [10] *vt* ridicule

riego *m* watering; (irrigación) irrigation

riel *m* rail

rienda *f* rein

riesgo *m* risk. **correr (el) ~ de** run the risk of

rifa *f* raffle. **~r** *vt* raffle

rifle *m* rifle

rigidez *f* rigidity; (fig) inflexibility

rígido *a* rigid; (fig) inflexible

rig|or *m* strictness; (exactitud) exactness; (de clima) severity. **de ~or** compulsory. **en ~or** strictly speaking. **~uroso** *a* rigorous

rima *f* rhyme. **~r** *vt/i* rhyme

rimbombante *a* resounding; *<lenguaje>* pompous; (fig, ostentoso) showy

rímel *m* mascara

rin *m* (Mex) rim

rincón *m* corner

rinoceronte *m* rhinoceros

riña *f* quarrel; (pelea) fight

riñón *m* kidney

río *m* river; (fig) stream. **~ abajo** downstream. **~ arriba** upstream. ● *vb* ⇒REÍR

riqueza *f* wealth; (fig) richness. **~s** *fpl* riches

ris|a *f* laugh. **desternillarse de ~a** split one's sides laughing. **la ~a** laughter. **~otada** *f* guffaw. **~ueño** *a* smiling; (fig) cheerful

rítmico *a* rhythmic(al)

ritmo *m* rhythm; (fig) rate

rit|o *m* rite; (fig) ritual. **~ual** *a & m* ritual

rival *a & m & f* rival. **~idad** *f* rivalry. **~izar** [10] *vi* rival

riz|ado *a* curly. **~ar** [10] *vt* curl; ripple *<agua>*. **~o** *m* curl; (en agua) ripple

róbalo *m* bass

robar *vt* steal *<cosa>*; rob *<banco>*; (raptar) kidnap

roble *m* oak (tree)

robo *m* theft; (de banco, museo) robbery; (en vivienda) burglary

robusto *a* robust

roca *f* rock

roce *m* rubbing; (señal) mark; (fig, entre personas) regular contact; (Pol) friction. **tener un ~ con uno** have a brush with s.o.

rociar [20] *vt* spray

rocín *m* nag

rocío *m* dew

rodaballo *m* turbot

rodaja *f* slice. **en ~s** sliced

roda|je *m* (de película) shooting; (de coche) running in. **~r** [2] *vt* shoot *<película>*; run in *<coche>*. ● *vi* roll; *<coche>* run; (hacer una película) shoot

rode|ar *vt* surround; (LAm) round up *<ganado>*. □ **~arse** *vpr* surround o.s. (**de** with). **~o** *m* detour; (de ganado) round-up. **andar con ~os** beat about the bush. **sin ~os** plainly

rodill|a *f* knee. **ponerse de ~as** kneel down. **~era** *f* knee-pad

rodillo *m* roller; (Culin) rolling-pin

roe|dor *m* rodent. **~r** [37] *vt* gnaw

rogar [2 & 12] *vt/i* beg; (Relig) pray; **se ruega a los Sres. pasajeros... passengers are requested.... se ruega no fumar** please do not smoke

roj|izo *a* reddish. **~o** *a & m* red. **ponerse ~o** blush

roll|izo *a* plump; *<bebé>* chubby. **~o** *m* roll; (de cuerda) coil; (Culin, rodillo) rolling-pin; (fig, ⊡, pesadez) bore

romance *a* Romance. ● *m* (idilio) romance; (poema) ballad

romano *a & m* Roman. **a la ~a** (Culin) (deep-)fried in batter

rom|anticismo *m* romanticism. **~ántico** *a* romantic

romería *f* pilgrimage; (LAm, multitud) mass

romero *m* rosemary

romo *a* blunt; *<nariz>* snub

rompe|cabezas *m invar* puzzle; (de piezas) jigsaw (puzzle). **~olas** *m invar* breakwater

romp|er (*pp* **roto**) *vt* break; tear *<hoja, camisa etc>*; break off *<relaciones etc>*. ● *vi* break; *<novios>* break up. **~er a** burst out. □ **~erse** *vpr* break

ron *m* rum

ronc|ar [7] *vi* snore. **~o** *a* hoarse

roncha *f* lump; (por alergia) rash

ronda *f* round; (patrulla) patrol; (serenata) serenade. **~r** *vt* patrol. ● *vi* be on patrol; (merodear) hang around

ronqu|era *f* hoarseness. **~ido** *m* snore

ronronear *vi* purr

roñ|a *f* (suciedad) grime. **~oso** *a* dirty; (oxidado) rusty; (tacaño) mean

rop|a *f* clothes, clothing. **~a blanca** linen, underwear. **~a de cama** bedclothes. **~a interior** underwear. **~aje** *m* robes; (excesivo) heavy clothing. **~ero** *m* wardrobe

ros|a *a invar* pink. ● *f* rose. ● *m* pink. **~áceo** *a* pinkish. **~ado** *a* pink; *<mejillas>* rosy. ● *m* (vino) rosé. **~al** *m* rose-bush

rosario *m* rosary; (fig) series

ros|ca *f* (de tornillo) thread; (de pan) roll; (bollo) type of doughnut. **~co** *m* roll. **~quilla** *f* type of doughnut

rostro *m* face

rota|ción *f* rotation. **~r** *vt/i* rotate. □ **~rse** *vpr* take turns. **~tivo** *a* rotary

roto *a* broken

rótula *f* kneecap

rotulador *m* felt-tip pen

rótulo *m* sign; (etiqueta) label; (logotipo) logo

rotundo *a* categorical

rotura *f* tear; (grieta) crack

rozadura *f* scratch

rozagante *a* (LAm) healthy

rozar [10] *vt* rub against; (ligeramente) brush against; (raspar) graze. □ **~se** *vpr* rub; (con otras personas) mix

Rte. *abrev* (**Remite(nte)**) sender

rubéola *f* German measles

rubí *m* ruby

rubicundo *a* ruddy

rubio *a* *<pelo>* fair; *<persona>* fairhaired; *<tabaco>* Virginia

rubor *m* blush; (Mex, cosmético) blusher. □ **~izarse** [10] *vpr* blush

rúbrica *f* (de firma) flourish; (firma) signature; (título) heading

rudeza *f* roughness

rudiment|ario *a* rudimentary. **~os** *mpl* rudiments

rueca *f* distaff

rueda *f* wheel; (de mueble) castor; (de personas) ring; (Culin) slice. **~ de prensa** press conference

ruedo *m* edge; (redondel) bullring

ruego *m* request; (súplica) entreaty. ● *vb* ⇒ROGAR

rufián *m* pimp; (granuja) rogue

rugby *m* rugby

rugi|do *m* roar. ~**r** [14] *vi* roar

ruibarbo *m* rhubarb

ruido *m* noise. ~**so** *a* noisy; (fig) sensational

ruin *a* despicable; (tacaño) mean

ruin|a *f* ruin; (colapso) collapse. ~**oso** *a* ruinous

ruiseñor *m* nightingale

ruleta *f* roulette

rulo *m* curler

rumano *a* & *m* Romanian

rumbo *m* direction; (fig) course; (fig, esplendidez) lavishness. **con** ~ **a** in the direction of. ~**so** *a* lavish

rumia|nte *a* & *m* ruminant. ~**r** *vt* chew; (fig) brood over. ● *vi* ruminate

rumor *m* rumour; (ruido) murmur. ~**ear** *vt*. **se** ~**ea que** rumour has it that. ~**oso** *a* murmuring

runrún *m* (de voces) murmur; (de motor) whirr

ruptura *f* breakup; (de relaciones etc) breaking off; (de contrato) breach

rural *a* rural

ruso *a* & *m* Russian

rústico *a* rural; (de carácter) coarse. **en rústica** paperback

ruta *f* route; (fig) course

rutina *f* routine. ~**rio** *a* routine; *<trabajo>* monotonous

Ss

S.A. *abrev* (**Sociedad Anónima**) Ltd, plc, Inc (Amer)

sábado *m* Saturday

sábana *f* sheet

sabañón *m* chilblain

sabático *a* sabbatical

sab|elotodo *m* & *f invar* know-all ⚊. ~**er** [38] *vt* know; (ser capaz de) be able to, know how to; (enterarse de) find out. ● *vi* know. ~**er a** taste of. **hacer** ~**er** let know. **¡qué sé yo!** how should I know? **que yo sepa** as far as I know. **¿**~**es nadar?** can you swim?

un no sé qué a certain sth. **¡yo qué sé!** how should I know? **¡vete a** ~**er!** who knows? ~**er** *m* knowledge. ~**ido** *a* well-known. ~**iduría** *f* wisdom; (conocimientos) knowledge

sabi|endas. a ~ knowingly; (a propósito) on purpose. ~**hondo** *m* know-all ⚊. ~**o** *a* learned; (prudente) wise

sabor *m* taste, flavour; (fig) flavour. ~**ear** *vt* taste; (fig) savour

sabot|aje *m* sabotage. ~**eador** *m* saboteur. ~**ear** *vt* sabotage

sabroso *a* tasty; *<chisme>* juicy; (LAm, agradable) pleasant

sabueso *m* (perro) bloodhound; (fig, detective) detective

saca|corchos *m invar* corkscrew. ~**puntas** *m invar* pencil-sharpener

sacar [7] *vt* take out; put out *<parte del cuerpo>*; (quitar) remove; take *<foto>*; win *<premio>*; get *<billete, entrada>*; withdraw *<dinero>*; reach *<solución>*; draw *<conclusión>*; make *<copia>*. ~ **adelante** bring up *<niño>*; carry on *<negocio>*

sacarina *f* saccharin

sacerdo|cio *m* priesthood. ~**te** *m* priest

saciar *vt* satisfy; quench *<sed>*

saco *m* sack; (LAm, chaqueta) jacket. ~ **de dormir** sleeping-bag

sacramento *m* sacrament

sacrific|ar [7] *vt* sacrifice; slaughter *<res>*; put to sleep *<perro, gato>*. □ ~**arse** *vpr* sacrifice o.s. ~**io** *m* sacrifice; (de res) slaughter

sacr|ilegio *m* sacrilege. ~**ílego** *a* sacrilegious

sacudi|da *f* shake; (movimiento brusco) jolt, jerk; (fig) shock. ~**da eléctrica** electric shock. ~**r** *vt* shake; (golpear) beat. □ ~**rse** *vpr* shake off; (fig) get rid of

sádico *a* sadistic. ● *m* sadist

sadismo *m* sadism

safari *m* safari

sagaz *a* shrewd

Sagitario *m* Sagittarius

sagrado *a* *<lugar>* holy, sacred; *<altar, escrituras>*) holy; (fig) sacred

sal *f* salt. ● *vb* ⇒SALIR

sala f room; (en casa) living room; (en hospital) ward; (para reuniones etc) hall; (en teatro) house; (Jurid) courtroom. ~ **de embarque** departure lounge. ~ **de espera** waiting room. ~ **de estar** living room. ~ **de fiestas** nightclub

salado a salty; <agua del mar> salt; (no dulce) savoury; (fig) witty

salario m wage

salchich|a f (pork) sausage. ~**ón** m salami

sald|ar vt settle <cuenta>; (vender) sell off. ~**o** m balance. ~**os** mpl sales. **venta de** ~os clearance sale

salero m salt-cellar

salgo vb →SALIR

sali|da f departure; (puerta) exit, way out; (de gas, de líquido) leak; (de astro) rising; (Com, venta) sale; (chiste) witty remark; (fig) way out; ~**da de emergencia** emergency exit. ~**ente** a (Archit) projecting; <pómulo etc> prominent. ~**r** [52] vi leave; (ir afuera) go out; (Informática) exit; <revista etc> be published; (resultar) turn out; <astro> rise; (aparecer) appear. ~**r adelante** get by. □ ~**rse** vpr leave; <recipiente, líquido etc> leak. ~**rse con la suya** get one's own way

saliva f saliva

salmo m psalm

salm|ón m salmon. ~**onete** m red mullet

salón m living-room, lounge. ~ **de actos** assembly hall. ~ **de clases** classroom. ~ **de fiestas** dancehall

salpica|dera f (Mex) mudguard. ~**dero** m (Auto) dashboard. ~**dura** f splash; (acción) splashing. ~**r** [7] vt splash; (fig) sprinkle

sals|a f sauce; (para carne asada) gravy; (Mus) salsa. ~**a verde** parsley sauce. ~**era** f sauce-boat

salt|amontes m invar grasshopper. ~**ar** vt jump (over); (fig) miss out. ● vi jump; (romperse) break; <líquido> spurt out; (desprenderse) come off; <pelota> bounce; (estallar) explode. ~**eador** m highwayman. ~**ear** vt (Culin) sauté

salt|o m jump; (al agua) dive. ~**o de agua** waterfall. ~ **mortal** somersault.

de un ~**o** with one jump. ~**ón** a <ojos> bulging

salud f health. ● int cheers!; (LAm, al estornudar) bless you! ~**able** a healthy

salud|ar vt greet, say hello to; (Mil) salute. **lo** ~**a atentamente** (en cartas) yours faithfully. ~ **con la mano** wave. ~**o** m greeting; (Mil) salute. ~**os** mpl best wishes

salva f salvo. **una** ~ **de aplausos** a burst of applause

salvación f salvation

salvado m bran

salvaguardia f safeguard

salvaje a (planta, animal) wild; (primitivo) savage. ● m & f savage

salva|mento m rescue. ~**r** vt save, rescue; (atravesar) cross (recorrer); travel (fig) overcome. □ ~**rse** vpr save o.s. ~**vidas** m & f invar lifeguard. ● m lifebelt. **chaleco** m ~**vidas** life-jacket

salvo a safe. ● adv & prep except (for). **a** ~ out of danger. **poner a** ~ put in a safe place. ~ **que** unless. ~**conducto** m safe-conduct

San a Saint, St. ~ **Miguel** St Michael

sana|r vt cure. ● vi recover; heal <herida>. ~**torio** m sanatorium

sanci|ón f sanction. ~**onar** vt sanction

sandalia f sandal

sandía f watermelon

sándwich /ˈsaŋgwitʃ/ m (pl ~**s**, ~**es**) sandwich

sangr|ante a bleeding; (fig) flagrant ~**ar** vt/i bleed. ~**e** f blood. **a** ~**e fría** in cold blood

sangría f (bebida) sangria

sangriento a bloody

sangu|ijuela f leech. ~**íneo** a blood

san|idad f health. ~**itario** a sanitary. ● m (Mex) toilet. ~**o** a healthy; <mente> sound. ~**o y salvo** safe and sound. **cortar por lo** ~**o** settle things once and for all

santiamén m. **en un** ~ in an instant

sant|idad f sanctity. ~**ificar** [7] vt sanctify. □ ~**iguarse** [15] vpr cross o.s. **~o** *a* holy; (delante de nombre) Saint, St. ● *m* saint; (día) saint's day, name day. **~uario** *m* sanctuary. **~urrón** *a* sanctimonious

saña *f* viciousness. **con ~** viciously

sapo *m* toad

saque *m* (en tenis) service; (inicial en fútbol) kick-off. **~ de banda** throw-in; (en rugby) line-out. **~ de esquina** corner (kick)

saque|ar *vt* loot. **~o** *m* looting

sarampión *m* measles

sarape *m* (Mex) colourful blanket

sarc|asmo *m* sarcasm. **~ástico** *a* sarcastic

sardina *f* sardine

sargento *m* sergeant

sarpullido *m* rash

sartén *f or m* frying-pan (Brit), frypan (Amer)

sastre *m* tailor. **~ría** *f* tailoring; (tienda) tailor's (shop)

Sat|anás *m* Satan. **~ánico** *a* satanic

satélite *m* satellite

satinado *a* shiny

sátira *f* satire

satírico *a* satirical. ● *m* satirist

satisf|acción *f* satisfaction. **~acer** [31] *vt* satisfy; (pagar) pay; (gustar) please; meet *<gastos, requisitos>*. □ **~acerse** *vpr* satisfy o.s.; (vengarse) take revenge. **~actorio** *a* satisfactory. **~echo** *a* satisfied. **~echo de sí mismo** smug

satura|ción *f* saturation. **~r** *vt* saturate

Saturno *m* Saturn

sauce *m* willow. **~ llorón** weeping willow

sauna *f*, (LAm) **sauna** *m* sauna

saxofón *m*, **saxófono** *m* saxophone

sazona|do *a* ripe; (Culin) seasoned. **~r** *vt* ripen; (Culin) season

....
se

● *pronombre*

····➤ (en lugar de le, les) **se lo di** (a él) I gave it to him; (a ella) I gave it to her; (a usted, ustedes) I gave it to you; (a ellos, ellas) I gave it to them. **se lo**

compré I bought it for him (*or* her *etc*). **se lo quité** I took it away from him (*or* her *etc*). **se lo dije** I told him (*or* her *etc*)

····➤ (reflexivo) **se secó** (él) he dried himself; (ella) she dried herself; (usted) you dried yourself; (sujeto no humano) it dried itself. **se secaron** (ellos, ellas) they dried themselves; (ustedes) you dried yourselves. (con partes del cuerpo) **se lavó la cara** (él) he washed his face. (con efectos personales) **se limpian los zapatos** they clean their shoes

····➤ (recíproco) each other, one another. **se ayudan mucho** they help each other a lot. **no se hablan** they don't speak to each other

····➤ (cuando otro hace la acción) **va a operarse** she's going to have an operation. **se cortó el pelo** he had his hair cut

····➤ (enfático) **se bebió el café** he drank his coffee. **se subió al tren** he got on the train

⟹ **se** also forms part of certain pronominal verbs such as **equivocarse, arrepentirse, caerse** etc., which are treated under the respective entries

····➤ (voz pasiva) **se construyeron muchas casas** many houses were built. **se vendió rápidamente** it was sold very quickly

····➤ (impersonal) **antes se escuchaba más radio** people used to listen to the radio more in the past. **no se puede entrar** you can't get in. **se está bien aquí** it's very nice here

····➤ (en instrucciones) **sírvase frío** serve cold
....

sé *vb* ⇒SABER *y* SER

sea *vb* ⇒SER

seca|dor *m* drier; (de pelo) hairdrier. **~nte** *a* drying. ● *m* blotting-paper. **~r** [7] *vt* dry. □ **~rse** *vpr*; *<río etc>* dry up; *<persona>* dry o.s.

sección *f* section

seco *a* dry; *<frutos, flores>* dried; (flaco) thin; *<respuesta>* curt. **a secas** just. **en ~** (bruscamente) suddenly. **lavar en ~** dry-clean

secretar|ía f secretariat; (Mex, ministerio) ministry. **~io** m secretary; (Mex, Pol) minister

secreto a & m secret

secta f sect. **~rio** a sectarian

sector m sector

secuela f consequence

secuencia f sequence

secuestr|ar vt confiscate; kidnap <persona>; hijack <avión>. **~o** m seizure; (de persona) kidnapping; (de avión) hijack(ing)

secundar vt second, help. **~io** a secondary

sed f thirst. ● vb ⇒SER. tener **~** be thirsty. tener **~** de (fig) be hungry for

seda f silk. **~** dental dental floss

sedante a & m sedative

sede f seat; (Relig) see; (de organismo) headquarters; (de congreso, juegos etc) venue

sedentario a sedentary

sedici|ón f sedition. **~oso** a seditious

sediento a thirsty

seduc|ción f seduction. **~ir** [47] vt seduce; (atraer) attract. **~tor** a seductive. ● m seducer

seglar a secular. ● m layman

segrega|ción f segregation. **~r** [12] vt segregate

segui|da f. en **~da** immediately. **~do** a continuous; (en plural) consecutive. **~** de followed by. ● adv straight; (LAm, a menudo) often. todo **~do** straight ahead. **~dor** m follower; (en deportes) supporter. **~r** [5 & 13] vt follow. ● vi (continuar) continue; (por un camino) go on. **~** adelante carry on

según prep according to. ● adv it depends; (a medida que) as

segunda f (Auto) second gear; (en tren, avión etc) second class. **~o** a & m second

segur|amente adv certainly; (muy probablemente) surely. **~idad** f security; (ausencia de peligro) safety; (certeza) certainty; (aplomo) confidence. **~idad en sí mismo** self-confidence. **~idad social** social security. **~o** a safe; (cierto) certain, sure; (estable) secure; (de fiar) reliable. ● adv for certain. ●

m insurance; (dispositivo de seguridad) safety device. **~o de sí mismo** self-confident. **~o contra terceros** third-party insurance

seis a & m six. **~cientos** a & m six hundred

seísmo m earthquake

selec|ción f selection. **~cionar** vt select, choose. **~tivo** a selective. **~to** a selected; (fig) choice

sell|ar vt stamp; (cerrar) seal. **~o** m stamp; (precinto) seal; (fig, distintivo) hallmark; (LAm, en moneda) reverse

selva f forest; (jungla) jungle

semáforo m (Auto) traffic lights; (Rail) signal; (Naut) semaphore

semana f week. S**~** Santa Holy Week. **~l** a weekly. **~rio** a & m weekly

semántic|a f semantics. **~o** a semantic

semblante m face; (fig) look

sembrar [1] vt sow; (fig) scatter

semeja|nte a similar; (tal) such. ● m fellow man. **~nza** f similarity. a **~nza de** like. **~r** vi. **~** a resemble

semen m semen. **~tal** a stud. ● m stud animal

semestr|al a half-yearly. **~e** m six months

semi|circular a semicircular. **~círculo** m semicircle. **~final** f semifinal

semill|a f seed. **~ero** m seedbed; (fig) hotbed

seminario m (Univ) seminar; (Relig) seminary

sémola f semolina

senado m senate. **~r** m senator

sencill|ez f simplicity. **~o** a simple; (para viajar) single ticket; (disco) single; (LAm, dinero suelto) change

senda f, **sendero** m path

sendos a pl each

seno m bosom. **~** materno womb

sensaci|ón f sensation; (percepción, impresión) feeling. **~onal** a sensational

sensat|ez f good sense. **~o** a sensible

sensi|bilidad *f* sensibility. **~ble** *a* sensitive; (notable) notable; (lamentable) lamentable. **~tivo** *a* <*órgano*> sense

sensual *a* sensual. **~idad** *f* sensuality

senta|do *a* sitting (down); **dar algo por ~do** take something for granted. **~dor** *a* (LAm) flattering. **~r** [1] *vt* sit; (establecer) establish. ● *vi* suit; (de medidas) fit; <*comida*> agree with. □ **~rse** *vpr* sit (down)

sentencia *f* (Jurid) sentence. **~r** *vt* sentence (**a** to)

sentido *a* heartfelt; (sensible) sensitive. ● *m* sense; (dirección) direction; (conocimiento) consciousness. **~ común** common sense. **~ del humor** sense of humour. **~ único** one-way. **doble ~** double meaning. **no tener ~** not make sense. **perder el ~** faint. **sin ~** senseless

sentim|ental *a* sentimental. **~iento** *m* feeling; (sentido) sense; (pesar) regret

sentir [4] *vt* feel; (oír) hear; (lamentar) be sorry for. **lo siento mucho** I'm really sorry. ● *m* (opinión) opinion. □ **~se** *vpr* feel; (Mex, ofenderse) be offended

seña *f* sign. **~s** *fpl* (dirección) address; (descripción) description. **dar ~s de** show signs of

señal *f* signal; (letrero, aviso) sign; (telefónica) tone; (Com) deposit. **dar ~es de** show signs of. **en ~ de** as a token of. **~ado** *a* <*hora, día*> appointed. **~ar** *vt* signal; (poner señales en) mark; (apuntar) point out; <*manecilla, aguja*> point to; (determinar) fix. □ **~arse** *vpr* stand out

señor *m* man, gentleman; (delante de nombre propio) Mr; (tratamiento directo) sir. **~a** *f* lady, woman; (delante de nombre propio) Mrs; (esposa) wife; (tratamiento directo) madam. **el ~** Mr. **muy ~ mío** Dear Sir. **¡no ~!** certainly not!. **~ial** *a* <*casa*> stately. **~ita** *f* young lady; (delante de nombre propio) Miss; (tratamiento directo) miss. **~ito** *m* young gentleman

señuelo *m* lure

sepa *vb* ⇒SABER

separa|ción *f* separation. **~do** *a* separate. **por ~do** separately. **~r** *vt* separate; (de empleo) dismiss. □ **~rse** *vpr* separate; <*amigos*> part. **~tista** *a* & *m* & *f* separatist

septentrional *a* north(ern)

septiembre *m* September

séptimo *a* seventh

sepulcro *m* sepulchre

sepult|ar *vt* bury. **~ura** *f* burial; (tumba) grave. **~urero** *m* gravedigger

sequ|edad *f* dryness. **~ía** *f* drought

séquito *m* entourage; (fig) train

ser [39]

● *verbo intransitivo*

····▸ to be. **es bajo** he's short. **es abogado** he's a lawyer. **ábreme, soy yo** open up, it's me. **¿cómo es?** (como persona) what's he like?; (físicamente) what does he look like? **era invierno** it was winter

····▸ **ser de** (indicando composición) to be made of. **es de hierro** it's made of iron. (provenir de) to be from. **es de México** he's from Mexico. (pertenecer a) to belong to. **el coche es de Juan** the car belongs to Juan, it's Juan's car

····▸ (sumar) **¿cuánto es todo?** how much is that altogether? **son 40 dólares** that's 40 dollars. **somos 10** there are 10 of us

····▸ (con la hora) **son las 3** it's 3 o'clock. **~ía la una** it must have been one o'clock

····▸ (tener lugar) to be held. **~á en la iglesia** it will be held in the church

····▸ (ocurrir) to happen **¿dónde fue el accidente?** where did the accident happen? **me contó cómo fue** he told me how it happened

····▸ (en locuciones) **a no ~ que** unless. **como sea** no matter what. **cuando sea** whenever. **donde sea** wherever **¡eso es!** that's it! **es que** the thing is. **lo que sea** anything. **no sea que, no vaya a ~ que** in case. **o sea** in other words. **sea … sea …** either … or … **sea como sea** at all costs

● *nombre masculino*

····▶ being; (persona) person. **el** ~ **humano** the human being. **un** ~ **amargado** a bitter person. **los** ~**es queridos** the loved ones

seren|ar vt calm down. □ ~**arse** vpr calm down. ~**ata** f serenade. ~**idad** f serenity. ~**o** a serene; <cielo> clear; <mar> calm. ● m night watchman. **al** ~**o** in the open

seri|al m serial. ~**e** f series. **fuera de** ~**e** (fig) out of this world. **producción** f **en** ~**e** mass production

seri|edad f seriousness. ~**o** a serious; (confiable) reliable; **en** ~**o** seriously. **poco** ~**o** frivolous

sermón m sermon; (fig) lecture

serp|enteante a winding. ~**entear** vi wind. ~**iente** f snake. ~**iente de cascabel** rattlesnake

serr|ar [1] vt saw. ~**ín** m sawdust. ~**uchar** vt (LAm) saw. ~**ucho** m (hand)saw

servi|cial a helpful. ~**cio** m service; (conjunto) set; (aseo) toilet; ~**cio a domicilio** delivery service. ~**dor** m servant. **su** (**seguro**) ~**dor** (en cartas) yours faithfully. ~**dumbre** f servitude; (criados) servants, staff. ~**l** a servile

servilleta f napkin, serviette

servir [5] vt serve; (en restaurante) wait on. ● vi serve; (ser útil) be of use. □ ~**se** vpr help o.s. ~**se de** use. **no** ~ **de nada** be useless. **para** ~**le** at your service. **sírvase sentarse** please sit down

sesent|a a & m sixty. ~**ón** a & m sixty-year-old

seseo m pronunciation of the Spanish c as an s

sesión f session; (en el cine, teatro)

seso m brain

seta f mushroom

sete|cientos a & m seven hundred. ~**nta** a & m seventy. ~**ntón** a & m seventy-year-old

setiembre m September

seto m fence; (de plantas) hedge. ~ **vivo** hedge

seudónimo m pseudonym

sever|idad f severity; (de profesor etc) strictness. ~**o** a severe; <profesor etc> strict

sevillan|as fpl popular dance from Seville. ~**o** m person from Seville

sexo m sex

sext|eto m sextet. ~**o** a sixth

sexual a sexual. ~**idad** f sexuality

si m (Mus) B; (solfa) te. ● conj if; (dubitativo) whether; ~ **no** otherwise. **por** ~ (**acaso**) in case

sí¹ pron reflexivo (él) himself; (ella) herself; (de cosa) itself; (uno) oneself; (Vd) yourself; (ellos, ellas) themselves; (Vds) yourselves; (recíproco) each other

sí² adv yes. ● m consent

sida m Aids

sidra f cider

siembra f sowing; (época) sowing time

siempre adv always; (LAm, todavía) still; (Mex, por fin) after all. ~ **que** if; (cada vez) whenever. **como** ~ as usual. **de** ~ (acostumbrado) usual. **lo de** ~ the usual thing. **para** ~ for ever

sien f temple

siento vb ⇒SENTAR y SENTIR

sierra f saw; (cordillera) mountain range

siesta f nap, siesta

siete a & m seven

sífilis f syphilis

sifón m U-bend; (de soda) syphon

sigilo m stealth; (fig) secrecy

sigla f abbreviation

siglo m century; (época) age. **hace** ~**s que no escribe** he hasn't written for ages

significa|ción f significance. ~**do** a (conocido) well-known. ● m meaning; (importancia) significance. ~**r** [7] vt mean; (expresar) express. ~**tivo** a meaningful; (importante) significant

signo m sign. ~ **de admiración** exclamation mark. ~ **de interrogación** question mark

sigo vb ⇒SEGUIR

siguiente a following, next. **lo** ~ the following

sílaba f syllable

silb|ar *vt/i* whistle. ~**ato** *m*, ~**ido** *m* whistle

silenci|ador *m* silencer. ~**ar** *vt* hush up. ~**o** *m* silence. ~**oso** *a* silent

sill|a *f* chair; (de montar) saddle (Relig) see ~**a de ruedas** wheelchair. ~**ín** *m* saddle. ~**ón** *m* armchair

silueta *f* silhouette; (dibujo) outline

silvestre *a* wild

simb|ólico *a* symbolic(al). ~**olismo** *m* symbolism. ~**olizar** [10] *vt* symbolize

símbolo *m* symbol

sim|etría *f* symmetry. ~**étrico** *a* symmetric(al)

similar *a* similar (**a** to)

simp|atía *f* friendliness; (cariño) affection. ~**ático** *a* nice, likeable; *<ambiente>* pleasant. ~**atizante** *m* & *f* sympathizer. ~**atizar** [10] *vi* get on (well together)

simpl|e *a* simple; (mero) mere. ~**eza** *f* simplicity; (tontería) stupid thing; (insignificancia) trifle. ~**icidad** *f* simplicity. ~**ificar** [7] *vt* simplify. ~**ista** *a* simplistic. ~**ón** *m* simpleton

simula|ción *f* simulation. ~**r** *vt* simulate; (fingir) feign

simultáneo *a* simultaneous

sin *prep* without. ~ **saber** without knowing. ~ **querer** accidentally

sinagoga *f* synagogue

sincer|idad *f* sincerity. ~**o** *a* sincere

sincronizar [10] *vt* synchronize

sindica|l *a* (trade-)union. ~**lista** *m* & *f* trade-unionist. ~**to** *m* trade union

síndrome *m* syndrome

sinfín *m* endless number (**de** of)

sinfonía *f* symphony

singular *a* singular; (excepcional) exceptional. □ ~**izarse** *vpr* stand out

siniestro *a* sinister. ● *m* disaster; (accidente) accident

sinnúmero *m* endless number (**de** of)

sino *m* fate. ● *conj* but

sinónimo *a* synonymous. ● *m* synonym (**de** for)

sintaxis *f* syntax

síntesis *f invar* synthesis; (resumen) summary

sint|ético *a* synthetic. ~**etizar** [10] *vt* synthesize; (resumir) summarize

síntoma *f* sympton

sintomático *a* symptomatic

sinton|ía *f* tuning; (Mus) signature tune. ~**izar** [10] *vt* (con la radio) tune (in) to

sinvergüenza *m* & *f* crook

siquiera *conj* even if. ● *adv* at least. **ni** ~ not even

sirena *f* siren; (en cuentos) mermaid

sirio *a* & *m* Syrian

sirvient|a *f* maid. ~**e** *m* servant

sirvo *vb* ⇒SERVIR

sísmico *a* seismic

sismo *m* earthquake

sistem|a *m* system. **por** ~**a** as a rule. ~**ático** *a* systematic

sitiar *vt* besiege; (fig) surround

sitio *m* place; (espacio) space; (Mil) siege; (Mex, parada de taxi) taxi rank. **en cualquier** ~ anywhere. ~ **web** website

situa|ción *f* situation; (estado, condición) position. ~**r** [21] *vt* place, put; locate *<edificio>*. □ ~**rse** *vpr* be successful, establish o.s.

slip /es'lip/ *m* (*pl* ~**s**) underpants, briefs

smoking /es'mokin/ *m* (*pl* ~**s**) dinner jacket (Brit), tuxedo (Amer)

sobaco *m* armpit

sobar *vt* handle; knead *<masa>*

soberan|ía *f* sovereignty. ~**o** *a* sovereign; (fig) supreme. ● *m* sovereign

soberbi|a *f* pride; (altanería) arrogance. ~**o** *a* proud; (altivo) arrogant

soborn|ar *vt* bribe. ~**o** *m* bribe

sobra *f* surplus. **de** ~ more than enough. ~**s** *fpl* leftovers. ~**do** *a* more than enough. ~**nte** *a* surplus. ~**r** *vi* be left over; (estorbar) be in the way

sobre *prep* on; (encima de) on top of; (más o menos) about; (por encima de) above; (sin tocar) over. ~ **todo** above all, especially. ● *m* envelope. ~**car**

gar [12] *vt* overload. **~coger** [14] *vt* startle; (conmover) move. **~cubierta** *f* dustcover. **~dosis** *f invar* overdose. **~entender** [1] *vt* understand, infer. **~girar** *vt* (LAm) overdraw. **~giro** *m* (LAm) overdraft. **~humano** *a* superhuman. **~llevar** *vt* bear. **~mesa** *f*. de **~mesa** after-dinner. **~natural** *a* supernatural. **~nombre** *m* nickname. **~pasar** *vt* exceed. **~peso** *m* (LAm) excess baggage. **~poner** [34] *vt* superimpose. □ **~ponerse** *vpr* overcome. **~saliente** *a* (fig) outstanding. ● *m* excellent mark. **~salir** [52] *vi* stick out; (fig) stand out. **~saltar** *vt* startle. **~salto** *m* fright. **~sueldo** *m* bonus. **~todo** *m* overcoat. **~venir** [53] *vi* happen. **~viviente** *a* surviving. ● *m & f* survivor. **~vivir** *vi* survive. **~volar** *vt* fly over

sobriedad *f* moderation; (de estilo) simplicity

sobrin|a *f* niece. **~o** *m* nephew. **~os** (varones) nephews; (varones y mujeres) nieces and nephews

sobrio *a* moderate, sober

socavar *vt* undermine

soci|able *a* sociable. **~al** *a* social. **~aldemócrata** *m & f* social democrat. **~alismo** *m* socialism. **~alista** *a & m & f* socialist. **~edad** *f* society; (Com) company. **~edad anónima** limited company. **~o** *m* member; (Com) partner. **~ología** *f* sociology. **~ólogo** *m* sociologist

socorr|er *vt* help. **~o** *m* help

soda *f* (bebida) soda (water)

sodio *m* sodium

sofá *m* sofa, settee

sofistica|ción *f* sophistication. **~do** *a* sophisticated

sofo|cante *a* suffocating; (fig) stifling. **~r** [7] *vt* smother <fuego>; (fig) stifle. □ **~rse** *vpr* get upset

soga *f* rope

soja *f* soya (bean)

sojuzgar [12] *vt* subdue

sol *m* sun; (luz) sunlight; (Mus) G; (solfa) soh. **al ~** in the sun. **día** *m* **de ~** sunny day. **hace ~**, **hay ~** it is sunny. **tomar el ~** sunbathe

solamente *adv* only

solapa *f* lapel; (de bolsillo etc) flap. **~do** *a* sly

solar *a* solar. ● *m* plot

solariego *a* <casa> ancestral

soldado *m* soldier. **~ raso** private

solda|dor *m* welder; (utensilio) soldering iron. **~r** [2] *vt* weld, solder

soleado *a* sunny

soledad *f* solitude; (aislamiento) loneliness

solemn|e *a* solemn. **~idad** *f* solemnity

soler [2] *vi* be in the habit of. **suele despertarse a las 6** he usually wakes up at 6 o'clock

sol|icitar *vt* request, ask for; apply for <empleo>. **~ícito** *a* solicitous. **~icitud** *f* request; (para un puesto) application; (formulario) application form; (preocupación) concern

solidaridad *f* solidarity

solid|ez *f* solidity; (de argumento etc) soundness. □ **~ificarse** [7] *vpr* solidify

sólido *a* solid; <argumento etc> sound. ● *m* solid

soliloquio *m* soliloquy

solista *m & f* soloist

solitario *a* solitary; (aislado) lonely. ● *m* loner; (juego, diamante) solitaire

solloz|ar [10] *vi* sob. **~o** *m* sob

solo *a* (sin compañía) alone; (aislado) lonely; (sin ayuda) by oneself; (único) only; (Mus) solo; <café> black. ● *m* solo; (juego) solitaire. **a solas** alone

sólo *adv* only. **~ que** except that. **no ~... sino también** not only... but also.... **tan ~** only

solomillo *m* sirloin

soltar [2] *vt* let go of; (dejar ir) release; (dejar caer) drop; (dejar salir, decir) let out; give <golpe etc>. □ **~se** *vpr* come undone; (librarse) break loose

solter|a *f* single woman. **~o** *a* single. ● *m* bachelor

soltura *f* looseness; (fig) ease, fluency

solu|ble *a* soluble. **~ción** *f* solution. **~cionar** *vt* solve; settle <huelga, asunto>

solvente *a & m* solvent

sombr|a *f* shadow; (lugar sin sol) shade. **a la ～a** in the shade. **～eado** *a* shady

sombrero *m* hat. **～ hongo** bowler hat

sombrío *a* sombre

somero *a* superficial

someter *vt* subdue; subject *<persona>*; (presentar) submit. □ **～se** *vpr* give in

somn|oliento *a* sleepy. **～ífero** *m* sleeping-pill

somos *vb* ⇒SER

son *m* sound. ● *vb* ⇒SER

sonámbulo *m* sleepwalker. **ser ～** walk in one's sleep

sonar [2] *vt* blow; ring *<timbre>*. ● *vi* sound; *<timbre, teléfono etc>* ring; *<despertador>* go off; (Mus) play; (fig, ser conocido) be familiar. **～ a** sound like. □ **～se** *vpr* blow one's nose

sonde|ar *vt* sound out; explore *<espacio>*; (Naut) sound. **～o** *m* poll; (Naut) sounding

soneto *m* sonnet

sonido *m* sound

sonoro *a* sonorous; (ruidoso) loud

sonr|eír [51] *vi* smile. □ **～eírse** *vpr* smile. **～isa** *f* smile

sonroj|arse *vpr* blush. **～o** *m* blush

sonrosado *a* rosy, pink

sonsacar [7] *vt* wheedle out

soñ|ado *a* dream. **～ador** *m* dreamer. **～ar** [2] *vi* dream (**con** of). **¡ni ～arlo!** not likely!

sopa *f* soup

sopesar *vt* (fig) weigh up

sopl|ar *vt* blow; blow out *<vela>*; blow off *<polvo>*; (inflar) blow up. ● *vi* blow. **～ete** *m* blowlamp. **～o** *m* puff

soport|al *m* porch. **～ales** *mpl* arcade. **～ar** *vt* support; (fig) bear, put up with. **～e** *m* support

soprano *f* soprano

sor *f* sister

sorb|er *vt* sip; (con ruido) slurp; (absorber) absorb. **～ por la nariz** sniff. **～ete** *m* sorbet, water-ice. **～o** *m* (pequeña cantidad) sip; (trago grande) gulp

sordera *f* deafness

sórdido *a* squalid; *<asunto>* sordid

sordo *a* deaf; *<ruido etc>* dull. ● *m* deaf person. **hacerse el ～** turn a deaf ear. **～mudo** *a* deaf and dumb

soroche *m* (LAm) mountain sickness

sorpre|ndente *a* surprising. **～nder** *vt* surprise. □ **～nderse** *vpr* be surprised. **～sa** *f* surprise

sorte|ar *vt* draw lots for; (fig) avoid. **～o** *m* draw. **por ～o** by drawing lots

sortija *f* ring; (de pelo) ringlet

sortilegio *m* sorcery; (embrujo) spell

sos|egar [1 & 12] *vt* calm. **～iego** *m* calmness

soslayo. de ～ sideways

soso *a* tasteless; (fig) dull

sospech|a *f* suspicion. **～ar** *vt* suspect. ● *vi*. **～ de** suspect. **～oso** *a* suspicious. ● *m* suspect

sost|én *m* support; (prenda femenina) bra Ⓔ, brassière. **～ener** [40] *vt* support; bear *<peso>*; (sujetar) hold; (sustentar) maintain; (alimentar) sustain. □ **～enerse** *vpr* support o.s.; (continuar) remain. **～enido** *a* sustained; (Mus) sharp. ● *m* (Mus) sharp

sota *f* (de naipes) jack

sótano *m* basement

soviético *a* (Historia) Soviet

soy *vb* ⇒SER

Sr. *abrev* (**Señor**) Mr. **～a.** *abrev* (**Señora**) Mrs. **～ta.** *abrev* (**Señorita**) Miss

su *a* (de él) his; (de ella) her; (de animal, objeto) its; (de uno) one's; (de Vd) your; (de ellos, de ellas) their; (de Vds) your

suav|e *a* smooth; (fig) gentle; *<color, sonido>* soft; *<tabaco, sedante>* mild. **～idad** *f* smoothness, softness. **～izante** *m* conditioner; (para ropa) softener. **～izar** [10] *vt* smooth, soften

subalimentado *a* underfed

subarrendar [1] *vt* sublet

subasta *f* auction. **～r** *vt* auction

sub|campeón *m* runner-up. **～consciencia** *f* subconscious. **～consciente** *a & m* subconscious. **～continente** *m* subcontinent. **～desarrollado** *a* under-developed. **～director** *m* assistant manager

súbdito *m* subject

sub|dividir vt subdivide. ~**estimar** vt underestimate

subi|da f rise; (a montaña) ascent; (pendiente) slope. ~**do** a <color> intense. ~**r** vt go up; climb <mountain>; (llevar) take up; (aumentar) raise; turn up <radio, calefacción>. ● vi go up. ~**r a** get into <coche>; get on <autobús, avión, barco, tren>; (aumentar) rise. ~ **a pie** walk up. □ ~**rse** vpr climb up. ~**rse a** get on <tren etc>

súbito a sudden. **de** ~ suddenly

subjetivo a subjective

subjuntivo a & m subjunctive

subleva|ción f uprising. □ ~**rse** vpr rebel

sublim|ar vt sublimate. ~**e** a sublime

submarino a underwater. ● m submarine

subordinado a & m subordinate

subrayar vt underline

subsanar vt rectify; overcome <dificultad>; make up for <carencia>

subscri|bir vt (pp **subscrito**) sign. □ ~**birse** vpr subscribe (a to). ~**pción** f subscription

subsidi|ario a subsidiary. ~**o** m subsidy. ~**o de desempleo,** ~ **de paro** unemployment benefit

subsiguiente a subsequent

subsist|encia f subsistence. ~**ir** vi subsist; (perdurar) survive

substraer [41] vt take away

subterráneo a underground

subtítulo m subtitle

suburb|ano a suburban. ~**io** m suburb; (barrio pobre) depressed area

subvenci|ón f subsidy. ~**onar** vt subsidize

subver|sión f subversion. ~**sivo** a subversive. ~**tir** [4] vt subvert

succi|ón f suction. ~**onar** vt suck

suce|der vi happen; (seguir) ~ **a** follow. ● vt (substituir) succeed. **lo que** ~**de es que** the trouble is that. **¿qué** ~**de?** what's the matter? ~**sión** f succession. ~**sivo** a successive; (consecutivo) consecutive. **en lo** ~**sivo** in future. ~**so** m event; (incidente) incident. ~**sor** m successor

suciedad f dirt; (estado) dirtiness

sucinto a concise; <prenda> scanty

sucio a dirty; <conciencia> guilty. **en** ~ in rough

sucre m (unidad monetaria del Ecuador) sucre

suculento a succulent

sucumbir vi succumb (**a** to)

sucursal f branch (office)

Sudáfrica f South Africa

sudafricano a & m South African

Sudamérica f South America

sudamericano a & m South American

sudar vi sweat

sud|este m south-east. ~**oeste** m south-west

sudor m sweat

Suecia f Sweden

sueco a Swedish. ● m (persona) Swede; (lengua) Swedish. **hacerse el** ~ pretend not to hear

suegr|a f mother-in-law. ~**o** m father-in-law. **mis** ~**os** my in-laws

suela f sole

sueldo m salary

suelo m ground; (dentro de edificio) floor; (territorio) soil; (en la calle etc) road surface. ● vb ⇒SOLER

suelto a loose; <cordones> undone; (sin pareja) odd; <lenguaje> fluent. **con el pelo** ~ with one's hair down. ● m change

sueño m sleep; (lo soñado, ilusión) dream. **tener** ~ be sleepy

suerte f luck; (destino) fate; (azar) chance. **de otra** ~ otherwise. **de** ~ **que** so. **echar** ~**s** draw lots. **por** ~ fortunately. **tener** ~ be lucky

suéter m sweater, jersey

suficien|cia f (aptitud) aptitude; (presunción) smugness. ~**te** a enough, sufficient; (presumido) smug. ~**temente** adv sufficiently

sufijo m suffix

sufragio m (voto) vote

sufrimiento m suffering. ~**r** vt suffer; undergo <cambio>; have <accident>. ● vi suffer

suge|rencia f suggestion. ~**rir** [4] vt suggest. ~**stión** f (Psych) suggestion. **es pura** ~**stión** it's all in one's mind. ∼**stionable** *a* impression-able. ∼**stionar** *vt* influence. ∼**sti-vo** *a* (estimulante) stimulating; (atracti-vo) sexy

suicid|a *a* suicidal. ● *m & f* suicide victim; (fig) maniac. □ ∼**arse** *vpr* commit suicide. ∼**io** *m* suicide

Suiza *f* Switzerland

suizo *a & m* Swiss

suje|ción *f* subjection. **con** ∼ **a** in accordance with. ∼**tador** *m* bra 🇪, brassière. ∼**tapapeles** *m invar* paper-clip. ∼**tar** *vt* fasten; (agarrar) hold. □ ∼**tarse** *vpr*. ∼**se** a hold on to; (someterse) abide by. ∼**to** *a* fas-tened; (susceptible) subject (**a** to). ● *m* individual; (Gram) subject.

suma *f* sum; (Math) addition; (combina-ción) combination. **en** ∼ in short. ∼**mente** *adv* extremely. ∼**r** *vt* add (up); (totalizar) add up to. ● *vi* add up. □ ∼**rse** *vpr*. ∼**rse** a join in

sumario *a* brief; (Jurid) summary. ● *m* table of contents; (Jurid) pre-trial proceedings

sumergi|ble *a* submersible. ∼**r** [14] *vt* submerge

suministr|ar *vt* supply. ∼**o** *m* sup-ply; (acción) supplying

sumir *vt* sink; (fig) plunge

sumis|ión *f* submission. ∼**o** *a* sub-missive

sumo *a* great; (supremo) supreme. **a lo** ∼ at the most

suntuoso *a* sumptuous

supe *vb* ⇒SABER

superar *vt* surpass; (vencer) over-come; beat <*marca*>; (dejar atrás) get over. □ ∼**se** *vpr* better o.s.

superchería *f* swindle

superfici|al *a* superficial. ∼**e** *f* sur-face; (extensión) area. **de** ∼**e** surface

superfluo *a* superfluous

superior *a* superior; (más alto) high-er; (mejor) better; <*piso*> upper. ● *m* superior. ∼**idad** *f* superiority

superlativo *a & m* superlative

supermercado *m* supermarket

supersticí|ón *f* superstition. ∼**oso** *a* superstitious

supervis|ar *vt* supervise. ∼**ión** *f* supervision. ∼**or** *m* supervisor

superviv|encia *f* survival. ∼**ien-te** *a* surviving. ● *m & f* survivor

suplantar *vt* supplant

suplement|ario *a* supplementary. ∼**o** *m* supplement

suplente *a & m & f* substitute

súplica *f* entreaty; (Jurid) request

suplicar [7] *vt* beg

suplicio *m* torture

suplir *vt* make up for; (reemplazar) re-place

supo|ner [34] *vt* suppose; (significar) mean; involve <*gasto, trabajo*>. ∼**si-ción** *f* supposition

suprem|acía *f* supremacy. ∼**o** *a* supreme

supr|esión *f* suppression; (de im-puesto) abolition; (de restricción) lifting. ∼**imir** *vt* suppress; abolish <*impues-to*>; lift <*restricción*>; delete <*párra-fo*>

supuesto *a* supposed; <*falso*> false. ● *m* assumption. **¡por** ∼! of course!

sur *m* south; (viento) south wind

surc|ar [7] *vt* plough; cut through <*agua*>. ∼**o** *m* furrow; (de rueda) rut

surfear *vi* (Informática) surf

surgir [14] *vi* spring up; (elevarse) loom up; (aparecer) appear; <*difi-cultad, oportunidad*> arise

surrealis|mo *m* surrealism. ∼**ta** *a & m & f* surrealist

surti|do *a* well-stocked; (variado) as-sorted. ● *m* assortment, selection. ∼**dor** *m* (de gasolina) petrol pump (Brit), gas pump (Amer). ∼**r** *vt* supply; have <*efecto*>. □ ∼**rse** *vpr* provide o.s. (**de** with)

susceptib|ilidad *f* sensitivity. ∼**le** *a* susceptible; (sensible) sensitive

suscitar *vt* provoke; arouse <*curio-sidad, interés*>

suscr... ⇒SUBSCR...

susodicho *a* aforementioned

suspen|der *vt* suspend; stop <*trata-miento*>; call off <*viaje*>; (Escol) fail; (colgar) hang (**de** from). ∼**se** *m* sus-pense. **novela de** ∼**se** thriller. ∼**sión** *f* suspension. ∼**so** *m* fail; (LAm, en libro, película) suspense. **en** ∼**so** suspended

suspir|ar *vi* sigh. ∼**o** *m* sigh

sust... ⇒SUBST...

sustanci|a f substance. **~al** a substantial. **~oso** a substantial

sustantivo m noun

sustent|ación f support. **~ar** vt support; (alimentar) sustain; (mantener) maintain. **~o** m support; (alimento) sustenance

sustitu|ción f substitution; (permanente) replacement. **~ir** [17] vt substitute, replace. **~to** m substitute; (permanente) replacement

susto m fright

susurr|ar vi <persona> whisper; <agua> murmur; <hojas> rustle

sutil a fine; (fig) subtle. **~eza** f subtlety

suyo a & pron (de él) his; (de ella) hers; (de animal) its; (de Vd) yours; (de ellos, de ellas) theirs; (de Vds) yours. **un amigo ~** a friend of his, a friend of theirs, etc

T t

tabac|alera f (state) tobacco monopoly. **~o** m tobacco; (cigarillos) cigarettes

tabern|a f bar. **~ero** m barman; (dueño) landlord

tabique m partition wall; (Mex, ladrillo) brick

tabl|a f plank; (del suelo) floorboard; (de vestido) pleat; (índice) index; (gráfico, en matemática etc) table. **hacer ~as** (en ajedrez) draw. **~a de surf** surfboard. **~ado** m platform; (en el teatro) stage. **~ao** m place where flamenco shows are held. **~ero** m board. **~ero de mandos** dashboard

tableta f tablet; (de chocolate) bar

tabl|illa f splint; (Mex, de chocolate) bar. **~ón** m plank. **~ón de anuncios** notice board (esp Brit), bulletin board (Amer)

tabú m (pl **~es**, **~s**) taboo

tabular vt tabulate

taburete m stool

tacaño a mean

tacha f stain, blemish. **sin ~** unblemished; <conducta> irreproachable. **~r** vt (con raya) cross out; (Jurid) impeach. **~ de** accuse of

tácito a tacit

taciturno a taciturn; (triste) glum

taco m plug; (LAm, tacón) heel; (de billar) cue; (de billetes) book; (fig, lío) mess; (palabrota) swearword; (Mex, Culin) taco, filled tortilla

tacón m heel

táctic|a f tactics. **~o** a tactical

táctil a tactile

tacto m touch; (fig) tact

tahúr m card-sharp

Tailandia f Thailand

tailandés a & m Thai

taimado a sly

taj|ada f slice. **sacar ~ada** profit. **~ante** a categorical; <tono> sharp. **~ear** vt (LAm) slash. **~o** m cut; (en mina) face

tal a such. **de ~ manera** in such a way. **un ~** someone called. ● pron. **como ~** as such. **y ~** and things like that. ● adv. **con ~ de que** as long as. **~ como** the way. **~ para cual** ⊞ two of a kind. **~ vez** maybe. **¿qué ~?** how are you? **¿qué ~ es ella?** what's she like?

taladr|ar vt drill. **~o** m drill

talante m mood. **de buen ~** <estar> in a good mood; <ayudar> willingly

talar vt fell

talco m talcum powder

talega f, **talego** m sack

talento m talent; (fig) talented person

talismán m talisman

talla f carving; (de diamante etc) cutting; (estatura) height; (tamaño) size. **~do** m carving; (de diamante etc) cutting. **~dor** m carver; (cortador) cutter; (LAm, de naipes) dealer. **~r** vt carve; sculpt <escultura>; cut <diamante>; (Mex, restregar) scrub. □ **~rse** vpr (Mex) rub o.s.

tallarín m noodle

talle m waist; (figura) figure

taller m workshop; (de pintor etc) studio; (Auto) garage

tallo m stem, stalk

tal|ón *m* heel; (recibo) counterfoil; (cheque) cheque. **~onario** *m* receipt book; (de cheques) cheque book

tamal *m* (LAm) tamale

tamaño *a* such a. ● *m* size. **de ~ natural** life-size

tambalearse *vpr* (persona) stagger; <*cosa*> wobble

también *adv* also, too

tambor *m* drum. **~ del freno** brake drum. **~ilear** *vi* drum

tamiz *m* sieve. **~ar** [10] *vt* sieve

tampoco *adv* neither, nor, not either. **yo ~ fui** I didn't go either

tampón *m* tampon; (para entintar) ink-pad

tan *adv* so. **~... como** as... as. **¿qué ~...?** (LAm) how...?

tanda *f* group; (de obreros) shift

tang|ente *a* & *f* tangent. **~ible** *a* tangible

tango *m* tango

tanque *m* tank

tante|ar *vt* estimate; sound up <*persona*>; (ensayar) test; (fig) weigh up; (LAm, palpar) feel. ● *vi* (LAm) feel one's way. **~o** *m* estimate; (prueba) test; (en deportes) score

tanto *a* (en singular) so much; (en plural) so many; (comparación en singular) as much; (comparación en plural) as many. ● *pron* so much; (en plural) so many. ● *adv* so; (con verbo) so much. **hace ~ tiempo** it's been so long. **~... como** both...and. **¿qué ~...?** (LAm) how much...? **~ como** as well as; (cantidad) as much as. **~ más... cuanto que** all the more ... because. **~ si... como si** whether ... or. **a ~s de** sometime in. **en ~** meanwhile. **en ~ que** while. **entre ~** meanwhile. **hasta ~ que** until. **no es para ~** it's not as bad as all that. **otro ~** the same; (el doble) as much again. **por (lo) ~** therefore. ● *m* certain amount; (punto) point; (gol) goal. **estar al ~ de** be up to date with

tañer [22] *vi* peal

tapa *f* lid; (de botella) top; (de libro) cover. **~s** *fpl* savoury snacks. **~dera** *f* cover, lid; (fig) cover. **~r** *vt* cover; (abrigar) wrap up; (obturar) plug. **~rrabo(s)** *m invar* loincloth

tapete *m* (de mesa) table cover; (Mex, alfombra) rug

tapia *f* wall. **~r** *vt* enclose

tapi|cería *f* tapestry; (de muebles) upholstery. **~z** *m* tapestry. **~ar** [10] *vt* upholster <*muebles*>

tapón *m* stopper; (Tec) plug

taqu|igrafía *f* shorthand. **~ígrafo** *m* shorthand writer

taquill|a *f* ticket office; (fig, dinero) takings. **~ero** *a* box-office

tara *f* (peso) tare; (defecto) defect

tarántula *f* tarantula

tararear *vt/i* hum

tarda|nza *f* delay. **~r** *vt* take. ● *vi* (retrasarse) be late; (emplear mucho tiempo) take a long time. **a más ~r** at the latest. **sin ~r** without delay

tard|e *adv* late. ● *f* (antes del atardecer) afternoon; (después del atardecer) evening. **~e o temprano** sooner or later. **de ~e en ~e** from time to time. **en la ~e** (LAm), **por la ~e** in the afternoon. **~ío** *a* late

tarea *f* task, job

tarifa *f* rate; (en transporte) fare; (lista de precios) tariff

tarima *f* dais

tarjeta *f* card. **~ de crédito** credit card. **~ postal** postcard

tarro *m* jar; (Mex, taza) mug

tarta *f* cake; (con base de masa) tart. **~ helada** ice-cream gateau

tartamud|ear *vi* stammer. **~o** *a*. **es ~o** he stammers

tasa *f* valuation; (impuesto) tax; (índice) rate. **~r** *vt* value; (limitar) ration

tasca *f* bar

tatarabuel|a *f* great-great-grandmother. **~o** *m* great-great-grandfather. **~os** *mpl* great-great-grandparents

tatua|je *m* (acción) tattooing; (dibujo) tattoo. **~r** [21] *vt* tattoo

taurino *a* bullfighting

Tauro *m* Taurus

tauromaquia *f* bullfighting

taxi *m* taxi. **~ista** *m* & *f* taxi-driver

taz|a *f* cup. **~ón** *m* bowl

te *pron* (acusativo) you; (dativo) (to) you; (reflexivo) (to) yourself

té *m* tea; (LAm, reunión) tea party

teatr|al *a* theatre; (exagerado) theatrical. **~o** *m* theatre; (literatura) drama

tebeo *m* comic

tech|ado *m* roof. **~ar** *vt* roof. **~o** *m* (interior) ceiling; (LAm, tejado) roof. **~umbre** *f* roof

tecl|a *f* key. **~ado** *m* keyboard. **~ear** *vt* key in

técnica *f* technique

tecnicismo *m* technical nature; (palabra) technical term

técnico *a* technical. ● *m* technician; (en deportes) trainer

tecnol|ogía *f* technology. **~ógico** *a* technological

tecolote *m* (Mex) owl

teja *f* tile. **~s de pizarra** slates. **~do** *m* roof. **a toca ~** cash

teje|dor *m* weaver. **~r** *vt* weave; (hacer punto) knit

tejemaneje *m* 🗊 intrigue. **~s** *mpl* scheming

tejido *m* material; (Anat, fig) tissue. **~s** *mpl* textiles

tejón *m* badger

tela *f* material, fabric; (de araña) web; (en líquido) skin

telar *m* loom. **~es** *mpl* textile mill

telaraña *f* spider's web, cobweb

tele *f* 🗊 TV, telly

tele|comunicación *f* telecommunication. **~diario** *m* television news. **~dirigido** *a* remote-controlled; *<misil>* guided. **~férico** *m* cable-car

tel|efonear *vt/i* telephone. **~efónico** *a* telephone. **~efonista** *m & f* telephonist. **~éfono** *m* telephone. **al ~éfono** on the phone

tel|egrafía *f* telegraphy. **~égrafo** *m* telegraph. **~egrama** *m* telegram

telenovela *f* television soap opera

teleobjetivo *m* telephoto lens

telep|atía *f* telepathy. **~ático** *a* telepathic

telesc|ópico *a* telescopic. **~opio** *m* telescope

telesilla *m & f* chair-lift

telespectador *m* viewer

telesquí *m* ski-lift

televi|dente *m & f* viewer. **~sar** *vt* televise. **~sión** *f* television. **~sor** *m* television (set)

télex *m invar* telex

telón *m* curtain

tema *m* subject; (Mus) theme

templ|ar [1] *vi* shake; (de miedo) tremble; (de frío) shiver. **~or** *m* shaking; (de miedo) trembling; (de frío) shivering; **~or de tierra** earth tremor. **~oroso** *a* trembling

tem|er *vt* be afraid (of). ● *vi* be afraid. □ **~erse** *vpr* be afraid. **~erario** *a* reckless. **~eroso** *a* frightened. **~ible** *a* fearsome. **~or** *m* fear

témpano *m* floe

temperamento *m* temperament

temperatura *f* temperature

tempest|ad *f* storm. **~uoso** *a* stormy

templ|ado *a* (tibio) warm; *<clima, tiempo>* mild; (valiente) courageous. **~anza** *f* mildness. **~ar** *vt* temper; (calentar) warm up. **~e** *m* tempering; *<coraje>* courage; (humor) mood

templo *m* temple

tempora|da *f* season. **~l** *a* temporary. ● *m* storm

tempran|ero *a <frutos>* early. **ser ~ero** be an early riser. **~o** *a & adv* early

tenacidad *f* tenacity

tenacillas *fpl* tongs

tenaz *a* tenacious

tenaza *f*, **tenazas** *fpl* pliers; (de chimenea, Culin) tongs; (de cangrejo) pincer

tende|ncia *f* tendency. **~nte** *a*. **~nte a** aimed at. **~r** [1] *vt* spread (out); hang out *<ropa a secar>*; (colocar) lay. ● *vi* tend (**a** to). □ **~rse** *vpr* lie down

tender|ete *m* stall. **~o** *m* shopkeeper

tendido *a* spread out; *<ropa>* hung out; *<persona>* lying down. ● *m* (en plaza de toros) front rows

tendón *m* tendon

tenebroso *a* gloomy; *<asunto>* sinister

tenedor *m* fork; (poseedor) holder

tener [40]

● *verbo transitivo*

!■ El presente del verbo **tener** admite dos traducciones: *to have* y *to have got,* este último de uso más extendido en el inglés británico

····▶ to have. **¿tienen hijos?** do you have any children?, have you got any children? **no tenemos coche** we don't have a car, we haven't got a car. **tiene gripe** he has (the) flu, he's got (the) flu

····▶ to be <*dimensiones, edad*>. **tiene 1 metro de largo** it's 1 metre long. **tengo 20 años** I'm 20 (years old)

····▶ (sentir) **tener** + *nombre* to be + *adjective*. ∼ **celos** to be jealous. ∼ **frío** to be cold

····▶ (sujetar, sostener) to hold. **tenme la escalera** hold the ladder for me

····▶ (indicando estado) **tiene las manos sucias** his hands are dirty. **me tiene preocupada** I'm worried about him. **me tuvo esperando** he kept me waiting

····▶ (llevar puesto) to be wearing, to have on. **¡qué zapatos más elegantes tienes!** those are very smart shoes you're wearing! **tienes el suéter al revés** you have your sweater on inside out

····▶ (considerar) ∼ **a uno por algo** to think s.o. is sth. **lo tenía por tímido** I thought he was shy

● *verbo auxiliar*

····▶ ∼ **que hacer algo** to have to do sth. **tengo que irme** I have to go

····▶ **tener** + *participio pasado.* **tengo pensado comprarlo** I'm thinking of buying it. **tenía entendido otra cosa** I understood something else

····▶ (LAm, con expresiones temporales) **tienen 2 años de estar aquí** they've been here for 2 months. **tiene mucho tiempo sin verlo** she hasn't seen him for a long time

····▶ (en locuciones) **aquí tiene** here you are. **¿qué tienes?** what's the matter with you? **¿ y eso qué tiene?** (LAm) and what's wrong with that?

□ **tenerse** *verbo pronominal*

····▶ (sostenerse) **no podía** ∼**se en pie** (de cansancio) he was dead on his feet; (de borracho) he could hardly stand

····▶ (considerarse) to consider o.s. **se tiene por afortunado** he considers himself lucky

tengo *vb* ⇒TENER

teniente *m* lieutenant

tenis *m* tennis. ∼ **de mesa** table tennis. ∼**ta** *m & f* tennis player

tenor *m* sense; (Mus) tenor. **a** ∼ **de** according to

tens|ión *f* tension; (arterial) blood pressure; (Elec) voltage; (estrés) strain. ∼**o** *a* tense

tentación *f* temptation

tentáculo *m* tentacle

tenta|dor *a* tempting. ∼**r** [1] *vt* tempt; (palpar) feel

tentativa *f* attempt

tenue *a* thin; <*luz, voz*> faint; <*color*> subdued

teñi|r [5 & 22] *vt* dye; (fig) tinge (**de** with). □ ∼**rse** *vpr* dye one's hair

teología *f* theology

te|oría *f* theory. ∼**órico** *a* theoretical

tequila *f* tequila

terap|euta *m & f* therapist. ∼**éutico** *a* therapeutic. ∼**ia** *f* therapy

terc|er *a* véase TERCERO. ∼**ero** *a* (Auto) third (gear). ∼**era** *f* (Auto) third (gear). ∼**ero** *a* (*delante de nombre masculino en singular* **tercer**) third. ● *m* third party. ∼**io** *m* third

terciopelo *m* velvet

terco *a* obstinate

tergiversar *vt* distort

termal *a* thermal

térmico *a* thermal

termina|ción *f* ending; (conclusión) conclusion. ∼**l** *a & m* terminal. ∼**nte** *a* categorical. ∼**r** *vt* finish, end. ∼**r por** end up. □ ∼**rse** *vpr* come to an end

término *m* end; (palabra) term; (plazo) period. ∼ **medio** average. **dar** ∼ **a** finish off. **en primer** ∼ first of all. **en último** ∼ as a last resort. **estar en**

buenos ∼s con be on good terms with. **llevar a ∼** carry out

terminología *f* terminology

termita *f* termite

termo *m* Thermos (P) flask, flask

termómetro *m* thermometer

termo|nuclear *a* thermonuclear. **∼stato** *m* thermostat

terner|a *f* (carne) veal. **∼o** *m* calf

ternura *f* tenderness

terquedad *f* stubbornness

terrado *m* flat roof

terraplén *m* embankment

terrateniente *m & f* landowner

terraza *f* terrace; (balcón) balcony; (terrado) flat roof

terremoto *m* earthquake

terre|no *a* earthly. ● *m* land; (solar) plot (fig) field. **∼stre** *a* land; (Mil) ground

terrible *a* terrible. **∼mente** *adv* awfully

territori|al *a* territorial. **∼o** *m* territory

terrón *m* (de tierra) clod; (Culin) lump

terror *m* terror. **∼ífico** *a* terrifying. **∼ismo** *m* terrorism. **∼ista** *m & f* terrorist

terso *a* smooth

tertulia *f* gathering

tesina *f* dissertation

tesón *m* tenacity

tesor|ería *f* treasury. **∼ero** *m* treasurer. **∼o** *m* treasure; (tesorería) treasury; (libro) thesaurus

testaferro *m* figurehead

testa|mento *m* will. **T∼mento** (Relig) Testament. **∼r** *vi* make a will

testarudo *a* stubborn

testículo *m* testicle

testi|ficar [7] *vt/i* testify. **∼go** *m* witness. **∼go ocular, ∼go presencial** eyewitness. **ser ∼go de** witness. **∼monio** *m* testimony

teta *f* tit (Ⓘ o vulg); (de biberón) teat

tétanos *m* tetanus

tetera *f* (para el té) teapot

tetilla *f* nipple; (de biberón) teat

tétrico *a* gloomy

textil *a & m* textile

text|o *m* text. **∼ual** *a* textual; *<traducción>* literal; *<palabras>* exact

textura *f* texture

tez *f* complexion

ti *pron* you

tía *f* aunt; Ⓘ woman

tiara *f* tiara

tibio *a* lukewarm

tiburón *m* shark

tiempo *m* time; (atmosférico) weather; (Mus) tempo; (Gram) tense; (en partido) half. **a su ∼** in due course. **a ∼** in time. **¿cuánto ∼?** how long? **hace buen ∼** the weather is fine. **hace ∼** some time ago. **mucho ∼** a long time. **perder el ∼** waste time

tienda *f* shop (esp Brit), store (esp Amer); (de campaña) tent. **∼ de comestibles, ∼ de ultramarinos** grocer's (shop) (Brit), grocery store (Amer)

tiene *vb* ⇒TENER

tienta. andar a ∼s feel one's way

tierno *a* tender; (joven) young

tierra *f* land; (planeta, Elec) earth; (suelo) ground; (Geol) soil, earth; (LAm, polvo) dust. **por ∼** overland, by land

tieso *a* stiff; (engreído) conceited

tiesto *m* flowerpot

tifón *m* typhoon

tifus *m* typhus; (fiebre tifoidea) typhoid (fever)

tigre *m* tiger. **∼sa** *f* tigress

tijera *f*, **tijeras** *fpl* scissors; (de jardín) shears

tijeretear *vt* snip

tila *f* (infusión) lime tea

tild|ar *vt*. **∼ar de** (fig) brand as. **∼e** *f* tilde

tilo *m* lime(-tree)

timar *vt* swindle

timbal *m* kettledrum; (Culin) timbale, meat pie. **∼es** *mpl* (Mus) timpani

timbr|ar *vt* stamp. **∼e** *m* (sello) fiscal stamp; (Mex) postage stamp; (Elec) bell; (sonido) timbre

timidez *f* shyness

tímido *a* shy

timo *m* swindle

timón *m* rudder; (rueda) wheel; (fig) helm

tímpano *m* eardrum

tina *f* tub. ~**co** *m* (Mex) water tank. ~**ja** *f* large earthenware jar

tinglado *m* mess; (asunto) racket

tinieblas *fpl* darkness; (fig) confusion

tino *f* good sense; (tacto) tact

tint|a *f* ink. de buena ~**a** on good authority. ~**e** *m* dyeing; (color) dye; (fig) tinge. ~**ero** *m* ink-well

tintinear *vi* tinkle; *<vasos>* chink, clink

tinto *a* *<vino>* red

tintorería *f* dry cleaner's

tintura *f* dyeing; (color) dye

tío *m* uncle; 🆔 man. ~**s** *mpl* uncle and aunt

tiovivo *m* merry-go-round

típico *a* typical

tipo *m* type; (🆔, persona) person; (figura de mujer) figure; (figura de hombre) build; (Com) rate

tip|ografía *f* typography. ~**ográfico** *a* typographic(al)

tira *f* strip. la ~ de lots of

tirabuzón *m* corkscrew; (de pelo) ringlet

tirad|a *f* distance; (serie) series; (de periódico etc) print-run. de una ~**a** in one go. ~**o** *a* (barato) very cheap; (🆔, fácil) very easy. ~**or** *m* (asa) handle

tiran|ía *f* tyranny. ~**izar** [10] *vt* tyrannize. ~**o** *a* tyrannical. ● *m* tyrant

tirante *a* tight; (fig) tense; *<relaciones>* strained. ● *m* strap. ~**s** *mpl* braces (esp Brit), suspenders (Amer)

tirar *vt* throw; (desechar) throw away; (derribar) knock over; drop *<bomba>*; fire *<cohete>*; (imprimir) print. ● *vi* (disparar) shoot. ~ **a** tend to (be); (parecerse a) resemble. ~ **abajo** knock down. ~ **de** pull. a todo ~ at the most. ir **tirando** get by. □ ~**se** *vpr* throw o.s.; (tumbarse) lie down

tirita *f* (sticking) plaster

tiritar *vi* shiver (de with)

tiro *m* throw; (disparo) shot. ~ **libre** free kick. a ~ within range. errar el ~ miss. pegarse un ~ shoot o.s.

tiroides *m* thyroid (gland)

tirón *m* tug. de un ~ in one go

tirote|ar *vt* shoot at. ~**o** *m* shooting

tisana *f* herb tea

tisú *m* (*pl* ~**s**, ~**es**) tissue

títere *m* puppet. ~**s** *mpl* puppet show

titilar *vi* *<estrella>* twinkle

titiritero *m* puppeteer; (acróbata) acrobat

titube|ante *a* faltering; (fig) hesitant. ~**ar** *vi* falter. ~**o** *m* hesitation

titula|do *a* *<libro>* entitled; *<persona>* qualified. ~**r** *m* headline; (persona) holder. ● *vt* call. □ ~**rse** *vpr* be called; *<persona>* graduate

título *m* title; (académico) qualification; (Univ) degree. a ~ de as, by way of

tiza *f* chalk

tiz|nar *vt* dirty. ~**ne** *m* soot

toall|a *f* towel. ~**ero** *m* towel-rail

tobillo *m* ankle

tobogán *m* slide; (para la nieve) toboggan

tocadiscos *m invar* record-player

toca|do *a* touched 🆔. ● *m* headdress. ~**dor** *m* dressing-table. ~**nte** *a*. en lo ~**nte** a with regard to. ~**r** [7] *vt* touch; (palpar) feel; (Mus) play; ring *<timbre>*; (mencionar) touch on; *<barco>* stop at. ● *vi* ring; (corresponder a uno). te ~ **a ti** it's your turn. en lo que ~ a as for. □ ~**rse** *vpr* touch; *<personas>*; touch each other

tocayo *m* namesake

tocino *m* bacon

tocólogo *m* obstetrician

todavía *adv* still; (con negativos) yet. ~ **no** not yet

....

todo, toda

● *adjetivo*

····➤ (la totalidad) all. ~ **el vino** all the wine. ~**s los edificios** all the buildings. ~ **ese dinero** all that money. ~ **el mundo** everyone. (como adv) **está toda sucia** it's all dirty

····➤ (entero) whole. ~ **el día** the whole day, all day. **toda su familia** his whole family. ~ **el tiempo** the whole time, all the time

····▸ (cada, cualquiera) every. ~ **tipo de coche** every type of car. ~**s los días** every day

····▸ (enfático) **a toda velocidad** at top speed. **es** ~ **un caballero** he's a real gentleman

····▸ (en locuciones) **ante** ~ above all. **a** ~ **esto** meanwhile. **con** ~ even so. **del** ~ totally. ~ **lo contrario** quite the opposite

⇒ Para expresiones como **todo recto, todo seguido** etc., ver bajo el respectivo adjetivo

● *pronombre*

····▸ all; (todas las cosas) everything. **eso es** ~ that's all. **lo perdieron** ~ they lost everything. **quiere comprar** ~ he wants to buy everything

····▸ **todos, todas** all; (todo el mundo) everyone. **los compró** ~**s** he bought them all, he bought all of them. ~**s queríamos ir** we all wanted to go. **vinieron** ~**s** everyone came

● *nombre masculino*

····▸ **el/un** ~ the/a whole

toldo *m* awning

tolera|ncia *f* tolerance. ~**nte** *a* tolerant. ~**r** *vt* tolerate

toma *f* taking; (de universidad etc) occupation; (Med) dose; (de agua) intake; (Elec) socket; (LAm, acequia) irrigation channel. ● *int* well!, fancy that! ~ **de corriente** power point. ~**dura** *f*. ~**dura de pelo** hoax. ~**r** *vt* take; catch <*autobús, tren*>; occupy <*universidad etc*>; (beber) drink, have; (comer) eat, have. ● *vi* take; (esp LAm, beber) drink; (LAm, dirigirse) go. ~**r a bien** take well. ~**r a mal** take badly. ~**r en serio** take seriously. ~**rla con uno** pick on s.o. ~**r por** take for. ~ **y daca** give and take. **¿qué va a** ~**r?** what would you like? □ ~**rse** *vpr* take; (beber) drink, have; (comer) eat, have

tomate *m* tomato

tomillo *m* thyme

tomo *m* volume

ton: **sin** ~ **ni son** without rhyme or reason

tonad|a *f* tune; (canción) popular song; (LAm, acento) accent. ~**illa** *f* tune

tonel *m* barrel. ~**ada** *f* ton. ~**aje** *m* tonnage

tónic|a *f* trend; (bebida) tonic water. ~**o** *a* tonic; <*sílaba*> stressed. ● *m* tonic

tonificar [7] *vt* invigorate

tono *m* tone; (Mus, modo) key; (color) shade

tont|ería *f* silliness; (cosa) silly thing; (dicho) silly remark. **dejarse de** ~**erías** stop fooling around. ~**o** *a* silly. ● *m* fool, idiot; (payaso) clown. **hacer el** ~**o** act the fool. **hacerse el** ~**o** act dumb

topacio *m* topaz

topar *vi*. ~ **con** run into

tope *a* maximum. ● *m* end; (de tren) buffer; (Mex, Auto) speed bump. **hasta los** ~**s** crammed full. **ir a** ~ go flat out

tópico *a* trite. **de uso** ~ (Med) for external use only. ● *m* cliché

topo *m* mole

topogr|afía *f* topography. ~**áfico** *a* topographical

toque *m* touch; (sonido) sound; (de campana) peal; (de reloj) stroke. ~ **de queda** curfew. **dar los últimos** ~**s** put the finishing touches. ~**tear** *vt* fiddle with

toquilla *f* shawl

tórax *m invar* thorax

torcer [2 & 9] *vt* twist; (doblar) bend; wring out <*ropa*>. ● *vi* turn. □ ~**se** *vpr* twist

tordo *a* dapple grey. ● *m* thrush

tore|ar *vt* fight; (evitar) dodge. ● *vi* fight (bulls). ~**o** *m* bullfighting. ~**ro** *m* bullfighter

torment|a *f* storm. ~**o** *m* torture. ~**oso** *a* stormy

tornado *m* tornado

tornasolado *a* irridescent

torneo *m* tournament

tornillo *m* screw

torniquete *m* (Med) tourniquet; (entrada) turnstile

torno *m* lathe; (de alfarero) wheel. **en** ~ **a** around

toro *m* bull. ~**s** *mpl* bullfighting. **ir a los** ~**s** go to a bullfight

toronja *f* (LAm) grapefruit

torpe *a* clumsy; (estúpido) stupid

torpedo *m* torpedo

torpeza *f* clumsiness; (de inteligencia) slowness. **una ~** a blunder

torre *f* tower; (en ajedrez) castle, rook; (Elec) pylon; (edificio) tower block (Brit), apartment block (Amer)

torren|cial *a* torrential. **~te** *m* torrent; (circulatorio) bloodstream; (fig) flood

tórrido *a* torrid

torsión *f* twisting

torso *m* torso

torta *f* tart; (LAm, de verduras) pie; (golpe) slap, punch; (Mex, bocadillo) filled roll. **no entender ni ~** not understand a thing. **~zo** *m* slap, punch. **pegarse un ~zo** have a bad accident

tortícolis *f* stiff neck

tortilla *f* omelette; (Mex, de maíz) tortilla

tórtola *f* turtle-dove

tortuga *f* tortoise; (de mar) turtle

tortuoso *a* winding; (fig) devious

tortura *f* torture. **~r** *vt* torture

tos *f* cough. **~ ferina** whooping cough

tosco *a* crude; *<persona>* coarse

toser *vi* cough

tost|ada *f* piece of toast. **~adas** *fpl* toast; (Mex, de tortilla) fried tortillas. **~ado** *a* *<pan>* toasted; *<café>* roasted; *<persona, color>* tanned. **~ar** *vt* toast *<pan>*; roast *<café>*; tan *<piel>*

total *a* total. ● *adv* after all. **~ que** so, to cut a long story short. ● *m* total; (totalidad) whole. **~idad** *f* whole. **~itario** *a* totalitarian. **~izar** [10] *vt* total

tóxico *a* toxic

toxi|cómano *m* drug addict. **~na** *f* toxin

tozudo *a* stubborn

traba *f* catch; (fig, obstáculo) obstacle. **poner ~s a** hinder

trabaj|ador *a* hard-working. ● *m* worker. **~ar** *vt* work; knead *<masa>*. ● *vi* work (**de** as); *<actor>* act. **¿en qué ~as?** what do you do? **~o** *m* work. **costar ~o** be difficult. **~oso** *a* hard

trabalenguas *m invar* tongue-twister

traba|r *vt* (sujetar) fasten; (unir) join; (entablar) strike up. □ **~rse** *vpr* get stuck. **trabársele la lengua** get tongue-tied

trácala *m* (Mex) cheat. ● *f* (Mex) trick

tracción *f* traction

tractor *m* tractor

tradici|ón *f* tradition. **~onal** *a* traditional

traduc|ción *f* translation. **~ir** [47] *vt* translate (**a** into). **~tor** *m* translator

traer [41] *vt* bring; (llevar) carry; (causar) cause. **traérselas** be difficult

trafica|nte *m & f* dealer. **~r** [7] *vi* deal

tráfico *m* traffic; (Com) trade

traga|luz *m* skylight. **~perras** *f invar* slot-machine. **~r** [12] *vt* swallow; (comer mucho) devour; (soportar) put up with. **no lo trago** I can't stand him. □ **~rse** *vpr* swallow; (fig) swallow up

tragedia *f* tragedy

trágico *a* tragic. ● *m* tragedian

trag|o *m* swallow, gulp; (pequeña porción) sip; (fig, disgusto) blow; (LAm, bebida alcohólica) drink. **echar(se) un ~o** have a drink. **~ón** *a* greedy. ● *m* glutton

trai|ción *f* treachery; (Pol) treason. **~cionar** *vt* betray. **~cionero** *a* treacherous. **~dor** *a* treacherous. ● *m* traitor

traigo *vb* ⇒TRAER

traje *m* dress; (de hombre) suit. **~ de baño** swimming-costume. **~ de etiqueta**, **~ de noche** evening dress. ● *vb* ⇒TRAER

traj|ín *m* coming and going; (ajetreo) hustle and bustle. **~inar** *vi* bustle about

trama *f* weft; (fig, argumento) plot. **~r** *vt* weave; (fig) plot

tramitar *vt* negotiate

trámite *m* step. **~s** *mpl* procedure

tramo *m* (parte) section; (de escalera) flight

tramp|a *f* trap; (fig) trick. **hacer ~a** cheat. **~illa** *f* trapdoor

trampolín *m* trampoline; (de piscina) springboard; (rígido) diving board

tramposo *a* cheating. ● *m* cheat

tranca *f* bar. ~**r** *vt* bar

trance *m* moment; (hipnótico etc) trance

tranco *m* stride

tranquil|idad *f* peace; (de espíritu) peace of mind. **con** ~ calmly. ~**izar** [10] *vt* calm down; (reconfortar) reassure. ~**o** *a* calm; *<lugar>* quiet; *<conciencia>* clear. **estáte** ~**o** don't worry

transa|cción *f* transaction; (acuerdo) settlement. ~**r** *vi* (LAm) compromise

transatlántico *a* transatlantic. ● *m* (ocean) liner

transbord|ador *m* ferry. ~**ar** *vt* transfer. ~**o** *m* transfer. **hacer** ~**o** change (**en** at)

transcri|bir (*pp* **transcrito**) *vt* transcribe. ~**pción** *f* transcription

transcur|rir *vi* pass. ~**so** *m* course

transeúnte *m & f* passer-by

transfer|encia *f* transfer. ~**ir** [4] *vt* transfer

transforma|ción *f* transformation. ~**dor** *m* transformer. ~**r** *vt* transform

transfusión *f* transfusion

transgre|dir *vt* transgress. ~**sión** *f* transgression

transición *f* transition

transigir [14] *vi* give in, compromise

transistor *m* transistor

transita|ble *a* passable. ~**r** *vi* go

transitivo *a* transitive

tránsito *m* transit; (tráfico) traffic

transitorio *a* transitory

transmi|sión *f* transmission; (radio, TV) broadcast ~**sor** *m* transmitter. ~**sora** *f* broadcasting station. ~**tir** *vt* transmit; (radio, TV) broadcast; (fig) pass on

transparen|cia *f* transparency. ~**tar** *vt* show. ~**te** *a* transparent

transpira|ción *f* perspiration. ~**r** *vi* transpire; (sudar) sweat

transport|ar *vt* transport. ~**e** *m* transport. **empresa** *f* **de** ~**es** removals company

transversal *a* transverse. **una calle** ~ **a la Gran Vía** a street which crosses the Gran Vía

tranvía *m* tram

trapear *vt* (LAm) mop

trapecio *m* trapeze; (Math) trapezium

trapo *m* cloth. ~**s** *mpl* rags; (Ⓘ, ropa) clothes. **a todo** ~ out of control

tráquea *f* windpipe, trachea

traquete|ar *vt* bang, rattle; *<persona>* rush around. ~**o** *m* banging, rattle

tras *prep* after; (detrás) behind

trascende|ncia *f* significance; (alcance) implication. ~**ntal** *a* transcendental; (importante) important. ~**r** [1] *vi* (saberse) become known; (extenderse) spread

trasero *a* back, rear. ● *m* (Anat) bottom

trasfondo *m* background

traslad|ar *vt* move; transfer *<empleado etc>*; (aplazar) postpone. ~**o** *m* transfer; (copia) copy. (mudanza) removal. **dar** ~**o** notify

trasl|úcido *a* translucent. □ ~**ucirse** [11] *vpr* be translucent; (dejarse ver) show through; (fig, revelarse) be revealed. ~**uz** *m*. **al** ~**uz** against the light

trasmano. a ~ out of the way

trasnochar *vt* (acostarse tarde) go to bed late; (no acostarse) stay up all night; (no dormir) be unable to sleep

traspas|ar *vt* go through; (transferir) transfer; go beyond *<límite>*. **se** ~**a** for sale. ~**o** *m* transfer

traspié *m* trip; (fig) slip. **dar un** ~ stumble; (fig) slip up

trasplant|ar *vt* transplant. ~**e** *m* transplant

trastada *f* prank; (jugada) dirty trick

traste *m* fret. **dar al** ~ **con** ruin. **ir al** ~ fall through. ~**s** *mpl* (Mex) junk

trastero *m* storeroom

trasto *m* piece of junk. ●~**s** *mpl* junk

trastorn|ado a mad. ~ar vt upset; (volver loco) drive mad; (fig, 🔲, gustar mucho) delight. ▫ ~arse vpr get upset; (volverse loco) go mad. ~o m (incl Med) upset; (Pol) disturbance; (fig) confusion

trat|able a friendly; (Med) treatable. ~ado m treatise; (acuerdo) treaty. ~amiento m treatment; (título) title. ~ante m & f dealer. ~ar vt (incl Med) treat; deal with <asunto etc>; (manejar) handle; (de tú, de Vd) address (de as). ● vi deal (with). ~ar con have to do with; (Com) deal in. ~ar de be about; (intentar) try. ¿de qué se ~a? what's it about? ~o m treatment; (acuerdo) agreement; (título) title; (relación) relationship. ¡~o hecho! agreed! ~os mpl dealings

traum|a m trauma. ~ático a traumatic

través: a ~ de through; (de lado a lado) crossways

travesaño m crossbeam; (de portería) crossbar

travesía f crossing; (calle) side-street

trav|esura f prank. ~ieso a <niño> mischievous, naughty

trayecto m (tramo) stretch; (ruta) route; (viaje) journey. ~ria f trajectory; (fig) course

traz|a f (aspecto) appearance. ~as fpl signs. ~ado m plan. ~ar [10] vt draw; (bosquejar) sketch. ~o m stroke; (línea) line

trébol m clover. ~es mpl (en naipes) clubs

trece a & m thirteen

trecho m stretch; (distancia) distance; (tiempo) while. a ~s here and there. de ~ en ~ at intervals

tregua f truce; (fig) respite

treinta a & m thirty

tremendo a terrible; (extraordinario) terrific

tren m train. ~ de aterrizaje landing gear. ~ de vida lifestyle

tren|cilla f braid. ~za f braid; (de pelo) plait. ~zar [10] vt plait

trepa|dor a climbing. ~dora f climber. ~r vt/i climb. ▫ ~rse vpr.

~rse a climb <árbol>; climb onto <silla etc>

tres a & m three. ~cientos a & m three hundred. ~illo m three-piece suite; (Mus) triplet

treta f trick

tri|angular a triangular. ~ángulo m triangle

trib|al a tribal. ~u f tribe

tribuna f platform; (de espectadores) stand. ~l m court; (de examen etc) board; (fig) tribunal

tribut|ar vt pay. ~o m tribute; (impuesto) tax

triciclo m tricycle

tricolor a three-coloured

tricotar vt/i knit

tridimensional a three-dimensional

trig|al m wheat field. ~o m wheat

trigésimo a thirtieth

trigueño a olive-skinned; <pelo> dark blonde

trilla|do a (fig, manoseado) trite; (fig, conocido) well-known. ~r vt thresh

trilogía f trilogy

trimestr|al a quarterly. ~e m quarter; (Escol, Univ) term

trinar vi warble. **estar que trina** be furious

trinchar vt carve

trinchera f ditch; (Mil) trench; (abrigo) trench coat

trineo m sledge

trinidad f trinity

trino m warble

trío m trio

tripa f intestine; (fig, vientre) tummy, belly. ~s fpl (de máquina etc) parts, workings. **revolver las ~s** turn one's stomach

tripl|e a triple. ● m. el ~e (de) three times as much (as). ~icado a. por ~icado in triplicate. ~icar [7] vt treble

tripula|ción f crew. ~nte m & f member of the crew. ~r vt man

tris m. **estar en un ~** be on the point of

triste a sad; <paisaje, tiempo etc> gloomy; (fig, insignificante) miserable. ~za f sadness

triturar *vt* crush

triunf|al *a* triumphal. **~ante** *a* triumphant. **~ar** *vi* triumph (**de, sobre** over). **~o** *m* triumph

trivial *a* trivial. **~idad** *f* triviality

trizas. **hacer algo ~** smash sth to pieces. **hacerse ~** smash

trocear *vt* cut up, chop

trocha *f* narrow path; (LAm, rail) gauge

trofeo *m* trophy

tromba *f* whirlwind; (marina) waterspout. **~ de agua** heavy downpour

trombón *m* trombone

trombosis *f invar* thrombosis

trompa *f* horn, (de orquesta) French horn; (de elefante) trunk; (hocico) snout; (Anat) tube. **coger una ~** 🄵 get drunk. **~zo** *m* bump

trompet|a *f* trumpet; (músico) trumpet player; (Mil) trumpeter. **~illa** *f* ear-trumpet

trompo *m* (juguete) (spinning) top

tronar *vt* (Mex) shoot. ● *vi* thunder

tronchar *vt* bring down; (fig) cut short. **~se de risa** laugh a lot

tronco *m* trunk. **dormir como un ~** sleep like a log

trono *m* throne

trop|a *f* troops. **~el** *m* mob

tropez|ar [1 & 10] *vi* trip; (fig) slip up. **~ar con** run into. **~ón** *m* stumble; (fig) slip

tropical *a* tropical

trópico *a* tropical. ● *m* tropic

tropiezo *m* slip; (desgracia) hitch

trot|ar *vi* trot. **~e** *m* trot; (fig) toing and froing. **al ~e** at a trot; (de prisa) in a rush. **de mucho ~e** hard-wearing

trozo *m* piece, bit. **a ~s** in bits

trucha *f* trout

truco *m* trick. **coger el ~** get the knack

trueno *m* thunder; (estampido) bang

trueque *m* exchange; (Com) barter

trufa *f* truffle

truhán *m* rogue

truncar [7] *vt* truncate; (fig) cut short

tu *a* your

tú *pron* you

tuba *f* tuba

tubérculo *m* tuber

tuberculosis *f* tuberculosis

tub|ería *f* pipes; (oleoducto etc) pipeline. **~o** *m* tube. **~o de ensayo** test tube. **~o de escape** (Auto) exhaust (pipe). **~ular** *a* tubular

tuerca *f* nut

tuerto *a* one-eyed, blind in one eye. ● *m* one-eyed person

tuétano *m* marrow; (fig) heart. **hasta los ~s** completely

tufo *m* stench

tugurio *m* hovel

tul *m* tulle

tulipán *m* tulip

tulli|do *a* paralysed. **~r** [22] *vt* cripple

tumba *f* grave, tomb

tumb|ar *vt* knock over, knock down *<estructura>*; (fig, 🄵, en examen) fail. □ **~arse** *vpr* lie down. **~o** *m* jolt. **dar un ~o** tumble. **~ona** *f* sun lounger

tumor *m* tumour

tumulto *m* turmoil; (Pol) riot

tuna *f* prickly pear; (de estudiantes) student band

tunante *m & f* rogue

túnel *m* tunnel

túnica *f* tunic

tupé *m* toupee; (fig) nerve

tupido *a* thick

turba *f* peat; (muchedumbre) mob

turbado *a* upset

turbante *m* turban

turbar *vt* upset; (molestar) disturb. □ **~se** *vpr* be upset

turbina *f* turbine

turbi|o *a* cloudy; *<vista>* blurred; *<asunto etc>* shady. **~ón** *m* squall

turbulen|cia *f* turbulence; (disturbio) disturbance. **~te** *a* turbulent

turco *a* Turkish. ● *m* Turk; (lengua) Turkish

tur|ismo *m* tourism; (coche) car. **hacer ~** travel around. **~ista** *m & f* tourist. **~ístico** *a* tourist

turn|arse *vpr* take turns (**para** to). **~o** *m* turn; (de trabajo) shift. **de ~** on duty

turquesa f turquoise

Turquía f Turkey

turrón m nougat

tutear vt address as *tú*. □ ~**se** vpr be on familiar terms

tutela f (Jurid) guardianship; (fig) protection

tutor m guardian; (Escol) form master

tuve vb ⇒TENER

tuyo a & pron yours. un amigo ~ a friend of yours

Uu

u conj or

ubic|ar vt (LAm) place; (localizar) find. □ ~**arse** vpr (LAm) be situated; (orientarse) find one's way around

ubre f udder

Ud. abrev (**Usted**) you

uf int phew!; (de repugnancia) ugh!

ufan|arse vpr be proud (con, de of); (jactarse) boast (con, de about). ~**o** a proud

úlcera f ulcer

ulterior a later; <lugar> further

últimamente adv (recientemente) recently; (finalmente) finally

ultim|ar vt complete; (LAm, matar) kill. ~**átum** m ultimatum

último a last; (más reciente) latest; (más lejano) furthest; (más alto) top; (más bajo) bottom; (definitivo) final. ● m last one. **estar en las últimas** be on one's last legs; (sin dinero) be down to one's last penny. **por** ~ finally. **vestido a la última** dressed in the latest fashion

ultra a ultra, extreme

ultraj|ante a offensive. ~**e** m insult, outrage

ultramar m. **de** ~ overseas; <productos> foreign. ~**inos** mpl groceries. **tienda de** ~**inos** grocer's (shop) (Brit), grocery store (Amer)

ultranza. **a** ~ (con decisión) decisively; (extremo) out-and-out

ultravioleta a invar ultraviolet

umbilical a umbilical

umbral m threshold

un, una

● artículo indefinido

! The masculine article **un** is also used before feminine nouns which begin with stressed **a** or **ha**, e.g. **un alma piadosa, un hada madrina**

····▸ (en sing) a; (antes de sonido vocálico) an. **un perro** a dog. **una hora** an hour

····▸ **unos, unas** (cantidad incierta) some. **compré** ~**os libros** I bought some books. (cantidad cierta) **tiene** ~**os ojos preciosos** she has beautiful eyes. **tiene** ~**os hijos muy buenos** her children are very good. (en aproximaciones) about. **en** ~**as 3 horas** in about 3 hours

⇒ For further information see **uno**

un|ánime a unanimous. ~**animidad** f unanimity

undécimo a eleventh

ungüento m ointment

únic|amente adv only. ~**o** a only; (fig, incomparable) unique

unicornio m unicorn

unid|ad f unit; (cualidad) unity. ~**ad de disco** disk drive. ~**o** a united

unifica|ción f unification. ~**r** [7] vt unite, unify

uniform|ar vt standardize. ~**e** a & m uniform. ~**idad** f uniformity

unilateral a unilateral

uni|ón f union; (cualidad) unity; (Tec) joint. ~**r** vt join; mix <líquidos>. □ ~**rse** vpr join together; <caminos> converge; <compañías> merge

unísono m unison. **al** ~ in unison

univers|al a universal. ~**idad** f university. ~**itario** a university. ~**o** m universe

uno, una

● *adjetivo*

Note that **uno** becomes **un** before masculine nouns

····▸ one. **una peseta** one peseta. **un dólar** one dollar. **ni una persona** not one person, not a single person. **treinta y un años** thirty one years

● *pronombre*

····▸ one. **~ es mío** one (of them) is mine. **es la una** it's one o'clock. **se ayudan el ~ al otro** they help one another, they help each other. **lo que sienten el ~ por el otro** what they feel for each other

····▸ (🔲, alguien) someone. **le pregunté a ~** I asked someone

····▸ **unos, unas** some. **no tenía vasos así es que le presté ~s** she didn't have any glasses so I lent her some. **a ~s les gusta, a otros no** some like it, others don't. **los ~s a los otros** one another, each other.

····▸ (impersonal) you. **~ no sabe qué decir** you don't know what to say

untar *vt* grease; (cubrir) spread; (fig, 🔲, sobornar) bribe

uña *f* nail; (de animal) claw; (casco) hoof

uranio *m* uranium

Urano *m* Uranus

urban|idad *f* politeness. **~ismo** *m* town planning. **~ización** *f* development. **~izar** [10] *vt* develop. **~o** *a* urban

urbe *f* big city

urdir *vt* (fig) plot

urg|encia *f* urgency; (emergencia) emergency. **~ente** *a* urgent; *<carta>* express. **~ir** [14] *vi* be urgent.

urinario *m* urinal

urna *f* urn; (Pol) ballot box

urraca *f* magpie

URSS *abrev* (Historia) (**Unión de Repúblicas Socialistas Soviéticas**) USSR

Uruguay *m*. **el ~** Uruguay

uruguayo *a & m* Uruguayan

us|ado *a* (con estar) used; *<ropa etc>* worn; (con ser) secondhand. **~ar** *vt* use; (llevar) wear. □ **~arse** *vpr* (LAm) be in fashion. **~o** *m* use; (costumbre) custom. **al ~o de** in the style of

usted *pron* you. **~es** you

usual *a* usual

usuario *a* user

usur|a *f* usury. **~ero** *m* usurer

usurpar *vt* usurp

utensilio *m* utensil; (herramienta) tool

útero *m* womb, uterus

útil *a* useful. **~es** *mpl* implements; (equipo) equipment

utili|dad *f* usefulness. **~dades** *fpl* (LAm) profits. **~zación** *f* use, utilization. **~zar** [10] *vt* use, utilize

utopía *f* Utopia

uva *f* grape. **~ pasa** raisin. **mala ~** bad mood

V v

vaca *f* cow. **carne de ~** beef

vacaciones *fpl* holiday(s), vacation(s) (Amer). **de ~** on holiday, on vacation (Amer)

vacante *a* vacant. ● *f* vacancy

vaciar [20] *vt* empty; (ahuecar) hollow out; (en molde) cast

vacila|ción *f* hesitation. **~nte** *a* unsteady; (fig) hesitant. **~r** *vi* hesitate (🔲, bromear) tease; (LAm, divertirse) have fun

vacío *a* empty; (frívolo) frivolous. ● *m* empty space; (estado) emptiness; (en física) vacuum; (fig) void

vacuna *f* vaccine. **~ción** *f* vaccination. **~r** *vt* vaccinate

vacuno *a* bovine

vad|ear *vt* ford. **~o** *m* ford

vaga|bundear *vi* wander. **~bundo** *a* vagrant; *<perro>* stray. **niño ~** street urchin. ● *m* tramp, vagrant. **~ncia** *f* vagrancy; (fig) laziness. **~r** [12] *vi* wander (about)

vagina *f* vagina

vago *a* vague; (holgazán) lazy. ● *m* layabout

vag|ón *m* coach, carriage; (de mercancías) wagon. ~**ón restaurante** dining-car. ~**oneta** *f* small freight wagon; (Mex, para pasajeros) van

vaho *m* breath; (vapor) steam. ~**s** *mpl* inhalation

vain|a *f* sheath; (Bot) pod. ~**illa** *f* vanilla

vaiv|én *m* swinging; (de tren etc) rocking. ~**enes** *mpl* (fig, de suerte) swings

vajilla *f* dishes, crockery

vale *m* voucher; (pagaré) IOU. ~**dero** *a* valid

valenciano *a* from Valencia

valentía *f* bravery, courage

valer [42] *vt* be worth; (costar) cost; (fig, significar) mean. ● *vi* be worth; (costar) cost; (servir) be of use; (ser valedero) be valid; (estar permitido) be allowed. ~ **la pena** be worthwhile, be worth it. **¿cuánto vale?** how much is it? **no** ~ **para nada** be useless. **eso no me vale** (Mex, 🆃) I don't give a damn about that. **¡vale!** all right!, OK! 🆃

valeroso *a* courageous

valgo *vb* ⇒ VALER

valía *f* worth

validez *f* validity. **dar** ~ **a** validate

válido *a* valid

valiente *a* brave; (en sentido irónico) fine. ● *m* brave person

valija *f* suitcase. ~ **diplomática** diplomatic bag

valioso *a* valuable

valla *f* fence; (en atletismo) hurdle

valle *m* valley

valor *m* value, worth; (coraje) courage. **objetos** *mpl* **de** ~ valuables. **sin** ~ worthless. ~**es** *mpl* securities. ~**ación** *f* valuation. ~**ar** *vt* value

vals *m invar* waltz

válvula *f* valve

vampiro *m* vampire

vanagloriarse *vpr* boast

vandalismo *m* vandalism

vándalo *m* & *f* vandal

vanguardia *f* vanguard. **de** ~ (en arte, música etc) avant-garde

vani|dad *f* vanity. ~**doso** *a* vain. ~**o** *a* vain; (inútil) futile; *<palabras>* empty. **en** ~ in vain

vapor *m* steam, vapour; (Naut) steamer. **al** ~ (Culin) steamed. ~**iza-dor** *m* vaporizer. ~**izar** [10] vaporize

vaquer|o *m* cowherd, cowboy. ~**os** *mpl* jeans

vara *f* stick; (de autoridad) staff (medida) yard

varar *vi* run aground

varia|ble *a* & *f* variable. ~**ción** *f* variation. ~**do** *a* varied. ~**nte** *f* variant; (Auto) by-pass. ~**ntes** *fpl* hors d'oeuvres. ~**r** [20] *vt* change; (dar variedad a) vary. ● *vi* vary; (cambiar) change

varicela *f* chickenpox

variedad *f* variety

varilla *f* stick; (de metal) rod

varios *a* several

varita *f* wand

variz *f* (*pl* **varices**, (LAm) **várices**) varicose vein

var|ón *a* male. ● *m* man; (niño) boy. ~**onil** *a* manly

vasco *a* & *m* Basque

vaselina *f* Vaseline (P), petroleum jelly

vasija *f* vessel, pot

vaso *m* glass; (Anat) vessel

vástago *m* shoot; (descendiente) descendant

vasto *a* vast

vaticin|ar *vt* forecast. ~**io** *m* prediction, forecast

vatio *m* watt

vaya *vb* ⇒IR

Vd. *abrev* (**Usted**) you

vecin|al *a* local. ~**dad** *f* neighbourhood; (vecinos) residents; (Mex, edificio) tenement house. ~**dario** *m* neighbourhood; (vecinos) residents. ~**o** *a* neighbouring. ● *m* neighbour; (de barrio, edificio) resident

veda *f* close season. ~**do** *m* reserve. ~**do de caza** game preserve. ~**r** *vt* prohibit

vega *f* fertile plain

vegeta|ción f vegetation. ~l a & m plant, vegetable. ~r vi grow; <persona> vegetate. ~riano a & m vegetarian

vehemente a vehement

vehículo m vehicle

veinte a & m twenty

veinti|cinco a & m twenty-five. ~cuatro a & m twenty-four. ~dós a & m twenty-two. ~nueve a & m twenty-nine; ~ocho a & m twenty-eight. ~séis a & m twenty-six. ~siete a & m twenty-seven. ~trés a & m twenty-three. ~uno a & m (delante de nombre masculino **veintiún**) twenty-one

vejar vt ill-treat

veje|storio m old crock; (LAm, cosa) old relic. ~z f old age

vejiga f bladder

vela f (Naut) sail; (de cera) candle; (vigilia) vigil. **pasar la noche en** ~ have a sleepless night

velada f evening

vela|do a veiled; (Foto) exposed. ~r vt watch over; hold a wake over <difunto>; (encubrir) veil; (Foto) expose. ● vi stay awake. ~r por look after. □ ~rse vpr (Foto) get exposed

velero m sailing-ship

veleta f weather vane

vell|o m hair; (pelusa) down. ~ón m fleece

velo m veil

veloc|idad f speed; (Auto, Mec) gear. **a toda** ~idad at full speed. ~ímetro m speedometer. ~ista m & f sprinter

velódromo m cycle-track

veloz a fast, quick

vena f vein; (en madera) grain. **estar de/en** ~ be in the mood

venado m deer; (Culin) venison

vencedor a winning. ● m winner

venc|er [9] vt defeat; (superar) overcome. ● vi win; <pasaporte> expire. □ ~erse vpr collapse; (LAm, pasaporte) expire. ~ido a beaten; <pasaporte> expired; (Com, atrasado) in arrears. **darse por** ~ido give up. ~imiento m due date; (de pasaporte) expiry date

venda f bandage. ~je m dressing. ~r vt bandage

vendaval m gale

vende|dor a selling. ● m seller; (en tienda) salesperson. ~dor ambulante pedlar. ~r vt sell. **se** ~ for sale. □ ~rse vpr <persona> sell out

vendimia f grape harvest

veneciano a Venetian

veneno m poison; (malevolencia) venom. ~so a poisonous

venera|ble a venerable. ~ción f reverence. ~r vt revere

venéreo a venereal

venezolano a & m Venezuelan

Venezuela f Venezuela

venga|nza f revenge. ~r [12] vt avenge. □ ~rse vpr take revenge (de, por for) (en on). ~tivo a vindictive

vengo vb ⇒VENIR

venia f (permiso) permission. ~l a venial

veni|da f arrival; (vuelta) return. ~dero a coming. ~r [53] vi come. ~r bien suit. **la semana que viene** next week. ¡**venga**! come on!

venta f sale; (posada) inn. **en** ~ for sale

ventaj|a f advantage. ~oso a advantageous

ventan|a f (inc informática) window; (de la nariz) nostril. ~illa f window

ventarrón m 🆃 strong wind

ventila|ción f ventilation. ~dor m fan. ~r vt air

vent|isca f blizzard. ~olera f gust of wind. ~osa f sucker. ~osidad f wind, flatulence. ~oso a windy

ventrílocuo m ventriloquist

ventur|a f happiness; (suerte) luck. **a la** ~a with no fixed plan. **echar la buena** ~a **a uno** tell s.o.'s fortune. **por** ~a fortunately; (acaso) perhaps. ~oso a happy, lucky

Venus m Venus

ver [43] vt see; watch <televisión>. ● vi see. **a mi modo de** ~ in my view. **a** ~ let's see. **dejarse** ~ show. **no lo puedo** ~ I can't stand him. **no tener nada que** ~ **con** have nothing to do with. **vamos a** ~ let's see. **ya lo veo**

that's obvious. **ya ~emos** we'll see. □ **~se** *vpr* see o.s.; (encontrarse) find o.s.; *<dos personas>* meet; (LAm, parecer) look

veran|eante *m & f* holidaymaker, vacationer (Amer). **~ear** *vi* spend one's summer holiday. **~eo** *m*. **ir de ~eo** spend one's summer holiday. **lugar** *m* **de ~eo** summer resort. **~iego** *a* summer. **~o** *m* summer

vera|s. de ~s really; (verdadero) real. **~z** *a* truthful

verbal *a* verbal

verbena *f* (fiesta) fair; (baile) dance

verbo *m* verb. **~so** *a* verbose

verdad *f* truth. **¿~?** isn't it?, aren't they?, won't it? etc. **a decir ~** to tell the truth. **de ~** really. **~eramente** *adv* really. **~ero** *a* true; (fig) real

verd|e *a* green; *<fruta>* unripe; *<chiste>* dirty. ● *m* green; (hierba) grass. **~or** *m* greenness

verdugo *m* executioner; (fig) tyrant

verdu|lería *f* greengrocer's (shop). **~lero** *m* greengrocer

vereda *f* path; (LAm, acera) pavement (Brit), sidewalk (Amer)

veredicto *m* verdict

verg|onzoso *a* shameful; (tímido) shy. **~üenza** *f* shame; (bochorno) embarrassment. **¡es una ~üenza!** it's a disgrace! **me da ~üenza** I'm ashamed/embarrassed. **tener ~üenza** be ashamed/embarrassed

verídico *a* true

verifica|ción *f* verification. **~r** [7] *vt* check. □ **~rse** *vpr* take place; (resultar verdad) come true

verja *f* (cerca) railings; (puerta) iron gate

vermú *m*, **vermut** *m* vermouth

verosímil *a* likely; *<relato>* credible

verruga *f* wart

versa|do *a* versed. **~r** *vi.* **~ sobre** deal with

versátil *a* versatile; (fig) fickle

versión *f* version; (traducción) translation

verso *m* verse; (poema) poem

vértebra *f* vertebra

verte|dero *m* dump; (desagüe) drain **~r** [1] *vt* pour; (derramar) spill ● *vi* flow

vertical *a & f* vertical

vértice *f* vertex

vertiente *f* slope

vertiginoso *a* dizzy

vértigo *m* (Med) vertigo. **dar ~** make dizzy

vesícula *f* vesicle. **~ biliar** gall bladder

vespertino *a* evening

vestíbulo *m* hall; (de hotel, teatro) foyer

vestido *m* dress

vestigio *m* trace. **~s** *mpl* remains

vest|imenta *f* clothes. **~ir** [5] *vt* (llevar) wear; dress *<niño etc>*. ● *vi* dress. **~ir de** wear. □ **~irse** *vpr* get dressed. **~irse de** wear; (disfrazarse) dress up as. **~uario** *m* wardrobe; (en gimnasio etc) changing room (Brit), locker room (Amer)

vetar *vt* veto

veterano *a* veteran

veterinari|a *f* veterinary science. **~o** *a* veterinary. ● *m* vet ⏹, veterinary surgeon (Brit), veterinarian (Amer)

veto *m* veto

vez *f* time; (turno) turn. **a la ~** at the same time. **alguna ~** sometimes; (en preguntas) ever. **algunas veces** sometimes. **a su ~** in turn. **a veces** sometimes. **cada ~** each time. **cada ~ más** more and more. **de una ~** in one go. **de una ~ para siempre** once and for all. **de ~ en cuando** from time to time. **dos veces** twice. **en ~ de** instead of. **érase una ~, había una ~** once upon a time there was. **otra ~** again. **pocas veces, rara ~** seldom. **una ~ (que)** once

vía *f* road; (Rail) line; (Anat) tract; (fig) way. **estar en ~s de** be in the process of. ● *prep* via. **~ aérea** by air. **~ de comunicación** means of communication. **~ férrea** railway (Brit), railroad (Amer). **~ rápida** fast lane

viab|ilidad *f* viability. **~le** *a* viable

viaducto *m* viaduct

viaj|ante *m & f* commercial traveller. **~ar** *vi* travel. **~e** *m* journey; (corto) trip. ~**e de novios** honeymoon. **¡buen** ~**e!** have a good journey!. **estar de** ~ be away. **salir de** ~ go on a trip. ~**ero** *m* traveller; (pasajero) passenger

víbora *f* viper

vibra|ción *f* vibration. ~**nte** *a* vibrant. ~**r** *vt/i* vibrate

vicario *m* vicar

viceversa *adv* vice versa

vici|ado *a* <*texto*> corrupt; <*aire*> stale. ~**ar** *vt* corrupt; (estropear) spoil. ~**o** *m* vice; (mala costumbre) bad habit. ~**oso** *a* dissolute; <*círculo*> vicious

víctima *f* victim; (de un accidente) casualty

victori|a *f* victory. ~**oso** *a* victorious

vid *f* vine

vida *f* life; (duración) lifetime. **¡~ mía!** my darling! **de por** ~ for life. **en mi** ~ never (in my life). **estar con** ~ be still alive

vídeo *m*, (LAm) **video** *m* video; (cinta) videotape; (aparato) video recorder

videojuego *m* video game

vidri|era *f* stained glass window; (puerta) glass door; (LAm, escaparate) shop window. ~**ería** *f* glass works. ~**ero** *m* glazier. ~**o** *m* glass; (LAm, en ventana) window pane. **limpiar los** ~**os** clean the windows. ~**oso** *a* glassy

vieira *f* scallop

viejo *a* old. ● *m* old person

viene *vb* ⇒VENIR

viento *m* wind. **hacer** ~ be windy

vientre *m* stomach; (cavidad) abdomen; (matriz) womb; (intestino) bowels; (de vasija etc) belly

viernes *m invar* Friday. **V~ Santo** Good Friday

viga *f* beam; (de metal) girder

vigen|cia *f* validity. ~**te** *a* valid; <*ley*> in force. **entrar en** ~**cia** come into force

vigésimo *a* twentieth

vigía *f* watch-tower. ● *m & f* (persona) lookout

vigil|ancia *f* vigilance. ~**ante** *a* vigilant. ● *m & f* security guard;

(nocturno) watchman. ~**ar** *vt* keep an eye on. ● *vi* be vigilant; <*vigía*> keep watch. ~**ia** *f* vigil; (Relig) fasting

vigor *m* vigour; (vigencia) force. **entrar en** ~ come into force. ~**oso** *a* vigorous

vil *a* vile. ~**eza** *f* vileness; (acción) vile deed

villa *f* (casa) villa; (Historia) town. **la V~** Madrid

villancico *m* (Christmas) carol

villano *a* villanous; (Historia) peasant

vilo. en ~ in the air

vinagre *m* vinegar. ~**ra** *f* vinegar bottle. ~**ras** *fpl* cruet. ~**ta** *f* vinaigrette

vincular *vt* bind

vínculo *m* tie, bond

vindicar [7] *vt* (rehabilitar) vindicate

vine *vb* ⇒VENIR

vinicult|or *m* wine-grower. ~**ura** *f* wine growing

vino *m* wine. ~ **de la casa** house wine. ~ **de mesa** table wine. ~ **tinto** red wine

viñ|a *f* vineyard. ~**atero** *m* (LAm) wine-grower. ~**edo** *m* vineyard

viola *f* viola

viola|ción *f* violation; (de una mujer) rape. ~**r** *vt* violate; break <*ley*>; rape <*mujer*>

violen|cia *f* violence; (fuerza) force. □ ~**tarse** *vpr* get embarrassed. ~**to** *a* violent; (fig) awkward

violeta *a invar & f* violet

viol|ín *m* violin. ● *m & f* (músico) violinist. ~**lnista** *m & f* violinist. ~**ón** *m* double bass. ~**onc(h)elista** *m & f* cellist. ~**onc(h)elo** *m* cello

vira|je *m* turn. ~**r** *vt* turn. ● *vi* turn; (fig) change direction. ~**r brusca-mente** swerve

virg|en *a.* **ser** ~**en** be a virgin. ●*f* virgin. ~**inal** *a* virginal. ~**inidad** *f* virginity

Virgo *m* Virgo

viril *a* virile. ~**idad** *f* virility

virtu|al *a* virtual. ~**d** *f* virtue; (capacidad) power. **en** ~**d de** by virtue of. ~**oso** *a* virtuous. ● *m* virtuoso

viruela *f* smallpox

virulento *a* virulent

virus *m invar* virus

visa *f* (LAm) visa. ~**ado** *m* visa. ~**r** *vt* endorse

vísceras *fpl* entrails

viscoso *a* viscous

visera *f* visor; (de gorra) peak

visib|ilidad *f* visibility. ~**le** *a* visible

visillo *m* (cortina) net curtain

visi|ón *f* vision; (vista) sight. ~**onario** *a & m* visionary

visita *f* visit; (visitante) visitor; (invitado) guest. ~**nte** *m & f* visitor. ~**r** *vt* visit

vislumbrar *vt* glimpse

viso *m* sheen; (aspecto) appearance

visón *m* mink

visor *m* viewfinder

víspera *f* day before, eve

vista *f* sight, vision; (aspecto, mirada) look; (panorama) view. **apartar la** ~ look away. **a primera** ~, **a simple** ~ at first sight. **con** ~**s a** with a view to. **en** ~ **de** in view of. **estar a la** ~ be obvious. **hacer la** ~ **gorda** turn a blind eye. **perder la** ~ lose one's sight. **tener a la** ~ have in front of one. **volver la** ~ **atrás** look back. ~**zo** *m* glance. **dar/echar un** ~**zo a** glance at

visto *a* seen; (poco original) common (considerado) considered. ~ **que** since. **bien** ~ acceptable. **está** ~ **que** it's obvious that. **mal** ~ unacceptable. **por lo** ~ apparently. ● *vb* ⇒VESTIR. ~ **bueno** *m* approval. ~**so** *a* colourful, bright

visual *a* visual. **campo** ~ field of vision

vital *a* vital. ~**icio** *a* life; *<cargo>* held for life. ~**idad** *f* vitality

vitamina *f* vitamin

viticult|or *m* wine-grower. ~**ura** *f* wine growing

vitorear *vt* cheer

vítreo *a* vitreous

vitrina *f* showcase; (en casa) glass cabinet; (LAm, escaparate) shop window

viud|a *f* widow. ~**ez** *f* widowhood. ~**o** *a* widowed. ● *m* widower

viva *m* cheer. ~**cidad** *f* liveliness. ~**mente** *adv* vividly. ~**z** *a* lively

víveres *mpl* supplies

vivero *m* nursery; (de peces) hatchery; (de moluscos) bed

viveza *f* vividness; (de inteligencia) sharpness; (de carácter) liveliness

vívido *a* vivid

vividor *m* pleasure seeker

vivienda *f* housing; (casa) house; (piso) flat (Brit), apartment (esp Amer). **sin** ~ homeless

viviente *a* living

vivificar [7] *vt* (animar) enliven

vivir *vt* live through. ● *vi* live; (estar vivo) be alive. **¡viva!** hurray! **¡viva el rey!** long live the king! ● *m* life. ~ **de** live on. **de mal** ~ dissolute

vivisección *f* vivisection

vivo *a* alive; (viviente) living; *<color>* bright; (listo) clever; (fig) lively. ● *m* sharp operator

vocab|lo *m* word. ~**ulario** *m* vocabulary

vocación *f* vocation

vocal *a* vocal. ● *f* vowel. ● *m & f* member. ~**ista** *m & f* vocalist

voce|ar *vt* call *<mercancías>*; (fig) proclaim; (Mex) page *<persona>*. ● *vi* shout. ~**río** *m* shouting. ~**ro** *m* (LAm) spokeperson

vociferar *vi* shout

vola|dor *a* flying. ● *m* rocket. ~**ndas. en** ~**ndas** in the air. ~**nte** *a* flying. ● *m* (Auto) steering-wheel; (nota) note; (rehilete) shuttlecock. ~**r** [2] *vt* blow up. ● *vi* fly; (🖪, desaparecer) disappear

volátil *a* volatile

volcán *m* volcano. ~**ico** *a* volcanic

volcar [2 & 7] *vt* knock over; (vaciar) empty out; turn over *<molde>*. ● *vi* overturn. □ ~**se** *vpr* fall over; *<vehículo>* overturn; (fig) do one's utmost. ~**se en** throw o.s. into

vóleibol *m*, (Mex) **volibol** *m* volleyball

voltaje *m* voltage

volte|ar *vt* turn over; (en el aire) toss; ring *<campanas>*; (LAm) turn over *<colchón etc>*. □ ~**arse** *vpr* (LAm) turn around; *<carro>* overturn. ~**reta** *f* somersault

voltio *m* volt

voluble *a* (fig) fickle

volum|en *m* volume. **~inoso** *a* voluminous

voluntad *f* will; (fuerza de voluntad) willpower; (deseo) wish; (intención) intention. **buena ~** goodwill. **mala ~** ill will

voluntario *a* voluntary. ● *m* volunteer

voluptuoso *a* voluptuous

volver [2] (*pp* **vuelto**) *vt* turn; (de arriba a abajo) turn over; (devolver) restore. ● *vi* return; (fig) revert. **~ a hacer algo** do sth again. **~ en sí** come round. □ **~se** *vpr* turn round; (hacerse) become

vomit|ar *vt* bring up. ● *vi* be sick, vomit. **~ivo** *a* disgusting

vómito *m* vomit; (acción) vomiting

voraz *a* voracious

vos *pron* (LAm) you. **~otros** *pron* you; (reflexivo) yourselves

vot|ación *f* voting; (voto) vote. **~ante** *m & f* voter. **~ar** *vt* vote for. ● *vi* vote (**por** for). **~o** *m* vote; (Relig) vow

voy *vb* ⇒IR

voz *f* voice; (rumor) rumour; (palabra) word. **~ pública** public opinion. **a media ~** softly. **a una ~** unanimously. **dar voces** shout. **en ~ alta** loudly

vuelco *m* upset. **el corazón me dio un ~** my heart missed a beat

vuelo *m* flight; (acción) flying; (de ropa) flare. **al ~** in flight; (fig) in passing

vuelta *f* turn; (curva) bend; (paseo) walk; (revolución) revolution; (regreso) return; (dinero) change. **a la ~** on one's return. **a la ~ de la esquina** round the corner. **dar la ~ al mundo** go round the world. **dar una ~** go for a walk. **estar de ~** be back

vuelvo *vb* ⇒VOLVER

vuestro *a* your. ● *pron* yours. **un amigo ~** a friend of yours

vulg|ar *a* vulgar; <persona> common. **~aridad** *f* vulgarity. **~arizar** [10] *vt* popularize. **~o** *m* common people

vulnerable *a* vulnerable

Ww

wáter /'(g)water/ *m* toilet

Web *m* /'(g)web/. **el ~** the Web

whisky /'(g)wiski/ *m* whisky

Xx

xenofobia *f* xenophobia

xilófono *m* xylophone

Yy

y *conj* and

ya *adv* already; (ahora) now; (con negativos) any more; (para afirmar) yes, sure; (en seguida) immediately; (pronto) soon. **~ mismo** (LAm) right away. ● *int* of course! **~ no** no longer. **~ que** since. **¡~, ~!** oh sure!

yacaré *m* (LAm) alligator

yac|er [44] *vi* lie. **~imiento** *m* deposit; (de petróleo) oilfield

yanqui *m & f* American, Yank(ee)

yate *m* yacht

yegua *f* mare

yelmo *m* helmet

yema *f* (Bot) bud; (de huevo) yolk; (golosina) sweet. **~ del dedo** fingertip

yerba *f* (LAm) grass; (Med) herb

yergo *vb* ⇒ERGUIR

yermo *a* uninhabited; (no cultivable) barren. ● *m* wasteland

yerno *m* son-in-law

yerro *m* mistake. ● *vb* ⇒ERRAR

yeso *m* plaster; (mineral) gypsum

yo *pron* I. ~ **mismo** myself. ¿**quién**, ~? who, me? **soy** ~ it's me

yodo *m* iodine

yoga *m* yoga

yogur *m* yog(h)urt

yuca *f* yucca

yugo *m* yoke

Yugoslavia *f* Yugoslavia

yugoslavo *a* & *m* Yugoslav

yunque *m* anvil

yunta *f* yoke

Zz

zafarrancho *m* (confusión) mess; (riña) quarrel

zafarse *vpr* escape; get out of *<obligación etc>*; (Mex, dislocarse) dislocate

zafiro *m* sapphire

zaga *f* rear; (en deportes) defence. **a la** ~ behind

zaguán *m* hall

zaherir [4] *vt* hurt

zahorí *m* dowser

zaino *a* *<caballo>* chestnut; *<vaca>* black

zalamer|ía *f* flattery. ~**o** *a* flattering. ● *m* flatterer

zamarra *f* (piel) sheepskin; (prenda) sheepskin jacket

zamarrear *vt* shake

zamba *f* South American dance

zambulli|da *f* dive; (baño) dip. □ ~**rse** *vpr* dive

zamparse *vpr* gobble up

zanahoria *f* carrot

zancad|a *f* stride. ~**illa** *f* trip. hacer una ~**illa a uno** trip s.o. up

zanc|o *m* stilt. ~**udo** *a* long-legged; *<ave>* wading. ● *m* (LAm) mosquito

zanganear *vi* idle

zángano *m* drone. ● *m* & *f* (persona) idler

zangolotear *vt* shake. ● *vi* rattle; *<persona>* fidget

zanja *f* ditch; (para tuberías etc) trench. ~**r** *vt* (fig) settle

zapat|ear *vi* tap with one's feet. ~**ería** *f* shoe shop; (arte) shoemaking. ~**ero** *m* shoemaker; (el que remienda zapatos) cobbler. ~**illa** *f* slipper; (de deportes) trainer. ~ **de ballet** ballet shoe. ~**o** *m* shoe

zarand|a *f* sieve. ~**ear** *vt* (sacudir) shake

zarcillo *m* earring

zarpa *f* paw

zarpar *vi* set sail, weigh anchor

zarza *f* bramble. ~**mora** *f* blackberry

zarzuela *f* Spanish operetta

zigzag *m* zigzag. ~**uear** *vi* zigzag

zinc *m* zinc

zócalo *m* skirting-board; (pedestal) plinth; (Mex, plaza) main square

zodiaco *m*, **zodíaco** *m* zodiac

zona *f* zone; (área) area

zoo *m* zoo. ~**logía** *f* zoology. ~**lógico** *a* zoological

zoólogo *m* zoologist

zopenco *a* stupid. ● *m* idiot

zoquete *m* blockhead

zorr|a *f* vixen ~**illo** *m* (LAm) skunk.. ~**o** *m* fox

zorzal *m* thrush

zozobra *f* (fig) anxiety. ~**r** *vi* founder

zueco *m* clog

zumb|ar *vt* 🔲 give *<golpe etc>*. ● *vi* buzz. ~**ido** *m* buzzing

zumo *m* juice

zurci|do *m* darning. ~**r** [9] *vt* darn

zurdo *a* left-handed; *<mano>* left

zurrar *vt* (fig, 🔲, dar golpes) beat (up)

zutano *m* so-and-so

Aa

a /ə/, *stressed form* /eɪ/

before vowel sound or silent 'h' **an**

● *indefinite article*

····▸ un (*m*), una (*f*). **a problem** un problema. **an apple** una manzana. **have you got a pencil?** ¿tienes un lápiz?

❗ Feminine singular nouns beginning with stressed or accented *a* or *ha* take the article **un** instead of **una**, e.g. *un águila, un hada*

····▸ (when talking about prices and quantities) por. **30 miles an hour** 30 millas por hora. **twice a week** dos veces por semana, dos veces a la semana

❗ There are many cases in which **a** is not translated, such as when talking about people's professions, in exclamations, etc: **she's a lawyer** *es abogada*. **what a beautiful day!** *¡qué día más precioso!*. **have you got a car?** *¿tienes coche?* **half a cup** *media taza*

aback /əˈbæk/ *adv*. **be taken ∼** quedar desconcertado

abandon /əˈbændən/ *vt* abandonar. ● *n* abandono *m*, desenfado *m*. **∼ed** *a* abandonado. **∼ment** *n* abandono *m*

abashed /əˈbæʃt/ *a* confuso

abate /əˈbeɪt/ *vi* disminuir; <*storm etc*> calmarse

abattoir /ˈæbətwɑ:(r)/ *n* matadero *m*

abbess /ˈæbɪs/ *n* abadesa *f*

abbey /ˈæbɪ/ *n* abadía *f*

abbot /ˈæbət/ *n* abad *m*

abbreviat|e /əˈbri:vɪeɪt/ *vt* abreviar. **∼ion** /-ˈeɪʃn/ *n* abreviatura *f*; (act) abreviación *f*

abdicat|e /ˈæbdɪkeɪt/ *vt/i* abdicar. **∼ion** /-ˈeɪʃn/ *n* abdicación *f*

abdom|en /ˈæbdəmən/ *n* abdomen *m*. **∼inal** /-ˈdɒmɪnl/ *a* abdominal

abduct /æbˈdʌkt/ *vt* secuestrar. **∼ion** /-ʃn/ *n* secuestro *m*

abhor /əbˈhɔ:(r)/ *vt* (*pt* **abhorred**) aborrecer. **∼rence** /-ˈhɒrəns/ *n* aborrecimiento *m*. **∼rent** /-ˈhɒrənt/ *a* aborrecible

abide /əˈbaɪd/ *vt* (*pt* **abided**) soportar. ● *vi* (old use, *pt* **abode**) morar. □ **∼ by** *vt* atenerse a; cumplir <*promise*>

ability /əˈbɪlətɪ/ *n* capacidad *f*; (cleverness) habilidad *f*

abject /ˈæbdʒekt/ *a* (wretched) miserable

ablaze /əˈbleɪz/ *a* en llamas

able /ˈeɪbl/ *a* (**-er, -est**) capaz. **be ∼** poder; (know how to) saber. **∼-bodied** /-ˈbɒdɪd/ *a* sano, no discapacitado

ably /ˈeɪblɪ/ *adv* hábilmente

abnormal /æbˈnɔ:ml/ *a* anormal. **∼ity** /-ˈmælətɪ/ *n* anormalidad *f*

aboard /əˈbɔ:d/ *adv* a bordo. ● *prep* a bordo de

abode /əˈbəʊd/ ⇒ABIDE. ● *n* (old use) domicilio *m*

aboli|sh /əˈbɒlɪʃ/ *vt* abolir. **∼tion** /æbəˈlɪʃn/ *n* abolición *f*

abominable /əˈbɒmɪnəbl/ *a* abominable

aborigin|al /æbəˈrɪdʒənl/ *a & n* aborigen (*m & f*), indígena (*m & f*). **∼es** /-i:z/ *npl* aborígenes *mpl*

abort /əˈbɔ:t/ *vt* hacer abortar. **∼ion** /-ʃn/ *n* aborto *m* provocado; (fig) aborto *m*. **have an ∼ion** hacerse un aborto. **∼ive** *a* fracasado

abound /əˈbaʊnd/ *vi* abundar (**in** en)

about /əˈbaʊt/ *adv* (approximately) alrededor de; (here and there) por todas partes; (in existence) por aquí. **∼ here** por aquí. **be ∼ to** estar a punto de. ● *prep* sobre; (around) alrededor de; (somewhere in) en. **talk ∼** hablar de. **∼-face**, **∼-turn** *n* (fig) cambio *m* rotundo

above /ə'bʌv/ adv arriba. ● prep encima de; (more than) más de. ∼ **all** sobre todo. ∼ **board** a legítimo. ● adv abiertamente. ∼**-mentioned** a susodicho

abrasi|on /ə'breɪʒn/ n abrasión f. ∼**ve** /-sɪv/ a abrasivo

abreast /ə'brest/ adv. march four ∼ marchar en columna de cuatro en fondo. **keep** ∼ **of** mantenerse al corriente de

abroad /ə'brɔːd/ adv (be) en el extranjero; (go) al extranjero; (far and wide) por todas partes

abrupt /ə'brʌpt/ a brusco. ∼**ly** adv (suddenly) repentinamente; (curtly) bruscamente

abscess /'æbsɪs/ n absceso m

abscond /əb'skɒnd/ vi fugarse

absen|ce /'æbsəns/ n ausencia f; (lack) falta f. ∼**t** /'æbsənt/ a ausente. ∼**t-minded** /-'maɪndɪd/ a distraído. ∼**t-mindedness** n distracción f, despiste m. ∼**tee** /-'tiː/ n ausente m & f. ∼**teeism** n absentismo m, ausentismo (LAm)

absolute /'æbsəluːt/ a absoluto. ∼**ly** adv absolutamente

absolve /əb'zɒlv/ vt (from sin) absolver; (from obligation) liberar

absor|b /əb'zɔːb/ vt absorber. ∼**bent** /-bent/ a absorbente. ∼**bent cotton** n (Amer) algodón m hidrófilo. ∼**ption** /əb'zɔːpʃən/ n absorción f

abstain /əb'steɪn/ vi abstenerse (from de)

abstemious /əb'stiːmɪəs/ a abstemio

abstention /əb'stenʃn/ n abstención f

abstract /'æbstrækt/ a abstracto. ● n (summary) resumen m; (painting) cuadro m abstracto. ● /əb'strækt/ vt extraer; (summarize) resumir. ∼**ion** /-ʃn/ n abstracción f

absurd /əb'sɜːd/ a absurdo. ∼**ity** n absurdo m, disparate m

abundan|ce /ə'bʌndəns/ n abundancia f. ∼**t** a abundante

abus|e /ə'bjuːz/ vt (misuse) abusar de; (ill-treat) maltratar; (insult) insultar. ● /ə'bjuːs/ n abuso m; (insults) insultos mpl. ∼**ive** /ə'bjuːsɪv/ a injurioso

abysmal /ə'bɪzməl/ a 🄴 pésimo

abyss /ə'bɪs/ n abismo m

academic /ækə'demɪk/ a académico; (pej) teórico. ● n universitario m, catedrático m

academy /ə'kædəmɪ/ n academia f.

accelerat|e /ək'seləreɪt/ vt acelerar. ● vi acelerar; (Auto) apretar el acelerador. ∼**ion** /-'reɪʃn/ n aceleración f. ∼**or** n acelerador m

accent /'æksənt/ n acento m

accept /ək'sept/ vt aceptar. ∼**able** a aceptable. ∼**ance** n aceptación f; (approval) aprobación f

access /'ækses/ n acceso m. ∼**ible** /ək'sesəbl/ a accesible; <person> tratable

accession /æk'seʃn/ n (to power, throne etc) ascenso m; (thing added) adquisición f

accessory /ək'sesərɪ/ a accesorio. ● n accesorio m, complemento m; (Jurid) cómplice m & f

accident /'æksɪdənt/ n accidente m; (chance) casualidad f. **by** ∼ sin querer; (by chance) por casualidad. ∼**al** /-'dentl/ a accidental, fortuito. ∼**ally** /-'dentəlɪ/ adv sin querer; (by chance) por casualidad. ∼**-prone** a propenso a los accidentes

acclaim /ə'kleɪm/ vt aclamar. ● n aclamación f

accolade /'ækəleɪd/ n (praise) encomio m

accommodat|e /ə'kɒmədeɪt/ vt (give hospitality to) alojar; (adapt) acomodar; (oblige) complacer. ∼**ing** a complaciente. ∼**ion** /-'deɪʃn/ n, ∼**ions** npl (Amer) alojamiento m

accompan|iment /ə'kʌmpənɪmənt/ n acompañamiento m. ∼**ist** n acompañante m & f. ∼**y** /ə'kʌmpənɪ/ vt acompañar

accomplice /ə'kʌmplɪs/ n cómplice m & f

accomplish /ə'kʌmplɪʃ/ vt (complete) acabar; (achieve) realizar; (carry out) llevar a cabo. ∼**ed** a consumado. ∼**ment** n realización f; (ability) talento m; (thing achieved) triunfo m, logro m

accord /ə'kɔːd/ vi concordar. ● vt conceder. ● n acuerdo m; (harmony) armonía *f.* of one's own ~ espontáneamente. ~**ance** *n.* in ~ance with de acuerdo con. ~**ing** *adv.* ~ing to según. ~**ingly** *adv* en conformidad; (therefore) por consiguiente

accordion /ə'kɔːdɪən/ *n* acordeón *m*

accost /ə'kɒst/ *vt* abordar

account /ə'kaʊnt/ *n* cuenta *f*; (description) relato *m*. ~**s** *npl* (in business) contabilidad *f*. on ~ of a causa de. on no ~ de ninguna manera. on this ~ por eso. take into ~ tener en cuenta. ● *vt* considerar. □ ~ **for** *vt* dar cuenta de, explicar

accountan|cy /ə'kaʊntənsɪ/ *n* contabilidad *f*. ~**t** *n* contable *m & f*, contador *m* (LAm)

accumulat|e /ə'kjuːmjʊleɪt/ *vt* acumular. ● *vi* acumularse. ~**ion** /-'leɪʃn/ *n* acumulación *f*

accura|cy /'ækjərəsɪ/ *n* exactitud *f*, precisión *f*. ~**te** /-ət/ *a* exacto, preciso

accus|ation /ækjuː'zeɪʃn/ *n* acusación *f*. ~**e** /ə'kjuːz/ *vt* acusar

accustom /ə'kʌstəm/ *vt* acostumbrar. ~**ed** *a*. be ~ed (to) estar acostumbrado (a). get ~ed (to) acostumbrarse (a)

ace /eɪs/ *n* as *m*

ache /eɪk/ *n* dolor *m*. ● *vi* doler. my leg ~s me duele la pierna

achieve /ə'tʃiːv/ *vt* realizar; lograr *<success>*. ~**ment** *n* realización *f*; (feat) proeza *f*; (thing achieved) logro *m*

acid /'æsɪd/ *a & n* ácido (*m*). ~**ic** *a* /ə'sɪdɪk/ *a* ácido. ~ **rain** *n* lluvia *f* ácida

acknowledge /ək'nɒlɪdʒ/ *vt* reconocer. ~ **receipt of** acusar recibo de. ~**ment** *n* reconocimiento *m*; (Com) acuse *m* de recibo

acne /'æknɪ/ *n* acné *m*

acorn /'eɪkɔːn/ *n* bellota *f*

acoustic /ə'kuːstɪk/ *a* acústico. ~**s** *npl* acústica *f*

acquaint /ə'kweɪnt/ *vt*. ~ **s.o. with** poner a uno al corriente de. be ~ed with conocer *<person>*; saber *<fact>*. ~**ance** *n* conocimiento *m*; (person) conocido *m*

acquiesce /ækwɪ'es/ *vi* consentir (in en). ~**nce** *n* aquiescencia *f*, consentimiento *m*

acqui|re /ə'kwaɪə(r)/ *vt* adquirir; aprender *<language>*. ~**re a taste for** tomar gusto a. ~**sition** /ækwɪ'zɪʃn/ *n* adquisición *f*. ~**sitive** /ə'kwɪzətɪv/ *a* codicioso

acquit /ə'kwɪt/ *vt* (*pt* **acquitted**) absolver. ~**tal** *n* absolución *f*

acre /'eɪkə(r)/ *n* acre *m*

acrid /'ækrɪd/ *a* acre

acrimonious /ækrɪ'məʊnɪəs/ *a* cáustico, mordaz

acrobat /'ækrəbæt/ *n* acróbata *m & f*. ~**ic** /-'bætɪk/ *a* acrobático. ~**ics** *npl* acrobacia *f*

acronym /'ækrənɪm/ *n* acrónimo *m*, siglas *fpl*

across /ə'krɒs/ *adv & prep* (side to side) de un lado al otro; (on other side) al otro lado de; (crosswise) a través. it is 20 metres ~ tiene 20 metros de ancho. go *or* walk ~ atravesar, cruzar

act /ækt/ *n* acto *m*; (action) acción *f*; (in variety show) número *m*; (decree) decreto *m*. ● *vt* hacer *<part, role>*. ● *vi* actuar; (pretend) fingir. ~ as actuar de; *<object>* servir de. ~ for representar. ~**ing** *a* interino. ● *n* (of play) representación *f*; (by actor) interpretación *f*; (profession) profesión *f* de actor

action /'ækʃn/ *n* acción *f*; (Jurid) demanda *f*; (plot) argumento *m*. out of ~ (on sign) no funciona. put out of ~ inutilizar. take ~ tomar medidas ~ **replay** *n* repetición *f* de la jugada

activate /'æktɪveɪt/ *vt* activar

activ|e /'æktɪv/ *a* activo; (energetic) lleno de energía; *<volcano>* en actividad. ~**ist** *n* activista *m & f*. ~**ity** /-'tɪvətɪ/ *n* actividad *f*

act|or /'æktə(r)/ *n* actor *m*. ~**ress** /-trɪs/ *n* actriz *f*

actual /'æktʃʊəl/ *a* verdadero. ~**ly** *adv* en realidad, efectivamente; (even) incluso

acute /ə'kjuːt/ *a* agudo. ~**ly** *adv* agudamente

ad /æd/ *n* 🄵 anuncio *m*, aviso *m* (LAm)

AD /eɪ'diː/ *abbr* (= **Anno Domini**) d. de J.C.

Adam's apple /ˈædəmzˈæpl/ *n*
nuez *f* (de Adán)

adapt /əˈdæpt/ *vt* adaptar. ● *vi* adaptarse. ~**ability** /-əˈbɪləti/ *n*. adapta-
bilidad *f*. ~**able** /-əbl/ *a* adaptable.
~**ation** /ˌædæpˈteɪʃn/ *n* adaptación
f; (of book etc) versión *f*. ~**or** /əˈdæptə
(r)/ *n* (Elec, with several sockets) enchufe *m* múltiple; (Elec, for different sockets)
adaptador *m*

add /æd/ *vt* añadir. ● *vi* sumar. □ ~
up *vt* sumar; (fig) tener sentido. ~ **up**
to equivaler a

adder /ˈædə(r)/ *n* víbora *f*

addict /ˈædɪkt/ *n* adicto *m*; (fig) entusiasta *m & f*. ~**ed** /əˈdɪktɪd/ *a*. ~**ed**
to adicto a; (fig) fanático de. ~**ion**
/əˈdɪkʃn/ *n* (Med) dependencia *f*; (fig)
afición *f*. ~**ive** /əˈdɪktɪv/ *a* que crea
adicción; (fig) que crea hábito

addition /əˈdɪʃn/ *n* suma *f*. **in** ~
además. ~**al** *a* suplementario

address /əˈdres/ *n* dirección *f*; (on
form) domicilio *m*; (speech) discurso
m. ● *vt* poner la dirección en; (speak
to) dirigirse a. ~ **book** *n* libreta *f* de
direcciones. ~**ee** /ˌædreˈsiː/ *n* destinatario *m*

adept /ˈædept/ *a & n* experto (*m*)

adequa|cy /ˈædɪkwəsɪ/ *n* suficien-
cia *f*. ~**te** /-ət/ *a* suficiente, adecuado. ~**tely** *adv* suficientemente, adecuadamente

adhere /ədˈhɪə(r)/ *vi* adherirse (**to**
a); observar <*rule*>. ~**nce** /-rəns/ *n*
adhesión *f*; (to rules) observancia *f*

adhesi|on /ədˈhiːʒn/ *n* adherencia
f. ~**ve** /-sɪv/ *a & n* adhesivo (*m*)

adjacent /əˈdʒeɪsnt/ *a* contiguo

adjective /ˈædʒɪktɪv/ *n* adjetivo *m*

adjourn /əˈdʒɜːn/ *vt* aplazar; suspender <*meeting etc*>. ● *vi* suspen-
derse

adjust /əˈdʒʌst/ *vt* ajustar <*machine*>; (arrange) arreglar. ● *vi*. ~ (**to**)
adaptarse (a). ~**able** *a* ajustable.
~**ment** *n* adaptación *f*; (Tec) ajuste
m

administer /ədˈmɪnɪstə(r)/ *vt*
administrar

administrat|ion /ədmɪnɪˈstreɪʃn/
n administración *f*. ~**ive**
/ədˈmɪnɪstrətɪv/ *a* administrativo.

~**or** /ədˈmɪnɪstreɪtə(r)/ *n* administrador *m*

admirable /ˈædmərəbl/ *a* admirable

admiral /ˈædmərəl/ *n* almirante *m*

admir|ation /ˌædməˈreɪʃn/ *n* admi-
ración *f*. ~**e** /ədˈmaɪə(r)/ *vt* admirar.
~**er** /ədˈmaɪərə(r)/ *n* admirador *m*

admission /ədˈmɪʃn/ *n* admisión *f*;
(entry) entrada *f*

admit /ədˈmɪt/ *vt* (*pt* **admitted**) dejar entrar; (acknowledge) admitir, reconocer. ~ **to** confesar. **be** ~**ted** (to
hospital etc) ingresar. ~**tance** *n*
entrada *f*. ~**tedly** *adv* es verdad
que

admonish /ədˈmɒnɪʃ/ *vt* reprender;
(advise) aconsejar

ado /əˈduː/ *n* alboroto m; (trouble) dificultad *f*. **without more** *or* **further** ~
en seguida, sin más

adolescen|ce /ˌædəˈlesns/ *n*
adolescencia *f*. ~**t** *a & n* adolescente
(*m & f*)

adopt /əˈdɒpt/ *vt* adoptar. ~**ed** *a*
<*child*> adoptivo. ~**ion** /-ʃn/ *n* adop-
ción *f* .

ador|able /əˈdɔːrəbl/ *a* adorable.
~**ation** /ˌædəˈreɪʃn/ *n* adoración *f*.
~**e** /əˈdɔː(r)/ *vt* adorar

adorn /əˈdɔːn/ *vt* adornar. ~**ment** *n*
adorno *m*

adrift /əˈdrɪft/ *a & adv* a la deriva

adult /ˈædʌlt/ *a & n* adulto (*m*)

adulter|er /əˈdʌltərə(r)/ *n* adúltero
m. ~**ess** /-ɪs/ *n* adúltera *f*. ~**y** *n*
adulterio *m*

advance /ədˈvɑːns/ *vt* adelantar.
● *vi* adelantarse. ● *n* adelanto *m*. **in**
~ con anticipación, por adelantado.
~**d** *a* avanzado; <*studies*> superior

advantage /ədˈvɑːntɪdʒ/ *n* ventaja
f. **take** ~ **of** aprovecharse de; abusar
de <*person*>. ~**ous** /ˌædvənˈteɪdʒəs/
a ventajoso

advent /ˈædvənt/ *n* venida *f*. **A**~ *n*
adviento *m*

adventur|e /ədˈventʃə(r)/ *n*
aventura *f*. ~**er** *n* aventurero *m*.
~**ous** *a* <*person*> aventurero;
<*thing*> arriesgado; (fig, bold) audaz

adverb /ˈædvɜːb/ *n* adverbio *m*

adversary /'ædvəsərɪ/ n adversario m

advers|e /'ædvɜːs/ a adverso, contrario, desfavorable. ~**ity** /əd'vɜːsətɪ/ n infortunio m

advert /'ædvɜːt/ n Ⓔ anuncio m, aviso m (LAm). ~**ise** /'ædvətaɪz/ vt anunciar. ● vi hacer publicidad; (seek, sell) poner un anuncio. ~**isement** /əd'vɜːtɪsmənt/ n anuncio m, aviso m (LAm). ~**iser** /'ædvətaɪzə(r)/ n anunciante m & f

advice /əd'vaɪs/ n consejo m; (report) informe m

advis|able /əd'vaɪzəbl/ a aconsejable. ~**e** /əd'vaɪz/ vt aconsejar; (inform) avisar. ~**e against** aconsejar en contra de. ~**er** n consejero m; (consultant) asesor m. ~**ory** a consultivo

advocate /'ædvəkət/ n defensor m; (Jurid) abogado m. ● /'ædvəkeɪt/ vt recomendar

aerial /'eərɪəl/ a aéreo. ● n antena f

aerobics /eə'rəʊbɪks/ npl aeróbica f

aerodrome /'eərədrəʊm/ n aeródromo m

aerodynamic /eərəʊdaɪ'næmɪk/ a aerodinámico

aeroplane /'eərəpleɪn/ n avión m

aerosol /'eərəsɒl/ n aerosol m

aesthetic /iːs'θetɪk/ a estético

afar /ə'fɑː(r)/ adv lejos

affable /'æfəbl/ a afable

affair /ə'feə(r)/ n asunto m. (love) ~ aventura f, amorío m. ~**s** npl (business) negocios mpl

affect /ə'fekt/ vt afectar; (pretend) fingir. ~**ation** /æfek'teɪʃn/ n afectación f. ~**ed** a afectado, amanerado

affection /ə'fekʃn/ n cariño m. ~**ate** /-ət/ a cariñoso

affiliate /ə'fɪlɪeɪt/ vt afiliar

affirm /ə'fɜːm/ vt afirmar. ~**ative** /-ətɪv/ a afirmativo. ● n respuesta f afirmativa

afflict /ə'flɪkt/ vt afligir. ~**ion** /-ʃn/ n aflicción f, pena f

affluen|ce /'æfluəns/ n riqueza f. ~**t** a rico.

afford /ə'fɔːd/ vt permitirse; (provide) dar. **he can't** ~ **a car** no le alcanza el dinero para comprar un coche

affront /ə'frʌnt/ n afrenta f, ofensa f. ● vt afrentar, ofender

afield /ə'fiːld/ adv. **far** ~ muy lejos

afloat /ə'fləʊt/ adv a flote

afraid /ə'freɪd/ a. **be** ~ tener miedo (**of** a); (be sorry) sentir, lamentar

afresh /ə'freʃ/ adv de nuevo

Africa /'æfrɪkə/ n África f. ~**n** a & n africano (m). ~**n-American** a & n norteamericano (m) de origen africano

after /'ɑːftə(r)/ adv después; (behind) detrás. ● prep después de; (behind) detrás de. **it's twenty** ~ **four** (Amer) son las cuatro y veinte. **be** ~ (seek) andar en busca de. ● conj después de que. ● a posterior. ~**-effect** n consecuencia f, efecto m secundario. ~**math** /'ɑːftəmæθ/ n secuelas fpl. ~**noon** /-'nuːn/ n tarde f. ~**shave** n loción f para después de afeitarse. ~**thought** n ocurrencia f tardía. ~**wards** /-wədz/ adv después

again /ə'gen/ adv otra vez; (besides) además. **do** ~ volver a hacer, hacer otra vez. ~ **and** ~ una y otra vez

against /ə'genst/ prep contra; (in opposition to) en contra de, contra

age /eɪdʒ/ n edad f. **at four years of** ~ a los cuatro años. **under** ~ menor de edad. ~**s** npl Ⓔ siglos mpl. ● vt/i (pres p **ageing**) envejecer. ~**d** /'eɪdʒd/ a de … años. ~**d 10** de 10 años. ~**d** /'eɪdʒɪd/ a viejo, anciano

agency /'eɪdʒənsɪ/ n agencia f; (department) organismo m

agenda /ə'dʒendə/ n orden m del día

agent /'eɪdʒənt/ n agente m & f; (representative) representante m & f

aggravat|e /'ægrəveɪt/ vt agravar; (Ⓔ, irritate) irritar. ~**ion** /-'veɪʃn/ n agravación f; (Ⓔ, irritation) irritación f

aggress|ion /ə'greʃn/ n agresión f. ~**ive** a agresivo. ~**iveness** n agresividad f. ~**or** n agresor m

aggrieved /ə'griːvd/ a apenado, ofendido

aghast /ə'gɑːst/ a horrorizado

agil|e /'ædʒaɪl/ *a* ágil. **~ity** /ə'dʒɪlətɪ/ *n* agilidad *f*

aging /'eɪdʒɪŋ/ *a* envejecido. ● *n* envejecimiento *m*

agitat|e /'ædʒɪteɪt/ *vt* agitar. **~ed** *a* nervioso. **~ion** /-'teɪʃn/ *n* agitación *f*, excitación *f*. **~or** *n* agitador *m*

ago /ə'gəʊ/ *adv*. a long time **~** hace mucho tiempo. **3 days ~** hace 3 días

agon|ize /'ægənaɪz/ *vi* atormentarse. **~izing** *a* <*pain*> atroz; <*experience*> angustioso. **~y** *n* dolor *m* (agudo); (mental) angustia *f*

agree /ə'gri:/ *vt* acordar. ● *vi* estar de acuerdo; (of figures) concordar; (get on) entenderse. □ **~ on** *vt* acordar <*date, details*>. □ **~ with** *vt* (of food etc) sentarle bien a. **~able** /ə'gri:əbl/ *a* agradable. **be ~able** (willing) estar de acuerdo. **~d** *a* <*time, place*> convenido. **~ment** /-mənt/ *n* acuerdo *m*. **in ~ment** de acuerdo

agricultur|al /ægrɪ'kʌltʃərəl/ *a* agrícola. **~e** /'ægrɪkʌltʃə(r)/ *n* agricultura *f*

aground /ə'graʊnd/ *adv*. **run ~** (of ship) varar, encallar

ahead /ə'hed/ *adv* delante; (in time) antes de. **be ~** ir delante

aid /eɪd/ *vt* ayudar. ● *n* ayuda *f*. **in ~ of** a beneficio de

AIDS /eɪdz/ *n* sida *m*

ailment /'eɪlmənt/ *n* enfermedad *f*

aim /eɪm/ *vt* apuntar; (fig) dirigir. ● *vi* apuntar; (fig) pretender. ● *n* puntería *f*; (fig) objetivo *m*. **~less** *a*, **~lessly** *adv* sin objeto, sin rumbo

air /eə(r)/ *n* aire *m*. **be on the ~** (Radio, TV) estar en el aire. **put on ~s** darse aires. ● *vt* airear. **~ bag** *n* (Auto) bolsa *f* de aire. **~ base** *n* base *f* aérea. **~borne** *a* en el aire; (Mil) aerotransportado. **~-conditioned** *a* climatizado, con aire acondicionado. **~ conditioning** *n* aire *m* acondicionado. **~craft** *n* (*pl invar*) avión *m*. **~craft carrier** *n* portaaviones *m*. **~field** *n* aeródromo *m*. **A~ Force** *n* fuerzas *fpl* aéreas. **~ freshener** *n* ambientador *m*. **~gun** *n* escopeta *f* de aire comprimido. **~ hostess** *n* azafata *f*, aeromoza *f* (LAm). **~line** *n* línea *f* aérea.

~ mail *n* correo *m* aéreo. **~plane** *n* (Amer) avión *m*. **~port** *n* aeropuerto *m*. **~sick** *a* mareado (en un avión). **~tight** *a* hermético. **~ traffic controller** *n* controlador *m* aéreo. **~y** *a* (**-ier, -iest**) aireado; <*manner*> desenfadado

aisle /aɪl/ *n* nave *f* lateral; (gangway) pasillo *m*

ajar /ə'dʒɑ:(r)/ *a* entreabierto

alarm /ə'lɑ:m/ *n* alarma *f*. ● *vt* asustar. **~ clock** *n* despertador *m*. **~ist** *n* alarmista *m* & *f*

Albania /æl'beɪnɪə/ *n* Albania *f*. **~n** *a* & *n* albanés (*m*)

albatross /'ælbətrɒs/ *n* albatros *m*

album /'ælbəm/ *n* álbum *m*

alcohol /'ælkəhɒl/ *n* alcohol *m*. **~ic** /-'hɒlɪk/ *a* & *n* alcohólico (*m*)

alcove /'ælkəʊv/ *n* nicho *m*

ale /eɪl/ *n* cerveza *f*

alert /ə'lɜ:t/ *a* vivo; (watchful) vigilante. ● *n* alerta *f*. **on the ~** alerta. ● *vt* avisar

algebra /'ældʒɪbrə/ *n* álgebra *f*

Algeria /æl'dʒɪərɪə/ *n* Argelia *f*. **~n** *a* & *n* argelino (*m*)

alias /'eɪlɪəs/ *n* (*pl* **-ases**) alias *m*. ● *adv* alias

alibi /'ælɪbaɪ/ *n* (*pl* **-is**) coartada *f*

alien /'eɪlɪən/ *n* extranjero *m*. ● *a* ajeno. **~ate** /-eɪt/ *vt* enajenar. **~ation** /-'neɪʃn/ *n* enajenación *f*

alienat|e /'eɪlɪəneɪt/ *vt* enajenar. **~ion** /-'neɪʃn/ *n* enajenación *f*

alight /ə'laɪt/ *a* ardiendo; <*light*> encendido

align /ə'laɪn/ *vt* alinear. **~ment** *n* alineación *f*

alike /ə'laɪk/ *a* parecido, semejante. **look** *or* **be ~** parecerse. ● *adv* de la misma manera

alive /ə'laɪv/ *a* vivo. **~ with** lleno de

alkali /'ælkəlaɪ/ *n* (*pl* **-is**) álcali *m*. **~ne** *a* alcalino

all /ɔ:l/

● *adjective*

····▸ todo, -da; (pl) todos, -das. **~ day** todo el día. **~ the windows** todas las ventanas. **~ four of us went** fuimos los cuatro

● *pronoun*

····▶ (everything) todo. **that's ~** eso es todo. **I did ~ I could to persuade her** hice todo lo que pude para convencerla

····▶ (after pronoun) todo, -da; (pl) todos, -das. **he helped us ~** nos ayudó a todos

····▶ **all of** todo, -da, (pl) todos, -das. **~ of the paintings** todos los cuadros. **~ of the milk** toda la leche

····▶ (in phrases) **all in all** en general. **not at all** (in no way) de ninguna manera; (after thanks) de nada, no hay de qué. **it's not at ~ bad** no está nada mal. **I don't like it at ~** no me gusta nada

● *adverb*

····▶ (completely) completamente. **she was ~ alone** estaba completamente sola. **I got ~ dirty** me ensucié todo/toda. **I don't know him ~ that well** no lo conozco tan bien

····▶ (in scores) **the score was one ~** iban empatados uno a uno

····▶ (in phrases) **to be all for sth** estar completamente a favor de algo. **to be all in** ⊞ estar rendido

all-around /ɔːləˈraʊnd/ *a* (Amer) completo

allay /əˈleɪ/ *vt* aliviar *<pain>*; aquietar *<fears etc>*

all-clear /ɔːlˈklɪə(r)/ *n* fin *m* de (la) alarma; (permission) visto *m* bueno

alleg|ation /ælɪˈɡeɪʃn/ *n* alegato *m*. **~e** /əˈledʒ/ *vt* alegar. **~edly** /-ɪdlɪ/ *adv* según se dice, supuestamente

allegiance /əˈliːdʒəns/ *n* lealtad *f*

allegory /ˈælɪɡərɪ/ *n* alegoría *f*

allerg|ic /əˈlɜːdʒɪk/ *a* alérgico (**to** a). **~y** /ˈælədʒɪ/ *n* alergia *f*

alleviate /əˈliːvɪeɪt/ *vt* aliviar

alley /ˈælɪ/ (*pl* **-eys**), **~way** *ns* calle-juela *f*

alliance /əˈlaɪəns/ *n* alianza *f*

alligator /ˈælɪɡeɪtə(r)/ *n* caimán *m*

allocat|e /ˈæləkeɪt/ *vt* asignar; (share out) repartir. **~ion** /-ˈkeɪʃn/ *n* asignación *f*; (distribution) reparto *m*

allot /əˈlɒt/ *vt* (*pt* **allotted**) asignar. **~ment** *n* asignación *f*; (land) parcela *f*

allow /əˈlaʊ/ *vt* permitir; (grant) conceder; (reckon on) prever; (agree)

admitir. □ **~ for** *vt* tener en cuenta. **~ance** /əˈlaʊəns/ *n* concesión *f*; (pension) pensión *f*; (Com) rebaja *f*. **make ~ances for** ser indulgente con *<person>*; (take into account) tener en cuenta

alloy /ˈælɔɪ/ *n* aleación *f*

all: **~ right** *adj & adv* bien. ● *int* ¡vale!, ¡okey! (esp LAm), ¡órale! (Mex). **~-round** *a* completo

allusion /əˈluːʒn/ *n* alusión *f*

ally /ˈælaɪ/ *n* aliado *m*. ● /əˈlaɪ/ *vt*. **~ o.s.** aliarse (**with** con)

almighty /ɔːlˈmaɪtɪ/ *a* todopoderoso

almond /ˈɑːmənd/ *n* almendra *f*

almost /ˈɔːlməʊst/ *adv* casi

alms *npl* limosnas *fpl*

alone /əˈləʊn/ *a* solo. ● *adv* sólo, solamente

along /əˈlɒŋ/ *prep* por, a lo largo de. ● *adv*. **~ with** junto con. **all ~** todo el tiempo. **come ~** venga. **~side** /-ˈsaɪd/ *adv* (Naut) al costado. ● *prep* al lado de

aloof /əˈluːf/ *adv* apartado. ● *a* reservado

aloud /əˈlaʊd/ *adv* en voz alta

alphabet /ˈælfəbet/ *n* alfabeto *m*. **~ical** /-ˈbetɪkl/ *a* alfabético

Alps /ælps/ *npl*. **the ~** los Alpes

already /ɔːlˈredɪ/ *adv* ya

Alsatian /ælˈseɪʃn/ *n* pastor *m* alemán

also /ˈɔːlsəʊ/ *adv* también; (moreover) además

altar /ˈɔːltə(r)/ *n* altar *m*

alter /ˈɔːltə(r)/ *vt* cambiar. ● *vi* cambiarse. **~ation** /-ˈreɪʃn/ *n* modificación *f*; (to garment) arreglo *m*

alternate /ɔːlˈtɜːnət/ *a* alterno; (Amer) ⇒ALTERNATIVE. ● /ˈɔːltəneɪt/ *vt/i* alternar. **~ly** /ɔːlˈtɜːnətlɪ/ *adv* alternativamente

alternative /ɔːlˈtɜːnətɪv/ *a* alternativo. ● *n* alternativa *f*. **~ly** *adv* en cambio, por otra parte

although /ɔːlˈðəʊ/ *conj* aunque

altitude /ˈæltɪtjuːd/ *n* altitud *f*

altogether /ɔːltəˈɡeðə(r)/ *adv* completamente; (on the whole) en total

aluminium /ˈæljʊˈmɪnɪəm/, **alu-minum** /əˈluːmɪnəm/ (Amer) *n* aluminio *m*

always /ˈɔːlweɪz/ *adv* siempre

am /æm/ ⇒BE

a.m. *abbr* (= **ante meridiem**) de la mañana

amalgamate /əˈmælgəmeɪt/ *vt* amalgamar. ● *vi* amalgamarse

amass /əˈmæs/ *vt* acumular

amateur /ˈæmətə(r)/ *a & n* amateur (*m & f*). ∼**ish** *a* (pej) torpe, chapucero

amaz|e /əˈmeɪz/ *vt* asombrar. ∼**ed** *a* asombrado, estupefacto. **be** ∼**ed at** quedarse asombrado de, asombrarse de. ∼**ement** *n* asombro *m*. ∼**ing** *a* increíble

ambassador /æmˈbæsədə(r)/ *n* embajador *m*

ambigu|ity /æmbɪˈgjuːətɪ/ *n* ambigüedad *f*. ∼**ous** /æmˈbɪgjʊəs/ *a* ambiguo

ambiti|on /æmˈbɪʃn/ *n* ambición *f*. ∼**ous** /-ʃəs/ *a* ambicioso

ambivalent /æmˈbɪvələnt/ *a* ambivalente

amble /ˈæmbl/ *vi* andar despacio, andar sin prisa

ambulance /ˈæmbjʊləns/ *n* ambulancia *f*

ambush /ˈæmbʊʃ/ *n* emboscada *f*. ● *vt* tender una emboscada a

amen /ɑːˈmen/ *int* amén

amend /əˈmend/ *vt* enmendar. ∼**ment** *n* enmienda *f*. ∼**s** *npl*. **make** ∼**s** reparar

amenities /əˈmiːnətɪz/ *npl* servicios *mpl*; (of hotel, club) instalaciones *fpl*

America /əˈmerɪkə/ *n* (continent) América; (North America) Estados *mpl* Unidos, Norteamérica *f*. ∼**n** *a & n* americano (*m*); (North American) estadounidense (*m & f*), norteamericano (*m*). ∼**nism** *n* americanismo *m*

amiable /ˈeɪmɪəbl/ *a* simpático

amicable /ˈæmɪkəbl/ *a* amistoso

amid(st) /əˈmɪd(st)/ *prep* entre, en medio de

ammonia /əˈməʊnɪə/ *n* amoníaco *m*, amoniaco *m*

ammunition /æmjʊˈnɪʃn/ *n* municiones *fpl*

amnesty /ˈæmnəstɪ/ *n* amnistía *f*

amok /əˈmɒk/ *adv*. **run** ∼ volverse loco

among(st) /əˈmʌŋ(st)/ *prep* entre

amount /əˈmaʊnt/ *n* cantidad *f*; (total) total *m*, suma *f*. □ ∼ **to** *vt* sumar; (fig) equivaler a, significar

amp(ere) /ˈæmp(eə(r))/ *n* amperio *m*

amphibi|an /æmˈfɪbɪən/ *n* anfibio *m*. ∼**ous** /-əs/ *a* anfibio

amphitheatre /ˈæmfɪθɪətə(r)/ *n* anfiteatro *m*

ampl|e /ˈæmpl/ *a* (**-er, -est**) amplio; (enough) suficiente; (plentiful) abundante. ∼**y** *adv* ampliamente, bastante

amplif|ier /ˈæmplɪfaɪə(r)/ *n* amplificador *m*. ∼**y** /ˈæmplɪfaɪ/ *vt* amplificar

amputat|e /ˈæmpjʊteɪt/ *vt* amputar. ∼**ion** /-ˈteɪʃn/ *n* amputación *f*

amus|e /əˈmjuːz/ *vt* divertir. ∼**ed** *a* <expression> divertido. **keep s.o.** ∼**ed** entretener a uno. ∼**ement** *n* diversión *f*. ∼**ing** *a* divertido

an /ən, æn/ ⇒A

anaemi|a /əˈniːmɪə/ *n* anemia *f*. ∼**c** *a* anémico

anaesthe|tic /ænɪsˈθetɪk/ *n* anestésico *m*. ∼**tist** /əˈniːsθɪtɪst/ *n* anestesista *m & f*

anagram /ˈænəgræm/ *n* anagrama *m*

analogy /əˈnælədʒɪ/ *n* analogía *f*

analy|se /ˈænəlaɪz/ *vt* analizar. ∼**sis** /əˈnæləsɪs/ *n* (*pl* **-ses** /-siːz/) *n* análisis *m*. ∼**st** /ˈænəlɪst/ *n* analista *m & f*. ∼**tic(al)** /ænəˈlɪtɪk(əl)/ *a* analítico

anarch|ist /ˈænəkɪst/ *n* anarquista *m & f*. ∼**y** *n* anarquía *f*

anatom|ical /ænəˈtɒmɪkl/ *a* anatómico. ∼**y** /əˈnætəmɪ/ *n* anatomía *f*

ancest|or /ˈænsestə(r)/ *n* antepasado *m*. ∼**ral** /-ˈsestrəl/ *a* ancestral. ∼**ry** /ˈænsestrɪ/ *n* ascendencia *f*

anchor /ˈæŋkə(r)/ *n* ancla *f*. ● *vt* anclar; (fig) sujetar. ● *vi* anclar.

~**man** *n* (on TV) presentador *m*.
~**woman** *n* (on TV) presentadora *f*.

ancient /'eɪnʃənt/ *a* antiguo, viejo

ancillary /æn'sɪlərɪ/ *a* auxiliar

and /ənd, ænd/ *conj* y; (before i- and hi-) e. **bread** ~ **butter** pan *m* con mantequilla. **go** ~ **see him** ve a verlo. **more** ~ **more** cada vez más. **try** ~ **come** trata de venir

anecdot|al /ænɪk'dəʊtl/ *a* anecdótico. ~**e** /'ænɪkdəʊt/ *n* anécdota *f*

anew /ə'nju:/ *adv* de nuevo

angel /'eɪndʒl/ *n* ángel *m*. ~**ic** /æn'dʒelɪk/ *a* angélico

anger /'æŋgə(r)/ *n* ira *f*. ● *vt* enfadar, (esp LAm) enojar

angle /'æŋgl/ *n* ángulo *m*; (fig) punto *m* de vista. ~**r** /'æŋglə(r)/ *n* pescador *m*

Anglican /'æŋglɪkən/ *a* & *n* anglicano (*m*)

angr|ily /'æŋgrɪlɪ/ *adv* con enfado, (esp LAm) con enojo. ~**y** /'æŋgrɪ/ *a* (**-ier, -iest**) enfadado, (esp LAm) enojado. **get** ~**y** enfadarse, enojarse (esp LAm)

anguish /'æŋgwɪʃ/ *n* angustia *f*

animal /'ænɪməl/ *a* & *n* animal (*m*)

animat|e /'ænɪmeɪt/ *vt* animar. ~**ion** /-'meɪʃn/ *n* animación *f*

animosity /ænɪ'mɒsətɪ/ *n* animosidad *f*

ankle /'æŋkl/ *n* tobillo *m*. ~ **boot** botín *m*. ~ **sock** calcetín *m* corto

annexe /'æneks/ *n* anexo *m*

annihilat|e /ə'naɪəleɪt/ *vt* aniquilar. ~**ion** /-'leɪʃn/ *n* aniquilación *f*

anniversary /ænɪ'vɜːsərɪ/ *n* aniversario *m*

announce /ə'naʊns/ *vt* anunciar, comunicar. ~**ment** *n* anuncio *m*; (official) comunicado *m*. ~**r** *n* (Radio, TV) locutor *m*

annoy /ə'nɔɪ/ *vt* molestar. ~**ance** *n* molestia *m*. ~**ed** *a* enfadado, enojado (LAm). ~**ing** *a* molesto

annual /'ænjʊəl/ *a* anual. ● *n* anuario *m*. ~**ly** *adv* cada año

annul /ə'nʌl/ *vt* (*pt* **annulled**) anular. ~**ment** *n* anulación *f*

anonymous /ə'nɒnɪməs/ *a* anónimo

anorak /'ænəræk/ *n* anorac *m*

another /ə'nʌðə(r)/ *a* & *pron* otro. ~ **10 minutes** 10 minutos más. **in** ~ **way** de otra manera. **one** ~ el uno al otro; (*pl*) unos a otros

answer /'ɑːnsə(r)/ *n* respuesta *f*; (solution) solución *f*. ● *vt* contestar; escuchar, oír <*prayer*>. ~ **the door** abrir la puerta. ● *vi* contestar. □ ~ **back** *vi* contestar. □ ~ **for** *vt* ser responsable de. ~**able** *a* responsable. ~**ing machine** *n* contestador *m* automático

ant /ænt/ *n* hormiga *f*

antagoni|sm /æn'tægənɪzəm/ *n* antagonismo *m*. ~**stic** /-'nɪstɪk/ *a* antagónico, opuesto. ~**ze** /æn'tægənaɪz/ *vt* provocar la enemistad de

Antarctic /æn'tɑːktɪk/ *a* antártico. ● *n* **the** ~ la región antártica

antelope /'æntɪləʊp/ *n* antílope *m*

antenatal /'æntɪneɪtl/ *a* prenatal

antenna /æn'tenə/ (*pl* **-nae** /-niː/) (of insect etc) *n* antena *f*; (*pl* **-nas**) (of radio, TV) antena *f*

anthem /'ænθəm/ *n* himno *m*

anthology /æn'θɒlədʒɪ/ *n* antología *f*

anthropolog|ist /ænθrə'pɒlədʒɪst/ *n* antropólogo *m*. ~**y** *n* antropología *f*

anti-... /ænti/ *pref* anti... ~**aircraft** /-'eəkrɑːft/ *a* antiaéreo

antibiotic /æntɪbaɪ'ɒtɪk/ *a* & *n* antibiótico (*m*)

anticipat|e /æn'tɪsɪpeɪt/ *vt* anticiparse a; (foresee) prever; (forestall) prevenir. ~**ion** /-'peɪʃn/ *n* (foresight) previsión *f*; (expectation) expectativa *f*

anti: ~**climax** /-'klaɪmæks/ *n* decepción *f*. ~**clockwise** /-'klɒkwaɪz/ *adv* & *a* en sentido contrario al de las agujas del reloj

antidote /'æntɪdəʊt/ *m* antídoto *m*

antifreeze /'æntɪfriːz/ *n* anticongelante *m*

antiperspirant /æntɪ'pɜːspɪrənt/ *n* antitranspirante *m*

antiquated /'æntɪkweɪtɪd/ *a* anticuado

antique /æn'ti:k/ *a* antiguo. ● *n* antigüedad *f*. ~ **dealer** anticuario *m*. ~ **shop** tienda *f* de antigüedades

antiquity /æn'tɪkwətɪ/ *n* antigüedad *f*

anti: ~**septic** /-'septɪk/ *a* & *n* antiséptico (*m*). ~**social** /-'səʊʃl/ *a* antisocial

antlers /'æntləz/ *npl* cornamenta *f*

anus /'eɪnəs/ *n* ano *m*

anvil /'ænvɪl/ *n* yunque *m*

anxi|ety /æŋ'zaɪətɪ/ *n* ansiedad *f*; (worry) inquietud *f*; (eagerness) anhelo *m*. ~**ous** /'æŋkʃəs/ *a* inquieto; (eager) deseoso. ~**ously** *adv* con inquietud; (eagerly) con impaciencia

any /'enɪ/ *a* algún; (negative) ningún *m*; (whatever) cualquier; (every) todo. **at** ~ **moment** en cualquier momento. **have you** ~ **wine?** ¿tienes vino? ● *pron* alguno; (negative) ninguno. **have we** ~? ¿tenemos algunos? **not** ~ ninguno. ● *adv* (a little) un poco, algo. **is it** ~ **better?** ¿está algo mejor?

anybody /'enɪbɒdɪ/ *pron* alguien; (*after negative*) nadie. ~ **can do it** cualquiera puede hacerlo

anyhow /'enɪhaʊ/ *adv* de todas formas; (in spite of all) a pesar de todo; (badly) de cualquier manera

anyone /'enɪwʌn/ *pron* ⇒ANYBODY

anything /'enɪθɪŋ/ *pron* algo; (whatever) cualquier cosa; (*after negative*) nada. ~ **but** todo menos

anyway /'enɪweɪ/ *adv* de todas formas

anywhere /'enɪweə(r)/ *adv* en cualquier parte; (*after negative*) en ningún sitio. ~ **else** en cualquier otro lugar. ~ **you go** dondequiera que vayas

apart /ə'pɑ:t/ *adv* aparte; (separated) separado. ~ **from** aparte de. **come** ~ romperse. **take** ~ desmontar

apartheid /ə'pɑ:theɪt/ *n* apartheid *m*

apartment /ə'pɑ:tmənt/ *n* (Amer) apartamento *m*, piso *m*. ~ **building** *n* (Amer) edificio *m* de apartamentos, casa *f* de pisos

apath|etic /æpə'θetɪk/ *a* apático. ~**y** /'æpəθɪ/ *n* apatía *f*

ape /eɪp/ *n* mono *m*. ● *vt* imitar

aperitif /ə'perətɪf/ *n* aperitivo *m*

aperture /'æpətʃʊə(r)/ *n* abertura *f*

apex /'eɪpeks/ *n* ápice *m*

aphrodisiac /æfrə'dɪzɪæk/ *a* & *n* afrodisíaco (*m*), afrodisiaco (*m*)

apolog|etic /əpɒlə'dʒetɪk/ *a* lleno de disculpas. **be** ~**etic** disculparse. ~**ize** /ə'pɒlədʒaɪz/ *vi* disculparse (for de). ~**y** /ə'pɒlədʒɪ/ *n* disculpa *f*

apostle /ə'pɒsl/ *n* apóstol *m*

apostrophe /ə'pɒstrəfɪ/ *n* apóstrofo *m*

appal /ə'pɔ:l/ *vt* (*pt* **appalled**) horrorizar. ~**ling** *a* espantoso

apparatus /æpə'reɪtəs/ *n* aparato *m*

apparel /ə'pærəl/ *n* (Amer) ropa *f*

apparent /ə'pærənt/ *a* aparente; (clear) evidente. ~**ly** *adv* por lo visto

apparition /æpə'rɪʃn/ *n* aparición *f*

appeal /ə'pi:l/ *vi* apelar; (attract) atraer. ● *n* llamamiento *m*; (attraction) atractivo *m*; (Jurid) apelación *f*. ~**ing** *a* atrayente

appear /ə'pɪə(r)/ *vi* aparecer; (seem) parecer; (in court) comparecer. ~**ance** *n* aparición *f*; (aspect) aspecto *m*; (in court) comparecencia *f*

appease /ə'pi:z/ *vt* aplacar; (pacify) apaciguar

append /ə'pend/ *vt* adjuntar

appendicitis /əpendɪ'saɪtɪs/ *n* apendicitis *f*

appendix /ə'pendɪks/ *n* (*pl* **-ices** /-ɪsi:z/) (of book) apéndice *m*. (*pl* **-ixes**) (Anat) apéndice *m*

appetite /'æpɪtaɪt/ *n* apetito *m*

applau|d /ə'plɔ:d/ *vt/i* aplaudir. ~**se** /ə'plɔ:z/ *n* aplausos *mpl*. **round of** ~**se** aplauso *m*

apple /'æpl/ *n* manzana *f*. ~ **tree** *n* manzano *m*

appliance /ə'plaɪəns/ *n* aparato *m*. **electrical** ~ electrodoméstico *m*

applic|able /'æplɪkəbl/ *a* aplicable; (relevant) pertinente. ~**ant** /'æplɪkənt/ *n* candidato *m*, solicitante *m* & *f*. ~**ation** /æplɪ'keɪʃn/ *n* aplicación *f*; (request) solicitud *f*. ~**ation form** formulario *m* (de solicitud)

appl|ied /ə'plaɪd/ *a* aplicado. ~**y** /ə'plaɪ/ *vt* aplicar. ● *vi* aplicarse; (ask) presentar una solicitud. ~**y for** solicitar <*job etc*>

appoint /ə'pɔɪnt/ *vt* nombrar; (fix) señalar. ~**ment** *n* cita *f*

apprais|al /ə'preɪzl/ *n* evaluación *f*. ~**e** /ə'preɪz/ *vt* evaluar

appreciable /ə'priːʃəbl/ *a* (considerable) considerable

appreciat|e /ə'priːʃɪeɪt/ *vt* (value) apreciar; (understand) comprender; (be grateful for) agradecer. ~**ion** /-'eɪʃn/ *n* aprecio *m*; (gratitude) agradecimiento *m*. ~**ive** /ə'priːʃɪətɪv/ *a* agradecido

apprehen|sion /æprɪ'henʃn/ *n* (fear) recelo *f*. ~**sive** *a* aprensivo

apprentice /ə'prentɪs/ *n* aprendiz *m*. ● *vt*. be ~**d** to s.o. estar de aprendiz con uno. ~**ship** *n* aprendizaje *m*

approach /ə'prəʊtʃ/ *vt* acercarse a. ● *vi* acercarse. ● *n* acercamiento *m*; (to problem) enfoque *m*; (access) acceso *m*

appropriate /ə'prəʊprɪət/ *a* apropiado. ● /ə'prəʊprɪeɪt/ *vt* apropiarse de. ~**ly** /-ətlɪ/ *adv* apropiadamente

approv|al /ə'pruːvl/ *n* aprobación *f*. on ~**al** a prueba. ~**e** /ə'pruːv/ *vt/i* aprobar. ~**ingly** *adv* con aprobación

approximat|e /ə'prɒksɪmət/ *a* aproximado. ● /ə'prɒksɪmeɪt/ *vt* aproximarse a. ~**ely** /-ətlɪ/ *adv* aproximadamente. ~**ion** /-'meɪʃn/ *n* aproximación *f*

apricot /'eɪprɪkɒt/ *n* albaricoque *m*, chabacano *m* (Mex)

April /'eɪprəl/ *n* abril *m*. ~ **fool!** ¡inocentón!

apron /'eɪprən/ *n* delantal *m*

apt /æpt/ *a* apropiado. be ~ to tener tendencia a. ~**itude** /'æptɪtjuːd/ *n* aptitud *f*. ~**ly** *adv* acertadamente

aquarium /ə'kweərɪəm/ *n* (*pl* -**ums**) acuario *m*

Aquarius /ə'kweərɪəs/ *n* Acuario *m*

aquatic /ə'kwætɪk/ *a* acuático

aqueduct /'ækwɪdʌkt/ *n* acueducto *m*

Arab /'ærəb/ *a* & *n* árabe (*m* & *f*). ~**ian** /ə'reɪbɪən/ *a* árabe. ~**ic** /'ærəbɪk/ *a* & *n* árabe (*m*). ~**ic numerals** números *mpl* arábigos

arable /'ærəbl/ *a* cultivable

arbitrary /'ɑːbɪtrərɪ/ *a* arbitrario

arbitrat|e /'ɑːbɪtreɪt/ *vi* arbitrar. ~**ion** /-'treɪʃn/ *n* arbitraje *m*. ~**or** *n* árbitro *m*

arc /ɑːk/ *n* arco *m*

arcade /ɑː'keɪd/ *n* arcada *f*; (around square) soportales *mpl*; (shops) galería *f*

arch /ɑːtʃ/ *n* arco *m*. ● *vt* arquear. ● *vi* arquearse

archaeolog|ical /ɑːkɪə'lɒdʒɪkl/ *a* arqueológico. ~**ist** /ɑːkɪ'ɒlədʒɪst/ *n* arqueólogo *m*. ~**y** /ɑːkɪ'ɒlədʒɪ/ *n* arqueología *f*

archaic /ɑː'keɪɪk/ *a* arcaico

archbishop /ɑːtʃ'bɪʃəp/ *n* arzobispo *m*

archer /'ɑːtʃə(r)/ *n* arquero *m*. ~**y** *n* tiro *m* con arco

architect /'ɑːkɪtekt/ *n* arquitecto *m*. ~**ure** /-tʃə(r)/ *n* arquitectura *f*. ~**ural** /-'tektʃərəl/ *a* arquitectónico

archives /'ɑːkaɪvz/ *npl* archivo *m*

archway /'ɑːtʃweɪ/ *n* arco *m*

Arctic /'ɑːktɪk/ *a* ártico. ● *n*. the ~ el Ártico

ard|ent /'ɑːdənt/ *a* fervoroso; <*supporter, lover*> apasionado. ~**our** /'ɑːdə(r)/ *n* fervor *m*; (love) pasión *f*

arduous /'ɑːdjʊəs/ *a* arduo

are /ɑː(r)/ ⇒BE

area /'eərɪə/ *n* (Math) superficie *f*; (of country) zona *f*; (of city) barrio *m*

arena /ə'riːnə/ *n* arena *f*; (scene of activity) ruedo *m*

aren't /ɑːnt/ = **are not**

Argentin|a /ɑːdʒən'tiːnə/ *n* Argentina *f*. ~**ian** /-'tɪnɪən/ *a* & *n* argentino (*m*)

argu|able /'ɑːgjʊəbl/ *a* discutible. ~**e** /'ɑːgjuː/ *vi* discutir; (reason) razonar. ~**ment** /'ɑːgjʊmənt/ *n* disputa *f*; (reasoning) argumento *m*. ~**mentative** /ɑːgjʊ'mentətɪv/ *a* discutidor

arid /'ærɪd/ *a* árido

Aries /'eəriːz/ *n* Aries *m*

arise /ə'raɪz/ *vi* (*pt* **arose**, *pp* **arisen**) surgir (from de)

aristocra|cy /ˌærɪˈstɒkrəsɪ/ *n* aristocracia *f*. **~t** /ˈærɪstəkræt/ *n* aristócrata *m & f*. **~tic** /-ˈkrætɪk/ *a* aristocrático

arithmetic /əˈrɪθmətɪk/ *n* aritmética *f*

ark /ɑːk/ *n* (Relig) arca *f*

arm /ɑːm/ *n* brazo *m*; (of garment) manga *f*. **~s** *npl* armas *fpl*. ● *vt* armar

armament /ˈɑːməmənt/ *n* armamento *m*

arm: ~band *n* brazalete *m*. **~chair** *n* sillón *m*

armed /ɑːmd/ *a* armado. **~ robbery** *n* robo *m* a mano armada

armful /ˈɑːmfʊl/ *n* brazada *f*

armour /ˈɑːmə(r)/ *n* armadura *f*. **~ed** /ˈɑːməd/ *a* blindado. **~y** /ˈɑːmərɪ/ *n* arsenal *m*

armpit /ˈɑːmpɪt/ *n* sobaco *m*, axila *f*

army /ˈɑːmɪ/ *n* ejército *m*

aroma /əˈrəʊmə/ *n* aroma *m*

arose /əˈrəʊz/ ⇒ARISE

around /əˈraʊnd/ *adv* alrededor; (near) cerca. **all ~** por todas partes. ● *prep* alrededor de; (with time) a eso de

arouse /əˈraʊz/ *vt* despertar

arrange /əˈreɪndʒ/ *vt* arreglar; (fix) fijar. **~ment** *n* arreglo *m*; (agreement) acuerdo *m*. **~ments** *npl* (plans) preparativos *mpl*

arrears /əˈrɪəz/ *npl* atrasos *mpl*. **in ~** atrasado en el pago (with de)

arrest /əˈrest/ *vt* detener. ● *n* detención *f*. **under ~** detenido

arriv|al /əˈraɪvl/ *n* llegada *f*. **new ~al** recién llegado *m*. **~e** /əˈraɪv/ *vi* llegar

arrogan|ce /ˈærəgəns/ *n* arrogancia *f*. **~t** *a* arrogante. **~tly** *adv* con arrogancia

arrow /ˈærəʊ/ *n* flecha *f*

arse /ɑːs/ *n* (vulg) culo *m*

arsenal /ˈɑːsənl/ *n* arsenal *m*

arsenic /ˈɑːsnɪk/ *n* arsénico *m*

arson /ˈɑːsn/ *n* incendio *m* provocado. **~ist** *n* incendiario *m*

art¹ /ɑːt/ *n* arte *m*. **A~s** *npl* (Univ) Filosofía y Letras *fpl*. **fine ~s** bellas artes *fpl*

art² /ɑːt/ (old use, with thou) ⇒ARE

artery /ˈɑːtərɪ/ *n* arteria *f*

art gallery *n* museo *m* de arte, pinacoteca *f*; <commercial> galería *f* de arte

arthritis /ɑːˈθraɪtɪs/ *n* artritis *f*

article /ˈɑːtɪkl/ *n* artículo *m*. **~ of clothing** prenda *f* de vestir

articulat|e /ɑːˈtɪkjʊlət/ *a* <utterance> articulado; <person> que sabe expresarse. ● /ɑːˈtɪkjʊleɪt/ *vt/i* articular. **~ed lorry** *n* camión *m* articulado. **~ion** /-ˈleɪʃn/ *n* articulación *f*

artificial /ɑːtɪˈfɪʃl/ *a* artificial. **~ respiration** respiración *f* artificial

artillery /ɑːˈtɪlərɪ/ *n* artillería *f*

artist /ˈɑːtɪst/ *n* artista *m & f*. **~tic** /ɑːˈtɪstɪk/ *a* artístico. **~ry** /ˈɑːtɪstrɪ/ *n* arte *m*, habilidad *f*

as /æz, əz/ *adv & conj* como; (since) ya que; (while) mientras. **~ big ~** tan grande como. **~ far ~** (distance) hasta; (qualitative) en cuanto a. **~ far ~ I know** que yo sepa. **~ if** como si. **~ long ~** mientras. **~ much ~** tanto como. **~ soon ~** tan pronto como. **~ well** también

asbestos /æzˈbestɒs/ *n* amianto *m*, asbesto *m*

ascen|d /əˈsend/ *vt/i* subir. **A~sion** /əˈsenʃn/ *n*. **the A~sion** la Ascensión. **~t** /əˈsent/ *n* subida *f*

ascertain /æsəˈteɪn/ *vt* averiguar

ash /æʃ/ *n* ceniza *f*. ● *n*. **~ (tree)** fresno *m*

ashamed /əˈʃeɪmd/ *a* avergonzado (of de). **be ~ of s.o.** avergonzarse de uno

ashore /əˈʃɔː(r)/ *adv* a tierra. **go ~** desembarcar

ash: ~tray *n* cenicero *m*. **A~ Wednesday** *n* Miércoles *m* de Ceniza

Asia /ˈeɪʃə/ *n* Asia *f*. **~n** *a & n* asiático (*m*). **~tic** /-ɪˈætɪk/ *a* asiático

aside /əˈsaɪd/ *adv* a un lado. ● *n* (in theatre) aparte *m*

ask /ɑːsk/ *vt* pedir; hacer <question>; (invite) invitar. **~ about** enterarse de. **~ s.o. to do something** pedirle a uno que haga algo. □ **~ after** *vt* preguntar por. □ **~ for** *vt*. **~ for help**

pedir ayuda. ~ **for trouble** buscarse problemas. □ ~ **in** vt. ~ **s.o. in** invitar a uno a pasar

askew /ə'skju:/ adv & a torcido

asleep /ə'sli:p/ adv & a dormido. **fall** ~ dormirse

asparagus /ə'spærəgəs/ n espárrago m

aspect /'æspekt/ n aspecto m

asphalt /'æsfælt/ n asfalto m. ● vt asfaltar

aspir|ation /æspə'reɪʃn/ n aspiración f. ~**e** /əs'paɪə(r)/ vi aspirar

aspirin /'æsprɪn/ n aspirina f

ass /æs/ n asno m; (fig, 🔲) imbécil m; (Amer vulg) culo m

assassin /ə'sæsɪn/ n asesino m. ~**ate** /-eɪt/ vt asesinar. ~**ation** /-'eɪʃn/ n asesinato m

assault /ə'sɔ:lt/ n (Mil) ataque m; (Jurid) atentado m. ● vt asaltar

assembl|e /ə'sembl/ vt reunir; (Mec) montar. ● vi reunirse. ~**y** n reunión f, (Pol etc) asamblea f. ~**y line** n línea f de montaje

assent /ə'sent/ n asentimiento m. ● vi asentir

assert /ə'sɜ:t/ vt afirmar; hacer valer <one's rights>. ~**ion** /-ʃn/ n afirmación f. ~**ive** a positivo, firme

assess /ə'ses/ vt evaluar; (determine) determinar; fijar <tax etc>. ~**ment** n evaluación f

asset /'æset/ n (advantage) ventaja f. ~**s** npl (Com) bienes mpl

assign /ə'saɪn/ vt asignar; (appoint) nombrar. ~**ment** n asignación f; (mission) misión f; (task) función f; (for school) trabajo m

assimilate /ə'sɪmɪleɪt/ vt asimilar. ● vi asimilarse

assist /ə'sɪst/ vt/i ayudar. ~**ance** n ayuda f. ~**ant** n ayudante m & f; (shop) dependienta f, dependiente m. ● a auxiliar, adjunto

associat|e /ə'səʊʃɪeɪt/ vt asociar. ● vi asociarse. ● /ə'səʊʃɪət/ a asociado. ● n colega m & f; (Com) socio m. ~**ion** /-'eɪʃn/ n asociación f.

assort|ed /ə'sɔ:tɪd/ a surtido. ~**ment** n surtido m

assum|e /ə'sju:m/ vt suponer; tomar <power, attitude>; asumir <role, burden>. ~**ption** /ə'sʌmpʃn/ n suposición f

assur|ance /ə'ʃʊərəns/ n seguridad f; (insurance) seguro m. ~**e** /ə'ʃʊə(r)/ vt asegurar. ~**ed** a seguro

asterisk /'æstərɪsk/ n asterisco m

asthma /'æsmə/ n asma f. ~**tic** /-'mætɪk/ a & n asmático (m)

astonish /ə'stɒnɪʃ/ vt asombrar. ~**ed** adj asombrado. ~**ing** a asombroso. ~**ment** n asombro m

astound /ə'staʊnd/ vt asombrar. ~**ed** adj atónito. ~**ing** adj increíble

astray /ə'streɪ/ adv. **go** ~ extraviarse. **lead** ~ llevar por mal camino

astrology /ə'strɒlədʒɪ/ n astrología f

astronaut /'æstrənɔ:t/ n astronauta m & f

astronom|er /ə'strɒnəmə(r)/ n astrónomo m. ~**ical** /æstrə'nɒmɪkl/ a astronómico. ~**y** /ə'strɒnəmɪ/ n astronomía f

astute /ə'stju:t/ a astuto

asylum /ə'saɪləm/ n asilo m. **lunatic** ~ manicomio m

....

at /æt/, *unstressed form* /ət/

● *preposition*

····▸ (location) en. **she's at the office** está en la oficina. **at home** en casa. **call me at the office** llámame a la oficina

⟹ For translations of phrases such as **at the top, at the front of, at the back of** see entries **top, front** etc

····▸ (at the house of) en casa de. **I'll be at Rachel's** estaré en casa de Rachel, voy a estar donde Rachel (LAm)

····▸ (talking about time) **at 7 o'clock** a las siete. **at night** por la noche, de noche, en la noche (LAm). **at Christmas** en Navidad

····▸ (talking about age) a. **at six (years of age)** a los seis años

····▸ (with measurements, numbers etc) a. **at 60 miles an hour** a 60 millas por hora. **at a depth of** a una profundidad de. **three at a time** de tres en tres

⟹ For translations of phrasal verbs with **at**, such as **look at**, see entries for those verbs

....

ate /et/ ⇒EAT

atheis|m /'eɪθɪɪzəm/ n ateísmo m.
~**t** n ateo m

athlet|e /'æθliːt/ n atleta m & f. ~**ic**
/-'letɪk/ a atlético. ~**ics** npl atletismo m; (Amer, Sport) deportes mpl

Atlantic /ət'læntɪk/ a atlántico. ● n.
the ~ (Ocean) el (Océano) Atlántico

atlas /'ætləs/ n atlas m

ATM abbr (= **automated teller
machine**) cajero m automático

atmospher|e /'ætməsfɪə(r)/ n
atmósfera f; (fig) ambiente m. ~**ic**
/-'ferɪk/ a atmosférico

atom /'ætəm/ n átomo m. ~**ic**
/ə'tɒmɪk/ a atómico

atroci|ous /ə'trəʊʃəs/ a atroz. ~**ty**
/ə'trɒsəti/ n atrocidad f

attach /ə'tætʃ/ vt sujetar; adjuntar
<document etc>. be ~**ed to** (be fond of)
tener cariño a. ~**ment** n (affection)
cariño m; (tool) accesorio m

attack /ə'tæk/ n ataque m. ● vt/i
atacar. ~**er** n agresor m

attain /ə'teɪn/ vt conseguir. ~**able**
a alcanzable

attempt /ə'tempt/ vt intentar. ● n
tentativa f; (attack) atentado m

attend /ə'tend/ vt asistir a; (escort)
acompañar. ● vi prestar atención.
□ ~ **to** vt (look after) ocuparse de.
~**ance** n asistencia f; (people present)
concurrencia f

atten|tion /ə'tenʃn/ n atención f.
~**tion!** (Mil) ¡firmes! **pay** ~**tion** prestar atención. ~**tive** a atento

attic /'ætɪk/ n desván m

attire /ə'taɪə(r)/ n atavío m. ● vt
ataviar

attitude /'ætɪtjuːd/ n postura f

attorney /ə'tɜːnɪ/ n (pl -**eys**) (Amer)
abogado m

attract /ə'trækt/ vt atraer. ~**ion**
/-ʃn/ n atracción f; (charm) atractivo
m. ~**ive** a atractivo; (interesting) atrayente

attribute /ə'trɪbjuːt/ vt atribuir.
● /'ætrɪbjuːt/ n atributo m

aubergine /'əʊbəʒiːn/ n berenjena f

auction /'ɔːkʃn/ n subasta f. ● vt su-
bastar. ~**eer** /-ə'nɪə(r)/ n subasta-
dor m

audaci|ous /ɔː'deɪʃəs/ a audaz.
~**ty** /ɔː'dæsəti/ n audacia f

audible /'ɔːdəbl/ a audible

audience /'ɔːdɪəns/ n (at play, film)
público m; (TV) audiencia f; (interview)
audiencia f

audiovisual /ɔːdɪəʊ'vɪʒʊəl/ a audiovisual

audit /'ɔːdɪt/ n revisión f de cuentas.
● vt revisar

audition /ɔː'dɪʃn/ n audición f. ● vt
hacerle una audición a. ● vi dar una
audición (for para)

auditor /'ɔːdɪtə(r)/ n interventor m
de cuentas

auditorium /ɔːdɪ'tɔːrɪəm/ (pl
-**riums** or -**ria** /-rɪə/) n sala f, audi-
torio m

augment /ɔːg'ment/ vt aumentar

augur /'ɔːgə(r)/ vt augurar. **it** ~**s well**
es de buen agüero

August /'ɔːgəst/ n agosto m

aunt /ɑːnt/ n tía f

au pair /əʊ'peə(r)/ n chica f au pair

aura /'ɔːrə/ n aura f, halo m

auster|e /ɔː'stɪə(r)/ a austero. ~**ity**
/ɔː'sterəti/ n austeridad f

Australia /ɒ'streɪlɪə/ n Australia f.
~**n** a & n australiano (m)

Austria /'ɒstrɪə/ n Austria f. ~**n** a &
n austríaco (m)

authentic /ɔː'θentɪk/ a auténtico.
~**ate** /-keɪt/ vt autenticar. ~**ity**
/-ən'tɪsəti/ n autenticidad f

author /'ɔːθə(r)/ n autor m. ~**ess**
/-ɪs/ n autora f

authoritative /ɔː'θɒrɪtətɪv/ a auto-
rizado; (manner) autoritario

authority /ɔː'θɒrəti/ n autoridad f;
(permission) autorización f

authoriz|ation /ɔːθəraɪ'zeɪʃn/ n
autorización f. ~**e** /'ɔːθəraɪz/ vt autorizar

autobiography /ɔːtəʊbaɪ'ɒgrəfi/ n
autobiografía f

autograph /'ɔːtəgrɑːf/ n autógrafo
m. ● vt firmar, autografiar

automat|e /'ɔːtəmeɪt/ vt automati-
zar. ~**ic** /-'mætɪk/ a automático.
~**ion** /-'meɪʃn/ n automatización f.
~**on** /ɔː'tɒmətən/ n (pl -**tons** or -**ta**
/-tə/) autómata m

automobile /'ɔ:təməbi:l/ n (Amer) coche m, carro m (LAm), automóvil m

autonom|ous /ɔ:'tɒnəməs/ a autónomo. **~y** n autonomía f

autopsy /'ɔ:tɒpsɪ/ n autopsia f

autumn /'ɔ:təm/ n otoño m. **~al** /ɔ:'tʌmnəl/ a otoñal

auxiliary /ɔ:g'zɪlɪərɪ/ a & n auxiliar (m & f)

avail /ə'veɪl/ n. to no **~** inútil

availab|ility /əveɪlə'bɪlətɪ/ n disponibilidad f. **~le** /ə'veɪləbl/ a disponible

avalanche /'ævəlɑ:nʃ/ n avalancha f

avaric|e /'ævərɪs/ n avaricia f. **~ious** /-'rɪʃəs/ a avaro

avenue /'ævənju:/ n avenida f; (fig) vía f

average /'ævərɪdʒ/ n promedio m. on **~** por término medio. ● a medio

avers|e /ə'vɜ:s/ a. be **~e** to ser reacio a. **~ion** /-ʃn/ n repugnancia f

avert /ə'vɜ:t/ vt (turn away) apartar; (ward off) desviar

aviation /eɪvɪ'eɪʃn/ n aviación f

avid /'ævɪd/ a ávido

avocado /ævə'kɑ:dəʊ/ n (pl **-os**) aguacate m

avoid /ə'vɔɪd/ vt evitar. **~able** a evitable. **~ance** n el evitar

await /ə'weɪt/ vt esperar

awake /ə'weɪk/ vt/i (pt **awoke**, pp **awoken**) despertar. ● a despierto. wide **~** completamente despierto; (fig) despabilado. **~n** /ə'weɪkən/ vt/i despertar. **~ning** n el despertar

award /ə'wɔ:d/ vt otorgar; (Jurid) adjudicar. ● n premio m; (Jurid) adjudicación f; (scholarship) beca f

aware /ə'weə(r)/ a. be **~** of sth ser consciente de algo, darse cuenta de algo

awash /ə'wɒʃ/ a inundado

away /ə'weɪ/ adv (absent) fuera. far **~** muy lejos. ● a **~** match partido m fuera de casa

awe /ɔ:/ n temor m. **~-inspiring** a impresionante. **~some** /-səm/ a imponente

awful /'ɔ:fʊl/ a terrible, malísimo. feel **~** sentirse muy mal

awkward /'ɔ:kwəd/ a difícil; (inconvenient) inoportuno; (clumsy) desmañado; (embarrassed) incómodo. **~ness** n dificultad f; (discomfort) molestia f; (clumsiness) torpeza f

awning /'ɔ:nɪŋ/ n toldo m

awoke /ə'wəʊk/, **awoken** /ə'wəʊkən/ ⇨AWAKE

axe /æks/ n hacha f. ● vt (pres p **axing**) cortar con hacha; (fig) recortar

axis /'æksɪs/ n (pl **axes** /-i:z/) eje m

axle /'æksl/ n eje m

....

Bb

....

BA /bi:'eɪ/ abbr ⇨BACHELOR

babble /'bæbl/ vi balbucir; (chatter) parlotear; <stream> murmullar.

baboon /bə'bu:n/ n mandril m

baby /'beɪbɪ/ n niño m, bebé m. **~ buggy**, **~ carriage** n (Amer) cochecito m. **~ish** /'beɪbɪʃ/ a infantil. **~-sit** vi cuidar a los niños, hacer de canguro. **~-sitter** n baby sitter m & f, canguro m & f

bachelor /'bætʃələ(r)/ n soltero m. B**~ of Arts** (BA) licenciado m en filosofía y letras. B**~ of Science** (BSc) licenciado m en ciencias

back /bæk/ n espalda f; (of car) parte f trasera; (of chair) respaldo m; (of cloth) revés m; (of house) parte f de atrás; (of animal, book) lomo m; (of hand, document) dorso m; (football) defensa m & f. in the **~** of beyond en el quinto infierno. ● a trasero. the **~** door la puerta trasera. ● adv atrás; (returned) de vuelta. ● vt apoyar; (betting) apostar a; dar marcha atrás a <car>. ● vi retroceder; <car> dar marcha atrás. □ **~** **down** vi volverse atrás. □ **~** **out** vi retirarse. □ **~** **up** vt apoyar; (Comp) hacer una copia de seguridad de. **~ache** n dolor m de espalda. **~bone** n columna f vertebral; (fig) pilar m. **~date** /-'deɪt/ vt antedatar. **~er** n partidario m; (Com) financiador *m*. ~**fire** /-'faɪə(r)/ *vi* (Auto) petardear; (fig) fallar. **his plan** ~**fired on him** le salió el tiro por la culata. ~**ground** *n* fondo *m*; (environment) antecedentes *mpl*. ~**hand** *n* (Sport) revés *m*. ~**ing** *n* apoyo *m*. ~**lash** *n* reacción *f*. ~**log** *n* atrasos *mpl*. ~**side** /-'saɪd/ *n* 🔲 trasero *m*. ~**stage** /-'steɪdʒ/ *a* de bastidores. ● *adv* entre bastidores. ~**stroke** *n* (tennis etc) revés *m*; (swimming) estilo *m* espalda, estilo *m* dorso (Mex). ~**up** *n* apoyo *m*; (Comp) copia *f* de seguridad. ~**ward** /-wəd/ *a* <*step etc*> hacia atrás; (retarded) retrasado; (undeveloped) atrasado. ● *adv* (Amer) ⇒BACK-WARDS. ~**wards** *adv* hacia atrás; (fall) de espaldas; (back to front) al revés. **go** ~**wards and forwards** ir de acá para allá. ~**water** *n* agua *f* estancada; (fig) lugar *m* apartado

bacon /'beɪkən/ *n* tocino *m*

bacteria /bæk'tɪərɪə/ *npl* bacterias *fpl*

bad /bæd/ *a* (**worse, worst**) malo, (before masculine singular noun) mal; (serious) grave; (harmful) nocivo; <*language*> indecente. **feel** ~ sentirse mal

bade /beɪd/ ⇒BID

badge /bædʒ/ *n* distintivo *m*, chapa *f*

badger /'bædʒə(r)/ *n* tejón *m*. ● *vt* acosar

bad: ~**ly** *adv* mal. **want** ~**ly** desear muchísimo. ~**ly injured** gravemente herido. ~**ly off** mal de dinero. ~**-mannered** /-'mænəd/ *a* mal educado

badminton /'bædmɪntən/ *n* bádminton *m*

bad-tempered /bæd'tempəd/ *a* (always) de mal carácter; (temporarily) de mal humor

baffle /'bæfl/ *vt* desconcertar. ~**d** *a* perplejo

bag /bæg/ *n* bolsa *f*; (handbag) bolso *m*. ● *vt* (*pt* **bagged**) ensacar; (take) coger (esp Spain), agarrar (LAm). ~**s** *npl* (luggage) equipaje *m*. ~**s of** 🔲 montones de

baggage /'bægɪdʒ/ *n* equipaje *m*. ~**room** *n* (Amer) consigna *f*

baggy /'bægɪ/ *a* <*clothes*> holgado

bagpipes /'bægpaɪps/ *npl* gaita *f*

bail[1] /beɪl/ *n* fianza *f*. ● *vt* poner en libertad bajo fianza. ~ **s.o. out** pagar la fianza a uno

bail[2] *vt*. ~ **out** (Naut) achicar

bait /beɪt/ *n* cebo *m*

bak|e /beɪk/ *vt* cocer al horno. ● *vi* cocerse. ~**er** *n* panadero *m*. ~**ery** *n* panadería *f*

balance /'bæləns/ *n* equilibrio *m*; (Com) balance *m*; (sum) saldo *m*; (scales) balanza *f*; (remainder) resto *m*. ● *vt* equilibrar <*load*>; mantener en equilibrio <*object*>; nivelar <*budget*>. ● *vi* equilibrarse; (Com) cuadrar. ~**d** *a* equilibrado

balcony /'bælkənɪ/ *n* balcón *m*

bald /bɔːld/ *a* (**-er, -est**) calvo, pelón (Mex)

bale /beɪl/ *n* bala *f*, fardo *m*. ● *vi*. ~ **out** lanzarse en paracaídas

Balearic /bælɪ'ærɪk/ *a*. **the** ~ **Islands** las Islas *fpl* Baleares

ball /bɔːl/ *n* bola *f*; (tennis etc) pelota *f*; (football etc) balón *m*, pelota *f* (esp LAm); (of yarn) ovillo *m*; (dance) baile *m*

ballad /'bæləd/ *n* balada *f*

ballast /'bæləst/ *n* lastre *m*

ball bearing *n* cojinete *m* de bolas

ballerina /bælə'riːnə/ *f* bailarina *f*

ballet /'bæleɪ/ *n* ballet *m*. ~ **dancer** *n* bailarín *m* de ballet, bailarina *f* de ballet

balloon /bə'luːn/ *n* globo *m*

ballot /'bælət/ *n* votación *f*. ~ **box** *n* urna *f*. ~ **paper** *n* papeleta *f*.

ball: ~**point** *n*. ~**point** (pen) bolígrafo *m*, pluma *f* atómica (Mex). ~**room** *n* salón *m* de baile

bamboo /bæm'buː/ *n* bambú *m*

ban /bæn/ *vt* (*pt* **banned**) prohibir. ~ **s.o. from sth** prohibir algo a uno. ● *n* prohibición *f*

banal /bə'nɑːl/ *a* banal. ~**ity** /bə'nælətɪ/ *n* banalidad *f*

banana /bə'nɑːnə/ *n* plátano *m*

band /bænd/ *n* (strip) banda *f*. ● *n* (Mus) orquesta *f*; (military, brass) banda *f*. □ ~ **together** *vi* juntarse

bandage /'bændɪdʒ/ n venda f. ● vt vendar

Band-Aid /'bændeɪd/ n (Amer, P) tirita f, curita f (LAm)

B & B /'biːənbiː/ abbr (= **bed and breakfast**) cama f y desayuno; (place) pensión f

bandit /'bændɪt/ n bandido m

band: ~**stand** n quiosco m de música. ~**wagon** n. **jump on the** ~**wagon** (fig) subirse al carro

bandy /'bændɪ/ a (**-ier, -iest**) patizambo

bang /bæŋ/ n (noise) ruido m; (blow) golpe m; (of gun) estampido m; (of door) golpe m. ● vt (strike) golpear. ~ **the door** dar un portazo. ● adv exactamente. ● int ¡pum! ~**s** npl (Amer) flequillo m, cerquillo m (LAm), fleco m (Mex)

banger /'bæŋə(r)/ n petardo m; (🔲, Culin) salchicha f

bangle /'bæŋgl/ n brazalete m

banish /'bænɪʃ/ vt desterrar

banisters /'bænɪstəz/ npl pasamanos m

banjo /'bændʒəʊ/ n (pl **-os**) banjo m

bank /bæŋk/ n (Com) banco m; (of river) orilla f. ● vt depositar. ● vi (Aviat) ladearse. □ ~ **on** vt contar con. □ ~ **with** vi tener una cuenta con. ~ **card** n tarjeta f bancaria; (Amer) tarjeta f de crédito (expedida por un banco). ~**er** n banquero m. ~ **holiday** n día m festivo, día m feriado (LAm). ~**ing** n (Com) banca f. ~**note** n billete m de banco

bankrupt /'bæŋkrʌpt/ a & n quebrado (m). **go** ~ quebrar. ● vt hacer quebrar. ~**cy** /-rʌpsɪ/ n bancarrota f, quiebra f

bank statement n estado m de cuenta

banner /'bænə(r)/ n bandera f; (in demonstration) pancarta f

banquet /'bæŋkwɪt/ n banquete m

banter /'bæntə(r)/ n chanza f

bap /bæp/ n panecillo m blando

baptism /'bæptɪzəm/ n bautismo m; (act) bautizo m

Baptist /'bæptɪst/ n bautista m & f

baptize /bæp'taɪz/ vt bautizar

bar /bɑː(r)/ n barra f; (on window) reja f; (of chocolate) tableta f; (of soap) pastilla f; (pub) bar m; (Mus) compás m; (Jurid) abogacia f; (fig) obstáculo m. ● vt (pt **barred**) atrancar <door>; (exclude) excluir; (prohibit) prohibir. ● prep excepto

barbar|ian /bɑː'beərɪən/ a & n bárbaro (m). ~**ic** /bɑː'bærɪk/ a bárbaro

barbecue /'bɑːbɪkjuː/ n barbacoa f. ● vt asar a la parilla

barbed wire /bɑːbd 'waɪə(r)/ n alambre m de púas

barber /'bɑːbə(r)/ n peluquero m, barbero m

barbwire /'bɑːbˈwaɪə(r)/ n (Amer) ⇒BARBED WIRE

bare /beə(r)/ a (**-er, -est**) desnudo; (room) con pocos muebles; (mere) simple; (empty) vacío. ● vt desnudar; (uncover) descubrir. ~ **one's teeth** mostrar los dientes. ~**back** adv a pelo. ~**faced** a descarado. ~**foot** a descalzo. ~**headed** /-'hedɪd/ a descubierto. ~**ly** adv apenas.

bargain /'bɑːgɪn/ n (agreement) pacto m; (good buy) ganga f. ● vi negociar; (haggle) regatear. □ ~ **for** vt esperar, contar con

barge /bɑːdʒ/ n barcaza f. ● vi. ~ **in** irrumpir

baritone /'bærɪtəʊn/ n barítono m

bark /bɑːk/ n (of dog) ladrido m; (of tree) corteza f. ● vi ladrar

barley /'bɑːlɪ/ n cebada f

bar: ~**maid** n camarera f. ~**man** /-mən/ n camarero m, barman m

barmy /'bɑːmɪ/ a 🔲 chiflado

barn /bɑːn/ n granero m

barometer /bə'rɒmɪtə(r)/ n barómetro m

baron /'bærən/ n barón m. ~**ess** /-ɪs/ n baronesa f

barracks /'bærəks/ npl cuartel m

barrage /'bærɑːʒ/ n (Mil) barrera f; (dam) presa f. **a** ~ **of questions** un aluvión de preguntas

barrel /'bærəl/ n barril m; (of gun) cañón m

barren /'bærən/ a estéril

barrette /bə'ret/ n (Amer) pasador m

barricade /ˈbærɪˈkeɪd/ n barricada f. ● vt cerrar con barricadas

barrier /ˈbærɪə(r)/ n barrera f

barring /ˈbɑːrɪŋ/ prep salvo

barrister /ˈbærɪstə(r)/ n abogado m

bartender /ˈbɑːtendə(r)/ n (Amer) (male) camarero m, barman m; (female) camarera f

barter /ˈbɑːtə(r)/ n trueque m. ● vt trocar

base /beɪs/ n base f. ● vt basar. ~**ball** n béisbol m, beisbol m (Mex)

basement /ˈbeɪsmənt/ n sótano m

bash /bæʃ/ vt golpear. ● n golpe m. have a ~ ⊞ probar

bashful /ˈbæʃfl/ a tímido

basic /ˈbeɪsɪk/ a básico, fundamental. ~**ally** adv fundamentalmente

basin /ˈbeɪsn/ n (for washing) palangana f; (for food) cuenco m; (Geog) cuenca f

basis /ˈbeɪsɪs/ n (pl **bases** /-siːz/) base f

bask /bɑːsk/ vi asolearse; (fig) gozar (in de)

basket /ˈbɑːskɪt/ n cesta f; (big) cesto m. ~**ball** n baloncesto m, básquetbol m (LAm)

bass /beɪs/ a bajo. ● n (Mus) bajo m

bassoon /bəˈsuːn/ n fagot m

bastard /ˈbɑːstəd/ n bastardo m. you ~! (⊞ or vulg) ¡cabrón! (⊞ or vulg)

bat /bæt/ n (for baseball, cricket) bate m; (for table tennis) raqueta f; (mammal) murciélago m. off one's own ~ por sí solo. ● vt (pt **batted**) golpear. without ~**ting an eyelid** sin pestañear. ● vi batear

batch /bætʃ/ n (of people) grupo m; (of papers) pila f; (of goods) remesa f; (of bread) hornada f; (Comp) lote m

bated /ˈbeɪtɪd/ a. with ~ **breath** con aliento entrecortado

bath /bɑːθ/ n (pl -s /bɑːðz/) baño m; (tub) bañera f, tina f (LAm). ~**s** (swimming pool) piscina f, alberca f (LAm). have a ~, take a ~ (Amer) bañarse. ● vt bañar. ● vi bañarse

bathe /beɪð/ vt bañar. ● vi bañarse. ● n baño m. ~**r** n bañista m & f

bathing /ˈbeɪðɪŋ/ n baños mpl. ~ **costume**, ~ **suit** n traje m de baño

bathroom /ˈbɑːθrʊm/ n cuarto m de baño; (Amer, toilet) servicio m, baño m (LAm)

batsman /ˈbætsmən/ n (pl -**men**) bateador m

battalion /bəˈtælɪən/ n batallón m

batter /ˈbætə(r)/ vt (beat) apalear; (cover with batter) rebozar. ● n batido m para rebozar; (Amer, for cake) masa f. ~**ed** /ˈbætəd/ a <car etc> estropeado; <wife etc> maltratado

battery /ˈbætərɪ/ n (Mil, Auto) batería f; (of torch, radio) pila f

battle /ˈbætl/ n batalla f; (fig) lucha f. ● vi luchar. ~**field** n campo m de batalla. ~**ship** n acorazado m

bawl /bɔːl/ vt/i gritar

bay /beɪ/ n (Geog) bahía f. keep at ~ mantener a raya

bayonet /ˈbeɪənet/ n bayoneta f

bay window /beɪ ˈwɪndəʊ/ n ventana f salediza

bazaar /bəˈzɑː(r)/ n bazar m

BC abbr (= **before Christ**) a. de C., antes de Cristo

be /biː/

present **am, are, is**; past **was, were**; past participle **been**

● intransitive verb

! Spanish has two verbs meaning be, ser and estar. ■ See those entries for further information about the differences between them.

⋯➤ (position, changed condition or state) estar. **where is the library?** ¿dónde está la biblioteca? **she's tired** está cansada. **how are you?** ¿cómo estás?

⋯➤ (identity, nature or permanent characteristics) ser. **she's tall** es alta. **he's Scottish** es escocés. **I'm a journalist** soy periodista. **he's very kind** es muy bondadoso

⋯➤ (feel) **to be** + adjective tener + sustantivo. **to be cold/hot** tener frío/calor. **he's hungry/thirsty** tiene hambre/sed

⋯➤ (age) **he's thirty** tiene treinta años

····▸ (weather) **it's cold/hot** hace frío/calor. **it was 40 degrees** hacía 40 grados

● *auxiliary verb*

····▸ (in tenses) estar. **I'm working** estoy trabajando. **they were singing** estaban cantando, cantaban

····▸ (in tag questions) **it's a beautiful house, isn't it?** es una casa preciosa, ¿verdad? *or* ¿no? *or* ¿no es cierto?

····▸ (in short answers) **are you disappointed? - yes, I am** ¿estás desilusionado? - sí (,lo estoy). **I'm surprised, aren't you?** estoy sorprendido, ¿tú no?

····▸ (in passive sentences) **it was built in 1834** fue construido en 1834, se construyó en 1834. **she was told that ...** le dijeron que..., se le dijo que ...

❗ Note that passive sentences in English are often translated using the pronoun *se* or using the third person plural.

beach /biːtʃ/ *n* playa *f*

beacon /'biːkən/ *n* faro *m*

bead /biːd/ *n* cuenta *f*; (of glass) abalorio *m*

beak /biːk/ *n* pico *m*

beaker /'biːkə(r)/ *n* taza *f* (alta y sin asa)

beam /biːm/ *n* (of wood) viga *f*; (of light) rayo *m*; (Naut) bao *m*. ● *vt* emitir. ● *vi* irradiar; (smile) sonreír

bean /biːn/ *n* alubia *f*, frijol *m* (LAm); (broad bean) haba *f*; (of coffee) grano *m*

bear /beə(r)/ *vt* (*pt* **bore**, *pp* **borne**) llevar; parir <*niño*>; (endure) soportar. ~ **right** torcer a la derecha. ~ **in mind** tener en cuenta. □ ~ **with** *vt* tener paciencia con. ● *n* oso *m*. ~**able** *a* soportable

beard /bɪəd/ *n* barba *f*. ~**ed** *a* barbudo

bearer /'beərə(r)/ *n* portador *m*; (of passport) titular *m & f*

bearing /'beərɪŋ/ *n* comportamiento *m*; (relevance) relación *f*; (Mec) cojinete *m*. **get one's** ~**s** orientarse. **lose one's** ~**s** desorientarse

beast /biːst/ *n* bestia *f*; (person) bruto *m*. ~**ly** *a* (**-ier**, **-iest**) bestial; (T) horrible

beat /biːt/ *vt* (*pt* **beat**, *pp* **beaten**) (hit) pegar; (Culin) batir; (defeat) derrotar; (better) sobrepasar; batir <*record*>; (baffle) dejar perplejo. ~ **it** (T) largarse. ● *vi* <*heart*> latir. ● *n* latido *m*; (Mus) ritmo *m*; (of policeman) ronda *f*. □ ~ **up** *vt* darle una paliza a; (Culin) batir. ~ **up on** (Amer, (T)) darle una paliza a.. ~**er** *n* batidor *m*. ~**ing** *n* paliza *f*

beautician /bjuː'tɪʃn/ *n* esteticista *m & f*

beautiful /'bjuːtɪfl/ *a* hermoso. ~**ly** *adv* maravillosamente

beauty /'bjuːtɪ/ *n* belleza *f*. ~ **salon**, ~ **shop** (Amer) *n* salón *m* de belleza. ~ **spot** *n* (on face) lunar *m*; (site) lugar *m* pintoresco

beaver /'biːvə(r)/ *n* castor *m*

became /bɪ'keɪm/ ⇒BECOME

because /bɪ'knz/ *conj* porque. ● *adv*. ~ **of** por, a causa de

beckon /'bekən/ *vt/i*. ~ (**to**) hacer señas (a)

become /bɪ'kʌm/ *vi* (*pt* **became**, *pp* **become**) hacerse, llegar a ser, volverse, convertirse en. **what has** ~ **of her?** ¿qué es de ella?

bed /bed/ *n* cama *f*; (layer) estrato *m*; (of sea, river) fondo *m*; (of flowers) macizo *m*. **go to** ~ acostarse. ● *vi* (*pt* **bedded**). ~ **and breakfast** (B & B) cama y desayuno; (place) pensión *f*. ~**bug** *n* chinche *f*. ~**clothes** *npl*, ~**ding** *n* ropa *f* de cama, cobijas *fpl* (LAm)

bed: ~**room** *n* dormitorio *m*, cuarto *m*, habitación *f*, recámara *f* (Mex). ~**-sitter** /-'sɪtə(r)/ *n* habitación *f* con cama y uso de cocina y baño compartidos, estudio *m*. ~**spread** *n* colcha *f*. ~**time** *n* hora *f* de acostarse

bee /biː/ *n* abeja *f*; (Amer, social gathering) círculo *m*

beech /biːtʃ/ *n* haya *f*

beef /biːf/ *n* carne *f* de vaca, carne *f* de res (Mex). ● *vi* (T) quejarse. ~**burger** *n* hamburguesa *f*. ~**y** *a* (**-ier**, **-iest**) musculoso

bee: ~**hive** *n* colmena *f*. ~**line** *n*. **make a** ~**line for** ir en línea recta hacia

been /biːn/ ⇒BE

beer /bɪə(r)/ n cerveza f

beet /biːt/ n (Amer) remolacha f, betabel f (Mex)

beetle /biːtl/ n escarabajo m

beetroot /'biːtruːt/ n invar remolacha f, betabel f (Mex)

befall /bɪ'fɔːl/ vt (pt **befell**, pp **befallen**) ocurrirle a. ● vi ocurrir

before /bɪ'fɔː(r)/ prep (time) antes de; (place) delante de. ~ **leaving** antes de marcharse. ● adv (place) delante; (time) antes. **a week** ~ una semana antes. **the week** ~ la semana anterior. ● conj (time) antes de que. ~ **he leaves** antes de que se vaya. ~**hand** adv de antemano

befriend /bɪ'frend/ vt hacerse amigo de

beg /beg/ vt/i (pt **begged**) mendigar; (entreat) suplicar; (ask) pedir. ~ **s.o.'s pardon** pedir perdón a uno. **I** ~ **your pardon!** ¡perdone Vd! **I** ~ **your pardon?** ¿cómo?

began /bɪ'gæn/ ⇒BEGIN

beggar /'begə(r)/ n mendigo m

begin /bɪ'gɪn/ vt/i (pt **began**, pp **begun**, pres p **beginning**) comenzar, empezar. ~**ner** n principiante m & f. ~**ning** n principio m

begrudge /bɪ'grʌdʒ/ vt envidiar; (give) dar de mala gana

begun /bɪ'gʌn/ ⇒BEGIN

behalf /bɪ'hɑːf/ n. **on** ~ **of**, **in** ~ **of** (Amer) de parte de, en nombre de

behav|e /bɪ'heɪv/ vi comportarse, portarse. ~**e** (o.s.) portarse bien. ~**iour** /bɪ'heɪvjə(r)/ n comportamiento m

behead /bɪ'hed/ vt decapitar

behind /bɪ'haɪnd/ prep detrás de, atrás de (LAm). ● adv detrás; (late) atrasado. ● n 🔲 trasero m

beige /beɪʒ/ a & n beige (m)

being /'biːɪŋ/ n ser m. **come into** ~ nacer

belated /bɪ'leɪtɪd/ a tardío

belch /beltʃ/ vi eructar. □ ~ **out** vt arrojar <smoke>

belfry /'belfrɪ/ n campanario m

Belgi|an /'beldʒən/ a & n belga (m & f). ~**um** /'beldʒəm/ n Bélgica f

belie|f /bɪ'liːf/ n (trust) fe f; (opinion) creencia f. ~**ve** /bɪ'liːv/ vt/i creer. ~**ve in** creer en. **make** ~**ve** fingir

belittle /bɪ'lɪtl/ vt menospreciar <achievements>; denigrar <person>

bell /bel/ n campana f; (on door, bicycle) timbre m

belligerent /bɪ'lɪdʒərənt/ a beligerante

bellow /'beləʊ/ vt gritar. ● vi bramar. ~**s** npl fuelle m

bell pepper n (Amer) pimiento m

belly /'belɪ/ n barriga f

belong /bɪ'lɒŋ/ vi pertenecer (**to** a); (club) ser socio (**to** de); (have as usual place) ir. ~**ings** /bɪ'lɒŋɪŋz/ npl pertenencias fpl. **personal** ~**ings** efectos mpl personales

beloved /bɪ'lʌvɪd/ a querido

below /bɪ'ləʊ/ prep debajo de, abajo de (LAm); (fig) inferior a. ● adv abajo

belt /belt/ n cinturón m; (area) zona f. ● vt (fig) rodear; 🔲 darle una paliza a. ~**way** n (Amer) carretera f de circunvalación

bench /bentʃ/ n banco m

bend /bend/ n curva f. ● vt (pt & pp **bent**) doblar; torcer <arm, leg>. ● vi doblarse; <road> torcerse. □ ~ **down** vi inclinarse □ ~ **over** vi agacharse

beneath /bɪ'niːθ/ prep debajo de; (fig) inferior a. ● adv abajo

beneficial /benɪ'fɪʃl/ a provechoso

beneficiary /benɪ'fɪʃərɪ/ n beneficiario m

benefit /'benɪfɪt/ n provecho m, ventaja f; (allowance) prestación f; (for unemployed) subsidio m; (perk) beneficio m. ● vt (pt **benefited**, pres p **benefiting**) beneficiar. ● vi beneficiarse

benevolent /bə'nevələnt/ a benévolo

benign /bɪ'naɪn/ a benigno

bent /bent/ ⇒BEND. ● n inclinación f. ● a torcido; (🔲, corrupt) corrompido

bereave|d /bɪ'riːvd/ n. **the** ~**d** la familia del difunto. ~**ment** n pérdida f; (mourning) luto m

beret /'bereɪ/ n boina f

berry /'berɪ/ n baya f

berserk /bə'sɜːk/ *a*. **go** ~ volverse loco

berth /bɜːθ/ *n* litera *f*; (anchorage) amarradero *m*. **give a wide** ~ **to** evitar. ● *vt/i* atracar

beside /bɪ'saɪd/ *prep* al lado de. **be** ~ **o.s.** estar fuera de sí

besides /bɪ'saɪdz/ *prep* además de; (except) excepto. ● *adv* además

besiege /bɪ'siːdʒ/ *vt* sitiar, asediar; (fig) acosar

best /best/ *a* (el) mejor. **the** ~ **thing is to...** lo mejor es... ● *adv* mejor. **like** ~ preferir. **in** lo mejor. **at** ~ a lo más. **do one's** ~ hacer todo lo posible. **make the** ~ **of** contentarse con. ~ **man** *n* padrino *m* (de boda)

bestow /bɪ'stəʊ/ *vt* conceder

bestseller /best'selə(r)/ *n* éxito *m* de librería, bestseller *m*

bet /bet/ *n* apuesta *f*. ● *vt/i* (*pt* **bet** *or* **betted**) apostar

betray /bɪ'treɪ/ *vt* traicionar. ~**al** *n* traición *f*

better /'betə(r)/ *a & adv* mejor. ~ **off** en mejores condiciones; (richer) más rico. **get** ~ mejorar. **all the** ~ tanto mejor. **I'd** ~ **be off** me tengo que ir. **the** ~ **part of** la mayor parte de. ● *vt* mejorar; (beat) sobrepasar. ~ **o.s.** superarse. ● *n* superior *m*. **get the** ~ **of** vencer a. **my** ~**s** mis superiores *mpl*

between /bɪ'twiːn/ *prep* entre. ● *adv* en medio

beverage /'bevərɪdʒ/ *n* bebida *f*

beware /bɪ'weə(r)/ *vi* tener cuidado. ● *int* ¡cuidado!

bewilder /bɪ'wɪldə(r)/ *vt* desconcertar. ~**ment** *n* aturdimiento *m*

bewitch /bɪ'wɪtʃ/ *vt* hechizar; (delight) cautivar

beyond /bɪ'jɒnd/ *prep* más allá de; (fig) fuera de. ~ **doubt** sin lugar a duda. ● *adv* más allá

bias /'baɪəs/ *n* tendencia *f*; (prejudice) prejuicio *m*. ● *vt* (*pt* **biased**) influir en. ~**ed** *a* parcial

bib /bɪb/ *n* babero *m*

Bible /'baɪbl/ *n* Biblia *f*

biblical /'bɪblɪkl/ *a* bíblico

bibliography /bɪblɪ'ɒɡrəfɪ/ *n* bibliografía *f*

biceps /'baɪseps/ *n invar* bíceps *m*

bicker /'bɪkə(r)/ *vi* altercar

bicycle /'baɪsɪkl/ *n* bicicleta *f*

bid /bɪd/ *n* (offer) oferta *f*; (attempt) tentativa *f*. ● *vi* hacer una oferta. ● *vt* (*pt & pp* **bid**, *pres p* **bidding**) ofrecer; (*pt* **bid**, *pp* **bidden**, *pres p* **bidding**) mandar; dar <welcome, good day etc>. ~**der** *n* postor *m*. ~**ding** *n* (at auction) ofertas *fpl*; (order) mandato *m*

bide /baɪd/ *vt*. ~ **one's time** esperar el momento oportuno

bifocals /baɪ'fəʊklz/ *npl* gafas *fpl* bifocales, anteojos *mpl* bifocales (LAm)

big /bɪg/ *a* (**bigger**, **biggest**) grande, (before singular noun) gran. ● *adv*. **talk** ~ fanfarronear

bigam|ist /'bɪɡəmɪst/ *n* bígamo *m*. ~**ous** /'bɪɡəməs/ *a* bígamo. ~**y** *n* bigamia *f*

big-headed /-'hedɪd/ *a* engreído

bigot /'bɪɡət/ *n* fanático *m*. ~**ed** *a* fanático

bike /baɪk/ *n* 🄵 bici *f* 🄵

bikini /bɪ'kiːnɪ/ *n* (*pl* **-is**) bikini *m*

bile /baɪl/ *n* bilis *f*

bilingual /baɪ'lɪŋɡwəl/ *a* bilingüe

bill /bɪl/ *n* cuenta *f*; (invoice) factura *f*; (notice) cartel *m*; (Amer, banknote) billete *m*; (Pol) proyecto *m* de ley; (of bird) pico *m*

billet /'bɪlɪt/ *n* (Mil) alojamiento *m*. ● *vt* alojar

billfold /'bɪlfəʊld/ *n* (Amer) cartera *f*, billetera *f*

billiards /'bɪlɪədz/ *n* billar *m*

billion /'bɪlɪən/ *n* billón *m*; (Amer) mil millones *mpl*

bin /bɪn/ *n* recipiente *m*; (for rubbish) cubo *m* de basura, bote *m* de basura (Mex); (for waste paper) papelera *f*

bind /baɪnd/ *vt* (*pt* **bound**) atar; encuadernar <book>; (Jurid) obligar. ● *n* 🄵 lata *f*. ~**ing** *n* (of books) encuadernación *f*; (braid) ribete *m*

binge /bɪndʒ/ *n* 🄳 (of food) comilona *f*; (of drink) borrachera *f*. **go on a** ~ ir de juerga

bingo /'bɪŋɡəʊ/ *n* bingo *m*

binoculars /bɪ'nɒkjʊləz/ *npl* gemelos *mpl*

biograph|er /baɪˈɒgrəfə(r)/ n biógrafo m. **~y** n biografía f

biolog|ical /baɪəˈlɒdʒɪkl/ a biológico. **~ist** /baɪˈɒlədʒɪst/ n biólogo m. **~y** /baɪˈɒlədʒɪ/ n biología f

birch /bɜ:tʃ/ n (tree) abedul m

bird /bɜ:d/ n ave f; (small) pájaro m; (▣, girl) chica f

Biro /ˈbaɪərəʊ/ n (pl **-os**) (P) bolígrafo m

birth /bɜ:θ/ n nacimiento m. **give ~** dar a luz. **~ certificate** n partida f de nacimiento. **~ control** n control m de la natalidad. **~day** n cumpleaños m. **~mark** n marca f de nacimiento. **~place** n lugar m de nacimiento. **~ rate** n natalidad f

biscuit /ˈbɪskɪt/ n galleta f

bisect /baɪˈsekt/ vt bisecar

bishop /ˈbɪʃəp/ n obispo m; (Chess) alfil m

bit /bɪt/ ⇒BITE. ● n trozo m; (quantity) poco m; (of horse) bocado m; (Mec) broca f; (Comp) bit m

bitch /bɪtʃ/ n perra f; (▣, woman) bruja f ▣

bit|e /baɪt/ vt/i (pt **bit**, pp **bitten**) morder; (insect) picar. **~e one's nails** morderse las uñas. ● n mordisco m; (mouthful) bocado m; (of insect etc) picadura f. **~ing** /ˈbaɪtɪŋ/ a mordaz

bitter /ˈbɪtə(r)/ a amargo; (of weather) glacial. ● n cerveza f amarga. **~ly** adv amargamente. **it's ~ly cold** hace un frío glacial. **~ness** n amargor m; (resentment) amargura f

bizarre /bɪˈzɑ:(r)/ a extraño

black /blæk/ a (**-er**, **-est**) negro. **~ and blue** amoratado. ● n negro m; (coffee) solo, negro (LAm). ● vt ennegrecer; limpiar <shoes>. **~ out** vi desmayarse. **~ and white** n blanco y negro m. **~-and-white** adj en blanco y negro. **~berry** /-bərɪ/ n zarzamora f. **~bird** n mirlo m. **~board** n pizarra f. **~currant** /-ˈkʌrənt/ n grosella f negra. **~en** vt ennegrecer. **~ eye** n ojo m morado. **~list** vt poner en la lista negra. **~mail** n chantaje m. ● vt chantajear. **~mailer** n chantajista m & f.

~out n apagón m; (Med) desmayo m; (of news) censura f. **~smith** n herrero m

bladder /ˈblædə(r)/ n vejiga f

blade /bleɪd/ n (of knife, sword) hoja f. **~ of grass** brizna f de hierba

blame /bleɪm/ vt echar la culpa a. **be to ~** tener la culpa. ● n culpa f. **~less** a inocente

bland /blænd/ a (**-er**, **-est**) suave

blank /blæŋk/ a <page, space> en blanco; <cassette> virgen; <cartridge> sin bala; (fig) vacío. ● n blanco m

blanket /ˈblæŋkɪt/ n manta f, cobija f (LAm), frazada (LAm); (fig) capa f. ● vt (pt **blanketed**) (fig) cubrir (**in**, **with** de)

blare /bleə(r)/ vi sonar muy fuerte. ● n estrépito m

blasphem|e /blæsˈfi:m/ vt/i blasfemar. **~ous** /ˈblæsfəməs/ a blasfemo. **~y** /ˈblæsfəmɪ/ n blasfemia f

blast /blɑ:st/ n explosión f; (gust) ráfaga f; (sound) toque m. ● vt volar. **~ed** a maldito. **~-off** n (of missile) despegue m

blatant /ˈbleɪtnt/ a patente; (shameless) descarado

blaze /bleɪz/ n llamarada f; (of light) resplandor m; (fig) arranque m. ● vi arder en llamas; (fig) brillar

blazer /ˈbleɪzə(r)/ n chaqueta f

bleach /bli:tʃ/ n lejía f, cloro m (LAm), blanqueador m (LAm). ● vt blanquear; decolorar <hair>.

bleak /bli:k/ a (**-er**, **-est**) desolado; (fig) sombrío

bleat /bli:t/ n balido m. ● vi balar

bleed /bli:d/ vt/i (pt **bled** /bled/) sangrar

bleep /bli:p/ n pitido m

blemish /ˈblemɪʃ/ n mancha f

blend /blend/ n mezcla f. ● vt mezclar. ● vi combinarse. **~er** n licuadora f

bless /bles/ vt bendecir. **~ you!** (on sneezing) ¡Jesús!, ¡salud! (Mex). **~ed** /ˈblesɪd/ a bendito. **~ing** n bendición f; (advantage) ventaja f

blew /blu:/ ⇒BLOW

blight /blaɪt/ n añublo m, tizón m; (fig) plaga f. ● vt añublar, atizonar; (fig) destrozar

blind /blaɪnd/ a ciego. ~ **alley** callejón m sin salida. ● n persiana f; (fig) pretexto m. ● vt dejar ciego; (dazzle) deslumbrar. ~**fold** a & adv con los ojos vendados. ● n venda f. ● vt vendar los ojos a. ~**ly** adv a ciegas. ~**ness** n ceguera f

blink /blɪŋk/ vi parpadear; <light> centellear. ~**ers** npl (on horse) anteojeras fpl

bliss /blɪs/ n felicidad f. ~**ful** a feliz

blister /'blɪstə(r)/ n ampolla f

blizzard /'blɪzəd/ n ventisca f

bloated /'bləʊtɪd/ a hinchado (with de)

blob /blɒb/ n (drip) gota f; (stain) mancha f

bloc /blɒk/ n (Pol) bloque m

block /blɒk/ n bloque m; (of wood) zoquete m; (of buildings) manzana f, cuadra f (LAm). in ~ **letters** en letra de imprenta. ~ **of flats** edificio m de apartamentos, casa f de pisos. ● vt bloquear. ~**ade** /blɒ'keɪd/ n bloqueo m. ● vt bloquear. ~**age** /-ɪdʒ/ n obstrucción f. ~**head** n 🅸 zopenco m

bloke /bləʊk/ n 🅸 tipo m, tío m 🅸

blond /blɒnd/ a & n rubio (m), güero (m) (Mex 🅸). ~**e** a & n rubia (f), güera (f) (Mex 🅸)

blood /blʌd/ n sangre f. ~**bath** n masacre m. ~**-curdling** /-keːdlɪŋ/a horripilante. ~**hound** n sabueso m. ~ **pressure** n tensión f arterial. high ~ **pressure** hipertensión f. ~**shed** n derramamiento m de sangre. ~**shot** a sanguinolento; <eye> inyectado de sangre. ~**stream** n torrente m sanguíneo. ~**thirsty** a sanguinario. ~**y** a (-ier, -iest) sangriento; (stained) ensangrentado; 🆇 maldito

bloom /bluːm/ n flor f. ● vi florecer

blossom /'blɒsəm/ n flor f. ● vi florecer. ~ (out) **into** (fig) llegar a ser

blot /blɒt/ n borrón m. ● vt (pt **blotted**) manchar; (dry) secar. □ ~ **out** vt oscurecer

blotch /blɒtʃ/ n mancha f. ~**y** a lleno de manchas

blotting-paper /'blɒtɪŋ/ n papel m secante

blouse /blaʊz/ n blusa f

blow /bləʊ/ vt (pt **blew**, pp **blown**) soplar; fundir <fuse>; tocar <trumpet>. ● vi soplar; <fuse> fundirse; (sound) sonar. ● n golpe m. □ ~ **down** vt derribar. □ ~ **out** vi apagar <candle>. □ ~ **over** vi pasar. □ ~ **up** vt inflar; (explode) volar; (Photo) ampliar. vi (explode) estallar; (burst) reventar. ~**dry** vt secar con secador. ~**lamp** n soplete m. ~**out** n (of tyre) reventón m. ~ **torch** n soplete m

blue /bluː/ a (-er, -est) azul; <joke> verde. ● n azul m. out of the ~ totalmente inesperado. ~**s** npl. have the ~**s** tener tristeza. ~**bell** n campanilla f. ~**bottle** n moscarda f. ~**print** n plano m; (fig, plan) programa m

bluff /blʌf/ n (poker) farol m, bluff m (LAm), blof m (Mex). ● vt engañar. ● vi tirarse un farol, hacer un bluf (LAm), blofear (Mex)

blunder /'blʌndə(r)/ vi cometer un error. ● n metedura f de pata

blunt /blʌnt/ a desafilado; <person> directo, abrupto. ● vt desafilar. ~**ly** adv francamente

blur /blɜː(r)/ n impresión f indistinta. ● vt (pt **blurred**) hacer borroso

blurb /blɜːb/ n resumen m publicitario

blurt /blɜːt/ vt. ~ **out** dejar escapar

blush /blʌʃ/ vi ruborizarse. ● n rubor m

boar /bɔː(r)/ n verraco m. wild ~ jabalí m

board /bɔːd/ n tabla f, tablero m; (for notices) tablón m de anuncios, tablero m de anuncios (LAm); (blackboard) pizarra f; (food) pensión f; (Admin) junta f. ~ **and lodging** casa y comida. full ~ pensión f completa. **go by the** ~ ser abandonado. ● vt alojar; ~ **a ship** embarcarse. ● vi alojarse (**with** en casa de); (at school) ser interno. ~**er** n huésped m & f; (school) interno m. ~**ing card** n tarjeta f de embarque.

~**ing house** n casa f de huéspedes, pensión f. ~**ing pass** n ⇒~ING CARD. ~**ing school** n internado m

boast /bəʊst/ vt enorgullecerse de. ● vi jactarse. ● n jactancia f. ~**ful** a jactancioso

boat /bəʊt/ n barco m; (small) bote m, barca f

bob /bɒb/ vi (pt **bobbed**) menearse, subir y bajar. □ ~ **up** vi presentarse súbitamente

bobbin /'bɒbɪn/ n carrete m; (in sewing machine) canilla f, bobina f

bobby pin /'bɒbɪ/ n (Amer) horquilla f, pasador m (Mex). ~ **sox** /sɒks/ npl (Amer) calcetines mpl cortos

bobsleigh /'bɒbsleɪ/ n bob(sleigh) m

bode /bəʊd/ vi. ~ **well/ill** ser de buen/mal agüero

bodice /'bɒdɪs/ n corpiño m

bodily /'bɒdɪlɪ/ a físico, corporal. ● adv físicamente

body /'bɒdɪ/ n cuerpo m; (dead) cadáver m. ~**guard** n guardaespaldas m. ~**work** n carrocería f

bog /bɒg/ n ciénaga f. □ ~ **down** vt (pt **bogged**). **get** ~**ged down** empantanarse

boggle /'bɒgl/ vi sobresaltarse. **the mind** ~**s** uno se queda atónito

bogus /'bəʊgəs/ a falso

boil /bɔɪl/ vt/i hervir. **be** ~**ing hot** estar ardiendo; <weather> hacer mucho calor. ● n furúnculo m. □ ~ **away** vi evaporarse. □ ~ **down to** vt reducirse a. □ ~ **over** vi rebosar. ~**ed** a hervido; <egg> pasado por agua. ~**er** n caldera f. ~**er suit** n mono m, overol m (LAm)

boisterous /'bɔɪstərəs/ a ruidoso, bullicioso

bold /bəʊld/ a (-**er**, -**est**) audaz. ~**ly** adv con audacia, audazmente

Bolivia /bə'lɪvɪə/ n Bolivia f. ~**n** a & n boliviano (m)

bolster /'bəʊlstə(r)/ □ ~ **up** vt sostener

bolt /bəʊlt/ n (on door) cerrojo m; (for nut) perno m; (lightning) rayo m; (leap) fuga f. ● vt echar el cerrojo a <door>; engullir <food>. ● vi fugarse. ● adv. ~ **upright** rígido

bomb /bɒm/ n bomba f. ● vt bombardear. ~**ard** /bɒm'bɑːd/ vt bombardear ~**er** /'bɒmə(r)/ n (plane) bombardero m; (terrorist) terrorista m & f. ~**ing** /'bɒmɪŋ/ n bombardeo m. ~**shell** n bomba f

bond /bɒnd/ n (agreement) obligación f; (link) lazo m; (Com) bono m. ● vi (stick) adherirse. ~**age** /-ɪdʒ/ n esclavitud f

bone /bəʊn/ n hueso m; (of fish) espina f. ● vt deshuesar; quitar las espinas a <fish>. ~**dry** a completamente seco. ~ **idle** a holgazán

bonfire /'bɒnfaɪə(r)/ n hoguera f, fogata f

bonnet /'bɒnɪt/ n gorra f; (Auto) capó m, capote m (Mex)

bonus /'bəʊnəs/ n (payment) bonificación f; (fig) ventaja f

bony /'bəʊnɪ/ a (-**ier**, -**iest**) huesudo; <fish> lleno de espinas

boo /buː/ int ¡bu! ● vt/i abuchear

boob /buːb/ n (回, mistake) metedura f de pata. ● vi 回 meter la pata

booby /'buːbɪ/ : ~ **prize** n premio m al peor. ~ **trap** n trampa f; (bomb) bomba f trampa

book /bʊk/ n libro m; (of cheques etc) talonario m, chequera f; (notebook) libreta f; (exercise book) cuaderno m. ~**s** (mpl) (Com) cuentas fpl. ● vt (enter) registrar; (reserve) reservar. ● vi reservar. ~**case** n biblioteca f, librería f, librero m (Mex). ~**ing** n reserva f, reservación f (LAm). ~**ing office** n (in theatre) taquilla f, boletería f (LAm). ~**keeping** n contabilidad f. ~**let** /'bʊklɪt/ n folleto m. ~**maker** n corredor m de apuestas. ~**mark** n señal f. ~**seller** n librero m. ~**shop**, (Amer) ~**store** n librería f. ~**worm** n (fig) ratón m de biblioteca

boom /buːm/ vi retumbar; (fig) prosperar. ● n estampido m; (Com) boom m

boost /buːst/ vt estimular; reforzar <morale>. ● n empuje m. ~**er** n (Med) revacunación f. ~**er cable** n (Amer) cable m de arranque

boot /buːt/ n bota f; (Auto) maletero m, cajuela f (Mex). □ ~ **up** vt (Comp) cargar

booth /buːð/ n cabina f; (at fair) puesto m

booze /buːz/ vi 🔲 beber mucho. ● n 🔲 alcohol m

border /'bɔːdə(r)/ n borde m; (frontier) frontera f; (in garden) arriate m. □ ~ **on** vt lindar con. ~**line** n línea f divisoria. ~**line case** n caso m dudoso

bor|e /bɔː(r)/ ⇒BEAR. ● vt (annoy) aburrir; (Tec) taladrar. ● vi taladrar. ● n (person) pelmazo m; (thing) lata f. ~**ed** a aburrido. **be** ~**ed** estar aburrido. **get** ~**ed** aburrirse. ~**edom** /'bɔːdəm/ n aburrimiento m. ~**ing** a aburrido, pesado

born /bɔːn/ a nato. **be** ~ nacer

borne /bɔːn/ ⇒BEAR

borough /'bʌrə/ n municipio m

borrow /'bɒrəʊ/ vt pedir prestado

Bosnia /'bɒznɪə/**:** ~ **Herzegovina** /hɜːtsəgəʊ'viːnə/ n Bosnia Herzegovina f. ~**n** a & n bosnio (m)

boss /bɒs/ n 🔲 jefe m. ● vt. ~ (about) 🔲 dar órdenes a. ~**y** a mandón

botan|ical /bə'tænɪkl/ a botánico. ~**ist** /'bɒtənɪst/ n botánico m. ~**y** /'bɒtənɪ/ n botánica f

both /bəʊθ/ a & pron ambos (mpl), los dos (mpl). ● adv al mismo tiempo, a la vez. ~ **Ann and Brian came** tanto Ann como Bob vinieron

bother /'bɒðə(r)/ vt (inconvenience) molestar; (worry) preocupar. ~ **it!** ¡caramba! ● vi molestarse. ~ **about** preocuparse de. ~ **doing** tomarse la molestia de hacer. ● n molestia f

bottle /'bɒtl/ n botella, mamila f (Mex); (for baby) biberón m. ● vt embotellar. □ ~ **up** vt (fig) reprimir. ~**neck** n (traffic jam) embotellamiento m. ~ **opener** n abrebotellas m, destapador m (LAm)

bottom /'bɒtəm/ n fondo m; (of hill) pie m; (buttocks) trasero m. ● a de más abajo; <price> más bajo; <lip, edge> inferior. ~**less** a sin fondo

bough /baʊ/ n rama f

bought /bɔːt/ ⇒BUY

boulder /'bəʊldə(r)/ n canto m

bounce /baʊns/ vt hacer rebotar. ● vi rebotar; <person> saltar; 🔲

<cheque> ser rechazado. ● n rebote m

bound /baʊnd/ ⇒BIND. ● vi saltar. ● n (jump) salto m. ~**s** npl (limits) límites mpl. **out of** ~**s** zona f prohibida. ● a. **be** ~ **for** dirigirse a. ~ **to** obligado a; (certain) seguro de

boundary /'baʊndərɪ/ n límite m

bouquet /bʊ'keɪ/ n ramo m; (of wine) buqué m, aroma m

bout /baʊt/ n período m; (Med) ataque m; (Sport) encuentro m

bow¹ /bəʊ/ n (weapon, mus) arco m; (knot) lazo m, moño m (LAm)

bow² /baʊ/ n reverencia f; (Naut) proa f. ● vi inclinarse. ● vt inclinar

bowels /'baʊəlz/ npl intestinos mpl; (fig) entrañas fpl

bowl /bəʊl/ n (container) cuenco m; (for washing) palangana f; (ball) bola f. ● vt (cricket) arrojar. ● vi (cricket) arrojar la pelota. □ ~ **over** vt derribar

bowl: ~**er** n (cricket) lanzador m. ~**er** (hat) sombrero m de hongo, bombín m. ~**ing** n bolos mpl. ~**ing alley** n bolera f

bow tie /bəʊ 'taɪ/ n corbata f de lazo, pajarita f

box /bɒks/ n caja f; (for jewels etc) estuche m; (in theatre) palco m. ● vt boxear contra. ~ **s.o.'s ears** dar una manotada a uno. ● vi boxear. ~**er** n boxeador m. ~**ing** n boxeo m. **B~ing Day** n el 26 de diciembre. ~ **office** n taquilla f, boletería f (LAm). ~ **room** n trastero m

boy /bɔɪ/ n chico m, muchacho m; (young) niño m

boycott /'bɔɪkɒt/ vt boicotear. ● n boicoteo m

boy: ~**friend** n novio m. ~**hood** n niñez f. ~**ish** a de muchacho; (childish) infantil

bra /brɑː/ n sostén m, sujetador m, brasier m (Mex)

brace /breɪs/ n abrazadera f. ● vt asegurar. ~ **o.s.** prepararse. ~**s** npl tirantes mpl; (Amer, dental) aparato(s) m(pl)

bracelet /'breɪslɪt/ n pulsera f

bracken /'brækən/ n helecho m

bracket /'brækɪt/ n soporte m; (group) categoría f; (parenthesis) paréntesis *m.* **square** ～s corchetes *mpl.* ● *vt* poner entre paréntesis; (join together) agrupar

brag /bræg/ *vi* (*pt* **bragged**) jactarse (**about** de)

braid /breɪd/ *n* galón *m*; (Amer, in hair) trenza *f*

brain /breɪn/ *n* cerebro *m*. ● *vt* romper la cabeza a. ～**child** *n* invento *m*. ～ **drain** *n* 🄸 fuga *f* de cerebros. ～**storm** *n* ataque *m* de locura; (Amer, brainwave) idea *f* genial. ～**wash** *vt* lavar el cerebro. ～**wave** *n* idea *f* genial. ～**y** *a* (**-ier, -iest**) inteligente

brake /breɪk/ *n* freno *m*. ● *vt/i* frenar. ～ **fluid** *n* líquido *m* de freno. ～ **lights** *npl* luces *fpl* de freno

bramble /'bræmbl/ *n* zarza *f*

bran /bræn/ *n* salvado *m*

branch /brɑːntʃ/ *n* rama *f*; (of road) bifurcación *f*; (Com) sucursal *m*; (fig) ramo *m*. □ ～ **off** *vi* bifurcarse. □ ～ **out** *vi* ramificarse

brand /brænd/ *n* marca *f*. ● *vt* marcar; (label) tildar de

brandish /'brændɪʃ/ *vt* blandir

brand: ～ **name** *n* marca *f*. ～**-new** /-'njuː/ *a* flamante

brandy /'brændɪ/ *n* coñac *m*

brash /bræʃ/ *a* descarado

brass /brɑːs/ *n* latón *m*. **get down to** ～ **tacks** (fig) ir al grano. ～ **band** *n* banda *f* de música

brassière /'bræsjeə(r)/ *n* ⇒BRA

brat /bræt/ *n* (pej) mocoso *m*

bravado /brə'vɑːdəʊ/ *n* bravata *f*

brave /breɪv/ *a* (**-er, -est**) valiente. ● *n* (North American Indian) guerrero *m* indio. **the** ～ *npl* los valientes. ● *vt* afrontar. ～**ry** /-ərɪ/ *n* valentía *f*, valor *m*

brawl /brɔːl/ *n* alboroto *m*. ● *vi* pelearse

brazen /'breɪzn/ *a* descarado

Brazil /brə'zɪl/ *n* Brasil *m*. ～**ian** /-jən/ *a* & *n* brasileño (*m*)

breach /briːtʃ/ *n* infracción *f*, violación *f*; (of contract) incumplimiento *m*; (gap) brecha *f*. ～ **of the peace** alteración *f* del orden público. ● *vt* abrir una brecha en

bread /bred/ *n* pan *m*. **a loaf of** ～ un pan. ～**crumbs** *npl* migajas *fpl*; (Culin) pan *m* rallado, pan *m* molido (Mex)

breadth /bredθ/ *n* anchura *f*

breadwinner /'bredwɪnə(r)/ *n* sostén *m* de la familia

break /breɪk/ *vt* (*pt* **broke**, *pp* **broken**) romper; infringir, violar <*law*>; batir <*record*>; comunicar <*news*>; interrumpir <*journey*>. ● *vi* romperse; <*news*> divulgarse. ● *n* ruptura *f*; (interval) intervalo *m*; (🄸, chance) oportunidad *f*; (in weather) cambio *m*. □ ～ **away** *vi* escapar. □ ～ **down** *vt* derribar; analizar <*figures*>. *vi* estropearse, descomponerse (LAm); (Auto) averiarse; (cry) deshacerse en lágrimas. □ ～ **in** *vi* <*intruder*> entrar (para robar). □ ～ **into** *vt* entrar en (para robar) <*house etc*>; (start doing) ponerse a. □ ～ **off** *vi* interrumpirse. □ ～ **out** *vi* <*war, disease*> estallar; (run away) escaparse. □ ～ **up** *vi* romperse; <*band, lovers*> separarse; <*schools*> terminar. ～**able** *a* frágil. ～**age** /-ɪdʒ/ *n* rotura *f*. ～**down** *n* (Tec) falla *f*; (Med) colapso *m*, crisis *f* nerviosa; (of figures) análisis *f*. ～**er** *n* (wave) ola *f* grande

breakfast /'brekfəst/ *n* desayuno *m*. **have** ～ desayunar

break: ～**through** *n* adelanto *m*. ～**water** *n* rompeolas *m*

breast /brest/ *n* pecho *m*; (of chicken etc) pechuga *f*. (estilo *m*) ～**stroke** *n* braza *f*, (estilo *m*) pecho *m* (LAm)

breath /breθ/ *n* aliento *m*, respiración *f*. **be out of** ～ estar sin aliento. **hold one's** ～ aguantar la respiración. **under one's** ～ a media voz

breath|e /briːð/ *vt/i* respirar. ～**er** *n* descanso *m*, pausa *f*. ～**ing** *n* respiración *f*

breathtaking /'breθteɪkɪŋ/ *a* impresionante

bred /bred/ ⇒BREED

breed /briːd/ *vt* (*pt* **bred**) criar; (fig) engendrar. ● *vi* reproducirse. ● *n* raza *f*

breez|e /briːz/ *n* brisa *f*. ～**y** *a* de mucho viento

brew /bruː/ *vt* hacer *<beer>*; preparar *<tea>*. ● *vi* hacer cerveza; *<tea>* reposar; (fig) prepararse. ● *n* infusión *f*. ~**er** *n* cervecero *m*. ~**ery** *n* cervecería *f*, fábrica *f* de cerveza

bribe /braɪb/ *n* soborno *m*. ● *vt* sobornar. ~**ry** /'braɪbərɪ/ *n* soborno *m*

brick /brɪk/ *n* ladrillo *m*. ~**layer** *n* albañil *m*

bridal /'braɪdl/ *a* nupcial

bride /braɪd/ *m* novia *f*. ~**groom** *n* novio *m*. ~**smaid** /'braɪdzmeɪd/ *n* dama *f* de honor

bridge /brɪdʒ/ *n* puente *m*; (of nose) caballete *m*; (Cards) bridge *m*. ● *vt* tender un puente sobre. ~ **a gap** llenar un vacío

bridle /'braɪdl/ *n* brida *f*. ~ **path** *n* camino *m* de herradura

brief /briːf/ *a* (**-er, -est**) breve. ● *n* (Jurid) escrito *m*. ● *vt* dar instrucciones a. ~**case** *n* maletín *m*, portafolio(s) *m* (LAm). ~**ly** *adv* brevemente. ~**s** *npl* (man's) calzoncillos *mpl*; (woman's) bragas *fpl*, calzones *mpl* (LAm), pantaletas *fpl* (Mex)

brigade /brɪ'geɪd/ *n* brigada *f*

bright /braɪt/ *a* (**-er, -est**) brillante, claro; (clever) listo; (cheerful) alegre. ~**en** *vt* aclarar; hacer más alegre *<house etc>*. ● *vi* (weather) aclararse; *<face>* illuminarse

brillian|ce /'brɪljəns/ *n* brillantez *f*, brillo *m*. ~**t** *a* brillante

brim /brɪm/ *n* borde *m*; (of hat) ala *f*. □ ~ **over** *vi* (*pt* **brimmed**) desbordarse

brine /braɪn/ *n* salmuera *f*

bring /brɪŋ/ *vt* (*pt* **brought**) traer; (lead) llevar. □ ~ **about** *vt* causar. □ ~ **back** *vt* devolver. □ ~ **down** *vt* derribar. □ ~ **off** *vt* lograr. □ ~ **on** *vt* causar. □ ~ **out** *vt* sacar; lanzar *<product>*; publicar *<book>*. □ ~ **round/to** *vt* hacer volver en sí. □ ~ **up** *vt* (Med) vomitar; educar *<children>*; plantear *<question>*

brink /brɪŋk/ *n* borde *m*

brisk /brɪsk/ *a* (**-er, -est**) enérgico, vivo

bristle /'brɪsl/ *n* cerda *f*. ● *vi* erizarse

Brit|ain /'brɪtən/ *n* Gran Bretaña *f*. ~**ish** /'brɪtɪʃ/ *a* británico. ● *npl* the ~**ish** los británicos. ~**on** /'brɪtən/ *n* británico *m*

Brittany /'brɪtənɪ/ *n* Bretaña *f*

brittle /'brɪtl/ *a* frágil, quebradizo

broach /brəʊtʃ/ *vt* abordar

broad /brɔːd/ *a* (**-er, -est**) ancho. in ~ **daylight** a plena luz del día. ~ **bean** *n* haba *f* ~**cast** *n* emisión *f*. ● *vt* (*pt* **broadcast**) emitir. ● *vi* hablar por la radio. ~**caster** *n* locutor *m*. ~**casting** *n* radio-difusión *f*. ~**en** *vt* ensanchar. ● *vi* ensancharse. ~**ly** *adv* en general. ~**-minded** /-'maɪndɪd/ *a* de miras amplias, tolerante

broccoli /'brɒkəlɪ/ *n invar* brécol *m*

brochure /'brəʊʃə(r)/ *n* folleto *m*

broil /brɔɪl/ *vt* (Amer) asar a la parrilla. ~**er** *n* (Amer) parrilla *f*

broke /brəʊk/ ⇒BREAK. ● *a* 🆃 sin blanca, en la ruina

broken /'brəʊkən/ ⇒BREAK. ● *a* roto

broker /'brəʊkə(r)/ *n* corredor *m*

brolly /'brɒlɪ/ *n* 🆃 paraguas *m*

bronchitis /brɒŋ'kaɪtɪs/ *n* bronquitis *f*

bronze /brɒnz/ *n* bronce *m*. ● *a* de bronce

brooch /brəʊtʃ/ *n* broche *m*

brood /bruːd/ *n* cría *f*; (hum) prole *m*. ● *vi* empollar; (fig) meditar

brook /brʊk/ *n* arroyo *m*. ● *vt* soportar

broom /bruːm/ *n* escoba *f*. ~**stick** *n* palo *m* de escoba

broth /brɒθ/ *n* caldo *m*

brothel /'brɒθl/ *n* burdel *m*

brother /'brʌðə(r)/ *n* hermano *m*. ~**hood** *n* fraternidad *f*. ~**-in-law** (*pl* ~**s-in-law**) *n* cuñado *m*. ~**ly** *a* fraternal

brought /brɔːt/ ⇒BRING

brow /braʊ/ *n* frente *f*; (of hill) cima *f*. ~**beat** *vt* (*pt* **-beaten**, *pp* **-beat**) intimidar

brown /braʊn/ *a* (**-er, -est**) marrón, café (Mex); *<hair>* castaño; *<skin>*

moreno; (tanned) bronceado. ● *n* marrón *m*, café *m* (Mex). ● *vt* poner moreno; (Culin) dorar. ~ **bread** *n* pan *m* integral ~ **sugar** /braʊn 'ʃʊgə(r)/ *n* azúcar *m* moreno, azúcar *f* morena

browse /braʊz/ *vi* (in a shop) curiosear; <*animal*> pacer; (Comp) navegar. ~**r** (Comp) browser *m*, navegador *m*

bruise /bru:z/ *n* magulladura *f*. ● *vt* magullar; machucar <*fruit*>

brunch /brʌntʃ/ *n* Ⓔ desayuno *m* tardío

brunette /bru:'net/ *n* morena *f*

brunt /brʌnt/ *n*. bear *o* take the ~ of sth sufrir algo

brush /brʌʃ/ *n* cepillo *m*; (large) escoba; (for decorating) brocha *f*; (artist's) pincel; (skirmish) escaramuza *f*. ● *vt* cepillar. □ ~ **against** *vt* rozar. □ ~ **aside** *vt* rechazar. □ ~ **off** *vt* (rebuff) desairar. □ ~ **up (on)** *vt* refrescar

brusque /bru:sk/ *a* brusco. ~**ly** *adv* bruscamente

Brussels /'brʌslz/ *n* Bruselas *f*. ~ **sprout** *n* col *f* de Bruselas

brutal /'bru:tl/ *a* brutal. ~**ity** /-'tælətɪ/ *n* brutalidad *f*. ~**ly** *adv* brutalmente

brute /bru:t/ *n* bestia *f*. ~ **force** fuerza *f* bruta

BSc *abbr* ⇒BACHELOR

bubbl|e /'bʌbl/ *n* burbuja *f*. ● *vi* burbujear. □ ~ **over** *vi* desbordarse. ~**ly** *a* burbujeante

buck /bʌk/ *a* macho. ● *n* (deer) ciervo *m*; (Amer Ⓔ) dólar *m*. **pass the** ~ pasar la pelota

bucket /'bʌkɪt/ *n* balde *m*, cubo *m*, cubeta *f* (Mex)

buckle /'bʌkl/ *n* hebilla *f*. ● *vt* abrochar. ● *vi* torcerse

bud /bʌd/ *n* brote *m*. ● *vi* (*pt* **budded**) brotar.

Buddhis|m /'bʊdɪzəm/ *n* budismo *m*. ~**t** *a* & *n* budista (*m* & *f*)

budding /'bʌdɪŋ/ *a* (fig) en ciernes

buddy /'bʌdɪ/ *n* Ⓔ amigo *m*, cuate *m* (Mex)

budge /bʌdʒ/ *vt* mover. ● *vi* moverse

budgerigar /'bʌdʒərɪgɑ:(r)/ *n* periquito *m*

budget /'bʌdʒɪt/ *n* presupuesto *m*

buffalo /'bʌfələʊ/ *n* (*pl* -oes *or* -o) búfalo *m*

buffer /'bʌfə(r)/ *n* parachoques *m*

buffet[1] /'bʊfeɪ/ *n* (meal) buffet *m*; (in train) bar *m*

buffet[2] /'bʌfɪt/ *n* golpe *m*; (slap) bofetada *f*. ● *vt* (*pt* **buffeted**) golpear

bug /bʌg/ *n* bicho *m*; Ⓔ, (germ) microbio *m*; (device) micrófono *m* oculto. ● *vt* (*pt* **bugged**) ocultar un micrófono en; (Ⓔ, bother) molestar

buggy /'bʌgɪ/ *n*. **baby** ~ sillita *f* de paseo (plegable); (Amer) cochecito *m*

bugle /'bju:gl/ *n* corneta *f*

build /bɪld/ *vt/i* (*pt* **built**) construir. ● *n* (of person) figura *f*, tipo *m*. □ ~ **up** *vt/i* fortalecer; (increase) aumentar. ~**er** *n* (contractor) contratista *m* & *f*; (labourer) albañil *m*. ~**ing** *n* edificio *m*; (construction) construcción *f*. ~**up** *n* aumento *m*; (of gas etc) acumulación *f*

built /bɪlt/ ⇒BUILD. ~**-in** *a* empotrado. ~**-up area** *n* zona *f* urbanizada

bulb /bʌlb/ *n* bulbo *m*; (Elec) bombilla *f*, foco *m* (Mex)

Bulgaria /bʌl'geərɪə/ *n* Bulgaria *f*. ~**n** *a* & *n* búlgaro (*m*)

bulg|e /bʌldʒ/ *n* protuberancia *f*. ● *vi* pandearse. ~**ing** *a* abultado; <*eyes*> saltón

bulk /bʌlk/ *n* bulto *m*, volumen *m*. in ~ a granel; (loose) suelto. the ~ of la mayor parte de. ~**y** *a* voluminoso

bull /bʊl/ *n* toro *m*. ~**dog** *n* bulldog *m*. ~**dozer** /-dəʊzə(r)/ *n* bulldozer *m*

bullet /'bʊlɪt/ *n* bala *f*

bulletin /'bʊlətɪn/ *n* anuncio *m*; (journal) boletín *m*. ~ **board** *n* (Amer) tablón *m* de anuncios, tablero *m* de anuncios (LAm)

bulletproof /'bʊlɪtpru:f/ *a* a prueba de balas

bullfight /'bʊlfaɪt/ *n* corrida *f* (de toros). ~**er** *n* torero *m*. ~**ing** *n* (deporte *m* de) los toros

bull: ~**ring** *n* plaza *f* de toros. ~**'s-eye** *n* diana *f*. ~**shit** *n* (vulg) sandeces *fpl* Ⓔ, gillipolleces *fpl* Ⓧ

bully /'bʊlɪ/ n matón m. ● vt intimidar. ~**ing** n intimidación f

bum /bʌm/ n (🔲, backside) trasero m; (Amer 🔲) holgazán m

bumblebee /'bʌmblbi:/ n abejorro m

bump /bʌmp/ vt chocar contra. ● vi dar sacudidas. ● n (blow) golpe m; (jolt) sacudida f. □ ~ **into** vt chocar contra; (meet) encontrar.

bumper /'bʌmpə(r)/ n parachoques m. ● a récord. ~ **edition** n edición f especial

bun /bʌn/ n bollo m; (bread roll) panecillo m, bolillo m (Mex); (hair) moño m, chongo m (Mex)

bunch /bʌntʃ/ n (of people) grupo m; (of bananas, grapes) racimo m; (of flowers) ramo m

bundle /'bʌndl/ n bulto m; (of papers) legajo m. □ ~ **up** vt atar

bungalow /'bʌŋgələʊ/ n casa f de un solo piso

bungle /'bʌŋgl/ vt echar a perder

bunk /bʌŋk/ n litera f

bunker /'bʌŋkə(r)/ n carbonera f; (Golf, Mil) búnker m

bunny /'bʌnɪ/ n conejito m

buoy /bɔɪ/ n boya f. □ ~ **up** vt hacer flotar; (fig) animar

buoyant /'bɔɪənt/ a flotante; (fig) optimista

burden /'bɜ:dn/ n carga f. ● vt cargar (with de)

bureau /'bjʊərəʊ/ n (pl -eaux /-əʊz/) agencia f; (desk) escritorio m; (Amer, chest of drawers) cómoda f

bureaucra|cy /bjʊə'rɒkrəsɪ/ n burocracia f. ~**t** /'bjʊərəkræt/ n burócrata m & f. ~**tic** /-'krætɪk/ a burocrático

burger /'bɜ:gə(r)/ n 🔲 hamburguesa f

burgl|ar /'bɜ:glə(r)/ n ladrón m. ~**ar alarm** n alarma f antirrobo. ~**ary** n robo m (en casa o edificio). ~**e** /'bɜ:gl/ vt entrar a robar en. **we were** ~**ed** nos entraron a robar

burial /'berɪəl/ n entierro m

burly /'bɜ:lɪ/ a (-ier, -iest) corpulento

burn /bɜ:n/ vt (pt burned or burnt) quemar. ● vi quemarse. ● n quemadura f. □ ~ **down** vt incendiar. vi incendiarse

burnt /bɜ:nt/ ⇒BURN

burp /bɜ:p/ n 🔲 eructo m. ● vi 🔲 eructar

burrow /'bʌrəʊ/ n madriguera f. ● vt excavar

burst /bɜ:st/ vt (pt burst) reventar. ● vi reventarse. ~ **into tears** echarse a llorar. ~ **out laughing** echarse a reír. ● n (Mil) ráfaga f; (of activity) arrebato; (of applause) salva f

bury /'berɪ/ vt enterrar; (hide) ocultar

bus /bʌs/ n (pl **buses**) autobús m, camión m (Mex)

bush /bʊʃ/ n arbusto m; (land) monte m. ~**y** a espeso

business /'bɪznɪs/ n negocio m; (Com) negocios mpl; (profession) ocupación f; (fig) asunto m. **mind one's own** ~ ocuparse de sus propios asuntos. ~**like** a práctico, serio. ~**man** /-mən/ n hombre m de negocios. ~**woman** n mujer f de negocios

busker /'bʌskə(r)/ n músico m ambulante

bus stop n parada f de autobús, paradero m de autobús (LAm)

bust /bʌst/ n busto m; (chest) pecho m. ● vt (pt busted or bust) 🔲 romper. ● vi romperse. ● a roto. **go** ~ 🔲 quebrar

bust-up /'bʌstʌp/ n 🔲 riña f

busy /'bɪzɪ/ a (-ier, -iest) ocupado; <street> concurrido. **be** ~ (Amer) <phone> estar comunicando, estar ocupado (LAm). ● vt. ~ **o.s. with** ocuparse de. ~**body** n entrometido m

but /bʌt/ conj pero; (after negative) sino. ● prep menos. ~ **for** si no fuera por. **last** ~ **one** penúltimo

butcher /'bʊtʃə(r)/ n carnicero m. ● vt matar; (fig) hacer una carnicería con

butler /'bʌtlə(r)/ n mayordomo m

butt /bʌt/ n (of gun) culata f; (of cigarette) colilla f; (target) blanco m; (Amer 🔲, backside) trasero m. ● vi topar. □ ~ **in** vi interrumpir

butter /'bʌtə(r)/ *n* mantequilla *f*. ● *vt* untar con mantequilla. ~**cup** *n* ranúnculo *m*. ~**fingers** *n* manazas *m*, torpe *m*. ~**fly** *n* mariposa *f*; (swimming) estilo *m* mariposa

buttock /'bʌtək/ *n* nalga *f*

button /'bʌtn/ *n* botón *m*. ● *vt* abotonar. ● *vi* abotonarse. ~**hole** *n* ojal *m*. ● *vt* (fig) detener

buy /baɪ/ *vt/i* (*pt* **bought**) comprar. ● *n* compra *f*. ~**er** *n* comprador *m*

buzz /bʌz/ *n* zumbido *m*. ● *vi* zumbar. □ ~ **off** *vi* ⊠ largarse. ~**er** *n* timbre *m*

by /baɪ/ *prep* por; (near) cerca de; (before) antes de; (according to) según. ~ **and large** en conjunto, en general. ~ **car** en coche. ~ **oneself** por sí solo

bye /baɪ/, **bye-bye** /'baɪbaɪ/ *int* 🔲 ¡adiós!

by: ~**-election** *n* elección *f* parcial. ~**-law** *n* reglamento *m* (local). ~**pass** *n* carretera *f* de circunvalación. ● *vt* eludir; *<road>* circunvalar. ~**-product** *n* subproducto *m*. ~**stander** /-stændə(r)/ *n* espectador *m*

byte /baɪt/ *n* (Comp) byte *m*, octeto *m*

Cc

cab /kæb/ *n* taxi *m*; (of lorry, train) cabina *f*

cabaret /'kæbəreɪ/ *n* cabaret *m*

cabbage /'kæbɪdʒ/ *n* col *f*, repollo *m*

cabin /'kæbɪn/ *n* (house) cabaña *f*; (in ship) camarote *m*; (in plane) cabina *f*

cabinet /'kæbɪnɪt/ *n* (cupboard) armario *m*; (for display) vitrina *f*. **C~** (Pol) gabinete *m*

cable /'keɪbl/ *n* cable *m*. ~ **car** *n* teleférico *m*. ~ **TV** *n* televisión *f* por cable, cablevisión *f* (LAm)

cackle /'kækl/ *n* (of hen) cacareo *m*; (laugh) risotada *f*. ● *vi* cacarear; (laugh) reírse a carcajadas

cactus /'kæktəs/ *n* (*pl* **-ti** /-taɪ/ *or* **-tuses**) cacto *m*

caddie, **caddy** /'kædɪ/ *n* (golf) portador *m* de palos

cadet /kə'det/ *n* cadete *m*

cadge /kædʒ/ *vt/i* gorronear

café /'kæfeɪ/ *n* cafetería *f*

cafeteria /kæfɪ'tɪərɪə/ *n* restaurante *m* autoservicio

caffeine /'kæfiːn/ *n* cafeína *f*

cage /keɪdʒ/ *n* jaula *f*. ● *vt* enjaular

cake /keɪk/ *n* pastel *m*, tarta *f*; (sponge) bizcocho *m*. ~ **of soap** pastilla *f* de jabón

calamity /kə'læmətɪ/ *n* calamidad *f*

calcium /'kælsɪəm/ *n* calcio *m*

calculat|e /'kælkjʊleɪt/ *vt/i* calcular. ~**ion** /-'leɪʃn/ *n* cálculo *m*. ~**or** *n* calculadora *f*

calculus /'kælkjʊləs/ *n* (Math) cálculo *m*

calendar /'kælɪndə(r)/ *n* calendario *m*

calf /kɑːf/ *n* (*pl* **calves**) (animal) ternero *m*; (of leg) pantorrilla *f*

calibre /'kælɪbə(r)/ *n* calibre *m*

call /kɔːl/ *vt/i* llamar. ● *n* llamada *f*; (shout) grito *m*; (visit) visita *f*. **be on** ~ estar de guardia. **long-distance** ~ llamada *f* de larga distancia, conferencia *f*. □ ~ **back** *vt* hacer volver; (on phone) volver a llamar. *vi* volver; (on phone) volver a llamar. □ ~ **for** *vt* pedir; (fetch) ir a buscar. □ ~ **off** *vt* suspender. □ ~ **on** *vt* pasar a visitar. □ ~ **out** *vi* dar voces. □ ~ **together** *vt* convocar. □ ~ **up** *vt* (Mil) llamar al servicio militar; (phone) llamar. ~ **box** *n* cabina *f* telefónica. ~**er** *n* visita *f*; (phone) el que llama *m*. ~**ing** *n* vocación *f*

callous /'kæləs/ *a* insensible, cruel

calm /kɑːm/ *a* (**-er, -est**) tranquilo; *<sea>* en calma. ● *n* tranquilidad *f*, calma *f*. ● *vt* calmar. ● *vi* calmarse. ~ **down** *vi* tranquilizarse. *vt* calmar. ~**ly** *adv* con calma

calorie /'kælərɪ/ *n* caloría *f*

calves /kɑːvz/ *npl* ⇒CALF

camcorder /'kæmkɔːdə(r)/ *n* videocámara *f*, camcórder *m*

came /keɪm/ ⇒COME

camel /'kæml/ n camello m

camera /'kæmərə/ n cámara f, máquina f fotográfica ∼**man** /-mən/ n camarógrafo m, cámara m

camouflage /'kæməflɑːʒ/ n camuflaje m. ● vt camuflar

camp /kæmp/ n campamento m. ● vi acampar. **go** ∼**ing** hacer camping

campaign /kæm'peɪn/ n campaña f. ● vi hacer campaña

camp: ∼**bed** n catre m de tijera. ∼**er** n campista m & f; (vehicle) cámper m. ∼**ground** n (Amer) ⇒∼SITE. ∼**ing** n camping m. ∼**site** n camping m

campus /'kæmpəs/ n (pl **-puses**) campus m, ciudad f universitaria

can¹ /kæn/, unstressed form /kən/

negative **can't, cannot** (formal);
past **could**

● auxiliary verb

····▸ (be able to) poder. I ∼'t lift it no lo puedo levantar. **she says she** ∼ **come** dice que puede venir

····▸ (be allowed to) poder. ∼ I **smoke?** ¿puedo fumar?

····▸ (know how to) saber. ∼ **you swim?** ¿sabes nadar?

····▸ (with verbs of perception) not translated. I ∼'t **see you** no te veo. I ∼ **hear you better now** ahora te oigo mejor

····▸ (in requests) ∼ I **have a glass of water, please?** ¿me trae un vaso de agua, por favor?. ∼ I **have a kilo of cheese, please?** ¿me da un kilo de queso, por favor?

····▸ (in offers) ∼ I **help you?** ¿te ayudo?; (in shop) ¿lo/la atienden?

can² /kæn/ n lata f, bote m. ● vt (pt **canned**) enlatar. ∼**ned music** música f grabada

Canad|a /'kænədə/ n (el) Canadá m. ∼**ian** /kə'neɪdɪən/ a & n canadiense (m & f)

canal /kə'næl/ n canal m

Canaries /kə'neərɪz/ npl = CANARY ISLANDS

canary /kə'neərɪ/ n canario m. **C∼ Islands** npl. the **C∼ Islands** las Islas Canarias

cancel /'kænsl/ vt (pt **cancelled**) cancelar; anular <command, cheque>; (delete) tachar. ∼**lation** /-'leɪʃn/ n cancelación f

cancer /'kænsə(r)/ n cáncer m. **C∼** n (Astr) Cáncer m. ∼**ous** a canceroso

candid /'kændɪd/ a franco

candidate /'kændɪdeɪt/ n candidato m

candle /'kændl/ n vela f. ∼**stick** n candelero m

candour /'kændə(r)/ n franqueza f

candy /'kændɪ/ n (Amer) caramelo m, dulce f (LAm). ∼**floss** /-flɒs/ n algodón m de azúcar

cane /keɪn/ n caña f; (for baskets) mimbre m; (stick) bastón m; (for punishment) palmeta f. ● vt castigar con palmeta

canister /'kænɪstə(r)/ n bote m

cannabis /'kænəbɪs/ n cáñamo m índico, hachís m, cannabis m

cannibal /'kænɪbl/ n caníbal m. ∼**ism** n canibalismo m

cannon /'kænən/ n invar cañón m. ∼ **ball** n bala f de cañón

cannot /'kænət/ ⇒CAN¹

canoe /kə'nuː/ n canoa f, piragua f. ● vi ir en canoa

canon /'kænən/ n canon m; (person) canónigo m. ∼**ize** vt canonizar

can opener n abrelatas m

canopy /'kænəpɪ/ n dosel m

can't /kɑːnt/ ⇒CAN¹

cantankerous /kæn'tæŋkərəs/ a mal humorado

canteen /kæn'tiːn/ n cantina f; (of cutlery) juego m de cubiertos

canter /'kæntə(r)/ n medio galope m. ● vi ir a medio galope

canvas /'kænvəs/ n lona f; (artist's) lienzo m

canvass /'kænvəs/ vi hacer campaña, solicitar votos. ∼**ing** n solicitación f (de votos)

canyon /'kænjən/ n cañón m

cap /kæp/ n gorra f; (lid) tapa f; (of cartridge) cápsula f; (of pen) capuchón m.

● *vt* (*pt* **capped**) tapar, poner cápsula a; (outdo) superar

capab|ility /keɪpə'bɪlətɪ/ *n* capacidad *f*. **∼le** /'keɪpəbl/ *a* capaz

capacity /kə'pæsətɪ/ *n* capacidad *f*; (function) calidad *f*

cape /keɪp/ *n* (cloak) capa *f*; (Geog) cabo *m*

capital /'kæpɪtl/ *a* capital. **∼ letter** mayúscula *f*. ● *n* (town) capital *f*; (money) capital *m*. **∼ism** *n* capitalismo *m*. **∼ist** *a* & *n* capitalista (*m* & *f*.) **∼ize** *vt* escribir con mayúsculas <*word*>. ● *vi*. **∼ize on** aprovechar

capitulat|e /kə'pɪtʃʊleɪt/ *vi* capitular. **∼ion** /-'leɪʃn/ *n* capitulación *f*

Capricorn /'kæprɪkɔːn/ *n* Capricornio *m*

capsize /kæp'saɪz/ *vt* hacer volcar. ● *vi* volcarse

capsule /'kæpsjuːl/ *n* cápsula *f*

captain /'kæptɪn/ *n* capitán *m*; (of plane) comandante *m* & *f*. ● *vt* capitanear

caption /'kæpʃn/ *n* (heading) título *m*; (of cartoon etc) leyenda *f*

captivate /'kæptɪveɪt/ *vt* encantar

captiv|e /'kæptɪv/ *a* & *n* cautivo (*m*). **∼ity** /-'tɪvətɪ/ *n* cautiverio *m*, cautividad *f*

capture /'kæptʃə(r)/ *vt* capturar; atraer <*attention*>; (Mil) tomar. ● *n* apresamiento *m*; (Mil) toma *f*

car /kɑː(r)/ *n* coche *m*, carro *m* (LAm); (Amer, of train) vagón *m*

caramel /'kærəmel/ *n* azúcar *m* quemado; (sweet) caramelo *m*, dulce *m* (LAm)

caravan /'kærəvæn/ *n* caravana *f*

carbohydrate /kɑːbəʊ'haɪdreɪt/ *n* hidrato *m* de carbono

carbon /'kɑːbən/ *n* carbono *m*; (paper) carbón *m*. **∼ copy** copia *f* al carbón. **∼ dioxide** /daɪ'ɒksaɪd/ *n* anhídrido *m* carbónico. **∼ monoxide** /mə'nɒksaɪd/ *n* monóxido *m* de carbono

carburettor /kɑːbjʊ'retə(r)/ *n* carburador *m*

carcass /'kɑːkəs/ *n* cuerpo *m* de animal muerto; (for meat) res *f* muerta

card /kɑːd/ *n* tarjeta *f*; (for games) carta *f*; (membership) carnet *m*; (records) ficha *f*. **∼board** *n* cartón *m*

cardigan /'kɑːdɪgən/ *n* chaqueta *f* de punto, rebeca *f*

cardinal /'kɑːdɪnəl/ *a* cardinal. ● *n* cardenal *m*

care /keə(r)/ *n* cuidado *m*; (worry) preocupación *f*; (protection) cargo *m*. **∼ of** a cuidado de, en casa de. **take ∼** tener cuidado. **take ∼ of** cuidar de <*person*>; ocuparse de <*matter*>. ● *vi* interesarse. **I don't ∼** me da igual. □ **∼ about** *vt* preocuparse por. □ **∼ for** *vt* cuidar de; (like) querer

career /kə'rɪə(r)/ *n* carrera *f*. ● *vi* correr a toda velocidad

care: **∼free** *a* despreocupado. **∼ful** *a* cuidadoso; (cautious) prudente. **be ∼ful** tener cuidado. **∼fully** *adv* con cuidado. **∼less** *a* negligente; (not worried) indiferente. **∼lessly** *adv* descuidadamente. **∼lessness** *n* descuido *m*

caress /kə'res/ *n* caricia *f*. ● *vt* acariciar

caretaker /'keəteɪkə(r)/ *n* vigilante *m*; (of flats etc) portero *m*

car ferry *n* transbordador *m* de coches

cargo /'kɑːgəʊ/ *n* (*pl* **-oes**) carga *f*

Caribbean /kærɪ'biːən/ *a* caribeño. **the ∼ (Sea)** *n* el mar Caribe

caricature /'kærɪkətʃʊə(r)/ *n* caricatura *f*. ● *vt* caricaturizar

carnage /'kɑːnɪdʒ/ *n* carnicería *f*, matanza *f*

carnation /kɑː'neɪʃn/ *n* clavel *m*

carnival /'kɑːnɪvl/ *n* carnaval *m*

carol /'kærəl/ *n* villancico *m*

carousel /kærə'sel/ *n* tiovivo *m*, carrusel *m* (LAm); (for baggage) cinta *f* transportadora

carp /kɑːp/ *n invar* carpa *f*. □ **∼ at** *vi* quejarse de

car park *n* aparcamiento *m*, estacionamiento *m*

carpent|er /'kɑːpɪntə(r)/ *n* carpintero *m*. **∼ry** /-trɪ/ *n* carpintería *f*

carpet /'kɑːpɪt/ *n* alfombra *f*. **∼ sweeper** *n* cepillo *m* mecánico

carriage /'kærɪdʒ/ n coche m; (Mec) carro m; (transport) transporte m; (cost, bearing) porte m; (of train) vagón m. **~way** n calzada f, carretera f

carrier /'kærɪə(r)/ n transportista m & f; (company) empresa f de transportes; (Med) portador m. **~ bag** n bolsa f

carrot /'kærət/ n zanahoria f

carry /'kærɪ/ vt llevar; transportar <goods>; (involve) llevar consigo, implicar. ● vi <sounds> llegar, oírse. □ ~ **off** vt llevarse. □ ~ **on** vi seguir, continuar. □ ~ **out** vt realizar; cumplir <promise, threat>. **~ cot** n cuna f portátil

carsick /'kɑːsɪk/ a mareado (por viajar en coche)

cart /kɑːt/ n carro m; (Amer, in supermarket, airport) carrito m. ● vt acarrear; (🄵, carry) llevar

carton /'kɑːtən/ n caja f de cartón

cartoon /kɑː'tuːn/ n caricatura f, chiste m; (strip) historieta f; (film) dibujos mpl animados

cartridge /'kɑːtrɪdʒ/ n cartucho m

carve /kɑːv/ vt tallar; trinchar <meat>

cascade /kæs'keɪd/ n cascada f. ● vi caer en cascadas

case /keɪs/ n caso m; (Jurid) proceso m; (crate) cajón m; (box) caja f; (suitcase) maleta f, petaca f (Mex). in any ~ en todo caso. in ~ he comes por si viene. in ~ of en caso de

cash /kæʃ/ n dinero m efectivo. pay (in) ~ pagar al contado. ● vt cobrar. ~ **in (on)** aprovecharse de. ~ **desk** n caja f. ~ **dispenser** n cajero m automático

cashier /kæ'ʃɪə(r)/ n cajero m

cashpoint /'kæʃpɔɪnt/ n cajero m automático

casino /kə'siːnəʊ/ n (pl -os) casino m

cask /kɑːsk/ n barril m

casket /'kɑːskɪt/ n cajita f; (Amer) ataúd m, cajón m (LAm)

casserole /'kæsərəʊl/ n cacerola f; (stew) guiso m, guisado m (Mex)

cassette /kə'set/ n cassette m & f

cast /kɑːst/ vt (pt cast) arrojar; fundir <metal>; emitir <vote>. ● n

lanzamiento m; (in play) reparto m; (mould) molde m

castanets /kæstə'nets/ npl castañuelas fpl

castaway /'kɑːstəweɪ/ n náufrago m

caster /'kɑːstə(r)/ n ruedecita f. ~ **sugar** n azúcar m extrafino

Castil|le /kæ'stiːl/ n Castilla f. **~ian** /kæ'stɪlɪən/ a & n castellano (m)

cast: ~ **iron** n hierro m fundido. **~-iron** a (fig) sólido

castle /'kɑːsl/ n castillo m; (Chess) torre f

cast-offs /'kɑːstɒfs/ npl desechos mpl

castrat|e /kæ'streɪt/ vt castrar. **~ion** /-ʃn/ n castración f

casual /'kæʒʊəl/ a casual; <meeting> fortuito; <work> ocasional; <attitude> despreocupado; <clothes> informal, de sport. **~ly** adv de paso

casualt|y /'kæʒʊəltɪ/ n (injured) herido m; (dead) víctima f; (in hospital) urgencias fpl. **~ies** npl (Mil) bajas fpl

cat /kæt/ n gato m

Catalan /'kætəlæn/ a & n catalán (m)

catalogue /'kætəlɒg/ n catálogo m. ● vt catalogar

Catalonia /kætə'ləʊnɪə/ n Cataluña f

catalyst /'kætəlɪst/ n catalizador m

catamaran /kætəmə'ræn/ n catamarán m

catapult /'kætəpʌlt/ n catapulta f; (child's) tirachinas f, resortera f (Mex)

catarrh /kə'tɑː(r)/ n catarro m

catastroph|e /kə'tæstrəfɪ/ n catástrofe m. **~ic** /kætə'strɒfɪk/ a catastrófico

catch /kætʃ/ vt (pt caught) coger (esp Spain), agarrar; tomar <train, bus>; (unawares) sorprender, pillar; (understand) entender; contagiarse de <disease>. ~ **a cold** resfriarse. ~ **sight of** avistar. ● vi (get stuck) engancharse; <fire> prenderse. ● n (by goalkeeper) parada f; (of fish) pesca f; (on door) pestillo m; (on window) cerradura f. □ ~ **on** vi 🄵 hacerse popular. □ ~

up *vi* poner al día. ~ **up with** alcanzar; ponerse al corriente de *<news etc>*. ~**ing** *a* contagioso. ~**phrase** *n* eslogan *m*. ~**y** *a* pegadizo

categor|ical /ˌkætɪˈɡɒrɪkl/ *a* categórico. ~**y** /ˈkætɪɡərɪ/ *n* categoría *f*

cater /ˈkeɪtə(r)/ *vi* encargarse del servicio de comida. ~ **for** proveer a *<needs>*. ~**er** *n* proveedor *m*

caterpillar /ˈkætəpɪlə(r)/ *n* oruga *f*, azotador *m* (Mex)

cathedral /kəˈθiːdrəl/ *n* catedral *f*

catholic /ˈkæθəlɪk/ *a* universal. **C**~ *a* & *n* católico (*m*). **C**~**ism** /kəˈθɒlɪsɪzəm/ *n* catolicismo *m*

cat: ~**nap** *n* sueñecito *m*. **C**~**seyes** *npl* (P) catafaros *mpl*

cattle /ˈkætl/ *npl* ganado *m*

catwalk *n* pasarela *f*

Caucasian /kɔːˈkeɪʒən/ *n*. **a male** ~ (Amer) un hombre de raza blanca

caught /kɔːt/ ⇒CATCH

cauliflower /ˈkɒlɪflaʊə(r)/ *n* coliflor *f*

cause /kɔːz/ *n* causa *f*, motivo *m*. ● *vt* causar

cautio|n /ˈkɔːʃn/ *n* cautela *f*; (warning) advertencia *f*. ● *vt* advertir; (Jurid) amonestar. ~**us** /-ʃəs/ *a* cauteloso, prudente

cavalry /ˈkævəlrɪ/ *n* caballería *f*

cave /keɪv/ *n* cueva *f*. □ ~ **in** *vi* hundirse. ~**man** *n* troglodita *m*

cavern /ˈkævən/ *n* caverna *f*

caviare /ˈkævɪɑː(r)/ *n* caviar *m*

cavity /ˈkævətɪ/ *n* cavidad *f*; (in tooth) caries *f*

CD *abbr* (= **compact disc**) CD *m*. ~ **player** (reproductor *m* de) compact-disc *m*. ~**-ROM** *n* CD-ROM

cease /siːs/ *vt/i* cesar. ~**fire** *n* alto *m* el fuego, cese *m* del fuego (LAm)

cedar /ˈsiːdə(r)/ *n* cedro *m*

ceiling /ˈsiːlɪŋ/ *n* techo *m*

celebrat|e /ˈselɪbreɪt/ *vt* celebrar. ● *vi* divertirse. ~**ed** *a* célebre. ~**ion** /-ˈbreɪʃn/ *n* celebración *f*; (party) fiesta *f*

celebrity /sɪˈlebrɪtɪ/ *n* celebridad *f*

celery /ˈselərɪ/ *n* apio *m*

cell /sel/ *n* celda *f*; (Biol, Elec) célula *f*

cellar /ˈselə(r)/ *n* sótano *m*; (for wine) bodega *f*

cello /ˈtʃeləʊ/ *n* (*pl* -**os**) violonc(h)elo *m*, chelo *m*

Cellophane /ˈseləfeɪn/ *n* (P) celofán *m* (P)

celluloid /ˈseljʊlɔɪd/ *n* celuloide *m*

Celsius /ˈselsɪəs/ *a*. **20 degrees** ~ **20** grados centígrados *or* Celsio(s)

cement /sɪˈment/ *n* cemento *m*. ● *vt* cementar

cemetery /ˈsemətrɪ/ *n* cementerio *m*

cens|or /ˈsensə(r)/ *n* censor *m*. ● *vt* censurar. ~**ship** *n* censura *f*. ~**ure** /ˈsenʃə(r)/ *vt* censurar

census /ˈsensəs/ *n* censo *m*

cent /sent/ *n* centavo *m*

centenary /senˈtiːnərɪ/ *n* centenario *m*

centi|grade /ˈsentɪɡreɪd/ *a* centígrado. ~**litre** *n* centilitro *m*. ~**metre** *n* centímetro *m*. ~**pede** /-piːd/ *n* ciempiés *m*

central /ˈsentrəl/ *a* central; (of town) céntrico. ~ **heating** *n* calefacción *f* central. ~**ize** *vt* centralizar

centre /ˈsentə(r)/ *n* centro *m*. ● *vt* (*pt* **centred**) centrar. ● *vi* centrarse (on en)

century /ˈsentʃərɪ/ *n* siglo *m*

cereal /ˈsɪərɪəl/ *n* cereal *m*

ceremon|ial /serɪˈməʊnɪəl/ *a* & *n* ceremonial (*m*). ~**y** /ˈserɪmənɪ/ *n* ceremonia *f*

certain /ˈsɜːtn/ *a* cierto. **for** ~ seguro. **make** ~ **of** asegurarse de. ~**ly** *adv* desde luego. ~**ty** *n* certeza *f*

certificate /səˈtɪfɪkət/ *n* certificado *m*; (of birth, death etc) partida *f*

certify /ˈsɜːtɪfaɪ/ *vt* certificar

chafe /tʃeɪf/ *vt* rozar. ● *vi* rozarse

chaffinch /ˈtʃæfɪntʃ/ *n* pinzón *m*

chagrin /ˈʃæɡrɪn/ *n* disgusto *m*

chain /tʃeɪn/ *n* cadena *f*. ● *vt* encadenar. ~ **reaction** *n* reacción *f* en cadena. ~**smoker** *n* fumador *m* que siempre tiene un cigarrillo encendido. ~ **store** *n* tienda *f* de una cadena

chair /tʃeə(r)/ *n* silla *f*; (Univ) cátedra *f*. ● *vt* presidir. ~**lift** *n* telesquí *m*, telesilla *m* (LAm). **~man** /-mən/ *n* presidente *m*

chalet /'ʃæleɪ/ *n* chalé *m*

chalk /tʃɔːk/ *n* (Geol) creta *f*; (stick) tiza *f*, gis *m* (Mex)

challeng|e /'tʃælɪndʒ/ *n* desafío *m*; (fig) reto *m*. ● *vt* desafiar; (question) poner en duda. **~ing** *a* estimulante

chamber /'tʃeɪmbə(r)/ *n* (*old use*) cámara *f*. **~maid** *n* camarera *f*. **~ pot** *n* orinal *m*

champagne /ʃæm'peɪn/ *n* champaña *m*, champán *m*

champion /'tʃæmpɪən/ *n* campeón *m*. ● *vt* defender. **~ship** *n* campeonato *m*

chance /tʃɑːns/ *n* casualidad *f*; (likelihood) posibilidad *f*; (opportunity) oportunidad *f*; (risk) riesgo *m*. **by ~** por casualidad. ● *a* fortuito

chancellor /'tʃɑːnsələ(r)/ *n* canciller *m*; (Univ) rector *m*. **C~ of the Exchequer** Ministro *m* de Hacienda

chandelier /ʃændə'lɪə(r)/ *n* araña *f* (de luces)

chang|e /tʃeɪndʒ/ *vt* cambiar; (substitute) reemplazar. **~ one's mind** cambiar de idea. ● *vi* cambiarse. ● *n* cambio *m*; (coins) cambio *m*, sencillo *m* (LAm), feria *f* (Mex); (money returned) cambio *m*, vuelta *f*, vuelto *m* (LAm). **~eable** *a* cambiable; <*weather*> variable. **~ing room** *n* (Sport) vestuario *m*, vestidor *m* (Mex); (in shop) probador *m*

channel /'tʃænl/ *n* canal *m*; (fig) medio *m*. ● *vt* (*pt* **channelled**) acanalar; (fig) encauzar. **the (English) C~** el Canal de la Mancha. **C~ Islands** *npl.* **the C~ Islands** las islas Anglonormandas. **C~ Tunnel** *n.* **the C~ Tunnel** el Eurotúnel

chant /tʃɑːnt/ *n* canto *m*. ● *vt/i* cantar

chao|s /'keɪɒs/ *n* caos *m*. **~tic** /-'ɒtɪk/ *a* caótico

chap /tʃæp/ *n* 🔟 tipo *m*, tío *m* 🔟. ● *vt* (*pt* **chapped**) agrietar. ● *vi* agrietarse

chapel /'tʃæpl/ *n* capilla *f*

chaperon /'ʃæpərəʊn/ *n* acompañante *f*

chapter /'tʃæptə(r)/ *n* capítulo *m*

char /tʃɑː(r)/ *vt* (*pt* **charred**) carbonizar

character /'kærəktə(r)/ *n* carácter *m*; (in book, play) personaje *m*. **in ~** característico. **~istic** /-'rɪstɪk/ *a* típico. ● *n* característica *f*. **~ize** *vt* caracterizar

charade /ʃə'rɑːd/ *n* farsa *f*. **~s** *npl* (game) charada *f*

charcoal /'tʃɑːkəʊl/ *n* carbón *m* vegetal; (for drawing) carboncillo *m*

charge /tʃɑːdʒ/ *n* precio *m*; (Elec, Mil) carga *f*; (Jurid) acusación *f*; (task, custody) encargo *m*; (responsibility) responsabilidad *f*. **in ~ of** responsable de, encargado de. **the person in ~** la persona responsable. **take ~ of** encargarse de. ● *vt* pedir; (Elec, Mil) cargar; (Jurid) acusar. ● *vi* cargar; <*animal*> embestir (**at** contra)

charit|able /'tʃærɪtəbl/ *a* caritativo. **~y** /'tʃærɪtɪ/ *n* caridad *f*; (society) institución *f* benéfica

charm /tʃɑːm/ *n* encanto *m*; (spell) hechizo *m*; (on bracelet) dije *m*, amuleto *m*. ● *vt* encantar. **~ing** *a* encantador

chart /tʃɑːt/ *n* (Aviat, Naut) carta *f* de navegación; (table) tabla *f*

charter /'tʃɑːtə(r)/ *n* carta *f*. ● *vt* alquilar <*bus, train*>; fletar <*plane, ship*>. **~ flight** *n* vuelo *m* chárter

chase /tʃeɪs/ *vt* perseguir. ● *vi* correr (**after** tras). ● *n* persecución *f*. □ **~ away**, **~ off** *vt* ahuyentar

chassis /'ʃæsɪ/ *n* chasis *m*

chastise /tʃæs'taɪz/ *vt* castigar

chastity /'tʃæstətɪ/ *n* castidad *f*

chat /tʃæt/ *n* charla *f*, conversación *f* (LAm), plática *f* (Mex). ● *vi* (*pt* **chatted**) charlar, conversar (LAm), platicar (Mex)

chatter /'tʃætə(r)/ *n* charla *f*. ● *vi* charlar. **his teeth are ~ing** le castañetean los dientes. **~box** *n* parlanchín *m*

chauffeur /'ʃəʊfə(r)/ *n* chófer *m*

chauvinis|m /'ʃəʊvɪnɪzəm/ *n* patriotería *f*; (male) machismo *m*. **~t** *n* patriotero *m*; (male) machista *m*

cheap /tʃiːp/ *a* (**-er, -est**) barato; (poor quality) de baja calidad; <*rate*>

económico. ~**(ly)** *adv* barato, a bajo precio

cheat /'tʃiːt/ *vt* defraudar; (deceive) engañar. ● *vi* (at cards) hacer trampas. ● *n* trampa *f*; (person) tramposo *m*

check /tʃek/ *vt* comprobar; (examine) inspeccionar; (curb) frenar. ● *vi* comprobar. ● *n* comprobación *f;* (of tickets) control *m;* (curb) freno *m;* (Chess) jaque *m;* (pattern) cuadro *m;* (Amer, bill) cuenta *f;* (Amer, cheque) cheque *m.* □ ~ **in** *vi* registrarse; (at airport) facturar el equipaje, chequear el equipaje (LAm), registrar el equipaje (Mex). □ ~ **out** *vi* pagar la cuenta y marcharse. □ ~ **up** *vi* confirmar. □ ~ **up on** *vt* investigar. ~**book** *n* (Amer) ⇒CHEQUEBOOK. ~**ered** /'tʃekəd/ *a* (Amer) ⇒CHEQUERED

checkers /'tʃekəz/ *n* (Amer) damas *fpl*

check: ~**mate** *n* jaque *m* mate. ● *vt* dar mate a. ~**out** *n* caja *f.* ~**point** control *m.* ~**up** *n* chequeo *m*, revisión

cheek /tʃiːk/ *n* mejilla *f*; (fig) descaro *m.* ~**bone** *n* pómulo *m.* ~**y** *a* descarado

cheep /tʃiːp/ *vi* piar

cheer /tʃɪə(r)/ *n* alegría *f*; (applause) viva *m.* ~**s!** ¡salud!.● *vt* alegrar; (applaud) aplaudir. ● *vi* alegrarse; (applaud) aplaudir. ~ **up!** ¡anímate! ~**ful** *a* alegre

cheerio /tʃɪərɪ'əʊ/ *int* 🔲 ¡adiós!, ¡hasta luego!

cheerless /'tʃɪəlɪs/ *a* triste

cheese /tʃiːz/ *n* queso *m*

cheetah /'tʃiːtə/ *n* guepardo *m*

chef /ʃef/ *n* jefe *m* de cocina

chemical /'kemɪkl/ *a* químico. ● *n* producto *m* químico

chemist /'kemɪst/ *n* farmacéutico *m*; (scientist) químico *m.* ~**ry** *n* química *f.* ~**'s** **(shop)** *n* farmacia *f*

cheque /tʃek/ *n* cheque *m*, talón *m.* ~**book** *n* chequera *f*, talonario *m*

cherish /'tʃerɪʃ/ *vt* cuidar; (love) querer; abrigar *<hope>*

cherry /'tʃerɪ/ *n* cereza *f.* ~ **tree** *n* cerezo *m*

chess /tʃes/ *n* ajedrez *m.* ~**board** *n* tablero *m* de ajedrez

chest /tʃest/ *n* pecho *m*; (box) cofre *m*, cajón *m*

chestnut /'tʃesnʌt/ *n* castaña *f.* ● *a* castaño. ~ **tree** *n* castaño *m*

chest of drawers *n* cómoda *f*

chew /tʃuː/ *vt* masticar. ~**ing gum** *n* chicle *m*

chic /ʃiːk/ *a* elegante

chick /tʃɪk/ *n* polluelo *m.* ~**en** /'tʃɪkɪn/ *n* pollo *m.* ● *a* 🔲 cobarde. □ ~**en** **out** *vi* 🔲 acobardarse. ~**enpox** /'tʃɪkɪnpɒks/ *n* varicela *f.* ~**pea** *n* garbanzo *m*

chicory /'tʃɪkərɪ/ *n* (in coffee) achicoria *f*; (in salad) escarola *f*

chief /tʃiːf/ *n* jefe *m.* ● *a* principal. ~**ly** *adv* principalmente

chilblain /'tʃɪlbleɪn/ *n* sabañón *m*

child /tʃaɪld/ *n* (*pl* **children** /'tʃɪldrən/) niño *m*; (offspring) hijo *m.* ~**birth** *n* parto *m.* ~**hood** *n* niñez *f.* ~**ish** *a* infantil. ~**less** *a* sin hijos. ~**like** *a* ingenuo, de niño

Chile /'tʃɪlɪ/ *n* Chile *m.* ~**an** *a* & *n* chileno (*m*)

chill /tʃɪl/ *n* frío *m*; (illness) resfriado *m.* ● *a* frío. ● *vt* enfriar; refrigerar *<food>*

chilli /'tʃɪlɪ/ *n* (*pl* -**ies**) chile *m*

chilly /'tʃɪlɪ/ *a* frío

chime /tʃaɪm/ *n* carillón *m.* ● *vt* tocar *<bells>*; dar *<hours>.* ● *vi* repicar

chimney /'tʃɪmnɪ/ *n* (*pl* -**eys**) chimenea *f.* ~ **sweep** *n* deshollinador *m*

chimpanzee /tʃɪmpæn'ziː/ *n* chimpancé *m*

chin /tʃɪn/ *n* barbilla *f*

china /'tʃaɪnə/ *n* porcelana *f*

Chin|a /'tʃaɪnə/ *n* China *f.* ~**ese** /-'niːz/ *a* & *n* chino (*m*)

chink /tʃɪŋk/ *n* (crack) grieta *f*; (sound) tintín *m.* ● *vi* tintinear

chip /tʃɪp/ *n* pedacito *m*; (splinter) astilla *f*; (Culin) patata *f* frita, papa *f* frita (LAm); (in gambling) ficha *f*; (Comp) chip *m.* have a ~ **on** one's shoulder guardar rencor. ● *vt* (*pt* **chipped**) desportillar. □ ~ **in** *vi* 🔲 interrumpir; (with money) contribuir

chiropodist /kɪˈrɒpədɪst/ n callista m & f, pedicuro m

chirp /tʃɜːp/ n pío m. ● vi piar. ∼y a alegre

chisel /ˈtʃɪzl/ n formón m. ● vt (pt **chiselled**) cincelar

chivalr|ous /ˈʃɪvəlrəs/ a caballeroso. ∼y /-rɪ/ n caballerosidad f

chlorine /ˈklɔːriːn/ n cloro m

chock /tʃɒk/ n cuña f. ∼-a-block a, ∼-full a atestado

chocolate /ˈtʃɒklət/ n chocolate m; (individual sweet) bombón m, chocolate m (LAm)

choice /tʃɔɪs/ n elección f; (preference) preferencia f. ● a escogido

choir /ˈkwaɪə(r)/ n coro m

choke /tʃəʊk/ vt sofocar. ● vi sofocarse. ● n (Auto) choke m, estárter m, ahogador m (Mex)

cholera /ˈkɒlərə/ n cólera m

cholesterol /kəˈlestərɒl/ n colesterol m

choose /tʃuːz/ vt/i (pt **chose**, pp **chosen**) elegir, escoger. ∼y a 🔟 exigente

chop /tʃɒp/ vt (pt **chopped**) cortar. ● n (Culin) chuleta f. □ ∼ **down** vt talar. □ ∼ **off** vt cortar. ∼**per** n hacha f; (butcher's) cuchilla f. ∼**py** a picado

chord /kɔːd/ n (Mus) acorde m

chore /tʃɔː(r)/ n tarea f, faena f. **household** ∼**s** npl quehaceres mpl domésticos

chorus /ˈkɔːrəs/ n coro m; (of song) estribillo m

chose /tʃəʊz/, **chosen** /ˈtʃəʊzn/ ⇒CHOOSE

Christ /kraɪst/ n Cristo m

christen /ˈkrɪsn/ vt bautizar. ∼**ing** n bautizo m

Christian /ˈkrɪstjən/ a & n cristiano (m). ∼**ity** /krɪstɪˈænətɪ/ n cristianismo m. ∼ **name** n nombre m de pila

Christmas /ˈkrɪsməs/ n Navidad f. Merry ∼! ¡Feliz Navidad!, ¡Felices Pascuas! Father ∼ Papá m Noel. ● a de Navidad, navideño. ∼ **card** n tarjeta f de Navidad f. ∼ **day** n día m de Navidad. ∼ **Eve** n Nochebuena f. ∼ **tree** n árbol m de Navidad

chrom|e /krəʊm/ n cromo m. ∼**ium** /ˈkrəʊmɪəm/ n cromo m

chromosome /ˈkrəʊməsəʊm/ n cromosoma m

chronic /ˈkrɒnɪk/ a crónico; (🔟, bad) terrible

chronicle /ˈkrɒnɪkl/ n crónica f. ● vt historiar

chronological /krɒnəˈlɒdʒɪkl/ a cronológico

chubby /ˈtʃʌbɪ/ a (-ier, -iest) regordete; <person> gordinflón 🔟

chuck /tʃʌk/ vt 🔟 tirar. □ ∼ **out** vt tirar

chuckle /ˈtʃʌkl/ n risa f ahogada. ● vi reírse entre dientes

chug /tʃʌg/ vi (pt **chugged**) (of motor) traquetear

chum /tʃʌm/ n amigo m, compinche m, cuate m (Mex)

chunk /tʃʌŋk/ n trozo m grueso. ∼y a macizo

church /ˈtʃɜːtʃ/ n iglesia f. ∼**yard** n cementerio m

churn /ˈtʃɜːn/ n (for milk) lechera f, cántara f; (for making butter) mantequera f. ● vt agitar. □ ∼ **out** vt producir en profusión

chute /ʃuːt/ n tobogán m

cider /ˈsaɪdə(r)/ n sidra f

cigar /sɪˈgɑː(r)/ n puro m

cigarette /sɪgəˈret/ n cigarrillo m. ∼ **end** n colilla f. ∼ **holder** n boquilla f. ∼ **lighter** n mechero m, encendedor m

cinecamera /ˈsɪnɪkæmərə/ n tomavistas m, filmadora f (LAm)

cinema /ˈsɪnəmə/ n cine m

cipher /ˈsaɪfə(r)/ n (Math, fig) cero m; (code) clave f

circle /ˈsɜːkl/ n círculo m; (in theatre) anfiteatro m. ● vt girar alrededor de. ● vi dar vueltas

circuit /ˈsɜːkɪt/ n circuito m

circular /ˈsɜːkjʊlə(r)/ a & n circular (f)

circulat|e /ˈsɜːkjʊleɪt/ vt hacer circular. ● vi circular. ∼**ion** /-ˈleɪʃn/ n circulación f; (number of copies) tirada f

circumcise /ˈsɜːkəmsaɪz/ vt circuncidar

circumference /sə'kʌmfərəns/ n circunferencia f

circumstance /'sɜːkəmstəns/ n circunstancia f. ~s (means) npl situación f económica

circus /'sɜːkəs/ n circo m

cistern /'sɪstən/ n cisterna f

cite /saɪt/ vt citar

citizen /'sɪtɪzn/ n ciudadano m; (inhabitant) habitante m & f

citrus /'sɪtrəs/ n. ~ fruits cítricos mpl

city /'sɪtɪ/ n ciudad f; the C~ el centro m financiero de Londres

civic /'sɪvɪk/ a cívico

civil /'sɪvl/ a civil; (polite) cortés

civilian /sɪ'vɪlɪən/ a & n civil (m & f)

civiliz|ation /sɪvɪlaɪ'zeɪʃn/ n civilización f. ~ed /'sɪvəlaɪzd/ a civilizado.

civil: ~ **servant** n funcionario m (del Estado), burócrata m & f (Mex). ~ **service** n administración f pública. ~ **war** n guerra f civil

clad /klæd/ ⇒CLOTHE

claim /kleɪm/ vt reclamar; (assert) pretender. ● n reclamación f; (right) derecho m; (Jurid) demanda f

clairvoyant /kleə'vɔɪənt/ n clarividente m & f

clam /klæm/ n almeja f. ● vi (pt **clammed**). ~ up ⬚ ponerse muy poco comunicativo

clamber /'klæmbə(r)/ vi trepar a gatas

clammy /'klæmɪ/ a (-ier, -iest) húmedo

clamour /'klæmə(r)/ n clamor m. ● vi. ~ for pedir a gritos

clamp /klæmp/ n abrazadera f; (Auto) cepo m. ● vt sujetar con abrazadera; poner cepo a <car>. □ ~ **down on** vt reprimir

clan /klæn/ n clan m

clang /klæŋ/ n sonido m metálico

clap /klæp/ vt (pt **clapped**) aplaudir; batir <hands>. ● vi aplaudir. ● n palmada f; (of thunder) trueno m

clarif|ication /klærɪfɪ'keɪʃn/ n aclaración f. ~y /'klærɪfaɪ/ vt aclarar. ● vi aclararse

clarinet /klærɪ'net/ n clarinete m

clarity /'klærətɪ/ n claridad f

clash /klæʃ/ n choque m; (noise) estruendo m; (contrast) contraste m; (fig) conflicto m. ● vt golpear. ● vi encontrarse; <colours> desentonar

clasp /klɑːsp/ n cierre m. ● vt agarrar; apretar <hand>

class /klɑːs/ n clase f. **evening** ~ n clase nocturna. ● vt clasificar

classic /'klæsɪk/ a & n clásico (m). ~al a clásico. ~s npl estudios mpl clásicos

classif|ication /klæsɪfɪ'keɪʃn/ n clasificación f. ~y /'klæsɪfaɪ/ vt clasificar

class: ~**room** n aula f, clase f. ~y a ⬚ elegante

clatter /'klætə(r)/ n ruido m; (of train) traqueteo m. ● vi hacer ruido

clause /klɔːz/ n cláusula f; (Gram) oración f

claustrophobia /klɔːstrə'fəʊbɪə/ n claustrofobia f

claw /klɔː/ n garra f; (of cat) uña f; (of crab) pinza f. ● vt arañar

clay /kleɪ/ n arcilla f

clean /kliːn/ a (-er, -est) limpio; <stroke> bien definido. ● adv completamente. ● vt limpiar. ● vi limpiar. □ ~ up vt hacer la limpieza. ~er n persona f que hace la limpieza. ~liness /'klenlɪnɪs/ n limpieza f

cleans|e /klenz/ vt limpiar. ~er n producto m de limpieza; (for skin) crema f de limpieza. ~ing cream n crema f de limpieza

clear /klɪə(r)/ a (-er, -est) claro; (transparent) transparente; (without obstacles) libre; <profit> neto; <sky> despejado. **keep** ~ **of** evitar. ● adv claramente. ● vt despejar; liquidar <goods>; (Jurid) absolver; (jump over) saltar por encima de; quitar, levantar (LAm) <table>. □ ~ **off** vi ⬚, ~ **out** vi ⬚, (go away) largarse. □ ~ **up** vt (tidy) ordenar; aclarar <mystery>. vi <weather> despejarse. ~**ance** n (removal of obstructions) despeje m; (authorization) permiso m; (by security) acreditación f. ~**ing** n claro m. ~**ly** adv evidentemente.

~way *n* carretera *f* en la que no se permite parar

cleavage /'kli:vɪdʒ/ *n* escote *m*

clef /klef/ *n* (Mus) clave *f*

clench /klentʃ/ *vt* apretar

clergy /'klɜ:dʒɪ/ *n* clero *m*. **~man** /-mən/ *n* clérigo *m*

cleric /'klerɪk/ *n* clérigo *m*. **~al** *a* clerical; (of clerks) de oficina

clerk /klɑ:k/ *n* empleado *m*; (Amer, salesclerk) dependiente *m*, vendedor *m*

clever /'klevə(r)/ *a* (**-er, -est**) inteligente; (skilful) hábil. **~ly** *adv* inteligentemente; (with skill) hábilmente. **~ness** *n* inteligencia *f*

cliché /'kli:ʃeɪ/ *n* lugar *m* común *m*, cliché *m*

click /klɪk/ *n* golpecito *m*. ● *vi* chascar; ⊞ llevarse bien. ● *vt* chasquear

client /'klaɪənt/ *n* cliente *m*

cliff /klɪf/ *n* acantilado *m*

climat|e /'klaɪmət/ *n* clima *m*. **~ic** /-'mætɪk/ *a* climático

climax /'klaɪmæks/ *n* clímax *m*; (orgasm) orgasmo *m*

climb /klaɪm/ *vt* subir *<stairs>*; trepar *<tree>*; escalar *<mountain>*. ● *vi* subir. ● *n* subida *f*. □ **~ down** *vi* bajar; (fig) ceder. **~er** *n* (Sport) alpinista *m & f*, andinista *m & f* (LAm); (plant) trepadora *f*

clinch /klɪntʃ/ *vt* cerrar *<deal>*

cling /klɪŋ/ *vi* (*pt* **clung**) agarrarse; (stick) pegarse

clinic /'klɪnɪk/ *n* centro *m* médico; (private hospital) clínica *f*. **~al** *a* clínico

clink /klɪŋk/ *n* tintineo *m*. ● *vt* hacer tintinear. ● *vi* tintinear

clip /klɪp/ *n* *<fastener>* clip *m*; (for paper) sujetapapeles *m*; (for hair) horquilla *f*. ● *vt* (*pt* **clipped**) (cut) cortar; (join) sujetar. **~pers** /'klɪpəz/ *npl* (for hair) maquinilla *f* para cortar el pelo; (for nails) cortaúñas *m*. **~ping** *n* recorte *m*

cloak /kləʊk/ *n* capa *f*. **~room** *n* guardarropa *m*; (toilet) lavabo *m*, baño *m* (LAm)

clock /klɒk/ *n* reloj *m*. **~wise** *a/adv* en el sentido de las agujas del re-

loj. **~work** *n* mecanismo *m* de relojería. **like ~work** con precisión

clog /klɒg/ *n* zueco *m*. ● *vt* (*pt* **clogged**) atascar

cloister /'klɔɪstə(r)/ *n* claustro *m*

close¹ /kləʊs/ *a* (**-er, -est**) cercano; (together) apretado; *<friend>* íntimo; *<weather>* bochornoso; *<link etc>* estrecho; *<game, battle>* reñido. **have a ~ shave** (fig) escaparse de milagro. ● *adv* cerca. ● *n* recinto *m*

close² /kləʊz/ *vt* cerrar. ● *vi* cerrarse; (end) terminar. **~ down** *vt/i* cerrar. ● *n* fin *m*. **~d** *a* cerrado

closely /'kləʊslɪ/ *adv* estrechamente; (at a short distance) de cerca; (with attention) detenidamente; (precisely) rigurosamente

closet /'klɒzɪt/ *n* (Amer) armario *m*; (for clothes) armario *m*, closet *m* (LAm)

close-up /'kləʊsʌp/ *n* (Cinema etc) primer plano *m*

closure /'kləʊʒə(r)/ *n* cierre *m*

clot /klɒt/ *n* (Med) coágulo *m*; ⊞ tonto *m*. ● *vi* (*pt* **clotted**) cuajarse; *<blood>* coagularse

cloth /klɒθ/ *n* tela *f*; (duster) trapo *m*; (tablecloth) mantel *m*

cloth|e /kləʊð/ *vt* (*pt* **clothed** or **clad**) vestir. **~es** /kləʊðz/ *npl* ropa. **~espin**, **~espeg** (Amer) *n* pinza *f* (para tender la ropa). **~ing** *n* ropa *f*

cloud /klaʊd/ *n* nube *f*. ● **~ over** *vi* nublarse. **~y** *a* (**-ier, -iest**) nublado; *<liquid>* turbio

clout /klaʊt/ *n* bofetada *f*. ● *vt* abofetear

clove /kləʊv/ *n* clavo *m*. **~ of garlic** *n* diente *m* de ajo

clover /'kləʊvə(r)/ *n* trébol *m*

clown /klaʊn/ *n* payaso *m*. ● *vi* hacer el payaso

club /klʌb/ *n* club *m*; (weapon) porra *f*; (golf club) palo *m* de golf; (at cards) trébol *m*. ● *vt* (*pt* **clubbed**) aporrear. □ **~ together** *vi* contribuir con dinero (**to** para)

cluck /klʌk/ *vi* cloquear

clue /klu:/ *n* pista *f*; (in crosswords) indicación *f*. **not to have a ~** no tener la menor idea

clump /klʌmp/ *n* grupo *m*. ● *vt* agrupar

clums|iness /'klʌmzɪnɪs/ n torpeza f. **~y** /'klʌmzɪ/ a (**-ier**, **-iest**) torpe

clung /klʌŋ/ ⇒CLING

cluster /'klʌstə(r)/ n grupo m. ● vi agruparse

clutch /klʌtʃ/ vt agarrar. ● n (Auto) embrague m

clutter /'klʌtə(r)/ n desorden m. ● vt. **~** (**up**) abarrotar. **~ed** /'klʌtəd/ a abarratado de cosas

coach /kəʊtʃ/ n autocar m, autobús m; (of train) vagón m; (horse-drawn) coche m; (Sport) entrenador m. ● vt (Sport) entrenar

coal /kəʊl/ n carbón m

coalition /kəʊə'lɪʃn/ n coalición f

coarse /kɔːs/ a (**-er**, **-est**) grueso; <material> basto; (person, language) ordinario

coast /kəʊst/ n costa f. ● vi (with cycle) deslizarse sin pedalear; (with car) ir en punto muerto. **~al** a costero. **~guard** n guardacostas m. **~line** n litoral m

coat /kəʊt/ n abrigo m; (jacket) chaqueta f; (of animal) pelo m; (of paint) mano f. ● vt cubrir, revestir. **~hanger** n percha f, gancho m (LAm). **~ing** n capa f. **~ of arms** n escudo m de armas

coax /kəʊks/ vt engatusar

cobbler /'kɒblə(r)/ n zapatero m (remendón)

cobblestone /'kɒbəlstəʊn/ n adoquín m

cobweb /'kɒbweb/ n telaraña f

cocaine /kə'keɪn/ n cocaína f

cock /kɒk/ n (cockerel) gallo m; (male bird) macho m. ● vt amartillar <gun>; aguzar <ears>. **~erel** /'kɒkərəl/ n gallo m. **~-eyed** /-aɪd/ a 🔲 torcido

cockney /'kɒknɪ/ a & n (pl **-eys**) londinense (m & f) (del este de Londres)

cockpit /'kɒkpɪt/ n (in aircraft) cabina f del piloto

cockroach /'kɒkrəʊtʃ/ n cucaracha f

cocktail /'kɒkteɪl/ n cóctel m

cock-up /'kɒkʌp/ n 🔲 lío m

cocky /'kɒkɪ/ a (**-ier**, **-iest**) engreído

cocoa /'kəʊkəʊ/ n cacao m; (drink) chocolate m, cocoa f (LAm)

coconut /'kəʊkənʌt/ n coco m

cocoon /kə'kuːn/ n capullo m

cod /kɒd/ n invar bacalao m

code /kəʊd/ n código m; (secret) clave f; in **~** en clave

coeducational /kəʊedʒʊ'keɪʃənl/ a mixto

coerc|e /kəʊ'ɜːs/ vt coaccionar. **~ion** /-ʃn/ n coacción f

coffee /'kɒfɪ/ n café m. **~ bean** n grano m de café. **~ maker** n cafetera f. **~pot** n cafetera f

coffin /'kɒfɪn/ n ataúd m, cajón m (LAm)

cog /kɒg/ n diente m; (fig) pieza f

coherent /kəʊ'hɪərənt/ a coherente

coil /kɔɪl/ vt enrollar. ● n rollo m; (one ring) vuelta f

coin /kɔɪn/ n moneda f. ● vt acuñar

coincide /kəʊɪn'saɪd/ vi coincidir. **~nce** /kəʊ'ɪnsɪdəns/ n casualidad f. **~ntal** /kəʊɪnsɪ'dentl/ a casual

coke /kəʊk/ n (coal) coque m. **C~** (P) Coca-Cola f (P)

colander /'kʌləndə(r)/ n colador m

cold /kəʊld/ a (**-er**, **-est**) frío. be **~** <person> tener frío. it is **~** (weather) hace frío. ● n frío m; (Med) resfriado m. have a **~** estar resfriado. **~-blooded** /-'blʌdɪd/ a <animal> de sangre fría; <murder> a sangre fría. **~-shoulder** /-'ʃəʊldə(r)/ vt tratar con frialdad. **~ sore** n herpes m labial. **~ storage** n conservación f en frigorífico

coleslaw /'kəʊlslɔː/ n ensalada f de col

collaborat|e /kə'læbəreɪt/ vi colaborar. **~ion** /-'reɪʃn/ n colaboración f. **~or** n colaborador m

collaps|e /kə'læps/ vi derrumbarse; (Med) sufrir un colapso. ● n derrumbamiento m; (Med) colapso m. **~ible** /-əbl/ a plegable

collar /'kɒlə(r)/ n cuello m; (for animals) collar m. ● vt 🔲 hurtar. **~bone** n clavícula f

colleague /'kɒliːg/ n colega m & f

collect /kə'lekt/ vt reunir; (hobby) coleccionar, juntar (LAm); (pick up) recoger; cobrar <rent>. ● vi <people> reunirse; <things> acumularse. ∼ion /-ʃn/ n colección f; (in church) colecta f; (of post) recogida f. ∼or n coleccionista m & f

college /'kɒlɪdʒ/ n colegio m; (of art, music etc) escuela f; (Amer) universidad f

colli|de /kə'laɪd/ vi chocar. ∼sion /-'lɪʒn/ n choque m

colloquial /kə'ləʊkwɪəl/ a coloquial

Colombia /kə'lʌmbɪə/ n Colombia f. ∼n a & n colombiano (m)

colon /'kəʊlən/ n (Gram) dos puntos mpl; (Med) colon m

colonel /'kɜːnl/ n coronel m

colon|ial /kə'ləʊnɪəl/ a colonial. ∼ize /'kɒlənaɪz/ vt colonizar. ∼y /'kɒlənɪ/ n colonia f

colossal /kə'lɒsl/ a colosal

colour /'kʌlə(r)/ n color m. off ∼ (fig) indispuesto. ● a de color(es), en color(es) ● vt colorear; (dye) teñir. ∼-blind a daltoniano. ∼ed /'kʌləd/ a de color. ∼ful a lleno de color; (fig) pintoresco. ∼ing n color; (food colouring) colorante m. ∼less a incoloro

column /'kɒləm/ n columna f. ∼ist n columnista m & f

coma /'kəʊmə/ n coma m

comb /kəʊm/ n peine m. ● vt (search) registrar. ∼ one's hair peinarse

combat /'kɒmbæt/ n combate m. ● vt (pt **combated**) combatir

combination /kɒmbɪ'neɪʃn/ n combinación f

combine /kəm'baɪn/ vt combinar. ● vi combinarse. ● /'kɒmbaɪn/ n asociación f. ∼ **harvester** n cosechadora f

combustion /kəm'bʌstʃən/ n combustión f

come /kʌm/ vi (pt **came**, pp **come**) venir; (occur) pasar. □ ∼ **across** vt encontrarse con <person>; encontrar <object>. □ ∼ **apart** vi deshacerse. □ ∼ **away** vi (leave) salir; (become detached) salirse. □ ∼ **back** vi volver. □ ∼ **by** vt obtener. □ ∼ **down** vi bajar. □ ∼ **in** vi

entrar; (arrive) llegar. □ ∼ **into** vt entrar en; heredar <money>. □ ∼ **off** vi desprenderse; (succeed) tener éxito. vt. ∼ **off it!** ⊡ ¡no me vengas con eso! □ ∼ **on** vi (start to work) encenderse. ∼ **on, hurry up!** ¡vamos, date prisa! □ ∼ **out** vi salir. □ ∼ **round** vi (after fainting) volver en sí; (be converted) cambiar de idea; (visit) venir. □ ∼ **to** vt llegar a <decision etc>. □ ∼ **up** vi subir; (fig) surgir. □ ∼ **up with** vt proponer <idea>. ∼**back** n retorno m; (retort) réplica f

comedian /kə'miːdɪən/ n cómico m

comedy /'kɒmədɪ/ n comedia f

comet /'kɒmɪt/ n cometa m

comfort /'kʌmfət/ n comodidad f; (consolation) consuelo m. ● vt consolar. ∼**able** a cómodo. ∼**er** n (for baby) chupete m, chupón m (LAm); (Amer, for bed) edredón m

comic /'kɒmɪk/ a cómico. ● n cómico m; (periodical) revista f de historietas, tebeo m. ∼**al** a cómico. ∼ **strip** n tira f cómica

coming /'kʌmɪŋ/ n llegada f. ∼s and goings idas fpl y venidas. ● a próximo; <week, month etc> que viene

comma /'kɒmə/ n coma f

command /kə'mɑːnd/ n orden f; (mastery) dominio m. ● vt ordenar; imponer <respect>

commandeer /kɒmən'dɪə(r)/ vt requisar

command: ∼**er** n comandante m. ∼**ing** a imponente. ∼**ment** n mandamiento m

commando /kə'mɑːndəʊ/ n (pl -os) comando m

commemorat|e /kə'meməreɪt/ vt conmemorar. ∼**ion** /-'reɪʃn/ n conmemoración f. ∼**ive** /-ətɪv/ a conmemorativo

commence /kə'mens/ vt dar comienzo a. ● vi iniciarse

commend /kə'mend/ vt alabar. ∼**able** a loable. ∼**ation** /kɒmen'deɪʃn/ n elogio m

comment /'kɒment/ n observación f. ● vi hacer observaciones (on sobre)

commentary /'kɒməntrɪ/ n comentario m; (Radio, TV) reportaje m

commentat|e /'kɒmənteɪt/ *vi* narrar. **∼or** *n* (Radio, TV) locutor *m*

commerc|e /'kɒmɜːs/ *n* comercio *m*. **∼ial** /kə'mɜːʃl/ *a* comercial. ● *n* anuncio *m*; aviso *m* (LAm). **∼ialize** *vt* comercializar

commiserat|e /kə'mɪzəreɪt/ *vi* compadecerse (**with** de). **∼ion** /-'reɪʃn/ *n* conmiseración *f*

commission /kə'mɪʃn/ *n* comisión *f*. **out of** ∼ fuera de servicio. ● *vt* encargar; (Mil) nombrar oficial

commissionaire /kəmɪʃə'neə(r)/ *n* portero *m*

commit /kə'mɪt/ *vt* (*pt* **committed**) cometer; (entrust) confiar. ∼ **o.s.** comprometerse. **∼ment** *n* compromiso *m*

committee /kə'mɪtɪ/ *n* comité *m*

commodity /kə'mɒdətɪ/ *n* producto *m*, artículo *m*

common /'kɒmən/ *a* (**-er, -est**) común; (usual) corriente; (vulgar) ordinario. ● *n*. **in** ∼ en común. **∼er** *n* plebeyo *m*. ∼ **law** *n* derecho *m* consuetudinario. **∼ly** *adv* comúnmente. **C∼ Market** *n* Mercado *m* Común. **∼place** *a* banal. ● *n* banalidad *f*. ∼ **room** *n* sala *f* común, salón *m* común. **C∼s** *n*. the (House of) **C∼s** la Cámara de los Comunes. ∼ **sense** *n* sentido *m* común. **C∼wealth** *n*. the **C∼wealth** la Mancomunidad *f* Británica

commotion /kə'məʊʃn/ *n* confusión *f*

commune /'kɒmjuːn/ *n* comuna *f*

communicat|e /kə'mjuːnɪkeɪt/ *vt* comunicar. ● *vi* comunicarse. **∼ion** /-'keɪʃn/ *n* comunicación *f*. **∼ive** /-ətɪv/ *a* comunicativo

communion /kə'mjuːnɪən/ *n* comunión *f*

communis|m /'kɒmjʊnɪsəm/ *n* comunismo *m*. **∼t** *n* comunista *m & f*

community /kə'mjuːnətɪ/ *n* comunidad *f*. ∼ **centre** *n* centro *m* social

commute /kə'mjuːt/ *vi* viajar diariamente (entre el lugar de residencia y el trabajo). ● *vt* (Jurid) conmutar. **∼r** *n* viajero *m* diario

compact /kəm'pækt/ *a* compacto. ● /'kɒmpækt/ *n* (for powder) polvera *f*. ∼ **disc**, ∼ **disk** /'kɒmpækt/ *n* disco *m* compacto, compact-disc *m*. ∼ **disc player** *n* (reproductor *m* de) compact-disc

companion /kəm'pænɪən/ *n* compañero *m*. **∼ship** *n* compañía *f*

company /'kʌmpənɪ/ *n* compañía *f*; (guests) visita *f*; (Com) sociedad *f*

compar|able /'kɒmpərəbl/ *a* comparable. **∼ative** /kəm'pærətɪv/ *a* comparativo; (fig) relativo. ● *n* (Gram) comparativo *m*. **∼e** /kəm'peə(r)/ *vt* comparar. **∼ison** /kəm'pærɪsn/ *n* comparación *f*

compartment /kəm'pɑːtmənt/ *n* compartim(i)ento *m*

compass /'kʌmpəs/ *n* brújula *f*. **∼es** *npl* compás *m*

compassion /kəm'pæʃn/ *n* compasión *f*. **∼ate** /-ət/ *a* compasivo

compatible /kəm'pætəbl/ *a* compatible

compel /kəm'pel/ *vt* (*pt* **compelled**) obligar. **∼ling** *a* irresistible

compensat|e /'kɒmpənseɪt/ *vt* compensar; (for loss) indemnizar. ● *vi*. **∼e for sth** compensar algo. **∼ion** /-'seɪʃn/ *n* compensación *f*; (financial) indemnización *f*

compère /'kɒmpeə(r)/ *n* presentador *m*. ● *vt* presentar

compete /kəm'piːt/ *vi* competir

competen|ce /'kɒmpətəns/ *n* competencia *f*. **∼t** *a* competente

competit|ion /kɒmpə'tɪʃn/ *n* (contest) concurso *m*; (Sport) competición *f*, competencia *f* (LAm); (Com) competencia *f*. **∼ive** /kəm'petətɪv/ *a* competidor; <price> competitivo. **∼or** /kəm'petɪtə(r)/ *n* competidor *m*; (in contest) concursante *m & f*

compile /kəm'paɪl/ *vt* compilar

complacen|cy /kəm'pleɪsənsɪ/ *n* autosuficiencia *f*. **∼t** *a* satisfecho de sí mismo

complain /kəm'pleɪn/ *vi*. ∼ (**about**) quejarse (de). ● *vt*. ∼ **that** quejarse de que. **∼t** *n* queja *f*; (Med) enfermedad *f*

complement /'kɒmplɪmənt/ *n* complemento *m*. ● *vt* complementar. ∼**ary** /-'mentrɪ/ *a* complementario

complet|e /kəm'pliːt/ *a* completo; (finished) acabado; (downright) total. ● *vt* acabar; llenar *<a form>*. ∼**ely** *adv* completamente. ∼**ion** /-ʃn/ *n* finalización *f*

complex /'kɒmpleks/ *a* complejo. ● *n* complejo *m*

complexion /kəm'plekʃn/ *n* tez *f*; (fig) aspecto *m*

complexity /kəm'pleksətɪ/ *n* complejidad *f*

complicat|e /'kɒmplɪkeɪt/ *vt* complicar. ∼**ed** *a* complicado. ∼**ion** /-'keɪʃn/ *n* complicación *f*

compliment /'kɒmplɪmənt/ *n* cumplido *m*; (amorous) piropo *m*. ● *vt* felicitar. ∼**ary** /-'mentrɪ/ *a* halagador; (given free) de regalo. ∼**s** *npl* saludos *mpl*

comply /kəm'plaɪ/ *vi.* ∼ **with** conformarse con

component /kəm'pəʊnənt/ *a & n* componente (*m*)

compos|e /kəm'pəʊz/ *vt* componer. **be** ∼**ed of** estar compuesto de. ∼**er** *n* compositor *m*. ∼**ition** /kɒmpə'zɪʃn/ *n* composición *f*

compost /'kɒmpɒst/ *n* abono *m*

composure /kəm'pəʊʒə(r)/ *n* serenidad *f*

compound /'kɒmpaʊnd/ *n* compuesto *m*; (enclosure) recinto *m*. ● *a* compuesto; *<fracture>* complicado

comprehen|d /kɒmprɪ'hend/ *vt* comprender. ∼**sion** /kɒmprɪ'henʃn/ *n* comprensión *f*. ∼**sive** /kɒmprɪ'hensɪv/ *a* extenso; *<insurance>* contra todo riesgo. ∼**sive** (**school**) *n* instituto *m* de enseñanza secundaria

compress /'kɒmpres/ *n* (Med) compresa *f*. ● /kəm'pres/ *vt* comprimir. ∼**ion** /-'preʃn/ *n* compresión *f*

comprise /kəm'praɪz/ *vt* comprender

compromis|e /'kɒmprəmaɪz/ *n* acuerdo *m*, compromiso *m*, arreglo *m*. ● *vt* comprometer. ● *vi* llegar a un acuerdo. ∼**ing** *a* *<situation>* comprometido

compuls|ion /kəm'pʌlʃn/ *n* (force) coacción *f*; (obsession) compulsión *f*. ∼**ive** /kəm'pʌlsɪv/ *a* compulsivo. ∼**ory** /kəm'pʌlsərɪ/ *a* obligatorio

comput|er /kəm'pjuːtə(r)/ *n* ordenador *m*, computadora *f* (LAm). ∼**erize** *vt* computarizar, computerizar. ∼**er studies** *n*, ∼**ing** *n* informática *f*, computación *f*

comrade /'kɒmreɪd/ *n* camarada *m* & *f*

con /kɒn/ *vt* (*pt* **conned**) 🔲 estafar. ● *n* (fraud) estafa *f*; (objection) ⇒PRO

concave /'kɒŋkeɪv/ *a* cóncavo

conceal /kən'siːl/ *vt* ocultar

concede /kən'siːd/ *vt* conceder

conceit /kən'siːt/ *n* vanidad *f*. ∼**ed** *a* engreído

conceiv|able /kən'siːvəbl/ *a* concebible. ∼**e** /kən'siːv/ *vt/i* concebir

concentrat|e /'kɒnsəntreɪt/ *vt* concentrar. ● *vi* concentrarse (**on** en). ∼**ion** /-'treɪʃn/ *n* concentración *f*

concept /'kɒnsept/ *n* concepto *m*

conception /kən'sepʃn/ *n* concepción *f*

concern /kən'sɜːn/ *n* asunto *m*; (worry) preocupación *f*; (Com) empresa *f*. ● *vt* tener que ver con; (deal with) tratar de. **as far as I'm** ∼**ed** en cuanto a mí. **be** ∼**ed about** preocuparse por. ∼**ing** *prep* acerca de

concert /'kɒnsət/ *n* concierto *m*. ∼**ed** /kən'sɜːtɪd/ *a* concertado

concertina /kɒnsə'tiːnə/ *n* concertina *f*

concerto /kən'tʃɜːtəʊ/ *n* (*pl* **-os** or **-ti** /-tɪ/) concierto *m*

concession /kən'seʃn/ *n* concesión *f*

concise /kən'saɪs/ *a* conciso

conclu|de /kən'kluːd/ *vt/i* concluir. ∼**ding** *a* final. ∼**sion** /-ʃn/ *n* conclusión *f*. ∼**sive** /-sɪv/ *a* decisivo. ∼**sively** *adv* concluyentemente

concoct /kən'kɒkt/ *vt* confeccionar; (fig) inventar. ∼**ion** /-ʃn/ *n* mezcla *f*; (drink) brebaje *m*

concrete /'kɒŋkriːt/ *n* hormigón *m*, concreto *m* (LAm). ● *a* concreto

concussion /kən'kʌʃn/ n conmoción f cerebral

condemn /kən'dem/ vt condenar. ~ation /kɒndem'neɪʃn/ n condena f

condens|ation /kɒnden'seɪʃn/ n condensación f. ~e /kən'dens/ vt condensar. ● vi condensarse

condescend /kɒndɪ'send/ vi dignarse (to a). ~ing a superior

condition /kən'dɪʃn/ n condición f. on ~ that a condición de que. ● vt condicionar. ~al a condicional. ~er n (for hair) suavizante m, enjuague m (LAm)

condo /'kɒndəʊ/ n (pl -os) (Amer 🄯) ⇒CONDOMINIUM

condolences /kən'dəʊlənsɪz/ npl pésame m

condom /'kɒndɒm/ n condón m

condominium /kɒndə'mɪnɪəm/ n (Amer) apartamento m, piso m (en régimen de propiedad horizontal)

condone /kən'dəʊn/ vt condonar

conduct /kən'dʌkt/ vt llevar a cabo <business, experiment>; conducir <electricity>; dirigir <orchestra>. ● /'kɒndʌkt/ n conducta f. ~or /kən'dʌktə(r)/ n director m; (of bus) cobrador m. ~ress /kən'dʌktrɪs/ n cobradora f

cone /kəʊn/ n cono m; (for ice cream) cucurucho m, barquillo m (Mex)

confectionery /kən'fekʃənrɪ/ n productos mpl de confitería

confederation /kənfedə'reɪʃn/ n confederación f

confess /kən'fes/ vt confesar. ● vi confesarse. ~ion /-ʃn/ n confesión f

confetti /kən'fetɪ/ n confeti m

confide /kən'faɪd/ vt/i confiar

confiden|ce /'kɒnfɪdəns/ n confianza f; (self-confidence) confianza f en sí mismo; (secret) confidencia f. ~ce trick n estafa f, timo m. ~t /'kɒnfɪdənt/ a seguro de sí mismo. be ~t of confiar en

confidential /kɒnfɪ'denʃl/ a confidencial. ~ity /-denʃɪ'ælətɪ/ n confidencialidad f

confine /kən'faɪn/ vt confinar; (limit) limitar. ~ment n (imprisonment) prisión f

confirm /kən'fɜːm/ vt confirmar. ~ation /kɒnfə'meɪʃn/ n confirmación f. ~ed a inveterado

confiscat|e /'kɒnfɪskeɪt/ vt confiscar. ~ion /-'keɪʃn/ n confiscación f

conflict /'kɒnflɪkt/ n conflicto m. ● /kən'flɪkt/ vi chocar. ~ing /kən'flɪktɪŋ/ a contradictorio

conform /kən'fɔːm/ vi conformarse. ~ist n conformista m & f

confound /kən'faʊnd/ vt confundir. ~ed a 🄯 maldito

confront /kən'frʌnt/ vt hacer frente a; (face) enfrentarse con. ~ation /kɒnfrʌn'teɪʃn/ n confrontación f

confus|e /kən'fjuːz/ vt confundir. ~ed a confundido. get ~ed confundirse. ~ing a confuso. ~ion /-ʒn/ n confusión f

congeal /kən'dʒiːl/ vi coagularse

congest|ed /kən'dʒestɪd/ a congestionado. ~ion /-tʃən/ n congestión f

congratulat|e /kən'grætjʊleɪt/ vt felicitar. ~ions /-'leɪʃnz/ npl enhorabuena f, felicitaciones fpl (LAm)

congregat|e /'kɒŋɡrɪɡeɪt/ vi congregarse. ~ion /-'ɡeɪʃn/ n asamblea f; (Relig) fieles mpl, feligreses mpl

congress /'kɒŋɡres/ n congreso m. C~ (Amer) el Congreso. ~man /-mən/ n (Amer) miembro m del Congreso. ~woman n (Amer) miembro f del Congreso

conifer /'kɒnɪfə(r)/ n conífera f

conjugat|e /'kɒndʒʊɡeɪt/ vt conjugar. ~ion /-'ɡeɪʃn/ n conjugación f

conjunction /kən'dʒʌŋkʃn/ n conjunción f

conjur|e /'kʌndʒə(r)/ vi hacer juegos de manos. ● vt. □ ~e up vt evocar. ~er, ~or n prestidigitador m

conk /kɒŋk/ vi. ~ out 🄯 fallar; <person> desmayarse

conker /'kɒŋkə(r)/ n 🄯 castaña f de Indias

conman /'kɒnmæn/ n (pl -men) 🄯 estafador m, timador m

connect /kə'nekt/ vt conectar; (associate) relacionar. ● vi (be fitted) estar conectado (to a). □ ~ with vt <train> enlazar con. ~ed a unido;

(related) relacionado. **be ~ed with** tener que ver con, estar emparentado con. **~ion** /-ʃn/ n conexión f; (Rail) enlace m; (fig) relación f. **in ~ion with** a propósito de, con respecto a

connive /kə'naɪv/ vi. **~e at** ser cómplice en

connoisseur /kɒnə'sɜː(r)/ n experto m

connotation /kɒnə'teɪʃn/ n connotación f

conquer /'kɒŋkə(r)/ vt conquistar; (fig) vencer. **~or** n conquistador m

conquest /'kɒŋkwest/ n conquista f

conscience /'kɒnʃəns/ n conciencia f

conscientious /kɒnʃɪ'enʃəs/ a concienzudo

conscious /'kɒnʃəs/ a consciente; (deliberate) intencional. **~ly** adv a sabiendas. **~ness** n consciencia f; (Med) conocimiento m

conscript /'kɒnskrɪpt/ n recluta m & f, conscripto m (LAm). ● /kən'skrɪpt/ vt reclutar. **~ion** /kən'skrɪpʃn/ n reclutamiento m, conscripción f (LAm)

consecrate /'kɒnsɪkreɪt/ vt consagrar

consecutive /kən'sekjʊtɪv/ a sucesivo

consensus /kən'sensəs/ n consenso m

consent /kən'sent/ vi consentir. ● n consentimiento m

consequen|ce /'kɒnsɪkwəns/ n consecuencia f. **~t** a consiguiente. **~tly** adv por consiguiente

conservation /kɒnsə'veɪʃn/ n conservación f, preservación f. **~ist** n conservacionista m & f

conservative /kən'sɜːvətɪv/ a conservador; (modest) prudente, moderado. **C~** a & n conservador (m)

conservatory /kən'sɜːvətrɪ/ n invernadero m

conserve /kən'sɜːv/ vt conservar

consider /kən'sɪdə(r)/ vt considerar; (take into account) tomar en cuenta. **~able** a considerable. **~ably** adv considerablemente

considerat|e /kən'sɪdərət/ a considerado. **~ion** /-'reɪʃn/ n consideración f. **take sth into ~ion** tomar algo en cuenta

considering /kən'sɪdərɪŋ/ prep teniendo en cuenta. ● conj. **~ (that)** teniendo en cuenta que

consign /kən'saɪn/ vt consignar; (send) enviar. **~ment** n envío m

consist /kən'sɪst/ vi. **~ of** consistir en. **~ency** n consistencia f; (fig) coherencia f. **~ent** a coherente; (unchanging) constante. **~ent with** compatible con. **~ently** adv constantemente

consolation /kɒnsə'leɪʃn/ n consuelo m

console /kən'səʊl/ vt consolar. ● /'kɒnsəʊl/ n consola f

consolidate /kən'sɒlɪdeɪt/ vt consolidar

consonant /'kɒnsənənt/ n consonante f

conspicuous /kən'spɪkjʊəs/ a (easily seen) visible; (showy) llamativo; (noteworthy) notable

conspir|acy /kən'spɪrəsɪ/ n conspiración f. **~ator** /kən'spɪrətə(r)/ n conspirador m. **~e** /kən'spaɪə(r)/ vi conspirar

constable /'kʌnstəbl/ n agente m & f de policía

constant /'kɒnstənt/ a constante. **~ly** adv constantemente

constellation /kɒnstə'leɪʃn/ n constelación f

consternation /kɒnstə'neɪʃn/ n consternación f

constipat|ed /'kɒnstɪpeɪtɪd/ a estreñido. **~ion** /-'peɪʃn/ n estreñimiento m

constituen|cy /kən'stɪtjʊənsɪ/ n distrito m electoral. **~t** n (Pol) elector m. ● a constituyente, constitutivo

constitut|e /'kɒnstɪtjuːt/ vt constituir. **~ion** /-'tjuːʃn/ n constitución f. **~ional** /-'tjuːʃənl/ a constitucional. ● n paseo m

constrict /kən'strɪkt/ vt apretar. **~ion** /-ʃn/ n constricción f

construct /kən'strʌkt/ vt construir. **~ion** /-ʃn/ n construcción f. **~ive** a constructivo

consul /'kɒnsl/ n cónsul m & f. ∼**ate** /'kɒnsjʊlət/ n consulado m

consult /kən'sʌlt/ vt/i consultar. ∼**ancy** n asesoría. ∼**ant** n asesor m; (Med) especialista m & f; (Tec) consejero m técnico. ∼**ation** /kɒnsəl'teɪʃn/ n consulta f

consume /kən'sju:m/ vt consumir. ∼**r** n consumidor m. ● a de consumo

consummate /'kɒnsəmət/ a consumado. ● /'kɒnsəmeɪt/ vt consumar

consumption /kən'sʌmpʃn/ n consumo m

contact /'kɒntækt/ n contacto m. ● vt ponerse en contacto con. ∼ **lens** n lentilla f, lente f de contacto (LAm)

contagious /kən'teɪdʒəs/ a contagioso

contain /kən'teɪn/ vt contener. ∼ o.s. contenerse. ∼**er** n recipiente m; (Com) contenedor m

contaminat|e /kən'tæmɪneɪt/ vt contaminar. ∼**ion** /-'neɪʃn/ n contaminación f

contemplate /'kɒntəmpleɪt/ vt contemplar; (consider) considerar

contemporary /kən'tempərərɪ/ a & n contemporáneo (m)

contempt /kən'tempt/ n desprecio m. ∼**ible** a despreciable. ∼**uous** /-tjʊəs/ a desdeñoso

contend /kən'tend/ vt competir. ∼**er** n aspirante m & f (for a)

content /kən'tent/ a satisfecho. ● /'kɒntent/ n contenido m. ● /kən'tent/ vt contentar. ∼**ed** /kən'tentɪd/ a satisfecho. ∼**ment** /kən'tentmənt/ n satisfacción f. ∼**s** /'kɒntents/ n contenido m; (of book) índice m de materias

contest /'kɒntest/ n (competition) concurso m; (Sport) competición f, competencia f (LAm). ● /kən'test/ vt disputar. ∼**ant** /kən'testənt/ n concursante m & f

context /'kɒntekst/ n contexto m

continent /'kɒntɪnənt/ n continente m. the C∼ Europa f. ∼**al** /-'nentl/ a continental. ∼**al quilt** n edredón m

contingen|cy /kən'tɪndʒənsɪ/ n contingencia f. ∼**t** a & n contingente (m)

continu|al /kən'tɪnjʊəl/ a continuo. ∼**ally** adv continuamente. ∼**ation** /-'eɪʃn/ n continuación f. ∼**e** /kən'tɪnju:/ vt/i continuar, seguir. ∼**ed** a continuo. ∼**ity** /kɒntɪ'nju:ətɪ/ n continuidad f. ∼**ous** /kən'tɪnjʊəs/ a continuo. ∼**ously** adv continuamente

contort /kən'tɔ:t/ vt retorcer. ∼**ion** /-ʃn/ n contorsión f. ∼**ionist** /-ʃənɪst/ n contorsionista m & f

contour /'kɒntʊə(r)/ n contorno m

contraband /'kɒntrəbænd/ n contrabando m

contracepti|on /kɒntrə'sepʃn/ n anticoncepción f. ∼**ve** /-tɪv/ a & n anticonceptivo (m)

contract /'kɒntrækt/ n contrato m. ● /kən'trækt/ vt contraer. ● vi contraerse. ∼**ion** /kən'trækʃn/ n contracción f. ∼**or** /kən'træktə(r)/ n contratista m & f

contradict /kɒntrə'dɪkt/ vt contradecir. ∼**ion** /-ʃn/ n contradicción f. ∼**ory** a contradictorio

contraption /kən'træpʃn/ n 🔲 artilugio m

contrary /'kɒntrərɪ/ a contrario. the ∼ lo contrario. on the ∼ al contrario. ● adv. ∼ to contrariamente a. ● /kən'treərɪ/ a (obstinate) terco

contrast /'kɒntrɑ:st/ n contraste m. ● /kən'trɑ:st/ vt/i contrastar. ∼**ing** a contrastante

contravene /kɒntrə'vi:n/ vt contravenir

contribut|e /kən'trɪbju:t/ vt contribuir con. ● vi contribuir. ∼**e to** escribir para <newspaper>. ∼**ion** /kɒntrɪ'bju:ʃn/ n contribución f. ∼**or** n contribuyente m & f; (to newspaper) colaborador m

contrite /'kɒntraɪt/ a arrepentido, pesaroso

contriv|e /kən'traɪv/ vt idear. ∼**e to** conseguir. ∼**ed** a artificioso

control /kən'trəʊl/ vt (pt **controlled**) controlar. ● n control m.

~**ler** *n* director *m*. ~**s** *npl* (Mec) mandos *mpl*

controvers|ial /kɒntrə'vɜ:ʃl/ controvertido. ~**y** /'kɒntrəvɜ:sɪ/ *n* controversia *f*

conundrum /kə'nʌndrəm/ *n* adivinanza *f*

convalesce /kɒnvə'les/ *vi* convalecer. ~**nce** *n* convalecencia *f*

convector /kən'vektə(r)/ *n* estufa *f* de convección

convene /kən'vi:n/ *vt* convocar. ● *vi* reunirse

convenien|ce /kən'vi:nɪəns/ *n* conveniencia *f*, comodidad *f*. **all modern** ~**ces** todas las comodidades. **at your** ~**ce** según le convenga. ~**ces** *npl* servicios *mpl*, baños *mpl* (LAm). ~**t** *a* conveniente; *<place>* bien situado; *<time>* oportuno. **be** ~**t** convenir. ~**tly** *adv* convenientemente

convent /'kɒnvənt/ *n* convento *m*

convention /kən'venʃn/ *n* convención *f*. ~**al** *a* convencional

converge /kən'vɜ:dʒ/ *vi* converger

conversation /kɒnvə'seɪʃn/ *n* conversación *f*. ~**al** *a* familiar, coloquial.

converse /kən'vɜ:s/ *vi* conversar. ● /'kɒnvɜ:s/ *a* inverso. ● *n* lo contrario. ~**ly** *adv* a la inversa

conver|sion /kən'vɜ:ʃn/ *n* conversión *f*. ~**t** /kən'vɜ:t/ *vt* convertir. ● /'kɒnvɜ:t/ *n* converso *m*. ~**tible** /kən'vɜ:tɪbl/ *a* convertible. ● *n* (Auto) descapotable *m*, convertible *m* (LAm)

convex /'kɒnveks/ *a* convexo

convey /kən'veɪ/ *vt* transportar *<goods, people>*; comunicar *<idea, feeling>*. ~**or belt** *n* cinta *f* transportadora, banda *f* transportadora (LAm)

convict /kən'vɪkt/ *vt* condenar. ● /'kɒnvɪkt/ *n* presidiario *m*. ~**ion** /kən'vɪkʃn/ *n* condena *f*; (belief) creencia *f*

convinc|e /kən'vɪns/ *vt* convencer. ~**ing** *a* convincente

convoluted /'kɒnvəlu:tɪd/ *a* *<argument>* intrincado

convoy /'kɒnvɔɪ/ *n* convoy *m*

convuls|e /kən'vʌls/ *vt* convulsionar. **be** ~**ed with laughter** desternillarse de risa. ~**ion** /-ʃn/ *n* convulsión *f*

coo /ku:/ *vi* arrullar

cook /kʊk/ *vt* hacer, preparar. ● *vi* cocinar; *<food>* hacerse. ● *n* cocinero *m*. □ ~ **up** *vt* 🅸 inventar. ~**book** *n* libro *m* de cocina. ~**er** *n* cocina *f*, estufa *f* (Mex). ~**ery** *n* cocina *f*

cookie /'kʊkɪ/ *n* (Amer) galleta *f*

cool /ku:l/ *a* (**-er, -est**) fresco; (calm) tranquilo; (unfriendly) frío. ● *n* fresco *m*; 🆇 calma *f*. ● *vt* enfriar. ● *vi* enfriarse. □ ~ **down** *vi* *<person>* calmarse. ~**ly** *adv* tranquilamente

coop /ku:p/ *n* gallinero *m*. □ ~ **up** *vt* encerrar

co-op /'kəʊɒp/ *n* cooperativa *f*

cooperat|e /kəʊ'ɒpəreɪt/ *vi* cooperar. ~**ion** /-'reɪʃn/ *n* cooperación *f*. ~**ive** /kəʊ'ɒpərətɪv/ *a* cooperativo. ● *n* cooperativa *f*

co-opt /kəʊ'ɒpt/ *vt* cooptar

co-ordinat|e /kəʊ'ɔ:dɪneɪt/ *vt* coordinar. ● /kəʊ'ɔ:dɪnət/ *n* (Math) coordenada *f*. ~**es** *npl* prendas *fpl* para combinar. ~**ion** /kəʊɔ:dɪ'neɪʃn/ *n* coordinación *f*

cop /kɒp/ *n* 🅸 poli *m* & *f* 🅸, tira *m* & *f* (Mex, 🅸)

cope /kəʊp/ *vi* arreglárselas. ~ **with** hacer frente a

copious /'kəʊpɪəs/ *a* abundante

copper /'kɒpə(r)/ *n* cobre *m*; (coin) perra *f*; 🅸 poli *m* & *f* 🅸, tira *m* & *f* (Mex, 🅸). ● *a* de cobre

copy /'kɒpɪ/ *n* copia *f*; (of book, newspaper) ejemplar *m*. ● *vt* copiar. ~**right** *n* derechos *mpl* de reproducción

coral /'kɒrəl/ *n* coral *m*

cord /kɔ:d/ *n* cuerda *f*; (fabric) pana *f*; (Amer, Elec) cordón *m*, cable *m*

cordial /'kɔ:dɪəl/ *a* cordial. ● *n* refresco *m* (concentrado)

cordon /'kɔ:dn/ *n* cordón *m*. □ ~ **off** *vt* acordonar

core /kɔ:(r)/ *n* (of apple) corazón *m*; (of Earth) centro *m*; (of problem) meollo *m*

cork /kɔ:k/ *n* corcho *m*. ~**screw** *n* sacacorchos *m*

corn /kɔːn/ n (wheat) trigo m; (Amer) maíz m; (hard skin) callo m

corned beef /kɔːnd 'biːf/ n carne f de vaca en lata

corner /'kɔːnə(r)/ n ángulo m; (inside) rincón m; (outside) esquina f; (football) córner m. ●vt arrinconar; (Com) acaparar

cornet /'kɔːnɪt/ n (Mus) corneta f; (for ice cream) cucurucho m, barquillo m (Mex)

corn: ~**flakes** npl copos mpl de maíz. ~**flour** n maizena f (P)

Cornish /'kɔːnɪʃ/ a de Cornualles

cornstarch /'kɔːnstɑːtʃ/ n (Amer) maizena f (P)

corny /'kɔːnɪ/ a (🄵, trite) gastado

coronation /kɒrə'neɪʃn/ n coronación f

coroner /'kɒrənə(r)/ n juez m de primera instancia

corporal /'kɔːpərəl/ n cabo m. ●a corporal

corporate /'kɔːpərət/ a corporativo

corporation /kɔːpə'reɪʃn/ n corporación f; (Amer) sociedad f anónima

corps /kɔː(r)/ n (pl **corps** /kɔːz/) cuerpo m

corpse /kɔːps/ n cadáver m

corpulent /'kɔːpjʊlənt/ a corpulento

corral /kə'rɑːl/ n (Amer) corral m

correct /kə'rekt/ a correcto; *<time>* exacto. ●vt corregir. ~**ion** /-ʃn/ n corrección f

correspond /kɒrɪ'spɒnd/ vi corresponder; (write) escribirse. ~**ence** n correspondencia f. ~**ent** n corresponsal m & f

corridor /'kɒrɪdɔː(r)/ n pasillo m

corro|de /kə'rəʊd/ vt corroer. ●vi corroerse. ~**sion** /-ʒn/ n corrosión f. ~**sive** /-sɪv/ a corrosivo

corrugated /'kɒrəgeɪtɪd/ a ondulado. ~ **iron** n chapa f de zinc

corrupt /kə'rʌpt/ a corrompido. ●vt corromper. ~**ion** /-ʃn/ n corrupción f

corset /'kɔːsɪt/ n corsé m

cosmetic /kɒz'metɪk/ a & n cosmético (m)

cosmic /'kɒzmɪk/ a cósmico

cosmopolitan /kɒzmə'pɒlɪtən/ a & n cosmopolita (m & f)

cosmos /'kɒzmɒs/ n cosmos m

cosset /'kɒsɪt/ vt (pt **cosseted**) mimar

cost /kɒst/ vt (pt **cost**) costar; (pt **costed**) calcular el coste de, calcular el costo de (LAm).●n coste m, costo m (LAm). **at all** ~**s** cueste lo que cueste. **to one's** ~ a sus expensas. ~**s** npl (Jurid) costas fpl

Costa Rica /kɒstə'riːkə/ n Costa f Rica. ~**n** a & n costarricense (m & f), costarriqueño (m & f)

cost: ~**-effective** a rentable. ~**ly** a (-ier, -iest) costoso

costume /'kɒstjuːm/ n traje m; (for party, disguise) disfraz m

cosy /'kəʊzɪ/ a (-ier, -iest) acogedor. ●n cubreteras m

cot /kɒt/ n cuna f

cottage /'kɒtɪdʒ/ n casita f. ~ **cheese** n requesón m. ~ **pie** n pastel m de carne cubierta con puré

cotton /'kɒtn/ n algodón m; (thread) hilo m; (Amer) ⇒~ WOOL. □ ~ **on** vi 🄵 comprender. ~ **bud** n bastoncillo m, cotonete m (Mex). ~ **candy** n (Amer) algodón m de azúcar. ~ **swab** n (Amer) ⇒~ BUD. ~ **wool** n algodón m hidrófilo

couch /kaʊtʃ/ n sofá m

cough /kɒf/ vi toser. ●n tos f. □ ~ **up** vt 🄵 pagar. ~ **mixture** n jarabe m para la tos

could /kʊd/ pt of CAN[1]

couldn't /'kʊdnt/ = **could not**

council /'kaʊnsl/ n consejo m; (of town) ayuntamiento m. ~ **house** n vivienda f subvencionada. ~**lor** n concejal m

counsel /'kaʊnsl/ n consejo m; (pl invar) (Jurid) abogado m. ●vt (pt **counselled**) aconsejar. ~**ling** n terapia f de apoyo. ~**lor** n consejero m

count /kaʊnt/ n recuento m; (nobleman) conde m. ●vt/i contar. □ ~ **on** vt contar. ~**down** n cuenta f atrás

counter /'kaʊntə(r)/ n (in shop) mostrador m; (in bank, post office) ventanilla f; (token) ficha f. ●adv. ~ **to** en contra de. ●a opuesto. ●vt oponerse a; parar *<blow>*

counter... /'kaʊntə(r)/ *pref* contra.... ~**act** /-'ækt/ *vt* contrarrestar. ~**attack** *n* contraataque *m*. ● *vt/i* contraatacar. ~**balance** *n* contrapeso *m*. ● *vt/i* contrapesar. ~**clockwise** /-'klɒkwaɪz/ *a/adv* (Amer) en sentido contrario al de las agujas del reloj

counterfeit /'kaʊntəfɪt/ *a* falsificado. ● *n* falsificación *f*. ● *vt* falsificar

counterfoil /'kaʊntəfɔɪl/ *n* matriz *f*, talón *m* (LAm)

counter-productive /kaʊntə prə'dʌktɪv/ *a* contraproducente

countess /'kaʊntɪs/ *n* condesa *f*

countless /'kaʊntlɪs/ *a* innumerable

country /'kʌntrɪ/ *n* (native land) país *m*; (countryside) campo *m*; (Mus) (música *f*) country *m*. ~**-and-western** /-en'westən/ (música *f*) country *m*. ~**man** /-mən/ *n* (of one's own country) compatriota *m*. ~**side** *n* campo *m*; (landscape) paisaje *m*

county /'kaʊntɪ/ *n* condado *m*

coup /ku:/ *n* golpe *m*

couple /'kʌpl/ *n* (of things) par *m*; (of people) pareja *f*; (married) matrimonio *m*. **a** ~ **of** un par de

coupon /'ku:pɒn/ *n* cupón *m*

courage /'kʌrɪdʒ/ *n* valor *m*. ~**ous** /kə'reɪdʒəs/ *a* valiente

courgette /kʊə'ʒet/ *n* calabacín *m*

courier /'kʊrɪə(r)/ *n* mensajero *m*; (for tourists) guía *m & f*

course /kɔːs/ *n* curso *m*; (behaviour) conducta *f*; (Aviat, Naut) rumbo *m*; (Culin) plato *m*; (for golf) campo *m*. **in due** ~ a su debido tiempo. **in the** ~ **of** en el transcurso de, durante. **of** ~ claro, por supuesto. **of** ~ **not** claro que no, por supuesto que no

court /kɔːt/ *n* corte *f*; (tennis) pista *f*; cancha *f* (LAm); (Jurid) tribunal *m*. ● *vt* cortejar; buscar <*danger*>

courteous /'kɜːtɪəs/ *a* cortés

courtesy /'kɜːtəsɪ/ *n* cortesía *f*

courtier /'kɔːtɪə(r)/ *n* (old use) cortesano *m*

court: ~ martial *n* (*pl* ~**s martial**) consejo *m* de guerra. ~**-martial** *vt* (*pt* ~**-martialled**) juzgar en

consejo de guerra. ~**ship** *n* cortejo *m*. ~**yard** *n* patio *m*

cousin /'kʌzn/ *n* primo *m*. **first** ~ primo carnal. **second** ~ primo segundo

cove /kəʊv/ *n* ensenada *f*, cala *f*

Coventry /'kɒvntrɪ/ *n*. **send s.o. to** ~ hacer el vacío a uno

cover /'kʌvə(r)/ *vt* cubrir. ● *n* cubierta *f*; (shelter) abrigo *m*; (lid) tapa *f*; (for furniture) funda *f*; (pretext) pretexto *m*; (of magazine) portada *f*. □ ~ **up** *vt* cubrir; (fig) ocultar. ~ **charge** *n* precio *m* del cubierto. ~**ing** *n* cubierta *f*. ~**ing letter** *n* carta *f* adjunta

covet /'kʌvɪt/ *vt* codiciar

cow /kaʊ/ *n* vaca *f*

coward /'kaʊəd/ *n* cobarde *m*. ~**ice** /'kaʊədɪs/ *n* cobardía *f*. ~**ly** *a* cobarde.

cowboy /'kaʊbɔɪ/ *n* vaquero *m*

cower /'kaʊə(r)/ *vi* encogerse, acobardarse

coxswain /'kɒksn/ *n* timonel *m*

coy /kɔɪ/ *a* (**-er, -est**) (shy) tímido; (evasive) evasivo

crab /kræb/ *n* cangrejo *m*, jaiba *f* (LAm)

crack /kræk/ *n* grieta *f*; (noise) crujido *m*; (of whip) chasquido *m*; (drug) crack *m*. ● *a* 🄘 de primera. ● *vt* agrietar; chasquear <*whip, fingers*>; cascar <*nut*>; gastar <*joke*>; resolver <*problem*>. ● *vi* agrietarse. **get** ~**ing** 🄘 darse prisa. □ ~ **down on** *vt* 🄘 tomar medidas enérgicas contra

cracker /'krækə(r)/ *n* (Culin) cracker *f*, galleta *f* (salada); (Christmas cracker) sorpresa *f* (*que estalla al abrirla*)

crackle /'krækl/ *vi* crepitar. ● *n* crepitación *f*, crujido *m*

crackpot /'krækpɒt/ *n* 🄘 chiflado *m*

cradle /'kreɪdl/ *n* cuna *f*. ● *vt* acunar

craft /krɑːft/ *n* destreza *f*; (technique) arte *f*; (cunning) astucia *f*. ● *n invar* (boat) barco *m*

craftsman /'krɑːftsmən/ *n* (*pl* -**men**) artesano *m*. ~**ship** *n* artesanía *f*

crafty /'krɑːftɪ/ *a* (**-ier, -iest**) astuto

cram /kræm/ *vt* (*pt* **crammed**) rellenar. ～ **with** llenar de. ● *vi* (for exams) memorizar, empollar, zambutir (Mex)

cramp /kræmp/ *n* calambre *m*

cramped /kræmpt/ *a* apretado

crane /kreɪn/ *n* grúa *f*. ● *vt* estirar <*neck*>

crank /kræŋk/ *n* manivela *f*; (person) excéntrico *m*. ～**y** *a* excéntrico

cranny /'krænɪ/ *n* grieta *f*

crash /kræʃ/ *n* accidente *m*; (noise) estruendo *m*; (collision) choque *m*; (Com) quiebra *f*. ● *vt* estrellar. ● *vi* quebrar con estrépito; (have accident) tener un accidente; <*car etc*> estrellarse, chocar; (fail) fracasar. ～ **course** *n* curso *m* intensivo. ～ **helmet** *n* casco *m* protector. ～**-land** *vi* hacer un aterrizaje forzoso

crass /kræs/ *a* craso, burdo

crate /kreɪt/ *n* cajón *m*. ● *vt* embalar

crater /'kreɪtə(r)/ *n* cráter *m*

crav|e /kreɪv/ *vt* ansiar. ～**ing** *n* ansia *f*

crawl /krɔːl/ *vi* <*baby*> gatear; (move slowly) avanzar lentamente; (drag o.s.) arrastrarse. ～ **to** humillarse ante. ～ **with** hervir de. ● *n* (swimming) crol *m*. **at a** ～ a paso lento

crayon /'kreɪən/ *n* lápiz *m* de color; (made of wax) lápiz *m* de cera, crayola *f* (P), crayón *m* (Mex)

craz|e /kreɪz/ *n* manía *f*. ～**y** /'kreɪzɪ/ *a* (**-ier**, **-iest**) loco. **be** ～**y about** estar loco por

creak /kriːk/ *n* crujido *m*; (of hinge) chirrido *m*. ● *vi* crujir; <*hinge*> chirriar

cream /kriːm/ *n* crema *f*; (fresh) nata *f*, crema *f* (LAm). ● *a* (colour) color crema. ● *vt* (beat) batir. ～ **cheese** *n* queso *m* para untar, queso *m* crema (LAm). ～**y** *a* cremoso

crease /kriːs/ *n* raya *f*, pliegue *m* (Mex); (crumple) arruga *f*. ● *vt* plegar; (wrinkle) arrugar. ● *vi* arrugarse

creat|e /kriː'eɪt/ *vt* crear. ～**ion** /-ʃn/ *n* creación *f*. ～**ive** *a* creativo. ～**or** *n* creador *m*

creature /'kriːtʃə(r)/ *n* criatura *f*

crèche /kreʃ/ *n* guardería *f* (infantil)

credib|ility /kredə'bɪlətɪ/ *n* credibilidad *f*. ～**le** /'kredəbl/ *a* creíble

credit /'kredɪt/ *n* crédito *m*; (honour) mérito *m*. **take the** ～ **for** atribuirse el mérito de. ● *vt* (*pt* **credited**) acreditar; (believe) creer. ～ **s.o. with** atribuir a uno. ～ **card** *n* tarjeta *f* de crédito. ～**or** *n* acreedor *m*

creed /kriːd/ *n* credo *m*

creek /kriːk/ *n* ensenada *f*. **up the** ～ ⊠ en apuros

creep /kriːp/ *vi* (*pt* **crept**) arrastrarse; (plant) trepar. ● *n* 🄳 adulador. ～**s** /kriːps/ *npl*. **give s.o. the** ～**s** poner los pelos de punta a uno. ～**er** *n* enredadera *f*

cremat|e /krɪ'meɪt/ *vt* incinerar. ～**ion** /-ʃn/ *n* cremación *f*. ～**orium** /kremə'tɔːrɪəm/ *n* (*pl* **-ia** /-ɪə/) crematorio *m*

crept /krept/ ⇒CREEP

crescendo /krɪ'ʃendəʊ/ *n* (*pl* **-os**) crescendo *m*

crescent /'kresnt/ *n* media luna *f*; (street) calle *f* en forma de media luna

crest /krest/ *n* cresta *f*; (on coat of arms) emblema *m*

crevice /'krevɪs/ *n* grieta *f*

crew /kruː/ *n* tripulación *f*; (gang) pandilla *f*. ～ **cut** *n* corte *m* al rape

crib /krɪb/ *n* (Amer) cuna *f*; (Relig) belén *m*. ● *vt/i* (*pt* **cribbed**) copiar

crick /krɪk/ *n* calambre *m*; (in neck) tortícolis *f*

cricket /'krɪkɪt/ *n* (Sport) críquet *m*; (insect) grillo *m*

crim|e /kraɪm/ *n* delito *m*; (murder) crimen *m*; (acts) delincuencia *f*. ～**inal** /'krɪmɪnl/ *a & n* criminal (*m & f*)

crimson /'krɪmzn/ *a & n* carmesí (*m*)

cringe /krɪndʒ/ *vi* encogerse; (fig) humillarse

crinkle /'krɪŋkl/ *vt* arrugar. ● *vi* arrugarse. ● *n* arruga *f*

cripple /'krɪpl/ *n* lisiado *m*. ● *vt* lisiar; (fig) paralizar

crisis /'kraɪsɪs/ *n* (*pl* **crises** /-siːz/) crisis *f*

crisp /krɪsp/ *a* (**-er**, **-est**) (Culin) crujiente; <*air*> vigorizador. ～**s** *npl* patatas *fpl* fritas, papas *fpl* fritas (LAm) (de bolsa)

crisscross /'krɪskrɒs/ *a* entrecruzado. ● *vt* entrecruzar. ● *vi* entrecruzarse

criterion /kraɪ'tɪərɪən/ *n* (*pl* **-ia** /-ɪə/) criterio *m*

critic /'krɪtɪk/ *n* crítico *m*. ~**al** *a* crítico. ~**ally** *adv* críticamente; (ill) gravemente

critici|sm /'krɪtɪsɪzəm/ *n* crítica *f*. ~**ze** /'krɪtɪsaɪz/ *vt/i* criticar

croak /krəʊk/ *n* (of person) gruñido *m*; (of frog) canto *m*. ● *vi* gruñir; <*frog*> croar

Croat /'krəʊæt/ *n* croata *m* & *f*. ~**ia** /krəʊ'eɪʃə/ *n* Croacia *f*. ~**ian** *a* croata

crochet /'krəʊʃeɪ/ *n* crochet *m*, ganchillo *m*. ● *vt* tejer a crochet *or* a ganchillo

crockery /'krɒkərɪ/ *n* loza *f*

crocodile /'krɒkədaɪl/ *n* cocodrilo *m*. ~ **tears** *npl* lágrimas *fpl* de cocodrilo

crocus /'krəʊkəs/ *n* (*pl* **-es**) azafrán *m* de primavera

crook /krʊk/ *n* 🔲 sinvergüenza *m* & *f*. ~**ed** /'krʊkɪd/ *a* torcido, chueco (LAm); (winding) tortuoso; (dishonest) deshonesto

crop /krɒp/ *n* cosecha *f*; (haircut) corte *m* de pelo muy corto. ● *vt* (*pt* **cropped**) cortar. □ ~ **up** *vi* surgir

croquet /'krəʊkeɪ/ *n* croquet *m*

cross /krɒs/ *n* cruz *f*; (of animals) cruce *m*. ● *vt* cruzar; (oppose) contrariar. ~ **s.o.'s mind** ocurrírsele a uno. ● *vi* cruzar. ~ **o.s.** santiguarse. ● *a* enfadado, enojado (esp LAm). □ ~ **out** *vt* tachar. ~**bar** *n* travesaño *m*. ~**-examine** /-ɪg'zæmɪn/ *vt* interrogar. ~**-eyed** *a* bizco. ~**fire** *n* fuego *m* cruzado. ~**ing** *n* (by boat) travesía *f*; (on road) cruce *m* peatonal. ~**ly** *adv* con enfado, con enojo (esp LAm). ~**-purposes** /-'pɜːpəsɪz/ *npl*. **talk at** ~**-purposes** hablar sin entenderse. ~**-reference** /-'refrəns/ *n* remisión *f*. ~**roads** *n invar* cruce *m*. ~**-section** /-'sekʃn/ *n* sección *f* transversal; (fig) muestra *f* representativa. ~**walk** *n* (Amer) paso de peatones.

~**word** *n* ~**word** (**puzzle**) crucigrama *m*

crotch /krɒtʃ/ *n* entrepiernas *fpl*

crouch /kraʊtʃ/ *vi* agacharse

crow /krəʊ/ *n* cuervo *m*. **as the** ~ **flies** en línea recta. ● *vi* cacarear. ~**bar** *n* palanca *f*

crowd /kraʊd/ *n* muchedumbre *f*. ● *vt* amontonar; (fill) llenar. ● *vi* amontonarse; (gather) reunirse. ~**ed** *a* atestado

crown /kraʊn/ *n* corona *f*; (of hill) cumbre *f*; (of head) coronilla *f*. ● *vt* coronar

crucial /'kruːʃl/ *a* crucial

crucifix /'kruːsɪfɪks/ *n* crucifijo *m*. ~**ion** /-'fɪkʃn/ *n* crucifixión *f*

crucify /'kruːsɪfaɪ/ *vt* crucificar

crude /kruːd/ *a* (**-er, -est**) (raw) crudo; (rough) tosco; (vulgar) ordinario

cruel /'kruːəl/ *a* (**crueller, cruellest**) cruel. ~**ty** *n* crueldad *f*

cruet /'kruːɪt/ *n* vinagrera *f*

cruise /kruːz/ *n* crucero *m*. ● *vi* hacer un crucero; (of car) circular lentamente. ~**r** *n* crucero *m*

crumb /krʌm/ *n* miga *f*

crumble /'krʌmbl/ *vt* desmenuzar. ● *vi* desmenuzarse; (collapse) derrumbarse

crummy /'krʌmɪ/ *a* (**-ier, -iest**) 🗵 miserable

crumpet /'krʌmpɪt/ *n* bollo *m* blando

crumple /'krʌmpl/ *vt* arrugar. ● *vi* arrugarse

crunch /krʌntʃ/ *vt* hacer crujir; (bite) masticar. ~**y** *a* crujiente

crusade /kruː'seɪd/ *n* cruzada *f*. ~**r** *n* cruzado *m*

crush /krʌʃ/ *vt* aplastar; arrugar <*clothes*>. ● *n* (crowd) aglomeración *f*. **have a** ~ **on** 🔲 estar chiflado por

crust /krʌst/ *n* corteza *f*. ~**y** *a* <*bread*> de corteza dura

crutch /krʌtʃ/ *n* muleta *f*; (Anat) entrepiernas *fpl*

crux /krʌks/ *n* (*pl* **cruxes**). **the** ~ (**of the matter**) el quid (de la cuestión)

cry /kraɪ/ *n* grito *m*. **be a far** ~ **from** (fig) distar mucho de. ● *vi* llorar; (call out) gritar. □ ~ **off** *vi* echarse atrás, rajarse. ~**baby** *n* llorón *m*

crypt /krɪpt/ *n* cripta *f*

cryptic /'krɪptɪk/ *a* enigmático

crystal /'krɪstl/ *n* cristal *m*. ~**lize** *vi* cristalizarse

cub /kʌb/ *n* cachorro *m*. **C**~ (Scout) *n* lobato *m*

Cuba /'kju:bə/ *n* Cuba *f*. ~**n** *a & n* cubano (*m*)

cubbyhole /'kʌbɪhəʊl/ *n* cuchitril *m*

cub|e /kju:b/ *n* cubo *m*. ~**ic** *a* cúbico

cubicle /'kju:bɪkl/ *n* cubículo *m*; (changing room) probador *m*

cuckoo /'kʊku:/ *n* cuco *m*, cuclillo *m*

cucumber /'kju:kʌmbə(r)/ *n* pepino *m*

cuddl|e /'kʌdl/ *vt* abrazar. ● *vi* abrazarse. ● *n* abrazo *m*. ~**y** *a* adorable

cue /kju:/ *n* (Mus) entrada *f*; (in theatre) pie *m*; (in snooker) taco *m*

cuff /kʌf/ *n* puño *m*; (Amer, of trousers) vuelta *f*, dobladillo *m*; (blow) bofetada *f*. **speak off the** ~ hablar de improviso. ● *vt* abofetear. ~**link** *n* gemelo *m*, mancuerna *f* (Mex)

cul-de-sac /'kʌldəsæk/ *n* callejón *m* sin salida

culinary /'kʌlɪnərɪ/ *a* culinario

cull /kʌl/ *vt* sacrificar en forma selectiva *<animals>*

culminat|e /'kʌlmɪneɪt/ *vi* culminar. ~**ion** /-'neɪʃn/ *n* culminación *f*

culprit /'kʌlprɪt/ *n* culpable *m & f*

cult /kʌlt/ *n* culto *m*

cultivat|e /'kʌltɪveɪt/ *vt* cultivar. ~**ion** /-'veɪʃn/ *n* cultivo *m*

cultur|al /'kʌltʃərəl/ *a* cultural. ~**e** /'kʌltʃə(r)/ *n* cultura *f*; (Bot etc) cultivo *m*. ~**ed** *a* cultivado; *<person>* culto

cumbersome /'kʌmbəsəm/ *a* incómodo; (heavy) pesado

cunning /'kʌnɪŋ/ *a* astuto. ● *n* astucia *f*

cup /kʌp/ *n* taza *f*; (trophy) copa *f*

cupboard /'kʌbəd/ *n* armario *m*

curator /kjʊə'reɪtə(r)/ *n* (of museum) conservador *m*

curb /kɜ:b/ *n* freno *m*; (Amer) bordillo *m* (de la acera), borde *m* de la banqueta (Mex). ● *vt* refrenar

curdle /'kɜ:dl/ *vt* cuajar. ● *vi* cuajarse; (go bad) cortarse

cure /kjʊə(r)/ *vt* curar. ● *n* cura *f*

curfew /'kɜ:fju:/ *n* toque *m* de queda

curio|sity /kjʊərɪ'ɒsətɪ/ *n* curiosidad *f*. ~**us** /'kjʊərɪəs/ *a* curioso

curl /kɜ:l/ *vt* rizar, enchinar (Mex). ~ **o.s. up** acurrucarse. ● *vi* *<hair>* rizarse, enchinarse (Mex); *<paper>* ondularse. ● *n* rizo *m*, chino *m* (Mex). ~**er** *n* rulo *m*, chino *m* (Mex). ~**y** *a* (**-ier, -iest**) rizado, chino (Mex)

currant /'kʌrənt/ *n* pasa *f* de Corinto

currency /'kʌrənsɪ/ *n* moneda *f*

current /'kʌrənt/ *a & n* corriente (*f*); (existing) actual. ~ **affairs** *npl* sucesos de actualidad. ~**ly** *adv* actualmente

curriculum /kə'rɪkjʊləm/ *n* (*pl* **-la**) programa *m* de estudios. ~ **vitae** *n* currículum *m* vitae

curry /'kʌrɪ/ *n* curry *m*. ● *vt* preparar al curry

curse /kɜ:s/ *n* maldición *f*; (oath) palabrota *f*. ● *vt* maldecir. ● *vi* decir palabrotas

cursory /'kɜ:sərɪ/ *a* superficial

curt /kɜ:t/ *a* brusco

curtain /'kɜ:tn/ *n* cortina *f*; (in theatre) telón *m*

curtsey, **curtsy** /'kɜ:tsɪ/ *n* reverencia *f*. ● *vi* hacer una reverencia

curve /kɜ:v/ *n* curva *f*. ● *vi* estar curvado; *<road>* torcerse

cushion /'kʊʃn/ *n* cojín *m*, almohadón *m*. ● *vt* amortiguar *<blow>*; (fig) proteger

cushy /'kʊʃɪ/ *a* (**-ier, -iest**) 🄸 fácil

custard /'kʌstəd/ *n* natillas *fpl*

custody /'kʌstədɪ/ *n* custodia *f*. **be in** ~ (Jurid) estar detenido

custom /'kʌstəm/ *n* costumbre *f*; (Com) clientela *f*. ~**ary** /-ərɪ/ *a* acostumbrado. ~**er** *n* cliente *m*. ~**s** *npl* aduana *f*. ~**s officer** *n* aduanero *m*

cut /kʌt/ vt/i (pt **cut**, pres p **cutting**) cortar; reducir <prices>. ● n corte m; (reduction) reducción f. □ ~ **across** vt cortar camino por. □ ~ **back**, ~ **down** vt reducir. □ ~ **in** vi interrumpir. □ ~ **off** vt cortar; (phone) desconectar; (fig) aislar. □ ~ **out** vt recortar; (omit) suprimir. □ ~ **through** vt cortar camino por. □ ~ **up** vt cortar en pedazos

cute /kjuːt/ a (**-er**, **-est**) 🇺🇸 mono, amoroso (LAm); (Amer, attractive) guapo, buen mozo (LAm)

cutlery /'kʌtlərɪ/ n cubiertos mpl

cutlet /'kʌtlɪt/ n chuleta f

cut: ~-price, (Amer) **~-rate** a a precio reducido. **~-throat** a despiadado. **~ting** a cortante; <remark> mordaz. ● n (from newspaper) recorte m; (of plant) esqueje m

CV n (= **curriculum vitae**) currículum m (vitae)

cycl|e /'saɪkl/ n ciclo m; (bicycle) bicicleta f. ● vi ir en bicicleta. **~ing** n ciclismo m. **~ist** n ciclista m & f

cylind|er /'sɪlɪndə(r)/ n cilindro m. **~er head** (Auto) n culata f. **~rical** /-'lɪndrɪkl/ a cilíndrico

cymbal /'sɪmbl/ n címbalo m

cynic /'sɪnɪk/ n cínico m. **~al** a cínico. **~ism** /-sɪzəm/ n cinismo m

Czech /tʃek/ a & n checo (m). **~oslovakia** /-əslə'vækɪə/ n (History) Checoslovaquia f. **~ Republic** n. the **~ Republic** n la República Checa

....

Dd

....

dab /dæb/ vt (pt **dabbed**) tocar ligeramente. ● n toque m suave. a **~ of** un poquito de

dad /dæd/ n 🇺🇸 papá m. **~dy** n papi m. **~dy-long-legs** n invar (cranefly) típula f; (Amer, harvestman) segador m, falangio m

daffodil /'dæfədɪl/ n narciso m

daft /dɑːft/ a (**-er**, **-est**) 🇺🇸 tonto

dagger /'dægə(r)/ n daga f, puñal m

daily /'deɪlɪ/ a diario. ● adv diariamente, cada día

dainty /'deɪntɪ/ a (**-ier**, **-iest**) delicado

dairy /'deərɪ/ n vaquería f; (shop) lechería f

daisy /'deɪzɪ/ n margarita f

dam /dæm/ n presa f, represa f (LAm)

damag|e /'dæmɪdʒ/ n daño m; **~s** (npl, Jurid) daños mpl y perjuicios mpl. ● vt (fig) dañar, estropear. **~ing** a perjudicial

dame /deɪm/ n (old use) dama f; (Amer, 🇺🇸) chica f

damn /dæm/ vt condenar; (curse) maldecir. ● int 🇺🇸 ¡caray! 🇺🇸. ● a maldito. ● n I don't give a **~** (no) me importa un comino

damp /dæmp/ n humedad f. ● a (**-er**, **-est**) húmedo. ● vt mojar. **~ness** n humedad f

danc|e /dɑːns/ vt/i bailar. ● n baile m. **~e hall** n salón m de baile. **~er** n bailador m; (professional) bailarín m. **~ing** n baile m

dandelion /'dændɪlaɪən/ n diente m de león

dandruff /'dændrʌf/ n caspa f

dandy /'dændɪ/ n petimetre m

Dane /deɪn/ n danés m

danger /'deɪndʒə(r)/ n peligro m; (risk) riesgo m. **~ous** a peligroso

dangle /'dæŋgl/ vt balancear. ● vi suspender, colgar

Danish /'deɪnɪʃ/ a danés. ● m (Lang) danés m

dar|e /deə(r)/ vt desafiar. ● vi atreverse a. I **~** say probablemente. ● n desafío m. **~edevil** n atrevido m. **~ing** a atrevido

dark /dɑːk/ a (**-er**, **-est**) oscuro; <skin, hair> moreno. ● n oscuridad f; (nightfall) atardecer. in the **~** a oscuras. **~en** vt oscurecer. ● vi oscurecerse. **~ness** n oscuridad f. **~room** n cámara f oscura

darling /'dɑːlɪŋ/ a querido. ● n cariño m

darn /dɑːn/ vt zurcir

dart /dɑːt/ n dardo m. ● vi lanzarse; (run) precipitarse. **~board** n diana f. **~s** npl los dardos mpl

dash /dæʃ/ *vi* precipitarse. ● *vt* tirar; (break) romper; defraudar <hopes>. ● *n* (small amount) poquito *m*; (punctuation mark) guión *m*. □ ~ **off** *vi* marcharse apresuradamente. ~ **out** *vi* salir corriendo. ~**board** *n* tablero *m* de mandos

data /'deɪtə/ *npl* datos *mpl*. ~**base** *n* base *f* de datos. ~ **processing** *n* proceso *m* de datos

date /deɪt/ *n* fecha *f*; (appointment) cita *f*; (fruit) dátil *m*. **to** ~ hasta la fecha. ● *vt* fechar. ● *vi* datar; datar <remains>; (be old-fashioned) quedar anticuado. ~**d** *a* pasado de moda

daub /dɔːb/ *vt* embadurnar

daughter /'dɔːtə(r)/ *n* hija *f*. ~**-in-law** *n* nuera *f*

dawdle /'dɔːdl/ *vi* andar despacio; (waste time) perder el tiempo

dawn /dɔːn/ *n* amanecer *m*. ● *vi* amanecer; (fig) nacer. **it** ~**ed on me that** caí en la cuenta de que

day /deɪ/ *n* día *m*; (whole day) jornada *f*; (period) época *f*. ~**break** *n* amanecer *m*. ~ **care center** *n* (Amer) guardería *f* infantil. ~**dream** *n* ensueño *m*. ● *vi* soñar despierto. ~**light** *n* luz *f* del día. ~**time** *n* día *m*

daze /deɪz/ *vt* aturdir. ● *n* aturdimiento *m*. **in a** ~ aturdido. ~**d** *a* aturdido

dazzle /'dæzl/ *vt* deslumbrar

dead /ded/ *a* muerto; (numb) dormido. ● *adv* justo; (ⓘ, completely) completamente. ~ **beat** rendido. ~ **slow** muy lento. **stop** ~ parar en seco. ~**en** *vt* amortiguar <sound, blow>; calmar <pain>. ~ **end** *n* callejón *m* sin salida. ~**line** *n* fecha *f* tope, plazo *m* de entrega. ~**lock** *n* punto *m* muerto. ~**ly** *a* (-ier, -iest) mortal

deaf /def/ *a* (-er, -est) sordo. ~**en** *vt* ensordecer. ~**ness** *n* sordera *f*

deal /diːl/ *n* (agreement) acuerdo *m*; (treatment) trato *m*. **a good** ~ bastante. **a great** ~ **(of)** muchísimo. ● *vt* (*pt* **dealt**) dar <a blow, cards>. ● *vi* (cards) dar, repartir. □ ~ **in** *vt* comerciar en. □ ~ **out** *vt* repartir, distribuir. □ ~ **with** *vt* tratar con <person>; tratar de <subject>; ocu-

parse de <problem>. ~**er** *n* comerciante *m*. **drug** ~**er** traficante *m* & *f* de drogas

dean /diːn/ *n* deán *m*; (Univ) decano *m*

dear /dɪə(r)/ *a* (-er, -est) querido; (expensive) caro. ● *n* querido *m*. ● *adv* caro. ● *int*. **oh** ~! ¡ay por Dios! ~ **me!** ¡Dios mío! ~**ly** *adv* (pay) caro; (very much) muchísimo

death /deθ/ *n* muerte *f*. ~ **sentence** *n* pena *f* de muerte. ~ **trap** *n* lugar *m* peligroso.

debat|able /dɪ'beɪtəbl/ *a* discutible. ~**e** /dɪ'beɪt/ *n* debate *m*. ● *vt* debatir, discutir

debauchery /dɪ'bɔːtʃərɪ/ *vt* libertinaje *m*

debit /'debɪt/ *n* débito *m*. ● *vt* debitar, cargar. ~ **card** *n* tarjeta *f* de cobro automático

debris /'debriː/ *n* escombros *mpl*

debt /det/ *n* deuda *f*. **be in** ~ tener deudas. ~**or** *n* deudor *m*

decade /'dekeɪd/ *n* década *f*

decaden|ce /'dekədəns/ *n* decadencia *f*. ~**t** *a* decadente

decay /dɪ'keɪ/ *vi* descomponerse; <tooth> cariarse. ● *n* decomposición *f*; (of tooth) caries *f*

deceased /dɪ'siːst/ *a* difunto

deceit /dɪ'siːt/ *n* engaño *m*. ~**ful** *a* falso. ~**fully** *adv* falsamente

deceive /dɪ'siːv/ *vt* engañar

December /dɪ'sembə(r)/ *n* diciembre *m*

decen|cy /'diːsənsɪ/ *n* decencia *f*. ~**t** *a* decente; (ⓘ, good) bueno; (ⓘ, kind) amable. ~**tly** *adv* decentemente

decepti|on /dɪ'sepʃn/ *n* engaño *m*. ~**ve** /-tɪv/ *a* engañoso

decibel /'desɪbel/ *n* decibel(io) *m*

decide /dɪ'saɪd/ *vt/i* decidir. ~**d** *a* resuelto; (unquestionable) indudable. ~**dly** *adv* decididamente; (unquestionably) indudablemente

decimal /'desɪml/ *a* & *n* decimal (*m*). ~ **point** *n* coma *f* (decimal), punto *m* decimal

decipher /dɪ'saɪfə(r)/ *vt* descifrar

decis|ion /dɪ'sɪʒn/ *n* decisión *f*. ~**ive** /dɪ'saɪsɪv/ *a* decisivo; <manner> decidido

deck /dek/ n (Naut) cubierta f; (Amer, of cards) baraja f; (of bus) piso m. ● vt adornar. ~**chair** n tumbona f, silla f de playa

declar|ation /deklə'reɪʃn/ n declaración f. ~**e** /dɪ'kleə(r)/ vt declarar

decline /dɪ'klaɪn/ vt rehusar; (Gram) declinar. ● vi disminuir; (deteriorate) deteriorarse. ● n decadencia f; (decrease) disminución f

decode /di:'kəʊd/ vt descifrar

decompose /di:kəm'pəʊz/ vi descomponerse

décor /'deɪkɔ:(r)/ n decoración f

decorat|e /'dekəreɪt/ vt adornar, decorar (LAm); empapelar y pintar <room>. ~**ion** /-'reɪʃn/ n (act) decoración f; (ornament) adorno m. ~**ive** /-ətɪv/ a decorativo. ~**or** n pintor m decorador

decoy /'di:kɔɪ/ n señuelo m. ● /dɪ'kɔɪ/ vt atraer con señuelo

decrease /dɪ'kri:s/ vt/i disminuir. ● /'di:kri:s/ n disminución f

decree /dɪ'kri:/ n decreto m. ● vt decretar

decrepit /dɪ'krepɪt/ a decrépito

dedicat|e /'dedɪkeɪt/ vt dedicar. ~**ion** /-'keɪʃn/ n dedicación f

deduce /dɪ'dju:s/ vt deducir

deduct /dɪ'dʌkt/ vt deducir. ~**ion** /-ʃn/ n deducción f

deed /di:d/ n hecho m; (Jurid) escritura f

deem /di:m/ vt juzgar, considerar

deep /di:p/ a (**-er**, **-est**) adv profundo. ● adv profundamente. **be** ~ **in thought** estar absorto en sus pensamientos. ~**en** vt hacer más profundo. ● vi hacerse más profundo. ~**freeze** n congelador m, freezer m (LAm). ~**ly** adv profundamente

deer /dɪə(r)/ n invar ciervo m

deface /dɪ'feɪs/ vt desfigurar

default /dɪ'fɔ:lt/ vi faltar. ● n. **by** ~ en rebeldía

defeat /dɪ'fi:t/ vt vencer; (frustrate) frustrar. ● n derrota f. ~**ism** n derrotismo m. ~**ist** n derrotista a & (m & f)

defect /'di:fekt/ n defecto m. ● /dɪ'fekt/ vi desertar. ~ **to** pasar a.

~**ion** /dɪ'fekʃn/ n (Pol) defección f.

~**ive** /dɪ'fektɪv/ a defectuoso

defence /dɪ'fens/ n defensa f. ~**less** a indefenso

defen|d /dɪ'fend/ vt defender. ~**dant** n (Jurid) acusado m. ~**sive** /-sɪv/ a defensivo. ● n defensiva f

defer /dɪ'fɜ:(r)/ vt (pt **deferred**) aplazar. ~**ence** /'defərəns/ n deferencia f. ~**ential** /defə'renʃl/ a deferente

defian|ce /dɪ'faɪəns/ n desafío m. **in** ~**ce of** a despecho de. ~**t** a desafiante. ~**tly** adv con actitud desafiante

deficien|cy /dɪ'fɪʃənsɪ/ n falta f. ~**t** a deficiente. **be** ~**t in** carecer de

deficit /'defɪsɪt/ n déficit m

define /dɪ'faɪn/ vt definir

definite /'defɪnɪt/ a (final) definitivo; (certain) seguro; (clear) claro; (firm) firme. ~**ly** adv seguramente; (definitively) definitivamente

definition /defɪ'nɪʃn/ n definición f

definitive /dɪ'fɪnɪtɪv/ a definitivo

deflate /dɪ'fleɪt/ vt desinflar. ● vi desinflarse

deflect /dɪ'flekt/ vt desviar

deform /dɪ'fɔ:m/ vt deformar. ~**ed** a deforme. ~**ity** n deformidad f

defrost /di:'frɒst/ vt descongelar. ● vi descongelarse

deft /deft/ a (**-er**, **-est**) hábil. ~**ly** adv hábilmente f

defuse /di:'fju:z/ vt desactivar <bomb>; (fig) calmar

defy /dɪ'faɪ/ vt desafiar

degenerate /dɪ'dʒenəreɪt/ vi degenerar. ● /dɪ'dʒenərət/ a & n degenerado (m)

degrad|ation /degrə'deɪʃn/ n degradación f. ~**e** /dɪ'greɪd/ vt degradar

degree /dɪ'gri:/ n grado m; (Univ) licenciatura f; (rank) rango m. **to a certain** ~ hasta cierto punto

deign /deɪn/ vi. ~ **to** dignarse

deity /'di:ɪtɪ/ n deidad f

deject|ed /dɪ'dʒektɪd/ a desanimado. ~**ion** /-ʃn/ n abatimiento m

delay /dɪ'leɪ/ vt retrasar, demorar (LAm). ● vi tardar, demorar (LAm). ● n retraso m, demora f (LAm)

delegat|e /'delɪgeɪt/ *vt/i* delegar. ● /'delɪgət/ *n* delegado *m*. **~ion** /-'geɪʃn/ *n* delegación *f*

delet|e /dɪ'li:t/ *vt* tachar. **~ion** /-ʃn/ *n* supresión *f*

deliberat|e /dɪ'lɪbəreɪt/ *vt/i* deliberar. ● /dɪ'lɪbərət/ *a* intencionado; <steps etc> pausado. **~ely** *adv* a propósito. **~ion** /-'reɪʃn/ *n* deliberación *f*

delica|cy /'delɪkəsɪ/ *n* delicadeza *f*; (food) manjar *m*. **~te** /'delɪkət/ *a* delicado

delicatessen /delɪkə'tesn/ *n* charcutería *f*, salchichonería *f* (Mex)

delicious /dɪ'lɪʃəs/ *a* delicioso

delight /dɪ'laɪt/ *n* placer *m*. ● *vt* encantar. **~ed** *vi* deleitarse. **~ed** *a* encantado. **~ful** *a* delicioso

deliri|ous /dɪ'lɪrɪəs/ *a* delirante. **~um** /-əm/ *n* delirio *m*

deliver /dɪ'lɪvə(r)/ *vt* entregar; (distribute) repartir; (aim) lanzar; (Med) **he ~ed the baby** la asistió en el parto. **~ance** *n* liberación *f*. **~y** *n* entrega *f*; (of post) reparto *m*; (Med) parto *m*

delta /'deltə/ *n* (Geog) delta *m*

delude /dɪ'lu:d/ *vt* engañar. **~ o.s.** engañarse

deluge /'delju:dʒ/ *n* diluvio *m*

delusion /dɪ'lu:ʒn/ *n* ilusión *f*

deluxe /dɪ'lʌks/ *a* de lujo

delve /delv/ *vi* hurgar. **~ into** (investigate) ahondar en

demand /dɪ'mɑ:nd/ *vt* exigir. ● *n* petición *f*, pedido *m* (LAm); (claim) exigencia *f*; (Com) demanda *f*. **in ~** muy popular, muy solicitado. **on ~** a solicitud. **~ing** *a* exigente. **~s** *npl* exigencias *fpl*

demented /dɪ'mentɪd/ *a* demente

demo /'deməʊ/ *n* (*pl* **-os**) 🄸 manifestación *f*

democra|cy /dɪ'mɒkrəsɪ/ *n* democracia *f*. **~t** /'deməkræt/ *n* demócrata *m & f*. **D~t** *a & n* (in US) demócrata (*m & f*). **~tic** /demə'krætɪk/ *a* democrático

demoli|sh /dɪ'mɒlɪʃ/ *vt* derribar. **~tion** /demə'lɪʃn/ *n* demolición *f*

demon /'di:mən/ *n* demonio *m*

demonstrat|e /'demənstreɪt/ *vt* demostrar. ● *vi* manifestarse, hacer

una manifestación. **~ion** /-'streɪʃn/ *n* demostración *f*; (Pol) manifestación *f*. **~or** /'demənstreɪtə(r)/*n* (Pol) manifestante *m & f*; (marketing) demostrador *m*

demoralize /dɪ'mɒrəlaɪz/ *vt* desmoralizar

demote /dɪ'məʊt/ *vt* bajar de categoría

demure /dɪ'mjʊə(r)/ *a* recatado

den /den/ *n* (of animal) guarida *f*, madriguera *f*

denial /dɪ'naɪəl/ *n* denegación *f*; (statement) desmentimiento *m*

denim /'denɪm/ *n* tela *f* vaquera *or* de jeans, mezclilla (Mex) *f*. **~s** *npl* vaqueros *mpl*, jeans *mpl*, tejanos *mpl*, pantalones *mpl* de mezclilla (Mex)

Denmark /'denmɑ:k/ *n* Dinamarca *f*

denote /dɪ'nəʊt/ *vt* denotar

denounce /dɪ'naʊns/ *vt* denunciar

dens|e /dens/ *a* (**-er, -est**) espeso; <person> torpe. **~ely** *adv* densamente. **~ity** *n* densidad *f*

dent /dent/ *n* abolladura *f*. ● *vt* abollar

dental /'dentl/ *a* dental. **~ floss** /flɒs/ *n* hilo *m or* seda *f* dental. **~ surgeon** *n* dentista *m & f*

dentist /'dentɪst/ *n* dentista *m & f*. **~ry** *n* odontología *f*

dentures /'dentʃəz/ *npl* dentadura *f* postiza

deny /dɪ'naɪ/ *vt* negar; desmentir <rumour>; denegar <request>

deodorant /dɪ'əʊdərənt/ *a & n* desodorante (*m*)

depart /dɪ'pɑ:t/ *vi* partir, salir. **~ from** (deviate from) apartarse de

department /dɪ'pɑ:tment/ *n* departamento *m*; (Pol) ministerio *m*, secretaría *f* (Mex). **~ store** *n* grandes almacenes *mpl*, tienda *f* de departamentos (Mex)

departure /dɪ'pɑ:tʃə(r)/ *n* partida *f*; (of train etc) salida *f*

depend /dɪ'pend/ *vi* depender. **~ on** depender de. **~able** *u* digno de confianza. **~ant** /dɪ'pendənt/ *n* familiar *m & f* dependiente. **~ence** *n* dependencia *f*. **~ent** *a* dependiente. **be ~ent on** depender de

depict /dɪ'pɪkt/ vt representar; (in words) describir

deplete /dɪ'pli:t/ vt agotar

deplor|able /dɪ'plɔːrəbl/ a deplorable. **~e** /dɪ'plɔː(r)/ vt deplorar

deploy /dɪ'plɔɪ/ vt desplegar

deport /dɪ'pɔːt/ vt deportar. **~ation** /-'teɪʃn/ n deportación f

depose /dɪ'pəʊz/ vt deponer

deposit /dɪ'pɒzɪt/ vt (pt **deposited**) depositar. ● n depósito m

depot /'depəʊ/ n depósito m; (Amer) estación f de autobuses

deprav|ed /dɪ'preɪvd/ a depravado. **~ity** /dɪ'prævətɪ/ n depravación f

depress /dɪ'pres/ vt deprimir; (press down) apretar. **~ed** a deprimido. **~ing** a deprimente. **~ion** /-ʃn/ n depresión f

depriv|ation /deprɪ'veɪʃn/ n privación f. **~e** /dɪ'praɪv/ vt. **~e of** privar de. **~d** a carenciado

depth /depθ/ n profundidad f. **be out of one's ~** perder pie; (fig) meterse en honduras. **in ~** a fondo

deput|ize /'depjʊtaɪz/ vi. **~ize for** sustituir a. **~y** /'depjʊtɪ/ n sustituto m. **~y chairman** n vicepresidente m

derail /dɪ'reɪl/ vt hacer descarrilar. **~ment** n descarrilamiento m

derelict /'derəlɪkt/ a abandonado y en ruinas

deri|de /dɪ'raɪd/ vt mofarse de. **~sion** /dɪ'rɪʒn/ n mofa f. **~sive** /dɪ'raɪsɪv/ a burlón. **~sory** /dɪ'raɪsərɪ/ a <offer etc> irrisorio

deriv|ation /derɪ'veɪʃn/ n derivación f. **~ative** /dɪ'rɪvətɪv/ n derivado m. **~e** /dɪ'raɪv/ vt/i derivar

derogatory /dɪ'rɒgətrɪ/ a despectivo

descen|d /dɪ'send/ vt/i descender, bajar. **~dant** n descendiente m & f. **~t** n descenso m, bajada f; (lineage) ascendencia f

descri|be /dɪs'kraɪb/ vt describir. **~ption** /-'krɪpʃn/ n descripción f. **~ptive** /-'krɪptɪv/ a descriptivo

desecrate /'desɪkreɪt/ vt profanar

desert[1] /dɪ'zɜːt/ vt abandonar. ● vi (Mil) desertar. **~er** /dɪ'zɜːtə(r)/ n desertor m

desert[2] /'dezət/ a & n desierto (m)

deserts /dɪ'zɜːts/ npl lo merecido. **get one's just ~** llevarse su merecido

deserv|e /dɪ'zɜːv/ vt merecer. **~ing** a <cause> meritorio

design /dɪ'zaɪn/ n diseño m; (plan) plan m. **~s** (intentions) propósitos mpl. ● vt diseñar; (plan) planear

designate /'dezɪgneɪt/ vt designar

designer /dɪ'zaɪnə(r)/ n diseñador m; (fashion ~) diseñador m de modas. ● a <clothes> de diseño exclusivo

desirable /dɪ'zaɪərəbl/ a deseable

desire /dɪ'zaɪə(r)/ n deseo m. ● vt desear

desk /desk/ n escritorio m; (at school) pupitre m; (in hotel) recepción f; (Com) caja f. **~top publishing** n autoedición f, edición f electrónica

desolat|e /'desələt/ a desolado; (uninhabited) deshabitado. **~ion** /-'leɪʃn/ n desolación f

despair /dɪ'speə(r)/ n desesperación f. **be in ~** estar desesperado. ● vi. **~ of** desesperarse de

despatch /dɪ'spætʃ/ vt, n ⇒DISPATCH

desperat|e /'despərət/ a desesperado. **~ely** adv desesperadamente. **~ion** /-'reɪʃn/ n desesperación f

despicable /dɪ'spɪkəbl/ a despreciable

despise /dɪ'spaɪz/ vt despreciar

despite /dɪ'spaɪt/ prep a pesar de

despondent /dɪ'spɒndənt/ a abatido

despot /'despɒt/ n déspota m

dessert /dɪ'zɜːt/ n postre m. **~spoon** n cuchara f de postre

destination /destɪ'neɪʃn/ n destino m

destiny /'destɪnɪ/ n destino m

destitute /'destɪtjuːt/ a indigente

destroy /dɪ'strɔɪ/ vt destruir. **~er** n destructor m

destructi|on /dɪ'strʌkʃn/ n destrucción f. **~ve** /-ɪv/ a destructivo

desultory /'desəltrɪ/ a desganado

detach /dɪ'tætʃ/ vt separar. **~able** a separable. **~ed** a (aloof) distante; (house) no adosado. **~ment** n

desprendimiento *m*; (Mil) desta-
camento *m*; (aloofness) indiferencia *f*

detail /'di:teɪl/ *n* detalle *m*. **explain
sth in** ∼ explicar algo detalladamente. ● *vt* detallar; (Mil) destacar.
∼**ed** *a* detallado

detain /dɪ'teɪn/ *vt* detener; (delay) retener. ∼**ee** /dɪ:ter'ni:/ *n* detenido *m*

detect /dɪ'tekt/ *vt* percibir; (discover)
descubrir. ∼**ive** *n* (private) detective
m; (in police) agente *m & f*. ∼**or** *n* de-
tector *m*

detention /dɪ'tenʃn/ *n* detención *f*

deter /dɪ'tɜ:(r)/ *vt* (*pt* **deterred**) disuadir; (prevent) impedir

detergent /dɪ'tɜ:dʒənt/ *a & n* detergente (*m*)

deteriorat|e /dɪ'tɪərɪəreɪt/ *vi* dete-
riorarse. ∼**ion** /-'reɪʃn/ *n* deterioro *m*

determin|ation /dɪtɜ:mɪ'neɪʃn/ *n*
determinación *f*. ∼**e** /dɪ'tɜ:mɪn/ *vt*
determinar; (decide) decidir. ∼**ed** *a*
determinado; (resolute) decidido

deterrent /dɪ'terənt/ *n* fuerza *f* de
disuasión

detest /dɪ'test/ *vt* aborrecer. ∼**able**
a odioso

detonat|e /'detəneɪt/ *vt* hacer de-
tonar. ● *vi* detonar. ∼**ion** /-'neɪʃn/ *n*
detonación *f*. ∼**or** *n* detonador *m*

detour /'di:tʊə(r)/ *n* rodeo *m*; (Amer,
of transport) desvío *m*, desviación *f*.
● *vt* (Amer) desviar

detract /dɪ'trækt/ *vi*. ∼ **from** disminuir

detriment /'detrɪmənt/ *n*. **to the** ∼
of en perjuicio de. ∼**al** /-'mentl/ *a*
perjudicial

devalue /di:'vælju:/ *vt* desvalorizar

devastat|e /'devəsteɪt/ *vt* devastar.
∼**ing** *a* devastador; (fig) arrollador.
∼**ion** /-'steɪʃn/ *n* devastación *f*

develop /dɪ'veləp/ *vt* desarrollar;
contraer <*illness*>; urbanizar <*land*>.
● *vi* desarrollarse; (appear) surgir.
∼**ing** *a* <*country*> en vías de desarrollo. ∼**ment** *n* desarrollo *m*. **(new)**
∼**ment** novedad *f*

deviant /'di:vɪənt/ *a* desviado

deviat|e /'di:vɪeɪt/ *vi* desviarse.
∼**ion** /-'eɪʃn/ *n* desviación *f*

device /dɪ'vaɪs/ *n* dispositivo *m*;
(scheme) estratagema *f*

devil /'devl/ *n* diablo *m*

devious /'di:vɪəs/ *a* taimado

devise /dɪ'vaɪz/ *vt* idear

devoid /dɪ'vɔɪd/ *a*. **be** ∼ **of** carecer
de

devolution /di:və'lu:ʃn/ *n* descen-
tralización *f*; (of power) delegación *f*

devot|e /dɪ'vəʊt/ *vt* dedicar. ∼**ed** *a*
<*couple*> unido; <*service*> leal. ∼**ee**
/devə'ti:/ *n* partidario *m*. ∼**ion** /-ʃn/
n devoción *f*

devour /dɪ'vaʊə(r)/ *vt* devorar

devout /dɪ'vaʊt/ *a* devoto

dew /dju:/ *n* rocío *m*

dexterity /dek'sterətɪ/ *n* destreza *f*

diabet|es /daɪə'bi:ti:z/ *n* diabetes *f*.
∼**ic** /-'betɪk/ *a & n* diabético (*m*)

diabolical /daɪə'bɒlɪkl/ *a* diabólico

diagnos|e /'daɪəgnəʊz/ *vt* diag-
nosticar. ∼**is** /-'nəʊsɪs/ *n* (*pl* **-oses**
/-si:z/) diagnóstico *m*

diagonal /daɪ'ægənl/ *a & n* diagonal (*f*)

diagram /'daɪəgræm/ *n* diagrama *m*

dial /'daɪəl/ *n* cuadrante *m*; (on clock,
watch) esfera *f*; (on phone) disco *m*. ● *vt*
(*pt* **dialled**) marcar, discar (LAm)

dialect /'daɪəlekt/ *n* dialecto *m*

dialling: ∼ **code** *n* prefijo *m*, código *m* de la zona (LAm). ∼ **tone** *n* tono
m de marcar, tono *m* de discado
(LAm)

dialogue /'daɪəlɒg/ *n* diálogo *m*

dial tone *n* (Amer) ⇒DIALLING TONE

diameter /daɪ'æmɪtə(r)/ *n* diámetro *m*

diamond /'daɪəmənd/ *n* diamante
m; (shape) rombo *m*. ∼**s** *npl* (Cards)
diamantes *mpl*

diaper /'daɪəpə(r)/ *n* (Amer) pañal *m*

diaphragm /'daɪəfræm/ *n* diafragma *m*

diarrhoea /daɪə'rɪə/ *n* diarrea *f*

diary /'daɪərɪ/ *n* diario *m*; (book)
agenda *f*

dice /daɪs/ *n invar* dado *m*. ● *vt*
(Culin) cortar en cubitos

dictat|e /dɪk'teɪt/ *vt/i* dictar. ∼**ion**
/dɪk'teɪʃn/ *n* dictado *m*. ∼**or** *n* dicta-
dor *m*. ∼**orship** *n* dictadura *f*

dictionary /'dɪkʃənərɪ/ n diccionario m

did /dɪd/ ⇒DO

didn't /'dɪdnt/ = did not

die /daɪ/ vi (pres p **dying**) morir. be dying to morirse por. □ ~ **down** vi irse apagando. □ ~ **out** vi extinguirse

diesel /'diːzl/ n (fuel) gasóleo m. ~ **engine** n motor m diesel

diet /'daɪət/ n alimentación f; (restricted) régimen m. be on a ~ estar a régimen. ● vi estar a régimen

differ /'dɪfə(r)/ vi ser distinto; (disagree) no estar de acuerdo. ~**ence** /'dɪfrəns/ n diferencia f; (disagreement) desacuerdo m. ~**ent** /'dɪfrənt/ a distinto, diferente. ~**ently** adv de otra manera

difficult /'dɪfɪkəlt/ a difícil. ~**y** n dificultad f

diffus|e /dɪ'fjuːs/ a difuso. ● /dɪ'fjuːz/ vt difundir. ● vi difundirse. ~**ion** /-ʒn/ n difusión f

dig /dɪg/ n (poke) empujón m; (poke with elbow) codazo m; (remark) indirecta f. ~**s** npl ⏹ alojamiento m ● vt (pt **dug**, pres p **digging**) cavar; (thrust) empujar. ● vi cavar. □ ~ **out** vt extraer. □ ~ **up** vt desenterrar

digest /'daɪdʒest/ n resumen m. ● /daɪ'dʒest/ vt digerir. ~**ion** /-'dʒestʃn/ n digestión f. ~**ive** /-'dʒestɪv/ a digestivo

digger /'dɪgə(r)/ n (Mec) excavadora f

digit /'dɪdʒɪt/ n dígito m; (finger) dedo m. ~**al** /'dɪdʒɪtl/ a digital

dignified /'dɪgnɪfaɪd/ a solemne

dignitary /'dɪgnɪtərɪ/ n dignatario m

dignity /'dɪgnətɪ/ n dignidad f

digress /daɪ'gres/ vi divagar. ~ from apartarse de. ~**ion** /-ʃn/ n digresión f

dike /daɪk/ n dique m

dilapidated /dɪ'læpɪdeɪtɪd/ a ruinoso

dilate /daɪ'leɪt/ vt dilatar. ● vi dilatarse

dilemma /daɪ'lemə/ n dilema m

diligent /'dɪlɪdʒənt/ a diligente

dilute /daɪ'ljuːt/ vt diluir

dim /dɪm/ a (**dimmer**, **dimmest**) <light> débil; <room> oscuro; (⏹, stupid) torpe. ● vt (pt **dimmed**) atenuar. ~ one's headlights (Amer) poner las (luces) cortas or de cruce, poner las (luces) bajas (LAm). ● vi <light> irse atenuando

dime /daɪm/ n (Amer) moneda de diez centavos

dimension /daɪ'menʃn/ n dimensión f

diminish /dɪ'mɪnɪʃ/ vt/i disminuir

dimple /'dɪmpl/ n hoyuelo m

din /dɪn/ n jaleo m

dine /daɪn/ vi cenar. ~**r** n comensal m & f; (Amer, restaurant) cafetería f

dinghy /'dɪŋgɪ/ n bote m; (inflatable) bote m neumático

dingy /'dɪndʒɪ/ a (-ier, -iest) miserable, sucio

dining: /'daɪnɪŋ/~ **car** n coche m restaurante. ~ **room** n comedor m

dinner /'dɪnə(r)/ n cena f, comida f (LAm). have ~ cenar, comer (LAm). ~ **party** n cena f, comida f (LAm)

dinosaur /'daɪnəsɔː(r)/ n dinosaurio m

dint /dɪnt/ n. by ~ of a fuerza de

dip /dɪp/ vt (pt **dipped**) meter; (in liquid) mojar. ~ one's headlights poner las (luces) cortas or de cruce, poner las (luces) bajas (LAm). ● vi bajar. ● n (slope) inclinación f; (in sea) baño m. □ ~ **into** vt hojear <book>

diphthong /'dɪfθɒŋ/ n diptongo m

diploma /dɪ'pləʊmə/ n diploma m

diploma|cy /dɪ'pləʊməsɪ/ n diplomacia f. ~**t** /'dɪpləmæt/ n diplomático m. ~**tic** /-'mætɪk/ a diplomático

dipstick /'dɪpstɪk/ n (Auto) varilla f del nivel de aceite

dire /daɪə(r)/ a (-er, -est) terrible; <need, poverty> extremo

direct /dɪ'rekt/ a directo. ● adv directamente. ● vt dirigir; (show the way) indicar. ~**ion** /-ʃn/ n dirección f. ~**ions** npl instrucciones fpl. ~**ly** adv directamente; (at once) en seguida. ● conj ⏹ en cuanto. ~**or** n director m; (of company) directivo m

directory /dɪ'rektərɪ/ n guía f; (Comp) directorio m

dirt /dɜ:t/ *n* suciedad *f*. **~y** *a* (**-ier**, **-iest**) sucio. ● *vt* ensuciar

disab|ility /dɪsə'bɪlətɪ/ *n* invalidez *f*. **~le** /dɪs'eɪbl/ *vt* incapacitar. **~led** *a* minusválido

disadvantage /dɪsəd'vɑ:ntɪdʒ/ *n* desventaja *f*. **~d** *a* desfavorecido

disagree /dɪsə'gri:/ *vi* no estar de acuerdo (**with** con). **~ with** <*food, climate*> sentarle mal a. **~able** *a* desagradable. **~ment** *n* desacuerdo *m*; (quarrel) riña *f*

disappear /dɪsə'pɪə(r)/ *vi* desaparecer. **~ance** *n* desaparición *f*

disappoint /dɪsə'pɔɪnt/ *vt* decepcionar. **~ing** *a* decepcionante. **~ment** *n* decepción *f*

disapprov|al /dɪsə'pru:vl/ *n* desaprobación *f*. **~e** /dɪsə'pru:v/ *vi*. **~e of** desaprobar. **~ing** *a* de reproche

disarm /dɪs'ɑ:m/ *vt* desarmar. ● *vi* desarmarse. **~ament** *n* desarme *m*

disarray /dɪsə'reɪ/ *n* desorden *m*

disast|er /dɪ'zɑ:stə(r)/ *n* desastre *m*. **~rous** /-strəs/ *a* catastrófico

disband /dɪs'bænd/ *vt* disolver. ● *vi* disolverse

disbelief /dɪsbɪ'li:f/ *n* incredulidad *f*

disc /dɪsk/ *n* disco *m*

discard /dɪs'kɑ:d/ *vt* descartar; abandonar <*beliefs etc*>

discern /dɪ'sɜ:n/ *vt* percibir. **~ing** *a* exigente; <*ear, eye*> educado

discharge /dɪs'tʃɑ:dʒ/ *vt* descargar; cumplir <*duty*>; (Mil) licenciar. ● /'dɪstʃɑ:dʒ/ *n* descarga *f*; (Med) secreción *f*; (Mil) licenciamiento *m*

disciple /dɪ'saɪpl/ *n* discípulo *m*

disciplin|ary /dɪsə'plɪnərɪ/ *a* disciplinario. **~e** /'dɪsɪplɪn/ *n* disciplina *f*. ● *vt* disciplinar; (punish) sancionar

disc jockey /'dɪskdʒɒkɪ/ *n* pinchadiscos *m & f*

disclaim /dɪs'kleɪm/ *vt* desconocer. **~er** *n* (Jurid) descargo *m* de responsabilidad

disclos|e /dɪs'kləʊz/ *vt* revelar. **~ure** /-ʒə(r)/ *n* revelación *f*

disco /'dɪskəʊ/ *n* (*pl* **-os**) 🄵 discoteca *f*

discolour /dɪs'kʌlə(r)/ *vt* decolorar. ● *vi* decolorarse

discomfort /dɪs'kʌmfət/ *n* malestar *m*; (lack of comfort) incomodidad *f*

disconcert /dɪskən'sɜ:t/ *vt* desconcertar

disconnect /dɪskə'nekt/ *vt* separar; (Elec) desconectar

disconsolate /dɪs'kɒnsələt/ *a* desconsolado

discontent /dɪskən'tent/ *n* descontento *m*. **~ed** *a* descontento

discontinue /dɪskən'tɪnju:/ *vt* interrumpir

discord /'dɪskɔ:d/ *n* discordia *f*; (Mus) disonancia *f*. **~ant** /-'skɔ:dənt/ *a* discorde; (Mus) disonante

discotheque /'dɪskətek/ *n* discoteca *f*

discount /'dɪskaʊnt/ *n* descuento *m*. ● /dɪs'kaʊnt/ *vt* hacer caso omiso de; (Com) descontar

discourag|e /dɪs'kʌrɪdʒ/ *vt* desanimar; (dissuade) disuadir. **~ing** *a* desalentador

discourteous /dɪs'kɜ:tɪəs/ *a* descortés

discover /dɪs'kʌvə(r)/ *vt* descubrir. **~y** *n* descubrimiento *m*

discredit /dɪs'kredɪt/ *vt* (*pt* **discredited**) desacreditar. ● *n* descrédito *m*

discreet /dɪs'kri:t/ *a* discreto. **~ly** *adv* discretamente

discrepancy /dɪ'skrepənsɪ/ *n* discrepancia *f*

discretion /dɪ'skreʃn/ *n* discreción *f*

discriminat|e /dɪs'krɪmɪneɪt/ *vt* discriminar. **~e between** distinguir entre. **~ing** *a* perspicaz. **~ion** /-'neɪʃn/ *n* discernimiento *m*; (bias) discriminación *f*

discus /'dɪskəs/ *n* disco *m*

discuss /dɪ'skʌs/ *vt* discutir. **~ion** /-ʃn/ *n* discusión *f*

disdain /dɪs'deɪn/ *n* desdén *m*. **~ful** *a* desdeñoso

disease /dɪ'zi:z/ *n* enfermedad *f*

disembark /dɪsɪm'bɑ:k/ *vi* desembarcar

disenchant|ed /dɪsɪn'tʃɑːntɪd/ *a* desilusionado. **~ment** *n* desencanto *m*

disentangle /dɪsɪn'tæŋgl/ *vt* desenredar

disfigure /dɪs'fɪgə(r)/ *vt* desfigurar

disgrace /dɪs'greɪs/ *n* vergüenza *f*. ● *vt* deshonrar. **~ful** *a* vergonzoso

disgruntled /dɪs'grʌntld/ *a* descontento

disguise /dɪs'gaɪz/ *vt* disfrazar. ● *n* disfraz *m*. in **~** disfrazado

disgust /dɪs'gʌst/ *n* repugnancia *f*, asco *m*. ● *vt* dar asco a. **~ed** *a* indignado; (stronger) asqueado. **~ing** *a* repugnante, asqueroso

dish /dɪʃ/ *n* plato *m*. **wash** *or* do the **~es** fregar los platos, lavar los trastes (Mex). □ **~ up** *vt/i* servir. **~cloth** *n* bayeta *f*

disheartening /dɪs'hɑːtnɪŋ/ *a* desalentador

dishonest /dɪs'ɒnɪst/ *a* deshonesto. **~y** *n* falta *f* de honradez

dishonour /dɪs'ɒnə(r)/ *n* deshonra *f*

dish: **~ soap** *n* (Amer) lavavajillas *m*. **~ towel** *n* paño *m* de cocina. **~washer** *n* lavaplatos *m*, lavavajillas *m*. **~washing liquid** *n* (Amer) ⇒**~** SOAP

disillusion /dɪsɪ'luːʒn/ *vt* desilusionar. **~ment** *n* desilusión *f*

disinfect /dɪsɪn'fekt/ *vt* desinfectar. **~ant** *n* desinfectante *m*

disintegrate /dɪs'ɪntɪgreɪt/ *vt* desintegrar. ● *vi* desintegrarse

disinterested /dɪs'ɪntrəstɪd/ *a* desinteresado

disjointed /dɪs'dʒɔɪntɪd/ *a* inconexo

disk /dɪsk/ *n* disco *m*. **~ drive** (Comp) unidad *f* de discos. **~ette** /dɪs'ket/ *n* disquete *m*

dislike /dɪs'laɪk/ *n* aversión *f*. ● *vt*. I **~ dogs** no me gustan los perros

dislocate /'dɪsləkeɪt/ *vt* dislocar(se) *<limb>*

dislodge /dɪs'lɒdʒ/ *vt* sacar

disloyal /dɪs'lɔɪəl/ *a* desleal. **~ty** *n* deslealtad *f*

dismal /'dɪzməl/ *a* triste; (bad) fatal

dismantle /dɪs'mæntl/ *vt* desmontar

dismay /dɪs'meɪ/ *n* consternación *f*. ● *vt* consternar

dismiss /dɪs'mɪs/ *vt* despedir; (reject) rechazar. **~al** *n* despido *m*; (of idea) rechazo *m*

dismount /dɪs'maʊnt/ *vi* desmontar

disobe|dience /dɪsə'biːdɪəns/ *n* desobediencia *f*. **~dient** *a* desobediente. **~y** /dɪsə'beɪ/ *vt/i* desobedecer

disorder /dɪs'ɔːdə(r)/ *n* desorden *m*; (ailment) afección *f*. **~ly** *a* desordenado

disorganized /dɪs'ɔːgənaɪzd/ *a* desorganizado

disorientate /dɪs'ɔːrɪənteɪt/ *vt* desorientar

disown /dɪs'əʊn/ *vt* repudiar

disparaging /dɪs'pærɪdʒɪŋ/ *a* despreciativo

dispatch /dɪs'pætʃ/ *vt* despachar. ● *n* despacho *m*. **~ rider** *n* mensajero *m*

dispel /dɪs'pel/ *vt* (*pt* **dispelled**) disipar

dispens|able /dɪs'pensəbl/ *a* prescindible. **~e** *vt* distribuir; (Med) preparar. □ **~ with** *vt* prescindir de

dispers|al /dɪ'spɜːsl/ *n* dispersión *f*. **~e** /dɪ'spɜːs/ *vt* dispersar. ● *vi* dispersarse

dispirited /dɪs'pɪrɪtɪd/ *a* desanimado

display /dɪs'pleɪ/ *vt* exponer *<goods>*; demostrar *<feelings>*. ● *n* exposición *f*; (of feelings) demostración *f*

displeas|e /dɪs'pliːz/ *vt* desagradar. be **~ed with** estar disgustado con. **~ure** /-'pleʒə(r)/ *n* desagrado *m*

dispos|able /dɪs'pəʊzəbl/ *a* desechable. **~al** /dɪs'pəʊzl/ *n* (of waste) eliminación *f*. at s.o.'s **~al** a la disposición de uno. **~e of** /dɪs'pəʊz/ *vt* deshacerse de

disproportionate /dɪsprə'pɔːʃənət/ *a* desproporcionado

disprove /dɪs'pruːv/ *vt* desmentir *<claim>*; refutar *<theory>*

dispute /dɪs'pjuːt/ vt discutir. ●n disputa f. in ～ disputado

disqualif|ication /dɪskwɒlɪfɪ'keɪʃn/ n descalificación f. ～y /dɪs'kwɒlɪfaɪ/ vt incapacitar; (Sport) descalificar

disregard /dɪsrɪ'gɑːd/ vt no hacer caso de. ●n indiferencia f (for a)

disreputable /dɪs'repjʊtəbl/ a de mala fama

disrespect /dɪsrɪ'spekt/ n falta f de respeto

disrupt /dɪs'rʌpt/ vt interrumpir; trastornar <plans>. ～ion /-ʃn/ n trastorno m. ～ive a <influence> perjudicial, negativo

dissatis|faction /dɪsætɪs'fækʃn/ n descontento m. ～fied /dɪ'sætɪsfaɪd/ a descontento

dissect /dɪ'sekt/ vt disecar

dissent /dɪ'sent/ vi disentir. ●n disentimiento m

dissertation /dɪsə'teɪʃn/ n (Univ) tesis f

dissident /'dɪsɪdənt/ a & n disidente (m & f)

dissimilar /dɪ'sɪmɪlə(r)/ a distinto

dissolute /'dɪsəluːt/ a disoluto

dissolve /dɪ'zɒlv/ vt disolver. ●vi disolverse

dissuade /dɪ'sweɪd/ vt disuadir

distan|ce /'dɪstəns/ n distancia f. from a ～ce desde lejos. in the ～ce a lo lejos. ～t a distante, lejano; (aloof) distante

distaste /dɪs'teɪst/ n desagrado m. ～ful a desagradable

distil /dɪs'tɪl/ vt (pt distilled) destilar. ～lery /dɪs'tɪlərɪ/ n destilería f

distinct /dɪs'tɪŋkt/ a distinto; (clear) claro; (marked) marcado. ～ion /-ʃn/ n distinción f; (in exam) sobresaliente m. ～ive a distintivo

distinguish /dɪs'tɪŋgwɪʃ/ vt/i distinguir. ～ed a distinguido

distort /dɪs'tɔːt/ vt torcer. ～ion /-ʃn/ n deformación f

distract /dɪs'trækt/ vt distraer. ～ed a distraído. ～ion /-ʃn/ n distracción f; (confusion) aturdimiento m

distraught /dɪs'trɔːt/ a consternado, angustiado

distress /dɪs'tres/ n angustia f. ●vt afligir. ～ed a afligido. ～ing a penoso

distribut|e /dɪ'strɪbjuːt/ vt repartir, distribuir. ～ion /-'bjuːʃn/ n distribución f. ～or n distribuidor m; (Auto) distribuidor m (del encendido)

district /'dɪstrɪkt/ n zona f, región f; (of town) barrio m

distrust /dɪs'trʌst/ n desconfianza f. ●vt desconfiar de

disturb /dɪs'tɜːb/ vt molestar; (perturb) inquietar; (move) desordenar; (interrupt) interrumpir. ～ance n disturbio m; (tumult) alboroto m. ～ed a trastornado. ～ing a inquietante

disused /dɪs'juːzd/ a fuera de uso

ditch /dɪtʃ/ n zanja f; (for irrigation) acequia f. ●vt 🄵 abandonar

dither /'dɪðə(r)/ vi vacilar

ditto /'dɪtəʊ/ adv ídem

divan /dɪ'væn/ n diván m

dive /daɪv/ vi tirarse (al agua), zambullirse; (rush) meterse (precipitadamente). ●n (into water) zambullida f; (Sport) salto m (de trampolín); (of plane) descenso m en picado, descenso m en picada (LAm); (🄵, place) antro m. ～r n saltador m; (underwater) buzo m

diverge /daɪ'vɜːdʒ/ vi divergir. ～nt a divergente

divers|e /daɪ'vɜːs/ a diverso. ～ify vt diversificar. ～ity n diversidad f

diver|sion /daɪ'vɜːʃn/ n desvío m; desviación f; (distraction) diversión f. ～t /daɪ'vɜːt/ vt desviar; (entertain) divertir

divide /dɪ'vaɪd/ vt dividir. ●vi dividirse. ～d highway n (Amer) autovía f, carretera f de doble pista

dividend /'dɪvɪdend/ n dividendo m

divine /dɪ'vaɪn/ a divino

diving /'daɪvɪŋ/: ～ board n trampolín m. ～ suit n escafandra f

division /dɪ'vɪʒn/ n división f

divorce /dɪ'vɔːs/ n divorcio m. ●vt divorciarse de. get ～d divorciarse. ●vi divorciarse. ～e /dɪvɔː'siː/ n divorciado m

divulge /daɪ'vʌldʒ/ vt divulgar

DIY abbr ⇒DO-IT-YOURSELF

dizz|iness /'dızınıs/ *n* vértigo *m*. ~**y** *a* (**-ier**, **-iest**) mareado. **be** *or* **feel** ~**y** marearse

DJ *abbr* ⇒DISC JOCKEY

do /duː/, *unstressed forms* /dʊ, də/

3rd pers sing present **does**; past **did**; past participle **done**

● *transitive verb*

••••➤ hacer. **he does what he wants** hace lo que quiere. **to do one's homework** hacer los deberes. **to do the cooking** preparar la comida, cocinar. **well done!** ¡muy bien!

••••➤ (clean) lavar <*dishes*>. limpiar <*windows*>

••••➤ (as job) **what does he do?** ¿en qué trabaja?

••••➤ (swindle) estafar. **I've been done!** ¡me han estafado!

••••➤ (achieve) **she's done it!** ¡lo ha logrado!

● *intransitive verb*

••••➤ hacer. **do as you're told!** ¡haz lo que se te dice!

••••➤ (fare) **how are you doing?** (with a task) ¿qué tal te va? **how do you do?** (as greeting) mucho gusto, encantado

••••➤ (perform) **she did well/badly** le fue bien/mal

••••➤ (be suitable) **will this do?** ¿esto sirve?

••••➤ (be enough) ser suficiente, bastar. **one box will do** con una caja basta, con una caja es suficiente

● *auxiliary verb*

••••➤ (to form interrogative and negative) **do you speak Spanish?** ¿hablas español?. **I don't want to** no quiero. **don't shut the door** no cierres la puerta

••••➤ (in tag questions) **you eat meat, don't you?** ¿comes carne, ¿verdad? *or* ¿no? **he lives in London, doesn't he?** vive en Londres, ¿no? *or* ¿verdad? *or* ¿no es cierto?

••••➤ (in short answers) **do you like it?** - **yes, I do** ¿te gusta? - sí. **who wrote it?** - **I did** ¿quién lo escribió? - yo

••••➤ (emphasizing) **do come in!** ¡pase Ud!. **you do exaggerate!** ¡cómo exageras!

□ **do away with** *vt* abolir. □ **do in** *vt* (☒, kill) eliminar. □ **do up** *vt* abrochar <*coat etc*>; arreglar <*house*>. □ **do with** *vt* (need) (with can, could) necesitar; (expressing connection) **it has nothing to do with that** no tiene nada que ver con eso. □ **do without** *vt* prescindir de

docile /'dəʊsaɪl/ *a* dócil

dock /dɒk/ *n* (Naut) dársena *f*; (wharf, quay) muelle *m*; (Jurid) banquillo *m* de los acusados. ~**s** *npl* (port) puerto *m*. ● *vt* cortar <*tail*>; atracar <*ship*>. ● *vi* <*ship*> atracar. ~**er** *n* estibador *m*. ~**yard** *n* astillero *m*

doctor /'dɒktə(r)/ *n* médico *m*, doctor *m*

doctrine /'dɒktrɪn/ *n* doctrina *f*

document /'dɒkjʊmənt/ *n* documento *m*. ~**ary** /-'mentrɪ/ *a* & *n* documental (*m*)

dodg|e /dɒdʒ/ *vt* esquivar. ● *vi* esquivarse. ● *n* treta *f*. ~**ems** /'dɒdʒəmz/ *npl* autos *mpl* de choque. ~**y** *a* (**-ier**, **-iest**) 🆅 (awkward) difícil

does /dʌz/ ⇒DO

doesn't /'dʌznt/ = **does not**

dog /dɒg/ *n* perro *m*. ● *vt* (*pt* **dogged**) perseguir

dogged /'dɒgɪd/ *a* obstinado

doghouse /'dɒghaʊs/ *n* (Amer) casa *f* del perro. **in the** ~ 🆅 en desgracia

dogma /'dɒgmə/ *n* dogma *m*. ~**tic** /-'mætɪk/ *a* dogmático

do|ings *npl* actividades *fpl*. ~**it-yourself** /duːɪtjɔːˈself/ *n* bricolaje *m*

dole /dəʊl/ *n* 🆅 subsidio *m* de paro, subsidio *m* de desempleo. **on the** ~ parado, desempleado. □ ~ **out** *vt* distribuir

doleful /'dəʊlfl/ *a* triste

doll /dɒl/ *n* muñeca *f*

dollar /'dɒlə(r)/ *n* dólar *m*

dollop /'dɒləp/ *n* 🆅 porción *f*

dolphin /'dɒlfɪn/ *n* delfín *m*

domain /dəʊˈmeɪn/ *n* dominio *m*; (fig) campo *m*

dome /dəʊm/ *n* cúpula *f*

domestic /dəˈmestɪk/ *a* doméstico; <*trade, flights, etc*> nacional. ~**ated**

/də'mestıkeıtıd/ a <*animal*> domesticado. ~ **science** n economía f doméstica

domin|ance /'dɒmınəns/ n dominio m. ~**ant** a dominante. ~**ate** /-eıt/ vt/i dominar. ~**ation** /-'neıʃn/ n dominación f. ~**eering** a dominante

Dominican Republic /də'mınıkən/ n República f Dominicana

dominion /də'mınjən/ n dominio m

domino /'dɒmınəʊ/ n (pl -**oes**) ficha f de dominó. ~**es** npl (game) dominó m

donat|e /dəʊ'neıt/ vt donar. ~**ion** /-ʃn/ n donativo m, donación f

done /dʌn/ ⇒DO

donkey /'dɒŋkı/ n burro m, asno m. ~'s **years** 🔲 siglos mpl

donor /'dəʊnə(r)/ n donante m & f

don't /dəʊnt/ = **do not**

doodle /'du:dl/ vi/i garrapatear

doom /du:m/ n destino m; (death) muerte f. ● vt. be ~ed to ser condenado a

door /dɔ:(r)/ n puerta f. ~**bell** n timbre m. ~ **knob** n pomo m (de la puerta). ~**mat** n felpudo m. ~**step** n peldaño m. ~**way** n entrada f

dope /dəʊp/ n 🔲 droga f; (🔳, idiot) imbécil m. ● vt 🔲 drogar

dormant /'dɔ:mənt/ a aletargado, <*volcano*> inactivo

dormice /'dɔ:maıs/ ⇒DORMOUSE

dormitory /'dɔ:mıtrı/ n dormitorio m

dormouse /'dɔ:maʊs/ n (pl -**mice**) lirón m

DOS /dɒs/ abbr (= **disc-operating system**) DOS m

dos|age /'dəʊsıdʒ/ n dosis f. ~**e** /dəʊs/ n dosis f

dot /dɒt/ n punto m. on the ~ en punto

dote /dəʊt/ vi. ~ **on** adorar

dotty /'dɒtı/ a (-**ier**, -**iest**) 🔲 chiflado

double /'dʌbl/ a doble. ● adv el doble. ● n doble m; (person) doble m & f. at the ~ corriendo. ● vt doblar; redoblar <*efforts etc*>. ● vi doblarse.

~ **bass** /beıs/ n contrabajo m. ~ **bed** n cama f de matrimonio, cama f de doa plazas (LAm). ~ **chin** n papada f. ~**cross** /-'krɒs/ vt traicionar. ~-**decker** /-'dekə(r)/ n autobús m de dos pisos. ~ **Dutch** n 🔲 chino m. ~ **glazing** /-gleızıŋ/ n doble ventana f. ~**s** npl (tennis) dobles mpl

doubly /'dʌblı/ adv doblemente

doubt /daʊt/ n duda f. ● vt dudar; (distrust) dudar de. ~**ful** a dudoso. ~**less** adv sin duda

dough /dəʊ/ n masa f; (🔳, money) pasta f 🔲, lana f (LAm 🔲). ~**nut** n donut m, dona f (Mex)

dove /dʌv/ n paloma f

down /daʊn/ adv abajo. ~ **with** abajo. **come** ~ bajar. **go** ~ bajar; <*sun*> ponerse. ● prep abajo. ● a 🔲 deprimido. ● vt derribar; (🔲, drink) beber. ● n (feathers) plumón m. ~ **and out** a en la miseria. ~**cast** a abatido. ~**fall** n perdición f; (of king, dictator) caída f. ~**hearted** /-'hɑ:tıd/ a abatido. ~**hill** /-'hıl/ adv cuesta abajo. ~**load** /-'ləʊd/ vt (Comp) trasvasar. ~**market** /-'mɑ:kıt/ a <*newspaper*> popular; <*store*> barato. ~ **payment** n depósito m. ~**pour** n aguacero m. ~**right** a completo. ● adv completamente. ~**s** npl colinas fpl. ~**stairs** /-'steəz/ adv abajo. ● /-steəz/ a de abajo. ~**stream** adv río abajo. ~-**to-earth** /-tʊ'ɜ:θ/ a práctico. ~**town** /-'taʊn/ n centro m (de la ciudad). ● adv. go ~**town** ir al centro. ~ **under** adv en las antípodas; (in Australia) en Australia. ~**ward** /-wəd/ a & adv, ~**wards** adv hacia abajo

dowry /'daʊərı/ n dote f

doze /dəʊz/ vi dormitar. □ ~ **off** vi dormirse

dozen /'dʌzn/ n docena f. a ~ **eggs** una docena de huevos. ~**s of** 🔲 miles de, muchos

Dr /'dɒktə(r)/ abbr (= **Doctor**) Dr ~. **Broadley** (el) Doctor Broadley

drab /dræb/ a monótono

draft /drɑ:ft/ n borrador m; (Com) letra f de cambio; (Amer, Mil) reclutamiento m; (Amer, of air) corriente f de aire. ● vt redactar el borrador de; (Amer, conscript) reclutar

drag /dræg/ vt (pt **dragged**) arrastrar. ● n Ⓔ lata f

dragon /'drægən/ n dragón m. ~**fly** n libélula f

drain /dreɪn/ vt vaciar <tank, glass>; drenar <land>; (fig) agotar. ● vi escurrirse. ● n (pipe) sumidero m, resumidero m (LAm); (plughole) desagüe m. ~**board** (Amer), ~**ing board** n escurridero m

drama /'drɑːmə/ n drama m; (art) arte m teatral. ~**tic** /drə'mætɪk/ a dramático. ~**tist** /'dræmətɪst/ n dramaturgo m. ~**tize** /'dræmətaɪz/ vt adaptar al teatro; (fig) dramatizar

drank /dræŋk/ ⇒DRINK

drape /dreɪp/ vt cubrir; (hang) colgar. ~**s** npl (Amer) cortinas fpl

drastic /'dræstɪk/ a drástico

draught /drɑːft/ n corriente f de aire. ~ **beer** n cerveza f de barril. ~**s** npl (game) juego m de damas fpl. ~**y** a lleno de corrientes de aire

draw /drɔː/ vt (pt **drew**, pp **drawn**) tirar; (attract) atraer; dibujar <picture>; trazar <line>. ~ **the line** trazar el límite. ● vi (Art) dibujar; (Sport) empatar; ~ **near** acercarse. ● n (Sport) empate m; (in lottery) sorteo m. □ ~ **in** vi <days> acortarse. □ ~ **out** vt sacar <money>. □ ~ **up** vi pararse. vt redactar <document>; acercar <chair>. ~**back** n desventaja f. ~**bridge** n puente m levadizo

drawer /drɔː(r)/ n cajón m, gaveta f (Mex). ~**s** npl calzones mpl

drawing /'drɔːɪŋ/ n dibujo m. ~ **pin** n tachuela f, chincheta f, chinche f. ~ **room** n salón m

drawl /drɔːl/ n habla f lenta

drawn /drɔːn/ ⇒DRAW

dread /dred/ n terror m. ● vt temer. ~**ful** a terrible. ~**fully** adv terriblemente

dream /driːm/ n sueño m. ● vt/i (pt **dreamed** or **dreamt** /dremt/) soñar. □ ~ **up** vt idear. a ideal. ~**er** n soñador m

dreary /'drɪərɪ/ a (**-ier, -iest**) triste; (boring) monótono

dredge /dredʒ/ n draga f. ● vt dragar. ~**r** n draga f

dregs /dregz/ npl posos mpl, heces fpl; (fig) hez f

drench /drentʃ/ vt empapar

dress /dres/ n vestido m; (clothing) ropa f. ● vt vestir; (decorate) adornar; (Med) vendar. ● vi vestirse. □ ~ **up** vi ponerse elegante. ~ **up as** disfrazarse de. ~ **circle** n primer palco m

dressing /'dresɪŋ/ n (sauce) aliño m; (bandage) vendaje m. ~**down** /-'daʊn/ n rapapolvo m, reprensión f. ~ **gown** n bata f. ~ **room** n vestidor m; (in theatre) camarín m. ~ **table** n tocador m

dress: ~**maker** n modista m & f. ~**making** n costura f. ~ **rehearsal** n ensayo m general

drew /druː/ ⇒DRAW

dribble /'drɪbl/ vi <baby> babear; (in football) driblar, driblear

drie|d /draɪd/ a <food> seco; <milk> en polvo. ~**r** /'draɪə(r)/ n secador m

drift /drɪft/ vi ir a la deriva; <snow> amontonarse. ● n (movement) dirección f; (of snow) montón m

drill /drɪl/ n (tool) taladro m; (of dentist) torno m; (training) ejercicio m. ● vt taladrar, perforar; (train) entrenar. ● vi entrenarse

drink /drɪŋk/ vt/i (pt **drank**, pp **drunk**) beber, tomar (LAm). ● n bebida f. ~**able** a bebible; <water> potable. ~**er** n bebedor m. ~**ing water** n agua f potable

drip /drɪp/ vi (pt **dripped**) gotear. ● n gota f; (Med) goteo m intravenoso; (Ⓔ, person) soso m. ~**dry** /-'draɪ/ a de lava y pon. ~**ping** a. be ~**ping wet** estar chorreando

drive /draɪv/ vt (pt **drove**, pp **driven**) conducir, manejar (LAm) <car etc>. ~ **s.o. mad** volver loco a uno. ~ **s.o. to do sth** llevar a uno a hacer algo. ● vi conducir, manejar (LAm). ~ **at** querer decir. ~ **in** (in car) entrar en coche. ● n paseo m; (road) calle f; (private road) camino m de entrada; (fig) empuje m. ~**r** n conductor m, chofer m (LAm). ~**r's license** n (Amer) ⇒DRIVING LICENSE

drivel /'drɪvl/ n tonterías fpl

driving /'draɪvɪŋ/ n conducción f. ~ **licence** n permiso m de conducir, licencia *f* de conducción (LAm), licencia *f* (de manejar) (Mex). ~ **test** *n* examen *m* de conducir, examen *m* de manejar (LAm)

drizzle /'drɪzl/ *n* llovizna *f*. ● *vi* lloviznar

drone /drəʊn/ *n* zumbido *m*. ● *vi* zumbar

drool /dru:l/ *vi* babear

droop /dru:p/ *vi* inclinarse; *<flowers>* marchitarse

drop /drɒp/ *n* gota *f*; (fall) caída *f*; (decrease) descenso *m*. ● *vt* (*pt* **dropped**) dejar caer; (lower) bajar. ● *vi* caer. □ ~ **in on** *vt* pasar por casa de. □ ~ **off** *vi* (sleep) dormirse. □ ~ **out** *vi* retirarse; *<student>* abandonar los estudios. ~**out** *n* marginado *m*

drought /draʊt/ *n* sequía *f*

drove /drəʊv/ ⇒DRIVE. ● *n* manada *f*

drown /draʊn/ *vt* ahogar. ● *vi* ahogarse

drowsy /'draʊzɪ/ *a* soñoliento

drudgery /'drʌdʒərɪ/ *n* trabajo *m* pesado

drug /drʌg/ *n* droga *f*; (Med) medicamento *m*. ● *vt* (*pt* **drugged**) drogar. ~ **addict** *n* drogadicto *m*. ~**gist** *n* (Amer) farmacéutico *m*. ~**store** *n* (Amer) farmacia *f* (*que vende otros artículos también*)

drum /drʌm/ *n* tambor *m*; (for oil) bidón *m*. ● *vi* (*pt* **drummed**) tocar el tambor. ● *vt*. ~ **sth into s.o.** hacerle aprender algo a uno a fuerza de repetírselo. ~**mer** *n* tambor *m*; (in group) batería *f*. ~**s** *npl* batería *f*. ~**stick** *n* baqueta *f*; (Culin) muslo *m*

drunk /drʌŋk/ ⇒DRINK. ● *a* borracho. **get** ~ emborracharse. ● *n* borracho *m*. ~**ard** /-əd/ *n* borracho *m*. ~**en** *a* borracho

dry /draɪ/ *a* (**drier**, **driest**) seco. ● *vt* secar. ● *vi* secarse. □ ~ **up** *vi* *<stream>* secarse; *<funds>* agotarse. ~**-clean** *vt* limpiar en seco. ~**-cleaner's** tintorería *f*. ~**er** *n* ⇒DRIER

dual /'dju:əl/ *a* doble. ~ **carriage-way** *n* autovía *f*, carretera *f* de doble pista

dub /dʌb/ *vt* (*pt* **dubbed**) doblar *<film>*

dubious /'dju:bɪəs/ *a* dudoso; *<person>* sospechoso

duchess /'dʌtʃɪs/ *n* duquesa *f*

duck /dʌk/ *n* pato *m*. ● *vt* sumergir; bajar *<head>*. ● *vi* agacharse. ~**ling** /'dʌklɪŋ/ *n* patito *m*

duct /dʌkt/ *n* conducto *m*

dud /dʌd/ *a* inútil; *<cheque>* sin fondos

due /dju:/ *a* debido; (expected) esperado. ~ **to** debido a. ● *adv*. ~ **north** derecho hacia el norte. ~**s** *npl* derechos *mpl*

duel /'dju:əl/ *n* duelo *m*

duet /dju:'et/ *n* dúo *m*

duffel, **duffle** /'dʌfl/: ~ **bag** *n* bolsa *f* de lona. ~ **coat** *n* trenca *f*

dug /dʌg/ ⇒DIG

duke /dju:k/ *n* duque *m*

dull /dʌl/ *a* (**-er**, **-est**) *<weather>* gris; *<colour>* apagado; *<person, play, etc>* pesado; *<sound>* sordo

dumb /dʌm/ *a* (**-er**, **-est**) mudo; Ⅱ estúpido. ~**found** /dʌm'faʊnd/ *vt* pasmar

dummy /'dʌmɪ/ *n* muñeco *m*; (of tailor) maniquí *m*; (for baby) chupete *m*. ● *a* falso. ~ **run** prueba *f*

dump /dʌmp/ *vt* tirar, botar (LAm). ● *n* vertedero *m*; (Mil) depósito *m*; Ⅱ lugar *m* desagradable. **be down in the** ~**s** estar deprimido

dumpling /'dʌmplɪŋ/ *n* bola *f* de masa hervida

Dumpster /'dʌmpstə(r)/ *n* (Amer, P) contenedor *m* (*para escombros*)

dumpy /'dʌmpɪ/ *a* (**-ier**, **-iest**) regordete

dunce /dʌns/ *n* burro *m*

dung /dʌŋ/ *n* (manure) estiércol *m*

dungarees /dʌŋgə'ri:z/ *npl* mono *m*, peto *m*

dungeon /'dʌndʒən/ *n* calabozo *m*

dunk /dʌŋk/ *vt* remojar

dupe /dju:p/ *vt* engañar. ● *n* inocentón *m*

duplicat|e /'dju:plɪkət/ *a* & *n* duplicado (*m*). ● /'dju:plɪkeɪt/ *vt* duplicar;

(on machine) reproducir. **~ing machine**, **~or** n multicopista f

durable /'djʊərəbl/ a durable

duration /djʊ'reɪʃn/ n duración f

duress /djʊ'res/ n. **under** ~ bajo coacción

during /'djʊərɪŋ/ prep durante

dusk /dʌsk/ n anochecer m

dust /dʌst/ n polvo m. ● vt quitar el polvo a; (sprinkle) espolvorear (**with** con). **~bin** n cubo m de la basura, bote m de la basura (Mex). **~ cloth** (Amer), **~er** n trapo m. **~jacket** n sobrecubierta f. **~man** /-mən/ n basurero m. **~pan** n recogedor m. **~y** a (**-ier**, **-iest**) polvoriento

Dutch /dʌtʃ/ a holandés. ● n (Lang) holandés m. **the** ~ (people) los holandeses. **~man** /-mən/ m holandés m. **~woman** n holandesa f

duty /'djuːtɪ/ n deber m; (tax) derechos mpl de aduana. **on** ~ de servicio. **~free** /-'friː/ a libre de impuestos

duvet /'djuːveɪ/ n edredón m

dwarf /dwɔːf/ n (pl **-s** or **dwarves**) enano m

dwell /dwel/ vi (pt **dwelt** or **dwelled**) morar.□ ~ **on** vt detenerse en. **~ing** n morada f

dwindle /'dwɪndl/ vi disminuir

dye /daɪ/ vt (pres p **dyeing**) teñir. ● n tinte m

dying /'daɪɪŋ/ ⇒DIE

dynamic /daɪ'næmɪk/ a dinámico. **~s** npl dinámica f

dynamite /'daɪnəmaɪt/ n dinamita f. ● vt dinamitar

dynamo /'daɪnəməʊ/ n (pl **-os**) dínamo f, dínamo f, dinamo m (LAm), dínamo m (LAm)

dynasty /'dɪnəstɪ/ n dinastía f

Ee

E abbr (= **East**) E

each /iːtʃ/ a cada. ● pron cada uno. ~ **one** cada uno. ~ **other** uno a otro, el uno al otro. **they love** ~ **other** se aman

eager /'iːgə(r)/ a impaciente; (enthusiastic) ávido. **~ness** n impaciencia f; (enthusiasm) entusiasmo m

eagle /'iːgl/ n águila f

ear /ɪə(r)/ n oído m; (outer) oreja f; (of corn) espiga f. **~ache** n dolor m de oído. **~drum** n tímpano m

earl /ɜːl/ n conde m

early /'ɜːlɪ/ a (**-ier**, **-iest**) temprano; (before expected time) prematuro. ● adv temprano; (ahead of time) con anticipación

earn /ɜːn/ vt ganar; (deserve) merecer

earnest /'ɜːnɪst/ a serio. **in** ~ en serio

earnings /'ɜːnɪŋz/ npl ingresos mpl; (Com) ganancias fpl

ear: **~phone** n audífono m. **~ring** n pendiente m, arete m (LAm). **~shot** n. **within** ~shot al alcance del oído

earth /ɜːθ/ n tierra f. **the E~** (planet) la Tierra. ● vt (Elec) conectar a tierra. **~quake** n terremoto m

earwig /'ɪəwɪg/ n tijereta f

ease /iːz/ n facilidad f; (comfort) tranquilidad f. **at** ~ a gusto; (Mil) en posición de descanso. **ill at** ~ molesto. **with** ~ fácilmente. ● vt calmar; aliviar <pain>. ● vi calmarse; (lessen) disminuir

easel /'iːzl/ n caballete m

easily /'iːzɪlɪ/ adv fácilmente

east /iːst/ n este m. ● a este, oriental; <wind> del este. ● adv hacia el este.

Easter /'iːstə(r)/ n Semana f Santa; (Relig) Pascua f de Resurrección. ~ **egg** n huevo m de Pascua

east: **~erly** /-əlɪ/ a <wind> del este. **~ern** /-ən/ a este, oriental. **~ward**

/-wəd/, **~wards** *adv* hacia el este

easy /'i:zɪ/ *a* (**-ier, -iest**) fácil. ● *adv.* **go ~ on sth** 🔲 no pasarse con algo. **take it ~** tomarse las cosas con calma. ● *int* ¡despacio! **~ chair** *n* sillón *m*. **~going** /-'gəʊɪŋ/ *a* acomodadizo

eat /i:t/ *vt/i* (*pt* **ate**, *pp* **eaten**) comer. □ **~ into** *vt* corroer. **~er** *n* comedor *m*

eaves /i:vz/ *npl* alero *m*. **~drop** *vi* (*pt* **-dropped**). **~drop (on)** escuchar a escondidas

ebb /eb/ *n* reflujo *m*. ● *vi* bajar; (fig) decaer

ebony /'ebənɪ/ *n* ébano *m*

EC /i:'si:/ *abbr* (= **European Community**) CE *f* (Comunidad *f* Europea)

eccentric /ɪk'sentrɪk/ *a & n* excéntrico (*m*). **~ity** /eksen'trɪsətɪ/ *n* excentricidad *f*

echo /'ekəʊ/ *n* (*pl* **-oes**) eco *m*. ● *vi* hacer eco

eclipse /ɪ'klɪps/ *n* eclipse *m*. ● *vt* eclipsar

ecolog|ical /i:kə'lɒdʒɪkl/ *a* ecológico. **~y** /ɪ'kɒlədʒɪ/ *n* ecología *f*

econom|ic /i:kə'nɒmɪk/ *a* económico. **~ical** *a* económico. **~ics** *n* economía *f*. **~ist** /ɪ'kɒnəmɪst/ *n* economista *m & f*. **~ize** /ɪ'kɒnəmaɪz/ *vi* economizar. **~ize on sth** economizar algo. **~y** /ɪ'kɒnəmɪ/ *n* economía *f*

ecsta|sy /'ekstəsɪ/ *n* éxtasis *f*. **~tic** /ɪk'stætɪk/ *a* extático

Ecuador /'ekwədɔ:(r)/ *n* Ecuador *m*. **~ean** /ekwə'dɔ:rɪən/ *a & n* ecuatoriano (*m*)

edg|e /edʒ/ *n* borde *m*; (of knife) filo *m*; (of town) afueras *fpl*. **have the ~e on** 🔲 llevar la ventaja a. **on ~e** nervioso. ● *vt* ribetear; (move) mover poco a poco. ● *vi* avanzar cautelosamente. **~eways** *adv* de lado. **~y** *a* nervioso

edible /'edɪbl/ *a* comestible

edit /'edɪt/ *vt* dirigir *<newspaper>*; preparar una edición de *<text>*; editar *<film>*. **~ion** /ɪ'dɪʃn/ *n* edición *f*. **~or** *n* (of newspaper) director *m*; (of text) redactor *m*.

~orial /edɪ'tɔ:rɪəl/ *a* editorial. ● *n* artículo *m* de fondo

educat|e /'edʒʊkeɪt/ *vt* educar. **~ed** *a* culto. **~ion** /-'keɪʃn/ *n* educación *f*; (knowledge, culture) cultura *f*. **~ional** /-'keɪʃənl/ *a* instructivo

EEC /i:i:'si:/ *abbr* (= **European Economic Community**) CEE *f* (Comunidad *f* Económica Europea)

eel /i:l/ *n* anguila *f*

eerie /'ɪərɪ/ *a* (**-ier, -iest**) misterioso

effect /ɪ'fekt/ *n* efecto *m*. **in ~** efectivamente. **take ~** entrar en vigor. **~ive** *a* eficaz; (striking) impresionante; (real) efectivo. **~ively** *adv* eficazmente. **~iveness** *n* eficacia *f*

effeminate /ɪ'femɪnət/ *a* afeminado

efficien|cy /ɪ'fɪʃənsɪ/ *n* eficiencia *f*; (Mec) rendimiento *m*. **~t** *a* eficiente. **~tly** *adv* eficientemente

effort /'efət/ *n* esfuerzo *m*. **~less** *a* fácil

e.g. /i:'dʒi:/ *abbr* (= **exempli gratia**) p.ej., por ejemplo

egg /eg/ *n* huevo *m*. □ **~ on** *vt* 🔲 incitar. **~cup** *n* huevera *f*. **~plant** *n* (Amer) berenjena *f*. **~shell** *n* cáscara *f* de huevo

ego /'i:gəʊ/ *n* (*pl* **-os**) yo *m*. **~ism** *n* egoísmo *m*. **~ist** *n* egoísta *m & f*. **~centric** /i:gəʊ'sentrɪk/ *a* egocéntrico. **~tism** *n* egotismo *m*. **~tist** *n* egotista *m & f*

eh /eɪ/ *int* 🔲 ¡eh!

eiderdown /'aɪdədaʊn/ *n* edredón *m*

eight /eɪt/ *a & n* ocho (*m*). **~een** /eɪ'ti:n/ *a & n* dieciocho (*m*). **~eenth** *a* decimoctavo. ● *n* dieciochavo *m*. **~h** /eɪtθ/ *a & n* octavo (*m*) **~ieth** /'eɪtɪəθ/ *a* octogésimo. ● *n* ochentavo *m*. **~y** /'eɪtɪ/ *a & n* ochenta (*m*)

either /'aɪðə(r)/ *a* cualquiera de los dos; (negative) ninguno de los dos; (each) cada. ● *pron* uno u otro; (with negative) ni uno ni otro. ● *adv* (negative) tampoco. ● *conj* o. **~ Tuesday or Wednesday** o el martes o el miércoles; (with negative) ni el martes ni el miércoles

eject /ɪ'dʒekt/ *vt* expulsar

eke /i:k/ *vt.* ~ **out** hacer alcanzar <*re-sources*>. ~ **out a living** ganarse la vida a duras penas

elaborate /ɪˈlæbərət/ *a* complicado. ●/ɪˈlæbəreɪt/ *vt* elaborar. ●/ɪˈlæbəreɪt/ *vi* explicarse

elapse /ɪˈlæps/ *vi* transcurrir

elastic /ɪˈlæstɪk/ *a & n* elástico (*m*). ~ **band** *n* goma *f* (elástica), liga *f* (Mex)

elat|ed /ɪˈleɪtɪd/ *a* regocijado. ~**ion** /-ʃn/ *n* regocijo *m*

elbow /ˈelbəʊ/ *n* codo *m*. ● *vt* dar un codazo a

elder /ˈeldə(r)/ *a* mayor. ● *n* mayor *m & f*; (tree) saúco *m*. ~**ly** /ˈeldəlɪ/ *a* mayor, anciano

eldest /ˈeldɪst/ *a & n* mayor (*m & f*)

elect /ɪˈlekt/ *vt* elegir. ~ **to do** decidir hacer. ● *a* electo. ~**ion** /-ʃn/ *n* elección *f*. ~**or** *n* elector *m*. ~**oral** *a* electoral. ~**orate** /-ət/ *n* electorado *m*

electric /ɪˈlektrɪk/ *a* eléctrico. ~**al** *a* eléctrico. ~ **blanket** *n* manta *f* eléctrica. ~**ian** /ɪlekˈtrɪʃn/ *n* electricista *m & f*. ~**ity** /ɪlekˈtrɪsətɪ/ *n* electricidad *f*

electrify /ɪˈlektrɪfaɪ/ *vt* electrificar; (fig) electrizar

electrocute /ɪˈlektrəkjuːt/ *vt* electrocutar

electrode /ɪˈlektrəʊd/ *n* electrodo *m*

electron /ɪˈlektrɒn/ *n* electrón *m*

electronic /ɪlekˈtrɒnɪk/ *a* electrónico. ~ **mail** *n* correo *m* electrónico. ~**s** *n* electrónica *f*

elegan|ce /ˈelɪɡəns/ *n* elegancia *f*. ~**t** *a* elegante. ~**tly** *adv* elegantemente

element /ˈelɪmənt/ *n* elemento *m*. ~**ary** /-ˈmentrɪ/ *a* elemental. ~**ary school** *n* (Amer) escuela *f* primaria

elephant /ˈelɪfənt/ *n* elefante *m*

elevat|e /ˈelɪveɪt/ *vt* elevar. ~**ion** /-ˈveɪʃn/ *n* elevación *f*. ~**or** *n* (Amer) ascensor *m*

eleven /ɪˈlevn/ *a & n* once (*m*). ~**th** *a* undécimo. ● *n* onceavo *m*

elf /elf/ *n* (*pl* **elves**) duende *m*

eligible /ˈelɪdʒəbl/ *a* elegible. **be** ~ **for** tener derecho a

eliminat|e /ɪˈlɪmɪneɪt/ *vt* eliminar. ~**ion** /-ˈneɪʃn/ *n* eliminación *f*

élite /eɪˈliːt/ *n* elite *f*, élite *f*

ellip|se /ɪˈlɪps/ *n* elipse *f*. ~**tical** *a* elíptico

elm /elm/ *n* olmo *m*

elope /ɪˈləʊp/ *vi* fugarse con el amante

eloquen|ce /ˈeləkwəns/ *n* elocuencia *f*. ~**t** *a* elocuente

El Salvador /elˈsælvədɔ:(r)/ *n* El Salvador

else /els/ *adv.* **somebody** ~ otra persona. **everybody** ~ todos los demás. **nobody** ~ ningún otro, nadie más. **nothing** ~ nada más. **or** ~ o bien. **somewhere** ~ en otra parte. ~**where** *adv* en otra parte

elu|de /ɪˈluːd/ *vt* eludir. ~**sive** /-sɪv/ *a* esquivo

elves /elvz/ ⇒ELF

emaciated /ɪˈmeɪʃɪeɪtɪd/ *a* consumido

email, **e-mail** /ˈiːmeɪl/ *n* correo *m* electrónico, correo-e *m*. ● *vt* mandar por correo electrónico, emailear. ~ **address** *n* casilla *f* electrónica, dirección *f* de correo electrónico

emancipat|e /ɪˈmænsɪpeɪt/ *vt* emancipar. ~**ion** /-ˈpeɪʃn/ *n* emancipación *f*

embankment /ɪmˈbæŋkmənt/ *n* terraplén *m*; (of river) dique *m*

embargo /ɪmˈbɑːɡəʊ/ *n* (*pl* **-oes**) embargo *m*

embark /ɪmˈbɑːk/ *vi* embarcarse. ~ **on** (fig) emprender. ~**ation** /embɑːˈkeɪʃn/ *n* embarque *m*

embarrass /ɪmˈbærəs/ *vt* avergonzar. ~**ed** *a* avergonzado. ~**ing** *a* embarazoso. ~**ment** *n* vergüenza *f*

embassy /ˈembəsɪ/ *n* embajada *f*

embellish /ɪmˈbelɪʃ/ *vt* adornar. ~**ment** *n* adorno *m*

embers /ˈembəz/ *npl* ascuas *fpl*

embezzle /ɪmˈbezl/ *vt* desfalcar. ~**ment** *n* desfalco *m*

emblem /ˈembləm/ *n* emblema *m*

embrace /ɪmˈbreɪs/ *vt* abrazar; (fig) abarcar. ● *vi* abrazarse. ● *n* abrazo *m*

embroider /ɪm'brɔɪdə(r)/ *vt* bordar. ∼**y** *n* bordado *m*

embroil /ɪm'brɔɪl/ *vt* enredar

embryo /'embrɪəʊ/ *n* (*pl* **-os**) embrión *m*. ∼**nic** /-'ɒnɪk/ *a* embrionario

emend /ɪ'mend/ *vt* enmendar

emerald /'emərəld/ *n* esmeralda *f*

emerge /ɪ'mɜːdʒ/ *vi* salir. ∼**nce** /-əns/ *n* aparición *f*

emergency /ɪ'mɜːdʒənsɪ/ *n* emergencia *f*; (Med) urgencia *f*. **in an ∼** en caso de emergencia. **∼ exit** *n* salida *f* de emergencia

emigra|nt /'emɪɡrənt/ *n* emigrante *m* & *f*. ∼**te** /'emɪɡreɪt/ *vi* emigrar. ∼**tion** /-'ɡreɪʃn/ *n* emigración *f*

eminen|ce /'emɪnəns/ *n* eminencia *f*. ∼**t** *a* eminente. ∼**tly** *adv* eminentemente

emi|ssion /ɪ'mɪʃn/ *n* emisión *f*. ∼**t** *vt* (*pt* **emitted**) emitir

emoti|on /ɪ'məʊʃn/ *n* emoción *f*. ∼**onal** *a* emocional; <*person*> emotivo; (moving) conmovedor. ∼**ve** /ɪ'məʊtɪv/ *a* emotivo

empathy /'empəθɪ/ *n* empatía *f*

emperor /'empərə(r)/ *n* emperador *m*

empha|sis /'emfəsɪs/ *n* (*pl* ∼**ses** /-siːz/) énfasis *m*. ∼**size** /'emfəsaɪz/ *vt* enfatizar. ∼**tic** /ɪm'fætɪk/ *a* <*gesture*> enfático; <*assertion*> categórico

empire /'empaɪə(r)/ *n* imperio *m*

empirical /ɪm'pɪrɪkl/ *a* empírico

employ /ɪm'plɔɪ/ *vt* emplear. ∼**ee** /emplɔɪ'iː/ *n* empleado *m*. ∼**er** *n* patrón *m*. ∼**ment** *n* empleo *m*. ∼**ment agency** *n* agencia *f* de trabajo

empower /ɪm'paʊə(r)/ *vt* autorizar (**to do** a hacer)

empress /'emprɪs/ *n* emperatriz *f*

empty /'emptɪ/ *a* vacío; <*promise*> vano. **on an ∼y stomach** con el estómago vacío. ● *n* 🄔 envase *m* (vacío). ● *vt* vaciar. ● *vi* vaciarse

emulate /'emjʊleɪt/ *vt* emular

emulsion /ɪ'mʌlʃn/ *n* emulsión *f*

enable /ɪ'neɪbl/ *vt*. ∼ **s.o. to do sth** permitir a uno hacer algo

enact /ɪ'nækt/ *vt* (Jurid) decretar; (in theatre) representar

enamel /ɪ'næml/ *n* esmalte *m*. ● *vt* (*pt* **enamelled**) esmaltar

enchant /ɪn'tʃɑːnt/ *vt* encantar. ∼**ing** *a* encantador. ∼**ment** *n* encanto *m*

encircle /ɪn'sɜːkl/ *vt* rodear

enclave /'enkleɪv/ *n* enclave *m*

enclos|e /ɪn'kləʊz/ *vt* cercar <*land*>; (Com) adjuntar. ∼**ed** *a* <*space*> cerrado; (Com) adjunto. ∼**ure** /ɪn'kləʊʒə(r)/ *n* cercamiento *m*

encode /ɪn'kəʊd/ *vt* codificar, cifrar

encore /'ɒŋkɔː(r)/ *int* ¡otra! ● *n* bis *m*, repetición *f*

encounter /ɪn'kaʊntə(r)/ *vt* encontrar. ● *n* encuentro *m*

encourag|e /ɪn'kʌrɪdʒ/ *vt* animar; (stimulate) fomentar. ∼**ement** *n* ánimo *m*. ∼**ing** *a* alentador

encroach /ɪn'krəʊtʃ/ *vi*. ∼ **on** invadir <*land*>; quitar <*time*>

encyclopaedi|a /ɪnsaɪklə'piːdɪə/ *n* enciclopedia *f*. ∼**c** *a* enciclopédico

end /end/ *n* fin *m*; (furthest point) extremo *m*. **in the ∼** por fin. **make ∼s meet** poder llegar a fin de mes. **put an ∼ to** poner fin a. **no ∼ of** muchísimos. **on ∼** de pie; (consecutive) seguido. ● *vt/i* terminar, acabar

endanger /ɪn'deɪndʒə(r)/ *vt* poner en peligro. ∼**ed** *a* <*species*> en peligro

endearing /ɪn'dɪərɪŋ/ *a* simpático

endeavour /ɪn'devə(r)/ *n* esfuerzo *m*, intento *m*. ● *vi*. ∼ **to** esforzarse por

ending /'endɪŋ/ *n* fin *m*

endless /'endlɪs/ *a* interminable

endorse /ɪn'dɔːs/ *vt* endosar; (fig) aprobar. ∼**ment** *n* endoso *m*; (fig) aprobación *f*; (Auto) nota *f* de inhabilitación

endur|ance /ɪn'djʊərəns/ *n* resistencia *f*. ∼**e** /ɪn'djʊə(r)/ *vt* aguantar. ∼**ing** *a* perdurable

enemy /'enəmɪ/ *n* & *a* enemigo (*m*)

energ|etic /enə'dʒetɪk/ *a* enérgico. ∼**y** /'enədʒɪ/ *n* energía *f*

enforce /ɪnˈfɔːs/ vt hacer cumplir <*law*>; hacer valer <*claim*>. **~d** a forzado

engag|e /ɪnˈɡeɪdʒ/ vt emplear <*staff*>; captar <*attention*>; (Mec) hacer engranar. ● vi (Mec) engranar. **~e in** dedicarse a. **~ed** a prometido, comprometido (LAm); (busy) ocupado. **be ~ed** (of phone) estar comunicando, estar ocupado (LAm). **get ~ed** prometerse, comprometerse (LAm). **~ement** n compromiso m

engine /ˈendʒɪn/ n motor m; (of train) locomotora f. **~ driver** n maquinista m

engineer /endʒɪˈnɪə(r)/ n ingeniero m; (mechanic) mecánico m; (Amer, Rail) maquinista m. ● vt (contrive) fraguar. **~ing** n ingeniería f

England /ˈɪŋɡlənd/ n Inglaterra f

English /ˈɪŋɡlɪʃ/ a inglés. ● n (Lang) inglés m. ● npl. **the ~** los ingleses. **~man** /-mən/ n inglés m. **~woman** n inglesa f

engrav|e /ɪnˈɡreɪv/ vt grabar. **~ing** n grabado m

engrossed /ɪnˈɡrəʊst/ a absorto

engulf /ɪnˈɡʌlf/ vt envolver

enhance /ɪnˈhɑːns/ vt realzar; aumentar <*value*>

enigma /ɪˈnɪɡmə/ n enigma m. **~tic** /enɪɡˈmætɪk/ a enigmático

enjoy /ɪnˈdʒɔɪ/ vt. **I ~ reading** me gusta la lectura. **~ o.s.** divertirse. **~able** a agradable. **~ment** n placer m

enlarge /ɪnˈlɑːdʒ/ vt agrandar; (Photo) ampliar. ● vi agrandarse. **~ upon** extenderse sobre. **~ment** n (Photo) ampliación f

enlighten /ɪnˈlaɪtn/ vt ilustrar. **~ment** n. **the E~ment** el siglo de las luces

enlist /ɪnˈlɪst/ vt alistar; conseguir <*support*>. ● vi alistarse

enliven /ɪnˈlaɪvn/ vt animar

enorm|ity /ɪˈnɔːmətɪ/ n enormidad f. **~ous** /ɪˈnɔːməs/ a enorme. **~ously** adv enormemente

enough /ɪˈnʌf/ a & adv bastante. ● n bastante m, suficiente m. ● int ¡basta!

enquir|e /ɪnˈkwaɪə(r)/ vt/i preguntar. **~e about** informarse de. **~y** n pregunta f; (investigation) investigación f

enrage /ɪnˈreɪdʒ/ vt enfurecer

enrol /ɪnˈrəʊl/ vt (pt **enrolled**) inscribir, matricular <*student*>. ● vi inscribirse, matricularse

ensue /ɪnˈsjuː/ vi seguir

ensure /ɪnˈʃʊə(r)/ vt asegurar

entail /ɪnˈteɪl/ vt suponer; acarrear <*expense*>

entangle /ɪnˈtæŋɡl/ vt enredar. **~ment** n enredo m

enter /ˈentə(r)/ vt entrar en, entrar a (esp LAm); presentarse a <*competition*>; inscribirse en <*race*>; (write) escribir. ● vi entrar

enterpris|e /ˈentəpraɪz/ n empresa f; (fig) iniciativa f. **~ing** a emprendedor

entertain /entəˈteɪn/ vt entretener; recibir <*guests*>; abrigar <*ideas, hopes*>; (consider) considerar. **~ing** a entretenido. **~ment** n entretenimiento m; (show) espectáculo m

enthral /ɪnˈθrɔːl/ vt (pt **enthralled**) cautivar

enthuse /ɪnˈθjuːz/ vi. **~ over** entusiasmarse por

enthusias|m /ɪnˈθjuːzɪæzəm/ n entusiasmo m. **~t** n entusiasta m & f. **~tic** /-ˈæstɪk/ a entusiasta. **~tically** adv con entusiasmo

entice /ɪnˈtaɪs/ vt atraer

entire /ɪnˈtaɪə(r)/ a entero. **~ly** adv completamente. **~ty** /ɪnˈtaɪərətɪ/ n. **in its ~ty** en su totalidad

entitle /ɪnˈtaɪtl/ vt titular; (give a right) dar derecho a. **be ~d to** tener derecho a. **~ment** n derecho m

entity /ˈentɪtɪ/ n entidad f

entrails /ˈentreɪlz/ npl entrañas fpl

entrance /ˈentrəns/ n entrada f. ● /ɪnˈtrɑːns/ vt encantar

entrant /ˈentrənt/ n participante m & f; (in exam) candidato m

entreat /ɪnˈtriːt/ vt suplicar. **~y** n súplica f

entrenched /ɪnˈtrentʃt/ a <*position*> afianzado

entrust /ɪnˈtrʌst/ vt confiar

entry /'entrɪ/ n entrada f

entwine /ɪn'twaɪn/ vt entrelazar

enumerate /ɪ'nju:məreɪt/ vt enumerar

envelop /ɪn'veləp/ vt envolver

envelope /'envələup/ n sobre m

enviable /'envɪəbl/ a envidiable

envious /'envɪəs/ a envidioso

environment /ɪn'vaɪərənmənt/ n medio m ambiente. **~al** /-'mentl/ a ambiental

envisage /ɪn'vɪzɪdʒ/ vt prever; (imagine) imaginar

envision /ɪn'vɪʒn/ vt (Amer) prever

envoy /'envɔɪ/ n enviado m

envy /'envɪ/ n envidia f. ● vt envidiar

enzyme /'enzaɪm/ n enzima f

ephemeral /ɪ'femərəl/ a efímero

epic /'epɪk/ n épica f. ● a épico

epidemic /epɪ'demɪk/ n epidemia f. ● a epidémico

epilep|sy /'epɪlepsɪ/ n epilepsia f. **~tic** /-'leptɪk/ a & n epiléptico (m)

epilogue /'epɪlɒg/ n epílogo m

episode /'epɪsəʊd/ n episodio m

epitaph /'epɪtɑ:f/ n epitafio m

epitom|e /ɪ'pɪtəmɪ/ n personificación f, epítome m. **~ize** vt ser la personificación de

epoch /'i:pɒk/ n época f

equal /'i:kwəl/ a & n igual (m & f). **~ to** (a task) a la altura de. ● vt (pt **equalled**) ser igual a; (Math) ser. **~ity** /ɪ'kwɒlətɪ/ n igualdad f. **~ize** vt igualar. ● vi (Sport) emapatar. **~izer** n (Sport) gol m del empate. **~ly** adv igualmente; <share> por igual

equation /ɪ'kweɪʒn/ n ecuación f

equator /ɪ'kweɪtə(r)/ n ecuador m. **~ial** /ekwə'tɔ:rɪəl/ a ecuatorial

equilibrium /i:kwɪ'lɪbrɪəm/ n equilibrio m

equinox /'i:kwɪnɒks/ n equinoccio m

equip /ɪ'kwɪp/ vt (pt **equipped**) equipar. **~ sth with** proveer algo de. **~ment** n equipo m

equivalen|ce /ɪ'kwɪvələns/ n equivalencia f. **~t** a & n equivalente (m). **be ~t to** equivaler

equivocal /ɪ'kwɪvəkl/ a equívoco

era /'ɪərə/ n era f

eradicate /ɪ'rædɪkeɪt/ vt erradicar, extirpar

erase /ɪ'reɪz/ vt borrar. **~r** n goma f (de borrar)

erect /ɪ'rekt/ a erguido. ● vt levantar. **~ion** /-ʃn/ n construcción f; (Anat) erección f

ero|de /ɪ'rəʊd/ vt erosionar. **~sion** /-ʒn/ n erosión f

erotic /ɪ'rɒtɪk/ a erótico

err /ɜ:(r)/ vi errar; (sin) pecar

errand /'erənd/ n recado m, mandado m (LAm)

erratic /ɪ'rætɪk/ a desigual; <person> voluble

erroneous /ɪ'rəʊnɪəs/ a erróneo

error /'erə(r)/ n error m

erudit|e /'eru:daɪt/ a erudito. **~ion** /-'dɪʃn/ n erudición f

erupt /ɪ'rʌpt/ vi entrar en erupción; (fig) estallar. **~ion** /-ʃn/ n erupción f

escalat|e /'eskəleɪt/ vt intensificar. ● vi intensificarse. **~ion** /-leɪʃn/ n intensificación f. **~or** n escalera f mecánica

escapade /eskə'peɪd/ n aventura f

escap|e /ɪ'skeɪp/ vi escaparse. ● vt evitar. ● n fuga f; (of gas, water) escape m. **have a narrow ~e** escapar por un pelo. **~ism** /-ɪzəm/ n escapismo m

escort /'eskɔ:t/ n acompañante m; (Mil) escolta f. ● /ɪ'skɔ:t/ vt acompañar; (Mil) escoltar

Eskimo /'eskɪməʊ/ n (pl **-os** or invar) esquimal m & f

especial /ɪ'speʃl/ a especial. **~ly** adv especialmente

espionage /'espɪənɑ:ʒ/ n espionaje m

Esq. /ɪ'skwaɪə(r)/ abbr (= **Esquire**) (in address) E. Ashton, **~** Sr. Don E. Ashton

essay /'eseɪ/ n ensayo m; (at school) composición f

essence /'esns/ n esencia f. **in ~** esencialmente

essential /ɪ'senʃl/ a esencial. ● n elemento m esencial. **~ly** adv esencialmente

establish /ɪˈstæblɪʃ/ *vt* establecer. ~**ment** *n* establecimiento *m*. the E~ment los que mandan, el sistema

estate /ɪˈsteɪt/ *n* finca *f*; (housing estate) complejo *m* habitacional, urbanización *f*, fraccionamiento *m* (Mex); (possessions) bienes *mpl*. ~ **agent** *n* agente *m* inmobiliario. ~ **car** *n* ranchera *f*, (coche *m*) familiar *m*, camioneta *f* (LAm)

esteem /ɪˈstiːm/ *n* estimación *f*, estima *f*

estimat|e /ˈestɪmət/ *n* cálculo *m*; (Com) presupuesto *m*. ● /ˈestɪmeɪt/ *vt* calcular. ~**ion** /-ˈmeɪʃn/ *n* estima *f*, estimación *f*; (opinion) opinión *f*

estranged /ɪsˈtreɪndʒd/ *a* alejado

estuary /ˈestʃʊərɪ/ *n* estuario *m*

etc /etˈsetrə/ *abbr* (= **et cetera**) etc., etcétera

etching /ˈetʃɪŋ/ *n* aguafuerte *m*

etern|al /ɪˈtɜːnl/ *a* eterno. ~**ity** /-ətɪ/ *n* eternidad *f*

ether /ˈiːθə(r)/ *n* éter *m*

ethic /ˈeθɪk/ *n* ética *f*. ~**al** *a* ético. ~**s** *npl* ética *f*

ethnic /ˈeθnɪk/ *a* étnico

ethos /ˈiːθɒs/ *n* carácter *m* distintivo

etiquette /ˈetɪket/ *n* etiqueta *f*

etymology /etɪˈmɒlədʒɪ/ *n* etimología *f*

euphemism /ˈjuːfəmɪzəm/ *n* eufemismo *m*

euphoria /juːˈfɔːrɪə/ *n* euforia *f*

Europe /ˈjʊərəp/ *n* Europa *f*. ~**an** /-ˈpɪən/ *a* & *n* europeo (*m*). ~**an Union** *n* Unión *f* Europea

euthanasia /juːθəˈneɪzɪə/ *n* eutanasia *f*

evacuat|e /ɪˈvækjʊeɪt/ *vt* evacuar; desocupar <*building*>. ~**ion** /-ˈeɪʃn/ *n* evacuación *f*

evade /ɪˈveɪd/ *vt* evadir

evaluate /ɪˈvæljʊeɪt/ *vt* evaluar

evangelical /iːvænˈdʒelɪkl/ *a* evangélico

evaporat|e /ɪˈvæpəreɪt/ *vi* evaporarse. ~**ion** /-ˈreɪʃn/ *n* evaporación *f*

evasi|on /ɪˈveɪʒn/ *n* evasión *f*. ~**ve** /ɪˈveɪsɪv/ *a* evasivo

eve /iːv/ *n* víspera *f*

even /ˈiːvn/ *a* (flat, smooth) plano; <*colour*> uniforme; <*distribution*> equitativo; <*number*> par. get ~ **with** desquitarse con. ● *vt* nivelar. □ ~ **up** *vt* equilibrar. ● *adv* aun, hasta, incluso. ~ **if** aunque. ~ **so** aun así. **not** ~ ni siquiera

evening /ˈiːvnɪŋ/ *n* tarde *f*; (after dark) noche *f*. ~ **class** *n* clase *f* nocturna

event /ɪˈvent/ *n* acontecimiento *m*; (Sport) prueba *f*. **in the** ~ **of** en caso de. ~**ful** *a* lleno de acontecimientos

eventual /ɪˈventʃʊəl/ *a* final, definitivo. ~**ity** /-ˈælətɪ/ *n* eventualidad *f*. ~**ly** *adv* finalmente

ever /ˈevə(r)/ *adv* (negative) nunca, jamás; (at all times) siempre. **have you** ~ **been to Greece?** ¿has estado (alguna vez) en Grecia? ~ **after** desde entonces. ~ **since** desde entonces. ~ **so** 🅔 muy. **for** ~ para siempre. **hardly** ~ casi nunca. ~**green** *a* de hoja perenne. ● *n* árbol *m* de hoja perenne. ~**lasting** *a* eterno

every /ˈevrɪ/ *a* cada, todo. ~ **child** todos los niños. ~ **one** cada uno. ~ **other day** un día sí y otro no. ~**body** *pron* todos, todo el mundo. ~**day** *a* de todos los días. ~**one** *pron* todos, todo el mundo. ~**thing** *pron* todo. ~**where** *adv* (be) en todas partes, (go) a todos lados

evict /ɪˈvɪkt/ *vt* desahuciar. ~**ion** /-ʃn/ *n* desahucio *m*

eviden|ce /ˈevɪdəns/ *n* evidencia *f*; (proof) pruebas *fpl*; (Jurid) testimonio *m*; **give** ~**ce** prestar declaración. ~**ce of** señales de. **in** ~**ce** visible. ~**t** *a* evidente. ~**tly** *adv* evidentemente

evil /ˈiːvl/ *a* malvado. ● *n* mal *m*

evo|cative /ɪˈvɒkətɪv/ *a* evocador. ~**ke** /ɪˈvəʊk/ *vt* evocar

evolution /iːvəˈluːʃn/ *n* evolución *f*

evolve /ɪˈvɒlv/ *vt* desarrollar. ● *vi* evolucionar

ewe /juː/ *n* oveja *f*

exact /ɪɡˈzækt/ *a* exacto. ● *vt* exigir (from a). ~**ing** *a* exigente. ~**ly** *adv* exactamente

exaggerat|e /ɪgˈzædʒəreɪt/ *vt* exagerar. **~ion** /-ˈreɪʃn/ *n* exageración *f*

exam /ɪgˈzæm/ *n* examen *m*. **~ination** /ɪgzæmɪˈneɪʃn/ *n* examen *m*. **~ine** /ɪgˈzæmɪn/ *vt* examinar; interrogar *<witness>*. **~iner** *n* examinador *m*

example /ɪgˈzɑːmpl/ *n* ejemplo *m*. for **~** por ejemplo. **make an ~ of s.o.** darle un castigo ejemplar a uno

exasperat|e /ɪgˈzæspəreɪt/ *vt* exasperar. **~ing** *a* exasperante. **~ion** /-ˈreɪʃn/ *n* exasperación *f*

excavat|e /ˈekskəveɪt/ *vt* excavar. **~ion** /-ˈveɪʃn/ *n* excavación *f*

exceed /ɪkˈsiːd/ *vt* exceder. **~ingly** *adv* sumamente

excel /ɪkˈsel/ *vi* (*pt* **excelled**) sobresalir. ● *vt*. **~ o.s.** lucirse. **~lence** /ˈeksələns/ *n* excelencia *f*. **~lent** *a* excelente

except /ɪkˈsept/ *prep* menos, excepto. **~ for** si no fuera por. ● *vt* exceptuar. **~ing** *prep* con excepción de

exception /ɪkˈsepʃən/ *n* excepción *f*. take **~ to** ofenderse por. **~al** *a* excepcional. **~ally** *adv* excepcionalmente

excerpt /ˈeksɜːpt/ *n* extracto *m*

excess /ɪkˈses/ *n* exceso *m*. ● /ˈekses/ *a* excedente. **~ fare** suplemento *m*. **~ luggage** exceso *m* de equipaje. **~ive** *a* excesivo

exchange /ɪkˈstʃeɪndʒ/ *vt* cambiar. ● *n* intercambio *m*; (of money) cambio *m*. **(telephone) ~** central *f* telefónica

excise /ˈeksaɪz/ *n* impuestos *mpl* interos. ● /ekˈsaɪz/ *vt* quitar

excit|able /ɪkˈsaɪtəbl/ *a* excitable. **~e** /ɪkˈsaɪt/ *vt* emocionar; (stimulate) excitar. **~ed** *a* entusiasmado. get **~ed** entusiasmarse. **~ement** *n* emoción *f*; (enthusiasm) entusiasmo *m*. **~ing** *a* emocionante

excla|im /ɪkˈskleɪm/ *vi/t* exclamar. **~mation** /ekskləˈmeɪʃn/ *n* exclamación *f*. **~mation mark** *n* signo *m* de admiración *f*

exclu|de /ɪkˈskluːd/ *vt* excluir. **~sion** /-ʒən/ *n* exclusión *f*. **~sive** /ɪkˈskluːsɪv/ *a* exclusivo; *<club>* selecto. **~sive of** excluyendo. **~sively** *adv* exclusivamente

excruciating /ɪkˈskruːʃɪeɪtɪŋ/ *a* atroz, insoportable

excursion /ɪkˈskɜːʃn/ *n* excursión *f*

excus|able /ɪkˈskjuːzəbl/ *a* perdonable. **~e** /ɪkˈskjuːz/ *vt* perdonar.**~e from** dispensar de. **~e me!** ¡perdón! ● /ɪkˈskjuːs/ *n* excusa *f*

ex-directory /eksdɪˈrektərɪ/ *a* que no figura en la guía telefónica, privado (Mex)

execut|e /ˈeksɪkjuːt/ *vt* ejecutar. **~ion** /eksɪˈkjuːʃn/ *n* ejecución *f*. **~ioner** *n* verdugo *m*

executive /ɪgˈzekjʊtɪv/ *a & n* ejecutivo (*m*)

exempt /ɪgˈzempt/ *a* exento (**from** de). ● *vt* dispensar. **~ion** /-ʃn/ *n* exención *f*

exercise /ˈeksəsaɪz/ *n* ejercicio *m*. ● *vt* ejercer. ● *vi* hacer ejercicio. **~ book** *n* cuaderno *m*

exert /ɪgˈzɜːt/ *vt* ejercer. **~ o.s.** hacer un gran esfuerzo. **~ion** /-ʃn/ *n* esfuerzo *m*

exhale /eksˈheɪl/ *vt/i* exhalar

exhaust /ɪgˈzɔːst/ *vt* agotar. ● *n* (Auto) tubo *m* de escape. **~ed** *a* agotado. **~ion** /-stʃən/ *n* agotamiento *m*. **~ive** *a* exhaustivo

exhibit /ɪgˈzɪbɪt/ *vt* exponer; (fig) mostrar. ● *n* objeto *m* expuesto; (Jurid) documento *m*. **~ion** /eksɪˈbɪʃn/ *n* exposición. **~ionist** exhibicionista *m & f*. **~or** /ɪgˈzɪbɪtə(r)/ *n* expositor *m*

exhilarat|ing /ɪgˈzɪləreɪtɪŋ/ *a* excitante. **~ion** /-ˈreɪʃn/ *n* regocijo *m*

exhort /ɪgˈzɔːt/ *vt* exhortar

exile /ˈeksaɪl/ *n* exilio *m*; (person) exiliado *m*. ● *vt* desterrar

exist /ɪgˈzɪst/ *vi* existir. **~ence** *n* existencia *f*. in **~ence** existente

exit /ˈeksɪt/ *n* salida *f*

exorbitant /ɪgˈzɔːbɪtənt/ *a* exorbitante

exorcis|e /ˈeksɔːsaɪz/ *vt* exorcizar. **~m** /-sɪzəm/ *n* exorcismo *m*. **~t** *n* exorcista *m & f*

exotic /ɪgˈzɒtɪk/ *a* exótico

expand /ɪk'spænd/ *vt* expandir; (develop) desarrollar. ● *vi* expandirse

expanse /ɪk'spæns/ *n* extensión *f*

expansion /ɪk'spænʃn/ *n* expansión *f*

expatriate /eks'pætrɪət/ *a* & *n* expatriado (*m*)

expect /ɪk'spekt/ *vt* esperar; (suppose) suponer; (demand) contar con. I ~ so supongo que sí. ~**ancy** *n* esperanza *f*. life ~**ancy** esperanza *f* de vida. ~**ant** *a* expectante. ~**ant mother** *n* futura madre *f*

expectation /ekspek'teɪʃn/ *n* expectativa *f*

expedient /ɪk'spiːdɪənt/ *a* conveniente. ● *n* expediente *m*

expedition /ekspɪ'dɪʃn/ *n* expedición *f*

expel /ɪk'spel/ *vt* (*pt* **expelled**) expulsar

expend /ɪk'spend/ *vt* gastar. ~**able** *a* prescindible. ~**iture** /-ɪtʃə(r)/ *n* gastos *mpl*

expense /ɪk'spens/ *n* gasto *m*. at s.o.'s ~e a costa de uno. ~**es** *npl* (Com) gastos *mpl*. ~**ive** *a* caro

experience /ɪk'spɪərɪəns/ *n* experiencia. ● *vt* experimentar. ~**d** *a* con experiencia; <*driver*> experimentado

experiment /ɪk'sperɪmənt/ *n* experimento *m*. ● *vi* experimentar. ~**al** /-'mentl/ *a* experimental

expert /'ekspɜːt/ *a* & *n* experto (*m*). ~**ise** /ekspɜː'tiːz/ *n* pericia *f*. ~**ly** *adv* hábilmente

expir|e /ɪk'spaɪə(r)/ *vi* <*passport, ticket*> caducar; <*contract*> vencer. ~**y** *n* vencimiento *m*, caducidad *f*

expla|in /ɪk'spleɪn/ *vt* explicar. ~**nation** /eksplə'neɪʃn/ *n* explicación *f*. ~**natory** /ɪks'plænətərɪ/ *a* explicativo

explicit /ɪk'splɪsɪt/ *a* explícito

explode /ɪk'spləʊd/ *vt* hacer explotar. ● *vi* estallar

exploit /'eksplɔɪt/ *n* hazaña *f*. ● /ɪk'splɔɪt/ *vt* explotar. ~**ation** /eksplɔɪ'teɪʃn/ *n* explotación *f*

explor|ation /eksplə'reɪʃn/ *n* exploración *f*. ~**atory** /ɪk'splɒrətrɪ/

a exploratorio. ~**e** /ɪk'splɔː(r)/ *vt* explorar. ~**er** *n* explorador *m*

explosi|on /ɪk'spləʊʒn/ *n* explosión *f*. ~**ve** /-sɪv/ *a* & *n* explosivo (*m*)

export /ɪk'spɔːt/ *vt* exportar. ● /'ekspɔːt/ *n* exportación *f*; (item) artículo *m* de exportación. ~**er** /ɪks'pɔːtə(r)/ exportador *m*

expos|e /ɪk'spəʊz/ *vt* exponer; (reveal) descubrir. ~**ure** /-ʒə(r)/ *n* exposición *f*. die of ~**ure** morir de frío

express /ɪk'spres/ *vt* expresar. ● *a* expreso; <*letter*> urgente. ● *adv* (by express post) por correo urgente. ● *n* (train) rápido *m*, expreso *m*. ~**ion** *n* expresión *f*. ~**ive** *a* expresivo. ~**ly** *adv* expresadamente. ~**way** *n* (Amer) autopista *f*

expulsion /ɪk'spʌlʃn/ *n* expulsión *f*

exquisite /'ekskwɪzɪt/ *a* exquisito

exten|d /ɪk'stend/ *vt* extender; (prolong) prolongar; ampliar <*house*>. ● *vi* extenderse. ~**sion** /-ʃn/ *n* extensión *f*; (of road, time) prolongación *f*; (building) anejo *m*. ~**sive** /-sɪv/ *a* extenso. ~**sively** *adv* extensamente. ~**t** *n* extensión *f*; (fig) alcance. to a certain ~**t** hasta cierto punto

exterior /ɪk'stɪərɪə(r)/ *a* & *n* exterior (*m*)

exterminat|e /ɪk'stɜːmɪneɪt/ *vt* exterminar. ~**ion** /-'neɪʃn/ *n* exterminio *m*

external /ɪk'stɜːnl/ *a* externo

extinct /ɪk'stɪŋkt/ *a* extinto. ~**ion** /-ʃn/ *n* extinción *f*

extinguish /ɪk'stɪŋgwɪʃ/ *vt* extinguir. ~**er** *n* extintor *m*, extinguidor *m* (LAm)

extol /ɪk'stəʊl/ *vt* (*pt* **extolled**) alabar

extort /ɪk'stɔːt/ *vt* sacar por la fuerza. ~**ion** /-ʃn/ *n* exacción *f*. ~**ionate** /-ənət/ *a* exorbitante

extra /'ekstrə/ *a* de más. ● *adv* extraordinariamente. ● *n* suplemento *m*; (Cinema) extra *m* & *f*

extract /'ekstrækt/ *n* extracto *m*. ● /ɪk'strækt/ *vt* extraer. ~**ion** /ɪk'strækʃn/ *n* extracción *f*

extradit|e /'ekstrədaɪt/ *vt* extraditar. ~**ion** /-'dɪʃn/ *n* extradición *f*

extra: ~ordinary /ɪkˈstrɔːdnrɪ/ *a*
extraordinario. **~-sensory** /ekstrə
ˈsensərɪ/ *a* extrasensorial

extravagan|ce /ɪkˈstrævəgəns/ *n*
prodigalidad *f*; (of gestures, dress)
extravagancia *f*. **~t** *a* pródigo; *<be-
haviour>* extravagante. **~za** *n* gran
espectáculo *m*

extrem|e /ɪkˈstriːm/ *a & n* extremo
(*m*). **~ely** *adv* extremadamente.
~ist *n* extremista *m & f*

extricate /ˈekstrɪkeɪt/ *vt* desenredar, librar

extrovert /ˈekstrəvɜːt/ *n* extrovertido *m*

exuberan|ce /ɪgˈzjuːbərəns/ *n*
exuberancia *f*. **~t** *a* exuberante

exude /ɪgˈzjuːd/ *vt* rezumar

exult /ɪgˈzʌlt/ *vi* exultar. **~ation**
/egzʌlˈteɪʃn/ *n* exultación *f*

eye /aɪ/ *n* ojo *m*. keep an ~ on no
perder de vista. see ~ to ~ with s.o.
estar de acuerdo con uno. ● *vt* (*pt*
eyed, *pres p* **eyeing**) mirar. **~ball**
n globo *m* ocular. **~brow** *n* ceja *f*.
~drops *npl* colirio *m*. **~lash** *n*
pestaña *f*. **~lid** *n* párpado *m*.
~-opener *n* 🔲 revelación *f*.
~-shadow *n* sombra *f* de ojos.
~sight *n* vista *f*. **~sore** *n* (fig, 🔲)
monstruosidad *f*, adefesio *m*. **~wit-
ness** *n* testigo *m* ocular

F f

fable /ˈfeɪbl/ *n* fábula *f*

fabric /ˈfæbrɪk/ *n* tejido *m*, tela *f*

fabricate /ˈfæbrɪkeɪt/ *vt* inventar.
~ation /-ˈkeɪʃn/ *n* invención *f*

fabulous /ˈfæbjʊləs/ *a* fabuloso

facade /fəˈsɑːd/ *n* fachada *f*

face /feɪs/ *n* cara *f*, rostro *m*; (of
watch) esfera *f*, carátula *f* (Mex); (aspect) aspecto *m*. ~ **down(wards)** boca
abajo. ~ **up(wards)** boca arriba. in
the ~ of frente a. lose ~ quedar mal.
pull ~s hacer muecas. ● *vt* mirar hacia; *<house>* dar a; (confront) enfren-

tarse con. ● *vi* volverse. □ ~ **up to**
vt enfrentarse con. ~ **flannel** *n* paño *m* (para lavarse la cara). **~less** *a*
anónimo. ~ **lift** *n* cirugía *f* estética
en la cara

facetious /fəˈsiːʃəs/ *a* burlón

facial /ˈfeɪʃl/ *a* facial

facile /ˈfæsaɪl/ *a* superficial,
simplista

facilitate /fəˈsɪlɪteɪt/ *vt* facilitar

facility /fəˈsɪlɪtɪ/ *n* facilidad *f*

fact /fækt/ *n* hecho *m*. **as a matter of
~, in ~** en realidad, de hecho

faction /ˈfækʃn/ *n* facción *f*

factor /ˈfæktə(r)/ *n* factor *m*

factory /ˈfæktərɪ/ *n* fábrica *f*

factual /ˈfæktʃʊəl/ *a* basado en hechos, factual

faculty /ˈfækəltɪ/ *n* facultad *f*

fad /fæd/ *n* manía *f*, capricho *m*

fade /feɪd/ *vi* *<colour>* desteñirse;
<flowers> marchitarse; *<light>*
apagarse; *<memory, sound>* desva-
necerse

fag /fæg/ *n* (🇺🇸, chore) faena *f*; (🇬🇧, cigarette) cigarillo *m*, pitillo *m*

Fahrenheit /ˈfærənhaɪt/ *a*
Fahrenheit

fail /feɪl/ *vi* fracasar; *<brakes>* fallar;
(in an exam) suspender, ser reprobado
(LAm). he **~ed to arrive** no llegó. ● *vt*
suspender, ser reprobado en (LAm)
<exam>; suspender, reprobar (LAm)
<candidate>. ● *n*. **without ~** sin falta.
~ing *n* defecto *m*. ● *prep*. **~ing that,**
... si eso no resulta.... **~ure** /ˈfeɪ
ljə(r)/ *n* fracaso *m*

faint /feɪnt/ *a* (**-er, -est**) (weak) débil;
(indistinct) indistinto. **feel ~** estar mareado. **the ~est idea** la más remota
idea. ● *vi* desmayarse. ● *n* desmayo
m. **~-hearted** /-ˈhɑːtɪd/ *a* pusilánime, cobarde. **~ly** *adv* (weakly) débil-
mente; (indistinctly) indistintamente;
(slightly) ligeramente

fair /feə(r)/ *a* (**-er, -est**) (just) justo;
<weather> bueno; *<amount>* ra-
zonable; *<hair>* rubio, güero (Mex
🔲); *<skin>* blanco. ● *adv* limpio.
● *n* feria *f*. **~-haired** /-ˈheəd/ *a* rubio, güero (Mex 🔲). **~ly** *adv* (justly)
justamente; (rather) bastante. **~ness**

n justicia *f*. **in all ~ness** since-ramente. **~ play** *n* juego *m* limpio

fairy /'feərɪ/ *n* hada *f*. **~ story, ~ tale** *n* cuento *m* de hadas

faith /feɪθ/ *n* (trust) confianza *f*; (Relig) fe *f*. **~ful** *a* fiel. **~fully** *adv* fielmente. **yours ~fully** (in letters) (le saluda) atentamente

fake /feɪk/ *n* falsificación *f*; (person) farsante *m*. ● *a* falso. ● *vt* falsificar

falcon /'fɔːlkən/ *n* halcón *m*

Falkland Islands /'fɔːlklənd/ *npl*. **the Falkland Islands, the Falklands** las (Islas) Malvinas

fall /fɔːl/ *vi* (*pt* **fell**, *pp* **fallen**) caer; (decrease) bajar. ● *n* caída *f*; (Amer, autumn) otoño *m*; (in price) bajada *f*. □ **~ apart** *vi* deshacerse. □ **~ back on** *vt* recurrir a. □ **~ down** *vi* (fall) caerse. □ **~ for** *vt* 🔲 enamorarse de *<person>*; dejarse engañar por *<trick>*. □ **~ in** *vi* (Mil) formar filas. □ **~ off** *vi* caerse; (diminish) disminuir. □ **~ out** *vi* (quarrel) reñir (**with** con); (drop out) caerse; (Mil) romper filas. □ **~ over** *vi* caerse. *vt* tropezar con. □ **~ through** *vi* no salir adelante

fallacy /'fæləsɪ/ *n* falacia *f*

fallible /'fælɪbl/ *a* falible

fallout /'fɔːlaʊt/ *n* lluvia *f* radiactiva. **~ shelter** *n* refugio *m* antinuclear

fallow /'fæləʊ/ *a* en barbecho

false /fɔːls/ *a* falso. **~ alarm** *n* falsa alarma. **~hood** *n* mentira *f*. **~ly** *adv* falsamente. **~ teeth** *npl* dentadura *f* postiza

falsify /'fɔːlsɪfaɪ/ *vt* falsificar

falter /'fɔːltə(r)/ *vi* vacilar

fame /feɪm/ *n* fama *f*. **~d** *a* famoso

familiar /fə'mɪlɪə(r)/ *a* familiar. **the name sounds ~** el nombre me suena. **be ~ with** conocer. **~ity** /-'ærətɪ/ *n* familiaridad *f*. **~ize** *vt* familiarizar

family /'fæməlɪ/ *n* familia *f*. ● *a* de (la) familia, familiar. **~ tree** *n* árbol *m* genealógico

famine /'fæmɪn/ *n* hambre *f*, hambruna *f*

famished /'fæmɪʃt/ *a* hambriento

famous /'feɪməs/ *a* famoso

fan /fæn/ *n* abanico *m*; (Mec) ventilador *m*; (enthusiast) aficionado *m*; (of group, actor) fan *m* & *f*; (of sport, team) hincha *m* & *f*. ● *vt* (*pt* **fanned**) abanicar; avivar *<interest>*. □ **~ out** *vi* desparramarse en forma de abanico

fanatic /fə'nætɪk/ *n* fanático *m*. **~al** *a* fanático. **~ism** /-sɪzəm/ *n* fanatismo *m*

fan belt *n* correa *f* de ventilador, banda *f* del ventilador (Mex)

fanciful /'fænsɪfl/ *a* (imaginative) imaginativo; (impractical) extravagante

fancy /'fænsɪ/ *n* imaginación *f*; (liking) gusto *m*. **take a ~ to** tomar cariño a *<person>*; aficionarse a *<thing>*. ● *a* de lujo. ● *vt* (imagine) imaginar; (believe) creer; (🔲, want) apetecer a. **~ dress** *n* disfraz *m*

fanfare /'fænfeə(r)/ *n* fanfarria *f*

fang /fæŋ/ *n* (of animal) colmillo *m*; (of snake) diente *m*

fantasize /'fæntəsaɪz/ *vi* fantasear

fantastic /fæn'tæstɪk/ *a* fantástico

fantasy /'fæntəsɪ/ *n* fantasía *f*

far /fɑː(r)/ *adv* lejos; (much) mucho. **as ~ as** hasta. **as ~ as I know** que yo sepa. **by ~** con mucho. ● *a* (**further, furthest** *or* **farther, farthest**) lejano. **~ away** lejano

farc|e /fɑːs/ *n* farsa *f*. **~ical** *a* ridículo

fare /feə(r)/ *n* (on bus) precio *m* del billete, precio *m* del boleto (LAm); (on train, plane) precio *m* del billete, precio *m* del pasaje (LAm); (food) comida *f*

Far East /fɑː'riːst/ *n* Extremo *or* Lejano Oriente *m*

farewell /feə'wel/ *int* & *n* adiós (*m*)

far-fetched /fɑː'fetʃt/ *a* improbable

farm /fɑːm/ *n* granja *f*. ● *vt* cultivar. □ **~ out** *vt* encargar (*a terceros*). ● *vi* ser agricultor. **~er** *n* agricultor *m*, granjero *m*. **~house** *n* granja *f*. **~ing** *n* agricultura *f*. **~yard** *n* corral *m*

far: ~-off *a* lejano. **~-reaching** /fɑː'riːtʃɪŋ/ *a* trascendental. **~-sighted** /fɑː'saɪtɪd/ *a* con visión del futuro; (Med, Amer) hipermétrope

farther, **farthest** /'fɑːðə(r), 'fɑːðəst/ ⇒FAR

fascinat|e /'fæsmeɪt/ vt fascinar. ~**ed** a fascinado. ~**ing** a fascinante. ~**ion** /-'neɪʃn/ n fascinación f

fascis|m /'fæʃɪzəm/ n fascismo m. ~**t** a & n fascista (m & f)

fashion /'fæʃn/ n (manner) manera f; (vogue) moda f. **be in/out of** ~ estar de moda/estar pasado de moda. ~**able** a de moda

fast /fɑːst/ a (**-er, -est**) rápido; <clock> adelantado; (secure) fijo; <colours> sólido. ● adv rápidamente; (securely) firmemente. ~ **asleep** profundamente dormido. ● vi ayunar. ● n ayuno m

fasten /'fɑːsn/ vt sujetar; cerrar <case>; abrochar <belt etc>. ● vi <case> cerrar; <belt etc> cerrarse. ~**er**, ~**ing** n (on box, window) cierre m; (on door) cerrojo m

fat /fæt/ n grasa f. ● a (**fatter, fattest**) gordo; <meat> que tiene mucha grasa; (thick) grueso. **get** ~ engordar

fatal /'feɪtl/ a mortal; (fateful) fatídico. ~**ity** /fə'tælətɪ/ muerto m. ~**ly** adv mortalmente

fate /feɪt/ n destino m; (one's lot) suerte f. ~**d** a predestinado. ~**ful** a fatídico

father /'fɑːðə(r)/ n padre m. ~**hood** m paternidad f. ~**-in-law** m (pl ~**s-in-law**) m suegro m. ~**ly** a paternal

fathom /'fæðəm/ n braza f. ● vt. ~ (**out**) comprender

fatigue /fə'tiːg/ n fatiga f. ● vt fatigar

fat|ten vt. ~**ten (up)** cebar <animal>. ~**tening** a que engorda. ~**ty** a graso, grasoso (LAm). ● n 🄓 gordinflón m

fatuous /'fætjʊəs/ a fatuo

faucet /'fɔːsɪt/ n (Amer) grifo m, llave f (LAm)

fault /fɔːlt/ n defecto m; (blame) culpa f; (tennis) falta f; (Geol) falla f. **at** ~ culpable. ● vt encontrarle defectos a. ~**less** a impecable. ~**y** a defectuoso

favour /'feɪvə(r)/ n favor m. ● vt favorecer; (support) estar a favor de;

(prefer) preferir. ~**able** a favorable. ~**ably** adv favorablemente. ~**ite** a & n preferido (m). ~**itism** n favoritismo m

fawn /fɔːn/ n cervato m. ● a beige, beis. ● vi. ~ **on** adular

fax /fæks/ n fax m. ● vt faxear

fear /fɪə(r)/ n miedo m. ● vt temer. ~**ful** a (frightening) espantoso; (frightened) temeroso. ~**less** a intrépido. ~**some** /-səm/ a espantoso

feasib|ility /fiːzə'bɪlətɪ/ n viabilidad f. ~**le** /'fiːzəbl/ a factible; (likely) posible

feast /fiːst/ n (Relig) fiesta f; (meal) banquete m

feat /fiːt/ n hazaña f

feather /'feðə(r)/ n pluma f. ~**weight** n peso m pluma

feature /'fiːtʃə(r)/ n (on face) rasgo m; (characteristic) característica f; (in newspaper) artículo m; ~ (**film**) película f principal, largometraje m. ● vt presentar; (give prominence to) destacar

February /'februərɪ/ n febrero m

fed /fed/ ⇒FEED

feder|al /'fedərəl/ a federal. ~**ation** /fedə'reɪʃn/ n federación f

fed up a 🄓 harto (**with** de)

fee /fiː/ n (professional) honorarios mpl; (enrolment) derechos mpl; (club) cuota f

feeble /'fiːbl/ a (**-er, -est**) débil

feed /fiːd/ vt (pt **fed**) dar de comer a; (supply) alimentar. ● vi comer. ● n (for animals) pienso m; (for babies) comida f. ~**back** n reacción f

feel /fiːl/ vt (pt **felt**) sentir; (touch) tocar; (think) considerar. **do you** ~ **it's a good idea?** ¿te parece buena idea? ~ **as if** tener la impresión de que. ~ **hot/hungry** tener calor/hambre. ~ **like** (🄓, want) tener ganas de. ● n sensación f. **get the** ~ **of sth** acostumbrarse a algo. ~**er** n (of insect) antena f. ~**ing** n sentimiento m; (physical) sensación f

feet /fiːt/ ⇒FOOT

feign /feɪn/ vt fingir

feint /feɪnt/ n finta f

fell /fel/ ⇒FALL. ● vt derribar; talar <tree>

fellow /'feləʊ/ n ⊡ tipo m; (comrade) compañero m; (of society) socio m. ~ **countryman** n compatriota m. ~ **passenger/traveller** n compañero m de viaje

felony /'feləni/ n delito m grave

felt /felt/ n ⇒FEEL. ● n fieltro m

female /'fi:meɪl/ a hembra; <voice, sex etc> femenino. ● n mujer f; (animal) hembra f

femini|ne /'femənɪn/ a & n femenino (m). ~**nity** /-'nɪnəti/ n feminidad f. ~**st** a & n feminista m & f

fenc|e /fens/ n cerca f, cerco m (LAm). ● vt. ~**e** (**in**) encerrar, cercar. ● vi (Sport) practicar la esgrima. ~**er** n esgrimidor m. ~**ing** n (Sport) esgrima f

fend /fend/ vi. ~ **for o.s.** valerse por sí mismo. □ ~ **off** vt defenderse de

fender /'fendə(r)/ n rejilla f; (Amer, Auto) guardabarros m, salpicadera f (Mex)

ferment /fə'ment/ vt/i fermentar. ~**ation** /-'teɪʃn/ n fermentación f

fern /fɜːn/ n helecho m

feroci|ous /fə'rəʊʃəs/ a feroz. ~**ty** /fə'rɒsəti/ n ferocidad f

ferret /'ferɪt/ n hurón m. ● vi (pt **ferreted**) ~ **about** husmear. ● vt. ~ **out** descubrir

ferry /'feri/ n ferry m. ● vt transportar

fertil|e /'fɜːtaɪl/ a fértil. ~**ity** /-'tɪləti/ n fertilidad f. ~**ize** /'fɜːtəlaɪz/ vt fecundar, abonar <soil>. ~**izer** n fertilizante m

ferv|ent /'fɜːvənt/ a ferviente. ~**our** /-və(r)/ n fervor m

fester /'festə(r)/ vi enconarse

festival /'festɪvl/ n fiesta f; (of arts) festival m

festiv|e /'festɪv/ a festivo. **the** ~**e season** n las Navidades. ~**ity** /fe'stɪvəti/ n festividad f

fetch /fetʃ/ vt (go for) ir a buscar; (bring) traer; (be sold for) venderse en. ~**ing** a atractivo

fête /feɪt/ n fiesta f. ● vt festejar

fetish /'fetɪʃ/ n fetiche m

fetter /'fetə(r)/ vt encadenar

feud /fjuːd/ n contienda f

feudal /'fjuːdl/ a feudal. ~**ism** n feudalismo m

fever /'fiːvə(r)/ n fiebre f. ~**ish** a febril

few /fjuː/ a pocos. **a** ~ **houses** algunas casas. ● n pocos mpl. **a** ~ unos (pocos). **a good** ~, **quite a** ~ ⊡ muchos. ~**er** a & n menos. ~**est** a el menor número de

fiancé /fɪ'ɒnseɪ/ n novio m. ~**e** /fɪ'ɒnseɪ/ n novia f

fiasco /fɪ'æskəʊ/ n (pl -**os**) fiasco m

fib /fɪb/ n ⊡ mentirilla f. ● vi ⊡ mentir, decir mentirillas

fibre /'faɪbə(r)/ n fibra f. ~**glass** n fibra f de vidrio

fickle /'fɪkl/ a inconstante

ficti|on /'fɪkʃn/ n ficción f. (**works of**) ~**on** novelas fpl. ~**onal** a novelesco. ~**tious** /fɪk'tɪʃəs/ a ficticio

fiddle /'fɪdl/ n ⊡ violín m; (⊡, swindle) trampa f. ● vt ⊡ falsificar. ~ **with** juguetear con

fidget /'fɪdʒɪt/ vi (pt **fidgeted**) moverse, ponerse nervioso. ~ **with** juguetear con. ● n persona f inquieta. ~**y** a inquieto

field /fiːld/ n campo m. ~ **day** n. **have a** ~ **day** hacer su agosto. ~ **glasses** npl gemelos mpl. **F**~ **Marshal** n mariscal m de campo. ~ **trip** n viaje m de estudio. ~**work** n investigaciones fpl en el terreno

fiend /fiːnd/ n demonio m. ~**ish** a diabólico

fierce /fɪəs/ a (-**er**, -**est**) feroz; <attack> violento. ~**ly** adv <growl> con ferocidad; <fight> con fiereza

fiery /'faɪəri/ a (-**ier**, -**iest**) ardiente; <temper> exaltado

fifteen /fɪf'tiːn/ a & n quince (m). ~**th** a decimoquinto. ● n quinceavo m

fifth /fɪfθ/ a & n quinto (m)

fift|ieth /'fɪftɪəθ/ a quincuagésimo. ● n cincuentavo m. ~**y** a & n cincuenta (m). ~**y-**~**y** adv mitad y mitad, a medias. ● a. **a** ~**y-**~**y chance** una posibilidad de cada dos

fig /fɪg/ n higo m

fight /faɪt/ vi (pt **fought**) luchar; (quarrel) disputar. ● vt luchar contra. ● n pelea m; (struggle) lucha f; (quarrel) disputa *f*; (Mil) combate *m*. □ ~ **back** *vi* defenderse. □ ~ **off** *vt* rechazar *<attack>*; luchar contra *<illness>*. ~**er** *n* luchador *m*; (aircraft) avión *m* de caza. ~**ing** *n* luchas *fpl*

figment /'fɪgmənt/ *n*. ~ **of the imagination** producto *m* de la imaginación

figurative /'fɪgjʊrətɪv/ *a* figurado

figure /'fɪgə(r)/ *n* (number) cifra *f*; (person) figura *f*; (shape) forma *f*; (of woman) tipo *m*. ● *vt* imaginar; (Amer 🇺🇸, reckon) calcular. ● *vi* figurar. **that** ~**s** 🇺🇸 es lógico. □ ~ **out** *vt* entender. ~**head** *n* testaferro *m*, mascarón *m* de proa. ~ **of speech** *n* figura *f* retórica

filch /fɪltʃ/ *vt* 🇺🇸 hurtar

file /faɪl/ *n* (tool, for nails) lima *f*; (folder) carpeta *f*; (set of papers) expediente *m*; (Comp) archivo *m*; (row) fila *f*. **in single** ~ en fila india. ● *vt* archivar *<papers>*; limar *<metal, nails>*. ● ~ **in** *vi* entrar en fila. ~ **past** *vt* desfilar ante

filing cabinet /'faɪlɪŋ/ *n* archivador *m*

fill /fɪl/ *vt* llenar. ● *vi* llenarse. ● *n*. **eat one's** ~ hartarse de comer. **have had one's** ~ **of** estar harto de □ ~ **in** *vt* rellenar *<form, hole>*. □ ~ **out** *vt* rellenar *<form>*. *vi* (get fatter) engordar. □ ~ **up** *vt* llenar. *vi* llenarse

fillet /'fɪlɪt/ *n* filete *m*. ● *vt* (*pt* **filleted**) cortar en filetes *<meat>*; quitar la espina a *<fish>*

filling /'fɪlɪŋ/ *n* (in tooth) empaste *m*, tapadura *f* (Mex). ~ **station** *n* gasolinera *f*

film /fɪlm/ *n* película *f*. ● *vt* filmar. ~ **star** *n* estrella *f* de cine

filter /'fɪltə(r)/ *n* filtro *m*. ● *vt* filtrar. ● *vi* filtrarse. ~**-tipped** *a* con filtro

filth /fɪlθ/ *n* mugre *f*. ~**y** *a* mugriento

fin /fɪn/ *n* aleta *f*

final /'faɪnl/ *a* último; (conclusive) decisivo. ● *n* (Sport) final *f*. ~**s** *npl* (Schol) exámenes *mpl* de fin de curso

finale /fɪ'nɑːlɪ/ *n* final *m*

final|ist *n* finalista *m* & *f*. ~**ize** *vt* ultimar. ~**ly** *adv* (lastly) finalmente, por fin

financ|e /'faɪnæns/ *n* finanzas *fpl*. ● *vt* financiar. ~**ial** /faɪ'nænʃl/ *a* financiero; *<difficulties>* económico

find /faɪnd/ *vt* (*pt* **found**) encontrar. ~ **out** *vt* descubrir. ● *vi* (learn) enterarse. ~**ings** *npl* conclusiones *fpl*

fine /faɪn/ *a* (**-er, -est**) (delicate) fino; (excellent) excelente. ● *adv* muy bien. ● *n* multa *f*. ● *vt* multar. ~ **arts** *npl* bellas artes *fpl*. ~**ly** *adv* (cut) en trozos pequeños; *<adjust>* con precisión

finger /'fɪŋgə(r)/ *n* dedo *m*. ● *vt* tocar. ~**nail** *n* uña *f*. ~**print** *n* huella *f* digital. ~**tip** *n* punta *f* del dedo

finish /'fɪnɪʃ/ *vt/i* terminar, acabar. ~ **doing** terminar de hacer. ● *n* fin *m*; (of race) llegada *f*

finite /'faɪnaɪt/ *a* finito

Fin|land /'fɪnlənd/ *n* Finlandia *f*. ~**n** *n* finlandés *m*. ~**nish** *a* & *n* finlandés (*m*)

fiord /fjɔːd/ *n* fiordo *m*

fir /fɜː(r)/ *n* abeto *m*

fire /faɪə(r)/ *n* fuego *m*; (conflagration) incendio *m*. ● *vt* disparar *<gun>*; (dismiss) despedir; avivar *<imagination>*. ● *vi* disparar. ~ **alarm** *n* alarma *f* contra incendios. ~**arm** *n* arma *f* de fuego. ~ **brigade**, ~ **department** (Amer) *n* cuerpo *m* de bomberos. ~ **engine** *n* coche *m* de bomberos, carro *m* de bomberos (Mex). ~**-escape** *n* escalera *f* de incendios. ~ **extinguisher** *n* extintor *m*, extinguidor *m* (LAm). ~**fighter** *n* bombero *m*. ~**man** /-mən/ *n* bombero *m*. ~**place** *n* chimenea *f*. ~**side** *n* hogar *m*. ~ **truck** *n* (Amer) ⇒~ ENGINE. ~**wood** *n* leña *f*. ~**work** *n* fuego *m* artificial

firm /fɜːm/ *n* empresa *f*. ● *a* (**-er, -est**) firme. ~**ly** *adv* firmemente

first /fɜːst/ *a* primero, (before masculine singular noun) primer. **at** ~ **hand** directamente. ● *n* primero *m*. ● *adv* primero; (first time) por primera vez. ~ **of all** primero. ~ **aid** *n* primeros auxilios *mpl*. ~ **aid kit** *n* botiquín *m*. ~ **class** /-'klɑːs/ *adv* *<travel>* en primera clase. ~**-class** *a* de primera clase. ~ **floor** *n* primer piso *m*; (Amer) planta *f* baja. **F~ Lady** *n* (Amer) Primera Dama *f*. ~**ly** *adv* en

primer lugar. ∼ **name** n nombre m
de pila. ∼-**rate** /-'reɪt/ a excelente

fish /fɪʃ/ n (pl invar or -**es**) pez m; (as
food) pescado m. ● vi pescar. **go** ∼**ing**
ir de pesca. □∼ **out** vt sacar.
∼**erman** n pescador m. ∼**ing** n
pesca f. ∼**ing pole** (Amer), ∼**ing
rod** n caña f de pesca. ∼**monger** n
pescadero m. ∼ **shop** n pescadería
f. ∼**y** a <smell> a pescado; (Ⓘ, ques-
tionable) sospechoso

fission /'fɪʃn/ n fisión f

fist /fɪst/ n puño m

fit /fɪt/ a (**fitter**, **fittest**) (healthy) en
forma; (good enough) adecuado; (able)
capaz. ● n (attack) ataque; (of clothes)
corte m. ● vt (pt **fitted**) (adapt) adaptar; (be the right size for) quedarle bien
a; (install) colocar. ● vi encajar; (in certain space) caber; <clothes> quedarle
bien a uno. □∼ **in** vi caber. ∼**ful** a
irregular. ∼**ness** n salud f; (Sport)
(buena) forma f física. ∼**ting** a apropiado. ● n (of clothes) prueba f. ∼**ting
room** n probador m

five /faɪv/ a & n cinco (m)

fix /fɪks/ vt fijar; (mend, deal with) arreglar. ● n. **in a** ∼ en un aprieto. ∼**ed**
a fijo. ∼**ture** /'fɪkstʃə(r)/ n (Sport)
partido m

fizz /fɪz/ vi burbujear. ● n
efervescencia f. ∼**le** /fɪzl/ vi. ∼**le out**
fracasar. ∼**y** a efervescente; <water>
con gas

fjord /fjɔːd/ n fiordo m

flabbergasted /'flæbəgɑːstɪd/ a
estupefacto

flabby /'flæbɪ/ a flojo

flag /flæg/ n bandera f. ● vi (pt
flagged) (weaken) flaquear; <conver-
sation> languidecer

flagon /'flægən/ n botella f grande,
jarro m

flagpole /'flægpəʊl/ n asta f de
bandera

flagrant /'fleɪgrənt/ a flagrante

flair /fleə(r)/ n don m (**for** de)

flak|e /fleɪk/ n copo m; (of paint, metal)
escama f. ● vi desconcharse. ∼**y** a
escamoso

flamboyant /flæm'bɔɪənt/ a
<clothes> vistoso; <manner> extra-
vagante

flame /fleɪm/ n llama f. **go up in** ∼**s**
incendiarse

flamingo /flə'mɪŋgəʊ/ n (pl -**o(e)s**)
flamenco m

flammable /'flæməbl/ a inflamable

flan /flæn/ n tartaleta f

flank /flæŋk/ n (of animal) ijada f; (of
person) costado m; (Mil, Sport) flanco m

flannel /'flænl/ n franela f; (for face)
paño m (para lavarse la cara).

flap /flæp/ vi (pt **flapped**) ondear;
<wings> aletear. ● vt batir <wings>;
agitar <arms>. ● n (cover) tapa f; (of
pocket) cartera f; (of table) ala f. **get
into a** ∼ Ⓘ ponerse nervioso

flare /fleə(r)/ ● n llamarada f; (Mil)
bengala f; (in skirt) vuelo m. □ ∼ **up** vi
llamear; <fighting> estallar; <per-
son> encolerizarse

flash /flæʃ/ ● vi destellar. ● vt (aim
torch) dirigir; (flaunt) hacer ostentación de. ∼ **past** pasar como un rayo.
● n destello m; (Photo) flash m.
∼**back** n escena f retrospectiva.
∼**light** n (Amer, torch) linterna f. ∼**y**
a ostentoso

flask /flɑːsk/ n frasco m; (vacuum flask)
termo m

flat /flæt/ a (**flatter**, **flattest**) plano;
<tyre> desinflado; <refusal> categóri-
co; <fare, rate> fijo; (Mus) bemol.
● adv (Mus) demasiado bajo. ∼ **out** (at
top speed) a toda velocidad. ● n
(rooms) apartamento m, piso m; (Auto,
esp Amer) Ⓘ pinchazo m; (Mus) bemol
m. ∼**ly** adv categóricamente. ∼**ten**
vt allanar, aplanar

flatter /'flætə(r)/ vt adular. ∼**ing** a
<person> lisonjero; <clothes> favore-
cedor. ∼**y** n adulación f

flaunt /flɔːnt/ vt hacer ostentación
de

flavour /'fleɪvə(r)/ n sabor m. ● vt
sazonar. ∼**ing** n condimento m

flaw /flɔː/ n defecto m. ∼**less** a perfecto

flea /fliː/ n pulga f

fleck /flek/ n mancha f, pinta f

fled /fled/ ⇒FLEE

flee /fliː/ vi (pt **fled**) huir. ● vt huir
de

fleece /fliːs/ n vellón m. ● vt Ⓘ
desplumar

fleet /fliːt/ n flota f; (of cars) parque m móvil

fleeting /'fliːtɪŋ/ a fugaz

Flemish /'flemɪʃ/ a & n flamenco (m)

flesh /fleʃ/ n carne f. **in the ~** en persona

flew /fluː/ ⇒FLY

flex /fleks/ vt doblar; flexionar <muscle>. ●n (Elec) cable m

flexib|ility /fleksə'bɪlətɪ/ n flexibilidad f. **~le** /'fleksəbl/ a flexible

flexitime /'fleksɪtaɪm/, (Amer) **flextime** /'flekstaɪm/ n horario m flexible

flick /flɪk/ n golpecito m. ●vt dar un golpecito a. □ **~ through** vt hojear

flicker /'flɪkə(r)/ vi parpadear. ●n parpadeo m; (of hope) resquicio m

flies /flaɪz/ npl (①, on trousers) bragueta f

flight /flaɪt/ n vuelo m; (fleeing) huida f, fuga f. **~ of stairs** tramo m de escalera f. **take (to) ~** darse a la fuga. **~ attendant** n (male) sobrecargo m, aeromozo m (LAm); (female) azafata f, aeromoza f (LAm). **~-deck** n cubierta f de vuelo

flimsy /'flɪmzɪ/ a (-ier, -iest) flojo, débil, poco sólido

flinch /flɪntʃ/ vi retroceder (**from** ante)

fling /flɪŋ/ vt (pt **flung**) arrojar. ●n (love affair) aventura f; (wild time) juerga f

flint /flɪnt/ n pedernal m; (for lighter) piedra f

flip /flɪp/ vt (pt **flipped**) dar un golpecito a. ●n golpecito m. □ **~ through** vt hojear

flippant /'flɪpənt/ a poco serio

flipper /'flɪpə(r)/ n aleta f

flirt /flɜːt/ vi coquetear. ●n (woman) coqueta f; (man) coqueto m

flit /flɪt/ vi (pt **flitted**) revolotear

float /fləʊt/ vi flotar. ●vt hacer flotar; introducir en Bolsa <company>. ●n flotador m; (cash) caja f chica

flock /flɒk/ n (of birds) bandada f; (of sheep) rebaño m. ●vi congregarse

flog /flɒg/ vt (pt **flogged**) (beat) azotar; (①, sell) vender

flood /flʌd/ n inundación f; (fig) avalancha f. ●vt inundar. ●vi <building etc> inundarse; <river> desbordar. **~light** n foco m. ●vt (pt **~lit**) iluminar (con focos)

floor /flɔː(r)/ n suelo m; (storey) piso m; (for dancing) pista f. ●vt derribar; (baffle) confundir

flop /flɒp/ vi (pt **flopped**) dejarse caer pesadamente; (①, fail) fracasar. ●n ① fracaso m. **~py** a flojo. ●n ⇒**~PY DISK**. **~py disk** n disquete m, floppy (disk) m

floral /'flɔːrəl/ a floral

florid /'flɒrɪd/ a florido

florist /'flɒrɪst/ n florista m & f

flounder /'flaʊndə(r)/ vi (in water) luchar para mantenerse a flote; <speaker> quedar sin saber qué decir

flour /flaʊə(r)/ n harina f

flourish /'flʌrɪʃ/ vi florecer; <business> prosperar. ●vt blandir. ●n ademán m elegante; (in handwriting) rasgo m. **~ing** a próspero

flout /flaʊt/ vt burlarse de

flow /fləʊ/ vi fluir; <blood> correr; (hang loosely) caer. ●n flujo m; (stream) corriente f; (of traffic, information) circulación f. **~ chart** n organigrama m

flower /'flaʊə(r)/ n flor f. ●vi florecer, florear (Mex). **~ bed** n macizo m de flores. **~y** a florido

flown /fləʊn/ ⇒FLY

flu /fluː/ n gripe f

fluctuat|e /'flʌktjʊeɪt/ vi fluctuar. **~ion** /-'eɪʃn/ n fluctuación f

flue /fluː/ n tiro m

fluen|cy /'fluːənsɪ/ n fluidez f. **~t** a <style> fluido; <speaker> elocuente. **be ~t in a language** hablar un idioma con fluidez. **~tly** adv con fluidez

fluff /flʌf/ n pelusa f. **~y** a (-ier, -iest) velloso

fluid /'fluːɪd/ a & n fluido (m)

flung /flʌŋ/ ⇒FLING

fluorescent /flʊə'resnt/ a fluorescente

flush /flʌʃ/ vi ruborizarse. ●vt. **~ the toilet** tirar de la cadena, jalarle a la cadena (LAm). ●n (blush) rubor m

fluster /'flʌstə(r)/ vt poner nervioso

flute /fluːt/ n flauta f

flutter /'flʌtə(r)/ *vi* ondear; *<bird>* revolotear. ● *n* (of wings) revoloteo *m*; (fig) agitación *f*

flux /flʌks/ *n* flujo *m*. **be in a state of** ~ estar siempre cambiando

fly /flaɪ/ *vi* (*pt* **flew**, *pp* **flown**) volar; *<passenger>* ir en avión; *<flag>* flotar; (rush) correr. ● *vt* pilotar, pilotear (LAm) *<aircraft>*; transportar en avión *<passengers, goods>*; izar *<flag>*. ● *n* mosca *f*; (of trousers) ⇒FLIES. ~**ing** *a* volante. ~**ing visit** visita *f* relámpago. ● *n* (activity) aviación *f*. ~**leaf** *n* guarda *f*. ~**over** *n* paso *m* elevado

foal /fəʊl/ *n* potro *m*

foam /fəʊm/ *n* espuma *f*. ● *vi* espumar. ~ **rubber** *n* goma *f* espuma, hule *m* espuma (Mex)

fob /fɒb/ *vt* (*pt* **fobbed**). ~ **sth off onto s.o.** (palm off) encajarle algo a uno

focal /'fəʊkl/ *a* focal

focus /'fəʊkəs/ *n* (*pl* **-cuses** *or* **-ci** /-saɪ/) foco *m*; (fig) centro *m*. **in** ~ enfocado. **out of** ~ desenfocado. ● *vt* (*pt* **focused**) enfocar; (fig) concentrar. ● *vi* enfocar; (fig) concentrarse (**on** en)

fodder /'fɒdə(r)/ *n* forraje *m*

foe /fəʊ/ *n* enemigo *m*

foetus /'fiːtəs/ *n* (*pl* **-tuses**) feto *m*

fog /fɒg/ *n* niebla *f*

fog|gy *a* (**-ier**, **-iest**) nebuloso. **it is** ~**gy** hay niebla. ~**horn** *n* sirena *f* de niebla

foible /'fɔɪbl/ *n* punto *m* débil

foil /fɔɪl/ *vt* (thwart) frustrar. ● *n* papel *m* de plata

foist /fɔɪst/ *vt* encajar (**on** a)

fold /fəʊld/ *vt* doblar; cruzar *<arms>*. ● *vi* doblarse; (fail) fracasar. ● *n* pliegue *m*. (for sheep) redil *m*. ~**er** *n* carpeta *f*. ~**ing** *a* plegable

foliage /'fəʊlɪdʒ/ *n* follaje *m*

folk /fəʊk/ *n* gente *f*. ● *a* popular. ~**lore** /-lɔː(r)/ *n* folklore *m*. ~ **music** *n* música *f* folklórica; (modern) música *f* folk. ~**s** *npl* (one's relatives) familia *f*

follow /'fɒləʊ/ *vt/i* seguir. □ ~ **up** *vt* seguir. ~**er** *n* seguidor *m*. ~**ing** *n*

partidarios *mpl*. ● *a* siguiente. ● *prep* después de

folly /'fɒlɪ/ *n* locura *f*

fond /fɒnd/ *a* (**-er**, **-est**) (loving) cariñoso; *<hope>* vivo. **be** ~ **of s.o.** tener(le) cariño a uno. **be** ~ **of sth** ser aficionado a algo

fondle /'fɒndl/ *vt* acariciar

fondness /'fɒndnɪs/ *n* cariño *m*; (for things) afición *f*

font /fɒnt/ *n* pila *f* bautismal

food /fuːd/ *n* comida *f*. ~ **processor** *n* robot *m* de cocina

fool /fuːl/ *n* idiota *m* & *f* ● *vt* engañar. □ ~ **about** *vi* hacer payasadas. ~**hardy** *a* temerario. ~**ish** *a* tonto. ~**ishly** *adv* tontamente. ~**ishness** *n* tontería *f*. ~**proof** *a* infalible

foot /fʊt/ *n* (*pl* **feet**) pie *m*; (measure) pie *m* (= 30,48cm); (of animal, furniture) pata *f*. **get under s.o.'s feet** estorbar a uno. **on** ~ a pie. **on/to one's feet** de pie. **put one's** ~ **in it** meter la pata. ● *vt* pagar *<bill>*. ~**age** /-ɪdʒ/ *n* (of film) secuencia *f*. ~**ball** *n* (ball) balón *m*; (game) fútbol *m*, futbol *m* (Mex); (American ~**ball**) fútbol *m* americano, futbol *m* americano (Mex). ~**baller** *n* futbolista *m* & *f*. ~**bridge** *n* puente *m* para peatones. ~**hills** *npl* estribaciones *fpl*. ~**hold** *n* punto *m* de apoyo. ~**ing** *n* pie *m*. **on an equal** ~**ing** en igualdad de condiciones. ~**lights** *npl* candilejas *fpl*. ~**man** /-mən/ *n* lacayo *m*. ~**note** *n* nota *f* (al pie de la página). ~**path** *n* (in country) senda *f*; (in town) acera *f*, banqueta *f* (Mex). ~**print** *n* huella *f*. ~**step** *n* paso *m*. ~**wear** *n* calzado *m*

- -

for /fɔː(r)/, *unstressed form* /fə(r)/

● *preposition*

····▸ (intended for). para. **it's** ~ **my mother** es para mi madre. **she works** ~ **a multinational** trabaja para una multinacional

····▸ (on behalf of) por. **I did it** ~ **you** lo hice por ti

⇒ See entries **para** and **por** for further information

····▸ (expressing purpose). para. **I use it** ~ **washing the car** lo uso para limpiar el coche. **what ~?** ¿para qué?. **to go out ~ a meal** salir a comer fuera

····➤ (in favour of) a favor de. **are you ~ or against the idea?** estás a favor o en contra de la idea?

····➤ (indicating cost, in exchage for) por. **I bought it ~ 30 pounds** lo compré por 30 libras. **she left him ~ another man** lo dejó por otro. **thanks ~ everything** gracias por todo. **what's the Spanish ~ 'toad'?** ¿cómo se dice 'toad' en español?

····➤ (expressing duration) **he read ~ two hours** leyó durante dos horas. **how long are you going ~?** ¿por cuánto tiempo vas? **I've been waiting ~ three hours** hace tres horas que estoy esperando, llevo tres horas esperando

····➤ (in the direction of) para. **the train ~ Santiago** el tren para Santiago

● *conjunction*

····➤ (because) porque, pues (literary usage). **she left at once, ~ it was getting late** se fue en seguida, porque *or* pues se hacía tarde

forage /'fɒrɪdʒ/ *vi* forrajear. ● *n* forraje *m*

forbade /fə'bæd/ ⇒FORBID

forbearance /fɔː'beərəns/ *n* paciencia *f*

forbid /fə'bɪd/ *vt* (*pt* **forbade**, *pp* **forbidden**) prohibir (**s.o. to do a uno hacer**). **~ s.o. sth** prohibir algo a uno. **~ding** *a* imponente

force /fɔːs/ *n* fuerza *f*. **by ~** a la fuerza. **come into ~** entrar en vigor. **the ~s** las fuerzas *fpl* armadas. ● *vt* forzar; (compel) obligar (**s.o. to do sth** a uno a hacer algo). **~ on** imponer a. **~ open** forzar. **~d** *a* forzado. **~feed** *vt* alimentar a la fuerza. **~ful** *a* enérgico

forceps /'fɔːseps/ *n* fórceps *m*

forcibl|e /'fɔːsəbl/ *a* a la fuerza. **~y** *adv* a la fuerza

ford /fɔːd/ *n* vado *m* ● *vt* vadear

fore /fɔː(r)/ *a* anterior. ● *n*. **come to the ~** hacerse evidente

forearm /'fɔːrɑːm/ *n* antebrazo *m*

foreboding /fɔː'bəʊdɪŋ/ *n* presentimiento *m*

forecast /'fɔːkɑːst/ *vt* (*pt* **forecast**) pronosticar <*weather*>; prever <*result*>. ● *n* pronóstico *m*. **weather ~** pronóstico *m* del tiempo

forecourt /'fɔːkɔːt/ *n* patio *m* delantero

forefinger /'fɔːfɪŋgə(r)/ *n* (dedo *m*) índice *m*

forefront /'fɔːfrʌnt/ *n* vanguardia *f*. **in the ~** a la vanguardia

forego /fɔː'gəʊ/ *vt* (*pt* **forewent**, *pp* **foregone**) ⇒FORGO

foregone /'fɔːgɒn/ *a*. **~ conclusion** resultado *m* previsto

foreground /'fɔːgraʊnd/ *n*. **in the ~** en primer plano

forehead /'fɒrɪd/ *n* frente *f*

foreign /'fɒrən/ *a* extranjero; <*trade*> exterior; <*travel*> al extranjero, en el extranjero. **~er** *n* extranjero *m*

foreman /'fɔːmən/ (*pl* **-men** /-mən/) *n* capataz *m*

foremost /'fɔːməʊst/ *a* primero. ● *adv*. **first and ~** ante todo

forerunner /'fɔːrʌnə(r)/ *n* precursor *m*

foresee /fɔː'siː/ *vt* (*pt* **-saw**, *pp* **-seen**) prever. **~able** *a* previsible

foresight /'fɔːsaɪt/ *n* previsión *f*

forest /'fɒrɪst/ *n* bosque *m*

forestall /fɔː'stɔːl/ *vt* (prevent) prevenir; (preempt) anticiparse a

forestry /'fɒrɪstrɪ/ *n* silvicultura *f*

foretaste /'fɔːteɪst/ *n* anticipo *m*

foretell /fɔː'tel/ *vt* (*pt* **foretold**) predecir

forever /fə'revə(r)/ *adv* para siempre; (always) siempre

forewarn /fɔː'wɔːn/ *vt* advertir

forewent /fɔː'went/ ⇒FOREGO

foreword /'fɔːwɜːd/ *n* prefacio *m*

forfeit /'fɔːfɪt/ *n* (penalty) pena *f*; (in game) prenda *f*. ● *vt* perder; perder el derecho a <*property*>

forgave /fə'geɪv/ ⇒FORGIVE

forge /fɔːdʒ/ *n* fragua *f*. ● *vt* fraguar; (copy) falsificar. □ **~ ahead** *vi* adelantarse rápidamente. **~r** *n* falsificador *m*. **~ry** *n* falsificación *f*

forget /fə'get/ *vt* (*pt* **forgot**, *pp* **forgotten**) olvidar, olvidarse de. ● *vi* olvidarse (**about** de). I **forgot** se me olvidó. **~ful** *a* olvidadizo

forgive /fə'gɪv/ *vt* (*pt* **forgave**, *pp* **forgiven**) perdonar. **~** s.o. for sth perdonar algo a uno. **~ness** *n* perdón *m*

forgo /fɔː'gəʊ/ *vt* (*pt* **forwent**, *pp* **forgone**) renunciar a

fork /fɔːk/ *n* tenedor *m*; (for digging) horca *f*; (in road) bifurcación *f*. ●*vi* <*road*> bifurcarse. □ **~ out** *vt* 🔲 desembolsar, aflojar 🔲. **~lift truck** *n* carretilla *f* elevadora

forlorn /fə'lɔːn/ *a* <*hope, attempt*> desesperado; <*smile*> triste

form /fɔːm/ *n* forma *f*; (document) formulario *m*; (Schol) clase *f*. ●*vt* formar. ●*vi* formarse

formal /'fɔːml/ *a* formal; <*person*> formalista; <*dress*> de etiqueta. **~ity** /-'mælətɪ/ *n* formalidad *f*. **~ly** *adv* oficialmente

format /'fɔːmæt/ *n* formato *m*. ●*vt* (*pt* **formatted**) (Comp) formatear

formation /fɔː'meɪʃn/ *n* formación *f*

former /'fɔːmə(r)/ *a* anterior; (first of two) primero. ●*n*. the **~** el primero *m*, la primera *f*, los primeros *mpl*, las primeras *fpl*. **~ly** *adv* antes

formidable /'fɔːmɪdəbl/ *a* formidable

formula /'fɔːmjʊlə/ *n* (*pl* **-ae** /-iː/ or **-as**) fórmula *f*. **~te** /-leɪt/ *vt* formular

forsake /fə'seɪk/ *vt* (*pt* **forsook**, *pp* **forsaken**) abandonar

fort /fɔːt/ *n* fuerte *m*

forth /fɔːθ/ *adv*. and so **~** y así sucesivamente. **~coming** /-'kʌmɪŋ/ *a* próximo, venidero; (sociable) comunicativo. **~right** *a* directo. **~with** /-'wɪθ/ *adv* inmediatamente

fortieth /'fɔːtɪɪθ/ *a* cuadragésimo. ●*n* cuadragésima parte *f*

fortnight /'fɔːtnaɪt/ *n* quince días *mpl*, quincena *f*. **~ly** *a* bimensual. ●*adv* cada quince días

fortress /'fɔːtrɪs/ *n* fortaleza *f*

fortunate /'fɔːtʃənət/ *a* afortunado. be **~** tener suerte. **~ly** *adv* afortunadamente

fortune /'fɔːtʃuːn/ *n* fortuna *f*. **~-teller** *n* adivino *m*

forty /'fɔːtɪ/ *a* & *n* cuarenta (*m*). **~ winks** un sueñecito

forum /'fɔːrəm/ *n* foro *m*

forward /'fɔːwəd/ *a* <*movement*> hacia adelante; (advanced) precoz; (pert) impertinente. ●*n* (Sport) delantero *m*. ●*adv* adelante. **go ~** avanzar. ●*vt* hacer seguir <*letter*>; enviar <*goods*>. **~s** *adv* adelante

forwent /fɔː'went/ ⇒FORGO

fossil /'fɒsl/ *a* & *n* fósil (*m*)

foster /'fɒstə(r)/ *vt* (promote) fomentar; criar <*child*>. **~ child** *n* hijo *m* adoptivo

fought /fɔːt/ ⇒FIGHT

foul /faʊl/ *a* (**-er**, **-est**) <*smell*> nauseabundo; <*weather*> pésimo; <*person*> asqueroso; (dirty) sucio; <*language*> obsceno. ●*n* (Sport) falta *f*. ●*vt* contaminar; (entangle) enredar. **~ play** *n* (Sport) jugada *f* sucia; (crime) delito *m*

found /faʊnd/ ⇒FIND. ●*vt* fundar.

foundation /faʊn'deɪʃn/ *n* fundación *f*; (basis) fundamento. (cosmetic) base *f* (de maquillaje). **~s** *npl* (Archit) cimientos *mpl*

founder /'faʊndə(r)/ *n* fundador *m*. ●*vi* <*ship*> hundirse

fountain /'faʊntɪn/ *n* fuente *f*. **~ pen** *n* pluma *f* (estilográfica) *f*, estilográfica *f*

four /fɔː(r)/ *a* & *n* cuatro (*m*). **~fold** *a* cuádruple. ●*adv* cuatro veces. **~some** /-səm/ *n* grupo *m* de cuatro personas **~teen** /'fɔːtiːn/ *a* & *n* catorce (*m*). **~teenth** *a* & *n* decimocuarto (*m*). **~th** /fɔːθ/ *a* & *n* cuarto (*m*). **~-wheel drive** *n* tracción *f* integral

fowl /faʊl/ *n* ave *f*

fox /fɒks/ *n* zorro *m*, zorra *f*. ●*vt* 🔲 confundir

foyer /'fɔɪeɪ/ *n* (of theatre) foyer *m*; (of hotel) vestíbulo *m*

fraction /'frækʃn/ *n* fracción *f*

fracture /'fræktʃə(r)/ *n* fractura *f*. ●*vt* fracturar. ●*vi* fracturarse

fragile /'frædʒaɪl/ *a* frágil

fragment /'frægmənt/ *n* fragmento *m*. **~ary** /-ərɪ/ *a* fragmentario

fragran|ce /'freɪgrəns/ *n* fragancia *f*. **~t** *a* fragante

frail /freɪl/ a (**-er, -est**) frágil

frame /freɪm/ n (of picture, door, window) marco m; (of spectacles) montura f; (fig, structure) estructura f. ● vt enmarcar <picture>; formular <plan, question>; ⊞, (incriminate unjustly) incriminar falsamente. **~work** n estructura f; (context) marco m

France /frɑːns/ n Francia f

frank /fræŋk/ a franco. ● vt franquear. **~ly** adv francamente

frantic /'fræntɪk/ a frenético. **~ with** loco de

fratern|al /frə'tɜːnl/ a fraternal. **~ity** /frə'tɜːnɪtɪ/ n fraternidad f; (club) asociación f. **~ize** /'frætənaɪz/ vi fraternizar

fraud /frɔːd/ n fraude m; (person) impostor m. **~ulent** /-jʊlənt/a fraudulento

fraught /frɔːt/ a (tense) tenso. **~ with** cargado de

fray /freɪ/ n riña f

freak /friːk/ n fenómeno m; (monster) monstruo m. ● a anormal. **~ish** a anormal

freckle /'frekl/ n peca f. **~d** a pecoso

free /friː/ a (**freer** /'friːə(r)/, **freest** /'friːɪst/) libre; (gratis) gratuito. **~ of charge** gratis. ● vt (pt **freed**) (set at liberty) poner en libertad; (relieve from) liberar (**from/of** de); (untangle) desenredar. **~dom** n libertad f. **~hold** n propiedad f absoluta. **~ kick** n tiro m libre. **~lance** a & adv por cuenta propia. **~ly** adv libremente. **~mason** n masón m. **~-range** a <eggs> de granja. **~ speech** n libertad f de expresión. **~style** n estilo m libre. **~way** n (Amer) autopista f

freez|e /friːz/ vt (pt **froze**, pp **frozen**) helar; congelar <food, wages>. ● vi helarse; (become motionless) quedarse inmóvil. ● n (on wages, prices) congelación f. **~er** n congelador m. **~ing** a glacial. ● n. **~ing (point)** punto m de congelación f. **below ~ing** bajo cero

freight /freɪt/ n (goods) mercancías fpl. **~er** n buque m de carga

French /frentʃ/ a francés. ● n (Lang) francés m. ● npl. **the ~** (people) los

franceses. **~ fries** npl patatas fpl fritas, papas fpl fritas (LAm). **~man** /-mən/ n francés m. **~ window** n puerta f ventana. **~woman** f francesa f

frenz|ied /'frenzɪd/ a frenético. **~y** n frenesí m

frequency /'friːkwənsɪ/ n frecuencia f

frequent /frɪ'kwent/ vt frecuentar. ● /'friːkwənt/ a frecuente. **~ly** adv frecuentemente

fresh /freʃ/ a (**-er, -est**) fresco; (different, additional) nuevo; <water> dulce. **~en** vi refrescar. □ **~en up** vi <person> refrescarse. **~er** n ⊞ ⇒**~MAN**. **~ly** adv recientemente. **~man** n /-mən/ estudiante m de primer año. **~ness** n frescura f

fret /fret/ vi (pt **fretted**) preocuparse. **~ful** a (discontented) quejoso; (irritable) irritable

friction /'frɪkʃn/ n fricción f

Friday /'fraɪdeɪ/ n viernes m

fridge /frɪdʒ/ n ⊞ frigorífico m, nevera f, refrigerador m (LAm)

fried /fraɪd/ ⇒**FRY**. ● a frito

friend /frend/ n amigo m. **~liness** n simpatía f. **~ly** a (**-ier, -iest**) simpático. **~ship** n amistad f

fries /fraɪz/ npl ⇒**FRENCH FRIES**

frieze /friːz/ n friso m

frigate /'frɪgət/ n fragata f

fright /fraɪt/ n miedo m; (shock) susto m. **~en** vt asustar. □ **~ off** vt ahuyentar. **~ened** a asustado. **be ~ened** tener miedo (**of** de.) **~ful** a espantoso, horrible. **~fully** adv terriblemente

frigid /'frɪdʒɪd/ a frígido

frill /frɪl/ n volante m, olán m (Mex). **~s** npl (fig) adornos mpl. **with no ~s** sencillo

fringe /frɪndʒ/ n (sewing) fleco m; (ornamental border) franja f; (of hair) flequillo m, cerquillo m (LAm), fleco m (Mex); (of area) periferia f; (of society) margen m

fritter /'frɪtə(r)/ vt. □ **~ away** vt desperdiciar <time>; malgastar <money>

frivol|ity /frɪ'vɒlətɪ/ n frivolidad f. **~ous** /'frɪvələs/ a frívolo

fro /frəʊ/ ⇒TO AND FRO

frock /frɒk/ n vestido m

frog /frɒg/ n rana f. **have a ~ in one's throat** tener carraspera. **~man** /-mən/ n hombre m rana. **~spawn** n huevos mpl de rana

frolic /'frɒlɪk/ vi (pt **frolicked**) retozar

from /frɒm/, unstressed /frəm/ prep de; (indicating starting point) desde; (habit, conviction) por; **~ then on** a partir de ahí

front /frʌnt/ n parte f delantera; (of building) fachada f; (of clothes) delantera f; (Mil, Pol) frente f; (of book) principio m; (fig, appearance) apariencia f; (seafront) paseo m marítimo, malecón m (LAm). **in ~ of** delante de. ● a delantero; (first) primero. **~al** a frontal; <attack> de frente. **~ door** n puerta f principal

frontier /'frʌntɪə(r)/ n frontera f

front page n (of newspaper) primera plana f

frost /frɒst/ n (freezing) helada f; (frozen dew) escarcha f. **~bite** n congelación f. **~bitten** a congelado. **~ed** a <glass> esmerilado. **~ing** n (Amer) glaseado m. **~y** a <weather> helado; <night> de helada; (fig) glacial

froth /frɒθ/ n espuma f. ● vi espumar. **~y** a espumoso

frown /fraʊn/ vi fruncir el entrecejo ● n ceño m. □ **~ on** vt desaprobar.

froze /frəʊz/ ⇒FREEZE. **~n** /'frəʊzn/ ⇒FREEZE. ● a congelado; <region> helado

frugal /'fru:gl/ a frugal

fruit /fru:t/ n (Bot, on tree, fig) fruto m; (as food) fruta f. **~ful** /'fru:tfl/ a fértil; (fig) fructífero. **~ion** /fru:'ɪʃn/ n. **come to ~ion** realizarse. **~less** a infructuoso. **~ salad** n macedonia f de frutas. **~y** a que sabe a fruta

frustrat|e /frʌ'streɪt/ vt frustrar. **~ion** /-ʃn/ n frustración f. **~ed** a frustrado. **~ing** a frustrante

fry /fraɪ/ vt (pt **fried**) freír. ● vi freírse. **~ing pan** n sárten f, sartén m (LAm)

fudge /fʌdʒ/ n dulce m de azúcar

fuel /'fju:əl/ n combustible m

fugitive /'fju:dʒɪtɪv/ a & n fugitivo (m)

fulfil /fʊl'fɪl/ vt (pt **fulfilled**) cumplir (con) <promise, obligation>; satisfacer <condition>; hacer realidad <ambition>. **~ment** n (of promise, obligation) cumplimiento m; (of conditions) satisfacción f; (of hopes, plans) realización f

full /fʊl/ a (-**er**, -**est**) lleno; <bus, hotel> completo; <account> detallado. **at ~ speed** a máxima velocidad. **be ~ (up)** (with food) no poder más. ● n. **in ~** sin quitar nada. **to the ~** completamente. **write in ~** escribir con todas las letras. **~back** n (Sport) defensa m & f. **~-blown** /fʊl'bləʊn/ a verdadero. **~-fledged** /-'fledʒd/ a (Amer) ⇒FULLY-FLEDGED. **~ moon** n luna f llena. **~-scale** /-'skeɪl/ a <drawing> de tamaño natural; (fig) amplio. **~ stop** n punto m. **~-time** a <employment> de jornada completa. ● /-'taɪm/ adv a tiempo completo. **~y** adv completamente. **~-fledged** /-'fledʒd/ a <chick> capaz de volar; <lawyer, nurse> hecho y derecho

fulsome /'fʊlsəm/ a excesivo

fumble /'fʌmbl/ vi buscar (a tientas)

fume /fju:m/ vi despedir gases; (fig, be furious) estar furioso. **~s** npl gases mpl

fumigate /'fju:mɪgeɪt/ vt fumigar

fun /fʌn/ n (amusement) diversión f; (merriment) alegría f. **for ~** en broma. **have ~** divertirse. **make ~ of** burlarse de

function /'fʌŋkʃn/ n (purpose, duty) función f; (reception) recepción f. ● vi funcionar. **~al** a funcional

fund /fʌnd/ n fondo m. ● vt financiar

fundamental /fʌndə'mentl/ a fundamental. **~ist** a & n fundamentalista (m & f)

funeral /'fju:nərəl/ n entierro m, funerales mpl. **~ director** n director m de pompas fúnebres

funfair /'fʌnfeə(r)/ n feria f; (permanent) parque m de atracciones, parque m de diversiones (LAm)

fungus /'fʌŋgəs/ n (pl -**gi** /-gaɪ/) hongo m

funnel /'fʌnl/ n (for pouring) embudo m; (of ship) chimenea f

funn|ily /'fʌnɪlɪ/ adv (oddly) curiosamente. ~y a (-ier, -iest) divertido, gracioso; (odd) curioso, raro

fur /fɜ:(r)/ n pelo m; (pelt) piel f

furious /'fjʊərɪəs/ a furioso. ~ly adv furiosamente

furlough /'fɜ:ləʊ/ n (Amer) permiso m. on ~ de permiso

furnace /'fɜ:nɪs/ n horno m

furnish /'fɜ:nɪʃ/ vt amueblar, amoblar (LAm); (supply) proveer. ~ings npl muebles mpl, mobiliario m

furniture /'fɜ:nɪtʃə(r)/ n muebles mpl, mobiliario m. a piece of ~ un mueble

furrow /'fʌrəʊ/ n surco m

furry /'fɜ:rɪ/ a peludo

furthe|r /'fɜ:ðə(r)/ a más lejano; (additional) nuevo. ● adv más lejos; (more) además. ● vt fomentar. ~rmore adv además. ~st a más lejano. ● adv más lejos

furtive /'fɜ:tɪv/ a furtivo

fury /'fjʊərɪ/ n furia f

fuse /fju:z/ vt (melt) fundir; (fig, unite) fusionar. ~ the lights fundir los plomos. ● vi fundirse; (fig) fusionarse. ● n fusible m, plomo m; (of bomb) mecha f. ~box n caja f de fusibles

fuselage /'fju:zəlɑ:ʒ/ n fuselaje m

fusion /'fju:ʒn/ n fusión f

fuss /fʌs/ n (commotion) jaleo m. kick up a ~ armar un lío, armar una bronca. make a ~ of tratar con mucha atención. ● vi preocuparse. ~y a (-ier, -iest) (finicky) remilgado; (demanding) exigente

futil|e /'fju:taɪl/ a inútil, vano. ~ity /fju:'tɪlətɪ/ n inutilidad f

futur|e /'fju:tʃə(r)/ a futuro. ● n futuro m. in ~e de ahora en adelante. ~istic /fju:tʃə'rɪstɪk/ a futurista

fuzz /fʌz/ n pelusa f. ~y a <hair> crespo; <photograph> borroso

Gg

gab /gæb/ n. have the gift of the ~ tener un pico de oro

gabardine /gæbə'di:n/ n gabardina f

gabble /'gæbl/ vi hablar atropelladamente

gable /'geɪbl/ n aguilón m

gad /gæd/ vi (pt gadded). ~ about callejear

gadget /'gædʒɪt/ n chisme m

Gaelic /'geɪlɪk/ a & n gaélico (m)

gaffe /gæf/ n plancha f, metedura f de pata, metida f de pata (LAm)

gag /gæg/ n mordaza f; (joke) chiste m. ● vt (pt gagged) amordazar. ● vi hacer arcadas

gaiety /'geɪətɪ/ n alegría f

gaily /'geɪlɪ/ adv alegremente

gain /geɪn/ vt ganar; (acquire) adquirir; (obtain) conseguir. ● vi <clock> adelantar. ● n ganancia f; (increase) aumento m

gait /geɪt/ n modo m de andar

gala /'gɑ:lə/ n fiesta f. ~ performance (función f de) gala f

galaxy /'gæləksɪ/ n galaxia f

gale /geɪl/ n vendaval m

gall /gɔ:l/ n bilis f; (fig) hiel f; (impudence) descaro m

gallant /'gælənt/ a (brave) valiente; (chivalrous) galante. ~ry n valor m

gall bladder /'gɔ:lblædə(r)/ n vesícula f biliar

gallery /'gælərɪ/ n galería f

galley /'gælɪ/ n (ship) galera f; (ship's kitchen) cocina f. ~ (proof) n galerada f

gallivant /'gælɪvænt/ vi 🇬🇧 callejear

gallon /'gælən/ n galón m (imperial = 4,546l; Amer = 3,785l)

gallop /'gæləp/ n galope m. ● vi (pt galloped) galopar

gallows /'gæləʊz/ n horca f

galore /gə'lɔ:(r)/ a en abundancia

galvanize /'gælvənaɪz/ *vt* galvanizar

gambl|e /'gæmbl/ *vi* jugar. **~e on** contar con. ● *vt* jugarse. ● *n* (venture) empresa *f* arriesgada; (bet) apuesta *f*; (risk) riesgo *m*. **~er** *n* jugador *m*. **~ing** *n* juego *m*

game /geɪm/ *n* juego *m*; (match) partido *m*; (animals, birds) caza *f*. ● *a* valiente. **~** for listo para. **~keeper** *n* guardabosque *m*. **~s** *n* (in school) deportes *mpl*

gammon /'gæmən/ *n* jamón *m* fresco

gamut /'gæmət/ *n* gama *f*

gander /'gændə(r)/ *n* ganso *m*

gang /gæŋ/ *n* pandilla *f*; (of workmen) equipo *m*. □**~** **up** *vi* unirse (on contra)

gangling /'gæŋglɪŋ/ *a* larguirucho

gangrene /'gæŋgriːn/ *n* gangrena *f*

gangster /'gæŋstə(r)/ *n* bandido *m*, gángster *m & f*

gangway /'gæŋweɪ/ *n* pasillo *m*; (of ship) pasarela *f*

gaol /dʒeɪl/ *n* cárcel *f*. **~er** *n* carcelero *m*

gap /gæp/ *n* espacio *m*; (in fence, hedge) hueco *m*; (in time) intervalo *m*; (in knowledge) laguna *f*; (difference) diferencia *f*

gap|e /'geɪp/ *vi* quedarse boquiabierto; (be wide open) estar muy abierto. **~ing** *a* abierto; (person) boquiabierto

garage /'gærɑːʒ/ *n* garaje *m*, garage *m* (LAm), cochera *f* (Mex); (petrol station) gasolinera *f*; (for repairs, sales) taller *m*, garage *m* (LAm)

garbage /'gɑːbɪdʒ/ *n* basura *f*. **~ can** *n* (Amer) cubo *m* de la basura, bote *m* de la basura (Mex). **~ collector**, **~ man** *n* (Amer) basurero *m*

garble /'gɑːbl/ *vt* tergiversar, embrollar

garden /'gɑːdn/ *n* (of flowers) jardín *m*; (of vegetables/fruit) huerto *m*. ● *vi* trabajar en el jardín. **~er** /'gɑːdnə (r)/ *n* jardinero *m*. **~ing** *n* jardinería *f*; (vegetable growing) horticultura *f*

gargle /'gɑːgl/ *vi* hacer gárgaras

gargoyle /'gɑːgɔɪl/ *n* gárgola *f*

garish /'geərɪʃ/ *a* chillón

garland /'gɑːlənd/ *n* guirnalda *f*

garlic / 'gɑːlɪk/ *n* ajo *m*

garment /'gɑːmənt/ *n* prenda *f* (de vestir)

garnish /'gɑːnɪʃ/ *vt* adornar, decorar. ● *n* adorno *m*

garret /'gærət/ *n* buhardilla *f*

garrison /'gærɪsn/ *n* guarnición *f*

garrulous /'gærələs/ *a* hablador

garter /'gɑːtə(r)/ *n* liga *f*

gas /gæs/ *n* (*pl* **gases**) gas *m*; (anaesthetic) anestésico *m*; (Amer, petrol) gasolina *f*. ● *vt* (*pt* **gassed**) asfixiar con gas

gash /gæʃ/ *n* tajo *m*. ● *vt* hacer un tajo de

gasket /'gæskɪt/ *n* junta *f*

gas: **~ mask** *n* careta *f* antigás. **~ meter** *n* contador *m* de gas

gasoline /'gæsəliːn/ *n* (Amer) gasolina *f*

gasp /gɑːsp/ *vi* jadear; (with surprise) dar un grito ahogado. ● *n* exclamación *f*, grito *m*

gas: **~ ring** *n* hornillo *m* de gas. **~ station** *n* (Amer) gasolinera *f*

gastric /'gæstrɪk/ *a* gástrico

gate /geɪt/ *n* puerta *f*; (of metal) verja *f*; (barrier) barrera *f*

gate: **~crash** *vt* colarse en. **~crasher** *n* intruso *m* (*que ha entrado sin ser invitado*). **~way** *n* puerta *f*

gather /'gæðə(r)/ *vt* reunir <*people, things*>; (accumulate) acumular; (pick up) recoger; recoger <*flowers*>; (fig, infer) deducir; (sewing) fruncir. **~ speed** acelerar. ● *vi* <*people*> reunirse; <*things*> acumularse. **~ing** *n* reunión *f*

gaudy /'gɔːdɪ/ *a* (**-ier, -iest**) chillón

gauge /geɪdʒ/ *n* (measurement) medida *f*; (Rail) entrevía *f*; (instrument) indicador *m*. ● *vt* medir; (fig) estimar

gaunt /gɔːnt/ *a* descarnado; (from illness) demacrado

gauntlet /'gɔːntlɪt/ *n*. run the **~** of aguantar el acoso de

gauze /gɔːz/ *n* gasa *f*

gave /geɪv/ ⇒GIVE

gawky /'gɔːkɪ/ *a* (**-ier, -iest**) torpe

gawp /gɔ:p/ *vi.* ∼ **at** mirar como un tonto

gay /geɪ/ *a* (**-er, -est**) (⊞, homosexual) homosexual, gay ⊞; (dated; joyful) alegre

gaze /geɪz/ *vi.* ∼ (**at**) mirar (fijamente). ● *n* mirada *f* (fija)

gazelle /gə'zel/ *n* (*pl invar or* **-s**) gacela *f*

GB *abbr* ⇒GREAT BRITAIN

gear /gɪə(r)/ *n* equipo *m*; (Tec) engranaje *m*; (Auto) marcha *f*, cambio *m*. **in** ∼ engranado. **out of** ∼ desengranado. **change** ∼, **shift** ∼ (Amer) cambiar de marcha. ● *vt* adaptar. ∼**box** *n* (Auto) caja *f* de cambios

geese /gi:s/ ⇒GOOSE

gel /dʒel/ *n* gel *m*

gelatine /'dʒelətiːn/ *n* gelatina *f*

gelignite /'dʒelɪgnaɪt/ *n* gelignita *f*

gem /dʒem/ *n* piedra *f* preciosa

Gemini /'dʒemɪnaɪ/ *n* Géminis *mpl*

gender /'dʒendə(r)/ *n* género *m*

gene /dʒiːn/ *n* gen *m*, gene *m*

genealogy /dʒiːnɪ'ælədʒɪ/ *n* genealogía *f*

general /'dʒenərəl/ *a* general. ● *n* general *m*. **in** ∼ en general. ∼ **election** *n* elecciones *fpl* generales. ∼**ization** /-'zeɪʃn/ *n* generalización *f*. ∼**ize** *vt/i* generalizar. ∼ **knowledge** *n* cultura *f* general. ∼**ly** *adv* generalmente. ∼ **practitioner** *n* médico *m* de cabecera

generat|e /'dʒenəreɪt/ *vt* generar. ∼**ion** /-'reɪʃn/ *n* generación *f*. ∼**ion gap** *n* brecha *f* generacional. ∼**or** *n* generador *m*

genero|sity /dʒenə'rɒsətɪ/ *n* generosidad *f*. ∼**us** /'dʒenərəs/ *a* generoso; (plentiful) abundante

genetic /dʒɪ'netɪk/ *a* genético. ∼**s** *n* genética *f*

Geneva /dʒɪ'niːvə/ *n* Ginebra *f*

genial /'dʒiːnɪəl/ *a* simpático, afable

genital /'dʒenɪtl/ *a* genital. ∼**s** *npl* genitales *mpl*

genitive /'dʒenɪtɪv/ *a & n* genitivo (*m*)

genius /'dʒiːnɪəs/ *n* (*pl* **-uses**) genio *m*

genocide /'dʒenəsaɪd/ *n* genocidio *m*

genre /ʒɑːŋr/ *n* género *m*

gent /dʒent/ *n* ⊞ señor *m*. ∼**s** *n* aseo *m* de caballeros

genteel /dʒen'tiːl/ *a* distinguido

gentl|e /'dʒentl/ *a* (**-er, -est**) <*person*> dulce; <*murmur, breeze*> suave; <*hint*> discreto. ∼**eman** *n* señor *m*; (well-bred) caballero *m*. ∼**eness** *n* amabilidad *f*. ∼**y** *adv* amablemente

genuine /'dʒenjuɪn/ *a* verdadero; <*person*> sincero

geograph|er /dʒɪ'ɒgrəfə(r)/ *n* geógrafo *m*. ∼**ical** /dʒɪə'græfɪkl/ *a* geográfico. ∼**y** /dʒɪ'ɒgrəfɪ/ *n* geografía *f*

geolog|ical /dʒɪə'lɒdʒɪkl/ *a* geológico. ∼**ist** /dʒɪ'ɒlədʒɪst/ *n* geólogo *m*. ∼**y** /dʒɪ'ɒlədʒɪ/ *n* geología *f*

geometr|ic(al) /dʒɪə'metrɪk(l)/ *a* geométrico. ∼**y** /dʒɪ'ɒmətrɪ/ *n* geometría *f*

geranium /dʒə'reɪnɪəm/ *n* geranio *m*

geriatric /dʒerɪ'ætrɪk/ *a* <*patient*> anciano; <*ward*> de geriatría. ∼**s** *n* geriatría *f*

germ /dʒɜːm/ *n* microbio *m*, germen *m*

German /'dʒɜːmən/ *a & n* alemán (*m*). ∼**ic** /dʒɜː'mænɪk/ *a* germánico. ∼ **measles** *n* rubéola *f*. ∼**y** *n* Alemania *f*

germinate /'dʒɜːmɪneɪt/ *vi* germinar

gesticulate /dʒe'stɪkjʊleɪt/ *vi* hacer ademanes, gesticular

gesture /'dʒestʃə(r)/ *n* gesto *m*, ademán *m*; (fig) gesto *m*. ● *vi* hacer gestos

....

get /get/

past **got**; past participle **got, gotten** (Amer); present participle **getting**

● *transitive verb*

····▸ (obtain) conseguir, obtener. **did you get the job?** ¿conseguiste el trabajo?

····▸ (buy) comprar. **I got it in the sales** lo compré en las rebajas

····➤ (achieve, win) sacar. **she got very good marks** sacó muy buenas notas

····➤ (receive) recibir. **I got a letter from Alex** recibí una carta de Alex

····➤ (fetch) ir a buscar. **~ your coat** vete a buscar tu abrigo

····➤ (experience) llevarse. **I got a terrible shock** me llevé un shock espantoso

····➤ (⚠, understand) entender. **I don't ~ what you mean** no entiendo lo que quieres decir

····➤ (ask or persuade) **to ~ s.o. to do sth** hacer que uno haga algo

> Note that *hacer que* is followed by the subjunctive form of the verb

····➤ (cause to be done or happen) **I must ~ this watch fixed** tengo que llevar a arreglar este reloj. **they got the roof mended** hicieron arreglar el techo

● *intransitive verb*

····➤ (arrive, reach) llegar. **I got there late** llegué tarde. **how do you ~ to Paddington?** ¿cómo se llega a Paddington?

····➤ (become) **to ~ tired** cansarse. **she got very angry** se puso furiosa. **it's ~ting late** se está haciendo tarde

⟹ For translations of expressions such as **get better, get old** ɛɛɔ ɔntɾiɔɔ **better, old** etc. See also **got**

····➤ **to get to do sth** (manage to) llegar a. **did you ~ to see him?** ¿llegaste a verlo?

□ **get along** *vi* (manage) arreglárselas; (progress) hacer progresos. □ **get along with** *vt* llevarse bien con. □ **get at** *vt* (reach) llegar a; (imply) querer decir. □ **get away** *vi* salir; (escape) escaparse. □ **get back** *vi* volver. *vt* (recover) recobrar. □ **get by** *vi* (manage) arreglárselas; (pass) pasar. □ **get down** *vi* bajar. *vt* (make depressed) deprimir. □ **get in** *vi* entrar. *vt* entrar en; subir a *<car>* □ **get off** *vt* bajar(se) de *<train etc>*. *vi* (from train etc) bajarse; (Jurid) salir absuelto. □ **get on** *vi* (progress) hacer progresos; (succeed) tener éxito. *vt* subirse a *<train etc>*. □ **get on with** *vt* (be on good terms

with) llevarse bien con; (continue) seguir con. □ **get out** *vi* salir. *vt* (take out) sacar. □ **get out of** *vt* (fig) librarse de. □ **get over** *vt* reponerse de *<illness>*. □ **get round** *vt* soslayar *<difficulty etc>*; engatusar *<person>*. □ **get through** *vi* pasar; (on phone) comunicarse (to con). □ **get together** *vi* (meet up) reunirse. *vt* (assemble) reunir. □ **get up** *vi* levantarse; (climb) subir

geyser /'giːzə(r)/ *n* géiser *m*

ghastly /'gɑːstlɪ/ *a* (**-ier, -iest**) horrible

gherkin /'gɜːkɪn/ *n* pepinillo *m*

ghetto /'getəʊ/ *n* (*pl* **-os**) gueto *m*

ghost /gəʊst/ *n* fantasma *m*. **~ly** *a* espectral

giant /'dʒaɪənt/ *n* gigante *m*. ● *a* gigantesco

gibberish /'dʒɪbərɪʃ/ *n* jerigonza *f*

gibe /dʒaɪb/ *n* pulla *f*

giblets /'dʒɪblɪts/ *npl* menudillos *mpl*

gidd|iness /'gɪdɪnɪs/ *n* vértigo *m*. **~y** *a* (**-ier, -iest**) mareado. **be/feel ~y** estar/sentirse mareado

gift /gɪft/ *n* regalo *m*; (ability) don *m*. **~ed** *a* dotado de talento. **~-wrap** *vt* envolver para regalo

gigantic /dʒaɪˈgæntɪk/ *a* gigantesco

giggle /'gɪgl/ *vi* reírse tontamente. ● *n* risita *f*

gild /gɪld/ *vt* dorar

gills /gɪlz/ *npl* agallas *fpl*

gilt /gɪlt/ *n* dorado *m*. ● *a* dorado

gimmick /'gɪmɪk/ *n* truco *m*

gin / dʒɪn/ *n* ginebra *f*

ginger /'dʒɪndʒə(r)/ *n* jengibre *m*. ● *a* rojizo. **he has ~ hair** es pelirrojo. **~bread** *n* pan *m* de jengibre

gipsy /'dʒɪpsɪ/ *n* gitano *m*

giraffe /dʒɪˈrɑːf/ *n* jirafa *f*

girder /'gɜːdə(r)/ *n* viga *f*

girdle /'gɜːdl/ *n* (belt) cinturón *m*; (corset) corsé *m*

girl /gɜːl/ *n* chica *f*, muchacha *f*; (child) niña *f*. **~friend** *n* amiga *f*; (of boy) novia *f*. **~ish** *a* de niña; *<boy>* afeminado. **~ scout** *n* (Amer) exploradora *f*, guía *f*

giro /'dʒaɪrəʊ/ *n* (*pl* **-os**) giro *m* (bancario)

girth /gɜ:θ/ *n* circunferencia *f*

gist /dʒɪst/ *n* lo esencial

give /gɪv/ *vt* (*pt* **gave**, *pp* **given**) dar; (deliver) entregar; regalar <*present*>; prestar <*aid, attention*>. ~ o.s. to darse a. ● *vi* dar; (yield) ceder; (stretch) dar de sí. ● *n* elasticidad *f*. □ ~ **away** *vt* regalar; revelar <*secret*>. □ ~ **back** *vt* devolver. □ ~ **in** *vi* ceder. □ ~ **off** *vt* emitir. □ ~ **out** *vt* distribuir. (become used up) agotarse. □ ~ **up** *vt* renunciar a; (yield) ceder. ~ **up doing sth** dejar de hacer algo. ~ o.s. **up** entregarse (**to** a). *vi* rendirse. ~**n** /'gɪvn/ ⇒GIVE. ● *a* dado. ~**n name** *n* nombre *m* de pila

glacier /'glæsɪə(r)/ *n* glaciar *m*

glad /glæd/ *a* contento. be ~ alegrarse (**about** de). ~**den** *vt* alegrar

gladly /'glædlɪ/ *adv* alegremente; (willingly) con mucho gusto

glamo|rous /'glæmərəs/ *a* glamoroso. ~**ur** /'glæmə(r)/ *n* glamour *m*

glance /glɑ:ns/ *n* ojeada *f*. ● *vi*. ~ **at** dar un vistazo a

gland /glænd/ *n* glándula *f*

glar|e /gleə(r)/ *vi* <*light*> deslumbrar; (stare angrily) mirar airadamente. ● *n* resplandor *m*; (stare) mirada *f* airada. ~**ing** *a* deslumbrante; (obvious) manifiesto

glass /glɑ:s/ *n* (material) cristal *m*, vidrio *m*; (without stem or for wine) vaso *m*; (with stem) copa *f*; (for beer) caña *f*; (mirror) espejo *m*. ~**es** *npl* (spectacles) gafas *fpl*, lentes *fpl* (LAm), anteojos *mpl* (LAm). ~**y** *a* vítreo

glaze /gleɪz/ *vt* poner cristal(es) *or* vidrio(s) a <*windows, doors*>; vidriar <*pottery*>. ● *vi*. ~ (**over**) <*eyes*> vidriarse. ● *n* barniz *m*; (for pottery) esmalte *m*

gleam /gli:m/ *n* destello *m*. ● *vi* destellar

glean /gli:n/ *vt* espigar; recoger <*information*>

glee /gli:/ *n* regocijo *m*

glib /glɪb/ *a* de mucha labia; <*reply*> fácil

glid|e /glaɪd/ *vi* deslizarse; (plane) planear. ~**er** *n* planeador *m*. ~**ing** *n* planeo *m*

glimmer /'glɪmə(r)/ *n* destello *m*. ● *vi* destellar

glimpse /glɪmps/ *n*. catch a ~ of vislumbrar, ver brevemente. ● *vt* vislumbrar

glint /glɪnt/ *n* destello *m*. ● *vi* destellar

glisten /'glɪsn/ *vi* brillar

glitter /'glɪtə(r)/ *vi* brillar. ● *n* brillo *m*

gloat /gləʊt/ *vi*. ~ **on/over** regodearse sobre

glob|al /'gləʊbl/ *a* (worldwide) mundial; (all-embracing) global. ~**al warming** *n* calentamiento *m* global. ~**e** /gləʊb/ *n* globo *m*

gloom /glu:m/ *n* oscuridad *f*; (sadness, fig) tristeza *f*. ~**y** *a* (**-ier, -iest**) triste; (pessimistic) pesimista

glor|ify /'glɔ:rɪfaɪ/ *vt* glorificar. ~**ious** /'glɔ:rɪəs/ *a* espléndido; <*deed, hero etc*> glorioso. ~**y** /'glɔ:rɪ/ *n* gloria *f*

gloss /glɒs/ *n* lustre *m*. ~ (**paint**) (pintura *f* al *or* de) esmalte *m*. □ ~ **over** *vt* (make light of) minimizar; (cover up) encubrir

glossary /'glɒsərɪ/ *n* glosario *m*

glossy /'glɒsɪ/ *a* brillante

glove /glʌv/ *n* guante *m*. ~ **compartment** *n* (Auto) guantera *f*, gaveta *f*

glow /gləʊ/ *vi* brillar. ● *n* brillo *m*. ~**ing** /'gləʊɪŋ/ *a* incandescente; <*account*> entusiasta; <*complexion*> rojo

glucose /'glu:kəʊs/ *n* glucosa *f*

glue /glu:/ *n* cola *f*, goma *f* de pegar. ● *vt* (*pres p* **gluing**) pegar

glum /glʌm/ *a* (**glummer, glummest**) triste

glutton /'glʌtn/ *n* glotón *m*

gnarled /nɑ:ld/ *a* nudoso

gnash /næʃ/ *vt*. ~ **one's teeth** rechinar los dientes

gnat /næt/ *n* jején *m*, mosquito *m*

gnaw /nɔ:/ *vt* roer. ● *vi*. ~ **at** roer

gnome /nəʊm/ *n* gnomo *m*

go /gəʊ/

3rd pers sing present **goes**; past
went; past participle **gone**

● *intransitive verb*

····➤ ir. **I'm going to France** voy a Francia. **to go shopping** ir de compras. **to
go swimming** ir a nadar

····➤ (leave) irse. **we're going on Friday**
nos vamos el viernes

····➤ (work, function) *<engine, clock>* funcionar

····➤ (become) **to go deaf** quedarse
sordo. **to go mad** volverse loco. **his
face went red** se puso colorado

····➤ (stop) *<headache, pain>* irse (+ *me/
te/le*). **the pain's gone** se me ha ido el
dolor

····➤ (turn out, progress) ir. **everything's
going very well** todo va muy bien.
how did the exam go? ¿qué tal te fue
en el examen?

····➤ (match, suit) combinar. **the jacket
and the trousers go well together** la
chaqueta y los pantalones combinan
bien.

····➤ (cease to function) *<bulb, fuse>*
fundirse. **the brakes have gone** los
frenos no funcionan

● *auxiliary verb*

to be going to + *infinitive* ir a + *infinitivo*. **it's going to rain** va a llover.
she's going to win! ¡va a ganar!

● *noun* (*pl* **goes**)

····➤ (turn) turno *m*. **you have three
goes** tienes tres turnos. **it's your go**
te toca a ti

····➤ (attempt) **to have a go at doing sth**
intentar hacer algo. **have another go**
inténtalo de nuevo

····➤ (energy, drive) empuje *m*. **she has a
lot of go** tiene mucho empuje

····➤ (in phrases) **I've been on the go all
day** no he parado en todo el día. **to
make a go of sth** sacar algo adelante
□ **go across** *vt/vi* cruzar. □ **go
after** *vt* perseguir. □ **go away** *vi*
irse. □ **go back** *vi* volver. □ **go
back on** *vt* faltar a *<promise etc>*.
□ **go by** *vi* pasar. □ **go down** *vi* bajar; *<sun>* ponerse. □ **go for** *vt* (🔲,
attack) atacar. □ **go in** *vi* entrar.

□ **go in for** *vt* presentarse para
□ **go in for** *vt* presentarse para
<exam>; participar en *<competition>*.
□ **go off** *vi* (leave) irse; (go bad) pasarse; (explode) estallar; *<lights>*
apagarse. □ **go on** *vi* seguir; (happen)
pasar; (be switched on) encenderse,
prenderse (LAm). □ **go out** *vi* salir;
<fire, light> apagarse. □ **go over** *vt*
(check) revisar; (revise) repasar. □ **go
through** *vt* pasar por; (search) registrar; (check) examinar. □ **go up**
vi/vt subir. □ **go without** *vt* pasar
sin

goad /gəʊd/ *vt* aguijonear

go-ahead /'gəʊəhed/ *n* luz *f* verde.
● *a* dinámico

goal /gəʊl/ *n* (Sport) gol *m*; (objective)
meta *f*. ~**ie** /'gəʊli/ *n* 🔲, ~**keeper**
n portero *m*, arquero *m* (LAm).
~**post** *n* poste *m* de la portería,
poste *m* del arco (LAm)

goat /gəʊt/ *n* cabra *f*

gobble /'gɒbl/ *vt* engullir

goblin /'gɒblɪn/ *n* duende *m*

god /gɒd/ *n* dios *m*. **G~** *n* Dios *m*.
~**child** *n* ahijado *m*. ~**daughter** *n*
ahijada *f*. ~**dess** /*f*/ *n* diosa *f*.
~**father** *n* padrino *m*. ~**forsaken**
a olvidado de Dios. ~**mother** *n*
madrina *f*. ~**send** *n* beneficio *m*
inesperado. ~**son** *n* ahijado *m*

going /'gəʊɪŋ/ *n* camino *m*; (racing)
(estado *m* del) terreno *m*. **it is slow/
hard ~** es lento/difícil. ● *a* *<price>*
actual; *<concern>* en funcionamiento

gold /gəʊld/ *n* oro *m*. ● *a* de oro.
~**en** *a* de oro; (in colour) dorado; *<op-
portunity>* único. ~**en wedding** *n*
bodas *fpl* de oro. ~**fish** *n invar* pez
m de colores. ~**mine** *n* mina *f* de
oro; (fig) fuente *f* de gran riqueza.
~**-plated** /-'pleɪtɪd/ *a* chapado en
oro. ~**smith** *n* orfebre *m*

golf /gɒlf/ *n* golf *m*. ~**ball** *n* pelota *f* de
golf. ~ **club** *n* palo *m* de golf; (place)
club *m* de golf. ~**course** *n* campo *m*
de golf. ~**er** *n* jugador *m* de golf

gondola /'gɒndələ/ *n* góndola *f*

gone /gɒn/ ⇒GO. ● *a* pasado. ~ **six
o'clock** después de las seis

gong /gɒŋ/ *n* gong(o) *m*

good /gʊd/ *a* (**better, best**) bueno,
(before masculine singular noun)

buen. ~ **afternoon** buenas tardes. ~
evening (before dark) buenas tardes;
(after dark) buenas noches. ~ **morning**
buenos días. ~ **night** buenas noches.
as ~ as (almost) casi. **feel ~** sentirse
bien. **have a ~ time** divertirse. ● *n*
bien *m*. **for ~** para siempre. **it is no**
~ shouting es inútil gritar *etc*.
~**bye** /-'baɪ/ *int* ¡adiós! ● *n* adiós *m*.
say ~bye to despedirse de. ~**for-**
nothing /-fənʌθɪŋ/ *a & n* inútil (*m*).
G~ Friday *n* Viernes *m* Santo.
~**-looking** /-'lʊkɪŋ/ *a* guapo, buen
mozo *m* (LAm), buena moza *f* (LAm).
~**ness** *n* bondad *f*. ~**ness!**, ~**ness**
gracious!, ~**ness me!**, **my ~ness!**
¡Dios mío! ~**s** *npl* mercancías *fpl*.
~**will** /-'wɪl/ *n* buena voluntad *f*. ~**y**
n (Culin, 🇺🇸) golosina *f*; (in film) bueno
m

gooey /'guːɪ/ *a* (**gooier, gooiest**)
🇺🇸 pegajoso; (fig) sentimental

goofy /'guːfɪ/ *a* (Amer) necio

goose /guːs/ *n* (*pl* **geese**) oca *f*,
ganso *m*. ~**berry** /'gʊzbərɪ/ *n* uva *f*
espina, grosella *f* espinosa. ~**-flesh**
n, ~**-pimples** *npl* carne *f* de gallina

gore /gɔː(r)/ *n* sangre *f*. ● *vt* cornear

gorge /gɔːdʒ/ *n* (Geog) garganta *f*.
● *vt*. ~ **o.s.** hartarse (on de)

gorgeous /'gɔːdʒəs/ *a* precioso;
(splendid) magnífico

gorilla /gə'rɪlə/ *n* gorila *m*

gorse /gɔːs/ *n* aulaga *f*

gory /'gɔːrɪ/ *a* (**-ier, -iest**) 🇺🇸 sangriento

gosh /gɒʃ/ *int* ¡caramba!

go-slow /gəʊ'sləʊ/ *n* huelga *f* de celo, huelga *f* pasiva

gospel /'gɒspl/ *n* evangelio *m*

gossip /'gɒsɪp/ *n* (chatter) chismorreo *m*; (person) chismoso *m*. ● *vi* (*pt*
gossiped) (chatter) chismorrear; (repeat scandal) conta chismes

got /gɒt/ ⇒GET. **have ~** tener. **I've ~**
to do it tengo que hacerlo.

gotten /'gɒtn/ ⇒GET

gouge /gaʊdʒ/ *vt* abrir <*hole*>. □ ~
out *vt* sacar

gourmet /'gʊəmeɪ/ *n* gastrónomo *m*

govern /'gʌvən/ *vt/i* gobernar.
~**ess** *n* institutriz *f*. ~**ment** *n* go-
bierno *m*. ~**or** *n* gobernador *m*

gown /gaʊn/ *n* vestido *m*; (of judge,
teacher) toga *f*

GP *abbr* ⇒GENERAL PRACTITIONER

grab /græb/ *vt* (*pt* **grabbed**) agarrar

grace /greɪs/ *n* gracia *f*. ~**ful** *a* elegante

gracious /'greɪʃəs/ *a* (kind) amable;
(elegant) elegante

grade /greɪd/ *n* clase *f*, categoría *f*;
(of goods) clase *f*, calidad *f*; (on scale)
grado *m*; (school mark) nota *f*; (Amer,
class) curso *m*, año *m*

gradient /'greɪdɪənt/ *n* pendiente *f*,
gradiente *f* (LAm)

gradual /'grædʒʊəl/ *a* gradual. ~**ly**
adv gradualmente, poco a poco

graduat|e /'grædʒʊət/ *n* (Univ) li-
cenciado. ● /'grædʒʊeɪt/ *vi* licenciar-
se. ~**ion** /-'eɪʃn/ *n* graduación *f*

graffiti /grə'fiːtɪ/ *npl* graffiti *mpl*,
pintadas *fpl*

graft /grɑːft/ *n* (Med, Bot) injerto *m*;
(Amer 🇺🇸, bribery) chanchullos *mpl*.
● *vt* injertar

grain /greɪn/ *n* grano *m*

gram /græm/ *n* gramo *m*

gramma|r /'græmə(r)/ *n* gramática
f. ~**tical** /grə'mætɪkl/ *a* gramatical

gramme /græm/ *n* gramo *m*

grand /grænd/ *a* (**-er, -est**) magnífico; (🇺🇸, excellent) estupendo. ~**child**
n nieto *m*. ~**daughter** *n* nieta *f*.
~**eur** /'grændʒə(r)/ *n* grandiosidad
f. ~**father** *n* abuelo *m*. ~**father**
clock *n* reloj *m* de caja. ~**iose**
/'grændɪəʊs/ *a* grandioso.
~**mother** *n* abuela *f*. ~**parents**
npl abuelos *mpl*. ~ **piano** *n* piano *m*
de cola. ~**son** *n* nieto *m*. ~**stand**
/'grænstænd/ *n* tribuna *f*

granite /'grænɪt/ *n* granito *m*

granny /'grænɪ/ *n* 🇺🇸 abuela *f*

grant /grɑːnt/ *vt* conceder; (give) do-
nar; (admit) admitir (**that** que). **take**
for ~ed dar por sentado. ● *n* concesión *f*; (Univ) beca *f*

granule /'grænuːl/ *n* gránulo *m*

grape /greɪp/ *n* uva *f*. ~**fruit** *n invar*
pomelo *m*, toronja *f* (LAm)

graph 307 **grip**

graph /grɑːf/ n gráfica f

graphic /'græfɪk/ a gráfico. ~s npl diseño m gráfico; (Comp) gráficos mpl

grapple /'græpl/ vi. ~ with forcejear con; (mentally) lidiar con

grasp /grɑːsp/ vt agarrar. ● n (hold) agarro m; (fig) comprensión f. ~ing a avaro

grass /grɑːs/ n hierba f. ~hopper n saltamontes m. ~ roots npl base f popular. ● a de las bases. ~y a cubierto de hierba

grate /greɪt/ n rejilla f; (fireplace) chimenea f. ● vt rallar. ● vi rechinar; (be irritating) ser crispante

grateful /'greɪtfl/ a agradecido. ~ly adv con gratitud

grater /'greɪtə(r)/ n rallador m

gratif|ied /'grætɪfaɪd/ a contento. ~y /'grætɪfaɪ/ vt satisfacer; (please) agradar a. ~ying a agradable

grating /'greɪtɪŋ/ n reja f

gratitude /'grætɪtjuːd/ n gratitud f

gratuitous /grə'tjuːɪtəs/ a gratuito

gratuity /grə'tjuːətɪ/ n (tip) propina f

grave /greɪv/ n sepultura f. ● a (-er, -est) (serious) grave

gravel /'grævl/ n grava f

gravely /'greɪvlɪ/ adv (seriously) seriamente; (solemnly) con gravedad

grave: ~stone n lápida f. ~yard n cementerio m

gravitate /'grævɪteɪt/ vi gravitar

gravity /'grævətɪ/ n gravedad f

gravy /'greɪvɪ/ n salsa f

gray /greɪ/ a & n (Amer) ⇒GREY

graze /greɪz/ vi (eat) pacer. ● vt (touch) rozar; (scrape) raspar. ● n rasguño m

greas|e /griːs/ n grasa f. ● vt engrasar. ~eproof paper n papel m encerado or de cera. ~y a <hands> grasiento; <food> graso; <hair, skin> graso, grasoso (LAm)

great /greɪt/ a (-er, -est) grande, (before singular noun) gran; (𝕀, very good) estupendo. G~ Britain n Gran Bretaña f. ~-grandfather /-'græn fɑːðə(r)/ n bisabuelo m. ~-grandmother /-'grænmʌðə(r)/ n bisabuela f. ~ly adv (very) muy; (much) mucho

Greece /griːs/ n Grecia f

greed /griːd/ n avaricia f; (for food) glotonería f. ~y a avaro; (for food) glotón

Greek /griːk/ a & n griego (m)

green /griːn/ a (-er, -est) verde. ● n verde m; (grass) césped m. ~ belt n zona f verde. ~ card n (Amer) permiso m de residencia y trabajo. ~ery n verdor m. ~gage /-geɪdʒ/ n claudia f. ~grocer n verdulero m. ~house n invernadero m. the ~house effect el efecto invernadero. ~ light n luz f verde. ~s npl verduras fpl

greet /griːt/ vt saludar; (receive) recibir. ~ing n saludo m

gregarious /grɪ'geərɪəs/ a gregario; <person> sociable

grenade /grɪ'neɪd/ n granada f

grew /gruː/ ⇒GROW

grey /greɪ/ a (-er, -est) gris. have ~ hair ser canoso. ● n gris m. ~hound n galgo m

grid /grɪd/ n reja f; (Elec, network) red f; (on map) cuadriculado m

grief /griːf/ n dolor m. come to ~ <person> acabar mal; (fail) fracasar

grievance /'griːvns/ n queja f formal

grieve /griːv/ vt apenar. ● vi afligirse. ~ for llorar

grievous /'griːvəs/ a doloroso; (serious) grave. ~ bodily harm (Jurid) lesiones fpl (corporales) graves

grill /grɪl/ n parrilla f. ● vt asar a la parrilla; (𝕀, interrogate) interrogar

grille /grɪl/ n rejilla f

grim /grɪm/ a (grimmer, grimmest) severo

grimace /'grɪməs/ n mueca f. ● vi hacer muecas

grim|e /graɪm/ n mugre f. ~y a mugriento

grin /grɪn/ vt (pt grinned) sonreír. ● n sonrisa f (abierta)

grind /graɪnd/ vt (pt ground) moler <coffee, corn etc>; (pulverize) pulverizar; (sharpen) afilar; (Amer) picar, moler <meat>

grip /grɪp/ vt (pt gripped) agarrar; (interest) captar. ● n (hold) agarro m; (strength of hand) apretón m; (hairgrip) horquilla *f*, pasador *m* (Mex). **come to ~s with** entender *<subject>*

grisly /'grɪzlɪ/ *a* (**-ier, -iest**) horrible

gristle /'grɪsl/ *n* cartílago *m*

grit /grɪt/ *n* arenilla *f*; (fig) agallas *fpl*. ● *vt* (*pt* **gritted**) echar arena en *<road>*. **~ one's teeth** (fig) acorazarse

groan /grəʊn/ *vi* gemir. ● *n* gemido *m*

grocer /'grəʊsə(r)/ *n* tendero *m*, abarrotero *m* (Mex). **~ies** *npl* comestibles *mpl*. **~y** *n* tienda *f* de comestibles, tienda *f* de abarrotes (Mex)

groggy /'grɒgɪ/ *a* (weak) débil; (unsteady) inseguro; (ill) malucho

groin /grɔɪn/ *n* ingle *f*

groom /gru:m/ *n* mozo *m* de caballos; (bridegroom) novio *m*. ● *vt* almohazar *<horses>*; (fig) preparar

groove /gru:v/ *n* ranura *f*; (in record) surco *m*

grope /grəʊp/ *vi* (find one's way) moverse a tientas. **~ for** buscar a tientas

gross /grəʊs/ *a* (**-er, -est**) (coarse) grosero; (Com) bruto; (fat) grueso; (flagrant) flagrante. ● *n invar* gruesa *f*. **~ly** *adv* (very) enormemente

grotesque /grəʊ'tesk/ *a* grotesco

ground /graʊnd/ ⇒GRIND. ● *n* suelo *m*; (area) terreno *m*; (reason) razón *f*; (Amer, Elec) toma *f* de tierra. ● *vt* fundar *<theory>*; retirar del servicio *<aircraft>*. **~s** *npl* jardines *mpl*; (sediment) poso *m*. **~ beef** *n* (Amer) carne *f* picada, carne *f* molida. **~ cloth** *n* (Amer) ⇒SHEET. **~ floor** *n* planta *f* baja. **~ing** *n* base *f*, conocimientos *mpl* (in de). **~less** *a* infundado. **~sheet** *n* suelo *m* impermeable (de una tienda de campaña). **~work** *n* trabajo *m* preparatorio

group /gru:p/ *n* grupo *m*. ● *vt* agrupar. ● *vi* agruparse

grouse /graʊs/ *n invar* (bird) urogallo *m*. ● *vi* 🄸 rezongar

grovel /'grɒvl/ *vi* (*pt* **grovelled**) postrarse; (fig) arrastrarse

grow /grəʊ/ *vi* (*pt* **grew**, *pp* **grown**) crecer; (become) volverse, ponerse. ● *vt* cultivar. **~ a beard** dejarse (crecer) la barba. □ **~ up** *vi* hacerse ma-

yor. **~ing** *a* *<quantity>* cada vez mayor; *<influence>* creciente

growl /graʊl/ *vi* gruñir. ● *n* gruñido *m*

grown /grəʊn/ ⇒GROW. ● *a* adulto. **~-up** *a* & *n* adulto (*m*)

growth /grəʊθ/ *n* crecimiento *m*; (increase) aumento *m*; (development) desarrollo *m*; (Med) bulto *m*, tumor *m*

grub /grʌb/ *n* (larva) larva *f*; (🄸, food) comida *f*

grubby /'grʌbɪ/ *a* (**-ier, -iest**) mugriento

grudg|e /grʌdʒ/ *vt* ⇒BEGRUDGE. ● *n* rencilla *f*. **bear/have a ~e against s.o.** guardarle rencor a uno. **~ingly** *adv* de mala gana

gruelling /'gru:əlɪŋ/ *a* agotador

gruesome /'gru:səm/ *a* horrible

gruff /grʌf/ *a* (**-er, -est**) *<manners>* brusco; *<voice>* ronco

grumble /'grʌmbl/ *vi* rezongar

grumpy /'grʌmpɪ/ *a* (**-ier, -iest**) malhumorado

grunt /grʌnt/ *vi* gruñir. ● *n* gruñido *m*

guarant|ee /gærən'ti:/ *n* garantía *f*. ● *vt* garantizar. **~or** *n* garante *m* & *f*

guard /gɑ:d/ *vt* proteger; (watch) vigilar. ● *n* (vigilance, Mil group) guardia *f*; (person) guardia *m*; (on train) jefe *m* de tren. □ **~ against** *vt* evitar; protegerse contra *<risk>*. **~ed** *a* cauteloso. **~ian** /-ɪən/ *n* guardián *m*; (of orphan) tutor *m*

Guatemala /gwɑ:tə'mɑ:lə/ *n* Guatemala *f*. **~n** *a* & *n* guatemalteco (*m*)

guer(r)illa /gə'rɪlə/ *n* guerrillero *m*. **~ warfare** *n* guerrilla *f*

guess /ges/ *vt* adivinar; (Amer, suppose) suponer. ● *n* conjetura *f*. **~work** *n* conjeturas *fpl*

guest /gest/ *n* invitado *m*; (in hotel) huésped *m*. **~house** *n* casa *f* de huéspedes

guffaw /gʌ'fɔ:/ *n* carcajada *f*. ● *vi* reírse a carcajadas

guidance /'gaɪdəns/ *n* (advice) consejos *mpl*; (information) información *f*

guide /gaɪd/ *n* (person) guía *m* & *f*; (book) guía *f*. **Girl G~** exploradora *f*, guía f. ● vt guiar. ~book n guía f. ~dog n perro m guía, perro m lazarillo. ~d missile n proyectil m teledirigido. ~lines npl pauta f

guild /gɪld/ n gremio m

guile /gaɪl/ n astucia f

guillotine /'gɪlətiːn/ n guillotina f

guilt /gɪlt/ n culpa f; (Jurid) culpabilidad f. ~y a culpable

guinea pig /'gɪnɪ/ n (also fig) cobaya f

guitar /gɪ'tɑː(r)/ n guitarra f. ~ist n guitarrista m & f

gulf /gʌlf/ n (part of sea) golfo m; (gap) abismo m

gull /gʌl/ n gaviota f

gullet /'gʌlɪt/ n garganta f, gaznate m Ⓣ

gullible /'gʌləbl/ a crédulo

gully /'gʌlɪ/ n (ravine) barranco m

gulp /gʌlp/ vt. □ ~ (down) tragarse de prisa. ● vi tragar saliva. ● n trago m

gum /gʌm/ n (Anat) encía f; (glue) goma f de pegar; (for chewing) chicle m. ● vt (pt gummed) engomar

gun /gʌn/ n (pistol) pistola f; (rifle) fusil m, escopeta f; (artillery piece) cañón m. ● vt (pt gunned). □ ~ down vt abatir a tiros. ~fire n tiros mpl

gun: ~man /-mən/ n pistolero m, gatillero m (Mex). ~powder n pólvora f. ~shot n disparo m

gurgle /'gɜːgl/ vi <liquid> gorgotear; <baby> gorjear

gush /gʌʃ/ vi. ~ (out) salir a borbotones. ● n (of liquid) chorro m; (fig) torrente m

gusset /'gʌsɪt/ n entretela f

gust /gʌst/ n ráfaga f

gusto /'gʌstəʊ/ n entusiasmo m

gusty /'gʌstɪ/ a borrascoso

gut /gʌt/ n intestino m. ● vt (pt gutted) destripar; <fire> destruir. ~s npl tripas fpl; (Ⓣ, courage) agallas fpl

gutter /'gʌtə(r)/ n (on roof) canalón m, canaleta f; (in street) cuneta f; (fig, ✕) arroyo m

guttural /'gʌtərəl/ a gutural

guy /gaɪ/ n (Ⓣ, man) tipo m Ⓣ, tío m Ⓣ

guzzle /'gʌzl/ vt (drink) chupar Ⓣ; (eat) tragarse

gym /dʒɪm/ n Ⓣ (gymnasium) gimnasio m; (gymnastics) gimnasia f

gymnasium /dʒɪm'neɪzɪəm/ n gimnasio m

gymnast /'dʒɪmnæst/ n gimnasta m & f. ~ics /dʒɪm'næstɪks/ npl gimnasia f

gymslip /'dʒɪmslɪp/ n túnica f (de gimnasia)

gynaecolog|ist /gaɪnɪ'kɒlədʒɪst/ n ginecólogo m. ~y n ginecología f

gypsy /'dʒɪpsɪ/ n gitano m

gyrate /dʒaɪə'reɪt/ vi girar

Hh

haberdashery /'hæbədæʃərɪ/ n mercería f; (Amer, clothes) ropa f y accesorios mpl para caballeros

habit /'hæbɪt/ n costumbre f; (Relig, costume) hábito m. be in the ~ of (+ gerund) tener la costumbre de (+ infinitivo), soler (+ infinitivo). get into the ~ of (+ gerund) acostumbrarse a (+ infinitivo)

habitable /'hæbɪtəbl/ a habitable

habitat /'hæbɪtæt/ n hábitat m

habitation /hæbɪ'teɪʃn/ n habitación f

habitual /hə'bɪtjʊəl/ a habitual; <liar> inveterado. ~ly adv de costumbre

hack /hæk/ n (old horse) jamelgo m; (writer) escritorzuelo m. ● vt cortar. ~er n (Comp) pirata m informático

hackneyed /'hæknɪd/ a manido

had /hæd/ ⇒HAVE

haddock /'hædək/ n invar eglefino m

haemorrhage /'hemərɪdʒ/ n hemorragia f

haemorrhoids /'hemərɔɪdz/ npl hemorroides fpl

hag /hæg/ n bruja f

haggard /'hægəd/ a demacrado

hail /heɪl/ *n* granizo *m*. ● *vi* granizar. ● *vt* (greet) saludar; llamar *<taxi>*. □ ~ **from** *vt* venir de. ~**stone** *n* grano *m* de granizo

hair /heə(r)/ *n* pelo *m*. ~**band** *n* cinta *f*, banda *f* (Mex). ~**brush** *n* cepillo *m* (para el pelo). ~**cut** *n* corte *m* de pelo. **have a** ~**cut** cortarse el pelo. ~**do** *n* 🆃 peinado *m*. ~**dresser** *n* peluquero *m*. ~**dresser's** (**shop**) *n* peluquería *f*. ~**dryer** *n* secador *m*, secadora *f* (Mex). ~**grip** *n* horquilla *f*, pasador *m* (Mex). ~**pin** *n* horquilla *f*. ~**pin bend** *n* curva *f* cerrada. ~**raising** *a* espeluznante. ~**spray** *n* laca *f*, fijador *m* (para el pelo). ~**style** *n* peinado *m*. ~**y** *a* (**-ier, -iest**) peludo

half /hɑːf/ *n* (*pl* **halves**) mitad *f*. ● *a* medio. ~ **a dozen** media docena *f*. ~ **an hour** media hora *f*. ● *adv* medio, a medias. ~**hearted** /-'hɑːtɪd/ *a* poco entusiasta. ~**mast** /-'mɑːst/ *n*. **at** ~**mast** a media asta. ~ **term** *n* vacaciones *fpl* de medio trimestre. ~**time** *n* (Sport) descanso *m*, medio tiempo *m* (LAm). ~**way** *a* medio. ● *adv* a medio camino

hall /hɔːl/ *n* (entrance) vestíbulo *m*; (for public events) sala *f*, salón *m*. ~ **of residence** residencia *f* universitaria, colegio *m* mayor. ~**mark** /-mɑːk/ *n* (on gold, silver) contraste *m*; (fig) sello *m* (distintivo)

hallo /həˈləʊ/ *int* ⇒HELLO

Hallowe'en /ˈhæləʊˈiːn/ *n* víspera *f* de Todos los Santos

hallucination /həluːsɪˈneɪʃn/ *n* alucinación *f*

halo /ˈheɪləʊ/ *n* (*pl* **-oes**) aureola *f*

halt /hɔːlt/ *n*. **come to a** ~ pararse. ● *vt* parar. ● *vi* pararse

halve /hɑːv/ *vt* reducir a la mitad; (divide into halves) partir por la mitad

halves /hɑːvz/ ⇒HALF

ham /hæm/ *n* jamón *m*

hamburger /ˈhæmbɜːgə(r)/ *n* hamburguesa *f*

hammer /ˈhæmə(r)/ *n* martillo *m*. ● *vt* martill(e)ar

hammock /ˈhæmək/ *n* hamaca *f*

hamper /ˈhæmpə(r)/ *n* cesta *f*. ● *vt* estorbar

hamster /ˈhæmstə(r)/ *n* hámster *m*

hand /hænd/ *n* mano *f*; (of clock, watch) manecilla *f*; (worker) obrero *m*. **by** ~ a mano. **lend a** ~ echar una mano. **on** ~ a mano. **on the one** ~... **on the other** ~ por un lado... por otro. **out of** ~ fuera de control. **to** ~ a mano. ● *vt* pasar. □ ~ **down** *vt* pasar. □ ~ **in** *vt* entregar. □ ~ **over** *vt* entregar. □ ~ **out** *vt* distribuir. ~**bag** *n* bolso *m*, cartera *f* (LAm), bolsa *f* (Mex). ~**brake** *n* (in car) freno *m* de mano. ~**cuffs** *npl* esposas *fpl*. ~**ful** *n* puñado *m*; ((🆃), person) persona *f* difícil

handicap /ˈhændɪkæp/ *n* desventaja *f*; (Sport) hándicap *m*. ~**ped** *a* minusválido

handicraft /ˈhændɪkrɑːft/ *n* artesanía *f*

handkerchief /ˈhæŋkətʃɪf/ *n* (*pl* **-fs** *or* **-chieves** /-'tʃiːvz/) pañuelo *m*

handle /ˈhændl/ *n* (of door) picaporte *m*; (of drawer) tirador *m*; (of implement) mango *m*; (of cup, bag, jug) asa *f*. ● *vt* manejar; (touch) tocar. ~**bars** *npl* manillar *m*, manubrio *m* (LAm).

hand: ~**out** *n* folleto *m*; (of money, food) dádiva *f*. ~**shake** *n* apretón *m* de manos

handsome /ˈhænsəm/ *a* (good-looking) guapo, buen mozo, buena moza (LAm); (generous) generoso

handwriting /ˈhændraɪtɪŋ/ *n* letra *f*

handy /ˈhændɪ/ *a* (**-ier, -iest**) (useful) práctico; *<person>* diestro; (near) a mano. **come in** ~ venir muy bien. ~**man** *n* hombre *m* habilidoso

hang /hæŋ/ *vt* (*pt* **hung**) colgar; (*pt* **hanged**) (capital punishment) ahorcar. ● *vi* colgar; *<clothing>* caer. ● *n*. **get the** ~ **of sth** coger el truco de algo. □ ~ **about**, ~ **around** *vi* holgazanear. □ ~ **on** *vi* (wait) esperar. □ ~ **out** *vt* tender *<washing>*. □ ~ **up** *vi* (also telephone) colgar

hangar /ˈhæŋə(r)/ *n* hangar *m*

hang: ~**er** *n* (for clothes) percha *f*. ~**glider** *n* alta *f* delta, deslizador *m* (Mex). ~**over** (after drinking) resaca *f*. ~**up** *n* 🆃 complejo *m*

hankie, hanky /ˈhæŋkɪ/ *n* 🆃 pañuelo *m*

haphazard /hæp'hæzəd/ *a* fortuito. ~**ly** *adv* al azar

happen /'hæpən/ *vi* pasar, suceder, ocurrir. **if he** ~**s to come** si acaso viene. ~**ing** *n* acontecimiento *m*

happ|ily /'hæpɪlɪ/ *adv* alegremente; (fortunately) afortunadamente. ~**i-ness** *n* felicidad *f*. ~**y** *a* (**-ier, -iest**) feliz; (satisfied) contento

harass /'hærəs/ *vt* acosar. ~**ment** *n* acoso *m*

harbour /'hɑ:bə(r)/ *n* puerto *m*

hard /hɑ:d/ *a* (**-er, -est**) duro; (difficult) difícil. ● *adv* <*work*> mucho; (pull) con fuerza. ~ **done by** tratado injustamente. ~**-boiled egg** /-'bɔɪld/ *n* huevo *m* duro. ~ **disk** *n* disco *m* duro. ~**en** *vt* endurecer. ● *vi* endurecerse. ~**-headed** /-'hedɪd/ *a* realista

hardly /'hɑ:dlɪ/ *adv* apenas. ~ **ever** casi nunca

hard: ~**ness** *n* dureza *f*. ~**ship** *n* apuro *m*. ~ **shoulder** *n* arcén *m*, acotamiento *m* (Mex). ~**ware** *n* /-weə(r)/ ferretería *f*; (Comp) hardware *m*. ~**ware store** *n* (Amer) ferretería *f*. ~**-working** /-'wɜ:kɪŋ/ *a* trabajador

hardy /'hɑ:dɪ/ *a* (**-ier, -iest**) fuerte; (Bot) resistente

hare /heə(r)/ *n* liebre *f*

hark /hɑ:k/ *vi* escuchar. □ ~ **back to** *vt* volver a

harm /hɑ:m/ *n* daño *m*. **there is no** ~ **in asking** con preguntar no se pierde nada. ● *vt* hacer daño a <*person*>; dañar <*thing*>; perjudicar <*interests*>. ~**ful** *a* perjudicial. ~**less** *a* inofensivo

harmonica /hɑ:'mɒnɪkə/ *n* armónica *f*

harmon|ious /hɑ:'məʊnɪəs/ *a* armonioso. ~**y** /'hɑ:mənɪ/ *n* armonía *f*

harness /'hɑ:nɪs/ *n* arnés *m*. ● *vt* poner el arnés a <*horse*>; (fig) aprovechar

harp /hɑ:p/ *n* arpa *f*. ● *vi*. ~ **on** (**about**) machacar (con)

harpoon /hɑ:'pu:n/ *n* arpón *m*

harpsichord /'hɑ:psɪkɔ:d/ *n* clavicémbalo *m*, clave *m*

harrowing /'hærəʊɪŋ/ *a* desgarrador

harsh /hɑ:ʃ/ *a* (**-er, -est**) duro, severo; <*light*> fuerte; <*climate*> riguroso. ~**ly** *adv* severamente. ~**ness** *n* severidad *f*

harvest /'hɑ:vɪst/ *n* cosecha *f*. ● *vt* cosechar

has /hæz/ ⇒HAVE

hassle /'hæsl/ *n* 🔢 lío *m* 🔢, rollo *m* 🔢. ● *vt* (harass) fastidiar

hast|e /heɪst/ *n* prisa *f*, apuro *m* (LAm). **make** ~**e** darse prisa. ~**ily** /'heɪstɪlɪ/ *adv* de prisa. ~**y** /'heɪstɪ/ *a* (**-ier, -iest**) rápido; (rash) precipitado

hat /hæt/ *n* sombrero *m*

hatch /hætʃ/ *n* (for food) ventanilla *f*; (Naut) escotilla *f*. ● *vt* empollar <*eggs*>; tramar <*plot*>. ● *vi* salir del cascarón. ~**back** *n* coche *m* con tres/cinco puertas; (door) puerta *f* trasera

hatchet /'hætʃɪt/ *n* hacha *f*

hat|e /heɪt/ *n* odio *m*. ● *vt* odiar. ~**eful** *a* odioso. ~**red** /'heɪtrɪd/ *n* odio *m*

haughty /'hɔ:tɪ/ *a* (**-ier, -iest**) altivo

haul /hɔ:l/ *vt* arrastrar; transportar <*goods*>. ● *n* (catch) redada *f*; (stolen goods) botín *m*; (journey) recorrido *m*. ~**age** /-ɪdʒ/ *n* transporte *m*. ~**er** (Amer), ~**ier** *n* transportista *m* & *f*

haunt /hɔ:nt/ *vt* frecuentar; <*ghost*> rondar. ● *n* sitio *m* preferido. ~**ed** *a* <*house*> embrujado; <*look*> angustiado

....

have /hæv/, *unstressed forms* /həv, əv/

3rd pers sing present **has**; past **had**

● *transitive verb*

····▸ tener. **I** ~ **three sisters** tengo tres hermanas. **do you** ~ **a credit card?** ¿tiene una tarjeta de crédito?

····▸ (in requests) **can I** ~ **a kilo of apples, please?** ¿me da un kilo de manzanas, por favor?

····▸ (eat) comer. **I had a pizza** comí una pizza

⋯➤ (drink) tomar. **come and ∼ a drink** ven a tomar una copa

⋯➤ (smoke) fumar <*cigarette*>

⋯➤ (hold, organize) hacer <*party, meeting*>

⋯➤ (get, receive) **I had a letter from Tony yesterday** recibí una carta de Tony ayer. **we've had no news of her** no hemos tenido noticias suyas

⋯➤ (illness) tener <*flu, headache*>. **to ∼ a cold** estar resfriado, tener catarro

⋯➤ **to have sth done: we had it painted** lo hicimos pintar. **I had my hair cut** me corté el pelo

⋯➤ **to have it in for s.o.** tenerle manía a uno

● *auxiliary verb*

⋯➤ haber. **I've seen her already** ya la he visto, ya la vi (LAm)

⋯➤ **to have just done sth** acabar de hacer algo. **I've just seen her** acabo de verla

⋯➤ **to have to do sth** tener que hacer algo. **I ∼ to** *or* **I've got to go to the bank** tengo que ir al banco

⋯➤ (in tag questions) **you've met her, ∼n't you?** ya la conoces, ¿no? *or* ¿verdad? *or* ¿no es cierto?

⋯➤ (in short answers) **you've forgotten something - have I?** has olvidado algo - ¿sí?

haven /'heɪvn/ *n* puerto *m*; (refuge) refugio *m*

haversack /'hævəsæk/ *n* mochila *f*

havoc /'hævək/ *n* estragos *mpl*

hawk /hɔːk/ *n* halcón *m*

hawthorn /'hɔːθɔːn/ *n* espino *m*

hay /heɪ/ *n* heno *m*. **∼ fever** *n* fiebre *f* del heno. **∼stack** *n* almiar *m*. **∼wire** *a.* **go ∼wire** (plans) desorganizarse; <*machine*> estropearse

hazard /'hæzəd/ *n* riesgo *m*. **∼ous** *a* arriesgado

haze /heɪz/ *n* neblina *f*

hazel /'heɪzl/ *n* avellano *m*. **∼nut** *n* avellana *f*

hazy /'heɪzɪ/ *a* (**-ier, -iest**) nebuloso

he /hiː/ *pron* él

head /hed/ *n* cabeza *f*; (of family, government) jefe *m*; (of organization) director *m*; (of beer) espuma *f*. **∼s or**

tails cara o cruz. ● *a* principal. ● *vt* encabezar, cabecear <*ball*>. □ **∼ for** *vt* dirigirse a. **∼ache** *n* dolor *m* de cabeza. **∼er** *n* (football) cabezazo *m*. **∼first** /-'fɜːst/ *adv* de cabeza. **∼ing** *n* título *m*, encabezamiento *m*. **∼lamp** *n* faro *m*, foco *m* (LAm). **∼land** /-lənd/ *n* promontorio *m*. **∼line** *n* titular *m*. **the news ∼lines** el resumen informativo. **∼long** *adv* de cabeza; (precipitately) precipitadamente. **∼master** *n* director *m*. **∼mistress** *n* directora *f*. **∼on** /-'ɒn/ *a & adv* de frente. **∼phones** *npl* auriculares *mpl*, cascos *mpl*. **∼quarters** /-'kwɔːtəz/ *n* (of business) oficina *f* central; (Mil) cuartel *m* general. **∼strong** *a* testarudo. **∼teacher** /-'tiːtʃə(r)/ *n* director *m*. **∼y** *a* (**-ier, -iest**) <*scent*> embriagador

heal /hiːl/ *vt* curar. ● *vi* cicatrizarse

health /helθ/ *n* salud *f*. **∼y** *a* sano

heap /hiːp/ *n* montón *m*. ● *vt* amontonar.

hear /hɪə(r)/ *vt/i* (*pt* **heard** /hɜːd/) oír. **∼, ∼!** ¡bravo! **∼ about** oír hablar de. **∼ from** recibir noticias de. **∼ing** *n* oído *m*; (Jurid) vista *f*. **∼ing-aid** *n* audífono *m*. **∼say** *n* rumores *mpl*

hearse /hɜːs/ *n* coche *m* fúnebre

heart /hɑːt/ *n* corazón *m*. **at ∼** en el fondo. **by ∼** de memoria. **lose ∼** descorazonarse. **∼ache** *n* congoja *f*. **∼ attack** *n* ataque *m* al corazón, infarto *m*. **∼break** *n* congoja *f*. **∼breaking** *a* desgarrador. **∼burn** *n* ardor *m* de estómago. **∼felt** *a* sincero

hearth /hɑːθ/ *n* hogar *m*

heart: ∼ily *adv* de buena gana. **∼less** *a* cruel. **∼y** *a* (welcome) caluroso; <*meal*> abundante

heat /hiːt/ *n* calor *m*; (contest) (prueba *f*) eliminatoria *f*. ● *vt* calentar. ● *vi* calentarse. **∼ed** *a* (fig) acalorado. **∼er** *n* calentador *m*

heath /hiːθ/ *n* brezal *m*, monte *m*

heathen /'hiːðn/ *n & a* pagano (*m*)

heather /'heðə(r)/ *n* brezo *m*

heat: ∼ing *n* calefacción *f*. **∼stroke** *n* insolación *f*. **∼wave** *n* ola *f* de calor

heave /hiːv/ *vt* (lift) levantar; exhalar <*sigh*>; (⬚, throw) tirar. ● *vi* (pull) tirar, jalar (LAm); (⬚, retch) dar arcadas

heaven /'hevn/ *n* cielo *m*. ~**ly** *a* celestial; (astronomy) celeste; (⬚, excellent) divino

heav|ily /'hevɪlɪ/ *adv* pesadamente; (smoke, drink) mucho. ~**y** *a* (**-ier**, **-iest**) pesado; <*rain*> fuerte; <*traffic*> denso. ~**yweight** *n* peso *m* pesado

heckle /'hekl/ *vt* interrumpir

hectic /'hektɪk/ *a* febril

he'd /hiːd/ = **he had**, **he would**

hedge /hedʒ/ *n* seto *m* (vivo). ● *vi* escaparse por la tangente. ~**hog** *n* erizo *m*

heed /hiːd/ *vt* hacer caso de. ● *n*. take ~ tener cuidado

heel /hiːl/ *n* talón *m*; (of shoe) tacón *m*

hefty /'heftɪ/ *a* (**-ier**, **-iest**) (sturdy) fuerte; (heavy) pesado

heifer /'hefə(r)/ *n* novilla *f*

height /haɪt/ *n* altura *f*; (of person) estatura *f*; (of fame, glory) cumbre *f*. ~**en** *vt* elevar; (fig) aumentar

heir /eə(r)/ *n* heredero *m*. ~**ess** *n* heredera *f*. ~**loom** *n* reliquia *f* heredada

held /held/ ⇨HOLD

helicopter /'helɪkɒptə(r)/ *n* helicóptero *m*

hell /hel/ *n* infierno *m*

he'll /hiːl/ = **he will**

hello /hə'ləʊ/ *int* ¡hola!; (Telephone, caller) ¡oiga!, ¡bueno! (Mex); (Telephone, person answering) ¡diga!, ¡bueno! (Mex). say ~ to saludar

helm /helm/ *n* (Naut) timón *m*

helmet /'helmɪt/ *n* casco *m*

help /help/ *vt/i* ayudar. he cannot ~ laughing no puede menos de reír. ~ o.s. to servirse. it cannot be ~ed no hay más remedio. ● *n* ayuda *f*. ● *int* ¡socorro! ~**er** *n* ayudante *m*. ~**ful** *a* útil; <*person*> amable. ~**ing** *n* porción *f*. ~**less** *a* (unable to manage) incapaz; (defenceless) indefenso

hem /hem/ *n* dobladillo *m*

hemisphere /'hemɪsfɪə(r)/ *n* hemisferio *m*

hen /hen/ *n* (chicken) gallina *f*; (female bird) hembra *f*

hence /hens/ *adv* de aquí. ~**forth** *adv* de ahora en adelante

henpecked /'henpekt/ *a* dominado por su mujer

her /hɜː(r)/ *pron* (direct object) la; (indirect object) le; (*after prep*) ella. I know ~ la conozco. ● *a* su, sus *pl*

herb /hɜːb/ *n* hierba *f*. ~**al** *a* de hierbas

herd /hɜːd/ *n* (of cattle, pigs) manada *f*; (of goats) rebaño *m*. ● *vt* arrear. ~ **together** reunir

here /hɪə(r)/ *adv* aquí, acá (esp LAm). ~! (take this) ¡tenga! ~**abouts** /-ə'baʊts/ *adv* por aquí. ~**after** /-'ɑːftə(r)/ *adv* en el futuro. ~**by** /-'baɪ/ *adv* por este medio

heredit|ary /hɪ'redɪtərɪ/ *a* hereditario

here|sy /'herəsɪ/ *n* herejía *f*. ~**tic** *n* hereje *m* & *f*

herewith /hɪə'wɪð/ *adv* adjunto

heritage /'herɪtɪdʒ/ *n* herencia *f*; (fig) patrimonio *m*

hermetically /hɜː'metɪklɪ/ *adv*. ~ **sealed** herméticamente cerrado

hermit /'hɜːmɪt/ *n* ermitaño *m*, eremita *m*

hernia /'hɜːnɪə/ *n* hernia *f*

hero /'hɪərəʊ/ *n* (*pl* **-oes**) héroe *m*. ~**ic** /hɪ'rəʊɪk/ *a* heroico

heroin /'herəʊɪn/ *n* heroína *f*

hero: ~**ine** /'herəʊɪn/ *n* heroína *f*. ~**ism** /'herəʊɪzm/ *n* heroismo *m*

heron /'herən/ *n* garza *f* (real)

herring /'herɪŋ/ *n* arenque *m*

hers /hɜːz/ *poss pron* (el) suyo *m*, (la) suya *f*, (los) suyos *mpl*, (las) suyas *fpl*

herself /hɜː'self/ *pron* ella misma; (*reflexive*) se; (*after prep*) sí misma

he's /hiːz/ = **he is**, **he has**

hesit|ant /'hezɪtənt/ *a* vacilante. ~**ate** /-teɪt/ *vi* vacilar. ~**ation** /-'teɪʃn/ *n* vacilación *f*

heterosexual /hetərəʊ'seksjʊəl/ *a* & *n* heterosexual (*m* & *f*)

het up /het'ʌp/ *a* ⬚ nervioso

hew /hjuː/ *vt* (*pp* **hewed** or **hewn**) cortar; (cut into shape) tallar

hexagon /'heksəgən/ n hexágono m. ~al /-'ægənl/ a hexagonal

hey /heɪ/ int ¡eh!; (expressing dismay, protest) ¡oye!

heyday /'heɪdeɪ/ n apogeo m

hi /haɪ/ int Ⓣ ¡hola!

hibernat|e /'haɪbəneɪt/ vi hibernar. ~ion /-'neɪʃn/ n hibernación f

hiccough, hiccup /'hɪkʌp/ n hipo m. have (the) ~s tener hipo. ● vi hipar

hide /haɪd/ vt (pt hid, pp hidden) esconder. ● vi esconderse. ● n piel f; (tanned) cuero m. ~-and-seek /'haɪdnsiːk/ n. play ~-and-seek jugar al escondite, jugar a las escondidas (LAm)

hideous /'hɪdɪəs/ a (dreadful) horrible; (ugly) feo

hideout /'haɪdaʊt/ n escondrijo m

hiding /'haɪdɪŋ/ n (Ⓣ, thrashing) paliza f. go into ~ esconderse. ~ place n escondite m, escondrijo m

hierarchy /'haɪərɑːkɪ/ n jerarquía f

hieroglyphics /haɪərə'glɪfɪks/ n jeroglíficos mpl

hi-fi /'haɪfaɪ/ a de alta fidelidad. ● n equipo m de alta fidelidad, hi-fi m

high /haɪ/ a (-er, -est) alto; <ideals> elevado; <wind> fuerte; (Ⓣ, drugged) drogado, colocado Ⓣ; <voice> agudo; <meat> pasado. ● n alto nivel m. a (new) ~ un récord. ● adv alto. ~er education n enseñanza f superior. ~-handed /-'hændɪd/ a prepotente. ~ heels npl zapatos mpl de tacón alto. ~lands /-ləndz/ npl tierras fpl altas. ~-level a de alto nivel. ~light n punto m culminante. ● vt destacar; (Art) realzar. ~ly adv muy; <paid> muy bien. ~ly strung a nervioso. H~ness n (title) alteza f. ~-rise a <building> alto. ~ school n (Amer) instituto m, colegio m secundario. ~ street n calle f principal. ~-strung a (Amer) nervioso. ~way n carretera f

hijack /'haɪdʒæk/ vt secuestrar. ● n secuestro m. ~er n secuestrador

hike /haɪk/ n caminata f. ● vi ir de caminata. ~r n excursionista m & f

hilarious /hɪ'leərɪəs/ a muy divertido

hill /hɪl/ n colina f; (slope) cuesta f. ~side n ladera f. ~y a accidentado

hilt /hɪlt/ n (of sword) puño m. to the ~ (fig) totalmente

him /hɪm/ pron (direct object) lo, le (only Spain); (indirect object) le; (after prep) él. I know ~ lo/le conozco. ~self pron él mismo; (reflexive) se; (after prep) sí mismo

hind|er /'hɪndə(r)/ vt estorbar. ~rance /'hɪndrəns/ n obstáculo m

hindsight /'haɪnsaɪt/ n. with ~ retrospectivamente

Hindu /'hɪnduː/ n & a hindú (m & f). ~ism n hinduismo m

hinge /hɪndʒ/ n bisagra f

hint /hɪnt/ n indirecta f; (advice) consejo m. ● vi soltar una indirecta. ~ at dar a entender

hip /hɪp/ n cadera f

hippie /'hɪpɪ/ n hippy m & f

hippopotamus /hɪpə'pɒtəməs/ n (pl -muses or -mi /-maɪ/) hipopótamo m

hire /haɪə(r)/ vt alquilar <thing>; contratar <person>. ● n alquiler m. car ~ alquiler m de coches. ~ purchase n compra f a plazos

his /hɪz/ a su, sus pl. ● poss pron (el) suyo m, (la) suya f, (los) suyos mpl, (las) suyas fpl

Hispan|ic /hɪ'spænɪk/ a hispánico. ● n (Amer) hispano m. ~ist /'hɪspənɪst/ n hispanista m & f

hiss /hɪs/ n silbido. ● vt/i silbar

histor|ian /hɪ'stɔːrɪən/ n historiador m. ~ic(al) /hɪ'stɒrɪkl/ a histórico. ~y /'hɪstərɪ/ n historia f.

hit /hɪt/ vt (pt hit, pres p hitting) golpear <object>; pegarle a <person>; (collide with) chocar con; (affect) afectar. ~ it off with hacer buenas migas con. □ ~ on vt dar con. ● n (blow) golpe m; (success) éxito m

hitch /hɪtʃ/ vt (fasten) enganchar. ● n (snag) problema m. ~ a lift, ~ a ride (Amer) ⇒~HIKE. ~hike vi hacer autostop, hacer dedo, ir de aventón (Mex). ~hiker n autoestopista m & f

hither /'hɪðə(r)/ adv aquí, acá. ~ and thither acá y allá. ~to adv hasta ahora

hit-or-miss /hɪtɔː'mɪs/ a <approach> poco científico

hive /haɪv/ n colmena f

hoard /hɔːd/ vt acumular. ● n provisión f; (of money) tesoro m

hoarding /'hɔːdɪŋ/ n valla f publicitaria

hoarse /hɔːs/ a (-er, -est) ronco. ~ly adv con voz ronca

hoax /həʊks/ n engaño m. ● vt engañar

hob /hɒb/ n (of cooker) hornillos mpl, hornillas fpl (LAm)

hobble /'hɒbl/ vi cojear, renguear (LAm)

hobby /'hɒbɪ/ n pasatiempo m. ~horse n (toy) caballito m (de niño); (fixation) caballo m de batalla

hockey /'hɒkɪ/ n hockey m; (Amer) hockey m sobre hielo

hoe /həʊ/ n azada f. ● vt (pres p hoeing) azadonar

hog /hɒg/ n (Amer) cerdo m. ● vt (pt hogged) Ⅱ acaparar

hoist /hɔɪst/ vt levantar; izar <flag>. ● n montacargas m

hold /həʊld/ vt (pt held) tener; (grasp) coger (esp Spain), agarrar; (contain) contener; mantener <interest>; (believe) creer. ● vi mantenerse. ● n (influence) influencia f; (Naut, Aviat) bodega f. get ~ of agarrar; (fig, acquire) adquirir. □ ~ **back** vt (contain) contener. □ ~ **on** vi (stand firm) resistir; (wait) esperar. □ ~ **on to** vt (keep) guardar; (cling to) agarrarse a. □ ~ **out** vt (offer) ofrecer. vi (resist) resistir. □ ~ **up** vt (raise) levantar; (support) sostener; (delay) retrasar; (rob) atracar. ~all n bolsa f (de viaje). ~er n tenedor m; (of post) titular m; (wallet) funda f. ~up atraco m

hole /həʊl/ n agujero m; (in ground) hoyo m; (in road) bache m. ● vt agujerear

holiday /'hɒlɪdeɪ/ n vacaciones fpl; (public) fiesta f. go on ~ ir de vacaciones. ~maker n veraneante m & f

holiness /'həʊlɪnɪs/ n santidad f

Holland /'hɒlənd/ n Holanda f

hollow /'hɒləʊ/ a & n hueco (m)

holly /'hɒlɪ/ n acebo m

holocaust /'hɒləkɔːst/ n holocausto m

holster /'həʊlstə(r)/ n pistolera f

holy /'həʊlɪ/ a (-ier, -iest) santo, sagrado. H~ **Ghost** n, H~ **Spirit** n Espíritu m Santo. ~ **water** n agua f bendita

homage /'hɒmɪdʒ/ n homenaje m. pay ~ to rendir homenaje a

home /həʊm/ n casa f; (for old people) residencia f de ancianos; (native land) patria f. ● a <cooking> casero; (address) particular; <background> familiar; (Pol) interior; <match> de casa. ● adv. (at) ~ en casa. ~land n patria f. ~less a sin hogar. ~ly a (-ier, -iest) casero; (Amer, ugly) feo. ~-made a hecho en casa. ~ **page** n (Comp) página f frontal. ~sick a. be ~sick echar de menos a su familia/su país, extrañar a su familia/su país (LAm). ~ **town** n ciudad f natal. ~work n deberes mpl

homicide /'hɒmɪsaɪd/ n homicidio m

homoeopathic /həʊmɪəʊ'pæθɪk/ a homeopático

homogeneous /hɒməʊ'dʒiːnɪəs/ a homogéneo

homosexual /həʊməʊ'seksjʊəl/ a & n homosexual (m)

honest /'ɒnɪst/ a honrado; (frank) sincero. ~ly adv honradamente. ~y n honradez f

honey /'hʌnɪ/ n miel f. ~comb n panal m. ~moon n luna f de miel. ~suckle n madreselva f

honorary /'ɒnərərɪ/ a honorario

honour /'ɒnə(r)/ n honor m. ● vt honrar; cumplir (con) <promise>. ~able a honorable

hood /hʊd/ n capucha f; (car roof) capota f; (Amer, car bonnet) capó m, capote m (Mex)

hoodwink /'hʊdwɪŋk/ vt engañar

hoof /huːf/ n (pl hoofs or hooves) (of horse) casco m, pezuña f (Mex); (of cow) pezuña f

hook /hʊk/ n gancho m; (on garment) corchete m; (for fishing) anzuelo m. let s.o. off the ~ dejar salir a uno del atolladero. off the ~ <telephone> descolgado. ● vt. ~ed on Ⅱ adicto a.

□ ~ **up** *vt* enganchar. ~**ed** *a* <*tool*> en forma de gancho; <*nose*> aguileño

hookey /'hʊkɪ/ *n*. **play** ~ (Amer Ⅱ) faltar a clase, hacer novillos

hooligan /'hu:lɪgən/ *n* vándalo *m*, gamberro *m*

hoop /hu:p/ *n* aro *m*

hooray /hʊ'reɪ/ *int* & *n* ¡viva! (*m*)

hoot /hu:t/ *n* (of horn) bocinazo *m*; (of owl) ululato *m*. ● *vi* tocar la bocina; <*owl*> ulular

Hoover /'hu:və(r)/ *n* (P) aspiradora *f*. ● *vt* pasar la aspiradora por, aspirar (LAm)

hooves /hu:vz/ ⇒HOOF

hop /hɒp/ *vi* (*pt* **hopped**) saltar a la pata coja; <*frog, rabbit*> brincar, saltar; <*bird*> dar saltitos. ● *n* salto *m*; (flight) etapa *f*. ~(**s**) (Bot) lúpulo *m*

hope /həʊp/ *n* esperanza *f*. ● *vt/i* esperar. ~ **for** esperar. ~**ful** *a* (optimistic) esperanzado; (promising) esperanzador. ~**fully** *adv* con optimismo; (it is hoped) se espera. ~**less** *a* desesperado

horde /hɔ:d/ *n* horda *f*

horizon /hə'raɪzn/ *n* horizonte *m*

horizontal /hɒrɪ'zɒntl/ *a* horizontal. ~**ly** *adv* horizontalmente

hormone /'hɔ:məʊn/ *n* hormona *f*

horn /hɔ:n/ *n* cuerno *m*, asta *f*, cacho *m* (LAm); (of car) bocina *f*; (Mus) trompa *f*. ~**ed** *a* con cuernos

hornet /'hɔ:nɪt/ *n* avispón *m*

horoscope /'hɒrəskəʊp/ *n* horóscopo *m*

horrible /'hɒrəbl/ *a* horrible

horrid /'hɒrɪd/ *a* horrible

horrific /hə'rɪfɪk/ *a* horroroso

horrify /'hɒrɪfaɪ/ *vt* horrorizar

horror /'hɒrə(r)/ *n* horror *m*

hors-d'oeuvre /ɔ:'dɜ:vr/ *n* (*pl* -**s** /-'dɜ:vr/ entremés *m*, botana *f* (Mex)

horse /hɔ:s/ *n* caballo *m*. ~**back** *n*. **on** ~**back** a caballo. ~**power** *n* (unit) caballo *m* (de fuerza). ~**racing** *n* carreras *fpl* de caballos. ~**shoe** *n* herradura *f*

horticultur|al /hɔ:tɪ'kʌltʃərəl/ *a* hortícola. ~**e** /'hɔ:tɪkʌltʃə(r)/ *n* horticultura *f*

hose /həʊz/ *n* manguera *f*, manga *f*. ● *vt*. ~ **down** lavar (con manguera). ~**pipe** *n* manga *f*

hosiery /'həʊzɪərɪ/ *n* calcetería *f*

hospice /'hɒspɪs/ *n* residencia *f* para enfermos desahuciados

hospitable /hɒ'spɪtəbl/ *a* hospitalario

hospital /'hɒspɪtl/ *n* hospital *m*

hospitality /hɒspɪ'tælətɪ/ *n* hospitalidad *f*

host /həʊst/ *n* (master of house) anfitrión *m*; (Radio, TV) presentador *m*; (multitude) gran cantidad *f*; (Relig) hostia *f*

hostage /'hɒstɪdʒ/ *n* rehén *m*

hostel /'hɒstl/ *n* (for students) residencia *f*; (for homeless people) hogar *m*

hostess /'həʊstɪs/ *n* anfitriona *f*

hostil|e /'hɒstaɪl/ *a* hostil. ~**ity** /-'tɪlətɪ/ *n* hostilidad *f*

hot /hɒt/ *a* (**hotter**, **hottest**) caliente; <*weather, day*> caluroso; <*climate*> cálido; (Culin) picante; <*news*> de última hora. **be/feel** ~ tener calor. **get** ~ calentarse. **it is** ~ hace calor. ~**bed** *n* (fig) semillero *m*

hotchpotch /'hɒtʃpɒtʃ/ *n* mezcolanza *f*

hot dog *n* perrito *m* caliente

hotel /həʊ'tel/ *n* hotel *m*. ~**ier** /-ɪeɪ/ *n* hotelero *m*

hot: ~**house** *n* invernadero *m*. ~**plate** *n* placa *f*, hornilla *f* (LAm). ~**-water bottle** /-'wɔ:tə(r)/ *n* bolsa *f* de agua caliente

hound /haʊnd/ *n* perro *m* de caza. ● *vt* perseguir

hour /aʊə(r)/ *n* hora *f*. ~**ly** *a* <*rate*> por hora. ● *adv* (every hour) cada hora; (by the hour) por hora

house /haʊs/ *n* (*pl* -**s** /'haʊzɪz/) casa *f*, (Pol) cámara *f*. ● /haʊz/ *vt* alojar; (keep) guardar. ~**hold** *n* casa *f*. ~**holder** *n* dueño *m* de una casa. ~**keeper** *n* ama *f* de llaves. ~**maid** *n* criada *f*, mucama *f* (LAm). ~**-proud** *a* meticuloso. ~**warming** (party) *n* fiesta de inauguración de una casa. ~**wife** *n* ama *f* de casa. ~**work** *n* tareas *fpl* domésticas

housing /'haʊzɪŋ/ n alojamiento m. ~ **development** (Amer), ~ **estate** n complejo m habitacional, urbanización f

hovel /'hɒvl/ n casucha f

hover /'hɒvə(r)/ vi <bird, threat etc> cernerse; (loiter) rondar. ~**craft** n (pl invar or -**crafts**) aerodeslizador m

how /haʊ/ adv cómo. ~ **about a walk?** ¿qué te parece si damos un paseo? ~ **are you?** ¿cómo está Vd? ~ **do you do?** (in introduction) mucho gusto. ~ **long?** (in time) ¿cuánto tiempo? ~ **long is the room?** ¿cuánto mide de largo el cuarto? ~ **often?** ¿cuántas veces?

however /haʊ'evə(r)/ adv (nevertheless) no obstante, sin embargo; (with verb) de cualquier manera que (+ subjunctive); (with adjective or adverb) por... que (+ subjunctive). ~ **much it rains** por mucho que llueva

howl /haʊl/ n aullido. ● vi aullar

hp abbr ⇒HORSEPOWER

HP abbr ⇒HIRE-PURCHASE

hub /hʌb/ n (of wheel) cubo m; (fig) centro m

hubcap /'hʌbkæp/ n tapacubos m

huddle /'hʌdl/ vi apiñarse

hue /hju:/ n (colour) color m

huff /hʌf/ n. be in a ~ estar enfurruñado

hug /hʌg/ vt (pt **hugged**) abrazar. ● n abrazo m

huge /hju:dʒ/ a enorme. ~**ly** adv enormemente

hulk /hʌlk/ n (of ship) barco m viejo

hull /hʌl/ n (of ship) casco m

hullo /hə'ləʊ/ int ⇒HELLO

hum /hʌm/ vt/i (pt **hummed**) <person> canturrear; <insect, engine> zumbar. ● n zumbido m

human /'hju:mən/ a & n humano (m). ~ **being** n ser m humano. ~**e** /hju:'meɪn/ a humano. ~**itarian** /hju:mænɪ'teərɪən/ a humanitario. ~**ity** /hju:'mænətɪ/ n humanidad f

humbl|e /'hʌmbl/ a (-**er**, -**est**) humilde. ● vt humillar. ~**y** adv humildemente

humdrum /'hʌmdrʌm/ a monótono

humid /'hju:mɪd/ a húmedo. ~**ity** /hju:'mɪdətɪ/ n humedad f

humiliat|e /hju:'mɪlɪeɪt/ vt humillar. ~**ion** /-'eɪʃn/ n humillación f

humility /hju:'mɪlətɪ/ n humildad f

humo|rist /'hju:mərɪst/ n humorista m & f. ~**rous** /-rəs/ a humorístico. ~**rously** adv con gracia. ~**ur** /'hju:mə(r)/ n humor m. **sense of** ~**ur** sentido m del humor

hump /hʌmp/ n (of person, camel) joroba f; (in ground) montículo m. ● vt encorvar. ~ (about) (ℍ, carry) cargar

hunch /hʌntʃ/ vt encorvar. ● n presentimiento m; (lump) joroba f. ~**back** n jorobado m

hundred /'hʌndrəd/ a ciento, (before noun) cien. **one** ~ **and ninety-eight** ciento noventa y ocho. **two** ~ doscientos. **three** ~ **pages** trescientas páginas. **four** ~ cuatrocientos. **five** ~ quinientos. ● n ciento m. ~**s of** centenares de. ~**th** a & n centésimo (m). ~**weight** n 50,8kg; (Amer) 45,36kg

hung /hʌŋ/ ⇒HANG

Hungar|ian /hʌŋ'geərɪən/ a & n húngaro (m). ~**y** /'hʌŋgərɪ/ n Hungría f

hung|er /'hʌŋgə(r)/ n hambre f. ● vi. ~**er for** tener hambre de. ~**rily** /'hʌŋgrəlɪ/ adv ávidamente. ~**ry** a (-**ier**, -**iest**) hambriento. **be** ~**ry** tener hambre

hunk /hʌŋk/ n (buen) pedazo m

hunt /hʌnt/ vt cazar. ● vi cazar. ~ **for** buscar. ● n caza f. ~**er** n cazador m. ~**ing** n caza f. **go** ~**ing** ir de caza

hurl /hɜ:l/ vt lanzar

hurrah /hʊ'rɑ:/, **hurray** /hʊ'reɪ/ int & n ¡viva! (m)

hurricane /'hʌrɪkən/ n huracán m

hurr|ied /'hʌrɪd/ a apresurado. ~**iedly** adv apresuradamente. ~**y** vi darse prisa, apurarse (LAm). ● vt meter prisa a, apurar (LAm). ● n prisa f. **be in a** ~**y** tener prisa, estar apurado (LAm)

hurt /hɜ:t/ vt (pt **hurt**) hacer daño a, lastimar (LAm). ~ **s.o.'s feelings** ofender a uno. ● vi doler. **my head** ~**s** me duele la cabeza. ~**ful** a hiriente

hurtle /'hɜːtl/ vt ir volando. ● vi. ~ along mover rápidamente

husband /'hʌzbənd/ n marido m, esposo m

hush /hʌʃ/ vt acallar. ● n silencio m. □ ~ **up** vt acallar <affair>. ~**-hush** a 🄸 super secreto

husk /hʌsk/ n cáscara f

husky /'hʌskɪ/ a (**-ier, -iest**) (hoarse) ronco

hustle /'hʌsl/ vt (jostle) empujar. ● vi (hurry) darse prisa, apurarse (LAm). ● n empuje m

hut /hʌt/ n cabaña f

hutch /hʌtʃ/ n conejera f

hybrid /'haɪbrɪd/ a & n híbrido (m)

hydrangea /haɪ'dreɪndʒə/ n hortensia f

hydrant /'haɪdrənt/ n. (fire) ~ n boca f de riego, boca f de incendios (LAm)

hydraulic /haɪ'drɔːlɪk/ a hidráulico

hydroelectric /haɪdrəʊ'lektrɪk/ a hidroeléctrico

hydrofoil /'haɪdrəfɔɪl/ n hidrodeslizador m

hydrogen /'haɪdrədʒən/ n hidrógeno m

hyena /haɪ'iːnə/ n hiena f

hygien|e /'haɪdʒiːn/ n higiene f. ~**ic** /haɪ'dʒiːnɪk/ a higiénico

hymn /hɪm/ n himno m

hyper... /'haɪpə(r)/ pref hiper...

hyphen /'haɪfn/ n guión m. ~**ate** /-eɪt/ vt escribir con guión

hypno|sis /hɪp'nəʊsɪs/ n hipnosis f. ~**tic** /-'nɒtɪk/ a hipnótico. ~**tism** /'hɪpnətɪzəm/ n hipnotismo m. ~**tist** /'hɪpnətɪst/ n hipnotista m & f. ~**tize** /'hɪpnətaɪz/ vt hipnotizar

hypochondriac /haɪpə'kɒndrɪæk/ n hipocondríaco m

hypocri|sy /hɪ'pɒkrəsɪ/ n hipocresía f. ~**te** /'hɪpəkrɪt/ n hipócrita m & f. ~**tical** /hɪpə'krɪtɪkl/ a hipócrita

hypodermic /haɪpə'dɜːmɪk/ a hipodérmico. ● n hipodérmica f

hypothe|sis /haɪ'pɒθəsɪs/ n (pl **-theses** /-siːz/) hipótesis f. ~**tical** /-ə'θetɪkl/ a hipotético

hysteri|a /hɪ'stɪərɪə/ n histerismo m. ~**cal** /-'terɪkl/ a histérico. ~**cs** /hɪ'sterɪks/ npl histerismo m. **have** ~**cs** ponerse histérico; (laugh) morir de risa

I /aɪ/ pron yo

ice /aɪs/ n hielo m. ● vt helar; glasear <cake>. ● vi. ~ (**up**) helarse, congelarse. ~**berg** /-bɜːg/ n iceberg m. ~ **box** n (compartment) congelador; (Amer 🄸, refrigerator) frigorífico m, refrigerador m (LAm). ~**cream** n helado m. ~ **cube** n cubito m de hielo

Iceland /'aɪslənd/ n Islandia f

ice: ~ **lolly** polo m, paleta f helada (LAm). ~ **rink** n pista f de hielo. ~ **skating** n patinaje m sobre hielo

icicle /'aɪsɪkl/ n carámbano m

icing /'aɪsɪŋ/ n glaseado m

icon /'aɪkɒn/ n icono m

icy /'aɪsɪ/ a (**-ier, -iest**) helado; (fig) glacial

I'd /aɪd/ = **I had, I would**

idea /aɪ'dɪə/ n idea f

ideal /aɪ'dɪəl/ a & n ideal (m). ~**ism** n idealismo m. ~**ist** n idealista m & f. ~**istic** /-'lɪstɪk/ a idealista. ~**ize** vt idealizar. ~**ly** adv idealmente

identical /aɪ'dentɪkl/ a idéntico. ~ **twins** npl gemelos mpl idénticos, gemelos mpl (LAm)

identif|ication /aɪdentɪfɪ'keɪʃn/ n identificación f. ~**y** /aɪ'dentɪfaɪ/ vt identificar. ● vi. ~**y with** identificarse con

identity /aɪ'dentɪtɪ/ n identidad f. ~ **card** n carné m de identidad

ideolog|ical /aɪdɪə'lɒdʒɪkl/ a ideológico. ~**y** /aɪdɪ'ɒlədʒɪ/ n ideología f

idiocy /'ɪdɪəsɪ/ n idiotez f

idiom /'ɪdɪəm/ n locución f. ~**atic** /-'mætɪk/ a idiomático

idiot /'ɪdɪət/ n idiota m & f. ~**ic** /-'ɒtɪk/ a idiota

idle /'aɪdl/ a (**-er, -est**) ocioso; (lazy) holgazán; (out of work) desocupado; <machine> parado. ●vi <engine> andar al ralentí. ~**ness** n ociosidad f; (laziness) holgazanería f

idol /'aɪdl/ n ídolo m. ~**ize** vt idolatrar

idyllic /ɪ'dɪlɪk/ a idílico

i.e. abbr (= **id est**) es decir

if /ɪf/ conj si

igloo /'ɪglu:/ n iglú m

ignite /ɪg'naɪt/ vt encender. ●vi encenderse. ~**ion** /-'nɪʃn/ n ignición f; (Auto) encendido m. ~**ion key** n llave f de contacto

ignoramus /ɪgnə'reɪməs/ n (pl -**muses**) ignorante

ignoran|ce /'ɪgnərəns/ n ignorancia f. ~**t** a ignorante

ignore /ɪg'nɔ:(r)/ vt no hacer caso de; hacer caso omiso de <warning>

ill /ɪl/ a enfermo. ●adv mal. ●n mal m

I'll /aɪl/ = **I will**

ill: ~**-advised** /-əd'vaɪzd/ a imprudente. ~ **at ease** /-ət'i:z/ a incómodo. ~**-bred** /-'bred/ a mal educado

illegal /ɪ'li:gl/ a ilegal

illegible /ɪ'ledʒəbl/ a ilegible

illegitima|cy /ɪlɪ'dʒɪtɪməsɪ/ n ilegitimidad f. ~**te** /-ət/ a ilegítimo

illitera|cy /ɪ'lɪtərəsɪ/ n analfabetismo m. ~**te** /-ət/ a analfabeto

illness /'ɪlnɪs/ n enfermedad f

illogical /ɪ'lɒdʒɪkl/ a ilógico

illuminat|e /ɪ'lu:mɪneɪt/ vt iluminar. ~**ion** /-'neɪʃn/ n iluminación f

illus|ion /ɪ'lu:ʒn/ n ilusión f. ~**sory** /-serɪ/ a ilusorio

illustrat|e /'ɪləstreɪt/ vt ilustrar. ~**ion** /-'streɪʃn/ n ilustración f; (example) ejemplo m

illustrious /ɪ'lʌstrɪəs/ a ilustre

ill will /ɪl'wɪl/ n mala voluntad f

I'm /aɪm/ = **I am**

image /'ɪmɪdʒ/ n imagen f. ~**ry** n imágenes fpl

imagin|able /ɪ'mædʒɪnəbl/ a imaginable. ~**ary** a imaginario. ~**ation** /-'neɪʃn/ n imaginación f. ~**ative** a imaginativo. ~**e** /ɪ'mædʒɪn/ vt imaginar(se)

imbalance /ɪm'bæləns/ n desequilibrio m

imbecile /'ɪmbəsi:l/ n imbécil m & f

imitat|e /'ɪmɪteɪt/ vt imitar. ~**ion** /-'teɪʃn/ n imitación f. ●a de imitación. ~**or** n imitador m

immaculate /ɪ'mækjʊlət/ a inmaculado

immatur|e /ɪmə'tjʊə(r)/ a inmaduro. ~**ity** n inmadurez f

immediate /ɪ'mi:dɪət/ a inmediato. ~**ly** adv inmediatamente. ●conj en cuanto (+ subjunctive)

immens|e /ɪ'mens/ a inmenso. ~**ely** adv inmensamente; (Ⅰ, very much) muchísimo

immers|e /ɪ'mɜ:s/ vt sumergir. ~**ion** /-ʃn/ n inmersión f. ~**ion heater** n calentador m de inmersión

immigra|nt /'ɪmɪgrənt/ a & n inmigrante (m & f). ~**tion** /-'greɪʃn/ n inmigración f

imminent /'ɪmɪnənt/ a inminente

immobil|e /ɪ'məʊbaɪl/ a inmóvil. ~**ize** /-bɪlaɪz/ vt inmovilizar

immoderate /ɪ'mɒdərət/ a inmoderado

immodest /ɪ'mɒdɪst/ a inmodesto

immoral /ɪ'mɒrəl/ a inmoral. ~**ity** /ɪmə'rælətɪ/ n inmoralidad f

immortal /ɪ'mɔ:tl/ a inmortal. ~**ity** /-'tælətɪ/ n inmortalidad f. ~**ize** vt inmortalizar

immun|e /ɪ'mju:n/ a inmune (**to** a). ~**ity** n inmunidad f. ~**ization** /ɪmjʊnaɪ'zeɪʃn/ n inmunización f. ~**ize** /'ɪmjʊnaɪz/ vt inmunizar

imp /ɪmp/ n diablillo m

impact /'ɪmpækt/ n impacto m

impair /ɪm'peə(r)/ vt perjudicar

impale /ɪm'peɪl/ vt atravesar (**on** con)

impart /ɪm'pɑ:t/ vt comunicar <news>; impartir <knowledge>

impartial /ɪm'pɑ:ʃl/ a imparcial. ~**ity** /-ɪ'rælətɪ/ n imparcialidad f

impassable /ɪm'pɑ:səbl/ a <barrier etc> infranqueable; <road> intransitable

impassive /ɪm'pæsɪv/ a impasible

impatien|ce /ɪmˈpeɪʃəns/ *n* impaciencia *f*. ~**t** *a* impaciente. **get** ~**t** impacientarse. ~**tly** *adv* con impaciencia

impeccable /ɪmˈpekəbl/ *a* impecable

impede /ɪmˈpiːd/ *vt* estorbar

impediment /ɪmˈpedɪmənt/ obstáculo *m*. (**speech**) ~ *n* defecto *m* del habla

impending /ɪmˈpendɪŋ/ *a* inminente

impenetrable /ɪmˈpenɪtrəbl/ *a* impenetrable

imperative /ɪmˈperətɪv/ *a* imprescindible. ● *n* (Gram) imperativo *m*

imperceptible /ɪmpəˈseptəbl/ *a* imperceptible

imperfect /ɪmˈpɜːfɪkt/ *a* imperfecto. ~**ion** /ɪmpəˈfekʃn/ *n* imperfección *f*

imperial /ɪmˈpɪərɪəl/ *a* imperial. ~**ism** *n* imperialismo *m*

impersonal /ɪmˈpɜːsənl/ *a* impersonal

impersonat|e /ɪmˈpɜːsəneɪt/ *vt* hacerse pasar por; (mimic) imitar. ~**ion** /-ˈneɪʃn/ *n* imitación *f*. ~**or** *n* imitador *m*

impertinen|ce /ɪmˈpɜːtɪnəns/ *n* impertinencia *f*. ~**t** *a* impertinente

impervious /ɪmˈpɜːvɪəs/ *a*. ~ **to** impermeable a

impetuous /ɪmˈpetjʊəs/ *a* impetuoso

impetus /ˈɪmpɪtəs/ *n* ímpetu *m*

implacable /ɪmˈplækəbl/ *a* implacable

implant /ɪmˈplɑːnt/ *vt* implantar

implement /ˈɪmplɪmənt/ *n* instrumento *m*, implemento *m* (LAm). ● /ˈɪmplɪment/ *vt* implementar

implicat|e /ˈɪmplɪkeɪt/ *vt* implicar. ~**ion** /-ˈkeɪʃn/ *n* implicación *f*

implicit /ɪmˈplɪsɪt/ *a* (implied) implícito; (unquestioning) absoluto

implore /ɪmˈplɔː(r)/ *vt* implorar

imply /ɪmˈplaɪ/ *vt* (involve) implicar; (insinuate) dar a entender, insinuar

impolite /ɪmpəˈlaɪt/ *a* mal educado

import /ɪmˈpɔːt/ *vt* importar. ● /ˈɪmpɔːt/ *n* importación *f*; (item) artículo *m* de importación; (meaning) significación *f*

importan|ce /ɪmˈpɔːtəns/ *n* importancia *f*. ~**t** *a* importante

importer /ɪmˈpɔːtə(r)/ *n* importador *m*

impos|e /ɪmˈpəʊz/ *vt* imponer. ● *vi*. ~**e on** abusar de la amabilidad de. ~**ing** *a* imponente. ~**ition** /ɪmpəˈzɪʃn/ *n* imposición *f*; (fig) abuso *m*

impossib|ility /ɪmpɒsəˈbɪlətɪ/ *n* imposibilidad *f*. ~**le** /ɪmˈpɒsəbl/ *a* imposible

impostor /ɪmˈpɒstə(r)/ *n* impostor *m*

impoten|ce /ˈɪmpətəns/ *n* impotencia *f*. ~**t** *a* impotente

impound /ɪmˈpaʊnd/ *vt* confiscar

impoverished /ɪmˈpɒvərɪʃt/ *a* empobrecido

impractical /ɪmˈpræktɪkl/ *a* poco práctico

impregnable /ɪmˈpregnəbl/ *a* inexpugnable

impregnate /ˈɪmpregneɪt/ *vt* impregnar (with con, de)

impress /ɪmˈpres/ *vt* impresionar; (make good impression) causar una buena impresión a. ● *vi* impresionar

impression /ɪmˈpreʃn/ *n* impresión *f*. ~**able** *a* impresionable. ~**ism** *n* impresionismo *m*

impressive /ɪmˈpresɪv/ *a* impresionante

imprint /ˈɪmprɪnt/ *n* impresión *f*. ● /ɪmˈprɪnt/ *vt* imprimir

imprison /ɪmˈprɪzn/ *vt* encarcelar. ~**ment** *n* encarcelamiento *m*

improbab|ility /ɪmprɒbəˈbɪlətɪ/ *n* improbabilidad *f*. ~**le** /ɪmˈprɒbəbl/ *a* improbable

impromptu /ɪmˈprɒmptjuː/ *a* improvisado. ● *adv* de improviso

improper /ɪmˈprɒpə(r)/ *a* impropio; (incorrect) incorrecto

improve /ɪmˈpruːv/ *vt* mejorar. ● *vi* mejorar. ~**ment** *n* mejora *f*

improvis|ation /ɪmprəvaɪˈzeɪʃn/ *n* improvisación *f*. ~**e** /ˈɪmprəvaɪz/ *vt/i* improvisar

impuden|ce /'ɪmpjʊdəns/ n insolencia f. ~t a insolente

impuls|e /'ɪmpʌls/ n impulso m. on ~e sin reflexionar. ~ive a irreflexivo

impur|e /ɪm'pjʊə(r)/ a impuro. ~ity n impureza f

in /ɪn/ prep en; (within) dentro de. ~ a firm manner de una manera terminante. ~ an hour('s time) dentro de una hora. ~ doing al hacer. ~ so far as en la medida en que. ~ the evening por la tarde. ~ the rain bajo la lluvia. ~ the sun al sol. one ~ ten uno de cada diez. the best ~ the world el mejor del mundo. ● adv (inside) dentro; (at home) en casa. come ~ entrar. ● n. the ~s and outs of los detalles de

inability /mə'bɪlətɪ/ n incapacidad f

inaccessible /mæk'sesəbl/ a inaccesible

inaccura|cy /m'ækjʊrəsɪ/ n inexactitud f. ~te /-ət/ a inexacto

inactiv|e /m'æktɪv/ a inactivo. ~ity /-'tɪvətɪ/ n inactividad f

inadequa|cy /m'ædɪkwəsɪ/ a insuficiencia f. ~te /-ət/ a insuficiente

inadvertently /məd'vɜ:təntlɪ/ adv sin querer

inadvisable /məd'vaɪzəbl/ a desaconsejable

inane /ɪ'neɪn/ a estúpido

inanimate /m'ænɪmət/ a inanimado

inappropriate /mə'prəʊprɪət/ a inoportuno

inarticulate /mɑ:'tɪkjʊlət/ a incapaz de expresarse claramente

inattentive /mə'tentɪv/ a desatento

inaudible /m'ɔ:dəbl/ a inaudible

inaugurate /ɪ'nɔ:gjʊreɪt/ vt inaugurar

inborn /'mbɔ:n/ a innato

inbred /m'bred/ a (inborn) innato; <social group> endogámico

Inc /ɪŋk/ abbr (Amer) (= **Incorporated**) S.A., Sociedad Anónima

incalculable /m'kælkjʊləbl/ a incalculable

incapable /m'keɪpəbl/ a incapaz

incapacit|ate /mkə'pæsɪteɪt/ vt incapacitar. ~y n incapacidad f

incarcerate /m'kɑ:səreɪt/ vt encarcelar

incarnat|e /m'kɑ:nət/ a encarnado. ~ion /-'neɪʃn/ n encarnación f

incendiary /m'sendɪərɪ/ a incendiario. ~ **bomb** bomba f incendiaria

incense /'msens/ n incienso m. ● /m'sens/ vt enfurecer

incentive /m'sentɪv/ n incentivo m

incessant /m'sesnt/ a incesante. ~ly adv sin cesar

incest /'msest/ n incesto m. ~uous /m'sestjʊəs/ a incestuoso

inch /mtʃ/ n pulgada f. (= 2,54cm). ● vi. ~ **forward** avanzar lentamente

incidence /'msɪdəns/ n frecuencia f

incident /'msɪdənt/ n incidente m

incidental /msr'dentl/ a <effect> secundario; (minor) incidental. ~ly adv a propósito

incinerat|e /m'sməreɪt/ vt incinerar. ~or n incinerador m

incision /m'sɪʒn/ n incisión f

incite /m'saɪt/ vt incitar. ~ment n incitación f

inclination /mklɪ'neɪʃn/ n inclinación f. have no ~ to no tener deseos de

incline /m'klaɪn/ vt inclinar. be ~d to tener tendencia a. ● vi inclinarse. ● /'mklaɪn/ n pendiente f

inclu|de /m'klu:d/ vt incluir. ~ding prep incluso. ~sion /-ʒn/ n inclusión f. ~sive /-sɪv/ a inclusivo

incognito /mkɒg'ni:təʊ/ adv de incógnito

incoherent /mkəʊ'hɪərənt/ a incoherente

incom|e /'mkʌm/ n ingresos mpl. ~e **tax** n impuesto m sobre la renta. ~ing a <tide> ascendente

incomparable /m'kɒmpərəbl/ a incomparable

incompatible /mkəm'pætəbl/ a incompatible

incompeten|ce /m'kɒmpɪtəns/ n incompetencia f. ~t a incompetente

incomplete /mkəm'pli:t/ a incompleto

incomprehensible /ɪnkɒm-
prɪˈhensəbl/ a incomprensible

inconceivable /ɪnkənˈsiːvəbl/ a
inconcebible

inconclusive /ɪnkənˈkluːsɪv/ a no
concluyente

incongruous /ɪnˈkɒŋgrʊəs/ a
incongruente

inconsiderate /ɪnkənˈsɪdərət/ a
desconsiderado

inconsisten|cy /ɪnkənˈsɪstənsɪ/ n
inconsecuencia f. ~**t** a inconsecuente. **be** ~**t with** no concordar con

inconspicuous /ɪnkənˈspɪkjʊəs/
a que no llama la atención. ~**ly** adv
sin llamar la atención

incontinent /ɪnˈkɒntɪnənt/ a
incontinente

inconvenien|ce /ɪnkənˈviːnɪəns/
a inconveniencia f; (drawback)
inconveniente m. ~**t** a inconveniente

incorporate /ɪnˈkɔːpəreɪt/ vt
incorporar; (include) incluir; (Com)
constituir (en sociedad)

incorrect /ɪnkəˈrekt/ a incorrecto

increas|e /ˈɪnkriːs/ n aumento m
(in de). ● /ɪnˈkriːs/ vt/i aumentar.
~**ing** /ɪnˈkriːsɪŋ/ a creciente.
~**ingly** adv cada vez más

incredible /ɪnˈkredəbl/ a increíble

incredulous /ɪnˈkredjʊləs/ a
incrédulo

incriminat|e /ɪnˈkrɪmɪneɪt/ vt
incriminar. ~**ing** a comprometedor

incubat|e /ˈɪŋkjʊbeɪt/ vt incubar.
~**ion** /-ˈbeɪʃn/ n incubación f. ~**or** n
incubadora f

incur /ɪnˈkɜː(r)/ vt (pt **incurred**)
incurrir en; contraer <debts>

incurable /ɪnˈkjʊərəbl/ a <disease>
incurable; <romantic> empedernido

indebted /ɪnˈdetɪd/ a. **be** ~ **to s.o.**
estar en deuda con uno

indecen|cy /ɪnˈdiːsnsɪ/ n indecen-
cia f. ~**t** a indecente

indecisi|on /ɪndɪˈsɪʒn/ n indecisión
f. ~**ve** /-ˈsaɪsɪv/ a indeciso

indeed /ɪnˈdiːd/ adv en efecto; (really?) ¿de veras?

indefinable /ɪndɪˈfaɪnəbl/ a inde-
finible

indefinite /ɪnˈdefɪnət/ a indefinido.
~**ly** adv indefinidamente

indelible /ɪnˈdelɪbl/ a indeleble

indemni|fy /ɪnˈdemnɪfaɪ/ vt (insure)
asegurar; (compensate) indemnizar.
~**ty** /-ətɪ/ n (insurance) indemnidad f;
(payment) indemnización f

indent /ɪnˈdent/ vt sangrar <text>.
~**ation** /-ˈteɪʃn/ n mella f

independen|ce /ɪndɪˈpendəns/ n
independencia f. ~**t** a independiente. ~**tly** adv independientemente

in-depth /ɪnˈdepθ/ a a fondo

indescribable /ɪndɪˈskraɪbəbl/ a
indescriptible

indestructible /ɪndɪˈstrʌktəbl/ a
indestructible

indeterminate /ɪndɪˈtɜːmɪnət/ a
indeterminado

index /ˈɪndeks/ n (pl **indexes**) (in
book) índice m; (pl **indexes** or **indices**) (Com, Math) índice m. ● vt poner índice a; (enter in index) poner en
un índice. ~**-linked** /-ˈlɪŋkt/ a indexado

India /ˈɪndɪə/ n la India. ~**n** a & n
indio (m)

indicat|e /ˈɪndɪkeɪt/ vt indicar.
~**ion** /-ˈkeɪʃn/ n indicación f. ~**ive**
/ɪnˈdɪkətɪv/ a & n indicativo (m).
~**or** /ˈɪndɪkeɪtə(r)/ n indicador m;
(Auto) intermitente m

indices /ˈɪndɪsiːz/ ⇒INDEX

indict /ɪnˈdaɪt/ vt acusar. ~**ment** n
acusación f

indifferen|ce /ɪnˈdɪfrəns/ n indi-
ferencia f. ~**t** a indiferente; (not good)
mediocre

indigesti|ble /ɪndɪˈdʒestəbl/ a
indigesto. ~**on** /-tʃən/ n indigestión
f

indigna|nt /ɪnˈdɪgnənt/ a indigna-
do. ~**tion** /-ˈneɪʃn/ n indignación f

indirect /ɪndɪˈrekt/ a indirecto. ~**ly**
adv indirectamente

indiscre|et /ɪndɪˈskriːt/ a indiscre-
to. ~**tion** /-ˈkreʃn/ n indiscreción f

indiscriminate /ɪndɪˈskrɪmɪnət/ a
indistinto. ~**ly** adv indistintamente

indispensable /ɪndɪˈspensəbl/ a
indispensable, imprescindible

indisposed /ɪndɪˈspəʊzd/ a indispuesto

indisputable /ˌɪndɪ'spjuːtəbl/ *a* indiscutible

indistinguishable /ˌɪndɪ'stɪŋgwɪʃəbl/ *a* indistinguible (**from** de)

individual /ˌɪndɪ'vɪdjʊəl/ *a* individual. ●*n* individuo *m*. ~**ly** *adv* individualmente

indoctrinat|e /ɪn'dɒktrɪneɪt/ *vt* adoctrinar. ~**ion** /-'neɪʃn/ *n* adoctrinamiento *m*

indolen|ce /'ɪndələns/ *n* indolencia *f*. ~**t** *a* indolente

indomitable /ɪn'dɒmɪtəbl/ *a* indómito

indoor /'ɪndɔː(r)/ *a* interior; <*clothes etc*> de casa; (covered) cubierto. ~**s** *adv* dentro, adentro (LAm)

induc|e /ɪn'djuːs/ *vt* inducir. ~**ement** *n* incentivo *m*

indulge /ɪn'dʌldʒ/ *vt* satisfacer <*desires*>; complacer <*person*>. ●*vi*. ~ **in** permitirse. ~**nce** /-əns/ *n* (of desires) satisfacción *f*; (extravagance) lujo *m*. ~**nt** *a* indulgente

industrial /ɪn'dʌstrɪəl/ *a* industrial; <*unrest*> laboral. ~**ist** *n* industrial *m & f*. ~**ized** *a* industrializado

industrious /ɪn'dʌstrɪəs/ *a* trabajador

industry /'ɪndəstrɪ/ *n* industria *f*; (zeal) aplicación *f*

inebriated /ɪ'niːbrɪeɪtɪd/ *a* beodo, ebrio

inedible /ɪn'edɪbl/ *a* incomible

ineffective /ˌɪnɪ'fektɪv/ *a* ineficaz; <*person*> incompetente

ineffectual /ˌɪnɪ'fektjʊəl/ *a* ineficaz

inefficien|cy /ˌɪnɪ'fɪʃnsɪ/ *n* ineficacia *f*; (of person) incompetencia *f*. ~**t** *a* ineficaz; <*person*> incompetente

ineligible /ɪn'elɪdʒəbl/ *a* inelegible. be ~ **for** no tener derecho a

inept /ɪ'nept/ *a* inepto

inequality /ˌɪnɪ'kwɒlətɪ/ *n* desigualdad *f*

inert /ɪ'nɜːt/ *a* inerte. ~**ia** /ɪ'nɜːʃə/ *n* inercia *f*

inescapable /ˌɪnɪ'skeɪpəbl/ *a* ineludible

inevitabl|e /ɪn'evɪtəbl/ *a* inevitable. ●*n*. the ~**e** lo inevitable. ~**y** *adv* inevitablemente

inexact /ˌɪnɪg'zækt/ *a* inexacto

inexcusable /ˌɪnɪk'skjuːsəbl/ *a* imperdonable

inexpensive /ˌɪnɪk'spensɪv/ *a* económico, barato

inexperience /ˌɪnɪk'spɪərɪəns/ *n* falta *f* de experiencia. ~**d** *a* inexperto

inexplicable /ˌɪnɪk'splɪkəbl/ *a* inexplicable

infallib|ility /ˌɪnfælə'bɪlətɪ/ *n* infalibilidad *f*. ~**le** /ɪn'fæləbl/ *a* infalible

infam|ous /'ɪnfəməs/ *a* infame. ~**y** *n* infamia *f*

infan|cy /'ɪnfənsɪ/ *n* infancia *f*. ~**t** *n* niño *m*. ~**tile** /'ɪnfəntaɪl/ *a* infantil

infantry /'ɪnfəntrɪ/ *n* infantería *f*

infatuat|ed /ɪn'fætjʊeɪtɪd/ *a*. be ~**ed with** estar encaprichado con. ~**ion** /-'eɪʃn/ *n* encaprichamiento *m*

infect /ɪn'fekt/ *vt* infectar; (fig) contagiar. ~ **s.o. with sth** contagiarle algo a uno. ~**ion** /-ʃn/ *n* infección *f*. ~**ious** /-ʃəs/ *a* contagioso

infer /ɪn'fɜː(r)/ *vt* (*pt* **inferred**) deducir

inferior /ɪn'fɪərɪə(r)/ *a & n* inferior (*m & f*). ~**ity** /-'ɒrətɪ/ *n* inferioridad *f*

inferno /ɪn'fɜːnəʊ/ *n* (*pl* **-os**) infierno *m*

infertil|e /ɪn'fɜːtaɪl/ *a* estéril. ~**ity** /-'tɪlətɪ/ *n* esterilidad *f*

infest /ɪn'fest/ *vt* infestar

infidelity /ˌɪnfɪ'delətɪ/ *n* infidelidad *f*

infiltrat|e /'ɪnfɪltreɪt/ *vt* infiltrarse en. ●*vi* infiltrarse. ~**or** *n* infiltrado *m*

infinite /'ɪnfɪnət/ *a* infinito. ~**ly** *adv* infinitamente

infinitesimal /ˌɪnfɪnɪ'tesɪml/ *a* infinitesimal

infinitive /ɪn'fɪnətɪv/ *n* infinitivo *m*

infinity /ɪn'fɪnətɪ/ *n* (infinite distance) infinito *m*; (infinite quantity) infinidad *f*

infirm /ɪn'fɜːm/ *a* enfermizo. ~**ity** *n* enfermedad *f*

inflam|e /ɪn'fleɪm/ *vt* inflamar. ~**mable** /ɪn'flæməbl/ *a* inflamable. ~**mation** /-ə'meɪʃn/ *n* inflamación *f*

inflat|e /ɪnˈfleɪt/ *vt* inflar. **∼ion** /-ʃn/ *n* inflación *f*. **∼ionary** *a* inflacionario

inflection /ɪnˈflekʃn/ *n* inflexión *f*

inflexible /ɪnˈfleksəbl/ *a* inflexible

inflict /ɪnˈflɪkt/ *vt* infligir (on a)

influen|ce /ˈɪnfluəns/ *n* influencia *f*. **under the ∼ce** (⛝, drunk) borracho. ● *vt* influir (en). **∼tial** /-ˈenʃl/ *a* influyente

influenza /ɪnfluˈenzə/ *n* gripe *f*

influx /ˈɪnflʌks/ *n* afluencia *f*

inform /ɪnˈfɔːm/ *vt* informar. **keep ∼ed** tener al corriente. ● *vi*. **∼ on** s.o. delatar a uno

informal /ɪnˈfɔːml/ *a* informal; *<language>* familiar. **∼ity** /-ˈmælətɪ/ *n* falta *f* de ceremonia. **∼ly** *adv* (casually) de manera informal; (unofficially) informalmente

inform|ation /ɪnfəˈmeɪʃn/ *n* información *f*. **∼ation technology** *n* informática *f*. **∼ative** *a* /ɪnˈfɔːmətɪv/ informativo. **∼er** /ɪbˈfɔːmə(r)/ *n* informante *m*

infrared /ɪnfrəˈred/ *a* infrarrojo

infrequent /ɪnˈfriːkwənt/ *a* poco frecuente. **∼ly** *adv* raramente

infringe /ɪnˈfrɪndʒ/ *vt* infringir. **∼ on** violar. **∼ment** *n* violación *f*

infuriat|e /ɪnˈfjʊərɪeɪt/ *vt* enfurecer. **∼ing** *a* exasperante

ingen|ious /ɪnˈdʒiːnɪəs/ *a* ingenioso. **∼uity** /ɪndʒɪˈnjuːətɪ/ *n* ingeniosidad *f*

ingot /ˈɪŋɡət/ *n* lingote *m*

ingrained /ɪnˈɡreɪnd/ *a* (belief) arraigado

ingratiate /ɪnˈɡreɪʃɪeɪt/ *vt*. **∼ o.s. with** congraciarse con

ingratitude /ɪnˈɡrætɪtjuːd/ *n* ingratitud *f*

ingredient /ɪnˈɡriːdɪənt/ *n* ingrediente *m*

ingrowing /ˈɪnɡrəʊɪŋ/, **ingrown** /ˈɪnɡrəʊn/ *a*. **∼ nail** *n* uñero *m*, uña *f* encarnada

inhabit /ɪnˈhæbɪt/ *vt* habitar. **∼able** *a* habitable. **∼ant** *n* habitante *m*

inhale /ɪnˈheɪl/ *vt* aspirar. ● *vi* (when smoking) aspirar el humo. **∼r** *n* inhalador *m*

inherent /ɪnˈhɪərənt/ *a* inherente. **∼ly** *adv* intrínsecamente

inherit /ɪnˈherɪt/ *vt* heredar. **∼ance** /-əns/ *n* herencia *f*

inhibit /ɪnˈhɪbɪt/ *vt* inhibir. **∼ed** *a* inhibido. **∼ion** /-ˈbɪʃn/ *n* inhibición *f*

inhospitable /ɪnhəˈspɪtəbl/ *a* *<place>* inhóspito; *<person>* inhospitalario

inhuman /ɪnˈhjuːmən/ *a* inhumano. **∼e** /ɪnhjuːˈmeɪn/ *a* inhumano. **∼ity** /ɪnhjuːˈmænətɪ/ *n* inhumanidad *f*

initial /ɪˈnɪʃl/ *n* inicial *f*. ● *vt* (*pt* **initialled**) firmar con iniciales. ● *a* inicial. **∼ly** *adv* al principio

initiat|e /ɪˈnɪʃɪeɪt/ *vt* iniciar; promover *<scheme etc>*. **∼ion** /-ˈeɪʃn/ *n* iniciación *f*

initiative /ɪˈnɪʃətɪv/ *n* iniciativa *f*. **on one's own ∼** por iniciativa propia. **take the ∼** tomar la iniciativa

inject /ɪnˈdʒekt/ *vt* inyectar. **∼ion** /-ʃn/ *n* inyección *f*

injur|e /ˈɪndʒə(r)/ *vt* herir. **∼y** *n* herida *f*

injustice /ɪnˈdʒʌstɪs/ *n* injusticia *f*

ink /ɪŋk/ *n* tinta *f*

ink: ∼well *n* tintero *m*. **∼y** *a* manchado de tinta

inland /ˈɪnlənd/ *a* interior. ● /ɪnˈlænd/ *adv* tierra adentro. **I∼ Revenue** /ˈɪnlənd/ *n* Hacienda *f*

in-laws /ˈɪnlɔːz/ *npl* parientes *mpl* políticos

inlay /ɪnˈleɪ/ *vt* (*pt* **inlaid**) taracear, incrustar. ● /ˈɪnleɪ/ *n* taracea *f*, incrustación *f*

inlet /ˈɪnlet/ *n* (in coastline) ensenada *f*; (of river, sea) brazo *m*

inmate /ˈɪnmeɪt/ *n* (of asylum) interno *m*; (of prison) preso *m*

inn /ɪn/ *n* posada *f*

innate /ɪˈneɪt/ *a* innato

inner /ˈɪnə(r)/ *a* interior; (fig) íntimo. **∼most** *a* más íntimo. **∼ tube** *n* cámara *f*

innocen|ce /ˈɪnəsns/ *n* inocencia *f*. **∼t** *a & n* inocente (*m & f*)

innocuous /ɪˈnɒkjʊəs/ a inocuo
innovat|e /ˈɪnəveɪt/ vi innovar.
~**ion** /-ˈveɪʃn/ n innovación f. ~**ive**
/ˈɪnəvətɪv/ a innovador. ~**or** n innovador m
innuendo /ɪnjuːˈendəʊ/ n (pl -**oes**)
insinuación f
innumerable /ɪˈnjuːmərəbl/ a
innumerable
inoculat|e /ɪˈnɒkjʊleɪt/ vt inocular.
~**ion** /-ˈleɪʃn/ n inoculación f
inoffensive /ɪnəˈfensɪv/ a inofensivo
inopportune /ɪnˈɒpətjuːn/ a
inoportuno
input /ˈɪnpʊt/ n aportación f, aporte
m (LAm); (Comp) entrada f. ● vt (pt
input, pres p **inputting**) entrar
<data>
inquest /ˈɪnkwest/ n investigación f
judicial
inquir|e /ɪnˈkwaɪə(r)/ vt/i pre-
guntar. ~**e about** informarse de. ~**y**
n pregunta f; (investigation) investigación f
inquisition /ɪnkwɪˈzɪʃn/ n inquisi-
ción f
inquisitive /ɪnˈkwɪzətɪv/ a inquisi-
tivo
insan|e /ɪnˈseɪn/ a loco. ~**ity**
/ɪnˈsænətɪ/ n locura f
insatiable /ɪnˈseɪʃəbl/ a insaciable
inscri|be /ɪnˈskraɪb/ vt inscribir
<letters>; grabar <design>. ~**ption**
/-ɪpʃn/ n inscripción f
inscrutable /ɪnˈskruːtəbl/ a
inescrutable
insect /ˈɪnsekt/ n insecto m. ~**icide**
/ɪnˈsektɪsaɪd/ n insecticida f
insecur|e /ɪnsɪˈkjʊə(r)/ a inseguro.
~**ity** n inseguridad f
insensitive /ɪnˈsensətɪv/ a insensible
inseparable /ɪnˈsepərəbl/ a inseparable
insert /ˈɪnsɜːt/ n materia f insertada.
● /ɪnˈsɜːt/ vt insertar. ~**ion**
/ɪnˈsɜːʃn/ n inserción f
inside /ɪnˈsaɪd/ n interior m. ~ **out**
al revés; (thoroughly) a fondo. ● a interior. ● adv dentro, adentro (LAm).
● prep dentro de. ~**s** npl tripas fpl

insight /ˈɪnsaɪt/ n perspicacia f. **gain
an** ~ **into** llegar a comprender bien
insignificant /ɪnsɪgˈnɪfɪkənt/ a
insignificante
insincer|e /ɪnsɪnˈsɪə(r)/ a poco
sincero. ~**ity** /-ˈserətɪ/ n falta f de
sinceridad
insinuat|e /ɪnˈsɪnjʊeɪt/ vt insinuar.
~**ion** /-ˈeɪʃn/ n insinuación f
insipid /ɪnˈsɪpɪd/ a insípido
insist /ɪnˈsɪst/ vt insistir (**that** en
que). ● vi insistir. ~ **on** insistir en.
~**ence** /-əns/ n insistencia f. ~**ent**
a insistente. ~**ently** adv con
insistencia
insolen|ce /ˈɪnsələns/ n insolencia
f. ~**t** a insolente
insoluble /ɪnˈsɒljʊbl/ a insoluble
insolvent /ɪnˈsɒlvənt/ a insolvente
insomnia /ɪnˈsɒmnɪə/ n insomnio
m. ~**c** /-ˈæk/ n insomne m & f
inspect /ɪnˈspekt/ vt (officially)
inspeccionar; (look at closely) revisar,
examinar . ~**ion** /-ʃn/ n inspección
f. ~**or** n inspector m; (on train, bus) revisor m, inspector m (LAm)
inspir|ation /ɪnspəˈreɪʃn/ n inspi-
ración f. ~**e** /ɪnˈspaɪə(r)/ vt inspirar.
~**ing** a inspirador
instability /ɪnstəˈbɪlətɪ/ n inesta-
bilidad f
install /ɪnˈstɔːl/ vt instalar. ~**ation**
/-əˈleɪʃn/ n instalación f
instalment /ɪnˈstɔːlmənt/ n (payment) plazo m; (of publication) entrega f;
(of radio, TV serial) episodio m
instance /ˈɪnstəns/ n ejemplo m;
(case) caso m. **for** ~ por ejemplo. **in
the first** ~ en primer lugar
instant /ˈɪnstənt/ a instantáneo. ● n
instante m. ~**aneous** /ɪnstən
ˈteɪnɪəs/ a instantáneo
instead /ɪnˈsted/ adv en cambio. ~
of en vez de, en lugar de
instigat|e /ˈɪnstɪgeɪt/ vt instigar.
~**ion** /-ˈgeɪʃn/ n instigación f
instinct /ˈɪnstɪŋkt/ n instinto m.
~**ive** a instintivo
institut|e /ˈɪnstɪtjuːt/ n instituto m.
● vt instituir; iniciar <enquiry etc>.
~**ion** /-ˈtjuːʃn/ n institución f.
~**ional** a institucional

instruct /ɪn'strʌkt/ *vt* instruir; (order) mandar. ~ s.o. in sth enseñar algo a uno. ~**ion** /-ʃn/ *n* instrucción *f*. ~**ions** *npl* (for use) modo *m* de empleo. ~**ive** *a* instructivo. ~**or** *n* instructor *m*

instrument /'ɪnstrəmənt/ *n* instrumento *m*. ~**al** /ɪnstrə'mentl/ *a* instrumental. **be** ~**al in** jugar un papel decisivo en

insubordinat|e /ɪnsə'bɔːdɪnət/ *a* insubordinado. ~**ion** /-'neɪʃn/ *n* insubordinación *f*

insufferable /ɪn'sʌfərəbl/ *a* <*person*> insufrible; <*heat*> insoportable

insufficient /ɪnsə'fɪʃnt/ *a* insuficiente

insular /'ɪnsjʊlə(r)/ *a* insular; (narrow-minded) estrecho de miras

insulat|e /'ɪnsjʊleɪt/ *vt* aislar. ~**ion** /-'leɪʃn/ *n* aislamiento *m*

insulin /'ɪnsjʊlɪn/ *n* insulina *f*

insult /ɪn'sʌlt/ *vt* insultar. ● /'ɪnsʌlt/ *n* insulto *m*. ~**ing** /ɪn'sʌltɪŋ/ *a* insultante

insur|ance /ɪn'ʃʊərəns/ *n* seguro *m*. ~**e** /ɪn'ʃʊə(r)/ *vt* (Com) asegurar; (Amer) ⇒ENSURE

insurmountable /ɪnsə'maʊntəbl/ *a* insuperable

intact /ɪn'tækt/ *a* intacto

integral /'ɪntɪgrəl/ *a* integral

integrat|e /'ɪntɪgreɪt/ *vt* integrar. ● *vi* integrarse. ~**ion** /-'greɪʃn/ *n* integración *f*

integrity /ɪn'tegrəti/ *n* integridad *f*

intellect /'ɪntəlekt/ *n* intelecto *m*. ~**ual** /ɪntə'lektʃʊəl/ *a* & *n* intelectual (*m*)

intelligen|ce /ɪn'telɪdʒəns/ *n* inteligencia *f*. ~**t** *a* inteligente. ~**tly** *adv* inteligentemente

intelligible /ɪn'telɪdʒəbl/ *a* inteligible

intend /ɪn'tend/ *vt*. ~ **to do** pensar hacer

intens|e /ɪn'tens/ *a* intenso; <*person*> apasionado. ~**ely** *adv* intensamente; (very) sumamente. ~**ify** /-ɪfaɪ/ *vt* intensificar. ● *vi* intensificarse. ~**ity** /-ɪti/ *n* intensidad *f*

intensive /ɪn'tensɪv/ *a* intensivo. ~ **care** *n* cuidados *mpl* intensivos

intent /ɪn'tent/ *n* propósito *m*. ● *a* atento. ~ **on** absorto en. ~ **on doing** resuelto a hacer

intention /ɪn'tenʃn/ *n* intención *f*. ~**al** *a* intencional

intently /ɪn'tentli/ *adv* atentamente

interact /ɪntər'ækt/ *vi* relacionarse. ~**ion** /-ʃn/ *n* interacción *f*

intercept /ɪntə'sept/ *vt* interceptar. ~**ion** /-ʃn/ *n* interceptación *f*

interchange /ɪntə'tʃeɪndʒ/ *vt* intercambiar. ● /'ɪntətʃeɪndʒ/ *n* intercambio *m*; (road junction) cruce *m*. ~**able** /-'tʃeɪndʒəbl/ *a* intercambiable

intercity /ɪntə'sɪti/ *a* rápido interurbano *m*

intercourse /'ɪntəkɔːs/ *n* trato *m*; (sexual) acto *m* sexual

interest /'ɪntrest/ *n* interés *m*. ● *vt* interesar. ~**ed** *a* interesado. **be** ~**ed in** interesarse por. ~**ing** *a* interesante

interfere /ɪntə'fɪə(r)/ *vi* entrometerse. ~ **in** entrometerse en. ~ **with** afectar (a); interferir <*radio*>. ~**nce** /-rəns/ *n* intromisión *f*; (Radio) interferencia *f*

interior /ɪn'tɪərɪə(r)/ *a* & *n* interior (*m*)

interjection /ɪntə'dʒekʃn/ *n* interjección *f*

interlude /'ɪntəluːd/ *n* intervalo *m*; (theatre, music) interludio *m*

intermediary /ɪntə'miːdɪəri/ *a* & *n* intermediario (*m*)

interminable /ɪn'tɜːmɪnəbl/ *a* interminable

intermittent /ɪntə'mɪtnt/ *a* intermitente. ~**ly** *adv* con discontinuidad

intern /ɪn'tɜːn/ *vt* internar. ● /'ɪntɜːn/ *n* (Amer, doctor) interno *m*

internal /ɪn'tɜːnl/ *a* interno. ~**ly** *adv* internamente. **I~ Revenue Service** *n* (Amer) Hacienda *f*

international /ɪntə'næʃənl/ *a* internacional

Internet /'ɪntənet/ *n*. **the** ~ el Internet

interpret /ɪn'tɜːprɪt/ *vt/i* interpretar. ~**ation** /-'teɪʃn/ *n* interpretación *f*. ~**er** *n* intérprete *m* & *f*

interrogat|e /ɪn'terəgeɪt/ *vt* interrogar. ~**ion** /-'geɪʃn/ *n* interrogatorio *m*. ~**ive** /-'rɒgətɪv/ *a* interrogativo

interrupt /ɪntə'rʌpt/ *vt/i* interrumpir. ~**ion** /-ʃn/ *n* interrupción *f*

intersect /ɪntə'sekt/ *vt* cruzar. ● *vi* <*roads*> cruzarse; (geometry) intersecarse. ~**ion** /-ʃn/ *n* (roads) cruce *m*; (geometry) intersección *f*

intersperse /ɪntə'spɜːs/ *vt* intercalar

interstate (highway) /'ɪntə steɪt/ *n* (Amer) carretera *f* interestatal

intertwine /ɪntə'twaɪn/ *vt* entrelazar. ● *vi* entrelazarse

interval /'ɪntəvl/ *n* intervalo *m*; (theatre) descanso *m*. **at** ~**s** a intervalos

interven|e /ɪntə'viːn/ *vi* intervenir. ~**tion** /-'venʃn/ *n* intervención *f*

interview /'ɪntəvjuː/ *n* entrevista *f*. ● *vt* entrevistar. ~**ee** /-'iː/ *n* entrevistado *m*. ~**er** *n* entrevistador *m*

intestine /ɪn'testɪn/ *n* intestino *m*

intimacy /'ɪntɪməsɪ/ *n* intimidad *f*

intimate /'ɪntɪmət/ *a* íntimo. ● /'ɪntɪmeɪt/ *vt* (state) anunciar; (imply) dar a entender. ~**ly** /'ɪntɪmətlɪ/ *adv* íntimamente

intimidat|e /ɪn'tɪmɪdeɪt/ *vt* intimidar. ~**ion** /-'deɪʃn/ *n* intimidación *f*

into /'ɪntuː/, *before consonant* /'ɪntə/ *prep* en; <*translate*> a

intolerable /ɪn'tɒlərəbl/ *a* intolerable

intoleran|ce /ɪn'tɒlərəns/ *n* intolerancia *f*. ~**t** *a* intolerante

intoxicat|e /ɪn'tɒksɪkeɪt/ *vt* embriagar; (Med) intoxicar. ~**ed** *a* ebrio. ~**ing** *a* <*substance*> estupefaciente. ~**ion** /-'keɪʃn/ *n* embriaguez *f*; (Med) intoxicación *f*

intransitive /ɪn'trænsɪtɪv/ *a* intransitivo

intravenous /ɪntrə'viːnəs/ *a* intravenoso

intrepid /ɪn'trepɪd/ *a* intrépido

intrica|cy /'ɪntrɪkəsɪ/ *n* complejidad *f*. ~**te** /-ət/ *a* complejo

intrigu|e /ɪn'triːg/ *vt/i* intrigar. ● /'ɪntriːg/ *n* intriga *f*. ~**ing** /ɪn'triːgɪŋ/ *a* intrigante

intrinsic /ɪn'trɪnsɪk/ *a* intrínseco. ~**ally** *adv* intrínsecamente

introduc|e /ɪntrə'djuːs/ *vt* introducir; presentar <*person*>. ~**tion** /ɪntrə'dʌkʃn/ *n* introducción *f*; (to person) presentación *f*. ~**tory** /ɪntrə'dʌktərɪ/ *a* preliminar; <*course*> de introducción

introvert /'ɪntrəvɜːt/ *n* introvertido *m*

intru|de /ɪn'truːd/ *vi* entrometerse; (disturb) importunar. ~**der** *n* intruso *m*. ~**sion** /-ʒn/ *n* intrusión *f*. ~**sive** /-sɪv/ *a* impertinente

intuiti|on /ɪntjuː'ɪʃn/ *n* intuición *f*. ~**ve** /ɪn'tjuːɪtɪv/ *a* intuitivo

inundat|e /'ɪnʌndeɪt/ *vt* inundar. ~**ion** /-'deɪʃn/ *n* inundación *f*

invade /ɪn'veɪd/ *vt* invadir. ~**r** *n* invasor *m*

invalid /'ɪnvəlɪd/ *n* inválido *m*. ● /ɪn'vælɪd/ *a* inválido. ~**ate** /ɪn'vælɪdeɪt/ *vt* invalidar

invaluable /ɪn'væljʊəbl/ *a* inestimable, invalorable (LAm)

invariabl|e /ɪn'veərɪəbl/ *a* invariable. ~**y** *adv* invariablemente

invasion /ɪn'veɪʒn/ *n* invasión *f*

invent /ɪn'vent/ *vt* inventar. ~**ion** /-'venʃn/ *n* invención *f*. ~**ive** *a* inventivo. ~**or** *n* inventor *m*

inventory /'ɪnvəntrɪ/ *n* inventario *m*

invertebrate /ɪn'vɜːtɪbrət/ *n* invertebrado *m*

inverted commas /ɪnvɜːtɪd'kɒ məz/ *npl* comillas *fpl*

invest /ɪn'vest/ *vt* invertir. ● *vi*. ~ **in** hacer una inversión *f*

investigat|e /ɪn'vestɪgeɪt/ *vt* investigar. ~**ion** /-'geɪʃn/ *n* investigación *f*. **under** ~**ion** sometido a examen. ~**or** *n* investigador *m*

inveterate /ɪn'vetərət/ *a* inveterado

invidious /ɪn'vɪdɪəs/ *a* (hateful) odioso; (unfair) injusto

invigorating /ɪn'vɪgəreɪtɪŋ/ *a* vigorizante; (stimulating) estimulante

invincible /ɪn'vɪnsɪbl/ *a* invencible

invisible /ɪnˈvɪzəbl/ a invisible

invit|ation /ɪnvɪˈteɪʃn/ n invitación f. ~e /ɪnˈvaɪt/ vt invitar; (ask for) pedir. ● /ˈɪnvaɪt/ n 🔲 invitación f. ~ing /ɪnˈvaɪtɪŋ/ a atrayente

invoice /ˈɪnvɔɪs/ n factura f. ● vt. ~ s.o. (for sth) pasarle a uno factura (por algo)

involuntary /ɪnˈvɒləntərɪ/ a involuntario

involve /ɪnˈvɒlv/ vt (entail) suponer; (implicate) implicar. ~d in envuelto en. ~d a (complex) complicado. ~ment n participación f; (relationship) enredo m

inward /ˈɪnwəd/ a interior. ● adv hacia adentro. ~s adv hacia dentro

iodine /ˈaɪədiːn/ n yodo m

ion /ˈaɪən/ n ion m

iota /aɪˈəʊtə/ n (amount) pizca f

IOU /aɪəʊˈjuː/ abbr (= I owe you) pagaré m

IQ abbr (= intelligence quotient) CI m, cociente m intelectual

Iran /ɪˈrɑːn/ n Irán m. ~ian /ɪˈreɪnɪən/ a & n iraní (m)

Iraq /ɪˈrɑːk/ n Irak m. ~i a & n iraquí (m)

irate /aɪˈreɪt/ a colérico

Ireland /ˈaɪələnd/ n Irlanda f

iris /ˈaɪərɪs/ n (Anat) iris m; (Bot) lirio m

Irish /ˈaɪərɪʃ/ a irlandés. ● n (Lang) irlandés m. npl. the ~ (people) los irlandeses. ~man /-mən/ n irlandés m. ~woman n irlandesa f

iron /ˈaɪən/ n hierro m; (appliance) plancha f. ● a de hierro. ● vt planchar. □ ~ out vt allanar

ironic /aɪˈrɒnɪk/ a irónico. ~ally adv irónicamente

ironing board /ˈaɪənɪŋ/ n tabla f de planchar, burro m de planchar (Mex)

iron: ~monger /-mʌŋgə(r)/ n ferretero m. ~monger's n ferretería f

irony /ˈaɪərənɪ/ n ironía f

irrational /ɪˈræʃənl/ a irracional

irrefutable /ɪrɪˈfjuːtəbl/ a irrefutable

irregular /ɪˈregjʊlə(r)/ a irregular. ~ity /-ˈlærətɪ/ n irregularidad f

irrelevan|ce /ɪˈreləvəns/ n irrelevancia f. ~t a irrelevante

irreparable /ɪˈrepərəbl/ a irreparable

irreplaceable /ɪrɪˈpleɪsəbl/ a irreemplazable

irresistible /ɪrɪˈzɪstəbl/ a irresistible

irrespective /ɪrɪˈspektɪv/ a. ~ of sin tomar en cuenta

irresponsible /ɪrɪˈspɒnsəbl/ a irresponsable

irretrievable /ɪrɪˈtriːvəbl/ a irrecuperable

irreverent /ɪˈrevərənt/ a irreverente

irrevocable /ɪˈrevəkəbl/ a irrevocable

irrigat|e /ˈɪrɪgeɪt/ vt regar, irrigar. ~ion /-ˈgeɪʃn/ n riego m, irrigación f

irritable /ˈɪrɪtəbl/ a irritable

irritat|e /ˈɪrɪteɪt/ vt irritar. ~ed a <expression> de impaciencia; <skin> irritado. be ~ed with estar irritado con. ~ing a irritante. ~ion /-ˈteɪʃn/ n irritación f

IRS abbr (Amer) ⇒INTERNAL REVENUE SERVICE

is /ɪz/ ⇒BE

Islam /ˈɪzlɑːm/ n el Islam. ~ic /ɪzˈlæmɪk/ a islámico

island /ˈaɪlənd/ n isla f. ~er n isleño m

isolat|e /ˈaɪsəleɪt/ vt aislar. ~ion /-ˈleɪʃn/ n aislamiento m

Israel /ˈɪzreɪl/ n Israel m. ~i /ɪzˈreɪlɪ/ a & n israelí (m)

issue /ˈɪʃuː/ n tema m, asunto m; (of magazine etc) número m; (of stamps, bank notes) emisión f; (of documents) expedición f. take ~ with discrepar de. ● vt hacer público <statement>; expedir <documents>; emitir <stamps etc>; prestar <library book>

....

it /ɪt/

● pronoun

····▶ (as subject) generally not translated. **it's huge** es enorme. **where is** it? ¿dónde está? **it's all lies** son todas mentiras

····▶ (as direct object) lo (*m*), la (*f*). **he read it to me** me lo/la leyó. **give it to me** dámelo/dámela

····▶ (as indirect object) le. **I gave it another coat of paint** le di otra mano de pintura

····▶ (after a preposition) *generally not translated*. **there's nothing behind it** no hay nada detrás

! Note, however, that in some cases *él* or *ella* must be used
■ e.g. **he picked up the spoon and hit me with it** *agarró la cuchara y me golpeó con ella*

····▶ (at door) **who is it?** ¿quién es?. **it's me** soy yo; (on telephone) **who is it, please?** ¿quién habla, por favor?; (before passing on to sb else) ¿de parte de quién, por favor? **it's Carol** soy Carol (Spain), habla Carol

····▶ (in impersonal constructions) **it is well known that ...** bien se sabe que ... **it's five o'clock** son las cinco. **so it seems** así parece

····▶ **that's it** (that's right) eso es; (that's enough, that's finished) ya está

Italian /ɪ'tæljən/ *a & n* italiano (*m*)

Italics /ɪ'tælɪks/ *npl* (letra *f*) cursiva *f*

Italy /'ɪtəlɪ/ *n* Italia *f*

itch /ɪtʃ/ *n* picazón *f*. ●*vi* picar. **I'm ~ing to** estoy que me muero por. **my arm ~es** me pica el brazo. **~y** *a* que pica. **I've got an ~y nose** me pica la nariz

it'd /ɪtəd/ = **it had**, **it would**

item /'aɪtəm/ *n* artículo *m*; (on agenda) punto *m*. **news ~** *n* noticia *f*. **~ize** *vt* detallar

itinerary /aɪ'tɪnərərɪ/ *n* itinerario *m*

it'll /'ɪtl/ = **it will**

its /ɪts/ *a* su, sus (*pl*). ●*pron* (el) suyo *m*, (la) suya *f*, (los) suyos *mpl*, (las) suyas *fpl*

it's /ɪts/ = **it is**, **it has**

itself /ɪt'self/ *pron* él mismo, ella misma, ello mismo; (*reflexive*) se; (*after prep*) sí mismo, sí misma

I've /aɪv/ = **I have**

ivory /'aɪvərɪ/ *n* marfil *m*. **~ tower** *n* torre *f* de marfil

ivy /'aɪvɪ/ *n* hiedra *f*

Jj

jab /dʒæb/ *vt* (*pt* **jabbed**) pinchar; (thrust) hurgonear. ●*n* pinchazo *m*

jack /dʒæk/ *n* (Mec) gato *m*; (socket) enchufe *m* hembra; (Cards) sota *f*. □ **~ up** *vt* alzar con gato

jackal /'dʒækl/ *n* chacal *m*

jackdaw /'dʒækdɔ:/ *n* grajilla *f*

jacket /'dʒækɪt/ *n* chaqueta *f*; (casual) americana *f*, saco *m* (LAm), (Amer, of book) sobrecubierta *f*; (of record) funda *f*, carátula *f*

jack: **~ knife** *vi* <lorry> plegarse. **~pot** *n* premio *m* gordo. **hit the ~pot** sacar el premio gordo

jade /dʒeɪd/ *n* (stone) jade *m*

jagged /'dʒægɪd/ *a* <edge, cut> irregular; <rock> recortado

jaguar /'dʒægjʊə(r)/ *n* jaguar *m*

jail /dʒeɪl/ *n* cárcel *m*, prisión *f*. ●*vt* encarcelar. **~er** *n* carcelero *m*. **~house** *n* (Amer) cárcel *f*

jam /dʒæm/ *vt* (*pt* **jammed**) interferir con <radio>; atestar <road>. **~ sth into sth** meter algo a la fuerza en algo. ●*vi* <brakes> bloquearse; <machine> trancarse. ●*n* mermelada *f*; (ⅈ, situation) apuro *m*

jangle /'dʒæŋgl/ *n* sonido *m* metálico (y áspero). ●*vi* hacer ruido (metálico)

janitor /'dʒænɪtə(r)/ *n* portero *m*

January /'dʒænjʊərɪ/ *n* enero *m*

Japan /dʒə'pæn/ *n* (el) Japón *m*. **~ese** /dʒæpə'ni:z/ *a & n invar* japonés (*m*)

jar /dʒɑ:(r)/ *n* tarro *m*, bote *m*. ●*vi* (*pt* **jarred**) <clash> desentonar. ●*vt* sacudir

jargon /'dʒɑ:gən/ *n* jerga *f*

jaundice /'dʒɔ:ndɪs/ *n* ictericia *f*

jaunt /dʒɔ:nt/ n excursión f

jaunty /'dʒɔ:ntɪ/ a (**-ier**, **-iest**) garboso

jaw /dʒɔ:/ n mandíbula f. **~s** npl fauces fpl. **~bone** n mandíbula f, maxilar m; (of animal) quijada f

jay /dʒeɪ/ n arrendajo m. **~walk** vi cruzar la calle descuidadamente. **~walker** n peatón m imprudente

jazz /dʒæz/ n jazz m. □ **~ up** vt animar. **~y** a chillón

jealous /'dʒeləs/ a celoso; (envious) envidioso. **~y** n celos mpl

jeans /dʒi:nz/ npl vaqueros mpl, jeans mpl, tejanos mpl, pantalones mpl de mezclilla (Mex)

Jeep (P), **jeep** /dʒi:p/ n Jeep m (P)

jeer /dʒɪə(r)/ vi. **~ at** mofarse de; (boo) abuchear. ● n burla f; (boo) abucheo m

Jell-O /'dʒeləʊ/ n (P) (Amer) gelatina f (con sabor a frutas)

jelly /'dʒelɪ/ n (clear jam) jalea f; (pudding) ⇒JELL-O; (substance) gelatina f. **~fish** n (pl invar or **-es**) medusa f

jeopardize /'dʒepədaɪz/ vt arriesgar

jerk /dʒɜ:k/ n sacudida f; (Ⓧ, fool) idiota m & f. ● vt sacudir

jersey /'dʒɜ:zɪ/ n (pl **-eys**) jersey m, suéter m, pulóver m

jest /dʒest/ n broma f. ● vi bromear

Jesus /'dʒi:zəs/ n Jesús m

jet /dʒet/ n (stream) chorro m; (plane) avión m (con motor a reacción); (mineral) azabache m. **~-black** /-'blæk/ a azabache negro a invar. **~ lag** n jet lag m, desfase f horario. **have ~ lag** estar desfasado. **~-propelled** /-prə'peld/ a (de propulsión) a reacción

jettison /'dʒetɪsn/ vt echar al mar; (fig, discard) deshacerse de

jetty /'dʒetɪ/ n muelle m

Jew /dʒu:/ n judío m

jewel /'dʒu:əl/ n joya f. **~ler** n joyero m. **~lery** n joyas fpl

Jewish /'dʒu:ɪʃ/ a judío

jiffy /'dʒɪfɪ/ n momentito m. **do sth in a ~** hacer algo en un santiamén

jig /dʒɪg/ n (dance) giga f

jigsaw /'dʒɪgsɔ:/ n. **~** (**puzzle**) rompecabezas m

jilt /dʒɪlt/ vt dejar plantado

jingle /'dʒɪŋgl/ vt hacer sonar. ● vi tintinear. ● n tintineo m; (advert) jingle m (publicitario)

job /dʒɒb/ n empleo m, trabajo m; (piece of work) trabajo m. **it is a good ~ that** menos mal que. **~less** a desempleado

jockey /'dʒɒkɪ/ n jockey m

jocular /'dʒɒkjʊlə(r)/ a jocoso

jog /dʒɒg/ vt (pt **jogged**) empujar; refrescar <memory>. ● vi hacer footing, hacer jogging. **~er** n persona f que hace footing. **~ging** n footing m, jogging m. **go ~ging** salir a hacer footing or jogging

join /dʒɔɪn/ vt (link) unir; hacerse socio de <club>; hacerse miembro de <political group>; alistarse en <army>; reunirse con <another person>. ● n juntura. ● vi. **~ together** <parts> unirse; <roads etc> empalmar; <rivers> confluir. □ **~ in** vi participar (en). □ **~ up** vi (Mil) alistarse. **~er** n carpintero m

joint /dʒɔɪnt/ a conjunto. ● n (join) unión f, junta f; (Anat) articulación f. (Culin) trozo m de carne (para asar). **out of ~** descoyuntado. **~ account** n cuenta f conjunta. **~ly** adv conjuntamente. **~ owner** n copropietario m.

joist /dʒɔɪst/ n viga f

jok|e /dʒəʊk/ n (story) chiste m; (practical joke) broma f. ● vi bromear. **~er** n bromista m & f; (Cards) comodín m. **~y** a jocoso

jolly /'dʒɒlɪ/ a (**-ier**, **-iest**) alegre. ● adv Ⓣ muy

jolt /dʒɒlt/ vt sacudir. ● vi <vehicle> dar una sacudida. ● n sacudida f

jostle /'dʒɒsl/ vt empujar. ● vi empujarse

jot /dʒɒt/ n pizca f. ● vt (pt **jotted**). □ **~ down** vt apuntar (rápidamente). **~ter** n bloc m

journal /'dʒɜ:nl/ n (diary) diario m; (newspaper) periódico m; (magazine) revista f. **~ism** n periodismo m. **~ist** n periodista m & f

journey /'dʒɜ:nɪ/ n viaje m. go on a ∼ hacer un viaje. ● vi viajar

jovial /'dʒəʊvɪəl/ a jovial

joy /dʒɔɪ/ n alegría f. ∼ful a feliz. ∼ous a feliz. ∼rider n joven m que roba un coche para dar una vuelta. ∼stick n (Aviat) palanca f de mando; (Comp) mando m, joystick m

jubila|nt /'dʒu:bɪlənt/ a jubiloso. ∼tion /-'leɪʃn/ n júbilo m

jubilee /'dʒu:bɪli:/ n aniversario m especial

Judaism /'dʒu:deɪɪzəm/ n judaísmo m

judge /dʒʌdʒ/ n juez m. ● vt juzgar. ∼ment n juicio m

judicia|l /dʒu:'dɪʃl/ a judicial. ∼ry /-ərɪ/ n judicatura f

judo /'dʒu:dəʊ/ n judo m

jug /dʒʌg/ n jarra f

juggernaut /'dʒʌgənɔ:t/ n camión m grande

juggle /'dʒʌgl/ vi hacer malabarismos. ● vt hacer malabarismos con. ∼r n malabarista m & f

juic|e /dʒu:s/ n jugo m, zumo m. ∼y a jugoso, zumoso; <story etc> 🄸 picante

jukebox /'dʒu:kbɒks/ n máquina f de discos, rocola f (LAm)

July /dʒu:'laɪ/ n julio m

jumble /'dʒʌmbl/ vt. ∼ (up) mezclar. ● n (muddle) revoltijo m. ∼ sale n venta f de objetos usados m

jumbo /'dʒʌmbəʊ/ a gigante. ∼ jet n jumbo m

jump /dʒʌmp/ vt saltar. ∼ rope (Amer) saltar a la comba, saltar a la cuerda. ∼ the gun obrar prematuramente. ∼ the queue colarse. ● vi saltar; (start) sobresaltarse; <prices> alzarse. ∼ at an opportunity apresurarse a aprovechar una oportunidad. ● n salto m; (start) susto m; (increase) aumento m. ∼er n jersey m, suéter m, pulóver m; (Amer, dress) pichi m, jumper m & f (LAm). ∼er cables (Amer), ∼ leads npl cables mpl de arranque. ∼ rope (Amer) comba f, cuerda f, reata f (Mex). ∼suit n mono m. ∼y a nervioso

junction /'dʒʌŋkʃn/ n (of roads, rails) cruce m; (Elec) empalme m

June /dʒu:n/ n junio m

jungle /'dʒʌŋgl/ n selva f, jungla f

junior /'dʒu:nɪə(r)/ a (in age) más joven (to que); (in rank) subalterno. ● n menor m

junk /dʒʌŋk/ n trastos mpl viejos; (worthless stuff) basura f. ● vt 🄸 tirar. ∼ food n comida f basura, alimento m chatarra (Mex). ∼ie /'dʒʌŋkɪ/ n 🄸 drogadicto m, yonqui m & f 🄸. ∼ mail n propaganda f que se recibe por correo. ∼ shop n tienda f de trastos viejos

junta /'dʒʌntə/ n junta f militar

Jupiter /'dʒu:pɪtə(r)/ n Júpiter m

jurisdiction /dʒʊərɪs'dɪkʃn/ n jurisdicción f

jur|or /'dʒʊərə(r)/ n (miembro m de un) jurado m. ∼y n jurado m

just /dʒʌst/ a (fair) justo. ● adv exactamente, justo; (barely) justo; (only) sólo, solamente. ∼ as tall tan alto (as como). ∼ listen! ¡escucha! he has ∼ arrived acaba de llegar, recién llegó (LAm)

justice /'dʒʌstɪs/ n justicia f. J∼ of the Peace juez m de paz

justif|iable /dʒʌstɪ'faɪəbl/ a justificable. ∼iably adv con razón. ∼ication /dʒʌstɪfɪ'keɪʃn/ n justificación f. ∼y /'dʒʌstɪfaɪ/ vt justificar

jut /dʒʌt/ vi (pt jutted). ∼ (out) sobresalir

juvenile /'dʒu:vənaɪl/ a juvenil; (childish) infantil. ● n (Jurid) menor m & f

Kk

kaleidoscope /kə'laɪdəskəʊp/ n caleidoscopio m

kangaroo /kæŋgə'ru:/ n canguro m

karate /kə'rɑ:tɪ/ n kárate m, karate m (LAm)

keel /ki:l/ n (of ship) quilla f. □ ∼ over vi volcar(se)

keen /ki:n/ a (-er, -est) <interest, feeling> vivo; <wind, mind, analysis> penetrante; <eyesight> agudo; (eager) entusiasta. **I'm ~ on golf** me encanta el golf. **he's ~ on Shostakovich** le gusta Shostakovich. **~ly** *adv* vivamente; (enthusiastically) con entusiasmo. **~ness** *n* intensidad *f*; (enthusiasm) entusiasmo *m*.

keep /ki:p/ *vt* (*pt* **kept**) guardar; cumplir *<promise>*; tener *<shop, animals>*; mantener *<family>*; observar *<rule>*; (celebrate) celebrar; (delay) detener; (prevent) impedir. ● *vi* *<food>* conservarse; (remain) quedarse; (continue) seguir. **~ doing** seguir haciendo. ● *n* subsistencia *f*; (of castle) torreón *m*. **for ~s** ⊞ para siempre. □ **~ back** *vt* retener. ● *vi* no acercarse. □ **~ in** *vt* no dejar salir. □ **~ off** *vt* mantenerse alejado de *<land>*. '**~ off the grass**' 'prohibido pisar el césped'. □ **~ on** *vi* seguir. **~ on doing sth** seguir haciendo. □ **~ out** *vt* no dejar entrar. □ **~ up** *vt* mantener. □ **~ up with** *vt* estar al día en

kennel /'kenl/ *n* casa *f* del perro; (Amer, for boarding) residencia *f* canina. **~s** *n invar* residencia *f* canina

kept /kept/ ⇒KEEP

kerb /kɜ:b/ *n* bordillo *m* (de la acera), borde *m* de la banqueta (Mex)

kerosene /'kerəsi:n/ *n* queroseno *m*

ketchup /'ketʃʌp/ *n* salsa *f* de tomate

kettle /'ketl/ *n* pava *f*, tetera *f* (para calentar agua)

key /ki:/ *n* llave *f*; (of computer, piano) tecla *f*; (Mus) tono *m*. **be off ~** no estar en el tono. ● *a* clave. □ **~ in** *vt* teclear. **~board** *n* teclado *m*. **~hole** *n* ojo *m* de la cerradura. **~ring** *n* llavero *m*

khaki /'kɑ:kɪ/ *a* caqui

kick /kɪk/ *vt* dar una patada a *<person>*; patear *<ball>*. ● *vi* dar patadas; *<horse>* cocear. ● *n* patada *f*; (of horse) coz *f*; (⊞, thrill) placer *m*. □ **~ out** *vt* ⊞ echar. □ **~ up** *vt* armar *<fuss etc>*. **~off** *n* (Sport) saque *m* inicial. **~ start** *vt* arrancar (*con el pedal de arranque*) *<engine>*

kid /kɪd/ *n* (young goat) cabrito *m*; (⊞, child) niño *m*, chaval *m*, escuincle *m* (Mex). ● *vt* (*pt* **kidded**) tomar el pelo a. ● *vi* bromear

kidnap /'kɪdnæp/ *vt* (*pt* **kidnapped**) secuestrar. **~per** *n* secuestrador *m*. **~ping** *n* secuestro *m*

kidney /'kɪdnɪ/ *n* riñón *m*

kill /kɪl/ *vt* matar; (fig) acabar con. ● *n* matanza *f*. □ **~ off** *vt* matar. **~er** *n* asesino *m*. **~ing** *n* matanza *f*; (murder) asesinato *m*. **make a ~ing** (fig) hacer un gran negocio

kiln /kɪln/ *n* horno *m*

kilo /'ki:ləʊ/ *n* (*pl* **-os**) kilo *m*. **~gram(me)** /'kɪləgræm/ *n* kilogramo *m*. **~metre** /'kɪləmi:tə(r)/, /kɪ'lɒmɪtə(r)/ *n* kilómetro *m*. **~watt** /'kɪləwɒt/ *n* kilovatio *m*

kilt /kɪlt/ *n* falda *f* escocesa

kin /kɪn/ *n* familiares *mpl*

kind /kaɪnd/ *n* tipo *m*, clase *f*. **~ of** (⊞, somewhat) un poco. **in ~** en especie. **be two of a ~** ser tal para cual. ● *a* amable

kindergarten /'kɪndəgɑ:tn/ *n* jardín *m* de infancia

kind-hearted /kaɪnd'hɑ:tɪd/ *a* bondadoso

kindle /'kɪndl/ *vt* encender

kind|ly *a* (**-ier, -iest**) bondadoso. ● *adv* amablemente; (please) haga el favor de. **~ness** *n* bondad *f*; (act) favor *m*

king /kɪŋ/ *n* rey *m*. **~dom** *n* reino *m*. **~fisher** *n* martín *m* pescador. **~-size(d)** *a* extragrande

kink /kɪŋk/ *n* (in rope) vuelta *f*, curva *f*; (in hair) onda *f*. **~y** *a* ⊞ pervertido

kiosk /'ki:ɒsk/ *n* quiosco *m*

kipper /'kɪpə(r)/ *n* arenque *m* ahumado

kiss /kɪs/ *n* beso *m*. ● *vt* besar. ● *vi* besarse

kit /kɪt/ *n* avíos *mpl*. **tool ~** caja *f* de herramientas. □ **~ out** *vt* (*pt* **kitted**) equipar

kitchen /'kɪtʃɪn/ *n* cocina *f*

kite /kaɪt/ *n* cometa *f*, papalote *m* (Mex)

kitten /'kɪtn/ *n* gatito *m*

knack /næk/ *n* truco *m*

knapsack /'næpsæk/ *n* mochila *f*

knead /ni:d/ *vt* amasar

knee /ni:/ *n* rodilla *f*. **~cap** *n* rótula
f

kneel /ni:l/ *vi* (*pt* **kneeled** *or*
knelt). **~ (down)** arrodillarse; (be on
one's knees) estar arrodillado

knelt /nelt/ ⇒KNEEL

knew /nju:/ ⇒KNOW

knickers /'nɪkəz/ *npl* bragas *fpl*,
calzones *mpl* (LAm), pantaletas *fpl*
(Mex)

knife /naɪf/ *n* (*pl* **knives**) cuchillo
m. ● *vt* acuchillar

knight /naɪt/ *n* caballero *m*; (Chess)
caballo *m*. ● *vt* conceder el título de
Sir a. **~hood** *n* título *m* de Sir

knit /nɪt/ *vt* (*pt* **knitted** *or* **knit**) hacer, tejer (LAm). ● *vi* tejer, hacer
punto. **~ one's brow** fruncir el ceño.
~ting *n* tejido *m*, punto *m*. **~ting
needle** *n* aguja *f* de hacer punto,
aguja *f* de tejer

knives /naɪvz/ ⇒KNIFE

knob /nɒb/ *n* botón *m*; (of door, drawer
etc) tirador *m*. **~bly** *a* nudoso

knock /nɒk/ *vt* golpear; (criticize) criticar. ● *vi* golpear; (at door) llamar,
golpear (LAm). ● *n* golpe *m*. □ **~
about** *vt* maltratar. □ **~ down** *vt*
derribar; atropellar <*person*>. □ **~
off** *vt* hacer caer. *vi* (国, finish work)
terminar, salir del trabajo. □ **~ out**
vt (by blow) dejar sin sentido; (elimin-
ate) eliminar. □ **~ over** *vt* tirar;
atropellar <*person*>. **~er** *n* aldaba *f*.
~-kneed /-'ni:d/ *a* patizambo.
~out *n* (Boxing) nocaut *m*

knot /nɒt/ *n* nudo *m*. ● *vt* (*pt* **knot-
ted**) anudar

know /nəʊ/ *vt* (*pt* **knew**) saber; (be
acquainted with) conocer. **let s.o. ~ sth**
decirle algo a uno; (warn) avisarle
algo a uno. ● *vi* saber. **~ how to do
sth** saber hacer algo. **~ about** entender de <*cars etc*>. **~ of** saber de. ● *n*.
be in the ~ estar enterado. **~-all** *n n*
sabelotodo *m* & *f*. **~-how** *n* know-
how *m*, conocimientos *mpl* y experiencia. **~ingly** *adv* a sabiendas.
~-it-all *n* (Amer) ⇒~-ALL

knowledge /'nɒlɪdʒ/ *n* saber *m*;
(awareness) conocimiento *m*; (learning)
conocimientos *mpl*. **~able** *a*
informado

known /nəʊn/ ⇒KNOW. ● *a* conocido

knuckle /'nʌkl/ *n* nudillo *m*. □ **~
under** *vi* someterse

Korea /kə'rɪə/ *n* Corea *f*. **~n** *a* & *n*
coreano (*m*)

kudos /'kju:dɒs/ *n* prestigio *m*

Ll

lab /læb/ *n* 国 laboratorio *m*

label /'leɪbl/ *n* etiqueta *f*. ● *vt* (*pt*
labelled) poner etiqueta a; (fig, describe as) tachar de

laboratory /lə'bɒrətərɪ/ *n* laboratorio *m*

laborious /lə'bɔ:rɪəs/ *a* penoso

labour /'leɪbə(r)/ *n* trabajo *m*; (workers) mano *f* de obra; (Med) parto *m*. **in
~** de parto. ● *vi* trabajar. ● *vt* insistir en. **L~** *n* el partido *m* laborista.
● *a* laborista. **~er** *n* peón *m*

lace /leɪs/ *n* encaje *m*; (of shoe)
cordón *m*, agujeta *f* (Mex). ● *vt* (fasten)
atar

lacerate /'læsəreɪt/ *vt* lacerar

lack /læk/ *n* falta *f*. **for ~ of** por falta
de. ● *vt* faltarle a uno. **he ~s confidence** le falta confianza en sí mismo.
~ing *a*. **be ~ing** faltar. **be ~ing in**
no tener

lad /læd/ *n* muchacho *m*

ladder /'lædə(r)/ *n* escalera *f* (de mano); (in stocking) carrera *f*. ● *vt* hacerse una carrera en. ● *vi* hacérsele
una carrera a

laden /'leɪdn/ *a* cargado (**with** de)

ladle /'leɪdl/ *n* cucharón *m*

lady /'leɪdɪ/ *n* señora *f*. **young ~** señorita *f*. **~bird** *n*, **~bug** *n* (Amer)
mariquita *f*, catarina *f* (Mex). **~-in-
waiting** *n* dama *f* de honor. **~like**
a fino

lag /læg/ *vi* (*pt* **lagged**). **~ (behind)**
retrasarse. ● *vt* revestir <*pipes*>. ● *n*
(interval) intervalo *m*

lager /'lɑ:gə(r)/ *n* cerveza *f* (rubia)

lagging /'lægɪŋ/ *n* revestimiento *m*

lagoon /lə'gu:n/ *n* laguna *f*

laid /leɪd/ ⇒LAY

lain /leɪn/ ⇒LIE¹

lair /leə(r)/ n guarida f

lake /leɪk/ n lago m

lamb /læm/ n cordero m

lame /leɪm/ a (-er, -est) cojo, rengo (LAm); <excuse> pobre, malo

lament /lə'ment/ n lamento m. ● vt lamentar. ~able /'læməntəbl/ a lamentable

lamp /læmp/ n lámpara f

lamp: ~post n farol m. ~shade n pantalla f

lance /lɑːns/ n lanza f

land /lænd/ n tierra f; (country) país m; (plot) terreno m. ● vt desembarcar; (obtain) conseguir; dar <blow>. ● vi (from ship) desembarcar; <aircraft> aterrizar. □~ up vi ir a parar. ~ing n desembarque m; (Aviat) aterrizaje m; (top of stairs) descanso m. ~lady n casera f; (of inn) dueña f. ~lord n casero m, dueño m; (of inn) dueño m. ~mark n punto m destacado. ~scape /-skeɪp/ n paisaje m. ~slide n desprendimiento m de tierras; (Pol) victoria f arrolladora

lane /leɪn/ n (path, road) camino m, sendero m; (strip of road) carril m

language /'læŋgwɪdʒ/ n idioma m; (speech, style) lenguaje m

lank /læŋk/ a <hair> lacio. ~y a (-ier, -iest) larguirucho

lantern /'læntən/ n linterna f

lap /læp/ n (of body) rodillas fpl; (Sport) vuelta f. ● vi (pt lapped) <waves> chapotear. □~up beber a lengüetazos; (fig) aceptar con entusiasmo

lapel /lə'pel/ n solapa f

lapse /læps/ vi (decline) degradarse; (expire) caducar; <time> transcurrir. ~ into silence callarse. ● n error m; (of time) intervalo m

laptop /'læptɒp/ n. ~ (computer) laptop m, laptop f (LAm)

lard /lɑːd/ n manteca f de cerdo

larder /'lɑːdə(r)/ n despensa f

large /lɑːdʒ/ a (-er, -est) grande, (before singular noun) gran. ● n. at ~ en libertad. ~ly adv en gran parte

lark /lɑːk/ n (bird) alondra f; (joke) broma f; (bit of fun) travesura f. □~ about vt hacer el tonto 🄸

larva /'lɑːvə/ n (pl -vae /-viː/) larva f

laser /'leɪzə(r)/ n láser m. ~ beam n rayo m láser. ~ printer n impresora f láser

lash /læʃ/ vt azotar. □~ out vi atacar. ~ out against vt atacar. ● n latigazo m; (eyelash) pestaña f; (whip) látigo m

lashings /'læʃɪŋz/ npl. ~ of (🄳, cream etc) montones de

lass /læs/ n muchacha f

lasso /læ'suː/ n (pl -os) lazo m

last /lɑːst/ a último; <week etc> pasado. ~ Monday el lunes pasado. ~ night anoche. ● adv por último; (most recently) la última vez. he came ~ llegó el último. ● n último m; (remainder) lo que queda. ~ but one penúltimo. at (long) ~ por fin. ● vi/t durar. □~ out vi sobrevivir. ~ing a duradero. ~ly adv por último

latch /lætʃ/ n pestillo m

late /leɪt/ a (-er, -est) (not on time) tarde; (recent) reciente; (former) antiguo, ex. be ~ llegar tarde. in ~ July a fines de julio. the ~ Dr Phillips el difunto Dr. Phillips. ● adv tarde. ~ly adv últimamente

latent /'leɪtnt/ a latente

later /'leɪtə(r)/ adv más tarde

lateral /'lætərəl/ a lateral

latest /'leɪtɪst/ a último. ● n. at the ~ a más tardar

lathe /leɪð/ n torno m

lather /'lɑːðə(r)/ n espuma f

Latin /'lætɪn/ n (Lang) latín m. ● a latino. ~ America n América f Latina, Latinoamérica f. ~ American a & n latinoamericano f

latitude /'lætɪtjuːd/ n latitud m

latter /'lætə(r)/ a último; (of two) segundo. ● n. the ~ éste m, ésta f, éstos mpl, éstas fpl

laugh /lɑːf/ vi reír(se). ~ at reírse de. ● n risa f. ~able a ridículo. ~ing stock n hazmerreír m. ~ter n risas fpl

launch /lɔːntʃ/ vt lanzar; botar <new vessel>. ● n lanzamiento m; (of new vessel) botadura; (boat) lancha f (a motor). ~ing pad, ~ pad n plataforma f de lanzamiento

laund|er /'lɔːndə(r)/ *vt* lavar (y planchar). **~erette** /-et/, **L~romat** /'lɔːndrəmæt/ (Amer) (P) *n* lavandería *f* automática. **~ry** *n* (place) lavandería *f*; (dirty clothes) ropa *f* sucia; (clean clothes) ropa *f* limpia

lava /'lɑːvə/ *n* lava *f*

lavatory /'lævətərɪ/ *n* (cuarto *m* de) baño *m*. **public ~** servicios *mpl*, baños *mpl* (LAm)

lavish /'lævɪʃ/ *a* <lifestyle> de derroche; (meal) espléndido; (production) fastuoso. ● *vt* prodigar (**on** a)

law /lɔː/ *n* ley *f*; (profession, subject of study) derecho *m*. **~ and order** *n* orden *m* público. **~ court** *n* tribunal *m*

lawn /lɔːn/ *n* césped *m*, pasto *m* (LAm). **~mower** *n* cortacésped *f*, cortadora *f* de pasto (LAm)

lawsuit /'lɔːsuːt/ *n* juicio *m*

lawyer /'lɔjə(r)/ *n* abogado *m*

lax /læks/ *a* descuidado; <morals etc> laxo

laxative /'læksətɪv/ *n* laxante *m*

lay /leɪ/ ⇒LIE. ● *vt* (*pt* **laid**) poner <also table, eggs>; tender <trap>; formar <plan>. **~ hands on** echar mano a. **~ hold of** agarrar. ● *a* (non-clerical) laico; <opinion etc> profano. □ **~ down** *vt* dejar a un lado; imponer <condition>. □ **~ into** *vt* 🗵 dar una paliza a. □ **~ off** *vt* despedir <worker>. *vi* 🄸 terminar. □ **~ on** *vt* (provide) proveer. □ **~ out** *vt* (design) disponer; (display) exponer; gastar <money>. **~about** *n* holgazán. **~by** *n* área *f* de reposo

layer /'leɪə(r)/ *n* capa *f*

layette /leɪ'et/ *n* canastilla *f*

layman /'leɪmən/ *n* (*pl* **-men**) lego *m*

layout /'leɪaʊt/ *n* disposición *f*

laz|e /leɪz/ *vi* holgazanear; (relax) descansar. **~iness** *n* pereza *f*. **~y** *a* perezoso. **~ybones** *n* holgazán *m*

lead¹ /liːd/ *vt* (*pt* **led**) conducir; dirigir <team>; llevar <life>; encabezar <parade, attack>. **I was led to believe that ...** me dieron a entender que .... ● *vi* (go first) ir delante; (in race) aventajar. ● *n* mando *m*; (clue) pista

f; (leash) correa *f*; (wire) cable *m*. **be in the ~** llevar la delantera

lead² /led/ *n* plomo *m*; (of pencil) mina *f*. **~ed** *a* <fuel> con plomo

lead /liːd/: **~er** *n* jefe *m*; (Pol) líder *m* & *f*; (of gang) cabecilla *m*. **~ership** *n* dirección *f*. **~ing** *a* principal; (in front) delantero

leaf /liːf/ *n* (*pl* **leaves**) hoja *f*. □ **~ through** *vi* hojear **~let** /'liːflɪt/ *n* folleto *m*. **~y** *a* frondoso

league /liːg/ *n* liga *f*. **be in ~ with** estar aliado con

leak /liːk/ *n* (hole) agujero *m*; (of gas, liquid) escape *m*; (of information) filtración *f*; (in roof) gotera *f*; (in boat) vía *f* de agua. ● *vi* gotear; <liquid> salirse; <boat> hacer agua. ● *vt* perder; filtrar <information>. **~y** *a* <receptacle> agujereado; <roof> que tiene goteras

lean /liːn/ (*pt* **leaned** or **leant** /lent/) *vt* apoyar. ● *vi* inclinarse. □ **~ against** *vt* apoyarse en. □ **~ on** *vt* apoyarse en. □ **~ out** *vt* asomarse (**of** a). □ **~ over** *vi* inclinarse ● *a* (**-er, -est**) <person> delgado; <animal> flaco; <meat> magro. **~ing** *a* inclinado. **~-to** *n* colgadizo *m*

leap /liːp/ *vi* (*pt* **leaped** or **leapt** /lept/) saltar. ● *n* salto *m*. **~frog** *n*. **play ~frog** saltar al potro, jugar a la pídola, brincar al burro (Mex). ● *vi* (*pt* **-frogged**) saltar. **~ year** *n* año *m* bisiesto

learn /lɜːn/ *vt/i* (*pt* **learned** or **learnt**) aprender (**to do** a hacer). **~ed** /-ɪd/ *a* culto. **~er** *n* principiante *m* & *f*; (apprentice) aprendiz *m*. **~ing** *n* saber *m*

lease /liːs/ *n* arriendo *m*. ● *vt* arrendar

leash /liːʃ/ *n* correa *f*

least /liːst/ *a* (smallest amount of) mínimo; (slightest) menor; (smallest) más pequeño. ● *n*. **the ~** lo menos. **at ~** por lo menos. **not in the ~** en absoluto. ● *adv* menos

leather /'leðə(r)/ *n* piel *f*, cuero *m*

leave /liːv/ *vt* (*pt* **left**) dejar; (depart from) salir de. **~ alone** dejar de tocar <thing>; dejar en paz <person>. ● *vi* marcharse; <train> salir. ● *n* permiso *m*. □ **~ behind** *vt* dejar. □ **~ out**

vt omitir. □ ~ **over** *vt*. be left over quedar. **on** ~ (Mil) de permiso

leaves /liːvz/ ⇒LEAF

lecture /'lektʃə(r)/ *n* conferencia *f*; (Univ) clase *f*; (rebuke) sermón *m*. ● *vi* dar clase. ● *vt* (scold) sermonear. ~**r** *n* conferenciante *m* & *f*, conferencista *m* & *f* (LAm); (Univ) profesor *m* universitario

led /led/ ⇒LEAD¹

ledge /ledʒ/ *n* cornisa *f*; (of window) alféizar *m*

leek /liːk/ *n* puerro *m*

leer /'lɪə(r)/ *vi*. ~ **at** mirar impúdicamente. ● *n* mirada impúdica *f*

left /left/ ⇒LEAVE. *a* izquierdo. ● *adv* a la izquierda. ● *n* izquierda *f*. ~**-handed** /-'hændɪd/ *a* zurdo. ~ **luggage** *n* consigna *f*. ~**overs** *npl* restos *mpl*. ~**-wing** /-'wɪŋ/ *a* izquierdista

leg /leg/ *n* pierna *f*; (of animal, furniture) pata *f*; (of pork) pernil *m*; (of lamb) pierna *f*; (of journey) etapa *f*. **on its last** ~**s** en las últimas. **pull s.o.'s** ~ 🔲 tomarle el pelo a uno

legacy /'legəsɪ/ *n* herencia *f*

legal /'liːgl/ *a* (permitted by law) lícito; (recognized by law) legítimo; *<system etc>* jurídico. ~**ity** /liː'gælətɪ/ *n* legalidad *f*. ~**ize** *vt* legalizar. ~**ly** *adv* legalmente

legend /'ledʒənd/ *n* leyenda *f*. ~**ary** *a* legendario

legible /'ledʒəbl/ *a* legible

legislat|e /'ledʒɪsleɪt/ *vi* legislar. ~**ion** /-'leɪʃn/ *n* legislación *f*

legitimate /lɪ'dʒɪtɪmət/ *a* legítimo

leisure /'leʒə(r)/ *n* ocio *m*. **at your** ~ cuando le venga bien. ~**ly** *a* lento, pausado

lemon /'lemən/ *n* limón *m*. ~**ade** /-'neɪd/ *n* (fizzy) gaseosa *f* (de limón); (still) limonada *f*

lend /lend/ *vt* (*pt* **lent**) prestar. ~**ing** *n* préstamo *m*

length /leŋθ/ *n* largo *m*; (of time) duración *f*; (of cloth) largo *m*. **at** ~ (at last) por fin. **at (great)** ~ detalladamente. ~**en** /'leŋθən/ *vt* alargar. ● *vi* alargarse. ~**ways** *adv* a lo largo. ~**y** *a* largo

lenient /'liːnɪənt/ *a* indulgente

lens /lenz/ *n* lente *f*; (of camera) objetivo *m*. (**contact**) ~**es** *npl* lentillas *fpl*, lentes *mpl* de contacto (LAm)

lent /lent/ ⇒LEND

Lent /lent/ *n* cuaresma *f*

Leo /'liːəʊ/ *n* Leo *m*

leopard /'lepəd/ *n* leopardo *m*

leotard /'liːətɑːd/ *n* malla *f*

lesbian /'lezbɪən/ *n* lesbiana *f*. ● *a* lesbiano

less /les/ *a* & *n* & *adv* & *prep* menos. ~ **than** menos que; (with numbers) menos de. ~ **and** ~ cada vez menos. **none the** ~ sin embargo. ~**en** *vt/i* disminuir

lesson /'lesn/ *n* clase *f*

lest /lest/ *conj* no sea que (+ *subjunctive*)

let /let/ *vt* (*pt* **let**, *pres p* **letting**) dejar; (lease) alquilar. ~ **me do it** déjame hacerlo. ● *v aux*. ~**'s go!** ¡vamos!, ¡vámonos! ~**'s see** (vamos) a ver. ~**'s talk/drink** hablemos/bebamos. □ ~ **down** *vt* bajar; (deflate) desinflar; (fig) defraudar. □ ~ **go** *vt* soltar. □ ~ **in** *vt* dejar entrar. □ ~ **off** *vt* disparar *<gun>*; (cause to explode) hacer explotar; hacer estallar *<firework>*; (excuse) perdonar. □ ~ **out** *vt* dejar salir. □ ~ **through** *vt* dejar pasar. □ ~ **up** *vi* disminuir. ~**down** *n* desilusión *f*

lethal /'liːθl/ *a* *<dose, wound>* mortal; *<weapon>* mortífero

largarg|ic /lɪ'θɑːdʒɪk/ *a* letárgico. ~**y** /'leθədʒɪ/ *n* letargo *m*

letter /'letə(r)/ *n* (of alphabet) letra *f*; (written message) carta *f*. ~ **bomb** *n* carta *f* bomba. ~**box** *n* buzón *m*. ~**ing** *n* letras *fpl*

lettuce /'letɪs/ *n* lechuga *f*

let-up /'letʌp/ *n* interrupción *f*

leukaemia /luː'kiːmɪə/ *n* leucemia *f*

level /'levl/ *a* (flat, even) plano, parejo (LAm); *<spoonful>* raso. ~ **with** (at same height) al nivel de. ● *n* nivel *m*. ● *vt* (*pt* **levelled**) nivelar; (aim) apuntar. ~ **crossing** *n* paso *m* a nivel, crucero *m* (Mex)

lever /'liːvə(r)/ *n* palanca *f*. ● *vt* apalancar. ~ **open** abrir haciendo palanca. ~**age** /-ɪdʒ/ *n* apalancamiento *m*

levy /'levɪ/ vt imponer <tax>. ● n impuesto m

lewd /lu:d/ a (**-er, -est**) lascivo

liab|ility /laɪə'bɪlətɪ/ n responsabilidad f; (⬛, disadvantage) lastre m. ~**ili-ties** npl (debts) deudas fpl. ~**le** /'laɪəbl/ a. be ~**le to do** tener tendencia a hacer. ~**le for** responsable de. ~**le to** susceptible de; expuesto a <fine>

liais|e /lɪ'eɪz/ vi actuar de enlace (with con). ~**on** /-ɒn/ n enlace m

liar /'laɪə(r)/ n mentiroso m

libel /'laɪbl/ n difamación f. ● vt (pt **libelled**) difamar (por escrito)

liberal /'lɪbərəl/ a liberal; (generous) generoso. L~ (Pol) del Partido Liberal. ● n liberal m & f. ~**ly** adv liberalmente; (generously) generosamente

liberat|e /'lɪbəreɪt/ vt liberar. ~**ion** /-'reɪʃn/ n liberación f

liberty /'lɪbətɪ/ n libertad f. **take liberties** tomarse libertades. **take the ~ of** tomarse la libertad de

Libra /'li:brə/ n Libra f

librar|ian /laɪ'breərɪən/ n bibliotecario m. ~**y** /'laɪbrərɪ/ n biblioteca f

lice /laɪs/ ⇒LOUSE

licence /'laɪsns/ n licencia f, permiso m

license /'laɪsns/ vt autorizar. ● n (Amer) ⇒LICENCE. ~ **number** n (Amer) (número m de) matrícula f. ~ **plate** n (Amer) matrícula f, placa f (LAm)

lick /lɪk/ vt lamer; (⬛, defeat) dar una paliza a. ● n lametón m

licorice /'lɪkərɪs/ n (Amer) regaliz m

lid /lɪd/ n tapa f; (eyelid) párpado m

lie¹ /laɪ/ vi (pt **lay**, pp **lain**, pres p **lying**) echarse, tenderse; (be in lying position) estar tendido; (be) estar, encontrarse. ~ **low** quedarse escondido. □ ~ **down** vi echarse, tenderse

lie² /laɪ/ n mentira f. ● vi (pt **lied**, pres p **lying**) mentir

lie-in /laɪ'ɪn/ n. **have a ~** quedarse en la cama

lieutenant /lef'tenənt/ n (Mil) teniente m

life /laɪf/ n (pl **lives**) vida f. ~ **belt** n salvavidas m. ~**boat** n lancha f de salvamento; (on ship) bote m salvavidas. ~**buoy** n boya f salvavidas. ~**guard** n salvavidas m & f. ~ **jacket** n chaleco m salvavidas. ~**less** a sin vida. ~**like** a verosímil. ~**line** n cuerda f de salvamento; (fig) tabla f de salvación. ~**long** a de toda la vida. ~ **pre-server** n (Amer, buoy) ⇒~BUOY; (jacket) ⇒~ JACKET. ~ **ring** n (Amer) ⇒~ BELT. ~**saver** n (person) salvavidas m & f; (fig) salvación f. ~ **-size(d)** a (de) tamaño natural. ~**time** n vida f. ~ **vest** n (Amer) ⇒~ JACKET

lift /lɪft/ vt levantar. ● vi <fog> disiparse. ● n ascensor m. **give a ~ to** s.o. llevar a uno en su coche, dar aventón a uno (Mex). □ ~ **up** vt levantar. ~**-off** n despegue m

light /laɪt/ n luz f; (lamp) lámpara f, luz f; (flame) fuego m. **come to ~** salir a la luz. **have you got a ~?** ¿tienes fuego? **the ~s** npl (traffic signals) el semáforo; (on vehicle) las luces. ● a (**-er, -est**) (in colour) claro; (not heavy) ligero. ● vt (pt **lit** or **lighted**) encender, prender (LAm); (illuminate) iluminar. ● vi encenderse, prenderse (LAm). ~ **up** vt iluminar. ● vi iluminarse. ~ **bulb** n bombilla f, foco m (Mex). ~**en** vt (make less heavy) aligerar, aliviar (LAm); (give light to) iluminar; (make brighter) aclarar. ~**er** n (for cigarettes) mechero m, encendedor m. ~**-hearted** /-'hɑ:tɪd/ a alegre. ~**house** n faro m. ~**ly** adv ligeramente

lightning /'laɪtnɪŋ/ n. **flash of ~** relámpago m. ● a relámpago

lightweight a ligero, liviano (LAm)

like /laɪk/ a parecido. ● prep como. ● conj ⬛ como. ● vt. I ~ **chocolate** me gusta el chocolate. **they ~ swim-ming** (a ellos) les gusta nadar. **would you ~ a coffee?** ¿quieres un café? ~**able** a simpático.

like|lihood /'laɪklɪhʊd/ n probabilidad f. ~**ly** a (**-ier, -iest**) probable. **he is ~ly to come** es probable que venga. ● adv probablemente. **not ~ly!** ¡ni hablar! ~**n** vt comparar (to con, a). ~**ness** n parecido m. **be a**

good ~**ness** parecerse mucho.
~**wise** adv (also) también; (the same
way) lo mismo

liking /'laɪkɪŋ/ n (for thing) afición f;
(for person) simpatía f

lilac /'laɪlək/ a lila. ● n lila f; (color) lila m

lily /'lɪlɪ/ n lirio m; (white) azucena f

limb /lɪm/ n miembro m. **out on a** ~
aislado

lime /laɪm/ n (white substance) cal f;
(fruit) lima f. ~**light** n. **be in the**
~**light** ser el centro de atención

limerick /'lɪmərɪk/ n quintilla f
humorística

limit /'lɪmɪt/ n límite m. ● vt limitar.
~**ation** /-'teɪʃn/ n limitación f. ~**ed**
a limitado. ~**ed company** n sociedad f anónima

limousine /'lɪməzi:n/ n limusina f

limp /lɪmp/ vi cojear, renguear (LAm).
● n cojera f, renguera f (LAm). **have a**
~ cojear. ● a (-er, -est) flojo

linden /'lɪndn/ n (Amer) tilo m

line /laɪn/ n línea f; (track) vía f; (wrinkle) arruga f; (row) fila f; (of poem)
verso m; (rope) cuerda f; (of goods)
surtido m; (Amer, queue) cola f. **stand
in** ~ (Amer) hacer cola. **get in** ~
(Amer) ponerse en la cola. **cut in** ~
(Amer) colarse. **in** ~ **with** de acuerdo
con. ● vt forrar <skirt, box>; bordear
<streets etc>. □ ~ **up** vi alinearse; (in
queue) hacer cola. vt (form into line) poner en fila; (align) alinear. ~**d** /laɪnd/
a <paper> con renglones; (with fabric)
forrado

linen /'lɪnɪn/ n (sheets etc) ropa f
blanca; (material) lino m

liner /'laɪnə(r)/ n (ship) transatlántico
m

linger /'lɪŋɡə(r)/ vi tardar en marcharse. ~ (**on**) <smells etc> persistir.
□ ~ **over** vt dilatarse en

lingerie /'lænʒərɪ/ n lencería f

linguist /'lɪŋɡwɪst/ n políglota m &
f; lingüista m & f. ~**ic** /lɪŋ'ɡwɪstɪk/ a
lingüístico. ~**ics** n lingüística f

lining /'laɪnɪŋ/ n forro m

link /lɪŋk/ n (of chain) eslabón m; (connection) conexión f; (bond) vínculo m;
(transport, telecommunications) conexión

f, enlace m. ● vt conectar; relacionar
<facts, events>. □ ~ **up** vt/i conectar

lino /'laɪnəʊ/ n (pl **os**) linóleo m

lint /lɪnt/ n (Med) hilas fpl

lion /'laɪən/ n león m. ~**ess** /-nɪs/ n
leona f

lip /lɪp/ n labio m; (edge) borde m.
~**read** vi leer los labios. ~**salve** n
crema f para los labios. ~ **service**
n. **pay** ~ **service to** aprobar de boquilla, aprobar de los dientes para
afuera (Mex). ~**stick** n lápiz m de labios

liqueur /lɪ'kjʊə(r)/ n licor m

liquid /'lɪkwɪd/ a & n líquido (m)

liquidate /'lɪkwɪdeɪt/ vt liquidar

liquidize /'lɪkwɪdaɪz/ vt licuar. ~**r** n
licuadora f

liquor /'lɪkə(r)/ n bebidas fpl
alcohólicas

liquorice /'lɪkərɪs/ n regaliz m

liquor store n (Amer) tienda f de
bebidas alcohólicas

lisp /lɪsp/ n ceceo m. **speak with a** ~
cecear. ● vi cecear

list /lɪst/ n lista f. ● vt hacer una lista
de; (enter in a list) inscribir. ● vi (ship)
escorar

listen /'lɪsn/ vi escuchar. ~ **in (to)**
escuchar. ~ **to** escuchar. ~**er** n
oyente m & f

listless /'lɪstlɪs/ a apático

lit /lɪt/ ⇒LIGHT

literacy /'lɪtərəsɪ/ n alfabetismo m

literal /'lɪtərəl/ a literal. ~**ly** adv
literalmente

literary /'lɪtərərɪ/ a literario

literate /'lɪtərət/ a alfabetizado

literature /'lɪtərətʃə(r)/ n literatura f; (fig) folletos mpl

lithe /laɪð/ a ágil

litre /'li:tə(r)/ n litro m

litter /'lɪtə(r)/ n basura f; (of animals)
camada f. ● vt ensuciar; (scatter)
esparcir. ~**ed with** lleno de. ~ **bin**
n papelera f. ~**bug**, ~ **lout** n persona f que tira basura en lugares
públicos

little /'lɪtl/ a pequeño; (not much) poco.
a ~ **water** un poco de agua. ● pron
poco, poca. **a** ~ un poco. ● adv poco.

~ **by** ~ poco a poco. ~ **finger** n (dedo m) meñique m

live /lɪv/ vt/i vivir. □~ **down** vt lograr borrar. □~ **off** vt vivir a costa de <*family, friends*>; (feed on) alimentarse de. □~ **on** vt (feed o.s. on) vivir de. vi <*memory*> seguir presente; <*tradition*> seguir existiendo. □~ **up** vt. ~ **it up** 🎩 darse la gran vida. □~ **up to** vt vivir de acuerdo con; cumplir <*promise*>. ●/laɪv/ a vivo; <*wire*> con corriente; <*broadcast*> en directo

livelihood /'laɪvlɪhʊd/ n sustento m

lively /'laɪvlɪ/ a (-ier, -iest) vivo

liven up /'laɪvn/ vt animar. ●vi animar(se)

liver /'lɪvə(r)/ n hígado m

lives /laɪvz/ ⇒LIFE

livestock /'laɪvstɒk/ n animales mpl (de cría); (cattle) ganado m

livid /'lɪvɪd/ a lívido; (🎩, angry) furioso

living /'lɪvɪŋ/ a vivo. ●n vida f. make a ~ ganarse la vida. ~ **room** n salón m, sala f (de estar), living m (LAm)

lizard /'lɪzəd/ n lagartija f; (big) lagarto m

load /ləʊd/ n (also Elec) carga f; (quantity) cantidad f; (weight, strain) peso m. ~**s of** 🎩 montones de. ●vt cargar. ~**ed** a cargado

loaf /ləʊf/ n (pl **loaves**) pan m; (stick of bread) barra f de pan. ●vi. ~ (**about**) holgazanear

loan /ləʊn/ n préstamo m. on ~ prestado. ●vt prestar

loath|e /ləʊð/ vt odiar. ~**ing** n odio m (of a). ~**esome** /-'sæm/ a repugnante

lobby /'lɒbɪ/ n vestíbulo m; (Pol) grupo m de presión. ●vt ejercer presión sobre. ●vi. ~ **for sth** ejercer presión para obtener algo

lobe /ləʊb/ n lóbulo m

lobster /'lɒbstə(r)/ n langosta f, bogavante m

local /'ləʊkl/ a local. ~ (**phone**) **call** llamada f urbana. ●n (🎩, pub) bar m. the ~**s** los vecinos mpl

local: ~ **government** n administración f municipal. ~**ity**

/-'kælətɪ/ n localidad f. ~**ly** adv <*live, work*> en la zona

locat|e /ləʊ'keɪt/ vt (situate) situar, ubicar (LAm); (find) localizar, ubicar (LAm). ~**ion** /-ʃn/ n situación f, ubicación f (LAm). on ~**ion** fuera del estudio. to film on ~**ion** in Andalusia rodar en Andalucía

lock /lɒk/ n (of door etc) cerradura f; (on canal) esclusa f; (of hair) mechón m. ●vt cerrar con llave. ●vi cerrarse con llave. □~ **in** vt encerrar. □~ **out** vt cerrar la puerta a. □~ **up** vt encerrar <*person*>; cerrar con llave <*building*>

locker /'lɒkə(r)/ n armario m, locker m (LAm). ~ **room** n (Amer) vestuario m, vestidor m (Mex)

locket /'lɒkɪt/ n medallón m

lock: ~**out** /'lɒkaʊt/ n cierre m patronal, paro m patronal (LAm). ~**smith** n cerrajero m

locomotive /ləʊkə'məʊtɪv/ n locomotora f

lodg|e /lɒdʒ/ n (of porter) portería f. ●vt alojar; presentar <*complaint*>. ~**er** n huésped m. ~**ings** n alojamiento m; (room) habitación f alquilada

loft /lɒft/ n desván m, altillo m (LAm)

lofty /'lɒftɪ/ a (-ier, -iest) elevado; (haughty) altanero

log /lɒg/ n (of wood) tronco m; (as fuel) leño m; (record) diario m. sleep like a ~ dormir como un tronco. ●vt (pt **logged**) registrar. □~ **in**, ~ **on** vi (Comp) entrar (al sistema). □~ **off**, ~ **out** vi (Comp) salir (del sistema)

logarithm /'lɒgərɪðəm/ n logaritmo m

loggerheads /'lɒgəhedz/ npl. be at ~ **with** estar a matar con

logic /'lɒdʒɪk/ a lógica f. ~**al** a lógico. ~**ally** adv lógicamente

logistics /lə'dʒɪstɪks/ n logística f. ●npl (practicalities) problemas mpl logísticos

logo /'ləʊgəʊ/ n (pl **-os**) logo m

loin /lɔɪn/ n (Culin) lomo m. ~**s** npl entrañas fpl

loiter /'lɔɪtə(r)/ vi perder el tiempo

loll /lɒl/ vi repantigarse

loll|ipop /'lɒlɪpɒp/ *n* pirulí *m*. ∼**y** *n* polo *m*, paleta *f* (helada) (LAm)

London /'lʌndən/ *n* Londres *m*. ● *a* londinense. ∼**er** *n* londinense *m* & *f*

lone /ləʊn/ *a* solitario. ∼**ly** *a* (**-ier**, **-iest**) solitario. **feel** ∼**ly** sentirse muy solo. ∼**r** *n* solitario *m*. ∼**some** /-səm/ *a* solitario

long /lɒŋ/ *a* (**-er**, **-est**) largo. **a** ∼ **time** mucho tiempo. **how** ∼ **is it?** ¿cuánto tiene de largo? ● *adv* largo/ mucho tiempo. **as** ∼ **as** (while) mientras; (provided that) con tal que (+ *subjunctive*). **before** ∼ dentro de poco. **so** ∼! ¡hasta luego! **so** ∼ **as** (provided that) con tal que (+ *subjunctive*). □ ∼ **for** *vi* anhelar. ∼ **to do** estar deseando hacer. ∼**-distance** /-'dɪstəns/ *a* de larga distancia. ∼**-distance phone call** llamada *f* de larga distancia, conferencia *f*. ∼**er** *adv*. **no** ∼**er** ya no

long: ∼**-haul** /-'hɔːl/ *a* de larga distancia. ∼**ing** *n* anhelo *m*, ansia *f*

longitude /'lɒŋgɪtjuːd/ *n* longitud *f*

long: ∼ **jump** *n* salto *m* de longitud. ∼**-playing record** *n* elepé *m*. ∼**-range** *a* de largo alcance. ∼**-sighted** /-'saɪtɪd/ *a* hipermétrope. ∼**-term** *a* a largo plazo. ∼**-winded** /-'wɪndɪd/ *a* prolijo

loo /luː/ *n* 🅱 váter *m*, baño *m* (LAm)

look /lʊk/ *vt* mirar; representar *<age>*. ● *vi* mirar; (seem) parecer; (search) buscar. ● *n* mirada *f*; (appearance) aspecto *m*. **good** ∼**s** belleza *f*. □ ∼ **after** *vt* cuidar *<person>*; (be responsible for) encargarse de. □ ∼ **at** *vt* mirar; (consider) considerar. □ ∼ **down on** *vt* despreciar. □ ∼ **for** *vt* buscar. □ ∼ **forward to** *vt* esperar con ansia. □ ∼ **into** *vt* investigar. □ ∼ **like** *vt* parecerse a. □ ∼ **on** *vi* mirar. □ ∼ **out** *vi* tener cuidado. □ ∼ **out for** *vt* buscar; (watch) tener cuidado con. □ ∼ **round** *vi* volver la cabeza. □ ∼ **through** *vt* hojear. □ ∼ **up** *vt* buscar *<word>*; (visit) ir a ver. □ ∼ **up to** *vt* admirar. ∼**-alike** *n* 🅱 doble *m* & *f*. ∼**out** *n* (Mil, person) vigía *m*. **be on the** ∼**out for** andar a la caza de. ∼**s** *npl* belleza *f*

loom /luːm/ *n* telar *m*. ● *vi* aparecerse

looney, loony /'luːnɪ/ *a* & *n* 🅳 chiflado (*m*) 🅸, loco (*m*)

loop /luːp/ *n* (shape) curva *f*; (in string) lazada *f*. ● *vt* hacer una lazada con. ∼**hole** *n* (in rule) escapatoria *f*

loose /luːs/ *a* (**-er**, **-est**) suelto; *<garment, thread, hair>* flojo; (inexact) vago; (not packed) suelto. **be at a** ∼ **end** no tener nada que hacer. ∼**ly** *adv* sueltamente; (roughly) aproximadamente. ∼**n** *vt* aflojar

loot /luːt/ *n* botín *m*. ● *vt/i* saquear. ∼**er** *n* saqueador *m*

lop /lɒp/ *vt* (*pt* **lopped**). ∼ **off** cortar

lop-sided /-'saɪdɪd/ *a* ladeado

lord /lɔːd/ *n* señor *m*; (British title) lord *m*. (**good**) **L**∼! ¡Dios mío! **the L**∼ el Señor. **the** (**House of**) **L**∼**s** la Cámara de los Lores

lorry /'lɒrɪ/ *n* camión *m*. ∼ **driver** *n* camionero *m*

lose /luːz/ *vt/i* (*pt* **lost**) perder. ∼**r** *n* perdedor *m*

loss /lɒs/ *n* pérdida *f*. **be at a** ∼ estar perplejo. **be at a** ∼ **for words** no encontrar palabras

lost /lɒst/ ⇒LOSE. ● *a* perdido. **get** ∼ perderse. ∼ **property** *n*, ∼ **and found** (Amer) oficina *f* de objetos perdidos

lot /lɒt/ *n* (fate) suerte *f*; (at auction) lote *m*; (land) solar *m*. **a** ∼ (**of**) muchos. **quite a** ∼ **of** 🅸 bastante. ∼**s** (**of**) 🅸 muchos. **they ate the** ∼ se lo comieron todo

lotion /'ləʊʃn/ *n* loción *f*

lottery /'lɒtərɪ/ *n* lotería *f*

loud /laʊd/ *a* (**-er**, **-est**) fuerte; (noisy) ruidoso; (gaudy) chillón. **out** ∼ en voz alta. ∼**hailer** /-'heɪlə(r)/ *n* megáfono *m*. ∼**ly** *adv* *<speak>* en voz alta; *<shout>* fuerte; *<complain>* a voz en grito. ∼**speaker** /-'spiːkə(r)/ *n* altavoz *m*, altoparlante *m* (LAm)

lounge /laʊndʒ/ *vi* repantigarse. ● *n* salón *m*, sala *f* (de estar), living *m* (LAm)

lous|e /laʊs/ *n* (*pl* **lice**) piojo *m*. ∼**y** /'laʊzɪ/ *a* (**-ier**, **-iest**) (🅱, bad) malísimo

lout /laʊt/ *n* patán *m*

lov|able /'lʌvəbl/ a adorable. ~e /lʌv/ n amor m; (tennis) cero m. **be in ~e (with)** estar enamorado (de). **fall in ~e (with)** enamorarse (de). ● vt querer, amar <*person*>. **I ~e milk** me encanta la leche. **~e affair** n aventura f, amorío m

lovely /'lʌvlɪ/ a (**-ier, -iest**) <*appearance*> precioso, lindo (LAm); <*person*> encantador, amoroso (LAm)

lover /'lʌvə(r)/ n amante m & f

loving /'lʌvɪŋ/ a cariñoso

low /ləʊ/ a & adv (**-er, -est**) bajo. ● vi <*cattle*> mugir. **~er** vt bajar. **~er o.s.** envilecerse. **~-level** a a bajo nivel. **~ly** a (**-ier, -iest**) humilde

loyal /'lɔɪəl/ a leal, fiel. **~ty** n lealtad f

lozenge /'lɒzɪndʒ/ n (shape) rombo m; (tablet) pastilla f

LP abbr (= **long-playing record**) elepé m

Ltd /'lɪmɪtɪd/ abbr (= **Limited**) S.A., Sociedad Anónima

lubricate /'lu:brɪkeɪt/ vt lubricar

lucid /'lu:sɪd/ a lúcido

luck /lʌk/ n suerte f. **good ~!** ¡(buena) suerte! **~ily** adv por suerte. **~y** a (**-ier, -iest**) <*person*> con suerte. **be ~y** tener suerte. **~y number** número m de la suerte

lucrative /'lu:krətɪv/ a lucrativo

ludicrous /'lu:dɪkrəs/ a ridículo

lug /lʌg/ vt (pt **lugged**) 🄸 arrastrar

luggage /'lʌgɪdʒ/ n equipaje m. **~ rack** n rejilla f

lukewarm /'lu:kwɔ:m/ a tibio; (fig) poco entusiasta

lull /lʌl/ vt (soothe, send to sleep) adormecer; (calm) calmar. ● n periodo m de calma

lullaby /'lʌləbaɪ/ n canción f de cuna

lumber /'lʌmbə(r)/ n trastos mpl viejos; (wood) maderos mpl. ● vt. **~ s.o. with sth** 🄸 endilgar algo a uno. **~jack** n leñador m

luminous /'lu:mɪnəs/ a luminoso

lump /lʌmp/ n (swelling) bulto m; (as result of knock) chichón m; (in liquid) grumo m; (of sugar) terrón m. ● vt. **~ together** agrupar. **~ it** 🄸 aguantarse. **~ sum** n suma f global. **~y** a <*sauce*> grumoso; <*mattress, cushions*> lleno de protuberancias

lunacy /'lu:nəsɪ/ n locura f

lunar /'lu:nə(r)/ a lunar

lunatic /'lu:nətɪk/ n loco m

lunch /lʌntʃ/ n comida f, almuerzo m. **have ~** comer, almorzar

luncheon /'lʌntʃən/ n comida f, almuerzo m. **~ voucher** n vale m de comida

lung /lʌŋ/ n pulmón m

lunge /lʌndʒ/ n arremetida f. ● vi. **~ at** arremeter contra

lurch /lɜ:tʃ/ vi tambalearse. ● n. **leave in the ~** dejar plantado

lure /ljʊə(r)/ vt atraer

lurid /'ljʊərɪd/ a <*colour*> chillón; (shocking) morboso

lurk /lɜ:k/ vi merodear; (in ambush) estar al acecho

luscious /'lʌʃəs/ a delicioso

lush /lʌʃ/ a exuberante

lust /lʌst/ n lujuria f; (craving) deseo m. ● vi. **~ after** codiciar

lute /lu:t/ n laúd m

Luxembourg, Luxemburg /'lʌksəmbɜ:g/ n Luxemburgo m

luxuriant /lʌg'zjʊərɪənt/ a exuberante

luxur|ious /lʌg'zjʊərɪəs/ a lujoso. **~y** /'lʌkʃərɪ/ n lujo m. ● a de lujo

lying /'laɪɪŋ/ ⇒LIE¹, LIE². ● n mentiras fpl. ● a mentiroso

lynch /lɪntʃ/ vt linchar

lyric /'lɪrɪk/ a lírico. **~al** a lírico. **~s** npl letra f

M m

MA /em'eɪ/ abbr ⇒MASTER

mac /mæk/ n 🄸 impermeable m

macabre /mə'kɑ:brə/ a macabro

macaroni /mækə'rəʊnɪ/ n macarrones mpl

mace /meɪs/ n (staff) maza f; (spice) macis f. **M~** (P) (Amer) gas m para defensa personal

machine /mə'ʃi:n/ n máquina f. ~ **gun** n ametralladora f. ~**ry** n maquinaria f; (working parts, fig) mecanismo m

mackintosh /'mækɪntɒʃ/ n impermeable m

macro /'mækrəʊ/ n (pl **-os**) (Comp) macro m

macrobiotic /mækrəʊbaɪ'ɒtɪk/ a macrobiótico

mad /mæd/ a (**madder**, **maddest**) loco; (🔲, angry) furioso. be ~ **about** estar loco por

madam /'mædəm/ n señora f

mad: ~**cap** a atolondrado. ~**den** vt (make mad) enloquecer; (make angry) enfurecer

made /meɪd/ ⇒MAKE. ~**-to-measure** hecho a (la) medida

mad: ~**house** n manicomio m. ~**ly** adv (interested, in love etc) locamente; (frantically) como un loco. ~**man** /-mən/ n loco m. ~**ness** n locura f

Madonna /mə'dɒnə/ n. the ~ (Relig) la Virgen

maestro /'maɪstrəʊ/ n (pl **maestri** /-stri:/ or **-os**) maestro m

Mafia /'mæfɪə/ n mafia f

magazine /mægə'zi:n/ n revista f; (of gun) recámara f

magenta /mə'dʒentə/ a magenta, morado

maggot /'mægət/ n gusano m

magic /'mædʒɪk/ n magia f. ● a mágico. ~**al** a mágico. ~**ian** /mə'dʒɪʃn/ n mago m

magistrate /'mædʒɪstreɪt/ n juez m que conoce de faltas y asuntos civiles de menor importancia

magnet /'mægnɪt/ n imán m. ~**ic** /-'netɪk/ a magnético; (fig) lleno de magnetismo. ~**ism** n magnetismo m. ~**ize** vt imantar, magnetizar

magnif|ication /mægnɪfɪ'keɪʃn/ n aumento m. ~**y** /'mægnɪfaɪ/ vt aumentar. ~**ying glass** n lupa f

magnificen|ce /mæg'nɪfɪsns/ a magnificencia f. ~**t** a magnífico

magnitude /'mægnɪtju:d/ n magnitud f

magpie /'mægpaɪ/ n urraca f

mahogany /mə'hɒgənɪ/ n caoba f

maid /meɪd/ n (servant) criada f, sirvienta f; (girl, old use) doncella f. old ~ solterona f

maiden /'meɪdn/ n doncella f. ● a <voyage> inaugural. ~ **name** n apellido m de soltera

mail /meɪl/ n correo m; (armour) (cota f de) malla f. ● a correo. ● vt echar al correo <letter>; (send) enviar por correo. ~**box** n (Amer) buzón m. ~**ing list** n lista f de direcciones. ~**man** /-mən/ n (Amer) cartero m. ~ **order** n venta f por correo

maim /meɪm/ vt mutilar

main /meɪn/ n. (water/gas) ~ cañería f principal. in the ~ en su mayor parte. the ~**s** npl (Elec) la red f de suministro. ● a principal. ~ **course** n plato m principal, plato m fuerte. ~ **frame** n (Comp) unidad f central. ~**land** n. the ~**land** la masa territorial de un país excluyendo sus islas. ● a. ~**land China** (la) China continental. ~**ly** adv principalmente. ~ **road** n carretera f principal. ~**stream** a <culture> establecido. ~ **street** n calle f principal

maint|ain /meɪn'teɪn/ vt mantener. ~**enance** /'meɪntənəns/ n mantenimiento m

maisonette /meɪzə'net/ n (small house) casita f; (part of house) dúplex m

maize /meɪz/ n maíz m

majestic /mə'dʒestɪk/ a majestuoso

majesty /'mædʒəstɪ/ n majestad f

major /'meɪdʒə(r)/ a (important) muy importante; (Mus) mayor. a ~ **road** una calle prioritaria. ● n comandante m & f, mayor m & f (LAm). ● vi. ~ **in** (Amer, Univ) especializarse en

Majorca /mə'jɔːkə/ n Mallorca f

majority /mə'dʒɒrətɪ/ n mayoría f. ● a mayoritario

make /meɪk/ vt (pt **made**) hacer; (manufacture) fabricar; ganar <money>; tomar <decision>; llegar a <destination>. ~ **s.o. do sth** obligar a uno a hacer algo. **be made of** estar hecho de. **I** ~ **it two o'clock** yo tengo las dos. ~ **believe** fingir. ~ **do** (manage) arreglarse. ~ **do with** (content o.s.) contentarse con. ~ **it** llegar; (succeed) tener éxito. ● *n* marca *f*. ~ **for** *vt* dirigirse a. □ ~ **good** *vt* compensar; (repair) reparar. □ ~ **off** *vi* escaparse (with con). □ ~ **out** *vt* distinguir; (understand) entender; (write out) hacer; (assert) dar a entender. *vi* (cope) arreglárselas. □ ~ **up** *vt* (constitute) formar; (prepare) preparar; inventar *<story>*; ~ **it up** (become reconciled) hacer las paces. ~ **up** (one's face) maquillarse. □ ~ **up for** *vt* compensar. ~**believe** *a* fingido, simulado. *n* ficción *f*. ~**over** *n* (Amer) maquillaje *m*. ~**r** *n* fabricante *m* & *f*. ~**shift** *a* (temporary) provisional, provisorio (LAm); (improvised) improvisado. ~**up** *n* maquillaje *m*. put on ~**up** maquillarse.

making /'meɪkɪŋ/ *n*. he has the ~**s** of tiene madera de. in the ~ en vías de formación

maladjusted /mælə'dʒʌstɪd/ *a* inadaptado

malaria /mə'leərɪə/ *n* malaria *f*, paludismo *m*

Malaysia /mə'leɪzɪə/ *n* Malasia *f*. ~**n** *a* & *n* malaisio (*m*)

male /meɪl/ *a* macho; *<voice, attitude>* masculino. ● *n* macho *m*; (man) varón *m*

malevolent /mə'levələnt/ *a* malévolo

malfunction /mæl'fʌŋkʃn/ *vi* fallar, funcionar mal

malic|e /'mælɪs/ *n* mala intención *f*, maldad *f*. **bear s.o.** ~**e** guardar rencor a uno. ~**ious** /mə'lɪʃəs/ *a* malintencionado. ~**iously** *adv* con malevolencia

malignant /mə'lɪgnənt/ *a* maligno

mallet /'mælɪt/ *n* mazo *m*

malnutrition /mælnju:'trɪʃn/ *n* desnutrición *f*

malpractice /mæl'præktɪs/ *n* mala práctica *f* (en el ejercicio de una profesión)

malt /mɔːlt/ *n* malta *f*

Malt|a /'mɔːltə/ *n* Malta *f*. ~**ese** /-'tiːz/ *a* & *n* maltés (*m*)

mammal /'mæml/ *n* mamífero *m*

mammoth /'mæməθ/ *n* mamut *m*. ● *a* gigantesco

man /mæn/ *n* (*pl* **men** /men/) hombre *m*; (Chess) pieza *f*. ~ **in the street** hombre *m* de la calle. ● *vt* (*pt* **manned**) encargarse de *<switchboard>*; tripular *<ship>*; servir *<guns>*

manacles /'mænəklz/ *n* (for wrists) esposas *fpl*; (for legs) grillos *mpl*

manag|e /'mænɪdʒ/ *vt* dirigir; administrar *<land, finances>*; (handle) manejar. ● *vi* (Com) dirigir; (cope) arreglárselas. ~**e to do** lograr hacer. ~**eable** *a* *<task>* posible de alcanzar; *<size>* razonable. ~**ement** *n* dirección *f*. ~**er** *n* director *m*; (of shop) encargado *m*; (of soccer team) entrenador *m*, director *m* técnico (LAm). ~**eress** /-'res/ *n* encargada *f*. ~**erial** /-'dʒɪərɪəl/ *a* directivo, gerencial (LAm). ~**ing director** *n* director *m* ejecutivo

mandate /'mændeɪt/ *n* mandato *m*

mandatory /'mændətərɪ/ *a* obligatorio

mane /meɪn/ *n* (of horse) crin(es) *f(pl)*; (of lion) melena *f*

mangle /'mæŋgl/ *n* rodillo *m* (escurridor). ● *vt* destrozar

man: ~**handle** *vt* mover a pulso; (treat roughly) maltratar. ~**hole** *n* registro *m*. ~**hood** *n* madurez *f*; (quality) virilidad *f*. ~**hour** *n* hora *f* hombre. ~**hunt** *n* persecución *f*

mania /'meɪnɪə/ *n* manía *f*. ~**c** /-ɪæk/ *n* maníaco *m*

manicure /'mænɪkjʊə(r)/ *n* manicura *f*, manicure *f* (LAm)

manifest /'mænɪfest/ *a* manifiesto. ● *vt* manifestar. ~**ation** /-'steɪʃn/ *n* manifestación *f*

manifesto /mænɪ'festəʊ/ *n* (*pl* **-os**) manifiesto *m*

manipulat|e /mə'nɪpjʊleɪt/ *vt* manipular. ~**ion** /-'leɪʃn/ *n* manipulación *f*. ~**ive** /-lətɪv/ *a* manipulador

man: ~**kind** *n* humanidad *f*. ~**ly** *a* viril. ~**made** *a* artificial

manner /'mænə(r)/ *n* manera *f*; (demeanour) actitud *f*; (kind) clase *f*. ~**ed** *a* amanerado. ~**s** *npl* modales *mpl*, educación *f*. bad ~**s** mala educación

manoeuvre /mə'nuːvə(r)/ *n* maniobra *f*. ● *vt/i* maniobrar

manor /'mænə(r)/ *n.* ~ **house** casa *f* solariega

manpower *n* mano *f* de obra

mansion /'mænʃn/ *n* mansión *f*

man: ~**-size(d)** *a* grande. ~**slaughter** *n* homicidio *m* sin premeditación

mantelpiece /'mæntlpi:s/ *n* repisa *f* de la chimenea

manual /'mænjʊəl/ *a* manual. ● *n* (handbook) manual *m*

manufacture /mænjʊ'fæktʃə(r)/ *vt* fabricar. ● *n* fabricación *f*. ~**r** *n* fabricante *m & f*

manure /mə'njʊə(r)/ *n* estiércol *m*

manuscript /'mænjʊskrɪpt/ *n* manuscrito *m*

many /'menɪ/ *a & pron* muchos, muchas. ~ **people** mucha gente. **a great/good** ~ muchísimos. **how** ~**?** ¿cuántos? **so** ~ tantos. **too** ~ demasiados

map /mæp/ *n* mapa *m*; (of streets etc) plano *m*

mar /mɑː(r)/ *vt* (*pt* **marred**) estropear

marathon /'mærəθən/ *n* maratón *m & f*

marble /'mɑːbl/ *n* mármol *m*; (for game) canica *f*

march /mɑːtʃ/ *vi* (Mil) marchar. ~ **off** *vi* irse. ● *n* marcha *f*

March /mɑːtʃ/ *n* marzo *m*

march-past /'mɑːtʃpɑːst/ *n* desfile *m*

mare /meə(r)/ *n* yegua *f*

margarine /mɑːdʒə'riːn/ *n* margarina *f*

margin /'mɑːdʒɪn/ *n* margen *f*. ~**al** *a* marginal

marijuana /mærɪ'hwɑːnə/ *n* marihuana *f*

marina /mə'riːnə/ *n* puerto *m* deportivo

marine /mə'riːn/ *a* marino. ● *n* (sailor) infante *m* de marina

marionette /mærɪə'net/ *n* marioneta *f*

marital status /mærɪtl 'steɪtəs/ *n* estado *m* civil

mark /mɑːk/ *n* marca *f*; (stain) mancha *f*; (Schol) nota *f*; (target) blanco *m*. ● *vt* (indicate) señalar, marcar; (stain) manchar; corregir *<exam>*. ~ **time** marcar el paso. □ ~ **out** *vt* (select) señalar; (distinguish) distinguir. ~**ed** *a* marcado. ~**edly** /-kɪdlɪ/ *adv* marcadamente. ~**er** *n* marcador *m*. ~**er** (**pen**) *n* rotulador *m*, marcador *m* (LAm)

market /'mɑːkɪt/ *n* mercado *m*. **on the** ~ en venta. ● *vt* comercializar. ~ **garden** *n* huerta *f*. ~**ing** *n* marketing *m*

marking /'mɑːkɪŋ/ *n* marcas *fpl*; (on animal, plant) mancha *f*

marksman /'mɑːksmən/ *n* (*pl* **-men**) tirador *m*. ~**ship** *n* puntería *f*

marmalade /'mɑːməleɪd/ *n* mermelada *f* (de cítricos)

maroon /mə'ruːn/ *a & n* granate (*m*). ● *vt* abandonar (en una isla desierta)

marquee /mɑː'kiː/ *n* toldo *m*, entoldado *m*; (Amer, awning) marquesina *f*

marriage /'mærɪdʒ/ *n* matrimonio *m*; (ceremony) casamiento *m*

married /'mærɪd/ *a* casado; *<life>* conyugal

marrow /'mærəʊ/ *n* (of bone) tuétano *m*; (vegetable) calabaza *f* verde alargada. ~ **squash** *n* (Amer) calabaza *f* verde alargada

marry /'mærɪ/ *vt* casarse con; (give or unite in marriage) casar. ● *vi* casarse. **get married** casarse (**to** con)

Mars /mɑːz/ *n* Marte *m*

marsh /mɑːʃ/ *n* pantano *m*

marshal /'mɑːʃl/ *n* (Mil) mariscal *m*; (Amer, police chief) jefe *m* de policía. ● *vt* (*pt* **marshalled**) reunir; poner en orden *<thoughts>*

marsh: ~ **mallow** /-'mæləʊ/ *n* malvavisco *m*, bombón *m* (LAm). ~**y** *a* pantanoso

martial /'mɑːʃl/ *a* marcial. ~ **arts** *npl* artes *fpl* marciales. ~ **law** *n* ley *f* marcial

martyr /'mɑːtə(r)/ *n* mártir *m & f*

marvel /'mɑːvl/ *n* maravilla *f*. ● *vi* (*pt* **marvelled**) maravillarse (**at** de). ~**lous** *a* maravilloso

Marxis|m /'mɑːksɪzəm/ *n* marxismo *m*. ~**t** *a & n* marxista (*m & f*)

marzipan /ˈmɑːzɪpæn/ n mazapán m

mascara /mæˈskɑːrə/ n rímel m (P)

mascot /ˈmæskɒt/ n mascota f

masculin|e /ˈmæskjʊlɪn/ a & n masculino (m). ~ity /-ˈlɪnətɪ/ n masculinidad f

mash /mæʃ/ n (Br ⚏, potatoes) puré m de patatas, puré m de papas (LAm). ● vt hacer puré de, moler (Mex). ~ed potatoes n puré m de patatas, puré m de papas (LAm)

mask /mɑːsk/ n máscara f; (Sport) careta f. ● vt ocultar

masochis|m /ˈmæsəkɪzəm/ n masoquismo m. ~t n masoquista m & f. ~tic /-ˈkɪstɪk/ a masoquista

mason /ˈmeɪsn/ n (stone ~) mampostero m. M~ (freemason) masón m. ~ry /ˈmeɪsnrɪ/ n albañilería f

masquerade /mɑːskəˈreɪd/ n mascarada f. ● vi. ~ as hacerse pasar por

mass /mæs/ n masa f; (Relig) misa f; (large quantity) montón m. the ~es las masas. ● vi concentrarse

massacre /ˈmæsəkə(r)/ n masacre f, matanza f. ● vt masacrar

mass|age /ˈmæsɑːʒ/ n masaje m. ● vt masajear. ~eur /mæˈsɜː(r)/ n masajista m. ~euse /mæˈsɜːz/ n masajista f

massive /ˈmæsɪv/ a masivo; (heavy) macizo; (huge) enorme

mass: ~ media n medios mpl de comunicación. ~-produce /-prə 'djuːs/ vt fabricar en serie

mast /mɑːst/ n mástil m; (for radio, TV) antena f repetidora

master /ˈmɑːstə(r)/ n amo m; (expert) maestro m; (in secondary school) profesor m; (of ship) capitán m; (master copy) original m. ~'s degree master m, maestría f. M~ of Arts (MA) poseedor m de una maestría en folosofía y letras. M~ of Science (MSc) poseedor m de una maestría en ciencias. ● vt llegar a dominar. ~ key n llave f maestra. ~mind n cerebro m. ● vt dirigir. ~piece n obra f maestra. ~stroke n golpe m

de maestro. ~y n dominio m; (skill) maestría f

masturbat|e /ˈmæstəbeɪt/ vi masturbarse. ~ion /-ˈbeɪʃn/ n masturbación f

mat /mæt/ n estera f; (at door) felpudo m. ● a (Amer) ⇒MATT

match /mætʃ/ n (Sport) partido m; (for fire) cerilla f, fósforo m (LAm), cerillo m (Mex); (equal) igual m. ● vt emparejar; (equal) igualar; <clothes, colours> hacer juego con. ● vi hacer juego. ~box n caja f de cerillas, caja f de fósforos (LAm), caja f de cerillos (Mex). ~ing a que hace juego. ~stick n cerilla f, fósforo m (LAm), cerillo m (Mex)

mate /meɪt/ n (of person) pareja f; (of animals, male) macho m; (of animals, female) hembra f; (assistant) ayudante m; (⚏, friend) amigo m, cuate m (Mex); (Chess) (jaque m) mate m. ● vi aparearse

material /məˈtɪərɪəl/ n material m; (cloth) tela f. ● a material. ~istic /-ˈlɪstɪk/ a materialista. ~ize vi materializarse. ~s npl materiales mpl

matern|al /məˈtɜːnl/ a maternal. ~ity /-ətɪ/ n maternidad f. ● a <ward> de obstetricia; <clothes> premamá, de embarazada

math /mæθ/ n (Amer) ⇒MATHS

mathematic|ian /mæθəməˈtɪʃn/ n matemático m. ~al /-ˈmætɪkl/ a matemático. ~s /-ˈmætɪks/ n matemática(s) f(pl)

maths /mæθs/ n matemática(s) f(pl)

matinée, matinee /ˈmætɪneɪ/ n (Theatre) función f de tarde; (Cinema) primera sesión f (de la tarde)

matrices /ˈmeɪtrɪsiːz/ ⇒MATRIX

matriculat|e /məˈtrɪkjʊleɪt/ vi matricularse. ~ion /-ˈleɪʃn/ n matrícula f

matrimon|ial /mætrɪˈməʊnɪəl/ a matrimonial. ~y /ˈmætrɪmənɪ/ n matrimonio m

matrix /ˈmeɪtrɪks/ n (pl **matrices**) matriz f

matron /ˈmeɪtrən/ n (married, elderly) matrona f; (in school) ama f de llaves; (former use, in hospital) enfermera f jefe

matt, **matte** (Amer) /mæt/ *a* mate

matted /'mætɪd/ *a* enmarañado y apelmazado

matter /'mætə(r)/ *n* (substance) materia *f*; (affair) asunto *m*; (pus) pus *m*. **as a** ∼ **of fact** en realidad. **no** ∼ no importa. **what is the** ∼? ¿qué pasa? **to make** ∼**s worse** para colmo (de males). ●*vi* importar. **it doesn't** ∼ no importa. ∼**-of-fact** /-əv'fækt/ *a* <*person*> práctico

mattress /'mætrɪs/ *n* colchón *m*

matur|e /mə'tjʊə(r)/ *a* maduro. ●*vi* madurar. ∼**ity** *n* madurez *f*

maudlin /'mɔːdlɪn/ *a* llorón

maul /mɔːl/ *vt* atacar (y herir)

mauve /məʊv/ *a & n* malva (*m*)

maverick /'mævərɪk/ *n* inconformista *m & f*

maxim /'mæksɪm/ *n* máxima *f*

maxim|ize /'mæksɪmaɪz/ *vt* maximizar. ∼**um** /-əm/ *a & n* máximo (*m*)

may /meɪ/, past **might**

●*auxiliary verb*

····▸ (expressing possibility) **he** ∼ **come** puede que venga, es posible que venga. **it** ∼ **be true** puede ser verdad. **she** ∼ **not have seen him** es posible que *or* puede que no lo haya visto

····▸ (asking for or giving permission) ∼ **I smoke?** ¿puedo fumar?, ¿se puede fumar? ∼ **I have your name and address, please?** ¿quiere darme su nombre y dirección, por favor?

····▸ (expressing a wish) ∼ **he be happy** que sea feliz

····▸ (conceding) **he** ∼ **not have much experience, but he's very hardworking** no tendrá mucha experiencia, pero es muy trabajador. **that's as** ∼ **be** puede ser

····▸**I** ∼ **as well stay** más vale quedarme

May /meɪ/ *n* mayo *m*

maybe /'meɪbɪ/ *adv* quizá(s), tal vez, a lo mejor

May Day *n* el primero de mayo

mayhem /'meɪhem/ *n* caos *m*

mayonnaise /meɪə'neɪz/ *n* mayonesa *f*, mahonesa *f*

mayor /meə(r)/ *n* alcalde *m*, alcaldesa *f*. ∼**ess** /-ɪs/ *n* alcaldesa *f*

maze /meɪz/ *n* laberinto *m*

me /miː/ *pron* me; (*after prep*) mí. **he knows** ∼ me conoce. **it's** ∼ soy yo

meadow /'medəʊ/ *n* prado *m*, pradera *f*

meagre /'miːgə(r)/ *a* escaso

meal /miːl/ *n* comida *f*. ∼**time** *n* hora *f* de comer

mean /miːn/ *vt* (*pt* **meant**) (intend) tener la intención de, querer; (signify) querer decir, significar. ∼ **to do** tener la intención de hacer. ∼ **well** tener buenas intenciones. **be meant for** estar destinado a. ●*a* (**-er, -est**) (miserly) tacaño; (unkind) malo; (Math) medio. ●*n* media *f*; (average) promedio *m*

meander /mɪ'ændə(r)/ *vi* <*river*> serpentear

meaning /'miːnɪŋ/ *n* sentido *m*. ∼**ful** *a* significativo. ∼**less** *a* sin sentido

meanness /'miːnnɪs/ *n* (miserliness) tacañería *f*; (unkindness) maldad *f*

means /miːnz/ *n* medio *m*. **by** ∼ **of** por medio de, mediante. **by all** ∼ por supuesto. **by no** ∼ de ninguna manera. ●*npl* (wealth) medios *mpl*, recursos *mpl*. ∼ **test** *n* investigación *f* de ingresos

meant /ment/ ⇒MEAN

meantime /'miːntaɪm/ *adv* mientras tanto, entretanto. ●*n*. **in the** ∼ mientras tanto, entretanto

meanwhile /'miːnwaɪl/ *adv* mientras tanto, entretanto

measl|es /'miːzlz/ *n* sarampión *m*. ∼**y** /'miːzlɪ/ *a* 🄵 miserable

measure /'meʒə(r)/ *n* medida *f*; (ruler) regla *f*. ●*vt/i* medir. ▢ ∼ **up to** *vt* estar a la altura de. ∼**ment** *n* medida *f*

meat /miːt/ *n* carne *f*. ∼**ball** *n* albóndiga *f*. ∼**y** *a* <*taste, smell*> a carne; <*soup, stew*> con mucha carne

mechan|ic /mɪ'kænɪk/ *n* mecánico *m*. ∼**ical** *a* mecánico. ∼**ics** *n* mecánica *f*. ∼**ism** /'mekənɪzəm/ *n* mecanismo *m.* ~**ize** /'mekənaız/ *vt* mecanizar

medal /'medl/ *n* medalla *f.* ~**list** /'medəlıst/ *n* medallista *m & f.* **be a gold** ~**list** ganar una medalla de oro

meddle /'medl/ *vi* meterse, entrometerse (**in** en). ~ **with** (tinker) toquetear

media /'mi:dɪə/ ⇒MEDIUM. ● *npl.* the ~ los medios de comunicación

mediat|e /'mi:dɪeɪt/ *vi* mediar. ~**ion** /-'eɪʃn/ *n* mediación *f.* ~**or** *n* mediador *m*

medical /'medɪkl/ *a* médico; <*student*> de medicina. ● *n* revisión *m* médica

medicat|ed /'medɪkeɪtɪd/ *a* medicinal. ~**ion** /-'keɪʃn/ *n* medicación *f*

medicin|al /mɪ'dɪsɪnl/ *a* medicinal. ~**e** /'medsɪn/ *n* medicina *f*

medieval /medrí:vl/ *a* medieval

mediocre /mi:dɪ'əʊkə(r)/ *a* mediocre

meditat|e /'medɪteɪt/ *vi* meditar. ~**ion** /-'teɪʃn/ *n* meditación *f*

Mediterranean /medɪtə'reɪnɪən/ *a* mediterráneo. ● *n.* the ~ el Mediterráneo

medium /'mi:dɪəm/ *n* (*pl* **media**) medio *m.* **happy** ~ término *m* medio. ● *a* mediano. ~-**size(d)** /-saɪz(d)/ *a* de tamaño mediano

medley /'medlɪ/ *n* (Mus) popurrí *m*; (mixture) mezcla *f*

meek /mi:k/ *a* (**-er, -est**) dócil

meet /mi:t/ *vt* (*pt* **met**) encontrar; (bump into s.o.) encontrarse con; (fetch) ir a buscar; (get to know, be introduced to) conocer. ● *vi* encontrarse; (get to know) conocerse; (have meeting) reunirse. ~ **up** *vi* encontrarse (**with** con). ❒ ~ **with** *vt* ser recibido con; (Amer, meet) encontrarse con. ~**ing** *n* reunión *f*; (accidental between two people) encuentro *m*

megabyte /'megəbaɪt/ *n* (Comp) megabyte *m*, megaocteto *m*

megaphone /'megəfəʊn/ *n* megáfono *m*

melanchol|ic /melən'kɒlɪk/ *a* melancólico. ~**y** /'melənkɒlɪ/ *n* melancolía *f.* ● *a* melancólico

mellow /'meləʊ/ *a* (**-er, -est**) <*fruit*> maduro; <*sound*> dulce; <*colour*> tenue; <*person*> apacible

melodrama /'melədrɑːmə/ *n* melodrama *m.* ~**tic** /melədrə'mætɪk/ *a* melodramático

melody /'melədɪ/ *n* melodía *f*

melon /'melən/ *n* melón *m*

melt /melt/ *vt* (make liquid) derretir; fundir <*metals*>. ● *vi* (become liquid) derretirse; <*metals*> fundirse. ❒ ~ **down** *vt* fundir

member /'membə(r)/ *n* miembro *m & f*; (of club) socio *m.* ~ **of staff** empleado *m.* **M**~ **of Congress** *n* (Amer) miembro *m & f* del Congreso. **M**~ **of Parliament** *n* diputado *m.* ~**ship** *n* calidad *f* de socio; (members) socios *mpl*, membresía *f* (LAm)

membrane /'membreɪn/ *n* membrana *f*

memento /mɪ'mentəʊ/ *n* (*pl* **-os** or **-oes**) recuerdo *m*

memo /'meməʊ/ *n* (*pl* **-os**) memorándum *m*, memo *m*

memoir /'memwɑː(r)/ *n* memoria *f*

memorable /'memərəbl/ *a* memorable

memorandum /memə'rændəm/ *n* (*pl* **-ums** or **-da** /-də/) memorándum *m*

memorial /mɪ'mɔːrɪəl/ *n* monumento *m.* ● *a* conmemorativo

memor|ize /'meməraɪz/ *vt* aprender de memoria. ~**y** /'memərɪ/ *n* (faculty) memoria *f*; (thing remembered) recuerdo *m.* **from** ~**y** de memoria. **in** ~**y of** a la memoria de

men /men/ ⇒MAN

menac|e /'menəs/ *n* amenaza *f*; (🄸, nuisance) peligro *m* público. ● *vt* amenazar. ~**ing** *a* amenazador

mend /mend/ *vt* reparar; arreglar <*garment*>. ~ **one's ways** enmendarse. ● *n* remiendo *m.* **be on the** ~ ir mejorando

menfolk /'menfəʊk/ *n* hombres *mpl*

menial /'mi:nɪəl/ *a* servil

meningitis /menɪn'dʒaɪtɪs/ *n* meningitis *f*

menopause /'menəpɔːz/ *n* menopausia *f*

menstruat|e /'menstrʊeɪt/ *vi* menstruar. **~ion** /-'eɪʃn/ *n* menstruación *f*

mental /'mentl/ *a* mental; *<hospital>* psiquiátrico. **~ity** /-'tælətɪ/ *n* mentalidad *f*. **~ly** *adv* mentalmente. **be ~ly ill** ser un enfermo mental

mention /'menʃn/ *vt* mencionar. **don't ~ it!** ¡no hay de qué! ● *n* mención *f*

mentor /'mentɔ:(r)/ *n* mentor *m*

menu /'menju:/ *n* menú *m*

meow /mɪ'aʊ/ *n & vi* ⇒MEW

mercenary /'mɜ:sɪnərɪ/ *a & n* mercenario (*m*)

merchandise /'mɜ:tʃəndaɪz/ *n* mercancias *fpl*, mercadería *f* (LAm)

merchant /'mɜ:tʃənt/ *n* comerciante *m*. ● *a <ship, navy>* mercante. **~ bank** *n* banco *m* mercantil

merci|ful /'mɜ:sɪfl/ *a* misericordioso. **~less** *a* despiadado

mercury /'mɜ:kjʊrɪ/ *n* mercurio *m*. **M~y** (planet) Mercurio *m*

mercy /'mɜ:sɪ/ *n* compasión *f*. **at the ~ of** a merced de

mere /mɪə(r)/ *a* simple. **~ly** *adv* simplemente

merge /mɜ:dʒ/ *vt* unir; fusionar *<companies>*. ● *vi* unirse; *<companies>* fusionarse. **~r** *n* fusión *f*

meridian /mə'rɪdɪən/ *n* meridiano *m*

meringue /mə'ræŋ/ *n* merengue *m*

merit /'merɪt/ *n* mérito *m*. ● *vt* (*pt* **merited**) merecer

mermaid /'mɜ:meɪd/ *n* sirena *f*

merr|ily /'merəlɪ/ *adv* alegremente. **~iment** /'merɪmənt/ *n* alegría *f*. **~y** /'merɪ/ *a* (**-ier, -iest**) alegre. **make ~** divertirse. **~y-go-round** *n* tiovivo *m*, carrusel *m* (LAm). **~y-making** *n* jolgorio *m*

mesh /meʃ/ *n* malla *f*

mesmerize /'mezməraɪz/ *vt* hipnotizar; (fascinate) cautivar

mess /mes/ *n* desorden *m*; (dirt) suciedad *f*; (Mil) rancho *m*. **make a ~ of** estropear. □ **~ up** *vt* desordenar; (dirty) ensuciar; estropear *<plans>*. □ **~ about** *vi* tontear. □ **~ with** *vt* (tinker with) manosear

mess|age /'mesɪdʒ/ *n* mensaje *m*; (when phoning) recado *m*. **~enger** /'mesɪndʒə(r)/ *n* mensajero *m*

Messiah /mɪ'saɪə/ *n* Mesías *m*

Messrs /'mesəz/ *npl*. **~ Smith** los señores Smith, los Sres. Smith

messy /'mesɪ/ *a* (**-ier, -iest**) en desorden; (dirty) sucio

met /met/ ⇒MEET

metabolism /mɪ'tæbəlɪzəm/ *n* metabolismo *m*

metal /'metl/ *n* metal. ● *a* de metal. **~lic** /mə'tælɪk/ *a* metálico

metaphor /'metəfə(r)/ *n* metáfora *f*. **~ical** /-'fɔrɪk/ *a* metafórico

mete /mi:t/ *vt*. **~ out** repartir; dar *<punishment>*

meteor /'mi:tɪə(r)/ *n* meteoro *m*. **~ic** /-'ɒrɪk/ *a* meteórico. **~ite** /'mi:tɪəraɪt/ *n* meteorito *m*

meteorolog|ical /mi:tɪərə'lɒdʒɪkl/ *a* meteorológico. **~ist** /-'rɒlədʒɪst/ *n* meteorólogo *m*. **~y** /-'rɒlədʒɪ/ *n* meteorología *f*

meter /'mi:tə(r)/ *n* contador *m*, medidor *m* (LAm); (Amer) ⇒METRE

method /'meθəd/ *n* método *m*. **~ical** /mɪ'θɒdɪkl/ *a* metódico. **M~ist** /'meθədɪst/ *a & n* metodista (*m & f*)

methylated /'meθɪleɪtɪd/ *a*. **~ spirit(s)** *n* alcohol *m* desnaturalizado

meticulous /mɪ'tɪkjʊləs/ *a* meticuloso

metre /'mi:tə(r)/ *n* metro *m*

metric /'metrɪk/ *a* métrico

metropoli|s /mɪ'trɒpəlɪs/ *n* metrópoli(s) *f*. **~tan** /metrə'pɒlɪtən/ *a* metropolitano

mettle /'metl/ *n*. **be on one's ~** (fig) estar dispuesto a dar lo mejor de sí

mew /mju:/ *n* maullido *m*. ● *vi* maullar

Mexic|an /'meksɪkən/ *a & n* mejicano (*m*), mexicano (*m*). **~o** /-kəʊ/ *n* Méjico *m*, México *m*

miaow /mi:'aʊ/ *n & vi* ⇒MEW

mice /maɪs/ ⇒MOUSE

mickey /'mɪkɪ/ *n*. **take the ~ out of** 🔲 tomar el pelo a

micro... /'maɪkrəʊ/ *pref* micro...

microbe /'maɪkrəʊb/ n microbio m
micro: ~**chip** n pastilla f. ~**film** n microfilme m. ~**phone** n micrófono m. ~**processor** /-'prəʊsesə(r)/ n microprocesador m. ~**scope** n microscopio m. ~**scopic** /-'skɒpɪk/ a microscópico. ~**wave** n microonda f. ~**wave oven** n horno m de microondas
mid- /mɪd/ pref. in ~ **air** en pleno aire. in ~ **March** a mediados de marzo
midday /mɪd'deɪ/ n mediodía m
middl|e /'mɪdl/ a de en medio. ● n medio m. **in the** ~**e** of en medio de. ~**e-aged** /-'eɪdʒd/ a de mediana edad. **M**~**e Ages** npl Edad f Media. ~**e class** n clase f media. ~**e-class** a de la clase media. **M**~**e East** n Oriente m Medio. ~**eman** n intermediario m. ~**e name** n segundo nombre m. ~**ing** a regular
midge /mɪdʒ/ n mosquito m
midget /'mɪdʒɪt/ n enano m. ● a minúsculo
Midlands /'mɪdləndz/ npl región f central de Inglaterra
midnight /'mɪdnaɪt/ n medianoche f
midriff /'mɪdrɪf/ n diafragma m
midst /mɪdst/ n. **in our** ~ entre nosotros. **in the** ~ **of** en medio de
midsummer /mɪd'sʌmə(r)/ n pleno verano m; (solstice) solsticio m de verano
midway /mɪd'weɪ/ adv a mitad de camino
Midwest /mɪd'west/ región f central de los EE.UU.
midwife /'mɪdwaɪf/ n comadrona f, partera f
midwinter /mɪd'wɪntə(r)/ n pleno invierno m
might /maɪt/ ⇒MAY. ● n (strength) fuerza f; (power) poder m. ~**y** a (strong) fuerte; (powerful) poderoso. ● adv 🗓 muy
migraine /'miːɡreɪn/ n jaqueca f
migra|nt /'maɪɡrənt/ a migratorio. ● n (person) emigrante m & f. ~**te** /maɪˈɡreɪt/ vi emigrar. ~**tion** /-'ɡreɪʃn/ n migración f
mild /maɪld/ a (**-er**, **-est**) <person> afable; <climate> templado; (slight) ligero; <taste, manner> suave

mildew /'mɪldjuː/ n moho m; (on plants) mildeu m, mildiu m
mildly /'maɪldlɪ/ adv (gently) suavemente; (slightly) ligeramente
mile /maɪl/ n milla f. ~**s better** 🗓 mucho mejor. ~**s too big** 🗓 demasiado grande. ~**age** /-ɪdʒ/ n (loosely) kilometraje m. ~**ometer** /maɪˈlɒmɪtə(r)/ n (loosely) cuentakilómetros m. ~**stone** n mojón m; (event, stage, fig) hito m
militant /'mɪlɪtənt/ a & n militante (m & f)
military /'mɪlɪtərɪ/ a militar
militia /mɪ'lɪʃə/ n milicia f
milk /mɪlk/ n leche f. ● a <product> lácteo; <chocolate> con leche. ● vt ordeñar <cow>. ~**man** /-mən/ n lechero m. ~ **shake** n batido m, (leche f) malteada f (LAm), licuado m con leche (LAm). ~**y** a lechoso. **M**~**y Way** n Vía f Láctea
mill /mɪl/ n molino m; (for coffee, pepper) molinillo m; (factory) fábrica f de tejidos de algodón. ● vt moler. □ ~ **about, mill around** vi dar vueltas
millennium /mɪ'lenɪəm/ n (pl **-ia** /-ɪə/ or **-iums**) milenio m
miller /'mɪlə(r)/ n molinero m
milli... /'mɪlɪ/ pref mili... ~**gram(me)** n miligramo m. ~**metre** n milímetro m
milliner /'mɪlɪnə(r)/ n sombrerero m
million /'mɪlɪən/ n millón m. **a** ~ **pounds** un millón de libras. ~**aire** /-'eə(r)/ n millonario m
millstone /'mɪlstəʊn/ n muela f (de molino); (fig, burden) carga f
mime /maɪm/ n mímica f. ● vt imitar, hacer la mímica de. ● vi hacer la mímica
mimic /'mɪmɪk/ vt (pt **mimicked**) imitar. ● n imitador m. ~**ry** n imitación f
mince /mɪns/ vt picar, moler (LAm) <meat>. **not to** ~ **matters/words** no andar(se) con rodeos. ● n carne f picada, carne f molida (LAm). ~ **pie** n pastelito m de Navidad (pastelito relleno de picadillo de frutos secos). ~**r** n máquina f de picar carne, máquina f de moler carne (LAm)

mind /maɪnd/ n mente f; (sanity) juicio m. **to my ~** a mi parecer. **be on one's mind** preocuparle a uno. **make up one's ~** decidirse.● vt (look after) cuidar (de); atender <shop>. **~ the steps!** ¡cuidado con las escaleras! **never ~ him** no le hagas caso. **I don't ~ the noise** no me molesta el ruido. **would you ~ closing the door?** ¿le importaría cerrar la puerta? ● vi. **never ~** no importa, no te preocupes. **I don't ~** (don't object) me da igual. **do you ~ if I smoke?** ¿le importa si fumo? **~ful** a atento (of a). **~less** a <activity> mecánico; <violence> ciego

mine¹ /maɪn/ poss pron (sing) mío, mía; (pl) míos, mías. **it is ~** es mío. **~ are blue** los míos/las mías son azules. **a friend of ~** un amigo mío/ una amiga mía

mine² /maɪn/ n mina f; (Mil) mina f. ● vt extraer. **~field** n campo m de minas. **~r** n minero m

mineral /'mɪnərəl/ a & n mineral (m). **~ water** n agua f mineral

mingle /'mɪŋɡl/ vi mezclarse

mini... /'mɪnɪ/ pref mini...

miniature /'mɪnɪtʃə(r)/ n miniatura f. ● a en miniatura

mini: ~bus n microbús m. **~cab** n taxi m (que se pide por teléfono)

minim|al /'mɪnɪml/ a mínimo. **~ize** vt reducir al mínimo. **~um** /-məm/ a & n (pl **-ima** /-mə/) mínimo (m)

mining /'maɪnɪŋ/ n minería f. ● a minero

miniskirt /'mɪnɪskɜːt/ n minifalda f

minist|er /'mɪnɪstə(r)/ n ministro m, secretario m (Mex); (Relig) pastor m. **~erial** /-'stɪərɪəl/ a ministerial. **~ry** n ministerio m, secretaría f (Mex)

mink /mɪŋk/ n visón m

minor /'maɪnə(r)/ a (also Mus) menor; <injury> leve; <change> pequeño; <operation> de poca importancia. ● n menor m & f de edad. **~ity** /maɪ'nɒrətɪ/ n minoría f. ● a minoritario

minstrel /'mɪnstrəl/ n juglar m

mint /mɪnt/ n (plant) menta f; (sweet) pastilla f de menta; (Finance) casa f de la moneda. **in ~ condition** como nuevo. ● vt acuñar

minus /'maɪnəs/ prep menos; (ﬁ, without) sin. ● n (sign) menos m. **five ~ three is two** cinco menos tres is igual a dos. **~ sign** n (signo m de) menos m

minute¹ /'mɪnɪt/ n minuto m. **the ~s** npl (of meeting) el acta f

minute² /maɪ'njuːt/ a diminuto; (detailed) minucioso

mirac|le /'mɪrəkl/ n milagro m. **~ulous** /mɪ'rækjʊləs/ a milagroso

mirage /'mɪrɑːʒ/ n espejismo m

mirror /'mɪrə(r)/ n espejo m; (driving ~) (espejo m) retrovisor m. ● vt reflejar

mirth /mɜːθ/ n regocijo m; (laughter) risas fpl

misapprehension /mɪsæprɪ'henʃn/ n malentendido m

misbehav|e /mɪsbɪ'heɪv/ vi portarse mal. **~iour** n mala conducta

miscalculat|e /mɪs'kælkjʊleɪt/ vt/i calcular mal. **~ion** /-'leɪʃn/ n error m de cálculo

miscarr|iage /'mɪskærɪdʒ/ n aborto m espontáneo. **~iage of justice** n injusticia f. **~y** vi abortar

miscellaneous /mɪsə'leɪnɪəs/ a heterogéneo

mischie|f /'mɪstʃɪf/ n (foolish conduct) travesura f; (harm) daño m. **get into ~f** hacer travesuras. **make ~f** causar daños. **~vous** /'mɪstʃɪvəs/ a travieso; <grin> pícaro

misconception /mɪskən'sepʃn/ n equivocación f

misconduct /mɪs'kɒndʌkt/ n mala conducta f

misdeed /mɪs'diːd/ n fechoría f

misdemeanour /mɪsdɪ'miːnə(r)/ n delito m menor, falta f

miser /'maɪzə(r)/ n avaro m

miserable /'mɪzərəbl/ a (sad) triste; (in low spirits) abatido; (wretched, poor) mísero; <weather> pésimo

miserly /'maɪzəlɪ/ a avariento

misery /'mɪzərɪ/ n (unhappiness) tristeza f; (pain) sufrimiento m

misfire /mɪs'faɪə(r)/ vi fallar

misfit /'mɪsfɪt/ n inadaptado m

misfortune /mɪsˈfɔːtʃuːn/ n desgracia f

misgiving /mɪsˈgɪvɪŋ/ n recelo m

misguided /mɪsˈgaɪdɪd/ a equivocado

mishap /ˈmɪshæp/ n percance m

misinform /mɪsɪnˈfɔːm/ vt informar mal

misinterpret /mɪsɪnˈtɜːprɪt/ vt interpretar mal

misjudge /mɪsˈdʒʌdʒ/ vt juzgar mal; (miscalculate) calcular mal

mislay /mɪsˈleɪ/ vt (pt **mislaid**) extraviar, perder

mislead /mɪsˈliːd/ vt (pt **misled** /mɪsˈled/) engañar. ~ing a engañoso

mismanage /mɪsˈmænɪdʒ/ vt administrar mal. ~ment n mala administración f

misplace /mɪsˈpleɪs/ vt (lose) extraviar, perder

misprint /ˈmɪsprɪnt/ n errata f

miss /mɪs/ vt (fail to hit) no dar en; (regret absence of) echar de menos, extrañar (LAm); perder <train, party>; perder <chance>. ~ **the point** no comprender. ● vi errar el tiro, fallar; <bullet> no dar en el blanco. ● n fallo m, falla f (LAm); (title) señorita f. □ ~ **out** vt saltarse <line>. ~**out on sth** perderse algo

misshapen /mɪsˈʃeɪpən/ a deforme

missile /ˈmɪsaɪl/ n (Mil) misil m

missing /ˈmɪsɪŋ/ a (lost) perdido. be ~ faltar. **go** ~ desaparecer. ~ **person** desaparecido m

mission /ˈmɪʃn/ n misión f. ~**ary** /ˈmɪʃənərɪ/ n misionero m

mist /mɪst/ n neblina f; (at sea) bruma f. □ ~ **up** vi empañarse

mistake /mɪˈsteɪk/ n error m. **make a** ~ cometer un error. **by** ~ por error. ● vt (pt **mistook**, pp **mistaken**) confundir. ~ **for** confundir con. ~**n** /-ən/ a equivocado. **be** ~**n** equivocarse

mistletoe /ˈmɪsltəʊ/ n muérdago m

mistreat /mɪsˈtriːt/ vt maltratar

mistress /ˈmɪstrɪs/ n (of house) señora f; (lover) amante f

mistrust /mɪsˈtrʌst/ vt desconfiar de. ● n desconfianza f. ~**ful** a desconfiado

misty /ˈmɪstɪ/ a (**-ier**, **-iest**) neblinoso; <day> de neblina. **it's** ~ hay neblina

misunderstand /mɪsʌndəˈstænd/ vt (pt **-stood**) entender mal. ~**ing** n malentendido m

misuse /mɪsˈjuːz/ vt emplear mal; malversar <funds>. ● /mɪsˈjuːs/ n mal uso m; (unfair use) abuso m; (of funds) malversación f

mite /maɪt/ n (insect) ácaro m

mitten /ˈmɪtn/ n mitón m

mix /mɪks/ vt mezclar. ● vi mezclarse; (go together) combinar. ~ **with** tratarse con <people>. ● n mezcla f. □ ~ **up** vt mezclar; (confuse) confundir. ~**ed** a <school etc> mixto; (assorted) mezclado. **be** ~**ed up** estar confuso. ~**er** n (Culin) batidora f; (TV, machine) mezcladora f. ~**ture** /ˈmɪkstʃə(r)/ n mezcla f. ~**-up** n lío m

moan /məʊn/ n gemido m. ● vi gemir; (complain) quejarse (**about** de)

moat /məʊt/ n foso m

mob /mɒb/ n turba f. ● vt (pt **mobbed**) acosar

mobil|e /ˈməʊbaɪl/ a móvil. ~**e home** n caravana f, trailer m (LAm). ~**e** (**phone**) n (teléfono m) móvil m, (teléfono m) celular m (LAm). ● n móvil m. ~**ize** /ˈməʊbɪlaɪz/ vt movilizar. ● vi movilizarse

mock /mɒk/ vt burlarse de. ● a <anger> fingido; <exam> de práctica. ~**ery** /ˈmɒkərɪ/ n burla f. **make a** ~**ery of sth** ridiculizar algo

model /ˈmɒdl/ n (example) modelo m; (mock-up) maqueta f; (person) modelo m. ● a (exemplary) modelo; <car etc> en miniatura. ● vt (pt **modelled**) modelar. ~ **s.o. on s.o.** tomar a uno como modelo

modem /ˈməʊdem/ n (Comp) módem m

moderat|e /ˈmɒdərət/ a & n moderado (m). ● /ˈmɒdəreɪt/ vt moderar. ~**ely** /ˈmɒdərətlɪ/ adv (fairly) medianamente. ~**ion** /-ˈreɪʃn/ n moderación f. **in** ~**ion** con moderación

modern /'mɒdn/ *a* moderno. ∼**ize** *vt* modernizar

modest /'mɒdɪst/ *a* modesto. ∼**y** *n* modestia *f*

modif|ication /mɒdɪfɪ'keɪʃn/ *n* modificación *f*. ∼**y** /-faɪ/ *vt* modificar

module /'mɒdjuːl/ *n* módulo *m*

moist /mɔɪst/ *a* (**-er, -est**) húmedo. ∼**en** /'mɔɪsn/ *vt* humedecer

moistur|e /'mɔɪstʃə(r)/ *n* humedad *f*. ∼**ize** *vt* hidratar. ∼**izer**, ∼**izing cream** *n* crema *f* hidratante

mole /məʊl/ *n* (animal) topo *m*; (on skin) lunar *m*

molecule /'mɒlɪkjuːl/ *n* molécula *f*

molest /mə'lest/ *vt* abusar (sexualmente) de

mollify /'mɒlɪfaɪ/ *vt* aplacar

mollusc /'mɒləsk/ *n* molusco *m*

mollycoddle /'mɒlɪkɒdl/ *vt* mimar

molten /'məʊltən/ *a* fundido; <*lava*> líquido

mom /mɒm/ *n* (Amer, 🔲) mamá *f* 🔲

moment /'məʊmənt/ *n* momento *m*. **at the** ∼ en este momento. **for the** ∼ de momento. ∼**ary** /'məʊməntərɪ/ *a* momentáneo

momentous /mə'mentəs/ *a* trascendental

momentum /mə'mentəm/ *n* momento *m*; (speed) velocidad *f*

mommy /'mɒmɪ/ *n* (Amer, 🔲) mamá *m* 🔲

monarch /'mɒnək/ *n* monarca *m*. ∼**y** *n* monarquía *f*

monastery /'mɒnəstərɪ/ *n* monasterio *m*

Monday /'mʌndeɪ/ *n* lunes *m*

money /'mʌnɪ/ *n* dinero *m*, plata *f* (LAm). ∼**box** *n* hucha *f*, alcancía *f* (LAm). ∼ **order** *n* giro *m* postal

mongrel /'mʌŋɡrəl/ *n* perro *m* mestizo, chucho *m* 🔲

monitor /'mɒnɪtə(r)/ *n* (Tec) monitor *m*. ● *vt* observar <*elections*>; seguir <*progress*>; (electronically) monitorizar; escuchar <*broadcast*>

monk /mʌŋk/ *n* monje *m*

monkey /'mʌŋkɪ/ *n* mono *m*. ∼**-nut** *n* cacahuete *m*, cacahuate *m* (Mex), maní *m* (LAm). ∼**wrench** *n* llave *f* inglesa

mono /'mɒnəʊ/ *n* monofonía *f*

monologue /'mɒnəlɒɡ/ *n* monólogo *m*

monopol|ize /mə'nɒpəlaɪz/ *vt* monopolizar; acaparar <*conversation*>. ∼**y** *n* monopolio *m*

monoton|e /'mɒnətəʊn/ *n* tono *m* monocorde. ∼**ous** /mə'nɒtənəs/ *a* monótono. ∼**y** *n* monotonía *f*

monsoon /mɒn'suːn/ *n* monzón *m*

monst|er /'mɒnstə(r)/ *n* monstruo *m*. ∼**rous** /-strəs/ *a* monstruoso

month /mʌnθ/ *n* mes *m*. £200 a ∼ 200 libras mensuales *or* al mes. ∼**ly** *a* mensual. ∼**ly payment** mensualidad *f*, cuota *f* mensual (LAm). ● *adv* mensualmente

monument /'mɒnjʊmənt/ *n* monumento *m*. ∼**al** /-'mentl/ *a* monumental

moo /muː/ *n* mugido *m*. ● *vi* mugir

mood /muːd/ *n* humor *m*. **be in a good/bad** ∼ estar de buen/mal humor. ∼**y** *a* (**-ier, -iest**) temperamental; (bad-tempered) malhumorado

moon /muːn/ *n* luna *f*. ∼**light** *n* luz *f* de la luna. ∼**lighting** *n* pluriempleo *m*. ∼**lit** *a* iluminado por la luna; <*night*> de luna

moor /mʊə(r)/ *n* páramo *m*; (of heather) brezal *m*. ● *vt* amarrar. ∼**ing** *n* (place) amarradero *m*. ∼**ings** *npl* (ropes) amarras *fpl*

moose /muːs/ *n invar* alce *m* americano

mop /mɒp/ *n* fregona *f*, trapeador *m* (LAm). ∼ **of hair** pelambrera *f*. ● *vt* (*pt* **mopped**). ∼ (**up**) limpiar

mope /məʊp/ *vi* estar abatido

moped /'məʊped/ *n* ciclomotor *m*

moral /'mɒrəl/ *a* moral. ● *n* (of tale) moraleja *f*

morale /mə'rɑːl/ *n* moral *f*

moral|ity /mɒ'rælətɪ/ *n* moralidad *f*. ∼**ly** *adv* moralmente. ∼**s** *npl* moralidad *f*

morbid /'mɔːbɪd/ *a* morboso

more /mɔː(r)/ *a* más. **two** ∼ **bottles** dos botellas más ● *pron* más. **you ate** ∼ **than me** comiste más que yo. **some** ∼ más. ∼ **than six** más de seis. **the** ∼ **he has, the** ∼ **he wants** cuánto más tiene, más quiere. ● *adv* más. ∼ **and** ∼ cada vez más. ∼ **or less** más o menos. **once** ∼ una vez más. **she doesn't live here any** ∼ ya no vive aquí. ∼**over** /mɔːˈrəʊvə(r)/ *adv* además

morgue /mɔːg/ *n* depósito *m* de cadáveres, morgue *f* (LAm)

morning /ˈmɔːnɪŋ/ *n* mañana *f*; (early hours) madrugada *f*. **at 11 o'clock in the** ∼ a las once de la mañana. **in the** ∼ por la mañana, en la mañana (LAm). **tomorrow/yesterday** ∼ mañana/ayer por la mañana *or* (LAm) en la mañana. (good) ∼**!** ¡buenos días!

Morocc|an /məˈrɒkən/ *a* & *n* marroquí (*m* & *f*). ∼**o** /-kəʊ/ *n* Marruecos *m*

moron /ˈmɔːrɒn/ *n* imbécil *m* & *f*

morose /məˈrəʊs/ *a* taciturno

Morse /mɔːs/ *n* Morse *m*. **in** ∼ **(code)** *n* en (código) morse

morsel /ˈmɔːsl/ *n* bocado *m*

mortal /ˈmɔːtl/ *a* & *n* mortal (*m*). ∼**ity** /-ˈtælətɪ/ *n* mortalidad *f*

mortar /ˈmɔːtə(r)/ *n* (all senses) mortero *m*

mortgage /ˈmɔːgɪdʒ/ *n* hipoteca *f*. ● *vt* hipotecar

mortify /ˈmɔːtɪfaɪ/ *vt* darle mucha vergüenza a

mortuary /ˈmɔːtjʊərɪ/ *n* depósito *m* de cadáveres, morgue *f* (LAm)

mosaic /məʊˈzeɪk/ *n* mosaico *m*

mosque /mɒsk/ *n* mezquita *f*

mosquito /mɒsˈkiːtəʊ/ *n* (*pl* **-oes**) mosquito *m*, zancudo *m* (LAm)

moss /mɒs/ *n* musgo *m*

most /məʊst/ *a* la mayoría de, la mayor parte de. ∼ **days** casi todos los días. ● *pron* la mayoría, la mayor parte. **at** ∼ como máximo. **make the** ∼ **of** aprovechar al máximo. ● *adv* más; (very) muy; (Amer, almost) casi. ∼**ly** *adv* principalmente

MOT *n*. ∼ **(test)** ITV *f*, inspección *f* técnica de vehículos

motel /məʊˈtel/ *n* motel *m*

moth /mɒθ/ *n* mariposa *f* de la luz, palomilla *f*; (in clothes) polilla *f*

mother /ˈmʌðə(r)/ *n* madre *f*. ● *vt* mimar. ∼**-in-law** *n* (*pl* ∼**s-in-law**) suegra *f*. ∼**land** *n* patria *f*. ∼**ly** *a*

maternal. ∼**-of-pearl** *n* nácar *m*, madreperla *f*. **M**∼**'s Day** *n* el día *m* de la Madre. ∼**-to-be** *n* futura madre *f*. ∼ **tongue** *n* lengua *f* materna

motif /məʊˈtiːf/ *n* motivo *m*

motion /ˈməʊʃn/ *n* movimiento *m*; (proposal) moción *f*. **put** *or* **set in** ∼ poner algo en marcha. ● *vt/i.* ∼ **(to)** **s.o. to** hacerle señas a uno para que. ∼**less** *a* inmóvil

motiv|ate /ˈməʊtɪveɪt/ *vt* motivar. ∼**ation** /-ˈveɪʃn/ *n* motivación *f*. ∼**e** /ˈməʊtɪv/ *n* motivo *m*

motley /ˈmɒtlɪ/ *a* variopinto

motor /ˈməʊtə(r)/ *n* motor *m*. ● *a* motor; (fem) motora, motriz. ∼ **bike** *n* 🇬🇧 motocicleta *f*, moto *f* 🇬🇧. ∼ **boat** *n* lancha *f* a motor. ∼ **car** *n* automóvil *m*. ∼ **cycle** *n* motocicleta *f*. ∼**cyclist** *n* motociclista *m* & *f*. ∼**ing** *n* automovilismo *m*. ∼**ist** *n* automovilista *m* & *f*. ∼**way** *n* autopista *f*

motto /ˈmɒtəʊ/ *n* (*pl* **-oes**) lema *m*

mould /məʊld/ *n* molde *m*; (fungus) moho *m*. ● *vt* moldear; formar *<character>*. ∼**ing** *n* (on wall etc) moldura *f* ∼**y** *a* mohoso

moult /məʊlt/ *vi* mudar de pelo/piel/plumas

mound /maʊnd/ *n* montículo *m*; (pile, fig) montón *m*

mount /maʊnt/ *vt* montar *<horse>*; engarzar *<gem>*; preparar *<attack>*. ● *vi* subir, crecer. ● *n*. montura *f*; (mountain) monte *m*. □ ∼ **up** *vi* irse acumulando

mountain /ˈmaʊntɪn/ *n* montaña *f*. ∼**eer** /maʊntɪˈnɪə(r)/ *n* alpinista *m* & *f*. ∼**eering** *n* alpinismo *m*. ∼**ous** *a* montañoso

mourn /mɔːn/ *vt* llorar. ● *vi* lamentarse. ∼ **for s.o.** llorar a uno. ∼**er** *n* doliente *m* & *f*. ∼**ful** *a* triste. ∼**ing** *n* duelo *m*, luto *m*. **be in** ∼**ing** estar de duelo

mouse /maʊs/ *n* (*pl* **mice**) ratón *m*. ∼**trap** *n* ratonera *f*

mousse /muːs/ *n* (Culin) mousse *f* *or* *m*; (for hair) mousse *f*

moustache /məˈstɑːʃ/ *n* bigote *m*

mouth /maʊθ/ n boca f; (of cave) entrada f; (of river) desembocadura f. **~ful** n bocado m. **~-organ** n armónica f. **~wash** n enjuague m bucal

move /muːv/ vt mover; (relocate) trasladar; (with emotion) conmover; (propose) proponer. **~ the television** cambiar de lugar la televisión. **~ house** mudarse de casa. ● vi moverse; (be in motion) estar en movimiento; (take action) tomar medidas. ● n movimiento m; (in game) jugada f; (player's turn) turno m; (removal) mudanza f. □ **~ away** vi alejarse. □ **~ in** vi instalarse. **~ in with s.o.** irse a vivir con uno. □ **~ over** vi correrse. **~ment** n movimiento m

movie /ˈmuːvɪ/ n (Amer) película f. **the ~s** npl el cine. **~ camera** n (Amer) tomavistas m, filmadora f (LAm)

moving /ˈmuːvɪŋ/ a en movimiento; (touching) conmovedor

mow /məʊ/ vt (pt **mowed** or **mown** /məʊn/) cortar <lawn>; segar <hay>. □ **~ down** vt acribillar. **~er** n (for lawn) cortacésped m

MP abbr ⇒MEMBER OF PARLIAMENT

Mr /ˈmɪstə(r)/ abbr (pl **Messrs**) (= **Mister**) Sr. **~ Coldbeck** Sr. Coldbeck

Mrs /ˈmɪsɪz/ abbr (pl **Mrs**) (= **Missis**) Sra. **~ Andrews** Sra. Andrews

Ms /mɪz/ abbr (title of married or unmarried woman)

MSc abbr ⇒MASTER

much /mʌtʃ/ a & pron mucho, mucha. ● adv mucho; (before pp) muy. **~ as** por mucho que. **~ the same** más o menos lo mismo. **how ~?** ¿cuánto?. **so ~** tanto. **too ~** demasiado

muck /mʌk/ n estiércol m; (fig, dirt) mugre f. □ **~ about** vi fam tontear

mud /mʌd/ n barro m, lodo m

muddle /ˈmʌdl/ vt embrollar. ● n desorden m; (mix-up) lío m. □ **~ through** vi salir del paso

muddy a lodoso; <hands etc> cubierto de lodo. **~guard** n guardabarros m, salpicadera f (Mex)

muffle /ˈmʌfl/ vt amortiguar <sound>. **~r** n (scarf) bufanda f; (Amer, Auto) silenciador m

mug /mʌg/ n taza f (alta y sin platillo), tarro m (Mex); (for beer) jarra f; (fam, face) cara f, jeta f fam; (fam, fool) idiota m & f. ● vt (pt **mugged**) asaltar. **~ger** n asaltante m & f. **~ging** n asalto m

muggy /ˈmʌgɪ/ a bochornoso

mule /mjuːl/ n mula f

mull /mʌl/ (Amer), **~ over** vt reflexionar sobre

multi|coloured /mʌltɪˈkʌləd/ a multicolor. **~national** /-ˈnæʃənl/ a & n multinacional (f)

multipl|e /ˈmʌltɪpl/ a múltiple. ● n múltiplo m. **~ication** /mʌltɪplɪˈkeɪʃn/ n multiplicación f. **~y** /ˈmʌltɪplaɪ/ vt multiplicar. ● vi (Math) multiplicar; (increase) multiplicarse

multitude /ˈmʌltɪtjuːd/ n. a **~ of problems** múltiples problemas

mum /mʌm/ n fam mamá f fam

mumble /ˈmʌmbl/ vt mascullar. ● vi hablar entre dientes

mummy /ˈmʌmɪ/ n (fam, mother) mamá f fam; (archaeology) momia f

mumps /mʌmps/ n paperas fpl

munch /mʌntʃ/ vt/i mascar

mundane /mʌnˈdeɪn/ a mundano

municipal /mjuːˈnɪsɪpl/ a municipal

mural /ˈmjʊərəl/ a & n mural (f)

murder /ˈmɜːdə(r)/ n asesinato m. ● vt asesinar. **~er** n asesino m

murky /ˈmɜːkɪ/ a (**-ier, -iest**) turbio

murmur /ˈmɜːmə(r)/ n murmullo m. ● vt/i murmurar

musc|le /ˈmʌsl/ n músculo m. **~ular** /ˈmʌskjʊlə(r)/ a muscular; <arm, body> musculoso

muse /mjuːz/ vi meditar (**on** sobre)

museum /mjuːˈzɪəm/ n museo m

mush /mʌʃ/ n papilla f

mushroom /ˈmʌʃrʊm/ n champiñón m; (Bot) seta f. ● vi aparecer como hongos

mushy /ˈmʌʃɪ/ a blando

music /ˈmjuːzɪk/ n música f. **~al** a musical. **be ~** tener sentido musical.

● *n* musical *m*. ∼**ian** /mju:'zıʃn/ *n* músico *m*

Muslim /'mʊzlım/ *a & n* musulmán (*m*)

mussel /'mʌsl/ *n* mejillón *m*

must /mʌst/ *v aux* deber, tener que; (expressing supposition) deber (de). **he** ∼ **be old** debe (de) ser viejo. **I** ∼ **have done it** debo (de) haberlo hecho. ● *n*. **be a** ∼ ser imprescindible

mustache /'mʌstæʃ/ *n* (Amer) bigote *m*

mustard /'mʌstəd/ *n* mostaza *f*

muster /'mʌstə(r)/ *vt* reunir

musty /'mʌstı/ *a* (**-ier, -iest**) que huele a humedad

mutation /mju:'teıʃn/ *n* mutación *f*

mute /mju:t/ *a* mudo

mutilate /'mju:tıleıt/ *vt* mutilar

mutiny /'mju:tını/ *n* motín *m*. ● *vi* amotinarse

mutter /'mʌtə(r)/ *vt/i* murmurar

mutton /'mʌtn/ *n* carne *f* de ovino

mutual /'mju:tʃʊəl/ *a* mutuo; (Ⅱ, common) común

muzzle /'mʌzl/ *n* (snout) hocico *m*; (device) bozal *m*

my /maı/ *a* (*sing*) mi; (*pl*) mis

myself /maı'self/ *pron* (*reflexive*) me; (used for emphasis) yo mismo *m*, yo misma *f*. **I cut** ∼ me corté. **I made it** ∼ lo hice yo mismo/misma. **I was by** ∼ estaba solo/sola

mysterious /mı'stıərıəs/ *a* misterioso. ∼**y** /'mıstərı/ *n* misterio *m*

mystical /'mıstıkl/ *a* místico

mystify /'mıstıfaı/ *vt* dejar perplejo

mystique /mı'sti:k/ *n* mística *f*

myth /mıθ/ *n* mito *m*. ∼**ical** *a* mítico. ∼**ology** /mı'θɒlədʒı/ *n* mitología *f*

Nn

N *abbr* (= **north**) N

nab /næb/ *vt* (*pt* **nabbed**) (🄳, arrest) pescar; (snatch) agarrar

nag /næg/ *vt* (*pt* **nagged**) fastidiar; (scold) estarle encima a. ● *vi* criticar

nail /neıl/ *n* clavo *m*; (of finger, toe) uña *f*. ∼ **polish** esmalte *m* para las uñas. ● *vt*. ∼ (**down**) clavar

naive /naı'i:v/ *a* ingenuo

naked /'neıkıd/ *a* desnudo. **to the** ∼ **eye** a simple vista

name /neım/ *n* nombre *m*; (of book, film) título *m*; (fig) fama *f*. **my** ∼ **is Chris** me llamo Chris. **good** ∼ buena reputación. ● *vt* ponerle nombre a; (appoint) nombrar. **a man** ∼**d Jones** un hombre llamado Jones. **she was** ∼**d after** *or* (Amer) **for her grandmother** le pusieron el nombre de su abuela. ∼**less** *a* anónimo. ∼**ly** *adv* a saber. ∼**sake** *n* (person) tocayo *m*

nanny /'nænı/ *n* niñera *f*

nap /næp/ *n* (sleep) sueñecito *m*; (after lunch) siesta *f*. **have a** ∼ echarse un sueño

napkin /'næpkın/ *n* servilleta *f*

nappy /'næpı/ *n* pañal *m*

narcotic /nɑ:'kɒtık/ *a & n* narcótico (*m*)

narrat|e /nə'reıt/ *vt* narrar. ∼**ive** /'nærətıv/ *n* narración *f*. ∼**or** /nə'reıtə(r)/ *n* narrador *m*

narrow /'nærəʊ/ *a* (**-er, -est**) estrecho, angosto (LAm). **have a** ∼ **escape** salvarse de milagro. ● *vt* estrechar; (limit) limitar. ● *vi* estrecharse. ∼**ly** *adv* (just) por poco. ∼**-minded** /-'maındıd/ *a* de miras estrechas

nasal /'neızl/ *a* nasal; <voice> gangoso

nasty /'nɑ:stı/ *a* (**-ier, -iest**) desagradable; (spiteful) malo (**to** con); <taste, smell> asqueroso; <cut> feo

nation /'neıʃn/ *n* nación *f*

national /'næʃənl/ *a* nacional. ● *n* ciudadano *m*. ∼ **anthem** *n* himno *m* nacional. ∼**ism** *n* nacionalismo *m*. ∼**ity** /næʃəˈnælətɪ/ *n* nacionalidad *f*. ∼**ize** *vt* nacionalizar. ∼**ly** *adv* a escala nacional

nationwide /ˈneɪʃnwaɪd/ *a & adv* a escala nacional

native /ˈneɪtɪv/ *n* natural *m & f*. **be a** ∼ **of** ser natural de. ● *a* nativo; *<country, town>* natal; *<language>* materno; *<plant, animal>* autóctono. **N**∼ **American** indio *m* americano

nativity /nəˈtɪvətɪ/ *n*. **the N**∼ la Natividad *f*

NATO /ˈneɪtəʊ/ *abbr* (= **North Atlantic Treaty Organization**) OTAN *f*

natter /ˈnætə(r)/ 🔲 *vi* charlar. ● *n* charla *f*

natural /ˈnætʃərəl/ *a* natural. ∼ **history** *n* historia *f* natural. ∼**ist** *n* naturalista *m & f*. ∼**ized** *a* *<citizen>* naturalizado. ∼**ly** *adv* (of course) naturalmente; (by nature) por naturaleza

nature /ˈneɪtʃə(r)/ *n* naturaleza *f*; (of person) carácter *m*; (of things) naturaleza *f*

naught /nɔːt/ *n* cero *m*

naughty /ˈnɔːtɪ/ *a* (**-ier, -iest**) malo, travieso

nause|a /ˈnɔːzɪə/ *n* náuseas *fpl*. ∼**ous** /-ɪəs/ *a* nauseabundo

nautical /ˈnɔːtɪkl/ *a* náutico. ∼ **mile** *n* milla *f* marina

naval /ˈneɪvl/ *a* naval; *<officer>* de marina

nave /neɪv/ *n* nave *f*

navel /ˈneɪvl/ *n* ombligo *m*

naviga|ble /ˈnævɪgəbl/ *a* navegable. ∼**te** /ˈnævɪgeɪt/ *vt* navegar por *<sea etc>*; gobernar *<ship>*. ● *vi* navegar. ∼**tion** /-ˈgeɪʃn/ *n* navegación *f*. ∼**tor** *n* oficial *m & f* de derrota

navy /ˈneɪvɪ/ *n* marina *f* de guerra. ∼ (**blue**) *a & n* azul (*m*) marino

NE *abbr* (= **north-east**) NE

near /nɪə(r)/ *adv* cerca. **draw** ∼ acercarse. ● *prep*. ∼ (**to**) cerca de. **go** ∼ (**to**) **sth** acercarse a algo. ● *a* cercano. ● *vt* acercarse a. ∼**by** *a* cercano. ∼**ly** *adv* casi. **he** ∼**ly died** por poco se muere, casi se muere. **not** ∼**ly** ni

con mucho. ∼**sighted** /-ˈsaɪtɪd/ *a* miope, corto de vista

neat /niːt/ *a* (**-er, -est**) *<person>* pulcro; *<room etc>* bien arreglado; (ingenious) hábil; *<whisky, gin>* solo; ; (Amer 🔲, great) fantástico 🔲. ∼**ly** *adv* pulcramente; *<organized>* cuidadosamente

necessar|ily /nesəˈserɪlɪ/ *adv* necesariamente. ∼**y** /ˈnesəserɪ/ *a* necesario

necessit|ate /nəˈsesɪteɪt/ *vt* exigir. ∼**y** /nɪˈsesətɪ/ *n* necesidad *f*. **the bare** ∼**ies** lo indispensable

neck /nek/ *n* (of person, bottle, dress) cuello *m*; (of animal) pescuezo *m*. ∼ **and** ∼ a la par, parejos (LAm). ∼**lace** /ˈnekləs/ *n* collar *m*. ∼**line** *n* escote *m*

nectar /ˈnektə(r)/ *n* néctar *m*

nectarine /ˈnektərɪn/ *n* nectarina *f*

née /neɪ/ *a* de soltera

need /niːd/ *n* necesidad *f* (**for** de). ● *vt* necesitar; (demand) exigir. **you** ∼ **not speak** no tienes que hablar

needle /ˈniːdl/ *n* aguja *f*. ● *vt* (🔲, annoy) pinchar

needless /ˈniːdlɪs/ *a* innecesario

needlework /ˈniːdlwɜːk/ *n* labores *fpl* de aguja; (embroidery) bordado *m*

needy /ˈniːdɪ/ *a* (**-ier, -iest**) necesitado

negative /ˈnegətɪv/ *a* negativo. ● *n* (of photograph) negativo *m*; (no) negativa *f*

neglect /nɪˈglekt/ *vt* descuidar *<house>*; desatender *<children>*; no cumplir con *<duty>*. ● *n* negligencia *f*. (**state of**) ∼ abandono *m*. ∼**ful** *a* negligente

neglig|ence /ˈneglɪdʒəns/ *n* negligencia *f*, descuido *m*. ∼**ent** *a* negligente. ∼**ible** /ˈneglɪdʒəbl/ *a* insignificante

negotia|ble /nɪˈgəʊʃəbl/ *a* negociable. ∼**te** /nɪˈgəʊʃɪeɪt/ *vt/i* negociar. ∼**tion** /-ˈeɪʃn/ *n* negociación *f*. ∼**tor** *n* negociador *m*

neigh /neɪ/ *vi* relinchar

neighbour /ˈneɪbə(r)/ *n* vecino *m*. ∼**hood** *n* vecindad *f*, barrio *m*. **in the** ∼**hood of** alrededor de. ∼**ing** *a* vecino

neither /'naɪðə(r)/ *a*. ∼ book ninguno de los libros. ● *pron* ninguno, -na. ● *conj*. neither...nor ni...ni. ∼ do I yo tampoco

neon /'ni:ɒn/ *n* neón *m*. ● *a* <*lamp etc*> de neón

nephew /'nevju:/ *n* sobrino *m*

Neptune /'neptju:n/ *n* Neptuno *m*

nerv|e /nɜ:v/ *n* nervio *m*; (courage) valor *m*; (calm) sangre *f* fría; (⊞, impudence) descaro *m*. ∼**es** *npl* (before exams etc) nervios *mpl*. get on s.o.'s ∼**es** ponerle los nervios de punta a uno. ∼**e-racking** *a* exasperante. ∼**ous** /'nɜ:vəs/ *a* nervioso. be/feel ∼**ous** estar nervioso. ∼**ousness** *n* nerviosismo *m*. ∼**y** /'nɜ:vɪ/ *a* nervioso; (Amer ⊞) descarado

nest /nest/ *n* nido *m*. ● *vi* anidar

nestle /'nesl/ *vi* acurrucarse

net /net/ *n* red *f*. the N∼ (Comp) la Red. ● *vt* (*pt* **netted**) pescar (con red) <*fish*>. ● *a* neto. ∼**ball** *n* baloncesto *m*

Netherlands /'neðələndz/ *npl*. the ∼ los Países Bajos

netting /'netɪŋ/ *n* redes *fpl*. wire ∼ tela *f* metálica

nettle /'netl/ *n* ortiga *f*

network /'netwɜ:k/ *n* red *f*; (TV) cadena *f*

neuro|sis /njʊə'rəʊsɪs/ *n* (*pl* -**oses** /-si:z/) neurosis *f*. ∼**tic** /-'rɒtɪk/ *a* & *n* neurótico (*m*)

neuter /'nju:tə(r)/ *a* & *n* neutro (*m*). ● *vt* castrar <*animals*>

neutral /'nju:trəl/ *a* neutral; <*col­our*> neutro; (Elec) neutro. ∼ (gear) (Auto) punto *m* muerto. ∼**ize** *vt* neutralizar

neutron /'nju:trɒn/ *n* neutrón *m*

never /'nevə(r)/ *adv* nunca; (more emphatic) jamás; (⊞, not) no. ∼ **again** nunca más. he ∼ smiles no sonríe nunca, nunca sonríe. I ∼ saw him ⊞ no lo vi. ∼**-ending** *a* interminable. ∼**theless** /-ðə'les/ *adv* sin embargo, no obstante

new /nju:/ *a* (-**er**, -**est**) nuevo. ∼**born** *a* recién nacido. ∼**comer** *n* recién llegado *m*. ∼**fangled** /-'fæŋgld/ *a* (pej) moderno. ∼**ly** *adv* recién. ∼**ly-weds** *npl* recién casados *mpl*

news /nju:z/ *n*. a piece of ∼ una noticia. good/bad ∼ buenas/malas noticias. the ∼ (TV, Radio) las noticias. ∼**agent** *n* vendedor *m* de periódicos. ∼**caster** *n* locutor *m*. ∼**dealer** *n* (Amer) ⇒∼AGENT. ∼**flash** *n* información *f* de última hora. ∼**letter** *n* boletín *m*, informativo *m*. ∼**paper** *n* periódico *m*, diario *m*. ∼**reader** *n* locutor *m*

newt /nju:t/ *n* tritón *m*

New Year /nju:'jɪə(r)/ *n* Año *m* Nuevo. **N∼'s Day** *n* día *m* de Año Nuevo. **N∼'s Eve** *n* noche *f* vieja, noche *f* de fin de Año

New Zealand /nju:'zi:lənd/ *n* Nueva Zeland(i)a *f*

next /nekst/ *a* próximo; <*week, month etc*> que viene, próximo; (adjoining) vecino; (following) siguiente. ● *adv* luego, después. ∼ to al lado de. when you see me ∼ la próxima vez que me veas. ∼ to nothing casi nada. ∼ door al lado (to de). ∼**-door** *a* de al lado. ∼ of kin *n* familiar(es) *m(pl)* más cercano(s)

nib /nɪb/ *n* plumilla *f*

nibble /'nɪbl/ *vt/i* mordisquear. ● *n* mordisco *m*

Nicaragua /nɪkə'rægjʊə/ *n* Nicaragua *f*. ∼**n** *a* & *n* nicaragüense (*m* & *f*)

nice /naɪs/ *a* (-**er**, -**est**) agradable; (likeable) simpático; (kind) amable; <*weather, food*> bueno. we had a ∼ time lo pasamos bien. ∼**ly** *adv* (kindly) amablemente; (politely) con buenos modales

niche /nɪtʃ, ni:ʃ/ *n* nicho *m*

nick /nɪk/ *n* corte *m* pequeño. in the ∼ of time justo a tiempo. ● *vt* (⊠ steal) afanar ⊠

nickel /'nɪkl/ *n* (metal) níquel *m*; (Amer) moneda *f* de cinco centavos

nickname /'nɪkneɪm/ *n* apodo *m*. ● *vt* apodar

nicotine /'nɪkəti:n/ *n* nicotina *f*

niece /ni:s/ *n* sobrina *f*

niggling /'nɪglɪŋ/ *a* <*doubt*> constante

night /naɪt/ *n* noche *f*; (evening) tarde *f*. **at** ~ por la noche, de noche. **good** ~ ¡buenas noches! ● *a* nocturno, de noche. ~**cap** *n* (drink) bebida *f* (tomada antes de acostarse). ~**club** *n* club *m* nocturno. ~**dress** *n* camisón *m*. ~**fall** *n* anochecer *m*. ~**gown**, ~**ie** /'naɪtɪ/ Ⓘ *n* camisón *m*. ~**life** *n* vida *f* nocturna. ~**ly** *a* de todas las noches. ~**mare** *n* pesadilla *f*. ~ **school** *n* escuela *f* nocturna. ~**-time** *n* noche *f*. ~**watchman** *n* sereno *m*

nil /nɪl/ *n* nada *f*; (Sport) cero *m*

nimble /'nɪmbl/ *a* (**-er, -est**) ágil

nine /naɪn/ *a & n* nueve (*m*). ~**teen** /naɪn'tiːn/ *a & n* diecinueve (*m*). ~**teenth** *a* decimonoveno. ● *n* diecinueveavo *m*. ~**tieth** /'naɪntɪəθ/ *a* nonagésimo. ● *n* noventavo *m*. ~**ty** *a & n* noventa (*m*)

ninth /'naɪnθ/ *a & n* noveno (*m*)

nip /nɪp/ *vt* (*pt* **nipped**) (pinch) pellizcar; (bite) mordisquear. ● *vi* (Ⓘ, rush) correr

nipple /'nɪpl/ *n* (of woman) pezón *m*; (of man) tetilla *f*; (of baby's bottle) tetina *f*, chupón *m* (Mex)

nippy /'nɪpɪ/ *a* (**-ier, -iest**) (Ⓘ, chilly) fresquito

nitrogen /'naɪtrədʒən/ *n* nitrógeno *m*

no /nəʊ/ *a* ninguno, (before masculine singular noun) ningún. **I have** ~ **money** no tengo dinero. **there's** ~ **food left** no queda nada de comida. **it has** ~ **windows** no tiene ventanas. **I'm** ~ **expert** no soy ningún experto. ~ **smoking** prohibido fumar. ~ **way!** Ⓘ ¡ni hablar! ● *adv & int* no. ● *n* (*pl* **noes**) no *m*

noble /'nəʊbl/ *a* (**-er, -est**) noble. ~**man** /-mən/ *n* noble *m*

nobody /'nəʊbədɪ/ *pron* nadie. **there's** ~ **there** no hay nadie

nocturnal /nɒk'tɜːnl/ *a* nocturno

nod /nɒd/ *vt* (*pt* **nodded**). ~ **one's head** asentir con la cabeza. ● *vi* (in agreement) asentir con la cabeza; (in greeting) saludar con la cabeza. □ ~ **off** *vi* dormirse

nois|e /nɔɪz/ *n* ruido *m*. ~**ily** *adv* ruidosamente. ~**y** *a* (**-ier, -iest**) ruidoso. **it's too** ~**y here** hay demasiado ruido aquí

nomad /'nəʊmæd/ *n* nómada *m & f*. ~**ic** /-'mædɪk/ *a* nómada

no man's land *n* tierra *f* de nadie

nominat|e /'nɒmɪneɪt/ *vt* (put forward) proponer; postular (LAm); (appoint) nombrar. ~**ion** /-'neɪʃn/ *n* nombramiento *m*; (Amer, Pol) proclamación *f*

non-... /nɒn/ *pref* no ...

nonchalant /'nɒnʃələnt/ *a* despreocupado

non-committal /nɒnkə'mɪtl/ *a* evasivo

nondescript /'nɒndɪskrɪpt/ *a* anodino

none /nʌn/ *pron* ninguno, ninguna. **there were** ~ **left** no quedaba ninguno/ninguna. ~ **of us** ninguno de nosotros. ● *adv* no, de ninguna manera. **he is** ~ **the happier** no está más contento

nonentity /nɒ'nentətɪ/ *n* persona *f* insignificante

non-existent /nɒnɪg'zɪstənt/ *a* inexistente

nonplussed /nɒn'plʌst/ *a* perplejo

nonsens|e /'nɒnsns/ *n* tonterías *fpl*, disparates *mpl*. ~**ical** /-'sensɪkl/ *a* disparatado

non-smoker /nɒn'sməʊkə(r)/ *n* no fumador *m*. **I'm a** ~ no fumo

non-stop /nɒn'stɒp/ *a* <*train*> directo; <*flight*> sin escalas. ● *adv* sin parar; (by train) directamente; (by air) sin escalas

noodles /'nuːdlz/ *npl* fideos *mpl*

nook /nʊk/ *n* rincón *m*

noon /nuːn/ *n* mediodía *m*

no-one /'nəʊwʌn/ *pron* nadie

noose /nuːs/ *n* soga *f*

nor /nɔː(r)/ *conj* ni, tampoco. **neither blue** ~ **red** ni azul ni rojo. **he doesn't play the piano,** ~ **do I** no sabe tocar el piano, ni yo tampoco

norm /nɔːm/ *n* norma *f*

normal /'nɔːml/ *a* normal. ~**cy** *n* (Amer) normalidad *f*. ~**ity** /-'mælətɪ/

n normalidad *f.* **~ly** *adv* normalmente

north /nɔːθ/ *n* norte *m.* ● *a* norte. ● *adv* hacia el norte. **N~ America** *n* América *f* del Norte, Norteamérica *f.* **N~ American** *a* & *n* norteamericano (*m*). **~east** *n* nor(d)este *m.* ● *a* nor(d)este. ● *adv* <*go*> hacia el nor(d)este. **it's ~east of Leeds** está al nor(d)este de Leeds. **~erly** /'nɔːðəlɪ/ *a* <*wind*> del norte. **~ern** /'nɔːðən/ *a* del norte. **~erner** *n* norteño *m.* **N~ern Ireland** *n* Irlanda *f* del Norte. **N~ Sea** *n* mar *m* del Norte. **~ward** /'nɔːθwəd/, **~wards** *adv* hacia el norte. **~west** *n* noroeste *m.* ● *a* noroeste. ● *adv* hacia el noroeste

Norw|ay /'nɔːweɪ/ *n* Noruega *f.* **~egian** /-'wiːdʒən/ *a* & *n* noruego (*m*)

nose /nəʊz/ *n* nariz *f.* **~bleed** *n* hemorragia *f* nasal. **~dive** *vi* descender en picado, descender en picada (LAm)

nostalgi|a /nɒ'stældʒə/ *n* nostalgia *f.* **~c** *a* nostálgico

nostril /'nɒstrɪl/ *n* ventana *f* de la nariz *f*

nosy /'nəʊzɪ/ *a* (**-ier, -iest**) 🄸 entrometido, metiche (LAm)

....

not /nɒt/

Cuando **not** va precedido del verbo auxiliar **do** or **have** o de un verbo modal como **should** etc se suele emplear la forma contraída **don't, haven't, shouldn't** etc

● *adverb*

····➤ no. **I don't know** no sé. **~ yet** todavía no. **~ me** yo no

····➤ (replacing a clause) **I suppose ~** supongo que no. **of course ~** por supuesto que no. **are you going to help me or ~?** ¿me vas a ayudar o no?

····➤ (emphatic) ni. **~ a penny more!** ¡ni un penique más!

····➤ (in phrases) **certainly ~** de ninguna manera . **~ you again!** ¡tú otra vez!

....

notabl|e /'nəʊtəbl/ *a* notable; <*author*> distinguido. **~y** /'nəʊtəblɪ/ *adv* notablemente; (in particular) particularmente

notch /nɒtʃ/ *n* muesca *f.* □ **~ up** *vt* apuntarse

note /nəʊt/ *n* (incl Mus) nota *f*; (banknote) billete *m.* **take ~s** tomar apuntes. ● *vt* (notice) observar; (record) anotar. □ **~ down** *vt* apuntar. **~book** *n* cuaderno *m.* **~d** *a* célebre. **~paper** *n* papel *m* de carta(s)

nothing /'nʌθɪŋ/ *pron* nada. **he eats ~** no come nada. **for ~** (free) gratis; (in vain) en vano. **~ else** nada más. **~ much happened** no pasó gran cosa. **he does ~ but complain** no hace más que quejarse

notice /'nəʊtɪs/ *n* (sign) letrero *m*; (item of information) anuncio *m*; (notification) aviso *m*; (of termination of employment) preaviso *m*; **~ (of dismissal)** despido *m.* **take ~ of** hacer caso a <*person*>. ● *vt* notar. ● *vi* darse cuenta. **~able** *a* perceptible. **~ably** *adv* perceptiblemente. **~board** *n* tablón *m* de anuncios, tablero *m* de anuncios (LAm)

notif|ication /nəʊtɪfɪ'keɪʃn/ *n* notificación *f.* **~y** /'nəʊtɪfaɪ/ *vt* informar; (in writing) notificar. **~y s.o. of sth** comunicarle algo a uno

notion /'nəʊʃn/ *n* (concept) concepto *m*; (idea) idea *f*

notorious /nəʊ'tɔːrɪəs/ *a* notorio

notwithstanding /nɒtwɪθ'stændɪŋ/ *prep* a pesar de. ● *adv* no obstante

nougat /'nuːgɑː/ *n* turrón *m*

nought /nɔːt/ *n* cero *m*

noun /naʊn/ *n* sustantivo *m*, nombre *m*

nourish /'nʌrɪʃ/ *vt* alimentar. **~ment** *n* alimento *m*

novel /'nɒvl/ *n* novela *f.* ● *a* original, novedoso. **~ist** *n* novelista *m* & *f.* **~ty** *n* novedad *f*

November /nəʊ'vembə(r)/ *n* noviembre *m*

novice /'nɒvɪs/ *n* principiante *m* & *f*

now /naʊ/ *adv* ahora. **~ and again, ~ and then** de vez en cuando. **right ~** ahora mismo. **from ~ on** a partir de ahora. ● *conj.* **~ (that)** ahora que. **~adays** /'naʊədeɪz/ *adv* hoy (en) día

nowhere /'nəʊweə(r)/ *adv* por ninguna parte, por ningún lado; (after motion towards) a ninguna parte, a ningún lado

nozzle /'nɒzl/ *n* (on hose) boca *f*; (on fire extinguisher) boquilla *f*

nuance /'njʊɑːns/ *n* matiz *m*

nuclear /'njuːklɪə(r)/ *a* nuclear

nucleus /'njuːklɪəs/ *n* (*pl* **-lei** /-lɪaɪ/) núcleo *m*

nude /njuːd/ *a & n* desnudo (*m*). in the ~ desnudo

nudge /nʌdʒ/ *vt* codear (ligeramente). ●*n* golpe *m* (suave) con el codo

nudi|st /'njuːdɪst/ *n* nudista *m & f*. ~ty /'njuːdətɪ/ *n* desnudez *f*

nuisance /'njuːsns/ *n* (thing, event) molestia *f*, fastidio *m*; (person) pesado *m*

null /nʌl/ *a* nulo

numb /nʌm/ *a* entumecido. go ~ entumecerse ●*vt* entumecer

number /'nʌmbə(r)/ *n* número *m*; (telephone number) número *m* de teléfono. a ~ of people varias personas. ●*vt* numerar; (count, include) contar. ~plate *n* matrícula *f*, placa *f* (LAm)

numer|al /'njuːmərəl/ *n* número *m*. ~ical /njuː'merɪkl/ *a* numérico. ~ous /'njuːmərəs/ *a* numeroso

nun /nʌn/ *n* monja *f*

nurse /nɜːs/ *n* enfermero *m*, enfermera *f*; (nanny) niñera *f*. ●*vt* cuidar; abrigar <*hope etc*>

nursery /'nɜːsərɪ/ *n* (for plants) vivero *m*; (day ~) guardería *f*. ~ **rhyme** *n* canción *f* infantil. ~ **school** *n* jardín *m* de infancia, jardín *m* infantil (LAm)

nursing home /'nɜːsɪŋ/ *n* (for older people) residencia *f* de ancianos (*con mayor nivel de asistencia médica*)

nut /nʌt/ *n* fruto *m* seco (nuez, almendra, avellana etc); (Tec) tuerca *f*. ~ **case** *n* 🔲 chiflado *m*. ~**crackers** *npl* cascanueces *m*. ~**meg** /-meg/ *n* nuez *f* moscada

nutri|ent /'njuːtrɪənt/ *n* nutriente *m*. ~**tion** /nju:'trɪʃn/ *n* nutrición *f*. ~**tious** /njuː'trɪʃəs/ *a* nutritivo

nuts /nʌts/ *a* (🔲, crazy) chiflado

nutshell /'nʌtʃel/ *n* cáscara *f* de nuez. in a ~ en pocas palabras

NW *abbr* (= **north-west**) NO

nylon /'naɪlɒn/ *n* nylon *m*

Oo

oaf /əʊf/ *n* zoquete *m*

oak /əʊk/ *n* roble *m*

OAP /əʊer'piː/ *abbr* (= **old-age pensioner**) *n* pensionista *m & f*, pensionado *m*

oar /ɔː(r)/ *n* remo *m*

oasis /əʊ'eɪsɪs/ *n* (*pl* **oases** /-siːz/) oasis *m*

oath /əʊθ/ *n* juramento *m*

oat|meal /'əʊtmiːl/ *n* harina *f* de avena; (Amer, flakes) avena *f* (en copos). ~**s** /əʊts/ *npl* avena *f*

obedien|ce /əʊ'biːdɪəns/ *n* obediencia *f*. ~**t** *a* obediente. ~**tly** *adv* obedientemente

obes|e /əʊ'biːs/ *a* obeso. ~**ity** *n* obesidad *f*

obey /əʊ'beɪ/ *vt/i* obedecer

obituary /ə'bɪtjʊərɪ/ *n* nota *f* necrológica, obituario *m*

object /'ɒbdʒɪkt/ *n* objeto *m*; (aim) objetivo *m*. ●/əb'dʒekt/ *vi* oponerse (to a). ~**ion** /əb'dʒekʃn/ *n* objeción *f*. ~**ionable** *a* censurable; (unpleasant) desagradable. ~**ive** /əb'dʒektɪv/ *a & n* objetivo (*m*)

oblig|ation /ɒblɪ'geɪʃn/ *n* obligación *f*. be under an ~ation to estar obligado a. ~**atory** /ə'blɪgətrɪ/ *a* obligatorio. ~**e** /ə'blaɪdʒ/ *vt* obligar. I'd be much ~ed if you could help me le quedaría muy agradecido si pudiera ayudarme. ●*vi* hacer un favor. ~**ing** *a* atento

oblique /ə'bliːk/ *a* oblicuo

obliterate /ə'blɪtəreɪt/ *vt* arrasar; (erase) borrar

oblivio|n /ə'blɪvɪən/ *n* olvido *m*. ~**us** /-vɪəs/ *a* (unaware) inconsciente (to, of de)

oblong /'ɒblɒŋ/ *a* oblongo. ●*n* rectángulo *m*

obnoxious /əb'nɒkʃəs/ *a* odioso

oboe /'əʊbəʊ/ *n* oboe *m*

obscen|e /əb'si:n/ *a* obsceno. **~ity** /əb'senətɪ/ *n* obscenidad *f*

obscur|e /əb'skjʊə(r)/ *a* oscuro. ● *vt* ocultar; impedir ver claramente <*issue*>. **~ity** *n* oscuridad *f*

obsequious /əb'si:kwɪəs/ *a* servil

observ|ant /əb'zɜ:vənt/ *a* observador. **~ation** /ɒbzə'veɪʃn/ *n* observación *f*. **~atory** /əb'zɜ:vətrɪ/ *n* observatorio *m*. **~e** /əb'zɜ:v/ *vt* observar. **~er** *n* observador *m*

obsess /əb'ses/ *vt* obsesionar. **~ed** /əb'sest/ *a* obsesionado. **~ion** /-ʃn/ *n* obsesión *f*. **~ive** *a* obsesivo

obsolete /'ɒbsəli:t/ *a* obsoleto

obstacle /'ɒbstəkl/ *n* obstáculo *m*

obstina|cy /'ɒbstɪnəsɪ/ *n* obstinación *f*. **~te** /-ət/ *a* obstinado. **~tely** *adv* obstinadamente

obstruct /əb'strʌkt/ *vt* obstruir; bloquear <*traffic*>. **~ion** /-ʃn/ *n* obstrucción *f*

obtain /əb'teɪn/ *vt* conseguir, obtener. **~able** *a* asequible

obtrusive /əb'tru:sɪv/ *a* <*presence*> demasiado prominente; <*noise*> molesto

obtuse /əb'tju:s/ *a* obtuso

obvious /'ɒbvɪəs/ *a* obvio. **~ly** *adv* obviamente

occasion /ə'keɪʒn/ *n* ocasión *f*. **~al** *a* esporádico. **~ally** *adv* de vez en cuando

occult /ɒ'kʌlt/ *a* oculto

occup|ant /'ɒkjʊpənt/ *n* ocupante *m* & *f*. **~ation** /ɒkjʊ'peɪʃn/ *n* ocupación *f*. **~ier** /'ɒkjʊpaɪə(r)/ *n* ocupante *m* & *f*. **~y** /'ɒkjʊpaɪ/ *vt* ocupar. **keep o.s. ~ied** entretenerse

occur /ə'kɜ:(r)/ *vi* (*pt* **occurred**) tener lugar, ocurrir; <*change*> producirse; (exist) encontrarse. **it ~red to me that** se me ocurrió que. **~rence** /ə'kʌrəns/ *n* (incidence) incidencia *f*. **it is a rare ~rence** no es algo frecuente

ocean /'əʊʃn/ *n* océano *m*

o'clock /ə'klɒk/ *adv*. **it is 7 ~** son las siete. **it's one ~** es la una

octagon /'ɒktəgən/ *n* octágono *m*

ootroctave /'ɒktɪv/ *n* octava *f*

October /ɒk'təʊbə(r)/ *n* octubre *m*

octopus /'ɒktəpəs/ *n* (*pl* **-puses**) pulpo *m*

odd /ɒd/ *a* (**-er, -est**) extraño, raro; <*number*> impar; (one of pair) desparejado. **smoke the ~ cigarette** fumarse algún que otro cigarrillo. **fifty-~** unos cincuenta, cincuenta y pico. **the ~ one out** la excepción. **~ity** *n* (thing) rareza *f*; (person) bicho *m* raro. **~ly** *adv* de una manera extraña. **~ly enough** por extraño que parezca. **~ment** *n* retazo *m*. **~s** *npl* probabilidades *fpl*; (in betting) apuesta *f*. **be at ~s** estar en desacuerdo. **~s and ends** *mpl* 🄳 cosas *fpl* sueltas

odious /'əʊdɪəs/ *a* odioso

odometer /ʊ'dɒmətə(r)/ *n* (Amer) cuentakilómetros *m*

odour /'əʊdə(r)/ *n* olor *m*

....

of /ɒv/, *unstressed form* /əv/

● *preposition*

····▸ de. **a pound of cheese** una libra de queso. **it's made of wood** es de madera. **a girl of ten** una niña de diez años

····▸ (in dates) de. **the fifth of November** el cinco de noviembre

····▸ (Amer, when telling the time) **it's ten (minutes) of five** son las cinco menos diez, son diez para las cinco (LAm)

❗ of is not translated in cases such as the following: **a**
■ **colleague of mine** *un colega mío;* **there were six of us** *éramos seis;* **that's very kind of you** *es Ud muy amable*

....

off /ɒf/ *prep* (from) de. **he picked it up ~ the floor** lo recogió del suelo; (distant from) **just ~ the coast of Texas** a poca distancia de la costa de Tejas. **2 ft ~ the ground** a dos pies del suelo; (absent from) **I've been ~ work for a week** hace una semana que no voy a trabajar. ● *adv* (removed) **the lid was ~** la tapa no estaba puesta; (distant) **some way ~** a cierta distancia; (leaving) **I'm ~** me voy; (switched off) <*light, TV*> apagado; <*water*> cortado; (cancelled) *<match>* cancelado; (not on duty) *<day>* libre. ● *adj.* be ~ *<meat>* estar malo, estar pasado; *<milk>* estar cortado. ~**-beat** *a* poco convencional. ~ **chance** *n.* on the ~ **chance** por si acaso

offen|ce /ə'fens/ *n* (breach of law) infracción *f*; (criminal ~ce) delito *m*; (cause of outrage) atentado *m*; (Amer, attack) ataque *m*. take ~ce ofenderse. ~**d** *vt* ofender. ~**der** *n* delincuente *m & f*. ~**sive** /-sɪv/ *a* ofensivo; (disgusting) desagradable

offer /'ɒfə(r)/ *vt* ofrecer. ~ to do sth ofrecerse a hacer algo. ● *n* oferta *f*. on ~ de oferta

offhand /ɒf'hænd/ *a* (brusque) brusco. say sth in an ~ way decir algo a la ligera. ● *adv* de improviso

office /'ɒfɪs/ *n* oficina *f*; (post) cargo *m*. doctor's ~ (Amer) consultorio *m*, consulta *m*. ~ **block** *n* edificio *m* de oficinas ~**r** *n* oficial *m & f*; (police ~r) policía *m & f*; (as form of address) agente

offici|al /ə'fɪʃl/ *a* oficial. ● *n* funcionario *m* del Estado; (of party, union) dirigente *m & f*. ~**ally** *adv* oficialmente. ~**ous** /ə'fɪʃəs/ *a* oficioso

offing /'ɒfɪŋ/ *n.* in the ~ en perspectiva

off: ~**-licence** *n* tienda *f* de vinos y licores. ~**-putting** *a* (disconcerting) desconcertante; (disagreeable) desagradable. ~**set** *vt* (*pt* **-set**, *pres p* **-setting**) compensar. ~**side** /ɒf'saɪd/ *a* (Sport) fuera de juego. ~**spring** *n invar* prole *f*. ~**-stage** /-'steɪdʒ/ *adv* fuera del escenario. ~**-white** *a* color hueso

often /'ɒfn/ *adv* a menudo, con frecuencia. how ~? ¿con qué frecuencia? more ~ con más frecuencia

ogle /'əʊgl/ *vt* comerse con los ojos

ogre /'əʊgə(r)/ *n* ogro *m*

oh /əʊ/ *int* ¡ah!; (expressing dismay) ¡ay!

oil /ɔɪl/ *n* aceite *m*; (petroleum) petróleo *m*. ● *vt* lubricar. ~**field** *n* yacimiento *m* petrolífero. ~ **painting** *n* pintura *f* al óleo; (picture) óleo *m.* ~ **rig** *n* plataforma *f* petrolífera. ~**y** *a* *<substance>* oleaginoso; *<food>* aceitoso

ointment /'ɔɪntmənt/ *n* ungüento *m*

OK /əʊ'keɪ/ *int* ¡vale!, ¡de acuerdo!, ¡bueno! (LAm). ● *a* ~, thanks bien, gracias. the job's ~ el trabajo no está mal

old /əʊld/ *a* (**-er, -est**) viejo; (not modern) antiguo; (former) antiguo; an ~ friend un viejo amigo. how ~ is she? ¿cuántos años tiene? she is ten years ~ tiene diez años. his ~er sister su hermana mayor. ~ **age** *n* vejez *f*. ~**-fashioned** /-'fæʃənd/ *a* anticuado

olive /'ɒlɪv/ *n* aceituna *f*.

Olympic /ə'lɪmpɪk/ *a* olímpico. the ~**s** *npl*, the ~ **Games** *npl* los Juegos Olímpicos

omelette /'ɒmlɪt/ *n* tortilla *f* francesa, omelette *m* (LAm)

omen /'əʊmen/ *n* agüero *m*

omi|ssion /ə'mɪʃn/ *n* omisión *f*. ~**t** /əʊ'mɪt/ *vt* (*pt* **omitted**) omitir

on /ɒn/ *prep* en, sobre; (about) sobre. ~ **foot** a pie. ~ **Monday** el lunes. ~ **seeing** al ver. I heard it ~ the radio lo oí por la radio. ● *adv* (light etc) encendido, prendido (LAm); (machine) en marcha; (tap) abierto. ~ **and** ~ sin cesar. and so ~ y así sucesivamente. have a hat ~ llevar (puesto) un sombrero. further ~ un poco más allá. what's ~ at the Odeon? ¿qué dan en el Odeon? go ~ continuar. later ~ más tarde

once /wʌns/ *adv* una vez; (formerly) antes. at ~ inmediatamente. ~ **upon a time there was...** érase una vez.... ~ **and for all** de una vez por todas. ● *conj* una vez que

one /wʌn/ *a* uno, (before masculine singular noun) un. the ~ person I trusted la única persona en la que confiaba.● *n* uno *m*. ~ **by** ~ uno a uno.. ● *pron* uno (*m*), una (*f*). the blue ~ el/la azul. this ~ éste/ésta. ~ **another** el uno al otro.

onerous /'ɒnərəs/ *a* *<task>* pesado

one: ~**self** /-'self/ *pron* (reflexive) se; (*after prep*) sí (mismo); (emphatic use) uno mismo, una misma. by ~**self** solo. ~**-way** *a* *<street>* de sentido único; *<ticket>* de ida, sencillo

onion /'ʌnɪən/ *n* cebolla *f*

onlooker /'ɒnlʊkə(r)/ *n* espectador *m*

only /'əʊnlɪ/ *a* único. **she's an ~ child** es hija única. ● *adv* sólo, solamente. **~ just** (barely) apenas. **I've ~ just arrived** acabo de llegar. ● *conj* pero, sólo que

onset /'ɒnset/ *n* comienzo *m*; (of disease) aparición *f*

onslaught /'ɒnslɔːt/ *n* ataque *m*

onus /'əʊnəs/ *n* responsabilidad *f*

onward(s) /'ɒnwəd(z)/ *a* & *adv* hacia adelante

ooze /uːz/ *vt/i* rezumar

opaque /əʊ'peɪk/ *a* opaco

open /'əʊpən/ *a* abierto; *<question>* discutible. ● *n*. **in the ~** al aire libre. ● *vt/i* abrir. **~ing** *n* abertura *f*; (beginning) principio *m*. **~ly** *adv* abiertamente. **~-minded** /-'maɪndɪd/ *a* de actitud abierta

opera /'ɒprə/ *n* ópera *f*

operate /'ɒpəreɪt/ *vt* manejar, operar (Mex) *<machine>*. ● *vi* funcionar; *<company>* operar. **~ (on)** (Med) operar (a)

operatic /ɒpə'rætɪk/ *a* operístico

operation /ɒpə'reɪʃn/ *n* operación *f*; (Mec) funcionamiento *m*; (using of machine) manejo *m*. **he had an ~** lo operaron. **in ~** en vigor. **~al** *a* operacional

operative /'ɒpərətɪv/ *a*. **be ~** estar en vigor

operator *n* operador *m*

opinion /ə'pɪnɪən/ *n* opinión *f*. **in my ~** en mi opinión, a mi parecer

opponent /ə'pəʊnənt/ *n* adversario *m*; (in sport) contrincante *m* & *f*

opportun|e /'ɒpətjuːn/ *a* oportuno. **~ist** /ɒpə'tjuːnɪst/ *n* oportunista *m* & *f*. **~ity** /ɒpə'tjuːnətɪ/ *n* oportunidad *f*

oppos|e /ə'pəʊz/ *vt* oponerse a. **be ~ed to** oponerse a, estar en contra de. **~ing** *a* opuesto. **~ite** /'ɒpəzɪt/ *a* (contrary) opuesto; (facing) de enfrente. ● *n*. **the ~ite** lo contrario. **quite the ~ite** al contrario. ● *adv* enfrente. ● *prep* enfrente de. **~ite number** *n* homólogo *m*. **~ition** /ɒpə'zɪʃn/ *n* oposición *f*; (resistence) resistencia *f*

oppress /ə'pres/ *vt* oprimir. **~ion** /-ʃn/ *n* opresión *f*. **~ive** *a* (cruel) opresivo; *<heat>* sofocante

opt /ɒpt/ *vi*. **~ to** optar por. □ **~ out** *vi* decidir no tomar parte

optic|al /'ɒptɪkl/ *a* óptico. **~ian** /ɒp'tɪʃn/ *n* óptico *m*

optimis|m /'ɒptɪmɪzəm/ *n* optimismo *m*. **~t** *n* optimista *m* & *f*. **~tic** /-'mɪstɪk/ *a* optimista

option /'ɒpʃn/ *n* opción *f*. **~al** *a* facultativo

or /ɔː(r)/ *conj* o; (before o- and ho-) u; (*after negative*) ni. **~ else** si no, o bien

oral /'ɔːrəl/ *a* oral. ● *n* ① examen *m* oral

orange /'ɒrɪndʒ/ *n* naranja *f*; (colour) naranja *m*. ● *a* naranja. **~ade** /-'eɪd/ *n* naranjada *f*

orbit /'ɔːbɪt/ *n* órbita *f*. ● *vt* orbitar

orchard /'ɔːtʃəd/ *n* huerto *m*

orchestra /'ɔːkɪstrə/ *n* orquesta *f*; (Amer, in theatre) platea *f*. **~l** /-'kestrəl/ *a* orquestal. **~te** /-eɪt/ *vt* orquestar

orchid /'ɔːkɪd/ *n* orquídea *f*

ordain /ɔː'deɪn/ *vt* (Relig) ordenar; (decree) decretar

ordeal /ɔː'diːl/ *n* dura prueba *f*

order /'ɔːdə(r)/ *n* orden *m*; (Com) pedido *m*; (command) orden *f*. **in ~ that** para que. **in ~ to** para. ● *vt* (command) ordenar, mandar; (Com) pedir; (in restaurant) pedir, ordenar (LAm); encargar *<book>*; llamar, ordenar (LAm) *<taxi>*. **~ly** *a* ordenado. ● *n* camillero *m*

ordinary /'ɔːdɪnrɪ/ *a* corriente; (average) medio; (mediocre) ordinario

ore /ɔː(r)/ *n* mena *f*

organ /'ɔːgən/ *n* órgano *m*

organ|ic /ɔː'gænɪk/ *a* orgánico. **~ism** /'ɔːgənɪzəm/ *n* organismo *m*. **~ist** /'ɔːgənɪst/ *n* organista *m* & *f*. **~ization** /ɔːgənaɪ'zeɪʃn/ *n* organización *f*. **~ize** /'ɔːgənaɪz/ *vt* organizar. **~izer** *n* organizador *m*

orgasm /'ɔːgæzəm/ *n* orgasmo *m*

orgy /'ɔːdʒɪ/ *n* orgía *f*

Orient /'ɔːrɪənt/ *n* Oriente *m*. **~al** /-'entl/ *a* oriental

orientat|e /'ɔːrɪənteɪt/ *vt* orientar.
~**ion** /-'teɪʃn/ *n* orientación *f*

origin /'ɒrɪdʒɪn/ *n* origen *m*. ~**al**
/ə'rɪdʒənl/ *a* original. ~**ally** *adv*
originariamente. ~**ate** /ə'rɪdʒɪneɪt/
vi. ~**ate from** provenir de

ornament /'ɔːnəmənt/ *n* adorno *m*.
~**al** /-'mentl/ *a* de adorno

ornate /ɔː'neɪt/ *a* ornamentado;
<*style*> recargado

ornithology /ɔːnɪ'θɒlədʒɪ/ *n* ornitología *f*

orphan /'ɔːfn/ *n* huérfano *m*. ● *vt*. be
~**ed** quedar huérfano. ~**age** /-ɪdʒ/
n orfanato *m*

orthodox /'ɔːθədɒks/ *a* ortodoxo

oscillate /'ɒsɪleɪt/ *vi* oscilar

ostentatious /ɒsten'teɪʃəs/ *a*
ostentoso

osteopath /'ɒstɪəpæθ/ *n* osteópata
m & f

ostracize /'ɒstrəsaɪz/ *vt* hacerle
vacío a

ostrich /'ɒstrɪtʃ/ *n* avestruz *m*

other /'ʌðə(r)/ *a & pron* otro. ~ than
aparte de. **the** ~ **one** el otro. ~**wise**
adv de lo contrario, si no

otter /'ɒtə(r)/ *n* nutria *f*

ouch /aʊtʃ/ *int* ¡ay!

ought /ɔːt/ *v aux*. I ~ **to see it** debería verlo. **he** ~ **to have done it** debería haberlo hecho

ounce /aʊns/ *n* onza *f* (= 28.35 gr.)

our /'aʊə(r)/ *a* (*sing*) nuestro, nuestra, (*pl*) nuestros, nuestras. ~**s**
/'aʊəz/ *poss pron* (*sing*) nuestro,
nuestra; (*pl*) nuestros, nuestras.
~**s is red** el nuestro es rojo. **a friend
of** ~**s** un amigo nuestro. ~**selves**
/-'selvz/ *pron* (reflexive) nos; (used for
emphasis and after prepositions) nosotros
mismos, nosotras mismas. **we be-
haved** ~**selves** nos portamos bien.
we did it ~**selves** lo hicimos nosotros mismos/nosotras mismas

oust /aʊst/ *vt* desbancar; derrocar
<*government*>

out /aʊt/ *adv* (outside) fuera, afuera
(LAm). (not lighted, not on) apagado; (in
blossom) en flor; (in error) equivocado.
he's ~ (not at home) no está; **be** ~ **to**
estar resuelto a. ~ **of** *prep* (from inside) de; (outside) fuera, afuera (LAm).

five ~ **of six** cinco de cada seis. **made**
~ **of** hecho de. **we're** ~ **of bread** nos
hemos quedado sin pan. ~**break** *n*
(of war) estallido *m*; (of disease) brote
m. ~**burst** *n* arrebato *m*. ~**cast** *n*
paria *m & f*. ~**come** *n* resultado *m*.
~**cry** *n* protesta *f*. ~**dated** /-'deɪtɪd/
a anticuado. ~**do** /-'duː/ *vt* (*pt* -**did**,
pp -**done**) superar. ~**door** *a*
<*clothes*> de calle; <*pool*> descu-
bierto. ~**doors** /-'dɔːz/ *adv* al aire
libre

outer /'aʊtə(r)/ *a* exterior

out: ~**fit** *n* equipo *m*; (clothes)
conjunto *m*. ~**going** *a* <*minister
etc*> saliente; (sociable) abierto.
~**goings** *npl* gastos *mpl*. ~**grow**
/-'grəʊ/ *vt* (*pt* -**grew**, *pp* -**grown**)
crecer más que <*person*>. **he's**
~**grown his new shoes** le han quedado pequeños los zapatos nuevos.
~**ing** *n* excursión *f*

outlandish /aʊt'lændɪʃ/ *a* extravagante

out: ~**law** *n* forajido *m*. ● *vt* proscri-
bir. ~**lay** *n* gastos *mpl*. ~**let** *n* salida *f*; (Com) punto *m* de venta; (Amer,
Elec) toma *f* de corriente. ~**line** *n*
contorno *m*; (summary) resumen *m*;
(plan of project) esquema *m*.● *vt* trazar;
(summarize) esbozar. ~**live** /-'lɪv/ *vt*
sobrevivir a. ~**look** *n* perspectivas
fpl; (attitude) punto *m* de vista.
~**lying** *a* alejado. ~**number**
/-'nʌmbə(r)/ *vt* superar en número.
~**-of-date** *a* <*ideas*> desfasado;
<*clothes*> pasado de moda.
~**patient** *n* paciente *m* externo.
~**post** *n* avanzada *f*. ~**put** *n* pro-
ducción *f*; (of machine, worker) rendimiento *m*. ~**right** *adv* completamente; (frankly) abiertamente; <*kill*>
en el acto. ● *a* completo; <*refusal*>
rotundo. ~**set** *n* principio *m*.
~**side** *a & n* exterior (*m*). **at the**
~**side** como máximo. ● /-'saɪd/ *adv*
fuera, afuera (LAm). ● *prep* fuera de.
~**size** *a* de talla gigante. ~**skirts**
npl afueras *fpl*. ~**spoken**
/-'spəʊkn/ *a* directo, franco.
~**standing** /-'stændɪŋ/ *a* excepcional; <*debt*> pendiente. ~**stretched**
/aʊt'stretʃt/ *a* extendido. ~**strip**
/-'strɪp/ *vt* (*pt* -**stripped**) (run faster
than) tomarle la delantera a; (exceed)

sobrepasar. ~**ward** /-wəd/ a <ap-pearance> exterior; <sign> externo; <journey> de ida. ~**wardly** adv por fuera, exteriormente. ~**(s)** adv hacia afuera. ~**weigh** /-'weɪ/ vt ser mayor que. ~**wit** /-'wɪt/ vt (pt **-witted**) burlar

oval /'əʊvl/ a ovalado, oval. ● n óvalo m

ovary /'əʊvərɪ/ n ovario m

ovation /əʊ'veɪʃn/ n ovación f

oven /'ʌvn/ n horno m

over /'əʊvə(r)/ prep por encima de; (across) al otro lado de; (during) du-rante; (more than) más de. ~ **and above** por encima de. ● adv por enci-ma; (ended) terminado; (more) más; (in excess) de sobra. ~ **again** otra vez. ~ **and** ~ una y otra vez. ~ **here** por aquí. ~ **there** por allí. **all** ~ (finished) acabado; (everywhere) por todas partes

over... /'əʊvə(r)/ pref excesiva-mente, demasiado

over: ~**all** /-'ɔːl/ a global; <length, cost> total. ● adv en conjunto. ● /'əʊvərɔːl/ n, ~**alls** npl mono m, overol m (LAm); (Amer, dungarees) peto m, overol m. ~**awe** /-'ɔː/ vt inti-midar. ~**balance** /-'bæləns/ vi perder el equilibrio. ~**bearing** /-'beərɪŋ/ a dominante. ~**board** adv <throw> por la borda. ~**cast** /-'kɑːst/ a <day> nublado; <sky> cu-bierto. ~**charge** /-'tʃɑːdʒ/ vt cobrarle de más. ~**coat** n abrigo m. ~**come** /-'kʌm/ vt (pt **-came**, pp **-come**) superar, vencer. ~**crowded** /-'kraʊdɪd/ a abarro-tado (de gente). ~**do** /-'duː/ vt (pt **-did**, pp **-done**) exagerar; (Culin) re-cocer. ~**dose** n sobredosis f. ~**draft** n descubierto m. ~**draw** /-'drɔː/ vt (pt **-drew**, pp **-drawn**) gi-rar en descubierto. **be** ~**drawn** tener un descubierto. ~**due** /-'djuː/ a. **the book is a month** ~**due** el plazo de de-volución del libro venció hace un mes. ~**estimate** /-'estɪmeɪt/ vt sobreestimar. ~**flow** /-'fləʊ/ vi desbordarse. ● n /-fləʊ/ (excess) exce-so m; (outlet) rebosadero m. ~**grown** /-'grəʊn/ a demasiado grande; <gar-den> lleno de maleza. ~**haul** /-'hɔːl/ vt revisar. ● /-hɔːl/ n revisión f.

~**head** /-'hed/ adv por encima. ● /-hed/ a de arriba. ~**heads** /-hedz/ npl, ~**head** n (Amer) gastos mpl indirectos. ~**hear** /-'hɪə(r)/ vt (pt **-heard**) oír por casualidad. ~**joyed** /-'dʒɔɪd/ a encantado. ~**land** a/adv por tierra. ~**lap** /-'læp/ vi (pt **-lapped**) traslaparse. ~**leaf** /-'liːf/ adv al dorso. ~**load** /-'ləʊd/ vt sobrecargar. ~**look** /-'lʊk/ vt <room> dar a; (not notice) pasar por alto; (disregard) disculpar. ~**night** /-'naɪt/ adv durante la noche. **stay** ~**night** quedarse a pasar la noche. ● a <journey> de noche; <stay> de una noche. ~**pass** n paso m eleva-do, paso m a desnivel (Mex). ~**pay** /-'peɪ/ vt (pt **-paid**) pagar demasia-do. ~**power** /-'paʊə(r)/ vt dominar <opponent>; <emotion> abrumar. ~**powering** /-'paʊərɪŋ/ a <smell> muy fuerte; <desire> irresistible. ~**priced** /-'praɪst/ a demasiado ca-ro. ~**rated** /-'reɪtɪd/ a sobrevalo-rado. ~**react** /-rɪ'ækt/ vi reaccionar en forma exagerada. ~**ride** /-'raɪd/ vt (pt **-rode**, pp **-ridden**) invalidar. ~**riding** /-'raɪdɪŋ/ a dominante. ~**rule** /-'ruːl/ vt anular; rechazar <objection>. ~**run** /-'rʌn/ vt (pt **-ran**, pp **-run**, pres p **-running**) invadir; exceder <limit>. ~**seas** /-'siːz/ a <trade> exterior; <investments> en el exterior; <visitor> extranjero. ● adv al extranjero. ~**see** /-'siː/ vt (pt **-saw**, pp **-seen**) supervisar. ~**seer** /-sɪə(r)/ n capataz m & f, su-pervisor m. ~**shadow** /-'ʃædəʊ/ vt eclipsar. ~**shoot** /-'ʃuːt/ vt (pt **-shot**) excederse. ~**sight** n descui-do m. ~**sleep** /-'sliːp/ vi (pt **-slept**) quedarse dormido. ~**step** /-'step/ vt (pt **-stepped**) sobrepasar. ~**step the mark** pasarse de la raya

overt /'əʊvɜːt/ a manifiesto

over: ~**take** /-'teɪk/ vt/i (pt **-took**, pp **-taken**) sobrepasar; (Auto) adelantar, rebasar (Mex). ~**throw** /-'θrəʊ/ vt (pt **-threw**, pp **-thrown**) derrocar. ~**time** n horas fpl extra

overture /'əʊvətjʊə(r)/ n obertura f

over: ~**turn** /-'tɜːn/ vt darle la vuel-ta a. ● vi volcar. ~**weight** /-'weɪt/ a demasiado gordo. **be** ~**weight** pesar demasiado. **~whelm** /-'welm/ *vt* aplastar; (with emotion) abrumar. **~whelming** *a* aplastante; (fig) abrumador. **~work** /-'wɜːk/ *vt* hacer trabajar demasiado. ● *vi* trabajar demasiado. ● *n* agotamiento *m*

owe /əʊ/ *vt* deber. **~ing to** debido a

owl /aʊl/ *n* búho *m*

own /əʊn/ *a* propio. my ~ house mi propia casa. ● *pron.* it's my ~ es mío (propio)/mía (propia). on one's ~ solo. get one's ~ back 🄸 desquitarse. ● *vt* tener. □ ~ **up** *vi*. 🄸 confesarse culpable. **~er** *n* propietario *m*, dueño *m*. **~ership** *n* propiedad *f*

oxygen /'ɒksɪdʒən/ *n* oxígeno *m*

oyster /'ɔɪstə(r)/ *n* ostra *f*

p *abbr* (= **pence, penny**) penique(s) *m(pl)*

p. (*pl* **pp.**) (= **page**) pág., p.

pace /peɪs/ *n* paso *m*. keep ~ with s.o. seguirle el ritmo a uno. ● *vi.* ~ up and down andar de un lado para otro. **~maker** *n* (runner) liebre *f*; (Med) marcapasos *m*

Pacific /pə'sɪfɪk/ *n.* the ~ (Ocean) el (Océano) Pacífico *m*

pacif|ist /'pæsɪfɪst/ *n* pacifista *m* & *f*. **~y** /'pæsɪfaɪ/ *vt* apaciguar

pack /pæk/ *n* fardo *m*; (of cigarettes) paquete *m*, cajetilla *f*; (of cards) baraja *f*; (of hounds) jauría *f*; (of wolves) manada *f*. a ~ of lies una sarta de mentiras. ● *vt* empaquetar; hacer <*suitcase*>; (press down) apisonar. ● *vi* hacer la maleta, empacar (LAm). **~age** /-ɪdʒ/ *n* paquete *m*. **~age holiday** *n* vacaciones *fpl* organizadas. **~ed** /pækt/ *a* lleno (de gente). **~et** /'pækɪt/ *n* paquete *m*

pact /pækt/ *n* pacto *m*, acuerdo *m*

pad /pæd/ *n* (for writing) bloc *m*. shoulder ~s hombreras *fpl*. ● *vt* (*pt* **padded**) rellenar

paddle /'pædl/ *n* pala *f*. ● *vi* mojarse los pies; (in canoe) remar (*con pala*)

paddock /'pædək/ *n* prado *m*

padlock /'pædlɒk/ *n* candado *m*. ● *vt* cerrar con candado

paed|iatrician /piːdɪə'trɪʃn/ *n* pediatra *m* & *f*. **~ophile** /'piːdəfaɪl/ *n* pedófilo *m*

pagan /'peɪgən/ *a* & *n* pagano (*m*)

page /peɪdʒ/ *n* página *f*; (attendant) paje *m*; (in hotel) botones *m*. ● *vt* llamar por megafonía/por buscapersonas

paid /peɪd/ ⇒PAY. ● *a.* put ~ to 🄸 acabar con

pail /peɪl/ *n* balde *m*, cubo *m*

pain /peɪn/ *n* dolor *m*. I have a ~ in my back me duele la espalda. *m.* be in ~ tener dolores. be a ~ in the neck 🄸 ser un pesado; (thing) ser una lata. ● *vt* doler. **~ful** *a* doloroso. it's very **~ful** duele mucho. **~killer** *n* analgésico *m*. **~less** *a* indoloro. **~staking** /'peɪnzteɪkɪŋ/ *a* concienzudo

paint /peɪnt/ *n* pintura *f*. ● *vt/i* pintar. **~er** *n* pintor *m*. **~ing** *n* (medium) pintura *f*; (picture) cuadro *m*

pair /peə(r)/ *n* par *m*; (of people) pareja *f*. a ~ of trousers unos pantalones. □ **~off, ~ up** *vi* formar parejas

pajamas /pə'dʒɑːməz/ *npl* (Amer) pijama *m*

Pakistan /pɑːkɪ'stɑːn/ *n* Pakistán *m*. **~i** *a* & *n* paquistaní (*m* & *f*)

pal /pæl/ *n* 🄸 amigo *m*

palace /'pælɪs/ *n* palacio *m*

palat|able /'pælətəbl/ *a* agradable. **~e** /'pælət/ *n* paladar *m*

pale /peɪl/ *a* (**-er, -est**) pálido. go ~, turn ~ palidecer. **~ness** *n* palidez *f*

Palestin|e /'pælɪstaɪn/ *n* Palestina *f*. **~ian** /-'stɪnɪən/ *a* & *n* palestino (*m*)

palette /'pælɪt/ *n* paleta *f*

palm /pɑːm/ *n* palma *f*. □ ~ **off** *vt* encajar (on a). **P~ Sunday** *n* Domingo *m* de Ramos

palpable /'pælpəbl/ *a* palpable

palpitat|e /'pælpɪteɪt/ *vi* palpitar. **~ion** /-'teɪʃn/ *n* palpitación *f*

pamper /'pæmpə(r)/ *vt* mimar

pamphlet /'pæmflɪt/ n folleto m

pan /pæn/ n cacerola f; (for frying) sartén f

panacea /pænə'sɪə/ n panacea f

Panama /'pænəmɑː/ n Panamá m. ~**nian** /-'meɪnɪən/ a & n panameño (m)

pancake /'pænkeɪk/ n crep(e) m, panqueque m (LAm)

panda /'pændə/ n panda m

pandemonium /pændɪ'məʊnɪəm/ n pandemonio m

pander /'pændə(r)/ vi. ~ **to** s.o. consentirle los caprichos a uno

pane /peɪn/ n vidrio m, cristal m

panel /'pænl/ n panel m; (group of people) jurado m. ~**ling** n paneles mpl

pang /pæŋ/ n punzada f

panic /'pænɪk/ n pánico m. ● vi (pt **panicked**) dejarse llevar por el pánico. ~**-stricken** a aterrorizado

panoram|a /pænə'rɑːmə/ n panorama m. ~**ic** /-'ræmɪk/ a panorámico

pansy /'pænzɪ/ n (Bot) pensamiento m

pant /pænt/ vi jadear

panther /'pænθə(r)/ n pantera f

panties /'pæntɪz/ npl bragas fpl, calzones mpl (LAm), pantaletas fpl (Mex)

pantihose /'pæntɪhəʊz/ npl ⇒PAN-TYHOSE

pantomime /'pæntəmaɪm/ n pantomima f

pantry /'pæntrɪ/ n despensa f

pants /pænts/ npl (man's) calzoncillos mpl; (woman's) bragas fpl, calzones mpl (LAm), pantaletas fpl (Mex); (Amer, trousers) pantalones mpl

pantyhose /'pæntɪhəʊz/ npl (Amer) panty m, medias fpl, pantimedias fpl (Mex)

paper /'peɪpə(r)/ n papel m; (newspaper) diario m, periódico m; (exam) examen m; (document) documento m. ● vt empapelar, tapizar (Mex). ~**back** n libro m en rústica. ~ **clip** n sujetapapeles m, clip m. ~**weight** n pisapapeles m. ~**work** n papeleo m, trabajo m administrativo

parable /'pærəbl/ n parábola f

parachut|e /'pærəʃuːt/ n paracaídas m. ● vi saltar en paracaídas. ~**ist** n paracaidista m & f

parade /pə'reɪd/ n desfile m; (Mil) formación f. ● vi desfilar. ● vt hacer alarde de

paradise /'pærədaɪs/ n paraíso m

paraffin /'pærəfɪn/ n queroseno m

paragraph /'pærəgrɑːf/ n párrafo m

Paraguay /'pærəgwaɪ/ n Paraguay m. ~**an** a & n paraguayo (m)

parallel /'pærəlel/ a paralelo. ● n paralelo m; (line) paralela f

paraly|se /'pærəlaɪz/ vt paralizar. ~**sis** /pə'ræləsɪs/ n (pl **-ses** /-siːz/) parálisis f

paranoia /pærə'nɔɪə/ n paranoia f

parapet /'pærəpɪt/ n parapeto m

paraphernalia /pærəfə'neɪlɪə/ n trastos mpl

parasite /'pærəsaɪt/ n parásito m

paratrooper /'pærətruːpə(r)/ n paracaidista m (del ejército)

parcel /'pɑːsl/ n paquete m

parch /pɑːtʃ/ vt resecar. be ~ed ▣ estar muerto de sed

parchment /'pɑːtʃmənt/ n pergamino m

pardon /'pɑːdn/ n perdón m; (Jurid) indulto m. I beg your ~ perdón. (I beg your) ~? ¿cómo?, ¿mande? (Mex). ● vt perdonar; (Jurid) indultar. ~ me? (Amer) ¿cómo?

parent /'peərənt/ n (father) padre m; (mother) madre f. my ~s mis padres. ~**al** /pə'rentl/ a de los padres

parenthesis /pə'renθəsɪs/ n (pl **-theses** /-siːz/) paréntesis m

parenthood /'peərənthʊd/ n el ser padre/madre

Paris /'pærɪs/ n París m

parish /'pærɪʃ/ n parroquia f; (municipal) distrito m. ~**ioner** /pə'rɪʃənə(r)/ n feligrés m

park /pɑːk/ n parque m. ● vt/i aparcar, estacionar (LAm)

parking: /'pɑːkɪŋ/~ **lot** n (Amer) aparcamiento m, estacionamiento m (LAm). ~ **meter** n parquímetro m

parkway /'pɑːkweɪ/ n (Amer) carretera f ajardinada

parliament /'pɑːləmənt/ n parlamento m. ~**ary** /-'mentrɪ/ a parlamentario

parlour /'pɑːlə(r)/ n salón m

parochial /pə'rəʊkɪəl/ a (fig) provinciano

parody /'pærədɪ/ n parodia f. ● vt parodiar

parole /pə'rəʊl/ n libertad f condicional

parrot /'pærət/ n loro m, papagayo m

parsley /'pɑːslɪ/ n perejil m

parsnip /'pɑːsnɪp/ n pastinaca f

part /pɑːt/ n parte f; (of machine) pieza f; (of serial) episodio m; (in play) papel m; (Amer, in hair) raya f. **take** ~ **in** tomar parte en, participar en. **for the most** ~ en su mayor parte. ● adv en parte. ● vt separar. ● vi separarse. □ ~ **with** vt desprenderse de

partial /'pɑːʃl/ a parcial. **be** ~ **to** tener debilidad por. ~**ly** adv parcialmente

participa|nt /pɑːtɪsɪpənt/ n participante m & f. ~**te** /-peɪt/ vi participar. ~**tion** /-'peɪʃn/ n participación f

particle /'pɑːtɪkl/ n partícula f

particular /pə'tɪkjʊlə(r)/ a particular; (precise) meticuloso; (fastidious) quisquilloso. **in** ~ en particular. ● n detalle m. ~**ly** adv particularmente; (specifically) específicamente

parting /'pɑːtɪŋ/ n despedida f; (in hair) raya f. ● a de despedida

partition /pɑː'tɪʃn/ n partición f; (wall) tabique m. ● vt dividir

partly /'pɑːtlɪ/ adv en parte

partner /'pɑːtnə(r)/ n socio m; (Sport) pareja f. ~**ship** n asociación f; (Com) sociedad f

partridge /'pɑːtrɪdʒ/ n perdiz f

part-time /pɑː'taɪm/ a & adv a tiempo parcial, de medio tiempo (LAm)

party /'pɑːtɪ/ n reunión f, fiesta f; (group) grupo m; (Pol) partido m; (Jurid) parte f

pass /pɑːs/ vt (hand, convey) pasar; (go past) pasar por delante de; (overtake) adelantar, rebasar (Mex); (approve) aprobar <exam, bill, law>; pronunciar <judgement>. ● vi pasar; <pain> pasarse; (Sport) pasar la pelota. □ ~ **away** vi fallecer. □ ~ **down** vt transmitir. □ ~ **out** vi desmayarse. □ ~ **round** vt distribuir. □ ~ **up** vt 🔢 dejar pasar. ● n (permit) pase m; (ticket) abono m; (in mountains) puerto m, desfiladero m; (Sport) pase m; (in exam) aprobado m. **make a** ~ **at** 🔢 intentar besar. ~**able** a pasable; <road> transitable

passage /'pæsɪdʒ/ n (voyage) travesía f; (corridor) pasillo m; (alleyway) pasaje m; (in book) pasaje m

passenger /'pæsɪndʒə(r)/ n pasajero m

passer-by /pɑːsə'baɪ/ n (pl **passers-by**) transeúnte m & f

passion /'pæʃn/ n pasión f. ~**ate** /-ət/ a apasionado. ~**ately** adv apasionadamente

passive /'pæsɪv/ a pasivo

Passover /'pɑːsəʊvə(r)/ n Pascua f de los hebreos

pass: ~**port** n pasaporte m. ~**word** n contraseña f

past /pɑːst/ a anterior; <life> pasado; <week, year> último. **in times** ~ en tiempos pasados. ● n pasado m. **in the** ~ (formerly) antes, antiguamente. ● prep por delante de; (beyond) más allá de. **it's twenty** ~ **four** son las cuatro y veinte. ● adv. **drive** ~ pasar en coche. **go** ~ pasar

paste /peɪst/ n pasta f; (glue) engrudo m; (wallpaper ~) pegamento m; (jewellery) estrás m

pastel /'pæstl/ a & n pastel (m)

pasteurize /'pɑːstʃəraɪz/ vt pasteurizar

pastime /'pɑːstaɪm/ n pasatiempo m

pastry /'peɪstrɪ/ n masa f; (cake) pastelito m

pasture /'pɑːstʃə(r)/ n pasto(s) mpl

pasty /'pæstɪ/ n empanadilla f, empanada f (LAm)

pat /pæt/ vt (pt **patted**) darle palmaditas. ● n palmadita f; (of butter) porción f

patch /pætʃ/ n (on clothes) remiendo m, parche m; (over eye) parche m. **a bad ~** una mala racha. ● vt remendar. □ ~ **up** vt hacerle un arreglo a

patent /'peɪtnt/ a patente. ● n patente f. ● vt patentar. ~ **leather** n charol m. ~**ly** adv. **it's ~ly obvious that...** está clarísimo que...

patern|al /pə'tɜːnl/ a paterno. ~**ity** /-ətɪ/ n paternidad f

path /pɑːθ/ n (pl -s /pɑːðz/) sendero m; (Sport) pista f; (of rocket) trayectoria f; (fig) camino m

pathetic /pə'θetɪk/ a (pitiful) patético; <excuse> pobre. **don't be so ~** no seas tan pusilánime

patien|ce /'peɪʃns/ n paciencia f. ~**t** a & n paciente (m & f). **be ~t with s.o.** tener paciencia con uno. ~**tly** adv pacientemente

patio /'pætɪəʊ/ n (pl -os) patio m

patriot /'pætrɪət/ n patriota m & f. ~**ic** /-'ɒtɪk/ a patriótico. ~**ism** n patriotismo m

patrol /pə'trəʊl/ n patrulla f. ● vt/i patrullar

patron /'peɪtrən/ n (of the arts) mecenas m & f; (of charity) patrocinador m; (customer) cliente m & f. ~**age** /'pætrənɪdʒ/ n (sponsorship) patrocinio m; (of the arts) mecenazgo m. ~**ize** /'pætrənaɪz/ vt ser cliente de; (fig) tratar con condescendencia. ~**izing** a condescendiente

pattern /'pætn/ n diseño m; (sample) muestra f; (in dressmaking) patrón m

paunch /pɔːntʃ/ n panza f

pause /pɔːz/ n pausa f. ● vi hacer una pausa

pave /peɪv/ vt pavimentar; (with flagstones) enlosar. ~**ment** n pavimento m; (at side of road) acera f, banqueta f (Mex)

paving stone /'peɪvɪŋstəʊn/ n losa f

paw /pɔː/ n pata f

pawn /pɔːn/ n (Chess) peón m; (fig) títere m. ● vt empeñar. ~**broker** n prestamista m & f

pay /peɪ/ vt (pt **paid**) pagar; prestar <attention>; hacer <compliment, visit>. ~ **cash** pagar al contado. ● vi

pagar; (be profitable) rendir. ● n paga f. **in the ~ of** al servicio de. □ ~ **back** vt devolver; pagar <loan>. □ ~ **in** vt ingresar, depositar (LAm). □ ~ **off** vt cancelar, saldar <debt>. vi valer la pena. □ ~ **up** vi pagar. ~**able** a pagadero. ~**ment** n pago m. ~**roll** n nómina f

pea /piː/ n guisante m, arveja f (LAm), chícharo m (Mex)

peace /piːs/ n paz f. ~ **of mind** tranquilidad f. ~**ful** a tranquilo. ~**maker** n conciliador m

peach /piːtʃ/ n melocotón m, durazno m (LAm)

peacock /'piːkɒk/ n pavo m real

peak /piːk/ n cumbre f; (of career) apogeo m; (maximum) máximo m. ~ **hours** npl horas fpl de mayor demanda (o consumo etc)

peal /piːl/ n repique m. ~**s of laughter** risotadas fpl

peanut /'piːnʌt/ n cacahuete m, maní m (LAm), cacahuate m (Mex)

pear /peə(r)/ n pera f. ~ (**tree**) peral m

pearl /pɜːl/ n perla f

peasant /'peznt/ n campesino m

peat /piːt/ n turba f

pebble /'pebl/ n guijarro m

peck /pek/ vt picotear. ● n picotazo m; (kiss) besito m

peculiar /pɪ'kjuːlɪə(r)/ a raro; (special) especial. ~**ity** /-'ærətɪ/ n rareza f; (feature) particularidad f

pedal /'pedl/ n pedal m. ● vi pedalear

pedantic /pɪ'dæntɪk/ a pedante

peddle /'pedl/ vt vender por las calles

pedestal /'pedɪstl/ n pedestal m

pedestrian /pɪ'destrɪən/ n peatón m. ~ **crossing** paso m de peatones. ● a pedestre; (dull) prosaico

pedigree /'pedɪgriː/ linaje m; (of animal) pedigrí m. ● a <animal> de raza

peek /piːk/ vi mirar a hurtadillas

peel /piːl/ n piel f, cáscara f. ● vt pelar <fruit, vegetables>. ● vi pelarse

peep /piːp/ vi. ~ **at** echarle un vistazo a. ● n (look) vistazo m; (bird sound) pío m

peer /pɪə(r)/ *vi* mirar. ∼ **at** escudriñar. ● *n* (equal) par *m* & *f*; (contemporary) coetáneo *m*; (lord) par *m*. ∼**age** /-ɪdʒ/ *n* nobleza *f*

peg /peg/ *n* (in ground) estaca *f*; (on violin) clavija *f*; (for washing) pinza *f*; (hook) gancho *m*; (for tent) estaquilla *f*. **off the** ∼ de confección. ● *vt* (*pt* **pegged**) sujetar (*con estacas, etc*); fijar <*precios*>

pejorative /pɪ'dʒɒrətɪv/ *a* peyorativo, despectivo

pelican /'pelɪkən/ *n* pelícano *m*

pellet /'pelɪt/ *n* bolita *f*; (for gun) perdigón *m*

pelt /pelt/ *n* pellejo *m*. ● *vt*. ∼ **s.o. with sth** lanzarle algo a uno. ● *vi*. ∼ **with rain**, ∼ **down** llover a cántaros

pelvis /'pelvɪs/ *n* pelvis *f*

pen /pen/ (for writing) pluma *f*; (ballpoint) bolígrafo *m*; (sheep ∼) redil *m*; (cattle ∼) corral *m*

penal /'piːnl/ *a* penal. ∼**ize** *vt* sancionar. ∼**ty** /'penltɪ/ *n* pena *f*; (fine) multa *f*; (in soccer) penalty *m*; (in US football) castigo *m*. ∼**ty kick** *n* (in soccer) penalty *m*

penance /'penəns/ *n* penitencia *f*

pence /pens/ ⇒PENNY

pencil /'pensl/ *n* lápiz *m*. ● *vt* (*pt* **pencilled**) escribir con lápiz. ∼**-sharpener** *n* sacapuntas *m*

pendulum /'pendjʊləm/ *n* péndulo *m*

penetrat|e /'penɪtreɪt/ *vt/i* penetrar. ∼**ing** *a* penetrante. ∼**ion** /-'treɪʃn/ *n* penetración *f*

penguin /'peŋgwɪn/ *n* pingüino *m*

penicillin /penɪ'sɪlɪn/ *n* penicilina *f*

peninsula /pə'nɪnsjʊlə/ *n* península *f*

penis /'piːnɪs/ *n* pene *m*

pen: ∼knife /'pennaɪf/ *n* (*pl* **penknives**) navaja *f*. ∼**-name** *n* seudónimo *m*

penn|iless /'penɪlɪs/ *a* sin un céntimo. ∼**y** /'penɪ/ *n* (*pl* **pennies** or **pence**) penique *m*

pension /'penʃn/ *n* pensión *f*; (for retirement) pensión *f* de jubilación. ∼**er** *n* jubilado *m*

pensive /'pensɪv/ *a* pensativo

Pentecost /'pentɪkɒst/ *n* Pentecostés *m*

penthouse /'penthaʊs/ *n* penthouse *m*

pent-up /pent'ʌp/ *a* reprimido; (confined) encerrado

penultimate /pen'ʌltɪmət/ *a* penúltimo

people /'piːpl/ *npl* gente *f*; (citizens) pueblo *m*. ∼ **say** (**that**) se dice que, dicen que. **English** ∼ los ingleses. **young** ∼ los jóvenes. **the** ∼ (nation) el pueblo. ● *vt* poblar

pepper /'pepə(r)/ *n* pimienta *f*; (vegetable) pimiento *m*. ● *vt* (intersperse) salpicar (**with** de). ∼**box** *n* (Amer) pimentero *m*. ∼**corn** *n* grano *m* de pimienta. ∼**mint** *n* menta *f*; (sweet) caramelo *m* de menta. ∼**pot** *n* pimentero *m*

per /pɜː(r)/ *prep* por. ∼ **annum** al año. ∼ **cent** ⇒PERCENT. ∼ **head** por cabeza, por persona. **ten miles** ∼ **hour** diez millas por hora

perceive /pə'siːv/ *vt* percibir; (notice) darse cuenta de

percent, per cent /pə'sent/ *n* (*no pl*) porcentaje *m*. ● *adv* por ciento. ∼**age** /-ɪdʒ/ *n* porcentaje *m*

percepti|ble /pə'septəbl/ *a* perceptible. ∼**on** /-ʃn/ *n* percepción *f*. ∼**ve** /-tɪv/ *a* perspicaz

perch /pɜːtʃ/ *n* (of bird) percha *f*; (fish) perca *f*. ● *vi* <*bird*> posarse. ∼ **on** <*person*> sentarse en el borde de

percolat|e /'pɜːkəleɪt/ *vi* filtrarse. ∼**or** *n* cafetera *f* eléctrica

percussion /pə'kʌʃn/ *n* percusión *f*

perfect /'pɜːfɪkt/ *a* perfecto; <*place, day*> ideal. ● /pə'fekt/ *vt* perfeccionar. ∼**ion** /pə'fekʃn/ *n* perfección *f*. **to** ∼**ion** a la perfección. ∼**ly** /'pɜːfɪktlɪ/ *adv* perfectamente

perform /pə'fɔːm/ *vt* desempeñar <*function, role*>; ejecutar <*task*>; realizar <*experiment*>; representar <*play*>; (Mus) interpretar. ∼ **an operation** (Med) operar. ● *vi* <*actor*> actuar; <*musician*> tocar; (produce results) <*vehicle*> responder; <*company*> rendir. ∼**ance** /-əns/ *n* ejecución *f*; (of play) representación *f*; (of actor, musician) interpretación *f*; (of team) actuación *f*; (of car) rendimiento *m*. **~er** *n* (actor) actor *m*; (entertainer) artista *m* & *f*

perfume /'pɜːfjuːm/ *n* perfume *m*

perhaps /pə'hæps/ *adv* quizá(s), tal vez, a lo mejor

peril /'perəl/ *n* peligro *m*. **~ous** *a* arriesgado, peligroso

perimeter /pə'rɪmɪtə(r)/ *n* perímetro *m*

period /'pɪərɪəd/ *n* período *m*; (in history) época *f*; (lesson) clase *f*; (Amer, Gram) punto *m*; (menstruation) período *m*, regla *f*. ● *a* de (la) época. **~ic** /-'ɒdɪk/ *a* periódico. **~ical** /pɪərɪ'ɒdɪkl/ *n* revista *f*. **~ically** *adv* periódico

peripher|al /pə'rɪfərəl/ *a* secundario; (Comp) periférico. **~y** /pə'rɪfərɪ/ *n* periferia *f*

perish /'perɪʃ/ *vi* perecer; (rot) deteriorarse. **~able** *a* perecedero. **~ing** *a* 🄸 glacial

perjur|e /'pɜːdʒə(r)/ *vr*. **~e o.s.** perjurarse. **~y** *n* perjurio *m*

perk /pɜːk/ *n* gaje *m*. □ **~ up** *vt* reanimar. *vi* reanimarse

perm /pɜːm/ *n* permanente *f*. ● *vt*. **have one's hair ~ed** hacerse la permanente

permanen|ce /'pɜːmənəns/ *n* permanencia *f*. **~t** *a* permanente. **~tly** *adv* permanentemente

permissible /pə'mɪsəbl/ *a* permisible

permission /pə'mɪʃn/ *n* permiso *m*

permit /pə'mɪt/ *vt* (*pt* **permitted**) permitir. ● /'pɜːmɪt/ *n* permiso *m*

peroxide /pə'rɒksaɪd/ *n* peróxido *m*

perpendicular /pɜːpən'dɪkjʊlə(r)/ *a* & *n* perpendicular (*f*)

perpetrat|e /'pɜːpɪtreɪt/ *vt* cometer. **~or** *n* autor *m*

perpetua|l /pə'petʃʊəl/ *a* perpetuo. **~te** /pə'petʃʊeɪt/ *vt* perpetuar

perplex /pə'pleks/ *vt* dejar perplejo. **~ed** *a* perplejo

persecut|e /'pɜːsɪkjuːt/ *vt* perseguir. **~ion** /-'kjuːʃn/ *n* persecución *f*

persever|ance /pɜːsɪ'vɪərəns/ *n* perseverancia *f*. **~e** /pɜːsɪ'vɪə(r)/ *vi* perseverar, persistir

Persian /'pɜːʃn/ *a* persa. **the ~ Gulf** *n* el golfo Pérsico

persist /pə'sɪst/ *vi* persistir. **~ence** /-əns/ *n* persistencia *f*. **~ent** *a* persistente; (continual) continuo

person /'pɜːsn/ *n* persona *f*. **in ~** en persona. **~al** *a* personal; <call> particular; <property> privado. **~al assistant** *n* secretario *m* personal. **~ality** /-'nælətɪ/ *n* personalidad *f*. **~ally** *adv* personalmente. **~nel** /pɜːsə'nel/ *n* personal *m*. **P~** (department) sección *f* de personal

perspective /pə'spektɪv/ *n* perspectiva *f*

perspir|ation /pɜːspə'reɪʃn/ *n* transpiración *f*. **~e** /pəs'paɪə(r)/ *vi* transpirar

persua|de /pə'sweɪd/ *vt* convencer, persuadir. **~e s.o. to do sth** convencer a uno para que haga algo. **~sion** *n* /-ʃn/ persuasión *f*. **~sive** /-sɪv/ *a* persuasivo

pertinent /'pɜːtɪnənt/ *a* pertinente. **~ly** *adv* pertinentemente

perturb /pə'tɜːb/ *vt* perturbar

Peru /pə'ruː/ *n* el Perú *m*

peruse /pə'ruːz/ *vt* leer cuidadosamente

Peruvian /pə'ruːvɪan/ *a* & *n* peruano (*m*)

perver|se /pə'vɜːs/ *a* retorcido; (stubborn) obstinado. **~sion** *n* perversión *f*. **~t** /pə'vɜːt/ *vt* pervertir. ● /'pɜːvɜːt/ *n* pervertido *m*

pessimis|m /'pesɪmɪzəm/ *n* pesimismo *m*. **~t** *n* pesimista *m* & *f*. **~tic** /-'mɪstɪk/ *a* pesimista

pest /pest/ *n* plaga *f*; (🄸, person, thing) peste *f*

pester /'pestə(r)/ *vt* importunar

pesticide /'pestɪsaɪd/ *n* pesticida *f*

pet /pet/ *n* animal *m* doméstico; (favourite) favorito *m*. ● *a* preferido. **my ~ hate** lo que más odio. ● *vt* (*pt* **petted**) acariciar

petal /'petl/ *n* pétalo *m*

petition /pɪ'tɪʃn/ *n* petición *f*

pet name *n* apodo *m*

petrified /'petrɪfaɪd/ a (terrified) muerto de miedo; (Geol) petrificado

petrol /'petrəl/ n gasolina f. ~ **pump** n surtidor m. ~ **station** n gasolinera f. ~ **tank** n depósito m de gasolina ~**eum** /pɪ'trəʊlɪəm/ n petróleo m.

petticoat /'petɪkəʊt/ n enagua f; (slip) combinación f

petty /'petɪ/ a (-ier, -iest) insignificante; (mean) mezquino. ~**y cash** n dinero m para gastos menores

petulant /'petjʊlənt/ a irritable

pew /pju:/ n banco m (de iglesia)

phantom /'fæntəm/ n fantasma m

pharma|ceutical /fɑ:mə'sju:tɪkl/ a farmacéutico. ~**cist** /'fɑ:məsɪst/ n farmacéutico m. ~**cy** /'fɑ:məsɪ/ n farmacia f

phase /feɪz/ n etapa f. □ ~ **out** vt retirar progresivamente

PhD abbr (= **Doctor of Philosophy**) n doctorado m; (person) Dr., Dra.

pheasant /'feznt/ n faisán m

phenomen|al /fɪ'nɒmɪnl/ a fenomenal. ~**on** /-mən/ n (pl -**ena** /-inə/) fenómeno m

philistine /'fɪlɪstaɪn/ a & n filisteo (m)

philosoph|er /fɪ'lɒsəfə(r)/ n filósofo m. ~**ical** /-ə'sɒfɪkl/ a filosófico. ~**y** /fɪ'lɒsəfɪ/ n filosofía f

phlegm /flem/ n flema f. ~**atic** /fleg'mætɪk/ a flemático

phobia /'fəʊbɪə/ n fobia f

phone /fəʊn/ n 🄸 teléfono m. ● vt/i llamar (por teléfono). ~ **back** (call again) volver a llamar; (return call) llamar (más tarde). ~ **book** n guía f telefónica, directorio m (LAm). ~ **booth**, ~ **box** n cabina f telefónica. ~ **call** n llamada f (telefónica). ~ **card** n tarjeta f telefónica. ~ **number** n número m de teléfono

phonetic /fə'netɪk/ a fonético. ~**s** n fonética f

phoney /'fəʊnɪ/ a (-ier, -iest) 🄸 falso

phosph|ate /'fɒsfeɪt/ n fosfato m. ~**orus** /'fɒsfərəs/ n fósforo m

photo /'fəʊtəʊ/ n (pl -**os**) 🄸 foto f. take a ~ sacar una foto. ~**copier** /-kɒpɪə(r)/ n fotocopiadora f.

~**copy** n fotocopia f. ● vt fotocopiar. ~**genic** /-'dʒenɪk/ a fotogénico. ~**graph** /-grɑ:f/ n fotografía f. ● vt fotografiar, sacarle una fotografía a. ~**grapher** /fə'tɒgrəfə(r)/ n fotógrafo m. ~**graphic** /-'græfɪk/ a fotográfico. ~**graphy** /fə'tɒgrəfɪ/ n fotografía f

phrase /freɪz/ n frase f. ● vt expresar. ~ **book** n manual m de conversación

physi|cal /'fɪzɪkl/ a físico. ~**cian** /fɪ'zɪʃn/ n médico m. ~**cist** /'fɪzɪsɪst/ n físico m. ~**cs** /'fɪzɪks/ n física f. ~**ology** /fɪzɪ'ɒlədʒɪ/ n fisiología f. ~**otherapist** /fɪzɪəʊ'θerəpɪst/ n fisioterapeuta m & f. ~**otherapy** /fɪzɪəʊ'θerəpɪ/ n fisioterapia f. ~**que** /fɪ'zi:k/ n físico m

pian|ist /'pɪənɪst/ n pianista m & f. ~**o** /pɪ'ænəʊ/ n (pl -**os**) piano m

pick /pɪk/ (tool) pico m. ● vt escoger; cortar <flowers>; recoger <fruit, cotton>; abrir con una ganzúa <lock>. ~ a quarrel buscar camorra. ~ holes in criticar. □ ~ **on** vt meterse con. □ ~ **out** vt escoger; (identify) reconocer. □ ~ **up** vt recoger; (lift) levantar; (learn) aprender; adquirir <habit, etc>; contagiarse de <illness>. ● vi mejorar; <sales> subir. ~**axe** n pico m

picket /'pɪkɪt/ n (group) piquete m. ~ **line** n piquete m. ● vt formar un piquete frente a

pickle /'pɪkl/ n (in vinegar) encurtido m; (Amer, gherkin) pepinillo m; (relish) salsa f (a base de encurtidos). ● vt encurtir

pick: ~**pocket** n carterista m & f. ~**-up** n (truck) camioneta f

picnic /'pɪknɪk/ n picnic m

picture /'pɪktʃə(r)/ n (painting) cuadro m; (photo) foto f; (drawing) dibujo m; (illustration) ilustración f; (film) película f; (fig) descripción f. ● vt imaginarse. ~**sque** /-'resk/ a pintoresco

pie /paɪ/ n empanada f; (sweet) pastel m, tarta f

piece /pi:s/ n pedazo m, trozo m; (part of machine) pieza f; (coin) moneda f; (in chess) figura f. a ~ of advice un consejo. a ~ of furniture un mueble. a ~ of news una noticia. take to ~s

desmontar. □ ~ **together** *vt* juntar.
~**meal** *a* gradual; (unsystematic) poco
sistemático. ● *adv* poco a poco

pier /pɪə(r)/ *n* muelle *m*; (with amuse-
ments) *paseo con atracciones sobre un
muelle*

pierc|e /pɪəs/ *vt* perforar. ~**ing** *a*
penetrante

piety /'paɪətɪ/ *n* piedad *f*

pig /pɪg/ *n* cerdo *m*, chancho *m* (LAm)

pigeon /'pɪdʒɪn/ *n* paloma *f*; (Culin)
pichón *m*. ~**-hole** *n* casillero *m*; (fig)
casilla *f*

piggy /'pɪgɪ/ *n* cerdito *m*. ~**back** *n*.
give s.o. a ~**back** llevar a uno a
cuestas. ~ **bank** *n* hucha *f*

pig-headed /-'hedɪd/ *a* terco

pigment /'pɪgmənt/ *n* pigmento *m*

pig|sty /'pɪgstaɪ/ *n* pocilga *f*. ~**tail** *n*
(plait) trenza *f*; (bunch) coleta *f*

pike /paɪk/ *n invar* (fish) lucio *m*

pilchard /'pɪltʃəd/ *n* sardina *f*

pile /paɪl/ *n* (heap) montón *m*; (of fabric) pelo *m*. ● *vt* amontonar. ~ **it on**
exagerar. ● *vi* amontonarse. □ ~ **up**
vt amontonar. ● *vi* amontonarse. ~**s**
/paɪlz/ *npl* (Med) almorranas *fpl*.
~**-up** *n* choque *m* múltiple

pilgrim /'pɪlgrɪm/ *n* peregrino.
~**age** /-ɪdʒ/ *n* peregrinación *f*

pill /pɪl/ *n* pastilla *f*

pillar /'pɪlə(r)/ *n* columna *f*. ~ **box** *n*
buzón *m*

pillow /'pɪləʊ/ *n* almohada *f*. ~**case**
n funda *f* de almohada

pilot /'paɪlət/ *n* piloto *m*. ● *vt* pilotar.
~ **light** *n* fuego *m* piloto

pimple /'pɪmpl/ *n* grano *m*, espinilla
f (LAm)

pin /pɪn/ *n* alfiler *m*; (Mec) perno *m*.
~**s and needles** hormigueo *m*.
● *vt* (*pt* **pinned**) prender con alfi-
leres; (fix) sujetar

PIN /pɪn/ *n* (= **personal identifica-
tion number**) PIN *m*

pinafore /'pɪnəfɔː(r)/ *n* delantal *m*.
~ **dress** *n* pichi *m*, jumper *m* & *f*
(LAm)

pincers /'pɪnsəz/ *npl* tenazas *fpl*

pinch /pɪntʃ/ *vt* pellizcar; (🔲, steal)
hurtar. ● *vi* <shoe> apretar. ● *n* pe-

llizco *m*; (small amount) pizca *f*. **at a** ~
si fuera necesario

pine /paɪn/ *n* pino *m*. ● *vi*. ~ **for sth**
suspirar por algo. □ ~ **away** *vi*
languidecer de añoranza. ~**apple**
/'paɪnæpl/ *n* piña *f*

ping-pong /'pɪŋpɒŋ/ *n* ping-pong *m*

pink /pɪŋk/ *a* & *n* rosa (*m*), rosado
(*m*)

pinnacle /'pɪnəkl/ *n* pináculo *m*

pin: ~**point** *vt* determinar con precisión *f*. ~**stripe** *n* raya *f* fina

pint /paɪnt/ *n* pinta *f* (= 0.57 litros)

pioneer /paɪə'nɪə(r)/ *n* pionero *m*

pious /'paɪəs/ *a* piadoso

pip /pɪp/ *n* (seed) pepita *f*; (time signal)
señal *f*

pipe /paɪp/ *n* tubo *m*; (Mus) caramillo
m; (for smoking) pipa *f*. ● *vt* llevar por
tuberías. ~**-dream** *n* ilusión *f*.
~**line** *n* conducto *m*; (for oil) oleoducto *m*. **in the** ~**line** en preparación
f

piping /'paɪpɪŋ/ *n* tubería *f*. ● *adv*. ~
hot muy caliente, hirviendo

pira|cy /'paɪərəsɪ/ *n* piratería *f*. ~**te**
/'paɪərət/ *n* pirata *m*

Pisces /'paɪsiːz/ *n* Piscis *m*

piss /pɪs/ *vi* 🔲 mear. □ ~ **off** *vi* 🔲. ~
off! ¡vete a la mierda! ~**ed** /pɪst/ *a*
(🔲, drunk) como una cuba; (Amer, fed
up) cabreado

pistol /'pɪstl/ *n* pistola *f*

piston /'pɪstən/ *n* pistón *m*

pit /pɪt/ *n* hoyo *m*; (mine) mina *f*; (Amer,
in fruit) hueso *m*

pitch /pɪtʃ/ *n* (substance) brea *f*; (degree) grado *m*; (Mus) tono *m*; (Sport)
campo *m*. ● *vi* (throw) lanzar; armar
<tent>. ● *vi* <ship> cabecear.
~**-black** /-'blæk/ *a* oscuro como boca de lobo. ~**er** *n* jarra *f*

pitfall /'pɪtfɔːl/ *n* trampa *f*

pith /pɪθ/ *n* (of orange, lemon) médula *f*;
(fig) meollo *m*

pitiful /'pɪtɪfl/ *a* lastimoso

pittance /'pɪtns/ *n* miseria *f*

pity /'pɪtɪ/ *n* lástima *f*, pena *f*; (compassion) piedad *f*. **it's a** ~ **you can't come**
es una lástima que no puedas venir.
● *vt* tenerle lástima a

pivot /'pɪvət/ n pivote m. ● vi pivotar; (fig) depender (**on** de)

placard /'plækɑːd/ n pancarta f; (sign) letrero m

placate /pləˈkeɪt/ vt apaciguar

place /pleɪs/ n lugar m; (seat) asiento m; (in firm, team) puesto m; (⊞, house) casa f. **feel out of ~** sentirse fuera de lugar. **take ~** tener lugar. ● vt poner, colocar; (identify) identificar. **be ~d** (in race) colocarse. **~-mat** n mantel m individual

placid /'plæsɪd/ a plácido

plague /pleɪg/ n peste f; (fig) plaga f. ● vt atormentar

plaice /pleɪs/ n invar platija f

plain /pleɪn/ a (**-er, -est**) (clear) claro; (simple) sencillo; (candid) franco; (ugly) feo. **in ~ clothes** de civil. ● adv totalmente. ● n llanura f. **~ly** adv claramente; (frankly) francamente; (simply) con sencillez

plait /plæt/ vt trenzar. ● n trenza f

plan /plæn/ n plan m; (map) plano m; (of book, essay) esquema f. ● vt (pt **planned**) planear; planificar <strategies>. **I'm ~ning to go to Greece** pienso ir a Grecia

plane /pleɪn/ n (tree) plátano m; (level) nivel m; (Aviat) avión m; (tool) cepillo m. ● vt cepillar

planet /'plænɪt/ n planeta m. **~ary** a planetario

plank /plæŋk/ n tabla f

planning /'plænɪŋ/ n planificación f. **family ~** planificación familiar. **town ~** urbanismo m

plant /plɑːnt/ n planta f; (Mec) maquinaria f; (factory) fábrica f. ● vt plantar; (place in position) colocar. **~ation** /plænˈteɪʃn/ n plantación f

plaque /plæk/ n placa f

plasma /'plæzmə/ n plasma m

plaster /'plɑːstə(r)/ n yeso m; (on walls) revoque m; (sticking plaster) tirita f (P), curita f (P) (LAm); (for setting bones) yeso m, escayola f. ● vt revocar; rellenar con yeso <cracks>

plastic /'plæstɪk/ a & n plástico (m)

Plasticine /'plæstɪsiːn/ n (P) plastilina f (P)

plastic surgery /plæstɪkˈsɜːdʒərɪ/ n cirugía f estética

plate /pleɪt/ n plato m; (of metal) chapa f; (silverware) vajilla f de plata; (in book) lámina f. ● vt recubrir (**with** de)

platform /'plætfɔːm/ n plataforma f; (Rail) andén m

platinum /'plætɪnəm/ n platino m

platitude /'plætɪtjuːd/ n lugar m común

platonic /pləˈtɒnɪk/ a platónico

plausible /'plɔːzəbl/ a verosímil; <person> convincente

play /pleɪ/ vt jugar a <game, cards>; jugar a, jugar (LAm) <football, chess>; tocar <instrument>; (act role) representar el papel de. ● vi jugar. ● n juego m; (drama) obra f de teatro. □ ~ **down** vt minimizar. □ ~ **up** vi ⊞ <child> dar guerra; <car, TV> no funcionar bien. **~er** n jugador m; (Mus) músico m. **~ful** a juguetón. **~ground** n parque m de juegos infantiles; (in school) patio m de recreo. **~group** n jardín m de la infancia. **~ing card** n naipe m. **~ing field** n campo m de deportes. **~pen** n corralito m. **~wright** /-raɪt/ n dramaturgo m

plc abbr (= **public limited company**) S.A.

plea /pliː/ n súplica f; (excuse) excusa f; (Jurid) defensa f

plead /pliːd/ vt (Jurid) alegar; (as excuse) pretextar. ● vi suplicar. **~ with** suplicarle a. **~ guilty** declararse culpable

pleasant /'pleznt/ a agradable

pleas|e /pliːz/ int por favor. ● vt complacer; (satisfy) contentar. ● vi agradar; (wish) querer. **~ed** a (satisfied) satisfecho; (happy) contento. **~ed with** satisfecho de. **~ing** a agradable; (news) grato. **~ure** /'pleʒə(r)/ n placer m

pleat /pliːt/ n pliegue m

pledge /pledʒ/ n cantidad f prometida

plent|iful /'plentɪfl/ a abundante. **~y** /'plentɪ/ n abundancia f. ● pron. **~y of** muchos, -chas; (of sth uncountable) mucho, -cha

pliable /'plaɪəbl/ a flexible

pliers /'plaɪəz/ npl alicates mpl

plight /plaɪt/ n situación f difícil

plimsolls /'plɪmsəlz/ npl zapatillas fpl de lona

plod /plɒd/ vi (pt **plodded**) caminar con paso pesado

plot /plɒt/ n complot m; (of novel etc) argumento m; (piece of land) parcela f. ● vt (pt **plotted**) tramar; (mark out) trazar. ● vi conspirar

plough /plaʊ/ n arado m. ● vt/i arar. □ ~ **into** vt estrellarse contra. □ ~ **through** vt avanzar laboriosamente por

ploy /plɔɪ/ n treta f

pluck /plʌk/ vt arrancar; depilarse <eyebrows>; desplumar <bird>. ~ **up courage** to armarse de valor para. ● n valor m. ~**y** a (-**ier**, -**iest**) valiente

plug /plʌg/ n (in bath) tapón m; (Elec) enchufe m; (spark ~) bujía f. ● vt (pt **plugged**) tapar; (▢, advertise) hacerle propaganda a. □ ~ **in** vt (Elec) enchufar. ~**hole** n desagüe m

plum /plʌm/ n ciruela f

plumage /'plu:mɪdʒ/ n plumaje m

plumb|er /'plʌmə(r)/ n fontanero m, plomero m (LAm). ~**ing** n instalación f sanitaria, instalación f de cañerías

plume /plu:m/ n pluma f

plump /plʌmp/ a (-**er**, -**est**) rechoncho

plunge /plʌndʒ/ vt hundir <knife>; (in water) sumergir; (into state, condition) sumir. ● vi zambullirse; (fall) caer. ● n zambullida f

plural /'plʊərəl/ n plural m. ● a en plural

plus /plʌs/ prep más. ● a positivo. ● n signo m de más; (fig) ventaja f

plush /plʌʃ/ a lujoso

Pluto /'plu:təʊ/ n Plutón m

plutonium /plu:'təʊnɪəm/ n plutonio m

ply /plaɪ/ vt manejar <tool>; ejercer <trade>. ~ **s.o. with drink** dar continuamente de beber a uno. ~**wood** n contrachapado m

p.m. abbr (= **post meridiem**) de la tarde

pneumatic drill /nju:'mætɪk/ a martillo m neumático

pneumonia /nju:'məʊnjə/ n pulmonía f

poach /pəʊtʃ/ vt escalfar <egg>; cocer <fish etc>; (steal) cazar furtivamente. ~**er** n cazador m furtivo

PO box /pi:'əʊ/ n Apdo. postal

pocket /'pɒkɪt/ n bolsillo m; (of air, resistance) bolsa f. ● vt poner en el bolsillo. ~**book** n (notebook) libro m de bolsillo; (Amer, wallet) cartera f; (Amer, handbag) bolso m, cartera f (LAm), bolsa f (Mex). ~ **money** n dinero m de bolsillo, mesada f (LAm)

pod /pɒd/ n vaina f

poem /'pəʊɪm/ n poema f

poet /'pəʊɪt/ n poeta m. ~**ic** /-'etɪk/ a poético. ~**ry** /'pəʊɪtrɪ/ n poesía f

poignant /'pɔɪnjənt/ a conmovedor

point /pɔɪnt/ n (dot, on scale) punto m; (sharp end) punta f; (in time) momento m; (statement) observación; (on agenda, in discussion) punto m; (Elec) toma f de corriente. **to the** ~ pertinente. **up to a** ~ hasta cierto punto. **be on the** ~ **of** estar a punto de. **get to the** ~ ir al grano. **there's no** ~ (in) **arguing** no sirve de nada discutir. ● vt (aim) apuntar; (show) indicar. ● vi señalar. ~ **at/to sth** señalar algo. □ ~ **out** vt señalar. ~**blank** a & adv a quemarropa. ~**ed** a (chin, nose) puntiagudo; (fig) mordaz. ~**less** a inútil

poise /pɔɪz/ n porte m; (composure) desenvoltura f

poison /'pɔɪzn/ n veneno m. ● vt envenenar. ~**ous** a venenoso; <chemical etc> tóxico

poke /pəʊk/ vt empujar; atizar <fire>. ● vi hurgar; (pry) meterse. ● n golpe m. □ ~ **about** vi fisgonear. ~**r** /'pəʊkə(r)/ n atizador m; (Cards) póquer m

poky /'pəʊkɪ/ a (-**ier**, -**iest**) diminuto

Poland /'pəʊlənd/ n Polonia f

polar /'pəʊlə(r)/ a polar. ~ **bear** n oso m blanco

pole /pəʊl/ n palo m; (fixed) poste m; (for flag) mástil m; (Geog) polo m

police /pə'li:s/ n policía f. ~**man** /-mən/ n policía m, agente m. ~ **station** n comisaría f. ~**woman** n policía f, agente f

policy /'pɒlɪsɪ/ n política f; (insurance) póliza f (de seguros)

polish /'pɒlɪʃ/ n (for shoes) betún m; (furniture ∿) cera f para muebles; (floor ∿) abrillantador m de suelos; (shine) brillo m; (fig) finura f. ● vt darle brillo a; limpiar *<shoes>*; (refine) pulir. □ ∿ **off** vt despachar. ∿ed a pulido

Polish /'pəʊlɪʃ/ a & n polaco (m)

polite /pə'laɪt/ a cortés. ∿ly adv cortésmente. ∿ness n cortesía f

politic|al /pə'lɪtɪkl/ a político. ∿ian /pɒlɪ'tɪʃn/ n político m. ∿s /'pɒlətɪks/ n política f

poll /pəʊl/ n elección f; (survey) encuesta f. ● vt obtener *<votes>*

pollen /'pɒlən/ n polen m

polling booth n cabina f de votar

pollut|e /pə'luːt/ vt contaminar. ∿ion /-ʃn/ n contaminación f

polo /'pəʊləʊ/ n polo m. ∿ **neck** n cuello m vuelto

poly|styrene /pɒlɪ'staɪriːn/ n poliestireno m. ∿thene /'pɒlɪθiːn/ n plástico, polietileno m

pomp /pɒmp/ n pompa f. ∿ous a pomposo

pond /pɒnd/ n (natural) laguna f; (artificial) estanque m

ponder /'pɒndə(r)/ vt considerar. ∿ous a pesado

pony /'pəʊnɪ/ n poni m. ∿-**tail** n cola f de caballo

poodle /'puːdl/ n caniche m

pool /puːl/ n charca f; (artificial) estanque m; (puddle) charco m. (common fund) fondos mpl comunes; (snooker) billar m americano. (**swimming**) ∿ n piscina f, alberca f (Mex). ∿s npl quinielas fpl. ● vt aunar

poor /pʊə(r)/ a (-**er**, -**est**) pobre; *<quality, diet>* malo. **be in** ∿ **health** estar mal de salud. ∿**ly** a 🆒 malito. ● adv mal

pop /pɒp/ n (Mus) música f pop; (Amer 🆒, father) papá m. ● vt (pt **popped**) hacer reventar; (put) poner. □ ∿ **in** vi (visit) pasar por. □ ∿ **out** vi saltar; *<person>* salir un rato. □ ∿ **up** vi surgir, aparecer

popcorn /'pɒpkɔːn/ n palomitas fpl

pope /pəʊp/ n papa m

poplar /'pɒplə(r)/ n álamo m (blanco)

poppy /'pɒpɪ/ n amapola f

popular /'pɒpjʊlə(r)/ a popular. ∿ity /-'lærətɪ/ n popularidad f. ∿ize vt popularizar

populat|e /'pɒpjʊleɪt/ vt poblar. ∿ion /-'leɪʃn/ n población f

porcelain /'pɔːsəlɪn/ n porcelana f

porch /pɔːtʃ/ n porche m

porcupine /'pɔːkjʊpaɪn/ n puerco m espín

pore /pɔː(r)/ n poro m

pork /pɔːk/ n carne f de cerdo m, carne f de puerco m (Mex)

porn /pɔːn/ n 🆒 pornografía f. ∿**ographic** /-ə'græfɪk/ a pornográfico. ∿**ography** /pɔː'nɒgrəfɪ/ n pornografía f

porpoise /'pɔːpəs/ n marsopa f

porridge /'pɒrɪdʒ/ n avena f (cocida)

port /pɔːt/ n puerto m; (Naut) babor m; (Comp) puerto m; (Culin) oporto m

portable /'pɔːtəbl/ a portátil

porter /'pɔːtə(r)/ n (for luggage) maletero m; (concierge) portero m

porthole /'pɔːthəʊl/ n portilla f

portion /'pɔːʃn/ n porción f; (part) parte f

portrait /'pɔːtrɪt/ n retrato m

portray /pɔː'treɪ/ vt representar. ∿**al** n representación f

Portug|al /'pɔːtjʊgl/ n Portugal m. ∿**uese** /-'giːz/ a & n portugués (m)

pose /pəʊz/ n pose f, postura f. ● vt representar *<threat>*; plantear *<problem, question>*. ● vi posar. ∿ **as** hacerse pasar por

posh /pɒʃ/ a 🆒 elegante

position /pə'zɪʃn/ n posición f; (job) puesto m; (situation) situación f. ● vt colocar

positive /'pɒzətɪv/ a positivo; (real) auténtico; (certain) seguro. ● n (Photo) positiva f. ∿**ly** adv positivamente

possess /pə'zes/ vt poseer. ∿**ion** /-ʃn/ n posesión f; (Jurid) bien m. ∿**ive** a posesivo

possib|ility /pɒsə'bɪlətɪ/ n posibilidad f. ∿**le** /'pɒsəbl/ a posible. ∿**ly** adv posiblemente

post /pəʊst/ n (pole) poste m; (job) puesto m; (mail) correo m. ● vt echar al correo *<letter>*; (send) enviar por correo. **keep s.o.** ~**ed** mantener a uno al corriente

post... /pəʊst/ *pref* post, pos

post: ~**age** /-ɪdʒ/ /-ɪdʒ/ *n* franqueo *m*. ~**al** *a* postal. ~**al order** *n* giro *m* postal. ~ **box** *n* buzón *m*. ~**card** *n* (tarjeta *f*) postal *f*. ~**code** *n* código *m* postal

poster /'pəʊstə(r)/ *n* cartel *m*, póster *m*

posterity /pɒs'terətɪ/ *n* posteridad *f*

posthumous /'pɒstjʊməs/ *a* póstumo

post: ~**man** /-mən/ *n* cartero *m*. ~**mark** *n* matasellos *m*

post mortem /pəʊst'mɔːtəm/ *n* autopsia *f*

post office *n* oficina *f* de correos, correos *mpl*, correo *m* (LAm)

postpone /pəʊst'pəʊn/ *vt* aplazar, posponer. ~**ment** *n* aplazamiento *m*

postscript /'pəʊstskrɪpt/ *n* posdata *f*

posture /'pɒstʃə(r)/ *n* postura *f*

posy /'pəʊzɪ/ *n* ramillete *m*

pot /pɒt/ *n* (for cooking) olla *f*; (for jam, honey) tarro *m*; (for flowers) tiesto *m*; (in pottery) vasija *f*. ~**s and pans** cacharros *mpl*

potato /pə'teɪtəʊ/ *n* (*pl* **-oes**) patata *f*, papa *f* (LAm)

potent /'pəʊtnt/ *a* potente; <*drink*> fuerte

potential /pəʊ'tenʃl/ *a & n* potencial (*m*). ~**ly** *adv* potencialmente

pot: ~**hole** *n* cueva *f* subterránea; (in road) bache *m*. ~**holing** *n* espeleología *f*

potion /'pəʊʃn/ *n* poción *f*

pot-shot *n* tiro *m* al azar

potter /'pɒtə(r)/ *n* alfarero *m*. ●*vi* hacer pequeños trabajos agradables. ~**y** *n* (pots) cerámica *f*; (workshop, craft) alfarería *f*

potty /'pɒtɪ/ *a* (**-ier, -iest**) 🄳 chiflado. ●*n* orinal *m*

pouch /paʊtʃ/ *n* bolsa *f* pequeña; (for correspondence) valija *f*

poultry /'pəʊltrɪ/ *n* aves *fpl* de corral

pounce /paʊns/ *vi* saltar. ~ **on** abalanzarse sobre

pound /paʊnd/ *n* (weight) libra *f* (= 454g); (money) libra *f* (esterlina); (for cars) depósito *m*. ●*vt* (crush) machacar. ●*vi* aporrear; <*heart*> palpitar; <*sound*> retumbar

pour /pɔː(r)/ *vt* verter; echar <*salt*>. ~ (**out**) servir <*drink*>. ●*vi* <*blood*> manar; <*water*> salir; (rain) llover a cántaros. ☐ ~ **out** *vi* <*people*> salir en tropel. ~**ing** *a*. ~**ing rain** lluvia *f* torrencial

pout /paʊt/ *vi* hacer pucheros

poverty /'pɒvətɪ/ *n* pobreza *f*

powder /'paʊdə(r)/ *n* polvo *m*; (cosmetic) polvos *mpl*. ●*vt* empolvar. ~ **one's face** ponerse polvos en la cara. ~**y** *a* como polvo

power /'paʊə(r)/ *n* poder *m*; (energy) energía *f*; (electricity) electricidad *f*; (nation) potencia *f*. ●*vt*. ~**ed by** impulsado por ~ **cut** *n* apagón *m*. ~**ed** *a* con motor. ~**ful** *a* poderoso. ~**less** *a* impotente. ~ **plant**, ~-**station** *n* central *f* eléctrica

PR = **public relations**

practicable /'præktɪkəbl/ *a* practicable

practical /'præktɪkl/ *a* práctico. ~ **joke** *n* broma *f*. ~**ly** *adv* prácticamente

practi|ce /'præktɪs/ *n* práctica *f*; (custom) costumbre *f*; (exercise) ejercicio *m*; (Sport) entrenamiento *m*; (clients) clientela *f*. **he's out of** ~**ce** le falta práctica. **in** ~**ce** (in fact) en la práctica. ~**se** /'præktɪs/ *vt* practicar; ensayar <*act*>; ejercer <*profession*>. ●*vi* practicar; <*professional*> ejercer. ~**tioner** /-'tɪʃənə(r)/ *n* médico *m*

prairie /'preərɪ/ *n* pradera *f*

praise /preɪz/ *vt* (Relig) alabar; (compliment) elogiar. ●*n* (credit) elogios *mpl*. ~**worthy** *a* loable

pram /præm/ *n* cochecito *m*

prank /præŋk/ *n* travesura *f*

prawn /prɔːn/ *n* gamba *f*, camarón *m* (LAm)

pray /preɪ/ *vi* rezar (**for** por). ~**er** /preə(r)/ *n* oración *f*

pre.. /priː/ *pref* pre...

preach /priːtʃ/ *vt/i* predicar. ~**er** *n* predicador *m*; (Amer, minister) pastor *m*

pre-arrange /priːəˈreɪndʒ/ *vt* concertar de antemano

precarious /prɪˈkeərɪəs/ *a* precario. ~**ly** *adv* precariamente

precaution /prɪˈkɔːʃn/ *n* precaución *f*

precede /prɪˈsiːd/ *vt* preceder. ~**nce** /ˈpresədəns/ *n* precedencia *f*. ~**nt** /ˈpresədənt/ *n* precedente *m*

preceding /prɪˈsiːdɪŋ/ *a* anterior

precept /ˈpriːsept/ *n* precepto *m*

precinct /ˈpriːsɪŋkt/ *n* recinto *m*; (Amer, police district) distrito *m* policial; (Amer, voting district) circunscripción *f*. **pedestrian** ~ zona *f* peatonal. ~**s** (of city) límites *mpl*

precious /ˈpreʃəs/ *a* precioso. ● *adv* ▣ muy

precipice /ˈpresɪpɪs/ *n* precipicio *m*

precipitate /prɪˈsɪpɪteɪt/ *vt* precipitar. ● /prɪˈsɪpɪtət/ *n* precipitado *m*. ● /prɪˈsɪpɪtət/ *a* precipitado

precis|e /prɪˈsaɪs/ *a* (accurate) exacto; (specific) preciso; (meticulous) minucioso. ~**ely** *adv* con precisión. ~**!** ¡exacto! ~**ion** /-ˈsɪʒn/ *n* precisión *f*

preclude /prɪˈkluːd/ *vt* excluir

precocious /prɪˈkəʊʃəs/ *a* precoz. ~**ly** *adv* precozmente

preconce|ived /priːkənˈsiːvd/ *a* preconcebido. ~**ption** /-ˈsepʃn/ *n* preconcepción *f*

precursor /priːˈkɜːsə(r)/ *n* precursor *m*

predator /ˈpredətə(r)/ *n* depredador *m*. ~**y** *a* predador

predecessor /ˈpriːdɪsesə(r)/ *n* predecesor *m*, antecesor *m*

predicament /prɪˈdɪkəmənt/ *n* aprieto *m*

predict /prɪˈdɪkt/ *vt* predecir. ~**ion** /-ʃn/ *n* predicción *f*

preen /priːn/ *vt* arreglar. ~ **o.s.** atildarse

prefab /ˈpriːfæb/ *n* ▣ casa *f* prefabricada. ~**ricated** /-ˈfæbrɪkeɪtɪd/ *a* prefabricado

preface /ˈprefəs/ *n* prefacio *m*; (to event) prólogo *m*

prefect /ˈpriːfekt/ *n* (Schol) monitor *m*; (official) prefecto *m*

prefer /prɪˈfɜː(r)/ *vt* (*pt* **preferred**) preferir. ~ **sth to sth** preferir algo a algo. ~**able** /ˈprefrəbl/ *a* preferible. ~**ence** /ˈprefrəns/ *n* preferencia *f*. ~**ential** /-əˈrenʃl/ *a* preferente

pregnan|cy /ˈpregnənsɪ/ *n* embarazo *m*. ~**t** *a* embarazada

prehistoric /priːhɪˈstɒrɪk/ *a* prehistórico

prejudge /priːˈdʒʌdʒ/ *vt* prejuzgar

prejudice /ˈpredʒʊdɪs/ *n* prejuicio *m*. ● *vt* predisponer; (harm) perjudicar. ~**d** *a* lleno de prejuicios

preliminary /prɪˈlɪmɪnərɪ/ *a* preliminar

prelude /ˈpreljuːd/ *n* preludio *m*

premature /ˈpremətjʊə(r)/ *a* prematuro

premeditated /priːˈmedɪteɪtɪd/ *a* premeditado

premier /ˈpremɪə(r)/ *n* (Pol) primer ministro *m*

première /ˈpremɪeə(r)/ *n* estreno *m*

premise /ˈpremɪs/ *n* premisa *f*. ~**s** /ˈpremɪsɪz/ *npl* local *m*. **on the** ~**s** en el local

premium /ˈpriːmɪəm/ *n* (insurance ~) prima *f* de seguro. **be at a** ~ escasear

premonition /priːməˈnɪʃn/ *n* premonición *f*, presentimiento *m*

preoccup|ation /priːɒkjʊˈpeɪʃn/ *n* (obsession) obsesión *f*; (concern) preocupación *f*. ~**ied** /-ˈɒkjʊpaɪd/ *a* absorto; (worried) preocupado

preparat|ion /prepəˈreɪʃn/ *n* preparación *f*. ~**ions** *npl* preparativos *mpl*. ~**ory** /prɪˈpærətrɪ/ *a* preparatorio

prepare /prɪˈpeə(r)/ *vt* preparar. ● *vi* prepararse. ● *a* preparado (willing). **be** ~**d to** estar dispuesto a

preposition /prepəˈzɪʃn/ *n* preposición *f*

preposterous /prɪˈpɒstərəs/ *a* absurdo

prerequisite /priːˈrekwɪzɪt/ *n* requisito *m* esencial

prerogative /prɪˈrɒgətɪv/ *n* prerrogativa *f*

Presbyterian /prezbɪˈtɪərɪən/ *a* & *n* presbiteriano (*m*)

prescri|be /prɪˈskraɪb/ *vt* prescribir; (Med) recetar. **~ption** /-ˈɪpʃn/ *n* (Med) receta *f*

presence /ˈprezns/ *n* presencia *f*. **~ of mind** presencia *f* de ánimo

present /ˈpreznt/ *n* (gift) regalo *m*; (current time) presente *m*. at **~** actualmente. **for the ~** por ahora. ● *a* presente. ● /prɪˈzent/ *vt* presentar; (give) obsequiar. **~ s.o. with** obsequiar a uno con. **~able** /prɪˈzentəbl/ *a* presentable. **~ation** /prezn'teɪʃn/ *n* presentación *f*; (ceremony) ceremonia *f* de entrega. **~er** /prɪˈzentə(r)/ *n* presentador *m*. **~ly** /ˈprezntlɪ/ *adv* dentro de poco

preserv|ation /prezəˈveɪʃn/ *n* conservación *f*. **~ative** /prɪˈzɜːvətɪv/ *n* conservante *m*. **~e** /prɪˈzɜːv/ *vt* conservar; (maintain) mantener; (Culin) hacer conserva de. ● *n* coto *m*; (jam) confitura *f*. **wildlife ~e** (Amer) reserva *f* de animales

preside /prɪˈzaɪd/ *vi* presidir. **~ over** presidir

presiden|cy /ˈprezɪdənsɪ/ *n* presidencia *f*. **~t** *n* presidente *m*. **~tial** /-ˈdenʃl/ *a* presidencial

press /pres/ *vt* apretar; prensar *<grapes>*; (put pressure on) presionar; (iron) planchar. **be ~ed for time** andar escaso de tiempo. ● *vi* apretar; *<time>* apremiar; (fig) urgir. ● *n* (Mec, newspapers) prensa *f*; (printing) imprenta *f*. □ **~ on** *vi* seguir adelante (with con). **~ conference** *n* rueda *f* de prensa. **~ cutting** *n* recorte *m* de periódico. **~ing** *a* urgente. **~-up** *n* flexión *f*, fondo *m*

pressur|e /ˈpreʃə(r)/ *n* presión *f*. ● *vt* presionar. **~e-cooker** *n* olla *f* a presión. **~ize** *vt* presionar

prestig|e /preˈstiːʒ/ *n* prestigio *m*. **~ious** /-ˈstɪdʒəs/ *a* prestigioso

presum|ably /prɪˈzjuːməblɪ/ *adv*. **~...** supongo que..., me imagino que... **~e** /prɪˈzjuːm/ *vt* suponer. **~ptuous** /prɪˈzʌmptʃʊəs/ *a* impertinente

presuppose /priːsəˈpəʊz/ *vt* presuponer

preten|ce /prɪˈtens/ *n* fingimiento *m*; (claim) pretensión *f*; (pretext) pretexto *m*. **~d** /-ˈtend/ *vt/i* fingir. **~sion** /-ˈtenʃən/ *n* pretensión *f*. **~tious** /-ˈtenʃəs/ *a* pretencioso

pretext /ˈpriːtekst/ *n* pretexto *m*

pretty /ˈprɪtɪ/ *a* (**-ier, -iest**) *adv* bonito, lindo (esp LAm)

prevail /prɪˈveɪl/ *vi* predominar; (win) prevalecer. □ **~ on** *vt* persuadir

prevalen|ce /ˈprevələns/ *n* (occurrence) preponderancia *f*; (predominance) predominio *m*. **~t** *a* extendido

prevent /prɪˈvent/ *vt* (hinder) impedir; (forestall) prevenir, evitar. **~ion** /-ʃn/ *n* prevención *f*. **~ive** *a* preventivo

preview /ˈpriːvjuː/ *n* preestreno *m*; (trailer) avance *m*

previous /ˈpriːvɪəs/ *a* anterior. **~ to** antes de. **~ly** *adv* antes

prey /preɪ/ *n* presa *f*. **bird of ~** ave *f* de rapiña

price /praɪs/ *n* precio *m*. ● *vt* fijar el precio de. **~less** *a* inestimable; (🔲, amusing) muy divertido. **~y** *a* 🔲 carito

prick /prɪk/ *vt/i* pinchar. ● *n* pinchazo *m*

prickl|e /ˈprɪkl/ *n* (Bot) espina *f*; (of animal) púa *f*; (sensation) picor *m*. **~y** *a* espinoso; *<animal>* con púas; (touchy) quisquilloso

pride /praɪd/ *n* orgullo *m*. ● *vr*. **~ o.s. on** enorgullecerse de

priest /priːst/ *n* sacerdote *m*. **~hood** *n* sacerdocio *m*

prim /prɪm/ *a* (**primmer, primmest**) mojigato; (affected) remilgado

primar|ily /ˈpraɪmərɪlɪ/ *adv* en primer lugar. **~y** /ˈpraɪmərɪ/ *a* (principal) primordial; (first, basic) primario. **~ school** *n* escuela *f* primaria

prime /praɪm/ *vt* cebar *<gun>*; (prepare) preparar; aprestar *<surface>*. ● *a* principal; (first rate) excelente. **~ minister** *n* primer ministro *m*. ● *n*. **be in one's ~** estar en la flor de la vida. **~r** *n* (paint) imprimación *f*

primeval /praɪˈmiːvl/ *a* primigenio

primitive /ˈprɪmɪtɪv/ *a* primitivo

primrose /'prɪmrəʊz/ n primavera f

prince /prɪns/ n príncipe m. ~**ss** /prɪn'ses/ n princesa f

principal /'prɪnsəpl/ a principal. ● n (of school) director m; (of university) rector m. ~**ly** /'prɪnsɪpəlɪ/ adv principalmente

principle /'prɪnsəpl/ n principio m. in ~ en principio. on ~ por principio

print /prɪnt/ vt imprimir; (write in capitals) escribir con letras de molde. ~**ed matter** impresos mpl. ● n (characters) letra f; (picture) grabado m; (Photo) copia f; (fabric) estampado m. in ~ (published) publicado; (available) a la venta. out of ~ agotado. ~**er** /'prɪntə(r)/ n impresor m; (machine) impresora f. ~**ing** n impresión f; (trade) imprenta f. ~**out** n listado m

prior /'praɪə(r)/ n prior m. ● a previo. ~ **to** antes de. ~**ity** /praɪ'ɒrətɪ/ n prioridad f. ~**y** n priorato m

prise /praɪz/ vt. ~ **open** abrir haciendo palanca

prison /'prɪzn/ n cárcel m. ~**er** n prisionero m; (in prison) preso m; (under arrest) detenido m. ~ **officer** n funcionario m de prisiones

priva|cy /'prɪvəsɪ/ n privacidad f. ~**te** /'praɪvɪt/ a privado; (confidential) personal; <lessons, house> particular. in ~**te** en privado; (secretly) en secreto. ● n soldado m raso. ~**te detective** n detective m & f privado. ~**tely** adv en privado. ~**tion** /praɪ'veɪʃn/ n privación f

privilege /'prɪvəlɪdʒ/ n privilegio m. ~**d** a privilegiado. **be** ~**d to** tener el privilegio de

prize /praɪz/ n premio m. ● a <idiot etc> de remate. ● vt estimar

pro /prəʊ/ n. ~**s and cons** los pros m y los contras

probab|ility /prɒbə'bɪlətɪ/ n probabilidad f. ~**le** /'prɒbəbl/ a probable. ~**ly** adv probablemente

probation /prə'beɪʃn/ n período m de prueba; (Jurid) libertad f condicional

probe /prəʊb/ n sonda f; (fig) investigación f. ● vt sondar. ● vi. ~ **into** investigar

problem /'prɒbləm/ n problema m. ● a difícil. ~**atic** /-'mætɪk/ a problemático

procedure /prə'si:dʒə(r)/ n procedimiento m

proceed /prə'si:d/ vi proceder; (move forward) avanzar. ~**ings** npl (report) actas fpl; (Jurid) proceso m. ~**s** /'prəʊsi:dz/ npl. **the** ~**s** lo recaudado

process /'prəʊses/ n proceso m. in **the** ~ **of** en vías de. ● vt tratar; revelar <photo>; tramitar <order>. ~**ion** /prə'seʃn/ n desfile m; (Relig) procesión f

procla|im /prə'kleɪm/ vt proclamar. ~**mation** /prɒklə'meɪʃn/ n proclamación f

procure /prə'kjʊə(r)/ vt obtener

prod /prɒd/ vt (pt **prodded**) (with sth sharp) pinchar; (with elbow) darle un codazo a. ● n (with sth sharp) pinchazo m; (with elbow) codazo m

produc|e /prə'dju:s/ vt producir; surtir <effect>; sacar <gun>; producir <film>; poner en escena <play>. ● /'prɒdju:s/ n productos mpl. ~**er** /prə'dju:sə(r)/ n (TV, Cinema) productor m; (in theatre) director m; (manufacturer) fabricante m & f. ~**t** /'prɒdʌkt/ n producto m. ~**tion** /prə'dʌkʃn/ n (manufacture) fabricación f; (output) producción f; (of play) producción f. ~**tive** /prə'dʌktɪv/ a productivo. ~**tivity** /prɒdʌk'tɪvətɪ/ n productividad f

profess /prə'fes/ vt profesar; (pretend) pretender. ~**ion** /-'feʃn/ n profesión f. ~**ional** a & n profesional (m & f). ~**or** /-'fesə(r)/ n catedrático m; (Amer) profesor m

proficien|cy /prə'fɪʃənsɪ/ n competencia f. ~**t** a competente

profile /'prəʊfaɪl/ n perfil m

profit /'prɒfɪt/ n (Com) ganancia f; (fig) provecho m. ● vi. ~ **from** sacar provecho de. ~**able** a provechoso

profound /prə'faʊnd/ a profundo. ~**ly** adv profundamente

profus|e /prə'fju:s/ a profuso. ~**ely** adv profusamente

prognosis /prɒg'nəʊsɪs/ n (pl **-oses**) pronóstico m

program /'prəʊgræm/ *n* (Comp) programa *m*; (Amer, course) curso *m*. ∼**me** /'prəʊgræm/ *n* programa *m*. ● *vt* (*pt* **-med**) programar. ∼**mer** *n* programador *m*

progress /'prəʊgres/ *n* progreso *m*; (development) desarrollo *m*. **make** ∼ hacer progresos. **in** ∼ en curso. ● /prə'gres/ *vi* hacer progresos; (develop) desarrollarse. ∼**ion** /prə'greʃn/ *n* progresión *f*; (advance) evolución *f*. ∼**ive** /prə'gresɪv/ *a* progresivo; (reforming) progresista. ∼**ively** *adv* progresivamente

prohibit /prə'hɪbɪt/ *vt* prohibir; (prevent) impedir. ∼**ive** *a* prohibitivo

project /prə'dʒekt/ *vt* proyectar. ● *vi* (stick out) sobresalir. ● /'prɒdʒekt/ *n* proyecto *m*; (Schol) trabajo *m*; (Amer, housing ∼) complejo *m* de viviendas subvencionadas. ∼**or** /prə'dʒektə(r)/ *n* proyector *m*

prolific /prə'lɪfɪk/ *a* prolífico

prologue /'prəʊlɒg/ *n* prólogo *m*

prolong /prə'lɒŋ/ *vt* prolongar

prom /prɒm/ *n* (Amer) baile *m* del colegio. ∼**enade** /prɒmə'nɑːd/ *n* paseo *m* marítimo. ● *vi* pasearse.

prominen|ce /'prɒmɪnəns/ *n* prominencia *f*; (fig) importancia *f*. ∼**t** *a* prominente; (important) importante; (conspicuous) destacado

promiscu|ity /prɒmɪ'skjuːətɪ/ *n* promiscuidad *f*. ∼**ous** /prə'mɪskjʊəs/ *a* promiscuo

promis|e /'prɒmɪs/ *n* promesa *f*. ● *vt/i* prometer. ∼**ing** *a* prometedor; <*future*> halagüeño

promot|e /prə'məʊt/ *vt* promover; promocionar <*product*>; (in rank) ascender. ∼**ion** /-'məʊʃn/ *n* promoción *f*; (in rank) ascenso *m*

prompt /prɒmpt/ *a* rápido; (punctual) puntual. ● *adv* en punto. ● *n* (Comp) presto *m*. ● *vt* incitar; apuntar <*actor*>. ∼**ly** *adv* puntualmente

prone /prəʊn/ *a* (tendido) boca abajo. **be** ∼ **to** ser propenso a

pronoun /'prəʊnaʊn/ *n* pronombre *m*

pronounc|e /prə'naʊns/ *vt* pronunciar; (declare) declarar. ∼**ement** *n* declaración *f*. ∼**ed** *a* pronunciado; (noticeable) marcado

pronunciation /prənʌnsɪ'eɪʃn/ *n* pronunciación *f*

proof /pruːf/ *n* prueba *f*, pruebas *fpl*; (of alcohol) graduación *f* normal. ● *a*. ∼ **against** a prueba de. ∼**-reading** *n* corrección *f* de pruebas

propaganda /prɒpə'gændə/ *n* propaganda *f*

propagate /'prɒpəgeɪt/ *vt* propagar. ● *vi* propagarse

propel /prə'pel/ *vt* (*pt* **propelled**) propulsar. ∼**ler** *n* hélice *f*

proper /'prɒpə(r)/ *a* correcto; (suitable) apropiado; (Gram) propio; (⊡, real) verdadero. ∼**ly** *adv* correctamente; <*eat, work*> bien

property /'prɒpətɪ/ *n* propiedad *f*; (things owned) bienes *mpl*. ● *a* inmobiliario

prophe|cy /'prɒfəsɪ/ *n* profecía *f*. ∼**sy** /'prɒfɪsaɪ/ *vt/i* profetizar. ∼**t** /'prɒfɪt/ *n* profeta *m*. ∼**tic** /prə'fetɪk/ *a* profético

proportion /prə'pɔːʃn/ *n* proporción *f*. ∼**al** *a*, ∼**ate** /-ət/ *a* proporcional

propos|al /prə'pəʊzl/ *n* propuesta *f*; (of marriage) proposición *f* matrimonial. ∼**e** /prə'pəʊz/ *vt* proponer. ● *vi*. ∼**e to s.o.** hacerle una oferta de matrimonio a una. ∼**ition** /prɒpə'zɪʃn/ *n* propuesta *f*; (offer) oferta *f*

proprietor /prə'praɪətə(r)/ *n* propietario *m*

pro rata /'prəʊ'rɑːtə/ *adv* a prorrata

prose /prəʊz/ *n* prosa *f*

prosecut|e /'prɒsɪkjuːt/ *vt* procesar (**for** por); (carry on) proseguir. ∼**ion** /-'kjuːʃn/ *n* proceso *m*. **the** ∼ (side) la acusación. ∼**or** *n* fiscal *m* & *f*; (in private prosecutions) abogado *m* de la acusación

prospect /'prɒspekt/ *n* (possibility) posibilidad *f* (**of** de); (situation envisaged) perspectiva *f*. ∼**s** (chances) perspectivas *fpl*. ∼**ive** /prə'spektɪv/ *a* posible; (future) futuro. ∼**or** /prə'spektə(r)/ *n* prospector *m*. ∼**us** /prə'spektəs/ *n* folleto *m* informativo

prosper /'prɒspə(r)/ *vi* prosperar. ∼**ity** /-'sperətɪ/ *n* prosperidad *f*. ∼**ous** *a* próspero

prostitut|e /'prɒstɪtjuːt/ *n* prostituta *f*. ∼**ion** /-'tjuːʃn/ *n* prostitución *f*

prostrate /'prɒstreɪt/ *a* postrado

protagonist /prə'tægənɪst/ *n* protagonista *m* & *f*

protect /prə'tekt/ *vt* proteger. ∼**ion** /-ʃn/ *n* protección *f*. ∼**ive** *a* protector. ∼**or** *n* protector *m*

protein /'prəʊtiːn/ *n* proteína *f*

protest /'prəʊtest/ *n* protesta *f*. **in** ∼ (against) en señal de protesta (contra). **under** ∼ bajo protesta. ● /prə'test/ *vt/i* protestar

Protestant /'prɒtɪstənt/ *a* & *n* protestante (*m* & *f*)

protester /prə'testə(r)/ *n* manifestante *m* & *f*

protocol /'prəʊtəkɒl/ *n* protocolo *m*

protrud|e /prə'truːd/ *vi* sobresalir. ∼**ing** *a* <chin> prominente. ∼**ing eyes** ojos saltones

proud /praʊd/ *a* orgulloso. ∼**ly** *adv* con orgullo; (arrogantly) orgullosamente

prove /pruːv/ *vt* probar; demostrar <loyalty>. ● *vi* resultar. ∼**n** *a* probado

proverb /'prɒvɜːb/ *n* refrán *m*, proverbio *m*

provide /prə'vaɪd/ *vt* proporcionar; dar <accommodation>. ∼ **s.o. with sth** proveer a uno de algo. ● *vi*. ∼ **for** (allow for) prever; mantener <person>. ∼**d** *conj*. ∼**d (that)** con tal de que, siempre que

providen|ce /'prɒvɪdəns/ *n* providencia *f*. ∼**tial** /-'denʃl/ *a* providencial

providing /prə'vaɪdɪŋ/ *conj*. ∼ **that** con tal de que, siempre que

provinc|e /'prɒvɪns/ *n* provincia *f*; (fig) competencia *f*. ∼**ial** /prə'vɪnʃl/ *a* provincial

provision /prə'vɪʒn/ *n* provisión *f*; (supply) suministro *m*; (stipulation) disposición *f*. ∼**s** *npl* provisiones *fpl*, víveres *mpl*. ∼**al** *a* provisional

provo|cation /prɒvə'keɪʃn/ *n* provocación *f*. ∼**cative** /-'vɒkətɪv/ *a* provocador. ∼**ke** /prə'vəʊk/ *vt* provocar

prow /praʊ/ *n* proa *f*

prowess /'praʊɪs/ *n* destreza *f*; (valour) valor *m*

prowl /praʊl/ *vi* merodear. ∼**er** *n* merodeador *m*

proximity /prɒk'sɪmətɪ/ *n* proximidad *f*

prude /pruːd/ *n* mojigato *m*

pruden|ce /'pruːdəns/ *n* prudencia *f*. ∼**t** *a* prudente. ∼**tly** *adv* prudentemente

prudish /'pruːdɪʃ/ *a* mojigato

prune /pruːn/ *n* ciruela *f* pasa. ● *vt* podar

pry /praɪ/ *vi* curiosear. ∼ **into sth** entrometerse en algo. *vt* (Amer) ⇒PRISE

PS *n* (postscript) P.D.

psalm /sɑːm/ *n* salmo *m*

psychiatr|ic /saɪkɪ'ætrɪk/ *a* psiquiátrico. ∼**ist** /saɪ'kaɪətrɪst/ *n* psiquiatra *m* & *f*. ∼**y** /saɪ'kaɪətrɪ/ *n* psiquiatría *f*

psychic /'saɪkɪk/ *a* para(p)sicológico

psycho|analysis /saɪkəʊə'næləsɪs/ *n* (p)sicoanálisis *m*. ∼**logical** /saɪkə'lɒdʒɪkl/ *a* (p)sicológico. ∼**logist** /saɪ'kɒlədʒɪst/ *n* (p)sicólogo *m*. ∼**logy** /saɪ'kɒlədʒɪ/ *n* (p)sicología *f*. ∼**therapy** /-'θerəpɪ/ *n* (p)sicoterapia *f*

pub /pʌb/ *n* bar *m*

puberty /'pjuːbətɪ/ *n* pubertad *f*

pubic /'pjuːbɪk/ *a* pubiano, púbico

public /'pʌblɪk/ *a* público. ∼**an** *n* tabernero *m*. ∼**ation** /-'keɪʃn/ *n* publicación *f*. ∼ **holiday** *n* día *m* festivo, día *m* feriado (LAm). ∼ **house** *n* bar *m*. ∼**ity** /pʌb'lɪsətɪ/ *n* publicidad *f*. ∼**ize** /'pʌblɪsaɪz/ *vt* hacer público. ∼**ly** *adv* públicamente. ∼ **school** *n* colegio *m* privado; (Amer) instituto *m*, escuela *f* pública

publish /'pʌblɪʃ/ *vt* publicar. ∼**er** *n* editor *m*. ∼**ing** *n* publicación *f*. ∼**ing house** editorial *f*

pudding /'pʊdɪŋ/ *n* postre *m*; (steamed) budín *m*

puddle /'pʌdl/ *n* charco *m*

Puerto Ric|an /pwɜ:təʊ'ri:kən/ *a* & *n* portorriqueño (*m*), puertorriqueño (*m*). **~o** /-əʊ/ *n* Puerto Rico *m*

puff /pʌf/ *n* (of wind) ráfaga *f*; (of smoke) nube *f*; (action) soplo *m*; (on cigarette) chupada *f*, calada *f*. ● *vt/i* soplar. **~ at** dar chupadas a *<pipe>*. **~ out** (swell up) inflar, hinchar. **~ed** *a* (out of breath) sin aliento. **~ paste** (Amer), **~ pastry** *n* hojaldre *m*. **~y** *a* hinchado

pull /pʊl/ *vt* tirar de, jalar (LAm); desgarrarse *<muscle>*. **~ a face** hacer una mueca. **~ a fast one** hacer una mala jugada. ● *vi* tirar, jalar (LAm). **~ at** tirar de, jalar (LAm). ● *n* tirón *m*, jalón *m* (LAm); (pulling force) fuerza *f*; (influence) influencia *f*. □ **~ away** *vi* (Auto) alejarse. □ **~ back** *vi* retirarse. □ **~ down** *vt* echar abajo *<building>*; (lower) bajar. □ **~ in** *vi* (Auto) parar. □ **~ off** *vt* (remove) quitar; (achieve) conseguir. □ **~ out** *vt* sacar; retirar *<team>*. *vi* (Auto) salirse. □ **~ through** *vi* recobrar la salud. □ **~ up** *vi* (Auto) parar. *vt* (uproot) arrancar; (reprimand) regañar

pullover /'pʊləʊvə(r)/ *n* suéter *m*, pulóver *m*, jersey *m*

pulp /pʌlp/ *n* pulpa *f*; (for paper) pasta *f*

pulpit /'pʊlpɪt/ *n* púlpito *m*

pulse /pʌls/ *n* (Med) pulso *m*; (Culin) legumbre *f*

pummel /'pʌml/ *vt* (*pt* **pummelled**) aporrear

pump /pʌmp/ *n* bomba *f*; (for petrol) surtidor *m*. ● *vt* sacar con una bomba. □ **~ up** *vt* inflar

pumpkin /'pʌmpkɪn/ *n* calabaza *f*

pun /pʌn/ *n* juego *m* de palabras

punch /pʌntʃ/ *vt* darle un puñetazo a; (perforate) perforar; hacer *<hole>*. ● *n* puñetazo *m*; (vigour) fuerza *f*; (device) perforadora *f*; (drink) ponche *m*. **~ in** *vi* (Amer) fichar (al entrar al trabajo). **~ out** *vi* (Amer) fichar (al salir del trabajo)

punctual /'pʌŋktʃʊəl/ *a* puntual. **~ity** /-'ælətɪ/ *n* puntualidad *f*. **~ly** *adv* puntualmente

punctuat|e /'pʌŋktʃʊeɪt/ *vt* puntuar. **~ion** /-'eɪʃn/ *n* puntuación *f*

puncture /'pʌŋktʃə(r)/ *n* (in tyre) pinchazo *m*. **have a ~** pinchar. ● *vt* pinchar. ● *vi* pincharse

punish /'pʌnɪʃ/ *vt* castigar. **~ment** *n* castigo *m*

punk /pʌŋk/ *n* punk *m* & *f*, punki *m* & *f*; (Music) punk *m*; (Amer, hoodlum) vándalo *m*

punt /pʌnt/ *n* (boat) batea *f*. **~er** *n* apostante *m* & *f*

puny /'pju:nɪ/ *a* (**-ier**, **-iest**) enclenque

pup /pʌp/ *n* cachorro *m*

pupil /'pju:pl/ *n* alumno *m*; (of eye) pupila *f*

puppet /'pʌpɪt/ *n* marioneta *f*, títere *m*; (glove **~**) títere *m*

puppy /'pʌpɪ/ *n* cachorro *m*

purchase /'pɜ:tʃəs/ *vt* adquirir. ● *n* adquisición *f*. **~r** *n* comprador *m*

pur|e /'pjʊə(r)/ *a* (**-er**, **-est**) puro. **~ity** *n* pureza *f*

purgatory /'pɜ:gətrɪ/ *n* purgatorio *m*

purge /pɜ:dʒ/ *vt* purgar. ● *n* purga *f*

purif|ication /pjʊərɪfɪ'keɪʃn/ *n* purificación *f*. **~y** /'pjʊərɪfaɪ/ *vt* purificar

purist /'pjʊərɪst/ *n* purista *m* & *f*

puritan /'pjʊərɪtən/ *n* puritano *m*. **~ical** /-'tænɪkl/ *a* puritano

purple /'pɜ:pl/ *a* morado. ● *n* morado *m*, púrpura *f*

purport /pə'pɔ:t/ *vt*. **~ to be** pretender ser

purpose /'pɜ:pəs/ *n* propósito *m*; (determination) resolución *f*. **on ~** a propósito. **serve a ~** servir de algo. **~ful** *a* (resolute) resuelto. **~ly** *adv* a propósito

purr /pɜ:(r)/ *vi* ronronear

purse /pɜ:s/ *n* monedero *m*; (Amer) bolso *m*, cartera *f* (LAm), bolsa *f* (Mex)

pursu|e /pə'sju:/ *vt* perseguir, continuar con *<course of action>*. **~it** /pə'sju:t/ *n* persecución *f*; (pastime) actividad *f*

pus /pʌs/ *n* pus *m*

push /pʊʃ/ *vt* empujar; apretar (button). ● *vi* empujar. ● *n* empujón *m*; (effort) esfuerzo *m*. □ **~ back** *vt* hacer retroceder. □ **~ off** *vi* ☒ largarse. ~**chair** *n* sillita *f* de paseo, carreola *f* (Mex). ~**y** *a* (pej) ambicioso

pussy /ˈpʊsɪ/ (*pl* **-sies**), **pussycat** /ˈpʊsɪkæt/ *n* Ⓔ minino *m*

put /pʊt/ *vt* (*pt* **put**, *pres p* **putting**) poner; (with care, precision) colocar; (inside sth) meter; (express) decir. □ ~ **across** *vt* comunicar. □ ~ **away** *vt* guardar. □ ~ **back** *vt* volver a poner; retrasar <*clock*>. □ ~ **by** *vt* guardar; ahorrar <*money*>. □ ~ **down** *vt* (on a surface) dejar; colgar <*phone*>; (suppress) sofocar; (write) apuntar; (kill) sacrificar. □ ~ **forward** *vt* presentar <*plan*>; proponer <*candidate*>; adelantar <*clocks*>; adelantar <*meeting*>. □ ~ **in** *vt* (instal) poner; presentar <*claim*>. □ ~ **in for** *vt* solicitar. □ ~ **off** *vt* aplazar, posponer; (disconcert) desconcertar. □ ~ **on** *vt* (wear) ponerse; poner <*CD, music*>; encender <*light*>. □ ~ **out** *vt* (extinguish) apagar; (inconvenience) incomodar; extender <*hand*>; (disconcert) desconcertar. □ ~ **through** *vt* (phone) pasar (**to** con). □ ~ **up** *vt* levantar; aumentar <*rent*>; subir <*price*>; poner <*sign*>; alojar <*guest*>. □ ~ **up with** *vt* aguantar, soportar

putrid /ˈpjuːtrɪd/ *a* putrefacto

putt /pʌt/ *n* (golf) golpe *m* suave

puzzl|e /ˈpʌzl/ *n* misterio *m*; (game) rompecabezas *m*. ● *vt* dejar perplejo. ~**ed** *a* <*expression*> de desconcierto. **I'm** ~**ed about it** me tiene perplejo. ~**ing** *a* incomprensible; (odd) curioso

pygmy /ˈpɪgmɪ/ *n* pigmeo *m*

pyjamas /pəˈdʒɑːməz/ *npl* pijama *m*, piyama *m or f* (LAm)

pylon /ˈpaɪlɒn/ *n* pilón *m*

pyramid /ˈpɪrəmɪd/ *n* pirámide *f*

python /ˈpaɪθn/ *n* pitón *m*

Qq

quack /kwæk/ *n* (of duck) graznido *m*; (person) charlatán *m*. ~ **doctor** *n* curandero *m*

quadrangle /ˈkwɒdræŋgl/ *n* cuadrilátero *m*

quadruped /ˈkwɒdrʊped/ *n* cuadrúpedo *m*

quadruple /ˈkwɒdrʊpl/ *a* & *n* cuádruplo (*m*). ● *vt* cuadruplicar

quagmire /ˈkwægmaɪə(r)/ *n* lodazal *m*

quaint /kweɪnt/ *a* (**-er**, **-est**) pintoresco; (odd) curioso

quake /kweɪk/ *vi* temblar. ● *n* Ⓔ terremoto *m*

qualif|ication /kwɒlɪfɪˈkeɪʃn/ *n* título *m*; (requirement) requisito *m*; (ability) capacidad *f*; (Sport) clasificación *f*; (fig) reserva *f*. ~**ied** /ˈkwɒlɪfaɪd/ *a* cualificado; (with degree, diploma) titulado; (competent) capacitado. ~**y** /ˈkwɒlɪfaɪ/ *vt* calificar; (limit) limitar. ● *vi* titularse; (Sport) clasificarse. ~**y for sth** (be entitled to) tener derecho a algo

qualit|ative /ˈkwɒlɪtətɪv/ *a* cualitativo. ~**y** /ˈkwɒlɪtɪ/ *n* calidad *f*; (attribute) cualidad *f*

qualm /kwɑːm/ *n* reparo *m*

quandary /ˈkwɒndrɪ/ *n* dilema *m*

quanti|fy /ˈkwɒntɪfaɪ/ *vt* cuantificar. ~**ty** /-tɪ/ *n* cantidad *f*

quarantine /ˈkwɒrəntiːn/ *n* cuarentena *f*. ● *vt* poner en cuarentena

quarrel /ˈkwɒrəl/ *n* pelea *f*. ● *vi* (*pt* **quarrelled**) pelearse, discutir. ~**some** /-səm/ *a* pendenciero

quarry /ˈkwɒrɪ/ *n* (excavation) cantera *f*; (prey) presa *f*

quart /kwɔːt/ *n* cuarto *m* de galón

quarter /ˈkwɔːtə(r)/ *n* cuarto *m*; (of year) trimestre *m*; (district) barrio *m*. **a** ~ **of an hour** un cuarto de hora. ● *vt* dividir en cuartos; (Mil) acuartelar. ~**-final** *n* cuarto *m* de final. ~**ly** *a* trimestral. ● *adv* trimestralmente

quartz /kwɔːts/ n cuarzo m

quay /kiː/ n muelle m

queasy /'kwiːzɪ/ a mareado

queen /kwiːn/ n reina f. ~ **mother** n reina f madre

queer /kwɪə(r)/ a (**-er, -est**) extraño

quench /kwentʃ/ vt quitar <*thirst*>; sofocar <*desire*>

query /'kwɪərɪ/ n pregunta f. ● vt preguntar; (doubt) poner en duda

quest /kwest/ n busca f

question /'kwestʃən/ n pregunta f; (for discussion) cuestión f. **in** ~ en cuestión. **out of the** ~ imposible. **without** ~ sin duda. ● vt hacer preguntas a; <*police etc*> interrogar; (doubt) poner en duda. ~**able** a discutible. ~ **mark** n signo m de interrogación. ~**naire** /-'neə(r)/ n cuestionario m

queue /kjuː/ n cola f. ● vi (*pres p* **queuing**) hacer cola

quibble /'kwɪbl/ vi discutir; (split hairs) sutilizar

quick /kwɪk/ a (**-er, -est**) rápido. be ~! ¡date prisa! ● adv rápido. ~**en** vt acelerar. ● vi acelerarse. ~**ly** adv rápido. ~**sand** n arena f movediza. ~**-tempered** /-'tempəd/ a irascible

quid /kwɪd/ n invar 🔲 libra f (esterlina)

quiet /'kwaɪət/ a (**-er, -est**) tranquilo; (silent) callado; (discreet) discreto. ● n tranquilidad f. ● vt/i (Amer) ⇒QUIETEN. ~**en** vt calmar. ● n calmarse. ~**ly** adv tranquilamente; (silently) silenciosamente; (discreetly) discretamente. ~**ness** n tranquilidad f

quilt /kwɪlt/ n edredón m. ~**ed** a acolchado

quintet /kwɪn'tet/ n quinteto m

quirk /kwɜːk/ n peculiaridad f

quit /kwɪt/ vt (*pt* **quitted**) dejar. ~ **doing** (Amer, cease) dejar de hacer. ● vi (give in) abandonar; (stop) parar; (resign) dimitir

quite /kwaɪt/ adv bastante; (completely) totalmente; (really) verdaderamente. ~ (**so!**) ¡claro! ~ **a few** bastante

quits /kwɪts/ a. be ~ estar en paz. **call it** ~ darlo por terminado

quiver /'kwɪvə(r)/ vi temblar

quiz /kwɪz/ n (*pl* **quizzes**) serie f de preguntas; (game) concurso m. ● vt (*pt* **quizzed**) interrogar. ~**zical** a burlón

quota /'kwəʊtə/ n cuota f

quot|ation /kwəʊ'teɪʃn/ n cita f; (price) presupuesto m. ~**ation marks** npl comillas fpl. ~**e** /kwəʊt/ vt citar; (Com) cotizar. ● n 🔲 cita f; (price) presupuesto m. **in** ~**es** npl entre comillas

....

Rr

....

rabbi /'ræbaɪ/ n rabino m

rabbit /'ræbɪt/ n conejo m

rabi|d /'ræbɪd/ a feroz; <*dog*> rabioso. ~**es** /'reɪbiːz/ n rabia f

race /reɪs/ n (in sport) carrera f; (ethnic group) raza f. ● vt hacer correr <*horse*>. ● vi (run) correr, ir corriendo; (rush) ir de prisa. ~**course** n hipódromo m. ~**horse** n caballo m de carreras. ~ **relations** npl relaciones fpl raciales. ~**track** n hipódromo m

racial /'reɪʃl/ a racial

racing /'reɪsɪŋ/ n carreras fpl. ~ **car** n coche m de carreras

racis|m /'reɪsɪzəm/ n racismo m. ~**t** a & n racista (m & f)

rack[1] /ræk/ n (shelf) estante m; (for luggage) rejilla f; (for plates) escurreplatos m. ● vt. ~ **one's brains** devanarse los sesos

rack[2] /ræk/ n. **go to** ~ **and ruin** quedarse en la ruina

racket /'rækɪt/ n (for sports) raqueta; (din) alboroto m; (swindle) estafa f. ~**eer** /-ə'tɪə(r)/ n estafador m

racy /'reɪsɪ/ a (**-ier, -iest**) vivo

radar /'reɪdɑː(r)/ n radar m

radian|ce /'reɪdɪəns/ n resplandor m. ~**t** a radiante

radiat|e /'reɪdɪeɪt/ vt irradiar. ● vi divergir. ~**ion** /-'eɪʃn/ n radiación f. ~**or** n radiador m

radical /'rædɪkl/ a & n radical (m)

radio /'reɪdɪəʊ/ n (pl **-os**) radio f or m. ●vt transmitir por radio. ~**active** /reɪdɪəʊ'æktɪv/ a radiactivo. ~**activity** /-'tɪvətɪ/ n radiactividad f

radish /'rædɪʃ/ n rábano m

radius /'reɪdɪəs/ n (pl **-dii** /-dɪaɪ/) radio m

raffle /'ræfl/ n rifa f

raft /rɑːft/ n balsa f

rafter /'rɑːftə(r)/ n cabrio m

rag /ræg/ n andrajo m; (for wiping) trapo m. in ~s <person> andrajoso

rage /reɪdʒ/ n rabia f; (fashion) moda f. ●vi estar furioso; <storm> bramar

ragged /'rægɪd/ a <person> andrajoso; <clothes> hecho jirones

raid /reɪd/ n (Mil) incursión f; (by police, etc) redada f; (by thieves) asalto m. ●vt (Mil) atacar; <police> hacer una redada en; <thieves> asaltar. ~**er** n invasor m; (thief) ladrón m

rail /reɪl/ n barandilla f; (for train) riel m; (rod) barra f. **by** ~ por ferrocarril. ~**ing** n barandilla f; (fence) verja f. ~**road** n (Amer), ~**way** n ferrocarril m. ~**way station** n estación f de ferrocarril

rain /reɪn/ n lluvia f. ●vi llover. ~**bow** /-bəʊ/ n arco m iris. ~**coat** n impermeable m. ~**fall** n precipitación f. ~**y** a (**-ier, -iest**) lluvioso

raise /reɪz/ vt levantar; (breed) criar; obtener <money etc>; formular <question>; plantear <problem>; subir <price>. ●n (Amer) aumento m

raisin /'reɪzn/ n (uva f) pasa f

rake /reɪk/ n rastrillo m. ●vt rastrillar; (search) buscar en. □ ~ **up** vt remover

rally /'rælɪ/ vt reunir; (revive) reanimar. ●n reunión f; (Auto) rally m

ram /ræm/ n carnero m. ●vt (pt **rammed**) (thrust) meter por la fuerza; (crash into) chocar con

RAM /ræm/ n (Comp) RAM f

rambl|e /'ræmbl/ n excursión f a pie. ●vi ir de paseo; (in speech) divagar. □ ~**e on** vi divagar. ~**er** n excursionista m & f. ~**ing** a <speech> divagador

ramp /ræmp/ n rampa f

rampage /ræm'peɪdʒ/ vi alborotarse. ● /'ræmpeɪdʒ/ n. **go on the** ~ alborotarse

ramshackle /'ræmʃækl/ a desvencijado

ran /ræn/ ⇒RUN

ranch /rɑːntʃ/ n hacienda f

random /'rændəm/ a hecho al azar; (chance) fortuito. ●n. **at** ~ al azar

rang /ræŋ/ ⇒RING²

range /reɪndʒ/ n alcance m; (distance) distancia f; (series) serie f; (of mountains) cordillera f; (extent) extensión f; (Com) surtido m; (stove) cocina f económica. ●vi extenderse; (vary) variar. ~**r** n guardabosque m

rank /ræŋk/ n posición f, categoría f; (row) fila f; (for taxis) parada f. **the** ~ **and file** la masa f. ~**s** npl soldados mpl rasos. ●a (**-er, -est**) (smell) fétido; (fig) completo. ●vt clasificar. ●vi clasificarse

ransack /'rænsæk/ vt registrar; (pillage) saquear

ransom /'rænsəm/ n rescate m. **hold s.o. to** ~ exigir rescate por uno. ●vt rescatar; (redeem) redimir

rant /rænt/ vi despotricar

rap /ræp/ n golpe m seco. ●vt/i (pt **rapped**) golpear

rape /reɪp/ vt violar. ●n violación f

rapid /'ræpɪd/ a rápido. ~**s** npl rápidos mpl

rapist /'reɪpɪst/ n violador m

raptur|e /'ræptʃə(r)/ n éxtasis m. ~**ous** /-rəs/ a extático

rare /reə(r)/ a (**-er, -est**) raro; (Culin) poco hecho. ~**fied** /'reərɪfaɪd/ a enrarecido. ~**ly** adv raramente

raring /'reərɪŋ/ a ⏹. ~ **to** impaciente por

rarity /'reərətɪ/ n rareza f

rascal /'rɑːskl/ n granuja m & f

rash /ræʃ/ a (**-er, -est**) precipitado, imprudente. ●n erupción f

rasher /'ræʃə(r)/ n loncha f

rashly /'ræʃlɪ/ adv precipitadamente, imprudentemente

rasp /rɑːsp/ n (file) escofina f

raspberry /'rɑːzbrɪ/ n frambuesa f

rat /ræt/ n rata f

rate /reɪt/ n (ratio) proporción f; (speed) velocidad f; (price) precio m; (of interest) tipo m. **at any ~** de todas formas. **at this ~** así. **~s** npl (taxes) impuestos mpl municipales. ● vt valorar; (consider) considerar; (Amer, deserve) merecer. ● vi ser considerado

rather /'rɑːðə(r)/ adv mejor dicho; (fairly) bastante; (a little) un poco. ● int claro. **I would ~** not prefiero no

rating /'reɪtɪŋ/ n clasificación f; (sailor) marinero m; (number, TV) índice m

ratio /'reɪʃɪəʊ/ n (pl **-os**) proporción f

ration /'ræʃn/ n ración f. **~s** npl (provisions) víveres mpl. ● vt racionar

rational /'ræʃənəl/ a racional. **~ize** vt racionalizar

rattle /'rætl/ vi traquetear. ● vt (shake) agitar; ⟨t⟩ desconcertar. ● n traqueteo m; (toy) sonajero m. □ **~ off** vt (fig) decir de corrida

raucous /'rɔːkəs/ a estridente

ravage /'rævɪdʒ/ vt estragar

rave /reɪv/ vi delirar; (in anger) despotricar. **~ about sth** poner a algo por las nubes

raven /'reɪvn/ n cuervo m

ravenous /'rævənəs/ a voraz; ⟨person⟩ hambriento. **be ~** morirse de hambre

ravine /rə'viːn/ n barranco m

raving /'reɪvɪŋ/ a. **~ mad** loco de atar

ravishing /'rævɪʃɪŋ/ a (enchanting) encantador

raw /rɔː/ a (**-er, -est**) crudo; ⟨sugar⟩ sin refinar; (inexperienced) inexperto. **~ deal** n tratamiento m injusto, injusticia f. **~ materials** npl materias fpl primas

ray /reɪ/ n rayo m

raze /reɪz/ vt arrasar

razor /'reɪzə(r)/ n navaja f de afeitar; (electric) maquinilla f de afeitar

Rd /rəʊd/ abbr (= **Road**) C/, Calle f

re /riː/ prep con referencia a. ● pref re.

reach /riːtʃ/ vt alcanzar; (extend) extender; (arrive at) llegar a; (achieve) lograr; (hand over) pasar, dar. ● vi extenderse. ● n alcance m. **within ~ of** al alcance de; (close to) a corta

distancia de. □ **~ out** vi alargar la mano

react /rɪ'ækt/ vi reaccionar. **~ion** /rɪ'ækʃn/ n reacción f. **~ionary** a & n reaccionario (m). **~or** /rɪ'æktə(r)/ n reactor m

read /riːd/ vt (pt **read** /red/) leer; (study) estudiar; (interpret) interpretar. ● vi leer; ⟨instrument⟩ indicar. □ **~ out** vt leer en voz alta. **~able** a (clear) legible. **~er** n lector m

readily /'redɪlɪ/ adv (willingly) de buena gana; (easily) fácilmente

reading /'riːdɪŋ/ n lectura f

readjust /riːə'dʒʌst/ vt reajustar. ● vi readaptarse (**to** a)

ready /'redɪ/ a (**-ier, -iest**) listo, preparado. **get ~** prepararse. **~-made** a confeccionado

real /rɪəl/ a verdadero. ● adv (Amer ⟨t⟩) verdaderamente. **~ estate** n bienes mpl raíces, propiedad f inmobiliaria. **~ estate agent** ⇒REALTOR. **~ism** n realismo m. **~ist** n realista m & f. **~istic** /-'lɪstɪk/ a realista. **~ity** /rɪ'ælətɪ/ n realidad f. **~ization** /rɪəlaɪ'zeɪʃn/ n comprensión f. **~ize** /'rɪəlaɪz/ vt darse cuenta de; (fulfil, Com) realizar. **~ly** /'rɪəlɪ/ adv verdaderamente

realm /relm/ n reino m

realtor /'riːəltə(r)/ n (Amer) agente m inmobiliario

reap /riːp/ vt segar; (fig) cosechar

reappear /riːə'pɪə(r)/ vi reaparecer

rear /rɪə(r)/ n parte f de atrás. ● a posterior, trasero. ● vt (bring up, breed) criar. ● vi **~ (up)** ⟨horse⟩ encabritarse

rearguard /'rɪəgɑːd/ n retaguardia f

rearrange /riːə'reɪndʒ/ vt arreglar de otra manera

reason /'riːzn/ n razón f, motivo m. **within ~** dentro de lo razonable. ● vi razonar. **~able** a razonable. **~ing** n razonamiento m

reassur|ance /riːə'ʃʊərəns/ n promesa f tranquilizadora; (guarantee) garantía f. **~e** /riːə'ʃʊə(r)/ vt tranquilizar

rebate /'riːbeɪt/ n (discount) rebaja f

rebel /'rebl/ n rebelde m & f. ● /rɪ'bel/ vi (pt **rebelled**) rebelarse. ~**lion** /rɪ'belɪən/ n rebelión f. ~**lious** a rebelde

rebound /rɪ'baʊnd/ vi rebotar; (fig) recaer. ● /'riːbaʊnd/ n rebote m

rebuff /rɪ'bʌf/ vt rechazar. ● n desaire m

rebuild /riː'bɪld/ vt (pt **rebuilt**) reconstruir

rebuke /rɪ'bjuːk/ vt reprender. ● n reprimenda f

recall /rɪ'kɔːl/ vt (call s.o. back) llamar; (remember) recordar. ● n /'riːkɔːl/ (of goods, ambassador) retirada f; (memory) memoria f

recap /'riːkæp/ vt/i (pt **recapped**) Ⓣ resumir

recapitulate /riːkə'pɪtʃʊleɪt/ vt/i resumir

recapture /riː'kæptʃə(r)/ vt recobrar; (recall) hacer revivir

recede /rɪ'siːd/ vi retroceder

receipt /rɪ'siːt/ n recibo m. ~s npl (Com) ingresos mpl

receive /rɪ'siːv/ vt recibir. ~r n (of stolen goods) perista m & f; (part of phone) auricular m

recent /'riːsnt/ a reciente. ~ly adv recientemente

recept|ion /rɪ'sepʃn/ n recepción f; (welcome) acogida f. ~**ionist** n recepcionista m & f. ~**ive** /-tɪv/ a receptivo

recess /rɪ'ses/ n hueco m; (holiday) vacaciones fpl. ~**ion** /rɪ'seʃn/ n recesión f

recharge /riː'tʃɑːdʒ/ vt cargar de nuevo, recargar

recipe /'resəpɪ/ n receta f. ~ **book** n libro m de cocina

recipient /rɪ'sɪpɪənt/ n recipiente m & f; (of letter) destinatario m

recit|al /rɪ'saɪtl/ n (Mus) recital m. ~**e** /rɪ'saɪt/ vt recitar; (list) enumerar

reckless /'reklɪs/ a imprudente. ~**ly** adv imprudentemente

reckon /'rekən/ vt/i calcular; (consider) considerar; (think) pensar. □ ~ **on** vt (rely) contar con

reclaim /rɪ'kleɪm/ vt reclamar; recuperar <land>

reclin|e /rɪ'klaɪn/ vi recostarse. ~**ing** a acostado; <seat> reclinable

recluse /rɪ'kluːs/ n ermitaño m

recogni|tion /rekəg'nɪʃn/ n reconocimiento m. **beyond** ~**tion** irreconocible. ~**ze** /'rekəgnaɪz/ vt reconocer

recoil /rɪ'kɔɪl/ vi retroceder. ● /'riːkɔɪl/ n (of gun) culatazo m

recollect /rekə'lekt/ vt recordar. ~**ion** /-ʃn/ n recuerdo m

recommend /rekə'mend/ vt recomendar. ~**ation** /-'deɪʃn/ n recomendación f

reconcil|e /'rekənsaɪl/ vt reconciliar <people>; conciliar <facts>. ~**e o.s.** resignarse (to a). ~**iation** /-sɪlɪ'eɪʃn/ n reconciliación f

reconnaissance /rɪ'kɒnɪsns/ n reconocimiento m

reconnoitre /rekə'nɔɪtə(r)/ vt (pres p **-tring**) (Mil) reconocer

re: ~**consider** /riːkən'sɪdə(r)/ vt volver a considerar. ~**construct** /riːkən'strʌkt/ vt reconstruir

record /rɪ'kɔːd/ vt (in register) registrar; (in diary) apuntar; (Mus) grabar. ● /'rekɔːd/ n (document) documento m; (of events) registro m; (Mus) disco m; (Sport) récord m. **off the** ~ en confianza. ~**er** /rɪ'kɔːdə(r)/ n registrador m; (Mus) flauta f dulce. ~**ing** /rɪ'kɔːdɪŋ/ n grabación f. ~**-player** /'rekɔːd-/ n tocadiscos m invar

recount /rɪ'kaʊnt/ vt contar, relatar

re-count /'riːkaʊnt/ vt volver a contar; recontar <votes>. ● /'riːkaʊnt/ n (Pol) recuento m

recover /rɪ'kʌvə(r)/ vt recuperar. ● vi reponerse. ~**y** n recuperación f

recreation /rekrɪ'eɪʃn/ n recreo m. ~**al** a de recreo

recruit /rɪ'kruːt/ n recluta m. ● vt reclutar; contratar <staff>. ~**ment** n reclutamiento m

rectang|le /'rektæŋgl/ n rectángulo m. ~**ular** /-'tæŋgjʊlə(r)/ a rectangular

rectify /'rektɪfaɪ/ vt rectificar

rector /'rektə(r)/ n párroco m; (of college) rector m. ~**y** n rectoría f

recuperat|e /rɪ'ku:pəreɪt/ *vt* recuperar. ● *vi* reponerse. ~**ion** /-'reɪʃn/ *n* recuperación *f*

recur /rɪ'kɜ:(r)/ *vi* (*pt* **recurred**) repetirse. ~**rence** /rɪ'kʌrns/ *n* repetición *f*. ~**rent** /rɪ'kʌrənt/ *a* repetido

recycle /ri:'saɪkl/ *vt* reciclar

red /red/ *a* (**redder, reddest**) rojo. ● *n* rojo. **be in the** ~ estar en números rojos. ~**den** *vi* enrojecerse. ~**dish** *a* rojizo

redecorate /ri:'dekəreɪt/ *vt* pintar de nuevo

rede|em /rɪ'di:m/ *vt* redimir. ~**mption** /-'dempʃn/ *n* redención *f*

red: ~**-handed** /-'hændɪd/ *a.* **catch s.o.** ~**handed** agarrar a uno con las manos en la masa. ~ **herring** *n* (fig) pista *f* falsa. ~**-hot** *a* al rojo vivo

red light *n* luz *f* roja

redo /ri:'du:/ *vt* (*pt* **redid**, *pp* **redone**) rehacer

redouble /rɪ'dʌbl/ *vt* redoblar

red tape /red'teɪp/ *n* (fig) papeleo *m*

reduc|e /rɪ'dju:s/ *vt* reducir; aliviar *<pain>*. ● *vi* (Amer, slim) adelgazar. ~**tion** /rɪ'dʌkʃn/ *n* reducción *f*

redundan|cy /rɪ'dʌndənsɪ/ *n* superfluidad *f*; (unemployment) despido *m*. ~**t** superfluo. **she was made** ~**t** la despidieron por reducción de plantilla

reed /ri:d/ *n* caña *f*; (Mus) lengüeta *f*

reef /ri:f/ *n* arrecife *m*

reek /ri:k/ *n* mal olor *m*. ● *vi.* ~ **(of)** apestar a

reel /ri:l/ *n* carrete *m*. ● *vi* dar vueltas; (stagger) tambalearse. □ ~ **off** *vt* (fig) enumerar

refectory /rɪ'fektərɪ/ *n* refectorio *m*

refer /rɪ'fɜ:(r)/ *vt* (*pt* **referred**) remitir. ● *vi* referirse. ~ **to** referirse a; (consult) consultar. ~**ee** /refə'ri:/ *n* árbitro *m*; (for job) referencia *f*. ● *vi* (*pt* **refereed**) arbitrar. ~**ence** /'refrəns/ *n* referencia *f*. ~**ence book** *n* libro *m* de consulta. **in** ~**ence to, with** ~**ence to** con referencia a; (Com) re-specto a. ~**endum** /refə'rendəm/ *n* (*pl* **-ums** *or* **-da**) referéndum *m*

refill /ri:'fɪl/ *vt* volver a llenar. ● /'ri:fɪl/ *n* recambio *m*

refine /rɪ'faɪn/ *vt* refinar. ~**d** *a* refinado. ~**ry** /-ərɪ/ *n* refinería *f*

reflect /rɪ'flekt/ *vt* reflejar. ● *vi* reflejarse; (think) reflexionar. □ ~ **badly upon** perjudicar. ~**ion** /-ʃn/ *n* reflexión *f*; (image) reflejo *m*. ~**or** *n* reflector *m*

reflex /'ri:fleks/ *a* & *n* reflejo (*m*). ~**ive** /rɪ'fleksɪv/ *a* (Gram) reflexivo

reform /rɪ'fɔ:m/ *vt* reformar. ● *vi* reformarse. ● *n* reforma *f*

refrain /rɪ'freɪn/ *n* estribillo *m*. ● *vi* abstenerse (**from** de)

refresh /rɪ'freʃ/ *vt* refrescar. ~**ing** *a* refrescante. ~**ments** *npl* (food and drink) refrigerio *m*

refrigerat|e /rɪ'frɪdʒəreɪt/ *vt* refrigerar. ~**or** *n* frigorífico *m*, refrigerador *m* (LAm)

refuel /ri:'fju:əl/ *vt/i* (*pt* **refuelled**) repostar

refuge /'refju:dʒ/ *n* refugio *m*. **take** ~ refugiarse. ~**e** /refjʊ'dʒi:/ *n* refugiado *m*

refund /rɪ'fʌnd/ *vt* reembolsar. ● /'ri:fʌnd/ *n* reembolso *m*

refusal /rɪ'fju:zl/ *n* negativa *f*

refuse /rɪ'fju:z/ *vt* rehusar. ● *vi* negarse. ● /'refju:s/ *n* residuos *mpl*

refute /rɪ'fju:t/ *vt* refutar

regain /rɪ'geɪn/ *vt* recobrar

regal /'ri:gl/ *a* real

regard /rɪ'gɑ:d/ *vt* considerar; (look at) contemplar. **as** ~**s** en lo que se fiere a. ● *n* (consideration) consideración *f*; (esteem) estima *f*. ~**s** *npl* saludos *mpl*. **kind** ~**s** recuerdos. ~**ing** *prep* en lo que se refiere a. ~**less** *adv* a pesar de todo. ~**less of** sin tener en cuenta

regatta /rɪ'gætə/ *n* regata *f*

regime /reɪ'ʒi:m/ *n* régimen *m*

regiment /'redʒɪmənt/ *n* regimiento *m*. ~**al** /-'mentl/ *a* del regimiento

region /'ri:dʒən/ *n* región *f*. **in the** ~ **of** alrededor de. ~**al** *a* regional

register /'redʒɪstə(r)/ *n* registro *m*. ● *vt* registrar; matricular *<vehicle>*; declarar *<birth>*; certificar *<letter>*; facturar *<luggage>*. ● *vi* (enrol) inscribirse; (fig) producir impresión

registrar /redʒɪˈstrɑː(r)/ n secretario m del registro civil; (Univ) secretario m general

registration /redʒɪˈstreɪʃn/ n registración f; (in register) inscripción f. ~ **number** n (Auto) (número de) matrícula f

registry /ˈredʒɪstrɪ/ n. ~ **office** n registro m civil

regret /rɪˈgret/ n pesar m; (remorse) arrepentimiento m. ● vt (pt **regretted**) lamentar. I ~ **that** siento (que). ~**table** a lamentable

regula|r /ˈregjʊlə(r)/ a regular; (usual) habitual. ● n Ⓔ cliente m habitual. ~**rity** /-ˈlærətɪ/ n regularidad f. ~**rly** adv con regularidad. ~**te** /ˈregjʊleɪt/ vt regular. ~**tion** /-ˈleɪʃn/ n regulación f; (rule) regla f

rehears|al /rɪˈhɜːsl/ n ensayo m. ~**e** /rɪˈhɜːs/ vt ensayar

reign /reɪn/ n reinado m. ● vi reinar

reindeer /ˈreɪndɪə(r)/ n invar reno m

reinforce /riːɪnˈfɔːs/ vt reforzar. ~**ment** n refuerzo m

reins /reɪnz/ npl riendas fpl

reiterate /riːˈɪtəreɪt/ vt reiterar

reject /rɪˈdʒekt/ vt rechazar. ● /ˈriːdʒekt/ n producto m defectuoso. ~**ion** /rɪˈdʒekʃn/ n rechazo m; (after job application) respuesta f negativa

rejoice /rɪˈdʒɔɪs/ vi regocijarse

rejoin /rɪˈdʒɔɪn/ vt reunirse con

rejuvenate /rɪˈdʒuːvəneɪt/ vt rejuvenecer

relapse /rɪˈlæps/ n recaída f. ● vi recaer; (into crime) reincidir

relat|e /rɪˈleɪt/ vt contar; (connect) relacionar. ● vi relacionarse (**to** con). ~**ed** a emparentado; <ideas etc> relacionado. ~**ion** /rɪˈleɪʃn/ n relación f; (person) pariente m & f. ~**ionship** n relación f; (blood tie) parentesco m; (affair) relaciones fpl. ~**ive** /ˈrelətɪv/ n pariente m & f. ● a relativo. ~**ively** adv relativamente

relax /rɪˈlæks/ vt relajar. ● vi relajarse. ~**ation** /-ˈseɪʃn/ n relajación f; (rest) descanso m; (recreation) recreo m. ~**ing** a relajante

relay /ˈriːleɪ/ n relevo m. ~ (**race**) n carrera f de relevos. ● /rɪˈleɪ/ vt transmitir

release /rɪˈliːs/ vt soltar; poner en libertad <prisoner>; estrenar <film>; (Mec) soltar; publicar <news>. ● n liberación f; (of film) estreno m; (record) disco m nuevo

relent /rɪˈlent/ vi ceder. ~**less** a implacable; (continuous) incesante

relevan|ce /ˈreləvəns/ n pertinencia f. ~**t** a pertinente

relia|bility /rɪlaɪəˈbɪlətɪ/ n fiabilidad f. ~**ble** /rɪˈlaɪəbl/ a <person> de confianza; <car> fiable. ~**nce** /rɪˈlaɪəns/ n dependencia f; (trust) confianza f. ~**nt** /rɪˈlaɪənt/ a confiado

relic /ˈrelɪk/ n reliquia f

relie|f /rɪˈliːf/ n alivio m; (assistance) socorro m. be on ~**f** (Amer) recibir prestaciones de la seguridad social. ~**ve** /rɪˈliːv/ vt aliviar; (take over from) relevar. ~**ved** a aliviado. feel ~**ved** sentir un gran alivio

religio|n /rɪˈlɪdʒən/ n religión f. ~**us** /rɪˈlɪdʒəs/ a religioso

relinquish /rɪˈlɪŋkwɪʃ/ vt abandonar, renunciar

relish /ˈrelɪʃ/ n gusto m; (Culin) salsa f. ● vt saborear

reluctan|ce /rɪˈlʌktəns/ n desgana f. ~**t** a mal dispuesto. be ~**t to** no tener ganas de. ~**tly** adv de mala gana

rely /rɪˈlaɪ/ vi. ~ **on** contar con; (trust) fiarse de; (depend) depender

remain /rɪˈmeɪn/ vi (be left) quedar; (stay) quedarse; (continue to be) seguir. ~**der** n resto m. ~**s** npl restos mpl; (left-overs) sobras fpl

remand /rɪˈmɑːnd/ vt. ~ **in custody** mantener bajo custodia. ● n. on ~ en prisión preventiva

remark /rɪˈmɑːk/ n observación f. ● vt observar. ~**able** a notable

remarry /riːˈmærɪ/ vi volver a casarse

remedy /ˈremədɪ/ n remedio m. ● vt remediar

remember /rɪˈmembə(r)/ vt acordarse de, recordar. ● vi acordarse

remind /rɪˈmaɪnd/ vt recordar. ~**er** n recordatorio m

reminisce /remɪ'nɪs/ *vi* rememorar los viejos tiempos. ~**nces** /-ənsɪz/ *npl* recuerdos *mpl*. ~**nt** /-'nɪsnt/ *a*. be ~**nt of** recordar

remnant /'remnənt/ *n* resto *m*; (of cloth) retazo *m*; (trace) vestigio *m*

remorse /rɪ'mɔːs/ *n* remordimiento *m*. ~**ful** *a* arrepentido. ~**less** *a* implacable

remote /rɪ'məʊt/ *a* remoto. ~ **control** *n* mando *m* a distancia. ~**ly** *adv* remotamente

remov|able /rɪ'muːvəbl/ *a* (detachable) de quita y pon; *<handle>* desmontable. ~**al** *n* eliminación *f*; (from house) mudanza *f*. ~**e** /rɪ'muːv/ *vt* quitar; (dismiss) destituir; (get rid of) eliminar

render /'rendə(r)/ *vt* rendir *<homage>*; prestar *<help etc>*. ~ **sth useless** hacer que algo resulte inútil

rendezvous /'rɒndɪvuː/ *n* (*pl* **-vous** /-vuːz/) cita *f*

renegade /'renɪɡeɪd/ *n* renegado

renew /rɪ'njuː/ *vt* renovar; (resume) reanudar. ~**al** *n* renovación *f*

renounce /rɪ'naʊns/ *vt* renunciar a

renovat|e /'renəveɪt/ *vt* renovar. ~**ion** /-'veɪʃn/ *n* renovación *f*

renown /rɪ'naʊn/ *n* renombre *m*. ~**ed** *a* de renombre

rent /rent/ *n* alquiler *m*. ●*vt* alquilar. ~**al** *n* alquiler *m*. **car** ~ (Amer) alquiler *m* de coche

renunciation /rɪnʌnsɪ'eɪʃn/ *n* renuncia *f*

reopen /riː'əʊpən/ *vt* volver a abrir. ●*vi* reabrirse

reorganize /riː'ɔːɡənaɪz/ *vt* reorganizar

rep /rep/ *n* (Com) representante *m* & *f*

repair /rɪ'peə(r)/ *vt* arreglar, reparar; arreglar *<clothes, shoes>*. ●*n* reparación *f*; (patch) remiendo *m*. **in good** ~ en buen estado. **it's beyond** ~ ya no tiene arreglo

repatriate /riː'pætrɪeɪt/ *vt* repatriar

repay /riː'peɪ/ *vt* (*pt* **repaid**) reembolsar; pagar *<debt>*; corresponder a *<kindness>*. ~**ment** *n* pago *m*

repeal /rɪ'piːl/ *vt* revocar. ●*n* revocación *f*

repeat /rɪ'piːt/ *vt* repetir. ●*vi* repetir(se). ●*n* repetición *f*. ~**edly** *adv* repetidas veces

repel /rɪ'pel/ *vt* (*pt* **repelled**) repeler. ~**lent** *a* repelente

repent /rɪ'pent/ *vi* arrepentirse. ~**ant** *a* arrepentido

repercussion /riːpə'kʌʃn/ *n* repercusión *f*

repertoire /'repətwɑː(r)/ *n* repertorio *m*

repetit|ion /repɪ'tɪʃn/ *n* repetición *f*. ~**ious** /-'tɪʃəs/ *a*, ~**ive** /rɪ'petətɪv/ *a* repetitivo

replace /rɪ'pleɪs/ *vt* reponer; cambiar *<battery>*; (take the place of) sustituir. ~**ment** *n* sustitución *f*; (person) sustituto *m*

replay /'riːpleɪ/ *n* (Sport) repetición *f* del partido; (recording) repetición *f* inmediata

replenish /rɪ'plenɪʃ/ *vt* reponer

replica /'replɪkə/ *n* réplica *f*

reply /rɪ'plaɪ/ *vt/i* responder, contestar. ~ **to sth** responder a algo, contestar algo. ●*n* respuesta *f*

report /rɪ'pɔːt/ *vt* *<reporter>* informar sobre; informar de *<accident>*; (denounce) denunciar. ●*vi* informar; (present o.s.) presentarse. ●*n* informe *m*; (Schol) boletín *m* de notas; (rumour) rumor *m*; (in newspaper) reportaje *m*. ~ **card** (Amer) *n* boletín *m* de calificaciones. ~**edly** *adv* según se dice. ~**er** *n* periodista *m* & *f*, reportero *m*

reprehensible /reprɪ'hensəbl/ *a* reprensible

represent /reprɪ'zent/ *vt* representar. ~**ation** /-'teɪʃn/ *n* representación *f*. ~**ative** *a* representativo. ●*n* representante *m* & *f*; (Amer, in government) diputado *m*

repress /rɪ'pres/ *vt* reprimir. ~**ion** /-ʃn/ *n* represión *f*. ~**ive** *a* represivo

reprieve /rɪ'priːv/ *n* indulto *m*; (fig) respiro *m*. ●*vt* indultar

reprimand /'reprɪmɑːnd/ *vt* reprender. ●*n* reprensión *f*

reprisal /rɪ'praɪzl/ *n* represalia *f*

reproach /rɪ'prəʊtʃ/ *vt* reprochar. ●*n* reproche *m*. ~**ful** *a* de reproche

reproduc|e /riːprə'djuːs/ *vt* reproducir. ●*vi* reproducirse. ~**tion**

/-'dʌkʃn/ n reproducción f. ~**tive** /-'dʌktɪv/ a reproductor

reprove /rɪ'pru:v/ vt reprender

reptile /'reptaɪl/ n reptil m

republic /rɪ'pʌblɪk/ n república f. ~**an** a & n republicano (m). R~ a & n (in US) republicano (m)

repugnan|ce /rɪ'pʌgnəns/ n repugnancia f. ~**t** a repugnante

repuls|e /rɪ'pʌls/ vt rechazar, repulsar. ~**ion** /-ʃn/ n repulsión f. ~**ive** a repulsivo

reput|able /'repjʊtəbl/ a acreditado, reputado. ~**ation** /repjʊ'teɪʃn/ n reputación f

request /rɪ'kwest/ n petición f. • vt pedir

require /rɪ'kwaɪə(r)/ vt requerir; (need) necesitar; (demand) exigir. ~**d** a necesario. ~**ment** n requisito m

rescue /'reskju:/ vt rescatar, salvar. • n rescate m. ~**r** n salvador m

research /rɪ'sɜ:tʃ/ n investigación f. • vt investigar. ~**er** n investigador m

resembl|ance /rɪ'zembləns/ n parecido m. ~**e** /rɪ'zembl/ vt parecerse a

resent /rɪ'zent/ vt guardarle rencor a *<person>*. she ~ed his success le molestaba que él tuviera éxito. ~**ful** a resentido. ~**ment** n resentimiento m

reserv|ation /rezə'veɪʃn/ n reserva f; (booking) reserva f. ~**e** /rɪ'zɜ:v/ vt reservar. • n reserva f; (in sports) suplente m & f. ~**ed** a reservado. ~**oir** /'rezəvwɑ:(r)/ n embalse m

reshuffle /ri:'ʃʌfl/ n (Pol) reorganización f

residen|ce /'rezɪdəns/ n residencia f. ~**t** a & n residente (m & f). ~**tial** /rezɪ'denʃl/ a residencial

residue /'rezɪdju:/ n residuo m

resign /rɪ'zaɪn/ vt/i dimitir. ~ o.s. to resignarse a. ~**ation** /rezɪg'neɪʃn/ n resignación f; (from job) dimisión f. ~**ed** a resignado

resilien|ce /rɪ'zɪlɪəns/ n elasticidad f; (of person) resistencia f. ~**t** a elástico; *<person>* resistente

resin /'rezɪn/ n resina f

resist /rɪ'zɪst/ vt resistir. • vi resistirse. ~**ance** n resistencia f. ~**ant** a resistente

resolut|e /'rezəlu:t/ a resuelto. ~**ion** /-'lu:ʃn/ n resolución f

resolve /rɪ'zɒlv/ vt resolver. ~ to do resolver a hacer. • n resolución f

resort /rɪ'zɔ:t/ n recurso m; (place) lugar m turístico. in the last ~ como último recurso. □ ~ to vt recurrir a.

resource /rɪ'sɔ:s/ n recurso m. ~**ful** a ingenioso

respect /rɪ'spekt/ n (esteem) respeto m; (aspect) respecto m. with ~ to con respecto a. • vt respetar. ~**able** a respetable. ~**ful** a respetuoso. ~**ive** a respectivo. ~**ively** adv respectivamente

respiration /respə'reɪʃn/ n respiración f

respite /'respaɪt/ n respiro m

respon|d /rɪ'spɒnd/ vi responder. ~**se** /rɪ'spɒns/ n respuesta f; (reaction) reacción f

responsib|ility /rɪspɒnsə'bɪlətɪ/ n responsabilidad f. ~**le** /rɪ'spɒnsəbl/ a responsable; *<job>* de responsabilidad. ~**ly** adv con formalidad

responsive /rɪ'spɒnsɪv/ a que reacciona bien. ~ to sensible a

rest /rest/ vt descansar; (lean) apoyar. • vi descansar; (lean) apoyarse. • n descanso m; (Mus) pausa f; (remainder) resto m, lo demás; (people) los demás, los otros mpl. to have a ~ tomarse un descanso. □ ~ up vi (Amer) descansar

restaurant /'restərɒnt/ n restaurante m

rest: ~**ful** a sosegado. ~**ive** a impaciente. ~**less** a inquieto

restor|ation /restə'reɪʃn/ n restablecimiento m; (of building, monarch) restauración f. ~**e** /rɪ'stɔ:(r)/ vt restablecer; restaurar *<building>*; devolver *<confidence, health>*

restrain /rɪ'streɪn/ vt contener. ~ o.s. contenerse. ~**ed** a (moderate) moderado; (in control of self) comedido. ~**t** n restricción f; (moderation) compostura f

restrict /rɪ'strɪkt/ *vt* restringir. ~**ion** /-ʃn/ *n* restricción *f*. ~**ive** *a* restrictivo

rest room *n* (Amer) baño *m*, servicio *m*

result /rɪ'zʌlt/ *n* resultado *m*. as a ~ of como consecuencia de. ● *vi*. ~ from resultar de. ~ in dar como resultado

resume /rɪ'zjuːm/ *vt* reanudar. ● *vi* reanudarse

résumé /'rezjʊmeɪ/ *n* resumen *m*; (Amer, CV) currículum *m*, historial *m* personal

resurrect /rezə'rekt/ *vt* resucitar. ~**ion** /-ʃn/ *n* resurrección *f*

resuscitat|e /rɪ'sʌsɪteɪt/ *vt* resucitar. ~**ion** /-'teɪʃn/ *n* resucitación *f*

retail /'riːteɪl/ *n* venta *f* al por menor. ● *a & adv* al por menor. ● *vt* vender al por menor. ● *vi* venderse al por menor. ~**er** *n* minorista *m & f*

retain /rɪ'teɪn/ *vt* retener; conservar *<heat>*

retaliat|e /rɪ'tælɪeɪt/ *vi* desquitarse; (Mil) tomar represalias. ~**ion** /-'eɪʃn/ *n* represalias *fpl*

retarded /rɪ'tɑːdɪd/ *a* retrasado

rethink /riː'θɪŋk/ *vt* (*pt* **rethought**) reconsiderar

reticen|ce /'retɪsns/ *n* reticencia *f*. ~**t** *a* reticente

retina /'retɪnə/ *n* retina *f*

retinue /'retɪnjuː/ *n* séquito *m*

retir|e /rɪ'taɪə(r)/ *vi* (from work) jubilarse; (withdraw) retirarse; (go to bed) acostarse. ~**ed** *a* jubilado. ~**ement** *n* jubilación *f*. ~**ing** *a* retraído

retort /rɪ'tɔːt/ *vt/i* replicar. ● *n* réplica *f*

retrace /riː'treɪs/ *vt*. ~ one's steps volver sobre sus pasos

retract /rɪ'trækt/ *vt* retirar *<statement>*. ● *vi* retractarse

retrain /riː'treɪn/ *vi* hacer un curso de reciclaje

retreat /rɪ'triːt/ *vi* retirarse. ● *n* retirada *f*; (place) refugio *m*

retrial /riː'traɪəl/ *n* nuevo juicio *m*

retriev|al /rɪ'triːvl/ *n* recuperación *f*. ~**e** /rɪ'triːv/ *vt* recuperar. ~**er** *n* (dog) perro *m* cobrador

retro|grade /'retrəgreɪd/ *a* retrógrado. ~**spect** /-spekt/ *n*. in ~ en retrospectiva. ~**spective** /-'spektɪv/ *a* retrospectivo

return /rɪ'tɜːn/ *vi* volver, regresar; *<symptom>* reaparecer. ● *vt* devolver; corresponder a *<affection>*. ● *n* regreso *m*, vuelta *f*; (Com) rendimiento *m*; (to owner) devolución *f*. in ~ for a cambio de. many happy ~s! ¡feliz cumpleaños! ~ ticket *n* billete *m or* (LAm) boleto *m* de ida y vuelta, boleto *m* redondo (Mex). ~**s** *npl* (Com) ingresos *mpl*

reun|ion /riː'juːnɪən/ *n* reunión *f*. ~**ite** /riːjuː'naɪt/ *vt* reunir

rev /rev/ *n* (Auto, 🔲) revolución *f*. ● *vt/i*. ~ (up) (*pt* **revved**) (Auto, 🔲) acelerar(se)

reveal /rɪ'viːl/ *vt* revelar. ~**ing** *a* revelador

revel /'revl/ *vi* (*pt* **revelled**) tener un jolgorio. ~ in deleitarse en. ~**ry** *n* jolgorio *m*

revelation /revə'leɪʃn/ *n* revelación *f*

revenge /rɪ'vendʒ/ *n* venganza *f*. take ~ vengarse. ● *vt* vengar

revenue /'revənjuː/ *n* ingresos *mpl*

revere /rɪ'vɪə(r)/ *vt* venerar. ~**nce** /'revərəns/ *n* reverencia *f*.

Reverend /'revərənd/ *a* reverendo

reverent /'revərənt/ *a* reverente

reverie /'revərɪ/ *n* ensueño *m*

revers|al /rɪ'vɜːsl/ *n* inversión *f*. ~**e** /rɪ'vɜːs/ *a* inverso. ● *n* contrario *m*; (back) revés *m*; (Auto) marcha *f* atrás. ● *vt* invertir; anular *<decision>*; (Auto) dar marcha atrás a. ● *vi* (Auto) dar marcha atrás

revert /rɪ'vɜːt/ *vi*. ~ to volver a; (Jurid) revertir a

review /rɪ'vjuː/ *n* revisión *f*; (Mil) revista *f*; (of book, play, etc) crítica *f*. ● *vt* examinar *<situation>*; reseñar *<book, play, etc>*; (Amer, for exam) repasar

revis|e /rɪ'vaɪz/ *vt* revisar; (Schol) repasar. ~**ion** /rɪ'vɪʒn/ *n* revisión *f*; (Schol) repaso *m*

revive /rɪ'vaɪv/ vt resucitar <*person*>

revolt /rɪ'vəʊlt/ vi sublevarse. ● n revuelta f. ~**ing** a asqueroso

revolution /revə'luːʃn/ n revolución f. ~**ary** a & n revolucionario (m). ~**ize** vt revolucionar

revolv|e /rɪ'vɒlv/ vi girar. ~**r** n revólver m. ~**ing** /rɪ'vɒlvɪŋ/ a giratorio

revue /rɪ'vjuː/ n revista f

revulsion /rɪ'vʌlʃn/ n asco m

reward /rɪ'wɔːd/ n recompensa f. ● vt recompensar. ~**ing** a gratificante

rewrite /riː'raɪt/ vt (pt **rewrote**, pp **rewritten**) volver a escribir or redactar; (copy out) escribir otra vez

rhetoric /'retərɪk/ n retórica f. ~**al** /rɪ'tɒrɪkl/ a retórico

rheumatism /'ruːmətɪzəm/ n reumatismo m

rhinoceros /raɪ'nɒsərəs/ n (pl **-oses** or invar) rinoceronte m

rhubarb /'ruːbɑːb/ n ruibarbo m

rhyme /raɪm/ n rima f; (poem) poesía f. ● vt/i rimar

rhythm /'rɪðəm/ n ritmo m. ~**ic(al)** /'rɪðmɪk(l)/ a rítmico

rib /rɪb/ n costilla f

ribbon /'rɪbən/ n cinta f

rice /raɪs/ n arroz m. ~ **pudding** n arroz con leche

rich /rɪtʃ/ a (**-er, -est**) rico. ● n ricos mpl. ~**es** npl riquezas fpl

ricochet /'rɪkəʃeɪ/ vi rebotar

rid /rɪd/ vt (pt **rid**, pres p **ridding**) librar (of de). **get ~ of** deshacerse de. ~**dance** /'rɪdns/ n. **good ~dance!** ¡adiós y buen viaje!

ridden /'rɪdn/ ⇒RIDE

riddle /'rɪdl/ n acertijo m. ● vt acribillar. **be ~d with** estar lleno de

ride /raɪd/ vi (pt **rode**, pp **ridden**) (on horseback) montar a caballo; (go) ir (en bicicleta, a caballo etc). ● vt montar a <*horse*>; ir en <*bicycle*>; (Amer) ir en <*bus, tren*>; recorrer <*distance*>. ● n (on horse) cabalgata f; (in car) paseo m en coche. **take s.o. for a ~** 🄸 engañarle a uno. ~**r** n (on horse) jinete m; (cyclist) ciclista m & f

ridge /rɪdʒ/ n (of hills) cadena f; (hilltop) cresta f

ridicul|e /'rɪdɪkjuːl/ n burlas fpl. ● vt ridiculizar. ~**ous** /rɪ'dɪkjʊləs/ a ridículo

rife /raɪf/ a difundido

rifle /'raɪfl/ n fusil m

rift /rɪft/ n grieta f; (fig) ruptura f

rig /rɪg/ vt (pt **rigged**) (pej) amañar. ● n (at sea) plataforma f de perforación. ▫ ~ **up** vt improvisar

right /raɪt/ a <*answer*> correcto; (morally) bueno; (not left) derecho; (suitable) adecuado. **be ~** <*person*> tener razón; <*clock*> estar bien. **it is ~** (just, moral) es justo. **put ~** rectificar. **the ~ person for the job** la persona indicada para el puesto. ● n (entitlement) derecho m; (not left) derecha f; (not evil) bien m. ~ **of way** (Auto) prioridad f. **be in the ~** tener razón. **on the ~** a la derecha. ● vt enderezar; (fig) reparar. ● adv a la derecha; (directly) derecho; (completely) completamente. ~ **away** adv inmediatamente. ~ **angle** n ángulo m recto. ~**eous** /'raɪtʃəs/ a recto; <*cause*> justo. ~**ful** /'raɪtfl/ a legítimo. ~**-handed** /-'hændɪd/ a diestro. ~**-hand man** n brazo m derecho. ~**ly** adv justamente. ~ **wing** a (Pol) derechista

rigid /'rɪdʒɪd/ a rígido

rig|orous /'rɪgərəs/ a riguroso. ~**our** /'rɪgə(r)/ n rigor m

rim /rɪm/ n borde m; (of wheel) llanta f; (of glasses) montura f

rind /raɪnd/ n corteza f; (of fruit) cáscara f

ring[1] /rɪŋ/ n (circle) círculo m; (circle of metal etc) aro m; (on finger) anillo m; (on finger with stone) sortija f; (Boxing) cuadrilátero m; (bullring) ruedo m; (for circus) pista f; ● vt cercar

ring[2] /rɪŋ/ n (of bell) toque m; (tinkle) tintineo m; (telephone call) llamada f. ● vt (pt **rang**, pp **rung**) hacer sonar; (telephone) llamar por teléfono. ~ **the bell** tocar el timbre. ● vi sonar. ~ **back** vt/i volver a llamar. ▫ ~ **up** vt llamar por teléfono

ring: ~**leader** /'rɪŋliːdə(r)/ n cabecilla m & f. ~ **road** n carretera f de circunvalación

rink /rɪŋk/ n pista f

rinse /rɪns/ vt enjuagar. ● n aclarado m; (of dishes) enjuague m; (for hair) tintura f (no permanente)

riot /'raɪət/ n disturbio m; (of colours) profusión f. **run** ∼ desenfrenarse. ● vi causar disturbios

rip /rɪp/ vt (pt **ripped**) rasgar. ● vi rasgarse. ● n rasgón m. □ ∼ **off** vt (pull off) arrancar; (⊠, cheat) robar

ripe /raɪp/ a (**-er, -est**) maduro. ∼**n** /'raɪpn/ vt/i madurar

rip-off /'rɪpɒf/ n ⊠ timo m

ripple /'rɪpl/ n (on water) onda f

ris|e /raɪz/ vi (pt **rose**, pp **risen**) subir; <sun> salir; <river> crecer; <prices> subir; <land> elevarse; (get up) levantarse. ● n subida f; (land) altura f; (increase) aumento m; (to power) ascenso m. **give** ∼**e to** ocasionar. ∼**er** n. **early** ∼**er** n madrugador m. ∼**ing** n. ● a <sun> naciente; <number> creciente; <prices> en alza

risk /rɪsk/ n riesgo m. ● vt arriesgar. ∼**y** a (**-ier, -iest**) arriesgado

rite /raɪt/ n rito m

ritual /'rɪtʃʊəl/ a & n ritual (m)

rival /'raɪvl/ a & n rival (m). ∼**ry** n rivalidad f

river /'rɪvə(r)/ n río m

rivet /'rɪvɪt/ n remache m. ∼**ing** a fascinante

road /rəʊd/ n (in town) calle f; (between towns) carretera f; (route, way) camino m. ∼ **map** n mapa m de carreteras. ∼**side** n borde m de la carretera. ∼**works** npl obras fpl. ∼**worthy** a <vehicle> apto para circular

roam /rəʊm/ vi vagar

roar /rɔː(r)/ n rugido m; (laughter) carcajada f. ● vt/i rugir. ∼ **past** <vehicles> pasar con estruendo. ∼ **with** laughter reírse a carcajadas. ∼**ing** a <trade etc> activo

roast /rəʊst/ vt asar; tostar <coffee>. ● a & n asado (m). ∼ **beef** n rosbif f

rob /rɒb/ vt (pt **robbed**) atracar, asaltar <bank>; robarle a <person>. ∼ **of** (deprive of) privar de. ∼**ber** n ladrón m; (of bank) atracador m. ∼**bery** n robo m; (of bank) atraco m

robe /rəʊb/ n bata f; (Univ etc) toga f

robin /'rɒbɪn/ n petirrojo m

robot /'rəʊbɒt/ n robot m, autómata m

robust /rəʊ'bʌst/ a robusto

rock /rɒk/ n roca f; (crag, cliff) peñasco m. ● vt mecer; (shake) sacudir. ● vi mecerse; (shake) sacudirse. ● n (Mus) música f rock. ∼**-bottom** /-'bɒtəm/ a ⊞ bajísimo

rocket /'rɒkɪt/ n cohete m

rock: ∼**ing-chair** n mecedora f. ∼**y** a (**-ier, -iest**) rocoso; (fig, shaky) bamboleante

rod /rɒd/ n vara f; (for fishing) caña f; (metal) barra f

rode /rəʊd/ ⇒RIDE

rodent /'rəʊdnt/ n roedor m

rogue /rəʊg/ n pícaro m

role /rəʊl/ n papel m

roll /rəʊl/ vt hacer rodar; (roll up) enrollar; allanar <lawn>; aplanar <pastry>. ● vi rodar; <ship> balancearse; (on floor) revolcarse. **be** ∼**ing** in money ⊞ nadar en dinero ● n rollo m; (of ship) balanceo m; (of drum) redoble m; (of thunder) retumbo m; (bread) panecillo m, bolillo m (Mex). □ ∼ **over** vi (turn over) dar una vuelta. □ ∼ **up** vt enrollar; arremangar <sleeve>. vi ⊞ llegar. ∼**-call** n lista f

roller /'rəʊlə(r)/ n rodillo m; (wheel) rueda f; (for hair) rulo m. ∼**-coaster** n montaña f rusa. ∼**-skate** n patín m de ruedas. ∼**-skating** patinaje m (sobre ruedas)

rolling /'rəʊlɪŋ/ a ondulado. ∼**-pin** n rodillo m

ROM /rɒm/ n (= **read-only memory**) ROM f

Roman /'rəʊmən/ a & n romano (m). ∼ **Catholic** a & n católico (m) (romano)

romance /rəʊ'mæns/ n novela f romántica; (love) amor m; (affair) aventura f

Romania /ruː'meɪnɪə/ n Rumania f, Rumanía f. ∼**n** a & n rumano (m)

romantic /rəʊ'mæntɪk/ a romántico

Rome /rəʊm/ n Roma f

romp /rɒmp/ vi retozar

roof /ruːf/ n techo m, tejado m; (of mouth) paladar m. ● vt techar. ~**rack** n baca f. ~**top** n tejado m

rook /rʊk/ n grajo m; (in chess) torre f

room /ruːm/ n cuarto m, habitación f; (bedroom) dormitorio m; (space) espacio m; (large hall) sala f. ~**y** a espacioso

roost /ruːst/ vi posarse. ~**er** n gallo m

root /ruːt/ n raíz f. take ~ echar raíces; <idea> arraigarse. ● vi echar raíces. ~ **about** vi hurgar. □ ~ **for** vt Ⓔ alentar. □ ~ **out** vt extirpar

rope /rəʊp/ n cuerda f. know the ~s estar al corriente. ● vt atar; (Amer, lasso) enlazar. □ ~ **in** vt agarrar

rose¹ /rəʊz/ n rosa f; (nozzle) roseta f

rose² /rəʊz/ ⇒RISE

rosé /ˈrəʊzeɪ/ n (vino m) rosado m

rot /rɒt/ vt (pt rotted) pudrir. ● vi pudrirse. ● n putrefacción f

rota /ˈrəʊtə/ n lista f (de turnos)

rotary /ˈrəʊtərɪ/ a rotatorio

rotat|e /rəʊˈteɪt/ vt girar; (change round) alternar. ● vi girar; (change round) alternarse. ~**ion** /-ʃn/ n rotación f

rote /rəʊt/ n. by ~ de memoria

rotten /ˈrɒtn/ a podrido; Ⓔ pésimo Ⓔ; <weather> horrible

rough /rʌf/ a (-er, -est) áspero; <person> tosco; (bad) malo; <ground> accidentado; (violent) brutal; (approximate) aproximado; <diamond> bruto. ● adv duro. ~ **copy**, ~ **draft** borrador m. ● vt. ~ **it** vivir sin comodidades. ~**age** /ˈrʌfɪdʒ/ n fibra f. ~**-and-ready** a improvisado. ~**ly** adv bruscamente; (more or less) aproximadamente

roulette /ruːˈlet/ n ruleta f

round /raʊnd/ a (-er, -est) redondo. ● n círculo m; (of visits, drinks) ronda f; (of competition) vuelta f; (Boxing) asalto m. ● prep alrededor de. ● adv alrededor. ~ **about** (approximately) aproximadamente. **come** ~ **to**, **go** ~ **to** (a friend etc) pasar por casa de. ● vt doblar <corner>. □ ~ **off** vt terminar; redondear <number>. □ ~ **up** vt rodear <cattle>; hacer una redada de

<suspects>. ~**about** n tiovivo m, carrusel m (LAm); (for traffic) glorieta f, rotonda f. ● a in directo. ~ **trip** n viaje m de ida y vuelta. ~**-up** n resumen m; (of suspects) redada f

rous|e /raʊz/ vt despertar. ~**ing** a enardecedor

route /ruːt/ n ruta f; (Naut, Aviat) rumbo m; (of bus) línea f

routine /ruːˈtiːn/ n rutina f. ● a rutinario

row¹ /rəʊ/ n fila f. ● vi remar

row² /raʊ/ n (Ⓔ, noise) bulla f Ⓔ; (quarrel) pelea f. ● vi Ⓔ pelearse

rowboat /ˈrəʊbəʊt/ (Amer) n bote m de remos

rowdy /ˈraʊdɪ/ a (-ier, -iest) n escandaloso, alborotador

rowing /ˈrəʊɪŋ/ n remo m. ~ **boat** n bote m de remos

royal /ˈrɔɪəl/ a real. ~**ist** a & n monárquico (m). ~**ly** adv magníficamente. ~**ty** n realeza f

rub /rʌb/ vt (pt rubbed) frotar. □ ~ **out** vt borrar

rubber /ˈrʌbə(r)/ n goma f, caucho m, hule m (Mex); (eraser) goma f (de borrar). ~ **band** n goma f (elástica). ~**-stamp** vt (fig) autorizar. ~**y** a parecido al caucho

rubbish /ˈrʌbɪʃ/ n basura f; (junk) trastos mpl; (fig) tonterías fpl. ~ **bin** n cubo m de la basura, bote m de la basura (Mex). ~**y** a sin valor

rubble /ˈrʌbl/ n escombros mpl

ruby /ˈruːbɪ/ n rubí m

rucksack /ˈrʌksæk/ n mochila f

rudder /ˈrʌdə(r)/ n timón m

rude /ruːd/ a (-er, -est) grosero, mal educado; (improper) indecente; (brusque) brusco. ~**ly** adv groseramente. ~**ness** n mala educación f

rudimentary /ruːdɪˈmentrɪ/ a rudimentario

ruffian /ˈrʌfɪən/ n rufián m

ruffle /ˈrʌfl/ vt despeinar <hair>; arrugar <clothes>

rug /rʌg/ n alfombra f, tapete m (Mex); (blanket) manta f de viaje

rugged /ˈrʌgɪd/ a <coast> escarpado; <landscape> escabroso

ruin /'ruːɪn/ n ruina f. ● vt arruinar; (spoil) estropear

rul|e /ruːl/ n regla f; (Pol) dominio m. **as a ~** por regla general. ● vt gobernar; (master) dominar; (Jurid) dictaminar. **~e out** vt descartar. **~ed paper** n papel m rayado. **~er** n (sovereign) soberano m; (leader) gobernante m & f; (measure) regla f. **~ing** a <class> dirigente. ● n decisión f

rum /rʌm/ n ron m

rumble /'rʌmbl/ vi retumbar; <stomach> hacer ruidos

rummage /'rʌmɪdʒ/ vi hurgar

rumour /'ruːmə(r)/ n rumor m. ● vt. **it is ~ed that** se rumorea que

rump steak /rʌmpsteɪk/ n filete m de cadera

run /rʌn/ vi (pt **ran**, pp **run**, pres p **running**) correr; <water> correr; (function) funcionar; (melt) derretirse; <makeup> correrse; <colour> desteñir; <bus etc> circular; (in election) presentarse. ● vt correr <race>; dirigir <business>; correr <risk>; (move, pass) pasar; tender <wire>; preparar <bath>. **~ a temperature** tener fiebre. ● n corrida f, carrera f; (outing) paseo m (en coche); (ski) pista f. **in the long ~** a la larga. **be on the ~** estar prófugo. □ **~ away** vi huir, escaparse. □ **~ down** vi bajar corriendo; <battery> descargarse. vt (Auto) atropellar; (belittle) denigrar. □ **~ in** vi entrar corriendo. □ **~ into** vt toparse con <friend>; (hit) chocar con. □ **~ off** vt sacar <copies>. □ **~ out** vi salir corriendo; <liquid> salirse; (fig) agotarse. □ **~ out of** vt quedarse sin. □ **~ over** vt (Auto) atropellar. □ **~ through** vt (review) ensayar; (rehearse) repasar. □ **~ up** vt ir acumulando <bill>. vi subir corriendo. **~away** n fugitivo m. **~ down** a <person> agotado

rung¹ /rʌŋ/ n (of ladder) peldaño m

rung² /rʌŋ/ ⇒RING

run: ~ner /'rʌnə(r)/ n corredor m; (on sledge) patín m. **~ner bean** n judía f escarlata. **~ner-up** n. **be ~er up** quedar en segundo lugar. **~ning** n. **be in the ~ning** tener posibilidades de ganar. ● a <water> corriente; <commentary> en directo. **four times**

~ning cuatro veces seguidas. **~ny** /'rʌnɪ/ a líquido; <nose> que moquea. **~way** n pista f de aterrizaje

rupture /'rʌptʃə(r)/ n ruptura f. ● vt romper

rural /'rʊərəl/ a rural

ruse /ruːz/ n ardid m

rush /rʌʃ/ n (haste) prisa f; (crush) bullicio m; (plant) junco m. ● vi precipitarse. ● vt apresurar; (Mil) asaltar. **~-hour** n hora f punta, hora f pico (LAm)

Russia /'rʌʃə/ n Rusia f. **~n** a & n ruso (m)

rust /rʌst/ n orín m. ● vt oxidar. ● vi oxidarse

rustle /'rʌsl/ vt hacer susurrar; (Amer) robar. ● vi susurrar □ **~ up** vt 🔢 preparar.

rust: ~proof a inoxidable. **~y (-ier, -iest)** oxidado

rut /rʌt/ n surco m. **be in a ~** estar anquilosado

ruthless /'ruːθlɪs/ a despiadado

rye /raɪ/ n centeno m

Ss

S abbr (= **south**) S

sabot|age /'sæbətɑːʒ/ n sabotaje m. ● vt sabotear. **~eur** /-'tɜː(r)/ n saboteador m

saccharin /'sækərɪn/ n sacarina f

sachet /'sæʃeɪ/ n bolsita f

sack /sæk/ n saco m. **get the ~** 🔢 ser despedido. ● vt 🔢 despedir.

sacrament /'sækrəmənt/ n sacramento m

sacred /'seɪkrɪd/ a sagrado

sacrifice /'sækrɪfaɪs/ n sacrificio m. ● vt sacrificar

sacrileg|e /'sækrɪlɪdʒ/ n sacrilegio m. **~ious** /-'lɪdʒəs/ a sacrílego

sad /sæd/ a (**sadder**, **saddest**) triste. **~den** vt entristecer

saddle /'sædl/ n silla f de montar.
● vt ensillar <horse>. ~ s.o. with sth
(fig) endilgarle algo a uno

sadist /'seɪdɪst/ n sádico m. ~tic
/sə'dɪstɪk/ a sádico

sadly /'sædlɪ/ adv tristemente; (fig)
desgraciadamente. ~ness n tristeza f

safe /seɪf/ a (-er, -est) seguro; (out of
danger) salvo; (cautious) prudente. ~
and sound sano y salvo. ● n caja f
fuerte. ~ deposit n caja f de seguridad. ~guard n salvaguardia f. ● vt
salvaguardar. ~ly adv sin peligro;
(in safe place) en lugar seguro. ~ty n
seguridad. f. ~ty belt n cinturón m
de seguridad. ~ty pin n imperdible
m

sag /sæg/ vi (pt sagged) <ceiling>
combarse; <bed> hundirse

saga /'sɑːgə/ n saga f

Sagittarius /sædʒɪ'teərɪəs/ n Sagitario m

said /sed/ ⇒SAY

sail /seɪl/ n vela f; (trip) paseo m (en
barco). set ~ zarpar. ● vi navegar;
(leave) partir; (Sport) practicar la vela;
(fig) deslizarse. go ~ing salir a navegar. vt gobernar <boat>. ~boat n
(Amer) barco m de vela. ~ing n
(Sport) vela f. ~ing boat n, ~ing
ship n barco m de vela. ~or n marinero m

saint /seɪnt/, before name /sənt/ n
santo m. ~ly a santo

sake /seɪk/ n. for the ~ of por. for
God's ~ por el amor de Dios

salad /'sæləd/ n ensalada f. ~ bowl
n ensaladera f. ~ dressing n aliño
m

salary /'sælərɪ/ n sueldo m

sale /seɪl/ n venta f; (at reduced prices)
liquidación f. for ~ (sign) se vende.
be for ~ estar a la venta. be on ~
(Amer, reduced) estar en liquidación.
~able a vendible. (for sale) estar a la
venta. ~s clerk n (Amer) dependiente m, dependienta f. ~sman /-mən/
n vendedor m; (in shop) dependiente
m. ~swoman n vendedora f; (in
shop) dependienta f

saliva /sə'laɪvə/ n saliva f

salmon /'sæmən/ n invar salmón m

saloon /sə'luːn/ n (on ship) salón m;
(Amer, bar) bar m; (Auto) turismo m

salt /sɔːlt/ n sal f. ● vt salar. ~ cellar n salero m. ~y a salado

salute /sə'luːt/ n saludo m. ● vt saludar. ● vi hacer un saludo

Salvadorean, **Salvadorian**
/sælvə'dɔːrɪən/ a & n salvadoreño
(m)

salvage /'sælvɪdʒ/ vt salvar

salvation /sæl'veɪʃn/ n salvación f

same /seɪm/ a igual (as que); (before
noun) mismo (as que). at the ~ time
al mismo tiempo. ● pron. the ~ lo
mismo. all the ~ de todas formas.
● adv. the ~ igual

sample /'sɑːmpl/ n muestra f. ● vt
degustar <food>

sanctify /'sæŋktɪfaɪ/ vt santificar.
~ion /'sæŋkʃn/ n sanción f. ● vt
sancionar. ~uary /'sæŋktʃʊərɪ/ n
(Relig) santuario m; (for wildlife) reserva f; (refuge) asilo m

sand /sænd/ n arena f. ● vt pulir
<floor>. □ ~ down vt lijar <wood>

sandal /'sændl/ n sandalia f

sand: ~castle n castillo m de arena. ~paper n papel m de lija. ● vt
lijar. ~storm n tormenta f de arena

sandwich /'sænwɪdʒ/ n bocadillo
m, sandwich m. ● vt. be ~ed between <person> estar apretujado
entre

sandy /'sændɪ/ a arenoso

sane /seɪn/ a (-er, -est) <person>
cuerdo; (sensible) sensato

sang /sæŋ/ ⇒SING

sanitary /'sænɪtrɪ/ a higiénico;
<system etc> sanitario. ~ towel, ~
napkin n (Amer) compresa f (higiéni-
ca)

sanitation /sænɪ'teɪʃn/ n higiene f;
(drainage) sistema m sanitario

sanity /'sænɪtɪ/ n cordura f; (good
sense) sensatez f

sank /sæŋk/ ⇒SINK

Santa (Claus) /'sæntə(klɔːz)/ n
Papá m Noel

sap /sæp/ n (in plants) savia f. ● vt (pt
sapped) minar

sapling /'sæplɪŋ/ n árbol m joven

sapphire /'sæfaɪə(r)/ n zafiro m

sarcas|m /'sɑːkæzəm/ n sarcasmo m. ∼**tic** /-'kæstɪk/ a sarcástico

sardine /sɑː'diːn/ n sardina f

sash /sæʃ/ n (over shoulder) banda f; (round waist) fajín m.

sat /sæt/ ⇒SIT

satchel /'sætʃl/ n cartera f

satellite /'sætəlaɪt/ n & a satélite (m). ∼ **TV** n televisión f por satélite

satin /'sætɪn/ n raso m. ● a de raso

satir|e /'sætaɪə(r)/ n sátira f. ∼**ical** /sə'tɪrɪkl/ a satírico. ∼**ize** /'sætəraɪz/ vt satirizar

satis|faction /sætɪs'fækʃn/ n satisfacción f. ∼**factorily** /-'fæktərɪlɪ/ adv satisfactoriamente. ∼**factory** /-'fæktərɪ/ a satisfactorio. ∼**fy** /'sætɪsfaɪ/ vt satisfacer; (convince) convencer. ∼**fying** a satisfactorio

saturat|e /'sætʃəreɪt/ vt saturar. ∼**ed** a saturado; (drenched) empapado

Saturday /'sætədeɪ/ n sábado m

Saturn /'sætən/ n Saturno m

sauce /sɔːs/ n salsa f; (cheek) descaro m. ∼**pan** /'sɔːspən/ n cazo m, cacerola f. ∼**r** /'sɔːsə(r)/ n platillo m

saucy /'sɔːsɪ/ a (-ier, -iest) descarado

Saudi /'saʊdɪ/ a & n saudita (m & f). ∼ **Arabia** /-ə'reɪbɪə/ n Arabia f Saudí

sauna /'sɔːnə/ n sauna f

saunter /'sɔːntə(r)/ vi pasearse

sausage /'sɒsɪdʒ/ n salchicha f

savage /'sævɪdʒ/ a salvaje; (fierce) feroz. ● n salvaje m & f. ● vt atacar. ∼**ry** n ferocidad f

sav|e /seɪv/ vt (rescue) salvar; ahorrar <money, time>; (prevent) evitar; (Comp) guardar. ● n (football) parada f. ● prep salvo, excepto. □ ∼**e up** vi/t ahorrar. ∼**er** n ahorrador m. ∼**ing** n ahorro m. ∼**ings** npl ahorros mpl

saviour /'seɪvɪə(r)/ n salvador m

savour /'seɪvə(r)/ vt saborear. ∼**y** a (appetizing) sabroso; (not sweet) no dulce

saw¹ /sɔː/ ⇒SEE¹

saw² /sɔː/ n sierra f. ● vt (pt **sawed**, pp **sawn**) serrar. ∼**dust** n serrín m. ∼**n** /sɔːn/ ⇒SAW²

saxophone /'sæksəfəʊn/ n saxofón m, saxófono m

say /seɪ/ vt/i (pt **said** /sed/) decir; rezar <prayer>. ● n. have a ∼ expresar una opinión; (in decision) tener voz en capítulo. have no ∼ no tener ni voz ni voto. ∼**ing** n refrán m

scab /skæb/ n costra f; (⚠, blackleg) esquirol m

scaffolding /'skæfəldɪŋ/ n andamios mpl

scald /skɔːld/ vt escaldar

scale /skeɪl/ n (also Mus) escala f; (of fish) escama f. ● vt (climb) escalar. ∼ **down** vt reducir (a escala) <drawing>; recortar <operation>. ∼**s** npl (for weighing) balanza f, peso m

scallion /'skæljən/ n (Amer) cebolleta f

scalp /skælp/ vt quitar el cuero cabelludo a

scamper /'skæmpə(r)/ vi. ∼ **away** irse correteando

scan /skæn/ vt (pt **scanned**) escudriñar; (quickly) echar un vistazo a; <radar> explorar

scandal /'skændl/ n escándalo m; (gossip) chismorreo m. ∼**ize** vt escandalizar. ∼**ous** a escandaloso

Scandinavia /skændɪ'neɪvɪə/ n Escandinavia f. ∼**n** a & n escandinavo (m)

scant /skænt/ a escaso. ∼**y** a (-ier, -iest) escaso

scapegoat /'skeɪpgəʊt/ n cabeza f de turco

scar /skɑː(r)/ n cicatriz f

scarc|e /skeəs/ a (-er, -est) escaso. be ∼e escasear. make o.s. ∼e ⚠ mantenerse lejos. ∼**ely** adv apenas. ∼**ity** n escasez f

scare /skeə(r)/ vt asustar. be ∼d tener miedo. be ∼d of sth tenerle miedo a algo. ● n susto m. ∼**crow** n espantapájaros m

scarf /skɑːf/ n (pl **scarves**) bufanda f; (over head) pañuelo m

scarlet /'skɑːlət/ a escarlata f. ∼ **fever** n escarlatina f

scarves /skɑːvz/ ⇒SCARF

scary /'skeərɪ/ *a* (**-ier, -iest**) que da miedo

scathing /'skeɪðɪŋ/ *a* mordaz

scatter /'skætə(r)/ *vt* (throw) esparcir; (disperse) dispersar. ● *vi* dispersarse. ~**ed** /'skætəd/ *a* disperso; (occasional) esporádico

scavenge /'skævɪndʒ/ *vi* escarbar (en la basura)

scenario /sɪ'nɑːrɪəʊ/ *n* (*pl* **-os**) perspectiva *f*; (of film) guión *m*

scen|e /siːn/ *n* escena *f*; (sight) vista *f*; (fuss) lío *m*. **behind the** ~**es** entre bastidores. ~**ery** /'siːnərɪ/ *n* paisaje *m*; (in theatre) decorado *m*. ~**ic** /'siːnɪk/ *a* pintoresco

scent /sent/ *n* olor *m*; (perfume) perfume *m*; (trail) pista *f*. ● *vt* intuir; (make fragrant) perfumar

sceptic /'skeptɪk/ *n* escéptico *m*. ~**al** *a* escéptico. ~**ism** /-sɪzəm/ *n* escepticismo *m*

sceptre /'septə(r)/ *n* cetro *m*

schedule /'ʃedjuːl, 'skedjuːl/ *n* programa *f*; (timetable) horario *m*. **behind** ~ atrasado. **it's on** ~ va de acuerdo a lo previsto. ● *vt* proyectar. ~**d flight** *n* vuelo *m* regular

scheme /skiːm/ *n* proyecto *m*; (plot) intriga *f*. ● *vi* (pej) intrigar

schizophrenic /skɪtsə'frenɪk/ *a & n* esquizofrénico (*m*)

scholar /'skɒlə(r)/ *n* erudito *m*. ~**ly** *a* erudito. ~**ship** *n* erudición *f*; (grant) beca *f*

school /skuːl/ *n* escuela *f*; (Univ) facultad *f*. ● *a* <age, holidays, year> escolar. ● *vt* instruir; (train) capacitar. ~**boy** *n* colegial *m*. ~**girl** *n* colegiala *f*. ~**ing** *n* instrucción *f*. ~**master** *n* (primary) maestro *m*; (secondary) profesor *m*. ~**mistress** *n* (primary) maestra *f*; (secondary) profesora *f*. ~**teacher** *n* (primary) maestro *m*; (secondary) profesor *m*

scien|ce /'saɪəns/ *n* ciencia *f*. **study** ~**ce** estudiar ciencias. ~**ce fiction** *n* ciencia *f* ficción. ~**tific** /-'tɪfɪk/ *a* científico. ~**tist** /'saɪəntɪst/ *n* científico *m*

scissors /'sɪsəz/ *npl* tijeras *fpl*

scoff /skɒf/ *vt* 🆒 zamparse. ● *vi*. ~ **at** mofarse de

scold /skəʊld/ *vt* regañar

scoop /skuːp/ *n* pala *f*; (news) primicia *f*. □ ~ **out** *vt* sacar; excavar <hole>

scooter /'skuːtə(r)/ *n* escúter *m*; (for child) patinete *m*

scope /skəʊp/ *n* alcance *m*; (opportunity) oportunidad *f*

scorch /skɔːtʃ/ *vt* chamuscar. ~**ing** *a* 🆒 de mucho calor

score /skɔː(r)/ *n* tanteo *m*; (Mus) partitura *f*; (twenty) veintena *f*. **on that** ~ en cuanto a eso. **know the** ~ 🆒 saber cómo son las cosas. ● *vt* marcar <goal>; anotarse <points>; (cut, mark) rayar; conseguir <success>. ● *vi* marcar

scorn /skɔːn/ *n* desdén *m*. ● *vt* desdeñar. ~**ful** *a* desdeñoso

Scorpio /'skɔːpɪəʊ/ *n* Escorpio *m*, Escorpión *m*

scorpion /'skɔːpɪən/ *n* escorpión *m*

Scot /skɒt/ *n* escocés *m*. ~**ch** /skɒtʃ/ *n* whisky *m*, güisqui *m*

scotch /skɒtʃ/ *vt* frustrar; acallar <rumours>

Scotch tape *n* (Amer) celo *m*, cinta *f* Scotch

Scot: ~land /'skɒtlənd/ *n* Escocia *f*. ~**s** *a* escocés. ~**tish** *a* escocés

scoundrel /'skaʊndrəl/ *n* canalla *f*

scour /'skaʊə(r)/ *vt* fregar; (search) registrar. ~**er** *n* estropajo *m*

scourge /skɜːdʒ/ *n* azote *m*

scout /skaʊt/ *n* explorador *m*. **Boy S**~ explorador *m*

scowl /skaʊl/ *n* ceño *m* fruncido. ● *vi* fruncir el ceño

scram /skræm/ *vi* 🆒 largarse

scramble /'skræmbl/ *vi* (clamber) gatear. ● *n* (difficult climb) subida *f* difícil; (struggle) rebatiña *f*. ~**d egg** *n* huevos *mpl* revueltos

scrap /skræp/ *n* pedacito *m*; (🆒, fight) pelea *f*. ● *vt* (*pt* **scrapped**) desechar. ~**book** *n* álbum *m* de recortes. ~**s** *npl* sobras *fpl*

scrape /skreɪp/ *n* (fig) apuro *m*. ● *vt* raspar; (graze) rasparse; (rub) rascar. □ ~ **through** *vi/t* aprobar por los pelos <exam>. □ ~ **together** *vt* reunir. ~**r** *n* rasqueta *f*

scrap: ～**heap** n montón m de deshechos. ～ **yard** n chatarrería f

scratch /skrætʃ/ vt rayar <furniture, record>; (with nail etc) arañar; rascarse <itch>. ● vi arañar. ● n rayón m; (from nail etc) arañazo m. **start from** ～ empezar desde cero. **be up to** ～ dar la talla

scrawl /skrɔːl/ n garabato m. ● vt/i garabatear

scream /skriːm/ vt/i gritar. ● n grito m

screech /skriːtʃ/ vi chillar; <brakes etc> chirriar. ● n chillido m; (of brakes etc) chirrido m

screen /skriːn/ n pantalla f; (folding) biombo m. ● vt (hide) ocultar; (protect) proteger; proyectar <film>

screw /skruː/ n tornillo m. ● vt atornillar. □ ～ **up** vt atornillar; entornar <eyes>; torcer <face>; (■, ruin) fastidiar. ～**driver** n destornillador m

scribble /skrɪbl/ vt/i garabatear. ● n garabato m

script /skrɪpt/ n escritura f; (of film etc) guión m

scroll /skrəʊl/ n rollo m (de pergamino)

scrounge /skraʊndʒ/ vt/i gorronear. ～**r** n gorrón m

scrub /skrʌb/ n (land) maleza f. ● vt/i (pt **scrubbed**) fregar

scruff /skrʌf/ n. **by the** ～ **of the neck** por el pescuezo. ～**y** a (-**ier**, -**iest**) desaliñado

scrup|le /skruːpl/ n escrúpulo m. ～**ulous** /-jʊləs/ a escrupuloso

scrutin|ize /skruːtɪnaɪz/ vt escudriñar; inspeccionar <document>. ～**y** /skruːtɪnɪ/ n examen m minucioso

scuffle /skʌfl/ n refriega f

sculpt /skʌlpt/ vt/i esculpir. ～**or** n escultor m. ～**ure** /-tʃə(r)/ n escultura f. ● vt/i esculpir

scum /skʌm/ n espuma f; (people, pej) escoria f

scupper /skʌpə(r)/ vt echar por tierra <plans>

scurry /skʌrɪ/ vi corretear

scuttle /skʌtl/ n cubo m del carbón. ● vt barrenar <ship>. ● vi. ～ **away** escabullirse rápidamente

scythe /saɪð/ n guadaña f

SE abbr (= **south-east**) SE

sea /siː/ n mar m. **at** ～ en el mar; (fig) confuso. **by** ～ por mar. ～**food** n mariscos mpl. ～ **front** n paseo m marítimo, malecón m (LAm). ～**gull** n gaviota f. ～**horse** n caballito m de mar

seal /siːl/ n sello m; (animal) foca f. ● vt sellar. □ ～ **off** vt acordonar <area>

sea level n nivel m del mar

sea lion n león m marino

seam /siːm/ n costura f; (of coal) veta f

seaman /siːmən/ n (pl -**men**) marinero m

seamy /siːmɪ/ a sórdido

seance /seɪɑːns/ n sesión f de espiritismo

search /sɜːtʃ/ vt registrar; buscar en <records>. ● n (for sth) búsqueda f; (of sth) registro m; (Comp) búsqueda f. **in** ～ **of** en busca de. □ ～ **for** vt buscar. ～**ing** a penetrante. ～**light** n reflector m. ～ **party** n partida f de rescate

sea: ～**shore** n orilla f del mar. ～**sick** a mareado. **be** ～**sick** marearse. ～**side** n playa f

season /siːzn/ n estación f; (period) temporada f. **high/low** ～ temporada f alta/baja. ● vt (Culin) sazonar. ～**al** a estacional; <demand> de estación. ～**ed** a (fig) avezado. ～**ing** n condimento m. ～ **ticket** n abono m (de temporada)

seat /siːt/ n asiento m; (place) lugar m; (in cinema, theatre) localidad f; (of trousers) fondillos mpl. **take a** ～ sentarse. ● vt sentar; (have seats for) <auditorium> tener capacidad para; <bus> tener asientos para. ～**belt** n cinturón m de seguridad

sea: ～**urchin** n erizo m de mar. ～**weed** n alga f marina. ～**worthy** a en condiciones de navegar

seclu|ded /sɪkluːdɪd/ a aislado. ～**sion** /-ʒn/ n aislamiento m

second /'sekənd/ *a & n* segundo (*m*). on ~ **thoughts** pensándolo bien. ● *adv* (in race etc) en segundo lugar. ● *vt* secundar. ~**s** *npl* (goods) artículos *mpl* de segunda calidad; (Ⅰ, more food) **have** ~**s** repetir. ● /sɪ'kɒnd/ *vt* (transfer) trasladar temporalmente. ~**ary** /'sekəndrɪ/ *a* secundario. ~**ary school** *n* instituto *m* (de enseñanza secundaria)

second: ~**-class** *a* de segunda (clase). ~**-hand** *a* de segunda mano. ~**ly** *adv* en segundo lugar. ~**-rate** *a* mediocre

secre|cy /'si:krəsɪ/ *n* secreto *m*. ~**t** *a & n* secreto (*m*). in ~**t** en secreto

secretar|ial /sekrə'teərɪəl/ *a* de secretario; <*course*> de secretariado. ~**y** /'sekrətrɪ/ *n* secretario *m*. S~**y of State** (in UK) ministro *m*: (in US) secretario *m* de Estado

secretive /'si:krɪtɪv/ *a* reservado

sect /sekt/ *n* secta *f*. ~**arian** /-'teərɪən/ *a* sectario

section /'sekʃn/ *n* sección *f*; (part) parte *f*

sector /'sektə(r)/ *n* sector *m*

secular /'sekjʊlə(r)/ *a* secular

secur|e /sɪ'kjʊə(r)/ *a* seguro; <*shelf*> firme. ● *vt* asegurar; (obtain) obtener. ~**ely** *adv* seguramente. ~**ity** *n* seguridad *f*; (for loan) garantía *f*

sedat|e /sɪ'deɪt/ *a* reposado. ● *vt* sedar. ~**ion** /sɪ'deɪʃn/ *n* sedación *f*. ~**ive** /'sedətɪv/ *a & n* sedante (*m*)

sediment /'sedɪmənt/ *n* sedimento *m*

seduc|e /sɪ'dju:s/ *vt* seducir. ~**er** *n* seductor *m*. ~**tion** /sɪ'dʌkʃn/ *n* seducción *f*. ~**tive** /sɪ'dʌktɪv/ *a* seductor

see /si:/ ● *vt* (*pt* **saw**, *pp* **seen**) ver; (understand) comprender; (escort) acompañar. ~**ing that** visto que. ~ **you later!** ¡hasta luego! ● *vi* ver. □ ~ **off** *vt* (say goodbye to) despedirse de. □ ~ **through** *vt* llevar a cabo; calar <*person*>. □ ~ **to** *vt* ocuparse de

seed /si:d/ *n* semilla *f*; (fig) germen *m*; (Amer, pip) pepita *f*. **go to** ~ granar; (fig) echarse a perder. ~**ling** *n* planta *f* de semillero. ~**y** *a* (**-ier**, **-iest**) sórdido

seek /si:k/ *vt* (*pt* **sought**) buscar; pedir <*approval*>. □ ~ **out** *vt* buscar

seem /si:m/ *vi* parecer

seen /si:n/ ⇒SEE

seep /si:p/ *vi* filtrarse

see-saw /'si:sɔ:/ *n* balancín *m*

seethe /si:ð/ *vi* (fig) estar furioso. I **was seething with anger** me hervía la sangre

see-through /'si:θru:/ *a* transparente

segment /'segmənt/ *n* segmento *m*; (of orange) gajo *m*

segregat|e /'segrɪgeɪt/ *vt* segregar. ~**ion** /-'geɪʃn/ *n* segregación *f*

seiz|e /si:z/ *vt* agarrar; (Jurid) incautar. ~**e on** *vt* aprovechar <*chance*>. □ ~**e up** *vi* (Tec) agarrotarse. ~**ure** /'si:ʒə(r)/ *n* incautación *f*; (Med) ataque *m*

seldom /'seldəm/ *adv* rara vez

select /sɪ'lekt/ *vt* escoger; (Sport) seleccionar. ● *a* selecto; (exclusive) exclusivo. ~**ion** /-ʃn/ *n* selección *f*. ~**ive** *a* selectivo

self /self/ *n* (*pl* **selves**). he's his old ~ **again** vuelve a ser el de antes. ~**-addressed** *a* con el nombre y la dirección del remitente. ~**-catering** *a* con facilidades para cocinar. ~**-centred** *a* egocéntrico. ~**-confidence** *n* confianza *f* en sí mismo. ~**-confident** *a* seguro de sí mismo. ~**-conscious** *a* cohibido. ~**-contained** *a* independiente. ~**-control** *n* dominio *m* de sí mismo. ~**-defence** *n* defensa *f* propia. ~**-employed** *a* que trabaja por cuenta propia. ~**-evident** *a* evidente. ~**-important** *a* presumido. ~**-indulgent** *a* inmoderado. ~**-interest** *n* interés *m* (personal). ~**ish** *a* egoísta. ~**ishness** *n* egoísmo *m*. ~**-pity** *n* autocompasión. ~**-portrait** *n* autorretrato *m*. ~**-respect** *n* amor *m* propio. ~**-righteous** *a* santurrón. ~**-sacrifice** *n* abnegación *f*. ~**-satisfied** *a* satisfecho de sí mismo. ~**-serve** (Amer), ~**-service** *a & n* autoservicio (*m*). ~**-sufficient** *a* independiente

sell /sel/ *vt* (*pt* **sold**) vender. ● *vi* venderse. □ ~ **off** *vt* liquidar. ~ **out** *vi*. **we've sold out of gloves** los guantes están agotados. ~**by date** *n* fecha *f* límite de venta. ~**er** *n* vendedor *m*

Sellotape /'seləteɪp/ *n* (P) celo *m*, cinta *f* Scotch

sell-out /'selaʊt/ *n* (performance) éxito *m* de taquilla; (⬜, betrayal) capitulación *f*

semblance /'sembləns/ *n* apariencia *f*

semester /sɪ'mestə(r)/ *n* (Amer) semestre *m*

semi... /'semɪ/ *pref* semi...

semi|breve /-bri:v/ *n* redonda *f*. ~**circle** *n* semicírculo *m*. ~**colon** /-'kəʊlən/ *n* punto *m* y coma. ~**detached** /-dɪ'tætʃt/ *a* <house> adosado. ~**final** /-'faɪnl/ *n* semifinal *f*

seminar /'seminɑ:(r)/ *n* seminario *m*

senat|e /'senɪt/ *n* senado *m*. **the S**~**e** (Amer) el Senado. ~**or** /-ətə(r)/ *n* senador *m*

send /send/ *vt/i* (*pt* **sent**) mandar, enviar. □ ~ **away** *vt* despedir. □ ~ **away for** *vt* pedir (por correo). □ ~ **for** *vt* enviar a buscar. □ ~ **off for** *vt* pedir (por correo). □ ~ **up** *vt* ⬜ parodiar. ~**er** *n* remitente *m*. ~**-off** *n* despedida *f*

senile /'si:naɪl/ *a* senil

senior /'si:nɪə(r)/ *a* mayor; (in rank) superior; <partner etc> principal. ● *n* mayor *m* & *f*. ~ **citizen** *n* jubilado *m*. ~ **high school** *n* (Amer) colegio *m* secundario. ~**ity** /-'ɒrəti/ *n* antigüedad *f*

sensation /sen'seɪʃn/ *n* sensación *f*. ~**al** *a* sensacional

sens|e /sens/ *n* sentido *m*; (common sense) juicio *m*; (feeling) sensación *f*. **make** ~**e** *vt* tener sentido. **make** ~**e of sth** entender algo. ~**eless** *a* sin sentido. ~**ible** /'sensəbl/ *a* sensato; <clothing> práctico. ~**itive** /'sensɪtɪv/ *a* sensible; (touchy) susceptible. ~**itivity** /-'tɪvəti/ *n* sensibilidad *f*. ~**ual** /'senʃʊəl/ *a* sensual. ~**uous** /'sensʊəs/ *a* sensual

sent /sent/ ⇒SEND

sentence /'sentəns/ *n* frase *f*; (judgment) sentencia *f*; (punishment) condena *f*. ● *vt*. ~ **to** condenar a

sentiment /'sentɪmənt/ *n* sentimiento *m*; (opinion) opinión *f*. ~**al** /-'mentl/ *a* sentimental. ~**ality** /-'tælətɪ/ *n* sentimentalismo *m*

sentry /'sentrɪ/ *n* centinela *f*

separa|ble /'sepərəbl/ *a* separable. ~**te** /'sepərət/ *a* separado; (independent) independiente. ● *vt* /'sepəreɪt/ separar. ● *vi* separarse. ~**tely** /'sepərətlɪ/ *adv* por separado. ~**tion** /-'reɪʃn/ *n* separación *f*. ~**tist** /'sepərətɪst/ *n* separatista *m* & *f*

September /sep'tembə(r)/ *n* se(p)tiembre *m*

septic /'septɪk/ *a* séptico

sequel /'si:kwəl/ *n* continuación *f*; (later events) secuela *f*

sequence /'si:kwəns/ *n* sucesión *f*; (of film) secuencia *f*

Serb /sɜ:b/ *a* & *n* ⇒SERBIAN. ~**ia** /'sɜ:bɪə/ *n* Serbia *f* ~**ian** *a* & *n* serbio (*m*)

serenade /serə'neɪd/ *n* serenata *f*. ● *vt* dar serenata a

serene /sɪ'ri:n/ *a* sereno

sergeant /'sɑ:dʒənt/ *n* sargento *m*

serial /'sɪərɪəl/ *n* serie *f*. ~**ize** *vt* serializar

series /'sɪəri:z/ *n* serie *f*

serious /'sɪərɪəs/ *a* serio. ~**ly** *adv* seriamente; (ill) gravemente. **take** ~**ly** tomar en serio

sermon /'sɜ:mən/ *n* sermón *m*

serum /'sɪərəm/ *n* (*pl* **-a**) suero *m*

servant /'sɜ:vənt/ *n* criado *m*

serve /sɜ:v/ *vt* servir; servir a <country>; cumplir <sentence>. ~ **as** servir de. **it** ~**s you right** ¡bien te lo mereces! ● *vi* servir; (in tennis) sacar. ● *n* (in tennis) saque *m*. ~**r** *n* (Comp) servidor *m*

service /'sɜ:vɪs/ *n* servicio *m*; (of car etc) revisión *f*. ● *vt* revisar <car etc>. ~ **charge** *n* (in restaurant) servicio *m*. ~**s** *npl* (Mil) fuerzas *fpl* armadas. ~ **station** *n* estación *f* de servicio

serviette /sɜ:vɪ'et/ *n* servilleta *f*

servile /'sɜ:vaɪl/ *a* servil

session /'seʃn/ *n* sesión *f*

set /set/ vt (pt **set**, pres p **setting**) poner; poner en hora *<clock etc>*; fijar *<limit etc>*; (typeset) componer. ~ **fire to** prender fuego a. ~ **free** vt poner en libertad. ● vi *<sun>* ponerse; *<jelly>* cuajarse. ● n serie f; (of cutlery etc) juego m; (tennis) set m; (TV, Radio) aparato m; (in theatre) decorado m; (of people) círculo m. ● a fijo. **be ~ on** estar resuelto a. □ ~ **back** vt (delay) retardar; (Ⅱ, cost) costar. □ ~ **off** vi salir. vt hacer sonar *<alarm>*; hacer explotar *<bomb>*. □ ~ **out** vt exponer *<argument>*. vi (leave) salir. □ ~ **up** vt establecer. ~**back** n revés m

settee /se'ti:/ n sofá m

setting /'setɪŋ/ n (of dial, switch) posición f

settle /'setl/ vt (arrange) acordar; arreglar *<matter>*; resolver *<dispute>*; pagar *<bill>*; saldar *<debt>*. ● vi (live) establecerse. □ ~ **down** vi calmarse; (become more responsible) sentar (la) cabeza. □ ~ **for** vt aceptar. □ ~ **up** vi arreglar cuentas. ~**ment** n establecimiento m; (agreement) acuerdo m; (of debt) liquidación f; (colony) colonia f. ~**r** n colono m

set: ~**to** n pelea f. ~**up** n Ⅱ sistema m; (con) tinglado m

seven /'sevn/ a & n siete (m). ~**teen** /sevn'ti:n/ a & n diecisiete (m). ~**teenth** a decimoséptimo. ● n diecisietavo m. ~**th** a & n séptimo (m). ~**tieth** /'sevəntɪɪθ/ a septuagésimo. ● n setentavo m. ~**ty** /'sevntɪ/ a & n setenta (m)

sever /'sevə(r)/ vt cortar; (fig) romper

several /'sevrəl/ a & pron varios

sever|e /sɪ'vɪə(r)/ a (**-er**, **-est**) severo; (serious) grave; *<weather>* riguroso. ~**ely** adv severamente. ~**ity** /sɪ'verətɪ/ n severidad f; (seriousness) gravedad f

sew /səʊ/ vt/i (pt **sewed**, pp **sewn**, or **sewed**) coser. □ ~ **up** vt coser

sew|age /'su:ɪdʒ/ n aguas fpl residuales. ~**er** /'su:ə(r)/ n cloaca f

sewing /'səʊɪŋ/ n costura f. ~**machine** n máquina f de coser

sewn /səʊn/ ⇒SEW

sex /seks/ n sexo m. **have ~** tener relaciones sexuales. ● a sexual. ~**ist** a

& n sexista (m & f). ~**ual** /'sekʃʊəl/ a sexual. ~**ual intercourse** n relaciones fpl sexuales. ~**uality** /-'ælətɪ/ n sexualidad f. ~**y** a (**-ier**, **-iest**) excitante, sexy, provocativo

shabby /'ʃæbɪ/ a (**-ier**, **-iest**) *<clothes>* gastado; *<person>* pobremente vestido

shack /ʃæk/ n choza f

shade /ʃeɪd/ n sombra f; (of colour) tono m; (for lamp) pantalla f; (nuance) matiz m; (Amer, over window) persiana f

shadow /'ʃædəʊ/ n sombra f. ● vt (follow) seguir de cerca a. ~**y** a (fig) vago

shady /'ʃeɪdɪ/ a (**-ier**, **-iest**) sombreado; (fig) turbio; *<character>* sospechoso

shaft /ʃɑ:ft/ n (of arrow) astil m; (Mec) eje m; (of light) rayo m; (of lift, mine) pozo m

shaggy /'ʃægɪ/ a (**-ier**, **-iest**) peludo

shake /ʃeɪk/ vt (pt **shook**, pp **shaken**) sacudir; agitar *<bottle>*; (shock) desconcertar. ~ **hands with** estrechar la mano a. ~ **one's head** negar con la cabeza; (Amer, meaning yes) asentir con la cabeza. ● vi temblar. □ ~ **off** vi deshacerse de. ● n sacudida f

shaky /'ʃeɪkɪ/ a (**-ier**, **-iest**) tembloroso; *<table etc>* inestable

shall /ʃæl/ v aux. **we ~ see** veremos. ~ **we go to the cinema?** ¿vamos al cine?

shallow /'ʃæləʊ/ a (**-er**, **-est**) poco profundo; (fig) superficial

sham /ʃæm/ n farsa f. ● a fingido

shambles /'ʃæmblz/ npl (Ⅱ, mess) caos m

shame /ʃeɪm/ n (feeling) vergüenza f. **what a ~!** ¡qué lástima! ● vt avergonzar. ~**ful** a vergonzoso. ~**less** a desvergonzado

shampoo /ʃæm'pu:/ n champú m. ● vt lavar

shan't /ʃɑ:nt/ = **shall not**

shape /ʃeɪp/ n forma f. ● vt formar; determinar *<future>*. ● vi tomar forma. ~**less** a informe

share /ʃeə(r)/ n porción f; (Com) acción f. ● vt compartir; (divide) dividir. ● vi compartir. ~ in sth participar en algo. □ ~ out vt repartir. ~holder n accionista m & f. ~-out n reparto m

shark /ʃɑːk/ n tiburón m

sharp /ʃɑːp/ a (-er, -est) <knife etc> afilado; <pin etc> puntiagudo; <pain, sound> agudo; <taste> ácido; <bend> cerrado; <contrast> marcado; (clever) listo; (Mus) sostenido. ● adv en punto. at seven o'clock ~ a las siete en punto. ~en vt (Mus) sostenido m. ~en vt afilar; sacar punta a <pencil>. ~ener n (Mec) afilador m; (for pencils) sacapuntas m. ~ly adv bruscamente

shatter /'ʃætə(r)/ vt hacer añicos. he was ~ed by the news la noticia lo dejó destrozado. ● vi hacerse añicos. ~ed /'ʃætəd/a (exhausted) agotado

shav|e /ʃeɪv/ vt afeitar, rasurar (Mex). ● vi afeitarse, rasurarse (Mex). ● n afeitada f, rasurada f (Mex). have a ~e afeitarse. ~er n maquinilla f (de afeitar). ~ing brush n brocha f de afeitar. ~ing cream n crema f de afeitar

shawl /ʃɔːl/ n chal m

she /ʃiː/ pron ella

sheaf /ʃiːf/ n (pl sheaves /ʃiːvz/) gavilla f

shear /ʃɪə(r)/ vt (pp shorn or sheared) esquilar. ~s /ʃɪəz/ npl tijeras fpl grandes

shed /ʃed/ n cobertizo m. ● vt (pt shed, pres p shedding) perder; derramar <tears>; despojarse de <clothes>. ~ light on arrojar luz sobre

she'd /ʃiː(ə)d/ = she had, she would

sheep /ʃiːp/ n invar oveja f. ~dog n perro m pastor. ~ish a avergonzado

sheer /ʃɪə(r)/ a (as intensifier) puro; (steep) perpendicular

sheet /ʃiːt/ n sábana f; (of paper) hoja f; (of glass) lámina f; (of ice) capa f

shelf /ʃelf/ n (pl shelves) estante m. a set of shelves unos estantes

shell /ʃel/ n concha f; (of egg) cáscara f; (of crab, snail, tortoise) caparazón m or

f; (explosive) proyectil m, obús m. ● vt pelar <peas etc>; (Mil) bombardear

she'll /'ʃiː(ə)l/ = SHE HAD, SHE WOULD

shellfish /'ʃelfɪʃ/ n invar marisco m; (collectively) mariscos mpl

shelter /'ʃeltə(r)/ n refugio m. take ~ refugiarse. ● vt darle cobijo a <fugitive>; (protect from weather) resguardar. ● vi refugiarse. ~ed /'ʃeltəd/ a <spot> abrigado; <life> protegido

shelv|e /ʃelv/ vt (fig) dar carpetazo a. ~ing n estantería f

shepherd /'ʃepəd/ n pastor m. ~ess /-'des/ n pastora f

sherbet /'ʃɜːbət/ n (Amer, water ice) sorbete m

sheriff /'ʃerɪf/ n (in US) sheriff m

sherry /'ʃerɪ/ n (vino m de) jerez m

she's /ʃiːz/ = she is, she has

shield /ʃiːld/ n escudo m. ● vt proteger

shift /ʃɪft/ vt cambiar; correr <furniture etc>. ● vi <wind> cambiar; <attention, opinion> pasar a; (Amer, change gear) cambiar de velocidad. ● n cambio m; (work) turno m; (workers) tanda f. ~y a (-ier, -iest) furtivo

shilling /'ʃɪlɪŋ/ n chelín m

shimmer /'ʃɪmə(r)/ vi rielar, relucir

shin /ʃɪn/ n espinilla f

shine /ʃaɪn/ vi (pt shone) brillar. ● vt sacar brillo a. ~ a light on sth alumbrar algo con una luz. ● n brillo m

shingle /'ʃɪŋɡl/ n (pebbles) guijarros mpl

shin|ing /'ʃaɪnɪŋ/ a brillante. ~y /'ʃaɪnɪ/ a (-ier, -iest) brillante

ship /ʃɪp/ n barco m, buque m. ● vt (pt shipped) transportar; (send) enviar; (load) embarcar. ~building n construcción f naval. ~ment n envío m. ~ping n transporte m; (ships) barcos mpl. ~shape a limpio y ordenado. ~wreck n naufragio m. ~wrecked a naufragado. be ~wrecked naufragar. ~yard n astillero m

shirk /ʃɜːk/ vt esquivar

shirt /ʃɜːt/ n camisa f. in ~-sleeves en mangas de camisa

shit /ʃɪt/ *n & int* (vulg) mierda (*f*). ● *vi* (vulg) (*pt* **shat**, *pres p* **shitting**) cagar

shiver /'ʃɪvə(r)/ *vi* temblar. ● *n* escalofrío *m*

shoal /ʃəʊl/ *n* banco *m*

shock /ʃɒk/ *n* (of impact) choque *m*; (of earthquake) sacudida *f*; (surprise) shock *m*; (scare) susto *m*; (Elec) descarga *f*; (Med) shock *m*. **get a ~** llevarse un shock. ● *vt* escandalizar; (apall) horrorizar. **~ing** *a* escandaloso; 🖭 espantoso

shod /ʃɒd/ ⇒SHOE

shoddy /'ʃɒdɪ/ *a* (**-ier**, **-iest**) mal hecho, de pacotilla

shoe /ʃuː/ *n* zapato *m*; (of horse) herradura *f*. ● *vt* (*pt* **shod**, *pres p* **shoeing**) herrar *<horse>*. **~horn** *n* calzador *m*. **~lace** *n* cordón *m* (de zapato). **~ polish** *n* betún *m*

shone /ʃɒn/ ⇒SHINE

shoo /ʃuː/ *vt* ahuyentar

shook /ʃʊk/ ⇒SHAKE

shoot /ʃuːt/ *vt* (*pt* **shot**) disparar; rodar *<film>*. ● *vi* (hunt) cazar. ● *n* (Bot) retoño *m*. □ **~ down** *vt* derribar. □ **~ out** *vi* (rush) salir disparado. □ **~ up** *vi* *<prices>* dispararse; (grow) crecer mucho

shop /ʃɒp/ *n* tienda *f*. **go to the ~s** ir de compras. **talk ~** hablar del trabajo. ● *vi* (*pt* **shopping**) hacer compras. **go ~ping** ir de compras. □ **~ around** *vi* buscar el mejor precio. **~ assistant** *n* dependiente *m*, dependienta *f*, empleado *m*, empleada *f* (LAm). **~keeper** *n* comerciante *m*, tendero *m*. **~lifter** *n* ladrón *m* (*que roba en las tiendas*). **~lifting** *n* hurto *m* (*en las tiendas*). **~per** *n* comprador *m*. **~ping** *n* (purchases) compras *fpl*. **do the ~ping** hacer la compra, hacer el mandado (Mex). **~ping bag** *n* bolsa *f* de la compra. **~ping cart** *n* (Amer) carrito *m* (de la compra). **~ping centre**, **~ping mall** (Amer) *n* centro *m* comercial. **~ping trolley** *n* carrito *m* de la compra. **~ steward** *n* enlace *m* sindical. **~ window** *n* escaparate *m*, vidriera *f* (LAm), aparador *m* (Mex)

shore /ʃɔː(r)/ *n* orilla *f*

shorn /ʃɔːn/ ⇒SHEAR

short /ʃɔːt/ *a* (**-er**, **-est**) corto; (not lasting) breve; *<person>* bajo; (curt) brusco. **a ~ time ago** hace poco. **be ~ of time/money** andar corto de tiempo/dinero. **Mick is ~ for Michael** Mick es el diminutivo de Michael. ● *adv* *<stop>* en seco. **we never went ~ of food** nunca nos faltó comida. ● *n*. **in ~** en resumen. **~age** /-ɪdʒ/ *n* escasez *f*, falta *f*. **~bread** *n* galleta *f* (*de mantequilla*). **~ circuit** *n* cortocircuito *m*. **~coming** *n* defecto *m*. **~ cut** *n* atajo *m*. **~en** *vt* acortar. **~hand** *n* taquigrafía *f*. **~ly** *adv* (soon) dentro de poco. **~ly before midnight** poco antes de la medianoche. **~s** *npl* pantalones *m* cortos, shorts *mpl*; (Amer, underwear) calzoncillos *mpl*. **~-sighted** /-'saɪtɪd/ *a* miope

shot /ʃɒt/ ⇒SHOOT. ● *n* (from gun) disparo *m*; tiro *m*; (in soccer) tiro *m*, disparo *m*; (in other sports) tiro *m*; (Photo) foto *f*. **be a good/poor ~** ser un buen/mal tirador. **be off like a ~** salir disparado. **~gun** *n* escopeta *f*

should /ʃʊd, ʃəd/ *v aux*. **I ~ go** debería ir. **you ~n't have said that** no deberías haber dicho eso. **I ~ like to see her** me gustaría verla. **if he ~ come** si viniese

shoulder /'ʃəʊldə(r)/ *n* hombro *m*. ● *vt* cargar con *<responsibility>*; ponerse al hombro *<burden>*. **~ blade** *n* omóplato *m*

shout /ʃaʊt/ *n* grito *m*. ● *vt/i* gritar. **~ at s.o.** gritarle a uno

shove /ʃʌv/ *n* empujón *m*. ● *vt* empujar; (🖭, put) poner. ● *vi* empujar. □ **~ off** *vi* 🖭 largarse

shovel /'ʃʌvl/ *n* pala *f*. ● *vt* (*pt* **shovelled**) palear *<coal>*; espalar *<snow>*

show /ʃəʊ/ *vt* (*pt* **showed**, *pp* **shown**) mostrar; (put on display) exponer; poner *<film>*. **I'll ~ you to your room** lo acompaño a su cuarto. ● *vi* (be visible) verse. ● *n* muestra *f*; (exhibition) exposición *f*; (in theatre) espectáculo *m*; (on TV, radio) programa *m*; (ostentation) pompa *f*. **be on ~** estar expuesto. □ **~ off** *vt* (pej) lucir, presumir de. *vi* presumir, lucirse.

▫ ~ **up** *vi* (be visible) notarse; (arrive) aparecer. *vt* (reveal) poner de manifiesto; (embarrass) hacer quedar mal. **~case** *n* vitrina *f*. **~down** *n* confrontación *f*

shower /'ʃaʊə(r)/ *n* (of rain) chaparrón *m*; (for washing) ducha *f*. **have a ~, take a ~** ducharse. ● *vi* ducharse

showjumping *n* concursos *mpl* hípicos.

shown /ʃəʊn/ ⇒SHOW

show: ~-off *n* fanfarrón *m*. **~room** *n* sala *f* de exposición *f*. **~y** *a* (**-ier, -iest**) llamativo; (attractive) ostentoso

shrank /ʃræŋk/ ⇒SHRINK

shred /ʃred/ *n* pedazo *m*; (fig) pizca *f*. ● *vt* (*pt* **shredded**) hacer tiras; destruir, triturar *<documents>*. **~der** *n* (for paper) trituradora *f*; (for vegetables) cortadora *f*

shrewd /ʃru:d/ *a* (**-er, -est**) astuto

shriek /ʃri:k/ *n* chillido *m*; (of pain) alarido *m*. ● *vt/i* chillar

shrift /ʃrɪft/ *n*. **give s.o. short ~** despachar a uno con brusquedad. **give sth short ~** desestimar algo de plano

shrill /ʃrɪl/ *a* agudo

shrimp /ʃrɪmp/ *n* gamba *f*, camarón *m* (LAm); (Amer, large) langostino *m*

shrine /ʃraɪn/ *n* (place) santuario *m*; (tomb) sepulcro *m*

shrink /ʃrɪŋk/ *vt* (*pt* **shrank**, *pp* **shrunk**) encoger. ● *vi* encogerse; *<amount>* reducirse; retroceder (recoil)

shrivel /'ʃrɪvl/ *vi* (*pt* **shrivelled**). **~ (up)** *<plant>* marchitarse; *<fruit>* resecarse y arrugarse

shroud /ʃraʊd/ *n* mortaja *f*; (fig) velo *m*. ● *vt* envolver

Shrove /ʃrəʊv/ *n*. **~ Tuesday** *n* martes *m* de carnaval

shrub /ʃrʌb/ *n* arbusto *m*

shrug /ʃrʌg/ *vt* (*pt* **shrugged**) encogerse de hombros

shrunk /ʃrʌŋk/ ⇒SHRINK. **~en** *a* encogido

shudder /'ʃʌdə(r)/ *vi* estremecerse. ● *n* estremecimiento *m*

shuffle /'ʃʌfl/ *vi* andar arrastrando los pies. ● *vt* barajar *<cards>*. **~ one's feet** arrastrar los pies

shun /ʃʌn/ *vt* (*pt* **shunned**) evitar

shunt /ʃʌnt/ *vt* cambiar de vía

shush /ʃʊʃ/ *int* ¡chitón!

shut /ʃʌt/ *vt* (*pt* **shut**, *pres p* **shutting**) cerrar. ● *vi* cerrarse. ● *a*. **be ~** estar cerrado. ▫ ~ **down** *vt/i* cerrar. ▫ ~ **up** *vt* cerrar; 🄸 hacer callar. *vi* callarse. **~ter** *n* contraventana *f*; (Photo) obturador *m*

shuttle /'ʃʌtl/ *n* lanzadera *f*; (Aviat) puente *m* aéreo; (space ~) transbordador *m* espacial. ● *vi*. ~ (back and forth) ir y venir. **~cock** *n* volante *m*. ~ **service** *n* servicio *m* de enlace

shy /ʃaɪ/ *a* (**-er, -est**) tímido. ● *vi* (*pt* **shied**) asustarse. **~ness** *n* timidez *f*

sick /sɪk/ *a* enfermo; *<humour>* negro; (🄸, fed up) harto. **be ~** estar enfermo; (vomit) vomitar. **be ~ of** (fig) estar harto de. **feel ~** sentir náuseas. **get ~** (Amer) caer enfermo, enfermarse (LAm). ~ **leave** *n* permiso *m* por enfermedad, baja *f* por enfermedad. **~ly** /'sɪklɪ/ *a* (**-lier, -liest**) enfermizo; *<taste, smell etc>* nauseabundo. **~ness** /'sɪknɪs/ *n* enfermedad *f*

side /saɪd/ *n* lado *m*; (of hill) ladera *f*; (of person) costado *m*; (team) equipo *m*; (fig) parte *f*. ~ **by ~** uno al lado del otro. **take ~s** tomar partido. ● *a* lateral. ▫ ~ **with** *vt* ponerse de parte de. **~board** *n* aparador *m*. ~ **dish** *n* acompañamiento *m*. **~-effect** *n* efecto *m* secundario; (fig) consecuencia *f* indirecta. **~line** *n* actividad *f* suplementaria. ~ **road** *n* calle *f* secundaria. **~-step** *vt* eludir. **~-track** *vt* desviar del tema. **~walk** *n* (Amer) acera *f*, vereda *f* (LAm), banqueta *f* (Mex). **~ways** *a* & *adv* de lado

siding /'saɪdɪŋ/ *n* apartadero *m*

sidle /'saɪdl/ *vi*. ~ **up to s.o.** acercarse furtivamente a uno

siege /si:dʒ/ *n* sitio *m*

sieve /sɪv/ *n* tamiz *m*. ● *vt* tamizar, cernir

sift /sɪft/ vt tamizar, cernir. ● vi. ~ through sth pasar algo por el tamiz

sigh /saɪ/ n suspiro. ● vi suspirar

sight /saɪt/ n vista f; (spectacle) espectáculo m; (on gun) mira f. **at first** ~ a primera vista. **catch** ~ **of** ver; (in distance) avistar. **lose** ~ **of** perder de vista. **see the** ~**s** visitar los lugares de interés. **within** ~ **of** (near) cerca de. ● vt ver; divisar <land>. ~**-seeing** n. **go** ~ ir a visitar los lugares de interés. ~**seer** /-si:ə(r)/ n turista m & f

sign /saɪn/ n (indication) señal f, indicio m; (gesture) señal f, seña f; (notice) letrero m; (Astr) signo m. ● vt firmar. □ ~ **on** vi (for unemployment benefit) anotarse para recibir el seguro de desempleo

signal /'sɪgnəl/ n señal f. ● vt (pt signalled) señalar. ● vi. ~ (to s.o.) hacer señas (a uno); (Auto) poner el intermitente, señalizar

signature /'sɪgnətʃə(r)/ n firma f. ~ **tune** n sintonía f

significan|ce /sɪg'nɪfɪkəns/ n importancia f. ~**t** a (important) importante; <fact, remark> significativo

signify /'sɪgnɪfaɪ/ vt significar

signpost /'saɪnpəʊst/ n señal f, poste m indicador

silen|ce /'saɪləns/ n silencio m. ● vt hacer callar. ~**cer** n (on gun and on car) silenciador m. ~**t** a silencioso; <film> mudo. **remain** ~**t** quedarse callado. ~**tly** adv silenciosamente

silhouette /sɪlu:'et/ n silueta f. ● vt. **be** ~**d** perfilarse (against contra)

silicon /'sɪlɪkən/ n silicio m. ~ **chip** n pastilla f de silicio

silk /sɪlk/ n seda f. ~**y** a (of silk) de seda; (like silk) sedoso

silly /'sɪlɪ/ a (-ier, -iest) tonto

silt /sɪlt/ n cieno m

silver /'sɪlvə(r)/ n plata f. ● a de plata. ~**-plated** a bañado en plata, plateado. ~**ware** /-weə(r)/ n platería f

simil|ar /'sɪmɪlə(r)/ a parecido, similar. ~**arity** /-'lærətɪ/ n parecido m. ~**arly** adv de igual manera. ~**e** /'sɪmɪlɪ/ n símil m

simmer /'sɪmə(r)/ vt/i hervir a fuego lento. □ ~ **down** vi calmarse

simpl|e /'sɪmpl/ a (-er, -est) sencillo, simple; <person> (humble) simple; (backward) simple. ~**e-minded** /-'maɪndɪd/ a ingenuo. ~**icity** /-'plɪsetɪ/ n simplicidad f, sencillez f. ~**ify** /'sɪmplɪfaɪ/ vt simplificar. ~**y** adv sencillamente, simplemente; (absolutely) realmente

simulate /'sɪmjʊleɪt/ vt simular

simultaneous /sɪml'teɪnɪəs/ a simultáneo. ~**ly** adv simultáneamente

sin /sɪn/ n pecado m. ● vi (pt sinned) pecar

since /sɪns/

● preposition

····▸ desde. **he's been living here** ~ **1991** vive aquí desde 1991. ~ **Christmas** desde Navidad. ~ **then** desde entonces. **I haven't been feeling well** ~ **Sunday** desde el domingo que no me siento bien. **how long is it** ~ **your interview?** ¿cuánto (tiempo) hace de la entrevista?

● adverb

····▸ desde entonces. **I haven't spoken to her** ~ no he hablado con ella desde entonces

● conjunction

····▸ desde que. **I haven't seen her** ~ **she left** no la he visto desde que se fue. ~ **coming to Manchester** desde que vine (or vino etc) a Manchester. **it's ten years** ~ **he died** hace diez años que se murió

····▸ (because) como, ya que. ~ **it was quite late, I decided to stay** como or ya que era bastante tarde, decidí quedarme

sincer|e /sɪn'sɪə(r)/ a sincero. ~**ely** adv sinceramente. **yours** ~**ely**, ~**ely (yours)** (in letters) (saluda) a usted atentamente. ~**ity** /-'serətɪ/ n sinceridad f

sinful /'sɪnfl/ a <person> pecador; <act> pecaminoso

sing /sɪŋ/ vt/i (pt **sang**, pp **sung**) cantar

singe /sɪndʒ/ vt (pres p **singeing**) chamuscar

singer /'sɪŋə(r)/ n cantante m & f

single /'sɪŋgl/ a solo; (not double) sencillo; <committee etc> soltero; <bed, room> individual, de una plaza (LAm); <ticket> de ida, sencillo. **not a** ~ **house** ni una sola casa. **every** ~ **day** todos los días sin excepción. ● n (ticket) billete m sencillo, boleto m de ida (LAm). □ ~ **out** vt escoger; (distinguish) distinguir. ~**-handed** /-'hæn dɪd/ a & adv sin ayuda. ~**s** npl (Sport) individuales mpl

singular /'sɪŋgjʊlə(r)/ n singular f. ● a singular; (unusual) raro; <noun> en singular

sinister /'sɪnɪstə(r)/ a siniestro

sink /sɪŋk/ vt (pt **sank**, pp **sunk**) hundir. ● vi hundirse. ● n fregadero m (Amer, in bathroom) lavabo m, lavamanos m. □ ~ **in** vi penetrar

sinner /'sɪnə(r)/ n pecador m

sip /sɪp/ n sorbo m. ● vt (pt **sipped**) sorber

siphon /'saɪfən/ n sifón m. ~ **(out)** sacar con sifón. □ ~ **off** vt desviar <money>

sir /sɜ:(r)/ n señor m. **S**~ n (title) sir m. **Dear S**~, (in letters) De mi mayor consideración:

siren /'saɪərən/ n sirena f

sister /'sɪstə(r)/ n hermana f; (nurse) enfermera f jefe. ~**-in-law** n (pl ~**s-in-law**) cuñada f

sit /sɪt/ vi (pt **sat**, pres p **sitting**) sentarse; <committee etc> reunirse en sesión. **be** ~**ting** estar sentado. ● vt sentar; hacer <exam>. □ ~ **back** vi (fig) relajarse. □ ~ **down** vi sentarse. **be** ~**ting down** estar sentado. □ ~ **up** vi (from lying) incorporarse; (straighten back) ponerse derecho. ~**-in** n (strike) encierro m, ocupación f

site /saɪt/ n emplazamiento m; (piece of land) terreno m; (archaeological) yacimiento m. **building** ~ n solar m. ● vt situar

sit: ~**ting** n sesión f; (in restaurant) turno m. ~**ting room** n sala f de estar, living m

situat|e /'sɪtjʊeɪt/ vt situar. ~**ion** /-'eɪʃn/ n situación f

six /sɪks/ a & n seis (m). ~**teen** /sɪk'sti:n/ a & n dieciséis (m). ~**teenth** a decimosexto. ● n dieciseisavo m. ~**th** a & n sexto (m). ~**tieth** /'sɪkstɪɪθ/ a sexagésimo. ● n sesentavo m. ~**ty** /'sɪkstɪ/ a & n sesenta (m)

size /saɪz/ n tamaño m; (of clothes) talla f; (of shoes) número m; (of problem, operation) magnitud f. **what** ~ **do you take?** (clothes) ¿qué talla tiene?; (shoes) ¿qué número calza?. □ ~ **up** vt 🔲 evaluar <problem>; calar <person>

sizzle /'sɪzl/ vi crepitar

skat|e /skeɪt/ n patín m. ● vi patinar. ~**eboard** n monopatín m, patineta f (Mex). ~**er** n patinador m. ~**ing** n patinaje m. ~**ing-rink** n pista f de patinaje

skeleton /'skelɪtn/ n esqueleto m. ~ **key** n llave f maestra

sketch /sketʃ/ n (drawing) dibujo m; (rougher) esbozo m; (TV, Theatre) sketch m. ● vt esbozar. ● vi dibujar. ~**y** a (**-ier**, **-iest**) incompleto

ski /ski:/ n (pl **skis**) esquí m. ● vi (pt **skied**, pres p **skiing**) esquiar. **go** ~**ing** ir a esquiar

skid /skɪd/ vi (pt **skidded**) patinar. ● n patinazo m

ski: ~**er** n esquiador m. ~**ing** n esquí m

skilful /'skɪlfl/ a diestro

ski-lift /'ski:lɪft/ n telesquí m

skill /skɪl/ n habilidad f; (technical) destreza f. ~**ed** a hábil; <worker> cualificado

skim /skɪm/ vt (pt **skimmed**) espumar <soup>; desnatar, descremar <milk>; (glide over) pasar casi rozando. ~ **milk** (Amer), ~**med milk** n leche f desnatada, leche f descremada. ~ **through** vt leer por encima

skimp /skɪmp/ vi. ~ **on sth** escatimar algo. ~**y** a (**-ier**, **-iest**) escaso; <skirt, dress> brevísimo

skin /skɪn/ n piel f. ● vt (pt **skinned**) despellejar. ~**-deep** a superficial. ~**-diving** n submarinismo m. ~**ny** a (**-ier**, **-iest**) flaco

skip /skɪp/ vi (pt **skipped**) vi saltar; (with rope) saltar a la comba, saltar a la cuerda. ● *vt* saltarse *<chapter>*; faltar a *<class>*. ● *n* brinco *m*; (container) contenedor *m* (*para escombros*). ∼**per** *n* capitán *m*. ∼**ping-rope**, ∼**rope** (Amer) *n* comba *f*, cuerda *f* de saltar, reata *f* (Mex)

skirmish /'skɜ:mɪʃ/ *n* escaramuza *f*

skirt /skɜ:t/ *n* falda *f*. ● *vt* bordear; (go round) ladear. ∼**ing-board** *n* rodapié *m*, zócalo *m*

skittle /'skɪtl/ *n* bolo *m*

skive off /skaɪv/ (*vi* 🄻, disappear) escurrir el bulto; (stay away from work) no ir a trabajar

skulk /skʌlk/ *vi* (hide) esconderse. ∼ **around** *vi* merodear

skull /skʌl/ *n* cráneo *m*; (remains) calavera *f*

sky /skaɪ/ *n* cielo *m*. ∼**lark** *n* alondra *f*. ∼**light** *n* tragaluz *m*. ∼**scraper** *n* rascacielos *m*

slab /slæb/ *n* (of concrete) bloque *m*; (of stone) losa *f*

slack /slæk/ *a* (**-er**, **-est**) flojo; *<person>* poco aplicado; *<period>* de poca actividad. ● *vi* flojear. ∼**en** *vt* aflojar. ● *vi* <person> descansar. ◻ ∼**en off** *vt/i* aflojar

slain /sleɪn/ ⇒SLAY

slake /sleɪk/ *vt* apagar

slam /slæm/ *vt* (*pt* **slammed**). ∼ **the door** dar un portazo. ∼ **the door shut** cerrar de un portazo. ∼ **on the brakes** pegar un frenazo; (🅇, criticize) atacar violentamente. ● *vi* cerrarse de un portazo

slander /'slɑːndə(r)/ *n* calumnia *f*. ● *vt* difamar

slang /slæŋ/ *n* argot *m*

slant /slɑːnt/ *vt* inclinar. ● *n* inclinación *f*

slap /slæp/ *vt* (*pt* **slapped**) (on face) pegarle una bofetada a; (put) tirar. ∼ **s.o. on the back** darle una palmada a uno en la espalda ● *n* bofetada *f*; (on back) palmada *f*. ● *adv* de lleno. ∼**dash** *a* descuidado; *<work>* chapucero

slash /slæʃ/ *vt* acuchillar; (fig) rebajar drásticamente. ● *n* cuchillada *f*

slat /slæt/ *n* tablilla *f*

slate /sleɪt/ *n* pizarra *f*. ● *vt* 🅇 poner por los suelos

slaughter /'slɔːtə(r)/ *vt* matar salvajemente; matar *<animal>*. ● *n* carnicería *f*; (of animals) matanza *f*

slave /sleɪv/ *n* esclavo *m*. ● *vi* ∼ (**away**) trabajar como un negro. ∼**-driver** *n* 🅇 negrero *m*. ∼**ry** /-ərɪ/ *n* esclavitud *f*

slay /sleɪ/ *vt* (*pt* **slew**, *pp* **slain**) dar muerte a

sleazy /'sliːzɪ/ *a* (**-ier**, **-iest**) 🅇 sórdido

sled /sled/ (Amer), **sledge** /sledʒ/ *n* trineo *m*

sledge-hammer *n* mazo *m*, almádena *f*

sleek /sliːk/ *a* (**-er**, **-est**) liso, brillante

sleep /sliːp/ *n* sueño *m*. go to ∼ dormirse. ● *vi* (*pt* **slept**) dormir. ● *vt* poder alojar. ∼**er** *n* (on track) traviesa *f*, durmiente *m*. be a **light/ heavy** ∼**er** tener el sueño ligero/pesado. ∼**ing bag** *n* saco *m* de dormir. ∼**ing pill** *n* somnífero *m*. ∼**less** *a*. have a ∼**less night** pasar la noche en blanco. ∼**walk** *vi* caminar dormido. ∼**y** *a* (**-ier**, **-iest**) soñoliento. be/feel ∼**y** tener sueño

sleet /sliːt/ *n* aguanieve *f*

sleeve /sliːv/ *n* manga *f*; (for record) funda *f*, carátula *f*. up one's ∼ en reserva. ∼**less** *a* sin mangas

sleigh /sleɪ/ *n* trineo *m*

slender /'slendə(r)/ *a* delgado; (fig) escaso

slept /slept/ ⇒SLEEP

slew /sluː/ ⇒SLAY

slice /slaɪs/ *n* (of ham) lonja *f*; (of bread) rebanada *f*; (of meat) tajada *f*; (of cheese) trozo *m*; (of sth round) rodaja *f*. ● *vt* cortar (en rebanadas, tajadas etc)

slick /slɪk/ *a* *<performance>* muy pulido. ● *n*. (oil) ∼ marea *f* negra

slid|e /slaɪd/ *vt* (*pt* **slid**) deslizar. ● *vi* (intentionally) deslizarse; (unintentionally) resbalarse. ● *n* resbalón *m*; (in playground) tobogán *m*, resbaladilla *f* (Mex); (for hair) pasador *m*, broche *m* (Mex); (Photo) diapositiva *f*. ∼**ing scale** *n* escala *f* móvil

slight /slaɪt/ a (**-er**, **-est**) ligero; (slender) delgado. ● vt desairar. ● n desaire m. ∼**est** a mínimo. **not in the** ∼**est** en absoluto. ∼**ly** adv un poco, ligeramente

slim /slɪm/ a (**slimmer**, **slimmest**) delgado. ● vi (pt **slimmed**) (become slimmer) adelgazar; (diet) hacer régimen

slim|e /slaɪm/ n limo m; (of snail, 🗵ug) baba f. ∼**y** a viscoso; (fig) excesivamente obsequioso

sling /slɪŋ/ n (Med) cabestrillo m. ● vt (pt **slung**) lanzar

slip /slɪp/ vt (pt **slipped**) deslizar. ∼ **s.o.'s mind** olvidársele a uno. ● vi resbalarse. **it** ∼**ped out of my hands** se me resbaló de las manos. **he** ∼**ped out the back door** se deslizó por la puerta trasera ● n resbalón m; (mistake) error m; (petticoat) combinación f; (paper) trozo m. **give s.o. the** ∼ lograr zafarse de uno. ∼ **of the tongue** n lapsus m linguae. ▢ ∼ **away** vi escabullirse. ▢ ∼ **up** vi 🆃 equivocarse

slipper /'slɪpə(r)/ n zapatilla f

slippery /'slɪpərɪ/ a resbaladizo

slip: ∼ **road** n rampa f de acceso. ∼**shod** /'slɪpʃɒd/ a descuidado. ∼**up** n 🆃 error m

slit /slɪt/ n raja f; (cut) corte m. ● vt (pt **slit**, pres p **slitting**) rajar; (cut) cortar

slither /'slɪðə(r)/ vi deslizarse

slobber /'slɒbə(r)/ vi babear

slog /slɒg/ vt (pt **slogged**) golpear. ● vi caminar trabajosamente. ● n golpetazo m; (hard work) trabajo m penoso. ▢ ∼ **away** vi sudar tinta 🆃

slogan /'sləʊgən/ n eslogan m

slop /slɒp/ vt (pt **slopped**) derramar. ● vi derramarse

slop|e /sləʊp/ vi inclinarse. ● vt inclinar. ● n declive m, pendiente f. ∼**ing** a inclinado

sloppy /'slɒpɪ/ a (**-ier**, **-iest**) <work> descuidado; <person> desaliñado

slosh /slɒʃ/ vi 🆃 chapotear

slot /slɒt/ n ranura f. ● vt (pt **slotted**) encajar

slot-machine n distribuidor m automático; (for gambling) máquina f tragamonedas

slouch /slaʊtʃ/ vi andar cargado de espaldas; (in chair) repanchigarse

Slovak /'sləʊvæk/ a & n eslovaco (m). ∼**ia** n Eslovaquia f

slovenly /'slʌvnlɪ/ a <work> descuidado; <person> desaliñado

slow /sləʊ/ a (**-er**, **-est**) lento. **be** ∼ <clock> estar atrasado. **in** ∼ **motion** a cámara lenta. ● adv despacio. ● vt retardar. ● vi ir más despacio. ▢ ∼ **down**, ∼ **up** vt retardar. vi ir más despacio. ∼**ly** adv despacio, lentamente

sludge /slʌdʒ/ n fango m

slug /slʌg/ n babosa f. ∼**gish** a lento

slum /slʌm/ n barrio m bajo

slumber /'slʌmbə(r)/ vi dormir

slump /slʌmp/ n baja f repentina; (in business) depresión f. ● vi bajar repentinamente; (collapse) desplomarse

slung /slʌŋ/ ⇒SLING

slur /slɜː(r)/ vt (pt **slurred**). ∼ **one's words** arrastrar las palabras. ● n. **a racist** ∼ un comentario racista

slush /slʌʃ/ n nieve f medio derretida

sly /slaɪ/ a (**slyer**, **slyest**) (crafty) astuto. ● n. **on the** ∼ a hurtadillas. ∼**ly** adv astutamente

smack /smæk/ n manotazo m. ● adv 🆃 ∼ **in the middle** justo en el medio. **he went** ∼ **into a tree** se dio contra un árbol. ● vt pegarle a (con la mano)

small /smɔːl/ a (**-er**, **-est**) pequeño, chico (LAm). ● n. **the** ∼ **of the back** la región lumbar. ∼ **ads** npl anuncios mpl (clasificados), avisos mpl (clasificados) (LAm). ∼ **change** n suelto m. ∼**pox** /-pɒks/ n viruela f. ∼ **talk** n charla f sobre temas triviales

smart /smɑːt/ a (**-er**, **-est**) elegante; (clever) listo; (brisk) rápido. ● vi escocer. ▢ ∼**en up** vt arreglar. vi <person> mejorar su aspecto, arreglarse. ∼**ly** adv elegantemente; (quickly) rápidamente

smash /smæʃ/ vt romper; (into little pieces) hacer pedazos; batir <record>. ● vi romperse; (collide) chocar (**into**

con). ● *n* (noise) estrépito *m*; (collision) choque *m*; (in sport) smash *m*. □ ~ **up** *vt* destrozar. ~**ing** *a* 🔲 estupendo

smattering /'smætərɪŋ/ *n* nociones *fpl*

smear /smɪə(r)/ *vt* untar (**with** de); (stain) manchar (**with** de); (fig) difamar. ● *n* mancha *f*

smell /smel/ *n* olor *m*; (sense) olfato *m*. ● *vt* (*pt* **smelt**) oler; *<animal>* olfatear. ● *vi* oler. ~ **of** sth oler a algo. ~**y** *a* maloliente. be ~**y** oler mal

smelt /smelt/ ⇒SMELL. ● *vt* fundir

smile /smaɪl/ *n* sonrisa *f*. ● *vi* sonreír. ~ **at** s.o. sonreírle a uno

smirk /smɜːk/ *n* sonrisita *f* (*de suficiencia etc*)

smith /smɪθ/ *n* herrero *m*

smithereens /smɪðə'riːnz/ *npl*. smash sth to ~ hacer algo añicos

smock /smɒk/ *n* blusa *f*, bata *f*

smog /smɒg/ *n* smog *m*

smok|e /sməʊk/ *n* humo *m*. ● *vt* fumar *<tobacco>*; ahumar *<food>*. ● *vi* fumar. ~**eless** *a* que arde sin humo. ~**er** *n* fumador *m*. ~**y** *a* <*room*> lleno de humo

smooth /smuːð/ *a* (**-er**, **-est**) *<texture/stone>* liso; *<skin>* suave; *<movement>* suave; *<sea>* tranquilo. ● *vt* alisar. □ ~ **out** *vt* allanar *<problems>*. ~**ly** *adv* suavemente; (without problems) sin problemas

smother /'smʌðə(r)/ *vt* asfixiar *<person>*. ~ s.o. with kisses cubrir a uno de besos

smoulder /'sməʊldə(r)/ *vi* arder sin llama

smudge /smʌdʒ/ *n* borrón *m*. ● *vi* tiznarse

smug /smʌg/ *a* (**smugger, smuggest**) pagado de sí mismo; *<expression>* de suficiencia

smuggl|e /'smʌgl/ *vt* pasar de contrabando. ~**er** *n* contrabandista *m & f*. ~**ing** *n* contrabando *m*

snack /snæk/ *n* tentempié *m*. ~ **bar** *n* cafetería *f*

snag /snæg/ *n* problema *m*

snail /sneɪl/ *n* caracol *m*. at a ~'s pace a paso de tortuga

snake /sneɪk/ *n* culebra *f*, serpiente *f*

snap /snæp/ *vt* (*pt* **snapped**) (break) romper. ~ one's fingers chasquear los dedos. ● *vi* romperse; *<dog>* intentar morder; (say) contestar bruscamente. ~ **at** *<dog>* intentar morder; (say) contestar bruscamente. ● *n* chasquido *m*; (Photo) foto *f*. ● *a* instantáneo. □ ~ **up** *vt* no dejar escapar *<offer>*. ~**py** *a* (**-ier, -iest**) 🔲 rápido. make it ~**py**! ¡date prisa! ~**shot** *n* foto *f*

snare /sneə(r)/ *n* trampa *f*

snarl /snɑːl/ *vi* gruñir

snatch /snætʃ/ *vt*. ~ sth from s.o. arrebatarle algo a uno; (steal) robar. ● *n* (short part) fragmento *m*

sneak /sniːk/ *n* soplón *m*. ● *vi* (*past & pp* **sneaked** *or* 🔲 **snuck**) ~ **in** entrar a hurtadillas. ~ **off** escabullirse. ~**ers** /'sniːkəz/ *npl* zapatillas *fpl* de deporte. ~**y** *a* artero

sneer /snɪə(r)/ *n* expresión *f* desdeñosa. ● *vi* hacer una mueca de desprecio. ~ **at** hablar con desprecio a

sneeze /sniːz/ *n* estornudo *m*. ● *vi* estornudar

snide /snaɪd/ *a* insidioso

sniff /snɪf/ *vt* oler. ● *vi* sorberse la nariz

snigger /'snɪgə(r)/ *n* risilla *f*. ● *vi* reírse (*por lo bajo*)

snip /snɪp/ *vt* (*pt* **snipped**) dar un tijeretazo a. ● *n* tijeretazo *m*

sniper /'snaɪpə(r)/ *n* francotirador *m*

snippet /'snɪpɪt/ *n* (of conversation) trozo *m*. ~s of information datos *mpl* aislados

snivel /'snɪvl/ *vi* (*pt* **snivelled**) lloriquear

snob /snɒb/ *n* esnob *m & f*. ~**bery** *n* esnobismo *m*. ~**bish** *a* esnob

snooker /'snuːkə(r)/ *n* snooker *m*

snoop /snuːp/ *vi* 🔲 husmear

snooze /snuːz/ *n* sueñecito *m*. ● *vi* dormitar

snore /snɔː(r)/ *n* ronquido *m*. ● *vi* roncar

snorkel /'snɔːkl/ *n* esnórkel *m*

snort /snɔːt/ *n* bufido *m*. ● *vi* bufar

snout /snaʊt/ n hocico m

snow /snəʊ/ n nieve f. ● vi nevar. **be ~ed in** estar aislado por la nieve. **be ~ed under with work** estar agobiado de trabajo. **~ball** n bola f de nieve. **~drift** n nieve f amontonada. **~fall** n nevada f. **~flake** n copo m de nieve. **~man** n muñeco m de nieve. **~plough** n quitanieves m. **~storm** n tormenta f de nieve. **~y** a <day, weather> nevoso; <landscape> nevado

snub /snʌb/ vt (pt snubbed) desairar. ● n desaire m. **~-nosed** a chato

snuck /snʌk/ ⇒SNEAK

snuff out /snʌf/ vt apagar <candle>

snug /snʌg/ a (snugger, snuggest) cómodo; (tight) ajustado

snuggle (up) /'snʌgl/ vi acurrucarse

so /səʊ/ adv (before a or adv) tan; (thus) así. ● conj (therefore) así que. **~ am I** yo también. **~ as to** para. **~ far** adv (time) hasta ahora. **~ far as I know** que yo sepa. **~ long!** ¡hasta luego! **and ~ on, and ~ forth** etcétera (etcétera). **I think ~** creo que sí. **or ~** más o menos **~ that** conj para que.

soak /səʊk/ vt remojar. ● vi remojarse. □ **~ in** vi penetrar. □ **~ up** vt absorber. **~ing** a empapado.

so-and-so /'səʊənsəʊ/ n fulano m

soap /səʊp/ n jabón m. ● vt enjabonar. **~ opera** n telenovela f, culebrón m. **~ powder** n jabón m en polvo. **~y** a jabonoso

soar /sɔː(r)/ vi <bird/plane> planear; (rise) elevarse; <price> dispararse. **~ing** a <inflation> galopante

sob /sɒb/ n sollozo m. ● vi (pt sobbed) sollozar

sober /'səʊbə(r)/ a (not drunk) sobrio

so-called /'səʊkɔːld/ a llamado; (pej) supuesto

soccer /'sɒkə(r)/ n fútbol m, futbol m (Mex)

sociable /'səʊʃəbl/ a sociable

social /'səʊʃl/ a social; (sociable) sociable. **~ism** n socialismo m. **~ist** a & n socialista (m & f). **~ize** vt socializar. **~ security** n seguridad f

social. **~ worker** n asistente m social

society /sə'saɪətɪ/ n sociedad f

sociolog|ical /səʊsɪə'lɒdʒɪkl/ a sociológico. **~ist** /-'ɒlədʒɪst/ n sociólogo m. **~y** /-'ɒlədʒɪ/ n sociología f

sock /sɒk/ n calcetín m

socket /'sɒkɪt/ n (of joint) hueco m; (of eye) cuenca f; (wall plug) enchufe m; (for bulb) portalámparas m

soda /'səʊdə/ n soda f. **~-water** n soda f

sodium /'səʊdɪəm/ n sodio m

sofa /'səʊfə/ n sofá m

soft /sɒft/ a (-er, -est) blando; <light, colour> suave; (gentle) dulce, tierno; (not strict) blando. **~ drink** n refresco m. **~en** /'sɒfn/ vt ablandar; suavizar <skin>. ● vi ablandarse. **~ly** adv dulcemente; <speak> bajito. **~ware** /-weə(r)/ n software m

soggy /'sɒgɪ/ a (-ier, -iest) empapado

soil /sɔɪl/ n tierra f; (Amer, dirt) suciedad f. ● vt ensuciar

solar /'səʊlə(r)/ a solar

sold /səʊld/ ⇒SELL

solder /'sɒldə(r)/ vt soldar

soldier /'səʊldʒə(r)/ n soldado m. □ **~ on** vi 🖅 seguir al pie del cañón

sole /səʊl/ n (of foot) planta f; (of shoe) suela f. ● a único, solo. **~ly** adv únicamente

solemn /'sɒləm/ a solemne

solicitor /sə'lɪsɪtə(r)/ n abogado m; (notary) notario m

solid /'sɒlɪd/ a sólido; <gold etc> macizo; (unanimous) unánime; <meal> sustancioso. ● n sólido m. **~s** npl alimentos mpl sólidos. **~arity** /sɒlɪ'dærətɪ/ n solidaridad f. **~ify** /sə'lɪdɪfaɪ/ vi solidificarse

solitary /'sɒlɪtrɪ/ a solitario

solitude /'sɒlɪtjuːd/ n soledad f

solo /'səʊləʊ/ n (pl -os) (Mus) solo m. **~ist** n solista m & f

solstice /'sɒlstɪs/ n solsticio m

solu|ble /'sɒljʊbl/ a soluble. **~tion** /sə'luːʃn/ n solución f

solve /sɒlv/ vt solucionar <problem>; resolver <mystery>. **~nt** /-vənt/ a & n solvente (m)

sombre /'sɒmbə(r)/ *a* sombrío

some /sʌm/, *unstressed form* /səm/

● *adjective*

····▸ (unspecified number) unos, unas. **he ate ~ olives** comió unas aceitunas

····▸ (unspecified amount) *not translated*. **I have to buy ~ bread** tengo que comprar pan. **would you like ~ coffee?** ¿quieres café?

····▸ (certain, not all) algunos, -nas. **I like ~ modern writers** algunos escritores modernos me gustan

····▸ (a little) algo de. **I eat ~ meat, but not much** como algo de carne, pero no mucho

····▸ (considerable amount of) **we've known each other for ~ time** ya hace tiempo que nos conocemos

····▸ (expressing admiration) **that's ~ car you've got!** ¡vaya coche que tienes!

● *pronoun*

····▸ (a number of things or people) algunos, -nas, unos, unas. **~ are mine and ~ aren't** algunos *or* unos son míos y otros no. **aren't there any apples? we bought ~ yesterday** ¿no hay manzanas? compramos algunas ayer

····▸ (part of an amount) **he wants ~** quiere un poco. **~ of what he said** parte *or* algo de lo que dijo

····▸ (certain people) algunos, -nas . **~ say that...** algunos dicen que...

● *adverb*

····▸ (approximately) unos, unas, alrededor de. **there were ~ fifty people there** había unas cincuenta personas, había alrededor de cincuenta personas

some: **~body** /-bədɪ/ *pron* alguien. **~how** *adv* de algún modo. **~how or other** de una manera u otra. **~one** *pron* alguien

somersault /'sʌməsɔːlt/ *n* salto *m* mortal. ● *vi* dar un salto mortal

some: **~thing** *pron* algo *m*. **~thing like** (approximately) alrededor de. **~time** *a* ex. ● *adv* algún día. **~time next week** un día de la semana que viene. **~times** *adv* a veces. **~where** *adv* en alguna parte, en algún lado

son /sʌn/ *n* hijo *m*

sonata /sə'nɑːtə/ *n* sonata *f*

song /sɒŋ/ *n* canción *f*

sonic /'sɒnɪk/ *a* sónico

son-in-law /'sʌnɪnlɔː/ *n* (*pl* **sons-in-law**) yerno *m*

sonnet /'sɒnɪt/ *n* soneto *m*

son of a bitch *n* (*pl* **sons of bitches**) (esp Amer 🅧) hijo *m* de puta

soon /suːn/ *adv* (**-er, -est**) pronto; (in a short time) dentro de poco. **~ after** poco después. **~er or later** tarde o temprano. **as ~ as** en cuanto; **as ~ as possible** lo antes posible. **the ~er the better** cuanto antes mejor

soot /sʊt/ *n* hollín *m*

sooth|e /suːð/ *vt* calmar; aliviar *<pain>*. **~ing** *a* *<medicine>* calmante; *<words>* tranquilizador

sooty /'sʊtɪ/ *a* cubierto de hollín

sophisticated /sə'fɪstɪkeɪtɪd/ *a* sofisticado; (complex) complejo

sophomore /'sɒfəmɔː(r)/ *n* (Amer) estudiante *m* & *f* de segundo curso (*en la universidad*)

sopping /'sɒpɪŋ/ *a*. **~ (wet)** empapado

soppy /'sɒpɪ/ *a* (**-ier, -iest**) 🄸 sentimental

soprano /sə'prɑːnəʊ/ *n* (*pl* **-os**) soprano *f*

sordid /'sɔːdɪd/ *a* sórdido

sore /'sɔː(r)/ *a* (**-er, -est**) dolorido; (Amer 🄸, angry) **be ~ at s.o.** estar picado con uno. **~ throat** *n* dolor *m* de garganta. **I've got a ~ throat** me duele la garganta. ● *n* llaga *f*.

sorrow /'sɒrəʊ/ *n* pena *f*, pesar *m*

sorry /'sɒrɪ/ *a* (**-ier, -ier**) arrepentido; (wretched) lamentable. **I'm ~** lo siento. **be ~ for s.o.** (pity) compadecer a uno. **I'm ~ you can't come** siento que no puedas venir. **say ~** pedir perdón. **~!** (apologizing) ¡lo siento! ¡perdón!. **~?** (asking s.o. to repeat) ¿cómo?

sort /sɔːt/ *n* tipo *m*, clase *f*; (🄸, person) tipo *m*. **a ~ of** una especie de. ● *vt* clasificar. □ **~ out** *vt* (organize) ordenar; organizar *<finances>*; (separate out) separar; solucionar *<problem>*

so-so /'səʊsəʊ/ *a* regular

soufflé /'suːfleɪ/ n suflé m

sought /sɔːt/ ⇨SEEK

soul /səʊl/ n alma f

sound /saʊnd/ n sonido m; (noise) ruido m. ● vt tocar. ● vi sonar; (seem) parecer (as if que). it ~s interesting suena interesante.. ● a (-er, -est) sano; <argument> lógico; (secure) seguro. ● adv. ~ asleep profundamente dormido. ~ barrier n barrera f del sonido. ~ly adv sólidamente; (asleep) profundamente. ~proof a insonorizado. ~track n banda f sonora

soup /suːp/ n sopa f

sour /'saʊə(r)/ a (-er, -est) agrio; <milk> cortado

source /sɔːs/ n fuente f

south /saʊθ/ n sur m. ● a sur a invar; <wind> del sur. ● adv <go> hacia el sur. it's ~ of está al sur de. S~ Africa n Sudáfrica f. S~ America n América f (del Sur), Sudamérica f. S~ American a & n sudamericano (m). ~-east n sudeste m, sureste m. ~erly /'sʌðəlɪ/ <wind> del sur. ~ern /'sʌðən/ a del sur, meridional. ~erner n sureño m. ~ward /-wəd/, ~wards adv hacia el sur. ~-west n sudoeste m, suroeste m

souvenir /suːvə'nɪə(r)/ n recuerdo m

sovereign /'sɒvrɪn/ n & a soberano (m)

Soviet /'səʊvɪət/ a (History) soviético. the ~ Union n la Unión f Soviética

sow[1] /səʊ/ vt (pt sowed, pp sowed or sown /səʊn/) sembrar

sow[2] /saʊ/ n cerda f

soy (esp Amer), **soya** /'sɔɪə/ n. ~ bean n soja f

spa /spɑː/ n balneario m

space /speɪs/ n espacio m; (room) espacio m, lugar m. ● a <research etc> espacial. ● vt espaciar. □ ~ out vt espaciar. ~craft, ~ship n nave f espacial

spacious /'speɪʃəs/ a espacioso

spade /speɪd/ n pala f. ~s npl (Cards) picas fpl

spaghetti /spə'getɪ/ n espaguetis mpl

Spain /speɪn/ n España f

span /spæn/ n (of arch) luz f; (of time) espacio m; (of wings) envergadura f. ● vt (pt spanned) extenderse sobre. ● a ⇨SPICK

Spaniard /'spænjəd/ n español m

spaniel /'spænjəl/ n spaniel m

Spanish /'spænɪʃ/ a español; (Lang) castellano, español. ● n (Lang) castellano m, español m. npl. the ~ (people) los españoles

spank /spæŋk/ vt pegarle a (en las nalgas)

spanner /'spænə(r)/ n llave f

spare /speə(r)/ vt. if you can ~ the time si tienes tiempo. can you ~ me a pound? ¿tienes una libra que me des? ~ no effort no escatimar esfuerzos. have money to ~ tener dinero de sobra. ● a (not in use) de más; (replacement) de repuesto; (free) libre. ~ (part) n repuesto m. ~ room n cuarto m de huéspedes. ~ time n tiempo m libre. ~ tyre n neumático m de repuesto

sparingly /'speərɪŋlɪ/ adv <use> con moderación

spark /spɑːk/ n chispa f. ● vt provocar <criticism>; suscitar <interest>. ~ing plug n (Auto) bujía f

sparkl|e /'spɑːkl/ vi centellear. ● n destello m. ~ing a centelleante; <wine> espumoso

spark plug n (Auto) bujía f

sparrow /'spærəʊ/ n gorrión m

sparse /spɑːs/ a escaso. ~ly adv escasamente

spasm /'spæzəm/ n espasmo m; (of cough) acceso m. ~odic /-'mɒdɪk/ a espasmódico; (Med) irregular

spat /spæt/ ⇨SPIT

spate /speɪt/ n racha f

spatial /'speɪʃl/ a espacial

spatter /'spætə(r)/ vt salpicar (with de)

spawn /spɔːn/ n huevas fpl. ● vt generar. ● vi desovar

speak /spiːk/ vt/i (pt spoke, pp spoken) hablar. ~ for s.o. hablar en nombre de uno. □ ~ up vi hablar más fuerte. ~er n (in public) orador m; (loudspeaker) altavoz m; (of language) hablante m & f

spear /spɪə(r)/ n lanza f. ~**head** vt (lead) encabezar

special /'speʃl/ a especial. ~**ist** /'speʃəlɪst/ n especialista m & f. ~**ity** /-ɪ'rælətɪ/ n especialidad f. ~**ization** /-əlaɪ'zeɪʃn/ n especialización f. ~**ize** /-əlaɪz/ vi especializarse. ~**ized** a especializado. ~**ly** adv especialmente. ~**ty** n (Amer) especialidad f

species /'spiːʃiːz/ n especie f

specif|ic /spə'sɪfɪk/ a específico. ~**ically** adv específicamente; <state> explícitamente. ~**ication** /-ɪ'keɪʃn/ n especificación f. ~**y** /'spesɪfaɪ/ vt especificar

specimen /'spesɪmɪn/ n muestra f

speck /spek/ n (of dust) mota f; (in distance) punto m

specs /speks/ npl ⚏ ⇒SPECTACLES

spectac|le /'spektəkl/ n espectáculo m. ~**les** npl gafas fpl, lentes fpl (LAm), anteojos mpl (LAm). ~**ular** /-'tækjʊlə(r)/ a espectacular

spectator /spek'teɪtə(r)/ n espectador m

spectr|e /'spektə(r)/ n espectro m. ~**um** /'spektrəm/ n (pl **-tra** /-trə/) espectro m; (of views) gama f

speculat|e /'spekjʊleɪt/ vi especular. ~**ion** /-'leɪʃn/ n especulación f. ~**or** n especulador m

sped /sped/ ⇒SPEED

speech /spiːtʃ/ n (faculty) habla f; (address) discurso m. ~**less** a mudo

speed /spiːd/ n velocidad f; (rapidity) rapidez f. ● vi (pt **speeded**) (drive too fast) ir a exceso de velocidad. □ ~ **off,** ~ **away** (pt **sped**) vi alejarse a toda velocidad. □ ~ **by** (pt **sped**) vi <time> pasar volando. □ ~ **up** (pt **speeded**) vt acelerar. vi acelerarse. ~**boat** n lancha f motora. ~ **limit** n velocidad f máxima. ~**ometer** /spiː'dɒmɪtə(r)/ n velocímetro m. ~**way** n (Amer) autopista f. ~**y** a (**-ier, -iest**) rápido

spell /spel/ n (magic) hechizo m; (of weather, activity) período m. **go through a bad** ~ pasar por una mala racha. ● vt/i (pt **spelled** or **spelt**) escribir. □ ~ **out** vt deletrear; (fig) explicar. ~**ing** n ortografía f

spellbound /'spelbaʊnd/ a embelesado

spelt /spelt/ ⇒SPELL

spend /spend/ vt (pt **spent** /spent/) gastar <money>; pasar <time>; dedicar <care>. ● vi gastar dinero

sperm /spɜːm/ n (pl **sperms** or **sperm**) esperma f; (individual) espermatozoide m

spew /spjuː/ vt/i vomitar

spher|e /sfɪə(r)/ n esfera f. ~**ical** /'sferɪkl/ a esférico

spice /spaɪs/ n especia f

spick /spɪk/ a. ~ **and span** limpio y ordenado

spicy /'spaɪsɪ/ a picante

spider /'spaɪdə(r)/ n araña f

spik|e /spaɪk/ n (of metal etc) punta f. ~**y** a puntiagudo

spill /spɪl/ vt (pt **spilled** or **spilt**) derramar. ● vi derramarse. ~ **over** vi <container> desbordarse; <liquid> rebosar

spin /spɪn/ vt (pt **spun**, pres p **spinning**) hacer girar; hilar <wool>; centrifugar <washing>. ● vi girar. ● n. **give sth a** ~ hacer girar algo. **go for a** ~ (Auto) ir a dar un paseo en coche

spinach /'spɪnɪdʒ/ n espinacas fpl

spindly /'spɪndlɪ/ a larguirucho

spin-drier /spɪn'draɪə(r)/ n centrifugadora f (de ropa)

spine /spaɪn/ n columna f vertebral; (of book) lomo m; (on animal) púa f. ~**less** a (fig) sin carácter

spinning wheel /'spɪnɪŋ/ n rueca f

spin-off /'spɪnɒf/ n resultado m indirecto; (by-product) producto m derivado

spinster /'spɪnstə(r)/ n soltera f

spiral /'spaɪərəl/ a espiral; <shape> de espiral. ● n espiral f. ● vi (pt **spiralled**) <unemployment> escalar; <prices> dispararse. ~ **staircase** n escalera f de caracol

spire /spaɪə(r)/ n aguja f

spirit /'spɪrɪt/ n espíritu m. **be in good** ~s estar animado. **in low** ~s abatido. ~**ed** a animado, fogoso. ~**s** npl (drinks) bebidas fpl alcohólicas (de *alta graduación).* ~**ual** /'spɪrɪtjʊəl/ *a* espiritual

spit /spɪt/ *vt* (*pt* **spat** *or* (Amer) **spit**, *pres p* **spitting**) escupir. ● *vi* escupir. **it's** ~**ting** caen algunas gotas. ● *n* saliva *f*; (for roasting) asador *m*

spite /spaɪt/ *n* rencor *m*. **in** ~ **of** a pesar de. ● *vt* fastidiar. ~**ful** *a* rencoroso

spittle /'spɪtl/ *n* baba *f*

splash /splæʃ/ *vt* salpicar. ● *vi* <*person*> chapotear. ● *n* salpicadura *f*. **a** ~ **of paint** un poco de pintura. □ ~ **about** *vi* chapotear. □ ~ **down** *vi* <*spacecraft*> amerizar. □ ~ **out** *vi* gastarse un dineral (**on** en)

splend|id /'splendɪd/ *a* espléndido. ~**our** /-ə(r)/ *n* esplendor *m*

splint /splɪnt/ *n* tablilla *f*

splinter /'splɪntə(r)/ *n* astilla *f*. ● *vi* astillarse

split /splɪt/ *vt* (*pt* **split**, *pres p* **splitting**) partir; fisionar <*atom*>; reventar <*trousers*>; (divide) dividir. ● *vi* partirse; (divide) dividirse. **a** ~**ting headache** un dolor de cabeza espantoso. ● *n* (in garment) descosido *m*; (in wood, glass) rajadura *f*. □ ~ **up** *vi* separarse. ~ **second** *n* fracción *f* de segundo

splutter /'splʌtə(r)/ *vi* chisporrotear; <*person*> farfullar

spoil /spɔɪl/ *vt* (*pt* **spoilt** *or* **spoiled**) estropear, echar a perder; (indulge) consentir, malcriar. ~**s** *npl* botín *m*. ~**-sport** *n* aguafiestas *m* & *f*

spoke[1] /spəʊk/ ⇒SPEAK

spoke[2] /spəʊk/ *n* (of wheel) rayo *m*

spoken /spəʊkən/ ⇒SPEAK

spokesman /'spəʊksmən/ *n* (*pl* **-men**) portavoz *m*

sponge /spʌndʒ/ *n* esponja *f*. ● *vt* limpiar con una esponja. ~ **off**, ~ **on** *vt* vivir a costillas de. ~ **cake** *n* bizcocho *m*

sponsor /'spɒnsə(r)/ *n* patrocinador *m*; (of the arts) mecenas *m* & *f*; (surety) garante *m*. ● *vt* patrocinar. ~**ship** *n* patrocinio *m*; (of the arts) mecenazgo *m*

spontaneous /spɒn'teɪnɪəs/ *a* espontáneo. ~**ously** *adv* espontáneamente

spoof /spuːf/ *n* Ⓘ parodia *f*

spooky /'spuːkɪ/ *a* (**-ier**, **-iest**) Ⓘ espeluznante

spool /spuːl/ *n* carrete *m*

spoon /spuːn/ *n* cuchara *f*. ~**ful** *n* cucharada *f*

sporadic /spə'rædɪk/ *a* esporádico

sport /spɔːt/ *n* deporte *m*. ~**s car** *n* coche *m* deportivo. ~**s centre** *n* centro *m* deportivo. ~**sman** /-mən/ *n*, (*pl* **-men**), ~**swoman** *n* deportista *m* & *f*

spot /spɒt/ *n* mancha *f*; (pimple) grano *m*; (place) lugar *m*; (in pattern) lunar *m*. **be in a** ~ Ⓘ estar en apuros. **on the** ~ allí mismo; <*decide*> en ese mismo momento. ● *vt* (*pt* **spotted**) manchar; (Ⓘ, notice) ver, divisar; descubrir <*mistake*>. ~ **check** *n* control *m* hecho al azar. ~**less** *a* <*clothes*> impecable; <*house*> limpísimo. ~**light** *n* reflector *m*; (in theatre) foco *m*. ~**ted** *a* moteado; <*material*> de lunares. ~**ty** *a* (**-ier**, **-iest**) <*skin*> lleno de granos; <*youth*> con la cara llena de granos

spouse /spaʊz/ *n* cónyuge *m* & *f*

spout /spaʊt/ *n* pico *m*; (jet) chorro *m*

sprain /spreɪn/ *vt* hacerse un esguince en. ● *n* esguince *m*

sprang /spræŋ/ ⇒SPRING

spray /spreɪ/ *n* (of flowers) ramillete *m*; (from sea) espuma *f*; (liquid in spray form) espray *m*; (device) rociador *m*. ● *vt* rociar

spread /spred/ *vt* (*pt* **spread**) (stretch, extend) extender; desplegar <*wings*>; difundir <*idea, news*>. ~ **butter on a piece of toast** untar una tostada con mantequilla. ● *vi* extenderse; <*disease*> propagarse; <*idea, news*> difundirse. ● *n* (of ideas) difusión *f*; (of disease, fire) propagación *f*; (Ⓘ, feast) festín *m*. □ ~ **out** *vi* (move apart) desplegarse

spree /spriː/ *n*. **go on a shopping** ~ ir de expedición a las tiendas

sprightly /'spraɪtlɪ/ *a* (**-ier**, **-iest**) vivo

spring /sprɪŋ/ n (season) primavera f; (device) resorte m; (in mattress) muelle m, resorte m (LAm); (elasticity) elasticidad f; (water) manantial m. ● a primaveral. ● vi (pt **sprang**, pp **sprung**) saltar; (issue) brotar. ∼ from sth <problem> provenir de algo. □ ∼ **up** vi surgir. ∼**board** n trampolín m. ∼**clean** /-'kli:n/ vi hacer una limpieza general. ∼ **onion** n cebolleta f. ∼**time** n primavera f. ∼**y** a (**-ier, -iest**) <mattress, grass> mullido

sprinkle /'sprɪŋkl/ vt salpicar; (with liquid) rociar. ● n salpicadura f; (of liquid) rociada f. ∼**r** n regadera f

sprint /sprɪnt/ n carrera f corta. ● vi (Sport) esprintar; (run fast) correr. ∼**er** n corredor m

sprout /spraʊt/ vi brotar. ● n brote m. (Brussels) ∼**s** npl coles fpl de Bruselas

sprung /sprʌŋ/ ⇒SPRING

spud /spʌd/ n 𝕋 patata f, papa f (LAm)

spun /spʌn/ ⇒SPIN

spur /spɜː(r)/ n espuela f; (stimulus) acicate m. **on the** ∼ **of the moment** sin pensarlo. ● vt (pt **spurred**). ∼ (**on**) espolear; (fig) estimular

spurn /spɜːn/ vt desdeñar; (reject) rechazar

spurt /spɜːt/ vi <liquid> salir a chorros. ● n chorro m; (of activity) racha f

spy /spaɪ/ n espía m & f. ● vt descubrir, ver. ● vi espiar. ∼ **on s.o.** espiar a uno

squabble /'skwɒbl/ vi reñir

squad /skwɒd/ n (Mil) pelotón m; (of police) brigada f; (Sport) equipo m. ∼ **car** m coche m patrulla. ∼**ron** /'skwɒdrən/ n (Mil, Aviat) escuadrón m; (Naut) escuadra f

squalid /'skwɒlɪd/ a miserable

squall /skwɔːl/ n turbión m

squalor /'skwɒlə(r)/ n miseria f

squander /'skwɒndə(r)/ vt derrochar; desaprovechar <opportunity>

square /skweə(r)/ n cuadrado m; (in town) plaza f. ● a cuadrado; <meal> decente; (𝕋, old-fashioned) chapado a la antigua. ● vt (settle) arreglar; (Math) elevar al cuadrado. ● vi (agree) cuadrar. □ ∼ **up**. vi arreglar cuentas (with con). ∼**ly** adv directamente

squash /skwɒʃ/ vt aplastar; (suppress) acallar. ● n. **it was a terrible** ∼ íbamos (or iban) terriblemente apretujados; (drink) orange ∼ naranjada f; (Sport) squash m; (vegetable) calabaza f. ∼**y** a blando

squat /skwɒt/ vi (pt **squatted**) ponerse en cuclillas; (occupy illegally) ocupar sin autorización. ● a rechoncho y bajo. ∼**ter** n ocupante m & f ilegal, okupa m & f

squawk /skwɔːk/ n graznido m. ● vi graznar

squeak /skwiːk/ n chillido m; (of door) chirrido m. ● vi chillar; <door> chirriar; <shoes> crujir. ∼**y** a chirriante

squeal /skwiːl/ n chillido m ● vi chillar

squeamish /'skwiːmɪʃ/ a impresionable, delicado

squeeze /skwiːz/ vt apretar; exprimir <lemon etc>. ● vi. ∼ **in** meterse. ● n estrujón m; (of hand) apretón m

squid /skwɪd/ n calamar m

squiggle /'skwɪgl/ n garabato m

squint /skwɪnt/ vi bizquear; (trying to see) entrecerrar los ojos. ● n estrabismo m

squirm /skwɜːm/ vi retorcerse

squirrel /'skwɪrəl/ n ardilla f

squirt /skwɜːt/ vt <liquid> echar un chorro de. ● vi salir a chorros. ● n chorrito m

St /sənt/ abbr (= **saint**) /sənt/ S, San(to); (= **street**) C/, Calle f

stab /stæb/ vt (pt **stabbed**) apuñalar. ● n puñalada f; (pain) punzada f. **have a** ∼ **at sth** intentar algo

stabili|ty /stə'bɪlətɪ/ n estabilidad f. ∼**ze** /'steɪbɪlaɪz/ vt/i estabilizar

stable /'steɪbl/ a (**-er, -est**) estable. ● n caballeriza f, cuadra f

stack /stæk/ n montón m. ● vt. ∼ (**up**) amontonar

stadium /'steɪdɪəm/ n (pl **-diums** or **-dia** /-dɪə/) estadio m

staff /stɑːf/ n (stick) palo m; (employees) personal m. **teaching** ∼ personal m docente. **a member of** ∼ un empleado

stag /stæg/ *n* ciervo *m*. **~-night**, **~-party** *n* (before wedding) fiesta *f* de despedida de soltero; (men-only party) fiesta *f* para hombres

stage /steɪdʒ/ *n* (in theatre) escenario *f*; (platform) plataforma *f*; (phase) etapa *f*. **the ~** (profession, medium) el teatro. ● *vt* poner en escena *<play>*; (arrange) organizar; (pej) orquestar. **~coach** *n* diligencia *f*

stagger /'stægə(r)/ *vi* tambalearse. ● *vt* dejar estupefacto; escalonar *<holidays etc>*. **~ing** *a* asombroso

stagna|nt /'stægnənt/ *a* estancado. **~te** /stæg'neɪt/ *vi* estancarse

staid /steɪd/ *a* serio, formal

stain /steɪn/ *vt* manchar; (colour) teñir. ● *n* mancha *f*; (dye) tintura *f*. **~ed glass window** *n* vidriera *f* de colores. **~less steel** *n* acero *m* inoxidable. **~ remover** *n* quitamanchas *m*

stair /steə(r)/ *n* escalón *m*. **~s** *npl* escalera *f*. **~case**, **~way** *n* escalera *f*

stake /steɪk/ *n* estaca *f*; (wager) apuesta *f*; (Com) intereses *mpl*. **be at ~** estar en juego. ● *vt* estacar; jugarse *<reputation>*. **~ a claim** reclamar

stala|ctite /'stæləktaɪt/ *n* estalactita *f*. **~gmite** /'stæləgmaɪt/ *n* estalagmita *f*

stale /steɪl/ *a* (**-er**, **-est**) no fresco; *<bread>* duro; *<smell>* viciado. **~mate** *n* (Chess) ahogado *m*; (deadlock) punto *m* muerto

stalk /stɔːk/ *n* tallo *m*. ● *vt* acechar. ● *vi* irse indignado

stall /stɔːl/ *n* (in stable) compartimiento *m*; (in market) puesto *m*. **~s** *npl* (in theatre) platea *f*, patio *m* de butacas. ● *vt* parar *<engine>*. ● *vi* *<engine>* pararse; (fig) andar con rodeos

stallion /'stæljən/ *n* semental *m*

stalwart /'stɔːlwət/ *a* *<supporter>* leal, incondicional

stamina /'stæmɪnə/ *n* resistencia *f*

stammer /'stæmə(r)/ *vi* tartamudear. ● *n* tartamudeo *m*

stamp /stæmp/ *vt* (with feet) patear; (press) estampar; (with rubber stamp) sellar; (fig) señalar. ● *vi* dar patadas en el suelo. ● *n* sello *m*, estampilla *f*

(LAm), timbre *m* (Mex); (on passport) sello *m*; (with foot) patada *f*; (mark) marca *f*, señal *f*. □ **~ out** *vt* (fig) erradicar. **~ed addressed envelope** *n* sobre *m* franqueado con su dirección

stampede /stæm'piːd/ *n* estampida *f*. ● *vi* salir en estampida

stance /stɑːns/ *n* postura *f*

stand /stænd/ *vi* (*pt* **stood**) estar de pie, estar parado (LAm); (rise) ponerse de pie, pararse; (be) encontrarse; (Pol) presentarse como candidato (**for** en). **the offer ~s** la oferta sigue en pie. **~ to reason** ser lógico. ● *vt* (endure) soportar; (place) colocar. **~ a chance** tener una posibilidad. ● *n* posición *f*, postura *f*; (for lamp etc) pie *m*, sostén *m*; (at market) puesto *m*; (booth) quiosco *m*; (Sport) tribuna *f*. **make a ~ against** sth oponer resistencia a algo. □ **~ back** *vi* apartarse. □ **~ by** *vi* estar preparado. *vt* (support) apoyar. □ **~ down** *vi* retirarse. □ **~ for** *vt* significar. □ **~ in for** *vt* suplir a. □ **~ out** *vi* destacarse. □ **~ up** *vi* ponerse de pie, pararse (LAm). □ **~ up for** *vt* defender. **~ up for oneself** defenderse. □ **~ up to** *vt* resistir a

standard /'stændəd/ *n* norma *f*; (level) nivel *m*; (flag) estandarte *m*. ● *a* estándar *a invar*, normal. **~ize** *vt* estandarizar. **~ lamp** *n* lámpara *f* de pie. **~s** *npl* principios *mpl*

stand: **~-by** *n* (at airport) stand-by *m*. **be on ~-by** *<police>* estar en estado de alerta. **~-in** *n* suplente *m* & *f*. **~ing** *a* de pie, parado (LAm); (permanent) permanente *f*. ● *n* posición *f*; (prestige) prestigio *m*. **~off** *n* (Amer, draw) empate *m*; (deadlock) callejón *m* sin salida. **~point** *n* punto *m* de vista. **~still** *n*. **be at a ~still** estar paralizado. **come to a ~still** *<vehicle>* parar; *<city>* quedar paralizado

stank /stæŋk/ ⇒STINK

staple /'steɪpl/ *a* principal. ● *n* grapa *f*. ● *vt* sujetar con una grapa. **~r** *n* grapadora *f*

star /stɑː(r)/ *n* (incl Cinema, Theatre) estrella *f*; (asterisk) asterisco *m*. ● *vi* (*pt* **starred**). **~ in a film** protagonizar una película. **~board** *n* estribor *m*.

starch /stɑːtʃ/ n almidón m; (in food) fécula f. ● vt almidonar. ~y a <food> a base de féculas

stardom /'stɑːdəm/ n estrellato m

stare /steə(r)/ n mirada f fija. ● vi. ~ (at) mirar fijamente

starfish /'stɑːfɪʃ/ n estrella f de mar

stark /stɑːk/ a (-er, -est) escueto. ● adv completamente

starling /'stɑːlɪŋ/ n estornino m

starry /'stɑːrɪ/ a estrellado

start /stɑːt/ vt empezar, comenzar; encender <engine>; arrancar <car>; (cause) provocar; abrir <business>. ● vi empezar; <car etc> arrancar; (jump) dar un respingo. to ~ with (as linker) para empezar. ~ off by doing sth empezar por hacer algo. ● n principio m; (Sport) ventaja f; (jump) susto m. make an early ~ (on journey) salir temprano. ~er n (Auto) motor m de arranque; (Culin) primer plato m. ~ing-point n punto m de partida

startle /'stɑːtl/ vt asustar

starv|ation /stɑː'veɪʃn/ n hambre f, inanición f. ~e /stɑːv/ vt hacer morir de hambre. ● vi morirse de hambre. I'm ~ing me muero de hambre

state /steɪt/ n estado m. be in a ~ estar agitado. the S~ los Estados mpl Unidos. ● vt declarar; expresar <views>; (fix) fijar. ● a del Estado; (Schol) público; (with ceremony) de gala. ~ly a (-ier, -iest) majestuoso. ~ly home n casa f solariega. ~ment n declaración f; (account) informe m. ~sman /-mən/ n estadista m

static /'stætɪk/ a estacionario. ● n (interference) estática f

station /'steɪʃn/ n estación f; (on radio) emisora f; (TV) canal m. ● vt colocar; (Mil) estacionar. ~ary a estacionario. ~er's (shop) n papelería f. ~ery n artículos mpl de papelería. ~ wagon n (Amer) ranchera f, (coche m) familiar m, camioneta f (LAm)

statistic /stə'tɪstɪk/ n estadística f. ~al a estadístico. ~s n (science) estadística f

statue /'stætʃuː/ n estatua f

stature /'stætʃə(r)/ n talla f, estatura f

status /'steɪtəs/ n posición f social; (prestige) categoría f; (Jurid) estado m

statut|e /'stætʃuːt/ n estatuto m. ~ory /-ʊtrɪ/ a estatutario

staunch /stɔːnʃ/ a (-er, -est) leal

stave /steɪv/ n (Mus) pentagrama m. □ ~ off vt evitar

stay /steɪ/ n (of time) estancia f, estadía f (LAm); (Jurid) suspensión f. ● vi quedarse; (reside) alojarse. I'm ~ing in a hotel estoy en un hotel. □ ~ in vi quedarse en casa. □ ~ up vi quedarse levantado

stead /sted/ n. in s.o.'s ~ en lugar de uno. stand s.o. in good ~ resultarle muy útil a uno. ~ily adv firmemente; (regularly) regularmente. ~y a (-ier, -iest) firme; (regular) regular; <flow> continuo; <worker> serio

steak /steɪk/ n. a ~ un filete. some ~ carne para guisar

steal /stiːl/ vt (pt stole, pp stolen) robar. ~ in vi entrar a hurtadillas

stealth /stelθ/ n. by ~ sigilosamente. ~y a sigiloso

steam /stiːm/ n vapor m. let off ~ (fig) desahogarse. ● vt (cook) cocer al vapor. ● vi echar vapor. □ ~ up vi empañarse. ~ engine n máquina f de vapor. ~er n (ship) barco m de vapor. ~roller n apisonadora f. ~y a lleno de vapor

steel /stiːl/ n acero m. ● vt. ~ o.s. armarse de valor. ~ industry n industria f siderúrgica

steep /stiːp/ ● a (-er, -est) empinado; <increase> considerable; <price> 🔢 excesivo

steeple /'stiːpl/ n aguja f, campanario m

steeply /'stiːplɪ/ adv abruptamente; <increase> considerablemente

steer /stɪə(r)/ vt dirigir; gobernar <ship>. ● vi (in ship) estar al timón. ~ clear of evitar. ~ing n (Auto) dirección f. ~ing wheel n volante m

stem /stem/ n (of plant) tallo m; (of glass) pie m; (of word) raíz f. ● vt (pt stemmed) contener <bleeding>. ● vi. ~ from provenir de

stench /stentʃ/ *n* hedor *m*

stencil /'stensl/ *n* plantilla *f*

stenographer /ste'nɒɡrəfə(r)/ *n* estenógrafo *m*

step /step/ *vi* (*pt* **stepped**). ~ **in** sth pisar algo. □ ~ **aside** *vi* hacerse a un lado. □ ~ **down** *vi* retirarse. □ ~ **in** *vi* (fig) intervenir. □ ~ **up** *vt* intensificar; redoblar *<security>*. ● *n* paso *m*; (stair) escalón *m*; (fig) medida *f*. **take** ~**s** tomar medidas. **be in** ~ llevar el paso. **be out of** ~ no llevar el paso. ~**brother** *n* hermanastro *m*. ~**daughter** *n* hijastra *f*. ~**father** *n* padrastro *m*. ~**ladder** *n* escalera *f* de tijera. ~**mother** *n* madrastra *f*. ~**ping-stone** *n* peldaño *m*. ~**sister** *n* hermanastra *f*. ~**son** *n* hijastro *m*

stereo /'sterɪəʊ/ *n* (*pl* -**os** estéreo *m*. ● *a* estéreo *a invar*. ~**type** *n* estereotipo *m*

steril|e /'steraɪl/ *a* estéril. ~**ize** /'sterɪlaɪz/ *vt* esterilizar

sterling /'stɜːlɪŋ/ *n* libras *fpl* esterlinas. ● *a* *<pound>* esterlina

stern /stɜːn/ *n* (of boat) popa *f*. ● *a* (-**er**, -**est**) severo

stethoscope /'steθəskəʊp/ *n* estetoscopio *m*

stew /stjuː/ *vt/i* guisar. ● *n* estofado *m*, guiso *m*

steward /'stjuːəd/ *n* administrador *m*; (on ship) camarero *m*; (air steward) sobrecargo *m*, aeromozo *m* (LAm). ~**ess** /-'des/ *n* camarera *f*; (on aircraft) auxiliar *f* de vuelo, azafata *f*

stick /stɪk/ *n* palo *m*; (for walking) bastón *m*; (of celery etc) tallo *m*. ● *vt* (*pt* **stuck**) (glue) pegar; (⬚, put) poner; (thrust) clavar; (⬚, endure) soportar. ● *vi* pegarse; (jam) atascarse. □ ~ **out** *vi* sobresalir. □ ~ **to** *vt* ceñirse a. □ ~ **up for** *vt* ⬚ defender. ~**er** *n* pegatina *f*. ~**ing plaster** *n* esparadrapo *m*; (individual) tirita *f*, curita *f* (LAm). ~**ler** /'stɪklə(r)/ *n*. **be a** ~**ler for** insistir en. ~**y** /'stɪkɪ/ *a* (-**ier**, -**iest**) *<surface>* pegajoso; *<label>* engomado

stiff /stɪf/ *a* (-**er**, -**est**) rígido; *<joint, fabric>* tieso; *<muscle>* entumecido; (difficult) difícil; *<manner>* estirado; *<drink>* fuerte. **have a** ~ **neck** tener

tortícolis. ~**en** *vi* (become rigid) agarrotarse; (become firm) endurecerse. ~**ly** *adv* rígidamente.

stifl|e /'staɪfl/ *vt* sofocar. ~**ing** *a* sofocante

stiletto (**heel**) /stɪ'letəʊ/ *n* (*pl* -**os**) tacón *m* de aguja

still /stɪl/ *a* inmóvil; (peaceful) tranquilo; *<drink>* sin gas. **sit** ~, **stand** ~ quedarse tranquilo. ● *adv* todavía, aún; (nevertheless) sin embargo. ~**born** *a* nacido muerto. ~ **life** *n* (*pl* -**s**) bodegón *m*. ~**ness** *n* tranquilidad *f*

stilted /'stɪltɪd/ *a* rebuscado; *<conversation>* forzado

stilts /stɪlts/ *npl* zancos *mpl*

stimul|ant /'stɪmjʊlənt/ *n* estimulante *m*. ~**ate** /-leɪt/ *vt* estimular. ~**ation** /-'leɪʃn/ *n* estímulo *m*. ~**us** /-əs/ *n* (*pl* -**li** /-laɪ/) estímulo *m*

sting /stɪŋ/ *n* picadura *f*; (organ) aguijón *m*. ● *vt/i* (*pt* **stung**) picar

stingy /'stɪndʒɪ/ *a* (-**ier**, -**iest**) tacaño

stink /stɪŋk/ *n* hedor *m*. ● *vi* (*pt* **stank** *or* **stunk**, *pp* **stunk**) apestar, oler mal

stipulat|e /'stɪpjʊleɪt/ *vt/i* estipular. ~**ion** /-'leɪʃn/ *n* estipulación *f*

stir /stɜː(r)/ *vt* (*pt* **stirred**) remover, revolver; (move) agitar; estimular *<imagination>*. ● *vi* moverse. ~ **up trouble** armar lío ⬚. ● *n* revuelo *m*, conmoción *f*

stirrup /'stɪrəp/ *n* estribo *m*

stitch /stɪtʃ/ *n* (in sewing) puntada *f*; (in knitting) punto *m*; (pain) dolor *m* costado. **be in** ~**es** ⬚ desternillarse de risa. ● *vt* coser

stock /stɒk/ *n* (Com, supplies) existencias *fpl*; (Com, variety) surtido *m*; (livestock) ganado *m*; (Culin) caldo *m*. ~**s and shares**, ~**s and bonds** (Amer) acciones *fpl*. **out of** ~ agotado. **take** ~ **of** sth (fig) hacer un balance de algo. ● *a* estándar *a invar*; (fig) trillado. ● *vt* surtir, abastecer (**with** de). □ ~ **up** *vi* abastecerse (**with** de). ~**broker** /-brəʊkə(r)/ *n* corredor *m* de bolsa. **S**~ **Exchange** *n* bolsa *f*. ~**ing** *n* media *f*. ~**pile** *n* reservas *fpl.* ● *vt* almacenar. **∼-still** *a* inmóvil. **∼-taking** *n* (Com) inventario *m*. **∼y** *a* (**-ier, -iest**) bajo y fornido

stodgy /'stɒdʒɪ/ (**-dgier, -dgiest**) *a* pesado

stoke /stəʊk/ *vt* echarle carbón (*or* leña) a

stole /stəʊl/ ⇒STEAL

stolen /'stəʊlən/ ⇒STEAL

stomach /'stʌmək/ *n* estómago *m*. ● *vt* soportar. **∼-ache** *n* dolor *m* de estómago

ston|e /stəʊn/ *n* piedra *f*; (in fruit) hueso *m*; (weight, *pl* **stone**) *unidad de peso equivalente a 14 libras o 6,35 kg*. ● *a* de piedra. ● *vt* apedrear. **∼e-deaf** *a* sordo como una tapia. **∼y** *a* <*silence*> sepulcral

stood /stʊd/ ⇒STAND

stool /stuːl/ *n* taburete *m*

stoop /stuːp/ *vi* agacharse; (fig) rebajarse. ● *n.* **have a ∼** ser cargado de espaldas

stop /stɒp/ *vt* (*pt* **stopped**) (halt, switch off) parar; (cease) terminar; (prevent) impedir; (interrupt) interrumpir. **∼ doing sth** dejar de hacer algo. **∼ it!** ¡basta ya! ● *vi* <*bus*> parar, detenerse; <*clock*> pararse. **it's ∼ped raining** ha dejado de llover. ● *n* (bus etc) parada *f*; (break on journey) parada *f*. **put a ∼ to sth** poner fin a algo. **come to a ∼** detenerse. **∼gap** *n* remedio *m* provisional. **∼over** *n* escala *f*. **∼page** /'stɒpɪdʒ/ *n* suspensión *f*, paradero *m* (LAm); (of work) huelga *f*, paro *m* (LAm); (interruption) interrupción *f*. **∼per** *n* tapón *m*. **∼watch** *n* cronómetro *m*

storage /'stɔːrɪdʒ/ *n* almacenamiento *m*

store /stɔː(r)/ *n* provisión *f*; (depot) almacén *m*; (Amer, shop) tienda *f*; (fig) reserva *f*. **in ∼** en reserva. ● *vt* (for future) poner en reserva; (in warehouse) almacenar. □ **∼ up** *vt* (fig) ir acumulando. **∼keeper** *n* (Amer) tendero *m*, comerciante *m & f*. **∼room** *n* almacén *m*; (for food) despensa *f*

storey /'stɔːrɪ/ *n* (*pl* **-eys**) piso *m*, planta *f*

stork /stɔːk/ *n* cigüeña *f*

storm /stɔːm/ *n* tempestad *f*. ● *vi* rabiar. ● *vt* (Mil) asaltar. **∼y** *a* tormentoso; <*sea, relationship*> tempestuoso

story /'stɔːrɪ/ *n* historia *f*; (in newspaper) artículo *m*; (rumour) rumor *m*; (Ⓕ, lie) mentira *f*, cuento *m*. **∼-teller** *n* cuentista *m & f*

stout /staʊt/ *a* (**-er, -est**) robusto, corpulento. ● *n* cerveza *f* negra

stove /stəʊv/ *n* estufa *f*

stow /stəʊ/ *vt* guardar; (hide) esconder. □ **∼ away** *vi* viajar de polizón. **∼away** *n* polizón *m & f*

straggl|e /'strægl/ *vi* rezagarse. **∼y** *a* desordenado

straight /streɪt/ *a* (**-er, -est**) recto; (tidy) en orden; (frank) franco; <*hair*> lacio; (Ⓕ, conventional) convencional. **be ∼** estar derecho. ● *adv* <*sit up*> derecho; (direct) directamente; (without delay) inmediatamente. **∼ away** en seguida, inmediatamente. **∼ on** todo recto. **∼ out** sin rodeos. ● *n* recta *f*. **∼en** *vt* enderezar. □ **∼en up** *vt* ordenar. **∼forward** /-'fɔːwəd/ *a* franco; (easy) sencillo

strain /streɪn/ *n* (tension) tensión *f*; (injury) torcedura *f*. ● *vt* forzar <*voice, eyesight*>; someter a demasiada tensión <*relations*>; (sieve) colar. **∼ one's back** hacerse daño en la espalda. **∼ a muscle** hacerse un esguince. **∼ed** *a* forzado; <*relations*> tirante. **∼er** *n* colador *m*. **∼s** *npl* (Mus) acordes *mpl*

strait /streɪt/ *n* estrecho *m*. **be in dire ∼s** estar en grandes apuros. **∼jacket** *n* camisa *f* de fuerza

strand /strænd/ *n* (thread) hebra *f*. **a ∼ of hair** un pelo. ● *vt.* **be ∼ed** <*ship*> quedar encallado. **I was left ∼ed** me abandonaron a mi suerte

strange /streɪndʒ/ *a* (**-er, -est**) raro, extraño; (not known) desconocido. **∼ly** *adv* de una manera rara. **∼ly enough** aunque parezca mentira. **∼r** *n* desconocido *m*; (from another place) forastero *m*

strangle /'stræŋgl/ *vt* estrangular

strap /stræp/ *n* correa *f*; (of garment) tirante *m*. ● *vt* (*pt* **strapped**) atar con una correa

strat|egic /strə'ti:dʒɪk/ a estratégico. **~egy** /'strætədʒɪ/ n estrategia f

straw /strɔ:/ n paja f; (drinking ~) pajita f, paja f, popote m (Mex). **the last ~** el colmo. **~berry** /-bərɪ/ n fresa f; (large) fresón m

stray /streɪ/ vi (wander away) apartarse; (get lost) extraviarse; (deviate) desviarse (**from** de). ● a <animal> (without owner) callejero; (lost) perdido. ● n (without owner) perro m/gato m callejero; (lost) perro m/gato m perdido

streak /stri:k/ n lista f, raya f; (in hair) reflejo m; (in personality) veta f

stream /stri:m/ n arroyo m; (current) corriente f. **a ~ of** una sarta de insultos. ● vi correr. □ **~ out** vi <people> salir en tropel. **~er** n (paper) serpentina f; (banner) banderín m. **~line** vt dar línea aerodinámica a; (simplify) racionalizar. **~lined** a aerodinámico

street /stri:t/ n calle f. **~car** n (Amer) tranvía m. **~ lamp** n farol m. **~ map**, **~ plan** n plano m

strength /streŋθ/ n fuerza f; (of wall etc) solidez f. **~en** vt reforzar <wall>; fortalecer <muscle>

strenuous /'strenjʊəs/ a enérgico; (arduous) arduo; (tiring) fatigoso

stress /stres/ n énfasis f; (Gram) acento m; (Mec, Med, tension) tensión f. ● vt insistir en

stretch /stretʃ/ vt estirar; (extend) extender; forzar <truth>; estirar <resources>. ● vi estirarse; (when sleepy) desperezarse; (extend) extenderse; (be elastic) estirarse. ● n (period) período m; (of road) tramo m. **at a ~** sin parar. □ **~ out** vi <person> tenderse. **~er** n camilla f

strict /strɪkt/ a (-er, -est) estricto; <secrecy> absoluto. **~ly** adv con severidad; <rigorously> terminantemente. **~ly speaking** en rigor

stridden /strɪdn/ ⇒STRIDE

stride /straɪd/ vi (pt **strode**, pp **stridden**) andar a zancadas. ● n zancada f. **take sth in one's ~** tomarse algo con calma. **~nt** /'straɪdnt/ a estridente

strife /straɪf/ n conflicto m

strike /straɪk/ vt (pt **struck**) golpear; encender <match>; encontrar <gold, oil>; <clock> dar. **it ~s me as odd** me parece raro. ● vi golpear; (go on strike) declararse en huelga; (be on strike) estar en huelga; (attack) atacar; <clock> dar la hora. ● n (of workers) huelga f, paro m; (attack) ataque m. **come out on ~** ir a la huelga. □ **~ off**, **~ out** vt tachar. **~ up a friendship** trabar amistad. **~r** n huelguista m & f; (Sport) artillero m

striking /'straɪkɪŋ/ a <resemblance> sorprendente; <colour> llamativo

string /strɪŋ/ n cordel m, mecate m (Mex); (Mus) cuerda f; (of lies, pearls) sarta f; (of people) sucesión f. □ **~ along** vt 🄸 engañar

stringent /'strɪndʒənt/ a riguroso

strip /strɪp/ vt (pt **stripped**) desnudar <person>; deshacer <bed>. ● vi desnudarse. ● n tira f; (of land) franja f. **~ cartoon** n historieta f

stripe /straɪp/ n raya f. **~d** a a rayas, rayado

strip lighting n luz f fluorescente

strive /straɪv/ vi (pt **strove**, pp **striven**). **~ to** esforzarse por

strode /strəʊd/ ⇒STRIDE

stroke /strəʊk/ n golpe m; (in swimming) brazada f; (Med) ataque m de apoplejía; (of pen etc) trazo m; (of clock) campanada f; (caress) caricia f. **a ~ of luck** un golpe de suerte. ● vt acariciar

stroll /strəʊl/ vi pasearse. ● n paseo m. **~er** n (Amer) sillita f de paseo, cochecito m

strong /strɒŋ/ a (-er, -est) fuerte. **~hold** n fortaleza f; (fig) baluarte m. **~ly** adv (greatly) fuertemente; <protest> enérgicamente; (deeply) profundamente. **~room** n cámara f acorazada

strove /strəʊv/ ⇒STRIVE

struck /strʌk/ ⇒STRIKE

structur|al /'strʌktʃərəl/ a estructural. **~e** /'strʌktʃə(r)/ n estructura f

struggle /'strʌgl/ vi luchar; (thrash around) forcejear. ● n lucha f

strum /strʌm/ vt (pt **strummed**) rasguear

strung /strʌŋ/ ⇒STRING

strut /strʌt/ n (in building) puntal m.
● vi (pt **strutted**) pavonearse

stub /stʌb/ n (of pencil, candle) cabo m;
(counterfoil) talón m; (of cigarette) colilla. □ ~ **out** (pt **stubbed**) vt apagar

stubble /'stʌbl/ n rastrojo m; (beard)
barba f de varios días

stubborn /'stʌbən/ a terco

stuck /stʌk/ ⇒STICK. ● a. the drawer
is ~ el cajón se ha atascado. the door
is ~ la puerta se ha atrancado. ~-**up**
a ⏐ estirado

stud /stʌd/ n tachuela f; (for collar) gemelo m.

student /'stju:dənt/ n estudiante m
& f; (at school) alumno m. ~ **driver** n
(Amer) persona que está aprendiendo
a conducir

studio /'stju:dɪəʊ/ n (pl -**os**) estudio
m. ~ **apartment**, ~ **flat** n estudio
m

studious /'stju:dɪəs/ a estudioso

study /'stʌdɪ/ n estudio m. ● vt/i
estudiar

stuff /stʌf/ n ⏐ cosas fpl. what's this
~ **called**? ¿cómo se llama esta cosa?.
● vt rellenar; disecar <animal>;
(cram) atiborrar; (put) meter de prisa.
~ **o.s.** ⏐ darse un atracón. ~**ing** n
relleno m. ~**y** a (-**ier**, -**iest**) mal
ventilado; (old-fashioned) acartonado.
it's ~**y** in here está muy cargado el
ambiente

stumble /'stʌmbl/ vi tropezar. ~**e
across**, ~**e on** vt dar con. ~**ing-
block** n tropiezo m, impedimento m

stump /stʌmp/ n (of limb) muñón m;
(of tree) tocón m

stun /stʌn/ vt (pt **stunned**) (daze)
aturdir; (bewilder) dejar atónito.
~**ning** a sensacional

stung /stʌŋ/ ⇒STING

stunk /stʌŋk/ →STINK

stunt /stʌnt/ n ⏐ ardid m publicitario. ● vt detener, atrofiar. ~**ed** a
(growth) atrofiado; (body) raquítico.
~**man** n especialista m. ~**woman**
n especialista f

stupendous /stju:'pendəs/ a estupendo

stupid /'stju:pɪd/ a (foolish) tonto; (un-

intelligent) estúpido. ~**ity** /-'pɪdətɪ/ n
estupidez f. ~**ly** adv estúpidamente

stupor /'stju:pə(r)/ n estupor m

sturdy /'stɜ:dɪ/ a (-**ier**, -**iest**) robusto

stutter /'stʌtə(r)/ vi tartamudear.
● n tartamudeo m

sty /staɪ/ n (pl **sties**) pocilga f; (Med)
orzuelo m

style /staɪl/ n estilo m; (fashion) moda f; (design, type) diseño m. **in** ~ a lo
grande. ● vt diseñar. ~**ish** a elegante. ~**ist** n estilista m & f. hair
~**ist** estilista m & f

stylus /'staɪləs/ n (pl -**uses**) aguja f
(de tocadiscos)

suave /swɑ:v/ a elegante y desenvuelto

subconscious /sʌb'kɒnʃəs/ a & n
subconsciente (m)

subdivide /sʌbdɪ'vaɪd/ vt subdi-
vidir

subdued /səb'dju:d/ a apagado

subject /'sʌbdʒɪkt/ a sometido. ~ **to**
sujeto a. ● n (theme) tema m; (Schol)
asignatura f, materia f (LAm); (Gram)
sujeto m; (Pol) súbdito m. ●
/səb'dʒekt/ vt someter. ~**ive**
/səb'dʒektɪv/ a subjetivo

subjunctive /səb'dʒʌŋktɪv/ a & n
subjuntivo (m)

sublime /sə'blaɪm/ a sublime

submarine /sʌbmə'ri:n/ n submarino m

submerge /səb'mɜ:dʒ/ vt sumergir.
● vi sumergirse

submission /səb'mɪʃn/ n su-
misión f. ~**t** /səb'mɪt/ vt (pt **sub-
mitted**) (subject) someter; presentar
<application>. ● vi rendirse

subordinate /sə'bɔ:dɪnət/ a & n
subordinado (m). ● /sə'bɔ:dɪneɪt/ vt
subordinar

subscribe /səb'skraɪb/ vi suscri-
bir. ~**be to** suscribirse a <maga-
zine>. ~**ber** n suscriptor m. ~**ption**
/-rɪpʃn/ n (to magazine) suscripción f

subsequent /'sʌbsɪkwənt/ a posterior, subsiguiente. ~**ly** adv poste-
riormente

subside /səb'saɪd/ vi <land> hundirse; <flood> bajar; <storm, wind>

amainar. **~nce** /'sʌbsɪdəns/ *n* hundimiento *m*

subsidiary /səb'sɪdɪərɪ/ *a* secundario; *<subject>* complementario. ● *n* (Com) filial

subsid‖ize /'sʌbsɪdaɪz/ *vt* subvencionar, subsidiar (LAm). **~y** /'sʌbsədɪ/ *n* subvención *f*, subsidio *m*

substance /'sʌbstəns/ *n* sustancia *f*

substandard /sʌb'stændəd/ *a* de calidad inferior

substantial /səb'stænʃl/ *a* (sturdy) sólido; *<meal>* sustancioso; (considerable) considerable

substitut‖e /'sʌbstɪtjuːt/ *n* (person) substituto *m*; (thing) sucedáneo *m*. ● *vt/i* sustituir. **~ion** /-'tjuːʃn/ *n* sustitución *f*

subterranean /sʌbtə'reɪnjən/ *a* subterráneo

subtitle /'sʌbtaɪtl/ *n* subtítulo *m*

subtle /'sʌtl/ *a* (**-er, -est**) sutil; (tactful) discreto. **~ty** *n* sutileza *f*

subtract /səb'trækt/ *vt* restar. **~ion** /-ʃn/ *n* resta *f*

suburb /'sʌbɜːb/ *n* barrio *m* residencial de las afueras, colonia *f*, the **~s** las afueras *fpl*. **~an** /sə'bɜːbən/ *a* suburbano. **~ia** /sə'bɜːbɪə/ *n* zonas residenciales de las afueras de una ciudad

subversive /səb'vɜːsɪv/ *a* subversivo

subway /'sʌbweɪ/ *n* paso *m* subterráneo; (Amer) metro *m*

succeed /sək'siːd/ *vi* *<plan>* dar resultado; *<person>* tener éxito. **~ in doing** lograr hacer. ● *vt* suceder

success /sək'ses/ *n* éxito *m*. **~ful** *a <person>* de éxito, exitoso (LAm). the **~ful applicant** el candidato que obtenga el puesto. **~fully** *a* satisfactoriamente. **~ion** /-ʃn/ *n* sucesión *f*. **for 3 years in ~ion** durante tres años consecutivos. **in rapid ~ion** uno tras otro. **~ive** *a* sucesivo. **~or** *n* sucesor *m*

succulent /'sʌkjʊlənt/ *a* suculento

succumb /sə'kʌm/ *vi* sucumbir

such /sʌtʃ/ *a* tal (+ *noun*), tan (+ *adj*). **~ a big house** una casa tan grande. ● *pron* tal. **~ and ~** tal o

cual. **~ as** como. **~ as it is** tal como es

suck /sʌk/ *vt* chupar *<sweet, thumb>*; sorber *<liquid>*. □ **~ up** *vt <vacuum cleaner>* aspirar; *<pump>* succionar. □ **~ up to** *vt* 🄸 dar coba a. **~er** *n* (plant) chupón *m*; (🄸, person) imbécil *m*

suckle /'sʌkl/ *vt* amamantar

suction /'sʌkʃn/ *n* succión *f*

sudden /'sʌdn/ *a* repentino. **all of a ~** de repente. **~ly** *adv* de repente

suds /sʌdz/ *npl* espuma *f* de jabón

sue /suː/ *vt* (*pres p* **suing**) demandar (**for** por)

suede /sweɪd/ *n* ante *m*

suet /'suːɪt/ *n* sebo *m*

suffer /'sʌfə(r)/ *vt* sufrir; (tolerate) aguantar. ● *vi* sufrir; (be affected) resentirse

suffic‖e /sə'faɪs/ *vi* bastar. **~ient** /sə'fɪʃnt/ *a* suficiente, bastante. **~iently** *adv* (lo) suficientemente

suffix /'sʌfɪks/ *n* (*pl* **-ixes**) sufijo *m*

suffocat‖e /'sʌfəkeɪt/ *vt* asfixiar. ● *vi* asfixiarse. **~ion** /-'keɪʃn/ *n* asfixia *f*

sugar /'ʃʊgə(r)/ *n* azúcar *m* & *f*. **~ bowl** *n* azucarero *m*. **~y** *a* azucarado.

suggest /sə'dʒest/ *vt* sugerir. **~ion** /-tʃən/ *n* sugerencia *f*

suicid‖al /suːɪ'saɪdl/ *a* suicida. **~e** /'suːɪsaɪd/ *n* suicidio *m*. **commit ~e** suicidarse

suit /suːt/ *n* traje *m*; (woman's) traje *m* de chaqueta; (Cards) palo *m*; (Jurid) pleito *m*. ● *vt* venirle bien a, convenirle a; *<clothes>* quedarle bien a; (adapt) adaptar. **be ~ed to** *<thing>* ser apropiado para. **I'm not ~ed to this kind of work** no sirvo para este tipo de trabajo. **~able** *a* apropiado, adecuado. **~ably** *adv <dressed>* apropiadamente; *<qualified>* adecuadamente. **~case** *n* maleta *f*, valija *f* (LAm)

suite /swiːt/ *n* (of furniture) juego *m*; (of rooms) suite *f*

sulk /sʌlk/ *vi* enfurruñarse

sullen /'sʌlən/ *a* hosco

sulphur /'sʌlfə(r)/ *n* azufre *m*. ~**ic acid** /sʌl'fjʊərɪk/ *n* ácido *m* sulfúrico

sultan /'sʌltən/ *n* sultán *m*

sultana /sʌl'tɑːnə/ *n* pasa *f* de Esmirna

sultry /'sʌltrɪ/ *a* (-**ier**, -**iest**) <*weather*> bochornoso; (fig) sensual

sum /sʌm/ *n* (of money) suma *f*, cantidad *f*; (Math) suma *f*. ● □ ~ **up** (*pt* **summed**) *vt* resumir. ● *vi* recapitular

summar|ily /'sʌmərɪlɪ/ *adv* sumariamente. ~**ize** *vt* resumir. ~**y** *n* resumen *m*

summer /'sʌmə(r)/ *n* verano *m*. ~ **camp** *n* (in US) colonia *f* de vacaciones. ~**time** *n* verano *m*. ~**y** *a* veraniego

summit /'sʌmɪt/ *n* (of mountain) cumbre *f*. ~ **conference** *n* conferencia *f* cumbre

summon /'sʌmən/ *vt* llamar; convocar <*meeting, s.o. to meeting*>; (Jurid) citar. □ ~ **up** *vt* armarse de. ~**s** *n* (Jurid) citación *f*. ● *vt* citar

sumptuous /'sʌmptjʊəs/ *a* suntuoso

sun /sʌn/ *n* sol *m*. ~**bathe** *vi* tomar el sol, asolearse (LAm). ~**beam** *n* rayo *m* de sol. ~**burn** *n* quemadura *f* de sol. ~**burnt** *a* quemado por el sol

Sunday /'sʌndeɪ/ *n* domingo *m*

sunflower /'sʌnflaʊə(r)/ *n* girasol *m*

sung /sʌŋ/ ⇒SING

sunglasses /'sʌnglɑːsɪz/ *npl* gafas *fpl* de sol, lentes *mpl* de sol (LAm)

sunk /sʌŋk/ ⇒SINK. ~**en** /'sʌŋkən/ ● *a* hundido

sun: ~**light** *n* luz *f* del sol. ~**ny** *a* (-**ier**, -**iest**) <*day*> de sol; (place) soleado. **it is** ~**ny** hace sol. ~**rise** *n*. at ~**rise** al amanecer. salida *f* del sol. ~**roof** *n* techo *m* corredizo. ~**set** *n* puesta *f* del sol. ~**shine** *n* sol *m*. ~**stroke** *n* insolación *f*. ~**tan** *n* bronceado *m*. get a ~**tan** broncearse. ~**tan lotion** *n* bronceador *m*

super /'suːpə(r)/ *a* Ⓣ genial, super *a invar*

superb /suː'pɜːb/ *a* espléndido

supercilious /suːpə'sɪlɪəs/ *a* desdeñoso

superficial /suːpə'fɪʃl/ *a* superficial

superfluous /suː'pɜːfluəs/ *a* superfluo

superhighway /'suːpəhaɪweɪ/ *n* (Amer, Auto) autopista *f*; (Comp) **information** ~ autopista *f* de la comunicación

superhuman /suːpə'hjuːmən/ *a* sobrehumano

superintendent /suːpərɪn'tendənt/ *n* director *m*; (Amer, of building) portero *m*; (of police) comisario *m*; (in US) superintendente *m & f*

superior /suː'pɪərɪə(r)/ *a & n* superior (*m*). ~**ity** /-'ɒrətɪ/ *n* superioridad *f*

superlative /suː'pɜːlətɪv/ *a* inigualable. ● *n* superlativo *m*

supermarket /'suːpəmɑːkɪt/ *n* supermercado *m*

supernatural /suːpə'nætʃrəl/ *a* sobrenatural

superpower /'suːpəpaʊə(r)/ *n* superpotencia *f*

supersede /suːpə'siːd/ *vt* reemplazar, sustituir

supersonic /suːpə'sɒnɪk/ *a* supersónico

superstitio|n /suːpə'stɪʃn/ *n* superstición *f*. ~**us** *a* /-əs/ supersticioso

supervis|e /'suːpəvaɪz/ *vt* supervisar. ~**ion** /-'vɪʒn/ *n* supervisión *f*. ~**or** *n* supervisor *m*

supper /'sʌpə(r)/ *n* cena *f* (ligera), comida *f* (ligera) (LAm)

supple /sʌpl/ *a* flexible

supplement /'sʌplɪmənt/ *n* suplemento *m*; (to diet, income) complemento *m*. ● *vt* complementar <*diet, income*>. ~**ary** /-'mentərɪ/ *a* suplementario

suppl|ier /sə'plaɪə(r)/ *n* (Com) proveedor *m*. ~**y** /sə'plaɪ/ *vt* suministrar; proporcionar <*information*>. ~**y s.o. with sth** <*equipment*> proveer a uno de algo; (in business) abastecer a uno de algo. ● *n* suministro *m*. ~**y and demand**

oferta *f* y demanda. ~**ies** *npl* provisiones *mpl,* víveres *mpl*; (Mil) pertrechos *mpl.* **office** ~**ies** artículos *mpl* de oficina

support /sə'pɔːt/ *vt* (hold up) sostener; (back) apoyar; mantener <*family*>. ● *n* apoyo *m*; (Tec) soporte *m.* ~**er** *n* partidario *m*; (Sport) hincha *m* & *f*

suppos|e /sə'pəʊz/ *vt* suponer; imaginarse; (think) creer. **I'm** ~**ed to start work at nine** se supone que tengo que empezar a trabajar a las nueve. ~**edly** *adv* supuestamente. ~**ition** /sʌpə'zɪʃn/ *n* suposición *f*

suppress /sə'pres/ *vt* reprimir <*feelings*>; sofocar <*rebellion*>. ~**ion** /-ʃn/*n* represión *f*

suprem|acy /suː'preməsɪ/ *n* supremacía *f.* ~**e** /suː'priːm/ *a* supremo

sure /ʃʊə(r)/ *a* (**-er, -est**) seguro. **make** ~ **that** asegurarse de que. ● *adv* ¡claro!. ~**ly** *adv* (undoubtedly) seguramente; (gladly) desde luego. ~**ly you don't believe that!** ¡no te creerás eso! ~**ty** /-ətɪ/ *n* garantía *f*

surf /sɜːf/ *n* oleaje *m*; (foam) espuma *f.* ● *vi* hacer surf. ● *vt* (Comp) surfear, navegar

surface /'sɜːfɪs/ *n* superficie *f.* ● *a* superficial. ● *vt* recubrir (**with** de). ● *vi* salir a la superficie; <*problems*> aflorar

surfboard /'sɜːfbɔːd/ *n* tabla *f* de surf

surfeit /'sɜːfɪt/ *n* exceso *m*

surf: ~**er** *n* surfista *m* & *f* ~**ing** *n* surf *m*

surge /sɜːdʒ/ *vi* <*crowd*> moverse en tropel; <*sea*> hincharse. ● *n* oleada *f*; (in demand, sales) aumento *m*

surg|eon /'sɜːdʒən/ *n* cirujano *m.* ~**ery** *n* cirugía *f*; (consulting room) consultorio *m*; (consulting hours) consulta *f.* ~**ical** *a* quirúrgico

surly /'sɜːlɪ/ *a* (**-ier, -iest**) hosco

surmise /sə'maɪz/ *vt* conjeturar

surmount /sə'maʊnt/ *vt* superar

surname /'sɜːneɪm/ *n* apellido *m*

surpass /sə'pɑːs/ *vt* superar

surplus /'sɜːpləs/ *a* & *n* excedente (*m*)

surpris|e /sə'praɪz/ *n* sorpresa *f.* ● *vt* sorprender. ~**ed** *a* sorprendido.

~**ing** *a* sorprendente. ~**ingly** *adv* sorprendentemente

surrender /sə'rendə(r)/ *vt* entregar. ● *vi* rendirse. ● *n* rendición *f*

surreptitious /sʌrəp'tɪʃəs/ *a* furtivo

surround /sə'raʊnd/ *vt* rodear; (Mil) rodear, cercar. ~**ing** *a* circundante. ~**ings** *npl* alrededores *mpl*; (environment) ambiente *m*

surveillance /sɜː'veɪləns/ *n* vigilancia *f*

survey /'sɜːveɪ/ *n* inspección *f*; (report) informe *m*; (general view) vista *f* general. ● /sə'veɪ/ *vt* inspeccionar; (measure) medir; (look at) contemplar. ~**or** *n* topógrafo *m*, agrimensor *m*; (of building) perito *m*

surviv|al /sə'vaɪvl/ *n* supervivencia *f.* ~**e** /sə'vaɪv/ *vt/i* sobrevivir. ~**or** *n* superviviente *m* & *f*

susceptible /sə'septəbl/ *a.* ~ **to** propenso a

suspect /sə'spekt/ *vt* sospechar; sospechar de <*person*>. ● /'sʌspekt/ *a* & *n* sospechoso (*m*)

suspen|d /sə'spend/ *vt* suspender. ~**ders** *npl* (Amer, braces) tirantes *mpl.* ~**se** /-s/ *n* (in film etc) suspense *m*, suspenso *m* (LAm). **keep s.o. in** ~**se** mantener a uno sobre ascuas. ~**sion** /-ʃn/ *n* suspensión *f.* ~**sion bridge** *n* puente *m* colgante

suspici|on /sə'spɪʃn/ *n* (belief) sospecha *f*; (mistrust) desconfianza *f.* ~**ous** /-ʃəs/ *a* desconfiado; (causing suspicion) sospechoso

sustain /sə'steɪn/ *vt* sostener; mantener <*conversation, interest*>; (suffer) sufrir

SW *abbr* (= **south-west**) SO

swab /swɒb/ *n* (specimen) muestra *f*, frotis *m*

swagger /'swægə(r)/ *vi* pavonearse

swallow /'swɒləʊ/ *vt/i* tragar. ● *n* trago *m*; (bird) golondrina *f*

swam /swæm/ ⇒SWIM

swamp /swɒmp/ *n* pantano *m*, ciénaga *f.* ● *vt* inundar. ~**y** *a* pantanoso

swan /swɒn/ *n* cisne *m*

swap /swɒp/ vt/i (pt **swapped**) intercambiar. ~ sth for sth cambiar algo por algo. ● n cambio m

swarm /swɔːm/ n enjambre m. ● vi <bees> enjambrar; (fig) hormiguear

swarthy /ˈswɔːðɪ/ a (-ier, -iest) moreno

swat /swɒt/ vt (pt **swatted**) matar (con matamoscas etc)

sway /sweɪ/ vi balancearse; (gently) mecerse. ● vt (influence) influir en

swear /sweə(r)/ vt/i (pt **swore**, pp **sworn**) jurar. ~word n palabrota f

sweat /swet/ n sudor m, transpiración f. ● vi sudar

sweat|er /ˈswetə(r)/ n jersey m, suéter m. ~shirt n sudadera f. ~suit n (Amer) chándal m, equipo m de deportes

swede /swiːd/ n nabo m sueco

Swede /swiːd/ n sueco m. ~n /ˈswiːdn/ n Suecia f. ~ish a sueco. ● n (Lang) sueco m. ● npl. the ~ (people) los suecos

sweep /swiːp/ vt (pt **swept**) barrer; deshollinar <chimney>. ● vi barrer. ● n barrido m. ~ away vt (carry away) arrastrar; (abolish) erradicar. ~er n barrendero m. ~ing a <gesture> amplio; <changes> radical; <statement> demasiado general

sweet /swiːt/ a (-er, -est) dulce; (fragrant) fragante; (pleasant) agradable; (kind, gentle) dulce; (cute) rico. have a ~ tooth ser dulcero. ● n caramelo m, dulce m (Mex); (dish) postre m. ~en vt endulzar. ~heart n enamorado m; (as form of address) amor m. ~ly adv dulcemente. ~ potato n boniato m, batata f

swell /swel/ vt (pt **swelled**, pp **swollen** or **swelled**) hinchar; (increase) aumentar. ● vi hincharse; (increase) aumentar. ● a (Amer Ⅱ) fenomenal. ● n (of sea) oleaje m. ~ing n hinchazón m

sweltering /ˈsweltərɪŋ/ vi sofocante

swept /swept/ ⇒SWEEP

swerve /swɜːv/ vi virar bruscamente

swift /swɪft/ a (-er, -est) veloz, rápido; <reply> rápido. ● n (bird) vencejo m. ~ly adv rápidamente

swig /swɪg/ vt (pt **swigged**) Ⅱ beber a grandes tragos. ● n Ⅱ trago m

swim /swɪm/ vi (pt **swam**, pp **swum**) nadar. ● n baño m. ~mer n nadador m. ~ming n natación f. ~ming bath(s) n(pl) piscina f cubierta, alberca f techada (Mex). ~ming pool n piscina f, alberca f (Mex). ~ming trunks npl bañador m, traje m de baño ~suit n traje m de baño, bañador m

swindle /ˈswɪndl/ vt estafar. ● n estafa f. ~r n estafador m

swine /swaɪn/ npl cerdos mpl. ● n (pl **swine**) (Ⅱ, person) canalla m & f

swing /swɪŋ/ vt (pt **swung**) balancear; (object on rope) hacer oscilar. ● vi (dangle) balancearse; (swing on a swing) columpiarse; <pendulum> oscilar. ~ open/shut abrirse/cerrarse. ● n oscilación f, vaivén m; (seat) columpio m; (in opinion) cambio m. in full ~ en plena actividad

swipe /swaɪp/ vt darle un golpe a; (✖, snatch) birlar. ● n golpe m

Swiss /swɪs/ a suizo (m). ● npl. the ~ los suizos

switch /swɪtʃ/ n (Elec) interruptor m; (exchange) intercambio m; (Amer, Rail) agujas fpl.● vt cambiar; (deviate) desviar. □ ~ off vt (Elec) apagar <light, TV, heating>; desconectar <electricity>. □ ~ on vt encender, prender (LAm); arrancar <engine>. ~board n centralita f

Switzerland /ˈswɪtsələnd/ n Suiza f

swivel /ˈswɪvl/ vi (pt **swivelled**) girar. ● vt hacer girar

swollen /ˈswəʊlən/ ⇒SWELL. ● a hinchado

swoop /swuːp/ vi <bird> abatirse; <police> llevar a cabo una redada. ● n (of bird) descenso m en picado or (LAm) en picada; (by police) redada f

sword /sɔːd/ n espada f

swore /swɔː(r)/ ⇒SWEAR

sworn /swɔːn/ ⇒SWEAR. ● a <enemy> declarado; <statement> jurado

swot /swɒt/ *vt/i* (*pt* **swotted**) (Schol, 🔲) empollar, estudiar como loco. ● *n* (Schol, 🔲) empollón *m*, matado *m* (Mex)

swum /swʌm/ ⇒SWIM

swung /swʌŋ/ ⇒SWING

syllable /'sɪləbl/ *n* sílaba *f*

syllabus /'sɪləbəs/ *n* (*pl* **-buses**) plan *m* de estudios; (of a particular subject) programa *m*

symbol /'sɪmbl/ *n* símbolo *m*. **∼ic(al)** /-'bɒlɪk(l)/ *a* simbólico. **∼ism** *n* simbolismo *m*. **∼ize** *vt* simbolizar

symmetr|ical /sɪ'metrɪkl/ *a* simétrico. **∼y** /'sɪmətrɪ/ *n* simetría *f*

sympath|etic /sɪmpə'θetɪk/ *a* comprensivo; (showing pity) compasivo. **∼ize** /'sɪmpəθaɪz/ *vi* comprender; (commiserate) **∼ize with s.o.** compadecer a uno. **∼y** /'sɪmpəθɪ/ *n* comprensión *f*; (pity) compasión *f*; (condolences) pésame *m*

symphony /'sɪmfənɪ/ *n* sinfonía *f*

symptom /'sɪmptəm/ *n* síntoma *m*. **∼atic** /-'mætɪk/ *a* sintomático

synagogue /'sɪnəgɒg/ *n* sinagoga *f*

synchronize /'sɪŋkrənaɪz/ *vt* sincronizar

syndicate /'sɪndɪkət/ *n* agrupación *f*; (Amer, TV) agencia *f* de distribución periodística

synonym /'sɪnənɪm/ *n* sinónimo *m*. **∼ous** /-'nɒnɪməs/ *a* sinónimo

syntax /'sɪntæks/ *n* sintaxis *f*

synthesi|s /'sɪnθəsɪs/ *n* (*pl* **-theses** /-siːz/) síntesis *f*. **∼ze** /-aɪz/ *vt* sintetizar

synthetic /sɪn'θetɪk/ *a* sintético

syringe /'sɪrɪndʒ/ *n* jeringa *f*, jeringuilla *f*

syrup /'sɪrəp/ *n* (sugar solution) almíbar *m*; (with other ingredients) jarabe *m*; (medicine) jarabe *m*

system /'sɪstəm/ *n* sistema *m*, método *m*; (Tec, Mec, Comp) sistema *m*. **the digestive ∼** el aparato digestivo. **∼atic** /-ə'mætɪk/ *a* sistemático. **∼atically** /-ə'mætɪklɪ/ *adv* sistemáticamente. **∼s analyst** *n* analista *m & f* de sistemas

T t

tab /tæb/ *n* (flap) lengüeta *f*; (label) etiqueta *f*

table /'teɪbl/ *n* mesa *f*; (list) tabla *f*. **∼cloth** *n* mantel *m*. **∼ mat** *n* salvamanteles *m*. **∼spoon** *n* cuchara *f* grande; (measure) cucharada *f* (grande)

tablet /'tæblɪt/ *n* pastilla *f*; (pill) comprimido *m*

table tennis *n* tenis *m* de mesa, ping-pong *m*

tabloid /'tæblɔɪd/ *n* tabloide *m*

taboo /tə'buː/ *a & n* tabú (*m*)

tacit /'tæsɪt/ *a* tácito

taciturn /'tæsɪtɜːn/ *a* taciturno

tack /tæk/ *n* tachuela *f*; (stitch) hilván *m*. ● *vt* clavar con tachuelas; (sew) hilvanar. ● *vi* (Naut) virar □ **∼ on** *vt* añadir.

tackle /'tækl/ *n* (equipment) equipo *m*; (soccer) entrada *f* fuerte; (US football, Rugby) placaje *m*. **fishing ∼** aparejo *m* de pesca. ● *vt* abordar <*problem*>; (in soccer) entrarle a; (in US football, Rugby) placar

tacky /'tækɪ/ *a* pegajoso

tact /tækt/ *n* tacto *m*. **∼ful** *a* diplomático

tactic|al /'tæktɪkl/ *a* táctico. **∼s** *npl* táctica *f*

tactless /'tæktləs/ *a* indiscreto

tadpole /'tædpəʊl/ *n* renacuajo *m*

tag /tæg/ *n* (label) etiqueta *f*. □ **∼ along** (*pt* **tagged**) *vt* 🔲 seguir

tail /teɪl/ *n* (of horse, fish, bird) cola *f*; (of dog, pig) rabo *m*. **∼s** *npl* (tailcoat) frac *m*; (of coin) cruz *f*. ● *vt* seguir. □ **∼ off** *vi* disminuir.

tailor /'teɪlə(r)/ *n* sastre *m*. **∼ed** /'teɪləd/ *a* entallado. **∼-made** *n* hecho a (la) medida

taint /teɪnt/ *vt* contaminar

take /teɪk/ *vt* (*pt* **took**, *pp* **taken**) tomar, coger (esp Spain), agarrar (esp LAm); (capture) capturar; (endure) aguantar; (require) requerir; llevar

<time>; tomar *<bath>*; tomar *<medicine>*; (carry) llevar; aceptar *<cheque>*. I ~ a size 10 uso la talla 14. ● *n* (Cinema) toma *f*. □ ~ **after** *vt* parecerse a. □ ~ **away** *vt* llevarse; (confiscate) quitar. □ ~ **back** *vt* retirar *<statement etc>*. □ ~ **in** *vt* achicar *<garment>*; (understand) asimilar; (deceive) engañar. □ ~ **off** *vt* (remove) quitar, sacar; quitarse *<shoes, jacket>*; (mimic) imitar. *vi* (Aviat) despegar. □ ~ **on** *vt* contratar *<employee>*. □ ~ **out** *vt* sacar. □ ~ **over** *vt* tomar posesión de; hacerse cargo de *<job>*. *vi* (assume control) asumir el poder. □ ~ **up** *vt* empezar a hacer *<hobby>*; aceptar *<challenge>*; subir *<hem>*; llevar *<time>*; ocupar *<space>*. ~-**off** *n* despegue *m*. ~-**over** *n* (Com) absorción *f*

takings /'teɪkɪŋz/ *npl* recaudación *f*; (at box office) taquilla *f*

talcum powder /'tælkəm/ *n* polvos *mpl* de talco, talco *m* (LAm)

tale /teɪl/ *n* cuento *m*

talent /'tælənt/ *n* talento *m*. ~**ed** *a* talentoso

talk /tɔːk/ *vt/i* hablar. ~ **to s.o.** hablar con uno. ~ **about** hablar de. ● *n* conversación *f*; (lecture) charla *f*. □ ~ **over** *vt* discutir. ~**ative** /-ətɪv/ *a* hablador

tall /tɔːl/ *a* (**-er, -est**) alto. ~ **story** *n* 🔟 cuento *m* chino

tally /'tælɪ/ *vi* coincidir (**with** con)

talon /'tælən/ *n* garra *f*

tambourine /tæmbə'riːn/ *n* pandereta *f*

tame /teɪm/ *a* (**-er, -est**) *<animal>* (by nature) manso; (tamed) domado. ● *vt* domar *<wild animal>*

tamper /'tæmpə(r)/ *vi*. ~ **with** tocar; (alter) alterar, falsificar

tampon /'tæmpɒn/ *n* tampón *m*

tan /tæn/ *vi* (*pt* **tanned**) broncearse. ● *n* bronceado *m*. **get a** ~ broncearse. ● *a* habano

tang /tæŋ/ *n* sabor *m* fuerte

tangent /'tændʒənt/ *n* tangente *f*

tangerine /tændʒə'riːn/ *n* mandarina *f*

tangible /'tændʒəbl/ *a* tangible

tangle /'tæŋgl/ *vt* enredar. **get** ~**d** (**up**) enredarse. ● *n* enredo *m*, maraña *f*

tango /'tæŋgəʊ/ *n* (*pl* **-os**) tango *m*

tank /tæŋk/ *n* depósito *m*; (Auto) tanque *m*; (Mil) tanque *m*

tanker /'tæŋkə(r)/ *n* (ship) buque *m* cisterna; (truck) camión *m* cisterna

tantrum /'tæntrəm/ *n* berrinche *m*, rabieta *f*

tap /tæp/ *n* grifo *m*, llave *f* (LAm); (knock) golpecito *m*. ● *vt* (*pt* **tapped**) (knock) dar un golpecito en; interceptar *<phone>*. ● *vi* dar golpecitos (**on** en). ~ **dancing** *n* claqué *m*

tape /teɪp/ *n* cinta *f*; (Med) esparadrapo *m*. ● *vt* (record) grabar. ~-**measure** *n* cinta *f* métrica

taper /'teɪpə(r)/ *vt* afilar. ● *vi* afilarse. □ ~ **off** *vi* disminuir

tape recorder *n* magnetofón *m*, magnetófono *m*

tapestry /'tæpɪstrɪ/ *n* tapiz *m*

tar /tɑː(r)/ *n* alquitrán *m*. ● *vt* (*pt* **tarred**) alquitranar

target /'tɑːgɪt/ *n* blanco *m*; (fig) objetivo *m*

tarmac /'tɑːmæk/ *n* pista *f*. **T**~ *n* (Amer, P) asfalto *m*

tarnish /'tɑːnɪʃ/ *vt* deslustrar; empañar *<reputation>*

tart /tɑːt/ *n* pastel *m*; (individual) pastelillo *m*; (🔞, woman) prostituta *f*, fulana *f* 🔟. ● *vt*. ~ **o.s. up** 🔟 engalanarse. ● *a* (**-er, -est**) ácido

tartan /'tɑːtn/ *n* tartán *m*, tela *f* escocesa

task /tɑːsk/ *n* tarea *f*. **take to** ~ reprender

tassel /'tæsl/ *n* borla *f*

tast|e /teɪst/ *n* sabor *m*, gusto *m*; (liking) gusto *m*. ● *vt* probar. ● *vi*. ~**e of** saber a. ~**eful** *a* de buen gusto. ~**eless** *a* soso; (fig) de mal gusto. ~**y** *a* (**-ier, -iest**) sabroso

tat /tæt/ *n* ⇒TIT FOR TAT

tatter|ed /'tætəd/ *a* hecho jirones. ~**s** /'tætəz/ *npl* andrajos *mpl*

tattoo /tæ'tuː/ *n* (on body) tatuaje *m*. ● *vt* tatuar

tatty /'tætɪ/ *a* (**-ier, -iest**) gastado, estropeado

taught /tɔːt/ ⇒TEACH

taunt /tɔːnt/ *vt* provocar mediante burlas. ● *n* pulla *f*

Taurus /'tɔːrəs/ *n* Tauro *m*

taut /tɔːt/ *a* tenso

tavern /'tævən/ *n* taberna *f*

tax /tæks/ *n* impuesto *m*. ● *vt* imponer contribuciones a *<person>*; gravar *<thing>*; (strain) poner a prueba. ~**able** *a* imponible. ~**ation** /-'seɪʃn/ *n* impuestos *mpl*; (system) sistema *m* tributario. ~ **collector** *n* recaudador *m* de impuestos. ~-**free** *a* libre de impuestos

taxi /'tæksɪ/ *n* (*pl* -**is**) taxi *m*. ● *vi* (*pt* **taxied**, *pres p* **taxiing**) *<aircraft>* rodar por la pista

taxpayer /'tækspeɪə(r)/ *n* contribuyente *m* & *f*

tea /tiː/ *n* té *m*; (afternoon tea) merienda *f*, té *m*. ~ **bag** *n* bolsita *f* de té

teach /tiːtʃ/ *vt* (*pt* **taught**) dar clases de, enseñar *<subject>*; dar clase a *<person>*. ~ **school** (Amer) dar clase(s) en un colegio. ● *vi* dar clase(s). ~**er** *n* profesor *m*; (primary) maestro *m*. ~**ing** *n* enseñanza *f*. ● *a* docente

tea: ~**cup** *n* taza *f* de té. ~ **leaf** *n* hoja *f* de té

team /tiːm/ *n* equipo *m*. □ ~ **up** *vi* asociarse (**with** con). ~ **work** *n* trabajo *m* de equipo

teapot /'tiːpɒt/ *n* tetera *f*

tear[1] /teə(r)/ *vt* (*pt* **tore**, *pp* **torn**) romper, rasgar. ● *vi* romperse, rasgarse. ● *n* rotura *f*; (rip) desgarrón *m*. □ ~ **along** *vi* ir a toda velocidad. □ ~ **apart** *vt* desgarrar. □ ~ **off**, ~ **out** *vt* arrancar. □ ~ **up** *vt* romper

tear[2] /tɪə(r)/ *n* lágrima *f*. be in ~s estar llorando. ~**ful** *a* lloroso *<farewell>* triste. ~ **gas** *n* gas *m* lacrimógeno

tease /tiːz/ *vt* tomarle el pelo a

tea: ~ **set** *n* juego *m* de té. ~**spoon** *n* cucharita *f*, cucharilla *f*; (amount) cucharadita *f*

teat /tiːt/ *n* (of animal) tetilla *f*; (for bottle) tetina *f*

tea towel /'tiːtaʊəl/ *n* paño *m* de cocina

techni|cal /'teknɪkl/ *a* técnico. ~**cality** *n* /-'kælətɪ/ *n* detalle *m* técnico. ~**cally** *adv* técnicamente. ~**cian** /tek'nɪʃn/ *n* técnico *m*. ~**que** /tek'niːk/ *n* técnica *f*

technolog|ical /teknə'lɒdʒɪkl/ *a* tecnológico. ~**y** /tek'nɒlədʒɪ/ *n* tecnología *f*

teddy bear /'tedɪ/ *n* osito *m* de peluche

tedi|ous /'tiːdɪəs/ *a* tedioso. ~**um** /'tiːdɪəm/ *n* tedio *m*

teem /tiːm/ *vi* abundar (**with** en), estar repleto (**with** de)

teen|age /'tiːneɪdʒ/ *a* adolescente; (for teenagers) para jóvenes. ~**ager** *n* adolescente *m* & *f*. ~**s** /tiːnz/ *npl* adolescencia *f*

teeny /'tiːnɪ/ *a* (-**ier**, -**iest**) 🛈 chiquito

teeter /'tiːtə(r)/ *vi* balancearse

teeth /tiːθ/ ⇒TOOTH. ~**e** /tiːð/ *vi*. he's ~ing le están saliendo los dientes. ~**ing troubles** *npl* (fig) problemas *mpl* iniciales

tele|communications /telɪkə mjuːnɪ'keɪʃnz/ *npl* telecomunicaciones *fpl*. ~**gram** /'telɪgræm/ *n* telegrama *m*. ~**pathic** /telɪ'pæθɪk/ *a* telepático. ~**pathy** /tə'lepəθɪ/ *n* telepatía *f*

telephon|e /'telɪfəʊn/ *n* teléfono *m*. ● *vt* llamar por teléfono. ~**e booth**, ~ **box** *n* cabina *f* telefónica. ~**e call** *n* llamada *f* telefónica. ~**e directory** *n* guía *f* telefónica. ~**e exchange** *n* central *f* telefónica. ~**ist** /tɪ'lefənɪst/ *n* telefonista *m* & *f*

tele|sales /'telɪseɪlz/ *npl* televentas *fpl*. ~**scope** *n* telescopio *m*. ~**scopic** /-'skɒpɪk/ *a* telescópico. ~**text** *n* teletex(to) *m*

televis|e /'telɪvaɪz/ *vt* televisar. ~**ion** /'telɪvɪʒn/ *n* (medium) televisión *f*. ~**ion** (**set**) *n* televisor *m*

telex /'teleks/ *n* télex *m*

tell /tel/ *vt* (*pt* **told**) decir; contar *<story, joke>*; (distinguish) distinguir. ~ **the difference** notar la diferencia. ~ **the time** decir la hora. ● *vi* (produce an effect) tener efecto; (know) saber. □ ~ **off** *vt* regañar. ~**ing** *a* revelador. **~-tale** n soplón m. ● a revelador

telly /'telɪ/ n 🄻 tele f

temp /temp/ n empleado m eventual or temporal

temper /'tempə(r)/ n (mood) humor m; (disposition) carácter m; (fit of anger) cólera f. **be in a ~** estar furioso. **lose one's ~** perder los estribos. **~ament** /'temprəmənt/ n temperamento m. **~amental** /-'mentl/ a temperamental. **~ate** /'tempərət/ a templado. **~ature** /'temprɪtʃə(r)/ n temperatura f. **have a ~ature** tener fiebre

tempestuous /tem'pestjʊəs/ a tempestuoso

temple /'templ/ n templo m; (Anat) sien f

tempo /'tempəʊ/ n (pl **-os** or **tempi**) ritmo m

temporar|ily /'tempərərəlɪ/ adv temporalmente, temporariamente (LAm). **~y** /'tempərərɪ/ a temporal, provisional; <job> eventual, temporal

tempt /tempt/ vt tentar. **~ation** /-'teɪʃn/ n tentación f. **~ing** a tentador

ten /ten/ a & n diez (m)

tenaci|ous /tɪ'neɪʃəs/ a tenaz. **~ty** /tɪ'næsətɪ/ n tenacidad f

tenan|cy /'tenənsɪ/ n inquilinato m. **~t** n inquilino m, arrendatorio m

tend /tend/ vi. **~ to** tender a. ● vt cuidar (de). **~ency** /'tendənsɪ/ n tendencia f

tender /'tendə(r)/ a tierno; (painful) sensible. ● n (Com) oferta f. **legal ~** n moneda f de curso legal. ● vt ofrecer, presentar. **~ly** adv tiernamente

tendon /'tendən/ n tendón m

tennis /'tenɪs/ n tenis m

tenor /'tenə(r)/ n tenor m

tens|e /tens/ a (**-er**, **-est**) (taut) tenso, tirante; <person> tenso. ● n (Gram) tiempo m. **~ion** /'tenʃn/ n tensión f; (between two parties) conflicto m

tent /tent/ n tienda f (de campaña), carpa f (LAm)

tentacle /'tentəkl/ n tentáculo m

tentative /'tentətɪv/ a <plan> provisional; <offer> tentativo; <person> indeciso

tenterhooks /'tentəhʊks/ npl. **be on ~** estar en ascuas

tenth /tenθ/ a & n décimo (m)

tenuous /'tenjʊəs/ a <claim> poco fundado; <link> indirecto

tenure /'tenjʊə(r)/ n tenencia f; (period of office) ejercicio m

tepid /'tepɪd/ a tibio

term /tɜːm/ n (of time) período m; (Schol) trimestre m; (word etc) término m. **~s** npl condiciones fpl; (Com) precio m. **on good/bad ~s** en buenas/malas relaciones. ● vt calificar de

termin|al /'tɜːmɪnl/ a terminal. ● (transport) terminal f; (Comp, Elec) terminal m. **~ate** /-eɪt/ vt poner fin a; poner término a <contract>; (Amer, fire) despedir. ● vi terminarse. **~ology** /-'nɒlədʒɪ/ n terminología f

terrace /'terəs/ n terraza f; (houses) hilera f de casas

terrain /tə'reɪn/ n terreno m

terrestrial /tɪ'restrɪəl/ a terrestre

terribl|e /'terəbl/ a espantoso. **~y** adv terriblemente

terrif|ic /tə'rɪfɪk/ a (🄻, excellent) estupendo; (🄻, huge) enorme. **~ied** /'terɪfaɪd/ a aterrorizado. **~y** /'terɪfaɪ/ vt aterrorizar. **~ying** a aterrador

territor|ial /terɪ'tɔːrɪəl/ a territorial. **~y** /'terɪtrɪ/ n territorio m

terror /'terə(r)/ n terror m. **~ism** n terrorismo m. **~ist** n terrorista m & f. **~ize** vt aterrorizar

terse /tɜːs/ a seco, lacónico

test /test/ n (of machine, drug) prueba f; (exam) prueba f, test m; (of blood) análisis m; (for eyes, hearing) examen m. ● vt probar, poner a prueba <product>; hacerle una prueba a <student>; evaluar <knowledge>; examinar <sight>

testament /'testəmənt/ n (will) testamento m. **Old/New T~** Antiguo/Nuevo Testamento

testicle /'testɪkl/ n testículo m

testify /'testɪfaɪ/ vt atestiguar. ● vi declarar

testimon|ial /testɪ'məʊnɪəl/ *n* recomendación *f.* **~y** /'testɪmənɪ/ *n* testimonio *m*

test: **~ match** *n* partido *m* internacional. **~ tube** *n* tubo *m* de ensayo, probeta *f*

tether /'teðə(r)/ *vt* atar. ● *n.* be at the end of one's **~** no poder más

text /tekst/ *n* texto *m.* **~book** *n* libro *m* de texto

textile /'tekstaɪl/ *a & n* textil (*m*)

texture /'tekstʃə(r)/ *n* textura *f*

Thames /temz/ *n* Támesis *m*

than /ðæn, ðən/ *conj* que; (with quantity) de

thank /θæŋk/ *vt* darle las gracias a, agradecer. **~ you** gracias. **~ful** *a* agradecido. **~fully** *adv* (happily) gracias a Dios. **~less** *a* ingrato. **~s** *npl* agradecimiento *m.* **~s!** 🔲 ¡gracias!. **~s to** gracias a

Thanksgiving (Day) /θæŋks 'gɪvɪŋ/ *n* (in US) el día de Acción de Gracias

that /ðæt, ðət/ *a* (*pl* **those**) ese, aquel, esa, aquella. ● *pron* (*pl* **those**) ése, aquél, ésa, aquélla. **~ is** es decir. **~'s not true** eso no es cierto. **~'s why** por eso. **is ~ you?** ¿eres tú? **like ~** así. ● *adv* tan. ● *rel pron* que; (with prep) el que, la que, el cual, la cual. ● *conj* que

thatched /θætʃt/ *a* <*roof*> de paja; <*cottage*> con techo de paja

thaw /θɔː/ *vt* descongelar. ● *vi* descongelarse; <*snow*> derretirse. ● *n* deshielo *m*

the *before vowel* /ðɪ/, *before consonant* /ðə/, *stressed form* /ðiː/

● *definite article*

····▸ el (*m*), la (*f*), los (*mpl*), las (*fpl*). **~ building** el edificio. **~ windows** las ventanas

❗ Feminine singular nouns beginning with a stressed or accented *a* or *ha* take the article *el* instead of *la*, e.g. **soul** el alma; **~ axe** el hacha. **~ eagle** el águila

Note that when *el* follows the prepositions *de* and *a*, it combines

to form *del* and *al*, e.g. **of ~ group** *del* grupo. **I went to ~ bank** *fui al banco*

····▸ (before an ordinal number in names, titles) *not translated.* **Henry ~ Eighth** Enrique Octavo. **Elizabeth ~ Second** Isabel Segunda

····▸ (in abstractions) lo. **~ impossible** lo imposible

theatr|e /'θɪətə(r)/ *n* teatro *m*; (Amer, movie theater) cine *m.* **~ical** /-'ætrɪkl/ *a* teatral

theft /θeft/ *n* hurto *m*

their /ðeə(r)/ *a* su, sus *pl.* **~s** /ðeəz/ *poss pron* (el) suyo *m*, (la) suya *f*, (los) suyos *mpl*, (las) suyas *fpl*

them /ðem, ðəm/ *pron* (accusative) los *m*, las *f*; (dative) les; (*after prep*) ellos *m*, ellas *f*

theme /θiːm/ *n* tema *m.* **~ park** *n* parque *m* temático. **~ song** *n* motivo *m* principal

themselves /ðəm'selvz/ *pron* ellos mismos *m*, ellas mismas *f*; (*reflexive*) se; (*after prep*) sí mismos *m*, sí mismas *f*

then /ðen/ *adv* entonces; (next) luego, después. **by ~** para entonces. **now and ~** de vez en cuando. **since ~** desde entonces. ● *a* entonces

theology /θɪ'ɒlədʒɪ/ *n* teología *f*

theor|etical /θɪə'retɪkl/ *a* teórico. **~y** /'θɪərɪ/ *n* teoría *f*

therap|eutic /θerə'pjuːtɪk/ *a* terapéutico. **~ist** /'θerəpɪst/ *n* terapeuta *m & f.* **~y** /θerəpɪ/ *n* terapia *f*

there /ðeə(r)/ *adv* ahí; (further away) allí, ahí; (less precise, further) allá. **~ is, ~ are** hay. **~ it is** ahí está. **down ~** ahí abajo. **up ~** ahí arriba. ● *int.* **~!** that's the last box ¡listo! ésa es la última caja. **~, ~, don't cry!** vamos, no llores. **~abouts** *adv* por ahí. **~fore** /-fɔː(r)/ *adv* por lo tanto.

thermometer /θə'mɒmɪtə(r)/ *n* termómetro *m*

Thermos /'θɜːməs/ *n* (P) termo *m*

thermostat /'θɜːməstæt/ *n* termostato *m*

thesaurus /θɪ'sɔːrəs/ *n* (*pl* **-ri** /-raɪ/) diccionario *m* de sinónimos

these /ðiːz/ *a* estos, estas. ● *pron* éstos, éstas

thesis /ˈθiːsɪs/ *n* (*pl* **theses** /-siːz/) tesis *f*

they /ðeɪ/ *pron* ellos *m*, ellas *f*. ～ **say that** dicen *or* se dice que

they'd /ðeɪ(ə)d/ = **they had**, **they would**

they'll /ðeɪl/ = **they will**

they're /ðeɪə(r)/ = **they are**

they've /ðeɪv/ = **they have**

thick /θɪk/ *a* (**-er**, **-est**) <*layer, sweater*> grueso, gordo; <*sauce*> espeso; <*fog, smoke*> espeso, denso; <*fur*> tupido; (🅸, stupid) burro. ● *adv* espesamente, densamente. ● *n*. **in the** ～ **of** en medio de. ～**en** *vt* espesar. ● *vi* espesarse. ～**et** /-ɪt/ *n* matorral *m*. ～**ness** *n* (of fabric) grosor *m*; (of paper, wood, wall) espesor *m*

thief /θiːf/ *n* (*pl* **thieves** /θiːvz/) ladrón *m*

thigh /θaɪ/ *n* muslo *m*

thimble /ˈθɪmbl/ *n* dedal *m*

thin /θɪn/ *a* (**thinner**, **thinnest**) <*person*> delgado, flaco; <*layer, slice*> fino; <*hair*> ralo

thing /θɪŋ/ *n* cosa *f*. **it's a good** ～ **(that)**… menos mal que…. **just the** ～ exactamente lo que se necesita. **poor** ～! ¡pobrecito!

think /θɪŋk/ *vt* (*pt* **thought**) pensar, creer. ● *vi* pensar (**about** en); (carefully) reflexionar; (imagine) imaginarse. **I** ～ **so** creo que sí. ～ **of s.o.** pensar en uno. **I hadn't thought of that** eso no se me ha ocurrido. ～ **over** *vt* pensar bien. ～ **up** *vt* idear, inventar. ～**er** *n* pensador *m*. ～**tank** *n* gabinete *m* estratégico

third /θɜːd/ *a* tercero, (before masculine singular noun) tercer. ● *n* tercio *m*, tercera parte *f*. ～ **(gear)** *n* (Auto) tercera *f*. ～**rate** *a* muy inferior. **T～ World** *n* Tercer Mundo *m*

thirst /θɜːst/ *n* sed *f*. ～**y** *a* sediento. **be** ～**y** tener sed

thirt|een /θɜːˈtiːn/ *a & n* trece (*m*). ～**teenth** *a* decimotercero. ● *n* treceavo *m* ～**ieth** /ˈθɜːtɪəθ/ *a* trigésimo. ● *n* treintavo *m*. ～**y** /ˈθɜːtɪ/ *a & n* treinta (*m*)

this /ðɪs/ *a* (*pl* **these**) este, esta. ～ **one** éste, ésta. ● *pron* (*pl* **these**) éste, ésta, esto. **like** ～ así

thistle /ˈθɪsl/ *n* cardo *m*

thong /θɒŋ/ *n* correa *f*; (Amer, sandal) chancla *f*

thorn /θɔːn/ *n* espina *f*. ～**y** *a* espinoso

thorough /ˈθʌrə/ *a* <*investigation*> riguroso; <*cleaning etc*> a fondo; <*person*> concienzudo. ～**bred** /-bred/ *a* de pura sangre. ～**fare** *n* vía *f* pública; (street) calle *f*. **no** ～**fare** prohibido el paso. ～**ly** *adv* <*clean*> a fondo; <*examine*> minuciosamente; (completely) perfectamente

those /ðəʊz/ *a* esos, esas, aquellos, aquellas. ● *pron* ésos, ésas, aquéllos, aquéllas

though /ðəʊ/ *conj* aunque. ● *adv* sin embargo. **as** ～ como si

thought /θɔːt/ ⇒THINK. ● *n* pensamiento *m*; (idea) idea *f*. ～**ful** *a* pensativo; (considerate) atento. ～**fully** *adv* pensativamente; (considerately) atentamente. ～**less** *a* desconsiderado

thousand /ˈθaʊznd/ *a & n* mil (*m*). ～**th** *a & n* milésimo (*m*)

thrash /θræʃ/ *vt* azotar; (defeat) derrotar

thread /θred/ *n* hilo *m*; (of screw) rosca *f*. ● *vt* enhebrar <*needle*>; ensartar <*beads*>. ～**bare** *a* gastado, raído

threat /θret/ *n* amenaza *f*. ～**en** *vt/i* amenazar. ～**ening** *a* amenazador

three /θriː/ *a & n* tres (*m*). ～**fold** *a* triple. ● *adv* tres veces

threshold /ˈθreʃhəʊld/ *n* umbral *m*

threw /θruː/ ⇒THROW

thrift /θrɪft/ *n* economía *f*, ahorro *m*. ～**y** *a* frugal

thrill /θrɪl/ *n* emoción *f*. ● *vt* emocionar. ～**ed** *a* contentísimo (**with** con). ～**er** *n* (book) libro *m* de suspense *or* (LAm) suspenso; (film) película *f* de suspense *or* (LAm) suspenso. ～**ing** *a* emocionante

thriv|e /θraɪv/ *vi* prosperar. ～**ing** *a* próspero

throat /θrəʊt/ *n* garganta *f*

throb /θrɒb/ *vi* (*pt* **throbbed**) palpitar; (with pain) dar punzadas; <*engine*> vibrar. **~bing** *a* <*pain*> punzante

throes /θrəʊz/ *npl*. **be in one's death** ~ estar agonizando

throne /θrəʊn/ *n* trono *m*

throng /θrɒŋ/ *n* multitud *f*

throttle /'θrɒtl/ *n* (Auto) acelerador *m* (*que se acciona con la mano*). ● *vt* estrangular

through /θruː/ *prep* por, a través de; (during) durante; (by means of) a través de; (Amer, until and including) **Monday** ~ **Friday** de lunes a viernes. ● *adv* de parte a parte, de un lado a otro; (entirely) completamente; (to the end) hasta el final. **be** ~ (finished) haber terminado. ● *a* <*train etc*> directo. **no** ~ **road** calle sin salida. **~out** /-'aʊt/ *prep* por todo; (time) durante todo. **~out his career** a lo largo de su carrera

throve /θrəʊv/ ⇒THRIVE

throw /θrəʊ/ *vt* (*pt* **threw**, *pp* **thrown**) tirar, aventar (Mex); lanzar <*grenade, javelin*>; (disconcert) desconcertar; Ⅱ hacer, dar <*party*>. ● *n* (of ball) tiro *m*; (of dice) tirada *f*. □ ~ **away** *vt* tirar. □ ~ **up** *vi* (vomit) vomitar.

thrush /θrʌʃ/ *n* tordo *m*

thrust /θrʌst/ *vt* (*pt* **thrust**) empujar; (push in) clavar. ● *n* empujón *m*; (of sword) estocada *f*

thud /θʌd/ *n* ruido *m* sordo

thug /θʌg/ *n* matón *m*

thumb /θʌm/ *n* pulgar *m*. ● *vt*. ~ **a lift** ir a dedo. **~tack** *n* (Amer) chincheta *f*, tachuela *f*, chinche *f* (Mex)

thump /θʌmp/ *vt* golpear. ● *vi* <*heart*> latir fuertemente. ● *n* golpazo *m*

thunder /'θʌndə(r)/ *n* truenos *mpl*, (of traffic) estruendo *m*. ● *vi* tronar. **~bolt** *n* rayo *m*. **~storm** *n* tormenta *f* eléctrica. **~y** *a* con truenos

Thursday /'θɜːzdeɪ/ *n* jueves *m*

thus /ðʌs/ *adv* así

thwart /θwɔːt/ *vt* frustrar

tic /tɪk/ *n* tic *m*

tick /tɪk/ *n* (sound) tic *m*; (insect) garrapata *f*, (mark) marca *f*, visto *m*, palomita *f* (Mex); (Ⅱ, instant) momentito

m. ● *vi* hacer tictac. ● *vt*. ~ (**off**) marcar

ticket /'tɪkɪt/ *n* (for bus, train) billete *m*, boleto *m* (LAm); (for plane) pasaje *m*, billete *m*; (for theatre, museum) entrada *f*; (for baggage, coat) ticket *m*; (fine) multa *f*. ~ **collector** *n* revisor *m*. ~ **office** *n* (transport) mostrador *m* de venta de billetes *or* (LAm) boletos; (in theatre) taquilla *f*, boletería *f* (LAm)

tickl|e /'tɪkl/ *vt* hacerle cosquillas a. ● *n* cosquilleo *m*. **~ish** /'tɪklɪʃ/ *a*. **be** **~ish** tener cosquillas

tidal wave /'taɪdl/ *n* maremoto *m*

tide /taɪd/ *n* marea *f*. **high/low** ~ marea alta/baja. □ ~ **over** *vt* ayudar a salir de un apuro

tid|ily /'taɪdɪlɪ/ *adv* ordenadamente. **~iness** *n* orden *m*. **~y** *a* (**-ier**, **-iest**) ordenado. ● *vt*/*i* ~**y** (**up**) ordenar, arreglar

tie /taɪ/ *vt* (*pres p* **tying**) atar, amarrar (LAm); hacer <*knot*>. ● *vi* (Sport) empatar. ● *n* (constraint) atadura *f*; (bond) lazo *m*; (necktie) corbata *f*; (Sport) empate *m*. ~ **in with** *vt* concordar con. □ ~ **up** *vt* atar. **be ~d up** (busy) estar ocupado

tier /tɪə(r)/ *n* hilera *f* superpuesta; (in stadium etc) grada *f*; (of cake) piso *m*

tiger /'taɪgə(r)/ *n* tigre *m*

tight /taɪt/ *a* (**-er**, **-est**) <*clothes*> ajustado, ceñido; (taut) tieso; <*control*> estricto; <*knot, nut*> apretado; (Ⅱ, drunk) borracho. **~en** *vt* apretar. □ **~en up** *vt* hacer más estricto. **~-fisted** /-'fɪstɪd/ *a* tacaño. **~ly** *adv* bien, fuerte; <*fastened*> fuertemente. **~rope** *n* cuerda *f* floja. **~s** *npl* (for ballet etc) leotardo(s) *m(pl)*; (pantyhose) medias *fpl*

tile /taɪl/ *n* (decorative) azulejo *m*; (on roof) teja *f*; (on floor) baldosa *f*. ● *vt* azulejar; tejar <*roof*>; embaldosar <*floor*>

till /tɪl/ *prep* hasta. ● *conj* hasta que. ● *n* caja *f*. ● *vt* cultivar

tilt /tɪlt/ *vt* inclinar. ● *vi* inclinarse. ● *n* inclinación *f*

timber /'tɪmbə(r)/ *n* madera *f* (*para construcción*)

time /taɪm/ *n* tiempo *m*; (moment) momento *m*; (occasion) ocasión *f*; (by clock) hora *f*; (epoch) época *f*; (rhythm) compás *m*. **at ~s** a veces. **for the ~ being** por el momento. **from ~ to ~** de vez en cuando. **have a good ~** divertirse, pasarlo bien. **in a year's ~** dentro de un año. **in no ~** en un abrir y cerrar de ojos. **in ~ a** tiempo; (eventually) con el tiempo. **arrive on ~** llegar a tiempo. **it's ~ we left** es hora de irnos. ● *vt* elegir el momento; cronometrar *<race>*. **~ bomb** *n* bomba *f* de tiempo. **~ly** *a* oportuno. **~r** *n* cronómetro *m*; (Culin) avisador *m*; (with sand) reloj *m* de arena; (Elec) interruptor *m* de reloj. **~s** /'taɪmz/ *prep*. **2 ~s 4 is 8** 2 (multiplicado) por 4 son 8. **~table** *n* horario *m*

timid /'tɪmɪd/ *a* tímido; (fearful) miedoso

tin /tɪn/ *n* estaño *m*; (container) lata *f*. **~ foil** *n* papel *m* de estaño

tinge /tɪndʒ/ *vt*. **be ~d with sth** estar matizado de algo. ● *n* matiz *m*

tingle /'tɪŋgl/ *vi* sentir un hormigueo

tinker /'tɪŋkə(r)/ *vi*. **~ with** juguetear con

tinkle /'tɪŋkl/ *vi* tintinear

tinned /tɪnd/ *a* en lata, enlatado

tin opener *n* abrelatas *m*

tint /tɪnt/ *n* matiz *m*

tiny /'taɪnɪ/ *a* (**-ier, -iest**) minúsculo, diminuto

tip /tɪp/ *n* punta *f*. ● *vt* (*pt* **tipped**) (tilt) inclinar; (overturn) volcar; (pour) verter; (give gratuity to) darle (una) propina a. □ **~ off** *vt* avisar. □ **~ out** *vt* verter. □ **~ over** *vi* caerse. *n* propina *f*; (advice) consejo *m* (práctico); (for rubbish) vertedero *m*. **~ped** *a* *<cigarette>* con filtro

tipsy /'tɪpsɪ/ *a* achispado

tiptoe /'tɪptəʊ/ *n*. **on ~** de puntillas

tiptop /'tɪptɒp/ *a* ① de primera. **in ~ condition** en excelente estado

tire /'taɪə(r)/ *n* (Amer) ⇒TYRE. ● *vt* cansar. ● *vi* cansarse. **~d** /'taɪəd/ *a* cansado. **get ~d** cansarse. **~d of** harto de. **~d out** agotado. **~less** *a* incansable; *<efforts>* inagotable. **~some** /-səm/ *a* *<person>* pesado; *<task>* tedioso

tiring /'taɪərɪŋ/ *a* cansado, cansador (LAm)

tissue /'tɪʃuː/ *n* (Anat, Bot) tejido *m*; (paper handkerchief) pañuelo *m* de papel. **~ paper** *n* papel *m* de seda

tit /tɪt/ *n* (bird) paro *m*; (▣, breast) teta *f*

titbit /'tɪtbɪt/ *n* exquisitez *f*

tit for tat *n*: **it was ~** fue ojo por ojo, diente por diente

title /'taɪtl/ *n* título *m*

to /tuː, tə/ *prep* a; (towards) hacia; (in order to) para; (as far as) hasta; (of) de. **give it ~ me** dámelo. **what did you say ~ him?** ¿qué le dijiste?; **I don't want ~** no quiero. **it's twenty ~ seven** (by clock) son las siete menos veinte, son veinte para las siete (LAm). ● *adv*. **pull ~** cerrar. **~ and fro** *adv* de un lado a otro

toad /təʊd/ *n* sapo *m*. **~stool** *n* hongo *m* (*no comestible*)

toast /təʊst/ *n* pan *m* tostado, tostadas *fpl*; (drink) brindis *m*. **a piece of ~** una tostada, un pan tostado (Mex). **drink a ~ to** brindar por. ● *vt* (Culin) tostar; (drink to) brindar por. **~er** *n* tostadora *f* (eléctrica), tostador *m*

tobacco /tə'bækəʊ/ *n* tabaco *m*. **~nist** /-ənɪst/ *n* estanquero *m*

toboggan /tə'bɒgən/ *n* tobogán *m*

today /tə'deɪ/ *n & adv* hoy (*m*)

toddler /'tɒdlə(r)/ *n* niño *m* pequeño (*entre un año y dos años y medio de edad*)

toe /təʊ/ *n* dedo *m* (del pie); (of shoe) punta *f*. **big ~** dedo *m* gordo (del pie). **on one's ~s** (fig) alerta. ● *vt*. **~ the line** acatar la disciplina

toffee /'tɒfɪ/ *n* toffee *m* (*golosina hecha con azúcar y mantequilla*)

together /tə'geðə(r)/ *adv* juntos; (at same time) a la vez. **~ with** junto con

toil /tɔɪl/ *vi* afanarse. ● *n* trabajo *m* duro

toilet /'tɔɪlɪt/ *n* servicio *m*, baño *m* (LAm). **~ paper** *n* papel *m* higiénico. **~ries** /'tɔɪlɪtrɪz/ *npl* artículos *mpl* de tocador. **~ roll** *n* rollo *m* de papel higiénico

token /'təʊkən/ *n* muestra *f*; (voucher) vale *m*; (coin) ficha *f*. ● *a* simbólico

told /təʊld/ ⇒TELL

tolera|ble /'tɒlərəbl/ a tolerable; (not bad) pasable. ∼**nce** /'tɒlərəns/ n to-lerancia f. ∼**nt** a tolerante. ∼**te** /-reɪt/ vt tolerar. ∼**tion** /-'reɪʃən/ n tolerancia f

toll /təʊl/ n (on road) peaje m, cuota f (Mex). **death** ∼ número m de muertos. ∼ **call** n (Amer) llamada f interurbana, conferencia f. ● vi doblar, tocar a muerto

tomato /tə'mɑːtəʊ/ n (pl -oes) tomate m, jitomate m (Mex)

tomb /tuːm/ n tumba f, sepulcro m. ∼**stone** n lápida f

tomorrow /tə'mɒrəʊ/ n & adv mañana (f). **see you** ∼! ¡hasta mañana!

ton /tʌn/ n tonelada f (= 1,016kg). ∼**s of** 🄸 montones de. **metric** ∼ tonelada f (métrica) (= 1,000kg)

tone /təʊn/ n tono m. □ ∼ **down** vt atenuar; moderar <language>. ∼**deaf** a que no tiene oído (musical)

tongs /tɒŋz/ npl tenacillas fpl

tongue /tʌŋ/ n lengua f. **say sth** ∼ **in cheek** decir algo medio burlándose. ∼**-tied** a cohibido. ∼**-twister** n trabalenguas m

tonic /'tɒnɪk/ a tónico. ● n (Med, fig) tónico m. ∼ (**water**) n tónica f

tonight /tə'naɪt/ adv & n esta noche (f); (evening) esta tarde (f)

tonne /tʌn/ n tonelada f (métrica)

tonsil /'tɒnsl/ n amígdala f. ∼**litis** /-'laɪtɪs/ n amigdalitis f

too /tuː/ adv (excessively) demasiado; (also) también. **I'm not** ∼ **sure** no estoy muy seguro. ∼ **many** demasiados. ∼ **much** demasiado

took /tʊk/ ⇒TAKE

tool /tuːl/ n herramienta f

tooth /tuːθ/ n (pl teeth) diente m; (molar) muela f. ∼**ache** n dolor m de muelas. ∼**brush** n cepillo m de dientes. ∼**paste** n pasta f dentífrica, pasta f de dientes. ∼**pick** n palillo m (de dientes)

top /tɒp/ n parte f superior, parte f de arriba; (of mountain) cima f; (of tree) copa f; (of page) parte f superior; (lid, of bottle) tapa f; (of pen) capuchón m; (spinning ∼) trompo m, peonza f. **be** ∼ **of the class** ser el primero de la cla-

se. **from** ∼ **to bottom** de arriba abajo. **on** ∼ **of** encima de; (besides) además de. ● a más alto; <shelf> superior; <speed> máximo; (in rank) superior; (leading) más destacado. ● vt (pt **topped**) cubrir; (exceed) exceder. □ ∼ **up** vt llenar. ∼ **floor** n último piso m. ∼ **hat** n chistera f. ∼**-heavy** /-'hevi/ a inestable (por ser más pesado en su parte superior)

topic /'tɒpɪk/ n tema m. ∼**al** a de actualidad

topless /tɒples/ a topless

topple /'tɒpl/ vi (Pol) derribar; (overturn) volcar. ● vi caerse

top secret /tɒp'siːkrɪt/ a secreto, reservado

torch /tɔːtʃ/ n linterna f; (flaming) antorcha f

tore /tɔː(r)/ ⇒TEAR¹

torment /'tɔːment/ n tormento m. ● /tɔː'ment/ vt atormentar

torn /tɔːn/ ⇒TEAR¹

tornado /tɔː'neɪdəʊ/ n (pl -oes) tornado m

torpedo /tɔː'piːdəʊ/ n (pl -oes) torpedo m. ● vt torpedear

torrent /'tɒrənt/ n torrente m. ∼**ial** /tə'renʃl/ a torrencial

torrid /'tɒrɪd/ a tórrido; <affair> apasionado

tortoise /'tɔːtəs/ n tortuga f. ∼**shell** n carey m

tortuous /'tɔːtjʊəs/ a tortuoso

torture /'tɔːtʃə(r)/ n tortura f. ● vt torturar

Tory /'tɔːrɪ/ a & n tory m & f

toss /tɒs/ vt tirar, lanzar <ball>; (shake) sacudir. ● vi. ∼ **and turn** (in bed) dar vueltas

tot /tɒt/ n pequeño m; (🄸, of liquor) trago m. ● vt (pt **totted**). ∼ **up** 🄸 sumar

total /'təʊtl/ a & n total (m). ● vt (pt **totalled**) ascender a un total de; (add up) totalizar. ∼**itarian** /təʊtælɪ'teərɪən/ a totalitario. ∼**ly** adv totalmente

totter /'tɒtə(r)/ vi tambalearse

touch /tʌtʃ/ vt tocar; (move) conmover; (concern) afectar. ● vi tocar; <wires> tocarse. ● n toque m; (sense) tacto m; (contact) contacto m. **be/get/**

stay in ~ **with** estar/ponerse/mantenerse en contacto con. □ ~ **down** vi <aircraft> aterrizar. □ ~ **up** vt retocar. ~**ing** a enternecedor. ~**y** a quisquilloso

tough /tʌf/ a (-**er**, -**est**) duro; (strong) fuerte, resistente; (difficult) difícil; (severe) severo. ~**en**. ~ (**up**) vt endurecer; hacer más fuerte <person>

tour /tʊə(r)/ n viaje m; (visit) visita f; (excursion) excursión f; (by team etc) gira f. **be on** ~ estar de gira. ● vt recorrer; (visit) visitar. ~ **guide** n guía de turismo

touris|m /'tʊərɪzəm/ n turismo m. ~**t** /'tʊərɪst/ n turista m & f. ● a turístico. ~**t office** n oficina f de turismo

tournament /'tɔːnəmənt/ n torneo m

tousle /'taʊzl/ vt despeinar

tout /taʊt/ vi. ~ (**for**) solicitar

tow /təʊ/ vt remolcar. ● n remolque m

toward(s) /tə'wɔːd(z)/ prep hacia. **his attitude** ~ **her** su actitud para con ella

towel /'taʊəl/ n toalla f

tower /'taʊə(r)/ n torre f. ● vi. ~ **above** <building> descollar sobre; <person> destacar sobre. ~ **block** n edificio m or bloque m de apartamentos. ~**ing** a altísimo; <rage> violento

town /taʊn/ n ciudad f; (smaller) pueblo m. **go to** ~ 🄸 no escatimar dinero. ~ **hall** n ayuntamiento m

toxic /'tɒksɪk/ a tóxico

toy /tɔɪ/ n juguete m. □ ~ **with** vt juguetear con <object>; darle vueltas a <idea>. ~**shop** n juguetería f

trac|e /treɪs/ n señal f, rastro m. ● vt trazar; (draw) dibujar; (with tracing paper) calcar; (track down) localizar. ~**ing paper** n papel m de calcar

track /træk/ n pista f, huellas fpl; (path) sendero m; (Sport) pista f. **the** ~(**s**) la vía férrea; (Rail) vía f. **keep** ~ **of** seguirle la pista a <person>. ● vt seguirle la pista a. □ ~ **down** vt localizar. ~ **suit** n equipo m (de deportes), chándal m

tract /trækt/ n (land) extensión f; (pamphlet) tratado m breve

traction /'trækʃn/ n tracción f

tractor /'træktə(r)/ n tractor m

trade /treɪd/ n comercio m; (occupation) oficio m; (exchange) cambio m; (industry) industria f. ● vt. ~ **sth for sth** cambiar algo por algo. ● vi comerciar. □ ~ **in** vt (give in part-exchange) entregar como parte del pago. ~ **mark** n marca f (de fábrica). ~**r** n comerciante m & f. ~ **union** n sindicato m

tradition /trə'dɪʃn/ n tradición f. ~**al** a tradicional

traffic /'træfɪk/ n tráfico m. ● vi (pt **trafficked**) comerciar (**in** en). ~ **circle** n (Amer) glorieta f, rotonda f. ~ **island** n isla f peatonal. ~ **jam** n embotellamiento m, atasco m. ~ **lights** npl semáforo m. ~ **warden** n guardia m, controlador m de tráfico

trag|edy /'trædʒɪdɪ/ n tragedia f. ~**ic** /'trædʒɪk/ a trágico

trail /treɪl/ vi arrastrarse; (lag) rezagarse. ● vt (track) seguir la pista de. ● n (left by animal, person) huellas fpl; (path) sendero m. **be on the** ~ **of s.o./ sth** seguir la pista de uno/algo ~**er** n remolque m; (Amer, caravan) caravana f, rulot m; (film) avance m

train /treɪn/ n (Rail) tren m; (of events) serie f; (of dress) cola f. ● vt capacitar <employee>; adiestrar <soldier>; (Sport) entrenar; educar <voice>; guiar <plant>; amaestrar <animal>. ● vi estudiar; (Sport) entrenarse. ~**ed** a (skilled) cualificado, calificado; <doctor> diplomado. ~**ee** /treɪ'niː/ n aprendiz m; (Amer, Mil) recluta m & f. ~**er** n (Sport) entrenador m; (of animals) amaestrador m. ~**ers** mpl zapatillas fpl de deporte. ~**ing** n capacitación f; (Sport) entrenamiento m

trait /treɪ(t)/ n rasgo m

traitor /'treɪtə(r)/ n traidor m

tram /træm/ n tranvía m

tramp /træmp/ vi. ~ (**along**) caminar pesadamente. ● n vagabundo m

trample /'træmpl/ vt pisotear. ● vi. ~ **on** pisotear

trampoline /'træmpəli:n/ *n* trampolín *m*

trance /trɑ:ns/ *n* trance *m*

tranquil /'træŋkwɪl/ *a* tranquilo. ~**lity** /-'kwɪləti/ *n* tranquilidad *f*; (of person) serenidad *f*. ~**lize** /'træŋkwɪlaɪz/ *vt* sedar, dar un sedante a. ~**lizer** *n* sedante *m*, tranquilizante *m*

transaction /træn'zækʃən/ *n* transacción *f*, operación *f*

transatlantic /trænzət'læntɪk/ *a* transatlántico

transcend /træn'send/ *vt* (go beyond) exceder

transcript /'trænskrɪpt/ *n* transcripción *f*

transfer /træns'fɜ:(r)/ *vt* (*pt* **transferred**) trasladar; traspasar <*player*>; transferir <*funds, property*>; pasar <*call*>. ●*vi* trasladarse. ●/'trænsfɜ:(r)/ *n* traslado *m*; (of player) traspaso *m*; (of funds, property) transferencia *f*; (paper) calcomanía *f*

transform /træns'fɔ:m/ *vt* transformar. ~**ation** /-ə'meɪʃn/ *n* transformación *f*. ~**er** *n* transformador *m*

transfusion /træns'fju:ʒn/ *n* transfusión *f*

transient /'trænzɪənt/ *a* pasajero

transistor /træn'zɪstə(r)/ *n* transistor *m*

transit /'trænsɪt/ *n* tránsito *m*. ~**ion** /træn'zɪʒn/ *n* transición *f*. ~**ive** /'trænsɪtɪv/ *a* transitivo

translat|e /trænz'leɪt/ *vt* traducir. ~**ion** /-ʃn/ *n* traducción *f*. ~**or** *n* traductor *m*

transmission /trænz'mɪʃn/ *n* transmisión *f*

transmit /trænz'mɪt/ *vt* (*pt* **transmitted**) transmitir. ~**ter** *n* transmisor *m*

transparen|cy /træns'pærənsɪ/ *n* transparencia *f*; (Photo) diapositiva *f*. ~**t** *a* transparente

transplant /træns'plɑ:nt/ *vt* trasplantar. ●/'trænsplɑ:nt/ *n* trasplante *m*

transport /træn'spɔ:t/ *vt* transportar. ●/'trænspɔ:t/ *n* transporte *m*. ~**ation** /-'teɪʃn/ *n* transporte *m*

trap /træp/ *n* trampa *f*. ●*vt* (*pt* **trapped**) atrapar; (jam) atascar; (cut off) bloquear. ~**door** *n* trampilla *f*

trapeze /trə'pi:z/ *n* trapecio *m*

trash /træʃ/ *n* basura *f*; (Amer, worthless people) escoria *f*. ~ **can** *n* (Amer) cubo *m* de la basura, bote *m* de la basura (Mex). ~**y** *a* <*souvenir*> de porquería; <*magazine*> malo

travel /'trævl/ *vi* (*pt* **travelled**) viajar; <*vehicle*> desplazarse. ●*vt* recorrer. ●*n* viajes *mpl*. ~ **agency** *n* agencia *f* de viajes. ~**ler** *n* viajero *m*. ~**ler's cheque** *n* cheque *m* de viaje *or* viajero. ~**ling expenses** *npl* gastos *mpl* de viaje

trawler /'trɔ:lə(r)/ *n* barca *f* pesquera

tray /treɪ/ *n* bandeja *f*

treacher|ous *a* traidor; (deceptive) engañoso. ~**y** *n* traición *f*

treacle /'tri:kl/ *n* melaza *f*

tread /tred/ *vi* (*pt* **trod**, *pp* **trodden**) pisar. ~ **on sth** pisar algo. ~ **carefully** andarse con cuidado. ●*n* (step) paso *m*; (of tyre) banda *f* de rodamiento

treason /'tri:zn/ *n* traición *f*

treasur|e /'treʒə(r)/ *n* tesoro *m*. ~**ed** /'treʒəd/ *a* <*possession*> preciado. ~**er** /'treʒərə(r)/ *n* tesorero *m*. ~**y** *n* erario *m*, tesoro *m*. **the T**~**y** el fisco, la hacienda pública. **Department of the T**~**y** (in US) Departamento *m* del Tesoro

treat /tri:t/ *vt* tratar; (Med) tratar. ~ **s.o.** (to meal etc) invitar a uno. ●*n* placer *m*; (present) regalo *m*

treatise /'tri:tɪz/ *n* tratado *m*

treatment /'tri:tmənt/ *n* tratamiento *m*

treaty /'tri:tɪ/ *n* tratado *m*

treble /'trebl/ *a* triple; <*clef*> de sol; <*voice*> de tiple. ●*vt* triplicar. ●*vi* triplicarse. ●*n* tiple *m* & *f*

tree /tri:/ *n* árbol *m*

trek /trek/ *n* caminata *f*. ●*vi* (*pt* **trekked**) caminar

trellis /'trelɪs/ *n* enrejado *m*

tremble /'trembl/ *vi* temblar

tremendous /trɪ'mendəs/ *a* formidable; (⎯, huge) tremendo. ~**ly** *adv* tremendamente

tremor /'tremə(r)/ *n* temblor *m*

trench /trentʃ/ *n* zanja *f*; (Mil) trinchera *f*

trend /trend/ *n* tendencia *f*; (fashion) moda *f*. **~y** *a* (**-ier, -iest**) 🔁 moderno

trepidation /trepɪ'deɪʃn/ *n* inquietud *f*

trespass /'trespəs/ *vi.* **~ on** entrar sin autorización (*en propiedad ajena*). **~er** *n* intruso *m*

trial /'traɪəl/ *n* prueba *f*; (Jurid) proceso *m*, juicio *m*; (ordeal) prueba *f* dura. **by ~ and error** por ensayo y error. **be on ~** estar a prueba; (Jurid) estar siendo procesado

triang|le /'traɪæŋgl/ *n* triángulo *m*. **~ular** /-'æŋgjʊlə(r)/ *a* triangular

trib|al /'traɪbl/ *a* tribal. **~e** /traɪb/ *n* tribu *f*

tribulation /trɪbjʊ'leɪʃn/ *n* tribulación *f*

tribunal /traɪ'bjuːnl/ *n* tribunal *m*

tributary /'trɪbjʊtrɪ/ *n* (Geog) afluente *m*

tribute /'trɪbjuːt/ *n* tributo *m*; (acknowledgement) homenaje *m*. **pay ~ to** rendir homenaje a

trick /trɪk/ *n* trampa *f*, ardid *m*; (joke) broma *f*; (feat) truco *m*; (in card games) baza *f*. **play a ~ on** gastar una broma a. **●** *vt* engañar. **~ery** *n* engaño *m*

trickle /'trɪkl/ *vi* gotear. **~ in** (fig) entrar poco a poco

trickster /'trɪkstə(r)/ *n* estafador *m*

tricky /'trɪkɪ/ *a* delicado, difícil

tricycle /'traɪsɪkl/ *n* triciclo *m*

tried /traɪd/ ⇒TRY

trifl|e /'traɪfl/ *n* nimiedad *f*; (Culin) postre de bizcocho, jerez, frutas y nata. **●** *vi.* □ **~e with** *vt* jugar con. **~ing** *a* insignificante

trigger /'trɪgə(r)/ *n* (of gun) gatillo *m*. **●** *vt.* **~ (off)** desencadenar

trim /trɪm/ *a* (**trimmer, trimmest**) (slim) esbelto; (neat) elegante. **●** *vt* (*pt* **trimmed**) (cut) recortar; (adorn) adornar. **●** *n* (cut) recorte *m*. **in ~** en buen estado. **~mings** *npl* recortes *mpl*

trinity /'trɪnɪtɪ/ *n.* **the (Holy) T~** la (Santísima) Trinidad

trinket /'trɪŋkɪt/ *n* chuchería *f*

trio /'triːəʊ/ *n* (*pl* **-os**) trío *m*

trip /trɪp/ (*pt* **tripped**) *vt* **~ (up)** hacerle una zancadilla a, hacer tropezar. **●** *vi* tropezar. **●** *n* (journey) viaje *m*; (outing) excursión *f*; (stumble) traspié *m*

tripe /traɪp/ *n* callos *mpl*, mondongo *m* (LAm), pancita *f* (Mex); (🔁, nonsense) paparruchas *fpl*

triple /'trɪpl/ *a* triple. **●** *vt* triplicar. **●** *vi* triplicarse. **~t** /'trɪplɪt/ *n* trillizo *m*

triplicate /'trɪplɪkət/ *a* triplicado. **in ~** por triplicado

tripod /'traɪpɒd/ *n* trípode *m*

trite /traɪt/ *a* trillado

triumph /'traɪʌmf/ *n* triunfo *m*. **●** *vi* triunfar (**over** sobre). **~al** /-'ʌmfl/ *a* triunfal. **~ant** /-'ʌmfnt/ *a* <*troops*> triunfador; <*moment*> triunfal; <*smile*> de triunfo

trivial /'trɪvɪəl/ *a* insignificante; <*concerns*> trivial. **~ity** /-'ælətɪ/ *n* trivialidad *f*

trod, trodden /trɒd, trɒdn/ ⇒TREAD

trolley /'trɒlɪ/ *n* (*pl* **-eys**) carretón *m*; (in supermarket, airport) carrito *m*; (for food, drink) carrito *m*, mesa *f* rodante. **~ car** *n* (Amer) tranvía *f*

trombone /trɒm'bəʊn/ *n* trombón *m*

troop /truːp/ *n* compañía *f*; (of cavalry) escuadrón *m*. **●** *vi.* **~ in** entrar en tropel. **~ out** salir en tropel. **~er** *n* soldado *m* de caballería; (Amer, state police officer) agente *m* & *f*. **~s** *npl* (Mil) tropas *fpl*

trophy /'trəʊfɪ/ *n* trofeo *m*

tropic /'trɒpɪk/ *n* trópico *m*. **~al** *a* tropical. **~s** *npl* trópicos *mpl*

trot /trɒt/ *n* trote *m*. **●** *vi* (*pt* **trotted**) trotar

trouble /'trʌbl/ *n* problemas *mpl*; (awkward situation) apuro *m*; (inconvenience) molestia *f*. **be in ~** estar en apuros. **get into ~** meterse en problemas. **look for ~** buscar camorra. **take the ~ to do sth** molestarse en hacer algo. **●** *vt* (bother) molestar; (worry) preocupar. **~-maker** *n* alborotador *m.* **~some** /-səm/ *a* problemático. **~ spot** n punto m conflictivo

trough /trɒf/ n (for drinking) abrevadero m; (for feeding) comedero m

troupe /tru:p/ n compañía f teatral

trousers /ˈtraʊzəz/ npl pantalón m, pantalones mpl

trout /traʊt/ n (pl **trout**) trucha f

trowel /ˈtraʊəl/ n (garden) desplantador m; (for mortar) paleta f

truant /ˈtru:ənt/ n. **play ~** hacer novillos

truce /tru:s/ n tregua f

truck /trʌk/ n camión m; (Rail) vagón m, furgón m; (Amer, vegetables, fruit) productos mpl de la huerta. **~ driver**, **~er** (Amer) n camionero m. **~ing** n transporte m por carretera

trudge /trʌdʒ/ vi andar penosamente

true /tru:/ a (-er, -est) verdadero; <story, account> verídico; <friend> auténtico, de verdad. **~ to sth/s.o.** fiel a algo/uno. **be ~** ser cierto. **come ~** hacerse realidad

truffle /ˈtrʌfl/ n trufa f; (chocolate) trufa f de chocolate

truly /ˈtru:lɪ/ adv verdaderamente; (sincerely) sinceramente. **yours ~** (in letters) cordiales saludos

trump /trʌmp/ n (Cards) triunfo m; (fig) baza f

trumpet /ˈtrʌmpɪt/ n trompeta f. **~er** n trompetista m & f, trompeta m & f

truncheon /ˈtrʌntʃən/ n porra f

trunk /trʌŋk/ n (of tree) tronco m; (box) baúl m; (of elephant) trompa f; (Amer, Auto) maletero m, cajuela f (Mex). **~s** npl bañador m, traje m de baño

truss /trʌs/. **truss (up)** vt atar

trust /trʌst/ n confianza f; (money, property) fondo m de inversiones; (institution) fundación f. **on ~** a ojos cerrados; (Com) al fiado. ● vi. **~ in s.o./sth** confiar en uno/algo. ● vt confiar en; (in negative sentences) fiarse; (hope) esperar. **~ed** a leal. **~ee** /trʌˈsti:/ n fideicomisario m. **~ful** a confiado. **~ing** a confiado. **~worthy**, **~y** a digno de confianza

truth /tru:θ/ n (pl **-s** /tru:ðz/) verdad f; (of account, story) veracidad f. **~ful** a veraz.

try /traɪ/ vt (pt **tried**) intentar; probar <food, product>; (be a strain on) poner a prueba; (Jurid) procesar. **~ to do sth** tratar de hacer algo, intentar hacer algo. **~ not to forget** procura no olvidarte. ● n tentativa f, prueba f; (Rugby) ensayo m. □ **~ on** vt probarse <garment>. □ **~ out** vt probar. **~ing** a duro; (annoying) molesto

tsar /zɑː(r)/ n zar m

T-shirt /ˈtiːʃɜːt/ n camiseta f

tub /tʌb/ n cuba f; (for washing clothes) tina f; (bathtub) bañera f; (for ice cream) envase m, tarrina f

tuba /ˈtjuːbə/ n tuba f

tubby /ˈtʌbɪ/ a (-ier, -iest) rechoncho

tube /tjuːb/ n tubo m; (▣, Rail) metro m; (Amer ▣, television) tele f. **inner ~** n cámara f de aire

tuberculosis /tjuːbɜːkjʊˈləʊsɪs/ n tuberculosis f

tub|ing /ˈtjuːbɪŋ/ n tubería f. **~ular** /-jʊlə(r)/ a tubular

tuck /tʌk/ n (fold) jareta f. ● vt plegar; (put) meter. □ **~ in(to)** vi (▣, eat) ponerse a comer. □ **~ up** vt arropar <child>

Tuesday /ˈtjuːzdeɪ/ n martes m

tuft /tʌft/ n (of hair) mechón m; (of feathers) penacho m; (of grass) mata f

tug /tʌg/ vt (pt **tugged**) tirar de. ● vi. **~ at sth** tirar de algo. ● n tirón m; (Naut) remolcador m. **~-of-war** n juego de tira y afloja

tuition /tjuːˈɪʃn/ n clases fpl

tulip /ˈtjuːlɪp/ n tulipán m

tumble /ˈtʌmbl/ vi caerse. ● n caída f. **~down** a en ruinas. **~-drier** n secadora f. **~r** n (glass) vaso m (de lados rectos)

tummy /ˈtʌmɪ/ n ▣ barriga f

tumour /ˈtjuːmə(r)/ n tumor m

tumult /ˈtjuːmʌlt/ n tumulto m. **~uous** /-ˈmʌltjʊəs/ a <applause> apoteósico

tuna /ˈtjuːnə/ n (pl **tuna**) atún m

tune /tjuːn/ n melodía f; (piece) tonada f. **be in ~** estar afinado. **be out of ~** estar desafinado. ● vt afinar, sintonizar *<radio, TV>*; (Mec) poner a punto. ● *vi.* ~ **in** (**to**) sintonizar (con). □ ~ **up** *vt/i* afinar. ~**ful** *a* melodioso. ~**r** *n* afinador *m*; (Radio) sintonizador *m*

tunic /'tju:nɪk/ *n* túnica *f*

tunnel /'tʌnl/ *n* túnel *m*. ● *vi* (*pt* **tunnelled**) abrir un túnel

turban /'tɜ:bən/ *n* turbante *m*

turbine /'tɜ:baɪn/ *n* turbina *f*

turbo /'tɜ:bəʊ/ *n* (*pl* **-os**) turbo(compresor) *m*

turbulen|ce /'tɜ:bjʊləns/ *n* turbulencia *f*. ~**t** *a* turbulento

turf /tɜ:f/ *n* (*pl* **turfs** or **turves**) césped *m*; (segment of grass) tepe *m*. □ ~ **out** *vt* 🔲 echar

turgid /'tɜ:dʒɪd/ *a* *<language>* ampuloso

turkey /'tɜ:kɪ/ *n* (*pl* **-eys**) pavo *m*

Turk|ey /'tɜ:kɪ/ *f* Turquía *f*. ~**ish** *a* & *n* turco (*m*)

turmoil /'tɜ:mɔɪl/ *n* confusión *f*

turn /tɜ:n/ *vt* hacer girar; volver *<head, page>*; doblar *<corner>*; (change) cambiar; (deflect) desviar. ~ **sth into sth** convertir *or* transformar algo en algo. ● *vi* *<handle>* girar, dar vueltas; *<person>* volverse, darse la vuelta. ~ **right** girar *or* doblar *or* torcer a la derecha. ~ **red** ponerse rojo. ~ **into sth** convertirse en algo. ● *n* vuelta *f*; (in road) curva *f*; (change) giro *m*; (sequence) turno *m*; (🔲, of illness) ataque *m*. **good** ~ favor *m*. **in** ~ a su vez. □ ~ **down** *vt* (fold) doblar; (reduce) bajar; (reject) rechazar. □ ~ **off** *vt* cerrar *<tap>*; apagar *<light, TV, etc>*. *vi* (from road) doblar. □ ~ **on** *vt* abrir *<tap>*; encender, prender (LAm) *<light etc>*. □ ~ **out** *vt* apagar *<light etc>*. *vi* (result) resultar. □ ~ **round** *vi* darse la vuelta. □ ~ **up** *vi* aparecer. *vt* (find) encontrar; levantar *<collar>*; subir *<hem>*; acortar *<trousers>*; poner más fuerte *<gas>*. ~**ed-up** *a* *<nose>* respingón. ~**ing** *n* (in town) bocacalle *f*. **we've missed the** ~**ing** nos hemos pasado la calle (*or* carretera). ~**ing-point** *n* momento *m* decisivo.

turnip /'tɜ:nɪp/ *n* nabo *m*

turn: ~**over** *n* (Com) facturación *f*; (of staff) movimiento *m*. ~**pike** *n* (Amer) autopista *f* de peaje. ~**stile** *n* torniquete *m*. ~**table** *n* platina *f*. ~**-up** *n* (of trousers) vuelta *f*, valenciana *f* (Mex)

turquoise /'tɜ:kwɔɪz/ *a* & *n* turquesa (*f*)

turret /'tʌrɪt/ *n* torrecilla *f*

turtle /'tɜ:tl/ *n* tortuga *f* de mar; (Amer, tortoise) tortuga *f*

turves /tɜ:vz/ ⇨TURF

tusk /tʌsk/ *n* colmillo *m*

tussle /'tʌsl/ *n* lucha *f*

tutor /'tju:tə(r)/ *n* profesor *m* particular

tuxedo /tʌk'si:dəʊ/ *n* (*pl* **-os**) (Amer) esmoquin *m*, smoking *m*

TV /ti:'vi:/ *n* televisión *f*, tele *f* 🔲

twang /twæŋ/ *n* tañido *m*; (in voice) gangueo *m*

tweet /twi:t/ *n* piada *f*. ● *vi* piar

tweezers /'twi:zəz/ *npl* pinzas *fpl*

twel|fth /twelfθ/ *a* duodécimo. ● *n* doceavo *m*. ~**ve** /twelv/ *a* & *n* doce (*m*)

twent|ieth /'twentɪəθ/ *a* vigésimo. ● *n* veinteavo *m*. ~**y** /'twentɪ/ *a* & *n* veinte (*m*)

twice /twaɪs/ *adv* dos veces. ~ **as many people** el doble de gente

twiddle /'twɪdl/ *vt* (hacer) girar

twig /twɪg/ *n* ramita *f*. ● *vi* (*pt* **twigged**) 🔲 caer, darse cuenta

twilight /'twaɪlaɪt/ *n* crepúsculo *m*

twin /twɪn/ *a* & *n* gemelo (*m*), mellizo (*m*) (LAm)

twine /twaɪn/ *n* cordel *m*, bramante *m*

twinge /twɪndʒ/ *n* punzada *f*; (of remorse) punzada *f*

twinkle /'twɪŋkl/ *vi* centellear. ● *n* centelleo *m*; (in eye) brillo *m*

twirl /twɜ:l/ *vt* (hacer) girar. ● *vi* girar. ● *n* vuelta *f*

twist /twɪst/ *vt* retorcer; (roll) enrollar; girar *<knob>*; tergiversar *<words>*; (distort) retorcer. ~ **one's ankle** torcerse el tobillo. ● *vi* *<rope, wire>* enrollarse; *<road, river>* serpentear. ● *n* torsión *f*; (curve) vuelta *f*

twit /twɪt/ *n* 🔲 imbécil *m*

twitch /twɪtʃ/ *vi* moverse. ● *n* tic *m*

twitter /'twɪtə(r)/ *vi* gorjear

two /tu:/ *a & n* dos (*m*). ∼**-bit** *a* (Amer) de tres al cuarto. ∼**-faced** *a* falso, insincero. ∼**fold** *a* doble. ● *adv* dos veces. ∼**pence** /'tʌpəns/ *n* dos peniques *mpl*. ∼**-piece** (**suit**) *n* traje *m* de dos piezas. ∼**-way** *a* <*traffic*> de doble sentido

tycoon /taɪ'ku:n/ *n* magnate *m*

tying /'taɪɪŋ/ ⇒TIE

type /taɪp/ *n* tipo *m*. ● *vt/i* escribir a máquina. ∼**-cast** *a* <*actor*> encasillado. ∼**script** *n* texto *m* mecanografiado, manuscrito *m* (*de una obra, novela etc*). ∼**writer** *n* máquina *f* de escribir. ∼**written** *a* escrito a máquina, mecanografiado

typhoon /taɪ'fu:n/ *n* tifón *m*

typical /'tɪpɪkl/ *a* típico. ∼**ly** *adv* típicamente

typify /'tɪpɪfaɪ/ *vt* tipificar

typi|ng /'taɪpɪŋ/ *n* mecanografía *f*. ∼**st** *n* mecanógrafo *m*

tyran|nical /tɪ'rænɪkl/ *a* tiránico. ∼**ny** /'tɪrəni/ *n* tiranía *f*. ∼**t** /'taɪərənt/ *n* tirano *m*

tyre /'taɪə(r)/ *n* neumático *m*, llanta *f* (LAm)

Uu

udder /'ʌdə(r)/ *n* ubre *f*

UFO /'ju:fəʊ/ *abbr* (= **unidentified flying object**) OVNI *m* (*objeto volante no identificado*)

ugly /'ʌɡlɪ/ *a* (**-ier, -iest**) feo

UK /ju:'keɪ/ *abbr* (= **United Kingdom**) Reino *m* Unido

Ukraine /ju:'kreɪn/ *n* Ucrania *f*

ulcer /'ʌlsə(r)/ *n* úlcera *f*; (external) llaga *f*

ultimate /'ʌltɪmət/ *a* (eventual) final; (utmost) máximo. ∼**ly** *adv* en última instancia; (in the long run) a la larga

ultimatum /ʌltɪ'meɪtəm/ *n* (*pl* **-ums**) ultimátum *m*

ultra... /'ʌltrə/ *pref* ultra... ∼**violet** /-'vaɪələt/ *a* ultravioleta

umbilical cord /ʌm'bɪlɪkl/ *n* cordón *m* umbilical

umbrella /ʌm'brelə/ *n* paraguas *m*

umpire /'ʌmpaɪə(r)/ *n* árbitro *m*. ● *vt* arbitrar

umpteen /'ʌmptiːn/ *a* 🔲 tropecientos 🔲. ∼**th** *a* 🔲 enésimo

un... /ʌn/ *pref* in..., des..., no, poco, sin

UN /ju:'en/ *abbr* (= **United Nations**) ONU *f* (*Organización de las Naciones Unidas*)

unable /ʌn'eɪbl/ *a.* be ∼ to no poder; (be incapable of) ser incapaz de

unacceptable /ʌnək'septəbl/ *a* <*behaviour*> inaceptable; <*terms*> inadmisible

unaccompanied /ʌnə'kʌmpənɪd/ *a* <*luggage*> no acompañado; <*person, instrument*> solo; <*singing*> sin acompañamiento

unaccustomed /ʌnə'kʌstəmd/ *a* desacostumbrado. be ∼ to *a* no estar acostumbrado a

unaffected /ʌnə'fektɪd/ *a* natural

unaided /ʌn'eɪdɪd/ *a* sin ayuda

unanimous /ju:'nænɪməs/ *a* unánime. ∼**ly** *adv* unánimemente; <*elect*> por unanimidad

unarmed /ʌn'ɑːmd/ *a* desarmado

unattended /ʌnə'tendɪd/ *a* sin vigilar

unattractive /ʌnə'træktɪv/ *a* poco atractivo

unavoidabl|e /ʌnə'vɔɪdəbl/ *a* inevitable. ∼**y** *adv*. I was ∼y delayed no pude evitar llegar tarde

unaware /ʌnə'weə(r)/ *a.* be ∼ of ignorar, no ser consciente de. ∼**s** /-eəz/ *adv* desprevenido

unbearabl|e /ʌn'beərəbl/ *a* insoportable, inaguantable. ∼**y** *adv* inaguantablemente

unbeat|able /ʌn'bi:təbl/ *a* <*quality*> insuperable; <*team*> invencible. ∼**en** *a* no vencido; <*record*> insuperado

unbelievabl|e /ʌnbɪˈliːvəbl/ *a* increíble. **~y** *adv* increíblemente

unbiased /ʌnˈbaɪəst/ *a* imparcial

unblock /ʌnˈblɒk/ *vt* desatascar

unbolt /ʌnˈbəʊlt/ *vt* descorrer el pestillo de

unborn /ʌnˈbɔːn/ *a* que todavía no ha nacido

unbreakable /ʌnˈbreɪkəbl/ *a* irrompible

unbroken /ʌnˈbrəʊkən/ *a* (intact) intacto; (continuous) ininterrumpido

unbutton /ʌnˈbʌtn/ *vt* desabotonar, desabrochar

uncalled-for /ʌnˈkɔːldfɔː(r)/ *a* fuera de lugar

uncanny /ʌnˈkænɪ/ *a* (-ier, -iest) raro, extraño

uncertain /ʌnˈsɜːtn/ *a* incierto; (hesitant) vacilante. **be ~ of/about sth** no estar seguro de algo. **~ty** *n* incertidumbre *f*

uncharitable /ʌnˈtʃærɪtəbl/ *a* severo

uncivilized /ʌnˈsɪvɪlaɪzd/ *a* incivilizado

uncle /ˈʌŋkl/ *n* tío *m*

unclean /ʌnˈkliːn/ *a* impuro

unclear /ʌnˈklɪə(r)/ *a* poco claro

uncomfortable /ʌnˈkʌmfətəbl/ *a* incómodo

uncommon /ʌnˈkɒmən/ *a* poco común

uncompromising /ʌnˈkɒmprəmaɪzɪŋ/ *a* intransigente

unconcerned /ʌnkənˈsɜːnd/ *a* indiferente

unconditional /ʌnkənˈdɪʃənl/ *a* incondicional

unconnected /ʌnkəˈnektɪd/ *a* (unrelated) sin conexión. **the events are ~** estos acontecimientos no guardan ninguna relación (entre sí)

unconscious /ʌnˈkɒnʃəs/ *a* (Med) inconsciente. **~ly** *adv* inconscientemente

unconventional /ʌnkənˈvenʃənl/ *a* poco convencional

uncork /ʌnˈkɔːk/ *vt* descorchar

uncouth /ʌnˈkuːθ/ *a* zafio

uncover /ʌnˈkʌvə(r)/ *vt* destapar; revelar   <*plot, scandal*>

undaunted /ʌnˈdɔːntɪd/ *a* impertérrito

undecided /ʌndɪˈsaɪdɪd/ *a* indeciso

undeniabl|e /ʌndɪˈnaɪəbl/ *a* innegable. **~y** *adv* sin lugar a dudas

under /ˈʌndə(r)/ *prep* debajo de; (less than) menos de; <*heading*> bajo; (according to) según; (expressing movement) por debajo de. ● *adv* debajo, abajo

under... *pref* sub...

under: **~carriage** *n* (Aviat) tren *m* de aterrizaje. **~charge** *vt* /-ˈtʃɑːdʒ/ cobrarle de menos a. **~clothes** *npl* ropa *f* interior. **~coat**, **~coating** (Amer) *n* (paint) pintura *f* base; (first coat) primera mano *f* de pintura. **~cover** *a* /-ˈkʌvə(r)/ secreto. **~current** *n* corriente *f* submarina. **~dog** *n*. **the ~dog** el que tiene menos posibilidades. **the ~dogs** *npl* los de abajo. **~done** *a* /-ˈdʌn/ <*meat*> poco hecho. **~estimate** /-ˈestɪmeɪt/ *vt* (underrate) subestimar. **~fed** /-ˈfed/ *a* subalimentado. **~foot** /-ˈfʊt/ *adv* debajo de los pies. **~go** *vt* (*pt* **-went**, *pp* **-gone**) sufrir. **~graduate** /-ˈɡrædjʊət/ *n* estudiante *m* & *f* universitario (no licenciado). **~ground** /-ˈɡraʊnd/ *adv* bajo tierra; (in secret) clandestinamente. ● /-ˈɡraʊnd/ *a* subterráneo; (secret) clandestino. ● *n* metro *m*. **~growth** *n* maleza *f*. **~hand** /-ˈhænd/ *a* (secret) clandestino; (deceptive) fraudulento. **~lie** /-ˈlaɪ/ *vt* (*pt* **-lay**, *pp* **-lain**, *pres p* **-lying**) subyacer a. **~line** /-ˈlaɪn/ *vt* subrayar. **~lying** /-ˈlaɪɪŋ/ *a* subyacente. **~mine** /-ˈmaɪn/ *vt* socavar. **~neath** /-ˈniːθ/ *prep* debajo de, abajo de (LAm). ● *adv* por debajo. **~paid** /-ˈpeɪd/ *a* mal pagado. **~pants** *npl* calzoncillos *mpl*. **~pass** *n* paso *m* subterráneo; (for traffic) paso *m* inferior. **~privileged** /-ˈprɪvəlɪdʒd/ *a* desfavorecido. **~rate** /-ˈreɪt/ *vt* subestimar. **~rated** /-ˈreɪtɪd/ *a* no debidamente apreciado. **~shirt** *n* (Amer) camiseta *f* (interior).

understand /ʌndəˈstænd/ *vt* (*pt* **-stood**) entender; (empathize with) comprender, entender. ● *vi* entender, comprender. ~**able** *a* comprensible. ~**ing** *a* comprensivo. ● *n* (grasp) entendimiento *m*; (sympathy) comprensión *f*; (agreement) acuerdo *m*

under: ~**statement** *n* subestimación *f*. ~**take** /-'teɪk/ (*pt* -**took**, *pp* -**taken**) emprender <*task*>; asumir <*responsibility*>. ~**take to do sth** comprometerse a hacer algo. ~**taker** *n* director *m* de pompas fúnebres. ~**taking** /-'teɪkɪŋ/ *n* empresa *f*; (promise) promesa *f*. ~**tone** *n*. **in an** ~**tone** en voz baja. ~**value** /-'vælju:/ *vt* subvalorar. ~**water** /-'wɔːtə(r)/ *a* submarino. ● *adv* debajo del agua. ~**wear** *n* ropa *f* interior. ~**weight** /-'weɪt/ *a* de peso más bajo que el normal. ~**went** /-'went/ ⇨UNDERGO. ~**world** *n* (criminals) hampa *f*. ~**write** /-'raɪt/ *vt* (*pt* -**wrote**, *pp* -**written**) (Com) asegurar; (guarantee financially) financiar

undeserved /ʌndɪ'zɜːvd/ *a* inmerecido

undesirable /ʌndɪ'zaɪərəbl/ *a* indeseable

undignified /ʌn'dɪgnɪfaɪd/ *a* indecoroso

undisputed /ʌndɪs'pjuːtɪd/ *a* <*champion*> indiscutido; <*facts*> innegable

undo /ʌn'duː/ *vt* (*pt* -**did**, *pp* -**done**) desabrochar <*button, jacket*>; abrir <*zip*>; desatar <*knot, laces*>

undoubted /ʌn'daʊtɪd/ *a* indudable. ~**ly** *adv* indudablemente, sin duda

undress /ʌn'dres/ *vt* desvestir, desnudar. ● *vi* desvestirse, desnudarse

undue /ʌn'djuː/ *a* excesivo

undulate /'ʌndjʊleɪt/ *vi* ondular

unduly /ʌn'djuːlɪ/ *adv* excesivamente

unearth /ʌn'ɜːθ/ *vt* desenterrar; descubrir <*document*>

unearthly /ʌn'ɜːθlɪ/ *a* sobrenatural. **at an** ~ **hour** a estas horas intempestivas

uneasy /ʌn'iːzɪ/ *a* incómodo

uneconomic /ʌniːkə'nɒmɪk/ *a* poco económico

uneducated /ʌn'edjʊkeɪtɪd/ *a* sin educación

unemploy|ed /ʌnɪm'plɔɪd/ *a* desempleado, parado. ~**ment** *n* desempleo *m*, paro *m*

unending /ʌn'endɪŋ/ *a* interminable, sin fin

unequal /ʌn'iːkwəl/ *a* desigual

unequivocal /ʌnɪ'kwɪvəkl/ *a* inequívoco

unethical /ʌn'eθɪkl/ *a* poco ético, inmoral

uneven /ʌn'iːvn/ *a* desigual

unexpected /ʌnɪk'spektɪd/ *a* inesperado; <*result*> imprevisto. ~**ly** *adv* <*arrive*> de improviso; <*happen*> de forma imprevista

unfair /ʌn'feə(r)/ *a* injusto; improcedente <*dismissal*>. ~**ly** *adv* injustamente

unfaithful /ʌn'feɪθfl/ *a* infiel

unfamiliar /ʌnfə'mɪlɪə(r)/ *a* desconocido. **be** ~ **with** desconocer

unfasten /ʌn'fɑːsn/ *vt* desabrochar <*clothes*>; (untie) desatar

unfavourable /ʌn'feɪvərəbl/ *a* desfavorable

unfeeling /ʌn'fiːlɪŋ/ *a* insensible

unfit /ʌn'fɪt/ *a*. **I'm** ~ no estoy en forma. ~ **for human consumption** no apto para el consumo

unfold /ʌn'fəʊld/ *vt* desdoblar; desplegar <*wings*>; (fig) revelar. ● *vi* <*leaf*> abrirse; <*events*> desarrollarse

unforeseen /ʌnfɔː'siːn/ *a* imprevisto

unforgettable /ʌnfə'getəbl/ *a* inolvidable

unforgivable /ʌnfə'gɪvəbl/ *a* imperdonable

unfortunate /ʌn'fɔːtʃənət/ *a* desafortunado; (regrettable) lamentable. ~**ly** *adv* desafortunadamente; (stronger) por desgracia, desgraciadamente

unfounded /ʌn'faʊndɪd/ *a* infundado

unfriendly /ʌn'frendlɪ/ *a* poco amistoso; (stronger) antipático

unfurl /ʌn'fɜːl/ *vt* desplegar

ungainly /ʌnˈgeɪnlɪ/ *a* desgarbado

ungrateful /ʌnˈgreɪtfl/ *a* desagradecido, ingrato

unhapp|iness /ʌnˈhæpmes/ *n* infelicidad *f*, tristeza *f*. ~**y** *a* (**-ier**, **-iest**) infeliz, triste; (unsuitable) inoportuno. **be ~y about sth** no estar contento con algo

unharmed /ʌnˈhɑːmd/ *a* <*person*> ileso

unhealthy /ʌnˈhelθɪ/ *a* (**-ier**, **-iest**) <*person*> de mala salud; <*complexion*> enfermizo; <*conditions*> poco saludable

unhurt /ʌnˈhɜːt/ *a* ileso

unification /juːnɪfɪˈkeɪʃn/ *n* unificación *f*

uniform /ˈjuːnɪfɔːm/ *a* & *n* uniforme (*m*). ~**ity** /-ˈfɔːmətɪ/ *n* uniformidad *f*

unify /ˈjuːnɪfaɪ/ *vt* unir

unilateral /juːnɪˈlætərəl/ *a* unilateral

unimaginable /ʌnɪˈmædʒɪnəbl/ *a* inimaginable

unimaginative /ʌnɪˈmædʒɪnətɪv/ *a* <*person*> poco imaginativo

unimportant /ʌnɪmˈpɔːtnt/ *a* sin importancia

uninhabited /ʌnɪnˈhæbɪtɪd/ *a* deshabitado; <*island*> despoblado

unintelligible /ʌnɪnˈtelɪdʒəbl/ *a* ininteligible

unintentional /ʌnɪnˈtenʃənl/ *a* involuntario

union /ˈjuːnjən/ *n* unión *f*; (trade union) sindicato *m*; (student ~) asociación *f* de estudiantes. **U~ Jack** *n* bandera *f* del Reino Unido

unique /juːˈniːk/ *a* único

unison /ˈjuːnɪsn/ *n*. **in ~** al unísono

unit /ˈjuːnɪt/ *n* unidad *f*; (of furniture etc) módulo *m*; (in course) módulo *m*

unite /juːˈnaɪt/ *vt* unir. ● *vi* unirsc. **U~d Kingdom** *n* Reino *m* Unido. **U~d Nations** *n* Organización *f* de las Naciones Unidas (ONU). **U~d States (of America)** *n* Estados *mpl* Unidos (de América)

unity /ˈjuːnɪtɪ/ *n* unidad *f*

univers|al /juːnɪˈvɜːsl/ *a* universal. ~**e** /ˈjuːnɪvɜːs/ *n* universo *m*

university /juːnɪˈvɜːsətɪ/ *n* universidad *f*. ● *a* universitario

unjust /ʌnˈdʒʌst/ *a* injusto. ~**ified** /-ɪfaɪd/ *a* injustificado

unkind /ʌnˈkaɪnd/ *a* poco amable; (cruel) cruel; <*remark*> hiriente

unknown /ʌnˈnəʊn/ *a* desconocido

unlawful /ʌnˈlɔːfl/ *a* ilegal

unleaded /ʌnˈledɪd/ *a* <*fuel*> sin plomo

unleash /ʌnˈliːʃ/ *vt* soltar

unless /ʌnˈles, ənˈles/ *conj* a menos que, a no ser que

unlike /ʌnˈlaɪk/ *prep* diferente de. (in contrast to) a diferencia de. ~**ly** *a* improbable

unlimited /ʌnˈlɪmɪtɪd/ *a* ilimitado

unlisted /ʌnˈlɪstɪd/ *a* (Amer) que no figura en la guía telefónica, privado (Mex)

unload /ʌnˈləʊd/ *vt* descargar

unlock /ʌnˈlɒk/ *vt* abrir (con llave)

unluck|ily /ʌnˈlʌkɪlɪ/ *adv* desgraciadamente. ~**y** *a* (**-ier**, **-iest**) <*person*> sin suerte, desafortunado. **be ~y** tener mala suerte; (bring bad luck) traer mala suerte

unmarried /ʌnˈmærɪd/ *a* soltero

unmask /ʌnˈmɑːsk/ *vt* desenmascarar

unmentionable /ʌnˈmenʃənəbl/ *a* inmencionable

unmistakable /ʌnmɪˈsteɪkəbl/ *a* inconfundible

unnatural /ʌnˈnætʃərəl/ *a* poco natural; (not normal) anormal

unnecessar|ily /ʌnˈnesəsərɪlɪ/ *adv* innecesariamente. ~**y** *a* innecesario

unnerve /ʌnˈnɜːv/ *vt* desconcertar

unnoticed /ʌnˈnəʊtɪst/ *a* inadvertido

unobtainable /ʌnəbˈteɪnəbl/ *a* imposible de conseguir

unobtrusive /ʌnəbˈtruːsɪv/ *a* discreto

unofficial /ʌnəˈfɪʃl/ *a* no oficial. ~**ly** *adv* extraoficialmente

unpack /ʌnˈpæk/ *vt* sacar las cosas de <*bags*>; deshacer, desempacar (LAm) <*suitcase*>. ● *vi* deshacer las maletas

unpaid /ʌnˈpeɪd/ a *<work>* no retribuido, no remunerado; *<leave>* sin sueldo

unperturbed /ʌnpəˈtɜːbd/ a impasible. **he carried on ~** siguió sin inmutarse

unpleasant /ʌnˈpleznt/ a desagradable

unplug /ʌnˈplʌg/ vt desenchufar

unpopular /ʌnˈpɒpjʊlə(r)/ a impopular

unprecedented /ʌnˈpresɪdentɪd/ a sin precedentes

unpredictable /ʌnprɪˈdɪktəbl/ a imprevisible

unprepared /ʌnprɪˈpeəd/ a no preparado; (unready) desprevenido

unprofessional /ʌnprəˈfeʃənəl/ a poco profesional

unprofitable /ʌnˈprɒfɪtəbl/ a no rentable

unprotected /ʌnprəˈtektɪd/ a sin protección; *<sex>* sin el uso de preservativos

unqualified /ʌnˈkwɒlɪfaɪd/ a sin título; (fig) absoluto

unquestion|able /ʌnˈkwestʃən əbl/ a incuestionable, innegable. **~ing** a *<obedience>* ciego; *<loyalty>* incondicional

unravel /ʌnˈrævl/ vt (pt **unravelled**) desenredar; desentrañar *<mystery>*

unreal /ʌnˈrɪəl/ a irreal. **~istic** /-ˈlɪstɪk/ a poco realista

unreasonable /ʌnˈriːzənəbl/ a irrazonable

unrecognizable /ʌnrekəg ˈnaɪzəbl/ a irreconocible

unrelated /ʌnrɪˈleɪtɪd/ a *<facts>* no relacionados (entre sí); *<people>* no emparentado

unreliable /ʌnrɪˈlaɪəbl/ a *<person>* informal; *<machine>* poco fiable; *<information>* poco fidedigno

unrepentant /ʌnrɪˈpentənt/ a impenitente

unrest /ʌnˈrest/ n (discontent) descontento m; (disturbances) disturbios mpl

unrivalled /ʌnˈraɪvld/ a incomparable

unroll /ʌnˈrəʊl/ vt desenrollar. ● vi desenrollarse

unruffled /ʌnˈrʌfld/ *<person>* sereno

unruly /ʌnˈruːlɪ/ a *<class>* indisciplinado; *<child>* revoltoso

unsafe /ʌnˈseɪf/ a inseguro

unsatisfactory /ʌnsætɪsˈfæktərɪ/ a insatisfactorio

unsavoury /ʌnˈseɪvərɪ/ a desagradable

unscathed /ʌnˈskeɪðd/ a ileso

unscheduled /ʌnˈʃedjuːld/ a no programado, no previsto

unscrew /ʌnˈskruː/ vt destornillar; desenroscar *<lid>*

unscrupulous /ʌnˈskruːpjʊləs/ a inescrupuloso

unseemly /ʌnˈsiːmlɪ/ a indecoroso

unseen /ʌnˈsiːn/ a *<danger>* oculto; (unnoticed) sin ser visto

unselfish /ʌnˈselfɪʃ/ a *<act>* desinteresado; *<person>* nada egoísta

unsettle /ʌnˈsetl/ vt desestabilizar *<situation>*; alterar *<plans>*. **~d** a agitado; *<weather>* inestable; (undecided) pendiente (de resolución)

unshakeable /ʌnˈʃeɪkəbl/ a inquebrantable

unshaven /ʌnˈʃeɪvn/ a sin afeitar, sin rasurar (Mex)

unsightly /ʌnˈsaɪtlɪ/ a feo

unskilled /ʌnˈskɪld/ a *<work>* no especializado; *<worker>* no cualificado, no calificado

unsociable /ʌnˈsəʊʃəbl/ a insociable

unsolved /ʌnˈsɒlvd/ a no resuelto; *<murder>* sin esclarecerse

unsophisticated /ʌnsəˈfɪstɪkeɪ tɪd/ a sencillo

unsound /ʌnˈsaʊnd/ a poco sólido

unspecified /ʌnˈspesɪfaɪd/ a no especificado

unstable /ʌnˈsteɪbl/ a inestable

unsteady /ʌnˈstedɪ/ a inestable, poco firme

unstuck /ʌnˈstʌk/ a despegado. **come ~** despegarse; (fail) fracasar

unsuccessful /ʌnsəkˈsesfʊl/ a *<attempt>* infructuoso. **be ~** no tener éxito, fracasar

unsuitable /ʌn'su:təbl/ *a* <*clothing*> poco apropiado, poco adecuado; <*time*> inconveniente. **she is ~ for the job** no es la persona indicada para el trabajo

unsure /ʌn'ʃʊə(r)/ *a* inseguro

unthinkable /ʌn'θɪŋkəbl/ *a* inconcebible

untid|iness /ʌn'taɪdməs/ *n* desorden *m*. **~y** *a* (**-ier, -iest**) desordenado; <*appearance, writing*> descuidado

untie /ʌn'taɪ/ *vt* desatar, desamarrar (LAm)

until /ən'tɪl, ʌn'tɪl/ *prep* hasta. ● *conj* hasta que

untold /ʌn'təʊld/ *a* incalculable

untouched /ʌn'tʊtʃt/ *a* intacto

untried /ʌn'traɪd/ *a* no probado

untrue /ʌn'tru:/ *a* falso

unused /ʌn'ju:zd/ *a* nuevo. ● /ʌn'ju:st/ *a*. **~ to** no acostumbrado a

unusual /ʌn'ju:ʒʊəl/ *a* poco común, poco corriente. **it's ~ to see so many people** es raro ver a tanta gente. **~ly** *adv* excepcionalmente, inusitadamente

unveil /ʌn'veɪl/ *vt* descubrir

unwanted /ʌn'wɒntɪd/ *a* superfluo; <*child*> no deseado

unwelcome /ʌn'welkəm/ *a* <*news*> poco grato; <*guest*> inoportuno

unwell /ʌn'wel/ *a* indispuesto

unwieldy /ʌn'wi:ldɪ/ *a* pesado y difícil de manejar

unwilling /ʌn'wɪlɪŋ/ *a* mal dispuesto. **be ~** no querer

unwind /ʌn'waɪnd/ *vt* (*pt* **unwound**) desenrollar. ● *vi* (🄵, relax) relajarse

unwise /ʌn'waɪz/ *a* poco sensato

unworthy /ʌn'wɜ:ðɪ/ *a* indigno

unwrap /ʌn'ræp/ *vt* (*pt* **unwrapped**) desenvolver

unwritten /ʌn'rɪtn/ *a* no escrito; <*agreement*> verbal

up /ʌp/ *adv* arriba; (upwards) hacia arriba; (higher) más arriba. **~ here** aquí arriba. **~ there** allí arriba. **~ to** hasta. **he's not ~ yet** todavía no se ha levantado. **be ~ against** enfren-

tarse con. **come ~** subir **go ~** subir. **he's not ~ to the job** no tiene las condiciones necesarias para el trabajo. **it's ~ to you** depende de ti. **what's ~?** ¿qué pasa? ● *prep*. **go ~ the stairs** subir la escalera. **it's just ~ the road** está un poco más allá. ● *vt* (*pt* **upped**) aumentar. ● *n*. **~s and downs** *npl* altibajos *mpl*; (of life) vicisitudes *fpl*. **~bringing** /'ʌpbrɪŋɪŋ/ *n* educación *f*. **~date** /ʌp'deɪt/ *vt* poner al día. **~grade** /ʌp'greɪd/ *vt* elevar de categoría <*person*>; mejorar <*equipment*>. **~heaval** /ʌp'hi:vl/ *n* trastorno *m*. **~hill** /ʌp'hɪl/ *adv* cuesta arriba. **~hold** /ʌp'həʊld/ *vt* (*pt* **upheld**) mantener <*principle*>; confirmar <*decision*>. **~holster** /ʌp'həʊlstə(r)/ *vt* tapizar. **~holstery** *n* tapicería *f*. **~keep** *n* mantenimiento *m*. **~market** /ʌp'mɑ:kɪt/ *a* de categoría

upon /ə'pɒn/ *prep* sobre. **once ~ a time** érase una vez

upper /'ʌpə(r)/ *a* superior. **~ class** *n* clase *f* alta

up: ~right *a* vertical; <*citizen*> recto. **place sth ~right** poner algo de pie. **~rising** /'ʌpraɪzɪŋ/ *n* levantamiento *m*. **~roar** *n* tumulto *m*

upset /ʌp'set/ *vt* (*pt* **upset**, *pres p* **upsetting**) (hurt) disgustar; (offend) ofender; (distress) alterar; desbaratar <*plans*>. ● *a* (hurt) disgustado; (distressed) alterado; (offended) ofendido; (disappointed) desilusionado. ● /'ʌpset/ *n* trastorno *m*. **have a stomach ~** estar mal del estómago

up: ~shot *n* resultado *m*. **~side down** /ʌpsaɪd'daʊn/ *adv* al revés (*con la parte de arriba abajo*); (in disorder) patas arriba. **turn sth ~side down** poner algo boca abajo. **~stairs** /ʌp'steəz/ *adv* arriba. **go ~stairs** subir. ● /'ʌpsteəz/ *a* de arriba. **~start** *n* advenedizo *m*. **~state** *adv* (Amer). **I live ~state** vivo en el norte del estado. **~stream** /ʌp'stri:m/ *adv* río arriba. **~take** *n*. **be quick on the ~take** agarrar las cosas al vuelo. **~-to-date** /ʌptə'deɪt/ *a* al día; <*news*> de última hora. **~turn** *n* repunte *m*, mejora *f*.

~**ward** /'ʌpwəd/ a <*movement*> ascendente; <*direction*> hacia arriba. ● *adv* hacia arriba. ~**wards** *adv* hacia arriba

uranium /jʊ'reɪnɪəm/ n uranio m

Uranus /'jʊərənəs/, /jʊə'reɪnəs/ n Urano m

urban /'ɜːbən/ a urbano

urchin /'ɜːtʃɪn/ n pilluelo m

urge /ɜːdʒ/ vt instar. ~ s.o. to do sth instar a uno a que haga algo. ● n impulso m; (wish, whim) ganas fpl. □ ~ **on** vt animar

urgen|cy /'ɜːdʒənsɪ/ n urgencia f. ~**t** a urgente. ~**tly** adv urgentemente, con urgencia

urin|ate /'jʊərɪneɪt/ vi orinar. ~**e** /'jʊərɪn/ n orina f

Uruguay /jʊərəgwaɪ/ n Uruguay m. ~**an** a & n uruguayo (m)

us /ʌs, əs/ pron nos; (after prep) nosotros m, nosotras f

US(A) /juːes'eɪ/ abbr (= **United States (of America)**) EE.UU. (only written), Estados mpl Unidos

usage /'juːzɪdʒ/ n uso m

use /juːz/ vt usar; utilizar <*service, facilities*>; consumir <*fuel*>. ● /juːs/ n uso m, empleo m. be of ~ servir. it is no ~ es inútil. □ ~ **up** vt agotar, consumir. ~**d** /juːzd/ a usado. ● /juːst/ v mod ~ **to**. he ~**d** to say decía, solía decir. there ~**d** to be (antes) había. ● a /juːst/. be ~**d** to estar acostumbrado a. ~**ful** /'juːsfl/ a útil. ~**fully** adv útilmente. ~**less** a inútil; <*person*> incompetente. ~**r** /-zə(r)/ n usuario m. drug ~ n consumidor m de drogas

usher /'ʌʃə(r)/ n (in theatre etc) acomodador m. □ ~ **in** vt hacer pasar; marcar el comienzo de <*new era*>. ~**ette** /-'ret/ n acomodadora f

USSR abbr (History) (= **Union of Soviet Socialist Republics**) URSS

usual /'juːʒʊəl/ a usual; (habitual) acostumbrado, habitual; <*place, route*> de siempre. as ~ como de costumbre, como siempre. ~**ly** adv normalmente. he ~**ly** wakes up early suele despertarse temprano

utensil /juː'tensl/ n utensilio m

utilize /'juːtɪlaɪz/ vt utilizar

utmost /'ʌtməʊst/ a sumo. ● n. do one's ~ hacer todo lo posible (**to** para)

utter /'ʌtə(r)/ a completo. ● vt pronunciar <*word*>; dar <*cry*>. ~**ly** adv totalmente

U-turn /'juːtɜːn/ n cambio m de sentido

....

Vv

....

vacan|cy /'veɪkənsɪ/ n (job) vacante f; (room) habitación f libre. ~**t** a <*building*> desocupado; <*seat*> libre; <*post*> vacante; <*look*> ausente

vacate /və'keɪt/ vt dejar

vacation /və'keɪʃn/ n (Amer) vacaciones fpl. go on ~ ir de vacaciones. ~**er** n (Amer) veraneante m & f

vaccin|ate /'væksɪneɪt/ vt vacunar. ~**ation** /-'neɪʃn/ n vacunación f. ~**e** /'væksiːn/ n vacuna f

vacuum /'vækjʊəm/ n vacío m. ~ **cleaner** n aspiradora f

vagina /və'dʒaɪnə/ n vagina f

vague /veɪg/ a (**-er, -est**) vago; <*outline*> borroso; <*person, expression*> despistado. ~**ly** adv vagamente

vain /veɪn/ a (**-er, -est**) vanidoso; (useless) vano. **in** ~ en vano

Valentine's Day /'væləntaɪmz/ n el día de San Valentín

valiant /'vælɪənt/ a valeroso

valid /'vælɪd/ a válido. ~**ate** /-eɪt/ vt dar validez a; validar <*contract*>. ~**ity** /-'ɪdətɪ/ n validez f

valley /'vælɪ/ n (pl **-eys**) valle m

valour /'vælə(r)/ n valor m

valu|able /'væljʊəbl/ a valioso. ~**ables** npl objetos mpl de valor. ~**ation** /-'eɪʃn/ n valoración f. ~**e** /'væljuː/ n valor m. ● vt valorar; tasar, valorar, avaluar (LAm) <*property*>. ~**e added tax** n impuesto m sobre el valor añadido

valve /vælv/ n válvula f

vampire /'væmpaɪə(r)/ n vampiro m

van /væn/ n furgoneta f, camioneta f; (Rail) furgón m

vandal /'vændl/ n vándalo m. ~**ism** n vandalismo m. ~**ize** vt destruir

vanilla /və'nɪlə/ n vainilla f

vanish /'vænɪʃ/ vi desaparecer

vanity /'vænɪtɪ/ n vanidad f. ~ **case** n neceser m

vapour /'veɪpə(r)/ n vapor m

varia|ble /'veərɪəbl/ a variable. ~**nce** /-əns/ n. at ~**ce** en desacuerdo. ~**nt** n variante f. ~**tion** /-'eɪʃn/ n variación f

vari|ed /'veərɪd/ a variado. ~**ety** /və'raɪətɪ/ n variedad f. ~**ety show** n espectáculo m de variedades. ~**ous** /'veərɪəs/ a (several) varios; (different) diversos

varnish /'vɑːnɪʃ/ n barniz m; (for nails) esmalte m. ● vt barnizar; pintar <nails>

vary /'veərɪ/ vt/i variar

vase /vɑːz/, (Amer) /veɪs/ n (for flowers) florero m; (ornamental) jarrón m

vast /vɑːst/ a vasto, extenso; <size> inmenso. ~**ly** adv infinitamente

vat /væt/ n cuba f

VAT /viː'eɪ'tiː/ abbr (= **value added tax**) IVA m

vault /vɔːlt/ n (roof) bóveda f; (in bank) cámara f acorazada; (tomb) cripta f. ● vt/i saltar

VCR n = **videocassette recorder**

VDU n = **visual display unit**

veal /viːl/ n ternera f

veer /vɪə(r)/ vi dar un viraje, virar

vegeta|ble /'vedʒɪtəbl/ a vegetal. ● n verdura f. ~**rian** /vedʒɪ'teərɪən/ a & n vegetariano (m). ~**tion** /vedʒɪ'teɪʃn/ n vegetación f

vehement /'viːəmənt/ a vehemente. ~**tly** adv con vehemencia

vehicle /'viːɪkl/ n vehículo m

veil /veɪl/ n velo m

vein /veɪn/ n vena f; (in marble) veta f

velocity /vɪ'lɒsɪtɪ/ n velocidad f

velvet /'velvɪt/ n terciopelo m

vendetta /ven'detə/ n vendetta f

vend|ing machine /'vendɪŋ/ n distribuidor m automático. ~**or** /'vendə(r)/ n vendedor m

veneer /və'nɪə(r)/ n chapa f, enchapado m; (fig) barniz m, apariencia f

venerate /'venəreɪt/ vt venerar

venereal /və'nɪərɪəl/ a venéreo

Venetian blind /və'niːʃn/ n persiana f veneciana

Venezuela /venə'zweɪlə/ n Venezuela f. ~**n** a & n venezolano (m)

vengeance /'vendʒəns/ n venganza f. with a ~ (fig) con ganas

venom /'venəm/ n veneno m. ~**ous** a venenoso

vent /vent/ n (conducto m de) ventilación; (air ~) respiradero m. give ~ to dar rienda suelta a. ● vt descargar

ventilat|e /'ventɪleɪt/ vt ventilar. ~**ion** /-'eɪʃn/ n ventilación f

ventriloquist /ven'trɪləkwɪst/ n ventrílocuo m

venture /'ventʃə(r)/ n empresa f. ● vt aventurar. ● vi atreverse

venue /'venjuː/ n (for concert) lugar m de actuación

Venus /'viːnəs/ n Venus m

veranda /və'rændə/ n galería f

verb /vɜːb/ n verbo m. ~**al** a verbal.

verdict /'vɜːdɪkt/ n veredicto m; (opinion) opinión f

verge /vɜːdʒ/ n borde m. □ ~ **on** vt rayar en

verify /'verɪfaɪ/ vt (confirm) confirmar; (check) verificar

vermin /'vɜːmɪn/ n alimañas fpl

versatil|e /'vɜːsətaɪl/ a versátil. ~**ity** /-'tɪlətɪ/ n versatilidad f

verse /vɜːs/ n estrofa f; (poetry) poesías fpl. ~**d** /vɜːst/ a. be well-~ed in ser muy versado en. ~**ion** /'vɜːʃn/ n versión f

versus /'vɜːsəs/ prep contra

vertebra /'vɜːtɪbrə/ n (pl -**brae** /-briː/) vértebra f. ~**te** /-brət/ n vertebrado m

vertical /'vɜːtɪkl/ a & n vertical (f). ~**ly** adv verticalmente

vertigo /'vɜːtɪgəʊ/ n vértigo m

verve /vɜːv/ n brío m

very /'verɪ/ adv muy. ~ **much** muchísimo. ~ **well** muy bien. the ~ **first**

el primero de todos. ● *a* mismo. **the ~ thing** exactamente lo que hace falta

vessel /'vesl/ *n* (receptacle) recipiente *m*; (ship) navío *m*, nave *f*

vest /vest/ *n* camiseta *f*; (Amer) chaleco *m*.

vestige /'vestɪdʒ/ *n* vestigio *m*

vet /vet/ *n* veterinario *m*; (Amer 🅸, veteran) veterano *m*. ● *vt* (*pt* **vetted**) someter a investigación *<applicant>*

veteran /'vetərən/ *n* veterano *m*

veterinary /'vetərɪnərɪ/ *a* veterinario. **~ surgeon** *n* veterinario *m*

veto /'vi:təʊ/ *n* (*pl* **-oes**) veto *m*. ● *vt* vetar

vex /veks/ *vt* fastidiar

via /'vaɪə/ *prep* por, por vía de

viable /'vaɪəbl/ *a* viable

viaduct /'vaɪədʌkt/ *n* viaducto *m*

vibrat|e /vaɪ'breɪt/ *vt/i* vibrar. **~ion** /-ʃn/ *n* vibración *f*

vicar /'vɪkə(r)/ *n* párroco *m*. **~age** /-rɪdʒ/ *n* casa *f* del párroco

vice /vaɪs/ *n* vicio *m*; (Tec) torno *m* de banco

vice versa /vaɪsɪ'vɜːsə/ *adv* viceversa

vicinity /vɪ'sɪnɪtɪ/ *n* vecindad *f*. **in the ~ of** cerca de

vicious /'vɪʃəs/ *a* *<attack>* feroz; *<dog>* fiero; *<rumour>* malicioso. **~ circle** *n* círculo *m* vicioso

victim /'vɪktɪm/ *n* víctima *f*. **~ize** *vt* victimizar

victor /'vɪktə(r)/ *n* vencedor *m*

Victorian /vɪk'tɔːrɪən/ *a* victoriano

victor|ious /vɪk'tɔːrɪəs/ *a* *<army>* victorioso; *<team>* vencedor. **~y** /'vɪktərɪ/ *n* victoria *f*

video /'vɪdɪəʊ/ *n* (*pl* **-os**) vídeo *m*, video *m* (LAm). **~ camera** *n* videocámara *f*. **~(cassette) recorder** *n* magnetoscopio *m*. **~tape** *n* videocassette *f*

vie /vaɪ/ *vi* (*pres p* **vying**) rivalizar

Vietnam /vjet'næm/ *n* Vietnam *m*. **~ese** *a* & *n* vietnamita (*m* & *f*)

view /vju:/ *n* vista *f*; (mental survey) visión *f* de conjunto; (opinion) opinión *f*. **in my ~** a mi juicio. **in ~ of** en vista de. **on ~** expuesto. ● *vt* ver *<scene,*

property>; (consider) considerar. **~er** *n* (TV) televidente *m* & *f*. **~finder** *n* visor *m*. **~point** *n* punto *m* de vista

vigilance *n* vigilancia *f*. **~ant** *a* vigilante

vigo|rous /'vɪgərəs/ *a* enérgico; *<growth>* vigoroso. **~ur** /'vɪgə(r)/ *n* vigor *m*

vile /vaɪl/ *a* (base) vil; *<food>* asqueroso; *<weather, temper>* horrible

village /'vɪlɪdʒ/ *n* pueblo *m*; (small) aldea *f*. **~r** *n* vecino *m* del pueblo; (of small village) aldeano *m*

villain /'vɪlən/ *n* maleante *m* & *f*; (in story etc) villano *m*

vindicate /'vɪndɪkeɪt/ *vt* justificar

vindictive /vɪn'dɪktɪv/ *a* vengativo

vine /vaɪn/ *n* (on ground) vid *f*; (climbing) parra *f*

vinegar /'vɪnɪgə(r)/ *n* vinagre *m*

vineyard /'vɪnjəd/ *n* viña *f*

vintage /'vɪntɪdʒ/ *n* (year) cosecha *f*. ● *a* *<wine>* añejo; *<car>* de época

vinyl /'vaɪnɪl/ *n* vinilo *m*

viola /vɪ'əʊlə/ *n* viola *f*

violat|e /'vaɪəleɪt/ *vt* violar. **~ion** /-'leɪʃn/ *n* violación *f*

violen|ce /'vaɪələns/ *n* violencia *f*. **~t** *a* violento. **~tly** *adv* violentamente

violet /'vaɪələt/ *a* & *n* violeta (*f*); (colour) violeta (*m*)

violin /'vaɪəlɪn/ *n* violín *m*. **~ist** *n* violinista *m* & *f*

VIP /vi:aɪ'pi:/ *abbr* (= **very important person**) VIP *m*

viper /'vaɪpə(r)/ *n* víbora *f*

virgin /'vɜːdʒɪn/ *a* & *n* virgen (*f*)

Virgo /'vɜːgəʊ/ *n* Virgo *f*

virile /'vɪraɪl/ *a* viril

virtual /'vɜːtʃʊəl/ *a*. **traffic is at a ~ standstill** el tráfico está prácticamente paralizado. **~ reality** *n* realidad *f* virtual. **~ly** *adv* prácticamente

virtue /'vɜːtʃu:/ *n* virtud *f*. **by ~ of** en virtud de

virtuous /'vɜːtʃʊəs/ *a* virtuoso

virulent /'vɪrʊlənt/ *a* virulento

virus /'vaɪərəs/ *n* (*pl* **-uses**) virus *m*

visa /'vi:zə/ *n* visado *m*, visa *f* (LAm)

vise /vaɪs/ *n* (Amer) torno *m* de banco

visib|ility /vɪzɪ'bɪlətɪ/ n visibilidad f. **~le** /'vɪzɪbl/ a visible; <sign, improvement> evidente

vision /'vɪʒn/ n visión f; (sight) vista f

visit /'vɪzɪt/ vt visitar; hacer una visita a <person>. ● vi hacer visitas. **~ with s.o.** (Amer) ir a ver a uno. ● n visita f. **pay s.o. a ~** hacerle una visita a uno. **~or** n visitante m & f; (guest) visita f

visor /'vaɪzə(r)/ n visera f

visual /'vɪʒʊəl/ a visual. **~ize** vt imaginar(se); (foresee) prever

vital /'vaɪtl/ a (essential) esencial; <factor> de vital importancia; <organ> vital. **~ity** /vaɪ'tælətɪ/ n vitalidad f

vitamin /'vɪtəmɪn/ n vitamina f.

vivacious /vɪ'veɪʃəs/ a vivaz

vivid /'vɪvɪd/ a vivo. **~ly** adv intensamente; (describe) gráficamente

vivisection /vɪvɪ'sekʃn/ n vivisección f

vocabulary /və'kæbjʊlərɪ/ n vocabulario m

vocal /'vəʊkl/ a vocal. **~ist** n cantante m & f

vocation /vəʊ'keɪʃn/ n vocación f. **~al** a profesional

vociferous /və'sɪfərəs/ a vociferador

vogue /vəʊg/ n moda f, boga f

voice /vɔɪs/ n voz f. ● vt expresar

void /vɔɪd/ a (not valid) nulo. ● n vacío m

volatile /'vɒlətaɪl/ a volátil; <person> imprevisible

volcan|ic /vɒl'kænɪk/ a volcánico. **~o** /vɒl'keɪnəʊ/ n (pl **-oes**) volcán m

volley /'vɒlɪ/ n (pl **-eys**) (of gunfire) descarga f cerrada; (sport) volea f. **~ball** n vóleibol m

volt /vəʊlt/ n voltio m. **~age** /-ɪdʒ/ n voltaje m

volume /'vɒljuːm/ n volumen m; (book) tomo m

voluntar|ily /'vɒləntərəlɪ/ adv voluntariamente. **~y** a voluntario; <organization> de beneficencia

volunteer /vɒlən'tɪə(r)/ n voluntario m. ● vt ofrecer. ● vi. **~ (to)** ofrecerse (a)

vomit /'vɒmɪt/ vt/i vomitar. ● n vómito m

voracious /və'reɪʃəs/ a voraz

vot|e /vəʊt/ n voto m; (right) derecho m al voto; (act) votación f. ● vi votar. **~er** n votante m & f. **~ing** n votación f

vouch /vaʊtʃ/ vi. **~ for s.o.** responder por uno. **~er** /-ə(r)/ n vale m

vow /vaʊ/ n voto m. ● vi jurar

vowel /'vaʊəl/ n vocal f

voyage /'vɔɪɪdʒ/ n viaje m; (by sea) travesía f

vulgar /'vʌlgə(r)/ a (coarse) grosero, vulgar; (tasteless) de mal gusto. **~ity** /-'gærətɪ/ n vulgaridad f

vulnerable /'vʌlnərəbl/ a vulnerable

vulture /'vʌltʃə(r)/ n buitre m

vying /'vaɪɪŋ/ ⇒VIE

W w

W abbr (= **West**) O

wad /wɒd/ n (of notes) fajo m; (tied together) lío m; (papers) montón m

waddle /'wɒdl/ vi contonearse

wade /weɪd/ vi caminar (por el agua etc)

wafer /'weɪfə(r)/ n galleta f de barquillo

waffle /'wɒfl/ n Ⓤ palabrería f. ● vi Ⓤ divagar; (in essay, exam) meter paja Ⓤ. ● n (Culin) gofre m, wafle m (LAm)

waft /wɒft/ vi flotar

wag /wæg/ vt (pt **wagged**) menear. ● vi menearse

wage /weɪdʒ/ n sueldo m. **~s** npl salario m, sueldo m. **~r** n apuesta f

waggle /'wægl/ vt menear. ● vi menearse

wagon /'wægən/ n carro m; (Rail) vagón m; (Amer, delivery truck) furgoneta f de reparto

wail /weɪl/ vi llorar

waist /weɪst/ n cintura f. **~coat** n chaleco m. **~line** n cintura f

wait /weɪt/ *vi* esperar; (at table) servir. ～ **for** esperar. ～ **on s.o.** atender a uno. ●*vt* (await) esperar *<chance, turn>*. ～ **table** (Amer) servir a la mesa. **I can't ～ to see him** me muero de ganas de verlo. ●*n* espera *f*. **lie in ～** acechar

waiter /'weɪtə(r)/ *n* camarero *m*, mesero *m* (LAm)

wait: ～ing-list *n* lista *f* de espera. **～ing-room** *n* sala *f* de espera

waitress /'weɪtrɪs/ *n* camarera *f*, mesera *f* (LAm)

waive /weɪv/ *vt* renunciar a

wake /weɪk/ *vt* (*pt* **woke**, *pp* **woken**) despertar. ●*vi* despertarse. ●*n* (Naut) estela *f*. **in the ～ of** como resultado de. □ ～ **up** *vt* despertar. *vi* despertarse

Wales /weɪlz/ *n* (el país de) Gales

walk /wɔːk/ *vi* andar, caminar; (not ride) ir a pie; (stroll) pasear. ●*vt* andar por *<streets>*; llevar de paseo *<dog>*. ●*n* paseo *m*; (long) caminata *f*; (gait) manera *f* de andar. □ ～ **out** *vi* salir; *<workers>* declararse en huelga. □ ～ **out on** *vt* abandonar. **～er** *n* excursionista *m* & *f*

walkie-talkie /wɔːkɪ'tɔːkɪ/ *n* walkie-talkie *m*

walk: ～ing-stick *n* bastón *m*. **W～man** /-mən/ *n* Walkman *m* (P). **～-out** *n* retirada *en señal de protesta*; (strike) abandono *m* del trabajo

wall /wɔːl/ *n* (interior) pared *f*; (exterior) muro *m*

wallet /'wɒlɪt/ *n* cartera *f*, billetera *f*

wallop /'wɒləp/ *vt* (*pt* **walloped**) ⊡ darle un golpazo a.

wallow /'wɒləʊ/ *vi* revolcarse

wallpaper /'wɔːlpeɪpə(r)/ *n* papel *m* pintado

walnut /'wɔːlnʌt/ *n* nuez *f*; (tree) nogal *m*

walrus /'wɔːlrəs/ *n* morsa *f*

waltz /wɔːls/ *n* vals *m*. ●*vi* valsar

wand /wɒnd/ *n* varita *f* (mágica)

wander /'wɒndə(r)/ *vi* vagar; (stroll) pasear; (digress) divagar. ●*n* vuelta *f*, paseo *m*. **～er** *n* trotamundos *m*

wane /weɪn/ *vi* *<moon>* menguar; *<interest>* decaer. ●*n*. **be on the ～** *<popularity>* estar decayendo

wangle /wæŋgl/ *vt* ⊡ agenciarse

want /wɒnt/ *vt* querer; (need) necesitar. ●*vi*. ～ **for** carecer de. ●*n* necesidad *f*; (lack) falta *f*. **～ed** *a <criminal>* buscado

war /wɔː(r)/ *n* guerra *f*. **at ～** en guerra

warble /'wɔːbl/ *vi* trinar, gorjear

ward /wɔːd/ *n* (in hospital) sala *f*; (child) pupilo *m*. □ ～ **off** *vt* conjurar *<danger>*; rechazar *<attack>*

warden /'wɔːdn/ *n* guarda *m*

warder /'wɔːdə(r)/ *n* celador *m* (*de una cárcel*)

wardrobe /'wɔːdrəʊb/ *n* armario *m*; (clothes) guardarropa *f*, vestuario *m*

warehouse /'weəhaʊs/ *n* depósito *m*, almacén *m*

wares /weəz/ *npl* mercancía(s) *f(pl)*

war: ～fare *n* guerra *f*. **～head** *n* cabeza *f*, ojiva *f*

warm /wɔːm/ *a* (**-er, -est**) *<water, day>* tibio, templado; *<room>* caliente; *<climate, wind>* cálido; *<clothes>* de abrigo; *<welcome>* caluroso. **be ～** *<person>* tener calor. **it's ～ today** hoy hace calor. ●*vt*. ～ **(up)** calentar *<room>*; recalentar *<food>*; (fig) animar. ●*vi*. ～ **(up)** calentarse; (fig) animarse. **～-blooded** /-'blʌdɪd/ *a* de sangre caliente. **～ly** *adv* (heartily) calurosamente. **～th** *n* calor *m*; (of colour, atmosphere) calidez *f*

warn /wɔːn/ *vt* advertir. **～ing** *n* advertencia *f*; (notice) aviso *m*

warp /wɔːp/ *vt* alabear. **～ed** /'wɔːpt/ *a <wood>* alabeado; *<mind>* retorcido

warrant /'wɒrənt/ *n* orden *f* judicial; (search ～) orden *f* de registro; (for arrest) orden *f* de arresto. ●*vt* justificar. **～y** *n* garantía *f*

warrior /'wɒrɪə(r)/ *n* guerrero *m*

warship /'wɔːʃɪp/ *n* buque *m* de guerra

wart /wɔːt/ *n* verruga *f*

wartime /'wɔːtaɪm/ *n* tiempo *m* de guerra

wary /'weərɪ/ *a* (**-ier, -iest**) cauteloso. **be ～ of** recelar de

was /wəz, wɒz/ ⇒BE

wash /wɒʃ/ *vt* lavar; fregar, lavar (LAm) *<floor>*. ～ **one's face** lavarse la cara. ● *vi* lavarse. ● *n* (in washing machine) lavado *m*. **have a** ~ lavarse. **I gave the car a** ~ lavé el coche. □ ~ **out** *vt* (clean) lavar; (rinse) enjuagar. □ ~ **up** *vi* fregar los platos, lavar los trastes (Mex); (Amer, wash face and hands) lavarse. ~**able** *a* lavable. ~**basin**, ~**bowl** (Amer) *n* lavabo *m*. ~**er** *n* arandela *f*. ~**ing** *n* lavado *m*; (dirty clothes) ropa *f* para lavar; (wet clothes) ropa *f* lavada. **do the** ~**ing** lavar la ropa, hacer la colada. ~**ing-machine** *n* máquina *f* de lavar, lavadora *f*. ~**ing-powder** *n* jabón *m* en polvo. ~**ing-up** *n*. **do the** ~**ing-up** lavar los platos, fregar (los platos). ~**ing-up liquid** *n* lavavajillas *m*. ~**out** *n* ⊞ desastre *m*. ~**room** *n* (Amer) baños *mpl*, servicios *mpl*

wasp /wɒsp/ *n* avispa *f*

waste /weɪst/ ● *a* <*matter*> de desecho; <*land*> (barren) yermo; (uncultivated) baldío. ● *n* (of materials) desperdicio *m*; (of time) pérdida *f*; (refuse) residuos *mpl*. ● *vt* despilfarrar <*electricity, money*>; desperdiciar <*talent, effort*>; perder <*time*>. ● *vi*. ~**disposal unit** *n* trituradora *f* de desperdicios. ~**ful** *a* poco económico; <*person*> despilfarrador. ~**paper basket** *n* papelera *f*

watch /wɒtʃ/ *vt* mirar; observar <*person, expression*>; ver <*TV*>; (keep an eye on) vigilar; (take heed) tener cuidado con. ● *vi* mirar. ● *n* (observation) vigilancia *f*; (period of duty) guardia *f*; (timepiece) reloj *m*. ~ **out** *vi* (be careful) tener cuidado; (look carefully) estarse atento. ~**dog** *n* perro *m* guardián. ~**man** /-mən/ *n* (*pl* -**men**) vigilante *m*.

water /'wɔːtə(r)/ *n* agua *f*. ● *vt* regar <*plants etc*>. ● *vi* <*eyes*> llorar. **make s.o.'s mouth** ~ hacérsele la boca agua, hacérsele agua la boca (LAm). ~ **down** *vt* diluir; aguar <*wine*>. ~**colour** *n* acuarela *f*. ~**cress** *n* berro *m*. ~**fall** *n* cascada *f*; (large) catarata *f*. ~**ing-can** *n* regadera *f*. ~**lily** *n* nenúfar *m*. ~**logged** /-lɒgd/ *a* anegado; <*shoes*> empapado. ~**proof** *a* impermeable; <*watch*> sumergible. ~**-skiing** *n* esquí *m*

acuático. ~**tight** *a* hermético; <*boat*> estanco; <*argument*> irrebatible. ~**way** *n* canal *m* navegable. ~**y** *a* acuoso; <*eyes*> lloroso

watt /wɒt/ *n* vatio *m*

wave /weɪv/ *n* onda *f*; (of hand) señal *f*; (fig) oleada *f*. ● *vt* agitar; (curl) ondular <*hair*>. ● *vi* (signal) hacer señales con la mano; ondear <*flag*>. ~**band** *n* banda *f* de frecuencia. ~**length** *n* longitud *f* de onda

waver /'weɪvə(r)/ *vi* (be indecisive) vacilar; (falter) flaquear

wavy /'weɪvɪ/ *a* (-**ier**, -**iest**) ondulado

wax /wæks/ *n* cera *f*. ● *vi* <*moon*> crecer. ~**work** *n* figura *f* de cera. ~**works** *npl* museo *m* de cera

way /weɪ/ *n* (route) camino *m*; (manner) manera *f*, forma *f*, modo *m*; (direction) dirección *f*; (habit) costumbre *f*. **it's a long** ~ **from here** queda muy lejos de aquí. **be in the** ~ estorbar. **by the** ~ a propósito. **either** ~ de cualquier manera. **give** ~ (collapse) ceder, romperse; (Auto) ceder el paso. **in a** ~ en cierta manera. **in some** ~**s** en ciertos modos. **make** ~ dejar paso a. **no** ~! ¡ni hablar! **on my** ~ **to** de camino a. **out of the** ~ remoto; (extraordinary) fuera de lo común. **that** ~ por allí. **this** ~ por aquí. ~ **in** *n* entrada *f*. ~**lay** /weɪ'leɪ/ *vt* (*pt* -**laid**) abordar. ~ **out** *n* salida *f*. ~**out** *a* ultramoderno, original. ~**s** *npl* costumbres *fpl*

we /wiː/ *pron* nosotros *m*, nosotras *f*

weak /wiːk/ *a* (-**er**, -**est**) débil; <*structure*> poco sólido; <*performance, student*> flojo; <*coffee*> poco cargado; <*solution*> diluido; <*beer*> suave; (pej) aguado. ~**en** *vt* debilitar. ● *vi* <*resolve*> flaquear. ~**ling** *n* alfeñique *m*. ~**ness** *n* debilidad *f*

wealth /welθ/ *n* riqueza *f*. ~**y** *a* (-**ier**, -**iest**) rico

weapon /'wepən/ *n* arma *f*

wear /weə(r)/ *vt* (*pt* **wore**, *pp* **worn**) llevar; vestirse de <*black, red, etc*>; (usually) usar. **I've got nothing to** ~ no tengo nada que ponerme. ● *vi* (through use) gastarse; (last) durar. ● *n* uso *m*; (damage) desgaste *m*; ~ **and tear** desgaste *m* natural. □ ~

out *vt* gastar; (tire) agotar. *vi* gastarse

weary /'wɪərɪ/ *a* (**-ier, -iest**) cansado. ● *vt* cansar. ● *vi* cansarse. ~ **of** cansarse de

weather /'weðə(r)/ *n* tiempo *m*. **what's the ~ like?** ¿qué tiempo hace?. **the ~ was bad** hizo mal tiempo. **be under the ~** 🄸 no andar muy bien 🄸. ● *vt* (survive) sobrellevar. **~-beaten** *a* curtido. ~ **forecast** *n* pronóstico *m* del tiempo. **~-vane** *n* veleta *f*

weave /wi:v/ *vt* (*pt* **wove**, *pp* **woven**) tejer; entretejer *<threads>*. ~ **one's way** abrirse paso. ● *vi* *<person>* zigzaguear; *<road>* serpentear. **~r** *n* tejedor *m*

web /web/ *n* (of spider) telaraña *f*; (of intrigue) red *f*. **~b site** *n* (Comp) sitio web *m*

wed /wed/ *vt* (*pt* **wedded**) casarse con. ● *vi* casarse.

we'd /wi:d/, /wɪəd/ = **we had**, **we would**

wedding /'wedɪŋ/ *n* boda *f*, casamiento *m*. **~-cake** *n* pastel *m* de boda. **~-ring** *n* anillo *m* de boda

wedge /wedʒ/ *n* cuña *f*

Wednesday /'wenzdeɪ/ *n* miércoles *m*

wee /wi:/ *a* 🄸 pequeñito. ● *n*. **have a ~** 🄸 hacer pis 🄸

weed /wi:d/ *n* mala hierba *f*. ● *vt* desherbar. □ ~ **out** *vt* eliminar. **~killer** *n* herbicida *m*. **~y** *a* *<person>* enclenque; (Amer, lanky) larguirucho 🄸

week /wi:k/ *n* semana *f*. **~day** *n* día *m* de semana. **~end** *n* fin *m* de semana. **~ly** *a* semanal. ● *n* semanario *m*. ● *adv* semanalmente

weep /wi:p/ *vi* (*pt* **wept**) llorar

weigh /weɪ/ *vt/i* pesar. ~ **anchor** levar anclas. □ ~ **down** *vt* (fig) oprimir. □ ~ **up** *vt* pesar; (fig) considerar

weight /weɪt/ *n* peso *m*; (sport) pesa *f*. **put on ~** engordar. **lose ~** adelgazar. **~-lifting** *n* halterofilia *f*, levantamiento *m* de pesos

weir /wɪə(r)/ *n* presa *f*

weird /wɪəd/ *a* (**-er**, **-est**) raro, extraño; (unearthly) misterioso

welcom|e /'welkəm/ *a* bienvenido. **you're ~e!** (after thank you) ¡de nada! ● *n* bienvenida *f*; (reception) acogida *f*. ● *vt* dar la bienvenida a; (appreciate) alegrarse de. **~ing** *a* acogedor

weld /weld/ *vt* soldar. ● *n* soldadura *f*. **~er** *n* soldador *m*

welfare /'welfeə(r)/ *n* bienestar *m*; (aid) asistencia *f* social. **W~ State** *n* estado *m* benefactor

well /wel/ *adv* (**better**, **best**) bien. ~ **done!** ¡muy bien!, ¡bravo! **as ~** también. **as ~ as** además de. **we may as ~ go tomorrow** más vale que vayamos mañana. **do ~** (succeed) tener éxito. **very ~** muy bien. ● *a* bien. **I'm very ~** estoy muy bien. ● *int* (introducing, continuing sentence) bueno; (surprise) ¡vaya!; (indignation, resignation) bueno. ~ **I never!** ¡no me digas! ● *n* pozo *m*

we'll /wi:l/, /wɪəl/ = **WE WILL**

well: ~-behaved /-bɪ'heɪvd/ *a* que se porta bien, bueno. **~-educated** /-'edjʊkeɪtɪd/ *a* culto.

wellington (boot) /'welɪŋtən/ *n* bota *f* de goma *or* de agua; (Amer, short boot) botín *m*

well: ~-known /-'nəʊn/ *a* conocido. ~ **off** *a* adinerado. **~-stocked** /-'stɒkt/ *a* bien provisto. **~-to-do** /-tə'du:/ *a* adinerado

Welsh /welʃ/ *a* & *n* galés (*m*). **the ~** *n* los galeses

went /went/ ⇒GO

wept /wept/ ⇒WEEP

were /wɜ:(r), wə(r)/ ⇒BE

we're /wɪə(r)/ = **we are**

west /west/ *n* oeste *m*. **the W~** el Occidente *m*. ● *a* oeste; *<wind>* del oeste. ● *adv* *<go>* hacia el oeste, al oeste. **it's ~ of York** está al oeste de York. **~erly** /-əlɪ/ *a* *<wind>* del oeste. **~ern** /-ən/ *a* occidental. ● *n* (film) película *f* del Oeste. **~erner** *n* occidental *m* & *f*. **W~ Indian** *a* & *n* antillano (*m*). **W~ Indies** *npl* Antillas *fpl*. **~ward(s)** /-wəd(z)/ *adv* hacia el oeste

wet /wet/ *a* (**wetter**, **wettest**) mojado; (rainy) lluvioso; (🄸, person) soso. '~ **paint**' 'pintura fresca'. **get ~** mojarse. **he got his feet ~** se mojó los pies. ● *vt* (*pt* **wetted**) mojar; (dampen) humedecer. ~ **o.s.** orinarse.

~ blanket *n* aguafiestas *m & f.* **~ suit** *n* traje *m* de neopreno

we've /wiːv/ = WE HAVE

whack /wæk/ *vt* 🔲 golpear. ● *n* 🔲 golpe *m*.

whale /weɪl/ *n* ballena *f.* **we had a ~ of a time** 🔲 lo pasamos bomba 🔲

wham /wæm/ *int* ¡zas!

wharf /wɔːf/ *n* (*pl* **wharves** or **wharfs**) muelle *m*

what /wɒt/

● *adjective*

····▸ (in questions) qué. **~ perfume are you wearing?** ¿qué perfume llevas?. **~ colour are the walls?** ¿de qué color son las paredes?

····▸ (in exclamations) qué. **~ a beautiful house!** ¡qué casa más linda!. **~ a lot of people!** ¡cuánta gente!

····▸ (in indirect speech) qué. **I'll ask him ~ bus to take** le preguntaré qué autobús hay que tomar. **do you know ~ time it leaves?** ¿sabes a qué hora sale?

● *pronoun*

····▸ (in questions) qué. **~ is it?** ¿qué es? **~ for?** ¿para qué?. **~'s the problem?** ¿cuál es el problema? **~'s he like?** ¿cómo es? **what?** (say that again) ¿cómo?, ¿qué?

····▸ (in indirect questions) qué. **I didn't know ~ to do** no sabía qué hacer

····▸ (relative) lo que. **I did ~ I could** hice lo que pude. ● **I need is a new car** lo que necesito es un coche nuevo

····▸ (in phrases) **~ about me?** ¿y yo qué? **~ if she doesn't come?** ¿y si no viene?

whatever /wɒt'evə(r)/ *a* cualquiera. ● *pron* (todo) lo que, cualquier cosa que

whatsoever /wɒtsəʊ'evə(r)/ *a & pron* = **whatever**

wheat /wiːt/ *n* trigo *m*

wheel /wiːl/ *n* rueda *f.* **at the ~** al volante. ● *vt* empujar <*bicycle etc*>; llevar (*en silla de ruedas etc*) <*person*>. **~barrow** *n* carretilla *f.* **~chair** *n* silla *f* de ruedas

wheeze /wiːz/ *vi* respirar con dificultad

when /wen/ *adv* cuándo. ● *conj* cuando. **~ever** /-'evə(r)/ *adv* (every time that) cada vez que, siempre que; (at whatever time) **we'll go ~ever you're ready** saldremos cuando estés listo

where /weə(r)/ *adv & conj* donde; (interrogative) dónde. **~ are you going?** ¿adónde vas? **~ are you from?** ¿de dónde eres?. **~abouts** /-əbaʊts/ *adv* en qué parte. ● *n* paradero *m.* **~as** /-'æz/ *conj* por cuanto; (in contrast) mientras (que). **~ver** /weər'evə(r)/ *adv* (in questions) dónde; (no matter where) en cualquier parte. ● *conj* donde (+ *subjunctive*), dondequiera (+ *subjunctive*)

whet /wet/ *vt* (*pt* **whetted**) abrir <*appetite*>

whether /'weðə(r)/ *conj* si. **I don't know ~ she will like it** no sé si le gustará. **~ you like it or not** te guste o no te guste

which /wɪtʃ/ *a* (in questions) (*sing*) qué, cuál; (*pl*) qué, cuáles. **~ one** cuál. **~ one of you** cuál de ustedes. ● *pron* (in questions) (*sing*) cuál; (*pl*) cuáles; (relative) que; (object) el cual, la cual, lo cual, los cuales, las cuales. **~ever** /-'evə(r)/ *a* cualquier. ● *pron* cualquiera que, el que, la que; (in questions) cuál; (*pl*) cuáles

while /waɪl/ *n* rato *m.* **a ~ ago** hace un rato. ● *conj* mientras; (although) aunque. □ **~ away** *vt* pasar <*time*>

whilst /waɪlst/ *conj* ⇒WHILE

whim /wɪm/ *n* capricho *m*

whimper /'wɪmpə(r)/ *vi* gimotear. ● *n* quejido *m*

whine /waɪn/ *vi* <*person*> gemir; <*child*> lloriquear; <*dog*> aullar

whip /wɪp/ *n* látigo *m*; (for punishment) azote *m.* ● *vt* (*pt* **whipped** /wɪpt/) fustigar, pegarle a (*con la fusta*) <*horse*>; azotar <*person*>; (Culin) batir

whirl /wɜːl/ *vi* girar rápidamente. **~pool** *n* remolino *m.* **~wind** *n* torbellino *m*

whirr /wɜː(r)/ *n* zumbido *m.* ● *vi* zumbar

whisk /wɪsk/ *vt* (Culin) batir. ● *n* (Culin) batidor *m.* **~ away** llevarse

whisker /'wɪskə(r)/ *n* pelo *m.* **~s** *npl* (of cat etc) bigotes *mpl*

whisky /'wɪskɪ/ n whisky m, güisqui m

whisper /'wɪspə(r)/ vt susurrar.
● vi cuchichear. ● n susurro m

whistle /'wɪsl/ n silbido m; (loud)
chiflado m; (instrument) silbato m, pito
m. ● vi silbar; (loudly) chiflar

white /waɪt/ a (-er, -est) blanco. go
~ ponerse pálido. ● n blanco; (of egg)
clara f. ~ **coffee** n café m con leche. ~**-collar worker** n empleado
m de oficina. ~ **elephant** n objeto
m inútil y costoso. ~**-hot** a <metal>
al rojo blanco. ~ **lie** n mentirijilla f.
~**n** vt/i blanquear. ~**wash** n cal f;
(cover-up) tapadera f 🔲. ● vt blanquear, encalar

Whitsun /'wɪtsn/ n Pentecostés m

whiz /wɪz/ vi (pt **whizzed**). ~ by, ~
past pasar zumbando. ~**-kid** n 🔲
lince m 🔲

who /huː/ pron (in questions) quién;
(pl) quiénes; (as relative) que; **the girl**
~ **lives there** la chica que vive allí.
those ~ **can't come tomorrow** los
que no puedan venir mañana.
~**ever** /huː'evə(r)/ pron quienquiera que; (interrogative) quién

whole /həʊl/ a. **the** ~ **country** todo el
país. **there's a** ~ **bottle left** queda
una botella entera. ● n todo m,
conjunto m; (total) total m. **on the** ~
en general. ~**-hearted** /-'hɑːtɪd/ a
<support> incondicional; <approval>
sin reservar. ~**meal** a integral.
~**sale** n venta f al por mayor. ● a &
adv al por mayor. ~**some** /-səm/ a
sano

wholly /'həʊlɪ/ adv completamente

whom /huːm/ pron que, a quien; (in
questions) a quién

whooping cough /'huːpɪŋ/ n tos f
convulsa

whore /hɔː(r)/ n puta f

whose /huːz/ pron de quién; (pl) de
quiénes. ● a (in questions) de quién;
(pl) de quiénes; (relative) cuyo; (pl)
cuyos

why /waɪ/ adv por qué. ~ **not?** ¿por
qué no? **that's** ~ **I couldn't go** por eso
no pude ir. ● int ¡vaya!

wick /wɪk/ n mecha f

wicked /'wɪkɪd/ a malo; (mischievous)
travieso; (🔲, very bad) malísimo

wicker /'wɪkə(r)/ n mimbre m & f.
● a de mimbre. ~**work** n artículos
mpl de mimbre

wicket /'wɪkɪt/ n (cricket) rastrillo m

wide /waɪd/ a (-er, -est) ancho;
<range, experience> amplio; (off target)
desviado. **it's four metres** ~ tiene
cuatro metros de ancho. ● adv. open
~! abra bien la boca. ~ **awake** a
completamente despierto; (fig) despabilado. **I left the door** ~ **open** dejé la
puerta abierta de par en par. ~**ly**
adv extensamente; (believed) generalmente; (different) muy. ~**n** vt
ensanchar. ● vi ensancharse.
~**spread** a extendido; (fig) difundido

widow /'wɪdəʊ/ n viuda f. ~**er** n
viudo m.

width /wɪdθ/ n anchura f. **in** ~
de ancho

wield /wiːld/ vt manejar; ejercer
<power>

wife /waɪf/ n (pl **wives**) mujer f,
esposa f

wig /wɪg/ n peluca f

wiggle /'wɪgl/ vt menear. ● vi menearse

wild /waɪld/ a (-er, -est) <animal>
salvaje; <flower> silvestre; <country>
agreste; (enraged) furioso; <idea>
extravagante; (with joy) loco. **a** ~
guess una conjetura hecha totalmente al azar. **I'm not** ~ **about the
idea** la idea no me enloquece. ● adv
en estado salvaje. **run** ~ <children>
criarse como salvajes. ~**s** npl
regiones fpl salvajes. ~**erness**
/'wɪldənɪs/ n páramo m. ~**fire** n.
spread like ~**fire** correr como un re-
guero de pólvora. ~**goose chase**
n empresa f inútil. ~**life** n fauna f.
~**ly** adv violentamente; (fig) locamente

will /wɪl/

● auxiliary verb

past would; contracted forms I'll,
you'll, etc = I will, you will, etc.;
won't = will not

····▷ (talking about the future)

! The Spanish future tense is
not always the first option for
■ translating the English future
tense. The present tense of *ir*
+ *a* + *verb* is commonly used
instead, particularly in Latin
American countries. **he'll be
here on Tuesday** *estará el
martes, va a estar el martes;*
she won't agree *no va a
aceptar, no aceptará*

••••➤ (in invitations and requests) ~ **you
have some wine?** ¿quieres (un poco
de) vino? **you'll stay for dinner, won't
you?** te quedas a cenar, ¿no?

••••➤ (in tag questions) **you** ~ **be back
soon, won't you?** vas a volver
pronto, ¿no?

••••➤ (in short answers) **will it be ready by
Monday? - yes, it** ~ ¿estará listo para
el lunes? - sí

● *noun*

••••➤ (mental power) voluntad *f*

••••➤ (document) testamento *m*

willing /'wɪlɪŋ/ *a* complaciente. ~ **to**
dispuesto a. **~ly** *adv* de buena gana
willow /'wɪləʊ/ *n* sauce *m*
will-power /'wɪlpaʊə(r)/ *n* fuerza *f*
de voluntad
wilt /wɪlt/ *vi* marchitarse
win /wɪn/ *vt* (*pt* **won**, *pres p* **winning**) ganar; (achieve, obtain) conseguir. ● *vi* ganar. ● *n* victoria *f*. □ ~
over *vt* ganarse a
wince /wɪns/ *vi* hacer una mueca de
dolor
winch /wɪntʃ/ *n* cabrestante *m*. ● *vt*
levantar con un cabrestante
wind¹ /wɪnd/ *n* viento *m*; (in stomach)
gases *mpl*. ~ **instrument** instrumento *m* de viento. ● *vt* dejar sin
aliento; <*blow*> cortarle la respiración a
wind² /waɪnd/ *vt* (*pt* **wound**) (wrap
around) enrollar; dar cuerda a <*clock
etc*>. ● *vi* <*road etc*> serpentear. □ ~
up *vt* dar cuerda a <*watch, clock*>;
(fig) terminar, concluir
wind /wɪnd/ : **~-cheater** *n* cazado-
ra *f*. **~fall** *n* (fig) suerte *f* inesperada
winding /'waɪndɪŋ/ *a* tortuoso

windmill /'wɪndmɪl/ *n* molino *m* (de
viento)
window /'wɪndəʊ/ *n* ventana *f*; (in
shop) escaparate *m*, vitrina *f* (LAm),
vidriera *f* (LAm), aparador *m* (Mex); (of
vehicle, booking-office) ventanilla *f*;
(Comp) ventana *f*, window *m*. ~ **box**
n jardinera *f*. **~-shop** *vi* mirar los
escaparates. **~sill** *n* alféizar *m or* repisa *f* de la ventana
wind /wɪnd/ : **~-pipe** *n* tráquea *f*.
~screen *n*, **~shield** *n* (Amer) pa-
rabrisas *m*. **~screen wiper** *n*
limpiaparabrisas *m*. **~-swept** *a*
azotado por el viento. **~y** *a* (**-ier**,
-iest) <*day*> ventoso, de viento. **it's
~y** hace viento
wine /waɪn/ *n* vino *m*. **~-cellar** *n*
bodega *f*. **~glass** *n* copa *f* de vino.
~-growing *n* vinicultura *f*. ● *a*
vinícola. ~ **list** *n* lista *f* de vinos.
~-tasting *n* cata *f* de vinos
wing /wɪŋ/ *n* ala *f*; (Auto) aleta *f*.
under one's ~ bajo la protección de
uno. **~er** *n* (Sport) ala *m & f*. **~s** *npl*
(in theatre) bastidores *mpl*
wink /wɪŋk/ *vi* guiñar el ojo; <*light
etc*> centellear. ● *n* guiño *m*. **not to
sleep a** ~ no pegar ojo
win: **~ner** *n* ganador *m*. **~ning-
post** *n* poste *m* de llegada. **~nings**
npl ganancias *fpl*
wint|er /'wɪntə(r)/ *n* invierno *m*.
● *vi* invernar. **~ry** *a* invernal
wipe /waɪp/ *vt* limpiar, pasarle un
trapo a; (dry) secar. ~ **one's nose**
limpiarse la nariz. ● *n*. **give sth a** ~
limpiar algo, pasarle un trapo a algo.
□ ~ **out** *vt* (cancel) cancelar; (destroy)
destruir; (obliterate) borrar. □ ~ **up** *vt*
limpiar
wir|e /'waɪə(r)/ *n* alambre *m*; (Elec)
cable *m*. **~ing** *n* instalación *f* eléctrica
wisdom /'wɪzdəm/ *n* sabiduría *f*. ~
tooth *n* muela *f* del juicio
wise /waɪz/ *a* (**-er**, **-est**) sabio; (sensible) prudente; <*decision, choice*>
acertado. **~ly** *adv* sabiamente; (sens-
ibly) prudentemente
wish /wɪʃ/ *n* deseo *m*; (greeting) saludo *m*. **make a** ~ pedir un deseo.
best ~es, John (in letters) saludos de

John, un abrazo de John. ● *vt* desear. ～ **s.o.** well desear buena suerte a uno. I ～ I were rich ¡ojalá fuera rico! he ～ed he hadn't told her lamentó habérselo dicho. ～**ful thinking** *n* ilusiones *fpl*

wistful /'wɪstfl/ *a* melancólico

wit /wɪt/ *n* gracia *f*; (intelligence) ingenio *m*. **be at one's ～s' end** no saber más qué hacer

witch /wɪtʃ/ *n* bruja *f*. ～**craft** *n* brujería *f*.

with /wɪð/ *prep* con; (cause, having) de. **come ～ me** ven conmigo. **take it ～ you** llévalo contigo; (formal) llévelo consigo. **the man ～ the beard** el hombre de la barba. **trembling ～ fear** temblando de miedo

withdraw /wɪð'drɔː/ *vt* (*pt* **withdrew**, *pp* **withdrawn**) retirar. ● *vi* apartarse. ～**al** *n* retirada *f*. ～**n** *a* <person> retraído

wither /'wɪðə(r)/ *vi* marchitarse

withhold /wɪð'həʊld/ *vt* (*pt* **withheld**) retener; (conceal) ocultar (**from** a)

within /wɪð'ɪn/ *prep* dentro de. ● *adv* dentro. ～ **sight** a la vista

without /wɪð'aʊt/ *prep* sin. ～ **paying** sin pagar

withstand /wɪð'stænd/ *vt* (*pt* -**stood**) resistir

witness /'wɪtnɪs/ *n* testigo *m*; (proof) testimonio *m*. ● *vt* presenciar; atestiguar <signature>. ～**box** *n* tribuna *f* de los testigos

witt|icism /'wɪtɪsɪzəm/ *n* ocurrencia *f*. ～**y** /'wɪtɪ/ *a* (**-ier**, **-iest**) gracioso

wives /waɪvz/ ⇒WIFE

wizard /'wɪzəd/ *n* hechicero *m*

wizened /'wɪznd/ *a* arrugado

wobbl|e /'wɒbl/ *vi* <chair> tambalearse; <bicycle> bambolearse; <voice, jelly, hand> temblar. ～**y** *a* <chair etc> cojo

woe /wəʊ/ *n* aflicción *f*

woke /wəʊk/, **woken** /'wəʊkən/ ⇒WAKE

wolf /wʊlf/ *n* (*pl* **wolves** /wʊlvz/) lobo *m*

woman /'wʊmən/ *n* (*pl* **women**) mujer *f*

womb /wuːm/ *n* matriz *f*

women /'wɪmɪn/ *npl* ⇒WOMAN

won /wʌn/ ⇒WIN

wonder /'wʌndə(r)/ *n* maravilla *f*; (bewilderment) asombro *m*. **no ～** no es de extrañarse (**that** que). ● *vt* (ask oneself) preguntarse. I ～ **whose book this is** me pregunto de quién será este libro; (in polite requests) I ～ **if you could help me?** ¿me podría ayudar? ～**ful** *a* maravilloso. ～**fully** *adv* maravillosamente

won't /wəʊnt/ = **will not**

wood /wʊd/ *n* madera *f*; (for burning) leña *f*; (area) bosque *m*. ～**ed** *a* poblado de árboles, boscoso. ～**en** *a* de madera. ～**land** *n* bosque *m*. ～**wind** /-wɪnd/ *n* instrumentos *mpl* de viento de madera. ～**work** *n* carpintería *f*; (in room etc) maderaje *m*. ～**worm** *n* carcoma *f*. ～**y** *a* leñoso

wool /wʊl/ *n* lana *f*. **pull the ～ over s.o.'s eyes** engañar a uno. ～**len** *a* de lana. ～**ly** *a* (**-ier**, **-iest**) de lana; (unclear) vago. ● *n* jersey *m*

word /wɜːd/ *n* palabra *f*; (news) noticia *f*. **by ～ of mouth** de palabra. I **didn't say a ～** yo no dije nada. **in other ～s** es decir. ● *vt* expresar. ～**ing** *n* redacción *f*; (of question) formulación *f*. ～ **processor** *n* procesador *m* de textos. ～**y** *a* prolijo

wore /wɔː(r)/ ⇒WEAR

work /wɜːk/ *n* trabajo *m*; (arts) obra *f*. **be out of ～** estar sin trabajo, estar desocupado. ● *vt* hacer trabajar; manejar <machine>. ● *vi* trabajar; <machine> funcionar; <student> estudiar; <drug etc> surtir efecto. □ ～ **off** *vt* desahogar. □ ～ **out** *vt* resolver <problem>; (calculate) calcular; (understand) entender. *vi* (succeed) salir bien; (Sport) entrenarse. □ ～ **up** *vt*. **get ～ed up** exaltarse. ～**able** *a* <project, solution> factible. ～**er** *n* trabajador *m*; (manual) obrero *m*; (in office, bank) empleado *m*. ～**ing** *a* <day> laborable; <clothes etc> de trabajo. **in ～ing order** en estado de funcionamiento. ～**ing class** *n* clase *f* obrera. ～**ing-class** *a* de la clase obrera. ～**man** /-mən/ *n* (*pl* -**men**) obrero *m*. ～**manship** *n* destreza *f*. ～**s** *npl* (building) fábrica *f*;

(Mec) mecanismo *m*. ~**shop** *n* taller *m*

world /wɜːld/ *n* mundo *m*. out of this ~ maravilloso. ●*a* mundial. **W~ Cup** *n*. the **W~** Cup la Copa del Mundo. ~**ly** *a* mundano. ~**wide** *a* universal. **W~ Wide Web** *n* World Wide Web *m*

worm /wɜːm/ *n* gusano *m*, lombriz *f*

worn /wɔːn/ ⇒WEAR. ●*a* gastado. ~**-out** *a* gastado; *<person>* rendido

worr|ied /ˈwʌrɪd/ *a* preocupado. ~**y** /ˈwʌrɪ/ *vt* preocupar; (annoy) molestar. ●*vi* preocuparse. ●*n* preocupación *f*. ~**ying** *a* inquietante

worse /wɜːs/ *a* peor. get ~ empeorar. ●*adv* peor; (more) más. ~**n** *vt/i* empeorar

worship /ˈwɜːʃɪp/ *n* culto *m*; (title) Su Señoría. ●*vt* (*pt* **worshipped**) adorar

worst /wɜːst/ *a* peor. he's the ~ in the class es el peor de la clase. ●*adv* peor. ●*n*. the ~ lo peor

worth /wɜːθ/ *n* valor *m*. ●*a*. be ~ valer. it's ~ trying vale la pena probarlo. it was ~ my while (me) valió la pena. ~**while** /-ˈwaɪl/ *a* que vale la pena. ~**y** /ˈwɜːðɪ/ *a* meritorio; (respectable) respetable; (laudable) loable

would /wʊd/ *v aux*. (in conditional sentences) ~ you go? ¿irías tú? he ~ come if he could vendría si pudiera; (in reported speech) I thought you'd forget pensé que te olvidarías; (in requests, invitations) ~ you come here, please? ¿quieres venir aquí? ~ you switch the television off? ¿podrías apagar la televisión?; (be prepared to) he ~n't listen to me no me quería escuchar

wound[1] /wuːnd/ *n* herida *f*. ●*vt* herir

wound[2] /waʊnd/ ⇒WIND[2]

wove, woven /wəʊv, ˈwəʊvn/ ⇒WEAVE

wow /waʊ/ *int* ¡ah!

wrangle /ˈræŋɡl/ *vi* reñir. ●*n* riña *f*

wrap /ræp/ *vt* (*pt* **wrapped**) envolver. ●*n* bata *f*; (shawl) chal *m*. ~**per** *n*, ~**ping** *n* envoltura *f*

wrath /rɒθ/ *n* ira *f*

wreak /riːk/ *vt* sembrar. ~ **havoc** causar estragos

wreath /riːθ/ *n* (*pl* **-ths** /-ðz/) corona *f*

wreck /rek/ *n* (ship) restos *mpl* de un naufragio; (vehicle) restos *mpl* de un avión siniestrado. be a nervous ~ tener los nervios destrozados. ●*vt* provocar el naufragio de *<ship>*; destrozar *<car>*; (Amer, demolish) demoler; (fig) destrozar. ~**age** /-ɪdʒ/ *n* restos *mpl*; (of building) ruinas *fpl*

wrench /rentʃ/ *vt* arrancar; (sprain) desgarrarse; dislocarse *<joint>*. ●*n* tirón *m*; (emotional) dolor *m* (*causado por una separación*); (tool) llave *f* inglesa

wrestl|e /ˈresl/ *vi* luchar. ~**er** *n* luchador *m*. ~**ing** *n* lucha *f*

wretch /retʃ/ *n* (despicable person) desgraciado *m*; (unfortunate person) desdichado *m* & *f*. ~**ed** /-ɪd/ *a* desdichado; *<weather>* horrible

wriggle /ˈrɪɡl/ *vi* retorcerse. ~ out of escaparse de

wring /rɪŋ/ *vt* (*pt* **wrung**) retorcer *<neck>*. ~ out of (obtain from) arrancar. □ ~ out *vt* retorcer

wrinkl|e /ˈrɪŋkl/ *n* arruga *f*. ●*vt* arrugar. ●*vi* arrugarse. ~**y** *a* arrugado

wrist /rɪst/ *n* muñeca *f*. ~**watch** *n* reloj *m* de pulsera

writ /rɪt/ *n* orden *m* judicial

write /raɪt/ *vt/i* (*pt* **wrote**, *pp* **written**, *pres p* **writing**) escribir. □ ~ **down** *vt* anotar. □ ~ **off** *vt* cancelar *<debt>*. ~**-off** *n*. the car was a ~-off el coche fue declarado un siniestro total. ~**r** *n* escritor *m*

writhe /raɪð/ *vi* retorcerse

writing /ˈraɪtɪŋ/ *n* (script) escritura *f*; (handwriting) letra *f*. in ~ por escrito. ~**s** *npl* obra *f*, escritos *mpl*. ~ **desk** *n* escritorio *m*. ~ **pad** *n* bloc *m*. ~ **paper** *n* papel *m* de escribir

written /ˈrɪtn/ ⇒WRITE

wrong /rɒŋ/ *a* equivocado, incorrecto; (not just) injusto; (mistaken) equivocado. be ~ no tener razón; (be mistaken) equivocarse. what's ~? ¿qué pasa? it's ~ to steal robar está mal. what's ~ with that? ¿qué hay de

malo en eso?. ● *adv* mal. go ∼ equivocarse; <*plan*> salir mal. ● *n*
injusticia *f*; (evil) mal *m*. in the ∼
equivocado. ● *vt* ser injusto con.
∼**ful** *a* injusto. ∼**ly** *adv* mal; (unfairly)
injustamente

wrote /rəʊt/ ⇒WRITE

wrought iron /rɔːt/ *n* hierro *m*
forjado

wrung /rʌŋ/ ⇒WRING

wry /raɪ/ *a* (**wryer, wryest**) irónico.
make a ∼ face torcer el gesto

···

X x

···

xerox /'zɪərɒks/ *vt* fotocopiar, xe-
rografiar

Xmas /'krɪsməs/ *n abbr* (**Christmas**) Navidad *f*

X-ray /'eksreɪ/ *n* (ray) rayo *m* X;
(photograph) radiografía *f*. ∼**s** *npl* rayos *mpl*. ● *vt* hacer una radiografía
de

xylophone /'zaɪləfəʊn/ *n* xilofón *m*,
xilófono *m*

···

Y y

···

yacht /jɒt/ *n* yate *m*. ∼**ing** *n* navegación *f* a vela

yank /jæŋk/ *vt* 🄴 tirar de (violentamente)

Yankee /'jæŋkɪ/ *n* 🄴 yanqui *m & f*

yap /jæp/ *vi* (*pt* **yapped**) <*dog*>
ladrar (*con ladridos agudos*)

yard /jɑːd/ *n* patio *m*; (Amer, garden)
jardín *m*; (measurement) yarda *f* (=
0.9144 metre)

yarn /jɑːn/ *n* hilo *m*; (🄴, tale) cuento
m

yawn /jɔːn/ *vi* bostezar. ● *n* bostezo
m

year /jɪə(r)/ *n* año *m*. be three ∼s old
tener tres años. ∼**ly** *a* anual. ● *adv*
cada año

yearn /'jɜːn/ *vi*. ∼ to do sth anhelar
hacer algo. ∼ for sth añorar algo.
∼**ing** *n* anhelo *m*, ansia *f*

yeast /jiːst/ *n* levadura *f*

yell /jel/ *vi* gritar. ● *n* grito *m*

yellow /'jeləʊ/ *a & n* amarillo (*m*)

yelp /jelp/ *n* gañido *m*. ● *vi* gañir

yes /jes/ *int & n* sí (*m*)

yesterday /'jestədeɪ/ *adv & n* ayer
(*m*). the day before ∼ anteayer *m*. ∼
morning ayer por la mañana, ayer en
la mañana (LAm)

yet /jet/ *adv* todavía, aún; (already) ya.
as ∼ hasta ahora; (as a linker) sin embargo. ● *conj* pero

Yiddish /'jɪdɪʃ/ *n* yídish *m*

yield /jiːld/ *vt* (surrender) ceder; producir <*crop/mineral*>; dar <*results*>.
● *vi* ceder. '**yield**' (Amer, traffic sign) ceda el paso. ● *n* rendimiento *m*

yoga /'jəʊɡə/ *n* yoga *m*

yoghurt /'jɒɡət/ *n* yogur *m*

yoke /jəʊk/ *n* (fig also) yugo *m*

yokel /'jəʊkl/ *n* palurdo *m*

yolk /jəʊk/ *n* yema *f* (de huevo)

···

you /juː/

● *pronoun*

····▸ (as the subject) (familiar form) (*sing*)
tú, vos (River Plate and parts of Central
America); (*pl*) vosotros, -tras (Spain),
ustedes (LAm); (formal) (*sing*) usted;
(*pl*) ustedes

In Spanish the subject
pronoun is usually only used
to give emphasis or mark
contrast.

····▸ (as the direct object) (familiar form)
(*sing*) te; (*pl*) os (Spain), los, las (LAm);
(formal) (*sing*) lo *or* (Spain) le, la; (*pl*)
los *or* (Spain) les, las. I love ∼ te quiero

····▸ (as the indirect object) (familiar form)
(*sing*) te; (*pl*) os (Spain), les (LAm); (formal) (*sing*) le; (*pl*) les. I sent ∼ the
book yesterday te mandé el libro
ayer

The pronoun se replaces the
indirect object pronoun le or
les when the latter is used

with the direct object pronoun (*lo, la* etc), e.g. **I gave it to** ~ *se lo di*

····➤ (when used after a preposition) (familiar form) (*sing*) ti, vos (River Plate and parts of Central America); (*pl*) vosotros, -tras (Spain), ustedes (LAm); (formal) (*sing*) usted; (*pl*) ustedes

····➤ (generalizing) uno, tú (esp Spain). ~ **feel very proud** uno se siente muy orgulloso, te sientes muy orgulloso (esp Spain). ~ **have to be patient** hay que tener paciencia

you'd /juːd/, /jʊəd/ = **you had**, **you would**

you'll /juːl/, /jʊəl/ = **you will**

young /jʌŋ/ *a* (**-er, -est**) joven. my ~**er sister** mi hermana menor. **he's a year** ~**er than me** tiene un año menos que yo. ~ **lady** *n* señorita *f*. ~ **man** *n* joven *m*. ~**ster** /-stə(r)/ *n* joven *m*

your /jɔː(r)/ *a* (belonging to one person) (*sing, familiar*) tu; (*pl, familiar*) tus; (*sing, formal*) su; (*pl, formal*) sus; (belonging to more than one person) (*sing, familiar*) vuestro, -tra, su (LAm); (*pl, familiar*) vuestros, -tras, sus (LAm); (*sing, formal*) su; (*pl, formal*) sus

you're /jʊə(r)/, /jɔː(r)/ = **you are**

yours /jɔːz/ *poss pron* (belonging to one person) (*sing, familiar*) tuyo, -ya; (*pl, familiar*) tuyos, -yas; (*sing, formal*) suyo, -ya; (*pl, formal*) suyos, -yas. (belonging to more than one person) (*sing, familiar*) vuestro, -tra; (*pl, familiar*) vuestros, -tras, suyos, -yas (LAm); (*sing, formal*) suyo, -ya; (*pl, formal*) suyos, -yas **an aunt of** ~ una tía tuya; ~ **is here** el tuyo está aquí

yoursel|f /jɔːˈself/ *pron* (*reflexive*). (emphatic use) ① tú mismo, tú misma; (formal) usted mismo, usted misma. **describe** ~**f** descríbete; (Ud form) descríbase. **stop thinking about** ~**f** deja de pensar en tí mismo; (formal) deje de pensar en sí mismo; **by** ~**f** solo, sola. ~**ves** /jɔːˈselvz/ *pron* vosotros mismos, vosotras mismas (familiar), ustedes mismos, ustedes mismas (LAm familiar), ustedes mismos, ustedes mismas (formal); (*re-*

flexive). **behave** ~**ves** ¡portaos bien (familiar), ¡pórtense bien! (LAm familiar), ¡pórtense bien! (formal). **by** ~**ves** solos, solas

youth /juːθ/ *n* (*pl* **youths** /juːðz/) (early life) juventud *f*; (boy) joven *m*; (young people) juventud *f*. ~**ful** *a* joven, juvenil. ~ **hostel** *n* albergue *m* juvenil

you've /juːv/ = **you have**

Yugoslav /ˈjuːɡəslɑːv/ *a* & *n* yugoslavo (*m*). ~**ia** /-ˈslɑːvɪə/ *n* Yugoslavia *f*

Zz

zeal /ziːl/ *n* fervor *m*, celo *m*

zeal|ot /ˈzelət/ *n* fanático *m*. ~**ous** /-əs/ *a* ferviente; (worker) que pone gran celo en su trabajo

zebra /ˈzebrə/ *n* cebra *f*. ~ **crossing** *n* paso *m* de cebra

zenith /ˈzenɪθ/ *n* cenit *m*

zero /ˈzɪərəʊ/ *n* (*pl* **-os**) cero *m*

zest /zest/ *n* entusiasmo *m*; (peel) cáscara *f*

zigzag /ˈzɪɡzæɡ/ *n* zigzag *m*. ● *vi* (*pt* **zigzagged**) zigzaguear

zilch /zɪltʃ/ *n* ⊠ nada de nada

zinc /zɪŋk/ *n* cinc *m*

zip /zɪp/ *n* cremallera *f*, cierre *m* (LAm), zíper *m* (Mex). ● *vt*. ~ (**up**) cerrar (la cremallera). **Z**~ **code** *n* (Amer) código *m* postal. ~ **fastener** *n* cremallera *f*. ~**per** *n/vt* ⇒ZIP

zodiac /ˈzəʊdɪæk/ *n* zodíaco *m*, zodiaco *m*

zombie /ˈzɒmbɪ/ *n* zombi *m* & *f*

zone /zəʊn/ *n* zona *f*. **time** ~ *n* huso *m* horario

zoo /zuː/ *n* zoo *m*, zoológico *m*. ~**logical** /zuːəˈlɒdʒɪkl/ *a* zoológico. ~**logist** /zuːˈɒlədʒɪst/ *n* zoólogo *m*. ~**logy** /zuːˈɒlədʒɪ/ *n* zoología *f*

zoom /zuːm/. □ ~ **in** *vi* (Photo) hacer un zoom in (**on** sobre). □ ~ **past** *vi/t* pasar zumbando. ~ **lens** *n* teleobjetivo *m*, zoom *m*

zucchini /zʊˈkiːnɪ/ *n* (*invar or* ~**s**) (Amer) calabacín *m*

Spanish verbs

Regular verbs:

in -ar (*e.g.* **comprar**)
Present: compr|o, ~as, ~a, ~amos,
~áis, ~an
Future: comprar|é, ~ás, ~á, ~emos,
~éis, ~án
Imperfect: compr|aba, ~abas, ~aba,
~ábamos, ~abais, ~aban
Preterite: compr|é, ~aste, ~ó, ~amos,
~asteis, ~aron
Present subjunctive: compr|e, ~es, ~e,
~emos, ~éis, ~en
Imperfect subjunctive: compr|ara,
~aras ~ara, ~áramos, ~arais, ~aran
compr|ase, ~ases, ~ase, ~ásemos,
~aseis, ~asen
Conditional: comprar|ía,
~ías, ~ía, ~íamos, ~íais,
~ían
Present participle: comprando
Past participle: comprado
Imperative: compra, comprad

in -er (*e.g.* **beber**)
Present: beb|o, ~es, ~e, ~emos, ~éis,
~en
Future: beber|é, ~ás, ~á, ~emos, ~éis,
~án
Imperfect: beb|ía, ~ías, ~ía, ~íamos,
~íais, ~ían
Preterite: beb|í, ~iste, ~ió, ~imos,
~isteis, ~ieron
Present subjunctive: beb|a, ~as, ~a,
~amos, ~áis, ~an
Imperfect subjunctive: beb|iera,
~ieras, ~iera, ~iéramos, ~ierais,
~ieran beb|iese, ~ieses, ~iese,
~iésemos, ~ieseis, ~iesen
Conditional: beber|ía, ~ías, ~ía,
~íamos, ~íais, ~ían
Present participle: bebiendo
Past participle: bebido
Imperative: bebe, bebed

in -ir (*e.g.* **vivir**)
Present: viv|o, ~es, ~e, ~imos, ~ís,
~en
Future: vivir|é, ~ás, ~á, ~emos, ~éis,
~án
Imperfect: viv|ía, ~ías, ~ía, ~íamos,
~íais, ~ían
Preterite: viv|í, ~iste, ~ió, ~imos,
~isteis, ~ieron
Present subjunctive: viv|a, ~as, ~a,
~amos, ~áis, ~an
Imperfect subjunctive: viv|iera,
~ieras, ~iera, ~iéramos, ~ierais,
~ieran
viv|iese, ~ieses, ~iese, ~iésemos,
~ieseis, ~iesen
Conditional: vivir|ía, ~ías, ~ía,
~íamos, ~íais, ~ían
Present participle: viviendo
Past participle: vivido
Imperative: vive, vivid

Irregular verbs:

[1] cerrar
Present: cierro, cierras, cierra,
cerramos, cerráis, cierran
Present subjunctive: cierre, cierres,
cierre, cerremos,
cerréis, cierren
Imperative: cierra, cerrad

[2] contar, mover
Present: cuento, cuentas, cuenta,
contamos, contáis, cuentan
muevo, mueves, mueve, movemos,
movéis, mueven
Present subjunctive: cuente, cuentes,
cuente, contemos, contéis, cuenten
mueva, muevas, mueva, movamos,
mováis, muevan
Imperative: cuenta, contad mueve,
moved

[3] jugar
Present: juego, juegas, juega,
jugamos, jugáis, juegan
Preterite: jugué, jugaste, jugó,
jugamos, jugasteis, jugaron
Present subjunctive: juegue, juegues,
juegue, juguemos, juguéis, jueguen

[4] sentir
Present: siento, sientes, siente,
sentimos, sentís, sienten
Preterite: sentí, sentiste, sintió,
sentimos, sentisteis, sintieron
Present subjunctive: sienta, sientas,
sienta, sintamos, sintáis, sientan
Imperfect subjunctive: sint|iera,
~ieras, ~iera, ~iéramos, ~ierais,

~ieran
sint|iese, ~ieses, ~iese, ~iésemos,
~ieseis, ~iesen
Present participle: sintiendo
Imperative: siente, sentid

[5] pedir
Present: pido, pides, pide, pedimos,
pedís, piden
Preterite: pedí, pediste, pidió,
pedimos, pedisteis, pidieron
Present subjunctive: pid|a, ~as, ~a,
~amos, ~áis, ~an
Imperfect subjunctive: pid|iera,
~ieras, ~iera, ~iéramos, ~ierais,
~ieran
pid|iese, ~ieses, ~iese, ~iésemos,
~ieseis, ~iesen
Present participle: pidiendo
Imperative: pide, pedid

[6] dormir
Present: duermo, duermes, duerme,
dormimos, dormís, duermen
Preterite: dormí, dormiste, durmió,
dormimos, dormisteis, durmieron
Present subjunctive: duerma,
duermas, duerma, durmamos,
durmáis, duerman
Imperfect subjunctive: durm|iera,
~ieras, ~iera, ~iéramos, ~ierais,
~ieran
durm|iese, ~ieses, ~iese, ~iésemos,
~ieseis, ~iesen
Present participle: durmiendo
Imperative: duerme, dormid

[7] dedicar
Preterite: dediqué, dedicaste, dedicó,
dedicamos, dedicasteis, dedicaron
Present subjunctive: dediqu|e, ~es,
~e, ~emos, ~éis, ~en

[8] delinquir
Present: delinco, delinques, delinque,
delinquimos, delinquís, delinquen
Present subjunctive: delinc|a, ~as, ~a,
~amos, ~áis, ~an

[9] vencer, esparcir
Present: venzo, vences, vence,
vencemos, vencéis, vencen
esparzo, esparces, esparce,
esparcimos, esparcís, esparcen
Present subjunctive:
venz|a, ~as, ~a, ~amos, ~áis, ~an
esparz|a, ~as, ~a, ~amos, ~áis, ~an

[10] rechazar
Preterite: rechacé, rechazaste,

rechazó, rechazamos, rechazasteis,
rechazaron
Present subjunctive: rechac|e, ~es,
~e, ~emos, ~éis, ~en

[11] conocer, lucir
Present: conozco, conoces, conoce,
conocemos, conocéis, conocen
luzco, luces, luce, lucimos, lucís,
lucen
Present subjunctive:
conozc|a, ~as, ~a, ~amos, ~áis, ~an
luzc|a, ~as, ~a, ~amos, ~áis, ~an

[12] pagar
Preterite: pagué, pagaste, pagó,
pagamos, pagasteis, pagaron
Present subjunctive: pagu|e, ~es, ~e,
~emos, ~éis, ~en

[13] distinguir
Present: distingo, distingues,
distingue, distinguimos, distinguís,
distinguen
Present subjunctive: disting|a, ~as,
~a, ~amos, ~áis, ~an

[14] acoger, afligir
Present: acojo, acoges, acoge,
acogemos, acogéis, acogen aflijo,
afliges, aflige, afligimos, afligís,
afligen
Present subjunctive:
acoj|a, ~as, ~a, ~amos, ~áis, ~an
aflij|a, ~as, ~a, ~amos, ~áis, ~an

[15] averiguar
Preterite: averigüé, averiguaste,
averiguó, averiguamos,
averiguasteis, averiguaron
Present subjunctive: averigü|e, ~es,
~e, ~emos, ~éis, ~en

[16] agorar
Present: agüero, agüeras, agüera,
agoramos, agoráis, agüeran
Present subjunctive: agüere, agüeres,
agüere, agoremos, agoréis, agüeren
Imperative: agüera, agorad

[17] huir
Present: huyo, huyes, huye, huimos,
huís, huyen
Preterite: huí, huiste, huyó, huimos,
huisteis, huyeron
Present subjunctive:
huy|a, ~as, ~a, ~amos, ~áis, ~an
Imperfect subjunctive:
huy|era, ~eras, ~era, ~éramos,
~erais, ~eran

huy|ese, ~eses, ~ese, ~ésemos,
~eseis, ~esen
Present participle: huyendo
Imperative: huye, huid

[18] creer
Preterite: creí, creíste, creyó, creímos,
creísteis, creyeron
Imperfect subjunctive: crey|era,
~eras, ~era, ~éramos, ~erais,
~eran crey|ese, ~eses, ~ese,
~ésemos, ~eseis, ~esen
Present participle: creyendo
Past participle: creído

[19] argüir
Present: arguyo, arguyes, arguye,
argüimos, argüís, arguyen
Preterite: argüí, argüiste, arguyó,
argüimos, argüisteis, arguyeron
Present subjunctive: arguy|a, ~as, ~a,
~amos, ~áis, ~an
Imperfect subjunctive: arguy|era,
~eras, ~era, ~éramos, ~erais,
~eran arguy|ese, ~eses, ~ese,
~ésemos, ~eseis, ~esen
Present participle: arguyendo
Imperative: arguye, argüid

[20] vaciar
Present: vacío, vacías, vacía,
vaciamos, vaciáis, vacían
Present subjunctive: vacíe, vacíes,
vacíe, vaciemos, vaciéis, vacíen
Imperative: vacía, vaciad

[21] acentuar
Present: acentúo, acentúas, acentúa,
acentuamos, acentuáis, acentúan
Present subjunctive:
acentúe, acentúes, acentúe,
acentuemos, acentuéis, acentúen
Imperative: acentúa, acentuad

[22] atañer, engullir
Preterite:
atañ|í, ~iste, ~ó, ~imos, ~isteis,
~eron
engull|í ~iste, ~ó, ~imos, ~isteis,
~eron
Imperfect subjunctive:
atañ|era, ~eras, ~era, ~éramos,
~erais, ~eran
atañ|ese, ~eses, ~ese, ~ésemos,
~eseis, ~esen
engull|era, ~eras, ~era, ~éramos,
~erais, ~eran engull|ese, ~eses,
~ese, ~ésemos, ~eseis, ~esen
Present participle: atañendo

engullendo

[23] aislar, aullar
Present: aíslo, aíslas, aísla, aislamos,
aisláis, aíslan
aúllo, aúllas, aúlla, aullamos,
aulláis, aúllan
Present subjunctive: aísle, aísles,
aísle, aislemos, aisléis, aíslen
aúlle, aúlles, aúlle, aullemos,
aulléis, aúllen
Imperative: aísla, aislad
aúlla, aullad

[24] abolir
Present: abolimos, abolís
Present subjunctive: not used
Imperative: abolid

[25] andar
Preterite: anduv|e, ~iste, ~o, ~imos,
~isteis, ~ieron
Imperfect subjunctive: anduv|iera,
~ieras, ~iera, ~iéramos, ~ierais,
~ieran anduv|iese, ~ieses, ~iese,
~iésemos, ~ieseis, ~iesen

[26] dar
Present: doy, das, da, damos,
dais, dan
Preterite: di, diste, dio, dimos, disteis,
dieron
Present subjunctive: dé, des, dé,
demos, deis, den
Imperfect subjunctive: diera, dieras,
diera, diéramos, dierais, dieran
diese, dieses, diese, diésemos,
dieseis, diesen

[27] estar
Present: estoy, estás, está, estamos,
estáis, están
Preterite: estuv|e, ~iste, ~o, ~imos,
~isteis, ~ieron
Present subjunctive: esté, estés, esté,
estemos, estéis, estén
Imperfect subjunctive: estuv|iera,
~ieras, ~iera, ~iéramos, ~ierais,
~ieran
estuv|iese, ~ieses, ~iese, ~iésemos,
~ieseis, ~iesen
Imperative: está, estad

[28] caber
Present: quepo, cabes, cabe, cabemos,
cabéis, caben
Future: cabr|é, ~ás, ~á, ~emos, ~éis,
~án
Preterite: cup|e, ~iste, ~o, ~imos,
~isteis, ~ieron

Present subjunctive: quep|a, ~as, ~a,
~amos, ~áis, ~an
Imperfect subjunctive: cup|iera,
~ieras, ~iera, ~iéramos, ~ierais,
~ieran
cup|iese, ~ieses, ~iese, ~iésemos,
~ieseis, ~iesen
Conditional: cabr|ía, ~ías, ~ía,
~íamos, ~íais, ~ían

[29] caer

Present: caigo, caes, cae, caemos,
caéis, caen
Preterite: caí, caiste, cayó, caímos,
caísteis, cayeron
Present subjunctive: caig|a, ~as, ~a,
~amos, ~áis, ~an
Imperfect subjunctive:
cay|era, ~eras, ~era, ~éramos,
~erais, ~eran
cay|ese, ~eses, ~ese, ~ésemos,
~eseis, ~esen
Present participle: cayendo
Past participle: caído

[30] haber

Present: he, has, ha, hemos, habéis,
han
Future: habr|é ~ás, ~á, ~emos, ~éis,
~án
Preterite: hub|e, ~iste, ~o, ~imos,
~isteis, ~ieron
Present subjunctive: hay|a, ~as, ~a,
~amos, ~áis, ~an
Imperfect subjunctive: hub|iera,
~ieras, ~iera, ~iéramos, ~ierais,
~ieran
hub|iese, ~ieses, ~iese, ~iésemos,
~ieseis, ~iesen
Conditional: habr|ía, ~ías, ~ía,
~íamos, ~íais, ~ían
Imperative: he, habed

[31] hacer

Present: hago, haces, hace, hacemos,
hacéis, hacen
Future: har|é, ~ás, ~á, ~emos, ~éis,
~án
Preterite: hice, hiciste, hizo, hicimos,
hicisteis, hicieron
Present subjunctive:
hag|a, ~as, ~a, ~amos, ~áis, ~an
Imperfect subjunctive:
hic|iera, ~ieras, ~iera, ~iéramos,
~ierais, ~ieran
hic|iese, ~ieses, ~iese, ~iésemos,
~ieseis, ~iesen
Conditional: har|ía,

~ías, ~ía, ~íamos, ~íais, ~ían
Past participle: hecho
Imperative: haz, haced

[32] placer

Present subjunctive: plazca
Imperfect subjunctive: placiera,
placiese

[33] poder

Present: puedo, puedes,
puede, podemos, podéis, pueden
Future: podr|é, ~ás, ~á, ~emos, ~éis,
~án
Preterite: pud|e, ~iste, ~o, ~imos,
~isteis, ~ieron
Present subjunctive:
pueda, puedas, pueda, podamos,
podáis, puedan
Imperfect subjunctive: pud|iera,
~ieras, ~iera, ~iéramos, ~ierais,
~ieran
pud|iese, ~ieses, ~iese, ~iésemos,
~ieseis, ~iesen
Conditional: podr|ía, ~ías, ~ía,
~íamos, ~íais, ~ían
Past participle: pudiendo

[34] poner

Present: pongo, pones, pone,
ponemos, ponéis, ponen
Future: pondr|é, ~ás, ~á, ~emos,
~éis, ~án
Preterite: pus|e, ~iste,
~o, ~imos, ~isteis, ~ieron
Present subjunctive: pong|a, ~as, ~a,
~amos, ~áis, ~an
Imperfect subjunctive: pus|iera,
~ieras, ~iera, ~iéramos, ~ierais,
~ieran
pus|iese, ~ieses, ~iese, ~iésemos,
~ieseis, ~iesen
Conditional: pondr|ía, ~ías, ~ía,
~íamos, ~íais, ~ían
Past participle: puesto
Imperative: pon, poned

[35] querer

Present: quiero, quieres,
quiere, queremos, queréis, quieren
Future: querr|é, ~ás, ~á, ~emos, ~éis,
~án
Preterite: quis|e, ~iste, ~o, ~imos,
~isteis, ~ieron
Present subjunctive:
quiera, quieras, quiera, queramos,
queráis,
quieran
Imperfect subjunctive: quis|iera,

~ieras, ~iera, ~iéramos, ~ierais,
~ieran
quisǀiese, ~ieses, ~iese, ~iésemos,
~ieseis, ~iesen
Conditional: querrǀía, ~ías, ~ía,
~íamos, ~íais, ~ían
Imperative: quiere, quered

[36] raer
Present: raigo/rayo, raes, rae, raemos,
raéis, raen
Preterite: raí, raíste, rayó, raímos,
raísteis, rayeron
Present subjunctive:
raigǀa, ~as, ~a, ~amos, ~áis, ~an
rayǀa, ~as, ~a, ~amos, ~áis, ~an
Imperfect subjunctive:
rayǀera, ~eras, ~era, ~éramos,
~erais, ~eran rayǀese, ~eses, ~ese,
~ésemos, ~eseis, ~esen
Present participle: rayendo
Past participle: raído

[37] roer
Present: roo, roes, roe, roemos, roéis,
roen
Preterite: roí, roíste, royó, roímos,
roísteis, royeron
Present subjunctive: roǀa, ~as, ~a,
~amos, ~áis, ~an
Imperfect subjunctive:
royǀera, ~eras, ~era, ~éramos,
~erais, ~eran
royǀese, ~eses, ~ese, ~ésemos,
~eseis, ~esen
Present participle: royendo
Past participle: roído

[38] saber
Present: sé, sabes, sabe, sabemos,
sabéis, saben
Future: sabrǀé, ~ás, ~á, ~emos, ~éis,
~án
Preterite: supǀe, ~iste,
~o, ~imos, ~isteis, ~ieron
Present subjunctive: sepǀa, ~as, ~a,
~amos, ~áis, ~an
Imperfect subjunctive: supǀiera,
~ieras, ~iera, ~iéramos, ~ierais,
~ieran
supǀiese, ~ieses, ~iese, ~iésemos,
~ieseis, ~iesen
Conditional: sabrǀía, ~ías, ~ía,
~íamos, ~íais, ~ían

[39] ser
Present: soy, eres, es, somos, sois, son
Imperfect: era, eras, era, éramos,
erais, eran
Preterite: fui, fuiste, fue, fuimos,
fuisteis, fueron
Present subjunctive: seǀa, ~as, ~a,
~amos, ~áis, ~an
Imperfect subjunctive: fuǀera, ~eras,
~era, ~éramos, ~erais, ~eran
fuǀese, ~eses, ~ese, ~ésemos,
~eseis, ~esen
Imperative: sé, sed

[40] tener
Present: tengo, tienes,
tiene, tenemos, tenéis,
tienen
Future: tendrǀé, ~ás, ~á, ~emos, ~éis,
~án
Preterite: tuvǀe, ~iste, ~o, ~imos,
~isteis, ~ieron
Present subjunctive: tengǀa, ~as, ~a,
~amos, ~áis, ~an
Imperfect subjunctive: tuvǀiera,
~ieras, ~iera, ~iéramos, ~ierais,
~ieran
tuvǀiese, ~ieses, ~iese, ~iésemos,
~ieseis, ~iesen
Conditional: tendrǀía, ~ías, ~ía,
~íamos, ~íais, ~ían
Imperative: ten, tened

[41] traer
Present: traigo, traes, trae, traemos,
traéis, traen
Preterite: trajǀe, ~iste, ~o, ~imos,
~isteis, ~eron
Present subjunctive: traigǀa, ~as, ~a,
~amos, ~áis, ~an
Imperfect subjunctive:
trajǀera, ~eras, ~era, ~éramos,
~erais, ~eran trajǀese, ~eses, ~ese,
~ésemos, ~eseis, ~esen
Present participle: trayendo
Past participle: traído

[42] valer
Present: valgo, vales, vale, valemos,
valéis, valen
Future: valdǀré, ~ás, ~á, ~emos, ~éis,
~án
Present subjunctive: valgǀa, ~as, ~a,
~amos ~áis, ~an
Conditional: valdǀría, ~ías, ~ía,
~íamos, ~íais, ~ían
Imperative: vale, valed

[43] ver
Present: veo, ves, ve,vemos,
veis, ven
Imperfect: veǀía, ~ías, ~ía, ~íamos,

~íais, ~ían

Preterite: vi, viste, vio, vimos, visteis,
vieron

Present subjunctive: ve|a, ~as, ~a,
~amos, ~áis, ~an

Past participle: visto

[44] yacer

Present: yazco, yaces, yace, yacemos,
yacéis, yacen

Present subjunctive: yazc|a, ~as, ~a,
~amos, ~áis, ~an

Imperative: yace, yaced

[45] asir

Present: asgo, ases, ase, asimos, asís,
asen

Present subjunctive: asg|a, ~as, ~a,
~amos, ~áis, ~an

[46] decir

Present: digo, dices, dice, decimos,
decís, dicen

Future: dir|é, ~ás, ~á, ~emos, ~éis,
~án

Preterite: dij|e, ~iste, ~o, ~imos,
~isteis, ~eron

Present subjunctive: dig|a, ~as, ~a,
~amos, ~áis, ~an

Imperfect subjunctive:
dij|era, ~eras, ~era, ~éramos,
~erais,~eran
dij|ese, ~eses, ~ese, ~ésemos,
~eseis, ~esen

Conditional: dir|ía, ~ías, ~ía,
~íamos, ~íais, ~ían

Present participle: dicho

Imperative: di, decid

[47] reducir

Present: reduzco, reduces, reduce,
reducimos, reducís, reducen

Preterite: reduj|e, ~iste, ~o, ~imos,
~isteis, ~eron

Present subjunctive: reduzc|a, ~as,
~a, ~amos, ~áis, ~an

Imperfect subjunctive: reduj|era,
~eras, ~era, ~éramos, ~erais,
~eran
reduj|ese, ~eses, ~ese, ~ésemos,
~eseis, ~esen

[48] erguir

Present: yergo, yergues, yergue,
erguimos, erguís, yerguen

Preterite: erguí, erguiste, irguió,
erguimos, erguisteis, irguieron

Present subjunctive: yerg|a, ~as, ~a,
~amos, ~áis, ~an

Imperfect subjunctive: irgu|iera,
~ieras, ~iera, ~iéramos, ~ierais,
~ieran
irgu|iese, ~ieses, ~iese, ~iésemos,
~ieseis, ~iesen

Present participle: irguiendo

Imperative: yergue, erguid

[49] ir

Present: voy, vas, va, vamos, vais, van

Imperfect: iba, ibas, iba, íbamos,
ibais, iban

Preterite: fui, fuiste, fue, fuimos,
fuisteis, fueron

Present subjunctive: vay|a, ~as, ~a,
~amos, ~áis, ~an

Imperfect subjunctive:
fu|era, ~eras, ~era, ~éramos,
~erais, ~eran fu|ese, ~eses, ~ese,
~ésemos, ~eseis, ~esen

Present participle: yendo

Imperative: ve, id

[50] oír

Present: oigo, oyes, oye, oímos, oís,
oyen

Preterite: oí, oíste, oyó, oímos, oísteis,
oyeron

Present subjunctive: oig|a, ~as, ~a,
~amos, ~áis, ~an

Imperfect subjunctive:
oy|era, ~eras, ~era, ~éramos,
~erais, ~eran
oy|ese, ~eses, ~ese, ~ésemos,
~eseis, ~esen

Present participle: oyendo

Past participle: oído

Imperative: oye, oíd

[51] reír

Present: río, ríes, ríe, reímos, reís,
ríen

Preterite: reí, reíste, rió, reímos,
reísteis, rieron

Present subjunctive: ría, rías, ría,
riamos, riáis, rían

Present participle: riendo

Past participle: reído

Imperative: ríe, reíd

[52] salir

Present: salgo, sales, sale, salimos,
salís, salen

Future: saldr|é, ~ás, ~á, ~emos, ~éis,
~án

Present subjunctive: salg|a, ~as, ~a,
~amos, ~áis, ~an

Conditional: saldr|ía,
~ías, ~ía, ~íamos, ~íais, ~ían

Imperative: sal, salid

[53] venir

Present: vengo, vienes, viene,
    venimos, venís, vienen
Future: vendr│é, ~ás, ~á, ~emos, ~éis,
    ~án
Preterite: vin│e, ~iste, ~o, ~imos,
    ~isteis, ~ieron
Present subjunctive: veng│a, ~as, ~a,
    ~amos, ~áis, ~an
Imperfect subjunctive: vin│iera,
    ~ieras, ~iera, ~iéramos, ~ierais,
    ~ieran
    vin│iese, ~ieses, ~iese, ~iésemos,
    ~ieseis, ~iesen
Conditional: vendr│ía, ~ías, ~ía,
    ~íamos, ~íais, ~ían
Present participle: viniendo
Imperative: ven, venid

Spanish
Grammar

JOHN BUTT

Introduction

Spanish is the main language of twenty-one countries and it will soon have 400 million speakers, so anyone who knows both it and English can communicate with a significant proportion of the Earth's inhabitants. Since each Spanish-speaking country has its own accents, colloquialisms and peculiarities of grammar and vocabulary, and since no one agrees about which country speaks the best Spanish, it is occasionally a problem to know which words foreign students should learn. For example, a ball-point pen is **un bolígrafo** in Spain, **una birome** in Argentina, **un lapicero** in Peru and Central America, **un esfero** in Colombia and **una pluma** or **una pluma atómica** in Mexico, although in this, as in many similar cases, the word used in Spain is understood by many people everywhere.

This problem should not be exaggerated. The problem of variety mainly affects familiar or popular vocabulary and slang. Variations in Spanish pronunciation are no great problem: they never amount to more than fairly minor regional differences of accent, so one does not run into the kind of problem that can face Americans or Englishmen in the countryside of Scotland or Ireland. The basic grammar of Spanish is moreover amazingly uniform considering the tremendous size of the Spanish-speaking world. And, above all, virtually every-body—except perhaps in remote villages—knows generally-used words. For example, Mexicans often say **cuate** for *friend*, but they all know and also use the word **amigo**, just as Americans who say *buddy* and Britons and Australians who say *chum*, *pal* or *mate* all share the common word *friend*—which is obviously the word any foreign learner of English would learn first.

As far as possible the examples given in this book avoid regional forms and reflect the sort of Spanish used in the media and by educated people when talking to people from other Spanish-speaking countries. Nevertheless, where differences are unavoidable the language used is that of Spain and important Latin-American variants are noted where they arise. As a result this basic grammar should be equally useful to students of the Spanish of Europe and of Latin America.

Grammatical terms written with capital letters (e.g. Subjunctive, Indicative, Mood) are explained in the Glossary on p.320. The description of pronunciation given on pp. 214–221 is rather more detailed than is usual in this kind of book, since many of the pocket grammars, dictionaries and phrase-books on sale in the English-speaking world contain badly misleading accounts of the sounds of Spanish.

Incorrect forms —i.e. forms that learners must avoid — appear in bold italics and are marked with an asterisk, e.g. **'quizá viene mañana'* for the correct **quizá venga mañana** *perhaps he's coming tomorrow*.

The American-English spelling 'preterit' (British 'preterite') is used throughout the book. In other cases where American and British English spelling differs, both forms are shown, e.g. *flavor*/(British *flavour*).

Contents

Verbs

Spanish verbs have different forms that show *Tense*[1]
(Present, Future, various kinds of Past Tense,

---

[1] Grammatical terms beginning with a capital letter are defined
in the Glossary on p. 320.

Conditional, etc.), *Mood* (Indicative, Imperative or Subjunctive), *Person* (first, second or third) and *Number* (singular or plural). There are also three Non-Finite Forms of verbs: the *Gerund*, the *Past Participle* and the *Infinitive*. The latter, which always ends in **-r**, is the Dictionary Form of the verb.

FORMS OF VERBS

The various forms of Spanish Regular and Irregular verbs are shown on pp. 239–302.

■ Tense

Spanish tenses are of two basic kinds: Simple Tenses, consisting of a single word, and Compound Tenses, consisting of an appropriate form of the verb **haber** plus a Past Participle:

Simple Tenses	**bebo, beberé, bebí** *I drink, I'll drink, I drank*
Compound Tenses	**he bebido, había bebido** *I have drunk, I had drunk*

All the various tenses of verbs can also appear in the Continuous Form, made from the verb **estar** *to be* plus the Gerund, which always ends in **-ndo**:

estoy bebiendo *I'm (in the middle of) drinking*
estaba bebiendo *I was drinking*
he estado bebiendo *I have been drinking*

The Continuous form is discussed further on pp.13–16.

■ Mood

Verbs appear either in the Indicative Mood, used for making statements as explained on p.18, the Subjunctive Mood, explained on pp.20–35, or the Imperative Mood, which is used for making orders or requests and is explained on pp. 36–40.

■ Person and Number

Spanish verbs are unlike English verbs in that their endings show the Person and Number of their Subject:

hablo *I speak*	**hablamos** *we speak*
hablas *you speak*	**habláis** (Spain only) *you (plural) speak*
habla *he/she speaks, you* (singular) *speak*	**hablan** *they/you* (plural) *speak*

As a result, a verb on its own can form a Spanish sentence: **voy** means *I'm going*, **duermen** means *they're sleeping*. The Spanish words for *I, you, he/she/it, we, they* have special uses that are discussed later (p.107).

TYPES OF VERB

As far as the task of learning their various forms is concerned, there are three broad types of Spanish verb:

■ Regular Verbs

The vast majority of Spanish verbs are regular. If one knows the endings of the various tense forms and the spelling rules shown on p.249, one can predict every form of every regular verb.

Regular verbs are divided into three Conjugations according to whether their Infinitive ends in **-ar**, **-er** or **-ir**. Three commonly encountered regular verbs are **hablar** *to speak* (first conjugation), **beber** *to drink* (second conjugation), **vivir** *to live* (third conjugation). The various forms of these three verbs in all their tenses are shown on pp.239–249, and these forms should be learned first.

■ Radical Changing Verbs

The endings of Radical Changing Verbs are the same as for regular verbs, but their stem vowels change in certain forms, cf. **dormir** *to sleep*, **duermo** *I sleep*, **durmió** *he slept*, etc. These irregularities appear only in the Present Tenses (Indicative and Subjunctive), in the **tú** Imperative and, in the case of some **-ir** verbs, in the Preterit, the Imperfect Subjunctive and the Gerund. Radical changing verbs are quite numerous and many are in everyday use. The most important are listed on pp.253–302.

■ Irregular verbs

Some Spanish verbs are truly irregular: some of their forms are unpredictable and must be learned separately. These verbs are not very numerous, but they include the most common verbs in the language like 'to go', 'to come', 'to be', 'to have', 'to put', and they must therefore be memorized thoroughly. The irregularities are usually most obvious in the Present Indicative and the Preterit: with some exceptions one can usually predict most of the other forms from these two sets of forms.

Irregular verbs are listed on pp.253–302.

USES OF THE INDICATIVE TENSES

Present Indicative Tense

Present Indicative forms like **hablo**, **bebes**, **vivimos** mean *I speak*, *you drink*, *we live* and also *I'm speaking*, *you're drinking*, *we're living*. They are also often used for future actions and occasionally for past ones as well. This imprecision can sometimes be removed by using the Present Continuous forms of the verb to stress the idea that an action is actually in progress in the present: see p.13.

The main uses of the simple Present Indicative tense are:

■ To show that an action happens habitually or is timeless (i.e. is an eternal truth):

> **Me peino todos los días** *I do my hair every day* (habit)
> **Los españoles comen mucho ajo** *The Spanish eat a lot of garlic* (habit)
> **Trabajas demasiado** *You work too much* (habit)
> **El carbón de piedra produce calor** *Coal produces heat* (timeless)

■ To show that something is happening in the present:

> **Hoy hace mucho calor** *It's very hot today*
> **¿Qué haces hoy?** *What are you doing today?*
> **¡Cómo llueve!** *Look at the rain!* (literally *how it's raining*)
> **Nos hospedamos en el Hotel Palace** *We're staying at the Palace Hotel*

It is more appropriate to use the Present Continuous if we need to stress the fact that the action is in progress *at this very moment*:

> **Roberto está pintando la puerta** *Roberto is (in the middle of) painting the door*

■ To show that an event is imminent, i.e. is just about to happen:

> **¡Socorro! ¡Que me caigo!** *Help! I'm falling!*
> **¿Le pago ahora?** *Do I pay you now?/Shall I pay you now?*
> **¡Que se va el tren!** *The train's leaving!*
> **¿Vienes conmigo?** *Are you coming with me?*

■ To show that an event in the future is scheduled or pre-arranged. In this case it is often like the English present form ending in *-ing* in *next year **we're going** to Miami*:

> **La fiesta es mañana a las ocho** *The party's tomorrow at eight o'clock*

> **Te llamo esta noche a las nueve** *I'll call you tonight at nine*
> **En diciembre voy a París** *In December I'm going to Paris*
> **El avión sale mañana a las ocho** *The plane leaves tomorrow at eight*

■ As a past tense (the 'Historic Present'). The present is often used as an alternative to the Preterit tense to make narrative in the past sound exciting. This is found both in formal literary styles and in informal speech:

> **Unos días después empieza la Guerra Civil** *A few days later the Civil War began* (literally *begins*)
> **Entra y me dice . . .** *She/He comes in and says to me . . .* (familiar style)

■ The present tense is also used in sentences of the type '*I've spoken/been speaking French since I was a girl*', '*it's the first time we've seen her in years*'. See p.205.

The Preterit Tense

■ To look back on an event as completed in the past. It is therefore used to report the fact that event A happened and *finished*, *then* event B happened, *then* event C, and so on.

> **Se sentó, sacó un cigarrillo y lo encendió** *He sat down, took out a cigarette and lit it*
> **Anoche vi dos veces a tu madre** *I saw your mother twice last night*
> **Fue intérprete y después profesor** *He was an interpreter and then a teacher*
> **El viernes estuve en casa de la abuela** *on Friday I visited grandmother's house*

■ For events that lasted for a specific period of time and then ended:

Fue presidente durante ocho años *He was President for eight years*

Su enfermedad duró varios meses *Her/his illness lasted several months*

Estuve esperando varias horas or **Esperé varias horas** *I waited several hours* (the Continuous stresses the action as long drawn-out)

English speakers often have difficulty in distinguishing between the Preterit and the Imperfect (see next section), especially in sentences of the following kind:

Tuve que decírselo *I had to tell it to him* (and I did)

Tenía que decírselo *I had to tell it to him* (I may or may not have done)

Fue un día magnífico *It was a magnificent day* (all day)

Era un día magnífico *It was a lovely day* (at the time, but perhaps it rained later during the day)

The last example shows how the Preterit of **ser**—**fue**—indicates a different point of view compared with the Imperfect **era**. The Preterit looks back on the event after it finished, whereas the Imperfect describes an event while it was still going on. This is clear in English with most verbs other than *to be*. Compare *what **did you do** in the garden yesterday?* (looks back on the event as finished, therefore Preterit: **¿qué hiciste ayer en el jardín?**) and *what **were you doing** in the garden yesterday?* (the action is described as not yet finished at the time, therefore Imperfect: **¿qué hacías ayer en el jardín?**).

The Imperfect Tense

■ To show that an event was not yet completed. The Imperfect is therefore used for events that *were continuing* when something else happened:

> **Ignacio estaba en la habitación cuando se hundió el techo** *Ignacio was in the room when the roof caved in*
>
> **Llovía muy fuerte, así que cerré la ventana** *It was raining very hard, so I shut the window*
>
> **Esta puerta era azul** *This door was blue* (i.e. at the time)
>
> **Ana tenía diecinueve años cuando se casó** *Ana was nineteen when she got married*
>
> **Cuando yo era pequeño yo adoraba a mi madre** *When I was little I adored my mother*

As these examples show, the Imperfect gives us no clear information about whether the event continued or when it ended: Ignacio probably left the room after the roof collapsed, but the point is that he was still there when it happened. As a general rule, if an English verb can be rewritten using *was* and the *-ing* form, Spanish will use the Imperfect: **Ana llevaba una falda azul cuando la vi** *Ana was wearing a blue skirt when I saw her*. But, as the examples above show, this rule does not usually apply to the verb *to be*.

■ To express habitual or timeless events in the past, i.e. events that had no clearly defined end even though they may no longer be happening now:

> **De niño yo tenía ojos azules** *I had/used to have blue eyes as a child*
>
> **Mi madre era vegetariana** *My mother was/used to be a vegetarian*
>
> **Yo iba todos los días a casa de mi amigo** *I went/used to go to my friend's house every day*
>
> **Londres era más grande que Nueva York** *London was/used to be bigger than New York*

As a general rule, if the meaning of the English verb can be expressed by the formula *used to . . .* Spanish will use the Imperfect Tense.

■ To denote something that was just going to happen (usually the same as **iba a . . .** *was going to*):

> **Yo me marchaba cuando sonó el teléfono** *I was leaving when the phone rang*

The Perfect Tense

Spanish distinguishes between the Perfect Tense and the Preterit, much the same as English does between the Perfect *I have seen* and the Simple Past *I saw*. The Perfect Tense is common in written styles everywhere and it is constantly heard in speech in Spain, but in some Latin-American varieties of spoken Spanish the Preterit may more or less completely replace the Perfect, although practice varies from country to country. The Perfect Tense is used:

■ For past events that have happened in a period of time that has not yet ended. Compare **fui dos veces el año pasado** *I went twice **last** year* and **he ido dos veces este año** *I **have been** twice **this** year* (this year hasn't ended yet):

> **La bolsa ha subido mucho hoy** *The stock market has gone up a lot today*
> **Ha llovido menos durante este siglo** *It has rained less this century*
> **No han contestado todavía** *They haven't replied yet*
> **Hemos estado trabajando toda la mañana** *We've been working all morning*

Latin Americans often use the Preterit in this context:

la bolsa subió mucho hoy, no contestaron todavía, estuvimos trabajando . . . , etc.

■ To show that the effects of a past event linger in or are relevant to the present. Compare **estuvo enfermo** *he was unwell* (in the past, but now he's recovered) and **ha estado enfermo** *he's been unwell* (that's why he's pale, late for work, irritable, etc.):

> **Alguien ha fumado/ha estado fumando en esta habitación. Huele a humo** *Someone has smoked/been smoking in this room. It smells of smoke*
> **Está contento porque lo/le² han ascendido** *He's pleased because they've promoted him*

Latin Americans may also prefer the Preterit tense in these cases.

■ In Spain, optionally, to show that an event happened today (i.e. since midnight). This is the 'Perfect of Recency':

> **Me he levantado temprano** *I got up early* (*today*)
> **Quién ha llamado?** *Who phoned (just now)?*
> **Perdona, no he podido hacerlo** *Sorry, I couldn't do it (today)*
> **Hemos ido al parque esta mañana** *We went to the park this morning*

If the event is very recent, the Perfect is usual in Spain, but for events earlier in the day the Preterit or the Perfect may be used. Latin Americans use the Preterit: **me levanté temprano**, **¿Quién llamó?**, etc.

---

² **Lo/le** shows that either pronoun can be used here for *him*, **lo** being more common in Latin America, and **le** preferred in Spain (although **lo** is also widely used).

The Pluperfect Tense

In general, the same as the English Pluperfect form (*had* + Past Participle), i.e. to show that an event in the past had finished before the next one started:

> **Ya habían dejado dos mensajes en el contestador cuando yo llegué** *They had already left two messages on the answering machine when I arrived*
>
> **La policía encontró el revólver que el asesino había comprado dos días antes** *The police found the revolver that the murderer had bought two days before*

The Future Tense

As was mentioned earlier, future time can be expressed by the simple Present Tense when the event is felt to be pre-scheduled or pre-arranged: **la película empieza a las ocho** *The film starts at eight*. Furthermore, the Future Tense forms shown here are often replaced by **ir a** + the Infinitive in informal styles, especially in Latin-American speech, e.g. **si me habla de esa manera, me enojaré** *if he talks like that to me I'll get angry* becomes **si me habla de esa manera, me voy a enojar/voy a enojarme**[3].

The Future Tense is used:

- For future events that are not pre-scheduled or fixtures:

> **Algún día se casará con ella** *He'll marry her one day*
>
> **Ya te cansarás** *You'll get tired eventually/in the end*

---

[3] In Spain **enfadarse** is the normal word for *to get angry*.

> **Para entonces yo ya no estaré aquí** *By then I won't be here any more*

■ For approximations, guesses and suppositions:

> **Miguel tendrá unos cincuenta años** *(I guess) Miguel's about fifty*
> **Estará durmiendo a estas horas** *(I guess) he'll be sleeping at this time*

Latin Americans tend to prefer the construction **deber** or **deber de** + Infinitive (which is also used in Spain): **debe (de) tener unos cincuenta años, debe (de) estar durmiendo . . .** The **de** is often dropped, but learners should retain it so as to distinguish between suppositions and obligations. Compare **debes hacerlo** *you've got to do it* (obligation).

■ In questions, to express wonder or amazement:

> **¿Qué habrá sido de él?** *What (on earth) can have happened to him?*
> **¿Quién será éste?** *I wonder who this is?*

The Conditional Tense

■ As an equivalent of the English *would* form in conditions:

> **En ese caso te dejarían en paz** *In that case they would leave you in peace*
> **El pastel estaría mejor con menos azúcar** *The cake would be better with less sugar*
> **Eso sí costaría más!** *That **would** cost more!*

■ With **poder, querer,** to make polite requests or express polite wishes:

> **¿Podría usted abrir la ventana un poquito?** *Could you open the window a bit?*

> **Querría terminarlo antes de las ocho** *I'd like to finish it before eight*

- To express the future in the past (i.e. the same as **iba a** + Infinitive):

> **Aquel día empezó la que sería su última película** *That day he began what would be his last film*
>
> **Yo sabía que no me devolvería el dinero** *I knew he wouldn't/wasn't going to give the money back to me*

- To express guesses or suppositions about the past:

> **Aquella semana la habríamos visto más de cinco veces** *That week we must have seen her more than five times*
>
> **Pesaría unos cien kilos** *It must have weighed about 100 kilos*

Deber or (preferably) **deber de** + Infinitive is more usual in this construction: **debía de pesar más de cien kilos**.

Note: the -**ra** form of the Imperfect Subjunctive is constantly found as an alternative for the Conditional of **haber** and **querer**:

> **Te hubiera/habría ayudado antes** *I would have helped you sooner*
>
> **Quisiera/querría verte mañana** *I'd like to see you tomorrow*

Continuous Forms of the Tenses

Spanish Continuous forms of the tenses (all formed with **estar** + the Gerund) either (a) stress that an event is, was or will be actually in progress at the time spoken of, or (b) in the case of the Preterit and Perfect Tenses, show that it continued for a certain amount of time in the past before ending.

As far as the Present, Imperfect and Future Continuous Tenses are concerned, English-speakers must remember to use the Continuous only for events actually *in progress*. The following is definitely *not* good Spanish: *'*mañana estoy viajando a Los Ángeles*' tomorrow I'm (in the middle of) traveling (British travelling) to Los Angeles,* correctly **mañana viajo a Los Ángeles.**

The Continuous is used:

■ In all tenses except the Preterit, Perfect and Pluperfect, to stress that an event is, was or will be actually in progress. Usually the non-Continuous tenses can also be used, but the Continuous is preferred nowadays when the event is actually in progress at the time:

> **Esto se está convirtiendo en una pesadilla** *This is turning into a nightmare*
> **Yo estaba durmiendo cuando sonó el despertador** *I was sleeping when the alarm clock went off*
> **Miguel está leyendo** *Miguel's reading*
> **Lo que pasó fue que ella estaba deseando irse** *What happened was that she wanted/was wanting to leave*
> **No puedes ir a las cinco porque estarás haciendo tus deberes** *You can't go at five o'clock because you'll be doing you're homework*

■ To show that an event is surprising or temporary:

> **¡¿Pero qué tonterías le has estado contando?!** *But what nonsense have you been telling him?!*
> **Es una zapatería, pero últimamente están vendiendo periódicos** *It's a shoe-shop, but lately they're selling newspapers*

María estaba trabajando de intérprete *Maria was working as an interpreter* (at the time, temporarily)

■ To emphasize the idea of repetitive actions that are or were still continuing:

Está bebiendo mucho últimamente *He's drinking a lot lately*

Siempre estaba pensando en ella *He was always thinking of her*

■ In the Preterit, Perfect or Pluperfect Tenses, to show that an event (a) lasted a certain length of time and (b) that it finished:

Anoche estuvimos viendo la televisión *We watched TV last night*

Te he estado esperando toda la mañana *I've been waiting for you all morning*

Había estado leyendo durante horas *He had been reading for hours*

Here the non-Continuous forms **vimos, he esperado, había leído** would not emphasize the long drawn-out nature of the events.

The Spanish Continuous *cannot* be used (at least in standard forms of the language):

■ For events that are not actually in progress:

Yo creo que este libro defiende una postura revolucionaria *I think that this book is defending/defends a revolutionary position* (not **está defendiendo**, which means *is in the middle of defending*)

Yo iba a verme con ella al día siguiente *I was seeing her the following day* (it hadn't happened yet)

Vamos mañana *We're going tomorrow* (it hasn't happened yet)

> **Su padre[4] está enfermo de muerte** *His father is dying* (i.e. he is fatally ill. **Está muriendo** would mean that he is actually dying at this moment)
>
> **Está sentado** *He's sitting down* (**está sentándose** has the unlikely meaning *he's in the middle of sitting down*)

■ Normally, for events that are not really actions but conditions or states:

> **Llevaba una pajarita de seda** *He was wearing a silk bow-tie*
>
> **Parecías más joven aquella noche** *You were looking younger that night*
>
> **Un aroma delicado flotaba en el aire** *A delicate smell was floating in the air*

■ Never with the verb **estar**. One cannot say *'estar estando'*, although **estar siendo** occasionally occurs:

> **Está siendo debatido en este momento** *It's being debated at this moment*

■ In standard varieties of Spanish, the Continuous is not used with the verbs **ir** *to go* and **venir** *to come*:

> **¿Adónde van ustedes?** *Where are you going?*
>
> **Ya vienen** *They're coming*

Less Common Tense Forms

The following forms are occasionally found, all of them (except for **tengo hecho**, etc.) being more common in writing than in speech:

■ **Tener** 'to have' is sometimes used to form compound tenses instead of **haber**. This is only possible if the verb

---

[4] Latin Americans tend to use **papá** for *father* and **mamá** for *mother*, but these words mean *daddy* and *mummy* in Spain.

has a direct object, and the difference between **lo he ter-minado** and **lo tengo terminado** is about the same as between *I've finished it* and *I've **got it** finished*: the latter emphasizes successful completion or acquisition of some-thing—

> **Ya tengo pintadas tres de las paredes** *I've got three of the walls painted*
>
> **Ya tenemos compradas las flores** *We've got the flowers bought/We've bought the flowers*

As the examples show, the past participle agrees in number and gender with the direct object of the verb.

■ The **-ra** form, used for the Imperfect Subjunctive in normal styles, is often found in flowery writing, but not in spoken Spanish, as an alternative for the Pluperfect in Relative Clauses. This is especially common in Latin America but is gaining ground in Spain:

> **Se casó con la que *fuera* la esposa de su padre** *He married the woman who had been his father's wife* (everyday style . . . **había sido la esposa . . .**)

■ **-ra** forms (and sometimes also **-se** forms) of verbs fre-quently appear after **después de que** *after* and **desde que** *since* instead of the Preterit tense:

> **Este es el primer discurso que pronuncia desde que lo/le nombraran presidente** *This is the first speech he has delivered since he was appointed President*

This use of the **-ra** forms rather than the Preterit after **desde que** and **después de que** is the preferred construc-tion in Spain, but the Preterit is possible, as this example from the Colombian novelist Gabriel García Márquez shows:

> **. . . su simple evocación le causaba un estre-mecimiento de pavor hasta mucho después**

de que se casó, y tuvo hijos . . . *the mere mention of him caused her a shudder of fear until long after she had married and had children*

However, the Subjunctive is obligatory after **después de que** and **desde que** when they point to events that are or were still in the future. See pp.29–30.

■ The Preterit of **haber** + the Past Participle is occasionally used to form the Anterior Preterit tense (**Pretérito anterior**). This is found only in literary styles before words meaning *as soon as* or *when*, to emphasize that an event *had just* finished before the next started. It can be replaced by the Pluperfect or, much more commonly, by the Preterit:

Apenas hubo terminado la cena, todos los invitados se fueron *Scarcely had supper finished when all the guests departed* (more usually **apenas terminó** . . .)

MOOD

The Indicative Mood

The uses of the various tenses of the Indicative Mood have already been discussed. The Indicative Mood is overwhelmingly the most commonly used verbal mood: in most types of Spanish well over 85% of the verbs are in the Indicative mood.

The Indicative is used:

■ In all Main Clauses (see Glossary) other than those that give orders (which require the Imperative mood):

En invierno no hacía mucho frío *It wasn't very cold in Winter*

No me gusta el sabor de la cerveza *I don't like
the taste of beer*

Me voy a comprar unos zapatos *I'm going to buy
some shoes*

■ In Subordinate Clauses after statements meaning *it is
true/correct/a fact/certain* **that** . . .

**Es verdad/cierto/correcto/un hecho que los
limones son agrios** *It's true/certain/correct/a
fact that lemons are sour*

But the Subjunctive is normally used when such statements are negated or denied: **no es cierto que los
limones *sean* dulces** *It isn't true that lemons are sweet.*

■ After statements that express beliefs or opinions:

Creo que llegan el martes *I think that they're
coming on Tuesday*

Parece que no pudo solucionarlo *It seems he
didn't manage to solve it*

Again, the Subjunctive is normally used when such statements are denied: **no creo que *lleguen* el martes** *I don't
think they're coming on Tuesday*

■ When the clause is introduced by a Subordinator (see
Glossary) that refers to a time when the action has or had
happened: compare **yo estaba viendo la televisión
cuando llegaron**[5] *I was watching TV when they arrived.*
This is discussed below on pp.29 ff.

■ In Relative Clauses, when the antecedent (the thing
referred to by the Relative Pronoun) is known to exist (see
p.34):

Conozco una cafetería donde sirven té inglés *I
know a café where they serve English tea*

[5] In Spain one usually says **ver la televisión** *to 'see' TV*,
although **mirar** *'to watch'* is heard in Latin America

■ After **si** *if* in 'open' conditions: **si llueve me quedo en casa** *if it rains I'm staying at home.* Conditional Sentences are explained on p.40.

The Subjunctive Mood

The basic function of the Subjunctive is not to make statements of fact, but either (a) to show that the speaker is reacting emotionally in some way to the event referred to or (b) that the event mentioned in a Subordinate Clause is still not a reality (e.g. because it hasn't happened yet). Most learners of Spanish postpone the Subjunctive until the last moment, but there are good reasons for tackling it early, since it is common in all styles of language.

The Subjunctive can be explained under five headings:

(a) Cases in which it appears in Subordinate Clauses (see Glossary) introduced by **que**, following some statement indicating want, necessity, possibility, emotional reaction, fear, doubt, etc.

(b) Cases in which it appears after a number of words which are mostly Subordinators (see Glossary), for example **cuando** *when*, **apenas** *scarcely*, **quizá** *perhaps*, **posiblemente** *possibly*, **antes de que** *before*, **después de que** *after*, **con tal de que** *provided that*, etc . . .

(c) Cases in which it appears in Relative Clauses, e.g. **quiero comprar una casa que *tenga* muchas ventanas** *I want to buy a house that has a lot of windows*.

(d) Cases in which the Subjunctive can appear in the Main Clause of a sentence, i.e. cases in which the Subjunctive could stand as the first word in a sentence (rare—the Imperative excepted).

(e) Cases in which it appears in the if-clause of Conditional Sentences, e.g. **si *tuviera* más tiempo lo**

haría mejor *if I had more time I'd do it better.* This is discussed on p.40.

Forms of the subjunctive

The Subjunctive has three simple tense forms (the fourth tense form, the Future Subjunctive, is virtually obsolete. See below).

Present:

> **(que) yo hable** *that I should speak . . .*
> **(que) él diga** *that he should say . . .*

-**ra** Past:

> **(que) yo fuera** *that I should have been . . .*
> **(que) usted pensara** *that you should have thought . . .*

-**se** Past:

> **(que) yo fuese** *that I should have been . . .*
> **(que) usted pensase** *that you should have thought . . .*

The Subjunctive can also appear in compound tenses:

Perfect:

> **(que) yo haya hablado** *that I should have spoken . . .*
> **(que) él haya dicho** *that he should have said . . .*

Pluperfect:

> **(que) yo hubiera/hubiese hablado** *that I should have spoken* (before then)
> **(que) él hubiera/hubiese dicho** *that he should have said* (before then)

Continuous forms are also possible, e.g. **(que) yo esté hablando** *that I should be (in the middle of) speaking,* etc.

These are formed from the appropriate tense of the Subjunctive of **estar** + the Gerund.

The English translations shown above are very approximate and misleading. The Spanish Subjunctive cannot usually be translated clearly into English since the latter language has lost most of its Subjunctive forms.

■ The Future Subjunctive

This is virtually obsolete. It is formed by replacing the last **a** in the **-ra** Imperfect Subjunctive by **e**: **hablare hablares hablare habláremos hablareis hablaren, comiere, comieres, comiere, comiéremos, comiereis, comieren**, etc.

It is nowadays rarely seen outside legal documents and similar very formal texts. In all other cases it is replaced by the Present or Imperfect Subjunctive, so foreign learners will not need to use it.

■ Equivalence of the **-ra** and **-se** Subjunctives

When they are used as Subjunctives, the **-ra** forms and the **-se** forms are interchangeable, the **-ra** forms being nowadays much more frequent than the **-se** forms:

> **Yo quería que me *llamaras* = Yo quería que me *llamases* I wanted you to call me**

In this book, unless otherwise stated, whenever the **-ra** form appears the **-se** form could have been used, and vice-versa.

Tense Agreement with the Subjunctive

The basic rules, which apply to ninety per cent of Spanish sentences, are:

Tense of verb in Main Clause	*Tense of Subjunctive in Subordinate Clause*
Present	Present
Future	" "
Perfect	Present (sometimes Imperfect)
Conditional	Imperfect (**-ra** or **-se**)
Imperfect	" "
Preterit	" "
Pluperfect	" "

> **Es/será/ha sido necesario que vengas** *It is/will be/has been necessary for you to come*
> **Sería/era/fue/había sido necesario que vinieras/vinieses** *It would be/was/had been necessary for you to come*

Replacement of a finite verb by an infinitive

When the subject of the Main Clause in a sentence and the subject of the Subordinate Clause refer to the same person or thing, the Infinitive is often used and not the Finite verb form: **quiero hacerlo** *I want to do it* (**yo** is the subject of both **querer** and **hacer**), but **quiero que él lo haga** *I want him to do it*.

In this respect English differs sharply from Spanish in allowing the Infinitive to refer to a new subject: *I prefer him to go*. The fact that Spanish does not allow this (with the few exceptions mentioned below) is the chief reason why it constantly uses the Subjunctive: **yo prefiero que él vaya**.

The use of the Infinitive is also found after certain Subordinators (note the appearance of **que** when the Infinitive is not used):

¿Te voy a ver antes de irme? *Will I see you before I go?*

¿Te voy a ver antes de que te vayas? *Will I see you before **you** go?*

Lo hizo sin darse cuenta *He did it without realizing*

Lo hizo sin que yo me diera cuenta *He did it without **my** realizing*

Other Subordinators that allow this are:

con tal de (que) *provided that*
después de (que) *after*
en caso de (que) *in the event of*
hasta (que) *until*
para (que)/a (que) *in order to*
a pesar de (que) *in spite of*

But most Subordinators require a Finite verb form (Subjunctive or Indicative) whether the subjects are the same or not:

Lo haré cuando termine esto *I'll do it when I finish (or he/she/you finish(es)) this* (never ***'lo haré cuando terminar esto'**)

Nos vamos en cuanto/apenas terminemos esto *We're going as soon as we finish this*

No digo nada, aunque sé la verdad *I'm saying nothing although I know the truth*

Lo hace bien porque sabe mucho *He does it well because he knows a lot*

The rules that determine whether the Finite verb is in the Indicative or Subjunctive are discussed below.

Subjunctive in clauses introduced by *que*

The Subjunctive is required in Subordinate Clauses after the word **que** when this word is introduced by a statement meaning:

■ Wanting, wishing, requesting

> **Quiero que me contestes** *I want you to answer*
>
> **Estaba deseando que se fueran** *He was wanting them to go*
>
> **Mi sueño de que mi hijo fuera médico** *My dream that my son would be a doctor*
>
> **Pidió que lo/le dejaran en paz** *He asked them to leave him in peace*
>
> **Prefiero que ustedes me lo entreguen a domicilio** *I prefer you to deliver it to me at home*

■ Ordering, obliging, causing, recommending, insisting

> **Le dijeron que se quedara** *They told him to stay*
>
> **Les ordenó que cargasen sus fusiles** *He ordered them to load their rifles*
>
> **El médico le recomendó que dejara de fumar** *The doctor recommended him to stop smoking*
>
> **Hizo que se quedaran en casa** *He made them stay at home*
>
> **Insistió en que se hiciera así** *He insisted that it should be done like this*

The verbs **ordenar, mandar, hacer, recomendar, aconsejar** *to advise*, **obligar** *to oblige* can optionally take the Infinitive: **les ordenó/mandó apagar las luces** or **ordenó/mandó que apagaran las luces** *he ordered them to put out the lights*; **los hizo quedarse en casa** *he made them stay at home*; **te recomiendo no hacerlo** *I recommend you not to do it*.

Decir que with the indicative mood means *to tell* (i.e. *inform*) *someone that*: **le dijeron que se quedaba** *they told him he that he was staying*.

■ Allowing and forbidding

> **No permito que mi hija viaje sola** *I don't allow my daughter to travel alone*

> **Les prohíbe que fumen en casa** *He forbids them to smoke at home*

And similarly **dejar** *to let*, **tolerar/aguantar** *to tolerate*, **oponerse a que** *to oppose*. However, **permitir, prohibir** and **dejar** also allow the infinitive construction: **no le permito/dejo a mi hija viajar sola, les prohíbe fumar en casa**

■ Needing

> **Es necesario/preciso que nos pongamos en contacto con ellos** *It's necessary that we contact them*
> **Hace falta que trabajen más** *They need to work more*

■ Possibility and impossibility

> **Es posible/probable/previsible que no lo terminen a tiempo** *It's possible/probable/likely that they won't finish it on time*
> **No puede ser que tenga tanto dinero** *It can't be (possible) that he's got so much money*

Use of the subjunctive with words meaning *perhaps* is discussed later in this section.

■ Emotional reactions, e.g. surprise, pleasure, displeasure, puzzlement

> **Me irrita que tengas esa actitud** *It irritates me that you have that attitude*
> **Fue increíble que no se diesen cuenta** *It was incredible that they didn't realize*
> **Estoy hasta la coronilla de que siempre tengamos tanto trabajo** *I'm sick to death of the fact that we have so much work*
> **Siento mucho que no puedan venir** *I'm sorry you/they can't come*

Nos extrañaba que no hubiese escrito *It puzzled us that he hadn't written*

■ The verb **quejarse de que** *to complain that* usually takes the Indicative: **siempre se queja de que tiene frío** *he's always complaining that he feels cold.*

■ Value judgments, i.e. any phrase meaning *it's good/bad that . . .* , *it's natural/logical/preferable/undesirable/satisfying that . . .* , etc.:

Conviene que llueva de vez en cuando *It's good that it rains from time to time*

Era absurdo que lo dejasen sin pintar *It was absurd for them to leave it unpainted*

Es natural que usted se sienta cansado *It's natural that you should feel tired*

Es importante que sepamos la verdad *It's important for us to know the truth*

The expression **menos mal que . . .** *it's a good thing that . . .* takes the Indicative: **menos mal que lo hiciste ayer** *it's a good thing you did it yesterday.*

■ Denial of truth, opinion, appearance or knowledge

No es verdad que la haya llamado *It isn't true that he called her*

No parece que esté dispuesta a hacerlo *It doesn't seem that she's prepared to do it*

No creo que sea posible *I don't think it's possible*

No sabía que fueras tan inteligente *I didn't know you were so intelligent*

No es que sea incorrecto, sino que es increíble *It isn't that it's incorrect but that it's incredible*

But these verbs take the indicative when they are positive: **es verdad que la ha llamado** *It's true that he called her*, etc. The indicative is also possible with **no saber que** when the thing referred to is not an opinion but a fact: **no**

sabía que ya había pagado *I didn't know that he'd already paid.*

■ Doubt

> **Dudo que sepas hacerlo** *I doubt you know how to do it*

■ Fear

> **Temo que la paz no sea posible** *I fear peace isn't possible*
>
> **Tengo miedo de que me muerda ese perro** *I'm scared that dog's going to bite me*

The indicative is usual after **temerse** when it expresses a regret: **me temo que he cometido un error** *I fear I've made a mistake.*

■ Hoping, depending on, sympathizing with, avoiding, explaining the cause of something:

> **Espero que ustedes estén bien** *I hope you're well*
>
> **Dependo de que me dé dinero periódicamente** *I depend on him giving me money regularly*
>
> **Esto sólo hacía que él se riera más** *This only made him laugh more*
>
> **Comprendo que no quieras hablar de ello** *I understand you not wanting to talk about it*
>
> **Intentaba evitar que su suegra se enterase** *He was trying to avoid his mother-in-law finding out*
>
> **Esto explicaba el que prefiriera quedarse en casa** *This explained the fact that he preferred to stay at home*

■ *The fact that . . .*

Use of the Subjunctive is common after **el hecho de que** . . . *the fact that*, and also after **el que** . . . or **que** . . . when they mean the same as **el hecho de que**. The question of when the Subjunctive is used after these words is complex, but the general rule is that the Subjunctive is usual except when **el hecho de que** is preceded by a preposition:

> **El hecho de que los gramáticos no siempre estén de acuerdo deja perplejos a muchos estudiantes** *The fact that the grammarians aren't always in agreement leaves many students perplexed*
> **El que lo hayamos visto tres veces no puede ser una coincidencia** *The fact that we've seen him/it three times can't be a coincidence*
> **Que fuera él quien lo hizo no debería sorprender a nadie** *The fact that he was the one who did it should surprise no one*

but

> **No quiso contestar por el hecho de que no se fiaba de la policía** *He refused to answer due to the fact that he didn't trust the police*

Use of the subjunctive after subordinators

The Subjunctive is required in certain cases after clauses introduced by Subordinators, e.g. words that introduce clauses and mean *when, as soon as, in order to, after, without, as long as,* etc. Most, but not all, of these are phrases that include the word **que**.

The Subjunctive is used after these words whenever the action that follows them has not or had not yet happened at the time referred to in the Main Clause. Compare **me acosté cuando llegó mamá** *I went to bed when* (i.e. *after*) *mother arrived* and **me acostaré cuando llegue mamá** *I'll go to bed when mother arrives* (she hasn't arrived yet).

With some subordinators the Subjunctive is always necessary: these include **antes de que** *before*, **sin que** *without*, **para que** and **a que** *in order to*, **con tal de que** and **a**

condición de que *provided that*. In a few cases the Indicative is always used, but with most subordinators either the Indicative or the Subjunctive is used, according to whether the event has or has not happened at the time:

> **Te llamaré en cuanto/apenas llegue** *I'll call you as soon as I arrive/he arrives*
>
> **Te llamé en cuanto/apenas llegó** *I called you as soon as he arrived*
>
> **Bebíamos champán siempre que nos traía una botella** *We drank champagne whenever he brought us a bottle*
>
> **Beberemos champán siempre que nos traigas una botella** *We'll drink champagne whenever/provided you bring us a bottle*
>
> **Lo compré después de que lo repararon[6]** *I bought it after they fixed it*
>
> **Lo compraré después de que lo reparen/hayan reparado** *I'll buy it after they've fixed it*

The following list includes the most common subordinators. Those marked 'variable' obey the rule just explained, while the others either always or never take the Subjunctive:

> **cuando** *when* (variable)
> **antes de que** *before* (always)
> **después de que** *after* (variable, but see p.17)
> **desde que** *since, from the moment that* (variable, but see p.17)
> **a partir del momento en que** *from the time that* (variable)

---

[6] However, as explained on page 17, the -ra form is common in Spain after **después de que** and **desde que** *since*, to refer to any event in the past: **después de que lo repararan**, **desde que la viera** *since he had seen her*.

según *as* (as in *he answered the letters as they arrived* **contestaba a las cartas según iban llegando**) (variable)

a medida que *as* (as **según**, but implies *without delay*; variable)

tan pronto como, nada más, en cuanto, nomás (the latter in Lat. Am. only), **apenas** all meaning *as soon as*, *scarcely* (variable)

a que, para que, a fin de que, con el objeto de que *in order to* (always)

no sea que, no fuera que *lest*, *in order that . . . not* (always)

de ahí que *hence the fact that* (always)

sin que *without* (always)

de manera que, de modo que, de forma que *in such a way that*, *so* (indicating manner or result) (variable)

en caso de que *in the event of . . .* (always)
por si *in case* (usually indicative)
suponiendo que *supposing that* (always)

hasta que *until* (variable)
siempre que *whenever*, *every time that* (variable)
mientras (que) when it means *provided that*, *as long as*, always takes the Subjunctive. When it means *while* and refers to some future event it optionally takes the Subjunctive **tú puedes descansar mientras que yo trabajo/trabaje** *you can rest while I work*; otherwise it takes the Indicative

con tal de que, siempre que, a condición de que *provided that* (always)

salvo que, excepto que, a menos que *unless* (nearly always take Subjunctive)

aunque *although* takes the Subjunctive when it refers to an uncertainty: **dile que venga aunque esté enfermo** *tell him to come even if he is sick.* It takes the indicative when it refers to past events: **fuimos al parque, aunque llovía a cántaros** *we went to the park although it was pouring with rain*

a pesar de que, **pese a que** *despite the fact that* (variable)

puesto que, **ya que**, **en vista de que**, **debido a que** *seeing that*, *in view of the fact that*, *due to the fact that* (never)

pues *because* (literary styles only; see p.189), *well . . . , in that case* (never)

como (see p. 187)

como si *as if* (always)

porque *because.* Only takes Subjunctive after the phrase **no porque** . . . *not because* . . . and also when it means an emphatic *simply because* or *just because*: **no voy a quedarme en casa sólo porque tú me lo digas** *I'm not staying at home simply because you tell me to* (you may not have said it yet, but even if you do . . .). **Porque** plus the subjunctive occasionally means *in order that* after a few verbs, especially those meaning *to make an effort*: **se esforzaba para que/porque todo el mundo lo aceptara** *he was making an effort to get everyone to accept it/him*

Subjunctive after words meaning 'perhaps'

■ After **a lo mejor,** which is colloquial (like *maybe* in British English), the appropriate tense of an Indicative verb form is used:

A lo mejor pensaba que no estabas en casa
Maybe he thought you weren't at home
A lo mejor es ella *Maybe it's her*

■ After **quizá**[7], **tal vez** (Lat. Am. **talvez**), **acaso** (literary style) and **posiblemente** *possibly,* the Subjunctive is always correct. However, modern Spanish increasingly prefers the Indicative in certain circumstances, and the following remarks reflect current tendencies:

The Present Subjunctive must be used if the event refers to the future:

> **Quizá/tal vez/acaso llegue mañana** *Perhaps it'll arrive tomorrow* (not *'**quizá llega mañana**')
> **Quizá/tal vez/posiblemente sea mejor** . . .
> *Perhaps/possibly it would be better* . . .

Either the Present Subjunctive or Present Indicative can be used if the verb refers to the present, the Subjunctive being more formal or rather more hesitant or hypothetical:

> **Quizá/tal vez sea/es verdad que** . . . *Perhaps it's true that*

An Indicative past tense or the Imperfect Subjunctive may be used if the event is in the past, the Subjunctive being slightly more hesitant:

> **Quizá pensaba/pensara/haya pensado que
> nadie se enteraría** *Perhaps he thought no one would find out*

The Imperfect Subjunctive or the Imperfect of **ir a** . . . is used for a future in the past:

> **Quizá/posiblemente me lo diera/iba a dar
> cuando llegase al día siguiente** *Perhaps/*

---

[7] The form **quizás** is generally avoided in writing.

> *possibly he would give it to me when he arrived the next day* (not **'Quizá me lo daba'*)

■ The word **igual** is nowadays constantly heard in Spain with the meaning *maybe* or *probably*, but it is not used in writing or formal speech. It always takes the Indicative mood.

The subjunctive in relative clauses

The Subjunctive must be used in relative clauses when the thing referred to by the relative pronoun does not exist or is not yet known to exist. Compare **quiero vivir en un país donde nunca *haga* frío** *I want to live in a country where it's never cold* (we don't know yet which country) and **los guatemaltecos viven en un país donde nunca *hace* frío** *the Guatemalans live in a country where it's never cold*. Further examples:

> **Nunca hubo guerra que no fuera un desastre**
> *There was never a war that wasn't a disaster*
> **Tienes que hablar con alguien que te comprenda** *You have to talk to someone who understands you*
> **Dame algo que no tenga alcohol** *Give me something/anything that doesn't have alcohol in it*

This construction requires practice since English does not make the distinction clear. Compare **va a casarse con una mujer que *tiene* mucho dinero** *he's going to marry a woman who has a lot of money* (Indicative, because he has found her) and **quiere casarse con una mujer que *tenga* mucho dinero** *he wants to marry a woman who has a lot of money* (Subjunctive: he's still looking for her).

There are a number of words and phrases that correspond to English words ending in *-ever*, e.g. *whatever, whenever, however, whoever, wherever*. These take the Subjunctive and can be conveniently included under discussion of the Subjunctive in relative clauses:

> **sea lo que seá** *whatever it is*
> **Tome lo que usted quiera** *Take whatever you like*
> **Pueden comer cuando quieran** *You can eat whenever you like*
> **Hazlo como quieras** *Do it however you like*
> **sea quien sea/quienquiera que sea** *whoever it is*
> **sea cual sea** *whichever it is*
> **esté donde esté/dondequiera que esté** *wherever he is*

The Subjunctive is also found in relative clauses—at least in formal styles—after a superlative when the idea of *ever* is stressed:

> **la temperatura más alta que se haya registrado en treinta años** *the highest temperature that has **ever** been recorded in thirty years*

but

> **Éstos son los mejores zapatos que tengo** *These are the best shoes I've got*

The subjunctive in main clauses

The Subjunctive can also appear in Main Clauses, i.e. it is possible for a Subjunctive verb to be the only verb in the sentence. This occurs:

■ In all forms of the **usted/ustedes** imperative: **dígame** *tell me*, **dénmelo** *give it to me*, **no me diga** *don't tell me*.

■ In the *negative* form of the **tú** and **vosotros** imperatives: **no me digas (tú)**, **no me digáis (vosotros)** *don't tell me*.

■ In third and first-person imperatives: **que pasen** *let them come in*, **pensemos** *let's think*.

■ After **ojalá** *let's hope that* . . . and after **quién** when it means *if only*: **¡Ojalá no llueva!** *Let's hope it doesn't rain!*, **¡Quién tuviera tanto dinero como tú!** *If only I had as much money as you!*

The imperative

The Imperative mood is used for orders and requests.

There are four second-person forms of the Imperative corresponding to the four pronouns meaning *you*: **tú**, **usted**, **vosotros/vosotras** and **ustedes**. There are also first-person plural imperatives (*let's go, let's wait*) and third-person imperatives (*let him go, let it be*). These are discussed below.

Vosotros/vosotras is not used in Latin America, where the only form used for *you* in the plural, whether one is speaking to intimate friends, little children, strangers or even animals, is **ustedes**.

■ The **tú** imperative is formed by removing the **-s** of the second-person singular of the present indicative: **habla** s*peak*, **cuenta** *count/tell* (from **contar**), **escribe** *write*. There are eight common exceptions:

decir *to say*	**di**
hacer *to make*	**haz**
ir *to go*	**ve**
poner *to put*	**pon**
salir *to go out*	**sal**
ser *to be*	**sé**[8]
tener *to have*	**ten**
venir *to come*	**ven**

The imperative of **estar** *to be* is usually formed (but not in every Latin-American region) from the Pronominal Form of the verb (see Glossary): **¡Estate quieto!**[9] *Sit still!*

These forms of the **tú** imperative are used only for *positive* orders. All *negative* orders in Spanish are based on the Present Subjunctive: **no hables** *don't speak!*, **no escribas**

---

[8] The accent distinguishes it from the pronoun **se**.

[9] **Quieto** = 'still', **callado** = 'quiet'.

don't write!; **sal** *leave!/get out!*, **no salgas** *don't leave/don't go out.*

In Argentina and in most of Central America (but not in Mexico) the pronoun **vos** replaces **tú** in ordinary speech. The imperative forms used vary from country to country, but in Argentina and in most other places they are created by dropping the **-d** from the standard Spanish **vosotros** imperative (see below): **decí, vení, contestame** (standard forms **di, ven, contéstame**). In the negative the standard Subjunctive forms should be used: **no digas, no vengas, no me contestes.**

■ The **vosotros/vosotras** Imperative is considered archaic in Latin America (and in the Canary Islands) and it is replaced by the **ustedes** form; but it is constantly heard in Spain. It is used for two or more close friends, children, family members or animals. It is formed by replacing the **-r** of the Infinitive by **-d**: **hablad** *speak!*, **venid** *come!*, **id** *go!* This form ending in **-d** is often nowadays replaced in familiar styles by the Infinitive: **hablar, venir, ir**, etc. However, careful speakers may consider this slovenly, so foreigners should use the **-d** forms.

All *negative* imperatives are based on the present Subjunctive, so one says **no habléis** *don't speak!*, **no vengáis** *don't come!*, **no vayáis** *don't go!*

■ The **usted** imperative is used when addressing a stranger (other than a child or another young person if you are also young), and the **ustedes** form is used for addressing more than one stranger (in Spain) or for more than one person, friend or stranger, in Latin America. All the **usted** and **ustedes** imperative forms, positive and negative, are identical to the third-person Present Subjunctive: **venga (usted)** *come!*, **contesten (ustedes)** *answer!*, **¡No se queden atrás!** *Don't fall behind!*

Object pronouns with the imperative

In the case of positive imperatives, Object Forms of
Personal Pronouns are attached to the imperative as
suffixes, in the order shown on page 113.

> **Dime la verdad** *Tell me the truth* (**tú**)
> **Llámala ahora** *Call her now* (**tú**)
> **Siéntate** *Sit down* (**tú**)
> **Decídnoslo** *Tell it to us* (**vosotros**)
> **Deme** *Give me*[10] (**usted**)
> **Déselo** *Give it to him/her/them* (**usted**)
> **Envíenmelos** *Send them to me* (**ustedes**)

Note that an accent is often necessary to show that the
stress is not shifted when the pronouns are added: **da** *give*
(**tú** form), **dame** *give me*, **dámelo** *give me it/give it to me*.

When the pronoun **os** is added to a **vosotros** imperative, the **d** is dropped: **lavad** + **os** = **lavaos** *get washed*;
also **callaos** *be quiet*, **decidíos** *make up your minds* (from
decidid + **os**; note accent). There is one exception: **idos**
go away (instead of ***'íos'**). Familiar speech nowadays
usually avoids these forms by using the Infinitive—
lavaros, callaros, decidiros, iros—although non-fluent
foreigners should not do this. The **vosotros** form is
replaced by the **ustedes** form in Latin America: **lávense,
cállense, decídanse, váyanse**, etc.

Personal pronouns are put *before* negative imperatives in
the same order as above:

> **No me digas la verdad** *Don't tell me the truth* (**tú**)
> **No la llames ahora** *Don't call her now* (**tú**)
> **No te sientes** *Don't sit down* (**tú**)
> **No nos lo digáis** *Don't tell it to us* (**vosotros**)

---

[10] Or **déme**. There is some disagreement about whether the
accent of **dé**, the third-person present subjunctive of **dar**, should be
retained when one pronoun is attached to it. The accent is required
on the word **dé** when it stands alone to avoid confusion with **de** *of*.

No se lo dé *Don't give it to him/her/them* (**usted**)
No nos los envíen *Don't send them to us* (**ustedes**)

Third-person imperatives

These translate English forms like *let him . . .* , *tell him/her to . . .* , etc. They consist of **que** plus the third-person present Subjunctive:

Que diga quién es *Tell him to say who he is*
Que vuelvan más tarde *Tell them to come back later*

The Passive **se** construction (see p.73) used with the Subjunctive forms an imperative often used in recipes, instructions and official forms to give impersonal orders:

Pónganse en una cacerola las patatas (Lat.-Am. **papas**) **y los tomates** *Put the potatoes and tomatoes in a saucepan*

Ponga en una cacerola las patatas, etc. would have meant the same thing.

First-person imperatives

The first-person plural of the Present Subjunctive translates the English *let's . . .* , *let us . . .* :

Pensemos un poco antes de hacerlo *Let's think a bit before doing it*

When the pronoun **nos** is added to this imperative form, the final -s of the verb is dropped:

Sentémonos *Let's sit down.*

The verb **ir** is unusual in that the Present Indicative is used for *let's go*: **vamos, vámonos**

Other forms of the imperative

■ There is a tendency to use the Infinitive for second-person Imperatives, singular and plural, especially in written instructions but also sometimes in speech: **re-llenar el cupón y enviarlo a . . .** *fill in the coupon and send it to . . .*, **no fumar** *no smoking*, **tirar** *pull!* Grammarians and schoolteachers disapprove of this, but it is becoming increasingly frequent.

■ The ordinary Present Indicative is often used for the Imperative, but it can sound angry: **¡Te duermes en seguida o me voy a enfadar!** (Lat-Am. **me voy a enojar**) *you're going to sleep right now or I'm going to get mad!*

■ The Imperative may be softened or replaced in polite speech by one of the following constructions, which are more friendly in tone:

> **¿Podría usted guardar mi maleta?** *Could you look after my suitcase?*
>
> **¿Le importaría llamar a mi mujer?** *Would you mind phoning my wife?*
>
> **¿Quisiera hacerme el favor de llamarme cuando sepa algo?** *Would you call me when you know something?*
>
> **Hagan el favor de permanecer sentados** *Please remain seated*
>
> **¿Me da una cerveza?** *Would you give me a beer, please?* (Question form used for polite request)

CONDITIONS

There are three basic kinds of Conditional Sentence in Spanish:

■ Conditions that do not require the Subjunctive in the *if*-clause[11]. These are conditions in which the condition is

---

[11] The Spanish for *if* is **si**. However, foreign learners are often confused by the widespread tendency to use **si** simply as a way of turning a remark into a protest: **¡Si te lo dije anoche!** *But I told you last night!*

equally likely or unlikely to be fulfilled. The verbs are in the Indicative Mood, and their tense is the same as in their English equivalents:

> **Si me das dinero, te compraré un helado** *If you give me some money I'll buy you an ice-cream*
> **Si te pones esa corbata, no voy contigo** *If you put that tie on, I'm not going with you*

The Imperfect Indicative is used if these conditions are reported by someone, but the Imperfect Indicative is not used in any other kinds of Conditional Sentence[12]:

> **Me dijo que no iría conmigo si me ponía esa corbata** *She said she wouldn't go with me if I put that tie on*

Como + Subjunctive is sometimes used instead of **si** in this kind of condition. This is particularly common in threats and apparently more frequent in Spain than Latin America:

> **Como vuelvas a hacerlo, llamo a la policía** *If you do it again, I'm calling the police*

■ Conditions that require the Imperfect Subjunctive in the *if*-clause and the Conditional in the other clause. The condition is less likely to be met or impossible to meet:

> **Si yo tuviera veinte años menos, sería feliz** *If I were twenty years younger, I'd be happy* (impossible)
> **Si trabajaras más te darían mejores notas** *If you worked harder they'd give you better grades/marks* (some doubt about whether it's possible)

The best styles of Spanish prefer the **-ra** form of the Imperfect Subjunctive in the *if*-clause of these sentences, although the **-se** form is common in speech.

[12] Except in familiar speech as an occasional alternative for the Conditional Tense, although beginners should avoid this.

■ Conditions that require the Pluperfect Subjunctive in the *if*-clause and the Pluperfect Conditional in the other clause. In this case the condition was not fulfilled:

> **Si se hubiera casado con ella, habría sido rico**
> *If he had married her he would have been rich* (but he didn't)

> **Si te hubiera visto, te habría saludado** *If I had seen you I would have said hello to you* (but I didn't)

Either the Conditional or the **-ra** form of **haber** can be used in the second clause (e.g. **hubiera saludado** or **habría saludado**).

The **si** and the Subjunctive in this kind of clause are occasionally replaced by **de** + Infinitive, but only if the verbs in each clause are in the same person:

> **De haberte visto, te habría saludado** *Had I seen you, I'd have said hello*

NON-FINITE VERB FORMS (SEE GLOSSARY)

The infinitive

This non-finite form always ends in **-ar**, **-er**, **-ir** or **-ír**: **andar** *to walk*, **convencer** *to convince*, **insistir** *to insist*, **reír** *to laugh*.

It is used:

■ After Modal Verbs (see p.60), e.g. **poder** *to be able*, **deber** *must*, **tener que** *to have to*, **hay que** *it's necessary to*, **saber** *to know how to*:

> **No puedo salir hoy** *I can't go out today*

Debiste llamarla *You should have called her*
Tenemos que esperar *We've got to wait*
Habrá que hacerlo *It'll be necessary to do it*
No sé nadar *I don't know how to swim*

■ After prepositions and prepositional phrases

Ha ido a América a estudiar *He's gone to study in America*
Tosía por haber fumado demasiado *He was coughing from having smoked too much*
Corrió hasta no poder más *He ran until he could (run) no more*
Roncaba sin darse cuenta *He was snoring without realizing*
lejos de pensar que . . . *far from thinking that . . .*
En lugar de ir a España . . . *Instead of going to Spain*

If the subject of the Infinitive and the subject of the Main Clause do not refer to the same thing or person, the Infinitive cannot be used (at least in careful Spanish): **tosía porque ella había fumado demasiado** *he was coughing because she had smoked too much* (not **'por ella haber fumado demasiado'*).

After some prepositions, the Spanish Infinitive may have a passive meaning: **una carta sin terminar** *an unfinished letter*, **cosas por hacer** *things to be done*.

■ After many other verbs

With some verbs no preposition is required before the Infinitive, and with other verbs a preposition is necessary. This list shows the construction with some of the most common verbs. Where no preposition is shown none is required, e.g. **quiero hacerlo** *I want to do it*:

abstenerse de *to abstain from*
acabar de: acabo de verla *I've just seen her*
acabar por *to end by*
acercarse a *to approach*
aconsejar *to advise*
acordarse de *to remember*
acostumbrar a *to be accustomed to*
acusar de *to accuse of*
admitir *to admit*
afirmar *to claim/state*
alegrarse de *to be happy at/to*
amenazar or **amenazar con** *to threaten*
anhelar *to long to*
animar a *to encourage to*
aparentar *to seem to, to have the look of . . .*
aprender a *to learn to*
arrepentirse de *to regret/repent*
asegurar *to assure/insure*
asombrarse de *to be surprised at*
asustarse de *to be frightened by*
atreverse a *to dare to*
autorizar a *to authorize to*
avergonzarse de *to be ashamed of*
ayudar a *to help to*
buscar *to seek to*
cansarse de *to tire of*
cesar de *to cease from*
comenzar a *to begin to*
comprometerse a *to undertake to*
condenar a *to condemn to*
conducir a *to lead to*
confesar *to confess*
conseguir *to succeed in*
consentir en *to consent to*
consistir en *to consist of*
contar con *count on*

contribuir a *to contribute to*
convenir en *to agree to*
convidar a *to invite to*
cuidar de *to take care to*
deber *must*
decidir *to decide to*
decidirse a *to make up one's mind to*
declarar *to declare*
dejar *to let/allow*: **me dejó hacerlo** *he let me do it*
dejar de *to stop/leave off, e.g.* **dejó de fumar** *he stopped smoking*
demostrar *to demonstrate*
depender de *depend on*
desafiar a *to challenge to*
desear *to desire/wish to*
desesperarse de *to despair of*
dignarse *to deign to*
disponerse a *to get ready to*
disuadir de *to dissuade from*
divertirse en *to amuse oneself by*
dudar *to doubt*
dudar en *to hesitate over*
echar(se) a *to begin to*
empeñarse en *to insist on*
empezar a *to begin to*
empezar por *to begin by*
enfadarse de *to get angry at*
enojarse de *to get angry at*
enseñar a *to show how to/teach how to*
escoger *to choose to*
esforzarse por *to strive to*
esperar *to hope/expect/wait*
evitar *to avoid*
fingir *to pretend to*
forzar a *to force to*

guardarse de *to take care not to*
habituarse a *to get used to*
hartarse de *to get tired of*
imaginar(se) *to imagine*
impedir *to prevent from*
incitar a *to incite to*
inclinar a *to incline to*
insistir en *to insist on*
intentar *to try to*
interesarse en (or **por**) *to be interested in*
invitar a *to invite to*[13]
jactarse de *to boast of*
jurar *to swear to*
juzgar *to judge*
limitarse a *to limit oneself to*
luchar por *to struggle to*
llevar a *to lead to*
lograr *to succeed in*
mandar *to order to*
mandar a *to send to*
maravillarse de *to marvel at*
merecer *to deserve to*
meterse a *to start to*
mover a *to move to*
necesitar *to need to*
negar *to deny*
negarse a *to refuse to*
obligar a *to oblige to*
ofrecerse a *to offer to*
olvidar, olvidarse de, olvidársele a uno[14] *to forget*
oponerse a *to oppose/resist*

[13] Note one special use of this verb in bars, restaurants etc.: **te invito** *I'm paying for you*, **¿Quién invita?** *Who's paying for us?*
[14] Note construction: **me olvidé de decirte** or **se me olvidó decirte** *I forgot to tell you.*

optar por *to opt to/for*
ordenar *to order to*
parar de[15] *to stop*
parecer *to seem to*
pasar a *to go on to*
pasar de *to pass from, to be uninterested in*
pedir *to ask to*
pensar: pienso hacerlo *I plan to do it*
pensar en *to think about*
permitir *to allow to*
poder *to be able to*
preferir *to prefer to*
prepararse a *to get ready to*
pretender *to claim to*
procurar *to try hard to*
prohibir *to prohibit from*
prometer *to promise to*
quedar en *to agree to*
querer *to want to*
recordar *to remember*[16]
renunciar a *to renounce*
resignarse a *to resign oneself to*
resistirse a *to resist*
resolver *to resolve to*
sentir *to regret/be sorry for*
soler: solía ir *he used to go*
solicitar *to apply to*
soñar con *to dream of*
sorprenderse de *to be surprised that*
tardar en *to be late in/be a long time*
temer *to fear to*
tender a *to tend to*

[15] **Pararse** means *to come to a halt* in Spain, *to stand up* in Latin America.
[16] Note alternatives: **recordar algo** or **acordarse de algo** *to remember something*.

> **tener que** *to have to*
> **terminar de** *to finish*
> **terminar por** *to finish by*
> **tratar de** *to try to*
> **vacilar en** *to hesitate over*
> **venir de** *to come from . . .*
> **volver a (hacer)** *to (do) again*

The Infinitive is normally only possible with the above verbs when the subject of both verbs is the same. Compare

> **Soñaba con ser bombero** *He dreamt of being a fireman*

and

> **Soñaba con que su hijo *fuese* bombero** *He dreamt of his son being a fireman.*

Verbs of permitting and forbidding allow either construction:

> **Te permito hacerlo/Te permito que lo hagas** *I allow you to do it*
> **Te prohibía ir/Te prohibía que fueses** *He forbade you to go.*

■ With verbs of stating, believing, claiming

In this case the Infinitive construction is *optionally* allowed when both verbs share the same subject:

> **Dice ser de Madrid/Dice que es de Madrid** *He says he's from Madrid* (he is talking about himself)
> **Afirmaba haberlos visto/que los había visto** *He claimed to have seen them*
> **Parecía conocerla/Parecía que la conocía** *He seemed to recognize her/It seemed that he recognized her*

Similarly with **pretender** *to claim*, **imaginar** *to imagine*, **creer** *to believe*, **recordar/acordarse de** *to remember*, **reconocer** *to recognize*, **admitir** *to admit*, **confesar** *to confess*.

■ After **ver** *to see* and **oír** *to hear*

> **Le oí decir que tenía mucho dinero** *I heard him say that he had a lot of money*
> **Te vi entrar en su casa** *I saw you enter his/her house*

For the possible use of the Gerund as an alternative to the Infinitive in this construction, see p.53.

■ In the common construction **al** + Infinitive, which translates *on doing something . . . , when . . .* **al llegar a Madrid** *. . . on arriving at Madrid . . .*

> **al levantarse** . . . *on getting up . . .*

■ After Subordinators (other than **cuando** *when*, **en cuanto**, *as soon as*, **apenas** *as soon as/scarcely* and a few others mentioned on p.24) when the subject of the first verb is identical to the subject of the second verb: Compare **comí antes de salir de casa** *I ate before leaving home* and **comí antes de que tú salieras de casa** *I ate before **you** left home*:

> **Entró sin hacer ruido** *He entered without making any noise*
> **Redecoraremos la casa en lugar de venderla** *We'll redecorate the house instead of selling it*

■ In combination with an adjective, and with noun phrases

> **Es difícil hacerlo** *It's difficult to do it*
> **Parecía imposible equivocarse** *It seemed impossible to make a mistake*
> **Cuesta trabajo pensar eso** *It's hard to think that*

If the Infinitive has no object and is not followed by **que**, **de** is required:

> **Es que ella es difícil *de* olvidar** *The fact is she's difficult to forget*
> **Sería imposible *de* probar** *It would be impossible to prove*

But this construction is usually avoided and **es que es difícil olvidarla, sería difícil probarlo,** etc. are used instead.

■ As a noun. In this case it often corresponds to the English form ending in *-ing*. When used as a noun, the Spanish Infinitive is masculine and singular:

> **No me gusta esperar** *I don't like waiting*
> **Cansa mucho viajar en avión** *Traveling* (British *travelling*) *in planes makes one very tired*
> **Sería mejor dejarlos aquí** *It would be better to leave them here*

This kind of sentence must never be translated using the Spanish Gerund: **'hablando da sed'* is definitely not possible for **(el) hablar da sed** *talking makes you thirsty*.

Use of the Definite Article with the Infinitive in such sentences is more or less optional, although it is common in literary styles at the head of a sentence or clause:

> **(El) decir esto le iba a causar muchos problemas** *Saying this was to cause him many problems*
> **Los médicos afirman que (el) comer mucho ajo es bueno para el corazón** *Doctors claim that eating a lot of garlic is good for the heart*

■ To make a quick answer to a question

> **—¿Qué hacemos? —Pensar** *'What are we going to do?' 'Think.'*

■ In familiar speech, as an alternative for the Imperative

This construction is discussed under the Imperative, p.36 ff.

■ In combination with **que**, or with the prepositions **por** or **a,** as an alternative for a relative clause.

The construction with **a** is commonly seen, but foreigners should use it only in set phrases like the ones shown:

> **Tengo mucho que hacer** *I've got a lot to do*
> **Queda mucho que/por hacer** *There's a lot left to do*
> **total a pagar** *total to pay/payable*
> **asuntos a tratar** *matters to be discussed*

> **Para** is used after verbs of wanting, needing:

> **Quieren algo para comer** *They want something to eat*
> **Necesito dinero para vivir** *I need money to live*

The gerund

The Gerund always ends in **-ndo**. It is formed:

In the case of all **-ar** verbs, by replacing the **-ar** by **-ando**: **hablar—hablando** *talking*, **andar—andando** *walking*.

In the case of most **-er** and **-ir** verbs, by replacing the Infinitive ending by **-iendo**: **comer—comiendo**, **vivir - viviendo, ser -siendo,** etc.

-iendo is written **-yendo** when it follows another vowel: **destruir—destruyendo** *destroying*, **creer— creyendo** *believing*, **caer—cayendo** *falling*, **oír—oyendo** *hearing*. The Gerund of **ir** is regularly formed: **yendo** *going*.

-iendo becomes **-endo** after **ñ** or **ll**: **gruñir— gruñendo** *growling*, **reñir—riñendo** *scolding*, **engullir— engullendo** *gobbling up, swallowing whole*.

Poder, venir, morir and **dormir,** and all verbs conjugated like **pedir, sentir** and **reír** base their Gerund on the stem of the third-person Preterit:

Infinitive	3rd-person Preterit	Gerund
poder	**pudo**	**pudiendo** *being able*
venir	**vino**	**viniendo** *coming*
repetir	**repitió**	**repitiendo** *repeating,*
pedir	**pidió**	**pidiendo** *asking for*
sentir	**sintió**	**sintiendo** *feeling*
corregir	**corrigió**	**corrigiendo** *correcting*
freír	**frió**	**friendo** *frying*
dormir	**durmió**	**durmiendo** *sleeping*
morir	**murió**	**muriendo** *dying*

The gerund of **decir** is not based on the preterite form (**dijo**): **diciendo** *saying.*

The Gerund is used:

■ To show that an action is simultaneous with another:

> **Entró riendo** *He came in laughing*
> **Se lo diré, pero no estando aquí este señor** *I'll tell you, but not while this gentleman is here*

■ To show the method by which something is done

> **Se hizo rico vendiendo vídeos ilegales** *He got rich selling illegal videos*
> **Verás el jardín asomándote al balcón** *You'll see the garden by looking out of the window*
> **Me molestaba cada cinco minutos diciéndome que no tenía dinero** *He bothered me every five minutes saying that he didn't have any money*

■ With **estar** to make the Continuous Form of verbs: **está trabajando** *he's (in the middle of) working.* This is discussed on p.13 ff.

■ With verbs meaning *see, imagine, paint, draw, photograph, meet, find, catch, surprise, remember*:

> **Los cogieron robando manzanas** *They caught them stealing apples*
>
> **Le sacaron una foto cenando con el presidente** *They took a photo of him/her having dinner with the President*
>
> **La vi jugando en el parque** *I saw her playing in the park*

Other verbs found with this construction are **recordar** *to remember*, **describir** *to describe*, **dibujar** *to sketch*, **pintar** *to paint*, **mostrar** *to show*, **representar** *to represent*.

With the verb **ver** *to see* the Infinitive is used if the action is complete: **lo/le vi bajarse del autobús** *I saw him get out of the bus* but **la vi jugando en el jardín** *I saw her (while she was) playing in the garden*.

The Infinitive is used after **oír** *to hear*: **te oyeron entrar** *they heard you come in*. The Infinitive is also always used with the verbs **venir** *to come* and **ir** *to go*: **la veíamos venir** *we could see her coming*, **lo/le vi ir hacia la puerta** *I saw him go towards the door*.

With **ver** and **oír** the idea of ongoing action can be stressed in colloquial language by using **que** + Imperfect Indicative: **la vi que iba en bicicleta** *I saw her riding a bicycle*.

■ With **venir** and **ir** to show that an event is drawn out over a period of time:

> **Iba apuntando todo lo que decían** *He was noting down everything they were saying*
>
> **Los problemas vienen siendo cada vez más complicados** *The problems are getting more and more complicated*

■ With **llevar** *to carry* to translate the idea of *to do something for n days/months/years*, etc.

> **Lleva varios días pintando la casa** *He's been painting his house for several days*

See page 205 for more remarks on this construction.

■ Occasionally as alternative for **aunque** *although* or **a pesar de que** *despite*

> **Un día se confesó que, amando inmensamente a su hija, le tenía envidia** *One day she admitted to herself that, despite loving her daughter immensely, she envied her*

■ As an alternative to **porque** *because* or **ya que** *since*:

> **Calló, viendo que el otro no le hacía caso** *He fell silent, seeing that the other was not paying attention to him*

■ In combination with **como**, as an alternative to **como si** *as if*

> **Se agachó como preparándose para saltar** *He squatted down, as if preparing to jump*
> **Emitió una tosecilla, como llamándonos al orden** *He made a slight cough, as if calling us to order*

The gerund as a participle

English regularly uses the *-ing* form of verbs to form an adjective: *an exhausting task*, *a surprising attitude*, *a freezing wind*. The Spanish Gerund is not possible in these cases: an adjective or a participle in -**nte** must be used (if one exists: see below): **una tarea agotadora, una actitud sorprendente, un viento helado**. The only exceptions are the two invariable adjectives **hirviendo** and **ardiendo**—**agua hirviendo** *boiling water*, **un árbol ardiendo** *a burning tree*.

English also constantly uses the *-ing* form to replace a relative pronoun plus a finite verb: *passengers waiting for* *the train, a woman driving a car*. In Spanish a Relative Pronoun and a Finite Verb must be used: **los pasajeros que esperan el tren, una mujer que conduce/conducía un coche**. The only exception that need concern beginners is captions to pictures: **una foto de una mujer dando de comer a un niño** *a photo of a woman feeding a child*.

In general, foreign students should respect the rule that the Spanish Gerund is basically a kind of adverb and must therefore modify a verb. If there is no verb, as in the phrase *a plane carrying passengers* there can be no Gerund: **un avión que lleva/llevaba pasajeros**, not **'un avión llevando pasajeros'*.

The past participle

Forms

| from **-ar** verbs | by replacing the **-ar** by **-ado** |
| from **-er** and **-ir** verbs | by replacing the ending by **-ido** |

hablar	*to speak*	**hablado**	*spoken*
comer	*to eat*	**comido**	*eaten*
ser	*to be*	**sido**	*been*
vivir	*to live*	**vivido**	*lived*
ir	*to go*	**ido**	*gone*

When the Infinitive ends in **-ír**, **-aer** or **-eer** the Past Participle ending is written with an accent: **reír—reído** *to laugh*, **traer—traído** *to bring*, **creer—creído** *to believe*. Verbs whose Infinitive ends in **-uir** do not have an accent: **construir—construido** *to build*.

The following forms are irregular:

abrir	*to open*	**abierto**	*opened*
absolver	*to absolve*	**absuelto**	*absolved*

cubrir	*to cover*	**cubierto**	*covered*
decir	*to say*	**dicho**	*said*
descomponer	*to put out of order*	**descompuesto**	*disordered*
describir	*to describe*	**descrito**	*described*
descubrir	*to discover*	**descubierto**	*discovered*
devolver	*to give back*	**devuelto**	*given back*
encubrir	*to cover up/ conceal*	**encubierto**	*concealed*
envolver	*to wrap up*	**envuelto**	*wrapped up*
escribir	*to write*	**escrito**	*written*
freír	*to fry*	**frito**	*fried*
hacer	*to make/do*	**hecho**	*made/done*
imponer	*to impose*	**impuesto**	*imposed*
inscribirse	*to sign on*	**inscrito**	*signed on*
morir	*to die*	**muerto**	*dead/died*
poner	*to put*	**puesto**	*put*
posponer	*to postpone*	**pospuesto**	*postponed*
prever	*to predict*	**previsto**	*foreseen*
resolver	*to resolve*	**resuelto**	*resolved*
revolver	*to turn over/ around*	**revuelto**	*turned over/ scrambled*
romper	*to break*	**roto**	*broken*
suponer	*to suppose*	**supuesto**	*supposed*
ver	*to see*	**visto**	*seen*
volver	*to return*	**vuelto**	*returned*

Another kind of irregularity involves a distinction between the verbal past participle and the past participle used as an adjective. The forms in the second column are used to form the Compound Tenses (e.g. **ha absorbido** *it has absorbed*, **habían soltado** *they had set free*), while the words in the third column form adjectives: **estaba absorto en su trabajo** *he was engrossed/absorbed in his work*, **unos papeles sueltos** *some loose sheets of paper*.

Infinitive	Verbal	Adjectival	
absorber	absorbido	absorto	*absorbed*
bendecir	bendecido	bendito	*blessed*
confesar	confesado	confeso	*confessed*
confundir	confundido	confuso	*confused*
despertar	despertado	despierto	*woken up*
elegir	elegido	electo	*chosen/elect*
imprimir	imprimido	impreso	*printed*
maldecir	maldecido	maldito	*cursed*
prender	prendido	preso	*taken prisoner*
presumir	presumido	presunto	*presumed*
proveer	proveído	provisto	*equipped with*
soltar	soltado	suelto	*let out*
suspender	suspendido	suspenso	*failed (exams)*

Uses of the past participle

The uses of the Spanish Past Participle resemble that of the English past participle. The main uses are:

■ In combination with the appropriate form of **haber**, to form Compound Tenses (e.g. the Perfect, Pluperfect, etc.):

> **Los científicos han descubierto una nueva droga** *Scientists have discovered a new drug*

> **No se habían dado cuenta** *They hadn't realized*

In these tenses the participle is invariable in form: it does not agree with either the subject or the object of the verb. The use of the Compound Tenses is discussed on p. 9 ff.

■ In combination with the verb **ser,** and also sometimes with the verb **estar,** to form the Passive Voice of verbs (which is discussed further on pp.64 ff):

El nuevo proyecto será presentado por el ministro de Obras Públicas *The new project will be presented by the Minister for Public Works*

As in English, the passive participle frequently appears without the verb *to be:*

Han encontrado a las niñas perdidas *They've found the lost girls (i.e. the girls that were lost)*

Preguntados sobre el aumento a los mínimos para este año, los portavoces contestaron que . . . *Asked about the increase in minimum salaries for this year, the spokespersons replied that . . .*

As the examples show, the participle must agree in number and gender with the noun it refers to.

■ To form adverbial phrases which describe the manner or appearance of the subject of a verb. As the examples show, this construction is used with a much wider range of participles than in English:

Gritó alborozado *He shouted in glee/gleefully*

Me miraba fascinada *She looked at me in fascination*

Salió contrariado del cuarto *He came/went out of the room in an upset state*

Llegados a este punto, podríamos preguntarnos si . . . *Having got this far, we might ask ourselves whether . . .*

un autor nacido en España y muerto en Francia *an author who was born in Spain and died in France*

■ To form absolute participle clauses, i.e. ones that do not depend on the finite verb in the sentence:

Cometido este acto de vandalismo, se guardó la navaja *Having committed this act of vandalism, he put away his knife*

Pero, una vez compradas las flores y la tarjeta, me di cuenta de que me había olvidado de su dirección *But, having bought the flowers and the card, I realized that I'd forgotten her address*

Adjectival participles

Many Spanish verbs have an adjectival participle formed by adding **-ante** to **-ar** verbs, and **-iente** (or, in some cases, **-ente**) to **-er** and **-ir** verbs:

preocupar *to worry*	**preocupante** *worrying*
cambiar *to change*	**cambiante** *changing/fickle*
excitar *to arouse*	**excitante** *arousing*
crecer *to grow*	**creciente** *growing*
sorprender *to surprise*	**sorprendente** *surprising*
conducir *to lead/drive*	**conducente a** *leading to*
consistir en *to consist of*	**consisente en** *consisting of*
existir *to exist*	**existente** *existing*

There are a few irregular forms, the most common being

convencer *to convince*	**convincente** *convincing*
dormir *to sleep*	**durmiente** *sleeping*
herir *to wound*	**hiriente** *wounding*
provenir de *to come from*	**proveniente de** *coming from*
seguir *to follow*	**siguiente** *following*

The suffix **-nte** is very productive, although many of the new formations are seen only in newspaper and technical language. But foreigners should not attempt to invent new words by using it: many verbs, for no obvious reason, do not form adjectives in **-nte**, e.g.

aburrir *to bore*	**aburrido** *boring*
asombrar *to amaze*	**asombroso** *amazing*
aterrar *to terrify*	**aterrador** *terrifying*
cansar *to tire*	**cansado** *tiring*

confiar *to trust*   **confiado** *trusting*
venir *to come*   **venidero** *coming*

MODAL VERBS (SEE GLOSSARY)

These are **poder** *to be able*, **deber** *must*, **querer** *to want*,
tener que *to have to*, **haber que** *to be necessary*, **saber** *to
know how to*, **soler** *to be accustomed to*. They are followed
by an Infinitive, although **poder + que** + Subjunctive is
used to mean *it is possible that* and **querer** requires the
Subjunctive when its subject is not the same as that of the
following verb. **Saber** is also followed by **que** and an
indicative tense when it means *to know* rather than *to know
how to*.

■ Poder

This differs little in meaning and use from the English
can, may:

> **No puedo ir hoy** *I can't go today*
> **Podría llover** *It might rain*
> **Puede que la situación mejore** *It may be that the
> situation will improve* (Lat. Am. also **pueda
> que** . . .)

The Preterit often means *managed to* (i.e. *could and did*)
whereas the Imperfect means *was able* (*but may not have*)

> **No pudo abrir la puerta** *He didn't manage to get
> the door open*
> **Como no podía hacerlo, pidió ayuda** *Since he
> couldn't do it, he asked for help*

The Preterit can also refer to something that could have
happened but definitely did not:

> **Tuviste suerte. Te pudiste matar** *You were lucky.
> You could have got killed*

■ **Deber**

This translates *must*. As in English, it may indicate obligation or likelihood: *you must do it/you've got to do it, he must be fifty*. The strict rule is that when it refers to likelihood it should be followed by **de**:

> **Debe de tener cincuenta años** *He must be fifty* (guess)
>
> **Debían de pensar que no era verdad** *They must have been thinking that it wasn't true* (guess)
>
> **Debes hacerlo ahora** *You've got to do it now* (obligation)
>
> **Deberías llamarlos ahora mismo** *You ought to call them right now* (obligation)

The form **deber de** is never used for obligations, but the form without **de** is constantly used nowadays for both meanings, which can be confusing for learners. When it is used for suppositions, **deber (de)** does not appear in the Future or Conditional tense: **deben (de) ser las cinco** *(I guess) it must be five o'clock*, not **'deberán (de) ser . . . '* or **'deberían (de) ser . . . '*

The Imperfect of **deber** either implies *was/were supposed to . . .* or it may be a familiar alternative for the Conditional: *ought to do it*: **debías hacerlo tú** *you were supposed to do it/you ought to do it* (i.e. **deberías hacerlo tú**). The Preterit of **deber** may mean *should have done it but didn't*, or *must have done it*:

> **Debí haberme ido, pero me quedé** *I should have left, but I stayed*
>
> **Debió de pensar que estamos todos locos** *He must have thought we're all mad*

The idea of *had to* (i.e. *was obliged to and did*) is translated by the Preterit of **tener que**:

> **Tuve que ponerme un suéter porque tenía frío** *I had to put on a sweater because I was cold*

■ Tener que

Tener que implies a strong obligation:

> **Tienes que decirnos la verdad** *You've got to tell us the truth*
> **Tuve que dárselo** *I was obliged to give it to him (and did)*

■ Haber que

Haber que (Present Indicative **hay que**) is an impersonal verb followed by the Infinitive and meaning *it is necessary to*:

> **Hay que añadir un poco de agua** *It's necessary to/We'll have to add a bit of water*
> **Hubo que encerrar al perro** *it was necessary to shut the dog in*

■ Haber de

Haber de is much used in Mexico for suppositions, where standard Spanish uses **deber de**, e.g. **ha de tener más de cincuenta años** for **debe de tener más de cincuenta años** or **tendrá más de cincuenta años** *he must be more than fifty*. In Spain **haber de** is a rather old-fashioned form that usually expresses a mild obligation: **si viene has de decirle lo que ha pasado** *if he comes you must tell him what has happened*; . . . **debes/tienes que decirle** . . . are more usual.

■ Querer

This verb translates *to want*. It also means *to love*, but in the latter sense it can refer only to human beings and animals: **quiero a mis padres, a mi perro** *I love my parents, my dog* but **adoro las novelas de amor** *I love novels about love*.

The conditional form, **querría** or, more commonly, **quisiera**, is used to make polite requests:

Quisiera/querría expresar mi agradecimiento a los organizadores . . . *I'd like to express my gratitude to the organizers*

The Imperfect means *wanted to*. The Preterit has two mutually exclusive meanings that can only be clarified by context. It usually implies *tried to . . .* (i.e. *wanted to but couldn't*):

Quiso acercarse al Rey, pero no pudo *He tried to get close to the King was, but he couldn't manage it*

However, it may imply *wanted to and did* when some idea of getting one's own way is involved: **lo dije porque quise, nada más** *I said it because I felt like it, and that's that*. The negative of the Preterit means *refused* (i.e. *didn't want to and didn't*): **no quiso decir su nombre** *he refused to give his name*.

■ **Saber**

The basic meaning of **saber** is *to know* (a fact); it must be distinguished from **conocer** *to know* (a person or place). Combined with an Infinitive it means *to know how to*, as in

Casi me ahogué por no saber nadar *I nearly drowned because of not knowing how to swim*
Me despidieron porque no sabía escribir a máquina *They fired me because I couldn't type*

■ **Soler**

This basically means *to be accustomed to*, *usually*. It is not used in the future or conditional tenses:

Solía limpiar mi coche (Lat. Am. **carro/auto**) **todos los días** *I used to clean my car every day*
Suele hacer menos calor en septiembre *It's usually less hot in September*

THE PASSIVE

The Passive construction makes the Direct Object of an Active sentence into the Subject of a Passive one. Active: *I chose the red one.* Passive: *the red one was chosen by me.*

The Spanish Passive is formed in one of two ways:

(a) In a way similar to English, by using the verb meaning *to be* (**ser,** or occasionally **estar**) + the Past Participle, which must agree in number and gender:

> **Mis dos novelas fueron publicadas el año pasado** *My two novels were published last year*
> **El proyecto fue rechazado por el comité** *The project was rejected by the committee*

(b) By using the Passive **se** construction:

> **Mis dos novelas se publicaron el año pasado** *My two novels were published last year*

Construction (a) and construction (b) are usually interchangeable, but only if the preposition **por** does not appear. In other words, if **se** is used we cannot go on to say *by* whom or what the action was done. For this reason one should not say **'el proyecto se rechazó por el comité'*. The Passive with **se** is further discussed at pp. 73–4.

The following points about the Spanish Passive with **ser** should be noted:

■ It is only used in written Spanish (where it is common, especially in newspapers)

This is a bold generalization, but English-speaking learners of Spanish will do well to avoid the Passive with **ser** when speaking Spanish and to master first the use of the much more common Passive **se** (p.73). Usually a simple active construction produces the best and most idiomatic Spanish: passive sentences like **estoy muy con-**

tento porque *fui besádo por* una actriz muy famosa
I'm really happy because I was kissed by a famous actress
sound natural to English-speakers but they are very
clumsy in Spanish. The active construction is more normal: **. . . porque me besó una actriz muy famosa** . . .
because a very famous actress kissed me.

Examples of the passive from written Spanish:

> **El derrumbamiento del edificio fue causado por
> un terremoto** *The collapse of the building was
> caused by an earthquake*
> **Los hechos serán investigados por las autori-
> dades** *The facts will be investigated by the
> authorities*
> **Varias personas han sido expulsadas del par-
> tido** *Several people have been expelled from the
> party*

■ It must *never* be used when the subject of the verb **ser**
would be the Indirect Object

English allows two passive versions of sentences like
*they gave fifty dollars **to** me*: *fifty dollars were given to me* or *I
was given fifty dollars*. The second of these two construction is *never* possible in Spanish and the best translation in
both cases is **me dieron cincuenta dólares** *they gave me
fifty dollars*. **'Fui dado cincuenta dólares'* is definitely
not Spanish. Further examples

> **Nunca me contaban la verdad** *I was never told
> the truth/They never told me the truth.*
> **Me preguntaron varias cosas** *I was asked sev-
> eral things/They asked me several things*
> **Le enviaron una carta** *He/She was sent a
> letter/They sent him/her a letter*

Fue enviada una carta can only mean *a letter was sent.*

■ *Never* with verbs combined with a preposition. Compare
*this bed has been slept **in*** and **alguien ha dormido en esta**

cama (*someone has slept in this bed*), never *'**esta cama ha sido dormido en'** which is emphatically not Spanish.

■ Usually only with the Preterit, Perfect and Future tenses of **ser**

Sentences like **fue interrogado por la policía** *he was interrogated by the police*, **ha sido interrogado . . .** and **será interrogado . . .** sound more natural than **es interrogado por la policía** *he is interrogated . . .* or **era interrogado por la policía** *he was being interrogated . . .* (although **estaba siendo interrogado . . .** is not unusual). Use of the Present or Imperfect of **ser** with the Passive is rather more common in Latin America than in Spain.

Use of *estar* to form the passive

■ A passive construction may be formed with **estar**

Use of **estar** draws attention to the state something is in, whereas use of **ser** describes the event that caused the state. Compare

> **La ciudad estaba inundada por las lluvias** *The city was covered in water as a result of the rains* (describes the state the city was in)
>
> **La ciudad fue inundada por las lluvias** *The city was flooded by the rain* (describes an event)

PRONOMINAL ('REFLEXIVE') VERBS

Pronominal verbs are verbs like **llamarse** *to be called*, **defenderse** *to defend oneself/to 'get by'*, **inhibirse** *to be inhibited*, **irse** *to go away*. These verbs are often called 'reflexive verbs', but the name is inaccurate. 'Reflexive' refers to only one of the various meanings of the Pronominal forms of verbs.

Pronominal verbs have an object pronoun that is of the same person and number as the subject of the verb:

> **(Yo) me lavo** *I wash (myself)*
> **(Tú) te vas** *You go away*
> **(Él/ella/usted) se cayó** *He/she/you fell over*
> **(Nosotros) nos queremos** *We love one another*
> **(Vosotros) os arrepentisteis** *You repented*
> **(Ellos/ellas/ustedes) se imaginan** *They/you
> imagine*

As the examples show, the third-person pronoun used for singular and plural is **se**. This pronoun may variously be translated *himself/herself/itself/yourself/themselves/yourselves*, but it also has several other uses.

Pronominal verbs have many uses in Spanish—far more than in French—and some of them are rather subtle. The picture is made more complicated by the fact that, as explained on p. 114, the pronoun **le** becomes **se** before **lo/la/los/las**, as in **se lo dije a mi madre** *I told it to my mother* (instead of the impossible * **'le lo dije a mi madre'**). This is an entirely different use of **se** not related to the issues discussed in this section.

The various uses of Pronominal verbs are best clarified by considering cases in which the subject of the verb is animate (human or some other animal) and cases in which the subject is inanimate.

Pronominal verbs with animate (human or animal) subjects

In this case the Pronominal form of verbs is used:

■ To show that the action is *not* done to someone or something else. Compare **asustas** *you frighten/you're frightening* (i.e. for someone else) and *te* **asustas** *you get frightened* (no one else involved). English often requires translation by *get . . .* + adjective or by *become*. Further examples:

Casó a su hija con un abogado *He married his daughter off to a lawyer*

Su hija se casó con un abogado *His daughter married/got married to a lawyer*

Convence cuando habla así *He's convincing (to others) when he talks like that*

Se convence cuando habla así *He gets convinced when he talks like that*

Se divorciaron al cabo de tres años *They got divorced after three years*

Me matriculé para el curso de inglés *I registered for the course of English*

Me canso fácilmente *I get tired easily*

Se irrita por nada *He gets irritable over nothing*

No te enojes/enfades *Don't get cross*

■ Simply to give the verb a different meaning altogether:

admirar *to admire*	**admirarse** *to be surprised*
despedir *to fire*	**despedirse** *to say good-bye*
dormir *to sleep*	**dormirse** *to go to sleep*
fumar *to smoke*	**fumarse** *to skip a class, meeting* (colloquial)
guardar *to guard*	**guardarse de** *to refrain from*

Some verbs are only found in the pronominal form. The following are common:

abstenerse *to abstain*
acatarrarse *to get a cold*
arrepentirse *to repent*
atreverse a *to dare*
enfermarse *to get ill* (but **enfermar** is used in Spain with the same meaning)
quejarse de *to complain about*
suicidarse *to commit suicide*

There are also certain commonly occurring verbs in which the pronominal form merely has a special nuance that needs separate explanation for each verb. A list of these appears on pp.75 ff.

■ To show that an action is done *to* or *for* oneself: this is the 'reflexive' use of pronominal verbs.The action can be accidental or deliberate. The subject is human or animal for the obvious reason that cups, doors etc. don't usually do things to themselves:

> **Me rasqué** *I scratched myself*
> **Te peinaste** *You did your hair* (literally *you combed yourself*)
> **Mario se ensució** *Mario got himself dirty*
> **Ustedes se van a matar haciendo eso** *You're going to kill yourselves doing that*
> **Se quitó el sombrero** *He took off his hat*
> **Se sacó el dinero del bolsillo** *He took the money out of his (own) pocket*

■ When the verb is plural, to mean *to do something to or for one another*:

This is the 'reciprocal' use of the pronominal form, and again the subjects are usually humans or other animals since doors or bricks don't usually do things to one another:

> **Se escriben todas las semanas** *They write to one another every week*
> **Se daban golpes** *They were hitting one another*
> **Nos respetamos el uno al otro** *We respect one another*

The phrase **el uno al otro** or (when more than two subjects are involved) **los unos a los otros** *one another* may be added to clarify the meaning. **La una a la otra** and **las unas a las otras** are used only when only females are involved.

■ To give the sentence a passive meaning. This is rare with animate subjects because of the clash of meanings with the other uses of the Pronominal form listed above. However, it occurs when the noun does not refer to specific individuals, as in **se ven muchos turistas en agosto** *a lot of tourists are seen in August*. This construction is very common with inanimate subjects (see below).

When the noun refers to specific individuals, a special construction exists which makes Passive **se** unambiguous with human subjects:

> **Se detuvo *a* un narcotraficante** *A drug-pusher was arrested*
>
> **Se admiraba mucho *a* estos profesores** *These teachers were much admired*

In this case the verb is always singular and the preposition **a** is put before the noun. This construction avoids the problem raised by **estos profesores se admiraban mucho**, which would mean *these teachers admired themselves a lot* or . . . *admired one another a lot*.

Students must not confuse this construction with Passive **se** used with nouns referring to inanimate things, as described on page 73. It is possible to rewrite **se admiraba mucho a estos profesores** as **se les[17] admiraba mucho** *they were admired a lot*. But this is not possible when the original sentence refers to an inanimate thing, as in **se venden manzanas** *apples are sold*, which can only be rewritten **se venden** *they are sold*, not ** 'se las vende'*. This is discussed in more detail in note (c) on page 74.

---

[17] There is a tendency everywhere to use **le/les** for *him/her/you* (i.e. **usted** or **ustedes**)/*them* in this construction rather than **lo/la/los/las**, although the latter is not incorrect.

■ With singular intransitive verbs (like *to go*, *to arrive*, *to be*), as an equivalent of English impersonal sentences that have the subject *one*, *people* or *you* used impersonally:

> **En España se duerme por la tarde** *In Spain people sleep in the afternoon*
> **Por esta carretera se llega al castillo medieval** *Along this road one arrives at the medieval castle*
> **Se está mejor al sol** *One's better off in the sun*

This construction cannot be used with a verb that already has **se** attached for some other reason. In this case the pronoun **uno** *one* is required or, in less formal language, **tú**:

> **Si uno se levanta tarde, se pierde lo mejor del día** *If one gets up late one misses the best part of the day* (**levantarse** *to get up* is already a pronominal verb)
> **Uno se olvida de esas cosas/Te olvidas de esas cosas** *One forgets such things/you forget such things* (**olvidarse de** *to forget*)

■ With singular transitive verbs which in English would have the pronoun *people*, *one*, *you*.

This construction is sometimes difficult to distinguish from the Passive use of **se** described later. If the sentence contains no noun or pronoun that could be understood as the subject, the impersonal meaning is intended. Thus, if we are talking about olive oil, the sentence **en España se come mucho** means *a lot of it is eaten in Spain* (passive: implied subject *olive oil*). But if the conversation is on general eating habits, the same sentence means *people eat a lot in Spain* (impersonal: the verb has no subject):

> **Se habla de ello, pero no lo creo** *People talk about it, but I don't believe it*
> **En este país se escribe y se lee poco** *In this country people don't write or read much*

■ With a few verbs, to give the meaning *to get something done*

> **Me voy a hacer un traje** *I'm going to get a suit made* (or *I'm going to make myself a suit*)
>
> **El rey se construyó un palacio de mármol** *The king built (i.e. had himself built) a marble palace*
>
> **Me tuve que operar de apendicitis** *I had to have an operation for appendicitis*
>
> **Me peino en Vidal Sassoon** *I get my hair done at Vidal Sassoon's*

This construction is not used in some parts of Latin America, where **mandar** plus the Infinitive is used to express the idea of ordering something to be done: **mandó construir un palacio** *he had a palace built* (this construction is also possible in Spain).

■ With verbs meaning *eat, drink* or other types of consumption, *know, see, learn* and one or two others, to emphasize the quantity consumed, learned, seen, etc. This device is optional (but usual) and is only possible when a specific quantity is mentioned:

> **Me bebí tres vasos de ron** *I drank three glasses of rum*
>
> **Te has comido una pizza entera** *You've eaten a whole pizza*
>
> **Se leyó el libro entero** *He read the whole book*
>
> **Se lo creyó todo** *He believed every word of it*

Pronominal verbs with inanimate subjects (neither human nor animals)

In this case the verb can only be third-person (since stones, trees, etc. can't speak for themselves). The Pronominal form of the verb shows

■ That the verb has no outside subject (i.e. that the verb is Intransitive). Compare **abrió la puerta** *he/she opened the door* and **se abrió la puerta** *the door opened*.

> **Esta madera se está pudriendo** *This wood is going rotten*
> **El agua se ha enfriado** *The water's got cold*
> **Se le hinchó la mano** *His hand swelled up*

This construction does not apply to all verbs. Several non-pronominal verbs can also refer to more or less spontaneous actions (i.e. actions that have no external subject):

> **La situación ha mejorado** *The situation has improved*
> **El globo reventó** *The balloon burst*
> **La hierba ha crecido** *The grass has grown*
> **Las cantidades han aumentado** *The quantities have increased*

■ To make the passive. This is much more common with inanimate than with human and other animal subjects:

> **Se rehogan la cebolla y el ajo en aceite caliente** *The onion and garlic are sautéed/lightly fried in hot oil*
> **Se compran libros de ocasión** *Second-hand books bought*
> **Esas cosas no debieron decirse** *Those things shouldn't have been said*

> **Se acepta la propuesta de la oposición** *The opposition's proposal is accepted*

Three important points about this construction are:

(a) The verb should agree in number with the subject. Foreign students should respect this rule whatever they may hear or see: sentences like **'se compra libros de ocasión'* are usually considered incorrect.

(b) This construction should not be followed by **por** + the agent of the action. If the person or thing that performed the action must be mentioned, only the Passive with **ser** (p.64) can be used: **el programa fue diseñado por J. González** *the program* (British *programme*) *was designed by J. González* is correct and **'el programa se diseñó por J. González'* is generally considered to be bad Spanish.

(c) The noun in this construction cannot be replaced by a pronoun. In other words one cannot change **se solucionó el problema** *the problem was solved* into **'se lo solucionó'* for *it was solved*, which is **se solucionó**. Use of an object pronoun is only possible if the original sentence referred to a human being and included the preposition **a** (the construction described on p.70). The following examples should make this clear:

> **Se admira mucho** *a* **Cervantes** *Cervantes is admired a great deal*
>
> **Se** *le* **admira mucho** *He is admired a lot*
>
> **Su novela se publicó el año pasado** *His novel was published last year*
>
> **Se publicó el año pasado** *It was published last year*
>
> **Se** *le* **puede ver** *He/she can be seen*
>
> **Se puede ver** (or) **puede verse** *It can be seen*

Unclassifiable pronominal verbs (subject either animate or inanimate)

A number of Spanish pronominal verbs are unclassifiable. The pronominal form merely has an extra nuance of meaning and these verbs must be learned as separate items. This type of verb raises problems that are not appropriate for a grammar of this size, so the following list includes only a brief description of some frequently encountered forms:

Infinitive	*non-Pronominal*	*Pronominal*
aparecer	*to appear*	*to materialize* (ghosts, visions)
bajar	*to go down stairs* *drop* (prices, etc.)	*to get out of* *to get down from* (trees, etc.)
caer	*to fall/drop*	*to fall down/over*
conocer	*to know* (a person)	*to know only too well*
dejar	*to leave something*	*to leave behind accidentally*
devolver	*to give back, to vomit*	parts of Lat. Am. *to come back*
encontrar	*to find*	*to find by chance*
estar	*to be* (somewhere)	*to stay put in a place*
ir	*to go*	*to go away, leave*
llegar	*to arrive*	*to approach*
llevar	*to carry, wear*	*to take away*
marchar	*to march*	*to go away*
morir	*to die*	same, but used of loved ones or for lingering deaths
parecer	*to seem*	*to resemble*
pasar	*to pass* (by) *to spend time*	*to go over the mark*

Infinitive	*non-Pronominal*	*Pronominal*
regresar	to come back	to return before time (only Lat. Am.)
salir	to leave, exit (normally)	to walk out, (fluid, gas) to leak
subir	go up stairs rise (prices, temperature)	get in (cars, etc.) climb (trees, etc.)
volver	to come back (normally)	to turn back, return before time

In some cases the difference is more or less simply stylistic, the non-pronominal form being rather more formal:

> **Olvidé decírtelo/Me olvidé de decírtelo/Se me olvidó decírtelo** *I forgot to tell you*
> **Espera/Espérate** *Wait!*
> **Calla/Cállate** *Be quiet!*
> **(Me) gasté todo el dinero que traía** *I spent all the money I had*
> **(Se) inventa cada cuento . . .** *He makes up all sorts of stories . . .*

Often the pronominal form suggests an unplanned or accidental action. Compare

> **La lluvia cae del cielo** *Rain falls from the sky* (natural)
> **(Se) cayó de la mesa** *It fell off the table*
> **Me caí en la calle** *I fell over in the street*

Ser, estar and 'there is'/'there are'

Spanish has two words that both translate as *to be*. They can only rarely be used interchangeably

ESTAR

The verb **estar** must be used:

■ To indicate *where* an object or person is (but not where something is *happening*, in which case use **ser**, as explained below):

> **Madrid está en España** *Madrid's in Spain*
> **Dile que no estoy** *Tell him I'm not at home*
> **¿Dónde está la piscina[18]?** *Where's the swimming-pool?*

■ With adjectives and participles to show the state or condition that something or someone is in, not an inherent characteristic. The condition or state is usually temporary—but not always, as the word **muerto** shows:

> **Estoy cansado/deprimido/contento** *I'm tired/depressed/pleased*
> **Está muerto/vivo** *He's dead/alive*
> **La ventana estaba rota** *The window was broken*
> **Las manzanas están verdes** *The apples are unripe* (**las manzanas son verdes** = *apples are green*)

[18] **Piscina = la alberca** in much of Latin America.

> **Estoy con gripe** *I've got the flu*
> **Estoy bien** *I'm feeling fine*

Compare **la nieve está negra** *the snow's black* (because of the soot, dirt) and **la nieve es blanca** *snow is white* (its natural state), or **eres muy guapa** *you're very attractive* and **estás muy guapa** *you're **looking** very attractive*.

■ To show that someone's or something's condition has altered (e.g. since you last saw it):

> **Manuel está calvo** *Manuel has gone bald*
> **Me han dicho que estás casado** *They tell me you're married*
> **¡Qué delgada está!** *Hasn't she got thin!*

Use of **ser** implies something more long-standing: **es casado** *he's a married man*, **es delgada** *she's thin/a thin person*.

■ To describe the taste or appearance of something:

> **Esta sopa está muy buena/rica** *This soup tastes very good/appetizing*
> **Está muy vieja** *She's looking very old*

SER

Ser must be used

■ To link two nouns or a pronoun and a noun:

> **La cebolla es una planta** *The onion is a plant*
> **Mario es profesor** *Mario is a teacher*
> **Yo soy psicólogo** *I'm a psychologist*
> **Esto es un problema** *This is a problem*

The pronoun may be implicit in the verb:

> **Era un hermoso día** *It was a lovely day*
> **Son estudiantes** *They're students*
> **Son las ocho** *It's eight o'clock*

The verb **estar** + a Noun or Pronoun means *to be at home*, *to be there*:

> **Está Mario** *Mario's there*
> **No está** *He's not at home*

Exceptions to this rule are so rare that beginners can ignore them, although the phrase **está un día hermoso** *it's a lovely day* is commonly heard in Spain.

■ To indicate *where* or *when* an event is happening

> **¿Dónde es la fiesta/clase/conferencia?** *Where's the party/class/lecture (being held)?*
> **La Guerra Civil fue en 1936** *The Civil War was in 1936*

But **estar** must be used for location of a thing: **¿Dónde está la habitación?** *Where's the room?*

■ With adjectives and participles, to show that a quality is an intrinsic part of something's nature rather than its condition or state:

> **Soy americano** *I'm American*
> **Eso es diferente** *That's different*
> **Son míos** *They're mine*
> **Son muy grandes** *They're very tall/big*
> **La Tierra es redonda** *The earth is round*

It is true that in such cases **ser** usually refers to a *permanent* quality, compare **soy rubio** *I'm blond* and **estoy irritado** *I'm irritated*. But **muerto** *dead* takes **estar** and the following possibly temporary states take **ser** in standard Spanish:

> **Soy feliz/desgraciado** *I'm happy/unhappy*
> **Soy rico/pobre** *I'm rich/poor* (or **estoy rico/pobre** for a temporary condition)
> **Soy consciente** *I'm aware* (**estoy consciente** in Lat. America)

Note however the phrase **estoy feliz y contento** *I'm happy and contented*. **Estar feliz/desgraciado** is commonly heard in Latin America, but it is usually avoided in writing.

■ In the phrase **ser de** *to be from, to be made from*

> **Soy de Madrid** *I'm from Madrid*
> **Es de oro** *It's made of gold*

CHANGES OF MEANING WITH *SER* AND *ESTAR*

Some adjectives change meaning according to which verb is used:

Adjective	Meaning with **ser**	Meaning with **estar**
aburrido	boring	bored
bueno	good	tasty
cansado	tiresome	tired
consciente	aware	conscious (not knocked out)
despierto	sharp-witted	awake
interesado	self-seeking	interested
listo	clever/smart	ready
malo	bad	ill
orgulloso	proud/haughty	proud (of something)
rico	rich	delicious
verde	green/smutty	unripe
vivo	alert	alive

THERE IS/THERE ARE

The Spanish for *there is/are* is **hay**. This is a special form of the verb **haber**, and the usual forms of this verb are used for the other tenses of **hay**. When used with this meaning, the verb is always third-person and always singular (although use of the plural for *there were/will be*, e.g. **habían/habrán muchos** for **había/habrá muchos** *there were/will be a lot* is extremely common in spoken Latin-American Spanish and also in Castilian as spoken by Catalans. It should be avoided in writing and it is not accepted in Spain). Examples

> **Hay cinco árboles** *There are five trees*
> **Había varias personas** *There were several people*
> **Hubo una tremenda explosión** *There was a tremendous explosion*

■ When **haber** refers back to some noun already mentioned in the sentence it normally requires an object pronoun:

> **Hay un error, o si no *lo* hay, entonces estas cifras son increíbles** *There's a mistake, or if there isn't then these figures are incredible*

■ The basic meaning of **haber** is *exist*. If the meaning is *is there* (i.e. rather than somewhere else) the verb **estar** is used:

> **Está Antonio** *Antonio is there/There's Antonio*
> **Para eso está el diccionario** *That's what the dictionary is there for*

Compare

> **¿Quién hay que sepa ruso?** *Who is there (i.e. who exists) who knows Russian?*

Articles

THE DEFINITE ARTICLE

The four forms of the Spanish Definite Article (the equivalent of *the*) are:

	singular	*plural*
masculine	**el**	**los**
feminine	**la**	**las**

There is also a 'neuter article', **lo**, discussed on pp. 145 ff.

These words stand in front of a noun and agree in number and gender with it: **el hombre** *the man*, **los hombres** *the men*, **la ventana** *the window* (fem.), **las ventanas** *the windows*.

■ When a feminine noun begins with a stressed **a-** sound, the masculine article is used in the singular, but the noun remains feminine and the feminine articles, definite and indefinite, are used in the plural: **el/un águila** *the/an eagle*, but **las águilas** *the eagles*. The following are some common nouns beginning with stressed **a-** or **ha-**:

África	*Africa*
Asia	*Asia*
el agua	*water*
el/un alma	*soul*
el/un ama de casa	*housewife*
el asma	*asthma*
el hambre	*hunger*

el hampa	*criminal underworld*
el/un abra	*mountain pass* (Lat. Am., Spain **el puerto**)
el/un alza	*rise/increase*
el/un ancla	*anchor*
el/un área	*area*
el/un arma	*weapon*
el/un aula	*lecture room/seminar room*
el/un haba	*bean*
el/un habla	*language/speech form*
el/un hacha	*ax/*(British *axe*)
el/un hada	*fairy*
el/un haya	*beech tree*

If any word comes between these nouns and the article, the normal feminine form reappears: **el agua** *the* water, but *la* **misma agua** *the same water*. **La/una** is always used before *adjectives* beginning with stressed **a**: **la/una amplia área** *the/a wide area*.

Feminine words beginning with an *unstressed* **a-** sound take the normal feminine articles:

> **la/una amnistía** *the/an amnesty*
> **la/una hamaca** *the/a hammock*

La is used before letters of the alphabet beginning with stressed **a-**: **la a, la hache**.

■ **A** *to* and **el** compound to form **al**. **De** *of* and **el** compound to form **del**: **voy al mercado** *I'm going to market*, **vengo del banco** *I've just come from the bank*. This is not done if the article is part of a proper name: **los lectores de** *El País* *the readers of El País*, **vamos a El Paso** *we're going to El Paso*.

USES OF THE DEFINITE ARTICLE

Article usage is subtle, prone to exceptions and may vary slightly between regions, but the general rule is that the

Spanish Definite Article is used as in English except that:

■ It is required before countable nouns that are generalizations:

> **Las ardillas son animales** *Squirrels* (in general) *are animals*
> **Me gustan las fresas** *I like strawberries* (i.e. strawberries in general)

■ It is used before abstractions or substances in general when they are the subject or object of a verb or when they stand on their own:

> **la astronomía** *astronomy*
> **la democracia** *democracy*
> **el espacio** *space*
> **la gripe** *flu*
> **el oxígeno** *oxygen*
> **El odio destruye todo** *Hatred destroys everything*
> **Admiro la generosidad** *I admire generosity*

Such nouns often appear without the article after prepositions, especially when they are the second noun in the combination noun + **de** + noun and the English translation could be a compound noun (two nouns joined together): **una lección de filosofía** *a philosophy lesson*, **una carta de amor** *a love letter*, **una fábrica de pan** *a bread factory*.

The article is also not used with nouns describing abstractions and substances after **con** *with* and **sin** *without*: **con entusiasmo** *with enthusiasm*, **sin dinero** *without money*, **los españoles nunca comen nada sin pan** *the Spanish never eat anything without bread*.

■ Articles are omitted before quantities and abstractions that refer only to a part, not to the whole (partitive nouns):

> **Trae azúcar** *Bring some sugar*

> **No he puesto sal** *I haven't put any salt in*
> **Repartieron armas** *They distributed weapons*

See the section on Translation Traps for further remarks on the Spanish equivalents of *some* and *any*.

■ The Definite Article replaces Possessive Adjectives (**mi** *my*, **tu** *your*, **su** *his*, etc.) with parts of the body and with personal belongings, especially when these are the object of a verb or whenever an Indirect Object Pronoun identifies the owner:

> **Mario levantó la mano** *Mario raised his hand*
> **Le robaron la cartera** *They stole his/her note-book/wallet*
> **Yo me quité las botas** *I took off my boots*
> **Te torciste el tobillo** *You twisted your ankle*
> **Póngase el sombrero** *Put on your hat*

■ The article should be used before each noun when more than one occurs, whenever the nouns refer to different things or people:

> **el perro y el gato** *the dog and cat*
> **el padre y la madre de Antonio** *Antonio's father and mother*

but

> **el presidente y secretario del comité** *the chairman and secretary of the committee* (same person)

■ It is used before titles like **señor, señora, señorita**, but not when the person is directly addressed and not before foreign titles:

> **Buenos días, señor/señora Rodríguez** *Good morning Mr/Mrs Rodríguez*
> **Le dije buenos días al señor/a la señora Morán/a míster Brown** *I said Good Day to Sr/Sra Morán/to Mister Brown*

■ It is used before the names of a few countries. There is much disagreement on this matter, but students should note the following points:

(a) Always use the article when a country is modified by an adjective or some other word or phrase that does not form part of its official name: **la España contemporánea** *modern Spain*, **el México de los aztecas** *The Mexico of the Aztecs*, but **Gran Bretaña** *Great Britain*, **Corea del Norte** *North Korea*. The United States is either **Estados Unidos** (singular, the usual form) or **Los Estados Unidos** (plural):

> **Estados Unidos denuncia la actitud de Ruritania** or (less commonly) **Los Estados Unidos denuncian . . .** *USA denounces the attitude of Ruritania*

(b) Use the article with **la India** *India*, **el Reino Unido** *the United Kingdom* and **El Salvador**. The article is more often than not used with **el Líbano** *Lebanon* and, in Latin America, with **la Argentina**. It is also frequent in Latin America with **Perú, Ecuador, Paraguay, Uruguay, Brasil**.

■ It is used with names of languages, except after the verb **hablar** and, usually, after **aprender**: **el español es una lengua latina** *Spanish is a Latin language*, **domina el chino** *he's totally fluent in Chinese*, but **hablo/aprendo inglés** *I speak/am learning English*.

■ The article is used with days of the week and seasons (but not after **en**):

> **Viene los lunes** *He comes on Mondays*
> **Las hojas caen durante el otoño** *The leaves fall during Fall/Autumn*
> **El invierno es la peor estación** *Winter is the worst season*

but

> **En invierno nieva mucho** *It snows a lot in Winter*

■ It is used before the names of streets and squares:

> **Vivo en la Plaza de España** *I live in the Plaza de España*
> **un pequeño hotel de la calle de las Monjas** *a little hotel on Nuns' street*

■ It is used before percentages:

> **El cinco por ciento de los mexicanos . . .** *five percent of Mexicans*

■ It is omitted before the second of two nouns joined by **de** when these form a compound noun. Compare:

> **una voz de mujer** *a woman's voice*
> **la voz de la mujer** *the voice of the woman*
>
> **el agua de manantial** *spring water*
> **el agua del manantial** *the water from the spring*

THE INDEFINITE ARTICLE

The forms of the Spanish Definite Article (the equivalent of *a/an*) are:

	singular	plural
masculine	**un**	**unos**
feminine	**una**	**unas**

Un is used before feminine nouns beginning with stressed **a**, e.g. **un arma** *a weapon,* **un área** *an area.* See p.82.

The Indefinite Article is used in much the same way as its English counterpart, except that:

■ It is omitted after **ser,** and after verbs meaning *to become,* before the names of professions and, often, before words denoting sex:

> **Es profesora** *She's a teacher*
> **Quiere hacerse diplomático** *He wants to become a diplomat*
> **No digo eso sólo porque yo sea mujer** *I don't say that just because I'm a woman*

But it is retained if the noun is qualified or modified by some word or phrase:

> **Es un profesor magnífico** *He's a magnificent teacher*
> **Es una mujer inteligente** *She's an intelligent woman*

■ It is omitted after **tener** *to have*, **llevar** *to wear*, **sacar** *to take out* and a few other common verbs, when the direct object is something of which we usually only have one:

> **Tiene mujer/secretaria/paraguas** *He's got a wife/secretary/umbrella*
> **Mi casa tiene jardín y garaje** *My house has a garden and garage*
> **Busca novia** *He's looking for a girlfriend*
> **Lleva corbata** *He's wearing a tie*

but **tengo un dólar** *I've got a dollar*, **tengo una hermana** *I've got a sister* (because in both cases it would be normal to have more than one). But the article reappears if the noun is qualified: **lleva *una* corbata de seda** *he's wearing a silk tie*, **tiene *una* mujer muy atractiva**[19] *he has a very attractive wife*.

■ It is usually omitted after **sin** *without*, **con** *with* and **como** when it means *for/as*:

---

[19] **Guapo/guapa** is the usual word in Spain for *good-looking*, but it tends to mean *brave/tough* in Latin America, where **buen mozo/buena moza** is often used for *good-looking*. **Atractivo** is used internationally.

un sobre sin estampilla (Spain sin sello) *an envelope without a stamp*
un hombre con pasaporte *a man with a passport*
Me lo dio como regalo *He gave it to me as a present*
Ha venido como asesor *He's come as an adviser*

But it is used before **con** when it means *accompanied by*:
ha venido con un amigo *he's come with a friend*.

■ It is not used before **otro** *another*, or after **qué** *what*, **medio** *half* and **tal** *such a*:

Hay otra película que quiero ver *There's another movie/film I want to see*
¡Qué pena! *What a pity!*
medio kilo *half a kilo*
tal día *such a day*

■ It is used with percentages:

Los precios subieron en un cinco por ciento *Prices rose five percent*

USES OF *UNOS/UNAS*

Spanish is unusual in that the Indefinite Article has a plural form. This is used:

■ To mean *approximately*

Trajeron unos mil kilos *They brought about 1000 kilos*

■ To mean *a/an* before nouns that do not appear in the singular, or to mean *a pair of* before nouns like *scissors, shoes, pants* that either come in pairs or are symmetrically shaped:

unos zapatos de cuero *a pair of leather shoes*
unas tijeras *a pair of scissors*

unos pantalones *a pair of pants* (Brit. *trousers*)

In the case of nouns that always appear in the plural, e.g. **los celos** *jealousy*, **las vacaciones** *vacation/holidays*, **las ganas** *urge/desire*, and before nouns that would mean a profession if the Indefinite Article were omitted, **unos/unas** must be used whenever **un/una** would be used before a singular noun:

unas vacaciones magníficas *a magnificent vacation/holiday*

Yo tenía unas ganas terribles *I had a terrible urge*

Sentía unos celos incontrolables *She/he felt an uncontrollable jealousy*

Sois/son unos payasos *You're a bunch of clowns (in the way you act)*

Compare

Sois/son payasos *You're clowns* (profession).

■ To mean *a few, a couple of*:

Me dejó unos libros *He left/lent me a few books*

Dale unas pesetas *Give him a couple of pesetas*

Unas veces sí, otras no *Sometimes yes, others no*

Nouns

GENDER OF NOUNS

Spanish nouns are either masculine or feminine and
this has major consequences for the shape of any adjectives,
articles or pronouns that may be associated with a noun.

The gender of nouns is not related to questions of sex,
except when the nouns refer to human beings or to a few
well-known animals. There are few absolutely foolproof
rules for predicting the gender of the other nouns in the
language, so the best rule is to learn every noun with its
definite article, which will soon become instinctive. It
must be remembered that the grammatical gender of
nouns referring to objects and abstractions is basically
arbitrary and has nothing to with their meaning. The fact
that **el árbol** *tree* is masculine in Spanish is arbitrary:
'tree' is femininc in the closely-related languages
Portuguese and French.

The following generalizations can be made:

■ Nouns referring to men or boys are masculine, and
nouns referring to women or girls are feminine:

el hombre *man*	**la mujer** *woman*
el modelo *male model*	**la modelo** *female model*
el juez *male judge*	**la juez** *female judge*

This generalization also applies to a few domestic and

well-known wild animals that have special forms to denote the female of the species:

el caballo *horse*	**la yegua** *mare*
el león *lion*	**la leona** *lioness*
el toro *bull*	**la vaca** *cow*

A longer list of these words appears below at p.97.

There are only a few words that are of invariable gender and apply to human beings of either sex, e.g.:

el bebé *baby*
el genio *genius*
el personaje *character* (in film, etc.),
la estrella *star* (in films, etc.)
la persona *person*
la víctima *victim*
la visita *visitor* (and *visit*)

■ Apart from those already mentioned and few others like **el lobo/la loba** *wolf/she-wolf*, **el gato/la gata** *tom-cat/she-cat*, **el perro/la perra** *dog/bitch*, the names of animals are of fixed arbitrary gender. The gender of these nouns must be learned separately from the dictionary:

la ardilla *squirrel*
el avestruz *ostrich*
la culebra *grass snake*
el lagarto *lizard*
la langosta *lobster*
el salmón *salmon*

The invariable words **macho** *male* and **hembra** *female* can be added if necessary:

el salmón hembra *the female salmon*
las ardillas macho *the male squirrels*

■ Nouns referring to inanimate things (and to plants) are of fixed gender. As was mentioned before, the gender of these words cannot be deduced from the meaning of the word: compare **el cuarto** (masculine) and **la habitación** (feminine) which both mean *room*.

However, the ending of a Spanish nouns that does not refer to a human being often gives a clue to the likely gender of a word:

■ Nouns ending in **-o** are masculine, e.g. **el libro** *book*, **el hombro** *shoulder*. Common exceptions are:

> **la foto** *photo*
> **la libido** *libido*
> **la mano** *hand*
> **la moto** *motor-cycle*
> **la radio** *radio* (in Spain and Argentina, but masculine in northern Latin America)

■ Nouns ending in **-r** are masculine, except **la flor** *flower*, **la coliflor** *cauliflower*, **la labor** *labor*/(Brit. *labour*):

> **el bar** *bar*
> **el calor** *heat*
> **el color** *color/colour*
> **el valor** *value*

■ Nouns ending in a stressed vowel are masculine:

> **(el) Canadá** *Canada*
> **el bisturí** *scalpel*
> **el tisú** *tissue*
> **el sofá** *sofa/couch*

■ Nouns ending in **-aje** are masculine:

> **el viaje** *journey*
> **el equipaje** *baggage*
> **el paisaje** *landscape*

■ Nouns ending in **-ie** are feminine:

> **la intemperie** *bad weather*
> **la serie** *series*

■ Other nouns ending in **-e** are unpredictable and must be learned separately:

> **el arte** (masculine) *art*
> **las artes** (feminine) *the arts*
> **la fuente** *fountain*
> **el puente** *bridge*
> **la parte** *part*
> **el parte** *bulletin*

■ Nouns ending in **-a** are feminine, with the important exceptions listed at (a) through (c) below:

> **la cama** *bed*
> **la casa** *house*
> **la mariposa** *butterfly*
> **la pera** *pear*

Exceptions:

(a)   **el alerta** *alert*
> **el cometa** *comet*
> **el día** *day*
> **el insecticida** *insecticide*
> **el mañana** *the morrow/tomorrow* (cf. **la mañana** *morning*)
> **el mapa** *map*
> **el mediodía** *noon*
> **el planeta** *planet*
> **el tranvía** *street-car/tram*
> **el vodka** *vodka*
> **el yoga** *yoga*

(b) Compound nouns consisting of a verb + a noun:

> **el montacargas** *freight elevator/service lift*
> **el guardarropa** *check room/cloakroom*

(c) Words ending in **-ma** that are of Greek origin. These are usually words that have a faintly technical or 'intellectual' character, e.g.

el aroma *aroma*
el clima *climate*
el coma *coma*
el crucigrama *crossword puzzle*
el diagrama *diagram*
el dilema *dilemma*
el diploma *diploma*
el dogma *dogma*
el enigma *enigma*
el esquema *scheme*
el fantasma *ghost*
el panorama *panorama*
el pijama *pajamas/pyjamas* (feminine in Latin America)
el plasma *plasma*
el poema *poem*
el problema *problem*
el programa *program/programme*
el síntoma *symptom*
el sistema *system*
el telegrama *telegram*
el tema *theme/topic/subject*

Words that end in **-ma** and are not of Greek origin are feminine, e.g. **la cama** *bed*, **la forma** *shape*, **la lima** *lime* (the fruit) or *file* (i.e. for wood or fingernails). Two words that are of Greek origin but are nevertheless feminine are **la lágrima** *tear* (i.e. the sort that one weeps) and **la estratagema** *stratagem*.

■ Nouns ending in **-tad, -dad** and **-tud** are feminine:

la ciudad *city*
la libertad *liberty*
la verdad *truth*
la virtud *virtue*

■ Nouns ending in **-ción** are feminine:

> la **intuición** *intuition*
> la **nación** *nation*
> la **reproducción** *reproduction*

■ Nouns ending in **-is** are feminine:

> la **tesis** *thesis*
> la **crisis** *crisis*
> la **apendicitis** *appendicitis*

Exceptions: **el análisis** *analysis*, **el énfasis** *emphasis*, **el éxtasis** *ecstasy*, **el oasis** *oasis*, **los paréntesis** *brackets*.

■ Feminine words beginning with *stressed* **a-** or **ha-** take the masculine definite article in the singular despite always being feminine in gender: **el agua** *water*, **el alma** *soul*. See p. 82 for discussion.

■ Some words have different meanings according to gender:

el **capital** *capital (money)*	la **capital** *capital (city)*
el **cólera** *cholera*	la **cólera** *wrath/anger*
el **coma** *coma*	la **coma** *comma*
el **cometa** *comet*	la **cometa** *kite* (the sort you fly)
el **corte** *cut*	la **corte** *the Court*
el **cura** *priest*	la **cura** *cure*
el **editorial** *editorial*	la **editorial** *publishing house*
el **frente** *front (military)*	la **frente** *forehead*
el **guardia** *policeman*	la **guardia** *guard*
el **mañana** *tomorrow/morrow*	la **mañana** *morning*
el **margen** *margin*	la **margen** *riverbank*
el **orden** *order* (opposite of *disorder*)	la **orden** *order* (=*command* or *religious order*)
el **Papa** *Pope*	la **papa** (Lat. Am.) *potato*[20]
el **parte** *bulletin*	la **parte** *part*

[20] The word used in Spain is **la patata**.

el **pendiente** *earring*	la **pendiente** *slope*
el **pez** *fish*	la **pez** *pitch (i.e. tar)*
el **policía** *policeman*	la **policía** *police force*
el **radio** *radius/radium*	la **radio** *radio* (masc. from Colombia northwards)

FORMS OF NOUNS REFERRING TO FEMALES

The following remarks apply to nouns referring to female human beings and to those few animals for which there is a special word denoting the female.

■ There are special words for the female of some persons and animals:

el **actor**/la **actriz** *actor/actress*
el **alcalde**/la **alcaldesa** *mayor/mayoress*
el **caballo**/la **yegua** *stallion/mare*
el **macho**/el **cabrío** *billy-goat* la **cabra** *she-goat*
el **carnero**/la **oveja** *ram/ewe (sheep)*
el **conde**/la **condesa** *count/countess*
el **duque**/la **duquesa** *duke/duchess*
el **emperador**/la **emperatriz** *emperor/empress*
el **gallo**/la **gallina** *rooster/hen (chicken)*
el **héroe**/la **heroína** *hero/heroine*
el **león**/la **leona** *lion/lioness*
el **marido**/la **mujer** *husband/wife*[21] or *woman*
el **padre**/la **madre** *father/mother*
el **príncipe**/la **princesa** *prince/princess*
el **rey**/la **reina** *king/queen*
el **toro**/la **vaca** *bull/cow*
el **yerno**/la **nuera** *son-in-law/daughter-in-law*

[21] In Latin America el **esposo**/la **esposa** should be used for *husband/wife*, the word **mujer** being reserved for *woman*.

el varón/la hembra *male/female*[22]

With the exception of **la oveja** *sheep/ewe*, **la gallina** *chicken/hen*, **la cabra** *goat/she-goat* and **el toro** *bull*[23], the masculine form of words referring to humans and animals also refers to mixed groups or the species in general:

> **los reyes** *kings/the king and queen/kings* and *queens*
> **los hermanos** *brothers/brothers and sisters*
> **los padres** *fathers/parents*
> **los tíos** *uncles/uncles and aunts*
> **los zorros** *male foxes/foxes*

■ With the exceptions shown, words referring to females are formed from the words referring to males in various ways, according to the ending:

> **-és > -esa**
> **el francés—la francesa** *Frenchman/woman*
> **el inglés—la inglesa** *Englishman/woman*
>
> **-o > -a**
> **el abogado—la abogada** *lawyer*
> **el americano—la americana** *American*
> **el cerdo** *pig*—**la cerda** *sow*
> **el gitano** *gypsy*—**la gitana** *gypsy woman*
> **el perro** *dog*—**la perra** *bitch*
> **el psicólogo—la psicóloga** *psychologist*

Exceptions: **el/la miembro** *member*, **el/la modelo** *model*, **el/la soldado** *soldier*, **el/la piloto** *pilot, racing driver*.

---

[22] **Varón** is a polite word for *male*. **Macho** is used for animals and, pejoratively, for the type of man who tries to dominate women.

[23] **Las vacas** = *cows*. *Cattle* is **el ganado vacuno**. **El ganado** includes cows, horses, sheep, donkeys and pigs, and can be made specific with adjectives like **caballar** (horses), **lanar** (sheep), **menor** (sheep, goats, pigs), etc. These terms are rather technical in style.

-**a** no change

> **el artista—la artista** *artist*
> **el belga—la belga** *Belgian*

-**í** no change

> **el iraní—la iraní** *Iranian*
> **el marroquí—la marroquí** *Moroccan*

-**e** usually no change, but a few change -**e** to -**a** (although the invariable forms are common and are more formal in style) :

> **el estudiante—la estudiante** *student*
> **el amante—la amante** *lover*
> **el principiante—la principianta** *beginner*

-**ón** > -**ona**

> **el preguntón—la preguntona** *inquisitive person*
> **el campeón—la campeona** *champion*
> **el león—la leona** *lioness*

Some words denoting professions tend to be invariable in formal language, especially in Spain, but they may form their feminine with -**a** in informal speech, although usage is at present in flux. The formal form is safer and is felt to be more respectful:

masculine	*formal/informal fem.*
el jefe *boss*	**la jefe/la jefa**
el juez *judge*	**la juez/la jueza**
el médico *doctor*	**la médico/la médica**
el primer ministro *prime minister*	**la primer ministro/la primera ministra**
el arquitecto *architect*	**la arquitecto/la arquitecta**
el sargento *sergeant*	**la sargento/la sargenta**

PLURAL OF NOUNS

The plural of Spanish nouns is formed as follows:

■ Nouns ending in an unstressed vowel or in stressed **e** add **-s**:

la **casa** *house*	las **casas** *houses*
el **libro** *book*	los **libros** *books*
el **puente** *bridge*	los **puentes** *bridges*
la **tribu** *tribe*	las **tribus** *tribes*
el **café** *coffee*	los **cafés** *coffees*
el **té** *tea*	los **tés** *teas*

■ Nouns ending in a stressed vowel other than **-e** add **-es**:

el **iraní** *Iranian*	los **iraníes** *Iranians*
el **marroquí** *Moroccan*	los **marroquíes** *Moroccans*
el **tabú** *taboo*	los **tabúes** *taboos*

Exceptions:

el **menú** *menu*	los **menús** *menus*
el **papá** *father*	los **papás** *fathers*
el **sofá** *sofa*	los **sofás** *sofas*
el **tisú** *paper tissue*	los **tisús** *tissues*
la **mamá** *mother*	las **mamás** *mothers*

There is a growing tendency in informal spoken language to make the plural of all nouns ending in a stressed vowel by simply adding **-s**.

■ Nouns ending in a consonant add **-es**:

el **inglés** *Englishman*	los **ingleses** *Englishmen*
la **nación** *nation*	las **naciones** *nations*
la **red** *net/network*	las **redes** *nets/networks*

As the examples show, an accent written on a vowel disappears after **-es** is added, unless the vowel is **í** or **ú**:

    el baúl *trunk (for storage)*   **los baúles** *trunks*
    el país *country*   **los países** *countries*

Nouns whose singular ends in -**en** require an accent on the second vowel from last in the plural to show that the stress has not shifted:

    la imagen *image*   **las imágenes** *images*
    el origen *origin*   **los orígenes** *origins*
    la virgen *virgin*   **las vírgenes** *virgins*

■ Many recent foreign borrowings add -s in the plural even though they end with a consonant:

    el bit *bit* (in computing) **los bits** *bits*
    el iceberg *iceberg*   **los icebergs** *the icebergs*
    el show *show*   **los shows** *shows*

■ The following do not change in the plural:

  (a) Nouns whose singular ends in an *unstressed* vowel + -**s**:

    la crisis *crisis*   **las crisis** *crises*
    el lunes *Monday*   **los lunes** *Mondays*
    el miércoles *Wednesday* **los miércoles**
                                    Wednesdays
    la tesis *thesis*   **las tesis** *theses*

  (b) Nouns ending in -**x**:

    el fax *fax*   **los fax** *faxes*

  (c) A few foreign words which must be learned separately:

    el déficit *deficit*   **los déficit** *deficits*
    el láser *laser*   **los láser** *lasers*

■ In the case of compound nouns consisting of two nouns, only the first noun is pluralized:

    el año luz *light year*   **los años luz** *light*
                                       years

el hombre rana *frogman*	**los hombres rana** *frogmen*
el perro guía *guide-dog*	**los perros guía** *guide-dogs*
la ciudad estado *city-state*	**las ciudades estado** *city-states*
la idea clave *key idea*	**las ideas clave** *key ideas*

One important exception is **el país miembro—los países miembros** *member country/member countries.*

■ The following plurals are irregular:

Three nouns show a shift in the position of the accent:

el carácter *character*	**los caracteres** *characters*
el espécimen *specimen*	**los especímenes** *specimens*
el régimen *regimes*	**los regímenes** *regimes*

The plural of the word **lord** *lord* (British title) is **los lores** *lords.*

COLLECTIVE NOUNS

Collective Nouns (see Glossary) are treated as singular, whereas familiar English often treats them as plural.

La minoría votó por el partido nacionalista *The minority voted for the nationalist party*
La mayoría es cristiana *The majority are christian*
El público se está irritando *The audience are/is getting irritated*
El pueblo está descontento *The people are discontented*
La policía es . . . *The police are . . .*

This applies even to collective numerals (see p.196 for more details):

> **Un billón de pesetas fue invertido** *A billion[24] pesetas were invested*
> **La primera treintena** *the first thirty or so*

However, plural agreement is optionally possible when a singular collective noun and a plural non-collective noun are joined by **de**:

> **Una treintena de personas perdieron** (or **perdió**) **la vida**
> **La mayoría de los indígenas son católicos** *The majority of the natives are Catholics*

---

[24] A million million in Spain. The American billion (1000 million) is much used in Latin America.

Personal Pronouns

FORMS OF PERSONAL PRONOUNS

Spanish Personal Pronouns can take different forms depending on Person (1st, 2nd or 3rd), Number (singular or plural) and grammatical function (Subject, Prepositional or Object). In the case of second-person pronouns, there are also different forms depending on the degree of familiarity.

SUBJECT PRONOUNS

yo	*I*
tú	*you* (familiar)
vos	*you* (familiar, Argentina and Central America; see below)
usted	*you* (formal)
él	*he/it*

ella	*she/it*
ello	*it* (neuter gender, explained on p.145)
nosotros	*we* (masculine or masc. and feminine mixed)
nosotras	*we* (feminine only)
vosotros	*you* (familiar, masculine or masc. and feminine mixed. Spain only)
vosotras	*you* (familiar, feminine only. Spain only)
ustedes	*you* (plural. Only formal use in Spain, both formal and familiar in Latin America)
ellos	*they* (masculine or masc. and feminine mixed)
ellas	*they* (feminine only)

Nosotros *we* (object form **nos**) is used to refer to male persons or to males and females mixed. **Nosotras** is used by females when referring to themselves and other females. See below for **vosotros/vosotras**.

OBJECT PRONOUNS

me	*me*
te	*you* (for **tú** or **vos**)
lo	*him/it/you* (**usted**) masculine Direct Object only
la	*her/it/you* (**usted**) feminine Direct Object only
le	*her/it/you* (**usted**) masculine or feminine Indirect Object
nos	*us*
os	*you* informal plural, Spain only
los	*them/you* (**ustedes**) masculine or mixed masc. and fem. Direct Object
las	*them* feminine Direct Object
les	*them/you* (**ustedes**) masculine or feminine Indirect Objects only

> **se**   3rd-person reflexive pronoun, singular or
>   plural, discussed on pp.66 ff

Masculine plural pronouns are always used for groups of people or objects when at least one of them is masculine: **hay dos profesores y treinta profesoras. *Los* he contado** *there are two male teachers and thirty female. I counted them.*

Le and **les** become **se** whenever they precede **lo, la, los** or **las**: see p.114 for details.

Usted and **ustedes** take third-person object pronouns, so **yo la vi ayer** can mean *I saw her/it yesterday* or *I saw you yesterday.* Adding **a usted** or **a ustedes** removes any ambiguity in this case and also makes the form even more formal and polite—**yo las vi a ustedes** *I saw you* (plural)—but it is rarely necessary to do this since context normally makes the meaning clear.

PREPOSITIONAL FORMS OF PERSONAL PRONOUNS

Only the first and second-person singular Personal Pronouns and the so-called 'reflexive' pronoun **se** have special forms, used after most prepositions:

> **de/a/por mí**[25] *of/to/by me*
> **para/contra ti** (no accent!) *for/against you*
> **de sí mismo/de sí misma** *of himself/of herself*

When the preposition is **con** a special form is used:

> **conmigo** *with me*: **ven conmigo** *come with me*
> **contigo** *with you*: **fue contigo** *he/she went with you*
> **consigo** *with himself/herself/yourself/themselves/*
> *yourselves*: **llevan el dinero consigo** *they're*
> *carrying the money on them(selves)*

For the rest of the pronouns the ordinary subject forms

[25] The accent distinguishes it from **mi** *my*.

are used: **contra él/ella/usted** *against him/her/you*, **de nosotros/vosotros/ustedes/ellos/ellas** *of us/you/them*, **con ellos/ustedes** *with them/you*.

The ordinary subject forms **yo** and **tú** are also used after **entre** *between* (**entre tú y yo** *between you and me*), **según** *according to* (**según tú** *according to you*), **excepto**, **menos** and **salvo** *except* (i.e. **excepto tú, menos yo** *except you, except me*), **hasta** when it means *even* (and not *as far as* or *up to*), and **incluso** *even*.

SUBJECT PRONOUNS

These pronouns are required only in special circumstances since Spanish verbs already include their subject pronouns in the ending: **fumo** means *I smoke, I'm smoking*, **fuiste** means *you went*. **Yo fumo** means *I* (and not someone else) *smoke*, **tú fuiste** means *you* (and not someone else) *went*. The pronouns must therefore not be used unnecessarily: '*****¿Sabes lo que le ha pasado a Ana? *Ella* se ha roto el brazo**' *Do you know what's happened to Ana? She's broken her arm* does not make good sense in Spanish because it wrongly stresses the *she*; the **ella** must be deleted. The subject pronouns are used

■ When there is a switch from one pronoun to another, as in

> **Yo estoy aquí todo el día trabajando mientras que tú no haces nada** *I'm here all day working while* ***you*** *do nothing*
>
> **Te confundiste. Yo soy Juan. Él es Antonio** *You made a mistake. I'm Juan.* ***He's*** *Antonio*

Sometimes the switch is implied rather than explicit **yo sé la respuesta** *I know the answer* (implies *but you don't/he doesn't, etc.*).

■ When the subject pronoun stands in isolation (i.e. without a verb):

> —¿**Quién va con Pedro?** —**Yo** *'Who's going with Pedro?' 'Me'*
>
> —¿**Quién fue el primero?** —**Tú y ella** *'Who was first?' 'You and her'*

■ In the case of all pronouns except **yo, tú** and **se**, after prepositions (see above).

■ In the case of **usted** and **ustedes**, from time to time in order to be emphatically polite:

> **No se olvide usted de que tiene que estar aquí mañana a las ocho en punto** *Please don't forget that you must be here tomorrow at eight o'clock sharp*

FORMAL AND INFORMAL MODES OF ADDRESS

■ **Tú** (and the corresponding object and prepositional forms **te** and **ti**) is used to address anyone with whom one is on first-name terms, e.g. relatives, friends, colleagues, children, and also animals. The only exception to the rule about first names might be employees with whom one is not on familiar terms: **Antonia, haga el favor de preparar la cena** *Antonia, please prepare dinner* (speaking to a cook or maid).

Spanish **tú** is used much more widely than French **vous** or German **Sie**: Spaniards under about forty use it even to total strangers of their own age or younger, but it should not be used to older strangers or persons in authority. Latin Americans are generally less ready to use **tú** than Spaniards.

■ **Vos** (object form **te**, possessive adjective **tu**, prepositional form **vos**) is used instead of **tú** in many parts of Latin America, but the only places where this usage is accepted as correct by all social groups are Argentina and most of Central America (but not Mexico). **Vos** tends to be considered 'unrefined' elsewhere in Latin America (if it is used at all), and it is not heard in Spain.

■ **Vosotros** (and the object form **os**) is used only in Spain to address more than one person when one normally addresses them individually as **tú**. Two or more females are addressed as **vosotras**. Latin Americans use **ustedes** (see below).

■ **Usted** (object forms **lo/la/le**) is used everywhere to address strangers, especially older strangers, and persons in authority. It is always used for people with whom one is not on first-name terms. The verb is always in the third-person singular.

Ustedes (object forms **los/las/les**) is used in Latin America to address two or more people, regardless of one's relationship with them. Latin-Americans use it for small children and even for animals. In Spain it is used to address two persons whom one normally addresses individually as **usted**. The verb is always in the third-person plural.

OBJECT PRONOUNS

The object forms have two basic functions:

(a) To denote the Direct Object (see Glossary) of an action

> **Me criticaron** *They criticized me*
> **Me llamó** *He/she/you called me*
> **Te admiran** *They admire you*
> **No lo sé** *I don't know it*
> **Nos persiguen** *They're persecuting us,*
> **Él os respeta** (Lat. Am. **Él los/las respeta**) *He respects you* (plural)

(b) To denote the Indirect Object (see Glossary) of an action

> **Le dicen** *They say to him/her/you*
> **Usted les mandó una carta** *You sent a letter to them*
> **Dame algo** *Give me something*
> **Dile** *Tell him/her*
> **Nos dice** *He says to us*
> **Os envían** *They send to you* (i.e. **a vosotros**)
> **Les da dinero** *He gives money to them* (or *to you* = **a ustedes**)

It should be noted that the term *Indirect Object* includes not only the meaning *to . . .* but also *from* after verbs meaning removal or taking off/away from, and in some cases it can be translated *for*:

> **Me compró una camisa** *He bought a shirt off me* (or *for me*)
> **Les confiscaron el dinero que llevaban** *They confiscated (i.e. took off them) the money they were carrying*
> **Me robaron cien dólares** *They stole $100 from me*
> **Te escribiré el ensayo** *I'll write the essay for you*

Object Pronouns are also used to show the person affected by something done to his/her body or to some intimate possession:

> **Me sacó una muela** *He took one of my teeth out*
> **Te vas a romper una uña** *You're going to break a finger-nail*
> **Le has manchado la falda** *You've stained her skirt*

The third-person pronouns used for the Indirect Object are unusual in that they differ from the corresponding Third-Person Direct Object Pronouns:

3rd-Person Direct Object Forms

Lo vieron *They saw him/it/you* **(usted)**
La vieron *They saw her/it/you* **(usted)**
Los vieron *They saw them/you* (masculine)
Las vieron *They saw them/you* (feminine)

3rd-Person Indirect Object Forms

Le dijeron *They said **to** him/her/you*
Les dijeron *They said **to** them/you*
Le torcieron el brazo *They twisted his/her/your
  arm*
Le/les have no separate feminine form.

FURTHER REMARKS ON THE USE OF *LE* AND *LES*

The relationship between **le/les** and **lo/la/los/las** is rather
complicated, since **le** and **les** are quite often used as *Direct*
Object pronouns as well as for Indirect Objects. This happens:

■ In Central and Northern Spain, and in the standard
written language of Spain, when the pronoun refers to a
human male and is singular:

> **Le vimos** *We saw **him*** (elsewhere **lo vimos**)
> **Lo vimos** *We saw **it***

Le is usual among the 'best' speakers in Spain (academ-
ics, schoolteachers, newsreaders, editors of quality publications, most writers), but the Academy in fact prefers **lo
vimos** for both *we saw him* and *we saw it*. The **lo** construction is slowly spreading in Spain and is easier for
beginners to remember. In Northern Spain one constantly
also hears **le/les** used for human female direct objects (i.e.
instead of **la**), but this is not approved usage.

Use of **les** for plural human direct objects is also very
common in speech in central and northern Spain and is
seen in writing in Spain, but it is not approved by the

Academy and other authorities; **los/las** should be used:
los vi ayer *I saw them (masc.) yesterday*, **las vi ayer** *I saw them (fem.) yesterday*.

■ With the following common verbs: (the list is not exhaustive)

> **creer** *to believe* (when its object is human): **yo le creo** *I believe him/her*
> **disgustar** *to displease*
> **gustar** *to please*: **les gusta** *they like it*
> **importar** *to matter to* . . .
> **interesar** *to interest*
> **llenar** when it means *fulfill* (British *fulfil*) in sentences like **ser ama de casa no le llena** *being a housewife doesn't fulfill her*. Compare **lo/la llena** *he fills it up*.
> **pegar** *to beat*: **su marido le pega mucho** *her husband beats her a lot*

■ **Le/les** are also preferred for third-person *human* direct objects in a number of other constructions, and in most parts of the Spanish-speaking world, although this topic is rather advanced for a grammar of this type. The most common cases are:

> (a) Optionally (but usually) after Impersonal **se**:
>
> **Se le** (or **lo**) **reconoció** *He was recognized*
>
> (b) Optionally when the direct object is **usted(es)** (but **lo/las/los/las** are also correct). Latin-American speakers from some regions may, for example, say
>
> **Perdone, señor, no quería molestar***le* *Excuse me, sir, I didn't want to bother you*

even though they would use **lo** in other contexts.

> (c) Often when the subject of the verb is non-human and non-animal. Compare

>> ***Le* espera una catástrofe** *A catastrophe awaits her*

and

>> ***La* espera su hermana** *Her sister is waiting for her*

Usage fluctuates in some of these cases, especially in Latin America. Colombians especially tend to prefer **lo/la/los/las** where others may use **le**.

ORDER AND POSITION OF OBJECT PRONOUNS

When two or more object pronouns appear in a sentence there are strict rules governing their order and their position in relation to the verb.

>The order of object pronouns is:

>| | | | |
>|----|----|----|---------|
>| se | te | me | le lo/la |
>| os | nos | les los/las | |

In other words, **se** (discussed on p.66 ff) always comes first, **te/os** always precedes all the rest, **me/nos** always precedes any pronoun beginning with **l**, and **le/les** precedes **lo/la/los/las** (and then becomes **se** as explained after the examples).

This order applies whether the pronouns appear before the verb or as suffixes:

>> **Te lo dijo** *He told it to you*
>> **Os la entregaron** *They delivered it to you*, Lat. Am. **Se lo entregaron**
>> **No te me pongas difícil** *Don't get difficult 'on me'*
>> **Me lo enseñó** *He showed it to me*
>> **Nos los enviaron** *They sent them to us*
>> **Se te dijo** *It was said to you* (see p.73)
>> **Se lo comuniqué a usted** *I informed you*
>> **Quiero regalártelo** *I want to present it to you/make a present of it to you*

No pueden dárnoslo *They can't give it to us*

Note: Whenever **le** or **les** immediately precede **lo, la, los** or **las, le/les** become **se**. This is the so-called 'rule of two l's': two Spanish object pronouns beginning with **l** can *never* stand side-by-side:

Se lo dije (never *'*le lo dije') *I told him/her/you/them*
Se los dieron (never *'*les los dieron') *They gave them to him/her/you/them*

The overworked pronoun **se** can therefore (among other things) stand for **a él** *to him*, **a ella** *to her*, **a usted** *to you*, **a ellos** *to them* (masc.), **a ellas** *to them* (fem.) and **a ustedes** *to you* (plural). Usually context makes the meaning clear, but if real ambiguity arises one adds one of the phrases just listed:

Se lo dije a ella *I told **her***
Se lo quité a ellos *I took it off/from **them*** (masc.)
Se lo daré a ustedes *I'll give it to **you***

These additional phrases should not be used unless emphasis or clarity are absolutely essential.

Familiar Latin-American speech very frequently shows that **se** stands for **les** and not **le** by adding **-s** to the Direct Object pronoun: **se** *los* **dije** = **se lo dije a ellos/ellas/ustedes** *I told it to them/you*. This is not accepted in written Spanish and is not heard in Spain.

POSITION OF OBJECT PRONOUNS

Object Personal Pronouns are placed:

■ *Before* all finite verb forms (i.e. forms other than the Gerund and Infinitive) *except* the positive Imperative. The pronouns appear in the order given above. No word can come between the pronouns and the verb:

Me lo deben *They/you owe it to me*

Yo no la conozco *I don't know her*
Te lo has olvidado *You've forgotten it* (**olvidarse**
  = *to forget*)
Siempre la recordaremos *We'll always remember
  her*
No me lo tires *Don't throw it away for me*
No nos lo digan *Don't tell it to us*

■ *Attached to* positive Imperatives in the order given
above:

Dímelo *Tell it to me*
Contestadme (Lat. Am. **Contéstenme**) *Answer
  me* (plural)
Dénselo a ella *Give* (plural) *it to her* (see p.114 for
  se)

The position of the stress does not change, so a written
accent is required when the stress falls more than two syllables from the end of the word formed after the pronouns
are added: **organizo** *I organize*, **organízamelo** *organize it
for me*.

■ *Attached to* Infinitives and Gerunds in the order given
above:

Sería una buena idea vendérnoslo *It would be a
  good idea to sell it to us*
No creo que sea posible explicárselo *I don't
  think it's possible to explain it to him* (**selo** for
  *lelo')
Está pintándomelo *He's painting it for me*
Me llamó pidiéndome dinero *He called me asking for money*

As the examples show, a written accent may be required
to show that the stress has not shifted.

However, if the Infinitive or the Gerund is preceded by
a Finite Verb (see Glossary), pronouns may be optionally
put in front of the latter:

No puede decírmelo/No me lo puede decir *He can't tell it to me*

Queríamos guardártelo/Te lo queríamos guardar *We wanted to keep it for you*

Voy a hacerlo/Lo voy a hacer *I'm going to do it*

Estaba esperándonos/Nos estaba esperando *She/he was waiting for us*

Iba diciéndoselo/Se lo iba diciendo *He was going along saying it to himself/to her/to them, etc.*

The second of these constructions is more usual in everyday language, but it is not possible with all verbs. The best advice for beginners is to use it only with the following verbs:

Verbs followed by Infinitive

acabar de *to have just . . .*
conseguir *to manage to*
deber *must*
empezar a *to begin to*
ir a *to be going to*
parecer *to seem to*
poder *to be able*
preferir *to prefer to*
querer *to want*
saber *to know how to*
soler *to habitually . . .*
tener que *to have to*
tratar de *to try to*
volver a *to . . . again* (**volvió a hacerlo/lo volvió a hacer** *he did it again*)

Verbs followed by Gerund

andar: **anda contándoselo a todo el mundo** or **se lo anda contando** . . . *he goes around telling everyone*

estar: está haciéndolo or **lo está haciendo** *he's doing it*

seguir: sigue haciéndolo or **lo sigue haciendo** *he's still doing it*

In cases of doubt the suffixed construction is always correct, but it is slightly more formal. The non-suffixed construction should not be used if any word comes between the finite verb and the Infinitive or Gerund: **intentó muchas veces verla** *he often tried to see her*, not *'**la intentó muchas veces ver**'. The suffixed forms should also be used with the Imperative: **vuelve a llamarlos** *call them again*, **ve a verlos** *go and see them*.

REDUNDANT PRONOUNS

Spanish often apparently unnecessarily uses Personal Pronouns when the thing or person is also referred to by a noun in the sentence.

This happens:

■ When the Direct Object noun precedes the verb:

Los libros te *los* mando por correo *I'll send you the books by post* (cf. **te mando los libros por correo**)

■ When the sentence contains a noun that is the Indirect Object:

***Se* lo diré a tu padre** *I'll tell your father* (not *'**lo diré a tu padre**')

Esto *les* parecía bien a sus colegas *This seemed OK to his colleagues*

***Le* robaron mil dólares a Miguel** *They stole 1000 dollars from Miguel*

However, a redundant pronoun is not used when a *Direct* Object comes after the verb. It should be remembered that the presence of the preposition **a** *to* does not necessarily show that the noun is the Indirect Object, since **a** also precedes human *direct* objects in Spanish (see p.157):

> **Vi a Miguel** *I saw Miguel* (not *"lo vi a Miguel'*, which, however, is normal in relaxed styles in Argentina and common in spoken Latin-American Spanish elsewhere)
> **La policía seguía a los ladrones** *The police were following the thieves*

EMPHASIS OF PERSONAL PRONOUNS

Subject Pronouns are emphasized simply by using the subject pronoun, since, as is explained on p.107, a Finite Verb in Spanish already contains its subject pronoun:

> **Lo sé** *I know it*
> **Yo lo sé** *I know it (but he doesn't, etc.)*

Object pronouns, direct and indirect, are emphasized by adding **a mí, a ti, a él/ella/usted, a nosotros/as, a vosotros/as** or **a ellos/ellas/ustedes**:

> **A mí nunca me dicen nada** *They never tell **me** anything*
> **A ella sí que la admiro** *I do admire **her*** (emphatic use of **sí**)
> **A ustedes sí los vi** *I did see **you***

TRANSLATING *IT'S ME, IT'S YOU*, ETC.

> **Soy yo** *It's me;* **Eres tú/Es usted** *It's you*
> **Son ellos** *It's them*
> **Son ustedes los que hacen más ruido** *You (plural) are the ones who make most noise*
> **Somos nosotras las que estamos más disgustadas** *It's we women who are most fed up*

I Indefinite Pronouns

This chapter discusses a series of miscellaneous pronouns that unlike the Personal Pronouns do not refer to specific individuals,

El que, la que, los que, las que

These mean *the one(s) that* or *the one(s) who/those that/who*. If the verb is in the subjunctive, the idea of **anyone** *who* is strengthened:

> **El que dice eso es tonto** *The person/man who says that is stupid*
> **El que diga eso . . .** *Anyone who says that . . .*
> **La que dijo eso** *The girl/woman who said that*
> **Los que vinieron ayer** *the ones who came yesterday*

El que is not always an indefinite pronoun since it can refer to specific persons or objects:

> **Antonio es el que lleva la boina azul** *Antonio's the one wearing the blue beret*
> **Esta cerveza es la que menos me gusta** *This beer's the one I like least*

For other uses of **el que**, see the Index.

Quien/quienes (no accent)

Quien may replace **el que/la que** and **quienes** may replace **los que/las que**, but only when they refer to humans:

> **Quienes/los que piensen así** *Those who think/anyone who thinks like that . . .*
> **No te fíes nunca de quien no dice la verdad** *Never trust the person who doesn't tell the truth*

For other uses of **quien/quienes** and also of **quién/quiénes** see the Index.

El de, la de, los de, las de

These mean *the one(s) belonging to*, or *the one(s) from*:

> **El coche de María es más grande que el de Antonio** *Marías's car is bigger than Antonio's*
> **Las de allí son mejores que las de aquí** *The ones* (fem.) *from there are better than the ones from here*

Lo que, lo de

These are neuter equivalents of **el que, el de**. They are required when they do not refer to a specific noun:

> **Lo que me irrita** *What/the thing that irritates me*
> **Le sorprendió lo que dijo Ana** *What Ana said surprised him*
> **Lo de Gabriel es increíble** *That business of/about Gabriel is incredible*

Alguien

This invariable word is equivalent to *someone* or, in questions, *anyone* (but in negative sentences **nadie** is required; see p.154):

> **Alguien entró** *Someone came in*
> **Vi a alguien en la calle** *I saw someone in the street*

> **¿Conoces a alguien que sepa ruso?** *Do you know anyone who knows Russian?*

Algo

This invariable word translates *something* or, in questions, *anything* (but **nada** is required in negative sentences; see p.154):

> **Me recuerda algo** *It reminds me of something*
> **¿Tienes algo para mi dolor de cabeza?** *Have you got anything for my headache?*

Alguno

This can be used either as a pronoun or an adjective.

As an adjective it appears before plural nouns with the meaning *some but not others*:

> **En algunos casos . . .** *In some cases*
> **Algunas mariposas tienen alas muy bonitas** *Some butterflies have very pretty wings*

It can also be used as an adjective before singular nouns that do not refer to quantities or substances, in which case it roughly translates *one or other, the odd . . . , one or two . . .* When it comes directly before a singular *masculine* noun it loses its final vowel:

> **En algún momento de mi vida . . .** *At some time or other in my life*
> **¿Has encontrado alguna falta?** *Have you found some mistake/any mistakes?*

Alguno is *not* used before non-countable nouns or quantities of objects when the meaning is 'an unspecified amount of':

> **Necesito pan** *I want some bread*
> **Trajo agua** *He brought some water*

> **Tengo que comprar flores** *I've got to buy some flowers*

Used as a pronoun, **alguno** *some of them, the odd . . . , some people, some things*

> **De vez en cuando salía con alguna de sus amigas** *Now and again she went out with the odd girlfriend/with some girlfriend or other*
> **Algunos dicen que . . .** *Some people say that . . .*

For further remarks on the Spanish equivalent of the English 'some' see the chapter on 'Translation Traps'.

Cualquier(a)

This word can also function as an adjective or pronoun. As an adjective it means *any* in the sense of *it doesn't matter which*. When it comes directly before a noun it loses its final **-a**:

> **en cualquier caso . . .** *in any case . . .*
> **cualquiera que sea la respuesta . . .** *whatever the reply*

It can be put after the noun, in which case it may sound faintly pejorative:

> **Podríamos ir a un cine cualquiera para pasar el rato** *We could go to any cinema to kill time*

As a pronoun it is often followed by **de** and means *any of*:

> **Puedes usar cualquiera de estas dos habitaciones** *You can use any/either of these two rooms*

The plural is **cualesquiera**:

> **cualesquiera que sean sus razones . . .** *whatever his reasons* (also **sean cuáles sean sus razones**)

Uno

This corresponds to the English impersonal pronoun *one*:

> **Si uno tiene que pagar dos veces más, no vale la pena** *If one has to pay twice as much, it isn't worth it*

A female speaker referring to herself would say **una**.

In everyday language **tú** tends to replace **uno** in this kind of sentence:

> **Si tienes que pagar dos veces más, no vale la pena** *If you have to pay twice as much, it isn't worth it*

Uno (or **tú**) must be used to form an impersonal form of a verb that already has **se**:

> **A veces uno tiene que contentarse con lo que tiene** *Sometimes one has to put up with what one has* (never *'**se tiene que contentarse**'* since a verb cannot have two **se**'s)

| Relative Pronouns

These introduce Relative Clauses (see Glossary). There are several possibilities in Spanish, but the most frequent solutions are:

When no preposition precedes:	**que**
When a preposition precedes:	**el que** (people or things)
	quien/quienes (people)
	el cual (see below)
whose	**cuyo**

El que, el cual and **cuyo** agree in number and gender with the noun or pronoun that they refer to:

	Singular	*Plural*
Masculine	**el que, el cual, cuyo**	**los que, los cuales, cuyos**
Feminine	**la que, la cual, cuya**	**las que, las cuales, cuyas**

Quien has a plural, **quienes**, but no separate feminine form.

■ No preposition:

> **el perro que mordió a mi hermana** *the dog that bit my sister*
>
> **la mujer que vi ayer** *the woman that/whom I saw yesterday*
>
> **la carta que recibí de mi nieto** *the letter that I got from my grandson*

■ With preposition

el bolígrafo[26] **con el que lo escribí** *the ball-point pen that I wrote it with*
los novelistas a los que/a quienes me refiero *the novelists I'm referring to*
la mujer con la que/con quien se casó *the woman he got married to*

■ Familiar English usually omits a relative pronoun that is the Direct Object of a verb or is accompanied by a Preposition, but Spanish never does this:

el libro *que* leí *the book I read*
el cine *al que* fuimos *the cinema we went to*

■ English constantly puts prepositions at the end of relative clauses. This is *never* possible in Spanish:

la mesa encima de la que había dejado el plato *the table he'd left the plate on* (Spanish must say *the table on which he had left the plate*)
los pronombres de los que estoy hablando *the pronouns I'm talking about*

■ **El cual**

This is a substitute for **el que**, but it is less used nowadays as it tends to sound rather heavy in familiar styles:

muchachos y muchachas, algunos de los cuales llevaban sombrero *boys and girls, some of whom were wearing hats*
los puntos a los cuales/a los que me he referido *the points that I have referred to*

■ **Cuyo**

This word means *whose*. It agrees in number and gender with the thing possessed, not with the possessor:

---

[26] See the preface for a selection of Latin-American words for *ballpoint pen*.

la señora cuyo bolso encontré en el metro[27] *the lady whose bag I found in the subway/underground*

Tolstoy, cuyas novelas figuran entre las más leídas del mundo *Tolstoy, whose novels figure among the most widely read in the world*

---

[27] **El metro = el subte** in Argentina.

Adjectives

Spanish adjectives (with rare exceptions) agree in number, and a majority also agree in gender, with the noun or pronoun they modify: **un edificio blanco** *a white building* (masc.), **una casa blanca** *a white house* (fem.), **tres edificios blancos/tres casas blancas** *three white buildings/three white houses*, etc.

FORMATION OF PLURAL OF ADJECTIVES

■ Add **-s** to an unstressed vowel:

> **grande—grandes** *big*
> **roja—rojas** *red* (fem.)

■ Add **-es** to a consonant or to a stressed vowel:

> **individual—individuales** *individual*
> **iraquí—iraquíes**[28] *Iraqi*

-**z** is changed to **c** if -**es** is added:

> **feroz—feroces** *ferocious*
> **feliz—felices** *happy*

FORMATION OF THE FEMININE OF ADJECTIVES:

■ Adjectives ending in -**o**: the -**o** changes to -**a**

---

[28] Familiar speech often simply adds -**s** to adjectives ending in a stressed vowel, but formal styles require -**es**.

	Masculine	Feminine	
Singular	**bueno**	**buena**	*good*
Plural	**buenos**	**buenas**	
Singular	**fantástico**	**fantástica**	*fantastic*
Plural	**fantásticos**	**fantásticas**	

■ Adjectives ending in any vowel other than **-o** have no separate feminine:

	Masc. or Fem. Singular	Masc. or Fem. Plural	
	inherente	**inherentes**	*inherent*
	grande	**grandes**	*big*
	indígena	**indígenas**	*native*
	hindú	**hindúes**	*Hindu*[29]

Exceptions: Adjectives ending in **-ote, -ete**:

	Masculine	Feminine	
Singular	**grandote**	**grandota**	*huge*
Plural	**grandotes**	**grandotas**	

Adjectives ending in consonants have no separate feminine forms:

	Singular	Plural	
	natural	**naturales**	*natural*
	feliz	**felices**	*happy*
	gris	**grises**	*gray/*(Brit. *grey*)

But the following exceptions must be noted:

■ Adjectives ending in **-és**:

	Masculine	Feminine	
Singular	**francés**	**francesa**	*French*
Plural	**franceses**	**francesas**	

[29] Or, in Latin America, (Asian) *Indian*, since **indio** is always taken to mean Amerindian in the Americas.

Exception:

cortés	**cortés**	*courteous*
corteses	**corteses**	

■ Adjectives ending in **-n** or **-or**:

	Masculine	Feminine	
Singular	**chiquitín**	**chiquitina**	*tiny*
Plural	**chiquitines**	**chiquitinas**	
Singular	**revelador**	**reveladora**	*revealing*
Plural	**reveladores**	**reveladoras**	

But comparative adjectives ending in **-or** have no separate feminine form:

Singular	Plural	
mejor	**mejores**	*better*
anterior	**anteriores**	*former/preceding*
exterior	**exteriores**	*outer/exterior*
inferior	**inferiores**	*lower/inferior*
interior	**interiores**	*inner/interior*
mayor	**mayores**	*greater*
menor	**menores**	*smaller*
superior	**superiores**	*upper/superior*
peor	**peores**	*worse*
posterior	**posteriores**	*later/subsequent*
ulterior	**ulteriores**	*ulterior/further.*

The following two adjectives also have no separate feminine forms:

Singular	Plural	
marrón	**marrones**	*brown*
afín	**afines**	*related by affinity*

■ **español** and **andaluz**:

	Masculine	Feminine	
Singular	**español**	**española**	*Spanish*
Plural	**españoles**	**españolas**	

Singular	**andaluz**	**andaluza**	*Andalusian*
Plural	**andaluces**	**andaluzas**	

INVARIABLE ADJECTIVES

A small number of adjectives are invariable (at least in literature and careful speech), i.e. they have no separate plural or feminine form, e.g. **las camisas rosa** *pink shirts*, **los rayos ultravioleta** *ultraviolet rays*. The following are the most common:

alerta	*alert*, optional plural **alertas**
ardiendo	*burning*
escarlata	*scarlet*
hembra	*female* (**los ratones hembra** *female mice*)
hirviendo	*boiling*
macho	*male* (**las ratas macho** *male rats*)
malva	*mauve*
modelo	*model* (i.e. *exemplary*)
naranja	*orange*
tabú	*taboo*
violeta	*violet*

Two-word color adjectives of the form *navy blue*, *deep brown*, *signal red* are also invariable:

> **los ojos verde oscuro** *dark green eyes*
> **los zapatos azul marino** *navy blue shoes*
> **las corbatas azul claro** *light blue ties*

In the case of adjectives joined by a hyphen, only the second element agrees:

> **las negociaciones anglo-francesas** *Anglo-French negotiations*

SHORT FORMS OF ADJECTIVES

Grande *big* becomes **gran** immediately before any singular noun: **un gran libro** *a big/great book*, but **dos grandes libros** *two big books*.

The following lose their final -o before a singular *masculine* noun:

bueno *good*	**un buen momento** *a good moment*
malo *bad*	**un mal ejemplo** *a bad example*
tercero *third*	**el tercer día** *the third day*
primero *first*	**el primer año** *the first year*

The adjective/pronouns **alguno** *some* and **ninguno** *none/no* also lose their final vowel before a singular *masculine* noun, and **cualquiera** *any* loses its vowel before any singular noun. They should be sought in the index.

Santo *saint* becomes **san** before the names of male saints not beginning with **Do-** or **To-**: **San José** *St Joseph*, but **Santo Domingo**, **Santo Toribio**. It is not abbreviated when it means *holy*: **el Santo Padre** *the Holy Father*.

AGREEMENT OF ADJECTIVES

Adjectives agree in number and, when possible, in gender with the noun or pronoun they refer to. Mixed groups of feminine and masculine nouns are treated as masculine:

> **tres profesores españoles** *three Spanish teachers* (males, or males and females)
> **tres profesoras españolas** *three female Spanish teachers*

Exceptions to this rule are:

■ Adjectives placed before nouns, which usually agree only with the first noun:

> **su notoria inteligencia y perspicacia** *his well-known intelligence* and *clear-sightedness*

■ Adjectives used as adverbs are always in the masculine singular form:

> **Estamos fatal** *We're feeling awful/We're in a real mess*
> **María habla muy claro** *Maria speaks very clearly*

■ Adjectives that do not refer to any specific noun or pronoun. These are always masculine singular in form:

> **Eso es fantástico** *That's fantastic*
> **Es muy bueno lo que has hecho** *What you've done is really good*

COMPARISON OF ADJECTIVES

■ The Comparative (see Glossary) is formed by using **más** *more* or **menos** *less*. *Than* is **que**:

> **Eres más grande que yo** *You're bigger than me*
> **El terremoto fue más violento que el anterior**
> *The earthquake was more violent than the previous one*
> **Esta silla está menos sucia que la otra** *This seat is less dirty than the other*

There are four special forms which replace **más** + the adjective:

bueno *good*	**mejor** *better*
grande *big*	**mayor** (or **más grande**) *bigger/greater*
malo *bad*	**peor** *worse*
pequeño *small*	**menor** (or **más pequeño**) *smaller*

These must not be used with **más**: **ella es mejor actriz que su hermana** *she's a better actress than her sister*.

Mayor and **menor** usually mean *greater* and *lesser* rather than *bigger* and *smaller*, but **mayor** is also used of physical size: **esta aula es mayor/más grande que la otra** *this lecture room is bigger than the other* (**más grande** is more usual in everyday language).

■ **Más de** or **menos de** must be used before numbers or quantities:

> **Su hijo tiene más de cuarenta años** *His son is more than forty*
>
> **No traigas menos de un kilo** *Don't bring less than a kilo*

The correct number and gender of **del que** (**del/de la/de los/de las que**) must be used if the **que** precedes a verb phrase:

> **Pone más azúcar del que le recomienda el médico** *He puts in more sugar than the doctor recommends him*
>
> **Siempre le da más flores de las que ella se espera** *He always gives her more flowers than she expects*

The form **de lo que** must be used if there is no noun with which **el que** could agree:

> **Es menos tonta de lo que parece** *She's less stupid than she looks*
>
> **más de lo que tú piensas** . . . *more than you think* . . .

■ *As . . . as* is expressed by **tan . . . como** (*not* **'tan que'*).

> **Una jirafa es tan alta como un elefante** *A giraffe is as tall as an elephant*
>
> **Este problema no es tan complicado como el anterior** *This problem isn't as complicated as the one before*

■ *The more . . . the more, the less . . . the less*

The standard formula, normal in speech in Spain, is
cuanto más . . . más or **cuanto menos . . . menos**.
Cuanto is often replaced by **mientras** in Latin-American
speech or, in Mexico and some other places, by **entre**:

> **Cuanto más trabajas, más/menos te dan** *The
> more you work, the more/the less they give you*

■ The Superlative (see Glossary) is usually expressed by
using a definite article with the Comparative:

> **Tú eres *el* más fuerte** *You're* (masculine) *the
> strongest*
> **Eres *la* mujer menos sincera que he conocido**
> *You're the least sincere woman I've met/known*

The definite article is omitted:

(1) When a possessive (e.g. **mi, tu, su, nuestro,** etc.)
precedes: **fue nuestro peor momento** *it was our worst
moment*, **es mi mejor amigo** *he's my best friend*. The article is retained if **de** follows: **ésta ha sido la peor de mis
películas** *this was the worst of my films*.

(2) When the adjective does not refer to any specific
noun: **sería menos complicado dejarlo como es** *it
would be less/least complicated to leave it as it is*

(3) After **el que** *the one who*:

> **Ana fue la que más colorada se puso** *Ana
> was the one who blushed most*
> **Éste es el que menos estropeado está** *This is
> the one that's least spoilt*

THE SUFFIX -*ÍSIMO*

The suffix -**ísimo** (fem. -**ísima**, plural -**ísimos/ísimas**)
strongly intensifies the meaning of an adjective: **es
grande** *it's big*, **es grandísimo** *it's enormous*.

It is added after removing a final vowel (if there is one):

> **duro** *hard*   **durísimo** *extremely hard*
> **fácil** *easy*   **facilísimo** *extremely easy*

Adjectives whose masculine singular end in **-go, -co** or **-z** require spelling changes:

> **rico** *rich*   **riquísimo** *tremendously rich*[30]
> **vago** *vague/lazy*   **vaguísimo** *very vague/bone idle*
> **feliz** *happy*   **felicísimo** *really happy*

POSITION OF ADJECTIVES

The question of whether a Spanish adjective appears before a noun, as in **un trágico incidente** or after, as in **un incidente trágico** (both translatable as *a tragic incident*) is one of the subtler points of the language. Hard and fast rules are difficult to formulate, but the following guidelines should help to train the ear of beginners.

An adjective *follows* the noun:

■ If it is used for the purposes of contrast. Sometimes the other term in the contrast is missing, but if a contrast is implied, the adjective must follow the noun:

> **Quiero comprar una camisa** *azul* I want to buy a blue shirt (i.e. and not a red/green one, etc. Implied contrast)
> **Debiste casarte con una mujer** *paciente* You should have married a patient woman
> **El pan** *blanco* **cuesta más** White bread costs more (i.e. contrasted with others)

---

[30] **Rico** with **estar** means *tastes good*: **el pastel está muy rico** *the cake's delicious*.

■ If it is a scientific, technical or other adjective that is not meant to express any emotional or subjective impression:

> **la fusión nuclear** *nuclear fusion*
> **un programa gráfico** *a graphics program/programme*
> **la física cuántica** *quantum physics*
> **la vida extraterrestre** *extra-terrestrial life*
> **un líquido caliente** *a hot liquid*

■ With very rare exceptions, if it denotes religion, ideology or place of origin:

> **un niño católico** *a Catholic child*
> **unas actitudes democráticas** *democratic attitudes*
> **un libro francés** *a French book*

An adjective *precedes* the noun:

■ If it is an adjective used so often with a specific noun that it virtually forms a set phrase. Swear-words also fall into the this class:

> **el feroz león africano** *the fierce African lion*
> **la árida meseta castellana** *the arid Castilian plain*
> **los majestuosos Andes** *the majestic Andes*
> **mi adorada esposa** *my beloved wife*
> **este maldito sacacorchos** *this damned corkscrew*

■ If it is one of the following common adjectives:

> **ambos** *both*
> **llamado** *so-called*
> **mero** *mere*
> **mucho** *a lot of*
> **otro** *another*
> **pleno** *total, mid-*
> **poco** *little/few*
> **tanto** *so much*

The following adjectives *may* precede the noun, and usually do in emotional, poetic or high-flown styles:

■ Any adjective denoting the speaker's emotional reaction to something:

> **un triste incidente** *a sad incident*
> **un feliz encuentro** *a happy encounter*
> **un sensacional descubrimiento** *a sensational discovery*

■ Adjectives describing shape, color, size, appearance. These especially tend to precede the noun in poetic or emotional styles:

> **la enorme mole del Everest** *the enormous mass of mount Everest*
> **una remota galaxia** *a remote galaxy*
> **la blanca luna** *the white moon*

■ **Grande** and **pequeño** usually precede the noun, although **grande** tends to follow when it is necessary to restrict its meaning to *big/large* rather than *great*:

> **un pequeño problema** *a slight problem*
> **un gran poeta** *a great poet*
> **un gran libro** *a big/great book*
> **un libro grande** *a big book*

Demonstrative Pronouns & Adjectives

These are words that translate *this, these, that, those*. Spanish differs from English in having two words for *that/those*, one resembling the old English *yonder* in that it points to distant things.

	masculine	*feminine*	
singular	**este**	**esta**	*this, this one*
plural	**estos**	**estas**	*these, these ones*
	(neuter form **esto**: see below)		
singular	**ese**	**esa**	*that, that one*
plural	**esos**	**esas**	*those, those ones*
	(neuter form **eso**: see below)		
singular	**aquel**	**aquella**	*that, that one* (far)
plural	**aquellos**	**aquellas**	*those, those ones* (far)
	(neuter form **aquello**: see p.140)		

When these are used as pronouns, i.e. when they mean *this **one**, those **ones***, etc., they may be written with an accent. According to a ruling made by the Royal Spanish Academy in 1959, the accent can be omitted except in those very rare cases where confusion could arise, as in **esta llama** *this flame* and **ésta llama** *this woman is calling*, or **este vale** *this receipt/IOU*, and **éste vale** *this one is okay*. This ruling of the Academy has not met with universal approval and many of the best publishers and most ordinary people always put an accent on the pronouns. In this book the accent is always written on the pronoun forms. The accent must *never* be written on a demonstrative *adjective*: **un libro como ése** or (according to the Academy) **un libro como ese** *a book like that one* (pronoun) is correct, but ****'*éste libro*' for **este libro** *this book* (adjective) looks very bad. The neuter forms **esto, eso,** and **aquello** are *never* written with an accent.

Difference between *ese* and *aquel*

Aquel and **ese** must be used correctly when a contrast is made between *there* and *further over there*:

> **Ponlo en el estante. No en ése sino en aquél**
> *Put it on the shelf. Not that one but that one over there*

If no such contrast is involved, either **aquel** or **ese** may be used for things that are far from the speaker. **Aquel** is also often used for things that are in the distant past.

> **¿Ven ustedes esas/aquellas montañas?** *Do you see those mountains (over there)?*
> **en aquella/esa época** *at that time* (**aquella** if we are talking of a remote past)

The former . . . the latter

The difference between **ese** and **aquel** is often exploited to mean *the former, the latter,* **aquel** meaning *the former:*

> **Había dos grandes grupos políticos, los Conservadores y los Liberales, aquéllos de tendencias clericales y éstos enconados enemigos de la Iglesia** *There were two large political groups, the Conservatives and the Liberals, the former clerical in tendency and the latter bitter enemies of the Church*

Use of the Neuter Demonstrative Pronouns

These are **esto** *this*, **eso** *that* and **aquello** *that*; **eso** can usually replace **aquello**. These refer to no noun in particular:

> **Eso es horrible** *That's horrible*
> **No quiero hablar de eso/aquello** *I don't want to talk about that* (**aquello** suggests something further in the past)

The following patterns should be noted:

> **Éste es *un* problema** *This one* (male or masculine object) *is a problem*
> **Esto es *un* problema** *This* (i.e. business, matter) *is a problem*
> **Éste es *el* problema** *This is the problem*

| Possessives

There are two sets of possessive adjectives. The Short
Forms can function only as adjectives and appear only
directly before a noun phrase; these words translate the
English *my, your, his, her, its*, etc. The Long Forms function as adjectives or pronouns and translate the English
mine, yours, ours, theirs, etc. They cannot appear directly
before a noun phrase.

THE SHORT FORMS

	Singular	Plural	
	mi	**mis**	*my*
	tu	**tus**	*your* (= **de ti**)
	su	**sus**	*his, her, its*
			your (= **de usted**)
masc.	**nuestro**	**nuestros**	*our*
fem.	**nuestra**	**nuestras**	
masc.	**vuestro**	**vuestros**	*your* (= **de vosotros**)
fem.	**vuestra**	**vuestras**	
	su	**sus**	*their*
			your (= **de ustedes**)

These agree in number and, where possible, in gender,
with the thing possessed, not with the possessor:

mi hijo *my son*	**mis hijos** *my sons/my children*
tu agenda *your diary*	**tus agendas** *your diaries*
su lápiz *his/her/your/ their pencil*	**sus lápices** *his/her/your/ their pencils*

nuestro coche *our car*	**nuestros coches** *our cars*
nuestra hija *our daughter*	**nuestras hijas** *our daughters*
vuestro amigo *your friend*	**vuestros amigos** *your friends*
vuestra mano *your hand*	**vuestras manos** *your hands*

Vuestro is used only in Spain: **su** replaces it in Latin America.

Su/sus has so many possible meanings that ambiguity occasionally arises. The identity of the possessor can be clarified by adding **de él, de ella, de usted, de ustedes, de ellos** or **de ellas** as required: **su casa de usted y no la de él** *your house, not his*. However, context nearly always makes such clarification unnecessary.

REPLACEMENT OF POSSESSIVE ADJECTIVES BY THE DEFINITE ARTICLE

Spanish Possessive Adjectives differ from their English counterparts in one major respect: they are replaced by the Definite Article when the sentence makes the identity of the possessor clear. This happens when:

■ An Indirect Object pronoun also refers to the possessor, as is normal when an action is done to someone's body or to some intimate possession:

> **Me estrechó la mano** *He/she shook my hand*
> **Le cortaron el pelo** *They cut his hair*
> **Me dejé el dinero en casa** *I've left my money at home*
> **Quítate la blusa** *take off your blouse*
> **Nos aparcó el coche** *He parked our car for us*

■ When the meaning of the sentence makes it obvious

who the possessor is (this replacement is optional, but usual):

> **María levantó la mano** *Maria raised her hand*
> **Mario puso la cartera en el maletín** *Mario put his notebook/wallet in his briefcase*
> **Dame la mano** *Give me your hand*

LONG FORMS

All of these forms agree in number and gender:

	singular	*plural*	
masculine	**mío**	**míos**	*mine*
feminine	**mía**	**mías**	
masculine	**tuyo**	**tuyos**	*yours (= de ti)*
feminine	**tuya**	**tuyas**	
masculine	**suyo**	**suyos**	*his/hers/its/*
feminine	**suya**	**suyas**	*(yours = **de usted** & **de ustedes**)/theirs*
masculine	**nuestro**	**nuestros**	*ours*
feminine	**nuestra**	**nuestras**	
masculine	**vuestro**	**vuestros**	*yours (= **de vosotros/de vosotras**)*
feminine	**vuestra**	**vuestras**	

Vuestro is replaced by **suyo** in Latin America.

The long forms are used:

■ To translate *a . . . of mine, a . . . of yours,* etc.

> **un amigo mío** *a friend of mine*
> **una tía nuestra** *an aunt of ours*
> **una carta suya** *a letter of his/hers/yours/theirs*

■ To translate *mine, yours,* etc.

> **Este saco es mío** *This jacket is mine* (Spain **esta chaqueta es mía**)
> **Esta casa es nuestra** *This house is ours*

The Definite Article is used (a) when the thing possessed is the Subject or Object of a verb, (b) if the possessive is preceded by a preposition:

> **De los tres dibujos yo prefiero el tuyo** *Of the three drawing I prefer yours*
> **La mía está abajo** *Mine is downstairs* (refers to some feminine object)
> **Estamos hablando del suyo** *We're talking about his/hers/yours/theirs* (refers to some masculine object)

The definite article is not used after the verb **ser** when the thing referred to is owned by the person involved, e.g. **ese reloj es mío** *that watch is mine*. The article is used when the thing referred to does not literally belong to the person involved: **ese asiento debe de ser el tuyo** *that seat must be yours*.

USE OF POSSESSIVES AFTER PREPOSITIONS AND PREPOSITIONAL PHRASES

Colloquial language in Latin-America tends to use long forms of possessives after prepositional phrases, i.e. **delante mío** for **delante de mí** *in front of me*, **detrás nuestro** for **detrás de nosotros/nosotras** *behind us*. This is avoided in standard Spanish and is frowned upon in Spain: the prepositional forms of pronouns should be used (see p.106). However, the possessive construction appears even in the best authors in Argentina.

Neuter Pronouns and Articles

Spanish has a series of words of neuter gender, so called because they do not refer to any specific masculine or feminine noun.

■ **Esto** *this*, **eso** *that*, **aquello** *that* see p.140.

■ **Ello**

Ello is most frequently used after prepositions. It translates *it* when this word does not refer to any specific noun or pronoun. Compare

> **No sé nada de él** *I don't know anything about him/it* (i.e. some male person or some masculine noun)

and

> **No sé nada de ello** *I don't know anything about it* (the situation or problem in general)

■ **Lo**

Lo has various uses. It may be

(a) a third-person masculine Direct Object personal pronoun as in **lo admiro** *I admire him/it:* see p.111.

(b) the Direct Object counterpart of **ello**. This is discussed in the next section.

(c) the neuter article, discussed after the next section.

■ **Lo** as a neuter third-person pronoun

This is the Direct Object form of **ello** and it is used to translate *it* when this does not refer to any noun or pronoun:

> **Su padre había muerto, pero él no lo sabía todavía** *His father had died but he didn't know (it) yet*

Lo is usually required after **ser** and **estar** when these refer back to something already mentioned in the sentence:

> **Dicen que es tonta, pero no lo es** *They say she's stupid, but she isn't*
> **Parece que estoy contento pero no lo estoy** *It looks as if I'm pleased, but I'm not*

For the use of **lo** with **hay** *there is/are*, see p.81.

■ **Lo** used to make abstract nouns from adjectives

Lo + a masculine singular adjective usually corresponds to an English phrase consisting of adjective + *thing*:

> **Lo increíble fue que** *The incredible thing was . . .*
> **lo más importante . . .** *the most important thing*
> **Lo mejor sería no mencionarlo** *The best thing to do would be not to mention it*

■ **Lo** + adverbs or adjectives to translate *how . . .* + adjective or adverb

Lo + an adverb, or **lo** + an adjective that agrees in number and gender, conveniently translates *how* after words implying admiration, blame, surprise, knowledge, etc.

> **Me sorprende lo bien que lo hizo** *I'm surprised at how well he did it*
> **Mira lo blancas que están estas sábanas** *Look how white these sheets are*
> **Ahora me doy cuenta de lo difícil que es** *Now I realize how difficult it is*

The word **cuán** is occasionally used instead in literary styles, but it is very rare in spoken Spanish:

> **Ahora me doy cuenta de cuán difícil es**

■ **Lo más** or **lo menos** + adverb can be used to translate the idea of *as . . . possible*:

> **Hágalo lo mejor posible** *Do it as well as possible*
> **Lo comió lo más deprisa que pudo** *He ate it as fast as he could*

| Adverbs

ADVERBS FORMED FROM ADJECTIVES

The usual way of forming an adverb from an adjective is by adding the suffix -**mente** to the singular form of an adjective (to the feminine form if it has one):

igual *equal*	**igualmente** *equally/likewise*
fantástico *fantastic*	**fantásticamente** *fantastically*

If the adjective has an accent, this remains unchanged:

increíble *incredible*	**increíblemente** *incredibly*
esporádico *sporadic*	**esporádicamente** *sporadically*

■ If two adverbs ending in -**mente** are joined by **y/e** *and*, **o/u** *or*, **ni** *nor/and not*, **pero/sino** *but*, the first drops the suffix -**mente**:

> **Se puede justificar económica y (p)sicológicamente** *It can be justified economically and psychologically*
>
> **Contestó irónica pero inteligentemente** *She/he replied ironically but intelligently*

■ Adverbs ending in -**mente** are used sparingly, rarely more than one to a sentence. One adverb ending in -**mente** should not be used to modify another.

> **Se defendieron con un valor increíble** *They defended themselves incredibly bravely* (not *"increíblemente valientemente"*)

■ There are alternative ways of expressing an adverbial idea, and these are preferred if the original sounds clumsy:

inteligentemente—con inteligencia *intelligently*
decididamente—de una manera decidida *decid-edly*
increíblemente—de forma increíble *incredibly*
rápidamente—deprisa *quickly*
etc.

OTHER ADVERBS

A large number of Spanish adverbs are independent words not formed from adjectives. These must be learned separately:

abajo *downstairs/down*
arriba *upstairs/up*
(a)dentro *inside*
(a)fuera *outside*
adelante *forward*
atrás *back*
adrede *on purpose*
ahora *now*
apenas *scarcely*
así *thus*
bien *well*
despacio *slowly*
igual *in the same way*
mal *badly*
mañana *tomorrow*
mucho *much/a lot*
poco *not much*
etc.

Even more numerous are adverbial phrases formed from a preposition + a noun; these must be learned separately. The following are typical:

a contrapelo *unwillingly*

> **a gritos** *while shouting*
> **a mano** *by hand*
> **a menudo** *often*
> **a oscuras** *in the dark*
> **a propósito** *on purpose*
> **a ratos** *occasionally*
> **a veces** *sometimes*
> **con ganas** *eagerly*
> **de noche/de día** *by night/day*
> **en balde/en vano** *pointlessly/for nothing*
> **en cambio** *on the other hand*

RECIÉN

The adverb **recién** deserves special mention. It means *just, only* in Latin America: **llegó recién** *he's just arrived* (= **acaba de llegar**), **recién entonces** (colloquial usage) *only then* (= **sólo entonces**). In Spain it means *recently, newly* and appears only in combination with participles : **recién pintado** *just painted/recently painted*.

ADJECTIVES AS ADVERBS

Some adjectives may be used as adverbs, in which case they are invariably masculine singular:

> **Trabaja muy duro** *He works very hard*
> **Hable claro** *Speak clearly*
> **Estamos fatal** *We're feeling dreadful/We're in a dreadful mess*

■ Very often normal adjectives can replace adverbs when the adjective really applies to the subject of the verb and not to the verb itself. The result is not always easily translated. The adjective agrees in number and gender with the subject of the verb:

> **Andaban cansados y tristes** *They were walking along (looking) tired and sad*
> **Vivían amargados** *They led bitter lives*
> **Me miró asustada** *She looked at me in alarm*

COMPARATIVE AND SUPERLATIVE OF ADVERBS

The comparative of adverbs is formed by using **más** *more* or **menos** *less*. **Que** is *than*:

> **fácilmente** *easily*   **más fácilmente** more easily
> **a menudo** often   **más a menudo** more often

The only irregular forms are

> **bien** *well*—**mejor** *better*
> **mal** *badly*—**peor** *worse*
> **mucho**—*much* **más** *more*
> **poco**—*little* **menos**—*less*

These latter forms do not agree in number when they are adverbs. Compare **son mejores** *they're better* (adjective) and **están mejor** *they're better off/in better condition* (adverb).

■ The superlative of adverbs is usually formed with **el que** or **quien**:

> **Ella es la que lo hará más fácilmente** *She's the one who will do it most/more easily*
> **Antonio es quien mejor canta** *Antonio sings best*
> **Tú eres el que más sabe de todo esto** *You know most about all this*

ADVERBS OF PLACE

The following are particularly frequent:

aquí *here*	**ahí** *(just) there* **allí** *there*
allá *there*	**acá** *here*
(a)dentro *inside*	**(a)fuera** *outside*
abajo *down/downstairs*	**arriba** *up/upstairs*
adelante *forward*	**atrás** *backwards/back*
delante *in front*	**detrás** *behind*

Aquí is the equivalent of *here*. **Ahí** means *just there* (*close by you*) and **allí** indicates somewhere further away; the distinction should be maintained.

Allá and **acá** are less common in Spain but they are obligatory everywhere when they follow **más**:

> **un poquito más allá/acá** *a bit more that/this way*

Acá replaces **aquí** in many regions of Latin America, especially in Argentina and neighbouring countries.

■ The forms **adentro**, **afuera** are, in the standard language, generally used only to express motion, and the forms **dentro** and **fuera** are used to indicate static position:

> **Fue adentro** *He went inside* (motion)
> **Estaba dentro/fuera** *He was inside/outside* (static position)

But this distinction is lost in Latin America, where the forms beginning with **a-** are generally used for static position and motion too: **estaba adentro/afuera**

The prepositional phrases are **dentro de** and **fuera de**:

> **dentro/fuera de la casa** *inside/outside the house*

However, the forms **adentro de**, **afuera de** are commonly heard in Latin America and are accepted in writing in Argentina.

Prepositional phrases are discussed at p.159 ff.

POSITION OF ADVERBS

■ When an adverb or adverbial phrase modifies a verb it generally follows the latter:

> **Canta bien** *He sings well*
> **Hablaba a gritos** *He was talking at the top of his voice*
> **El presidente consiguió también que se modificara la ley** *The President also managed to get the law modified*

■ When an adverb modifies a Modal Verb (see Glossary) plus a participle or Infinitive, the adverb should not be inserted between the modal and the non-finite form:

> **Lo ha hecho siempre/Siempre lo ha hecho** *He's always done it* (never *'**lo ha siempre hecho**')
> **Por fin voy a verla/Voy a verla por fin** *I'm finally going to see her*

■ When an adverb modifies a whole phrase and not just the verb, it usually precedes the whole phrase (as in English):

> **Normalmente viene a las tres** *Normally he comes at three*

| Negation

■ The following are the words most commonly used to make negative statements:

apenas	*hardly, scarcely*
nada	*nothing*
nadie	*no one*
ni	*nor, not even*
ninguno	*none*
no	*not*
nunca or **jamás**	*never*

■ Negating a verb

The basic patterns are as follows. Note that if a negative word *follows* a verb, the verb must also be *preceded* by a negative word: this is the so-called double negative construction:

Positive	Negative
Vamos *We're going*	**No vamos** *We aren't going*
Lo han comprado *They've bought it*	**No lo han comprado** *They haven't bought it*
Tengo algo *I have something*	**No tengo nada** *I don't have anything*
Conozco a alguien *I know someone*	**No conozco a nadie** *I don't know anyone*
Ana o María *Ana or Maria*	**ni Ana ni María** *neither Ana nor Maria*
Vino con él o con ella *He came with him or with her*	**No vino ni con él ni con ella** *He didn't come with him or with her* (i.e. with neither of them)

algún día *some day*

Lo/le vi con alguna chica
I saw him with some girl

ningún día *no day*

No lo/le vi con ninguna chica *I didn't see him with any girl*

Siempre llueve *It always rains* **No llueve nunca** *It never rains* (or **nunca llueve**)

■ Negatives may be combined:

Apenas conoce a nadie *He hardly knows anyone*

Nunca sale con nadie *He never goes out with anyone*

Nadie compra nada *No one buys anything*

No te he visto nunca en ninguna parte con ninguna de ellas *I've never seen you anywhere with any of those girls/women*

■ Spanish negative words are also used in comparisons, where English uses *anyone, anything, ever*:

Está más guapa que nunca *She's more attractive than ever*

Se acuesta antes que nadie *He goes to bed before anyone else*

Es más impresionante que nada que yo haya visto hasta ahora *It's more impressive than anything I've seen up until now*

■ **Ni**, or **ni siquiera** translate *not . . . even*

Ni (siquiera) pienses en llamarme *Don't even think about calling me*

Ni siquiera se acordó del cumpleaños de su mujer *He didn't even remember his wife's birthday*

■ **Ninguno** may be used as an adjective or a pronoun. Its forms are:

	Singular	Plural
Masculine	**ninguno**	**ningunos**
Feminine	**ninguna**	**ningunas**

But when it comes before a singular masculine noun it loses its final **-o**:

> **Ningún presidente americano se atrevería a decir eso** *No American President would dare to say that*
>
> **Ninguna mujer inteligente defiende el machismo** *No intelligent woman defends machismo*
>
> **¿Libros? No tengo ninguno** *Books? I haven't got a single one*

■ **Nomás** is much used in Latin America (but not in Spain) to mean *just, barely*

> **Los vimos en la entrada nomás** *We saw them right in the entrance* (Spain **en la misma entrada**)
>
> **Te llamaré nomás llegue a casa** *I'll call you as soon as I get home* (Spain **nada más llegue . . .** , **en cuanto llegue . . .**)

■ No words should be inserted between the auxiliary verb **haber** and the Past Participle in Compound tenses:

> **No lo he hecho nunca** *I've never done it* (not *"**no lo he nunca hecho**')

| Personal *A*

In Spanish, certain kinds of noun and pronoun must be preceded by **a** when they are the **Direct Object** of a verb. This happens:

■ When the Direct Object represents a *known* human being or animal:

> **Vi a Antonio** *I saw Antonio*
> **Admiro a ese profesor** *I admire that teacher*
> **Llama al camarero**[31] *Call the waiter*
> **Conozco a alguien que sabe chino** *I know someone who knows Chinese*
> **Arrestaron al narcotraficante** *They arrested the drug-pusher*
> **Criticaron al gobierno** *They criticized the government* (collective noun standing for known human beings)
> **Voy a lavar al perro** *I'm going to wash the dog*

Compare **voy a lavar el coche** *I'm going to wash the car*—never *'. . . **al coche**' since the car is non-human. In the case of an unknown human being or animal, **a** is usually omitted; the more impersonal the object the less likely is the use of **a**:

> **Vi (a) un hombre en la calle** *I saw a man in the road*
> **Odio las serpientes** *I hate snakes*

■ In those cases in which word order does not make it clear which is the object and which is the subject of the

---

[31] **Camarero = el mesero** in much of Latin America.

verb. This usually happens in Relative Clauses where the word order is usually Verb-Subject:

> **una medida que afecta al problema** *a measure that affects the problem* (since **. . . que afecta el problema** could mean either *. . . that affects the problem* or *. . . that the problem affects*)

> **Se llamaba al director "Maxi"** *people called the director Maxi* (Impersonal **se**. The **a** avoids confusion with **. . . se llamaba Maxi** *the director's name was Maxi*)

Prepositions

Prepositions—words like *in, of, on, through, to, underneath, without*—stand in front of nouns or pronouns and relate them in various ways to the rest of the sentence: **en España** *in Spain*, **de María** *of Maria*, **encima de la mesa** *on (top) of the table*, etc.

■ Prepositions can also stand in front of verbs: *without looking, by shouting*. In English the verb form used in this case is the *-ing* form, but in Spanish the form used is always the Infinitive: **sin ver** *without seeing*, (**cansado**) **de hablar** *(tired) of talking*. Prepositions do not appear before a Gerund. A rare exception is **en** + Gerund, as in **en llegando** 'on arriving', but this construction is old-fashioned and is nowadays expressed by **al** + Infinitive, e.g. **al llegar a Madrid** *on arriving in Madrid*.

■ The prepositions **a** 'to' and **de** 'of' combine with the masculine singular Definite Article **el** to form **al** 'to the' and **del** 'of the'. No other combinations of these prepositions are used: compare **a él** 'to *him*' and **de él** 'of *him*'. The combined form is not used when the **el** is part of a proper name: **a El Ferrol** 'to El Ferrol', **de El Cairo** 'from Cairo'.

■ Prepositional phrases consist of more than one word, of which one is always a preposition. They function like prepositions: **a causa de** *because of*, **detrás de** *behind*. The more common of these are included with the simple prepositions in the following list.

ALPHABETICAL LIST OF SPANISH PREPOSITIONS AND THEIR USE

There are minor local variations between Spain and Latin America with respect to prepositional usage. These variations are more numerous in colloquial speech than in written language.

Prepositional usage is often dictated by apparently arbitrary rules and frequently does not correspond between languages: compare English *to dream of* someone, Spanish **soñar** *con* **alguien** (literally *'to dream with someone'*), or English *to try to*, Spanish **tratar** *de* (literally *'to try of'*).

a[32] *to* (after words denoting motion or giving, sending, showing, beginning, etc.)

> **Vamos a Caracas** *We're going to Caracas*
> **Volaron a Roma** *They flew to Rome*
> **Le dio cien dólares a su hijo** *He gave 100 dollars to his son*
> **Envíe esta carta al Ministerio** *Send this letter to the Ministry*
> **Voy a verla** *I'm going to see her*
> **Empezó a llorar** *He/she began to cry*
> **un viaje a la luna** *a journey to the moon*
> **un homenaje al rey** *a homage to the King*

at, but usually only when it means *towards*:

> **Apuntaba al blanco** *He was aiming at the target*
> **Tiraban piedras a la policía** *They were throwing stones at the police*

---

[32] The preposition *a* is also used in Spanish before human or animal direct objects: **vio a Miguel/a su hermana** *He saw Miguel/his sister.* This is discussed on p.157.

When the English word *at* means *in* or *close to* a place, as in *at the bus-stop*, *at the table*, *at Cambridge*, the Spanish translation is **en** (q.v.), although the following exceptions should be noted:

> **a la salida/entrada** *at the exit/entrance*
> **a la mesa** *at table* (cf. **en la/una *mesa*** *at the/a table*)
> **a mi espalda/derecha/izquierda** *at my back/right/left*
> **a pie de página** *at the foot of the page*

at, before numbers and in several set phrases

> **a las seis** *at six o'clock*
> **a las ocho y media** *at eight-thirty*
> **a doscientos kilómetros por hora** *at 200 km per hour*
> **a treinta kilómetros** *at a distance of thirty km*
> **a los treinta años** *at the age of thirty*
> **al mismo tiempo** *at the same time*
> **al amanecer** *at dawn*

by, *in the manner* of, in set phrases indicating the manner in which something is done

> **a mano, a pie, a caballo** *by hand, by/in pencil, by horse/on horseback*
> **escribir a máquina** *to type*
> **a empujones** *by pushing*
> **arroz a la catalana** *rice cooked Catalan-style*
> **vestido a la inglesa** *dressed in the English style*

in, in set phrases

> **al sol/a la sombra** *in the sun/shade*
> **a lo lejos** *in the distance*

on, in set phrases

> **a la derecha/izquierda** *on the right/left*
> **a la llegada de** *on the arrival of*

al día siguiente *on the next day*
al salir de casa *on leaving home*
estar a dieta *to be on a diet*

onto after verbs of motion

El gato saltó a la mesa *The cat jumped onto the table*

into after verbs of motion

Se tiró al agua *He dived into the water*
Entró corriendo al cuarto *He ran into the room*
(Spain . . . ***en** el cuarto*)

after in set phrases

Se cansa a los dos minutos *He gets tired after two minutes*
a los dos días de hacerlo *two days after doing it*

per

tres veces a la semana *three times per/a week*
cinco mil dólares al mes *$5,000 per/a month*

of, like, after words meaning *taste, smell, sound like, look like*

Sabe a ajo *It tastes of garlic*
Huele a pescado *It smells of fish*
un olor/sabor a vino *a smell/taste of wine*
Suena a mentira *It sounds like a lie*
Se parece a su madre *He looks like his mother*

from, away from, off (after words meaning *steal, take away from, buy, hear*)

Le compró un coche a su hermano *He bought a car off his brother*
Les roban dinero a los turistas *They steal money from the tourists*
Se lo oí decir a Miguel *I heard it from Miguel*

a bordo de *on board of*

a cambio de *in exchange for*

a causa de *because of*

> **a causa del ruido/calor** *because of the noise/heat*

a costa de *at the cost of*

a diferencia de *unlike*

> **a diferencia de algunos de sus amigos** *unlike some of his friends*

a espaldas de *behind the back of*

a excepción de *with the exception of*

a falta de *for lack of/for want of*

a favor de *in favor* (Brit. *favour*) *of*

a fin de *with the aim of*

a finales/a fines de *towards the end of*

> **a finales de junio** *towards the end of June*

a fuerza de *by dint of*

a juicio de *in the opinion of*

a mediados de *towards the middle of*

> **a mediados de julio** *in mid-July*

a modo de *in the manner of*

además de *as well as*

a la hora de *at the moment of*

a lo largo de *throughout/along*

> **a lo largo del río** *along (the length of) the river*
> **a lo largo del siglo** *throughout the century*

a partir de *starting from*

> **a partir de hoy** *from today*
> **a partir de ahora** *from now on*

a pesar de *despite, in spite of*

>**No me lo dio, a pesar de toda su generosidad**
>*He didn't give it to me, despite all his generosity*

a por (Spain only) same as **por** (q.v.) when the latter means *in search of*

>**Voy a por el médico** *I'm going for the doctor/to fetch the doctor*

a principios de *towards the beginning of*

a prueba de . . . *proof*

>**a prueba de bomba** *bomb-proof*

a punto de *on the verge of*

>**Estaba a punto de decirlo** *He was on the verge of saying it*

a raíz de (literary) *immediately after/as an immediate result of*

>**a raíz de la Guerra Civil** *immediately after the Civil War*

a riesgo de *at the risk of*

a través de *through/across*

>**a través del llano** *across the plain*

a vista de *in the sight/presence of*

a voluntad de *at the discretion of*

>**El servicio es a voluntad del cliente** *The service charge is at the customer's discretion*

acerca de *about* (= *on the subject of*)

>**Me preguntó qué pensaba acerca de todo eso** *He asked me what I thought of/about all that*

además de *as well as*

al alcance de *within reach of*

al cabo de *at the end of*

>> **al cabo de una semana** *after a week/at the end of a week*

al contrario de *contrary to*

al corriente de *informed about/up to date with*

>> **No estoy al corriente de todo lo que ha pasado** *I'm not up to date with everything that's happened*

al estilo de *in the style of*

al frente de *at the head/forefront of*

al lado de *next to*

>> **Se sentó al lado de su jefe** *He sat next to his boss*

al nivel de *at the level of*

al tanto de = **al corriente de**

alrededor de *around*

>> **un viaje alrededor del mundo** *a journey round the world*
>> **alrededor de mil** *around/about 1,000*

ante *in the presence of, faced with*

>> **ante este problema** *faced with this problem*
>> **ante el juez** *in the presence of/before the judge*

In literary styles it may be an equivalent of **delante de** *in front of* (q.v.).

antes de *before* (time)

>> **Tienen que terminarlo antes de las doce** *They've got to finish it before 12 o'clock*

Compare **antes** *que* rather than: **cualquier cosa antes que tener que asistir a una de esas reuniones** *anything rather than have to go to one of those meetings.*

bajo *beneath, under*

Debajo de (q.v.) is the usual Spanish translation of *underneath*, although **bajo** is used in literary language to mean our *beneath* with words like **el cielo** *sky*, **el sol** *sun*, **el techo** *roof*: **bajo un cielo azul** *beneath a sky of blue*. **Bajo** is also required with social and political systems, with temperatures and in some set phrases:

> **debajo de la cama** *under the bed*
> **bajo un régimen totalitario** *under a totalitarian regime*
> **bajo cero** *below zero*
> **bajo órdenes** *under orders*
> **Estás bajo aviso** *You've been warned* (lit. 'You're under a warning')
> **bajo la condición de que** . . . *on condition that* . . .

cerca de *near*

> **Vivo cerca del puente** *I live near the bridge*

con *with*. The following special forms should be noted:

> **con + mí = conmigo** *with me*
> **con + ti = contigo** *with you*
> **con + sí = consigo** *with himself/herself/yourself, with themselves/yourselves*

> **Vine con mi tía** *I came with my aunt*
> **con amor** *with love, lovingly*
> **Vamos contigo** *We're going with you*
> **Lo abrió con el destornillador** *He opened it with the screwdrlver*
> **Es muy cariñoso con ellos** *He's very affectionate with/towards them*

> **Está enojada** (Spain **enfadada**) **con usted** *She's angry with you*

despite (same meaning as **a pesar de**)

> **Con todos sus esfuerzos, no lo consiguió**
> *Despite all his efforts he didn't achieve it*
> **Con ser su amigo, no habla bien de él** *Despite being his friend, he doesn't speak well of him*

if after an Infinitive (this construction is not particularly common)

> **Con trabajar un poquito más, aprobará el examen** *If he works a little more, he'll pass the examination*

into, against, to, when some idea of a collision or mutual encounter is involved

> **El autobús chocó con** (or **contra**) **un árbol** *The bus ran into a tree*
> **Me encontré con el jefe** *I ran into/unexpectedly met the boss*
> **Se ve con ella todos los días** *He sees/meets her* (US *meets with her*) *every day*
> **Yo me escribo con ella** *I write to her regularly/correspond with her*

with . . . in in phrases that mention the contents of some vessel or receptacle

> **un camión con frutas** *a truck/lorry loaded with fruit*
> **una botella con agua** *a bottle with water in it*

con motivo de *on the occasion of*

> **con motivo del quinto aniversario de . . .** *on the occasion of the fifth anniversary of*

con objeto de *with the object/intention of*

con relación a *in respect of/in relation to*

con respecto a *with respect/reference to/in comparison to*

The spelling of the word **el respeto** *respect* (shown to someone) should be noted.

contra *against*

> **Escribió un artículo contra el uso de las drogas**
> *He wrote an article against the use of drugs*
> **Se apoyó contra un árbol** *He leaned against a tree*

Adverbially, the phrase **en contra** is used: **votar en contra** *to vote against*.

de *of* (i.e. *belonging to* or *made of*). English may join nouns to form compound nouns where **de** is normally used in Spanish:

> **el Banco de España** *The Bank of Spain*
> **los zapatos de Antonio** *Antonio's shoes*
> **el ama de casa** *the housewife*
> **un talonario de cheques** *a checkbook* (British *cheque-book*)
> **la sopa de legumbres** *the vegetable soup*
> **la base de datos** *the database*
> **un chaleco de cuero** *a leather jacket*
> **Murió de paludismo** *He died of/from malaria*

from

> **una carta de mi madre** *a letter from my mother*
> **Es de Almería** *He comes from Almería* (**viene de**
> . . . means *he's coming from* . . .)
> **Hemos llegado ahora de Madrid** *We've just arrived from Madrid*
> **a partir de ahora** *starting from now*
> **la carretera que va de Madrid a Valencia** *the road that goes from Madrid to Valencia*

See also **desde**, which also means *from*.

off/down from

> **Se bajaron del autobús** *They got off the bus*
> **Bájate de ahí** *Come down from there*

by after verbs meaning *pull, take by, seize*

> **Me tiraba de la oreja** *He/she used to pull me by
> my ear*
> **Iban cogidos de la mano** *They were walking
> hand-in-hand*

measuring, costing, old, before quantities, years, etc.

> **una soga de cinco metros** *a rope measuring five
> meters/metres* (i.e. *five meters long*)
> **el menú de dos mil pesetas** *the 2,000 peseta
> menu*
> **un niño de tres años** *a three-year old child*
> **Tiene cien metros de largo/profundo** *It's 100
> meters/metres long/deep*

about in the sense of *concerning*, after verbs meaning *speak,
complain*, etc.

> **Me niego a hablar de eso** *I refuse to talk about
> that*
> **Se quejó de la mala comida** *He complained
> about the bad food*
> **Le informaron de lo que pasaba** *They informed
> him about what was happening*

like, as, in phrases referring to condition or state

> **trabajar de profesor/guía** *to work as a
> teacher/guide*
> **Vas de marqués por la vida** *You give yourself
> airs and graces* (literally *you go through life like a
> marquis*)

> **Se vistió de payaso** *He dressed up as a clown*
> **estar de broma** *to be joking, to be fooling about*

This use can also be translated as *for* or *on* in some phrases:

> **Se va de viaje** *He's going on a journey*
> **Se fueron de fin de semana** *They've gone away for the weekend*

in, after Superlative expressions

> **El mejor restaurante de España** *the best restaurant in Spain*

with to show the cause of some event

> **Saltaba de alegría** *They were jumping with joy*
> **Enfermó** (Latin America **se enfermó**) **de bronquitis** *He fell ill with bronchitis*

if before Infinitives

> **De ser verdad, provocará un escándalo** *If it's true, it'll cause a scandal*

than in the expression **más/menos de** *more/less than*, when a quantity follows (see p.133) and also before clauses (see p.133)

De also appears in many adverbial phrases, e.g.

> **de broma** *as a joke*
> **de golpe/de repente** *suddenly*
> **de maravilla** *fantastically well*
> **de nuevo** *again*
> **de paso** *on the way through*

The use of **de** before **que** is discussed on p.233.

de acuerdo con *in accordance with*

> **de acuerdo con el Código Penal** *in accordance with the Penal Code*

de parte de *on the part of, on behalf of*

—¿Puedo hablar con Antonio?—Claro. ¿De parte de quién? '*Can I speak to Antonio?' 'Of course. Who's speaking/Who shall I say is speaking?'*

de regreso a *on returning to*

debajo de *underneath*

> **debajo de la mesa** *underneath the table*

Latin Americans often say **abajo de,** but this is not used in Spain.

delante de *in front of*

> **No quiero decirlo delante de ella** *I don't want to say it in front of her*

dentro de *inside*

> **dentro de la casa** *inside the house*

Latin Americans often say **adentro de,** a form not accepted in Spain.

in, i.e. before deadline

> **Llegarán dentro de veinte minutos** *They'll arrive in twenty minutes*

Latin Americans often say **. . . en veinte minutos.**

desde *from* (a place), when some kind of motion is implied or distance is stressed

> **Se veía desde lejos** *It was visible from a distance*
> **Desde aquí hay más de cien kilómetros** *It's more than 100 km from here*
> **Han venido desde Barcelona** *They've come **all the way** from Barcelona* (cf. **. . . de Barcelona** *. . . from Barcelona*)

There is some overlap in meaning in this case with **de.**

since in time phrases

> **desde entonces** *since then*
> **desde marzo** *since March*
> **Desde niño siempre he creído en Dios** *I've
> always believed in God since I was a child*

For the phrase **desde hace**, as in **desde hace tres
años** *for three years*, see pp.206–7.

después de *after (time)*

detrás de *behind*

durante *during*

> **durante el siglo veinte** *during the twentieth cen-
> tury*

for in expressions of time

> **Durante varios días no hablaste de otra cosa**
> *You talked of nothing else for several days*
> **durante varias horas** *for several hours*

For other ways of expressing *for n days/minutes*, see p.
205 ff.

en This word combines the meanings of *in*, *into*, *on*, and
at. Spanish-speakers often have difficulty in distinguishing between these English words.

on   **El plato está en la mesa** *The plate's on the table*
       (or **encima de**[33])
       Lo vi en la televisión *I saw it on television*
       Flotaba en el agua *It was floating on/in the water*
       en la luna *on the moon*

in   **Está en el maletero de tu coche** *It's in the
       trunk/*(British *boot*) *of your car*

---

[33] **Encima de** is the clearest and most usual way of expressing
on top of a flat surface.

Nací en Caracas *I was born in Caracas*
en el campo *in the countryside*
en 1999/verano/abril/español *in
    1999/summer/April/Spanish*
en la mañana/tarde/noche *in the morning/after-
    noon/by night* (this is Latin-American Spanish:
    Spain uses **por** with these nouns)

In time phrases of the sort *he'll be here in five minutes*,
dentro de is more usual than **en** (at least in Spain): **llegará dentro de cinco minutos**.

into   **Entró corriendo en la habitación** *He ran into the
    room* (**entrar** is followed by **en** in Spain, usually in
    Latin America by **a**)
**Introduzca una moneda de cien pesetas en la
    ranura** *Put a 100-peseta coin into the slot*

at   with nouns denoting place, when motion is not
    implied

Estudié en Cambridge *I studied at Cambridge*
en la parada del autobús *at the bus-stop*
Me senté en una mesa del bar *I sat down at a
    table in the bar*
en el semáforo *at the traffic-lights*
en la puerta *at the door*

En is also used with certain festivals and special days

en Navidad *at Christmas*
en los fines de semana *at weekends*

at, by in estimates of quantity, value, price, quality or
characteristics

La casa fue valorada en doscientos mil dólares
    The house was valued at 200,000 dollars
Me tienen en poca estima *They hold a low opin-
    ion of me*

> **¿En cuánto lo estiman?** *How much do they estimate that it's worth?*
> **Ha bajado en un diez por ciento** *It's gone down by ten per cent*
> **La reconocí en la manera de hablar** *I recognized her by her way of speaking*

en busca de *in search of*

en caso de *in case of*

> **en caso de incendio** *in case of fire*

en contra de *in opposition to*

en cuanto a *as for . . . /concerning*

> **en cuanto a los demás . . .** *as far as the rest are concerned . . .*

en forma de *in the shape of*

en lugar de *instead of* (+ noun, pronoun or infinitive)

en medio de *in the middle of*

> **en medio de la calle** *in the middle of the street*

en torno a *around (the subject of)/concerning*

en vez de *instead of* (+ Infinitive)

en vista de *in view of*

> **en vista de lo ocurrido** *in view of what's happened*

encima de *on top of*

> **El libro está encima de la mesa** *The book's on the table*
> See also **en**, **sobre**

enfrente de *opposite*

> **La comisaría está enfrente del museo** *The police-station is opposite the museum*

entre *between*

> **entre tú y yo** *between you and me* (note that the
> prepositional forms of **tú** and **yo**—**ti** and **mí**—are
> not used when two pronouns follow **entre**)
> **entre los dos pinos** *between the two pinetrees*

among, through

> **El sol se veía apenas entre las nubes** *The sun
> was barely visible among/through the clouds*
> **Encontraron la sortija entre la hierba** *They found
> the ring among/in the grass*
> **Recuerdo haberla visto entre la gente que
> estaba en la fiesta** *I recall seeing her among the
> people that were at the party*

what with

> **Entre una cosa y otra, se me ha ido el día** *What
> with one thing and another my day has gone*

The phrases **entre semana** *on weekdays* and **entre sí**
among themselves or *to himself/herself/themselves* (as in **decía
entre sí** *he said to himself*) should be noted.

excepto *except*

Prepositional forms of pronouns are not used with this
word.

> **Vinieron todos, excepto Antonio** *They all came,
> except Antonio*
> **Excepto tú y yo** *except you and me*

frente a *opposite*

> **Aparcaron frente a la comisaría** *They parked in
> front of the police-station*

in contrast with

> **Frente a otros miembros de su partido, atacó la
> política de la nacionalización** *In contrast with*

> *other members of his party, he attacked the policy of nationalization*

fuera de *outside*

> **fuera de la casa** *outside the house*

Latin Americans often say **afuera de,** a form not accepted in Spain.

hacia *towards*

> **El cometa viaja hacia el sol** *The comet is traveling* (British *travelling*) *towards the Sun*
> **Se volvió hacia ella** *He turned towards her*
> **su actitud hacia sus padres** *his attitude towards his parents*

around (i.e. *approximately*) in time phrases

> **hacia mil novecientos** *around 1900*

hasta *as far as, until*

> **Caminaron hasta la estación** *They walked as far as the station*
> **Las obras continuarán hasta octubre** *The work will continue until October*
> **hasta mañana** *until tomorrow*
> **hasta luego** *good-bye/see you later* (lit. *until then*)

From Colombia northwards **hasta** can also mean *not until . . . not before . . .* :

> **Terminamos hasta ayer** (= **no terminamos hasta ayer**) *We didn't finish until yesterday*

junto a *next to, by*

> **Estuvo esperando junto a la puerta** *He waited by/next to the door*

lejos de *far from*

> **lejos de aquí** *far from here*

mas allá de *beyond*

> **más allá del mar** *beyond/on the other side of the sea*

mediante *by means of*

> **Intentaron solucionar el problema mediante una serie de medidas económicas** *They tried to solve the problem by a series of economic measures*

This word is rather literary, **con** being more usual in everyday language.

no obstante (literary) *notwithstanding* (same as **a pesar de**)

para *for*

This preposition must be carefully distinguished from **por**, which is also sometimes translatable as *for*.

> **Este dinero es para ti** *This money is for you*
> **Necesitamos habitaciones para ocho personas** *We need rooms for eight people*
> **¿Tienen ustedes algo para el dolor de muelas?** *Do you have something for toothache?*
> **¿Para qué lo hiciste?** *What did you do it for?*

to (when it means *in order to*) followed by Infinitive

> **Pon más ajo para darle más sabor** *Put in more garlic to give it more flavor/*(Brit. *flavour*)
> **Se fue de vacaciones para descansar** *He went away on vacation/holiday to rest*
> **Tiene suficiente dinero para vivir** *He's got enough money to live*

by in time phrases

> **Lo necesito para mañana** *I need it by tomorrow*
> **Para entonces ya no servirá** *It'll be no use by then*

for in expressions meaning *to need **for** n days*, etc.

> **Necesito el coche para dos días** *I need the car for two days*

on the point of (with Infinitive. Latin Americans use **por**)

> **Está para/por llover** *It's about to rain*

in . . . view

> **Para ella, él era el más atractivo de todos** *In her view, he was the most attractive of all*
> **Para mí que eso suena falso** *In my view, that sounds false*

towards after positive emotions (i.e. love, affection), in combination with **con**

> **el cariño que tenía para con sus hijos** *the affection he had for his children*

por   Various meanings

Although the English translation may sometimes be *for*, its meaning is not the same as **para** and the two words must be carefully distinguished.

As a result of, because of, for (when it means *because of*)

> **Tuvimos que cerrar las ventanas por los mosquitos** *We had to shut the windows because of the mosquitoes*
> **Muchas gracias por todo lo que has hecho** *Many thanks for* (i.e. *because of*) *all you have done*
> **Lo hice por ti** *I did it because of you/for your sake* (compare **lo hice para ti** *I did/made it for* (i.e. *to give to*) *you*
> **Te lo mereces por no decir la verdad** *You deserve it for not telling the truth*
> **La admiro por su generosidad** *I admire her for* (i.e. *because of*) *her generosity*

> **Lo hago por dinero** *I do it for money* (i.e. *because of*)
>
> **Llegamos tarde por la nieve** *We arrived late because of the snow*

words meaning *in return for*

> **Te dan doscientas pesetas por libra esterlina** *They give you 200 pesetas to the pound*
>
> **Cambió el coche por otro** *He changed his car for another*

per
> **dos mil kilómetros por hora** *2,000 km an/per hour*
>
> **dos pares de zapatos por persona** *two pairs of shoes per person*

The preposition **a** is used for time: **dos veces al día** *twice per day/a day*

for in the sense of substitution *for*

> **Me tomó por español** *He took me for* (i.e. *confused me with*) *a Spaniard*
>
> **Hazlo por mí** *Do it for* (i.e. *instead of*) *me*

for meaning *in support of*

> **Estamos luchando por la libertad** *We're fighting for freedom*
>
> **No estoy por la pornografía** *I don't support pornography*
>
> **Se esforzó mucho por su hijo** *He made a great effort for his son*

for in the meaning *to the value of*

> **una camisa de seda por cien dólares** *a 100-dollar silk shirt*
>
> **una factura por dos millones de pesos** *a bill for two million pesos*
>
> **Podrás venderlo por un millón** *You'll be able to sell it for a million*

for in the meaning *in search of*. In this case European Spanish regularly uses **a por**:

> **Tendré que ir (a) por gasolina** *I'll have to go for* (i.e. *to get*) *some gas/petrol*
>
> **Ir por lana y volver trasquilado** *To go for wool and come back shorn* (proverb used when a plan misfires)

by to indicate *by* whom or what something is done

> **Esta novela fue escrita por Juan Goytisolo** *This novel was written by Juan Goytisolo*
>
> **La iglesia fue destruida por un terremoto** *The cathedral was destroyed by an earthquake*

by = *by means of*

> **Los motores diesel funcionan por compresión** *Diesel engines work by compression*
>
> **Funciona por electricidad** *It works on/by electricity*
>
> **Más por chiripa que por otra cosa** *More by fluke than by anything else*
>
> **Consiguió el empleo por enchufe** *He got the job through connections/by influence*
>
> **por avión** *by plane* (but **en tren, en coche, en bicicleta**)
>
> **por teléfono/fax** *by phone/fax*

however in phrases of the type *however hard you work, however tall he is*

> **Por muy alto que seas, no lo alcanzarás** *You won't reach it, however tall you are*
>
> **Por más deprisa que andemos, no llegaremos a tiempo** *However fast we walk, we won't get there in time*

in, around when referring to places or time. In this case it implies approximate location or time

> **Vivo por aquí** *I live round here*
> **por ahí** *somewhere around there*
> **por enero** *around January*

along, through, via after words indicating motion

> **Andábamos por la calle** *We were walking along
> the street*
> **Pasaron por San Pedro** *They passed through
> San Pedro*
> **a Madrid por Segovia** *to Madrid via Segovia*

to before an Infinitive, in the sense of *in order to*.
This overlaps in meaning with the much more frequent
para. Por is used only when there is a personal or subjective motive, and *para* is usually optionally possible as well:

> **He venido por estar contigo** *I've come to be with
> you* (i.e. *because I **want** to be with you*)
> **Yo haría cualquier cosa por conseguir ese
> empleo** *I'd do anything to get that job*

por debajo de *under* (with figures, quantities)

> **muy por debajo de las cifras del año anterior**
> *well below last year's figures*

salvo = excepto, and like the latter word it does not take
prepositional forms of pronouns: **salvo/excepto tú**
except you.

según *according to*

> **según el parte meteorológico** *according to the
> weather forecast*
> **según tú** *according to you* (note that the preposi-
> tional forms of pronouns—**mí, ti**—are not used
> after this preposition)

depending on

> **según la cantidad que pongas** *depending on the
> quantity you put in*

> **según la persona con la que hables** *depending on the person you talk to*

sin *without*

> **Lo hice sin ayuda** *I did it without help*
> **sin dudar** *without hesitating*
> **sin nada/nadie** *without anything/anyone* (Spanish says *without nothing/no one*)

sobre *on top of*

There is some overlap between this use of **sobre** and **encima de** and **en**. **Sobre** is more specific than **en** in that its spatial meaning is clearly *on top of*, and it is somewhat more literary than **encima de**, which is the usual translation of *on top of*:

> **sobre/encima de/en la mesa** *on (top of) the table*

over with verbs like *fly*, *pass*

> **El avión voló sobre la ciudad** *The plane flew over the city*
> **Pasó sobre mi cabeza** *It passed over my head*

around (i.e. *roughly*) before times and quantities

> **sobre las tres** *around three o'clock*
> **Tenía sobre cinco metros de largo** *it was about 5 meters/metres long*

over, i.e. *more than, above,* with numbers

> **un aumento sobre el año pasado** *an increase over last year*
> **veinte grados sobre cero** *20 degrees above zero*

about in the meaning *on the subject of*

> **un programa sobre problemas ecológicos** *a program/*(British *programme) about ecological problems*
> **hablar sobre . . . .** *to talk on the subject of . . .*

on, over, above in the meaning of *overlooking*

> **una casa sobre el mar** *a house on/overlooking the sea*
> **el castillo que está construido sobre la ciudad** *the castle that is built overlooking the city*

over in the sense of superiority *over*

> **sobre todo** *above all*
> **la superioridad sobre** *superiority over . . .*

tras *after*

This word is literary and is replaced in everyday language by **detrás de** (space) or **después de** (time).

> **tras (después de) la victoria de los conservadores** *after the victory of the conservatives*
> **tras (detrás de) la puerta** *behind the door*
> **año tras año** *year after year* (set phrase)

PREPOSITION FINDER (ENGLISH-SPANISH)

This list gives the Spanish equivalents of the more common English prepositions. The Spanish words should be checked in the preceding alphabetical list:

about	= *on the subject of* **sobre, de, acerca de**
	= *roughly* **sobre, alrededor de**
	= *all over* **por**
above	**encima de, sobre**
according to	**según, de acuerdo con**
across	**a través de, por**
after	time **después de**
	place **detrás de**

among(st)	**entre**
(a)round	as in *walk round the tree* **alrededor de**
	= *approximately* **sobre, alrededor de**
as far back as	(= *since*) **desde**
at	place (no motion involved) **en**
	place (motion at, towards) **a, contra**
	time **a**
	with numbers **a, en**
before	time **antes de**
	place **delante de** (= *in front of*)
below	place **debajo de**
	numbers **bajo**; = *inferior to* **por debajo de**
beneath	**debajo de, bajo**
beside	**al lado de**
	= *as well as* **además de**
between	**entre**
by	= *done by* **por**
	time **para**
	= *near to* **junto a, al lado de**
	= *by transport* **por, en**
	= *by night* **por**
	= *by doing*, see Gerund,. p.52
by means of	**mediante, por**
during	**durante**
except	**excepto, salvo**
for	= *made/bought/designed/intended for* **para**
	= *as a result of, because of* **por**
	= *on behalf of* **por**
	= *instead of* **por, en lugar de**
	= *in search of* (**a**) **por**
	time (i.e. *for n days*) **durante, por**; see also p.205.

	= *in exchange for* **a cambio de**
	= *for a quantity, price* **por**
from	**desde, de**
	time **desde, a partir de**
in	time and place **en**
	after superlatives **de**
	= *within* a certain time **dentro de**
in front of	**delante de, ante**
inside	**dentro de, en**
into	**en**
of	**de**
on	**encima de, sobre, en**
	a after verbs of motion
	= *on* doing something **al** + Infinitive
on behalf of	**de parte de**
onto	**a**
out of	place **de**
	motive, reason for **por**
	number **sobre**
outside	**fuera de**
over	= *above* **sobre, encima de**
	= *across* **a través de**
	motive (e.g. *fall out over*) **por**
	number **sobre, encima de**
per	*per day, week* **a**
	per person **por**
since	**desde**
through	= *across* **a través de, entre**
	= *thanks to* **por**
	= *by means of* **mediante, por**

to	place **a**
	purpose (=*in order to*) **para; a** after verbs of motion
	after **bastante** *enough* **para**
towards	**hacia**
	= *emotion towards* **hacia, para con**
under	= *underneath* **debajo de**
	under *regime, orders* **bajo**
	with figures **por debajo de**
underneath	**debajo de**
upon	see *on*
via	**por**
with	**con**
	emotions *with* (= *arising from*) **de, con**
without	**sin**

| Conjunctions

These are words like *and, but, so,* used for joining words, phrases or clauses.

■ como

This word has several meanings:

(1) With the subjunctive, *if*: see p.41.

(2) To introduce Relative Clauses after words describing manner:

> **la manera como . . .** *the way that . . .*

(3) To mean *seeing that/as/since*. In this case it must come at the head of the phrase:

> **Como se nos hacía tarde, decidimos dejarlo para el día siguiente** *As/since it was getting late, we decided to leave it for the next day*

In this context **ya que** or **puesto que**, which both mean *seeing that . . .* can also be used.

Cómo (note accent) means *how* and is discussed on p. 202.

■ ni *nor, not even.* See p. 155.

■ o *or*

It is written and pronounced **u** before words beginning with and **o** sound:

> **sociedades u organizaciones** *societies or organizations*
>
> **mujeres u hombres** *men or women*

■ pero, sino

Spanish has two words for *but*. **Sino** is used in constructions that mean *not A but B*, and especially in the formula

no sólo . . . sino *not only . . . but*:

> **Esto no es vino, sino agua** *This isn't water but wine/This isn't water. It's wine*
>
> **no sólo en España, sino en Latinoamérica también** *not only in Spain but in Latin America too*

It sometimes means *except*:

> **No se podía hacer otra cosa sino disculparse** *There was nothing else to be done except/but to say sorry*
>
> **No podía ser sino un mensaje de sus tíos** *It could be nothing else except/but a message from his aunt and uncle*

The form **sino que** must be used when the words introduce a verb phrase:

> **No sólo hablaba alemán, sino que sabía otras cinco lenguas también** *He not only spoke German but he knew five other languages as well*

In other cases *but* is translated **pero**, which differs from **sino** in that it does not suggest incompatibility or replacement, but merely a limiting of meaning.

> **Ana no sabe francés, pero sí sabe escribir a máquina** *Ana doesn't know French, but she can type*
>
> **Te daré cincuenta dólares, pero no te voy a dar un regalo también** *I'll give you fifty dollars, but I'm not going to give you a present as well*
>
> **Es inteligente pero perezoso** *He's intelligent but lazy*

■ **porque** *because*

Porque means *because* and it must be distinguished in pronunciation and spelling from **por qué** *why*: Compare **yo comprendo, porque me lo explicaste** *I understand,* *because* *you explained it to me*, and **yo comprendo por qué me lo explicaste** *I understand **why** you explained it to me*.

The phrase **no porque** requires the subjunctive:

> **Lo hizo no porque realmente quisiera hacerlo sino porque se sentía presionado** *He did it not because he really wanted to, but because he felt pressured*

■ **puesto que, ya que** *since* (= *because*)

> **No ha sido posible terminarlo, ya que/puesto que no hay dinero** *It hasn't been possible to finish it, since there's no money*

■ **pues**

This may mean *because* when it is used as a conjunction, but this usage is literary, like the English *for* and it is not heard in spoken Spanish:

> **Se le entendía poco, pues** (i.e. **porque**) **hablaba muy bajo** *One could understand very little of what he said, for he spoke in a very low voice*

In everyday language it is very common in the meaning *in that case*: **si no te gusta, pues vete** *if you don't like, well, in that case go away*.

■ **que**

This word has numerous functions other than as a conjunction, and they must be clearly distinguished.

(1) It may be a Relative Pronoun, as in **la mujer que compró las flores** *the woman **who** bought the flowers*.

(2) It means *than* in comparisons: **eres más alto que yo** *you're taller **than** me*.

(3) **Qué** (note accent) is a separate word and translates *what* in direct and indirect questions: **no sé qué hacer** *I don't know **what** to do*.

The conjunction **que** introduces clauses in the same way as the English *that*:

> **El plomero**[34] **dice que viene esta tarde** *The plumber says he's coming this afternoon/evening*

Unlike its English counterpart, it is not omitted (at least in normal styles): **creo que es verdad** *I think it's true*.

See the chapter on Translation Traps for the phrase **de que**. See p.39 for imperatives phrases like **que venga** *tell him to come/let him come*.

■ **y** *and*

Pronounced as though it were written *i*: **mexicanos y norteamericanos** *Mexicans and Americans*. It is written and pronounced **e** before any word beginning with an **i** sound:

> **la agricultura e industria peruanas** *Peruvian agriculture and industry*
> **Vinieron Mario e Iris** *Mario and Iris came*
> **musulmanes e hindúes** *Muslims and Hindus*

but

> **carbón y hierro** *coal and iron* (because **hierro** begins with a *y* sound)

---

[34] The word for *plumber* in Spain is **el fontanero**.

Numbers, Time, Quantities

CARDINAL NUMBERS

1 un/uno/una
2 dos
3 tres
4 cuatro
5 cinco
6 seis
7 siete
8 ocho
9 nueve
10 diez
11 once
12 doce
13 trece
14 catorce
15 quince
16 dieciséis
17 diecisiete
18 dieciocho
19 diecinueve
20 veinte
21 veintiún/veintiuno/veintiuna
22 veintidós
23 veintitrés
24 veinticuatro
25 veinticinco
26 veintiséis

27 **veintisiete**
28 **veintiocho**
29 **veintinueve**
30 **treinta**
31 **treinta y un/uno/una**
32 **treinta y dos**
33 **treinta y tres**
34 **treinta y cuatro**
35 **treinta y cinco**
36 **treinta y seis**
37 **treinta y siete**
38 **treinta y ocho**
39 **treinta y nueve**
40 **cuarenta**
41 **cuarenta y un/uno/una**
50 **cincuenta**
60 **sesenta**
70 **setenta**
80 **ochenta**
90 **noventa**
100 **cien/ciento**
101 **ciento un/uno/una**
102 **ciento dos**
200 **doscientos/doscientas**
210 **doscientos diez/doscientas diez**
300 **trescientos/trescientas**
400 **cuatrocientos/cuatrocientas**
500 **quinientos/quinientas**
600 **seiscientos/seiscientas**
700 **setecientos/setecientas**
800 **ochocientos/ochocientas**
900 **novecientos/novecientas**
1.000 **mil**
1.050 **mil cincuenta**
1999 **mil novecientos noventa y nueve**
2.000 **dos mil**

66.000 sesenta y seis mil
1.000.000 un millón
1.000.000.000 an American billion: **mil millones**
1.000.000.000.000 a million millions: **un billón**[35]

■ Thousands are separated by periods/full-stops—**10.000** = **diez mil** *10,000*—and decimals are separated by commas: **10,25** = **diez coma veinticinco** = *ten point two five*. But Mexico uses our system—10,000; 10.25, etc.

■ 16 through 29 are written as one word.

■ **Mil** is not pluralized in numbers—**cinco mil** *5000*. It is, however, pluralized when it is used as a noun: **los miles de personas que creen eso** *the thousands of people who believe that*.When used thus **mil** is a masculine noun.

■ **Uno** becomes **un** before a masculine noun, **una** before a feminine noun:

> **Hay treinta y un libros** *There are thirty-one books*
> **Hay treinta y una cartas** *There are thirty-one letters*

but

> **¿Cuántos libros hay? Treinta y uno** *How many books are there? Thirty-one*

■ **Ciento** *one hundred* is used when another number follows—**ciento trece** *113*—but **cien** is used in all other cases: **hay más de cien** *there are more than 100*, **cien hombres** *100 men*.

However, **ciento** is used in percentages: **el quince por ciento** *15%*

---

[35] In Spain **un billón** is a million million, although for Latin-Americans it is often the same as the US billion (a thousand million). It is a good idea to get this point straight before discussing prices or the national debt!.

■ The hundreds (i.e. 100, 200, 300, 400, 500, 600, 700, 800 and 900) are written as one word and the suffixed form **-cientos** agrees in number with the thing counted:

> **doscient*a*s mujeres/mesas** *200 women/tables* (fem.)
> **quinient*o*s quince hombres/dólares** *515 men/dollars* (masc.)

The irregular forms **quinientos/as** *500*, **setecientos/as** *700*, and **novecientos/as** *900* should be noted.

■ **Millón** and **billón** are nouns, whereas other numbers are adjectives. They therefore required **de** before the thing counted: **ha costado un millón/billón de dólares** *it cost a million/billion dollars*, but **ha costado un millón tres mil dólares** *it cost one million three thousand dollars*

■ Telephone numbers are said by tens whenever possible, and one begins either by hundreds or by a single digit when there is an odd number of figures:

> **ocho treinta y siete veintidós quince** 837 2215
> or **ochocientos treinta y siete veintidós quince**

Cero is used for *zero*:

> **cero quince cuarenta veintiséis** 015 4026

ORDINAL NUMBERS

Ordinal Numbers higher than ten are rather a mouthful in Spanish and they are usually avoided in all but formal styles. One says **el quince aniversario** rather than **el decimoquinto aniversario** *the 15th anniversary*, or **el capítulo veintiséis** *chapter 26/the 26th chapter*. The higher the number, the rarer the ordinal form. For this reason only ordinal numbers up to 20th and a few other common forms are given here.

The forms ending in **-avo** should strictly speaking be

used only for fractions—**diez quinceavos** *ten fifteenths.*
But they are very commonly used in Latin America to
form the higher ordinal numbers, although this is not usually accepted in Spain.

primer(o)	*first*	
segundo	*second*	
tercer(o)	*third*	
cuarto	*fourth*	
quinto	*fifth*	
sexto	*sixth*	
séptlmo/sétimo	*seventh*	
octavo	*eighth*	
noveno	*ninth*	
décimo	*tenth*	
undécimo	*eleventh*	**onceavo**
duodécimo	*twelfth*	**doceavo**
decimotercero	*thirteenth*	**treceavo**
decimocuarto	*fourteenth*	**catorceavo**
decimoquinto	*fifteenth*	**quinceavo**
decimosexto	*sixteenth*	**dieciseisavo**
decimoséptimo	*seventeenth*	**diecisieteavo**
decimoctavo	*eighteenth*	**dieciochavo**
decimonoveno	*nineteenth*	**diecinueveavo**
vigésimo	*twentieth*	**veinteavo**
centésimo	*hundredth*	**centavo**
milésimo	*thousandth*	

■ All these are normal adjectives and agree in number and
gender:

> **los treinta primeros hombres** *the first thirty men*
> **la segunda calle a la derecha** *the second street
> on the right*

■ **Primero** and **tercero** lose their final vowel before a
singular masculine noun: **el primer/tercer día** *the*

first/third day, but **la primera/tercera semana** *the first/third week*.

APPROXIMATE NUMBERS

Approximate numbers are formed by adding **-ena** to the cardinal number after removing any final vowel. These numbers exist for 10, 15, the tens 20 through 50 and for 100. They are in common use, although **docena** *dozen* is not used as much as in English:

una decena	*about ten* (note irregular form)
una quincena	*about fifteen*
una veintena	*about twenty, a score*
una treintena	*about thirty*
una centena	*about a hundred* (note irregular form)

Note special form **un millar** *about a thousand*.

Like all collective nouns, these are normally grammatically *singular*: **la primera treintena** *the first thirty or so*, **ha venido una veintena** *about twenty have come*. When **de** + a plural noun follows, either agreement is possible: **una treintena de estudiantes se quedaron/se quedó en el aula** *about thirty students remained in the lecture hall*.

FRACTIONS

The following special words exist:

> **1/2 una mitad**
> **1/3 un tercio**
> **2/3 dos tercios**, etc.

For higher fractions the masculine ordinal number is used, although the feminine form is also found:

1/4 un cuarto
1/5 un quinto
3/7 tres séptimos
7/10 siete décimos
tres millonésimos/as *three millionths*

In non-mathematical language the word **parte** is added for values over *half*: **la tercera parte** *a third*, **la quinta parte** *a fifth*.

As was mentioned earlier, decimals are expressed with a comma (although Mexico follows our system):

3,75 = tres coma setenta y cinco

■ The main arithmetical signs are:

+ más	**: dividido por** or **entre**
− menos	**× (multiplicado) por**
² al cuadrado	**% por ciento**

Dos más ocho son diez $2 + 8 = 10$
Ocho dividido por dos (or **ocho entre dos**) **son cuatro** $8:2 = 4$
Tres multiplicado por cinco son quince $3 \times 5 = 15$
Nueve son tres al cuadrado $9 = 3^2$
el treinta por ciento 30%

TIME

¿Qué hora es? (Lat. Am. often **¿Qué horas son?**) *What's the time?*, **¿Qué hora tiene?** *What time do you have?/What's the time, please?*

Es la una	*it's one o'clock*
Es la una y cinco	*five past/five after one*
Son . . .	*It's . . .*
las dos	*two o'clock*
las once	*eleven o'clock*

las tres y cuarto	*three fifteen*
las cuatro y veinticinco	*four twenty-five*

(also in Lat. Am. **las cuatro con veinticinco minutos**)

las cinco y media	*five thirty*
las seis menos veinte	*twenty before/to six*
las siete menos cuarto	*a quarter before/to seven*
las ocho menos diez	*ten minutes before/to eight*
las nueve en punto	*nine o'clock exactly*
Son menos diez/y diez	*It's ten to/ten past*
Son pasadas las cinco	*It's past five o'clock*
Es medianoche	*It's midnight*
Es mediodía	*It's mid-day*
las siete de la tarde	*seven p.m.*[36]
las tres de la madrugada[37]	*three a.m.*

■ The twenty-four hour clock is much used for timetables and in official documents: **a las quince veinticinco** *at fifteen twenty-five, at three thirty-five p.m.*

■ **Por la mañana, por la tarde** *in the afternoon/evening,* **por la noche** *at night* (Latin Americans may use **en** or **a** for **por**). **Mañana por la mañana** *Tomorrow morning.*

---

[36] **La tarde** stretches from about 1p.m. to about 8 p.m. and therefore includes both our afternoon and evening.

[37] **La madrugada** is the hours between midnight and 6 a.m. **La mañana** corresponds to our *morning* and can also be used instead of *la madrugada*.

PREPOSITIONS ETC. WITH TIMES OF DAY

a *at*

> **Te veo a las ocho** *I'll see you at eight o'clock*

para *by*

> **Tienes que estar allí para las siete** *You have to be there by seven*

a partir de *from*

> **Las llamadas telefónicas cuestan menos a partir de la una** *Phone calls cost less from/after one o'clock*

al cabo de *after* (i.e. *at the end of*)

> **Al cabo de unos instantes se dio cuenta de que** *After a few moments she realized that* . . .

sobre/a eso de *about*

> **Llegaremos sobre/a eso de las ocho** *We'll arrive around eight*

hasta *until*

> **hasta las cinco** *until five o'clock*

a más tardar *at the latest*

> **Hay que llegar a las tres a más tardar**

DAYS, MONTHS, SEASONS

Days of the week

lunes *Monday*
martes *Tuesday*
miércoles *Wednesday*
jueves *Thursday*
viernes *Friday*

Months and seasons

enero *January*
febrero *February*
marzo *March*
abril *April*
mayo *May*

Days of the week	Months and seasons
sábado *Saturday*	**junio** *June*
domingo *Sunday*	**julio** *July*
	agosto *August*
hoy *today*	**se(p)tiembre** *September*
ayer *yesterday*	**octubre** *October*
anteayer *the day before yesterday*	**noviembre** *November*
mañana *tomorrow*	**diciembre** *December*
pasado mañana *the day after tomorrow*	**la primavera** *spring*
	el verano *summer*
al día siguiente *the following day*	**el otoño** *autumn/fall*
	el invierno *winter*

Days and months are all masculine and are usually written with a small letter, as are the seasons.

PREPOSITIONS WITH DAYS, MONTHS, SEASONS, ETC.

■ **En** is used for *in* in most cases:

> **en abril** *in April*
> **en el mes de agosto** *in the month of August*
> **en mil novecientos noventa y nueve** *in 1999*
> **en el siglo veinte** *in the twentieth century*
> **en los años ochenta** *in the eighties*

■ With days of the week no preposition is used:

> **Llegaron el martes** *They arrived on Tuesday*
> **Está cerrado los lunes** *It's closed on Mondays*

THE DATE

> **¿A cuántos estamos?** *What's the date?*
> **El once de febrero** *February 11*

No preposition is used and the cardinal numbers are used:

> **Llegué a Managua el quince de enero** *I arrived at Managua on January 15*
>
> **Llegaremos el primero** (sometimes also **el uno**) **de mayo** *We'll arrive on May 1*

AGE

> **¿Cuántos años tienes?** *How old are you?*
>
> **¿Qué tiempo tiene?** *How old's the baby?* (if it's possibly less than one)
>
> **¿Qué edad tiene?** *What's his/her age?*
>
> **Tengo cuarenta y ocho años** *I'm 48*
>
> **Mañana cumplo treinta años** *I'm thirty tomorrow*
>
> **El cumpleaños** *birthday*

MEASUREMENTS

> **¿Cuánto mides?** *How tall are you?*
>
> **¿Cuánto tiene de largo/longitud?** *How long is it?*
>
> **¿Cuánto mide?** *How high is it?*
>
> **¿Cuánto tiene de profundidad?** *How deep is it?*
>
> **Tiene cien metros de largo/alto/ancho/profundidad** *It's 100 meters/metres long/high/wide/deep*
>
> **¿Qué número calzas?** *What size shoes do you take?*
>
> **Mi talla es la cuarenta** *My size is 40* (European system used for dresses, suits)[38]

---

[38] 40 Continental European = 14 British, 12 American. There is much scope for confusion since all three systems are in use in the Spanish-speaking world. Mexico generally uses the American system and Spain the European.

| Questions

■ It is often possible in informal styles to turn a simple statement into a question simply by changing the intonation:

> **Tu mamá lo sabe** *Your mother knows*
> **¿Tu mamá lo sabe?** *Does your mother know?* (rising intonation)

■ Alternatively, the order of the verb and its subject can be reversed:

> **¿Lo sabe tu mamá?** *Does your mother know?*
> **¿Conoce Antonio a mi suegro?** *Does Antonio know my father-in-law?*

■ Spanish has a series of words that correspond to our question words:

> **¿cómo?** *how?*
> **¿cuál?/¿cuáles?** *which?*
> **¿cuándo?** *when?*
> **¿dónde?** *where?*
> **¿para qué?** *what for?*
> **¿por qué?** *why?* (contrast with **porque** *because*)
> **¿qué?** *what?/which?*
> **¿quién?/¿quiénes?** *who?*

These question words must be written with an accent and are pronounced as stressed words. This is the case in both Direct and Indirect Questions:

> **¿Cuándo viene?** *When's he coming?* (Direct Question)
> **No sé cuándo viene** *I don't know when he's coming* (Indirect Question)

After these words the verb is put before the subject:

> **¿Cómo van ustedes a Miami?** *How are you going to Miami?*[39]
>
> **¿Por qué dice eso tu jefe?** *Why does your boss say that?*

Who? must be translated by **quiénes** if we are certain that more than one person is involved:

> **¿Quién lo hizo?** *Who did it?*
>
> **¿Quiénes lo hicieron?** *Which persons did it?*

■ Translating *what?*

When the English word is followed by nothing, the Spanish word is **qué**:

> **Tenemos que hacer algo, pero no sabemos qué**
> *We have to do something, but we don't know what*

The English *what + to be* is translated **cuál + ser**, except when *what is?* really means *what is the definition of?* or *how many?*

> **¿Cuál fue la solución que él propuso?** *What was the solution that he suggested?*
>
> **¿Cuál es su profesión?** *What's your profession?*

but

> **¿Qué hora es?** *What's the time?*
>
> **¿Qué es un agujero negro?** *What is (the definition of) a Black Hole?*

When the English *what* precedes a verb other than **ser** it is translated **lo que**, but before an Infinitive by **qué**:

> **No sé lo que quieres** *I don't know what you want*

---

[39] Cubans may use ordinary word order here—**¿Cómo ustedes van . . . ?**, etc.

> **No sé qué decirles** *I don't know what to say to them*

When *what* stands before a noun, it is translated **qué**:

> **Dinero? ¿Qué dinero?** *Money? What money?*
> **No sé en qué canal es** *I don't know what/which channel it's on*

Many Latin-Americans use **cuál** in such sentences, e.g. **¿A cuáles libros te refieres?** for **¿A qué libros te refieres?** *what books are you referring to?*, but this is not done in Spain and is not the case in every Latin-American country.

■ Translating *which?*

When *which* stands alone, it is translated **cuál**, plural **cuáles** (although **quién**, plural **quienes** is more appropriate for human beings):

> **He leído alguno de estos libros, pero no recuerdo cuál** *I've read one or other of these books, but I can't remember which*

Which of? is **cuál de**, plural **cuáles de**. When *which* is an abbreviated form of *which of them* **cuál/cuáles** must also be used:

> **Puedes elegir tres de estos. ¿Cuáles prefieres?** *You can choose three of these. Which (ones of them) do you prefer?*

When *which* can be replaced by *what* it should be translated **qué**. See the previous section for examples.

For n Days/Weeks, Ago, Since and Similar Expressions

■ *for n days, weeks, etc.*

The most frequently used construction in everyday Spanish uses the regular verb **llevar**[40]. Note that Spanish uses the Present or the Imperfect tense where English uses the Perfect or Pluperfect tenses:

> ***Llevo*** **seis años estudiando español** *I have been studying Spanish for six years*
>
> ***Llevaba*** **seis años estudiando español** *I had been studying Spanish for six years*
>
> **Lleva años aquí** *He/she's been here for years*
>
> **Llevas varios días enfadado** *You've been angry for several days*
>
> **Llevábamos tres horas esperando** *We had been waiting for three hours*

The following constructions with **hacer** are more formal:

> **Estudio español desde hace seis años** *I have been studying Spanish for six years*

or

> **Hace seis años que estudio español**
>
> **Yo estudiaba español desde hacía seis años** *I had been studying Spanish for six years*

[40] Use of **tener**, e.g. **tengo seis años aquí** *I've been here six years*, is common in Latin America, but not in Spain.

or

Hacía seis años que yo estudiaba español

English-speakers are easily misled into thinking that a sentence like *he estado* **tres meses en Nueva York** *I was in New York for three months* means the same as *llevo* **tres meses en Nueva York** *I've been in New York for three months*. The former implies that the speaker has now left the city, whereas the latter clearly indicates that his/her stay is still continuing.

When the period of time is clearly finished, **durante** may be used:

> **La estuvo mirando durante tres minutos** *He gazed at her for three minutes*
> **Victoria reinó durante casi cuarenta años** *Victoria reigned for nearly forty years*

In some cases no preposition is used:

> **Estuve tres días en Barcelona** *I was in Barcelona (for) three days*

■ *Ago*

The usual construction uses **hacer**:

> **La vi hace tres días/Hace tres días que la vi** *I saw her three days ago*

■ *Since*

The use of the Present and Imperfect tenses should be noted:

> *Vivo* **aquí desde abril** *I've been living here since April*
> **Mi madre** *vive* **con mi tía desde que murió mi padre** *My mother's been living with my aunt since my father died*
> *Vivíamos* **allí desde el año anterior** *We had been living there since the year before*

Spaniards may use the Perfect and Pluperfect tenses in these sentences, but the Present or Imperfect are usually required by Latin-Americans. If the sentence is negated, the Perfect tense is used, or the Preterit in those regions (much of Latin America) where the Perfect is little used:

> **No la he visto/No la vi desde el domingo** *I haven't seen her since Sunday*

■ *The first time that . . . ,* etc.

Use of the Spanish Present and Imperfect tenses should be noted in these sentences:

> **Es la primera vez que *oigo* mencionar su nombre** *It is the first time I have heard his name mentioned*
>
> **Era la primera vez que *entraban* en ese edificio** *It was the first time they had entered that building*

| Affective Suffixes

'Affective' suffixes are suffixes like **-ito**, **-illo**, **-ón**, **-azo** that add various emotional overtones to a noun, adjective or adverb. In general, foreign learners should avoid using them until they are very fluent in the language, since they can sound silly or even insulting if misused. They are less frequent in some places than in others: Mexicans and Central Americans sprinkle their speech with diminutive suffixes, in Argentina and Spain they are less common (but still much used), and in some places diminutive forms are considered more appropriate in women's speech than men's.

DIMINUTIVE SUFFIXES

The main Diminutive Suffixes are **-ito**, **-ecito** (or **-ico** in some regions), **-illo**, **-ecillo**. Other suffixes like **-uelo**, **-iño**, **-ín** are also encountered, the latter two being regional in use

They are used:

■ To make one's speech especially friendly or affectionate

For this reason they are much used when talking to little children, but they are also often used between strangers in order to make the tone friendly. Compare

> **¿Le pongo un poco de sal?** *Shall I put some salt on it for you?* (neutral tone)
> **¿Le pongo un poquito de sal?** (same thing but more friendly)

> **Eres un comilón** (or **comelón**) *You eat a lot*
> **Eres un comiloncillo** *You sure like your food!* (more friendly)

Ahora se lo traigo *I'll bring it to you now*
Ahorita se lo traigo (same but more friendly).

Ahorita is especially common in Mexico, but Spaniards say **ahora mismo**)

■ To convey the idea of smallness, usually with some feeling of affection:

La casa tiene un jardincito *The house has a little backyard/garden*
¡Mira los pajaritos! *Look at the little birds!*
un cafetín *a little café*

■ Sometimes, especially in the case of **-illo**, to add a sarcastic tone:

¡Qué listillo eres! *Aren't you smart! What a know-all you are!* (sarcastic: **listo** = *clever*)
señorito (roughly) *a spoilt son from a rich family*
miedica *cowardly/'chicken'*

Sometimes diminutive suffixes simply change the original meaning without any emotional overtones:

el palo *a stick*	**el palillo** *a toothpick*
la tesis *thesis*	**la tesina** *dissertation*
la ventana *window*	**la ventanilla** *vehicle window*

AUGMENTATIVE SUFFIXES

The main Augmentative Suffixes are **-ón**, **-azo** and **-ote**. As their name suggests, they indicate increased size or intensity, often (especially in the first two cases) with some overtone of excess or unpleasantness:

mandón *bossy*
aburridón *really boring* (**aburrido** = *boring*)
dramón *a big melodrama* (sarcastic, cf. **el drama** *drama*)

> **un vinazo** *a really strong, heavy wine* (**el vino** = *wine*)
> **la palabrota** *swearword* (**la palabra** = *word*)
> **grandote** *enormous* (**grande** = *big*)

PEJORATIVE SUFFIXES

-ajo, -uco, -ucho, -astro are also sometimes added to nouns and adjectives to add an idea of unpleasantness:

> **el hotelucho** *flophouse/dump of a hotel*
> **la palabreja** *peculiar, horrible word*
> **la casuca, la casucha** *hovel/dingy house* (**la casa** = *house*)

| Word Order

Word order in questions is mentioned on p.203. Word order with adverbs is mentioned on p.153. Other useful points to remember are:

■ Spanish is unlike English in that it puts a Verb and an Object (if there is one) before the Subject rather than separate them by many intervening words. Spanish does not like to leave verb phrases dangling at the end of the sentence far from their subject. The position of the verbs in italics should be noted in these sentences:

> ***Rompió*** **la ventana el vecino que siempre lleva el sombrero amarillo** *The neighbor/*(Brit. *neighbour*) *who always wears the yellow hat broke the window*
>
> ***Ganó*** **el partido el equipo que más se había entrenado antes** *The team that had trained most before won the match*
>
> **Me fui porque me *revienta* tener que esperar varias horas en la parada del autobús** *I left because having to wait several hours at the bus-stop gets on my nerves*

The preceding rule is almost always applied in Subordinate and Relative Clauses. The verb is usually not left at the end of the sentence:

> **Esa es la moto que me vendió Alfredo** *That's the motor-bike that Alfredo sold me* (lit. *that sold me Alfredo*)
>
> **Quedará prohibido cuando entre en vigor la nueva ley** *It'll be prohibited when the new law*

> comes into effect (lit. *comes into effect the new law*)

■ After adverbs and adverbial phrases, the verb is often put before the subject:

> **Si bien *dice* el refrán que "ojos que no ven, corazón que no llora"** . . . *If the proverb is right* (literally *if well says the proverb that* . . .) *that 'what the eye doesn't see, the heart doesn't weep about'* . . .
>
> **Con la noche *llegan* a su fin las actividades del día** *At nightfall the day's activities come to an end*

■ An English preposition can appear at the end of a sentence, but Spanish prepositions *always* stand before the noun or pronoun that they refer to:

> **La chica a la que di el dinero** *The girl I gave the money **to*** . . .
>
> **Las escaleras por las que subieron** *The stairs they went **up***
>
> **alguien con quien salir** . . . *someone to go out **with*** . . .

■ No word ever comes between Object Pronouns and their verb:

> ***Me lo* diste ayer** *You gave it to me yesterday*
>
> ***Me* has defendido siempre** *You've always defended me*

■ There is a tendency, especially in colloquial speech, to put the most urgent information first. This is required in some contexts, e.g. **¡viene la policía!** *the police are coming!,* but normal word order would also be correct in the following sentences:

> **Dinero tiene, pero no es un millonario** *He's got money, but he's no millionaire* (literally *money he's got* . . .)

Invitada está, pero no sé si viene *She's invited—but I don't know if she'll come* (literally *invited she is . . .*)

Todos esos detalles ya me los explicaste ayer *You already explained all those details to me yesterday*

In the last example the Direct Object (**todos estos detalles**) is echoed or resumed by **los,** as explained on p.117.

| Pronunciation

The descriptions given in this section are approximate: it is not possible to give an exact picture in writing of the pronunciation of a foreign language. An attempted representation of the pronunciation is shown between square brackets, e.g. [elpérro] = **el perro** *dog*: the letters in the square brackets should be given their normal Spanish pronunciation, although a few special signs are used, explained below. Where two pronunciations are shown, the Latin-American version is first.

VOWELS

Spanish vowels are neither numerous nor complicated, but none of them is exactly like any English vowel sound. They are all *short* and do not vary in length or quality, whether stressed or not; compare the English pronunciation of *panorama,* which has three different *a* sounds, and the Spanish **panorama,** which has only one kind of *a.*

	Approximate equivalents	
	American English	Southern British
a	*father* (but much shorter)	*father*(shortened), *cut*
	The vowel must be as short as the *a* of *cat.*	
e	*egg*	*egg*
	Not like the *ay* of *day* (which is much too long and ends in a *y* sound), although the first part of this English diphthong is close to Spanish **e.** Spanish **e** is an equivalent of the French *e* in **un café**	

i	*seen* but much shorter and with no trace of a *y* sound at the end	same
o	no exact equivalent? *hot* (rounded) Not like the *o* of *note* (which is too long and ends in a *w* sound) but a very short version of the first part of this sound with rounded lips is good	
u	*good*, but with rounded lips same Not like *oo* of *food* (too long, lips not rounded and ends in a *w* sound)	

Examples: **cama, teme, sin, somos, luz**.

English-speakers, American and British, must learn to pronounce adjacent vowels without a trace of a pause (glottal stop), *y*, *r* or *w* sound between them: **sea o no** *whether it is or not* is [seaonó], not 'sayer-ou-nou', **lo ha hecho** *he's done it* = [loaécho], not 'lo-wa-echou'.

Vowels are not slurred when they are unstressed. **Beca** *(study) grant* is [béka] and nothing like the English word *baker*. The sound of the English *a* in *above* or *e* in *the* does not exist in Spanish.

DIPHTHONGS

American and Southern British

ai, ay	*aisle*
au	*cow*, but with rounded lips
ei, ey	*day*
eu	like *e* in *egg* followed by *w* of *well*
ie, ye	*ye*s
ia, ya	*y* of *yes* + Spanish **a**
iu	*y* of *yes* + Spanish **u**
oi, oy	*boy*

ou   *low* but with rounded lips

ua   *w* of *want* (with rounded lips) + Spanish **a**

ue   *went* with rounded lips

uy   Spanish **u** + *y* of *yes*

Examples: **hay** *there is/are*, **causa** *cause*, **ley** *law*,
Europa *Europe*, **bien** *well*, **ya** *already*, **la viuda** *widow*, **no
unió** *he did not join together* (pronounced [nounyó]),
Managua, **bueno** *good*, **muy** *very*.

Words are run together whenever possible without
pauses between them: **nos han dado una fortuna** =
[nosandaðounafortúna] *they've given us a fortune*. When
one word ends in a vowel and the next one begins with a
vowel a diphthong is formed if possible and identical vowels are run together to form a very slightly longer vowel.
English speakers must avoid inserting a pause or a *y* or *w*:

> **ha iniciado** [aynisyáðo]/[ayniθyáðo] *has initiated*
>   (**ay** as in English *eye*)
> **la apertura** [lapertúra] *the opening*
> **he indicado** [eyndikáðo] *I have indicated* (**ey** as *ay*
>   in English *day*)
> **he entrado** [entráðo] *I have entered*
> **si han dicho** [syandícho] *if they've said* (**sya** like
>   *cea* in English *oceanic*)
> **no implica** [noymplíka] *it doesn't imply*

TRIPHTHONGS

These arise when one of the above diphthongs is preceded
or followed by a *y* sound or a *w* sound:

American and British English

uai, uay *wise*, but with rounded lips
uei, uey *ways*, but with rounded lips

| iai | *yike* |
| iei | *Yates* |

Examples: **continuáis** *you continue*, **Paraguay**, **continuéis** *you continue* (Subjunctive form), **buey** *ox*, **y aire** [yáy-re] *and air*.

CONSONANTS

p, t, k and **ch** are pronounced as in American and British English except that no puff of breath follows them. A piece of tissue paper hung two inches from the lips should barely move when one says the Spanish words **pipa** *pipe*, **tú** *you*, **kilo** *kilogram*, **chacha** *housemaid* (familiar style, Spain)

t is always pronounced with the tongue against the front teeth and not as in English with the tongue on the ridge of gum behind the front teeth.

c is pronounced as Spanish **k** before **a, o** and **u: cama** *bed*, **cosa** *thing*, **el cura** *the priest*.

Before **e** and **i** it is pronounced the same as Spanish **z**, i.e. as *c* in *rice* in Latin America and [θ] (like the *th* of *think*) in Spain: **cinco** [sínko]/[θínko] *five*, **central** [sentrál]/[θentrál] *central*.

b and **v** are pronounced in nearly every position as [ß], a sound that does not exist in English. It is technically known as a voiced bilabial fricative and is made by holding the lips as for *b* and murmuring through them; it should be possible to produce the sound as long as you have breath. The sound of English *v* in *vat* does not exist in Spanish: the pairs of words **tuvo/tubo** [túßo] *he had/tube*, **iba/IVA** [íßa] *he was going/Value Added Tax*, **lavase/la base** [laßáse] *he washed/the base* sound exactly the same in Spanish.

The same two letters are pronounced like the *b* of *big*

only when they come after **n** (even between words) or when they occur after a pause): **son buenos** [sombwénos] *they're good*, **en Bolivia** [embolíßya] *in Bolivia*, **ambos** [ámbos] *both*. Note that **n** is pronounced **m** before **b** and **v**.

d is pronounced [ð] in nearly every position, i.e. like the English *th* in *this*, *then*: **lado** [láðo] *size*, **los dados** [losdáðos] *the dice*, **libertad** [lißertáð] *freedom*. **d** is, however, pronounced like the *d* of *dog* (but with the tongue against the front teeth) after **n** and **l** and after a pause: **han dicho** [andícho] *they've said*, **cuando** [kwándo] *when*, **falda** [fálda] *skirt*, **sal de mar** [saldemár] *sea salt*.

f is pronounced as in English.

g is pronounced like Spanish **j** before **e** and **i**: see notes on **j**. It is pronounced [ɣ] in nearly every other position, a sound that does not exist in English. It is technically known as a voiced velar fricative and is made by holding the mouth as for the *g* in *ago* and gently releasing air through the throat while murmuring; it should be possible to keep the sound up as long as you have breath: **hago** [áɣo] *I do*, **laguna** [laɣúna] *pond*, **Paraguay** [paraɣwáy].

The same letter is pronounced like the English *g* of *go* only after **n** and at the beginning of a word after a pause: **son grandes** [songrándes] *they're big*, **sin ganas** [singánas] *without enthusiasm/appetite*, **tengo** [téngo] *I have*. The **n** must be pronounced like the *ng* of *bring* when **g** follows it.

The combination **gue** and **gui** are pronounced as the Spanish **g** of **hago** plus **e** or **i**; the silent **u** merely shows that the **g** is not pronounced like Spanish **j**: **pague** [páɣe] *pay*, **la guirnalda** [laɣirnálda] *wreath*. In the combinations **güe** and **güi** the **u** is pronounced like *w*, cf. **desagüe** [desáɣwe] *drain*, **nicaragüense** [nikaraɣwénse] *Nicaraguan*.

h is always silent. Compare the pairs **asta/hasta**
spear/until, **ha/a** *has/to,* **hecho/echo** *done/I throw out,*
which are each pronounced identically. The rule in
Spanish is the reverse of English: in Spanish *not* dropping
one's aitches tends to sound illiterate.

j is pronounced in Spain and most of Argentina like the *ch*
in Scottish *loch* (phonetic sign [χ]). In most of the rest of
Latin America it is soft like the *h* in English *hat*. **G** is pronounced like **j** before **e** and **i**: **rojo** [rróχo] *red,* **ajo** [áχo]
garlic, **jarra** [χárra] *jar,* **general** [χenerál] *general,* **gente**
[χénte] *people,* **rígido** [rríχiδo] *rigid.*

l is always pronounced like the *l* in Southern British or
Southern Irish *leaf*. It is not pronounced like the *l* in the
English *cold*. Americans and Scots tend to use the latter
kind of *l* even at the beginning of words like *leaf,* so they
must take care over the Spanish sound: **lobo** *wolf,* **sal** *salt,*
natural, gol *goal* (in soccer).

ll varies from region to region. The correct pronunciation
in standard Spanish does not correspond to anything in
English: it is a palatal **l**, i.e. **l** pronounced with the tongue
spread flat against the roof of the mouth. Many English-
speakers pronounce it like the *li* in *million,* but this is the
Spanish sound **li** in words like **alianza** *alliance,* **exilio**
exile: the two words **polio** *polio* and **pollo** *chicken* sound
quite different. The best solution for English speakers is to
pronounce it always like the *y* of *yacht*—as millions of
Spanish speakers do. This may sound slovenly to some
speakers, but it is much better than the *li* of *million*. In
most of the Argentina and Uruguay it is pronounced like
the *s* of *pleasure.*

m is pronounced as in English, or sometimes like **n**
when it occurs at the end of a word, as in
referéndum.

n is pronounced as in English before a vowel or **d, t,**

another **n**, or when nothing follows it: **no**, **Londres** *London*, **antes** *before*, **innato** *innate*, **son** *they are*.

Before all other consonants it is pronounced with the mouth in the same position as for the following consonant, i.e.

before **k**, **j**, **g** and **c** when pronounced **k**, like *ng* in *song*: **con kilos** *with kilos*, **sin gusto** *without taste*, **lengua** *tongue/language*, **en Colombia**, **banco** *bank/bench*;

before **m**, **b**, **p**, **v**, like the *m* in *mouse*: **en Madrid**, **han bajado** *they've got down*, **en París**, **han visto** *they've seen*;

before **ll**, **y** and **ch**, like **ñ** (see below): **en llamas** *in flames*, **en Yepes**, **ancho** *wide*, **en Chile**;

before **f** it is pronounced with the tongue and lips in the position for pronouncing **f**: **son fuertes** *they're strong*, **en frente** *opposite*.

ñ is difficult for Americans and Britons. It is a palatal *n*, i.e. an *n* pronounced with the tongue flat against the roof of the mouth. It is not the same as the *ni* in *onion*, which is the Spanish **ni** in words like **Sonia**, **milenio** *millennium*. Students should try their pronunciation of the two words **huraño** [uráño] *shy/unsociable* and **uranio** [urányo] *uranium* on a native Spanish-speaker: if the difference of meaning is clear, all is well.

q is found only in the combination **que** and **qui**, which are pronounced [ke] and [ki]. See **k** (first item in list of consonants) for details: **parque** *park*, **quiso** *he wanted*

r between vowels and at the end of words is rather like the *d* in the American English *soda* or the *r* in Scottish English *carry*: i.e. a single flap of the tongue against the gum ridge. It is not like the *r* in American or British *red*, *rose*. **R** is never dropped, as it is in southern British English in words like *cart*, and it is never pronounced with the tongue curled back, as it is in the USA in words like *far*.

Examples **Carlos, bar,' cara** *face*, **mero** *mere*, **decir** *to say*.

At the beginning of a word and after **n, l** and **s** it is rolled like Spanish **rr**, e.g. in **Roma, alrededor** *around*, **honra** *honour*, **Israel**.

rr is a rolled **r** (three taps of the tongue). It is important to distinguish between **caro** *dear* and **carro** *car/cart*, **pero** *but* and **perro** *dog*.

s is pronounced like *s* in *hiss*, not as in *rose*.

w is found only in foreign words, where it is pronounced like Spanish **v/b** (see above): **kiwi** [kíßi] *kiwi fruit*, **Kuwait** [kußáyt].

x is the same as in English in Latin America, but in Spain it is often pronounced *s* before a consonant: **explicar** [eksplikár]/[esplikár] *explain*, but **taxi** [táksi].

y is like y in *yacht*. In Argentina it is like the *s* in *pleasure*.

z is always pronounced the same as the Spanish **c** when the latter occurs before **e** and **i**, i.e. like *ss* in *hiss* in Latin America and [θ] (as *th* in *think*) in Spain: **haz** [as]/[aθ] *do*, **las veces** [lasßéses]/[lasßéθes] *the times*.

STRESS (see Glossary)

The position of stress in a Spanish word is often variable and can change the meaning. See the section on Writing Accents (p.222) for details.

Spelling and Punctuation

This chapter presupposes a knowledge of Spanish pronunciation (explained in the previous chapter).

THE ALPHABET

The Spanish alphabet has the following letters:

a **a**	g **ge**	m **eme**	r **erre/ere**	y **i griega**
b **be**	h **hache**	n **ene**	s **ese**	z **zeta**
c **ce**	i **i**	ñ **eñe**	t **te**	
d **de**	j **jota**	o **o**	u **u**	
e **e**	k **ka**	p **pe**	v **uve**	
f **efe**	l **ele**	q **cu**	w **uve doble**	

Letters of the alphabet are all feminine: **la a, una ce**.

Ch and **ll** were counted as separate letters of the alphabet until the Association of Academies of Spanish decided to introduce normal alphabetical order in April 1994. As a result alphabetical order in dictionaries and directories printed before that date will differ from ours, e.g. **chato** came after **cubrir, llama** after **luz**.

WRITING ACCENTS

There are three written accents in Spanish: the acute accent, the dieresis and the **tilde**.

The dieresis occurs only in the combinations **güe** and

güi, where it shows that the **u** is not silent as in **nicaragüense** *Nicaraguan*, **el pingüino** *the penguin*.

The **tilde** appears only over **ñ**, and forms an entirely different letter, described on p.220.

■ The acute accent is used for three purposes:

(a) Occasionally to distinguish two words that are spelt the same, e.g. **sólo** *only* and **solo** *alone*.

(b) On question words: **¿cuándo vienes?** *when are you coming?*, **no sabe qué hacer** *he doesn't know what to do*. See p.202 for details.

(c) To show where the stress falls in unpredictably stressed words

This latter function is very important, since the position of stress in a Spanish word is crucial for the meaning: compare **hablo** *I speak* and **habló** *he spoke*.

An accent must be written on the stressed vowel:

(1) Whenever the stress falls more than two full vowels[41] from the end:

> **rápido** *fast*
> **las imágenes** *images*
> **dígamelo** *say it to me*
> **fácilmente** *easily*
> **cámbiate** *change your clothes* (third full vowel from end)

(2) Whenever the word ends in a vowel or **n** or **s** and the stress falls on the final vowel:

> **habló** *he spoke*
> **iraní** *Iranian*
> **cambié** *I changed*

---

[41] By 'full vowel' is meant **a**, **e** and **o** and also **i** when it is pronounced as in **sin** and not like *y* as in **Colombia**, and **u** when it is pronounced as in **uno** and not like *w* as in **continuo**.

la nación *the nation*
francés *French*

Compare the following words which are stressed on the last full vowel but one and therefore do not require an accent: **hablo** *I speak*, **cambio** *I change*, **dicen** *they say*, **la imagen** *the image*, **las naciones** *the nations*, **las series** *the series* (plural).

(3) When the word ends in a consonant other than **n** or **s** and it is *not* stressed on the last vowel:

> **el récord** *the record* (in sport, etc.)
> **el revólver** *the revolver*
> **fácil** *easy*

Compare the following words which are stressed on the last vowel and therefore do not require an accent: **la libertad** *freedom*, **natural** *natural*, **el complot** *conspiracy/plot*.

■ Words of one syllable (i.e. having only one fully pronounced vowel) are not written with an accent:

> **fui** [fwi] *I was*[42]
> **fue** [fwe] *he was*
> **vio** [byo] *he saw*
> **dio** [dyo] *he gave*
> **la fe** *faith*

The only exceptions are accents written to distinguish one word from another: see list below.

Words like **fió** *he entrusted*, **crié** *I bred/raised* have two syllables (i.e. the **i** is pronounced separately).

■ The following words are distinguished by an accent:

> **aun** *even*   **aún** *still/yet*[43]

[42] **fui, fue, vio** and **dio** were written with an accent until 1959.
[43] **Aun** should be pronounced as one syllable [awn] (aw like *ow* in *how*) and **aún** as two [a-ún].

de *of*	**dé** Present Subjunctive of **dar** *to give*
el *the*	**él** *he*
este *this*	**éste** *this one* (see p.138)
ese/aquel *that*	**ése/aquél** *that one* (see p.138)
mas *but* (poetic)	**más** *more*
mi *my*	**mí** *me* (after prepositions)
se pronoun	**sé** *I know*
si *if*	**sí** *yes*; *himself/herself/ yourself/themselves*, etc.
solo *alone*	**sólo** *only*
te *you*	**té** *tea*
tu *your*	**tú** *you*

DIPHTHONGS AND TRIPHTHONGS: SPELLING AND ACCENT RULES

■ Diphthongs consist of a *y* or *w* sound preceded or followed by a vowel. The pronunciation of the following diphthongs is shown on p.215:

> **au ua ai/ay ia/ya**
> **eu ue ei/ey ie/ye**
> **iu**
> **ou uo oi/oy io/yo**

The sound *y* is always written **y** at the end of words:

> **rey** *king*
> **doy** *I give*

The sound *y* is written either **y** or **hi** at the beginning of words:

> **el yate** *yacht*
> **la hierba** or **la yerba** *grass*

The sound *w* is always written **hu** at the beginning of a word or when it comes between vowels:

> **la huerta** [lawérta] *orchard*
> **ahuecar** [awekár] *to hollow out*

When the combinations of vowel plus **i** or **u** represent two separate vowels and not a diphthong, the **i** or **u** is written with an accent (even if **h** intervenes):

> **dúo** *duo*
> **el búho** *the owl*
> **hacías** *you were doing*
> **prohíben** *they prohibit*
> **se reúnen** *they hold a meeting*

■ Triphthongs consist of one of the above Diphthongs preceded or followed by a *y sound* or a *w* sound:

> **actuáis** [aktwáys] *you act*
> **buey** [bwey] *ox*

Diphthongs and Triphthongs count as one full vowel for the purpose of finding the stress accent:

Regular stress	Irregular
hacia *towards*	**ha**cía *he made*
dio *he gave*	**me fío** *I trust*
aire *air*	**aísla** *he isolates*
sois *you* (**vosotros**) *are*	**prohíbe** *he prohibits*

MISCELLANEOUS SPELLING RULES

The main traps set by the Spanish spelling system are:

■ **b** and **v** are pronounced the same, so words like **vello** *down* (i.e. very fine hair) and **bello** *beautiful* sound the same.

■ The sound **s** (as in English *hiss*) can be spelt three different ways in Latin America:

feroz *ferocious* [ferós]   **as** *ace* [as]   **haz** *do* [as]
hace *does* [áse]   **cinco** *five* [sínko]

The **z** and **c** in the above words are pronounced like *th* of *think* in central and northern Spain.

■ There is no certain way of predicting the spelling of the sound [χ] (like the *ch* in the Scottish *loch*). It is usually written **j** before **a**, **o**, **u** and **g** before **e** and **i**. But there are quite a few words in which the combination **je** occurs, e.g. **el viaje** *journey*, **el equipaje** *baggage*, **el paisaje** *countryside*, **Jesús** *Jesus*, **condujeron** *they drove*, etc.

■ **gue/güe** and **gui/güi**: see p.218.

■ **h** is a silent letter, so there is no difference in sound, for example, between **hecho** *done* and **echo** *I pour out*.

■ **que** and **qui**: the **u** is silent and the **q** is pronounced [k].

■ **r** and **rr**: see p.220

■ A number of alternative spellings exist, the most important of which are:

words beginning with **psic-** (the equivalent of our *psych-*) may be written **sic-**: **psicología** or **sicología** *psychology*, because the **p** is silent;

the words **septiembre** *September* and **séptimo** *seventh* can be spelt without the **p**;

words beginning with **ree-** may be spelt **re-**, e.g. **relegir** or **reelegir** *re-elect*.

In all cases the longer forms are more usual (at least in Spain).

PUNCTUATION

There are variations in punctuation rules depending on country and, to some extent, on publisher. Only the major differences between Spanish and English practice are mentioned.

■ A comma is used to separate decimals (but not in Mexico, which uses the same system as English):

> **12,75 doce coma setenta y cinco** *12.75*

■ A period (British 'full stop') is used to separate thousands

> **1.000.000 un millón** *a million*

Mexico uses our system.

■ In some publications double inverted commas (**las comillas**) are used to enclose quoted words, in others chevrons are used (**« »**):

> **Tuvieron problemas por "el fuerte carácter de la suegra"** or . . . **«por el fuerte carácter de la suegra»** *They had problems due to 'their mother-in-law's strong character'*

■ Question marks and exclamation marks must be written upside-down at the beginning of questions and exclamations as well as the right way up at the end:

> **Oye, ¿sabes qué hora es?** *Listen, d'you know what time it is?*
> **Pero, ¡qué tonto!** *But what a fool!*

As can be seen, the start of the question or exclamation does not always coincide with the start of the sentence.

A **raya** or double-length dash is used to mark off dialogue in novels and stories:

> **—Tengo un hijo tuyo —me dijo después—. Allí está.**
> **Y apuntó con el dedo a un muchacho largo con los ojos azorados.**
> **—¡Quítate el sombrero, para que te vea tu padre!**

'*I've got a son of yours*', he said to me afterwards. '*There he is.*'
   And he pointed to a tall boy with alarmed eyes.
   '*Take your hat off so your father can see you!*'

| Translation Traps

This section covers a number of important miscellaneous points that could not be neatly fitted in elsewhere in the book.

'afternoon'/'evening'
'American'/'Latin-American', 'Spanish-American'
'any'
aun and *aún*
'to become'
de que and *de*
'-ing' forms of English verbs
'to like'
'only'/'alone'
'some'
'Spanish'/'Castilian'
'would'
ya

Afternoon, evening

It is difficult to differentiate these words in Spanish, since **la tarde** runs from about 1 p.m. to after sunset and therefore includes our afternoon and evening. **La noche** begins around 8 or 9 p.m.

American, Latin-American, South American, Spanish-American

In Spain **americano** usually means the same as the English *American*. In Latin America the same word is usually taken to mean *Latin-American* and **norteamericano** is used for our *American*. The adjective **estadounidense** 'pertaining to the USA' is generally found only in newspaper styles.

América Latina or **Latinoamérica** is *Latin America* and is a preferred term since it stresses trans-national identity; the adjective is **latinoamericano**. However, these terms include Brazil, Haiti, Martinique and one or two other places that speak Latin-based languages, and there is no entirely satisfactory word for Spanish-speaking Latin America. **La América de habla española** *Spanish-speaking America* is long-winded, but **Hispanoamérica**, **hispanoamericano** strictly mean *Spanish-America(n)* and some people consider them unfair to the non-European or non-Spanish components of the populations.

América del sur, adjective **sudamericano** or **suramericano** (the latter frowned on by strict grammarians) means *South America* and does not include Central America or the Caribbean.

Any

This word is translated as follows:

(a) Before substances and countable nouns, in negative and interrogative sentences, no Spanish equivalent:

> **No tengo agua/flores** *I haven't got any water/flowers*
> **¿Hay?** *Is there any/Are there any?*
> **¿Hay americanos en tu clase?** *Are there any Americans in your class?*

(b) When it means *it doesn't matter which*: **cualquiera** (see p.122):

> **Puedes elegir cualquiera de ellos** *You can choose any of them*
> **en cualquier sitio y a cualquier hora** *in any place and at any time*

(c) In comparisons: **ninguno** (see p.155):

> **Ella es mejor que ninguno de los hombres**
> *She's better than any of the men*

(d) After **sin** *without*, no Spanish equivalent:

> **Ha venido sin dinero** *He's come without any*
> *money*

Aun and aún

Aun means *even*, as in **aun en ese caso no lo haría** *even in that case I wouldn't do it.* **Incluso**[44] means the same thing, and is nowadays more common.

Aún means the same as **todavía** *yet*: **todavía/aún no han llegado** *they haven't arrived yet.*

To become

There are several ways of translating this word and words similar to it in meaning (cf. *to get* angry, *to go* red, *to turn* nasty):

(a) Use a Pronominal Verb if one exists, e.g. **alegrarse** *to become cheerful*, **se cansó** *he/she got/became tired.*

(b) Use **ponerse** for short-lived changes of mood, appearance: **no te pongas así** *don't get like that*, **esto se pone difícil** *this is getting difficult*, **se puso colorada** *she went red.*

(c) Use **volverse** for more permanent changes: **te has vuelto muy reaccionario** *you've got very reactionary*, **se volvió loco** *he went mad.*

(d) Use **convertirse en** for total changes of nature, cf. English *to turn into*: **los alquimistas creían que el plomo podía convertirse en oro** *alchemists thought lead could become/turn into gold.*

[44] Many Latin Americans say **inclusive** for **incluso**.

(e) Use **hacerse** for conversions to a belief or changes of profession involving qualifications: **se hizo diseñador** *he became a designer*. **Hacerse** is also found in some set phrases with non-human subjects, e.g. **se ha hecho tarde** *it's got late*.

(f) Use **nombrar** for posts, offices, titles: **lo/le han nombrado Ministro de Asuntos Exteriores** *he's become the Minister for Foreign Affairs*.

de que and que

These both translate *that*: **dice que viene** *he says that he's coming*, **la idea de que viene . . .** *the idea that he's coming*.

De que must be used:

(a) After nouns, to show that what follows is a Subordinate Clause and not a Relative Clause. Compare **el argumento que él defiende es absurdo** *the argument that/which he's defending is absurd* (Relative Clause) and **el argumento *de que* la luna está hecha de queso es absurdo** *the argument that the Moon is made of cheese is absurd* (Subordinator). If the English word *which* could replace *that* in such sentences, **de que** cannot be used.

(b) Before clauses after prepositional phrases, verbs and adjectives that include **de**: Compare

> **antes de la salida del tren** *before the departure of the train*
>
> **antes de que salga el tren** *before the train leaves*
>
> **Estoy seguro de tu amor** *I'm sure of your love*
> **Estoy seguro de que me quieres** *I'm sure that you love me*
>
> **Se queja de que no la dejan dormir** *She complains that they don't let her sleep*

(c) **De que** must *not* be used after verbs meaning *to say, to think, to tell,* etc.

Dice que está enferma *She/he says that she's ill* (*never* *"dice de que está enferma'*)

'-ing' forms of English verbs

This English verb form has many different uses, either as an adjective, a noun, a participle or, sometimes, as a gerund. The following are some of the most common ways of translating the *-ing* form:

(a) When it is a noun it must be translated by the Infinitive or by a suitable Spanish noun:

> *Smoking is forbidden* **Prohibido fumar**
> *I like dancing* **Me gusta bailar**
> *hunting and fishing* **la caza y la pesca**

In compounds like *driving wheel, fishing rod, diving suit*, the *-ing* form is a noun and the translation must be learned separately: **el volante, la caña de pescar, la escafandra/el traje de buceo**.

(b) When it is an adjective it must be translated by an adjective:

> *A boring film* **una película aburrida**
> *An overwhelming majority* **una mayoría abrumadora**
> *A worrying problem* **un problema preocupante**

(c) After a preposition it is translated by the Infinitive:

> *Do it without complaining* **Hazlo sin quejarte**

But when the subject of the *-ing* form is not the same as the subject of the main verb, the Subjunctive or the Indicative may be required. See p.29 ff for more details:

> *I entered without him seeing me* **Entré sin que él me viera**

(d) When the -*ing* form shows when or how an action is done, use the Spanish Gerund:

> *I realized it while walking down the street* **Me di cuenta andando por la calle**
> *He stood looking at me* **Se quedó mirándome**
> *You'll get nothing by shouting like that* **No conseguirás nada gritando así**

(e) For the phrase '*on . . . -ing*' use **al** plus the Infinitive:

> *on entering the room* **al entrar en el cuarto**

(f) To translate 'standing', 'sitting', 'leaning' or other bodily positions, use the Past Participle:

> *I was sitting on the beach* **Yo estaba sentado en la playa**
> *She was leaning against the tree* **Estaba apoyada contra el árbol**
> *He was crouching in the corner* **Estaba agazapado en el rincón**

(g) After many verbs, the -*ing* form must be translated by an Infinitive, often with a preposition:

> *Stop shouting* **Deja de gritar**
> *Start writing* **Empiece a escribir**

See the list of verbs that take the Infinitive on p.44 ff.

To like

Spanish uses the verb **gustar,** which means *to please,* so the English subject must become the object in Spanish:

> **Me gusta el vino** *Wine pleases me = I like wine*
> **No me gusta** *It doesn't please me = I don't like it*
> **¿Te/Le gusta bailar?** *Does dancing please you? = Do you like dancing?*

Le gusta trabajar aquí *Working here pleases/him/her = (S)he likes working here*
¿Te gusto? *Do I please you? = Do you like me?*
Me gustas *You please me = I like you*

Only and *alone*

Solo (agrees in number and gender: **sola, solos, solas**) is an adjective meaning *alone*: **está sola** *she's on her own*. **Sólo** (with accent) means *only*, and is the same as **solamente**: **sólo sé español** *I only know Spanish*.

Some

This word may be translated in several different ways:

(a) Before substances and vague quantities of countable nouns: no Spanish equivalent

Pon azúcar *Put in some sugar*
Compra pan/flores *Buy some bread/flowers*
Hay patatas (Lat. Am. **papas**) *There are some potatoes*

(b) Before countable nouns when it means *a small number*: **unos/unas**:

Han venido unos ingleses *Some/a couple of English people have come*

(c) When *some* means *certain*, i.e. *some but not others*: **alguno** (discussed on p.121):

En algunos países está prohibido beber alcohol *In some countries drinking alcohol is forbidden*
Algún día podré comprarlo *I'll be able to buy it some day*

Spanish, Castilian

España is the country, and **español** is the adjective *Spanish*. **El español** is not *the* language of Spain, since Catalan, Basque and Galician also have official status and several other languages are recognized locally. **El castellano** *Castilian* is the official name for the language described in this book, although Castilian-speakers often call it **el español**, which may annoy speakers of the other languages.

What and which

See p.p. 203–4.

Would

This usually forms the Conditional tense in English, in which case it is translated by the Spanish Conditional tense:

> *If we sold more, prices* **would** *be lower* **Si vendiéramos más, los precios serían más bajos**

But *would* is occasionally used in English narrative to express habitual actions, in which case it must be translated by the Spanish Imperfect tense or by **soler** + Infinitive:

> *Each day he* **would** *get up* (= *used to get up*) *at six and he'd feed the chickens* **Todos los días se levantaba a las seis y daba de comer a las gallinas**
> *He* **would** (= *used to*) *ring her every night before going to bed* **Solía llamarla todas las noches, antes de acostarse**

Ya

This constantly-used word basically means:

already with a past tense: **ya ha llegado/ha llegado ya** *he's already arrived*;

right now with a present tense or imperative:**ya vienen** *they're coming right now*, **¡dímelo ya!** *tell me right now!*;

for sure/soon with a positive future tense: **no te preocupes: ya llegará** *don't worry, she'll come for sure/she'll be here soon*;

not . . . any more with a negative present or future: **ya no vienen/vendrán** *they're not coming any more*.

Verb Forms

FORMS OF REGULAR VERBS

As the following tables show, one adds the appropriate endings to the stem, which is the form left after removing the **-ar**, **-er** or **-ir** of the Infinitive:

Infinitive	Stem	Examples
hablar	**habl-**	**hablas** *you speak*
beber	**beb-**	**bebíamos** *we were drinking*
vivir	**viv-**	**vivieron** *they lived*

Each tense has a separate set of endings, which differ for each of the three conjugations, although the endings of certain tenses (e.g. the Future and Conditional) are identical for all verbs, and the differences between the endings of the **-ir** and **-er** conjugations are not numerous.

CONJUGATION OF REGULAR VERB **HABLAR** to speak

Infinitive	**hablar**
Gerund	**hablando**
Past Participle	**hablado**
Imperative	
Tú	**habla**
Vosotros/as	**hablad**
Usted	**hable**
Ustedes	**hablen**

INDICATIVE

Present

hablo	**hablamos**
hablas	**habláis**
habla	**hablan**

Imperfect

hablaba	**hablábamos**
hablabas	**hablabais**
hablaba	**hablaban**

Preterit

hablé	**hablamos**
hablaste	**hablasteis**
habló	**hablaron**

Present Continuous
estoy hablando
etc.

Imperfect Continuous
estaba hablando
etc.

Preterit Continuous
estuve hablando
etc.

See p.269 for the conjugation of **estar**.

Perfect
he hablado

hemos hablado

has hablado

habéis hablado

ha hablado

han hablado

Pluperfect
había hablado

habíamos hablado

habías hablado

habíais hablado

había hablado

habían hablado

Perfect Continuous
he estado hablando
etc.

Pluperfect Continuous
había estado hablando
etc.

Pretérito anterior
hube hablado

hubimos hablado

hubiste hablado

hubisteis hablado

hubo hablado

hubieron hablado

Future
hablaré   hablaremos

hablarás   hablaréis

hablará   hablarán

Future Perfect
habré hablado

habremos hablado

habrás hablado

habréis hablado

habrá hablado

habrán hablado

Future Continuous
estaré hablando
etc.

Future Perfect Continuous
habré estado hablando
etc.

Conditional
hablaría   hablaríamos

hablarías   hablaríais

hablaría   hablarían

Perfect Conditional
habría hablado

habríamos hablado

habrías hablado

habríais hablado

habría hablado

habrían hablado

The Perfect Conditional may also be formed with the -ra Imperfect Subjunctive of **haber,** *e.g.* **hubiera hablado,** *etc.*

Conditional Continuous	*Perfect Conditional Continuous*
estaría hablando	**habría estado hablando**
etc.	*or* **hubiera estado hablando**
	etc.

SUBJUNCTIVE

Present Subjunctive		*Present Subjunctive Continuous*
hable	**hablemos**	**esté hablando**
hables	**habléis**	*etc.*
hable	**hablen**	

Imperfect Subjunctives

-ra *form*		**-se** *form*	
hablara	**habláramos**	**hablase**	**hablásemos**
hablaras	**hablarais**	**hablases**	**hablaseis**
hablara	**hablaran**	**hablase**	**hablasen**

Imperfect Subjunctive Continuous
estuviera hablando *or* **estuviese hablando**
etc.   *etc.*

Perfect Subjunctive

haya hablado	**hayamos hablado**
hayas hablado	**hayáis hablado**
haya hablado	**hayan hablado**

Perfect Subjunctive Continuous
haya estado hablando
etc.

Pluperfect Subjunctive

hubiera hablado	**hubiéramos hablado**
hubieras hablado	**hubierais hablado**
hubiera hablado	**hubieran hablado**

   or **hubiese hablado** *etc.*

Perfect Subjunctive Continuous
haya estado hablando
etc.

Pluperfect Subjunctive Continuous
hubiera estado hablando
or **hubiese estado hablando**
etc.

Future Subjunctive

hablare	**habláremos**
hablares	**hablareis**
hablare	**hablaren**

CONJUGATION OF REGULAR VERB
BEBER *to drink*

Infinitive	**beber**
Gerund	**bebiendo**
Past Participle	**bebido**
Imperative	
Tú	**bebe**
Vosotros/as	**bebed**
Usted	**beba´**
Ustedes	**beban**

INDICATIVE

Present

bebo	**bebemos**
bebes	**bebéis**
bebe	**beben**

Imperfect

bebía	**bebíamos**
bebías	**bebíais**
bebía	**bebían**

Preterit

bebí	**bebimos**
bebiste	**bebisteis**
bebió	**bebieron**

Present Continuous
estoy bebiendo
etc.

Imperfect Continuous
estaba bebiendo
etc.

Preterit Continuous
estuve bebiendo
etc.

Perfect
he bebido	**hemos bebido**
has bebido	**habéis bebido**
ha bebido	**han bebido**

Pluperfect
había bebido	**habíamos bebido**
habías bebido	**habíais bebido**
había bebido	**habían bebido**

Perfect Continuous	*Pluperfect Continuous*
he estado bebiendo	**había estado bebiendo**
etc.	*etc.*

Pretérito anterior
hube bebido	**hubimos bebido**
hubiste bebido	**hubisteis bebido**
hubo bebido	**hubieron bebido**

Future
beberé	**beberemos**
beberás	**beberéis**
beberá	**beberán**

Future Perfect
habré bebido	**habremos bebido**
habrás bebido	**habréis bebido**
habrá bebido	**habrán bebido**

Future Continuous	*Future Perfect Continuous*
estaré bebiendo	**habré estado bebiendo**
etc.	*etc.*

Conditional
bebería	**beberíamos**
beberías	**beberíais**
bebería	**beberían**

Perfect Conditional
habría bebido   **habríamos bebido**
habrías bebido   **habríais bebido**
habría bebido   **habrían bebido**

The Perfect Conditional may also be formed with the **-ra**
Imperfect Subjunctive of **haber,** *e.g.* **hubiera bebido,** *etc.*

Conditional Continuous   *Conditional Perfect Continuous*
estaría bebiendo   **habría estado bebiendo**
etc.   *or* **hubiera estado bebiendo,** *etc.*
                                  etc.

SUBJUNCTIVE

Present Subjunctive   *Present Subjunctive Continuous*
beba   bebamos   **esté bebiendo**
bebas   bebáis   *etc.*
beba   beban

Imperfect Subjunctives
-ra *form*   **-se** *form*
bebiera   bebiéramos   **bebiese   bebiésemos**
bebieras   bebierais   **bebieses   bebieseis**
bebiera   bebieran   **bebiese   bebiesen**

Imperfect Continuous Subjunctive
estuviera bebiendo *or* **estuviese bebiendo**
etc.   *etc.*

Perfect Subjunctive
haya bebido   **hayamos bebido**
hayas bebido   **hayáis bebido**
haya bebido   **hayan bebido**

Pluperfect Subjunctive
hubiera bebido   **hubiéramos bebido**
hubieras bebido   **hubierais bebido**
hubiera bebido   **hubieran bebido**
or **hubiese bebido,** *etc.*

Perfect Subjunctive Continuous
haya estado bebiendo
etc.

Pluperfect Subjunctive Continuous
hubiera estado bebiendo
or **hubiese estado bebiendo**
etc.

Future Subjunctive

bebiere	**bebiéremos**
bebieres	**bebiereis**
bebiere	**bebieren**

CONJUGATION OF REGULAR VERB **VIVIR**
to live

■ *Only the endings marked with an asterisk differ from those of the* **-er** *conjugation.*

Infinitive	**vivir★**
Gerund	**viviendo**
Past Participle	**vivido**
Imperative	
Tú	**vive**
Vosotros/as	**vivid★**
Usted	**viva**
Ustedes	**vivan**

INDICATIVE

Present		*Imperfect*	
vivo	**vivimos★**	**vivía**	**vivíamos**
vives	**vivís★**	**vivías**	**vivíais**
vive	**viven**	**vivía**	**vivían**

Preterit	
viví	**vivimos**
viviste	**vivisteis**
vivió	**vivieron**

Present
estoy viviendo
etc.

Imperfect Continuous
estaba viviendo
etc.

Preterit Continuous
estuve viviendo
etc.

Perfect
he vivido
has vivido
ha vivido

hemos vivido
habéis vivido
han vivido

Pluperfect
había vivido
habías vivido
había vivido

habíamos vivido
habíais vivido
habían vivido

Perfect Continuous
he estado viviendo
etc.

Pluperfect Continuous
había estado viviendo
etc.

Pretérito anterior
hube vivido
hubiste vivido
hubo vivido

hubimos vivido
hubisteis vivido
hubieron vivido

Future
viviré★
vivirás★
vivirá★

viviremos★
viviréis★
vivirán★

Future Perfect
habré vivido
habrás vivido
habrá vivido

habremos vivido
habréis vivido
habrán vivido

Future Continuous
estaré viviendo
etc.

Future Perfect Continuous
habré estado viviendo
etc.

Conditional
viviría★   **viviríamos★**
vivirías★   **viviríais★**
viviría★   **vivirían★**

Conditional Perfect
habría vivido   **habríamos vivido**
habrías vivido   **habríais vivido**
habría vivido   **habrían vivido**

The Perfect Conditional may also be formed with the **-ra**
Imperfect Subjunctive of **haber**, *e.g.* **hubiera vivido**, *etc.*

Conditional Continuous   *Conditional Perfect Continuous*
estaría viviendo   **habría estado viviendo**
etc.   *etc.*

SUBJUNCTIVE

Present Subjunctive   *Present Subjunctive Continuous*
viva   **vivamos**   **esté viviendo**
vivas   **viváis**   *etc.*
viva   **vivan**

Imperfect Subjunctives

-ra *form*   **-se** *form*
viviera   **viviéramos**   **viviese**   **viviésemos**
vivieras   **vivierais**   **vivieses**   **vivieseis**
viviera   **vivieran**   **viviese**   **viviesen**

Imperfect Subjunctive Continuous
estuviera viviendo *or* **estuviese viviendo**
etc.   *etc.*

Perfect Subjunctive
haya vivido   **hayamos vivido**
hayas vivido   **hayáis vivido**
haya vivido   **hayan vivido**

Pluperfect Subjunctive

hubiera vivido	**hubiéramos vivido**
hubieras vivido	**hubierais vivido**
hubiera vivido	**hubieran vivido**
or **hubiese vivido** *etc.*	

Perfect Subjunctive Continuous Pluperfect Subjunctive Continuous

haya estado viviendo	**hubiera estado viviendo**
etc.	*or* **hubiese estado viviendo**
	etc.

Future Subjunctive

viviere	**viviéremos**
vivieres	**viviereis**
viviere	**vivieren**

SPELLING RULES AFFECTING CONJUGATION OF ALL SPANISH VERBS

- Infinitive ends in **-car**   **c > qu** before **e** or **i**. See **sacar** (no.52)

- Infinitive ends in **-gar**   **g > gu** before **e** or **i**. See **pagar** (no. 34)

- Infinitive ends in **-zar**   **z > c** before **e** or **i**. See **rezar** (no. 49)

- Infinitive ends in **-guar**   dieresis needed on **u** before **e**. See **averiguar** (no.7)

- Infinitive ends in **-cer**: a few verbs are conjugated like **vencer** (no. 61), i.e. **c > z** before **a** or **o**: these include **ejercer** *to exercise*, **convencer** *to convince*, **mecer** *to rock/sway*. **Escocer** *to sting* and **torcer** *to twist* are conjugated like **cocer** *to cook* (no.12). The rest, which are the vast majority, are conjugated like **parecer** (no. 35) and show a slight irregularity: **c > zc** before **a, o**.

■ Infinitive ends in vowel + **-er** or vowel + **-ir**: a *y* sound is written **y** between vowels. See **poseer** (no. 40) and **construir** (no. 13) for examples.

■ Infinitive ends in **-cir**. Check verb in list.

■ Infinitive ends in **-ger** or **-gir**: **g** > **j** before **o** or **a**. See **proteger** (no. 43).

■ Infinitive ends in **-ñer**, **-ñir** or **-llir**: diphthong **ió** in Preterit > **ó**; diphthong **ie** in Preterit and in Imperfect Subjunctive > **e**. See **tañer** (no. 57).

SPANISH VERBS: HINTS AND TIPS FOR LEARNERS

The Spanish verb system is complicated, but there are a number of short cuts that will save learners time and effort.

■ Compound Tense Formation: all verbs

The Compound Tenses (see Glossary) of all verbs are formed with the verb **haber** and the Past Participle, formed as explained on p. 55.

The most frequently used compound tenses are:

Perfect	**he hablado**	*I have spoken, etc.*
Pluperfect	**había hablado**	*I had spoken*
Future	**habré hablado**	*I will have spoken,*
Conditional	**habría** or **hubiera hablado**	*I would have spoken*

The Past Participle is invariable in form in these tenses. The full conjugation of the irregular verb **haber** appears on p.271.

■ Imperfect Indicative: only three verbs are irregular:

ser *to be*: **era eras era éramos erais eran**
ir *to go*: **iba ibas iba íbamos ibais iban**
ver *to see*: **veía veías veía veíamos veíais veían**
   (the *e* is unexpected)

In all other cases the endings of the Imperfect are added
to the stem left after removing the **-ar**, **-er** or **-ir** of the
Infinitive, e.g. **dar** *to give*: **daba, dabas, daba, dábamos,
dabais, daban**; **tener** *to have*: **tenía, tenías, tenía,
teníamos, teníais, tenían**.

■ Future and Conditional: with twelve exceptions, all
verbs form their Future by adding **-é -ás -á -emos -éis -
án** to their Infinitive, and all verbs form their Conditional
by adding **-ía -ías -ía -íamos -íais -ían** to their
Infinitive (the latter endings are the same as the endings of
the Imperfect Indicative of **-er** verbs). The exceptions are
the following verbs (and also any compound verbs based
on them, e.g. **componer** *to compose*). The Future and
Conditional endings are added to the slightly modified
form of the Infinitive shown in bold italics:

caber *cabr-* to fit in	**querer** *querr-* to want
decir *dir-* to say	**saber** *sabr-* to know
haber *habr-* auxiliary verb	**salir** *saldr-* to leave
hacer *har-* to do/to make	**tener** *tendr-* to have
poder *podr-* to be able	**valer** *valdr-* to be worth
poner *pondr-* to put	**venir** *vendr-* to come

■ The Present Subjunctive can be formed for nearly all
verbs by adding the following endings to the stem left
after removing the **-o** of the first-person Present
Indicative:

-ar verbs :	**-e**	**-es**	**-e**	**-emos**	**-éis**	**-en**
-er & -ir verbs:	**-a**	**-as**	**-a**	**-amos**	**-áis**	**-an**

Examples:

Infinitive	1st-person singular Present Indicative (stem in Italics)	Present Subjunctive
hablar *to speak*	*habl*o	*habl*e, etc.
comer *to eat*	*com*o	*com*a, etc.
vivir *to live*	*viv*o	*viv*a, etc.
contar *to tell*	*cuent*o	*cuent*e, etc.
perder *to lose*	*pierd*o	*pierd*a, etc.
pedir *to ask for*	*pid*o	*pid*a, etc.
hacer *to do*	*hag*o	*hag*a, etc.
tener *to have*	*teng*o	*teng*a, etc.

The main exceptions are the following verbs, which should be checked in the tables printed below:

> **dar** *to give* (unexpected accent in Subjunctive)
> **estar** *to be* (unexpected accents in Subjunctive)
> **haber**
> **ir** *to go*
> **morir** *to die* and **dormir** *to sleep*
> **saber** *to know*
> **sentir** *to feel* (and all verbs like it)
> **ser** *to be*

In the case of Radical-Changing verbs like **contar, mover, cerrar, perder** only the stressed vowel is altered: c**ue**ntos—contemos, p**ie**rda—perdamos, etc.

■ The Imperfect Subjunctive of all verbs is predictable: the endings are added to the stem left after the ending of the third-person singular Preterit is removed (but this stem may require separate learning in the case of Radical-Changing and Irregular verbs):

Infinitive	3rd-person Preterit (stem in italics)	Imperfect Subjunctive
hablar *to speak*	**habl**ó *he spoke*	**habl**ara, **habl**ase, etc.
sentir *to feel*	**sinti**ó *he felt*	**sinti**era, **sinti**ese, etc.
estar *to be*	**estuv**o *he was*	**estuvi**era, **estuvi**ese, etc.
tener *to have*	**tuv**o *he had/got*	**tuvi**era, **tuvi**ese, etc.
decir *to say*	**dij**o *he said*	**dij**era, **dij**ese, etc.

Note the loss of **i** after **j** in words like **dijera/dijese, trajera/trajese, produjera/produjese**.

■ The Imperative

The **vosotros** Imperative (not used in Latin America) is always regularly formed by replacing the -**r** of the Infinitive by -**d**: **hablar—hablad**, **ir—id**, **ser—sed**, etc.

The **Usted** and **Ustedes** Imperative are always identical to the 3rd-person Present Subjunctive, singular and plural respectively, e.g. **hacer—haga—hagan**.

The **tú** Imperative is always formed by dropping the -**s** from the 2nd-person singular of the Present Indicative: **cuentas** *you tell*—¡**cuenta!** *tell!*, **pides** *you ask for*—¡**pide!** *ask for!* There are a few important exceptions, shown on p.36.

TABLES OF IRREGULAR VERBS, TYPICAL RADICAL CHANGING VERBS AND EXAMPLES OF VERBS AFFECTED BY SPELLING CHANGES

The Indicative Present and Preterit and the Present Subjunctive are always shown in full, whether they are regular or not. The endings of the Future and Conditional tenses are the same for all verbs. The endings of the

Imperfect Indicative are all regular, with very few exceptions (**ir** and **ser**). The Imperfect Subjunctive endings are always the same as for regular verbs.

1. **Abolir** *to abolish*

This, and a few verbs like it, is a defective verb. Forms in which the ending does not begin with **i** are not used.

Infinitive **abolir**	*Gerund* **aboliendo**
Past Participle **abolido**	*Imperative* **abolid.** **Abole is not found*

INDICATIVE

Present	*Imperfect*	*Preterit*
not found	**abolía**	**abolí**
not found	etc.	**aboliste**
not found		**abolió**
abolimos		**abolimos**
abolís		**abolisteis**
not found		**abolieron**

Future	*Conditional*
aboliré	**aboliría**
etc.	etc.

SUBJUNCTIVE

Present	*Imperfect*
no forms in use	**aboliera/aboliese**
	etc.

2. **Adquirir** *to acquire*

Radical changing verb. Only **inquirir** *to enquire* is conjugated the same way.

Infinitive **adquirir**	*Gerund* **adquiriendo**
Past Participle **adquirido**	*Imperative* **adquiere adquirid**

INDICATIVE

Present	Imperfect	Preterit
adquiero	adquiría	adquirí
adquieres	etc.	adquiriste
adquiere		adquirió
adquirimos		adquirimos
adquirís		adquiristeis
adquieren		adquirieron

Future	Conditional
adquiriré	adquiriría
etc.	etc.

SUBJUNCTIVE

Present	Imperfect
adquiera	adquiriera/adquiriese
adquieras	etc.
adquiera	
adquiramos	
adquiráis	
adquieran	

3. **Aislar** *to isolate*

The **i** is written with an accent when it is stressed. The accent was introduced in 1959 and does not appear in books printed before then.

Infinitive **aislar**   *Gerund* **aislando**

Past Participle **aislado** *Imperative* **aísla aislad**

INDICATIVE

Present	Imperfect	Preterit
aíslo	aislaba	aislé
aíslas	etc.	aislaste
aísla		aisló
aislamos		aislamos
aisláis		aislasteis
aíslan		aislaron

Future
aislaré
etc.

Conditional
aislaría
etc.

SUBJUNCTIVE

Present
aísle
aísles
aísle
aislemos
aisléis
aíslen

Imperfect
aislara/aislase
etc.

4. **Andar** *to walk/go about*

Infinitive **andar**
Past Participle **andado**

Gerund **andando**
Imperative **anda andad**

Present	*Imperfect*	*Preterit*
ando	**andaba**	**anduve**
andas	etc.	**anduviste**
anda		**anduvo**
andamos		**anduvimos**
andáis		**anduvisteis**
andan		**anduvieron**

Future
andaré
etc.

Conditional
andaría
etc.

SUBJUNCTIVE

Present
ande
andes
ande
andemos
andéis
anden

Imperfect
anduviera/anduviese
etc.

5. **Argüir** *to argue* (*a point*)

The dieresis on the **u** shows that it is pronounced as *w*.

Infinitive **argüir**   *Gerund* **arguyendo**
Past Participle **argüido**   *Imperative* **arguye argüid**

INDICATIVE

Present	*Imperfect*	*Preterit*
arguyo	argüía	argüí
arguyes	etc.	argüiste
arguye		arguyó
argüimos		argüimos
argüís		argüisteis
arguyen		arguyeron

Future	*Conditional*
argüiré	argüiría
etc.	etc.

SUBJUNCTIVE

Present	*Imperfect*
arguya	arguyera/arguyese
arguyas	etc.
arguya	
arguyamos	
arguyáis	
arguyan	

6. **Asir** *to grasp/seize*

Infinitive **asir**   *Gerund* **asiendo**
Past Participle **asido**   *Imperative* **ase, asid**

Forms containing **g** are usually avoided.

INDICATIVE

Present	*Imperfect*	*Preterit*
(asgo)	asía	así
ases	etc.	asiste

Present, continued
ase
asimos
asís
asen

Preterit, continued
asió
asimos
asisteis
asieron

Future
asiré
etc.

Conditional
asiría
etc.

SUBJUNCTIVE

Present
(asga)
(asgas)
(asga)
(asgamos)
(asgáis)
(asgan)

Imperfect
asiera/asiese
etc.

7. **Averiguar** *to ascertain*

The dieresis shows that the **u** is not silent.

Infinitive **averiguar**
Past Participle **averiguado**

Gerund **averiguando**
Imperative **averigua averiguad**

INDICATIVE

Present
averiguo
averiguas
averigua
averiguamos
averiguáis
averiguan

Imperfect
averiguaba
etc.

Preterit
averigüé
averiguaste
averiguó
averiguamos
averiguasteis
averiguaron

Future
averiguaré
etc.

Conditional
averiguaría
etc.

SUBJUNCTIVE

Present	Imperfect
averigüe	averiguara/averiguase
averigües	etc.
averigüe	
averigüemos	
averigüéis	
averigüen	

8. Caber *to fit into*

Infinitive caber	*Gerund* cabiendo
Past Participle cabido	*Imperative* cabe cabed

INDICATIVE

Present	Imperfect	Preterit
quepo	cabía	cupe
cabes	etc.	cupiste
cabe		cupo
cabemos		cupimos
cabéis		cupisteis
caben		cupieron

Future	Conditional
cabré	cabría
etc.	etc.

SUBJUNCTIVE

Present	Imperfect
quepa	cupiera/cupiese
quepas	etc.
quepa	
quepamos	
quepáis	
quepan	

9. **Caer** *to fall*

Infinitive **caer**   *Gerund* **cayendo**
Past Participle **caído**   *Imperative* **cae caed**

INDICATIVE

Present	*Imperfect*	*Preterit*
caigo	caía	caí
caes	etc.	caíste
cae		cayó
caemos		caímos
caéis		caísteis
caen		cayeron

Future	*Conditional*
caeré	caeriá
etc.	etc.

SUBJUNCTIVE

Present	*Imperfect*
caiga	cayera/cayese
caigas	etc.
caiga	
caigamos	
caigáis	
caigan	

10. **Cambiar** *to change*

Regular: the **i** is always pronounced like **y**. However, many verbs ending in **-iar** are conjugated like **liar** (no. 28).

Infinitive **cambiar**   *Gerund* **cambiando**
Past Participle **cambiado**   *Imperative* **cambia cambiad**

INDICATIVE

Present	*Imperfect*	*Preterit*
cambio	cambiaba	cambié
cambias	etc.	cambiaste

Present, continued		*Preterit, continued*
cambia		**cambió**
cambiamos		**cambiamos**
cambiáis		**cambiasteis**
cambian		**cambiaron**

Future	*Conditional*
cambiaré	**cambiaría**
etc.	*etc.*

SUBJUNCTIVE

Present	*Imperfect*
cambie	**cambiara/cambiase**
cambies	*etc.*
cambie	
cambiemos	
cambiéis	
cambien	

11. **Cerrar** *to shut/close*

Radical changing verb.

Infinitive **cerrar**	*Gerund* **cerrando**
Past Participle **cerrado**	*Imperative* **cierra cerrad**

INDICATIVE

Present	*Imperfect*	*Preterit*
cierro	**cerraba**	**cerré**
cierras	*etc.*	**cerraste**
cierra		**cerró**
cerramos		**cerramos**
cerráis		**cerrasteis**
cierran		**cerraron**

Future	*Conditional*
cerraré	**cerraría**
etc.	*etc.*

SUBJUNCTIVE

Present	*Imperfect*
cierre	cerrara/cerrase
cierres	*etc.*
cierre	
cerremos	
cerréis	
cierren	

12. Cocer *to boil*

Radical changing verb conjugated like **mover** but with spelling change **c > z** before **o** or **a**.

Infinitive **cocer**   *Gerund* **cociendo**
Past Participle **cocido**   *Imperative* **cuece coced**

INDICATIVE

Present	*Imperfect*	*Preterit*
cuezo	cocía	cocí
cueces	*etc.*	cociste
cuece		coció
cocemos		cocimos
cocéis		cocisteis
cuecen		cocieron

Future	*Conditional*
coceré	cocería
etc.	*etc.*

SUBJUNCTIVE

Present	*Imperfect*
cueza	cociera/cociese
cuezas	*etc.*
cueza	
cozamos	
cozáis	
cuezan	

13. **Construir** *to build*

The **y** between vowels should be noted.

Infinitive **construir**　　　*Gerund* **construyendo**
Past Participle **construido**　　*Imperative* **construye construid**

INDICATIVE

Present	*Imperfect*	*Preterit*
construyo	construía	construí
construyes	etc.	construiste
construye		construyó
construimos		construlmos
construís		construisteis
construyen		construyeron

Future	*Conditional*
construiré	construiría
etc.	etc.

SUBJUNCTIVE

Present	*Imperfect*
construya	construyera/construyese
construyas	etc.
construya	
construyamos	
construyáis	
construyan	

14. **Contar** *to count/tell a story*

Radical changing verb.

Infinitive **contar**　　　*Gerund* **contando**
Past Participle **contado**　　*Imperative* **cuenta contad**

INDICATIVE

Present	*Imperfect*	*Preterit*
cuento	contaba	conté
cuentas	etc.	contaste

Present, continued		*Preterit, continued*
cuenta		**contó**
contamos		**contamos**
contáis		**contasteis**
cuentan		**contaron**

Future	*Conditional*
contaré	**contaría**
etc.	*etc.*

SUBJUNCTIVE

Present	*Imperfect*
cuente	**contara/contase**
cuentes	*etc.*
cuente	
contemos	
contéis	
cuenten	

15. **Continuar** *to continue*

The **u** is stressed when possible.

Infinitive **continuar**   *Gerund* **continuando**
Past Participle **continuado** *Imperative* **continúa continuad**

INDICATIVE

Present	*Imperfect*	*Preterit*
continúo	**continuaba**	**continué**
continúas	*etc.*	**continuaste**
continúa		**continuó**
continuamos		**continuamos**
continuáis		**continuasteis**
continúan		**continuaron**

Future		*Conditional*
continuaré		**continuaría**
etc.		*etc.*

SUBJUNCTIVE

Present	Imperfect
continúe	continuara/continuase
continúes	*etc.*
continúe	
continuemos	
continuéis	
continúen	

16. Dar *to give*

Infinitive **dar** *Gerund* **dando**
Past Participle **dado** *Imperative* **da dad**

INDICATIVE

Present	Imperfect	Preterit
doy	daba	di
das	dabas	diste
da	daba	dio *(no accent)*
damos	dábamos	dimos
dais	dabais	disteis
dan	daban	dieron

Future	Conditional
daré	daría
etc.	*etc.*

SUBJUNCTIVE

Present	Imperfect
dé	diera/diese
des	*etc.*
dé	
demos	
deis	
den	

17. Decir *to say*

Infinitive **decir** *Gerund* **diciendo**
Past Participle **dicho** *Imperative* **di decid**

INDICATIVE

Present	Imperfect	Preterit
digo	decía	dije
dices	etc.	dijiste
dice		dijo
decimos		dijimos
decís		dijisteis
dicen		dijeron

Future	Conditional
diré	diría
etc.	etc.

SUBJUNCTIVE

Present	Imperfect
diga	dijera/dijese
digas	etc.
diga	
digamos	
digáis	
digan	

18. **Discernir** *to discern*

Radical changing verb. This pattern (**e** > **ie**) is rare in the **-ir** conjugation but common in the **-er** conjugation.

Infinitive **discernir**   *Gerund* **discerniendo**
Past Participle **discernido**   *Imperative* **discierne discernid**

INDICATIVE

Present	Imperfect	Preterit
discierno	discernía	discerní
disciernes	etc.	discerniste
discierne		discernió
discernimos		discernimos
discernís		discernistels
disciernen		discernieron

Future	*Conditional*
discerniré	**discerniría**
etc.	etc.

SUBJUNCTIVE

Present	*Imperfect*
discierna	**discerniera/discerniese**
disciernas	etc.
discierna	
discernamos	
discernáis	
disciernan	

19. **Dormir** *to sleep*

Only **morir** *to die* (past. participle **muerto**) is conjugated similarly.

Infinitive **dormir**	*Gerund* **durmiendo**
Past Participle **dormido**	*Imperative* **duerme dormid**

INDICATIVE

Present	*Imperfect*	*Preterit*
duermo	**dormía**	**dormí**
duermes	etc.	**dormiste**
duerme		**durmió**
dormimos		**dormimos**
dormís		**dormisteis**
duermen		**durmieron**

Future	*Conditional*
dormiré	**dormiría**
etc.	etc.

SUBJUNCTIVE

Present	*Imperfect*
duerma	**durmiera/durmiese**
duermas	etc.
duerma	

Present, continued
durmamos
durmáis
duerman

20. Erguir(se) *to rear up/sit up straight*

Conjugated like **sentir** but with the normal spelling change **ie > ye** at the beginning of words.
The alternative forms are conjugated like **pedir**.

Infinitive **erguir**   *Gerund* **irguiendo**
Past Participle **erguido**   *Imperative* **yergue/irgue erguid**

INDICATIVE

Present	*Imperfect*	*Preterit*
yergo/irgo	**erguía**	**erguí**
yergues/irgues	*etc.*	**erguiste**
yergue/irgue		**irguió**
erguimos		**erguimos**
erguís		**erguisteis**
yerguen/irguen		**irguieron**

Future	*Conditional*
erguiré	**erguiría**
etc.	*etc.*

SUBJUNCTIVE

Present	*Imperfect*
yerga/irga	**irguiera/irguiese**
yergas/irgas	*etc.*
yerga/irga	
yergamos/irgamos	
yergáis/irgáis	
yergan/irgan	

21. Errar *to wander/err*

Conjugated like **cerrar** but with regular spelling change **ie > ye** at the beginning of words.

Infinitive **errar**   *Gerund* **errando**
Past Participle **errado** *Imperative* **yerra errad**

INDICATIVE

Present	*Imperfect*	*Preterit*
yerro	erraba	erré
yerras	etc.	erraste
yerra		erró
erramos		erramos
erráis		errasteis
yerran		erraron

Future	*Conditional*
erraré	erraría

SUBJUNCTIVE

Present	*Imperfect*
yerre	errara/errase
yerres	etc.
yerre	
erremos	
erréis	
yerren	

22. **Estar** *to be*

Infinitive **estar**   *Gerund* **estando**
Past Participle **estado** *Imperative* **estate estaos**

INDICATIVE

Present	*Imperfect*	*Preterit*
estoy	estaba	estuve
estás	etc.	estuviste
está		estuvo
estamos		estuvimos
estáis		estuvisteis
están		estuvieron

Future
estaré
etc.

Conditional
estaría
etc.

SUBJUNCTIVE

Present
esté
estés
esté
estemos
estéis
estén

Imperfect
estuviera/estuviese
etc.

23. Gruñir *to growl*

The diphthongs **ió** and **ie** become **ó** and **e** after **ñ**.

Infinitive **gruñir**
Past Participle **gruñido**

Gerund **gruñendo**
Imperative **gruñe gruñid**

INDICATIVE

Present
gruño
gruñes
gruñe
gruñimos
gruñís
gruñen

Imperfect
gruñía
etc.

Preterit
gruñí
gruñiste
gruñó
gruñimos
gruñisteis
gruñeron

Future
gruñiré
etc.

Conditional
gruñiría
etc.

SUBJUNCTIVE

Present
gruña
gruñas
gruña
gruñamos

Imperfect
gruñera/gruñese
etc.

Present, continued
gruñáis
gruñan

24. Haber (auxiliary verb or *there is/are*)

The 3rd-person present is **hay** when it means *there is/are.*

Infinitive **haber**   *Gerund* **habiendo**
Past Participle **habido**   *Imperative not found*

INDICATIVE

Present	*Imperfect*	*Preterit*
he	había	hube
has	etc.	hubiste
ha (hay)		hubo
hemos		hubimos
habéis		hubisteis
han		hubieron

Future	*Conditional*
habré	habría
etc.	etc.

SUBJUNCTIVE

Present	*Imperfect*
haya	hubiera/hubiese
hayas	etc.
haya	
hayamos	
hayáis	
hayan	

25. Hacer *to do/to make*

Infinitive **hacer**   *Gerund* **haciendo**
Past Participle **hecho**   *Imperative* **haz haced**

INDICATIVE

Present	Imperfect	Preterit
hago	hacía	hice
haces	*etc.*	hiciste
hace		hizo
hacemos		hicimos
hacéis		hicisteis
hacen		hicieron

Future	Conditional
haré	haría
etc.	*etc.*

SUBJUNCTIVE

Present	Imperfect
haga	hiciera/hiciese
hagas	*etc.*
haga	
hagamos	
hagáis	
hagan	

26. Ir *to go*

Infinitive ir	Gerund yendo
Past Participle ido	Imperative ve id

The **vosotros** imperative of **irse** is **idos**, not the expected **'ios'*.

INDICATIVE

Present	Imperfect	Preterit
voy	iba	fui *(no accent)*
vas	ibas	fuiste
va	iba	fue *(no accent)*
vamos	íbamos	fuimos
vais	ibais	fuisteis
van	iban	fueron

Future	Conditional
Future **iré** *etc.*	*Conditional* **iría** *etc.*

SUBJUNCTIVE

Present	*Imperfect*
vaya	**fuera/fuese**
vayas	*etc.*
vaya	
vayamos	
vayáis	
vayan	

27. **Jugar** *to play (a game)*

The only verb in which stressed **u** becomes **ue**.

Infinitive **jugar**	*Gerund* **jugando**
Past Participle **jugado**	*Imperative* **juega jugad**

INDICATIVE

Present	*Imperfect*	*Preterit*
juego	**jugaba**	**jugué**
juegas	*etc.*	**jugaste**
juega		**jugó**
jugamos		**jugamos**
jugáis		**jugasteis**
juegan		**jugaron**

Future	*Conditional*
jugaré	**jugaría**
etc.	*etc.*

SUBJUNCTIVE

Present	*Imperfect*
juegue	**jugara/jugase**
juegues	*etc.*
juegue	

Present, continued
juguemos
juguéis
jueguen

28. **Liar** *to tie up in a bundle*

The **i** may be stressed. Compare **cambiar**.

Infinitive **liar**   *Gerund* **liando**
Past Participle **liado**   *Imperative* **lía liad**

INDICATIVE

Present	*Imperfect*	*Preterit*
lío	**liaba**	**lié**
lías	*etc.*	**liaste**
lía		**lió**
liamos		**liamos**
liáis		**liasteis**
lían		**liaron**

Future	*Conditional*
liaré	**liaría**
etc.	*etc.*

SUBJUNCTIVE

Present	*Imperfect*
líe	**liara/liase**
líes	*etc.*
líe	
liemos	
liéis	
líen	

29. **Lucir** *to show off* (transitive)

c > zc before **o** or **a**.

Infinitive **lucir**   *Gerund* **luciendo**
Past Participle **lucido**   *Imperative* **luce lucid**

INDICATIVE

Present	Imperfect	Preterit
luzco	lucía	lucí
luces	etc.	luciste
luce		lució
lucimos		lucimos
lucís		lucisteis
lucen		lucieron

Future	Conditional
luciré	luciría

SUBJUNCTIVE

Present	Imperfect
luzca	luciera/luciese
luzcas	etc.
luzca	
luzcamos	
luzcáis	
luzcan	

30. Maldecir *to curse*

Conjugated like **decir** except for the Past Participle, Imperative, Future and Conditional.

Infinitive **maldecir**	*Gerund* **maldiciendo**
Past Participle **maldecido**	*Imperative* **maldice maldecid**

INDICATIVE

Present	Imperfect	Preterit
maldigo	maldecía	maldije
maldices	etc.	maldijiste
maldice		maldijo
maldecimos		maldijimos
maldecís		maldijisteis
maldicen		maldijeron

Future
maldeciré
etc.

Conditional
maldeciría
etc.

SUBJUNCTIVE

Present
maldiga
maldigas
maldiga
maldigamos
maldigáis
maldigan

Imperfect
maldijera/maldijese
etc.

31. **Mover** *to move*

Radical changing verb.

Infinitive **mover**
Past Participle **movido**

Gerund **moviendo**
Imperative **mueve, moved**

INDICATIVE

Present
muevo
mueves
mueve
movemos
movéis
mueven

Imperfect
movía
etc.

Preterit
moví
moviste
movió
movimos
movisteis
movieron

Future
moveré
etc.

Conditional
movería
etc.

SUBJUNCTIVE

Present
mueva
muevas
mueva
movamos

Imperfect
moviera/moviese
etc.

Present, continued
mováis
muevan

32. Oír *to hear*

Infinitive **oír**	*Gerund* **oyendo**
Past Participle **oído**	*Imperative* **oye oíd**

INDICATIVE

Present	*Imperfect*	*Preterit*
oigo	**oía**	**oí**
oyes	*etc.*	**oíste**
oye		**oyó**
oímos		**oímos**
oís		**oístels**
oyen		**oyeron**

Future	*Conditional*
oiré	**oiría**
etc.	*etc.*

SUBJUNCTIVE

Present	*Imperfect*
oiga	**oyera/oyese**
oigas	*etc.*
oiga	
oigamos	
oigáis	
oigan	

33. Oler *to smell*

Conjugated like **mover**, but the diphthong **ue** is always written **hue** at the beginning of a word.

Infinitive **oler**	*Gerund* **oliendo**
Past Participle **olido**	*Imperative* **huele oled**

INDICATIVE

Present	*Imperfect*	*Preterit*
huelo	olía	olí
hueles	etc.	oliste
huele		olió
olemos		olimos
oléis		olisteis
huelen		olieron

Future	*Conditional*
oleré	olería
etc.	etc.

SUBJUNCTIVE

Present	*Imperfect*
huela	oliera/oliese
huelas	etc.
huela	
olamos	
oláis	
huelan	

34. **Pagar** *to pay*

Regular -**ar** verb, but with spelling changes. The silent *u* keeps the **g** hard (like the **g** in **hago**).

Infinitive **pagar**	*Gerund* **pagando**
Past Participle **pagado**	*Imperative* **paga pagad**

INDICATIVE

Present	*Imperfect*	*Preterit*
pago	pagaba	pagué
pagas	etc.	pagaste
paga		pagó
pagamos		pagamos
pagáis		pagasteis
pagan		pagaron

Future	*Conditional*
pagaré	**pagaría**
etc.	*etc.*

SUBJUNCTIVE

Present	*Imperfect*
pague	**pagara/pagase**
pagues	*etc.*
pague	
paguemos	
paguéis	
paguen	

35. **Parecer** *to seem*

The change **c > zc** before **a** or **o** affects most verbs ending in **-cer** (common exceptions are **vencer, ejercer, torcer, cocer**).

Infinitive **parecer**	*Gerund* **pareciendo**
Past Participle **parecido**	*Imperative* **parece pareced**

INDICATIVE

Present	*Imperfect*	*Preterit*
parezco	**parecía**	**parecí**
pareces	*etc.*	**pareciste**
parece		**pareció**
parecemos		**parecimos**
parecéis		**parecistels**
parecen		**parecieron**

Future	*Conditional*
pareceré	**parecería**
etc.	*etc.*

SUBJUNCTIVE

Present	*Imperfect*
parezca	**pareciera/pareciese**
parezcas	*etc.*

Present, continued
parezca
parezcamos
parezcáis
parezcan

36. **Pedir** *to ask for*
Radical changing verb.

Infinitive **pedir**	*Gerund* **pidiendo**
Past Participle **pedido**	*Imperative* **pide pedid**

INDICATIVE

Present	*Imperfect*	*Preterit*
pido	**pedía**	**pedí**
pides	*etc.*	**pediste**
pide		**pidió**
pedimos		**pedimos**
pedís		**pedisteis**
piden		**pidieron**

Future	*Conditional*
pediré	**pediría**
etc.	*etc.*

SUBJUNCTIVE

Present	*Imperfect*
pida	**pidiera/pidiese**
pidas	*etc.*
pida	
pidamos	
pidáis	
pidan	

37. **Perder** *to lose*
Radical changing verb.

Infinitive **perder**	*Gerund* **perdiendo**
Past Participle **perdido**	*Imperative* **pierde perded**

INDICATIVE

Present	Imperfect	Preterit
pierdo	perdía	perdí
pierdes	etc.	perdiste
pierde		perdió
perdemos		perdimos
perdéis		perdisteis
pierden		perdieron

Future	Conditional
perderé	perdería
etc.	etc.

SUBJUNCTIVE

Present	Imperfect
pierda	perdiera/perdiese
pierdas	etc.
pierda	
perdamos	
perdáis	
pierdan	

38. Poder *to be able*

Infinitive **poder**	Gerund **pudiendo**
Past Participle **podido**	Imperative *not found*

INDICATIVE

Present	Imperfect	Preterit
puedo	podía	pude
puedes	etc.	pudiste
puede		pudo
podemos		pudimos
podéis		pudisteis
pueden		pudieron

Future	Conditional
podré	podría
etc.	etc.

SUBJUNCTIVE

Present	Imperfect
pueda	pudiera/pudiese
puedas	etc.
pueda	
podamos	
podáis	
puedan	

39. **Poner** *to put*

Infinitive **poner**	*Gerund* **poniendo**
Past Participle **puesto**	*Imperative* **pon poned**

The **tú** *imperative of compounds takes an accent:* **compón, pospón.**

INDICATIVE

Present	Imperfect	Preterit
pongo	ponía	puse
pones	etc.	pusiste
pone		puso
ponemos		pusimos
ponéis		pusisteis
ponen		pusieron

Future	Conditional
pondré	pondría
etc.	etc.

SUBJUNCTIVE

Present	Imperfect
ponga	pusiera/pusiese
pongas	etc.
ponga	
pongamos	
pongáis	
pongan	

40. **Poseer** *to possess*

Note unstressed **i** > **y** between vowels.

Infinitive **poseer**   *Gerund* **poseyendo**
Past Participle **poseído** *Imperative* **posee, poseed**

INDICATIVE

Present	*Imperfect*	*Preterit*
poseo	poseía	poseí
posees	etc.	poseíste
posee		poseyó
poseemos		poseímos
poseéis		poseísteis
poseen		poseyeron

Future	*Conditional*
poseeré	poseería
etc.	etc.

SUBJUNCTIVE

Present	*Imperfect*
posea	poseyera/poseyese
poseas	etc.
posea	
poseamos	
poseáis	
posean	

41. **Producir** *to produce*

c > **zc** before **a** and **o**, and irregular Preterit. All verbs
whose Infinitive ends in **-ducir** conjugate like this verb.

Infinitive **producir**   *Gerund* **produciendo**
Past Participle **producido** *Imperative* **produce producid**

INDICATIVE

Present	*Imperfect*	*Preterit*
produzco	producía	produje
produces	etc.	produjiste

Present, continued
produce
producimos
producís
producen

Preterit, continued
produjo
produjimos
produjisteis
produjeron

Future	*Conditional*
produciré	**produciría**
etc.	*etc.*

SUBJUNCTIVE

Present	*Imperfect*
produzca	**produjera/produjese**
produzcas	*etc.*
produzca	
produzcamos	
produzcáis	
produzcan	

42. **Prohibir** *to prohibit*

The **i** of the stem is written with an accent when it is stressed (this spelling rule was introduced in 1959 so the accent does not appear in texts printed before then).

Infinitive **prohibir** *Gerund* **prohibiendo**
Past Participle **prohibido** *Imperative* **prohíbe prohibid**

INDICATIVE

Present	*Imperfect*	*Preterit*
prohíbo	**prohibía**	**prohibí**
prohíbes	*etc.*	**prohibiste**
prohíbe		**prohibió**
prohibimos		**prohibimos**
prohibís		**prohibisteis**
prohíben		**prohibieron**

Future	*Conditional*
prohibiré	**prohibiría**
etc.	*etc.*

SUBJUNCTIVE

Present	*Imperfect*
prohíba	**prohibiera/prohibiese**
prohíbas	*etc.*
prohíba	
prohibamos	
prohibáis	
prohíban	

43. **Proteger** *to protect*

Regular verb with spelling changes.

Infinitive **proteger**	*Gerund* **protegiendo**
Past Participle **protegido**	*Imperative* **protege proteged**

INDICATIVE

Present	*Imperfect*	*Preterit*
protejo	**protegía**	**protegí**
proteges	*etc.*	**protegiste**
protege		**protegió**
protegemos		**protegimos**
protegéis		**protegisteis**
protegen		**protegieron**

Future	*Conditional*
protegeré	**protegería**
etc.	*etc.*

SUBJUNCTIVE

Present	*Imperfect*
proteja	**protegiera/protegiese**
protejas	*etc.*
proteja	

Present, continued
protejamos
protejáis
protejan

44. **Querer** *to want/love*

Infinitive **querer**   *Gerund* **queriendo**
Past Participle **querido**   *Imperative* **quiere quered**

INDICATIVE

Present	*Imperfect*	*Preterit*
quiero	quería	quise
quieres	etc.	quisiste
quiere		quiso
queremos		quisimos
queréis		quisisteis
quieren		quisieron

Future	*Conditional*
querré	querría
etc.	etc.

SUBJUNCTIVE

Present	*Imperfect*
quiera	quisiera/quisiese
quieras	etc.
quiera	
queramos	
queráis	
quieran	

45. **Regir** *to govern/direct*

Conjugated like **pedir** but with predictable spelling changes.

Infinitive **regir**   *Gerund* **rigiendo**
Past Participle **regido**   *Imperative* **rige regid**

INDICATIVE

Present	*Imperfect*	*Preterit*
rijo	regía	regí
riges	etc.	registe
rige		rigió
regimos		regimos
regís		registeis
rigen		rigieron

Future	*Conditional*
regiré	regiría
etc.	etc.

SUBJUNCTIVE

Present	*Imperfect*
rija	rigiera/rigiese
rijas	etc.
rija	
rijamos	
rijáis	
rijan	

46. **Reír** *to laugh*

Conjugated like **pedir**.

Infinitive **reír**	*Gerund* **riendo**
Past Participle **reído**	*Imperative* **ríe reíd**

INDICATIVE

Present	*Imperfect*	*Preterit*
río	reía	reí
ríes	etc.	reíste
ríe		rió
reímos		reímos
reís		reísteis
ríen		rieron

Future	*Conditional*
reiré	reiría
etc.	*etc.*

SUBJUNCTIVE

Present	*Imperfect*
ría	riera/riese
rías	*etc.*
ría	
riamos	
riáis	
rían	

47. **Reñir** *to scold*

Conjugated like **pedir,** but **ió** becomes **ó** and **ie** becomes **e** after **ñ.**

Infinitive **reñir**	*Gerund* **riñendo**
Past Participle **reñido**	*Imperative* **riñe reñid**

INDICATIVE

Present	*Imperfect*	*Preterit*
riño	reñía	reñí
riñes	*etc.*	reñiste
riñe		riñó
reñimos		reñimos
reñís		reñisteis
riñen		riñeron

Future	*Conditional*
reñiré	reñiría
etc.	*etc.*

SUBJUNCTIVE

Present	*Imperfect*
riña	riñera/riñese
riñas	*etc.*
riña	

Present, continued
riñamos
riñáis
riñan

48. **Reunir** *to bring together/call a meeting*

The **u** is written with an accent when stressed. The verb
rehusar *to refuse* is similar: **rehúso, rehúsa, rehusamos,**
etc. The accent was introduced in 1959 and is not seen in
books printed before then.

Infinitive **reunir**	*Gerund* **reuniendo**
Past Participle **reunido**	*Imperative* **reúne reunid**

INDICATIVE

Present	*Imperfect*	*Preterit*
reúno	**reunía**	**reuní**
reúnes	*etc.*	**reuniste**
reúne		**reunió**
reunimos		**reunimos**
reunís		**reunisteis**
reúnen		**reunieron**

Future	*Conditional*
reuniré	**reuniría**
etc.	*etc.*

SUBJUNCTIVE

Present	*Imperfect*
reúna	**reuniera/reuniese**
reúnas	*etc.*
reúna	
reunamos	
reunáis	
reúnan	

49. **Rezar** *to pray*

Regular **-ar** verb with spelling changes.

Infinitive **rezar**   *Gerund* **rezando**
Past Participle **rezado**   *Imperative* **reza rezad**

INDICATIVE

Present	*Imperfect*	*Preterit*
rezo	rezaba	recé
rezas	etc.	rezaste
reza		rezó
rezamos		rezamos
rezáis		rezasteis
rezan		rezaron

Future	*Conditional*
rezaré	rezaría
etc.	etc.

SUBJUNCTIVE

Present	*Imperfect*
rece	rezara/rezase
reces	etc.
rece	
recemos	
recéis	
recen	

50. **Roer** *to gnaw*

Infinitive **roer**   *Gerund* **royendo**
Past Participle **roído**   *Imperative* **roe roed**

INDICATIVE

Present	*Imperfect*	*Preterit*
roo	roía	roí
roes	etc.	roíste
roe		royó

Present, continued	*Preterit, continued*
roemos	**roímos**
roéis	**roísteis**
roen	**royeron**

The alternative first-person singular present forms **royo** *and* **roigo** *are rarely seen.*

Future	*Conditional*
roeré	**roería**
etc.	*etc.*

SUBJUNCTIVE

Present	*Imperfect*
roa (roiga, roya)	**royera/royese**
roas (roigas, royas)	*etc.*
roa (roiga, roya)	
roamos (roigamos, royamos)	
roáis (roigáis, royáis)	
roan (roigan, royan)	

Bracketed forms are rarely found.

51. **Saber** *to know*

Infinitive **saber**	*Gerund* **sabiendo**
Past Participle **sabido**	*Imperative* **sabe sabed**

INDICATIVE

Present	*Imperfect*	*Preterit*
sé	**sabía**	**supe**
sabes	*etc.*	**supiste**
sabe		**supo**
sabemos		**supimos**
sabéis		**supisteis**
saben		**supieron**

Future	*Conditional*
sabré	**sabría**
etc.	*etc.*

SUBJUNCTIVE

Present	*Imperfect*
sepa	**supiera/supiese**
sepas	etc.
sepa	
sepamos	
sepáis	
sepan	

52. **Sacar** *to take out/extract*

Regular **-ar** verb with spelling changes.

Infinitive **sacar**   *Gerund* **sacando**
Past Participle **sacado**   *Imperative* **saca sacad**

INDICATIVE

Present	*Imperfect*	*Preterit*
saco	sacaba	saqué
sacas	etc.	sacaste
saca		sacó
sacamos		sacamos
sacáis		sacasteis
sacan		sacaron

Future	*Conditional*
sacaré	sacaría
etc.	etc.

SUBJUNCTIVE

Present	*Imperfect*
saque	**sacara/sacase**
saques	etc.
saque	
saquemos	
saquéis	
saquen	

53. **Salir** *to go out/leave*

Infinitive **salir**   *Gerund* **saliendo**
Past Participle **salido**   *Imperative* **sal salid**

INDICATIVE

Present	*Imperfect*	*Preterit*
salgo	salía	salí
sales	etc.	saliste
sale		salió
salimos		salimos
salís		salisteis
salen		salieron

Future	*Conditional*
saldré	saldría
etc.	etc.

SUBJUNCTIVE

Present	*Imperfect*
salga	saliera/salieses
salgas	etc.
salga	
salgamos	
salgáis	
salgan	

54. **Seguir** *to follow*

Infinitive **seguir**   *Gerund* **siguiendo**
Past Participle **seguido**   *Imperative* **sigue seguid**

INDICATIVE

Present	*Imperfect*	*Preterit*
sigo	seguía	seguí
sigues	etc.	seguiste
sigue		siguió

Present, continued		*Preterit, continued*
seguimos		**seguimos**
seguís		**seguisteis**
siguen		**siguieron**

Future	*Conditional*
seguiré	**seguiría**
etc.	*etc.*

SUBJUNCTIVE

Present	*Imperfect*
siga	**siguiera/siguiese**
sigas	*etc.*
siga	
sigamos	
sigáis	
sigan	

55. **Sentir** *to feel*

Radical changing verb.

Infinitive **sentir**	*Gerund* **sintiendo**
Past Participle **sentido**	*Imperative* **siente sentid**

INDICATIVE

Present	*Imperfect*	*Preterit*
siento	**sentía**	**sentí**
sientes	*etc.*	**sentiste**
siente		**sintió**
sentimos		**sentimos**
sentís		**sentisteis**
sienten		**sintieron**

Future	*Conditional*
sentiré	**sentiría**
etc.	*etc.*

SUBJUNCTIVE

Present	*Imperfect*
sienta	sintiera/sintiese
sientas	*etc.*
sienta	
sintamos	
sintáis	
sientan	

56. **Ser** *to be*

Infinitive **ser**	*Gerund* **siendo**
Past Participle **sido**	*Imperative* **sé sed**

INDICATIVE

Present	*Imperfect*	*Preterit*
soy	era	fui
eres	eras	fuiste
es	era	fue
somos	éramos	fuimos
sois	erais	fuisteis
son	eran	fueron

The accent on the third-person Preterit forms **fuí** *and* **fué** *was abolished in the spelling reforms of 1959.*

Future	*Conditional*
seré	sería
etc.	*etc.*

SUBJUNCTIVE

Present	*Imperfect*
sea	fuera/fuese
seas	fueras/fueses
sea	fuera/fuese
seamos	fuéramos/fuésemos
seáis	fuerais/fueseis
sean	fueran/fuesen

57. **Tañer** *to chime*

ió is simplified to **ó** and **ie** to **e** as usual after **ñ**. This change also affects verbs ending in **-llir** like **bullir** *to seethe*.

Infinitive **tañer**	*Gerund* **tañendo**
Past Participle **tañido**	*Imperative* **tañe tañed**

INDICATIVE

Present	*Imperfect*	*Preterit*
taño	tañía	tañí
tañes	*etc.*	tañiste
tañe		tañó
tañemos		tañimos
tañéis		tañisteis
tañen		tañeron

Future	*Conditional*
tañeré	tañería
etc.	*etc.*

SUBJUNCTIVE

Present	*Imperfect*
taña	tañera/tañese
tañas	*etc.*
taña	
tañamos	
tañáis	
tañan	

58. **Tener** *to have*

Infinitive **tener**	*Gerund* **teniendo**
Past Participle **tenido**	*Imperative* **ten tened**

INDICATIVE

Present	*Imperfect*	*Preterit*
tengo	tenía	tuve
tienes	*etc.*	tuviste

Present continued	Preterit continued
tiene	tuvo
tenemos	tuvimos
tenéis	tuvisteis
tienen	tuvieron

Singular imperative of compounds ends in **-én: detener**
detain/stop **detén, retener** *retain* **retén.**

Future	Conditional
tendré	tendría
etc.	*etc.*

SUBJUNCTIVE

Present	Imperfect
tenga	tuviera/tuviese
tengas	*etc.*
tenga	
tengamos	
tengáis	
tengan	

59. **Traer** *to bring*

Infinitive **traer**	*Gerund* **trayendo**
Past Participle **traído**	*Imperative* **trae traed**

INDICATIVE

Present	Imperfect	Preterit
traigo	traía	traje
traes	*etc.*	trajiste
trae		trajo
traemos		trajimos
traéis		trajisteis
traen		trajeron

Future	Conditional
traeré	traería
etc.	*etc.*

SUBJUNCTIVE

Present	*Imperfect*
traiga	**trajera/trajese**
traigas	*etc.*
traiga	
traigamos	
traigáis	
traigan	

60. **Valer** *to be worth*

Infinitive **valer**	*Gerund* **valiendo**
Past Participle **valido**	*Imperative* **vale valed**

INDICATIVE

Present	*Imperfect*	*Preterit*
valgo	**valía**	**valí**
vales	*etc.*	**valiste**
vale		**valió**
valemos		**valimos**
valéis		**valisteis**
valen		**valieron**

Future	*Conditional*
valdré	**valdría**
etc.	*etc.*

SUBJUNCTIVE

Present	*Imperfect*
valga	**valiera/valiese**
valgas	*etc.*
valga	
valgamos	
valgáis	
valgan	

61. **Vencer** *to defeat*

Regular verb with spelling changes.

Infinitive **vencer**   *Gerund* **venciendo**
Past Participle **vencido**   *Imperative* **vence venced**

INDICATIVE

Present	*Imperfect*	*Preterit*
venzo	vencía	vencí
vences	*etc.*	venciste
vence		venció
vencemos		vencimos
vencéis		vencisteis
vencen		vencieron

Future	*Conditional*
venceré	vencería
etc.	*etc.*

SUBJUNCTIVE

Present	*Imperfect*
venza	venciera/venciese
venzas	*etc.*
venza	
venzamos	
venzáis	
venzan	

62. **Venir** *to come*

Infinitive **venir**   *Gerund* **viniendo**
Past Participle **venido**   *Imperative* **ven venid**

INDICATIVE

Present	*Imperfect*	*Preterit*
vengo	venía	vine
vienes	*etc.*	viniste
viene		vino
venimos		vinimos
venís		vinisteis
vienen		vinieron

Future	Conditional
vendré	**vendría**
etc.	*etc.*

SUBJUNCTIVE

Present	Imperfect
venga	**viniera/viniese**
vengas	*etc.*
venga	
vengamos	
vengáis	
vengan	

63. **Ver** *to see*

Infinitive **ver**	Gerund **viendo**
Past Participle **visto**	Imperative **ve ved**

INDICATIVE

Present	Imperfect	Preterit
veo	**veía**	**vi**
ves	*etc.*	**viste**
ve		**vio** *(no accent)*
vemos		**vimos**
veis		**visteis**
ven		**vieron**

Future	Conditional
veré	**vería**
etc.	*etc.*

SUBJUNCTIVE

Present	Imperfect
vea	**viera/viese**
veas	*etc.*
vea	

Present, continued
veamos
veáis
vean

64. Yacer *to lie (as in 'he lay there'. This verb is archaic.)*

Infinitive **yacer**   *Gerund* **yaciendo**
Past Participle **yacido**   *Imperative* **yace/yaz yaced**

INDICATIVE

Present	*Imperfect*	*Preterit*
yazco	**yacía**	**yací**
yaces	*etc.*	**yaciste**
yace		**yació**
yacemos		**yacimos**
yacéis		**yacisteis**
yacen		**yacieron**

The alternative first-person singular present forms **yago/yazgo**
are rarely seen.

Future	*Conditional*
yaceré	**yacería**

Present	*Imperfect*
yazca (yazga, yaga)	**yaciera/yaciese**
yazcas (yazgas, yagas)	*etc.*
etc.	

65. Zurcir *to darn*

Regular verb with spelling changes.

Infinitive **zurcir**   *Gerund* **zurciendo**
Past Participle **zurcido**   *Imperative* **zurce zurcid**

INDICATIVE

Present	*Imperfect*	*Preterit*
zurzo	zurcía	zurcí
zurces	etc.	zurciste
zurce		zurció
zurcimos		zurcimos
zurcís		zurcisteis
zurcen		zurcieron

Future	*Conditional*
zurciré	zurciría
etc.	etc.

SUBJUNCTIVE

Present	*Imperfect*
zurza	zurciera/zurciese
zurzas	etc.
zurza	
zurzamos	
zurzáis	
zurzan	

LIST OF IRREGULAR AND RADICAL CHANGING VERBS

A few regular verbs that are affected by regular spelling changes are included. Numerous rare or archaic verbs are omitted. The number identifies the model verbs printed on pp.254–302.

Pronominal (i.e. 'reflexive') infinitives are not shown unless the pronominal form is the more usual form.

abastecer to supply   **parecer (35)**
abolir to abolish   **(1)**
aborrecer to detest   **parecer (35)**

abrir *to open*	past participle **abierto**
absolver *to absolve*	**mover (31)** past participle **absuelto**
abstenerse *to abstain*	**tener (58)**
abstraer *to abstract*	**traer (59)**
acentuar *to accentuate*	**continuar (15)**
acertar *to hit the mark*	**cerrar (11)**
acontecer *to occur*	**parecer (35)**
acordar *to agree upon*	**contar (14)**
acostarse *to go to bed*	**contar (14)**
actuar *to act*	**continuar (15)**
adherir *to adhere*	**sentir (55)**
adolecer *to be ill*	**parecer (35)**
adormecer *to put to sleep*	**parecer (35)**
adquirir *to acquire*	**(2)**
advertir *to warn*	**sentir (55)**
aferrarse *to grasp*	**cerrar (11);** may be conjugated regularly
agradecer *to thank*	**parecer (35)**
agredir *to assault*	**abolir (1)**
agriar *to sour*	**cambiar (10)**
aguar *to spoil*	**averiguar (7)**
aislar *to isolate*	**aislar (3)**
alentar *to encourage*	**cerrar (11)**
aliar *to ally*	**liar (28)**
almorzar *to lunch*	**contar (14); z>c** before **e**
amanecer *to dawn*	**parecer (35)**
amnistiar *to amnesty*	**liar (28)**
ampliar *to enlarge*	**liar (28)**
andar *to walk*	**(4)**
anochecer *to grow dark*	**parecer (35)**
ansiar *to yearn for*	**liar (28)**
anteponer *to put in front*	**poner (39)**
aparecer *to appear*	**parecer (35)**
apetecer *to crave*	**parecer (35)**
apostar *to bet*	**contar (14)**

apretar *to squeeze*	**cerrar (11)**
aprobar *to approve, pass* (exam.)	**contar (14)**
argüir *to argue*	**(5)**
arraigar *to establish*	**pagar (34)**
arrendar *to lease*	**cerrar (11)**
arrepentirse *to repent*	**sentir (55)**
ascender *to ascend*	**perder (37)**
asentar *to settle*	**cerrar (11)**
asentir *to assent*	**sentir (55)**
asir *to grasp*	**(6)**
atender *to attend*	**perder (37)**
atenerse *to abide by*	**tener (58)**
atenuar *to attenuate*	**continuar (15)**
atraer *to attract*	**traer (59)**
atravesar *to cross*	**cerrar (11)**
atribuir *to attribute*	**construir (13)**
avenir *to reconcile*	**venir (62)**
aventar *to fan*	**cerrar (11)**
avergonzar *to shame*	**contar (14)**, **z>c** before **e**, and diphthong spelt **üe**, e.g. subjunctive **avergüence**
averiar *to spoil*	**liar (28)**
bendecir *to bless*	**maldecir (30)**
biografiar *to write biography*	**liar (28)**
caber *to fit in*	**(8)**
caer *to fall*	**(9)**
calentar *to heat*	**(11)**
carecer *to lack*	**parecer (35)**
cegar *to blind*	**cerrar (11)**; **g>gu** before **e**
ceñir *to girdle*	**reñir (47)**
cerrar *to close*	**cerrar (11)**
circunscribir *to circumscribe*	past participle **circunscrito**
cocer *to cook*	**(12)**

coger *to catch*	**proteger (43)**
colar *to filter*	**contar (14)**
colegir *to infer*	**regir (45)**
colgar *to hang*	**contar (14) g>gu before e**
comenzar *to begin*	**cerrar (11) z>c before e**
compadecer *to pity*	**parecer (35)**
comparecer *to appear*	**parecer (35)**
competir *to compete*	**pedir (36)**
complacer *to please*	**parecer (35)**
componer *to compose*	**poner (39)**
comprobar *to check*	**contar (14)**
comunicar *to communicate*	**sacar (52)**
concebir *to conceive*	**pedir (36)**
conceptuar *to deem*	**continuar (15)**
concernir *to concern*	**discernir (18);** third person only
concertar *to harmonize*	**cerrar (11)**
conciliar *to reconcile*	**cambiar (10)**
concluir *to terminate*	**construir (13)**
concordar *to reconcile*	**contar (14)**
condescender *to condescend*	**perder (37)**
conducir *to drive*	**producir (41)**
conferir *to confer*	**sentir (55)**
confesar *to confess*	**cerrar (11)**
confiar *to entrust*	**liar (28)**
confluir *to come together*	**construir (13)**
conmover *to move (emotionally)*	**mover (31)**
conocer *to know*	**parecer (35)**
conseguir *to achieve*	**seguir (54)**
consentir *to consent*	**sentir (55)**
consolar *to console*	**contar (14)**
consonar *to harmonize*	**contar (14)**
constituir *to constitute*	**construir (13)**
constreñir *to restrict*	**reñir (47)**

construir *to build* (13)
contar *to count, tell* (14)
contener *to contain* tener (58)
continuar *to continue* (15)
contradecir *to contradict* decir (17)
contraer *to contract* traer (59)
contrahacer *to forge* hacer (25)
contravenir *to contravene* venir (62)
contribuir *to contribute* construir (13)
convalecer *to convalesce* parecer (35)
convencer *to convince* vencer (61)
convenir *to agree* venir (62)
convertir *to convert* sentir (55)
corregir *to correct* regir (45)
corroer *to corrode* roer (50)
costar *to cost* contar (14)
crecer *to grow* parecer (35)
creer *to believe* poseer (40)
criar *to rear* liar (28)
cubrir *to cover* past participle **cubierto**
dar *to give* (16)
decaer *to decay* caer (9)
decir *to say* (17)
decrecer *to diminish* parecer (35)
deducir *to deduce* producir (41)
defender *to defend* perder (37)
deferir *to relegate* sentir (55)
demoler *to demolish* mover (31)
demostrar *to demonstrate* contar (14)
denegar *to reject* cerrar (11) g>gu before e
denostar *to revile* contar (14)
derretir *to melt* pedir (36)
desacertar *to be wrong* cerrar (11)
desacordar *to put out of* contar (14)
    tune
desafiar *to challenge* liar (28)

desalentar *to dishearten*   **cerrar (11)**
desandar *to retrace steps*   **andar (4)**
desaparecer *to disappear*   **parecer (35)**
desaprobar *to disapprove of*   **contar (14)**
desasosegar *to unsettle*   **cerrar (11) g>gu before e**
desatender *to disregard*   **perder (37)**
descender *to descend*   **perder (37)**
descolgar *to take down*   **contar (14) g>gu before e**
descollar *to stand out*   **contar (14)**
descomedirse *to be rude*   **pedir (36)**
descomponer *to break down into parts*   **poner (39)**
desconcertar *to disconcert*   **cerrar (11)**
desconocer *not to know*   **parecer (35)**
desconsolar *to distress*   **contar (14)**
descontar *to discount*   **contar (14)**
desconvenir *to disagree*   **venir (62)**
describir *to describe*   past participle **descrito**
descubrir *to discover*   past participle **descubierto**
desempedrar *to take up stones*   **cerrar (11)**
desenraizar *to uproot*   **aislar (3)**
desentenderse *to pretend not to know about*   **perder (37)**
desenterrar *to unearth*   **cerrar (11)**
desenvolver *to unwrap*   **mover (31)**; past participle **desenvuelto**
desfallecer *to weaken*   **parecer (35)**
deshacer *to unmake*   **hacer (25)**
desleír *to dissolve*   **reír (46)**
deslucir *to tarnish*   **lucir (29)**
desmembrar *to dismember*   **cerrar (11)**
desmentir *to deny*   **sentir (55)**

desmerecer *not to deserve*	**parecer (35)**
desobedecer *to disobey*	**parecer (35)**
desoír *to disregard*	**oír (32)**
despedir *to fire*	**pedir (36)**
despertar *to awake*	**cerrar (11)**
desplegar *to unfold*	**cerrar (11)**; **g>gu** before **e**; now often regular
despoblar *to depopulate*	**contar (14)**
desproveer *to deprive of*	**poseer (40)**; past participle **desprovisto** or **desproveído**
desterrar *to exile*	**cerrar (11)**
destituir *to dismiss*	**construir (13)**
destruir *to destroy*	**construir (13)**
desvariar *to rave*	**liar 28**
desvergonzarse *to lose all shame*	**contar (14)**; **z>c** before **e**; diphthong spelt **üe**
desviar *to divert, throw off course*	**liar (28)**
desvirtuar *to spoil*	**continuar (15)**
detener *to stop, detain*	**tener (58)**
detraer *to separate*	**traer (59)**
devolver *to give back*	**mover (31)**; past participle **devuelto**
diferir *to differ*	**sentir (55)**
digerir *to digest*	**sentir (55)**
diluir *to dilute*	**construir (13)**
discernir *to discern*	**(18)**
disentir *to dissent*	**sentir (55)**
disminuir *to diminish*	**construir (13)**
disolver *to dissolve*	**mover (31)**; past participle **disuelto**
disponer *to dispose*	**poner (39)**
distender *to distend*	**perder (37)**
distraer *to distract*	**traer (59)**
distribuir *to distribute*	**construir (13)**
divertir *to amuse*	**sentir (55)**

doler *to hurt*	**mover (31)**
dormir *to sleep*	**(19)**
efectuar *to effect*	**continuar (15)**
ejercer *to exercise*	**vencer (61)**
elegir *to elect, to choose*	**regir (45)**
embebecer *to fascinate*	**parecer (35)**
embellecer *to embellish*	**parecer (35)**
embestir *to charge (e.g. bull)*	**pedir (36)**
embravecer *to infuriate*	**parecer (35)**
embrutecer *to brutalize*	**parecer (35)**
empedrar *to pave*	**cerrar (11)**
empequeñecer *to dwarf*	**parecer (35)**
empezar *to start*	**cerrar (11); z>c before e**
empobrecer *to impoverish*	**parecer (35)**
enaltecer *to extol*	**parecer (35)**
enardecer *to impassion*	**parecer (35)**
encanecer *to get gray/grey hair*	**parecer (35)**
encarecer *to extol*	**parecer (35)**
encender *to ignite*	**perder (37)**
encerrar *to shut in*	**cerrar (11)**
encomendar *to commend*	**cerrar (11)**
encontrar *to find, meet*	**contar (14)**
encubrir *to cloak, hush up*	past participle **encubierto**
endurecer *to harden*	**parecer (35)**
enflaquecer *to make thin*	**parecer (35)**
enfriar *to chill*	**liar (28)**
enfurecer *to infuriate*	**parecer (35)**
engrandecer *to enlarge*	**parecer (35)**
engreírse *to grow smug*	**reír (46)**
engrosar *to swell (a quantity)*	**contar (14)**; now usually regular
enloquecer *to madden*	**parecer (35)**
enmendar *to emend*	**cerrar (11)**
enmudecer *to silence*	**parecer (35)**

ennegrecer *to blacken* — **parecer (35)**

ennoblecer *to ennoble* — **parecer (35)**

enorgullecer *to make proud* — **parecer (35)**

enriquecer *to enrich* — **parecer (35)**

ensombrecer *to darken* — **parecer (35)**

ensordecer *to deafen* — **parecer (35)**

entender *to understand* — **perder (37)**

enternecer *to soften* — **parecer (35)**

enterrar *to bury* — **cerrar (11)**

entreabrir *to half open* — past participle **entreabierto**

entreoír *to hear faintly* — **oír (32)**

entretener *to distract* — **tener (58)**

entrever *to glimpse* — **ver (63)** third-person present singular **entrevé**

entristecer *to sadden* — **parecer (35)**

envanecer *to make vain* — **parecer (35)**

envejecer *to age* — **parecer (35)**

enviar *to send* — **liar (28)**

envilecer *to debase* — **parecer (35)**

envolver *to wrap up* — **mover (31)** past participle **envuelto**

equivaler *to be equal* — **valer (60)**

erguir *to straighten up* — **(20)**

errar *to wander* — **(21)**

escabullirse *to slip away* — **gruñir (23)**

escalofriarse *to shiver* — **liar (28)**

escarmentar *to teach a lesson* — **cerrar (11)**

escarnecer *to scoff* — **parecer (35)**

escocer *to annoy, hurt* — **cocer (12)**

escribir *to write* — past participle **escrito**

esforzarse *to strive* — **contar (14)** z>c before **e**

esparcir *to strew, scatter* — **zurcir (65)**

espiar *to spy on* — **liar (28)**

establecer *to establish* — **parecer (35)**

estar *to be* (22)

estremecer *to shake* **parecer (35)**

europeizar *to Europeanize* **aislar (3)**

evacuar *to evacuate* **averiguar (7)** (no dieresis)

evaluar *to evaluate* **continuar (15)**

exceptuar *to except* **continuar (15)**

excluir *to exclude* **construir (13)**

expedir *to ship* **pedir (36)**

exponer *to expose* **poner (39)**

extasiar *to enrapture* **liar (28)**

extender *to extend* **perder (37)**

extraer *to extract* **traer (59)**

extraviar *to mislead* **liar (28)**

fallecer *to pass away* **parecer (35)**

favorecer *to favor/favour* **parecer (35)**

fiar *to entrust, give credit* **liar (28)**

florecer *to flourish* **parecer (35)**

fluctuar *to fluctuate* **continuar (15)**

fluir *to flow* **construir (13)**

fortalecer *to strengthen* **parecer (35)**

forzar *to force* **contar (14) z>c** before **e**

fotografiar *to photograph* **liar (28)**

fregar *to scrub* **cerrar (11) g>gu** before **e**

freír *to fry* **reír (46)**; past participle **frito**

fruncir *to pucker* **zurcir (65)**

gemir *to groan* **pedir (36)**

gloriar(se) *to glory* **liar (28)**

gobernar *to govern* **cerrar (11)**

graduar *to grade* **continuar (15)**

gruñir *to growl* (23)

guarecer *to protect* **parecer (35)**

guarnecer *to equip* **parecer (35)**

guiar *to guide* **liar (28)**

haber auxiliary for forming (24)
compound tenses, or
there *is/are*

habituar *to make accustomed to*	**continuar (15)**
hacer *to do, make*	**(25)**
hastiar *to weary*	**liar (28)**
heder *to reek*	**perder (37)**
helar *to freeze*	**cerrar (11)**
henchir *to cram, stuff*	**pedir (36)**
hender *to cleave*	**perder (37)**
hendir = **hender**	**discernir (18)**
herir *to wound*	**sentir (55)**
herrar *to shoe, brand*	**cerrar (11)**
hervir *to boil*	**sentir (55)**
holgar *to take one's ease*	**contar (14) g>gu** before **e**
hollar *to trample*	**contar (14)**
huir *to flee*	**construir (13)**
humedecer *to dampen*	**parecer (35)**
impedir *to impede*	**pedir (36)**
imponer *to impose*	**poner (39);** imperative singular **impón**
incensar *to incense*	**cerrar (11)**
incluir *to include*	**construir (13)**
indisponer *to indispose*	**poner (39)**
individuar *to individualize*	**continuar (15)**
inducir *to induce*	**producir (41)**
infatuar *to make big-headed*	**continuar (15)**
inferir *to infer*	**sentir (55)**
influir *to influence*	**construir (13)**
ingerir *to ingest*	**sentir (55)**
inquirir *to investigate*	**adquirir (2)**
insinuar *to hint*	**continuar (15)**
instituir *to institute*	**construir (13)**
instruir *to instruct*	**construir (13)**
interferir *to interfere*	**sentir (55)**
interponer *to interpose*	**poner (39)**
intervenir *to intervene*	**venir (62)**

introducir *to insert*	**producir (41)**
intuir *to intuit*	**construir (13)**
invertir *to invest*	**sentir (55)**
ir *to go*	**(26)**
izar *to raise (flag)*	**rezar (49)**. All verbs ending in **-izar** conjugate like **rezar**.
jugar *to play*	**(27)**
languidecer *to languish*	**parecer (35)**
leer *to read*	**poseer (40)**
liar *to tie up in a bundle*	**(28)**
llegar *to arrive*	**pagar (34)**
llover *to rain*	**mover (31)**; usually only 3rd person
lucir *to sport, show off*	**(29)**
maldecir *to curse*	**(30)**
manifestar *to manifest*	**cerrar (11)**
mantener *to maintain*	**tener (58)**
mecer *to rock (a child)*	**vencer (61)**
medir *to measure*	**pedir (36)**
mentar *to mention by name*	**cerrar (11)**
mentir *to lie*	**sentir (55)**
merecer *to merit*	**parecer (35)**
merendar *to eat an afternoon snack*	**cerrar (11)**
moler *to grind*	**mover (31)**
morder *to bite*	**mover (31)**
morir *to die*	**dormir (19)**; past participle **muerto**
mostrar *to die*	**contar (14)**
mover *to move*	**(31)**
mullir *to fluff up*	**gruñir (23)**
nacer *to be born*	**parecer (35)**
negar *to deny*	**cerrar (11) g>gu** before **e**
nevar *to snow*	**cerrar (11)**; usually 3rd person only

obedecer *to obey*	**parecer (35)**
obtener *to obtain*	**tener (58)**
ofrecer *to offer*	**parecer (35)**
oír *to hear*	**(32)**
oler *to smell*	**(33)**
oponer *to oppose*	**poner (39)**
oscurecer *to darken*	**parecer (35)**
pacer *to graze*	**parecer (35)**
padecer *to suffer*	**parecer (35)**
palidecer *to pale*	**parecer (35)**
parecer *to seem*	**(35)**
pedir *to ask for*	**(36)**
pensar *to think*	**cerrar (11)**
perecer *to perish*	**parecer (35)**
permanecer *to remain*	**parecer (35)**
perpetuar *to perpetuate*	**continuar (15)**
perseguir *to pursue*	**seguir (54)**
pertenecer *to belong*	**parecer (35)**
pervertir *to pervert*	**sentir (55)**
plegar *to fold*	**cerrar (11); g>gu** before **e**
poblar *to people/populate*	**contar (14)**
poder *to be able*	**(38)**
podrir *to rot*	variant of **pudrir**; **-u-** used for all forms save past participle **podrido**
poner *to put*	**(39)**
poseer *to possess*	**(40)**
posponer *to postpone*	**poner (39)**
predecir *to foretell*	**decir (17)**
predisponer *to predispose*	**poner (39)**
preferir *to prefer*	**sentir (55)**
prescribir *to prescribe*	past participle **prescrito**
presuponer *to presuppose*	**poner (39)**
prevalecer *to prevail*	**parecer (35)**
prevaler *to take advantage of*	**valer (60)**

prevenir *to prepare*	**venir (62)**
prever *to foresee*	**ver (63)**; third-pers. present singular **prevé**
probar *to prove*	**contar (14)**
producir *to produce*	**(41)**
proferir *to utter* (usually *cries, insults*)	**sentir (55)**
prohibir *to prohibit*	**(42)**
promover *to promote*	**mover (31)**
proponer *to propose*	**poner (39)**
proseguir *to continue*	**seguir (54)**
prostituir *to prostitute*	**construir (13)**
proteger *to protect*	**(43)**
proveer *to supply*	**poseer (40)**; past participle **provisto/proveído**
provenir *to arise from*	**venir (62)**
pudrir *to rot*	regular; see **podrir**
puntuar *to punctuate/mark*	**continuar (15)**
quebrar *to snap*	**cerrar (11)**
querer *to want/love*	**(44)**
reaparecer *to reappear*	**parecer (35)**
reblandecer *to soften*	**parecer (35)**
recaer *to relapse*	**caer (9)**
recocer *to warm up* (*food*)	**cocer (12)**
recomendar *to recommend*	**cerrar (11)**
reconocer *to recognize*	**parecer (35)**
reconvenir *to reprimand*	**venir (62)**
recordar *to remember/remind*	**contar (14)**
recostar(se) *to lean back*	**contar (14)**
redituar *to yield*	**continuar (15)**
reducir *to reduce*	**producir (41)**
reelegir *to re-elect*	**regir (45)**
referir *to refer*	**sentir (55)**
reforzar *to reinforce*	**contar (14)**; **z>c** before **e**

refregar *to rub/scrub*	**cerrar (11); g>gu** before **e**
regar *to water*	**cerrar (11); g>gu** before **e**
regir *to govern*	**(45)**
rehacer *to redo*	**hacer (25)**
rehusar *to refuse*	**reunir (48)**
reír *to laugh*	**(46)**
rejuvenecer *to rejuvenate*	**parecer (35)**
remendar *to mend*	**cerrar (11)**
remorder *to grieve* (transitive)	**mover (31)**
remover *to stir up/Lat. Am. to remove*	**mover (31)**
rendir *to yield*	**pedir (36)**
renegar *to deny strongly*	**cerrar (11); g>gu** before **e**
renovar *to renew*	**contar (14)**
reñir *to scold*	**(47)**
repetir *to repeat*	**pedir (36)**
replegar *to fold over*	**cerrar (11); g>gu** before **e**
reponer *to replace*	**poner (39)**
reprobar *to reprove*	**contar (14)**
reproducir *to reproduce*	**producir (41)**
requebrar *to flatter*	**cerrar (11)**
requerir *to require*	**sentir (55)**
resarcir *to compensate for*	**zurcir (65)**
resentirse *to resent*	**sentir (55)**
resfriar *to chill*	**liar (28)**
resollar *to wheeze*	**contar (14)**
resolver *to resolve*	**mover (31); past participle resuelto**
resonar *to echo*	**contar (14)**
resplandecer *to gleam*	**parecer (35)**
restablecer *to re-establish*	**parecer (35)**
restituir *to return*	**construir (13)**
retemblar *to shudder*	**cerrar (11)**
retener *to retain*	**tener (58)**

retorcer *to twist*   **cocer (12)**; **c>z** before **a, o**

retraer *to draw in*   **traer (59)**

retribuir *to pay*   **construir (13)**

reunir *to bring together*   **(48)**

reventar *to burst*   **cerrar (11)**

reverdecer *to grow green again*   **parecer (35)**

revertir *to revert*   **sentir (55)**

revestir *to put on (clothes)*   **pedir (36)**

revolar *to flutter about*   **contar (14)**

revolcarse *to knock over*   **contar (14) c>qu** before **e**

revolver *to turn over*   **mover (31)**; past participle **revuelto**

rezar *to pray*   **(49)**

robustecer *to strengthen*   **parecer (35)**

rociar *to sprinkle*   **liar (28)**

rodar *to roll*   **contar (14)**

roer *to gnaw*   **(50)**

rogar *to request*   **contar (14)**; **g>gu** before **e**

romper *to break*   past participle **roto**

saber *to know*   **(51)**

sacar *to take out*   **(52)**

salir *to come out/leave*   **(53)**

satisfacer *to satisfy*   **hacer (25)**

seducir *to seduce*   **producir (41)**

segar *to reap*   **cerrar (11) g>gu** before **e**

seguir *to follow*   **(54)**

sembrar *to show*   **cerrar (11)**

sentar *to seat*   **cerrar (11)**

sentir *to feel*   **(55)**

ser *to be*   **(56)**

serrar *to saw*   **cerrar (11)**

servir *to serve*   **pedir (36)**

situar *to situate*   **continuar (15)**

sobre(e)ntender *to infer*   **perder (37)**

sobreponer *to put on top*   **poner (39)**

sobresalir *to jut out*	**salir (53)**
sobrevenir *to happen suddenly*	**venir (62)**
sofreír *to fry lightly*	**reír (46)**; past participle **sofrito**
soldar *to solder*	**contar (14)**
soler *to be used to*	**mover (31)** future, conditional and past and future subjunctives not used
soltar *to release*	**contar (14)**; past participle **suelto**
sonar *to sound*	**contar (14)**
sonreír *to smile*	**reír (46)**
soñar *to dream*	**contar (14)**
sosegar *to calm*	**cerrar (11) g>gu** before **e**
sostener *to support*	**tener (58)**
subarrendar *to sublease*	**cerrar (11)**
subscribir	see **suscribir**
substituir	see **sustituir**
substraer	see **sustraer**
subvenir *to defray costs*	**venir (62)**
subvertir *to subvert*	**sentir (55)**
sugerir *to suggest*	**sentir (55)**
suponer *to suppose*	**poner (39)**
suscribir *to subscribe*	past participle **suscrito**
sustituir *to substitute*	**construir (13)**
sustraer *to remove*	**traer (59)**
tañer *to chime*	**(57)**
temblar *to tremble*	**cerrar (11)**
tender *to tend*	**perder (37)**
tener *to have*	**(58)**
tentar *to tempt*	**cerrar (11)**
teñir *to dye*	**reñir (47)**
torcer *to twist*	**cocer (12); c>z** before **a, o**
tostar *to toast*	**contar (14)**
traducir *to translate*	**producir (41)**
traer *to bring*	**(59)**

tra(n)scender *to transcend*	**perder (37)**
transcribir *to transcribe*	past participle **transcrito**
transferir *to transfer*	**sentir (55)**
transgredir *to transgress*	**abolir (1)**; sometimes regular
transponer *to transpose*	**poner (39)**
trasegar *to switch round*	**cerrar (11)**; **g>gu** before **e**
traslucir *to hint at*	**lucir (29)**
trastrocar *to switch round*	**contar (14)**; **c>qu** before **e**
trocar *to barter*	**contar (14)**; **c>qu** before **e**
tronar *to thunder*	**contar (14)**
tropezar *to stumble*	**cerrar (11)**; **z>c** before **e**
tullir *to maim*	**gruñir (23)**
vaciar *to empty*	**liar (28)**
valer *to be worth*	**(60)**
valuar *to value*	**continuar (15)**
variar *to vary*	**liar (28)**
vencer *to win/conquer*	**(61)**
venir *to come*	**(62)**
ver *to see*	**(63)**
verter *to pour out*	**perder (37)**
vestir *to clothe*	**pedir (36)**
volar *to fly*	**contar (14)**
volcar *to upset*	**contar (14)**; **c>qu** before **e**
volver *to return*	**mover (31)**; past participle **vuelto**
yacer *to lie* (i.e. *lie down*)	**(64)**
zaherir *to mortify*	**sentir (55)**
zambullir *to plunge*	**gruñir (23)**
zurcir *to darn* **(65)**	

Glossary of Grammatical Terms

A few terms not used in this book but often found in Spanish grammars are also included. Terms printed in bold characters are defined elsewhere in the glossary.

Abstract noun A **noun** that refers to something that is not a person or concrete object. The following are abstract nouns: *liberty, impatience, innocence*.

Accent Strictly speaking, the various signs written over certain vowels in Spanish and many other languages, e.g. in the words **café**, **averigüe**. It is often confusingly used to mean stress; see **Stressed Syllable.**

Active see **Passive**

Adjectival Participles Adjectives formed from some (but by no means all) Spanish verbs by adding -**ante**, -**ente** or -**iente**, e.g. **preocupante** *worrying*, **hiriente** *wounding*.

Adjective A word that describes a noun, e.g. *a good* book, **un** *buen* libro.

Adverb A word that describes a verb, an adjective or another adverb: *he did it* **well**, **lo hizo** *bien*; *terribly tired*, **terriblemente** cansado; *very quickly*, *muy* **deprisa**.

Agreement Agreement in Spanish is of three kinds:

(1) **Number agreement**: the fact that a singular noun or pronoun requires a singular adjective, verb or article, and a plural noun or pronoun a plural adjective, verb or article:

El buen alumno *trabaja* mucho *The good student works hard*

Los buenos alumnos *trabajan* mucho *The good students work hard*

(2) **Person agreement**: the fact that a first-person subject requires a first-person verb and so on:

Person	Singular	Plural
First	**Yo quiero** *I want*	**Nosotros queremos** *We want*
Second	**Tú quieres** *You want*	**Vosotros queréis** *You want*
Third	**Ella quiere** *She wants*	**Ellos quieren** *They want*

(3) **Gender agreement**: the fact that masculine nouns require masculine adjectives, articles or pronouns, and feminine nouns require feminine adjectives, articles or pronouns:

Masculine	*un* muchacho rubi*o* *a blond boy*
	este libro roj*o* *this red book*
Feminine	*una* muchacha rubi*a* *a blond girl*
	esta casa blanc*a* *this white house*

Anterior Preterit Tense See **Pretérito anterior**

Apposition Two nouns or noun phrases placed side by side so that the second expands the meaning of the first: *Don Quixote, **the greatest Spanish novel**.* The words in bold are said to be 'in apposition' to the first part of the phrase.

Articles Words meaning *the* or *a/an*. See **Definite Article** and **Indefinite Article**.

Attributive Adjective In Spanish, an adjective that specifies the type or purpose of a noun: **la industria** *hotelera the hotel industry*, **problemas sindicales** *trade-union problems*. English regularly expresses the same construction by joining nouns together, e.g. *police dog, baseball game*.

Auxiliary verb A verb used to form a **Compound Tense** The most common auxiliary verbs in English are *to have* as in *I **have** said*, and *to be* as in *I **am** saying*. The Spanish equivalents are **haber** as in **yo *he* dicho** and **estar** as in **yo *estoy* diciendo**.

Cardinal numbers The ordinary numbers used for counting, e.g. *one, two, three*, etc. See also **Ordinal Numbers**.

Ceceo See **Seseo**.

Clause A group of words that forms part of a sentence and includes a **Finite Verb:** *I'll finish it before she arrives* contains two clauses, *I'll finish it* and *before she arrives*. Often a sentence consists of only one clause, cf. *Jack ate an apple*. Among the types of clause mentioned in this grammar are **Main Clause, Subordinate Clause** and **Relative Clause**, each separately defined below.

Collective Noun A noun that, although it may be singular in form, refers to a group of people or things: *flock, crowd, committee, crew, majority, dozen*, etc.

Comparative Forms of adjectives and adverbs that indicate a *more* or *less* intense quality: *better, worse, more intelligent, less beautiful*, **mejor, peor, más inteligente, menos bello**, etc.

Compound noun A noun formed from two or more nouns joined together: *fire alarm, cat-hair, fish soup, database design textbook*. As the examples show, English can make complex compound nouns, but Spanish has only a few, e.g. **año luz** *light year*, **perro policía** *police-dog*. Generally Spanish creates such nouns either by using **de** *of*—**manual de diseño de bases de datos**—or by using an **Attributive Adjective** (q.v.): **problemas *estudiantiles*** *student problems*.

Compound tenses Tense forms of verbs created in English by using the verb *have* plus a past participle, and in Spanish by using **haber** plus a past participle: *I have done, had finished, I will have left,* **he hecho, había terminado, habré salido**.

Conditional Sentence One that includes a condition and a result, e.g. *if it rains we'll stay at home, if it had rained we would have stayed at home.* Occasionally the *if*-clause is omitted: *it would be have been nice* (i.e. if some condition or other had been met).

Conditional tense The tense of a verb used to express what might or could happen or have happened: *I would be angry, He would have realized,* **me enojaría, se habría dado cuenta**.

Conjugation The general pattern that a verb's forms follow. There are three conjugations in Spanish corresponding to **Infinitives** ending in -**ar**, -**er** and -**ir**. All regular verbs belong to one of these conjugations. Radical changing and irregular verbs follow one of these conjugations in most forms, but some forms are unpredictable.

Conjunction Words or phrases (**Relative Pronouns** excepted) that connect words, phrases and clauses within a sentence. In the following sentence the words in bold are conjunctions: *I bought a shirt **and** a tie, **but when** she saw them, Mary said **that** she didn't like them, **so** I took them back, **although** I liked them myself.*

Consonant Simply defined as all the sounds in a language that are not vowels, i.e. in English and Spanish the sounds corresponding to all the letters of the alphabet except *a, e, i, o, u* and *y* when the latter is pronounced like *i*. See also **Vowel and Semi-vowel**.

Continuous The name given to Spanish verb forms consisting of **estar** plus a gerund, e.g. **estoy fumando** *I'm smoking*. See also **Progressive**.

Definite Article in English *the*, in Spanish **el, la, los, las** when used with the same meaning as the English word.

Demonstrative Adjective A special type of adjective used to point to something: in English *this*, *that* and *those*, in Spanish **este/esta/estos/estas, ese/esa/esos/esas, aquel/aquella/aquellos/aquellas**.

Demonstrative Pronoun A special type of pronoun used to point to something, e.g. *I don't want **this** one, I want **that** one*. In Spanish they usually have the same form as **Demonstrative Adjectives**, but are usually distinguished in writing by an accent. See p.138.

Diphthong In Spanish, a combination of a **Vowel** (q.v.) and a **Semi-vowel** (q.v.), e.g. the **oy** in **soy** or the **ue** in **bueno**.

Direct Object A noun or pronoun that directly experiences the action of a verb: *He hit **me**, Jack saw **Mary**, I wrote **it***. See also **Indirect Object**.

Direct Question see **Indirect Question**.

Feminine see **Gender**

Finite Verb Form A verb form that shows **Tense**, **Person** and **Number**, e.g. *he walked* (Third-person, Past and Singular), **iremos** *we'll go* (First-person, Future and Plural). See also **Non-Finite Verb Form**.

First Person see **Person**

Future Perfect Tense Tense forms that refer to an event that *will have* happened by a certain time: *I **will have** **died** of hunger by the time you finish cooking dinner*.

Future Tense Strictly speaking, the tense form that refers to the future, usually taken in Spanish to mean forms like **hablaré, iremos**. The term is not very helpful because both Spanish and English have several different ways of expressing the future, cf. *we're going tomorrow,* *we'll go tomorrow, we're going to go tomorrow, we go tomorrow, we're to go tomorrow.*

Gender In Spanish, the fact that nouns and pronouns are either 'masculine' or 'feminine'. Gender is usually obvious if the word refers to a male or a female human being, but all Spanish nouns are either feminine or masculine, even when they refer to sexless objects: **el libro** *book*, **el fusil** *rifle*, **el árbol** *tree* are masculine nouns, **la cama** *bed*, **la cucaracha** *cockroach* and **la flor** *flower* are feminine. In the case of such nouns, grammatical gender has obviously got nothing to do with sex. See also **Agreement**.

Generic 'Referring to a whole class or every member of a set of things.' In the sentence *I hate beer/oysters/politics*, the three nouns are said to be generic nouns since they refer to substances, things or abstractions in general. Compare **Partitive**.

Gerund The Spanish verb form created by replacing the ending of the **Infinitive** by -ando or -iendo, depending on **Conjugation**, e.g. **hablando, durmiendo**. The gerund is one of the **Non-Finite Verb Forms** of Spanish and corresponds to some of the uses of the English verb form ending in *-ing*.

Historic Present The **Present Tense** used to make a past event sound dramatic, cf. *There I am resting after all my hard work when she walks in and tells me I'm lazy!*

Imperative See **Mood**.

Imperfect Subjunctive The name traditionally given to the simple (i.e. non-compound) verb forms of the past of the Spanish subjunctive. Examples: **hablara/ hablase, dijeran/dijesen**. See also **Mood**.

Imperfect Tense A Spanish past tense formed by adding a set of endings (-aba, -abas, -aba or -ía, -ías, -ía, etc.) to the **Stem** of the verb. It usually expresses either habitual actions in the past—**yo fumaba mucho** *I used to smoke a lot*—or events that were in progress at the time but had not yet ended, cf. *I was smoking a lot.*

Impersonal Pronouns Pronouns that refer to unidentifiable persons or things, e.g. *someone, something, anyone,* **alguien, algo, cualquiera,** etc.

Impersonal se One of the many uses of the pronoun **se** as a rough equivalent of the English *one, people*: **se vive mejor en España** *people live better in* Spain, **se come bien en Francia** *people eat well in France.* Compare **Passive se.**

Indefinite Article In English *a/an*, in Spanish **un/una/unos/unas** when used with the same meaning as their English counterparts.

Indicative Mood See **Mood.**

Indirect Object The noun or pronoun that acquires, hears or in some way receives the **Direct Object** (q.v.) of a verb. The word *him* or **le** is the Indirect Object in these sentences and the words in bold italics are the Direct Object: *I sent him **the letter**/***le** enviaron ***la carta****, she told him **the truth**/*ella **le** dijo ***la verdad***. In Spanish an Indirect Object can also lose as well as receive: **le** robaron ***mil pesetas*** *they stole 1,000 ptas from him*, **se le** cae el pelo *his hair's falling out* (literally *his hair is falling out* (**caerse**) *from him*).

Indirect Question A question included in a **Subordinate Clause** (q.v.) in a sentence. It is normally introduced by some such expression as *I wonder . . . , Do you know where . . . , I'll ask him when . . . .* Direct question: *When is he coming?,* Indirect Question *I don't know **when he is coming***.

Infinitive The 'dictionary form' of a verb, which always ends in -**r** in Spanish, e.g. **hablar, comer, vivir**. It often corresponds to the English form preceded by *to*— *to speak, to eat , to live*—and sometimes to the form ending in *-ing*, as in **fumar es malo para la salud** *smoking is bad for the health*. It is a **Non-Finite-Verb Form** (q.v.).

Interrogative A feature of words that ask questions, like *why?* (adverb), *when?* (adverb), *who?* (pronoun), *which?* (adjective), Spanish **¿por qué?, ¿cuándo?, ¿quién?, ¿qué?, ¿cuál?**

Intransitive Verb a verb that has no **Direct Object** present or implied: *I go, she came* are intransitive, as are their Spanish equivalents, **voy, vino**: one cannot go *someone* or come *something*. 'Transitive' and 'Intransitive' are often descriptions of the use of a verb rather than of its inherent nature, since many so-called intransitive verbs can take a direct object and then become transitive, cf. *he slept ten hours*, Spanish **durmió diez horas**, or Spanish **lo durmieron** *they put him to sleep*. See also **Transitive verbs**.

Irregular Verb A verb whose forms cannot always be predicted from the usual pattern. English *go-went-gone*, *sleep-slept*, Spanish **soy, eres, es** are typical examples.

Main Clause A Clause (q.v.) that could stand alone as a sentence. In *I stood up when she came in*, the words *I stood up* could form a sentence on their own and therefore form the Main Clause; *when she came in* cannot form a sentence without the addition of more words, and is therefore a **Subordinate Clause** (q.v.).

Masculine see **Gender**.

Modal Verbs A verb that indicates the 'mood' of another, e.g. *I **may** go* (possibility), *you **ought to** do it* (obligation), *she **can't** come* (possibility). The main

Spanish Modal Verbs are **poder, deber, tener que, soler**.

Mood The traditional name given to the three different forms that Spanish and English verbs can take according to the use being made of the verb:

Indicative Mood, used for making statements: *it's raining, you said it,* **yo hablo español**

Subjunctive Mood, almost obsolete in English, but much used in Spanish to show that the verb expresses something hoped, wanted, feared, approved, disapproved, possible or, after **Subordinators** (q.v.) something that has or had not yet happened, e.g. **quiero que *vayas*** *I want you to go*, **espero que *venga*** *I hope that he comes*, **antes de que *saliera* el avión** *before the plane left.* The subjunctive occasionally occurs in English, e.g. *if I **were** you, it is necessary that this **be** done quickly, if this **be** true.*

Imperative Mood: The form of a verb used to express a command or order: *tell me the truth,* **dime la verdad**.

Non-Finite Verb Forms Verb forms that cannot express Person, Tense or Number, e.g. *living, to live, lived*— three forms that do not tell us who lived when and how many people were involved. In Spanish the non-finite verb forms are the **Gerund**, the **Infinitive** and the **Past Participle**.

Noun A word that names a person, object or abstraction, e.g. *Peter, woman, table, hope, freedom.* See also **Abstract Noun, Collective Noun**.

Number In grammar, the state of being either singular (i.e. referring to only one person or thing) or plural (referring to more than one).

Object Pronouns in Spanish, pronouns like **me, te, nos, os** that refer either to the **Direct Object** or the **Indirect Object** (q.v.). **Le** and **les** are also object pronouns, although in standard Spanish they usually (but by no means always) refer only to the Indirect Object.

Ordinal Numbers Numerals that indicates the order in which something appears, e.g. *first/**primero**, second/**segundo**, hundredth/**centésimo***. Compare **Cardinal Number**.

Partitive 'Referring only to a part of something, not to the whole'. In *Don't forget to buy bread/oysters* the words *bread* and *oysters* are Partitive Nouns: they imply *some* bread, *some* oysters, not all the bread or oysters that exist. Compare **Generic**.

Passive The opposite of **Active**. An active sentence that can be made passive must contain a **Subject**, a **Transitive Verb** and optionally a **Direct Object**: *A car ran him down*/**Lo atropelló un coche**. The equivalent Passive Sentence makes the direct object into the subject: *He was run down by a car*/**Fue atropellado por un coche**. See also **Passive se**.

Passive se One of the uses of the Spanish pronoun **se** to make the equivalent of a **Passive** (q.v.) sentence: **estos libros se publicaron en España** *these books were published in Spain*.

Past Participle The part of the verb used to form **Compound Tenses** and **Passive** sentences. In English it usually ends in **-ed**, in Spanish **-ado** or **-ido**, although there are exceptions in both languages, cf. *broken*/**roto**, *seen*/**visto**. It is a **Non-Finite Verb Form** (q.v.).

Perfect Tense The **Compound Tense** formed in English with the present tense of *to have* plus the **Past Participle**, in Spanish from the present tense of **haber** plus the past participle, e.g. *he has seen*, **ha visto**. It is often called the **pretérito perfecto** in Spanish.

Perfect Tense Continuous (or Continuous Perfect Tense) The tense formed in English with the **Perfect Tense** of *to be* plus the *-ing* form, in Spanish with the perfect tense of **estar** plus the **Gerund**, e.g. *he has been thinking*, **ha estado pensando**.

Perfect of Recency The use of the **Perfect Tense** in Spanish (as opposed to the **Preterit Tense**) to show that an event occurred recently (e.g. since midnight). This is more typical of Spain than Latin America.

Person See **Agreement**

Personal a The term used in Spanish grammar to refer to the preposition **a** when used before **Direct Objects** that refer to human beings, e.g. **vi a Mario** *I saw Mario*. See p.157.

Personal Pronouns Subject pronouns and **Object Pronouns** referring to people or things, e.g. *I*/**yo**, *you*/**tú**/**usted**, *he*/**él**, or *me*/**me**, *him*/**lo**/**le**, *us*/**nos**, etc.

Phrase A meaningful group of words in a sentence that does not contain a **Finite Verb**, e.g. the bold words in *I arrived **at ten o'clock***.

Pluperfect Conditional The tense formed in Spanish by using the **Conditional** form of **haber** + the **Past Participle**: **habrían sido** *they would have been*. The **-ra** form of **haber** may also be used: **hubieran sido** *they would have been*.

Pluperfect Subjunctive The **Subjunctive** version of the Spanish **Pluperfect** (q.v.), formed from the **-ra** or **-se** form of **haber** + the **Past Participle**, e.g. **si me hubieras visto** *if you had seen me*.

Pluperfect Tense The tense formed in English with the past of **had** plus the **Past Participle**, e.g. *I had done*, and in Spanish with the **Imperfect** of **haber** and the **Past Participle**, e.g. **yo había hecho**.

Possessive Adjective An adjective that indicates possession, i.e. *my*/**mi**, *your*/**tu/vuestro/su**, *his*/**su**, *our*/**nuestro**, etc.

Possessive Pronoun A pronoun that indicates possession. English examples are *mine, yours, hers*; Spanish examples are **el mío, el tuyo, el suyo**, etc.

Prefix A letter or letters that usually have no meaning in isolation but are added at the beginning a word to change the meaning, e.g. *pre-* in *pre-school*, *re-* in *represent*.

Preposition A word used before a noun to relate it to the rest of the phrase or sentence, e.g. *on*/**en**, *with*/**con**, *without*/**sin**, *against*/**contra**, etc. In English a preposition can come at the end of a clause or sentence: *the girl he's going out **with***. In Spanish a preposition must precede the word it refers to: **la chica *con* la que sale**.

Prepositional Phrase A phrase used like a **Preposition**, e.g. *on behalf of*/**de parte de**, *in return for*/**a cambio de**.

Present Continuous The name usually given in Spanish grammar to the tense form based on the present of **estar** plus the **Gerund**, e.g. **está cantando** *he is singing*. See also **Progressive**.

Present Participle In Spanish, the name sometimes given to **Adjectival Participles** (q.v.). In English, the name sometimes given to the *-ing* form of verbs, e.g. *walking, riding*.

Present Tense The name given to the verb form that indicates events that are happening in the present, e.g. **hablo** *I speak/I'm speaking*. The name is misleading since in both languages this tense form can also be used for future, timeless and even past actions. See also **Present Continuous, Historic Present**.

Preterit (British spelling 'Preterite') The name given in English to the simple Past Tense in Spanish that denotes a completed action, e.g. **hablé** *I spoke*, **tuve** *I got*, **dijimos** *we said*. In Spanish this tense is often called the **pretérito indefinido**.

Pretérito anterior The Spanish name for the tense form made with the **Preterit** of **haber** and the **Past Participle**, e.g. **hubo hablado** *he had said*. It is nowadays used only in literary styles.

Progressive The name usually given to English verb forms made with *to be* and the *-ing* form of a verb, e.g. *he was singing, they are shouting*. The rough Spanish equivalent is the **Continuous**.

Pronominal verb A Spanish verb that has an **Object Pronoun** that is of the same person and number as the subject, e.g. **me afeito** *I'm shaving (myself)*, **te vas** *you're leaving*, **se murieron** *they died*. Traditionally these were called 'reflexive verbs', but the term **Reflexive** correctly refers to just one possible meaning of a Pronominal Verb, not to the *form* of the verb.

Pronoun A word, e.g. *he, she,* it, *they, I,* **yo, tú**, that stands for a noun.

Radical-changing verb In Spanish, verbs that have regular endings but unpredictable vowel changes in certain forms, e.g. **contar** *to tell*, **cuento** *I tell* but **contamos** *we tell*, or **pedir** *to ask for*, **pido** *I ask for*, **pedí** *I asked for*, **pidió** *he asked for*, etc.

Reciprocal One of the meanings that a plural Spanish **Pronominal Verb** can have. The action is done to or for *one another*, e.g. **se quieren** *they love one another*.

Reflexive One of the meanings of a Spanish **Pronominal Verb** which shows that an the action is done by the subject to him or herself, e.g. **me lavo** *I wash myself*.

Regular Verb A verb whose various forms are all predictable from the pattern used by its **Conjugation** (q.v.). Typical Spanish examples are **hablar, comer** and **vivir**, which have no irregularities or exceptions.

Relative Clause A clause that modifies or restricts the meaning of a noun or pronoun that occurred earlier in the sentence, e.g. *I was talking to the woman **who lives over the road**, That's the girl **that/whom I saw yesterday***. In Spanish Relative clauses are always introduced by a **Relative Pronoun** (q.v.), but the pronoun can sometimes be omitted in English, cf. *that's the girl I saw yesterday*.

Relative Pronoun A class of words that introduce a **Relative Clause (q.v.)**. English relative pronouns are *who, whom, which, that*; Spanish equivalents are **que, el que, quien, el cual**.

Second Person See **Person**

Semi-Vowel A special kind of vowel that acts like a consonant. There are two Spanish semi-vowels, one pronounced like the *y* of *yes* as in **bien**, the other like the *w* of *wood* as in **bueno**. When a semi-vowel is attached to a **Vowel**, a **Diphthong** is formed.

Seseo In Spanish pronunciation, the use of an s sound where Spaniards from Central and Northern Spain use a sound like the *th* of *think*, e.g. in words like **cinco** *five*, **atroz** *atrocious*. Most Andalusians and Canary Islanders and all Latin Americans use **seseo**. Use of the *th* sound is called **ceceo**.

Simple Tense A one-word tense form of a verb, e.g. *he does*, **sabe, toma**. It is the opposite of **Compound Tense** (q.v.).

Stem The part of a verb to which the various endings that indicate Tense, Person and Mood are added. The stem of *kissing* is *kiss*: *kissed, kisses*. The stem of **hablar** is

habl: **habl***amos*, **habl***aron*, **habl***ando* etc. Some irregular verbs have no single identifiable stem, e.g. **ser**—**soy, eres, fui**, etc.

Stressed Syllable The **Syllable** of a word spoken most loudly. Stress is crucial to meaning in both Spanish: and English: compare **hablo** *I speak* with **habló** *he spoke* or the two pronunciations of *invalid* in *the invalid had an invalid ticket*.

Subject The noun or pronoun that performs the action of verb or about which the verb phrase makes a statement: **Mary** *got up late*, **I** *am getting tired*, **Miguel conoce a Antonia**.

Subjunctive See **Mood**.

Subordinate Clause A clause in a sentence that depends on a **Main Clause** to make sense. In *Jane got up before the sun rose*, the subordinate clause *before the sun rose* cannot stand alone as a sentence, whereas the main clause *Jane got up* can.

Subordinator A **Conjunction** used to introduce a **Subordinate Clause**, e.g. *I did it **before** you did*, *Peter phoned **when** she arrived*, *I paid **although** I wasn't pleased*.

Suffix A letter or letters that (usually) have no meaning in isolation but are added to the end of a word to change the meaning, e.g. *-ness* in *smallness*, **-ito** in **perrito**.

Superlative The form of an adjective or adverb that shows that the quality referred to is the most intense of all: *Molly is the **brightest** student, you're the **best***, **Molly es la más inteligente, tú eres el mejor**. See also **Comparative**.

Syllable In Spanish, a portion or element of a word that contains one **Vowel** sound (**Diphthongs** and **Triphthongs** counting as one vowel). **Es** contains one syllable, **era** contains two and **habitación** contains four (**ió** being a diphthong and counting as one vowel).

Tense The form of a verb that indicates *when* the action takes place. *I went*/**yo iba/yo fui/yo he ido** are all past tenses of various kinds, *I'll go/I will go/I'm going to go* are different types of future tense.

Third Person See **Person**.

Transitive Verb A verb that can have a **Direct Object**. The following verbs are transitive: *I hit him*, **La vi** *I saw her*. *I yawned*/**bostecé** is **Intransitive** since we cannot yawn something or someone.

Triphthong The combination of a **Semi-Vowel**, a **Vowel** and another **Semi-Vowel**, e.g. **uéi** in **continuéis** (pronounced 'way').

Verb A word that explains what the **Subject** of a clause or sentence does: *I eat fish*, *You tell tall stories*.

Vowel The sounds of a language that are not classified as consonants and which, in the case of Spanish, can form a **Syllable** (q.v.) on their own or in combination with consonants. Spanish has five vowels: **a, e, i, o, u.** English has the same number of vowel signs, but they are pronounced in more than a dozen different ways.

| Index

Prepositional phrases like **en contra, con motivo de, debajo de** are listed in alphabetical order on pp.166–183. Only a few important English prepositions are included here. The rest are listed with their Spanish equivalents on pp. 183–6.

For individual Spanish verbs not listed here, see the list on pp. 303–319.

Also available from Oxford University Press

Oxford Take off in Spanish
Language learning course with almost 5 hours of audio
Book and 4 cassettes 0–19–860276–6
Book and 4 CDs 0–19–860296–0
Book only 0–19–860297–9
Also available in Latin American Spanish

Oxford Take off in Spanish Dictionary
0–19–860333–9
(available in the UK only)

Pocket Oxford Spanish Dictionary
The ideal dictionary for higher examinations
0–19–860281–2

The Oxford Starter Spanish Dictionary
Designed for absolute beginners
0–19–860330–4

The Oxford Colour Spanish Dictionary Plus
Colour headwords throughout
0–19–864562–7
0–19–864566–X (US edition)

Oxford Spanish Verbpack
0–19–860340–1

Oxford Spanish Wordpack
0–19–860337–1